D1263826

The Political Economy of Fiscal Federalism

The Political Economy of Fiscal Federalism

Edited by
Wallace E. Oates
Princeton University

Lexington Books
D.C. Heath and Company
Lexington, Massachusetts
Toronto

Library of Congress Cataloging in Publication Data

Main entry under title:

The Political economy of fiscal federalism.

   Papers presented at a conference sponsored by the International Seminar in Public Economics and the International Institute of Management, and held Jan. 8–10, 1976, at the International Institute of Management in Berlin.
   1. Intergovernmental fiscal relations—Congresses. 2. Finance, Public—Congresses. 3. Grants-in-aid—Congresses. I. Oates, Wallace E. II. International Seminar in Public Economics. III. International Institute of Management. IV. Title: Fiscal federalism.

HJ192.P63   336.1'85   76-24471
ISBN 0-669-00961-X

Published simultaneously in Canada.

Printed in the United States of America.

International Standard Book Number: 0-669-00961-X

Library of Congress Catalog Card Number: 76-24471

Contents

Preface

A critical dimension of the continuing evolution of the structures of modern governments is the changing roles of different levels of government and, not infrequently, the creation of yet new tiers of public decision making. In Italy and England, for example, attempts to rationalize the organization of the public sector have led to efforts to introduce new regional governments. On the North American scene, many jurisdictions have turned to metropolitan government and special districts in an attempt to make the public sector more effective in the provision of needed services. Evolving forms are, moreover, by no means limited to the more decentralized levels of government. One of the most fascinating of these "federal" phenomena is the emergence of a new upper-tier level of government in the European community.

In each of these cases, a central concern is the appropriate functions for each of these levels of government. What is the proper scope of decision making for each tier of the public sector? In view of the inevitable interplay of the different levels of government, what policy tools are available for coordinating the actions of the central and decentralized public agencies?

The search for answers to these questions has generated a considerable research effort in recent years. Economists, for example, have tried to set forth some basic principles for the organization of fiscal decision making in a multi-tiered system. At the policy level, however, the development of actual public institutions has been largely the result of a combination of economic and political pressures to which the existing forms of government have had to adapt. To understand the actual pattern of evolution of governmental structures must take us well beyond some first principles.

This book is itself the product of an interdisciplinary conference designed to bring together some of the more formal research efforts in fiscal federalism and the facts of the "federal experience." Drawing on recent events in a substantial range of countries, some with quite centralized governments and others with a greater role for lower levels in the public sector, the conference confronted the so-called principles of federal finance with the actual responses of public decision-makers to specific intergovernmental issues. The result was a lively, and sometimes rather heated, debate on the interpretation of both fact and theory in governmental structure and choices. This debate reflected the diversity of perspectives represented at the sessions: both economists and political scientists from seven different countries contributed papers and discussion. The character of the meetings was thus one of continuing interaction between the viewpoints from various disciplines, the experiences of different countries with their own governmental forms, and the formal analysis of fiscal systems, on the one hand, and the interpretation of actual events, on the other.

The organization of this book reflects the course of the conference. It begins with two introductory essays in Part I, one by an economist and the other by a political scientist, which provide a background and point of departure for the debate. These essays themselves suggest at the outset that principles of economic efficiency are likely to run head on into considerations of both social justice and political reality.

Part II presents a series of seven concise studies of actual governmental experience in six individual countries and in the European Community. These are not essays describing intergovernmental structure. Rather, each chapter is an analysis of the response in the public sector to a particular problem (or set of problems). As such, the chapters provide intriguing insights into the processes of public choice in a range of multilevel systems. In some cases, such as in France, the central government has been able to maintain a rather firm and direct hold over public investment by local authorities. In contrast, in Germany there has been much more difficulty in regulating local investments. Part II concludes with a study of the European community and its newly emerging upper-tier level of government. The application of the principles of federal finance to the creation of a "central" government raises a whole series of important, challenging issues. In addition to the determination of the appropriate range of fiscal functions for the new level of government, there remains the matter of the compensation of various jurisdictions which may suffer some economic injury from the formation of the "federation." This has been a major theme of Community policy.

Part III consists of six research papers on general problems in federal finance. Three of the essays relate to the "pure theory" of local finance, while the remaining papers have a more empirical bent. The concluding paper by Werner Pommerehne, the longest in the book, provides a rich source of data and other information for students of fiscal federalism.

The occasion for all these papers was the fourth in the series of International Seminars in Public Economics (ISPE), which was sponsored jointly by ISPE under its President, Richard Musgrave, and by the host, the International Institute of Management, in Berlin under its Director, Professor Dr. Fritz Scharpf. The conference was held in Berlin on January 8 to 10, 1976. I am most grateful to Professor Dr. Scharpf, Professor Dr. Bruno Frey, and Professor Dennis Mueller for their efforts in planning the conference and to Sue Anne Batey for administrative support. In addition, all the participants wish to thank the Conference Assistant, Ilana Trevor, for her help with the various logistical matters. Finally, I am deeply indebted to Ellen Seiler for her expert editorial assistance in the preparation of this book.

**Part I:
Introduction**

1

An Economist's Perspective on Fiscal Federalism

Wallace E. Oates

The federal system was created with the intention of combining the different advantages which result from the magnitude and the littleness of nations.

Alexis de Tocqueville
Democracy in America

De Tocqueville's observation on the origin of federal government takes on new dimensions from the perspective of recent economic events and research. In the realm of macroeconomic policy, for example, the importance of size has become increasingly apparent: the monetary and fiscal authorities of a small, highly "open" country in today's international economy have only a limited scope for independent action; in various limiting cases, they may lose entirely their control over the size of the domestic money supply and the availability of credit.[1] On the other hand, the "littleness" of fiscal jurisdictions continues to offer compelling advantages for the provision of a number of important public services. In fact, fiscal data covering recent decades for a large number of countries indicate a growth in the budgets of decentralized levels of government relative to that of the national authority.

Recent fiscal history has been, to a significant extent, the response to a continuing tension between the economic and political forces inducing greater centralization and the opposing centrifugal attractions of local fiscal control. In the United States, this has given birth to federal revenue sharing with state and local governments. On a larger scale, the ongoing drama in the European community reflects the pushes and pulls of the gains from economic unification versus the desirability of fiscal autonomy. The effort continues to forge new fiscal institutions to combine ". . . the different advantages which result from the magnitude and the littleness of nations."

These events have stimulated a renewal of interest in the study of multilevel finance that has resulted in the emergence of fiscal federalism as a subject of study in its own right. In this paper, I want to explore at a relatively general

3

level what the basic principles of economics have to say about the organization and functioning of the public sector in a federal system. I stress that the perspective will be on the *economics* of federalism in the more narrow and conventional sense; the subject is the implications of economic analysis for the traditional concerns of the economist—the allocation of resources and the distribution of income.

This will raise some controversial issues. We find, for example, that the objective of efficient resource allocation suggests that individuals should segregate themselves by communities according to their demands for public services. However, it is precisely this sort of segregation that, for political or even ethical reasons, we may be quite reluctant to tolerate. In some instances, then, economic analysis points in directions that may leave us uneasy because of their implied social and political consequences. Nevertheless, it is my purpose here simply to follow the economic logic to its own conclusions. Even where this leads to propositions that are "normatively" unsettling, the analysis is still likely to reveal some fundamental forces at work in the economic system with which we must contend, regardless of our objectives for social policy.

I should also emphasize that the term *federalism* for the economist is not to be understood in a narrow constitutional sense. In economic terms, all governmental systems are more or less federal; even in a formally unitary system, for example, there is typically a considerable extent of de facto fiscal discretion at decentralized levels. Instead of being dichotomously federal or nonfederal, governments vary along some multidimensional spectrum in the degree to which fiscal decision-making is decentralized. As Livingston (1952, p. 86) has argued, "The essence of federalism lies not in the institutional or constitutional structure but in the society itself" [see also Oates (1972, chap.1)]. For purposes of economic analysis, I find it more useful to envision a "centralized solution" to the problem of resource allocation in the public sector as one that emphasizes standardized levels of services across all jurisdictions, while the "federal" approach stresses greater scope for decentralized choice in the provision of these services.

Finally, I should point out that certain portions of this chapter have a strongly U.S. flavor. In particular, the local-finance literature has explored in great detail the mobility model, whose applicability seems largely confined to modern metropolitan areas in which individuals often work in one place and reside in another. These models predict a process of segregation by socioeconomic class, which seems to characterize urban areas in the United States rather better than in some other countries. The applicability of this line of analysis to certain other nations (or supranational bodies like the European community) is open to real question. However, other parts of the chapter deal with issues relevant to the intergovernmental structure of nearly all countries.

I. The Division of Fiscal Functions Among
   Levels of Government

There seems to be a consensus on the proposition that the primary responsibility for macroeconomic stabilization policies and for the redistribution of income and wealth must rest with the central government. The basic point is not that local governments in the aggregate have no impact on total demand or the distribution of income, but rather that the constraints on an individual local government leave it very little scope for an effective stabilization or redistributive policy within its jurisdiction.

On the macroeconomic side, local governments do not possess the power to create or destroy money. Moreover, any attempts to influence the level of local economic activity by deliberate fiscal measures will be dissipated by the deflection of most of the new demand to goods and services produced elsewhere; typically, the local economy is highly open, i.e., it has a large average and marginal propensity to import, so the local authority is unable to contain the new spending within its borders.

Similarly, the mobility of individual economic units among different localities places fairly narrow limits on the capacity for local income redistribution. For example, an aggressive policy to redistribute income from the rich to the poor in a particular locality, may, in the end, simply chase the relatively wealthy to other jurisdictions and attract those with low incomes. The likely outcome is a community homogeneous in poor residents (an unappealing prospect for most local jurisdiction).[2] The ability to redistribute income to a significant extent depends largely on impediments to mobility of the sort provided by national borders (and, in some instances, even these may not be fully adequate).

The Decentralization Theorem

Decentralized choice in the public sector comes into its own in Musgrave's allocation branch. Consider an economy composed of two communities in which a single public service is provided. For the moment, let us ignore the problem of mobility by assuming that each individual's location is permanently fixed in one or the other of these two localities. Finally, let us postulate that there are no spillover effects in the provision of the public service; the benefits from these outputs are confined solely to the residents of the community in which they are provided, so that, in Breton's (1965, p. 180) terminology, a "perfect mapping" exists.

The spirit of the *unitary solution* to the provision of the public service

would be to ensure a uniform level of the service over both communities. However, it is easy to see that in economic terms this will generally be inefficient. If
the demands in the two communities for the public service differ (and if there
are no economies of scale from centralized provision of the service), then we
can increase welfare by diversifying outputs in the two communities in accordance with local demands. I have elsewhere (1972, pp. 33–38, 54–63) described
this rather straightforward proposition as the decentralization theorem. Its
importance in the context of public-sector outputs is that, subject to certain
conditions, it establishes a presumption in favor of the *federal solution* to resource allocation in the government sector: the decentralized provision of public
services in response to local demands.

The conditions necessary for the validity of the proposition are also important: the absence of both spillover effects and any economies of scale. If, for
example, the central government can achieve cost savings by providing a uniform
service level across both localities, then this must be weighed against the potential welfare gains from diversified local outputs to ascertain the appropriate
level of government to provide the service. These kinds of tradeoffs constitute
the problem of determining the optimal size jurisdiction for providing a particular public service. This determination is further complicated by the presence of
several public services. In order to reduce the decision-making costs implicit in
a myriad of different levels of government, it will normally make sense to con-
solidate the provision of several services under the roof of one governmental
unit, although this may mean that the optimal jurisdiction size for each service
in isolation no longer corresponds precisely to the actual jurisdiction of the
responsible government.

In practice, however, possibly the most difficult dimension of this optimal-
jurisdiction problem has proved to be the geographical delineation of the benefits and costs. It is not clear, for example, just what the geographical range of
significant benefits is for functions like education and police services. For
instance, it can be argued that I have an "option value" for levels of public
outputs in other communities because I may at some point move to one of them.

Consumer Mobility and the Tiebout Model

A large portion of the local-finance literature has addressed the issues that arise
when consumers move among communities, at least in part in response to fiscal
differentials. The immediate appeal of the mobility model is the enhanced
potential that it offers for realizing the welfare gains from diversified local
outputs. We can envision a world in which different communities offer varying
levels of public services and in which each individual selects as a community of
residence a locality with a service level corresponding to his level of demand. By
"voting with their feet," individuals at the same time reveal their preferences
and promote an efficient allocation of resources with the public sector.

The origin of this line of analysis in the economics literature is the classic article by Tiebout (1956). Tiebout sketched out a model which, in contrast to Samuelson's allegations concerning the inefficiencies resulting from decentralized choice for public goods, showed that, for a particular class of public goods (those whose consumption is restricted to a specific geographical area), individual choice can, at least in principle, generate an efficient outcome. In Tiebout's world, perfectly mobile consumers, living solely on dividend income, choose to reside in communities that provide their desired levels of public outputs. The resulting solution closely parallels the market solution for private goods:

> Just as the consumer may be visualized as walking to a private market place to buy his goods, the prices of which are set, we place him in the position of walking to a community where the prices (taxes) of community services are set. Both trips take the consumer to market. There is no way in which the consumer can avoid revealing his preferences in a spatial economy. Spatial mobility provides the local public-goods counterpart to the private market's shopping trip [Tiebout (1956, p. 422)].

The Tiebout model, however, involves a number of heroic assumptions *and* omissions, the investigation of which spurred later research. It is quite striking, for example, that a paper which purports to describe individual location decisions in response to local services uses a nonspatial model and makes no mention of local taxation! In addition, a number of the assumptions verge on the outrageous: Tiebout's consumers, for example, are completely footloose in the sense that the location of their jobs or friends has no influence on their choice of a community of residence—the selection is made solely on fiscal criteria.

The large literature that has followed on Tiebout's paper has tried to relax some of these assumptions and to enrich the analysis. Buchanan and Goetz (1972) have shown that certain inefficiencies are likely where the individual must commute to a place of work. On another front, Schuler (1974) has begun the integration of the model into an explicitly spatial framework. However, rather than attempt a comprehensive survey of the work on the mobility model, I shall explore a couple of issues that I find of particular interest and relevance to the political economy of fiscal federalism.

The first concerns the tendencies in the mobility model to the formation of communities that are stratified by income class.[3] The Tiebout solution involves a sorting-out process in which individuals with similar demands for local services locate together; since we might generally expect the demand for local services to exhibit a positive income elasticity, this in itself should encourage a tendency toward segregation by income. However, there is a second inducement to income homogeneity implicit in the use of income-related taxes to finance local services. High-income residents in a particular community have a fiscal incentive to exclude those with lower incomes, since the latter will make only a relatively small contribution to the local treasury. We thus have both a taste element and a pecuniary incentive operating in the local public sector to produce a system of communities which are relatively homogeneous in income.

This segregation solution has some interesting implications. First, note how it removes the potential for any income redistribution through local budgets. Even though communities employ income-related taxes (such as property or personal income taxes), no redistribution whatsoever occurs in the limiting case of perfect income segregation, since everyone in a particular community has the same income.

A second intriguing aspect of this outcome is its apparent instability. It will generally be in the interest of a relatively poor individual to locate in a high-income community, where at the existing tax rate he will get a partial free ride from the larger tax payments of his neighbors. We can thus envision a process in which wealthy households establish a community with high levels of public outputs only to find themselves invaded by lower-income families seeking the pecuniary advantages of the large tax base—a continuing game of hide-and-seek with no stable solution.

How do we bring stability into this world? In the United States, at least, the answer to this is fairly clear: higher-income communities have adopted exclusionary zoning regulations specifically to keep out poorer families. Such ordinances typically require a minimum lot size and, perhaps, certain housing characteristics to ensure that only a wealthy family can afford to purchase or build a house. Zoning regulations have thus been the policy instrument to achieve a stable composition of the local community.

Until quite recently, there has been little formal economic analysis of zoning activities. In general, there seemed to be some presumption that the use of local property taxation introduced certain inefficiencies or distortions in the local housing market (as well as into local decisions concerning public services) and the introduction of zoning impediments to mobility among local jurisdictions probably made things even worse. However, Hamilton (1975) has demonstrated that this need not be the case; in fact, the Hamilton model shows that a system of many communities, each using property taxation and zoning ordinances that specify a minimum value for local houses, effectively converts the property tax into a pure benefit tax and restores all the efficiency properties of the Tiebout solution. Moreover, the equilibrium in the Hamilton model is a stable one: no household will have any incentive to relocate.

This is an intriguing result from the perspective of public policy. Our amended mobility model is one in which households segregate themselves, largely by income class, to consume desired levels of public outputs and effectively wall themselves in from potential lower-income entrants by means of exclusionary zoning ordinances. And the outcome is efficient resource allocation in the local public sector! What can hardly escape notice is that this is precisely the system that is presently under severe attack in the popular literature and in the courts in the United States. The tide of opinion contends that this system both fails to accommodate regional housing needs for lower-income households and gives rise to intolerable differences in the quality of public services (particularly schools) across different localities. We thus seem to have another of the (frequent) conflicts between economic efficiency and norms of social justice.

In concluding this section, let me comment briefly on the applicability of the mobility model. The model itself appears to make strong demands on consumer responses to local-sector differentials; households must undertake the expensive act of moving to satisfy their demands for local services. How realistic is this? As stated, it seems an unlikely description of the behavior of a typical household. Census data do indicate that the average family does, in fact, move surprisingly frequently; in the United States, for example, the 1970 census indicated that only about half the families sampled were living in the same house as in 1965. However, the vast majority of these moves are surely not motivated primarily by fiscal considerations; they are the result of a change in the location of employment or, perhaps, in family status. Whatever the motivation for the move, once the individual begins to survey the available alternatives, he can take into account the levels of local public services, particularly the quality of local schools and the degree of public safety. For an individual working in a central city, there typically exists a wide range of potential residential communities within the suburbs, and when choosing among these communities, he can be expected to devote significant attention to such things as the reputation of the local public school system.

The mobility model may thus provide a reasonable approximation to behavior *within metropolitan areas.* There is, moreover, a growing empirical literature whose findings are consistent with this view. However, the case for the mobility model is much weaker in a regional context; the constraint imposed by place of employment is probably sufficient in most cases to restrict the scope of choice among residential communities to a single metropolitan area (or even part of that area).

The Measurement of the Welfare Gains from Decentralized Public Choice

The economic rationale for a federal system is to be found in the capacity of decentralized government units to improve resource allocation in the public sector through the diversification of public outputs in accordance with local tastes. This, of course, has long been recognized. A more difficult and intriguing question is the order of magnitude of the economic gains to be realized from such diversification. How much is the decentralized provision of public outputs worth?

There is, in principle at least, a straightforward way to answer this question:

the measurement of the increase in consumers' surplus associated with varying levels of local public services. Let us suppose, for purposes of illustration, that we can divide the population in two groups, within each of which the demand for a particular public output is the same for all persons. In terms of Figure 1-1, each of the people in group 1 possesses a demand of D_1, while the demand curve for those in group 2 is D_2. Assuming that the public service can be provided at constant cost per head,[4] the desired level of consumption of people in group 1 is Q_1, and that of group 2 individuals is Q_2.

The spirit of the centralized solution to the provision of the public service is a standardized level of the service to everyone. In Figure 1-1 suppose that this uniform output is a compromise between the higher and lower demands at, say, Q_c. The welfare loss to each group 1 person is then simply the shaded triangle ABC, which represents the excess of costs to each person over his valuation of the "excessive" units of consumption. Similarly, there is a welfare loss to each group 2 individual equal to the shaded triangle CDE (in this case, the excess of marginal valuation over cost for the "lost" units of consumption.)[5]

Two points regarding Figure 1-1 are worthy of note. First, the extent of the welfare loss from centralized provision is obviously critically dependent on the variation in individual demands; if Q_1 and Q_2 were quite close, then Q_c could provide a close approximation to the most desired outputs for all individuals

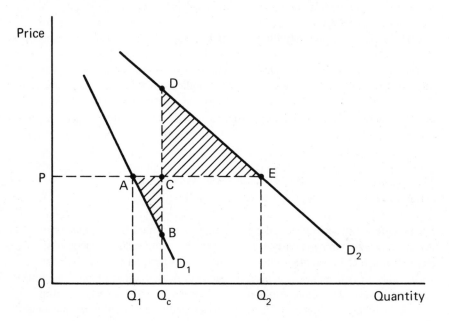

Figure 1-1. Welfare Losses from Centralization

with little resulting loss in consumer surplus. Second, note that the magnitude of the loss in consumer surplus varies inversely with the price elasticity of demand. The steeper the demand curves in Figure 1-1, the larger will be the area of the shaded triangles (which reflects the more rapid decline in the marginal valuation of additional units of consumption for group 1 persons or the increased marginal valuation of lost units for group 2 individuals).[6] The loss in welfare from imposing a uniform level of consumption of a public service over all jurisdictions will, therefore, depend on the extent of the variation in the most desired quantity among the localities and on the price elasticities of individual demands.

While this analysis suggests a direct way to measure the gains from diversified local outputs, it is not an easy matter to implement the technique for a number of reasons (not the least of which are the difficulties in measuring units of public output and in obtaining reliable estimates of individual demand functions). One recent illustrative attempt by Bradford and Oates (1974) generated an estimate of the welfare loss from imposing a standardized level of expenditure per pupil in all school districts in northeastern New Jersey. Assuming that each family was located in a municipality providing the family's most desired school budget, Bradford and Oates estimated a multiplicative demand function for school expenditures and then used this function to calculate the loss in consumer surplus resulting from the introduction of a hypothetical uniform level of spending equal simply to the existing average expenditure per pupil.[7] The computations indicated a substantial welfare loss from the hypothetical centralization of school spending: for a dollar transferred from a high-expenditure school district to a lower-spending district, the loss in consumer surplus was, *on average,* about 50 cents. Moreover, estimates of the price elasticity of demand for other local public services by Bergstrom and Goodman (1973) are typically quite low (on the order of –0.2), which suggests that welfare losses from uniform consumption may well be considerable.

Boss (1974) has recently presented an alternative, and extremely intriguing, approach to the measurement of the value of decentralized choice. Boss studied a fiscal-reform referendum to centralize the financing of local schools in Oregon. In brief, the proposal would have entailed the standardizing of school operating budgets on a statewide basis to replace existing local budget determination. The program also involved a radical shift away from local property taxation to statewide business and individual income taxation. The tax proposal was such that an estimated 85 percent of the taxpayers in Oregon would have enjoyed a net decrease in their tax payments. However; 58 percent of the voters going to the polls rejected the plan. Boss analyzed the referendum results on a county-by-county basis: for each county he calculated the median tax change and then used this to estimate a predicted "yes" vote. Interestingly, the predicted vote exhibited a high correlation with the actual vote, which suggests that the voters in Oregon did respond systematically to net tax gains. However, the predicted "yes" vote consistently exceeded the true vote (on average, by some 42 percent); Oregon voters apparently placed a positive value on local fiscal control. Boss went on to estimate this valuation and found that a voter typically would have required compensation on the order of $150 for the loss of local budget determination for schools.

While all these calculations are hedged by critical assumptions and qualifications, they do at least suggest that people attach some economic value to local fiscal choice and that the measurement of this valuation may not be a wholly intractable problem. This implies, moreover, that attempts to impose centrally determined uniform levels of public outputs can be expected to encounter opposition, not only of a formal political sort but also in terms of individual behavior seeking either private sources of services or alternative ways to obtain desired levels of outputs.[8]

II. Fiscal Equity in a Federal System

In the discussion of the mobility model, we examined some existing conflicts between economic efficiency and equity in the provision of local services. At a policy level, matters of fiscal equity have, in fact, weighed very heavily in the formulation of budgetary programs. Most countries rely, to a greater or lesser extent, on equalizing intergovernmental grants to compensate for perceived geographical inequities. These grants typically incorporate variables to reflect need and fiscal capacity in an attempt to reduce the differences among localities in their ability to provide acceptable levels of public outputs. A district, for example, with an abnormally large fraction of its population in the school-age years and with a relatively small tax base will typically receive more grant assistance per capita than a jurisdiction in a more favorable fiscal position. In this section, I want to examine further some of these issues of fiscal equity.

Horizontal Equity in a Federal System

The principle that people in equal positions should be treated equally is one of the traditional canons of equitable taxation. However, Buchanan (1950) pointed out some years ago that decentralized finance is likely to violate this principle. Since the size of the tax base per capita will vary from one jurisdiction to the next, it follows that different tax rates will be required to raise the same amount of revenue per head. A resident of a locality with a relatively large tax base will thus face a lower tax rate and have a lower tax bill than his counterpart in a district with a smaller tax base. Buchanan concluded that the central government could introduce either a geographically discriminating income tax or, preferably, a set of unconditional grants to local governments to restore the equal treatment of equals.

There is one important assumption implicit in all this: the absence of significant consumer mobility. If we pose this problem in terms of the mobility model, we find that it resolves itself. Suppose, for example, that one jurisdiction possesses a notable fiscal advantage over the others; this could take the form of a relatively large tax base or, alternatively, superior efficiency in the provision of a public output (such as the lower cost of maintaining clean air in a town located on a hill). In an environment of mobile individuals, the value of such differences will be capitalized into local property values. Consumers will bid for places in the fiscally advantaged community until the increased price of property exactly offsets the fiscal gain. Mobility thus ensures that equals will be treated equally, for whatever fiscal advantages are enjoyed will be paid for in the form of a higher actual (or imputed) rent. In the mobility model, horizontal equity is self-policing.

This suggests that significant horizontal inequities should be ironed out by market forces within the metropolitan economy. This may not be true, however, at the regional level, where the mobility model appears less applicable. Here the obstacles to mobility may permit unequal treatment of equals to persist. Such unequal treatment has provided some of the motivation for equalizing intergovernmental grants in many countries. If one examines the constitutions or basic legislation authorizing these grant programs, there typically appears some reference to assistance that allows all jurisdictions to provide an adequate level of services by an effort not appreciably different from the others. *Effort* in this sense is often interpreted to refer to the fraction of income paid in taxes. The basic idea seems to be that, if local services were financed through proportional taxation of income, then all jurisdictions *ought* to be able to provide some specified and adequate level of services with (roughly) the same tax rate.

Minimum Service Levels

The second major objective of many of these grant programs is to ensure the provision of certain minimally acceptable levels of public outputs in all localities. The economic rationalization for this objective is not wholly clear. It seems, however, to draw to some extent on both efficiency and equity arguments. On the efficiency side one can argue that many of these services have substantial spillover effects; it is in my interest, for example, that all residents of the country attain a basic proficiency in reading and writing. Moreover, as mentioned earlier, guaranteed service levels can have an option value in that I may find it desirable at some future date to reside in another community (although the force of this argument is blunted if there exists a wide choice among local jurisdictions).

In terms of equity, the basic notion seems to be that everyone should be assured a certain minimum level of public services; to deprive an individual of adequate schooling opportunities or safety is to do him an injustice. This is typically interpreted to mean that all localities should provide at least certain prescribed minimum levels of services.

While a society may deem such minimum service levels an explicit objective of economic and social policy, the curious part is that, in many countries, this objective has been pursued through the use of essentially lump-sum grants. Such grants may serve to equalize the fiscal capacity to provide such services, but they certainly do not ensure the attainment of the minimum level of public outputs. This requires further measures prescribing standards with which the localities must comply. Here again we find a basic source of tension in a federal system between economic efficiency, on the one hand, and equity considerations, on the other: efficiency points in the direction of a wide scope for decentralized choice in the public sector, while the desire to guarantee adequate service levels in all jurisdictions motivates centrally imposed constraints on local fiscal behavior.

Vertical Equity in a Federal System

We noted in the introduction that the primary responsibility for the redistribution of income must lie with the central government. The point I want to add here is simply that such redistribution is best accomplished by central-government taxation and transfers directly to individuals, not indirectly by intergovernmental grants. The obvious problem is that such grants represent transfers from one group of people to another, whereas a just distribution of income is normally defined over individuals. If, for example, the central government attempts to redistribute income from rich to poor by transferring funds to the governments of poorer jurisdictions, it is bound to find itself engaging in some perverse transfers, because there will no doubt be at least a few low-income individuals in the wealthy locality and some high-income persons in the poorer jurisdiction. Equalizing intergovernmental grants are not an adequate substitute for a nationwide negative income tax.

III. Public Revenues in a Federal System

In the concluding section I want to explore the subjects of taxation and revenue sharing in a federal system. The problems of the efficiency and incidence of a tax are typically a good deal more complicated at the local than at the national level because of the effects of the tax on the interjurisdictional flows of commodities and factors of production. Moreover, these flows impose certain types of constraints on local taxation that may not exist for the central government.

We have already noted the inability of a local government to employ strongly redistributive tax measures because of the resulting outmigration of the heavily taxed individuals. To the extent that we desire significantly progressive taxation, we must look primarily to the central government. Moreover, with a little ingenuity local governments may be able to shift a substantial portion of their tax burdens onto residents of other jurisdictions. The taxation of certain locally produced goods may, for example, be largely borne in the form of higher prices paid by outsiders. One particular favorite is the heavy taxation of tourists with excise taxes on hotel and restaurant bills and on other services to finance a major portion of the local budget. This "exporting" of local taxes appears not to be a trivial phenomenon: McLure (1967) has estimated that in the United States approximately 20 to 25 percent of state taxes are shifted onto the residents of other states.

In addition to these issues of incidence, local taxation has a relatively high potential for the distortion of patterns of resource use. The supply of capital, for example, *may* be quite price inelastic for the country as a whole, so that national taxation of capital will involve only minor deadweight losses. In contrast, the supply of capital to a single local jurisdiction is likely to be highly elastic; the same tax at the local level will divert units of capital elsewhere where they have a lower marginal product. Another interesting example involves heavy reliance on local sales taxes. To the extent that one jurisdiction pushes its tax rate above that of neighboring localities, it creates an incentive for consumers to waste the additional time and resources to travel elsewhere to purchase items available locally. There is, in fact, some evidence for the United States suggesting that even relatively small differentials in local sales-tax rates have had noticeable effects on the geographical purchasing patterns of consumers.[9]

What all this suggests is that the design of an efficient and equitable system of local taxation is an extremely demanding task. In particular, we may expect the usual sorts of income and commodity taxes to generate greater deadweight losses per unit of revenues at the local than the national level and, in addition, to induce certain anomalies in incidence through such things as tax exporting.[10]

The central government, largely free from some of these constraints, has distinct advantages in the field of taxation. Besides the capacity for a more progressive revenue structure and the avoidance of certain deadweight losses because of national uniformity, centralized taxation typically results in some cost savings from economies of scale in tax administration. In the United States, for instance, the administrative costs of the federal individual income tax amount to only about one-half of 1 percent of revenues. In contrast, at the state level these costs for income or sales taxation are roughly 1 to 2 percent of tax receipts [Pechman (1971, p. 53), Maxwell (1969, p. 102)].

Revenue Sharing

One way to realize some of these advantages of centralized taxation without relinquishing local expenditure authority is through revenue sharing: the central government can effectively act as a tax-collection agent for local governments. From this perspective revenue sharing is best seen as a substitution of centrally raised tax receipts for local revenues. The national revenue authority simply collects a prescribed level of taxes, which it then distributes in the form of lump-sum grants to local governments. It is important, however, that local authorities continue to raise some significant portion of their own revenues, for *at the margin*, fiscally responsible local choice requires that each community finance its own expenditures.

The popular case for revenue sharing has, however, taken a rather different tack; it has stressed the so-called fiscal mismatch between central and local governments. This argument focuses on the constraints on local budgets imposed by the relative income inelasticity of their tax systems. Because of growing demands for local services and their rising relative costs, the expansion in local spending necessary to keep pace with the growth in demand for public outputs is more than proportionate to the growth in income. However, most local revenue systems exhibit an income elasticity not much in excess of unity, so that revenue needs expand more rapidly than actual receipts at existing tax rates. The result is the persistent recurrence of a "revenue gap," with the implication that political obstacles to raising tax rates or instituting new taxes result in a systematic underprovision of public services.

Heller (1966, p. 118) made this point quite eloquently in the United States during the 1960s:

At the Federal level, economic growth and a powerful tax system, interacting under modern fiscal management, generate new revenues faster than they generate new demands on the Federal purse. But at the state-local level, the situation is reversed. Under the whiplash of prosperity, responsibilities are outstripping revenues.

From this vantage point, the appeal of revenue sharing is that it puts the highly elastic central revenue system at the disposal of local government: it matches growth in expenditure needs with an automatic growth in revenues and thereby moderates the revenue gaps and associated fiscal crises besetting local governments.

The difficulty with this argument is that its premise implies some rather strange behavior on the part of the taxpayer-voters. We normally assume that an individual's demand for public services (as for other commodities) depends on his tastes, his level of income, and the cost (here, a tax-price) to him of these services. There is no reason, in principle, to think that an individual's demand for public outputs is a function of the income elasticity of the revenue system. But this is what the fiscal-mismatch argument seems to imply: people will support increases in the public budget if they can be funded without increases in tax rates (that is, from increments to revenues resulting solely from growth in income), but they will not support this same budgetary expansion if it requires a rise in tax rates. In brief, the implication is that what people care about is not their tax *bill* but rather their tax *rate*. From this perspective, the argument simply is not consistent with our usual models of rational consumer behavior; instead, it implies the presence of a form of fiscal illusion.

The proposition is, however, an empirical one: Does a higher income elasticity of the tax structure result in a more rapid expansion over time in the public budget? To test this hypothesis, I have examined the growth in state and local budgets in the United States over the decade of the 1960s, a period of extraordinary budgetary increases, to see if those states and cities with relatively income-inelastic tax systems experienced comparatively small rises in expenditure. The approach was to take two samples (one consisting of the 48 coterminous states and the other of 33 large central cities) in which, after controlling for the effect of other explanatory variables by multiple-regression analysis, I examined the partial association between the growth in expenditure per capita over the decade 1960–1970 and a proxy variable for the income elasticity of the state's (or city's) revenue system [For a detailed description of the approach and findings, see Oates (1975)].

The findings showed a statistically significant positive coefficient on the tax variable (at a 0.05 level of significance), providing support for the hypothesis that the income elasticity of the tax structure does have some effect on the growth in the public budget. However, the magnitude of the estimated effect was not very large. Among the states, for example, the estimated coefficient indicates that a state government that generated 35 percent of its revenues through individual income taxes would, other things equal, have experienced an expansion in spending per capita over the period 1960–1970 of roughly $35 more than a state that relied wholly on sales and excise taxes. However, this compares to a mean increase in state expenditure per capita of $228 for the decade. It would be difficult, in my judgment, to regard this as a large effect, hardly of sufficient size to justify major fiscal reform.

If, as I am inclined to believe, the effect of revenue sharing on the size of local public budgets is quite modest, then the appropriate perspective on revenue sharing is to regard it as a substitution of central taxation for locally raised revenues. To evaluate the merits of the program, we must then look to the altered pattern of incidence, possible reductions in deadweight losses, and the cost savings from administering a more centralized system of taxation.

Finally, there is one further aspect of revenue sharing on which a "narrow" economic view may be less than adequate. An implicit assumption in the analysis is that the central government can act as a tax collector for local governments without impairing the local-expenditure prerogative. So long as the transfers of funds to local governments are truly of a lump-sum form, there is no reason in principle why the recipient should feel any constraints as to how he employs these resources. This, however, is no doubt rather naïve; so long as the central government is a major supplier of local funds, political realities can be expected to induce the central government to use this leverage to achieve some of its own objectives. In the United Kingdom, for example, central-government grants (primarily of a lump-sum form) now account for approximately two-thirds of local authority revenues, and this has given rise to widespread concern over the erosion of local autonomy and has generated renewed interest in additional sources of tax revenues at the local level. Important as it may be, this particular dimension of revenue sharing is difficult to incorporate into a purely economic analysis.

My objective in this chapter has been to provide an overview of the *economics* of fiscal federalism. I have tried to develop the implications of the basic principles of economics for the functioning of a multilevel public sector. Such an approach does generate a variety of insights which are useful for the analysis of public budgetary policy. But, as I have tried to emphasize at several points, it is difficult to cast the analytic net sufficiently wide to capture all the salient aspects of fiscal programs like revenue sharing. Moreover, the economic logic sometimes points in directions that can be quite discomforting in terms of their social implications. Nevertheless, in so doing, it often reveals certain basic tendencies in the system (toward, for example, segregation by income) with which public policy must come to terms irrespective of its goals.

Notes

1. For a useful survey of this literature, see Whitman (1970).

2. Pauly (1973) has argued that there may be a modest role for local redistributive policies.

3. This discussion draws on Bradford and Oates (1974).

4. If there are cost savings from joint consumption in larger groups, these must, of course, be weighed off against the gains in consumer surplus from more diversified consumption.

5. For an algebraic treatment of the measurement of these consumer surpluses, see Barzel (1969); for a summary of Barzel's analysis, see Oates (1972, pp. 59–63).

6. It is interesting that this is precisely the reverse of the case of the excess burden resulting from distorting taxes. In partial-equilibrium terms, the excess burden generated by an excise tax varies directly with the price elasticity of demand. The source of this difference is that under tax analysis we are varying price and are thus moving along the vertical axis in Figure 1–1, while for the problem here we are altering quantity on the horizontal axis.

7. This calculation ignores any spillover effects associated with education.

8. As one possible illustration, the elimination of the selective grammar schools in the United Kingdom may encourage residential patterns of the Tiebout type as a means to control the quality of neighborhood schools.

9. In a study of sales taxation in New York City, Hamovitch (1966) estimated that increases in the city's sales tax rate of 1 percentage point had led on past occasions to declines of about 6 percent in taxable sales. Likewise, a cross-sectional econometric study of 173 U.S. metropolitan areas by Mikesell (1970) revealed that an increase of 1 percentage point in the differential between city and suburban sales taxes is associated on average with approximately a 7 percent reduction in retail sales in the central city.

10. Some qualifications are in order. We noted earlier, for example, that in the mobility model, with the appropriate use of local zoning ordinances, local property taxation *can* be perfectly efficient. In addition, a heavier reliance on local land taxation appears to offer considerable potential for reducing the distorting effects of local taxes.

11. It is possible to try to rationalize this fiscal illusion in a kind of Downsian model of rational political ignorance [see Oates (1975)].

References

Barzel, Y. 1969. Two propositions on the optimum level of producing collective goods. *Public Choice* 6:31–37.

Bergstrom, T., and Goodman, R. 1973, Private demands for public goods. *American Economic Review* 63:280–296.

Boss, M. 1974. Economic theory of democracy: An empirical test. *Public Choice* 19:111–115.

Bradford, D., and Oates, W. 1974. Suburban exploitation of central cities and governmental structure. In *Redistribution through Public Choice,* H. Hochman and G. Peterson, eds. Columbia University Press, pp. 43–90.

Breton, A. 1965. A theory of government grants. *Canadian Journal of Economics and Political Science* 31:175–187.

Buchanan, J. 1950. Federalism and fiscal equity. *American Economic Review* 40:583–599.

Buchanan, J., and Goetz, C. 1972. Efficiency limits of fiscal mobility: An assessment of the Tiebout model. *Journal of Public Economics* 1:25–44.

Hamilton, B. 1975. Zoning and property taxation in a system of local governments. *Urban Studies* 12:205–211.

Hamovitch, W. 1966. Effects of increases in sales tax rates on taxable sales in New York City. In *Research Report of the Graduate School in Public Administration, New York University, Financing Government in New York City.* New York: New York University, pp. 619–633.

Heller, W. 1966. *New Dimensions of Political Economy.* Cambridge, Mass.: Harvard University Press.

Livingston, W. 1952. A note on the nature of federalism. *Political Science Quarterly* 67:81–95.

McLure, C. 1967. The interstate exporting of state and local taxes: Estimates for 1962. *National Tax Journal* 20:49–77.

Maxwell, J. 1969. *Financing State and Local Governments*, rev. ed. Washington, D.C.: The Brookings Institution.

Mikesell, J. 1970. Central cities and sales tax differentials: The border city problem. *National Tax Journal* 23:206–213.

Oates, W. 1972. *Fiscal Federalism.* New York: Harcourt Brace Jovanovich.

Oates, W. 1975. Automatic increases in tax revenues: The effect on the size of the public budget. In *Financing the New Federalism: Revenue Sharing, Conditional Grants, and Taxation*, W. Oates, ed. Baltimore: Johns Hopkins Press. pp. 139–160.

Pauly, M. 1973. Income redistribution as a local public good. *Journal of Public Economics* 2:35–58.

Pechman, J. 1971. *Federal Tax Policy*, rev. ed. Washington, D.C.: The Brookings Institution.

Schuler, R. 1974. The interaction between local government and urban residential location. *American Economic Review* 64:682–696.

Tiebout, C. 1956. A pure theory of local expenditures. *Journal of Political Economy* 64:416–424.

Whitman, M. Von N., 1970. Policies for internal and external balance. *Princeton Studies in International Finance* 9. Princeton, N.J.: Princeton University Press.

2

A Political Scientist's View of Fiscal Federalism

Samuel H. Beer

In recent years, the economist's tools of analysis have been widely applied to the study of politics and government. Various terms have been used to indicate this approach, such as *public choice theory* and *theory of collective action*, but probably the most favored is *political economy.* One of the subjects on which political economy has shed much light is the distribution of decision-making power among levels of government. The task of this chapter is to present a critique of what political economy has to say about this ancient problem of political science. As a political scientist, I will assuredly not try to instruct economists in the meaning of the basic conceptual tools of their trade. But it may be useful to economists to see (1) how a political scientist uses those tools and what questions he thinks they can help him answer and (2) at what points he feels impelled to raise doubts about the adequacy of this approach and to call on other resources of political science as helps toward explanation and prescription. The thrust of my argument is that although the economist's approach has greatly illuminated the subject of territorial centralization and decentralization, it suffers from inherent limitations that prevent it from coping adequately with major aspects of the subject.

Obviously, the subject I have taken goes beyond the scope indicated by my assigned title. Before turning to the substance of my argument, therefore, I must explain why I believe that the concept of fiscal federalism has, so to speak, burst its bonds and raised these larger and more important questions.

As Oates recognizes in Chapter 1 of this book, his use of the term *federalism* gives it a much broader meaning than that usually employed by political scientists. Not that they are agreed on a single meaning. Three hundred years of discussion of the topic have produced a multiplicity of meanings—so many indeed that one authority [Earle (1964)] can subtitle a book on federalism *Infinite Variety in Theory and Practice.* If, therefore, economists take some liberties with our terminology, we hardly dare complain.

Still, there are some points of fairly general agreement among political scientists. Usually when they say a polity is federal, they mean at least that its territorial division of powers is secured by some exceptional legal protection,

21

such as being specified in a written constitution that can be amended only by an extraordinary majority. So Benson (1961, p. 3) writes, a federal government is "a government in which the written constitution, or an inviolable statutory precedent, specifies that certain fundamental authority adheres to a central government and that other governmental authority belongs to smaller areas." Following this logic, discussions of American government usually mean by "federal" the division of power between the federal government and the state governments, the relation of the state government to its local governments being considered "unitary," since legally the latter are the creatures of the former.

For this reason, political scientists normally do not mean by federal just any decentralized polity, but on the contrary, a special kind of decentralization. Some, for instance, find in federalism a major agency of constitutionalism, contending that a federal division of power constitutes a safeguard of liberty that is missing from unitary systems because the latter can give to the decentralization of power no exceptional protection [see, Friedrich (1968, pp. 194-195)]. To say that the latter sort of system—the decentralized unitary system—has the same properties as the former—the constitutionally protected federal system—would stand on its head what these students of politics are trying to assert. In short, it is fair play for the economist to define federal just as he likes, so long as he is consistent in his usage. But it is my task modestly to warn him that he cannot then take some political scientist's conclusions about what the political scientist calls federal government and apply them to what he, the economist, calls federal government. In the usage of most political scientists, Oates is talking not about federalism but about the larger subject of multilevel government. To refer to this subject as federalism confuses the discussion for many readers.

My second and rather more complicated problem is with the term *fiscal*. I take the term to have the meaning of fiscal in the expression *fiscal policy*, i.e., "governmental tax and expenditure policies."[1] The fiscal aspect of multilevel government is obviously important. It includes such matters as the distribution of the power of taxation among levels of government, along with related questions, such as tax allocation, tax coordination, and tax equity. It includes the financial aspect of intergovernmental relations, which consist in the aid extended by one level of government to another. So conceived, multilevel finance can be treated as a separate subject of study.

Difficulties arise when such inquiry into multilevel finance is directed to problems of public policy, since many of the principal problems that are intimately related to multilevel finance cannot be confined within a purely fiscal view of their source or remedy. Consider the question of dealing with the externalities of pollution. Fiscal means can be used, of course. But a remedy might also require government action by coercive rule. One can conceive of a solution requiring a division of responsibilities between levels of government, finance coming from the national government and regulation being imposed by the subnational governments. In dealing with this problem, it would be futile to discuss only its fiscal aspects. And, in fact, my observation is that when economists are confronted by the need for a broader approach, they take it, even though they may say they are only talking about "fiscal federalism." Thus, when Oates is following out the logic of his admirable decentralization theorem, he does not exclude from his analysis the use of nonfiscal powers. For instance, in discussing how local governments might seek to stabilize the segregation solution to the movement of suburban populations, he takes up the probable use of exclusionary zoning powers. And generally, in applying the mobility model—a derivative of the decentralization theorem—to the actual behavior of metropolitan dispersion, it is clear that the public goods that will attract (or repel) citizen-consumers often consist of government action that involves no significant resource allocation but rather the control of the social milieu by regulation—for instance, with regard to such matters as school prayers, the drug culture, or crime in the street.

Similarly, when one steps back and asks what criteria should be used in determining what it is about a situation that makes it a problem, one must have difficulty accepting the limits of those traditionally central concerns of the economist—efficiency in the allocation of resources and equity in the distribution of income. Integral to the situation may be noneconomic features that are at least as important as the economic ones. The segregation solution—to continue with this example—as it actually takes shape in the settlement pattern of metropolitan areas of the United States is a problem of public policy, not only because it segregates income groups, but also, and I should say in a far more important way, because it segregates races. The equity that is violated is not just fiscal, and the social and political consequences of the situation are a good deal more dangerous than the purely economic ones.

My criticism is that the questions economists and others actually discuss under the heading of fiscal federalism have come to constitute a subject that cannot be confined within the denotation of that term. This broader subject, however, is not just another result of interdisciplinary spillover. It is not constituted merely by the fact that contemporary problems of public policy have, so to speak, added on other sorts of conditions to the fiscal and economic aspects of multilevel finance. This broader subject results rather from the application of the powerful, new methodology of political economy to the study of multilevel government in both its financial and nonfinancial aspects.

To call this subject *fiscal federalism* is to slight the contribution that economics, by means of the new political economy, has made in recent years to the study of this familiar subject of political science. The decentralization theorem itself, for example, is valid and illuminating whether the public good with which it is concerned is provided by taxing-spending measures or solely by regulation. It diverts attention from the broad merit and powerful uses of the idea to confine it to budgetary behavior and economic consequences. The political scientist is drawn into the discussion of its implications not simply because the economist's subject matter impinges on his subject matter, but rather because a method of analysis drawn from economics has shown great power in analyzing a familiar problem of his discipline. What economists and others actually talk about under the nominal heading of fiscal federalism is usually the broader and more interesting subject of the political economy of multilevel government. My task, therefore, is to present a political scientist's critique of that subject.

Rational Choice Theory

The basis of political economy, as I understand it, is the theory of rational choice. This theory is a general logic that has been applied in several fields but that has been largely developed by economists and can be most readily illustrated from economic analysis.[2] I shall first state briefly what I take the theory of rational choice to be and then try to follow out the logic of the theory in order to see what it implies for the territorial division of power.

"The major postulate of analytic theories of decision," writes Steinbrunner (1974, p. 28), "holds that decisions will be taken which maximize value (utility) given the constraints of the situation." This means in the first place that action is instrumentalist; that is, the individual thinks in terms of means and ends, allocating his scarce resources in such a way as to achieve the concrete goals that embody his values. But how does he choose among these goals which are often qualitatively different from one another? Modern economy theory rejects the old psychological hedonism that supposed that all goals sought by an individual had some common subjective property. Still, it is assumed that the individual will compare possible goals in the light of their utility to him. "As a customer you will buy a good because you feel it gives you satisfaction or 'utility,'" writes Samuelson (1970, pp. 410–414), who then goes on to show how, in a "process of rational choice," the consumer will so distribute his purchases as to achieve "maximum satisfaction or utility." The observable result of this pursuit of maximum utility is a rational, i.e., consistent, ordering of the individual's preferences among the various ways of employing his scarce means.

In seeking to maximize his utility, the individual from time to time makes decisions, i.e., conscious analytic mental operations. Each decision includes evaluation of the alternative courses of action that appear to be open in the situation. In these moments of calculation, the individual is receptive to and will seek and use all kinds of information throwing light on the most effective course of action. Ideally, he evaluates all possible courses of action in relation to all his values. Once these possibilities are surveyed and evaluated, the utility-maximizing course of action is chosen and followed out.

What the individual contributes to the process of decision is his sense of utility and his observing and calculating intelligence. To say that the individual pursues his utility by means of his intelligence is to say that only individuals feel, think, and choose. This is the postulate of methodological individualism. When two or more individuals seem to act as an entity, such collective action can be explained as the resultant of rational choice on the part of the individuals constituting the group. The action of others in a network of interpersonal relations can have a great deal of influence on what the individual does. But this influence can affect only his choice of means, not his ends. The drift is that the individual brings a pattern of fixed tastes or preferences to the marketplace of economics or politics.

Throughout the process of decision, the individual is guided by self-interest. It is *his* utility that he seeks to maximize. From this dominance of self-interest, it follows that when something is done in response to the wishes, real or presumed, of another, this has occurred because the donor thinks he is getting back more than he gave: the process is an exchange.

In sum, rational choice theory yields a model in which decision making is instrumentalist, utilitarian, periodic, open-minded, individualistic, and self-regarding. It follows that all interpersonal relations conforming to this model are relations of exchange.

The Confederal Polity

What does this model of rational decision making imply for the territorial division of powers? Oates has already drawn out some of the implications in his discussion of Tiebout's mobility model. I find nothing to disagree with in that discussion but do think there are other more radical implications that should be considered. For instance, when studying his analysis I get the feeling—perhaps because of the political scientist in me—that somewhere in the background is a very powerful central government. Who, for instance, is going to draw the boundaries of these local polities? The goal is perfect correspondence of tastes with polities in the provision of public goods. But that will surely require the creation of new local polities as well as merely movement among those which happen to exist in a particular country at a particular time.

In the spirit of Oates's decentralization theorem, I take the goal to be a correspondence of people and polities such that people with the same preferences for public services are in the same polity. If this is not the case, if some people prefer some mix not being offered by their polity, a further sorting out of people should take place to enable them to enjoy their preferred combination of benefits and costs in another polity. They would now be better off without having made anyone else worse off, and the whole society would have moved closer to a political equilibrium.

This solution can be achieved without supposing intervention by a central government and solely by the action of individuals and their democratically controlled governments, if we suppose three conditions: freedom of mobility, of partition, and of combination.

By mobility "voting with their feet," citizens would move from less to more desirable polities. But mobility alone would not take care of the individuals who were displeased with all the choices made available by existing local polities. To deal with this, the boundaries of the polities themselves must be subject to rational choice. This requirement implies freedom to partition; that is, that a dissatisfied group be able to secede in whole or in part from its polity and set up a new government to provide the service it prefers. Likewise, of course, there must be freedom of combination, so that the various local polities shall be able to provide for the services desired by a wider body of citizens.

Looking only at the local polities for the moment, it appears that mobility and partition will ultimately confer an extraordinary benefit upon each polity. We assume that these polities are democratically governed, i.e., on the basis of one man one vote with majority rule. But majority rule is a very poor way of maximizing utility among people who disagree. It means at least that the interests of the minority will be frustrated. Over a period of time, logrolling may offset this disadvantage. But freedom of partition opens another solution, since now the minority can secede with regard to its frustrated interests and provide for their satisfaction under a new government while, of course, also remaining under the old government with regard to those services on which they agree with its other members. Ultimately, each polity is homogeneous in its wishes, and its government's actions represent not majority rule but the rule of unanimity. The useful and interesting implication for the real world is that although we need hardly expect unanimity to be within human reach, the freedoms to move to and to create new polities corresponding to different preferences promise a substantial reduction in conflict and frustration.

In a contemporary social and economic context, such a process no doubt would lead to very considerable governmental fragmentation. In terms of rational choice theory, however, far from being a disadvantage, fragmentation performs useful functions.[3] It does not attempt to suppress conflict by such means as adjudication, i.e., subjecting the parties to some coercive rule derived from the legal system, constitution, or normative order. Rather, it eliminates conflict by enabling the parties to separate, so that each gets its way. In the respective polities and generally in the resulting political system thoroughgoing responsiveness reigns.

Except in some segmented Jeffersonian utopia, such local polities will confront external problems. This possibility, however, implies no need for hierarchical intervention from above but can be left to the local polities for recognition and remedy. Where a number of local governments are producing negative spillovers, e.g., pollution from their wastewater systems, a logical solution might well be to create a special district to cope with this harmful side effect. Where the spillover is positive, e.g., education, it might make sense for the beneficiary polities to create a school district through which they could extend "optimizing grants" to their respective school systems.[4] Similarly, such rational actors can be trusted to centralize services that can be more cheaply performed on a larger scale by a more inclusive jurisdiction.

This brief sketch is enough to show that the theory of rational choice has substantial and useful implications for political science and, specifically, for both the positive and the normative analysis of the problem of the territorial distribution of power. In a modern social and economic context, a polity so designed would surely be decentralized. It would also have other traits. It would tend to be very complex and highly fragmented territorially and functionally, its levels linked not hierarchically by command but coordinately by exchange. It would also be very flexible, indeed flexible to the point of continual change, as periodic comprehensive calculations of utility led to new combinations by polities and new partitions by their citizens in the search for a better all-round balance of welfare. In all these traits—responsiveness, fragmentation, specialization, contractual relations, and continual change—it resembles the model of the economic free market, which, like it, also derives from the theory of rational choice. As for a name, so loose and flexible a polity might appropriately be called *confederal*, meaning separate polities linked solely by compact.

The Suburban Phenomenon

Rational-choice theory can be widely used in the study of multilevel government.[5] In the previous sketch of the confederal polity, I have deliberately narrowed its focus in order to complement Oates's discussion. This focus also makes it easier to bring the theory to the test of fact by suggesting its applicability to the political development of metropolitan areas in the United States since World War II. Considering the usual fate of models, its predictions do not fare badly when set alongside the suburban phenomenon.

The rise of the suburbs has constituted a vast movement of decentralization. The new urban pattern is not only decentralized, it is also highly differentiated. The earlier observation that suburbs were uniformly made up of the same sort of middle-class people soon gave way to the perception that suburbs are economically and socially specialized. As Williams (1971, p. 98) has remarked: "There is a place for the young, the old; the rich, the poor; the Catholic, the bigoted, and the broadminded. There hardly exists a municipality which is a true sample of the greater metropolitan area." As the central cities thin out and lose population and their old heterogeneity, the characteristics of the suburb tend to become the dominant urban form.

In trying to explain these phenomena, some observers argued that the migrants were merely looking for better housing. The weight of research has shown, however, that houses are valued not only for their intrinsic qualities but also and especially as a means of access to a certain social and economic milieu. The suburbanites were, so to speak, shopping for a certain type of community. A crucial feature in the metropolitan area is that these specialized territorial clusters coincide with local polities, fully equipped with the powers of self-government. As Oates has observed, the local polities use their legal powers over zoning, housing, and taxation to screen migrants and thus to modify the purely free-market effects of community shopping. One result is the income segregation on which Oates comments and which appears to have increased markedly in the 1960s [see Williams (1975, especially p. 23, Table II)]. In this manner, the metropolitan area is an arena of conflict in which its constituent polities use their powers to defend and forward various interests of their residents. They discharge not only internal functions for their citizens but also external functions toward the outside world. While peaceful to the point of unanimity within, they turn a more anxious eye on the surrounding world. With some exaggeration, but also some truth, their behavior has been compared with that of sovereign states in the international arena [Holden (1964)].

These urban units not only take part in political conflict, they may also issue from it. Their new residents, of course, have sometimes moved from localities where they have been politically frustrated in their efforts to create the services and milieu they prefer. But also an entirely new jurisdiction can result from such a mismatch of preferences and power. As areas within a county become urbanized, they will normally come to want city-type services. If the county cannot or will not provide them, the urbanizing area may create its own vehicle of local services by incorporating as a new municipality. This step may take place by anticipation. Where a central city has the power of annexation, urbanizing areas on its fringes sometimes incorporate in order to avoid being absorbed. With regard to many new suburbs formed around such expanding cities, one authority [Williams (1971, p. 81)] observes that most represented "substantial efforts to create islands of municipal dissent."

A rather different rationale motivates the new incorporation that results when a business firm arranges to have the area in its immediate vicinity set up as a separate jurisdiction. In this case, the purpose is the avoidance of the heavier tax burden that would fall on the firm if it remained part of the larger local government unit which surrounds it—and from which it may well draw much of its work force. Such "phantom" incorporations for industrial and commercial reasons have long been familiar from Massachusetts to California.

In any case, whether for personal or business reasons, the immense diffusion of population among the suburbs of metropolitan areas after World War II was accomplished not only by a movement among existing local polities but also by the partition of existing polities and the creation of new ones. As Table 2-1 shows, between 1952 and 1962, when the surge to the suburbs crested, the number of municipalities increased at twice the rate that prevailed during the decade before or after.

The question of what functions these burgeoning local polities have chosen to reserve for their control is crucial for understanding the motivation of the

Table 2-1
Increase in Number of Municipalities 1942–1972

	Number of Municipalities	Increase During Previous Decade
1972	18,517	520
1962	17,997	1,219
1952	16,778	558
1942	16,220	—

Source: U.S. Bureau of the Census, *Census of Governments: 1972*, Vol. 1, *Governmental Organization* 1962, Vol. 1, *Governmental Organization; Historical Statistics of the United States: Colonial Times to 1957*, Washington, D.C. 1960, p. 694.

suburban movement and the territorial division of powers it tends to produce. Williams (1971, chap. 6) has illuminated the rationale with his distinction between life-style services and system-maintenance services. *Life style* applies to business units as well as households, but its meaning is most easily seen in relation to housing. Residential location gives access to certain neighbors, classified in various ways by ethnicity, income, social class, and so on. Preferences with regard to such social access in great part motivate choice of location and constitute a sphere over which exclusive control is accordingly sought. Education is a prime example, since it determines with what sort of children one's offspring will associate and be socialized. For similar reasons, libraries, recreational programs, cultural programs, and aspects of police and health programs acquire importance. Nor is this rationale confined to suburbs. Intracity decentralization also focuses on devolving similar functions on neighborhoods in the form of community control.

The life-style values are the principal motor from which the decentralizing movement gets its thrust. System-maintenance services, on the other hand, are the means to these ends. In themselves neutral with regard to life-style values, they are the services needed to make this highly interdependent system of specialized areas work. Transportation systems, meaning primarily roads and highways, are an obvious example. But water-supply and sewage-disposal systems and utilities perform similar functions, leading to interlocal centralized agencies.

In the provision of system-maintenance services, externalities and economies of scale often draw local polities into wider combinations. It is common for suburbs to purchase services, such as water or sanitation, from the county in which they are located or from a neighboring central city. A favored means of combination is the special district in which adjoining polities combine, usually to provide only a single specialized service, such as highways, mass transit, or wastewater management. Between 1942 and 1972, the number of special districts rose from 8,299 to 23,885.[6] Although the special district has other uses, this immense growth is to a considerable degree accounted for by its use in providing such interlocal centralized agencies in metropolitan areas.

The distinction between life-style and system-maintenance services is not identical with the distinction between services with internal and services with external effects. Yet the externalities of the system-maintenance services are surely more physical, more measurable, more easily isolated and identified and therefore more controllable than those of the life-style services, with their less tangible and more purely social externalities. As Oates remarks in the preceding chapter, it is hard to determine "just what the geographical range of *significant* benefits is for functions like education and police services." In this respect, there are technical reasons for centralizing the former more readily than the latter. But surely it is the high valuation given to life-style services that has been primarily responsible for the jealousy with which the suburbs have guarded their autonomy. A major expression has been their strong resistance to consolidation under metropolitan governments that would subject them to the majorities of heterogeneous populations. Since World War II, the number of metropolitan areas has greatly increased, reaching 263 by 1973. Yet in spite of many efforts, only some half-dozen or so have acquired areawide, general-purpose governments.

The political development of metropolitan areas in the United States since World War II has led to a pattern of settlement and governance in which the diversity of life styles embodied in the different communities and sustained by supportive public services represents, in a rough and ready way, a diversity of tastes and preferences among residents. The confederal polity model derived from rational choice theory and based on freedom of mobility, partition, and combination goes a long way to show what has happened and why it has happened. For this contribution to his discipline, the political scientist can only thank economics and economists.

Critique of the Confederal Polity

Crucial problems of contemporary American government and politics, however, quite escape the comprehension of rational choice theory. One is the technocracy problem. I use this slightly apocalyptic term *technocracy* in order to give emphasis to new traits developed in recent years by the bureaucratic elements of our political system—and of the political systems of advanced countries generally. These new traits of the bureaucratic component derive from what Mosher (1968, p. 105) calls the rise of "government by professionals," which he dates from the mid-1950s. The influence of science and professional knowledge on public policy and public servants goes back to the early days of the modern state in America and Europe. It is the vastly increased rate of growth of specialized sciences and fields of technology that has given "professional specialisms" their great and increasing influence on policy making during the past generation.

One aspect of this technocratic tendency has been a marked shift of initiative and influence from the private sector of politics—voters, pressure groups, and parties—to the public sector—government itself and its associated cadres of consultants. The growing complexity of the knowledge that is used in attempts to identify and solve current problems has meant a greater role for the expert in these tasks. With this shift of initiative and influence from the private to the public sector, there tends to be a reversal of the flow of power; often, instead of the lobby creating the program, it is the program that creates the lobby. Hence, the justifiable fear of government by professional and the concern to find some way to strengthen control by the voter.

Likewise troubling to some observers is the effect of the new professionalism upon multilevel government. In the fields of health, housing, urban renewal, highways, environment, welfare, education, and poverty, the federal government has drawn heavily upon specialized and technical knowledge in and around the bureaucracy for the conception and execution of new programs. For the most part, moreover, it has not administered these programs directly but rather has used conditional grants to secure the services of state and local governments for their administration. The centralizing influence that results, however, consists not only of the federal "strings" attached to the money. The greater presence of scientifically and professionally trained civil servants at all levels of government also tends to create strong vertical connections between bureaucratic cadres in specialized functional fields, which have their own ideas of what programs should be adopted and how they should be carried out. These new centralizing influences have had enough effect to give rise to a new term, *functional federalism*, to describe the new system of intergovernmental relationships. Nor has this change been recorded only with academic neutrality. From many mayors, governors, county supervisors—the generalists of state and local government—complaints have risen against the influence and the recalcitrance of narrow bureaucratic functionalists, who with no more than the usual hyperbole of American political rhetoric have been chastized as "balkanized bureaucracies," "vertical functional autocracies," and "feudal functional federalisms" [Wright (1972)].

Professionalism means the formation of an occupational skill by general concepts. The knowledge of the professional, as of the scientist, is theoretical. That is, it can be applied generally to similar problems wherever and whenever they exist. What the professional brings to government, therefore, is not just an interest in a specific problem at a certain time and place, but rather a preparation to deal with all such problems. His professional equipment directs him to work through and enlist the initiative of the widest possible jurisdiction. John Stuart Mill put the matter this way in a letter to De Tocqueville in 1835:

Up to now centralization has been the thing most foreign to the English temperament. Our habits or the nature of our temperament do not in the least draw us toward general ideas; but centralization is based on general ideas; that is, the desire for power to attend, in a uniform and general way, to the present and future needs of society [quoted in Maude (1966)].

A present-day view echoes this same analysis:

Professionals profess. They profess to know better than others the nature of certain matters, and to know better than their clients what ails them or their affairs . . . . Physicians consider it their prerogative to define the nature of disease and of health, and to determine how medical services ought to be distributed and paid for. Social workers are not content to develop a technique of case work; they concern themselves with social legislation. Every profession considers itself the proper body to set the terms in which some aspect of society, life or nature is to be thought of, and to define the general lines, or even the details, of public policy concerning it [Hughes (1963)].

There are two elements in this analysis of the centralizing, technocratic tendencies of professionalism. First, the generality of the professional's knowledge prepares him to apply his discipline to the wider public. The existence and use of such knowledge—general, scientific, widely applicable—is in no way foreign to rational choice theory. On the contrary, the information that the utility maximizer uses during his periodic reconsiderations is not just data but also presumably includes generalizations empirically founded. The Benthamite and Baconian background of this conception of mind assures its harmony with the scientific spirit. There is, however, also a second element, a value element, which endows the professional with the desire, indeed the obligation, to use his knowledge for the public. It is this crucial element of professional and technocratic behavior that rational choice theory does not comprehend, viz., altruism, the desire to do good to others even at some expense to yourself. "The concept of altruism," as Myrdal (1954, p. 47) observes, "became the rock on which the utilitarian philosophy was wrecked."

Action so motivated can be found in any occupation, and all I am asserting is that it not infrequently occurs among "public servants," as that name implies. In a fundamental sense, altruism of any kind is a centralizing and hierarchical force, since even when there is no hint of coercion or imposition, it means that one person has decided what is good for someone else. But what is to join the altruists together? One powerful force is a common body of professional knowledge. They now have the instrument for general solutions, as well as their altruistic commitment to make the widest possible use of their discipline. I am not saying that the object of altruism will necessarily welcome these well-meant attentions. Indeed, he may fear or detest them. There is such a thing as "altruism with teeth."

In a profession, public or private, the job definition itself is other-regarding. Moreover, a goal so defined can become a genuine personal motivation. The Webbs used to emphasize this point in those old discussions of how productive effort would be motivated in the coming socialist society.[7] Granting that an ideal of social service would have to take the place of the pursuit of riches, they pointed to civil servants, doctors, and other professional people as showing what this meant and how it could happen. The later growth and further spread of professionalism have lent support to their contention. Although the professionals in charge of public services may be strongly motivated by other-regarding concerns, however, that does not mean that they and the services they adminis-ter will be easily controlled by political or administrative superiors. Convinced of his own selfless commitment to professional standards and objectives, the public-spirited head of a nationalized industry can cause as much distortion of the national economic plan as any old-fashioned capitalist oligarch. To be self-righteous one need not be self-interested; quite the contrary.

The new technocrat professionally committed to his plan, like the old bureaucrat austerely pursuing his duty, is a stranger to the confederal polity. Theorists do sometimes try to force the facts to fit the theory by saying that altruism is really a pursuit of "symbolic" self-satisfaction. The sense of guilt from not doing one's duty and the glow of self-approval from meeting one's obli-gations are supposed to be incentives just like the costs and benefits of pay and promotion,[8] and so assimilable to them in one's "utility function." This view is the old hedonistic fallacy of the nineteenth-century utilitarians. It does not fit the facts of subjective experience and leads to ineffective management and con-trol. A person does feel satisfaction in doing his duty or in meeting the moral obligation of some altruistic imperative. But a reason he feels this satisfaction, this self-approval, is precisely that he did not act for it but for his duty. It is more faithful to everyday experience to recognize, as most modern psychology does, that ego-oriented motives are qualitatively different from other-oriented motives.[9]

The problem is to control bureaucratic autonomy, especially in its present technocratic phase. The confederal model offers the solution of dividing the bureaucratic forces and dispersing control over their incentives among several levels of government linked by contract. The reality, as the American experience with functional federalism amply attests, is that such a classic confederal tactic is weak and even dangerous in the face of the tendency of professionals to work together across intergovernmental boundaries for policy aims of their own. One cannot understand this technocratic thrust, nor cope with it effectively, if one does not also see how often and how far it rests upon the other-regarding impera-tives of professionalism. The preferences of an individual resulting from such values—essentially, from his conception of rights and duties—are not qualitatively like other preferences. The theorist misses the point if he bunches them all to-gether and calls them *utility*. The strength of rational choice theory is precisely that it identifies one major and distinctive sort of decision making. The explana-tory power of this approach has been amply demonstrated by economic analysis, and there are many aspects of political activity on which it sheds light, as I have tried to illustrate. This explanatory power, however, is lost if one tries to expand the theory to cover all behavior and all sorts of motivation. Oates's analysis of the mobility model, for instance, assumes that the individuals involved are motivated by fiscal self-interest. If he were to start from the assumption that the rich were altruists ready to assume the heavier tax burden resulting from an influx of poor people into their community, a pattern of settlement different from the segregation solution would follow.

There are different sorts of bureaucratic autonomy and so different problems of control, depending upon different sorts of motivation. Bureaucratic autonomy may arise from the self-interested pursuit of money and power and lead to careerism or even to corruption. That sort of problem requires different controls from the bureaucratic autonomy that springs from dedication to a professional conception of the public interest—the tendency toward technocracy. The careerist may combine with others, but he is a rugged individualist continually reassessing his chances, so his coalitions are likely to be temporary and shifting. By definition he can be bought off, but will he stay bought? As careerist he has nothing to offer except energy, which it is the quite conventional task of his superiors to elicit and direct by properly personalized incentives.

The overbearing technocrat, on the other hand, is perhaps more readily detected, because the root of his deviance is a publicly known profession. Yet he will be a hard man to restrain if you are asking him to deny his version of the public good. Ultimately, he may well have his price, but a genuine sense of duty may also raise it to an outrageous height. Moral values introduce a certain lumpiness into the process of political exchange, with its carefully graduated less and more. For the same reason, the coalitions of the technocrat have a solidarity not of a gang but of a guild, so that even when one member has been bought off or otherwise brought under control, the guild persists. This complicates the task of control because the guild has not only energy but also knowledge to offer the public. The task of a rational democracy is to utilize these resources without being dominated by them. The confederal polity is not up to this task. While it fragments the polity and the possibility of democratic control, the technocratic guilds, entrenched in the specialized services for system maintenance, will see to it that their conceptions of the public interest are promoted.

The Art of Associating Together

The problem is how to impose control by the private sector—ultimately the voters—upon the massive technocratic bureaucracies of the public sector. This task obviously requires participation in politics by the voters. As many, if not most, political scientists would also say, I shall contend that effective democratic control requires not merely participation but also some kind of association by voters with one another on a national scale (i.e., on a scale commensurate with the national thrust of the bureaucracies) and for a public purpose (i.e., a purpose that is more than the sum of individual goals in that it includes a conception of rights and duties). As rational choice theory does not comprehend the tendencies of bureaucracy that make such control necessary, so also it fails to see that such control is possible.

Rational choice theory has many illuminating things to say about political participation. Most of what it says, however, purports to show why voters will not participate. The argument is simple and, on the premises of rational choice theory, conclusive. Where the outcome will be determined by the action of thousands or millions of people, my individual action can make no difference. So why should I bother to vote, to join a party, or to subscribe to a pressure group? Among rational men, such a prospect will lead to total abstention. Rational choice theory, which sheds so much light on why individuals will welcome the provision of public goods, by the same logic clouds with inspissated gloom the prospect that they can control the use of these public goods.

The creation of a new polity itself poses problems for rational choice theory. The action of individuals when they move from a less to a more preferred location is, of course, intelligible. But how is one to explain the collective action of large numbers of persons which is necessary for partition or combination? In some instances, one can get around this difficulty by pointing to the role of suburb-building entrepreneurs. A few individuals or a large corporation, impelled by reasons of self-interest, may provide the individualized incentives that mobilize the large-scale action necessary for a new incorporation. Such political entrepreneurs have been individuals or organizations, private or public actors, businessmen or politicians. They have included many types, ranging from saloon keepers, who needed a municipality to grant them licenses, to a gigantic construction firm like Arthur Levitt and Sons, which created whole communities for profit [see Anton (1971)].

Given the existence of a small polity, it might be inferred from rational choice theory that smallness in numbers would encourage participation. To be sure, the numbers would have to be very small if the rational, calculating citizen were to be able to conclude that what he did would make a difference. The political situation would have to be such as to permit him to believe, for instance, that his vote might well break a tie or that the circle of acquaintances whom he could influence was large enough to swing an election. The evidence, however, does not support this hypothesis that smallness encourages participation. On the contrary, the turnout for local elections is generally very low when compared with the turnout for national elections [see, for example, Wirt (1975, p. 130)].

Sociological studies of small polities show that more complicated forces are at work. Indeed, because of the sociological context, small size may indirectly have an effect quite the opposite from what rational choice theory implies. In the less populous town or county, small size discourages participation in the sense that it tends to restrain citizens from making demands on government.[10] To put forward a demand is to invite conflict. But because of the small numbers involved, politics is highly personalized; hence, conflicts that arise in politics tend to spread to other relationships, subjecting them to intolerable strain. This prospect of the diffusion of hostility reacts on citizens to discourage the initial act of conflict-risking participation.

The voter may indeed report a sense of greater personal efficacy from taking part in the small polity. But the conditions that make this possible also make difficult the impersonal discussion of issues. The merits of a highway extension, regional sewage connection, or other system-maintenance step get mixed up with personal feelings toward the person who makes the proposal because of his neighborhood, his business, his ethnicity, his religion, or even his family. The considerations producing such a personalized politics are a mixed bag of straightforward economic calculation, fuzzy but strong social identifications, and presumed moral imperatives. Typically, in the very small American polity one finds a relative absence of interest-group competition. In its stead there are decision strategies emphasizing consensus and, as a result, strong resistance to change. In this way, small size itself impedes rational discourse and decision. While there is no doubt a place for the small polity with its special satisfactions,[11] it hardly seems the right building block on which to found effective democratic control of the wide-ranging bureaucratic organizations of the modern state.

Even at the level of the small polity, then, rational choice theory is an insufficient tool for analyzing political participation. When we try to understand the participation of millions in the national polity, these basic concepts of economics are even less adequate. Their logic still illuminates those interactions in national politics that constitute exchange relations, viz., the bargaining, brokering, and logrolling among individuals, groups, and governments. Two related aspects of political reality, however, are neglected: the other-regarding norms that lead people to take part and the other-regarding purposes that they pursue.

Political participation on such a large scale requires a very special political culture. To see this cultural basis, it is helpful to consult an observer who had an almost unique opportunity to compare large populations which at the time differed in this propensity. The observer is De Tocqueville, who understood the importance to popular governments of "the art of associating together" and who also was able to compare the French when they had not yet acquired this art with the Americans when they were first practicing it on a large scale. De Tocqueville sufficiently recognized the logic of rational choice theory to perceive that "the same social conditions that render associations so necessary to democratic nations also make their formation more difficult than elsewhere" (1838, p. 515 of 1969 edition). In an aristocratic society, he observed, effective action can be taken by only a few magnates, each of whom has great weight. But in a democratic country, the number of people associating together must be large. The moral development that enabled Americans to cope with this difficulty had both a technical and a normative aspect. De Tocqueville (1838, p. 522

of 1969 edition) spoke of a "habit," a "faculty," a "spirit," such that the art of associating became part of the "customs and *mores*" of the American democracy, leading its citizens to regard association as the "universal means" to achieve their ends.

What De Tocqueville revealed to his time escapes neither common sense nor political science today, viz., that in a democratic political culture one reason people vote and otherwise participate is a sense of civic duty. Hardly separable from such a moral imperative is the motivation to participate arising from identification with the political community as a whole or with some group, organized or unorganized, that is taking part in its politics. I do not need to argue against methodological individualism that groups are "real." The important point is that people feel and act as if they were real: that is, they feel as if their class, or race, or religion, or indeed their nation had done something, or failed to do something, and accordingly have a sense of triumph, pride, sorrow, anger, shame, or guilt in relation to the behavior of the collectivity. They are subject to "public affections," (Burke's phrase), which are quite distinct from private affections, but which motivate them strongly.[12]

Accordingly, voters vote because they feel they "ought to participate" and also because they take personal satisfaction in the act of voting [Almond and Verba (1963, pp. 19, 146, and *passim*)]. Both sorts of civic motivation—from moral values and from social and political identification—constitute attitudes that are distinguishable from motivations of personal advantage. Survey data have made it possible to measure the "sense of civic duty" among various groups of voters and its relation to their actual political participation.[13] A recent study of young people in the United States and Great Britain is worth mentioning specifically, since it explicitly posed the question of rational choice theory by asking for agreement or disagreement with the following assertion: "When you come right down to it, so many other people vote in national elections that it isn't very important whether the individual votes or not." In both countries, the respondents disagreed overwhelmingly, asserting that it was important for the individual to vote. Some of their reasons were indicated by strongly affirmative responses to such statements in a "civic duty index" as "Every person should devote himself to staying informed about politics and government, even if it means giving up some spare time" and "Every person has the duty to criticize the government when it does something wrong even if the matter does not concern him directly."[14]

The Role of Party Government

The task of the democratic polity is to utilize the resources of centralizing technocracy without being dominated by them. The principal means that "the art of associating together" has produced to perform this task is the political party. Not every political formation that has borne the name of party has been able to perform that task effectively, viz., link voters to government in such a way that their wishes control what it does. The requisites of successful "party government" have been exhaustively discussed by political scientists. I am not far from the mainstream of that discussion when I say that the effective political party will have two aspects, one pluralistic, the other monistic. It will be a coalition of groups of people, organized and unorganized, who give their votes to the candidates of the party in exchange for benefits they enjoy as individuals. In its monistic aspect, the party's adherents also share a commitment to a public purpose, supported by the affect of identification. The public purpose legitimates the interests favored by the party program, expressing what is common to them and generating further compatible initiatives. Identification yields the pleasures of partisanship and creates the habit of party voting. Such a political formation can organize mass participation in politics, aggregating the pluralisms of modern society with some prospect of giving direction to and exercising control over the large centralized bureaucracy that such a society will inevitably call forth.

The model of party government, if applied with a heavy hand, cannot be made to fit the fluid and miscellaneous realities of American politics. But if used with a proper sense of the fallibilities of models, it will bring out the possibilities of democratic control. The obvious illustration is the Democratic party as remade by Franklin Roosevelt. No doubt about it, in one important aspect, this political formation was a highly pluralistic coalition founded upon exchange. Laying the base for the new Democratic party, mainly in the cities of the North, Roosevelt added to traditional elements, such as the South and certain big-city machines, new strength from organized labor, farmers, recent immigrants, Negroes, old people, and intellectuals. Typically, for each of the constituent groups there was a program or set of programs that favored the interests of the group.

From the interaction of leader and followers, however, there emerged not only a powerful and long-lived coalition but also a coherent public purpose. In a recent study, Ladd and Hadley (1975, especially chap. I) give emphasis to this other aspect. In American politics, as they see it, parties have won majority status when they served as "the party of the new political agenda," representing "a public philosophy which attained wide-spread acceptance as positive, forward-looking, progressive." In becoming the new majority party, the Democrats did attract exceptionally strong support from certain economic and social groups. These authors stress, however, "the breadth of the conversions," pointing out that "we miss the larger dynamic of the conversion process if we fail to note the remarkable uniformity in increased support across the population spectrum" (p. 87). I am reminded of the comment of a restless reformer in 1937: "The trouble with Mr. Roosevelt is that he thinks he is the President of all the people."[15]

One cannot explain this party and its purposes solely or even largely in terms of the externalities of an advanced economy. In American political development, as in other countries, attempts to control the spillovers from the private and public sectors explain much centralization. This is a major rationale for the group politics that produced railroad regulation, pure food and drug acts, quarantine control, and water-pollution control. In accord with their source in market failures, the object of these efforts was to perfect the market. Government was prevailed upon to intervene to get the result that the free and rational action of individuals would produce, were it not for such aberrations as indivisibilities, decreasing-cost industries, and the gross inadequacies of market information. Some New Deal legislation can be explained in this way. But its novel and characteristic object was not to perfect the market but to change it—to alter the way it worked and to supplement its outcomes. The "public philosophy" by which it was proposed to do this consisted of a new conception of rights and duties and of the role of government in enforcing them.

A word about the more concrete character of that new conception of rights and duties is in order to make more intelligible its general function in the polity. There was definitely a tinge of income redistribution about it, though not necessarily with regard to results. North (1974, p. 168) concludes that "it is not at all clear that New Deal measures provided any significant redistribution of income." The welfare programs that were inaugurated by the Social Security Act of 1935 and expanded over later years did involve transfers from high- to low-income groups, especially if we can assume that the money came from progressive income taxation. There was even a redistributive element—the social principle—in the social insurance system. But the central achievement of the New Deal was not so much redistribution of income as redistribution of power. The characteristic measure here was the Wagner Act of 1935, which not only gave new guarantees to labor's right to organize, but also and especially imposed upon employers the obligation to bargain with labor organizations. This act transformed the position of the American workingman in his relations with his employer. What proportion of wage earners benefited materially from this act I do not know. I am confident that the act greatly increased the power of organized wage earners by increasing their number and their rights, and, indirectly in some degree, the power of the unorganized as well. The position of "the working stiff" was never the same again. Other programs had a similar effect. Some years later, Galbraith (1952) perceived this common character and identified it as "countervailing power." Mentioning the Wagner Act, Agricultural Adjustment Act, Wage Hour Act, and the Securities Exchange Commission, Galbraith observed that only this concept made fully comprehensible much of the domestic legislation of the previous twenty years and especially that of the New Deal.

A conception of rights and duties performs distinctive functions in a polity. If embodied in formal law, it will be the basis of a process of adjudication in which relationships are determined according to certain rules. A process of adjudication is not a process of exchange. The parties to the relationship that is being regulated do not arrive at the settlement by each giving up an equivalent, although some times there is a suggestion of exchange when judges talk of "balancing" rights because they cannot find a clear rule instructing them in the ordering of those rights. The political process typically partakes of the nature of both exchange and adjudication. Exchange is perhaps the more obvious aspect. Voters support a candidate who proposes to get certain benefits for them. By logrolling in a legislature, one politician votes for projects that another member wants in exchange for a similar favor from his fellow. When groups with conflicting interests make claims upon government, the politician, as broker, arranges a compromise by which each group makes concessions as a means of getting at least part of what he wants.

At the same time, however, these processes of exchange are accomplished without excessive damage or delay because they are conditioned by a generally accepted conception of rights and duties, substantive and procedural. The demands that a group may make upon government are intrinsically without limit. The capacities and resources available to the government are one constraint. But a further and major constraint is what in that time and place is regarded as a just and rightful claim. This is at once a subjective restraint on the demandants and an objective condition imposed by the attitudes of other participants. There was a time when an appropriation of $25,000 for free seed grain for drought-stricken farmers could be vetoed by Grover Cleveland on the grounds that "it is not the duty of government to support the people."[16] Times change and with them the demands that are legitimated by the reigning public philosophy.

Similarly, in compromising conflicts, the balance of mutual concessions that is arranged and accepted will be guided by and will need to find legitimation in such conceptions. The formation of majority coalitions, as Wilson (1975) has recently written, cannot be based solely on self-interested bargains but must also accord with certain "principles." "Persuading men who disagree to compromise their differences." he states by way of generalization, "can rarely be achieved solely by the parceling out of relative advantage; the belief is also required that what is being agreed to is right, proper, and defensible before public opinion."

In political settlements, the relation of adjudicatory and exchange elements is complex. The normative background does not only, as suggested above, shape the exchange process, it also makes it possible. After a bargain is struck, the actual delivery of benefits, economic or political, is not instantaneous but involves some delay on one side or the other. Mutual trust immensely facilitates exchange by assuring the risk-taking party that even if the objective chance to refuse performance presents itself to the other party, he will keep his word. In the economy, such trust, as Arrow (1970, p. 70) has observed, makes possible a whole range of mutually beneficial exchange that without it would hardly be feasible.[17] The same is true in the polity.

The Problem of the Politics of Redistribution

I do not mean to be nostalgic about the New Deal. Its revival would not solve our problems. Indeed, the massive centralization that it inaugurated and developed has become—as in history great measures of improvement often become— the source of many present woes. I used the New Deal rather to show how a political party can act as an instrument of other-regarding public choice.

For the study of multilevel finance, this point is of crucial importance. For it shows one major way that a democratic polity actually goes about mustering and exercising the political support necessary for a policy of redistribution. Among political economists, it is a commonplace to say that in a modern society the redistribution function must be performed by the central government. As Oates points out, an aggressive policy of income redistribution from rich to poor in a particular locality will very probably chase away the relatively few wealthy to other jurisdictions and attract those with low incomes. Moreover, the tendency toward the segregation solution that appears in his analysis of suburban mobility means that the redistribution problem becomes even more serious. In contrast with the older urban forms, the small town and the big city, the modern suburb tends to be socially and economically homogeneous. Such segregation deprives the local polity with poor residents of direct access to the resources of the better off who have moved or seceded. For where there was a mix of all income groups, even if taxes were only proportional and not progressive, there was a certain redistributive effect in that the resources of the better-off bore much of the cost of supporting the public services heavily utilized by the less well-off [see Fried et al. (1973, p. 288)]. Thus, suburban segregation, as well as interstate and interlocal competition, reduce the likelihood of redistribution by subnational governments.

For the political economist to say that the federal government ought to step in and do what the subnational governments will not or cannot afford to do, however, does not mean that anything will actually happen. If a policy of redistribution is to be adopted, there must be some political cause. In the American experience, it was the accomplishment of the new Democratic party of Roosevelt to provide such a cause. Its new public philosophy was embodied in the purpose of a political party, institutionalized in new legal arrangements, and internalized in new social sentiments and norms. A coalition based solely on exchange could not have produced such effects since by definition its members would help one another only in return for equivalents. Rational choice theory, with its stress on exchange, can point the way to central action to correct externalities and other market failures. It has little comprehension of the broader purposes that the polity should fulfill or of the motivations that would enable it to fulfill them.

Conclusion

In presenting this critique of the political economy of multilevel government, I have put forward these main points:

1. The new political economy based on rational choice theory goes a long way toward explaining the political development of metropolitan areas since World War II, especially the phenomenon of suburbanization.

2. The confederal polity that has tended to result from this development is an inadequte political basis for democratic control over the centralizing technocratic bureaucracies of the American governmental system.

3. In order to understand the threat of technocratic bureaucracy and how to cope with it, we must go beyond rational choice theory and draw on other intellectual resources of political science, in particular its appreciation of the role of motivation based on other-regarding norms and group identifications among both bureaucrats and voters.

4. Such a noneconomic conception of political action shows how nationwide aggregations of voters might arise with the political basis and public purpose necessary to impose democratic control and direction on technocratic power.

5. This approach to politics likewise shows how a democratic polity might be able to amass the political support to cope with other hard choices of public policy today, such as the problem of redistribution, which is insoluble in terms of rational choice theory.

6. The world of political exchange is real and important. It operates successfully, however, because of a normative background that impels people to participate, sustains their trust, and defines and legitimates the demands they may make on one another.

Notes

1. I take this meaning from Samuelson (1970, p. 331), who writes: "by a positive fiscal policy we mean the process of shaping *taxation* and *public expenditure* in order (1) to help dampen down the swings of the business cycle and (2) to contribute toward the maintenance of a growing high-employment economy free from excessive deflation."

2. "Embodiments of rational analysis," writes Steinbrunner (1974, p. 25), "can be found in formal axiom systems, in economic analysis, in historical accounts of political events, in discussions of substantive policy, and in common observation." In a larger sense, I hardly need say, rational choice theory descends from currents of modern thought that have been as much concerned with political as economic behavior—Hobbes and Bentham immediately come to mind—and in essence its strengths and weaknesses are the familiar strengths and weaknesses of the political philosophy of utilitarian individualism.

3. The benefits of "overlap and fragmentation of authority" in the territorial distribution of powers are developed by Ostrom (1974, p. 220 and *passim*), as well as in his other works, where in general what I have called *the confederal model* is put forward [see, in particular, Ostrom (1973 and 1971)].

4. On "optimizing grants," see Break (1967, chap. III, "Functional Grants-in-Aid").

5. Externalities are one major reason for having any government at all—that is, for "primary centralization." Moreover, as the interlocal flow of social costs and benefits increases, the same logic leads to "secondary centralization"—that is, to the intervention by a more inclusive jurisdiction. I have discussed these grounds for centralization and their relation to group politics in Beer (1973).

6. U.S. Bureau of the Census, *Statistical Abstract of the United States: 1973*, Washington, D.C., p. 412.

7. I have discussed this in my introduction to the 1975 edition of Sidney and Beatrice Webb (1920, p. xxix).

8. See, for example, Olson (1965, long footnote on p. 61). It begins: "In addition to monetary and social incentives, there are also erotic incentives, psychological incentives, moral incentives, and so on."

9. A similar though not identical distinction is made by an economist in a recent discussion of motivation in economic and political behavior. Developing his theory of "selective rationality," Leibenstein (1976a, p. 9) observes that "individuals are willing to forgo maximization in part because of standards of behavior" (which he also refers to as *superego considerations*). "The obverse of this idea," he continues, "is that individuals might be willing to put forth effort despite the fact that there is no counterpart gain involved in order to behave in accordance with their standards, or their sense of duty . . ." [See also Leibenstein (1976b, chaps. 5-10)]. As I have done, Leibenstein not only identifies conventional economic analysis with a theory of motivation that explains action in terms of utility maximization, but he also distinguishes such behavior from behavior proceeding from such motivations as "sense of duty," "standards of behavior," and "superego considerations."

10. I am relying very heavily on an excellent recent discussion of this question by Sokolow (1975).

11. The satisfactions of a sense of efficacy are given great emphasis in Dahl and Tufte (1973).

12. Burke (1790; 1935 edition, p. 75) attacks the "barbarous philosophy" of the French Revolution because its emphasis on reason leaves nothing which "engages the affections of the commonwealth." "These public affections," he continues, "combined with manners, are required sometimes as supplements, sometimes as correctives, always as aids to law."

13. See Key (1961, p. 324) and references given there. For a discussion of "civic duty," see also Campbell et al. (1960, *passim*). Leibenstein's (1976b, pp. 8, 9, 12) analysis of voting follows the same tack. "On the basis of traditional economics," he writes, "voting does not make sense." Some cost is in-

volved in voting, but there is no loss to the individual if he does not vote, since his vote will not determine the outcome. Yet many people do vote, the reason being "superego considerations." A similar motivation, he says, also accounts for other sorts of political activity inexplicable on grounds of economic reasoning, for instance, membership in political parties, trade unions, and other "voluntary and semivoluntary organizations."

14. This survey was made by Nelson Rosenbaum in 1972 and involved interviews with about a thousand teenage respondents respectively in Britain and the United States.

15. Maury Maverick, then a Congressman from San Antonio. He was chafing at Roosevelt's tactics with regard to what became the Wage Hour Bill of 1938.

16. The date was February 19, 1887; quoted in Nevins (1932, p. 332).

17. In this article, Arrow is critical of models that attempt to analyze political behavior "along the lines of economic theory" by starting from the assumption that in politics individuals are governed "by the same motives as in economics." Among the departures from atomistic behavior, he mentions "norms of social behavior, including ethical and moral codes" and specifies "trust in each other's word" as an example.

References

Almond, G., and Verba, S. 1963. *The Civic Culture: Political Attitudes and Democracy in Five Nations.* Princeton, N.J.: Princeton University Press.

Anton, T.J. 1971. Three models of community development in the United States. *Publius: The Journal of Federalism* 1, no. 1.

Arrow, K.J. 1970. The organization of economic activity: Issues pertinent to the choice of market versus non-market allocation. In *Public Expenditure and Policy Analysis*, R.H. Haveman and J. Margolis, eds. Chicago: Markham.

Beer, S.H. 1973. The modernization of American federalism. *Publius: The Journal of Federalism* 3, no. 2.

Benson, G.C. 1961. Values of decentralized government—1961. In *Essays in Federalism*, G.C. Benson et al. Claremont, Calif.: Institute for Studies in Federalism.

Break, G.F. 1967. *Intergovernmental Fiscal Relations in the United States.* Washington, D.C.: The Brookings Institution.

Burke, E. 1790. *Reflections on the French Revolution.* London: Everyman, 1935 edition.

Campbell, A., Converse, P., Miller, W., and Stokes, D. 1960. *The American Voter.* New York: Wiley.

Dahl, R.A., and Tufte, E.R. 1973. *Size and Democracy.* Stanford, Calif.: Stanford University Press.

Earle, V., ed. 1964. *Federalism: Infinite Variety in Theory and Practice.* Itasca, Ill.: Peacock.

Fried, E.R., et al. 1973. *Setting National Priorities: The 1974 Budget.* Washington, D.C.: The Brookings Institution.

Friedrich, C.J. 1968. *Constitutional Government and Democracy: Theory and Practice in Europe and America,* 4th edition. Waltham, Mass.: Blaisdell.

Galbraith, J.K. 1952. *American Capitalism: The Concept of Countervailing Power.* Boston: Houghton Mifflin.

Holden, M., Jr. 1964. The governance of the metropolis as a problem in diplomacy. *Journal of Politics* 26:627–647.

Hughes, E.C. 1963. Professions. *Daedalus* 92:656–657.

Key, V.O., Jr. 1961. *Public Opinion and American Democracy.* New York: Knopf.

Ladd, E.C., Jr., with C.D. Hadley. 1975. *Transformation of the American Party System: Political Coalitions from the New Deal to the 1970s.* New York: Norton.

Leibenstein, H. 1976a. Beyond economic man: On the interface between economics and politics. Paper prepared for delivery at the 1976 Edinburgh International Political Science Association Congress of August 16–21.

Leibenstein, H. 1976b. *Beyond Economic Man.* Cambridge, Mass.: Harvard University Press.

Maude, A. 1966. In *Encounter* 26:62.

Mosher, F.C. 1968. *Democracy and the Public Service.* New York: Oxford University Press.

Myrdal, G. 1954. *The Political Element in the Development of Economic Theory.* Cambridge, Mass.: Harvard University Press.

Nevins, A. 1932. *Grover Cleveland: A Study in Courage.* New York: Dodd, Mead.

North, D.C. 1974. *Growth and Welfare in the American Past: A New Economic History,* 2d ed. Englewood Cliffs, N.J.: Prentice-Hall.

Olson, M. 1965. *The Logic of Collective Action: Public Goods and the Theory of Groups.* Cambridge, Mass.: Harvard University Press.

Ostrom, V. 1971. *The Political Theory of a Compound Republic.* Blacksburg, Va.: Virginia Polytechnic Institute.

Ostrom, V. 1973. *The Intellectual Crisis in American Public Administration.* University, Ala.: University of Alabama Press.

Ostrom, V. 1974. Can federalism make a difference? In The federal polity, D.J. Elazar, ed. *Publius: The Journal of Federalism* 3, no. 2.

Samuelson, P.A. 1970. *Economics,* 8th ed. New York: McGraw-Hill.

Sokolow, A.D. 1975. Small community policy making and the new federalism. Paper prepared for delivery at the 1975 Annual Meeting of the American Political Science Association of September 2–5.

Steinbrunner, J.D. 1974. *The Cybernetic Theory of Decision: New Dimensions of Political Analysis.* Princeton, N.J.: Princeton University Press.

Tocqueville, A. de, 1838. *Democracy in America,* J.P. Mayer, ed., G. Lawrence, trans. New York: Doubleday, 1969 edition.

Webb, S., and Webb, B. 1920. *A Constitution for the Socialist Commonwealth of Great Britain,* S.H. Beer, ed. Cambridge, England: Cambridge University Press, 1975 edition.

Williams, O.P. 1971. *Metropolitan Political Analysis: A Social Access Approach* New York: Free Press.

Williams, O.P. 1975. The politics of urban space. In The suburban reshaping of american politics, E.M. Baker, ed. *Publius: The Journal of Federalism* 5, no. 1.

Wilson, J.Q. 1975. The rise of the bureaucratic state. *The Public Interest* 41:93.

Wirt, F.M. 1975. Suburbs and politics in America. In The suburban reshaping of american politics, E.M. Baker, ed. *Publius: The Journal of Federalism* 5, no. 1.

Wright, D. 1972. Policy control: The hidden issue in revenue sharing. In *Politics in 72: Trends in Federalism,* F.M. Carney and H.F. Way, eds. Belmont, Calif.: Wadsworth.

Part II
Studies in the Federal Response to
Political and Economic Pressures

3

The Political Economy of Devolution: The British Case

Alan Peacock

1. Introduction: Background

Worried by the growing support for the Scottish National Party (SNP) and for its Welsh counterpart Plaid Cymru (significantly known by its Welsh name), as instanced by the 1967 by-elections, Mr. Wilson, the then Prime Minister, appointed a Royal Commission on the Constitution under the chairmanship of Lord Crowther, a time-honoured method used by British governments to buy time.[1] Though its terms of reference were very wide and could have been interpreted as covering the whole range of constitutional problems, it was clearly understood that the main question facing the commission was whether, how, and to what extent government should be further devolved within the United Kingdom.

The commission were appointed in April 1969 but did not report until December 1973. By that time, its activities had been largely forgotten about, and when its 500-page report, together with a 200-page Memorandum of Dissent[2] and a considerable number of volumes of evidence and research reports appeared, the editor of the well-known journal *Public Administration* was tempted to recall David Hume's acerbic remark on the appearance of his *Treatise of Human Nature,* which fell "dead-born from the press." However, the polite Parliamentary gestures of approval for services rendered were in stark contrast to the close attention paid to various schemes of devolution based on the evidence and conclusions of the commission, which at the end of 1974 were officially offered for discussion. By then the Labour Government faced loss of support to Scottish and Welsh nationalists and to the Liberal party, which had a strong commitment to transfer of power from the center to the regions.

In essence the Labor Government has accepted the principal recommendations of the majority of the commission's members and is committed to setting up separate directly elected assemblies in Scotland and Wales. These assemblies will be endowed with considerable control over expenditure functions at present undertaken by the Scottish and Welsh offices—the central government's execu-

The views expressed in this article are the author's and do not necessarily reflect the position of the government of the United Kingdom.

49

tive "arm" in these regions—but will have very little discretion over means of finance. Though all members of the commission opposed the setting up of a federal government structure in the United Kingdom and rejected the demand of nationalist parties for Scottish and Welsh independence, two members of the commission, Lord Crowther-Hunt and myself, preferred a form of devolution that offered the same opportunities for control of the executive by regional assemblies in the English regions as well as in Scotland and Wales.

I have chosen to avoid giving a detailed description of the various schemes of devolution proposed, for I believe that the value of the devolution debate for an international audience lies more in examining the intellectual process leading to devolution proposals and less in a detailed examination of their content, interesting and relevant though this could be to other countries.

In section 2 below, I briefly review the place of the devolution debate within the framework of the recently developed economic theory of representative government. Having explained how a demand for devolution has arisen, section 3 describes how the Kilbrandon Commission (hereafter referred to as KC) went about the task of measuring its intensity. Section 4 reviews the two main sets of devolution schemes proposed and speculates on their economic impact. A final section 5 endeavors to draw some lessons from the devolution debate in the United Kingdom.

2. Models of Constitutional Change

The model of constitutional change that one could employ to explain the demand for devolution would depend on the questions one seeks to answer. Latterly, economists who have made the running in this area have been interested in developing positive models in which individuals try to induce governments to do what they want, i.e., reduce their frustration with government policy, by a series of signaling actions within a given jurisdiction or by mobility or the threat of mobility to other jurisdictions within the nation-state [see Breton (1974); Breton and Scott (1975)]. The signaling actions can range from direct engagement in politics to adjustment of economic behavior, but all these kinds of action—together with mobility—involve costs that have to be matched with benefits, and both the costs and benefits may be uncertain.

If Breton and others are right, the variance in the distribution of preferences of citizens for different types of services and their methods of finance will increase as the degree of centralization increases. By any standards, the United Kingdom has become a highly centralized state, as measured by the growth in the relative importance of central government finance not only of central but also of local government services. (I prefer this measure of the degree of centralization to the Breton/Scott use of the relative size of expenditure responsibilities at the center.) Local governments are still immediately responsible for important social services, such as housing and education up to university level, but their standards of services are strongly influenced by central government both through legislation and by sources of finance. Local governments are "creatures of the center" in another fundamental sense, for they have no separate constitutional existence; their powers are determined by Acts of Parliament, i.e., legislation enacted by the central government. It follows that citizens with preference systems differing markedly from those reflected in public expenditure and taxation would derive only a restricted net benefit by movement from one jurisdiction to another. In a study of local government in urban areas in both the United States and the United Kingdom, for instance, it has been shown [see Aronson (1974)] that fiscal factors affected the distribution of population in both countries but that the percentage of correct predictions is lower in the U.K. case. Aronson explains this by the fact that fiscal differences between towns, as measured by the coefficient of variation for tax rates and per capita expenditure, is not as great in England as in the United States. This could result, as Aronson asserts, from more homogenous individual preferences in England than in the United States, but I believe that his second reason is more important, namely, the effects of grants from the center to local governments, which are based on an equalizing formula.

Because of the high proportion of total central and local current governmental services financed from the center, roughly 84 percent in 1974, the efforts to influence their amount and composition must be concentrated on the political signaling system, which could influence central-government decisions. However, this part of the signaling system is highly restricted, for policies are decided and implemented by a Government formed by a majority party in a Parliament which itself is elected by a system of simple majority voting. It is also restricted by complete immunity of the higher civil service from direct electoral pressures, for this highly paid bureaucracy is not voted into office but is recruited by competitive examination for administrative posts that carry security of tenure. It is no surprise, therefore, that pressure-group action designed to exercise a *continuing* influence over politicians and bureaucrats has become of growing importance in the United Kingdom, of which the best-known examples are the activities of the Confederation of British Industries and the Trades Union Congress, which have almost acquired the status of "estates of the realm."

The growing demand for devolution suggests that the traditional signaling systems are not working as well as they should and that the deviation of individual and group preferences from those reflected in the existing amount and pattern of government services has become more marked. Thus the interesting feature of the British situation is that it appears to have engendered demands for *changes in the signaling system itself,* as expressed in the demand for proportional representation in national elections and for some system of devolved government.

This is an unusual situation in the United Kingdom, though Home Rule for Scotland was a lively subject of debate after the First World War. A Royal Commission, therefore, would be bound to proceed rather warily. Though the terms of reference of the KC were wide enough to make it possible to recommend a fundamental constitutional reform, its members chose to assume that, broadly speaking, the existing functions of government and particularly the economic functions should be taken as data but that their division between layers of government was the matter at issue.[3] Recommendations for devolution would therefore have to depend on wider considerations than reducing the deviation between collective and individual preferences as depicted in individualistic approaches to the theory of government, though such models can be extended, e.g., through postulating interdependent preference functions, to take account of distributional growth and stabilization aims calling for collective action.

The KC, therefore, had to act in a similar fashion to a political philosopher deploying a normative rather than a positive theory of constitutional change. The analogue in economics used to depict this approach is a constrained maximization policy model in which an objective function embodying several arguments has to be maximized subject to resource and other constraints.[4] The commission simply interpolated an additional argument into the objective function or, more modestly a political boundary condition, viz., alternative forms of devolved decision making, and then in a not particularly rigorous way formed a judgment on its effect on social welfare.

3. Measuring the Demand for Devolution

While a Royal Commission could in principle deliver its recommendations *ex cathedra* without reference to outside opinion on an issue such as constitutional reform, it would have to face strong criticism if it did not at least take evidence, as such commissions traditionally have done. The usual method is to issue an open invitation to the public to offer written evidence, though a commission may ask specific organizations and individuals to submit evidence and will reserve the right whom to call to give oral evidence, particularly if it is believed that otherwise it would not obtain a reasonable cross section of opinion. However, even if care is exercised, the taking of evidence is a very haphazard method of proceeding. Given equal individual interest in expressing views on devolution problems, the costs of doing so fall very unequally on different sections of the community. It comes as no surprise that most of the evidence was received from the literate middle classes, who bear lower costs in articulating their preferences and through various professional bodies ranging from local government officers' associations to churches that can have their expenses met by others, including the taxpayer or ratepayer. To some extent the KC reduced absolute, if not differential, individual costs by taking evidence in different parts of the country, but in practice this benefited Wales, Scotland, and Northern Ireland, where 30 meetings were held, in contrast to England, where only 2 meetings were held outside London. This clearly reflected the bias in membership towards the Celtic fringe, a bias reinforced by the appointment of Scottish, Welsh, and Northern Irish assistant commissioners but none from England.

After considerable argument, the commission agreed to supplement this traditional source of views by a detailed survey of attitudes toward devolution and other aspects of government [see social and community Planning Research (1973)]. The difficulties in using such a method for eliciting opinions on specific kinds of devolution are immense. It would have required the commission to prepare models of devolution in advance of the survey, which they were in no position to do. It would assume that these models and their implications for the respondent were fully articulated and understood, and even if these difficulties were overcome, and allowing for the risks of low response rates to complicated and difficult questions, there would be still left the problem of evaluating attitudes toward hypothetical alternative schemes. The attitudes survey, therefore, as well as probing general attitudes toward government, could trawl only opinions on devolution of the most general and abstract nature, such as eliciting reasons for wishing devolution and for preference between devolution to a regional administration and devolution requiring elected bodies. An illustration of these difficulties is given later.

In evaluating the evidence, the MR (Majority Report) and MD (Memorandum of Dissent) agreed on three main points: (1) there had developed a growing lack of communication between central government and the electorate; (2) the political power of individuals and their elected representatives in Parliament had declined, while that of the central administration and ad hoc bodies appointed on its recommendation had increased; and (3) in respect of (1) and (2) there was no marked difference of opinion on these matters between regions of the United Kingdom. But, on the vital question of remedies, the MR and MD disagreed on the interpretation of evidence.

The MR argued that the survey provided no substantial evidence in favor of a bigger share in political decision making as distinct from bringing the administrative apparatus more directly in touch with the people. The problem, in their view, was one of "a felt lack of communication" rather than "a felt lack of participation." Moreover, they believed that the survey pointed toward more "spontaneous" interest in devolution in Scotland and Wales than in English regions. The MD, on the other hand, made two technical criticisms of the survey, perhaps with the benefit of hindsight. First, it could not elicit the difference between discontent with the government of the day and discontent with the system of government itself, and second, it was not asked to set its findings against comparable information on attitudes, notably by national opinion polls and Gallup polls covering similar problems. It found ample evidence in the survey itself for a demand for more individual participation in the political decision-making process and no evidence that this demand varied in intensity between the Celtic nations and the English regions.

As a signatory of the MD, I believe, of course, that its analysis of the evidence in the survey and of other evidence is much sounder than those of the survey investigators themselves and of the MR. However, this is neither to say that the survey was not competently carried out nor that its interpretation was easy. As an indication of the inherent problem of investigation and interpretation, let me take one striking example. It is obvious that whoever were to take the decisions in a devolved system, attitudes toward forms of devolution would depend on the costs and benefits attached to any particular scheme. The impact effect might be to produce recognizable benefits derived from greater power over the amount and mix of publicly provided services, but these might be offset by costs in the form of adverse real income changes. Thus, a relatively poor region with complete responsibility for running its own services would pay the price in a fall in the positive "fiscal residuum," to use Buchanan's term, which would initially reduce per capita real incomes, and, in addition, it is conceivable that individual regional government services might lose the cost advantages associated with the scale of central government operation. Even then, it would be difficult to translate these effects into a cost and benefit calculus for other than some mythical "representative" individual, whereas any particular individual might be able to adjust his real income position *within* the new system through the new dimension introduced into the political signaling system, e.g., through the changing opportunities for tax avoidance or through political action with others to alter regional-government tax schedules. Further, the individual's judgment is not based solely on short-term considerations and therefore on the impact of the change in the governmental system within his own region. His judgment of the net present value of devolution will depend on whether, for example, other regions are endowed with comparable systems of government and how far the fiscal arrangements with the center would affect regional incomes. These factors would affect his judgment, not only because his utility might depend on how others in other regions were treated, but also because it might depend on his view on the opportunities to improve his position through interregional migration.

When the survey was taken, the KC had not even got to the stage of listing any possible "runners" for the devolution stakes. Even if it had, it would have been an impossible task to give respondents anything other than a very general idea of how they might be affected by any possible scheme. Furthermore, the costs to the individual of going through the process of cerebration that might have required him to undertake some rather sophisticated analysis would probably have reduced the response rate to a negligible percentage. Thus the attitudes survey could only offer general evidence on the *expectations* of respondents of the effects of devolution on themselves and others without being able to probe how these expectations were formed and how they might vary if individuals were offered a (hypothetical) choice of alternative schemes. I reproduce as Figure 3-1 one chart of the attitudes survey without comment in order to demonstrate these difficulties.

4. The Devolution Schemes

The final outcome of the commission's deliberations and of the government's proposals are only partly based on the evidence that we have examined, which is probably not surprising if only because of the inherent difficulties in basing proposals on attempts to reveal the electorate's preferences. I cannot possibly do more than summarize the main differences between, and the consequences of, two sets of proposals, those of the MR and those of the MD. And there is not space enough to comment on the intense speculation surrounding the constitutional aspects of these proposals. I shall concentrate exclusively on the possible economic effects of the alternative systems.

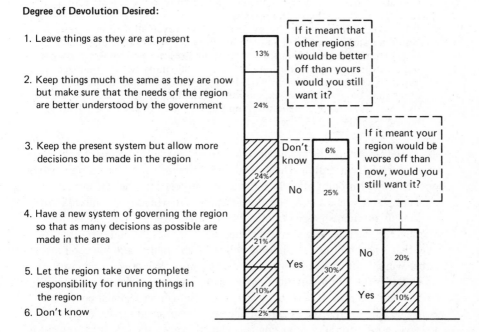

Degree of Devolution Desired:

1. Leave things as they are at present

2. Keep things much the same as they are now but make sure that the needs of the region are better understood by the government

3. Keep the present system but allow more decisions to be made in the region

4. Have a new system of governing the region so that as many decisions as possible are made in the area

5. Let the region take over complete responsibility for running things in the region

6. Don't know

Source: Commission on the Constitution, Research Papers No. 7, Chart 2, p. 98. Reprinted with permission of the Controller of Her Majesty's Stationery Office, 1973.

Figure 3-1. Proportions Wanting Devolution if Consequences Economically Bad for Region.

Table 3-1 summarizes the principal features of the various types of schemes, ignoring certain variations in them put forward by individual members and other constitutional matters (such as changes in House of Commons procedure and in relations between Westminster and the Channel Islands and the Isle of Man).

The MR proposals amount to saying this:

There is a general demand for a limited extension of the signaling system which indicates that the electorate could be predicted to support constitutional change. This demand varies according to region. Scotland and Wales prefer a change which requires a limited degree of *political* participation through regional legislatures which would give substantial freedom to vary the *composition* of social and environmental services but without requiring control over the total expenditure on these services or over the methods of their finance. English regions will be content with an improvement in communications between Government departments, Parliament, and their electorate. Devolved government only to Scotland and to Wales would have the following advantages:

a. It would reflect electorate's preferences;
b. It would cause the minimum of administrative disruption, given that Scotland and Wales already have separate Government Departments responsible for a large part of their administration;
c. Effects on economic objectives other than improved allocation of resources would be minimized, for macroeconomic policy would be constrained only by more spending freedom for a very limited segment of total spending by public authorities. Distributional effects would similarly be minimized. In any case, central government would be left with sufficient instruments, other than composition of expenditure, to make any corrections necessary to offset the effects of devolution on growth, stability, and income distribution [see MR (1973, chap. 8)].

As the Government's proposals follow these recommendations closely, they deserve particular attention. The general case made for partial devolution may be conceded, save for point (1), which I believe conflicts with the evidence, such as it is. However, there is a major unstated assumption, which is recognized in the government's statement [see Command Paper 6348 (1975)] that the position regarding the English regions must be considered separately, and this is the belief that a new political equilibrium will be established. There is a good case for believing that this assumption is untenable, and I shall now explain why.

Consider the "representative" canny Scot or go-getting Welshman weighing the costs and benefits of new-found freedom. Through his regional politicians he may be able to alter the pattern of devolved government service in a way that moves constraints on his optimizing behavior. However, the gain in movement to a more preferred position may be offset by a rise in the relative price of services, so increasing his budget constraint. This could happen in two ways: (1) from more "X-inefficiency" arising from lack of regional experience in expenditure control and project appraisal and perhaps from discrimination in favor of own-

Table 3–1
Principal Features of Devolution Proposals

	Majority Report	Memorandum of Dissent	Government Proposals
1. *Extent of Devolution*	Devolution to Scotland and Wales only.	Devolution to all regions.	Devolution to Scotland and Wales now. No decision on England.
2. *Rationale*	a. "Historically identifiable" nations—Scotland, Wales. b. Existing administrative devolution to build on, i.e., Scottish and Welsh offices. c. Demand "stronger" in Scotland and Wales.	a. Principle of political equality. b. Demand equally distributed throughout United Kingdom. c. Improved division of labor between central and regional government.	a. Same as for MR.
3. *Political Institutions*	a. Elected assemblies in Scotland and Wales by proportional representation. b. Executive authority vested in Ministers appointed from Assembly. c. Advisory councils for English regions. d. Representation in U.K. House of Commons for Scotland and Wales in proportion to population. e. Regional Committees in U.K. Parliament.	a. Elected assemblies in all regions by proportional representation. b. Executive authority in Assembly committees reflecting party composition. c. Representation in U.K. House of Commons for all regions on population basis. d. Possible reform of House of Lords to reflect regional representation.	a. Elected assemblies in Scotland and Wales by simple majority system. b. Scotland: executive authority vested in members of Assembly of the majority party. Wales: executive authority vested in Assembly committees reflecting party composition. c. No firm proposals at this stage. d. No change in representation of Scotland and Wales in House of Commons (central legislature).

(continued)

Table 3–1
Principal Features of Devolution Proposals

	Majority Report	Memorandum of Dissent	Government Proposals
4. *Financial Powers*	a. Responsibility for expenditure on all main social and environmental services within total agreed with central government. b. Substantial freedom in expenditure allocation within agreed total. c. No firm views on central-regional revenue sources.	a. Same as for MR, 4a. b. Same as for MR, 4b. c. Devolution of some taxing powers in order to promote regional political participation.	a. Same as for MR, 4a. b. Same as for MR, 4b. c. No new sources of regional revenue other than power to precept on local government taxes (the local rate).

region suppliers to government; and (2) from "scale" effects produced by operating services at a regional rather than national level, which would result in higher marginal and average costs. It has been argued [King (1973)] that the most important case for consideration of scale effects would be hospitals, which in recent years have absorbed nearly 20 percent of current and capital expenditure on "devolvable" services. Since the devolved governments will not be responsible for finance of these services, the loss in real income to members of the "Celtic fringe" would take the form of lower standards of service at the present level of finance available on a regional basis.

However, being no fool, our representative Scot or Welshman realizes that his devolved government has an important additional weapon that may yield a compensatory real income effect. His regional assembly, serviced by its bureaucracy, represents the creation of a new power base capable of exercising direct and continuous pressure on central government in a way denied other regions. Favorable bargains will be sought (1) in the financial allocation available to devolved governments and (2) in the way other policy instruments could be used to discriminate in favor of a particular region, e.g., siting of central-government defence establishments and purchasing policy. At the same time, pressure through regional representatives in the central legislature could be maintained, since regional representation is not to be reduced.

It is therefore difficult to believe that regions without the proposed Assemblies would not be concerned about a prospective political change that could put them at a relative disadvantage. Table 3-2 offers skeleton profiles of the regions of the United Kingdom which would bring the point home to them. Devolved government is being offered to two regions representing less than 14 percent of the total population of the United Kingdom, with a low relative population density where, admittedly, GDP per head is relatively low and unemployment is relatively high, but where the degree of economic disadvantage is not much greater than in some other regions, notably less than in the North region. More telling still is the fact that devolvable government expenditure per head in Scotland and Wales is much higher than in all other regions, though it is difficult to establish whether this reflects a concomitant difference in standards of services on offer. Though there is little firm evidence for recent years, there is little doubt that after deduction of allocable taxes Scotland and Wales are net gainers from the financial operations of the central government. The conclusion, therefore, that other regions will press hard for equality of political rights and thus for comparable power bases seems irresistible.[5]

Therefore, though it has been rejected for the present, this conclusion offers point for further consideration of the MD, which starts from a fundamentally different position. Its argument might be summarized as follows:

The demand for more political participation is widely distributed, contrary to the interpretation of evidence by the MR. Equality of political rights is equitable

Table 3-2
Regional Economic Profiles

Region	Population (in millions) (1973)	Population (% of U.K.) (1973)	Persons per sq. km. (1973)	Rel. Pop. Density (1973)	GDP (factor cost) per head (1972)	Rel. GDP per head (1972)	Unemployment (% av.) (1973)	Devolvable per Head (1969)	Rel. Devolvable Gov. Expenditure[a]
England:									
North	3.3	5.9	170	74.1	819	85.0	4.7	128.5	116.6
Yorkshire/Humberside	4.8	8.6	340	148.5	903	93.7	2.9	98.0	88.9
East Midlands	3.4	6.1	283	123.6	928	96.3	2.1	90.4	82.0
East Anglia	1.7	3.1	138	60.3	919	95.4	1.9	94.4	85.7
South East	17.3	31.1	632	275.9	1,117	115.8	1.5	94.4	85.7
South West	3.8	6.8	164	71.6	932	96.7	2.4	93.3	84.7
West Midlands	5.1	9.2	397	173.4	984	102.0	2.2	91.7	83.2
North West	6.8	12.2	845	369.0	900	93.3	3.6	104.6	94.6
Scotland	5.2	9.4	66	28.8	880	91.3	3.5	144.1	130.8
Wales	2.7	4.9	132	57.6	843	87.4	4.6	233.0	211.4
Northern Ireland	1.5	2.7	110	48.0	678	70.3	6.0	–	–[b]
United Kingdom	55.6	100.0	229	100.0	960	100.0	2.7	110.2[b]	100[b]

Sources: *HMSO Abstract of Regional Statistics: 1974* for Cols. 1–7. King (1973) for Cols. 8 and 9.

[a]"Devolvable" expenditure is total government expenditure *less* "unallocable" expenditure (mainly defence).
[b]Great Britain only.

in principle and, for the reasons given, a reasonable prediction of what ultimately will be politically acceptable. Moreover, it leaves the legislature free to take a much more active interest in important national and international issues and therefore to exert more pressure on the executive, for regional assemblies can concentrate on the redress of local grievances. It follows not only that there should be elected assemblies in all regions but that they should have some devolved taxing powers as well as freedom in expenditure allocation, so that regional political participation is fostered. To reinforce contact between different layers of government and to reduce centralizing tendencies, local government would have no direct link with the central government but would be represented in the functional committees of the regional assembly. Likewise, a proportion of elected representatives of the regional assemblies would be members of the House of Lords (the British Upper House), which would both raise the prestige of regional assemblies and offer the House of Lords a more positive role in the process of government [see MD (1973, chap. 6)].

Space prevents a detailed examination of the problems facing such a radical change in the structure of British government. It is clear that the MD is written on the assumption that dissemination of political power is an important argument in the community's objective function that must be assigned a considerable weight. At the same time, though it spells out its proposals in detail, it leaves at least partly unsolved the extent to which particular financial arrangements designed to further the aim of dissemination of power (e.g., taxing powers) will affect the values of the other arguments, notably stabilization and distributional objectives. A good deal of the official evidence to the KC by the Treasury and Inland Revenue argues for nothing more than token devolution of taxing powers and complete control over the total regional assembly budget because of the fear of surrender of budgetary instruments important for stabilization. I have argued elsewhere [Peacock (1973)] that this evidence rests on a fairly simplistic model of the role of fiscal policy in controlling fluctuations in income and employment. What must be emphasized is that the MD argues that such important issues as these cannot be resolved without much further study and that any precise proposals would take a generation to work out. This view is in stark contrast with that of the present government, which hopes to begin the process of (limited) devolution within the lifetime of the present Parliament.

5. Conclusion

Faced with the far-reaching consequences of the oil crisis for the pursuit of the traditional objectives of maintaining a high level of employment and controlling inflation and with the need to improve the poor growth performance of the U.K. economy, embarking on a major constitutional reform could hardly come at a more inopportune moment for the British government. However, as already indicated, its political survival and, indeed, that of any alternative government is estimated to depend upon making some concession to the demand for political and economic decentralization. At the same time, these concessions do not embody what would commonly be regarded as a major economic indicator of transfer of power, namely, the devolution of responsibility for financing a major part of decentralized expenditures, the main ground for rejection of transfer being the need to maintain centralized control of finance for economic stabilization purposes. As pointed out, this approach may be based on strong technical assumptions and a mistaken view of the strength of demand for devolution. It is arguable, first, whether or not devolution of financing power would make much difference to the central government's capability for preserving economic stability [see King (1967)]. Second, it is questionable, as section 4 has argued, whether or not the political inequalities created by the proposed system would be tolerated by the "losers" in the English regions.

The final paradox in the British situation is that the decision whether or not and how to devolve government seems certain to be taken in a way that could be regarded as contrary to the whole spirit of the growing demand for political participation. Such is the power of a British government in office and the strength of party discipline that an Act of Devolution can be passed in the central legislature by simple majority of members who themselves are elected by a simple majority system, and in a matter of months after a public statement of intention (such as a white paper). No referendum, special majority provisions, Presidential veto, or delays by an Upper House will stand in the way. When they finally come into being, the regional assemblies will be the creatures of Parliament and will have no independently guaranteed constitutional rights. In the home country, the "Mother of Parliaments" remains a matriarch.

Notes

1. The original Chairman, Lord Crowther, better known as Geoffrey Crowther, died in 1972 and was succeeded by Lord Kilbrandon, a Lord of Appeal. This is why the Commission is known today as the Kilbrandon Commission. The present author replaced Professor Donald Robertson of Glasgow in November 1970, who also died in the course of the commission's work.

2. The constitutional convention is that a substantial minority of members must dissent from the majority's findings before they can publish a minority report. There were only two signatories to the Memorandum of Dissent, Lord Crowther-Hunt (no relation of the original Chairman) and the author.

3. The author, in a prefatory note to the Memorandum of Dissent (MD), argued strongly that the problem of devolution embraced that of reexamining the allocation of functions between the public and private sector [see MD (1973), p. xi].

4. I am no authority on the latest developments in political philosophy. Surely someone has clothed political theories in this methodological garb. Thus Hobbes: objective function has one main argument—preservation of peace. Constraint—men are by nature querulous, therefore, in the absence of policy intervention, lawlessness and life "nasty, brutish and short." Appropriate policy instrument—firm dictatorial government.

5. At the time of writing, attempts are already being made to muster support for regional assemblies in England. For example, Members of Parliament with constituencies in the North of England are examining proposals for a regional assembly in the North. An attempt has also been made to revive the ancient Cornish Parliament.

References

Aronson, R. 1974. Financing public goods and the distribution of population in metropolitan areas: An analysis of fiscal migration in the United States and England. In *Economic Policies and Social Goals, York Studies in Economics*, A.J. Culyer, ed. London: Martin Robertson.

Breton, A. 1974. *The Economic Theory of Representative Government*, chaps. 5 and 6. Chicago: Aldine.

Breton, A., and Scott, A. 1974. A theory of the structure of the public sector. mimeographed, chap. 3.

Command Paper 6348. 1975. *Our Changing Democracy: Devolution to Scotland and Wales.* London: Her Majesty's Stationery Office.

King, D. 1973. Financial and economic aspects of regionalism and separatism. Research paper no. 10, Commission on the Constitution. London: Her Majesty's Stationery Office.

King, D. 1976. The fiscal implications of devolution. Lecture delivered to Institute for Fiscal Studies, London.

MD. 1973. Memorandum of dissent by Lord Crowther-Hunt and Professor Alan Peacock. Command paper no. 5460-I. London: Her Majesty's Stationery Office.

MR. 1973. Report of the Royal Commission on the Constitution. Command paper no. 5460. London: Her Majesty's Stationery Office.

Peacock, A. 1973. Economic policy and the finance of intermediate levels of government. Appendix A to MD (1973).

Social and Community Planning Research. 1973. Devolution and other aspects of government: An attitudes survey. Research paper no. 7, Commission on the Constitution. London: Her Majesty's Stationery Office.

4

France: Central-Government Control over Public Investment Expenditures

Rèmy Prud'homme

Introduction

France is said to be—with Japan—one of the most "centralized" countries of the nonsocialist developed world. Although intergovernmental relationships in France are complex and evolving, it is true that the role played by the central government is a key element of the system. I can therefore focus my analysis of the French system on central-government control (CGC).

The discussion will be limited to CGC over public expenditure. CGC over public income (i.e., over taxes) appears clearly in the statistical tables: about 85 percent of the taxes raised in France are raised by the central government. In addition, the nature of local-government taxation is decided by the central government. Local government cannot create a new tax; it cannot even change the rates of the various existing taxes; it can only change a sort of global rate of taxation. CGC over expenditures is not so tight and is more interesting.

I shall further restrict my analysis by focusing on investment expenditures. It must be noted that there is a complete dichotomy between investment expenditures and operating expenditures. Sources of finance and decision-making processes are entirely separate. To have a swimming pool built is one thing, but to get the fuel required to heat it is another. There are instances of completed equipment not being utilized for lack of operation funds. Needless to say, this separation makes it difficult to achieve an optimal combination of production factors. Although this difficulty is in itself an interesting problem, I shall not discuss it here. The reason for focusing on capital expenditures rather than on operating expenditures is that the former, although less important in money terms, are more "strategic" than the latter. Salaries, which constitute the bulk of operating expenditures, are largely predetermined. Investments, by contrast, can be chosen; they can be policy tools. At any rate, this is how the matter is seen in France. The political debate on public expenditures at both national and local levels concentrates on investments, as does the planning process.

I shall first examine briefly the nature of CGC on public investments, trying to explain who controls what and how. I shall then discuss the major objectives of this control and whether or not they are achieved. I shall also deal with the limits to CGC that make the system workable.

The Nature of Central-Government Control

CGC over public investment expenditures is either direct or indirect, according to the type of investment. Some investments, such as for universities and major highways, are undertaken, paid for, and of course decided on by the central government. Other types of investments, such as for primary schools or water-treatment plants, are undertaken and paid for by local governments. Local governments, however, are usually too poor to finance these investments and must have recourse to central-government subsidies and to borrowing, thus opening the door to CGC. The key points are (1) that decisions relative to subsidies and loans are made piecemeal (investment by investment), not as a whole, and (2) that loans are usually granted only when subsidies are granted. For a given local-government investment, sources of finance could be, for instance, as follows:

Local taxes	20
Central-government subsidy	20
Loan	60
Total	100

The loan is usually granted by the *Caisse des Dépots et Consignations*, a central-government–controlled financial organization; it will be granted more or less automatically once a central-government subsidy for this investment has been obtained, but it will not be granted if this particular investment has not received a central-government subsidy. No subsidy, no loan; and it is easy to conclude, no investment. This is the mechanism by which the central government controls indirectly local-government investments.

Local governments are no longer prevented from borrowing on financial markets. Over recent years, many cities have had recourse to banks. Some have even floated bonds abroad. But this is hardly a way of escaping CGC, for two reasons: (1) market rates are much higher than *Caisse des Dépots* rates, and (2) Ministry of Finance authorization is necessary for important bond issues.

Needless to say, local-government officials complain bitterly about CGC control of investments. To make matters worse (or to make them look worse), a value-added tax of about 15 percent is levied on the investment. In my example, the central government would therefore disburse only about 5 percent of the investment and yet be in a position to decide whether or not it will be made.

Functions of Central-Government Control

CGC over investments is not without a rationale. It serves at least four major objectives: (1) it is a tool for political control; (2) it enables the central government to carry out regional policies; (3) it enables the central government to carry out sectoral policies; and (4) it is used in macroeconomic policy making.

The French system obviously gives the central government considerable power. An attempt was made [Prud'homme (1974)] to explain the relationship with the following equation:

$$C_r = 1.139P_r + 1.855G_r - 0.037I_r - 430 \qquad R^2 = 0.980$$
$$(0.122) \quad (1.674) \quad (0.378)$$

where: C_r = central-government expenditures for public investments in region
   r during the 1966–1970 period
   P_r = population of region r in 1966
   G_r = population increase in region r over 1966–1970
   I_r = index of political influence of region r (relative number of
   representatives belonging to political parties in office)

The equation suggests that "political influence," as it was measured, does not influence the granting of subsidies and the allocation of directly controlled public investments between regions. It is likely, however, that at a finer level political muscle does play a role: A mayor who becomes minister usually gets things done for his city.

But the power given to the central government is not used primarily to "favor" areas that are politically well behaved. It is used, in a more subtle manner, to control political and social discontent. When difficulties and conflicts of an economic or political nature arise, well-chosen and promptly decided subsidies or investment will help calm minds and matters.

One other point to be made is that the power given by this system to the central government is more in the hands of the bureaucracy than in the hands of politicians. Ministers cannot possibly decide on every subsidy. Decisions are therefore taken by high civil servants, to whom local-government elected officials (mayors, councillors) must address themselves and from whom they must seek approval for their investment projects. The power thus given to civil servants is very extensive and goes a long way to explain the reasonably high quality of many French bureaucrats.

CGC over public investments has a second function: it enables the central government to carry out regional policies. First, it can be used to make sure that the level of public services is about equal in every location. The system in itself tends to create a fairly uniform pattern of quality. Napolean I used to boast: "At this very moment every pupil, in every French Lycée, is now working on

the same Tacitus version!" Things have somewhat changed since the time of
Napoleon I, but because they are produced all over France according to identical
mechanisms, primary schooling and hospital care, for example, are roughly
similar all over France. Differences in incomes between local governments are
not reflected in differences between public-services levels. CGC operates as a
filter, or as a siphon, between the two. While such a statement requires qualifications, the lack of quantitative studies on regional differences in the quality
of public services makes qualifications difficult. But this very lack of studies
suggests that the problem is not pressing, and it is a general belief (which I
share) that such differences, if they exist, are not very great.

CGC can go further than prevent differences in levels of public services. It
can be a tool to carry out the regional policy (*politique d'aménagement du
territoire*) of the central government. The French government has such a policy,
spelled out in official pronouncements and documents, and particularly in
the Five-Year Plans, aimed at reducing interregional disparities. One way to
promote the development of lagging regions is precisely to increase social-
overhead capital in those regions. CGC makes it possible to do that.

In other words, CGC can help change the explosive sequence largely
characteristic of the U.S. scene—income differentials, leading to similar public-
services differentials, leading to greater income differentials—into an implosive
sequence—income differentials, leading to a reversal of public-services differentials, leading to lesser income differentials.

This, however, is more a theoretical possibility than a French reality. My
equation suggested that central-government expenditures by regions were on the
average proportional to the population of the regions. Differences in per capita
expenditures could therefore be taken to represent voluntary distortions de-
picting the regional policy actually carried out by the central government. It
appears that the regions that had more than their share were not those that,
according to the announced policy, should have had more than their share. The
same calculations were made for the central- and local-government investment
expenditures by regions, and they led to the same conclusions.

A third function of CGC is to ensure that the distribution of public investments by type is in accordance with nationally determined needs or priorities.
This is done in two ways. The central government can and does manipulate the
"demand" for public investments by manipulating the rates of subsidies. The
20 percent rate quoted above is an example and an average. In fact, the rates of
subsidy range from 0 to 100 percent. The higher the rate, the more attractive
the investment for the local government. Figure 4-1 illustrates the choice to be
made by a local government between two types of investments, i and j. It is
assumed that the unit costs of i and j are identical; the indifference curves that
depict the satisfaction derived by the local community from mixes of i and j
happen to be symmetrical. Under a given budgetary constraint, L_1, the local
government would choose A on indifference curve I_1. Let us assume that in-

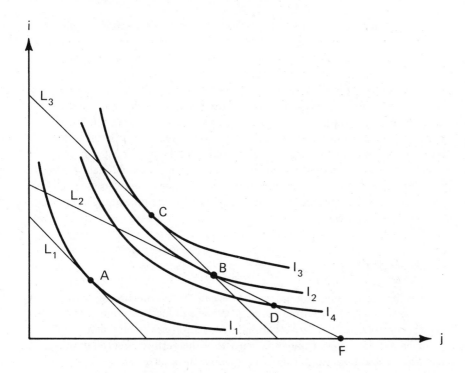

Figure 4–1. Subsidies for Local Investment

vestment i is subsidized at a 20 percent rate, and investment j at a 60 percent
rate. This modifies the absolute and relative prices of i and j for the local
government. Its budgetary constraint is moved to L_2. The local government will
then chose B on indifference curve I_2. Had the subsidy money thus given to
the local government taken the form of an unattached grant, the budgetary constraint would have been moved to L_3 and the choice made would have been C
on indifference curve I_3. It should be added that the French experience suggests
that local governments behave as subsidy-maximizers rather than satisfaction-
maximizers; they tend to choose a point that is situated somewhere between B
and F, such as D, on an indifference curve I_4, which is even lower than I_2.

The central government also manipulates the supply of public investments,
in that it decides the total amount of subsidy (and of direct investments) to be
spent on a particular type of investment. The rationale for this type of control
is that public services (public investments are taken to be a proxy for public
services), although delivered and consumed at a local level, are a legitimate concern of the central government. Each inhabitant being also a citizen, it is the
responsibility of the central government to make sure that for each type of
public service minimal levels are offered everywhere.

The fourth function of CGC is of a macroeconomic nature. It gives the central government, which is responsible for overall economic policy, an instrument to increase or decrease overall demand. Tax policy is not much used for that purpose in France. If operating expenditures are not very flexible, there remain investment expenditures. At a time of economic boom and inflation, investment expenditures will be cut; at a time of recession, they will be increased. High rates of economic growth are therefore associated with low—not high— rates of public investment. While the paucity of data makes it difficult to test this point and the quarterly figures that would be necessary for a lag analysis are not available, Figure 4-2, which plots rates of growth of GNP against rates of growth of central-government investments (excluding defence) for the last eight years, clearly shows that there is no positive correlation and suggests that there may be a negative one.

The Limits of CGC

CGC has therefore many advantages—for the central government. But each advantage is a disadvantage from the point of view of local governments: political control is seen as "colonialism," since national regional policies prevent dynamic areas from reaping the benefits of their efforts. Central-government guidance relative to types of investment does not maximize local-government satisfaction, as shown in Figure 4-1, and countercyclical use of public investments prevents local governments from serious investment planning. CGC is therefore resisted by local governments. In practice, CGC is not absolute, and several mechanisms have been developed to soften it.

The first such mechanism is called *deconcentration*. Deconcentration is the transfer of powers from high levels of the central-government bureaucracy to lower levels, as from a minister to a prefect. It is quite different from decentralization, which is the transfer of powers from central government to local government, as from a minister to a mayor. The prefect is appointed (and controlled) by the minister, whereas the mayor is locally elected. A number of deconcentration measures have been taken. In 1970 investments were classified by type, and it was decided that decisions, particularly decisions as to whether or not to grant a subsidy, relative to certain types of investments would no longer be taken in the Paris ministries but would be taken by the departmental or regional prefects. The decision makers have thus been brought closer to the "demand" for public services, at least for some types of investment.

Deconcentration procedures suggest that a dichotomy between central-government control and local-government control would be an oversimplification. Deconcentrated CGC is hardly CGC. In theory, local officials of the central-government bureaucracy are busy implementing central-government objectives and orders; in practice, they are influenced by local realities and problems. Some

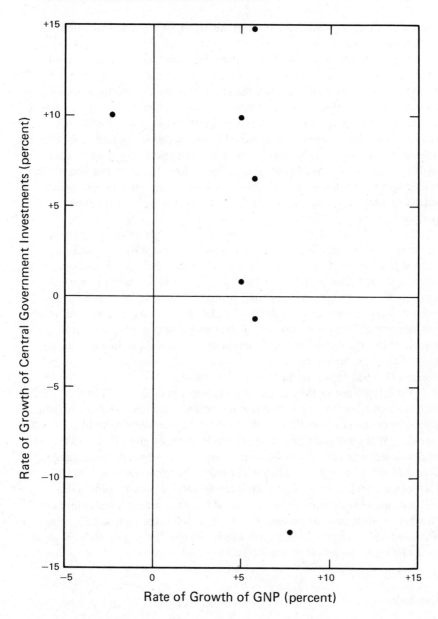

Figure 4–2. Growth Rates of GNP and Central-Government Investment

local officials have occasionally become advocates vis-à-vis Paris of "their" department or region.

A second limit to CGC is the role played by the "consultation" procedures of the planning process. The Five-Year Plans include a matrix of public investments by type and by region. Until the Sixth Plan, public investment was first divided between various types of investment, and then each type of investment was divided into regions. For the Sixth Plan (1971–1975) and the Seventh Plan (1976–1980), which is being prepared now, the process is reversed: public investment is divided into regions, and each region is asked how it wants to divide its share into types of investment. The process by which the demand for public investment thus "revealed" by the regions is adjusted to the priorities established by the central government is rather complex, but the wishes expressed by the regions are taken into account.

It should be added, however, that the role of the plan, even (or particularly) in the field of public investments, is not great, because the government is not obliged to follow it. In practice, what matters is the yearly budgetary process, which is largely divorced from the plan. The plan only provides those regions or those sectors that do not get their planned share with an argument in budgetary discussions: "According to the plan, we should get more." Although the Ministry of Finance knows how to deal with that type of argument, it does not much like the sort of pressure exerted by the plan. As of this writing, it is not definite that the matrix of public investments by type and region for the Seventh Plan will appear in the final text of the plan.

The importance of the budgetary process brings us to a third limit to CGC, which comes from the way investment projects are initiated. At an early point, someone identifies a "need" or a "demand" and comes up with an idea for an investment that will meet this demand. The idea is then given flesh and turned into a project proposal. Often the project proposal will be criticized, counterproposals will be prepared, and choices between projects will be made. Only then will the project go to higher levels for decision. In other words, a distinction can be made between the *power of initiative*, which is the ability to launch new ideas, and the *power of decision*, which is the right to kill them. The central government certainly has a large share of this power of decision. But its control over the power of initiative is definitely smaller.

Conclusion

The heart of the matter is that both central governments and local governments (as well as regional governments) have a legitimate concern for the provision of public services. Some public services are more "national" than others and some less. But most are at the same time "national" and "local." The solution therefore should not be looked for in an allocation of the various services to the various levels of governments. Each level of government should have its say for each type of public service. This complicates matters, because different levels of governments will have different priorities—and rightly so. The problem therefore becomes one of finding appropriate mechanisms to accommodate conflicting views.

Reference

Prud'homme, R. 1974. Critique de la politique d'aménagement du territoire. *Revue d'Economie Politique* 6:921–935.

5

Stabilization Policy, Grants-in-Aid, and the Federal System in Western Germany

Jack H. Knott

Introduction

Since the middle 1960s a public debate in Western Germany has taken place over the issue of whether and in what ways the federal government should try to influence local public investment decisions.[1] A central concern has been how to assure a closer correspondence between these local decisions and central fiscal-policy goals. Presently, if the federal government wants to alter public spending as a fiscal-policy measure, it must contend with the independent budget decisions of state and local governments over more than three-fourths of total public investment.

In part due to dissatisfaction with this state of affairs, the federal government is turning to a greater emphasis upon monetary policy.[2] In the past, however, monetary policy has not proved very effective because of the openness of the West German economy to interest-rate–induced capital flows. In addition, the independent position of the Bundesbank has left the central government with only an indirect control over this aspect of policy. For these reasons, an exclusive reliance upon monetary policy may not present an attractive alternative. Assuming, then, that the central government can be expected to continue its reliance upon fiscal policy,[3] this chapter treats two main themes: should the central government even concern itself with cycles in local public investment; and, if so, are intergovernmental grants-in-aid a useful instrument for trying to prevent them?

To the extent that local public expenditures vary procyclically, the business-cycle swings in the private economy are reinforced, thereby increasing the difficulty of pursuing fiscal policy on the federal level. In the German case, 90 percent of public investment is made in the construction industry, but during the period 1970–1973 the federal government made only slightly more than 16

The research described here was supported by Doctoral Fellowships from the University of California, Berkeley, and the International Institute of Management, Berlin. I am very grateful to my colleagues at the Institute in Berlin and want especially to thank Bernd Reissert and Fritz Scharpf for their patient and helpful comments during the course of my work. For help with the revision, I am indebted to Edward Gramlich.

percent of the total. Any federal investment program designed as a fiscal-policy measure that does not include state or local investments cannot have much impact on overall investment in the private economy [Barbier (1975)].

Cyclical swings in local expenditure may also cause disruption of local construction employment and the provision of local services. The joint federal-state-local stabilization program (*Konjunkturprogramm*) in September 1975, for example, was particularly designed to help alleviate unemployment in the construction industry. The provision of local services has not presented as great a problem as unemployment; nevertheless, in 1974–1975, the main theme of the budget speeches made before the local parliaments was the reduction of city financial capacity and service levels due to the continuing recession and decline in tax income [Der Staedtetag(1975)].

These are not only hypothetical concerns. Over the last 10 years, local and state investment expenditures and credit assumption have shown a pronouncedly procyclical development [Biehl et al. (1974)]. A main response to this trend is the provision in the Finance Reform of 1969 that prescribes the use of inter-governmental financial aid for economic stabilization. This measure made constitutional earlier extensive practice that had taken place in particular during the 1966–1967 recession.

Despite these constitutional and practical measures, the grant system and its applicability to fiscal policy remain very controversial issues. All the states and the federal government disfavor a further extension of these grants, and some of the states have set about testing the constitutionality of the way these grants have been implemented. Most recently, the federation has become even more disenchanted with the use of investment grants for fiscal-policy purposes, proposing to include them in the budget-cutting program for 1976 [Apel (1975)].

Part of the difficulty is based upon the rather complex system of budgetary and political relations between the states and the federal government. A further issue is whether investment grants can be varied in a way that satisfies the requirements of stabilization policy. Grants for above-surface construction, which are a prominent type of federal grant, require a minimum two-year planning phase plus a two- to three-year execution phase [Schmidz (1972)]. Smaller communities that do not possess a large array of investment projects may find it difficult to alter these plans in the short run. The familiar problem of a time lag between approval of an investment project and its execution also plagued the use of these investment grants as a stabilization measure. During the 1966–1967 recession, the construction industry started its recovery more than one-half year after general business activity had turned upward.

A somewhat different although related issue is whether stabilization policy should have altered these grants in the short run even if the practical capacity existed to do so. Stabilization does not represent the only goal or even the most important goal of investment policy. Officials involved in the Joint Task invest-ment areas, for example, see their task as promoting long-term growth, which, they argue, should not depend upon temporary ups or down in the private economy.[4] The grant system also serves the function of equalizing income among regions that have varying tax yields.[5] More local sources of income are not always sufficient to meet basic policy needs, whereas the central government controls a much broader tax base and has access to a larger credit market.

To extend the analysis of these issues, section 2 of this chapter contains a discussion of institutional factors that might support the phenomenon of cycles in local investment. It also examines why, in contrast to the United States, grants-in-aid have been considered a main avenue for preventing these cycles. Section 3 analyzes the 1967 recession and subsequent boom period in order to see how the local investment cycle has developed and what happened to grants-in-aid.

Section 4 then takes a closer look at state grants-in-aid to local governments. The issue of whether any differences existed between the anticyclical or procyclical behavior of individual states is examined. In addition, the response of local public investment to variations in grants is looked at, especially during the recession phase. Section 5, the final part of the chapter, comes back to the original two main issues and examines factors for and against the use of grants-in-aid for stabilization policy.

2. The Institutional Setting

Unlike more centralized systems, the federal government in Germany does not have the option to influence directly state or local spending decisions. The Basic Law stipulates that the federation and the states have independent budgetary powers insofar as the Basic Law does not prescribe otherwise. The Law does add, however, that both levels need to take account of macroeconomic equilibrium, to be accomplished by means of special federal laws requiring approval of the Bundesrat.[6]

Since the Finance Reform in 1969, federal legislation with Bundesrat approval may set ceilings on capital borrowing of all levels of government.[7] The ceilings are based on a weighted average of each government's actual credit assumption over the last three years. Because the Bundesrat must approve any such measure, however, a commonly stated opinion is that the restrictions did not severely hinder state investment spending.[8] They presumably did have a more positive impact on the capital market. In particular, the restrictions have raised questions about their possible contravention of the right of self-administration for the local governments [see Buechmann (1974)]. Another argument against them is that they cause disruption of local investment planning. Because actual credit is not taken up until very late in the planning of a construction project, it is argued, a limitation imposed at that time introduces undue strains with contractors and other clients.[9]

Under normal circumstances, the capital borrowing of local governments

is not regulated by federal legislation. Generally the state interior ministries
judge the debt capacity of the community, based upon the community's
financial strength, which is measured primarily in terms of tax revenue. During
times of recession, tax income naturally declines, reducing the financial strength
of the community. As this occurs, the debt authorities become less willing to
approve additional debt assumption. In response, the communities cut back on
investment spending, thereby reinforcing the business-cycle recession in the
private economy [Der Spiegel (1975)] .

Federal legislation with Bundesrat approval may also require that the states
and federal government freeze certain tax income at the Bundesbank.[10] Action
by the federal government may then later release these reserves, again with
Bundesrat approval, for the purpose of additional spending in times of recession. Significantly, the local governments are not included in this system. They
do build savings according to law, but these are not used for stabilization
purposes nor are they in any way controlled by central policy of the federal
government. The reciprocal of this measure, that is, the obligatory running of
current-account deficits during a recession, is not provided for by the Basic
Law.[11]

An additional potential avenue for influencing local investment decisions
is the use of intergovernmental grants-in-aid. For purposes of this book, only
tied-investment grants are analysed in detail; comparisons are made, however,
with untied or formula grants, which form part of the revenue-sharing and
equalization system in Western Germany.[12]

The main argument against the use of tied-investment grants on the federal
level is that constitutionally the federal government may not give financial aid
directly to local governments. Instead, it may give the money only to the states,
which make it part of their program of state aid. Under normal circumstances,
there is no obligation of the state to follow the policy direction set by the
federal government. The state may spend as much as it desires in these areas,
regardless of what the federal government prefers. The federal contribution
is also made only in limited spending areas and is relatively modest in comparison to the size of the states' grants programs for local investment.[13]

If the federal government decides upon a policy of increasing investment
grants during a recession, it will propose a special stabilization program (Konjunkturprogramm) that contains additional investments in these areas. To induce
state participation, it generally makes the additional funds provisional upon
matched spending by the state and local governments. This program will then
be discussed in the Finance Planning Council[14] and worked out into an administrative agreement. The Bundestag then has a period of 30 days in which to
reject the plan; otherwise it goes into effect.

Instances in which the federal government has attempted to reduce tied-
investment grants explicitly for stabilization reasons have occurred only once.
In 1973 the Planning Commissions in the Joint Task (Gemeinschaftsaufgaben)

spending areas agreed to a 10 percent shift in spending to the following year. The shift did not alter the regular, planned program, however, but had more of a symbolic character.[15]

This raises the issue of whether or not these grants have followed a destabilizing growth pattern. Studies of the stabilization effects of investment grants have all agreed that they have followed a more or less destabilizing, and hence procyclical, course [see Kock (1975) and Biehl et al. (1974)]. Federal tied grants to the states have shown only a slightly procyclical development; state tied grants to local government, on the other hand, have evidenced a pronounced procyclical trend. The other major types of grants-in-aid, the untied or formula grants, have also followed a procyclical tendency. From the state to the local level, untied grants developed procyclically but in a less pronounced way than the tied grants [Kock (1975)].

Examining the major types of stabilization instruments, it becomes apparent that in each case—grants-in-aid, debt ceilings, and stabilization reserves—the federal government exercises only either an indirect or marginal influence upon the local investment cycle. The state interior ministries exercise the key function of overseeing local debt levels but have done so in a way that encourages destabilizing behavior. The legal stipulation that the federal government give financial aid only to the states has further placed the states in a central position over the local communities. In this instance as well, the state grant programs have supported a destabilizing behavior on the part of the local governments. Moreover, the local communities have not as yet become part of the obligatory stabilization reserve system. In sum, the federal government cannot directly influence the local spending cycle. Major instruments that are available have marginal impact or, as in the case of credit policy, reinforce the local procyclical pattern. Section 3 takes a look at this pattern during the 1967 recession and subsequent boom.

3. The 1967 Recession and Subsequent Boom

Local governments have followed a rather procyclical investment pattern during the 1960s and early 1970s. As seen in Figure 5-1, especially during the 1966-1967 recession, investment declined considerably; again, in the boom phase, 1969-1972, investment surged ahead, registering growth rates over 15.0 percent per year. Since 1972 real public investment on the local level has not grown strongly, while outlays for personnel and other current budgetary items have climbed more rapidly.

A frequent explanation for the procyclical investment behavior of local governments puts an emphasis upon the income side, much as would be the case in a private household.[16] With higher income, the borrowing potential of the community increases. If 90 units of funds are needed, for example, but

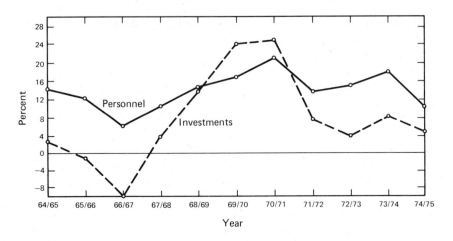

Source: Klein et al. (1975); Statistisches Bundesamt (1962–71); and own calculations

Figure 5–1. Local Government Investments for Construction and Personnel Expenditures (Percentage Annual Change, 1964–1975).

the local administration takes in 100, it can use the extra 10 units for investment, of which 5 to 8 units meet interest payments and around 2 units go for amortization. But, with this amount, the administration can spend another 90 units for investment. In other words, they key amount is the surplus of current income that allows the community to meet its debt payments.

During the 1966–1967 recession, overall local government income grew at 3.2 percent over the previous year. The average annual growth rate for the 10-year period 1964–1974 was 10.8 percent; for the boom years 1969–1971 it was 14.4 percent. Tax income declined more than overall income in 1966–1967, while revenue from grants-in-aid grew slightly faster than the total at 5.0 percent. As expected, the decline in current revenue caused a decline in credit assumption of –2.3 percent. Subsequently, the taking of credit again climbed sharply at an annual average growth rate of 23.0 percent.

Tax income as a source of local-expenditure financing, and, in particular, investment financing, has fallen consistently over the 10-year period. Taxes as a percentage of total income fell from 34.7 percent in 1961 to 29.7 percent in 1975. As a source of investment financing, the decline has been even more significant. In 1962 current income accounted for 36.7 percent of investment financing, while in 1974 the figure had fallen to 15.9 percent. Intergovernmental grants-in-aid have largely filled this gap, especially as a source of finance for local investments. The percentage share that tied grants comprise of local-investment financing increased from 15.0 percent in 1962 to 29.2 percent in 1974 [Klein and Gleitze (1975)] . For this reason, grants have become a major potential source for influencing local investment decisions.

Each federal state in Germany has a system of tax-equalization laws (*Finanzausgleichsgesetze*) that regulate to a large extent the untied and formula grants to the local communities. These untied grants followed a slightly procyclical trend over the last 10 years and have accounted for at least 50 percent or more of total grants-in-aid from the states. The main reason for the procyclical growth of these grants is that they are tied to tax revenue. Moreover, the percentage share of the tax revenue which the localities receive is not easily changed. Politically, the states cannot raise this percentage in recession times and lower it in boom times in order to even out the revenue flow for the communities.

In terms of overall figures, the federal government increased tied grants to states for local investment programs by 23.5 percent in 1966–1967, a very anticyclical development [Kock (1975)]. Looking at state grants to local governments, a much less favorable picture emerges. State tied grants for investment increased by an annual rate of only 1.8 percent. Although published figures are not generally available for individual programs, Hahn (1974) provides data on the percentage participation of the federation, the states, and the localities in the Low-Cost Housing Program from 1952–1972, which serve as an indication of developments in this spending area. These data are presented in Table 5–1.

In the first recession year, 1966, federal participation continued to fall according to a longer-term administrative agreement that foresaw a declining federal share. In the following year, owing to the passage of the stabilization programs, the federal share reversed course, climbing in volume by more than 500 percent. The concurrent sharp reduction of the states' contribution, however, more than leveled out this anticyclical spending of the federation. As Table 5–1 shows, the states reduced spending by 1380.07 DM in 1967, slightly more than the amount by which the federation increased its spending.

In summary, it appears that grants-in-aid did very little to offset destabilizing local spending, thereby reinforcing the local business cycle. Coupled with this was an even sharper decline in the revenue from taxes, causing local govern-

Table 5–1

Participation of the Federation, States, and Local Governments in Low-Cost Housing, 1966–1967

(In Million DM and Percent Annual Change)

	1966	1967	Annual Change	Percent Annual Change
Federal	246.89	1595.65	1348.76	546.3
State	3887.52	2507.45	-1380.07	-35.5
Local	222.77	205.16	-17.61	-7.7

Source: Adapted from Hahn (1974).

ments to reduce borrowing and investment. As in the analysis of fiscal-policy instruments, the federal states occupy a key position for the success of any federal stabilization strategy. Section 4 therefore takes a closer look at state grants-in-aid policies.

4. State Grants-in-Aid Policies

In the past, the aggregate of state spending has followed a destabilizing path. Yet the differences among states in wealth and population size raise the question of whether some states might pursue a less procyclical policy than others. North Rhine–Westphalia (NRW), for example, has a population of more than 16 million and produces a state domestic product that approaches that of many smaller foreign countries. The Saarland, on the other hand, has less than 2 million inhabitants and does not possess a large industrial infrastructure. Conceivably, the wealthier and more populous states pursue a less procyclical policy than the others.

The Public Choice literature argues indirectly that size is a factor that can hinder successful pursuit of stabilization policy. The economies of smaller governmental units are often too open to allow them to retain the benefits a stabilization policy might produce. Oates (1972), for example, argues that smaller governmental units have less incentive to follow stabilization policy because they end up paying the costs themselves while a share of the benefits accrues to others [see also Neumann (1971)]. Following this line of reasoning, the smaller federal states may not have as much incentive to take initiatives in the stabilization-policy field as do larger states.

In a similar manner, the Expert Commission for the Realignment of the Federal States (*Sachverstaendigenkommission zur Neuegliederung des Bundesgebietes*) proposed a reduction of the number of states to five or six more-or-less equal units in size and tax base.[17] The purpose would be to create units that could support the necessary governmental program without extraordinary funding from the federal level. A related issue is whether or not the new states could better fulfill the requirements of stabilization policy. Presumably, if the larger and wealthier states' spending was found to be less business-cycle sensitive, that would support the argument for realignment of the states along these lines.

A lack of adequate financing may also disincline a state to pursue stabilization policy. The relatively less wealthy states in Western Germany have argued that their general pressing policy needs preclude an active stabilization perspective [Kock (1975)]. Especially during periods of growth, restrictions on expenditures represent for poorer states cutbacks in essential public services and infrastructure development. During a recession phase, these same states face severe difficulty meeting regular costs even without spending additional stabilization funds.

The fiscal-policy performance of each state's grants-in-aid program is considered by looking at the yearly tied-investment grants given to the local governments within the state's jurisdiction from 1962 to 1971.[18] Two time blocs are particularly important in this regard: the recession years 1966–1967 and the boom years 1969–1971. The percentage growth in Gross National Product for 1966–1967 fell to 1 percent, while from 1969 to 1971 the average growth rate was 12.2 percent. The 1967 recession was short, lasting not much more than one year. The economy began to recover again strongly in 1968 with a GNP growth rate for that year of 9.0 percent. The high point of the subsequent boom phase was reached in 1970 with a GNP growth rate of 13.3 percent.

Table 5–2 shows the percentage change in growth rates for tied-investment grants to local governments for 1966–1967 and the average growth-rate change for 1969–1971 for each of the eight regular states, excluding the city-states.[19] For the period 1966–1967, the table shows a rather sharp division in grant policy between NRW, SH, LS, and BV as the one group (Group 1) and HS, RLP, BW, and SL as the other (Group 2). The first group has a 15.8 percent average increase in grants-in-aid for that year, while the second group reduces their grants on average –5.8 percent. All the states in the second group fall below the midpoint and/or the average growth rate for 1966–1967, while all the states in the first group lie above it. The difference between the average percentage growth rate of the two groups is 21.6 percent, without much variation within each group.

Dividing the states again according to growth rates above and below the mean for the boom period 1969–1971, the same two groups fall out. The states in the first group show an average growth rate of 9.5 percent, while the second

Table 5–2
Federal State Expenditure on Categorical Grants for Investment to Local Governments, 1966–1967 and 1969–1971
(Percent Annual Change in Extraordinary Budget)

Federal State	Year	
Group 1	1966–67	1969–71 (68/69–69/70 70/71)
North Rhine–Westphalia (NRW)	15.1	14.4
Schleswig-Holstein (SH)	15.9	9.6
Lower Saxony (LS)	16.6	7.6
Bavaria (BV)	15.4	6.4
Group 2		
Hessen (HS)	–2.9	24.8
Rhineland-Palatinate (RLP)	–6.9	18.4
Baden-Wuerttemberg (BW)	–1.0	18.4
Saarland (SL)	–12.4	16.6

Source: Adapted from *Statistisches Bundesamt* (1962–1971).

group has an average rate of 19.6 percent. For this period, the break is not so sharp nor is the variation around the mean so small. Despite this, the placement of each state in the two groupings does not change from one time period to the next, as can be seen from Figure 5-2.

The point of view that more financially secure and larger federal states pursue a less procyclical budget policy receives little support from the data on investment grants-in-aid to local governments during the time period 1962–1971. The less procyclical group contains such diverse states as NRW and SH. The former is the largest and one of the most wealthy, while the latter is next to the poorest and one of the smaller states in population. In the more procyclical group, a similar contrast in state characteristics is found. BS competes with NRW for first place in wealth and size, but the SL is West Germany's poorest and smallest regular federal state.[20]

In a similar manner, the proposal to realign the states into larger and more self-sufficient entities financially does not receive support from the data. The strongest case against realignment on the basis of stabilization policy is the differing performance of BW and NRW, two traditionally self-sufficient federal

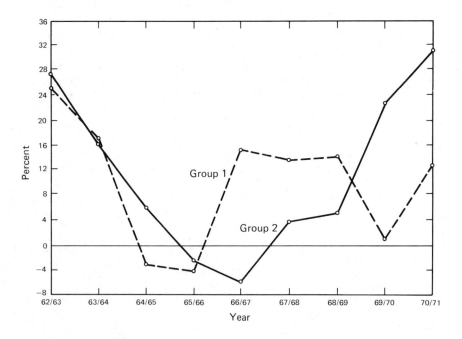

Source: Adapted from *Statistisches Bundesamt* (1962–1971).

Figure 5-2. Categorical Investment Grants of Group 1 and Group 2 States in Extraordinary Budget, 1962–1971 (Percentage Annual Change).

states. Both have a very similar per capita income, although the size of BW is somewhat smaller. The creation of all states comparable to BW, however, would not necessarily enhance the fiscal-policy performance of the states. A relatively poorer and smaller state, LS for example, has the highest growth rate for 1966–1967 and next to the lowest rate for 1969–1971.

The political party of the state government also does not determine the division of the states into these two groupings. BV is governed by the Christian Socialist Union (CSU), NRW by the Social Democrats (SPD), and SH by the Christian Democrats (CDU). In the second group, comparable party variations are found as well. HS has an SPD government, while BW is governed by the CDU.[21]

The federal grants taken together with the state grants do comprise a sizable proportion of total local public investment (TLPI), although the percentage shares vary from only 17.3 percent in LS to 42.9 percent in NRW for the year 1967. Presumably, those states in which intergovernmental investment grants comprise a larger percentage share of TLPI have a greater potential for influencing local-governmental fiscal-policy performance. Through the use of these grants, NRW, for example, should be able to influence local governmental investment behavior more substantially than would LS.

Table 5–3 presents the average percentage growth rates of investment grants and local investments for the recession years 1966–1967 and the boom years 1969–1971. The only real difference in local investment spending between the two groups takes place in the recession phase, 1966–1967. The less procyclical group shows an average falloff in local investment spending of –4.2 percent, despite a 15.8 percent average increase in state grants. The more procyclical grouping falls off even more sharply at –12.8 percent. Apparently, a rather

Table 5–3

Percentage Annual Change in State Categorical Grants for Investment and Total Local Public Investment in the Extraordinary Budget, 1966–1967 and 1969–1971

	1966–67	
	Grants	*Investments*
Group 1	15.8	–4.2
Group 2	–5.8	–12.8
	1968–69/69–70/70–71	
	Grants	*Investments*
Group 1	9.5	20.0
Group 2	19.6	22.7

Source: Adapted from *Statistisches Bundesamt* (1962–1971).

significant increase in investment grants during a recession does not deter a negative growth rate for local public investment. It does, however, prevent investments from falling off as far as they otherwise would have.

In the boom phase, only a very slight difference in investment spending
patterns between the two groups is found, despite the fact that grants-in-aid of
the second grouping grow twice as fast as those of the first. During the boom,
the percentage share that state investment grants represent of TLPI for the
first grouping is 31.9 percent; for the second grouping, the comparable figure is
33.9 percent. Because the potential for influencing local investment decisions
of the two groups is similar, the lack of difference in local public investment
spending in the boom phase seems to fall to the dynamics of local investment
decisions.

During the 1967 recession, all four states in the first grouping increase
grants-in-aid by approximately 15 to 16 percent. The range is only from 16.6
percent for LS to 15.1 percent for NRW. This lack of variation allows for holding
fiscal policy constant in a limited way, while at the same time varying the
percent that these grants represent of TLPI.

As Table 5–4 shows, the greater the percentage share of investment grants
on TLPI, the less the falloff in local investment during the recession years 1966–
1967. The two clearest cases are NRW and LS. The latter state's investment falls
off by twice the amount of the former state's investment. NRW's grants program
accounts for almost half of TLPI, but it still experiences a falloff in this investment of –3.0 percent, despite the state's policy of increasing investment grants
by 15.1 percent. Even a fairly large grant program accounting for almost 50
percent of local investments cannot guarantee an anticyclical local-governmental
spending policy.

A difference in grants as a percentage share of TLPI of 25.6 percent between
NRW and LS produces only a 3.0 percentage difference in investment growth. In
both cases, the growth rates are negative, despite large positive increases in state
grants. Nevertheless, all four investment growth patterns for these states lie

Table 5-4
**Categorical Grants for Investment as a Percentage of Total Local Investment
Expenditure in Extraordinary Budget, 1966–1967**

		(Percent annual change)			
	National Average	NRW	SH	BV	LS
% Grants	+7.9	15.1	15.9	15.4	16.6
% Investments	–8.0	–3.0	–3.4	–4.5	–6.0
Grants/% of I	33.9	42.9	35.7	31.8	17.3

Source: Adapted from *Statistisches Bundesamt* (1962–1971).

under the national average, some by more than 50 percent. If only local public investment is considered during the recession phase, the two groupings formed by grants-in-aid patterns (see Table 5-2) do not change.

The influence of intergovernmental grants upon local public investment during the 1962-1971 period is not great. During the boom period 1969-1971, local public investment in the first grouping of states grows at a rate comparable to local investment in the second grouping, despite a 50 percent slower growth in grants-in-aid. In the recession years, local public investment in both state groupings registers a negative growth, even though the grants in the first group increase by 15.0 percent. Apparently, to counteract business-cycle swings in local public investment requires a large grant program (up to 50 percent of local public investments) and a consciously anticyclical policy. Even meeting the requirements, however, does not predict success during the boom phase. Very likely it will prove difficult to cut expenditures in the grant program to the extent that they can be increased in the recession. At the same time, during the boom local governments readily utilize other sources of finance to pursue their own policy.

The explanation for the difference between the two state groupings remains puzzling based upon the criteria presented. The clearest difference exists for the 1966-1967 period, while the 1969-1971 period shows a more mixed result. The answer to this question, however, goes beyond the purposes of this chapter and offers a fitting subject for further research.

5. Summary and Conclusions

For at least two reasons, the federal government needs to concern itself with local investment decisions. Local governments make approximately two-thirds of the total public investment. On this basis alone, to the extent that the federal government intends to pursue fiscal policy with the budget, it must take account of these local expenditures. Furthermore, an analysis of the 1967 recession and subsequent boom has shown that local government have followed a destabilizing course in investment expenditure. Moreover, the major fiscal-policy instruments used by the federal government to deal with this development either had only a marginal positive effect or actually reinforced the local procyclical pattern.

In particular, the inclusion of the local governments in the system of obligatory stabilization reserves offers a direct way to improve their participation in investment stabilization programs. To some extent, it would also help to level out the cyclical nature of their tax revenue. This might be accomplished by including in the reserve system the local communities' share of revenue from the income tax.

The state laws that regulate debt assumption also need revision or amendment so that they provide for situations of economic disturbance. The new policy should at least allow for a constant increase in investment and corresponding debt in order not to reinforce the local business cycle. To realize this change, state and federal governments need to make sure that local revenue sources grow at a rate comparable to other levels of government. Because local governments do not have as much capacity for credit assumption as do other levels, the current-income part of revenue plays a more important role in determining cycles in local public investment.

The issue of whether and in what way to use grants-in-aid for influencing local investment is not easy to resolve because of the position of the federal states. The aggregate of tied grants has varied more procyclically than revenue-sharing grants at the state level. In at least one program, Low-Cost Housing, state action completely offset federal policy.

The further analysis of individual state differences raised more reservations of a different kind. Despite strong increases in tied grants in 1967 in some states, local investment within these state jurisdictions still showed a negative growth rate. In particular, the boom phase raised doubts about the effectiveness of tied grants as a stabilization instrument. Despite growth rates for tied grants that averaged more than twice as much for one group as the other, little difference appeared in local-investment growth rates. In other words, for tied grants to make a significant impact on the local investment cycle, the states need to vary these grants in a very anticyclical manner. Some further evidence suggested that if even a sharp variation in these grants is to have an effect on local investment, the share that tied grants represent of local investment also needs to be large.

A political and a budgetary factor work against the fulfillment of these two conditions. The National Association of Communities and spokesmen for the states have repeatedly emphasized that tied grants represent a reduction in local autonomy. Neither level is willing to accept an increase in federal tied grants. Moreover, on a regular yearly basis, tied grants are not varied for stabilization purposes. The yearly decisions over the growth rates of grants are taken in the individual ministries or planning committees on the criteria of substantive objectives of policy and normal budgetary constraints. Only under rather unusual economic circumstances will the finance ministry and the chancellor (minister president in the states) impose upon this pattern for stabilization purposes.[22] As analyzed in the introduction, longer-term substantive goals play a more important role in investment planning than does stabilization policy.

On the other hand, the same reasons that cause investment expenditure to vary procyclically also give the policy maker the option to vary these expenditures anticyclically. Approximately 90 percent of the federal budget in West Germany is legally or otherwise fixed; the investments represent that part of the budget that is new and variable. To take even these expenditures out of their flexible position would leave little room for discretionary policy.

In times of economic stress, stabilization policy must use grants-in-aid not as an exclusive instrument but only as part of a set of instruments. If the burden is primarily placed upon grants, the requirement of anticyclical variation becomes too great. The share that these grants should represent of local investment also raises questions about local autonomy. A preferable policy is to try to avoid procyclical swings in grant spending while at the same time bolstering the impact by other, complementary measures.

Notes

1. A recent form this debate has taken is a series of newspaper articles written by representatives of the cities, states, and national government [see Schmidt (1973); Weinberger (1973); and Wertz et al. (1973)].

2. This chapter is part of a larger study of economic policy and budgeting in Western Germany. The study is based upon over 50 open-ended interviews with officials and politicians involved in the budgetary process. The interviews were completed from April to November 1975 and were carried out on federal, state, and local levels of government. Most of the federal interviews were conducted in the Economics and Finance Ministries with officials at the section (*referat*) or division (*abteilung*) level. In addition, the budget director or another budgetary official in each state was interviewed, as well as representatives from the National Community Associations (*Spitzenverbaende*). Numerous respondents emphasized the shift to monetary policy during the discussions.

3. From an analysis of the listings of economic policy decisions given by the *Sachverstaendigenrat* (1970–1975), approximately 50 percent deal with tax or budgetary policy [see also Cowart (1975)].

4. The Joint Tasks (*Gemeinschaftsaufgaben*) were established constitutionally in 1969 with the Finance Reform and represent joint spending programs with the states and federal government in the areas of university construction, support for agriculture, and regional economic promotion. Despite these late constitutional arrangements, joint spending existed in these areas since 1957, 1956, and 1951, respectively.

5. This is especially the case for regional economic promotion but is also a general goal prescribed by the Basic Law (see Art. 106, par. 3, no. 2). For an excellent analysis of this aspect of the grants system, see Reissert (1975).

6. Basic Law, Art. 104, par. a, and 109. For a good commentary on these sections, see Maunz et al. (1973).

7. The most recent legislation is *"Die Verordnung ueber die Begrenzung der Kreditaufnahme"* of June 1973 (*Schuldendeckel-verordnung*). The original amendment to the Basic Law is Art. 109, par. 4, no. 2.

8. Many of the officials interviewed who deal with this aspect of policy hold this opinion.

9. This aspect was brought out by the interviews with officials on the local level of government.

10. See Art. 109, par. 4, no. 1 of the Basic Law.

11. Article 115 of the Basic Law does allow for the possibility during a recession of taking up more credit than that which covers investment expenditure. Nevertheless, the norm that credit must not exceed investments is strong and has never been exceeded on the federal level.

12. For a thorough description of these systems, see Rothweiler (1972). Basically, income and sales taxes are shared by the levels of government in a type of vertical equalization of income. In addition, wealthier states share tax revenue with less wealthy ones; and within each state jurisdiction, the state redistributes revenue among the local governments.

13. In a specific joint program, the planning commission, administrative officials, or law may determine each partner's share. In the Joint Tasks, for example, there are 50/50 matching requirements. Other additional spending by the states in the general spending area, however, is not prohibited. In programs for local governments, the aggregate state share for 1971 was four times that of the federal government. Variations in state spending, therefore, can have a much greater effect [see, in this regard, Kock (1975), especially p. 216].

14. The Finance Planning Council (*Finanzplanungsrat*) is a budgetary coordinating body set up under the Stability and Growth Law of 1967. Its membership consists of the finance ministers of the states and the federal government as well as three representatives of the National Community Associations.

15. This is the opinion expressed by the interviewed official in the Regional Policy Program.

16. This is the most frequent explanation offered to me during the interviews with budgetary officials involved in local governmental financial relations.

17. *Sachverstaendigenkommission* (1973). These proposals are based on Art. 29 of the Basic Law, which also foresees a realignment of the states. See also Scharpf (1974) and Ernst (1974).

18. I am indebted to Bernd Reissert, who recorded these data on yearly time-series sheets for each federal state and then kindly allowed me to use them in these analyses. The original data come from *Statistisches Bundesamt* (1962–1971). Note also that the state grant figures include federal funds as well because in the published statistics the amounts are recorded together. The federal contribution does not alter the differences in state policies, however, because federal grants are given largely according to a population formula [see Reissert (1975)].

19. The *Statistisches Bundesamt* (1962–1971) does not contain these figures for the city-states.

20. The SL, SH, and RLP are the least wealthy and smallest in population. The most wealthy and largest states are NRW, BW, and BV. LS is in the middle, and HS is a mixed case: small in population but near the top in per capita income.

21. For an analysis of party influence on economic policy, see Cowart (1975).

22. This is a short summary of more extensive material obtained from the interviews on this point.

References

Apel, H. 1975. *Massnahmen zur Verbesserung der Haushaltsstruktur und zur Verminderung der Kreditaufnahme. Bundesministerium der Finanzen. Referat Presse und Information.* Bonn, Sept. 8:2-8.

Barbier, H. 1975. *Der Rahmen fuer ein Konjunkturprogramm ist eng. Suddeutsche Zeitung.* July 2:17.

Biehl, D., Juettemeier, K.H., and Legler, H. 1974. *Zu den konjunkturellen Effekten der Laender-und Gemeindehaushalte in der Bundesrepublik Deutschland 1960-74. Die Weltwirtschaft,* Special edition, vol. 1. Kiel: Institut fuer Weltwirtschaft, pp. 29-49.

Beuchmann, W. 1974. *Planung, Kreditbeschraenkung und kommunale Selbstverwaltung. Archiv fuer Kommunalwissenschaften* 13, no. 2: 63-77.

Cowart, A.T. 1975. Policies as multiattribute phenomena: The case of economic policy making in Europe. Paper presented at European Consortium for Political Research, Annual Meeting, Workshop on Organizational Theory and Public Policy. April 7-13, London:16-21.

Ernst, W. 1974. *Wozu Neugliederung? Die Oeffentliche Verwaltung.* pp. 12ff.

Hahn, T. 1974. *Foederung des Sozialen Wohnungsbaues: Dargestellt unter Besonderer Beruecksichtigung der Aufstellung und Durchfuehrung der Jaehrlicher Wohnungsbauprogramm in Baden-Wuerttemberg.* Unpublished paper, pp. 29-35.

Klein, R., and Gleitze, J.M. 1975. *Gemeindefinanzbericht 1975. Der Staedtetag.* Stuttgart: Kohlhammer Verlag. January, special printing, pp. 8-9 and 13.

Kock, H. 1975. *Stabilitaetspolitik im foederalistischen System der Bundesrepublik Deutschland.* Cologne: Bund Verlag, pp. 99-110.

Maunz, T., Duerig, G., and Herzog, R. 1973. *Grundgesetz Kommentar.* Munich: Beck'sche Verlag.

Neumann, M. 1971. *Zur Oekonomischen Theorie des Foederalismus. Kyklos* 24: 493-511.

Oates, W.E. 1972. *Fiscal Federalism* New York: Harcourt Brace Jovanovich, pp. 3-64.

Reissert, B. 1975. *Die finanzielle Beteiligung des Bundes an Aufgaben der Laender und das Postulat der Einheitlichkeit der Lebensverhaeltnisse im Bundesgebiet.* Bonn-Bad Godesberg: Vorwaertsdruck.

Rothweiler, R.L. 1972. Revenue sharing in the Federal Republic of Germany. *Publius* 2:4-25.

Sachverstaendigenkommission fuer die Neugliederung des Bundesgebietes beim Bundesminister des Innern, 1973. Vorschlaege zue Neugliederung des Bundesgebietes gemaess Art. 29GG, Bonn.

Sachverstaendigenrat zur Begutachtung der gesamtwirtschaftlichen Entwicklung, 1970-75. Jahresgutachten. Stuttgart: *Kohlhammer Verlag,* pp. 32-34, 61-63, 90-93.

Scharpf, F. 1974. *Alternativen des deutschen Foederalismus: Fuer ein handlungsfaehiges Entwicklungsystem, Die Neue Gesellschaft* 3. Bonn-Bad Godesberg: Neue Gesellschaft, pp. 237-244.

Schmidt, H. 1973. *Theorie und Thesen der Finanzpolitik. Handelblatt,* Sept. 3.

Schmidt, H. 1972. *Schuldendeckel: Das falsche Instrument.* Handelsblatt, May 2.

Der Spiegel. 1975. *Was der Bund nicht hat.* pp. 27-28.

Der Staedtetag. 1975. *Ruecklaeufige Finanz- und Leistungskraft: Auszuege aus staedtischen Haushaltsreden 1975.* Special printing. Stuttgart: Kohlhammer Verlag, pp. 16-24.

Statistisches Bundesamt. 1962-71. Kommunal Finanzen, Finanzen und Steuern. Jahresabschluesse II. Reihe 1, Wiesbaden.

Weinberger, B. 1973. *Kein Kontrolrecht des Bundes ueber die Etats der Kommunen. Handelsblatt,* Oct. 5.

Wertz, H., Huber, L., and Rau, H. 1973. *Fuer die Bundeslaender ist ihre Finanzautonomie unantastbar. Handelsblatt,* Sept. 20.

6

The Interregional Income Gap as a Problem of Swiss Federalism

René L. Frey

Switzerland is considered to be one of the classic federal states. Her federal structure is accepted as a matter of course, hardly ever scientifically examined, and seldom really open to doubt. In the last few decades, no large study of Swiss federalism has been carried out except for a few publications on interregional fiscal relations. The turning point seems to have been reached a few years ago. The cantons united to form the Foundation for Confederal Collaboration (Stiftung für eidgenöss ische Zusammenarbeit), with the goal of a fundamental analysis of federalism [see, for example, its Hearings on Federalism (1973)]. A further incentive for scientific work on federalism stemmed from the preparatory work for the complete revision of the Swiss federal constitution.

In Switzerland, as in other countries, federalism is also seen primarily as a problem of constitutional law. Economists have not occupied themselves with federalism until recently—again excepting interregional fiscal relations. This changed only when the economic theory of federalism was developed by Tullock (1969), Olson (1969), and especially Oates (1972). A small number of economists whose orientation was toward public finance and regional economics have tried to put Swiss federalism on an economic basis. Their main influence has been to show that the economic theory of federalism might remove the conservative and backward flavor of Swiss federalism and justify it in a new way [e.g., Frey (1974); Frey et al. (1975)].

In this paper, just one of the many problems of federalism has been singled out in order to show how Swiss federalism works today: the problem of the interregional income gap. In section 1, changes in the distribution of income between the cantons are described. These changes were considered, from a political point of view, to be such serious deteriorations—mainly because they intensified migration (as discussed in section 2)—that they induced many countermeasures (sections 3 and 4). Section 5 contains some reflections on the effects of these measures on the diminution of the interregional income gap. The aim of this research is not to offer political solutions but to explain the functioning of Swiss federalism from the point of view of an economist.

1. The Regional Income Gap

Because official estimates of national income or national product by cantons do not yet exist in Switzerland, private studies must be depended upon to measure the regional income gap. For the years 1950, 1960, and 1965 the national-income estimates of Fischer (1967) are used; after 1969, those of the Union Bank of Switzerland are used.[1]

Changes in the income disparity between the cantons can be seen in Table 6-1. The coefficient of variation (standard deviation divided by the arithmetic mean) as a one-dimensional measure of distribution has developed in the following way:

1950: 19.5%	1969: 19.9%
	1970: 20.7%
	1971: 20.1%
1960: 16.8%	1972: 19.8%
	1973: 24.5%
1965: 15.5%	1974: 26.3%

The regional income gap narrowed in the 1950s and 1960s but seems to have widened again in recent years. This deterioration, incidentally, coincides with the slowing down of economic growth. Owing to the lack of statistics on regional purchasing power, it cannot be determined how far the measured income gap reflects differences in prices only. When thinking of the problems of the environment and the agglomerations, it is fair to say that the interregional welfare gap is smaller than the income gap.

In a growing economy, increases in the relative differences in per capita income by cantons mean even greater differences in money terms, of course. The absolute differences between the richest and the poorest cantons and between the five richest and the five poorest cantons are shown in Table 6-2 for 1950, 1969, and 1974.

Another measure of the regional income gap exists in the "time distance" between the cantons [Sicherl (1973)]. When the per capita income of the richest canton in 1950 (Basel-Stadt, with 5,100 Swiss francs) is converted into the purchasing power of 1974, one gets a per capita income equivalent to that of the poorest canton in 1974 (Appenzell I.R., with 11,200 Swiss francs). This means that it took the poorest canton 24 years to reach the 1950 economic level of the richest one. It would also be interesting to know in what year the richest canton in 1974 (Basel-Stadt, with 31,000 Swiss francs) reached the 1974 per capita income level of Apenzell I.R. For lack of statistics, it is impossible to compute this year, but it must have been before 1950.

According to a study by Williamson (1965), a reduction in the income gap, a regional convergence, is to be expected in a highly developed country like

Table 6–1

Canton	Per Capita Income in Thousands of Swiss Francs			Per Capita Income When National Average = 100		
	1950	1969	1974	1950	1969	1974
Zürich	4.3	12.5	21.6	118	117	121
Bern	3.5	9.8	16.3	96	92	91
Luzern	3.1	9.2	14.7	86	86	82
Uri	2.9	9.5	13.4	78	89	75
Schwyz	2.9	8.4	13.4	80	79	75
Obwalden	2.6	8.2	11.7	70	77	65
Nidwalden	3.3	9.1	14.0	89	85	78
Glarus	3.6	8.0	15.6	99	75	87
Zug	3.5	12.1	21.5	97	113	120
Fribourg	2.7	8.2	12.9	75	77	72
Solothurn	3.8	9.9	16.7	103	93	93
Basel-Stadt	5.1	16.0	31.1	139	150	174
Basel-Landschaft	3.8	12.0	18.5	105	112	103
Schaffhausen	3.7	10.0	17.4	101	93	97
Appenzell A.R.	2.9	9.7	15.1	80	91	84
Appenzell I.R.	2.6	6.8	11.2	70	64	63
St. Gallen	3.4	9.2	14.8	92	86	83
Graubünden	2.9	9.2	15.3	78	86	85
Aargau	3.5	10.4	17.0	97	97	95
Thurgau	3.4	9.4	15.6	94	88	87
Ticino	3.0	8.9	14.0	83	83	78
Vaud	3.7	11.0	17.3	100	103	97
Valais	2.4	8.3	13.6	64	78	76
Neuchâtel	4.4	10.2	17.4	119	95	97
Genève	4.6	13.4	25.0	127	125	140
Switzerland	3.7	10.7	17.9	100	100	100

Source: Fischer (1967), Union Bank of Switzerland (Various years).

Table 6–2

Differences between:	Differences in Per Capita Income in Thousands of Swiss Francs					
	Current Prices			1974 Prices		
	1950	1969	1974	1950	1969	1974
Richest and Poorest Cantons	2.7	9.2	19.9	5.9	12.9	19.9
5 Richest and 5 Poorest Cantons	1.9	4.8	10.0	4.1	6.7	10.0

Switzerland, so that the developments of the last few years may be called atypical. However, it remains to be seen whether our results are only a cyclical phenomenon, whether they result from lack of data or even erroneous data, or whether Williamson's theory will after all be proved incorrect.

2. The Income Gap and Interregional Migration

According to economic theory (assuming perfect rationality, full information, and no restrictions on regional mobility), differences in regional per capita income should induce migration from the poor to the rich cantons.[2] The reasons are twofold. On the one hand, there are pushing factors in the less developed regions, such as low income expectations, a narrow range of occupational possibilities, poor educational opportunities for the children, and other deficiencies in the social-overhead capital. On the other hand, the greater income possibilities, the wide range of infrastructural provisions, and the superior social amenities in the rich cantons operate as pulling factors [e.g., Siebert (1970); Richardson (1973)].

The first hypothesis we want to test is whether the interregional migration is indeed from the poor to the rich cantons. At first glance, this hypothesis is not confirmed for the period 1968–1973: there is no statistically significant correlation between migration and per capita income by cantons.[3] This is due in great part to the fact that migration is determined by the income of the place of work, but the place of residence may very well lie in another canton. If the two cantons Basel-Stadt and Basel-Landschaft, where this discrepancy is at its most marked, are combined, there is a statistically significant correlation, and per capita income can explain 33 percent of migration.[4] If labor-market regions are considered instead of cantons, the migration hypothesis may be even better confirmed[5] although based on data for another period).[6]

Further determining factors for migration, in addition to income differences, are the quality of the environment, the quantitative and qualitative provision of public goods and services, and—for the upper-income class—the tax burden. Unfortunately, only the tax burden can be statistically tested, but its inclusion does not lead to a better explanation of migration.[7] This means either that migrants ignore the tax burden or that they equate higher taxes with better public services.[8]

3. Strategies for Narrowing the Income Gap

In principle, there are three strategies for solving the problem of the increasing income gap between the cantons: (1) laissez-faire, or promotion of emigration from the poorer regions, trusting that after a while the marginal products of labor, and therefore the wages, will converge (so-called passive readjustment); (2) reduction of the attraction of rich regions, namely by a systematic internalization of all social costs of the growth of the agglomerations; and (3) aid to the poor regions by regional planning and investments in social-overhead capital, which presupposes regional income redistribution at the federal level (so-called active readjustment). In recent decades, strategy 1 has been followed de facto in Switzerland, even though in political circles almost everybody supported strategy 3 and a few measures were taken in this direction. Strategy 2, on the other hand, has hardly any followers. This political attitude can, to some extent, be explained in economic terms; for the rest, it can be traced back to institutional factors.

Let us look first at the economic (and fiscal) factors. The social costs of the growth of the agglomerations in Switzerland have only recently been recognized. Political ability to reduce the attraction of the highly developed agglomerations has long been very weak in Switzerland because the cantons and the local communities have more financial, fiscal, and other means at their disposal for which they are not responsible to the federal authorities than do the regional and local jurisdictions of other countries. According to the theory of public goods, a regional jurisdiction can not be expected to put itself into a disadvantageous position by slowing down its economic growth if it has no guarantee that the other regions will do the same [Olson (1965)]. Now that the social costs of the growth of the agglomeration have been politically recognized, the chances are somewhat increased that the problem of regional income disparity will be solved within the federal structure.

As mentioned above, certain institutional factors are important in explaining the regional policies of the last few years. First, the proportion of cantons with above-average per capita income has decreased, both in number and in population, as shown in Table 6-3. Second, the federal element in political decision making is very large in Switzerland. The two chambers of parliament have absolutely equal rights: the Nationrat is made up proportionate to the population of the cantons, while each canton has two seats (each of the six half-cantons having one seat) in the Ständerat. Any revision of the federal constitution requires not only the separate approval of both chambers but the approval of the majority of citizens (or, more exactly, of the electorate) and the majority of the cantons (Ständemehr). There have been fifty such plebiscites since 1958. The structural changes mentioned (the decreasing proportion of rich cantons and the increase in income disparity both absolutely and relatively) theoretically improve the ability of the poor cantons to force the rich cantons toward interregional redistribution. But if the results of the plebiscites are analyzed, this hypothesis cannot be confirmed.[9] It is possible, however, (although statistically untestable) that the interests of the poor cantons have already been taken into consideration during the preparation of the laws (e.g., in the form of higher subsidy rates or weaker regulations for poorer cantons).

Table 6–3

	Cantons with Per Capita Income above National Average		
Year	Cantons (Number)	Population (% of Total Population)	National Income (% of Swiss National Income)
1950	8	43	49
1960	8	44	51
1965	5	30	36
1969	6	39	46
1974	5	31	40

To summarize, both economic and institutional factors in Switzerland have improved the possibility that measures will be passed to reduce regional income disparities.

4. Instruments and Measures

Grants-in-aid are among the most important and longstanding instruments for the reduction of regional income disparity. Unconditional grants are relatively rare in Switzerland; they are confined to a small part of the cantonal participation in federal taxes. Considerably more important—and as a single instrument the most important—are the tied (conditional) grants in the form of federal transfers differentiated according to the financial ability of the cantons.

Swiss interregional fiscal relations are not very clear; a systematic reorganization is due. Political discussions to date have centered around the index of financial capacity (*Finanzindex*), which determines the subsidy rates and the contributions of the cantons in federal taxes.

Further, instruments for reducing regional disparities are protective customs duties for the benefit of agriculture and less developed regions and the location and pricing policies of public enterprises. A regional policy in the form of social-overhead investments in regions in need of development experienced an upward trend when a federal law on investment aid in mountain regions came into force in 1975. The confederation will provide a fund of 500 million Swiss francs to foster regional subcenters, hoping to narrow the gap between urban and rural, rich and poor, highly and less-developed regions.

Further incentives for regional policies favoring the poorer regions will come from a law on regional planning adopted in parliament in 1974 but not yet in force. It provides, among other things, an interregional compensation scheme (*volkswirtschaftlicher Ausgleich*). Funds will be raised mainly in the centers of agglomerations and transferred to agriculture and forestry for the costs they incur in regional planning. It will also compensate areas whose development is limited by regional-planning measures if they are not already at a certain level of economic development. A referendum was planned against the law of regional planning by small business and federalist circles. Opponents of the referendum fear that it will not only hinder the poor regions from reducing their distance from the rich cantons—in spite of the planned interregional-redistribution measures—but will also reduce their chances for further economic development.

Only when political discussions are beginning are two further instruments suggested that could contribute to the reduction of the regional income gap: charges for the internalization of social costs (environmental charges, etc.) and the interregional equalization of burdens (interjurisdictional transfers). In both cases, the aim is to prevent external effects and spillovers, which tend to lead to false levels and structures of public expenditures and, owing to biased incentives to migrate, to welfare losses.

This survey of regional-policy instruments and measures shows that the deterioration of the interregional distribution of income and the improved climate for interregional redistribution have led to corresponding political measures. How these measures will affect the aim of decreasing the income disparity between the cantons is difficult to estimate and is beyond the scope of this chapter. Much more to the point is what effects the measures have had so far, and how these effects are related to the structure of Swiss federalism.

5. Effects of Measures to Decrease the Income Gap

Wittmann (1971) tried to record statistically the formal regional incidence of the federal budget for the year 1967. He showed that the federal budget works in the desired direction: inhabitants of the poor cantons receive more payments from the federal government than they pay in the form of taxes. The balance is negative for the rich cantons, of course,[10] and it seems that there is an interregional redistribution of income operating in the right direction.

From the point of view of the reduction of the regional income gap, it is not the formal incidence that is relevant, however. The interregional distribution of income depends on the regional tax incidence and on who benefits from the public goods and services made possible by federal expenditures (regional expenditure incidence). While statistical studies on these modifications are not possible for Switzerland, it can fairly safely be said that, considering the one-sided structure of production combined with the small size of the Swiss cantons, especially the poor ones, the import rate of the poorer cantons is comparatively greater, and therefore a considerable part of the federal expenditure paid to them flows into the richer cantons. Conditioned by the economic structure, the rich cantons consequently manage to cancel at least part of the regional redistribution. This may explain why the rich cantons do not strongly resist the redistribution imposed on them.

So far, the economic gap between rich and poor cantons and the political measures resulting from variations in this gap have been examined. The question to be answered now is whether it is not so much the very poor cantons that profit most from the formal regional redistribution policy but the economically middle-class cantons. The hypothesis that these middle-class cantons push the poor ones forward in order to facilitate the passage of subsidy programs on the federal level and therefore sweep in a differential rent cannot be statistically proven for Switzerland. Apparently, the strong political power of the poor cantons can prevent this. This power can be traced back to institutional factors (*Ständerat* and *Ständemehr*), as already shown, as well as to the poor cantons' homogeneity of interests. The poor cantons are nonindustrial mountain regions strongly dependent on agriculture and tourism.

The interests of the middle-class cantons are, in contrast, considerably less homogeneous. Some are half-industrialized low-mountain cantons; some are markedly industrial cantons that lack a center of agglomeration, and some are cantons with an out-of-date economic structure. When there are concrete measures to influence the regional income gap, the middle-class cantons sometimes have the same interests as the rich cantons and at other times are in the position of the poor ones. But when general measures are to be decided on, such as the division of the cantons into classes for grants-in-aid (financially strong, average, and weak cantons with correspondingly low, medium, or high subsidy rates) or untied interregional transfers, these financially average cantons normally enter into a coalition with the poor cantons. For these groups, the regional redistribution policy is no zero-sum game. Their political strength enables them to force the financially strong cantons into the financing of the redistribution they desire. The reduction in the number of cantons with above-average per capita incomes since 1959 and the fact that party discipline is not very marked in Switzerland[11] facilitate this kind of regional policy.

One result of this silent coalition of the financially weak and average cantons is that they consider their classification in a class of grants-in-aid, once it is attained, to be a vested right. Of the seven class alterations since 1959, six were in their favor; only once was a canton graded down [Lehner (1971)]. Undoubtedly, this is an important explanation for the relative increase in the proportion of the transfers. Transfers from the federal government to the cantons almost doubled in the past two decades: from 17 percent in 1953 to 32 percent in 1972. The effect of these vested rights goes so far that care is taken that the index of financial capacity be revised when a canton would otherwise slip into a less favorable class because of earlier criteria. Certain cantons are considered as poor, and it is politically impossible to remove them from the group of poor cantons even when their economic situation has improved. A few years ago, population density was introduced as a criterion just to prevent this.

6. Conclusions

We have seen how the regional income gap and the migration thereby induced lead to political counteractions in Switzerland. An attempt is being made to narrow the gap by regional income redistribution, especially in the form of federal subsidies graded according to the financial capacity of the cantons and recently an increase in social-overhead investments by the federal government for the development of poor regions. The suppression of development in the rich regions by systematic internalization of the social costs of the agglomeration's growth is still at an early stage.

The explanation for this policy can, for the most part, be traced to the federal structure of Switzerland and, in particular, to the following facts:

The number of cantons with per capita income above the national average has greatly diminished in recent years. Furthermore, the variance has increased.

The poor cantons have above-average political (voting) power.

Their interests, as opposed to those of the middle-class and rich cantons, are largely homogeneous.

The poor cantons can, in coalition with the partly developed ones, outvote the rich cantons and force them to finance the regional redistribution programs.

The resistance of the rich cantons is amazingly weak, probably in large part because a considerable portion of the financial help flowing from the federal government to the poorer cantons flows back to them, owing to the one-sided economic structure of the poorer cantons.

Notes

1. While the two estimates do not correspond perfectly, the correlation is fairly good ($r = 0.88$ for Fischer 1965 and Union Bank 1969). Furthermore, the bank's method of estimating has changed slightly through the years. Unfortunately, it is not possible to determine to what extent a systematic bias results from these changes so that the intertemporal comparison is impossible. A survey by the Federal Bureau of Statistics did show, however, that these private estimates are satisfactory and therefore need not urgently be replaced by official ones.

2. Leaving a region is equivalent to the "exit" solution, as developed by

Hirschman (1970). The alternative reaction, "voice," is discussed below in connection with political measures for narrowing the interregional gap and thus eliminating or reducing the need for interregional mobility.

$$3. \qquad w_{68-73} = -47.3 + 4.13y_{72} \qquad r^2 = 0.09$$

where w_{68-73} = net immigration into cantons from 1968 to 1973 as percentage of 1971 population

y_{72} = national income per inhabitant of the cantons in 1972 in thousands of Swiss francs

Coefficients are not statistically significant at the 0.1 level.

$$4. \qquad w_{68-73} = -114.4 + 8.48y_{72}* \qquad r^2 = 0.33$$

where w_{68-73} is as defined in note 3, and $y_{72}*$ is as in note 3 except that Basel-Stadt and Basel-Landschaft have been combined into one "canton."

$$5. \qquad w_{50-60} = -228.5 + 32.15y_{65}** \qquad r^2 = 0.37$$

where w_{50-60} = net immigration into cantons between 1950 and 1960 as percentage of 1950 population

$y_{65}**$ = per capita income of the labor-market regions in 1965 in thousands of Swiss francs

[ORL-Institute (1971)].

6. Our estimates of migration functions take only the internal variables into consideration as explanatory variables. In the period under examination, the (economically determined) immigration of the labor force from Mediterranean areas was of great importance. The percentage of foreigners in Switzerland in 1950 was 8.3; in 1960, 13.5; and in 1970, 17.7.

$$7. \qquad w_{68-73} = -246.7 + 10.54y_{72}* + 12.11t^{25} \qquad r^2 = 0.28$$
$$w_{68-73}* = -86.3 + 7.68y_{72}* - 0.69t^{50} \qquad r^2 = 0.27$$

where t^{25} = tax burden as percentage of a labor income of 25,000 Swiss francs in 1972 (married man without children, cantonal and local taxes)

t^{50} = tax burden at 50,000 Swiss francs.

8. The tax burden of the poor cantons is, with a taxable income of

20,000 Swiss francs, significantly higher	$(r^2 = 0.29)$
50,000 Swiss francs, somewhat higher	$(r^2 = 0.20)$
100,000 Swiss francs, hardly higher	$(r^2 = 0.05)$

than average (calculated for the year 1973 on the basis of the Statistical Year Book of Switzerland). (Level of significance for r^2 at 0.05, 0.14; at 0.01, 0.24; and at 0.001, 0.36.)

9. The correlation between plebiscite results is as follows:

Financial issues: $x = 13.5 - 0.05y$ $r^2 = 0.02$
Economic issues: $x = 15.7 + 0.03y$ $r^2 = 0.01$
Other issues: $x = 8.1 - 0.05y$ $r^2 = 0.05$
All issues: $x = 37.5 - 0.07y$ $r^2 = 0.02$

x = number of plebiscites in which a canton had the winners, 1966–1975, and y = per capita income in 1969 in thousands of Swiss francs. (None of the coefficients is statistically significant.)

10. $S_{67} = 1330 - 133.3y_{69}$ $r^2 = 0.29$
            $S_{67} = 1942 - 245.0y_{65}$ $r = 0.37$
            $S_{67} = 1840 - 341.9y_{60}$ $r^2 = 0.39$

where S_{67} = balance from federal payments received and taxes of the canton in Swiss francs, and y_{69}, y_{65}, y_{60} = per capita income in 1969, 1965, and 1960 in thousands of Swiss francs. (All coefficients are statistically significant at the 0.01 level.)

11. The fronts are determined much more by the economic interests of the various industries and sectors. The same holds for public plebiscites. Often the cantonal parties express different recommendations to the voters than do their national party organizations.

References

Fischer, G. 1967. *Das Volkseinkommen der Kantone* 1950–1965. *Wirtschaft und Recht* 4:229–270.

Frey, R.L. 1974. *Der schweizerische Föderalismus—wirtschaftlich durchleuchtet. Zeitschrift für Schweizerisches Recht* 3/4:359–378.

Frey, R.L., Neugebauer, G., and Zumbühl, M. 1975. *Der schweizerische Föderalismus aus okonomischer Sicht.* Unpublished report.

Hirschmann, A.O. 1970. *Exit, Voice, and Loyalty: Responses to Decline in Firms, Organizations, and States.* Cambridge Mass.: Harvard University Press.

Lehner, D. 1971. *Der Finanzausgleich zwischen Bund und Kantonen im Hinblick auf eine Bundesfinanzreform.* Bern and Stuttgart: Haupt.

Oates, W.E. 1972, *Fiscal Federalism.* New York: Harcourt Brace Jovanovich.

Olson, M. 1965. *The Logic of Collective Action: Public Goods and the Theory of Groups.* Cambridge, Mass.: Harvard University Press.

Olson, M. 1969. The principle of "fiscal equivalence": The division of responsibilities among different levels of government. *American Economic Review* 2:479–487.

ORL-Institute. 1971. *Vademecum Raumplanung in der Schweiz.* Zurich: ORL.

Richardson, H.W. 1973. *Regional Growth Theory*. London: Macmillan.

Sicherl, P. 1973. Time-distance as a dynamic measure of disparities in social and economic development. *Kyklos* 3:559-575.

Siebert, H. 1970. *Regionales Wirtschaftswachstum und regionale Mobilität.* Tübingen: Mohr.

Stiftung für eidgenössische Zusammenarbeit. 1973. *Föderalismus Hearings.* Zurich: Benziger.

Tullock, G. 1969. Federalism: Problems of scale. *Public Choice* 6:19-29.

Union Bank of Switzerland. Yearly, *Switzerland, in figures.*

Williamson, J.G. 1965. Regional inequality and the process of national development: A description of the pattern. *Economic Development and Cultural Change* 1:3-45.

Wittmann, W. 1971. *Bundesstaatlicher Finanzausgleich: eine Globalbilanz.* Zurich: Redressement national.

7
The Federal-Provincial Dimensions of the 1973–1974 Energy Crisis in Canada

Albert Breton

1. Introduction

In most of the oil-consuming nations of the world, the energy crisis of 1973–1974 provoked shortages, sometimes accompanied by rationing and sometimes by queues, reductions in food production caused by the higher price of crude-oil–derived fertilizers, lower rates of growth of output, and/or balance-of-payments problems. In Canada, the crisis provoked a federal-provincial problem of some magnitude and, in the shorter run at least, I submit only very little else. It is largely for this reason, one must surmise, that the policy recommendations of economists and others who prescribed on this issue as if it had no federal-provincial dimensions were essentially unheeded.

Because the federal-provincial aspects of the energy crisis fairly well reflect the full panoply of issues pertaining to fiscal federalism in Canada, I focus on that question in trying to fulfill the task assigned to me of describing "the central problems inherent in the fiscal structure" of Canada. It would have been possible for me to choose a number of other areas of policy to achieve that goal, since there are very few policy problems in Canada that do not have an extremely important and often dominant federal-provincial component. Indeed, it seems that over the last decade most policy questions have acquired a stronger federal-provincial coloration than they have had in the past.

I devote the next section to a description of those features of the politico-economic environment that must be emphasized for an understanding of how the Canadian energy crisis emerged and how Canadian governments responded to it. Then in section 3 I examine the nature of the challenge and the particular response it elicited. I conclude with a brief statement on what appear to be the most serious difficulties posed by the fiscal structure that has emerged and is still emerging in Canada.

I would like to thank J. Bell, R. Bird, and D. Stevenson for their helpful comments. All remaining errors are mine.

105

2. The Background

To understand the history of the energy crisis in Canada, attention must first be directed to the British North America Act, an 1869 Act of the Imperial Parliament in London, which is also Canada's Constitution. This act gives the provinces the ownership of most natural resources (one exception is the fisheries) located in the provinces, including underground resources (B.N.A. Act, secs. 93 (13) and 109). Resources located outside the provinces, like those in the Northwest Territories and the offshore resources, are owned by the federal government—though some of the coastal provinces are challenging the federal ownership of offshore resources, and negotiations on this issue are continuing between the governments involved.

As landlords of the resources, the provinces can control minimum levels of production, as well as raise royalties and taxes, and therefore can have an important effect on matters pertaining to energy.

The federal government derives its powers in the energy field from a number of bases. It can rely on the "trade and commerce" clause of the B.N.A. Act which, given the interpretations of the courts, means that the central government has authority over international and interprovincial trade but not over intraprovincial trade.[1] This control allows the federal government to regulate maximum levels of production in the country.

The federal government can also rely on its taxing power and has historically used the corporation income tax to influence the rate, speed, and extent of exploration and development in the energy field. Finally, the central government derives jurisdiction from the "peace, order, and good government" clause of Section 91 of the B.N.A. Act, which confers to it preemptive authority in matters of general national concern.

There is no doubt, therefore, that the constitutional stage is so set that any problem in the energy field in Canada always has strong federal-provincial elements. When problems are as large as those of the crisis of 1973–1974, the full federal-provincial diplomatic machinery is set in motion.[2]

The second feature of the landscape that has to be highlighted if the events of 1973–1974 are to be understood is what we can call Canada's *energy policy*—in spite of the fact that Canada, like most other countries, has not had a comprehensive and articulated energy policy. I will take that term to mean the large number of administrative and regulatory measures that affect energy production and consumption in Canada.

The most important of these measures is surely the National Oil Policy, introduced and implemented in 1960. That measure divided the country into two separate markets. One market to the west of the Ottawa Valley—the Borden line, named after Henry Borden, the Chairman of the Royal Commission on Energy—comprised the four Western provinces and most of Ontario, while the other market to the east included a small part of eastern Ontario, Quebec, and four

Atlantic provinces. The Western market was supplied by Alberta oil and the Eastern market by Venezuelan and Middle Eastern oil.

The purpose of the Borden line was to guarantee a market to Alberta oil, which—in addition to being higher-cost oil—had for a number of years been in excess supply. It has been argued [Scott and Pearse (1974, p. 23)] that in exchange for this protective device, the large Alberta producers—which for the most part also supply oil to the United States—"arranged to open the Detroit and Midwestern U.S. markets to western Canadian crude." The Montreal and Eastern market continued to benefit from low-cost crude oil.

One reflection of the National Oil Policy was a transportation system for crude oil which reflected that policy. Indeed, the Eastern market was supplied by a pipeline built mainly across United States territory from Portland in Maine to Montreal, so as to ensure oil delivery in the winter, when the St. Lawrence Seaway froze over, as well as in the summer. The Western market was supplied by pipelines from Edmonton in Alberta and from Toledo in Ohio to Sarnia in Ontario. The legal division of the country into two markets was therefore compounded by a technical or physical division.

As a consequence of the National Oil Policy, Canada imports about 45 percent of her crude-oil requirements and exports about 50 percent of her crude-oil production, so that even if the country is, in net terms, virtually self-sufficient, it is equally true that changes in world supply and/or demand, which alter the world price of crude, have an immediate impact on oil prices in Canada. It is further the case that physical shortages in world markets—defined as shortfalls in supply relative to the previous period's demand—would affect Canada's Eastern market, because of the physical impossibility of moving oil from the West to the East.[3]

A last feature of the institutional landscape to which attention should be directed, because of the crucial role it played in the energy crisis of 1973-1974, is the nature of the equalization formula that regulates the unconditional grants paid from the federal Treasury to the provincial governments.[4]

The formula, which is still in force today, is a fairly simple one.[5] To describe it one needs two basic concepts. The first is that of a "revenue source base"—personal income, corporation income, general sales, motor fuel, water-power rentals, etc.—that is chosen to be as close as possible to the base used in all provinces. Call that base B_{ij} for province i and source j. Given B_{ij}, define the "national average provincial revenue rate:"

$$t_{cj} = \frac{\left(\sum_{i=1}^{10} t_{ij} B_{ij}\right)}{\left(\sum_{i=1}^{10} B_{ij}\right)} \tag{7.1}$$

t_{cj} is therefore the total revenue for all provinces from source j divided by the total base for all provinces for source j.

The equalization payments (in dollars) paid to province i are then equal to

$$E_i = P_i \sum_{j-1}^{n} t_{cj} \left(\frac{B_{cj}}{P_c} - \frac{B_{ij}}{P_i} \right) \tag{7.2}$$

if $E_i > 0$. Otherwise, $E_i = 0$, where $B_{cj} = \sum_{i=1}^{10} B_{ij}$, P_i is the population of province

i, and $P_c = \sum_{i=1}^{10} P_i$.

The formula simply says that for each tax source a province will receive a grant if its per capita base is less than the national average per capita base and that the grant will be proportional to the national average tax rate t_{cj} and to its population P_k; otherwise, it will receive nothing.

Substituting equation (7.1) into (7.2), and rearranging terms, yields

$$E_i = \sum_{j=1}^{n} \left(\sum_{i=1}^{10} t_{ij} B_{ij} \right) \left(\frac{P_i}{P_c} - \frac{B_{ij}}{B_{cj}} \right)$$

The total revenue of province i is therefore equal to

$$R_i = \sum_{j=1}^{n} t_{ij} B_{ij} + E_i$$

or

$$R_i = \sum_{j=1}^{n} t_{ij} B_{ij} + \left[\sum_{j=1}^{n} \left(\sum_{i=1}^{10} t_{ij} B_{ij} \right) \left(\frac{P_i}{P_c} - \frac{B_{ij}}{B_{cj}} \right) \right] \tag{7.3}$$

To analyze the effect of a change in the tax base, we must examine the effect of such a change in the province—call it a—in which the base changes and in all the other provinces separately. Assuming a change in base k, differentiate equation (7.3) partially with respect to B_{ak} to get

$$\frac{\delta R_a}{\delta B_{ak}} = t_{ak} + t_{ak}\left(\frac{P_a}{P_c} - \frac{B_{ak}}{B_{ck}}\right) - \left(\sum_{i=1}^{10} t_{ik} B_{ik}\right)\left(\frac{B_{ck} - B_{ak}}{B_{ck}^2}\right) \tag{7.4}$$

and

$$\left(\frac{\delta R_i}{\delta B_{ak}}\right)_{i \neq a} = t_{ak}\left(\frac{P_i}{P_c} - \frac{B_{ik}}{B_{ck}}\right) + \left(\sum_{i=1}^{10} t_{ik} B_{ik}\right)\left(\frac{B_{ik}}{B_{ck}^2}\right) \tag{7.5}$$

Equation (7.4) has three terms. The first, relating to the behavior of province a's own revenue when B_{ak} changes, is positive. The second and third term pertain to the equalization formula. Because in general $B_{ck} > B_{ak}$, the third term is negative. Therefore, whether a province gains on equalization payments and in total revenue when its tax base changes depends on whether $P_a/P_c \gtrless B_{ak}/B_{ck}$ in the second term. If the difference between P_a/P_c and B_{ak}/B_{ck} is sufficiently negative, a province could lose in the aggregate as a result of an increase in tax base k, although it could not be worse off when all tax bases are added up, since when $E_i < 0$, it is automatically set to zero.

In equation (7.5), the second term is always positive, so that the other provinces will gain as a result of a base change in a if $P_i/P_c > B_{ik}/B_{ck}$. An increase in B_{ak} will raise B_{ck} without changing B_{ik} and therefore will tend to make (7.5) positive whatever was its initial value.

For my purposes, it is necessary to take notice of only two facts. First, "oil royalties" and "other oil and gas revenues" are two of the bases that enter the equalization formula.[6] Second, oil is produced mainly in three Canadian provinces. Indeed, in 1972 Alberta produced 84 percent of Canada's petroleum, all but a fraction of the remainder coming from British Columbia and Saskatchewan.

3. The Events and the Response

Given the background I have described, a few conclusions follow immediately from the decision of the OPEC countries to raise the international price of crude oil in the second half of 1973 and in the early part of 1974 to a price that finally approached 400 percent of the mid-1973 price. First, because the Eastern market in Canada is totally dependent on foreign oil as a result of the National Oil Policy, the price in that market followed the world price. If that price had been allowed to rise for users of oil, the Canadian government would not have been able to prevent the price of crude from rising in the Western market, if for no other than political reasons. Indeed, given the current regional cleavages in Canada, it is impossible to imagine that Ontario and the provinces to the West would be able to use low-price oil while Quebec and the provinces to the East were required to consume high-price crude.

The government faced two alternatives. It could let the price of crude oil rise to the world level of about $12.50 a barrel, or it could freeze the price. The first option implied substantial increases in equalization payments to all provinces except Alberta and Saskatchewan. Indeed, a rise in the price of crude would have increased equalization payments from approximately $1.4 billion in 1974 to something in the neighborhood of $3.4 billion, or by $2 billion, as can be derived from equation (7.5) above. It would also have changed the status of Ontario from a "have" to a "have-not" province for equalization purposes.[7]

The other alternative of freezing the price of oil at $6 a barrel[8]—which the government chose to do—implied paying a subsidy to the Eastern market. The government decided to subsidize imports by paying a consumer subsidy equal to the differential between the world price and the frozen domestic price. The cost of this subsidy program has turned out to be approximately $2 billion per annum, or about the same as the increased cost of equalization would have been.[9] To finance the subsidy, the federal government imposed a tax on oil exported from the West. Since the United States is the only country that imports Canadian crude, the tax was set to equal the difference between the posted domestic price and the international price in the Chicago market.

One should perhaps note that there is very little economic ground on which to decide between the two options facing the government *given the nature of the equalization formula*. Indeed, the economic costs—as distinguished from the cash costs—of a price freeze may or may not have been larger than the dead-weight loss of the current equalization formula, but it is easy to believe that the difference is small, given that the equalization formula is an inefficient one from a resource-allocation point of view.

From a more general politicoeconomic viewpoint, it could be argued that the Canadian government made the correct decision, at least as long as one is willing to accept the view, as I do, that it is easier in the longer run to let the domestic price of crude oil rise to the international price and to eliminate the export tax—all exclusive decisions of the federal government—than it would be to transform, through bargaining between 11 governments, an equalization formula that added $2 billion additional transfer dollars to provincial coffers. It should be noted that this argument is partly based on a hope, since it may never come about, that the equalization formula is made more efficient and more rational from both an equity and an allocative standpoint.[10]

The decision to freeze the domestic price of crude was welcomed by the oil-consuming provinces, which together account for 78 percent of Canada's population, though it was far from appreciated by the oil-producing ones. And for good reasons, since the loss to these latter provinces was enormous: at $12.50 a barrel, Alberta's royalty revenues would have increased by $3.4 billion, those of

Saskatchewan by $0.5 billion, and those of British Columbia by $0.16 billion.[11]

To deal with the political and constitutional issues created by the freeze and the energy crisis generally, the Canadian government in December 1973 announced a series of measures of which the most important for this chapter's argument were (1) the abolishment of the Borden line dividing the country into two markets; (2) the building of a pipeline from Sarnia to Montreal and more easterly points to guarantee supplies in these provinces and to make possible the movement of Western crude to the Eastern market; (3) the sharing of the proceeds of the export tax with the producing provinces on a formula to be agreed upon at a meeting of the First Ministers (the Prime Minister of Canada and the Provincial Premiers); and (4) permission for the price of crude oil to rise in the more or less distant future.[12]

At the meeting of First Ministers in February 1974, it was agreed that the tax proceeds would be shared on a 50/50 basis between the federal government and the oil-producing provinces. That agreement lasted only until March 1975. At that date, the federal government claimed the entire revenues from the export tax to subsidize crude consumption in Eastern Canada. The complicated and time-consuming mechanisms required for the building of a pipeline have been set in motion, and it is expected that in two to four years the pipeline will be completed.

Most important, after protracted and painful negotiations between Ottawa and the provinces—the federal government wanting to increase the price of oil by $2 a barrel, Alberta holding out for a larger increase, and the oil-consuming provinces, led by Ontario, wanting to maintain the freeze—the price of crude oil was increased by $1.50 to $7.50 a barrel in June 1975. This decision was accompanied by an announcement by the government of Canada that it stood by its policy of allowing the domestic price of crude to move slowly to the world price level.

As if to underscore the federal-provincial nature of the energy problem in Canada, the decision by the federal government was followed by a decision by three provincial governments—Ontario, British Columbia, and Manitoba—to freeze the price of oil at $6 a barrel.[13] These are not decisions that can or have been sustained for very long, since the provinces do not want and/or are not in a position to pay a subsidy to the oil companies. Consequently, if the price were not allowed to rise, supplies would dry up.[14] But the response indicates the complex constitutional coloration of many relatively simple economic issues in Canada.

Finally, the equalization formula was amended to distinguish between two kinds of royalties from crude oil: those resulting from the price increases after 1974 and those which had been accruing before these increases. Only one-third of the revenues from the first source are now reckoned in the base in calculating equalization payments.

4. Conclusion

Instead of summarizing the content of this brief chapter, let me indicate one of the problems that the energy crisis, as well as many other federal-provincial problems that arise regularly, are beginning to make clear. The federal-provincial complications of the energy crisis of 1973–1974 in Canada have been almost exclusively complications that arose from the fact that important components of the federal-provincial machinery are uncoordinated. Decisions relating to a given issue—an equalization-payments formula, for example—are made without consideration of the fact that another decision pertaining to something else—a National Oil Policy—has been made in the past.

While it is easier to be critical in this area than to come forward with an integrated blueprint, the disjointedness of the federal-provincial process and the absence of an image of the whole system of interrelated institutions and policies—in spite of the existence of numerous federal-provincial secretariats, branches of government departments, and committees—is bound to put unnecessary stresses on a structure that, though robust and creative, surely has enough environmental problems already. At the same time, one is reminded that the almost unbelievable problem-solving capacity of the Canadian federal structure may be partly the result of the fact that Canadians insist on solving problems which, with a little more forethought, could have been avoided. Practice may not make perfect, but it is certainly a way of learning by doing!

Notes

1. Section 121 of the B.N.A. Act prohibits all restrictions on the free flow of trade between provinces.

2. The term *diplomatic* is taken from Simeon (1972), who shows that the analytical apparatus applied to diplomatic relations between countries is useful in understanding federal-provincial relations in Canada.

3. This is not strictly accurate. It is true that Canada's railway rolling stock does not permit important shipments of crude across the country, but in the early part of the winter of 1973–1974 the Canadian government, at a very high cost, shipped Western crude through the Panama Canal and the St. Lawrence Seaway to the Eastern market in anticipation of a harsh winter—which did not materialize!

4. The discussion that follows is largely based on Courchene and Beavis (1973) and also on Carter (1971).

5. The formula has been changed in recent years to allow inclusion of a large number of tax bases, but otherwise it has remained unchanged. The number of bases, equal to 16 in 1973, is now 23.

6. It is interesting to note that natural-resource revenues have been in-

cluded in the base, with a few other "standard" tax bases, since 1962. The "explosion" in bases included in the formula came about in 1967.

7. These estimates are from Courchene (1975).

8. The price of crude oil was not frozen until January 1974; between the summer of 1973 and January 1975, it rose from about $4.50 to $6 a barrel.

9. This number is taken from Hunter (1975, p. 45).

10. The equalization formula is revised every five years. The next revision is due in 1977.

11. The interest of British Columbia in these matters is greater than the above number indicates, since British Columbia's royalty income accrues from natural gas more than from crude oil, and the problems are not totally dissimilar between these two energy sources.

12. In addition, an Energy Supplies Allocation Board was created, as well as a publicly owned company—known as Petro-Can—oriented primarily to exploration and development. A number of measures to increase supplies were also announced.

13. In 1973 the Nova Scotia government amended its Gasoline Licensing Act to give power to the Public Utilities Board created under the act to set oil prices and to require wholesalers and retailers to file information with it on costs and prices. An increase in the price of oil allowed by the federal government therefore takes effect only after approval by the Public Utilities Board. The June 1975 increase was allowed to pass through.

14. The price freeze imposed by the provinces expired on November 15, 1975.

References

Carter, G.E. 1971. *Canadian Conditional Grants since World War II*. Toronto: Canadian Tax Foundation.

Courchene, T.J. 1975. Equalization payments and energy royalties. Mimeographed.

Courchene, T.J., and Beavis, D.A. 1973. Federal-provincial tax equalization: An evaluation. *Canadian Journal of Economics* 6:483-502.

Hunter, L. A. W. 1975. *Energy Policies of the World: Canada.* University of Delaware, Newark, Del.: Center for the Study of Marine Policy.

Scott, A.D., and Pearse, P.H. 1974. The political economy of energy development in Canada. In *The MacKenzie Pipeline*, P.H. Pearse, ed. Toronto: McClelland and Stewart. pp. 1-32.

Simeon, R. 1972. *Federal-Provincial Diplomacy: The Making of Recent Policy in Canada.* Toronto: University of Toronto Press.

8

Governmental Diversity: Bane of the Grants Strategy in the United States

Robert D. Reischauer

The federal government of the United States attempts to address a wide range of domestic problems—including poverty, educational deficiency, crime, pollution, and inadequate transportation systems—primarily by providing grants-in-aid to its state and local governments. In the past fifteen years, such grant programs have proliferated in number to over a thousand and have grown spectacularly in budgetary significance to the point where they now represent one-sixth of federal spending and almost one-fourth of state and local government receipts (see Table 8-1). However, this expansion has satisfied neither the recipient governments nor the Congress; instead, a consensus exists that the "grants strategy" both has failed to solve the country's domestic problems and has done little to strengthen the structure of fiscal federalism.

While there are numerous possible reasons for these apparent failures, this paper examines just one: the tremendous diversity of governmental arrangements in the United States. This diversity is inherent in the structure of American federalism and makes virtually impossible designing, generating support for, and implementing effective domestic grant programs.

Significant Aspects of Government Diversity

In a nation as physically large and populous as the United States, it is not surprising that subnational units of government are faced with very different sorts of problems, public service demands, and costs. It is surprising—but certainly not unique in federal systems—that the institutional arrangements that have evolved for providing public services are so diverse. Six basic types of government are found in the United States: states, counties, municipalities, townships, school districts, and special districts. From the perspective of the federal government, which is forced by Constitutional constraints to operate through existing governmental institutions rather than revise these structures, a number of characteristics of this diversity are important.

The views expressed herein are those of the author and should not be attributed to the Congressional Budget Office.

Table 8-1
Federal Aid to State and Local Governments

Fiscal Year	Amount (Billions of $)	Percent of Federal Government Expenditures	Percent of State and Local Government Receipts
1976	$59.8	16.0%	25.2%
1973	41.8	17.0	24.3
1970	24.0	12.2	19.4
1965	10.9	9.2	15.3
1960	7.0	7.6	14.7
1950	2.3	5.3	10.4

Source: U.S. Office of Management and Budget (1976, p. 264).

First, none of these governmental types is found everywhere in the nation. Residents of the District of Columbia are not served by a state government. County governments do not exist in two states (Rhode Island and Connecticut) and in 102 separate geographic areas in 21 other states. Municipal governments, which typically provide most local public services in closely settled areas, are nonexistent in rural areas as well as in some urban territories where strong county governments prevail. Townships—a type of local government that, like counties but unlike municipalities, exists to serve residents of geographic areas without regard to population concentration—are found throughout only one state (Indiana) and in parts of only 20 others. Separate independent school districts are the exclusive providers of elementary and secondary education in 30 states, do not exist in 5 others, and provide education in only parts of the remaining 15. Finally, special district governments, which generally have been created to perform a single governmental function, such as the conservation of natural resources or the provision of fire-protection services, are not found at all in one state (Alaska) and are lacking in parts of all others.

The second aspect of the structure of subnational government that has implications for a federal grants policy is the vast numbers of governments, their difference in scale, and their overlapping nature. With the exception of the states, there are thousands of each type of government, some providing services to millions of persons and others to fewer than a dozen (see Table 8-2). The vast majority of local governments provide services to relatively few people. In any single geographic area there are likely to be a number of types of active governments. In some cases, all six of the basic types of governments provide services; in others, as few as one or two are present. Generally, the governments' boundaries are not coterminous, that is they do not coincide.

A third, and by far the most important, aspect of this diversity is that the service and fiscal responsibilities imposed on various types of governments differ tremendously both among and within states. The most important state and local

Table 8-2
Characteristics of the Basic Types of State and Local Government (1972)

Governmental Type	Number	Percent of U.S. Population Served	Range of Populations Served	Population Served by Median Jurisdiction	Percent of Total State and Local Government	
					Direct General Expenditures	General Revenues
State	50	99.6	From 330 thousand to 20.6 million	2.9 million	37.1	53.3
County	3,044	88.4	From 164 to 7.0 million	Between 10,000 and 24,999	13.6	10.0
Municipality	18,517	65.1	From less than 5 to 7.9 million	Less than 1,000	21.1	17.0
Township	16,991	22.6	From less than 5 to 800,000[a]	Less than 1,000	2.3	2.2
School District	15,781	81.1[a]	From less than 10 to 986,000[a]	Between 600 and 1,149[a]	22.7	14.9
Special District	23,885	N.A.	N.A.	N.A.	3.1	2.6

Source: U.S. Bureau of the Census (1973).
N.A. means not available.
[a]Population data refers to public-school enrollment.

public service, elementary and secondary education, illustrates the variation in governments charged with providing a single service. In Hawaii, the state government alone provides elementary and secondary education, while in Maine schooling is provided in some areas by the state and in others by municipalities, townships, or separate school districts. A wide variety of other patterns exists elsewhere (see Table 8-3). Education is by no means an isolated case. Welfare-related programs are provided in some areas by state governments and in others by counties or by counties and municipalities; within different areas of some states police services are provided by the state, county, municipal, or township government.

The diversity in the provision of services is matched by the diversity of responsibilities for supplying financial support. The existence of large amounts of intergovernmental grants means that often the jurisdiction responsible for providing a particular service is not the one responsible for its fiscal support. For example, elementary and secondary education in both New Hampshire and Alabama is provided exclusively by local governments, but in Alabama less than one-fifth of the costs are borne by local governments, while in New Hampshire nine-tenths of the support is provided by localities. Similarly, welfare (AFDC) checks are written by local governments in both New York and Iowa, yet local governments in New York must provide over one-fourth of the funds needed to cover these checks, while local governments in Iowa must supply less than one-tenth of the funds.

Differences in service and fiscal responsibility translate into differences in the relative importance of the various types of governments. For example, state government is very important in Hawaii, where it is responsible for 89 percent of the state's direct service expenditures and 77 percent of its revenues; in Nebraska, where the similar percentages are 29 and 36, the state is not anywhere near as important a factor. Among local governments, counties are extremely

Table 8-3
Patterns of Responsibility for Providing Elementary and Secondary Education Services

Responsible Governments	Example
State	Hawaii
Counties	North Carolina
School Districts	Colorado
Counties and School Districts	Minnesota
Counties and Municipalities	Virginia
Municipalities and School Districts	New Hampshire
State, Counties, and Municipalities	Alaska
Counties, Municipalities, and School Districts	Tennessee
Municipalities, Townships, and School Districts	Connecticut
State, Municipalities, Townships, and School Districts	Maine
Counties, Municipalities, Townships, and School Districts	New York

Source: U.S. Bureau of the Census (1973).

important in North Carolina, where they are responsible for 70 percent of local government spending, but not so in Massachusetts, where 3 percent of such spending is in their hands. Municipalities and townships are responsible for 94 percent of local-government spending in Connecticut, but only 22 percent in Nebraska, for example.

A final critical aspect of the diversity of subnational government structure in the United States is the variation with respect to both the scope of government activity and the instruments used to raise revenues to support public services. No simple accepted view exists of the proper domain of state and local governments. Most, if not all, services provided by these governments are also available privately. In some areas, private vendors are the primary providers of such services as hospitals, fire protection, sanitation, housing, libraries, public transportation, higher education, and utilities (water, gas, and electricity) that elsewhere are supplied exclusively by the government sector. In general, a mixed situation prevails, but the levels of services provided publicly varies tremendously. To take some simple examples: welfare payments per recipient vary by over 6 to 1 among the states; California's system of public higher education provides twice as many slots per high school graduate as that of New Jersey; levels of elementary and secondary public-school services—as measured by per pupil spending—vary by a factor of 10 to 1 within nine states and by over 2 to 1 within all but seven.

The revenue sources relied upon by similar types of governments also vary widely. While income and sales taxes are the mainstay of most state governments, four states lack the former and ten the latter; one lacks both. At one time, local governments depended almost exclusively on property taxes, but this is increasingly less true. While the only tax avilable to counties in many states is the property levy, in Alabama county governments obtain more resources from sales and income taxes than they do from property levies. Many municipalities, including Philadelphia, Oklahoma City, Cincinnati, St. Louis, Kansas City, New Orleans, Louisville, Birmingham, and Phoenix, rely on property taxes for less than one-fourth of the revenues they raise. In some parts of the nation, local governments depend heavily upon profits from publicly owned utilities. Even where governments appear to depend upon the same basic type of tax, differences may be significant. Sales taxes, for example, may cover all retail sales or may exclude food, medicine, or clothing and may include certain services. Property taxes may be levied against the total value of the property, have flat exemptions (homestead exemptions), or give preference to certain classes of property owners, such as veterans or the aged.

Governmental Diversity and the Policy Makers

The diversity of governmental structure in the United States has not been subject to broad-scale policy debate or concern. Policy makers, like the average citizen, have generally ignored it and at most are familiar only with the structure of their own state and local government. When they do think on a broader scale, they are likely to assume that the structure with which they are familiar exists throughout the nation. In any case, policy makers tend to shy away from considering such "technicalities" as the structure of governments, because such considerations are likely to raise difficulties in the path of initiatives they want to propose.

The lack of familiarity of policy makers with the diversity of government structure has produced a situation in which flawed policy initiatives are put forward, and at times passed, on the basis of misunderstandings. Three recent policy issues illustrate this point. First, in 1971 the possibility arose that the courts would declare unconstitutional the prevailing systems of school finance, which relied heavily on locally levied property taxes. In response to this situation and to a simultaneous popular revolt against rising property-tax rates, the White House proposed a plan to replace local school property-tax revenues with revenues from a national value-added tax. It was not until the basic outlines of the plan were laid out by the President that policy makers realized that the diversity of existing methods of financing education made the plan unworkable. If each community were provided the resources needed to replace school property taxes, some jurisdictions would receive over $1,000 per pupil and significant tax relief while others would receive nothing from the new tax and their total tax burden would increase greatly. Alternatively, if a flat amount per pupil were provided to each state or to each government operating schools, some would receive more than enough to eliminate their school property taxes while others would not and would be forced to raise other taxes or reduce school spending. Once these problems were understood, the White House proposed the appropriate course of action: various commissions and panels were asked to study the problem and it ultimately died as a public issue.

A second example relates to the recent tribulations of New York City. In search of support in the Congress for federal aid, the city marshaled what it considered to be one of its strongest arguments—the tremendous welfare costs borne by the city. City officials expected that when others saw that this federal grant program forced the city to supplement $2 billion in state and federal aid with $1 billion in local resources, sympathy would certainly pour forth. If anything, the opposite occurred. City officials were not fully cognizant of the extent to which New York was peculiar. In 40 states, virtually all of the welfare costs borne by New York City are shouldered by state governments. Many federal legislators therefore saw New York's welfare burden not as a reason for federal intervention but rather as a further indication that the State of New York had not done all that it should to deal with the city's problems.

A third example can be found in the revenue-sharing legislation adopted in 1972. Because national aggregates indicate that slightly over one-third of all state and local direct government expenditures are made by state governments, federal legislators did not think it absurd that one-third of this large grant should be provided to states and two-thirds to local governments. However, the variety that exists among states with respect to their fiscal importance means that the state of Nebraska's grant relative to its fiscal responsibilities is over twice as large as that of Hawaii. In short, what appeared to policy makers to be neutral means of dividing resources between state and local governments was, in fact, far from that.

The Implications of Governmental Diversity

For a nation that has emphasized grants-in-aid as a mechanism for solving domestic problems, the diversity of governmental structure and policy makers' lack of understanding of this diversity have a number of important implications.

First, the federal government is faced with a dilemma in choosing the appropriate governments with which it should interact when it wishes to act on a particular domestic problem area. One option is to deal exclusively with one type of government: states, counties, municipalities, etc. However, this results in certain areas of the nation not being served by the grant program, because the type of government chosen does not exist there.

More serious is the possibility that in some parts of the country the chosen type of government may lack the experience, ability, or even the legal authority to carry out the intent of the grant program. This situation has occurred to some extent in the new manpower (CETA) and community-development block-grant programs that explicitly designate urban county governments as the recipient governments—all urban areas except within the largest cities. In some regions, these counties have had little or no previous experience with manpower or community-development programs. When faced with the new grant, they tend to create a new, and sometimes duplicative, service structure rather than turn the resources over to another type of government that previously was responsible for providing such programs within that particular geographic area.

Another option for the federal government is to deal with whatever government is responsible for the particular service. This approach also has a number of problems. First, a decision must be made as to whether responsibility is to be judged in terms of providing or of financially supporting the service. In many areas, a focus on service delivery would require interaction between the federal government and local governments; an emphasis on financial support would call for the federal government to interact with state authorities. The former might appear to be more logical if the federal government is concerned with augmenting services directed at a certain problem, but it is of course possible for the states to change their own local grant strategy to blunt, if not negate, the impact intended by the federal government. This approach may also have the drawback of requiring the federal government to deal with an extremely diverse group of governments with different legal powers, constraints, and capacities. In many service areas, it may be impossible to design a grant program that would fit the needs and limits of all, or even a majority, of the governments responsible for providing the particular service. Moreover, it is not at all certain that the federal government has a clear idea of which specific government has the prime responsibility for a particular service in each part of the nation. In fact, in some geographic areas duplicate services are provided by overlapping jurisdictions.

Such considerations partially explain the prevalence of "project grants," which require that the governments interested in a program and capable of providing the specified service apply for part of the resources of federal grant programs. This method allows the federal government to deal with the limited number of governments that have the appropriate responsibility, and it avoids the need to know which governments have this authority. Furthermore, the project method allows the grant to be tailored individually to the resources, legal authority, and experience of the applicant government, whether it is a county, municipality, special district, or whatever. While the "project grants" approach may circumvent some problems posed by the diversity of governmental structure, it has been severely criticized in recent years for several reasons: subjective elements can enter into the distribution of resources; a great deal of red tape is necessarily generated; small and unsophisticated jurisdictions have difficulty competing for projects; and the process leaves considerable control in the hands of federal administrators.

A final option for the federal government is to deal only with the states, relying on them to handle any necessary distribution to lower levels of governments. Until recently, this was the strategy followed by most federal grant programs. As recently as 1968, some 89 percent of federal grant funds were channeled to state governments, even though local governments supplied a large fraction of the services supported by those funds. For example, grants for such predominantly local services as elementary and secondary education, libraries, and law enforcement are provided to state governments, with only loose instructions as to how they should be distributed among the responsible localities.

This option may circumvent the problems of diversity and be more constitutionally correct, since local governments are creations of the states and not of the national government. But some suspect it is an option that guarantees that the objectives of a grant program will not be achieved. Many domestic problems brought to the Congress for action in recent years revolve around the distribution of income and the provision of public services to persons who have low incomes and/or who live in declining core cities. Generally, the affected local governments are too poor to tackle the problems alone or cannot deal with them because of the open nature of local economies. In many cases, state governments could deal with the problems but are unwilling to do so. In such instances, providing federal aid to the state for distribution to the appropriate local governments may be like asking the fox to guard the chicken coop.

The Safe Streets Act, which was spawned largely by concern over rising inner-city crime rates, is an example of this problem. Despite the fact that the bulk of law enforcement activity (87 percent of the employment and 85 percent of the direct expenditures) is conducted by local governments, the complex division of responsibility for providing these services among local governments left the federal government with little choice but to provide grants to states. While the states are required to pass a reasonable fraction through to their local governments, they are free within broad bounds to design their own patterns of distribution. Rather than focus the resources on the areas where the problems of crime are most acute—urban centers—most states have chosen to distribute the resources on a per capita basis. In some states, funds are allocated to local planning districts that have been gerrymandered to reduce further the influence large cities have over the funds once they are distributed to local governments. Thus, while over $2.5 billion has been spent on this program in the past eight years, it does not appear that the money generally has been used to address the primary problem toward which it was directed.

Dissatisfaction with the "project grant" approach and with the option of leaving federal grants in the hands of state governments has led recently to an increased effort to design mechanisms for dealing directly with the local governments that deliver services in the problem area. These efforts have met several obstacles caused by the diversity of governmental structure. First, the sheer numbers of governments involved make even the most simple programs difficult to administer. A tremendous amount of effort has been required to answer the questions and solve the problems of the 39,000 recipients of revenue sharing, a program that places very few restrictions on recipient governments and therefore was expected to pose little in the way of difficulties. Grants for a specific purpose—such as education or police protection—to a vast number of governments would probably swamp the bureaucracy with problems, questions, and demands from the recipient governments. A related issue involves program design. If thousands of small, unsophisticated jurisdictions are included as recipients, complex demands cannot be placed on them. Nor, given the diversity of governmental arrangements, can the program be too specific in what it requires recipients to do, because they may not have the power to conform. Even the general revenue-sharing program ran into this difficulty: in Illinois, many recipient townships were not empowered to engage in many of the activities required by the law; they spent as much as they deemed appropriate on services that were legal under the revenue-sharing law and their own charters but found it difficult to spend all the money granted to them.

A second obstacle to dealing directly with local governments is the difficulty in developing reasonable methods for allocating grant funds among their large numbers. The kinds of data needed to develop a sensible distribution formula are often unavailable. Considerable costs would have to be incurred to generate data that would allow the federal government to allocate grant funds to local governments in a way that followed the objectives of most programs. Faced with this situation, the federal government has taken a number of approaches. In some cases, clearly inadequate, but available, data have been used to distribute federal grants. This partially explains the use of population to allocate grants for such purposes as law-enforcement assistance, drug-abuse treatment, and other areas where the "need" or magnitude of the problem is correlated only weakly with population size. In other instances, hopelessly out-of-date information is used. For example, in the early 1970s the major federal grant for elementary and secondary education was being distributed according to data gathered in the 1960 census. A more recent approach has been to reduce the number of eligible jurisdictions to a manageable number for which data are available or can be generated at a reasonable cost. For example, the new manpower and community-development block-grant programs and the recently vetoed countercyclical revenue-sharing program require that the federal government deal only with the largest local governments; the smaller localities benefit from these programs only indirectly through the amounts provided to state governments. While this solution is reasonable, it threatens to undermine the political coalition supporting some grant programs. Governments cut out of direct participation are less willing to fight for larger appropriations or even continuation of the program because the benefits are uncertain from their perspective.

In recent years, increasing concern has been expressed about interjurisdictional fiscal disparities. Many think that these disparities, as they are manifested in the "urban fiscal crisis," will be one of the major domestic problems of the next decade. Preliminary attempts to resolve this problem have been stymied not only by political forces but also by the difficulties posed by the diversity of government structures. While a general consensus can be reached that the amount of aid received by each government under an equalization program should relate positively to the jurisdiction's needs and inversely to its fiscal capacity, there is little agreement on the operational meaning of these terms in a nation where service responsibilities and revenue instruments vary tremendously from jurisdiction to jurisdiction. If all governments relied on similar sources of revenue, a relatively noncontroversial "fiscal capacity index" could be constructed based on a weighted average of the various revenue bases. However, methods of raising revenue are diverse, so such an index necessarily would include revenue sources not used by some jurisdictions either by choice or by lack of legal authority. As a result, federal grant programs have fallen back on the use of per capita income as a crude measure of the relative fiscal capacity of different jurisdictions. In a nation where a relatively small fraction of state and local government revenue is derived directly from income taxes and where states and localities understandably try to export as much of their tax burden as possible, this solution is clearly unsatisfactory. In some local areas, there is no correlation between income and fiscal capacity as measured by revenue sources utilized by the jurisdictions [Reischauer (1974a, pp. 283–306)]. Table 8–4 lists the relative fiscal capacities of the states as measured both by representative

Table 8-4

State Fiscal Capacity and Revenue Requirements Indexes (1972), Per Capita, U.S. Average = 100

State	Representative Revenue System (Average Tax-rate Weights) (1972)	Personal Income by Place of Residence (1972)	Representative Service Requirements (Average Expenditure Weights) (1972)
Alabama	76	76	95
Alaska	131	115	105
Arizona	107	94	97
Arkansas	81	74	90
California	112	112	102
Colorado	106	101	97
Connecticut	112	119	108
Delaware	122	115	101
D.C.	126	128	97
Florida	112	98	98
Georgia	93	87	99
Hawaii	116	113	98
Idaho	88	82	93
Illinois	110	113	105
Indiana	97	96	100
Iowa	99	95	96
Kansas	101	100	97
Kentucky	84	80	94
Louisiana	93	78	97
Maine	84	81	91
Maryland	101	110	103
Massachusetts	98	106	101
Michigan	100	110	105
Minnesota	97	95	99
Mississippi	71	70	90
Missouri	96	95	99
Montana	106	90	93
Nebraska	106	98	95
Nevada	156	115	96
New Hampshire	115	94	96
New Jersey	112	118	105
New Mexico	92	77	93
New York	106	116	105
North Carolina	87	85	95
North Dakota	86	91	93
Ohio	96	101	101
Oklahoma	98	84	94
Oregon	106	95	96
Pennsylvania	95	100	98
Rhode Island	88	99	99

(continued)

Table 8-4 Continued

State	Representative Revenue System (Average Tax-rate Weights) (1972)	Personal Income by Place of Residence (1972)	Representative Service Requirements (Average Expenditure Weights) (1972)
South Carolina	74	77	94
South Dakota	89	83	91
Tennessee	84	82	95
Texas	99	90	98
Utah	83	82	95
Vermont	102	81	94
Virginia	92	97	99
Washington	101	101	99
West Virginia	81	80	92
Wisconsin	95	94	98
Wyoming	125	94	93

Source: Reischauer (1974b).

revenue systems and personal income. It also contains a relative-needs index based on a representative service system.

The same situation exists with respect to service requirements. Lacking a uniform set of services that are provided by all governments, "needs" have generally been measured by some gross proxy such as population. However, it is clear that the services provided by state and local governments and those which are supported by most grant programs are directed at very specific sub-groups of the population—and these are not distributed among jurisdictions in proportion to the general population. Given the crude way in which capacity and needs are measured, it is not surprising that services and tax burdens have not been equalized among jurisdictions, despite the large amounts of grants and larger amount of equalization rhetoric.

Conclusion

In concluding this discussion, two corollaries of the thesis that the diversity of American governmental structure dooms the grants strategy to failure should be pointed out. The first corollary is that intergovernmental frustration levels tend to rise rather than fall as grant levels increase. From the federal perspective, more is being done to solve a problem when grant levels increase; but, from the standpoint of the recipient jurisdiction and the public at large, the constraints imposed by the government structure may render the programs ineffective. The response of the federal government to the criticism that "things aren't working" is to tighten up the administrative control of the program, then blame the states for mismanagement. This, in turn, increases hostility at the state and local level. The second corollary is that the federal government will increasingly tend to rely on what is called the *incomes strategy*. Faced with its inability to use grants to solve domestic problems and a reluctance to demand structural changes, national policy makers will tend to design programs in which the federal government deals directly with citizens rather than dealing through intermediary state and local governments. This will reinforce the tendencies toward centralization already apparent in American federalism.

References

Reischauer, R.D. 1974a. In defense of the property tax: The case against an increased reliance on local nonproperty taxes. *Proceedings* (National Tax Institute of America).

Reischauer, R.D. 1974b. Rich governments—Poor governments. Unpublished manuscript.

U.S. Bureau of the Census. 1973. *1972 Census of Governments.* Washington: GPO.

U.S. Office of Management and Budget. 1976. *Budget of the United States: Fiscal Year 1977, Special Analyses.* Washington: GPO.

9

The Finances of the European Community: A Case Study in Embryonic Fiscal Federalism

Michael Emerson

Levels of Government

Fiscal federalism, which I take to mean the economics of multilevel government finance, is an important contemporary issue in the European Community.[1] The structure of government for the majority of the Community's population seems to be moving toward a three- and, for many people, a four-level system, each with its direct elections—local, national, and Community for most, plus regional/state for many.

There is already concern in some quarters that Europe may be becoming overgoverned. On the other hand, two factors objectively support some multiplication of levels of government. First, the size of the government sector in Europe has grown from about 10 percent of GNP at the turn of the century to 45 percent now. And second, the minimum size for serious bargaining in world trade and economic diplomacy and for efficient investment in certain research-and-development–intensive industries seems to have grown to around the 250-million-population level, while the optimal size of jurisdiction for managing many of the faster-growing public services seems to remain firmly at the lower levels of government. The case for fiscal federalism therefore seems, a priori, to be substantial.

The organization of different levels of government is changing, or is under serious pressure for change, within most member countries, quite apart from the case of the Community itself. The reorganization of local government is very widespread, mainly through the consolidation of small municipalities and the reshaping of the boundaries of urban agglomerations.

Tendencies favoring a regional or state level of government, while not universal, are quite pronounced. In Germany the federal form of government seems solidly entrenched. In Italy directly elected regional governments have recently been given significantly increased financial responsibilities. In the United Kingdom the devolution white paper of November 1975 proposes

The views expressed are not attributable to the Commission of the European Communities.

The author is most grateful to Mr. J. McKenna for help in preparation of this chapter.

directly elected assemblies for Scotland and Wales with large spending responsibilities. In France the issue remains a live one, although the last major proposal in favor of regional devolution was rejected in the referendum of 1969. Federalism has at times seemed close at hand in Belgium, although the last general election in 1973 was a setback for the federalists; a regionalization program is nonetheless being implemented.

Then there is the gradual emergence of the Community tier to the government structure, which is the subject of this chapter. In two fields, external trade and agricultural policy, the Community's responsibilities are analogous to those found in a federal state. In two further fields, aid to developing countries and regional policy, the Community's role has been recently growing to the extent of a significant minority degree of coresponsibility with member states. In other fields, the Community's role remains embryonic, or weakly organized, or still at the state of conception and debate. All this will be explored further in this chapter.

At the political level, the budgetary powers of the European Parliament have gradually increased. At present, Parliament has powers of amendment with the "last word" over the Council for some expenditures within narrow limits, the power of global reject, but no powers of legislative initiative (which the Treaties gave to the Commission). Direct election to the European Parliament, due now in May or June 1978, will be the next major move, and its possible effects on the Community finances will also be considered later on.

Institutions

A few words can situate the institutions that will be referred to later on. The Community institutions are:

1. *Parliament*
2. *Council*
3. *Court of Justice*

These three have no operational budgets beyond their administrative expenditures.

4. *Commission*, which administers, and whose budget contains, four funds: (a) *agricultural guarantee fund* (*FEOGA Guarantee*), (b) *agricultural guidance fund* (*FEOGA Guidance*), (c) *social fund*, (d) *regional development fund*, and various other direct programs of operational expenditure on nuclear and other research activities, including *Euratom*, energy and industry, food aid, and some other development aid.

The Commission also administers two legally distinct Community institutions, each of which have nonbudgetized financial operations of some size:

5. *European coal and steel community (ECSC)*
6. *European development fund (EDF)*

The only administratively independent financial agency is:

7. *European investment bank (EIB)*
   The *General Budget of the European Communities* includes 1, 2, 3, and 4, and the administrative expenses of 5 and 6.
   I shall also refer to some non-Community institutions that are wholly or predominantly creatures of EC member governments: the *European Space Agency* (ESA), in which member countries account for over 90 percent of its financing; some multigovernment public enterprises, for example, in the nuclear-fuels business (*Eurodif* and *Urenco*); and various multigovernmental aeronautics projects.
   Only a passing reference will be made to the Community's monetary institutions, which are governed by the Council and jointly administered by the Commission, the Monetary Committee, and the Committee of Governors of Central Banks. These are:

"*Snake*," a stable-exchange-rate parity club with 2¼ percent margins, of which Germany, France, Benelux, and Denmark are the present members (Ireland, Italy, and the United Kingdom are floating outside the "Snake"); some nonmember countries are associate members.

European Monetary Cooporation Fund (EMCF), which provides the Community's multilateral settlements system and short-term loan facilities between central banks, notably for "Snake" member countries.

A *medium-term loan facility* between member states, on which Italy has, since December 18, 1974, a 1.562-billion unit-of-account three-year loan outstanding.

A new "*Euroloan*" facility for the medium- to long-run recycling of OPEC surpluses to member states via the Community, whose activation was agreed on February 17, 1976 for five-year loans placed on the Eurodollar market of $300 million for Ireland and $1,000 million for Italy.

The Community's financial transactions are denominated in *units of account* (UA). The original unit of account was worth U.S. $1 and was converted into member-country currencies at IMF parity exchange rates; the General Budget still uses these exchange rates (for reasons referred to below), although a re-formed system using a new standard-basket European unit of account (EUA) is being progressively introduced; it is already adopted for the EDF, ECSC, and EIB. The EUA has a daily quotation and on January 1, 1976 was worth SDR

1.00462, or U.S. $ 1.16528. The agricultural funds use a further different set of "green" exchange rates, which are also commented on below.[2]

A number of interesting problems have arisen in managing and reforming the units of account, some of which are referred to in this chapter, and the reasons for which seem to arise from the fact that the Community is attempting something rather novel in the history of fiscal federalism—building up a fabric of integrated budgetary instruments before adopting a common currency. Indeed, in the mid-1960s it was widely believed that exchange-rate changes had become an institutional impossibility in the Community. The new EUA shows the Community adapting its operations to the reality of floating exchange rates, while at the same time attempting to advance with some of the mechanics of monetary integration; the EUA is due to have a parallel money function as well as serving as a budgetary unit of account.

Expenditure Functions

Present expenditure functions are summarized in Table 9-1, where the total for 1975 amounted to 8.5 billion UA, or a little under 1 percent of the Community GNP and a little over 2 percent of total public expenditure. In addition, further expenditure through ad hoc clubs in the area of advanced technology (space, aeronautics, nuclear) may account for approaching 1 billion UA more.

These activities will be reviewed under the following headings: (1) Community Democracy, Bureaucracy, and Justice; (2) Community External Relations; (3) Functioning of the Common Market; (4) Economies of Scale and Spillovers; and (5) Reallocative and Redistributive Activities.

1. Community Democracy, Bureaucracy, and Justice

The expenses under this heading are shown in Table 9-1. The Community institutions employ about 12,000 people.

2. Community External Relations

The fact that the Community does not have a defence sector is entirely atypical in the history of emerging federations. This has two indirect implications for the economic integration process. First, the absence of a common defence sector explains, perhaps, why the Community finds itself attempting to pursue economic integration without a federal government structure. Second, the financing of the defence sector has always in modern times been associated with, and often was responsible for, a large personal income tax, which gives to the federal or central government an automatic redistributive function of considerable size. Thus, the Community is also pursuing economic integration without automatic redistribution at a general macroeconomic level.

The Commission's recent contribution to the debate on European union suggests that defence could be identified as a field of "potential" Community competence if a Treaty of Union were to be aimed at in the foreseeable future. An earlier and more concrete step forward could be

"the development of a common policy on arms and equipment, possibly involving the setting up of a 'European Arms Agency,' which would bring about a more rational use of the available funds and the industrial and technological potentials of the member states. Experience has shown that the lack of a common policy in this field has meant that a number of industries are excessively dependent on sources outside the Community. This situation not only affects

Table 9-1

Expenditure of European Community Institutions 1973-1976

(In Millions of Units of Account)

	1973[a]	1974[a]	1975[a]	1976[b]	1978 Forecasts[c]
General Budget of the EC					
Administration:					
Commission	167	214	253	311	340
Council	25	41	50	64	
Parliament	23	33	42	51	128
Court of Justice	6	8	9	11	
Total	233	296	354	437	468
Interventions:					
Agriculture Funds	4,156	3,838	4,305	5,485	5,409
Social Fund	283	328	369	441	541
Regional Development Fund	–	–	150	300	750[d]
Research, Technology, Industry, and Energy (incl. *Euratom*)	75	109	126	188	332
Development Cooperation	48	260	312	237	707
Total	4,562	4,535	5,262	6,651	7,739
Other:					
Miscellaneous Aids, Subsidies, etc.	16	55	18	34	29
Contingency Reserve	63	23	36	24	–
Refund of Costs of Collection of Own Resources	250	309	390	429	494
Total General Budget	5,134	5,218	6,061	7,577	8,730

Table 9-1 Continued

	1973[a]	1974[a]	1975[a]	1976[b]	1978 Forecasts[c]
European Coal and Steel Community (ECSC)	406	557	(900)		
Interest and Other	98	141	} (200)[e]	–	–
Research, etc.	22	38		–	–
Gross Loans	286	378	700	–	–
European Investment Bank (EIB)	1,010	1,265	(1,306)		
Interest	143	198	} (300)[e]	–	–
Administration and Other	51	71		–	–
Gross Loans	816	996	1,006	–	–
European Development Fund (EDF)	167	172	182	–	3,390[d] (1976–1980)
Total Community Institutions	6,717	7,212	(8,449)	–	–

Sources: Official Journal of the European Communities: No. L 367, 31/12/73, *Supplementary Budget No. 4 of the E.C. for the Financial Year 1973*; No. 307, 27/ 12/74, *Supplementary Budgets Nos. 1 & 2*, 1974; No. L 1975, 7/7/75–*Supplementary Budget No. 2 of the E.C. for the Financial Year 1975*; No. L 66, 15/3/76, *General Budget of the E.C. for the Financial Year 1976*; *Draft General Budget of the European Communities for the Financial Year 1976*, Vol. 7, Part III, *Triennial Financial Forecasts 1976, 1977, 1978* (Commission of the European Communities, Brussels); European Investment Bank, *Annual Reports* 1973, 1974 and 1975 (Luxembourg); *ECSC Auditors' Reports* 1973, 1974 & 1975, Commission of the European Communities (Paul Gaudy, Luxembourg); The European Development Fund *End of Year Situation Reports*, 1973, 1974 & 1975 (Office for Official Publications of the European Communities, Luxembourg).
[a] Appropriations including supplementary budgets.
[b] Council decision of December 18, 1975.
[c] 1978 forecasts at 1975 prices unless otherwise indicated.
[d] Amounts fixed in nominal terms.
[e] Estimates.

the production of military equipment, and hence Europe's scope for independence, but also certain nonmilitary industries" (see *Bulletin of the EC, Supplement 5/75*).

There are some signs of movement in this area, with the European members of NATO and France agreeing in February 1976 to collaborate on defence procurement and joint equipment projects. The recent Tindemans report argues that "the European Union will remain incomplete as long as it does not have a defense policy" and, for the time being, recommends creation of a European Arms Agency (see *Bulletin of the EC, Supplement 1/76*).

Relations with developing countries have been the area in which the Community has made the fastest progress since enlargement. The reasons for this are several. There was in any case the need, following from enlargement, to integrate the former British dependencies into the pattern of economic relations already established for the associated exdependencies of the six. Also important was that in this area the member states were in some degree ready to pool their national roles into a new Community identity. Finally, the Community seems to have found in this case sufficient flexibility and imagination to negotiate an integrated agreement—the Lomé Convention signed with 46 African, Caribbean, and Pacific (ACP) countries on February 28, 1975—covering development aid, compensation for export commodity–price fluctuations, and unilateral preferential trade arrangements (in favor of the 46).

The Lomé Convention [see the EC Courier (1975)] contains five distinct financial instruments that in total amount to 3,900 million EUA for the period 1976-1980 (EDF grants, special loans, risk capital and STABEX, and EIB loans). The main characteristics of these headings are given in Table 9-2.

One of these, STABEX (an export earnings stabilization fund) merits some further description because of its originality, and because it is sometimes seen as a model for further worldwide arrangements in the context of UNCTAD and the North-South dialogue. The STABEX scheme will run as follows:

1. Transfers shall be paid where the export earnings of ACP countries for given products for a calendar year fall 7.5 percent (or 2.5 percent in some areas) below the average for the four preceding years.
2. The products covered are ground nuts, cocoa, coffee, cotton, coconut, palm oil and nuts, hides and skins, wood, bananas, tea, sisal, and iron ore.
3. Thirty-four out of the 46 ACP states count for the more favorable 2.5 percent clause by virtue of being "least-developed" land-locked, or islands.
4. The transfers will be usable for general purposes, and without interest.
5. The transfers shall be repayable under conditions that are broadly the reverse of those causing the original transfer, except that the payment conditions are not symmetrical and are biased to be favorable to the ACP states.
6. The balances outstanding at the end of the 5-year period may, taking into account the balance-of-payments situation of the states concerned, be either reconstituted or waived.

There have been other significant moves in the field of development cooperation (listed in Table 9-2). The food-aid program and the program of aid to non-ACP developing countries are currently being affected by the legislative process in a manner a bit reminiscent of the U.S. Presidential/Congressional tussle over aid budgets in the sixties; for 1976 the Commission opened with proposals for these two programs totalling 400 million UA. The Council then reduced this to 210 million UA, the Parliament then increased it back to 380 million UA, and the total finally and jointly adopted was 237 million UA.

The Community's endeavors to build up a comprehensive policy toward

Table 9-2
Principal Community Financial Instruments: Development Cooperation Sector

European Development Fund:			
EDF II (1964–1969)	Grant and loan and to associate developing countries.	800 mill. UA[a]	Similar to EDF IV(a–c)
EDF III (1971–1975)		1,000 mill. UA[a]	
EDF IV (1976–1980, Lomé)	Development assistance to 46 African, Caribbean and Pacific (ACP) countries:		
	a. Grant aid.	2,100 mill. EUA	Quite often matching EC member-state aid, no general ceiling to total project cost.
	b. Special loans.	430 mill. EUA	As per (a) above 1 % interest (interest-free for least-developed), typically 40-years maturity, 10-year grace period.
	c. Risk capital.	95 mill. EUA	Normally minority participation in share capital, or convertible loans.
	d. Export stabilization (STABEX).	390 mill. EUA	Unconditional transfers, reimbursable according to circumstances (see text).
European Investment Bank:			
Turkey 2nd. assoc. protocol (1973–76):	Development loans	25 mill. UA	Loans on EIB market terms.
	Special loans from member state contributions.	180 mill. UA old "Six" 47 mill. UA new "Three"	Loans of 30-years maturity, 8-year grace period, 2½–4½ % interest.
Greece 1st assoc. protocol (1962–67, 1974–)	Development loans.	125 mill. UA	Loans max. 30-years maturity, 7-year grace period, 2½ % interest for infrastructure, 4½ % interest for industrial projects.
1976–1980, Lomé	Development loans for ACP countries.	390 mill. EUA	Rate of interest reflecting EIB own resources less normally 3 % interest-rate subsidy financed from EDF IV (a) maturities ranging from 10 to 20 years, grace period 2–5 years according to type of project.

Maghreb (1977–81) probably	Development loans for ACP countries.	167 mill. EUA	Broadly as for EIB Lomé, 2 % interest-rate subsidy.
Portugal (1976–)	Development loans for ACP countries.	150 mill EUA	General 3 % interest subsidy (of 30 mill. UA from General Budget).
General Budget Development Cooperation Sector:			
Food Aid (Chapter 92)	Grants to least-favored developing countries, ACP and other.	Successively: 1976 295 mill. UA (Comm) / 1976 206 mill. UA (Council) / 1976 326 mill. UA (Parl.) / 1976 207 mill. UA (fin. dec.)	Grants in kind to beneficiaries, states or multilateral programmes; for resale on local markets. Cost split with FEOGA[b]
Fin. and Techn. aid to non-ACP developing countries (Chapter 90)	Grants to least-favored non-ACP developing countries.	Successively: 1976 105 mill. UA (Comm) / 1976 3.5 mill. UA (Council) / 1976 43.5 mill. UA (Parl.) / 1976 30 mill. UA (fin. dec.)	Details undecided.

Sources: *Draft General Budgets of the European Communities for 1976; European Investment Bank Annual Report, 1974* (Luxembourg); *The Courier, European Community–Africa–Caribbean–Pacific, No. 31* –Special Issue, March 1975, "EEC–ACP Convention of Lomé", Commission of the European Communities, 1975, Brussels; European Development Funds II and III *End of Year Statements*, Office for Official Publications of the European Communities, Luxembourg.

[a]Disbursements under these programmes are still continuing–the dates relate to commitments. Includes EIB allocation for these periods.
[b]The cost of food aid is split, FEOGA Guarantee taking the amount of normal export restitutions, the Food Aid Chapter 92 taking the remaining costs.

Mediterranean countries is reflected in a further bundle of aid and cooperation agreements, of which those with the associate states of Greece and Turkey are of long standing, while the programs for the Maghreb Group (Morocco, Algeria, and Tunisia) and Malta are new. Proposals have also been made as regards the Machrek Group (Syria, Jordan, Lebanon, and Egypt).

Finally, there is the case of Portugal, where the Community is offering economic assistance and trying to encourage a pluralist democratic outcome to the political struggle. The mechanics of Community aid are in the form of 150 million EUA long-term loans from the EIB, coupled with a 3 percent interest rebate to be financed from the General Budget.

3. Functioning of the Common Market

The mechanical functioning of the Common Market generates expenditure only in the agricultural sector; in other sectors it generates receipts (customs duties; see below). A common support price for oil also has its advocates in the Community, and the Rome European Council of December 1975 requested the Commission to propose a "mechanism" to protect existing energy resources in the Community.

Before the Common Market, all member countries intervened in their agricultural markets, and the Common Agricultural Policy (CAP) is the consequence of establishing free trade in agricultural produce while choosing a single set of integrated market-support instruments.

Since the workings of the agricultural guarantee fund are rather well known, the following remarks will not be fully proportional in length to the amount of money spent in this sector. Briefly, the CAP subsidies or taxes the difference between Community and world price. This basic "support price" system covers 72 percent of agricultural output, including the main cereals, beef, and dairy products. Fixed aids are given for certain products (durum wheat, olive oil, tobacco) for particular reasons. For the main products, the interplay of Community and world prices since 1968 is clearly portrayed in Figure 9-1. This has brought comparative stability of prices at a relatively high level and at a considerable budgetary cost—as the following figures (in millions of UA) from the 1976 budget show:

Milk products	1,941
Cereals	715
Beef and veal	680
Oils and fats	411
Tobacco	203
Wine	196
Sugar	170

Fruits and vegetables	113
Pigmeat	69
Other	140

The high level of budgetary cost has led, over the past year, to an intensive policy-review activity, first within the Commission and then in the Council (see *Bulletin of the EC*, Supplement 2/75).

The conclusions of the Commission and Council were not perhaps as radical as some were expecting but do nonetheless pinpoint the key areas of policy concern in the economics of the CAP. The milk surplus led to divided conclusions, one view envisioning an improved use of market-intervention methods, another view seeing the necessity for price policy to be used more actively to stabilize production. For the meat market, the problems of managing the production cycle are foremost. For cereals, the objective is to achieve a more economic set of relative prices, as between the cereals for bread and those for animal consumption.

An interesting episode has been the CAP's navigation through the storm of international monetary events starting with the big franc-mark crossrate changes in 1969 and, subsequently, through the period of generalized floating from August 1971 to the Smithsonian Agreement in December 1971, the creation of the "Snake in the Tunnel" in March 1972, the departure of the pound from the Snake in June 1972 and of the lira in February 1973, the concerted float of the Snake in March 1973, the further revaluations of the mark "within the Snake" in March and June 1973, and the French franc's temporary absence from the Snake between January 1974 and July 1975.

The problem has been that with a fixed-support–price mechanism for a common set of prices defined in terms of units of account, any exchange rate change will directly change the level of internal prices of farm produce. These consequences are not in principle different for other traded goods, but differences in degree are important: for other goods the price effects of exchange-rate changes are in part dissipated in their impact by time lags, pricing practices, and market imperfections. For agriculture, the price effects are fully and immediately perceived by consumers and farmers.

The price and income effects of the exchange-rate changes of the past few years were thus evaluated in certain cases as being politically unacceptable. Moreover, there was genuine uncertainty as to where the international monetary system was heading and whether certain exchange-rate changes might be reversed (as was indeed the case of the French franc in its leave of absence from the Snake), in which case the economic and political costs incurred by pushing up and then down certain farm prices and incomes would have been in vain.

For these reasons, a system of multiple exchange rates was set up for temporary use, whereby the exchange rates of the "green" unit of account (agricultural

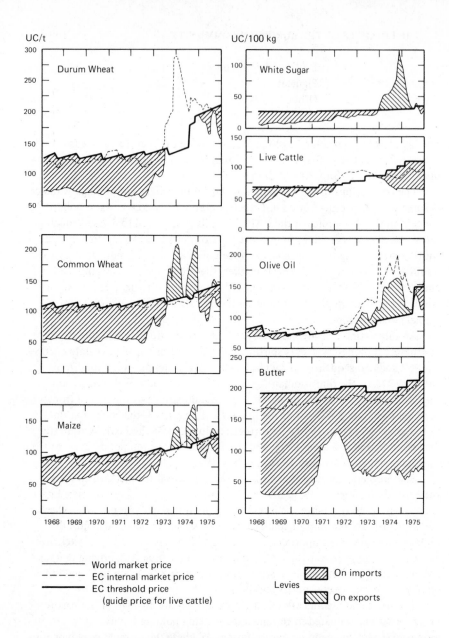

UC/t

UC/100 kg

Durum Wheat

White Sugar

Common Wheat

Live Cattle

Olive Oil

Maize

Butter

1968 1969 1970 1971 1972 1973 1974 1975   1968 1969 1970 1971 1972 1973 1974 1975

——————— World market price
– – – – – EC internal market price
——————— EC threshold price
  (guide price for live cattle)

Levies

On imports

On exports

Sources: *Bulletin of the E.C.*, supplement 2/75 'Stocktaking of the Common Agricultural Policy' (Office for Official Publications of the European Communities, Luxembourg), and E.C. Information Series '*Agricultural Markets-Prices*' (Commission of the European Communities, Brussels).

Note: the import or export levies correspond to the Community's variable border subsidies or taxes, which correspond to the difference between world and Community prices.

Figure 9-1. Threshold Prices, Levies and Internal Market Prices for Certain Agricultural Products

reference rate) could differ from the market exchange rates. In order to maintain undistorted trade flows, a system of border taxes and subsidies, known as *monetary compensatory amounts* (MCA), was established, compensating the differences between the market and green exchange rates.

One example may illustrate how the system works. On January 1, 1976, Germany had a level of internal farm prices at 110 percent of the Community price (i.e., an MCA of +10 percent), while the United Kingdom had a level of internal farm prices of 94 percent (i.e., an MCA of –6 percent).[3] For undistorted trade, the British buyer of food produce has to be indifferent on grounds of price as to its origin within the Community, subject only to transport costs. This is achieved, since when Britain buys from Germany, the importer pays 94, to which the Community intervention agencies add 6 on account of the British MCA, and 10 on account of the German MCA, the German producer receiving his 110. If the Community price is considered to be the economic price, the British consumer has been subsidised 6 percent and the German farmer 10 percent.[4]

Undistorted trade flows in the sense described do not mean, of course, undistorted conditions for production, which is why the Commission and Council are endeavoring to phase out the MCAs (see *Bulletin of the EC, Supplement 2/75*). Considerable progress has in fact been made in this direction. The maximum difference in Community farm prices was in July 1973, when the German MCA was +12 percent and the Italian MCA was –28 percent, a spread of 40 percent, compared with that of 16 percent, as indicated above. Policy has been increasingly to integrate a revision of the green exchange rates with the annual farm-price negotiations. In this way, reductions in the MCAs can be fitted coherently into a set of decisions that aim at adjusting prices in the light of cost increases at the Community and national levels and the market conditions for specific products.

While the objective is to restore the common level of prices and eliminate the multiple exchange-rate regime, the regime described has managed (with all its considerable budgetary complications) to accommodate for a period some very strong political pressures that could otherwise have been much more damaging to the very existence of the Community.

4. Economies of Scale and Spillovers

Here we are concerned with goods and services that risk being undersupplied, or inefficiently produced, or both, where there is inadequate Community-level public-sector intervention. There are the cases of advanced-technology goods that offer economies of scale at a 250-million population and the different category of goods and services where the benefits spill over across national frontiers to the extent that any single country may not take account of the full returns which the investment offers, as may be the case for cross-frontier transport infrastructure, for example.

In the textbooks of fiscal federalism, major examples of spillovers arise in the case of transport infrastructure. Transcontinental railways were among the important early achievements of the American, Canadian, and Australian federations, as more recently in the United States the interstate highways have been.

Europe's common-transport infrastructure is in some respects already relatively developed. However, there are deficiencies in the high-speed railway links (see *Bulletin of the EC*, 11/75, p. 69), and although the motorway links in the Benelux-France-Germany corner of Europe are increasing, they are not yet comprehensive. One Community financial instrument, the EIB's "common interest" operations, is designed to help finance projects of this sort. It has been active, for example, in motorway link-ups, transnational gas and oil pipelines, and electricity-generation projects feeding into more than one national grid. Some spectacular projects would seem to be natural cases for major Community financial participation, for example, the newly announced Rhone-Rhine canal link and the recently abandoned Channel Tunnel.

Apart from weaknesses in the physical infrastructure across frontiers, there are undoubtedly important regulatory functions that remain to be undertaken. By way of illustration, Table 9-3 gives the prices in December 1975 in Belgian francs per kilometer for selected scheduled international and national airflights of comparable distance. The United Kingdom–Continental case presumably reflects the absence of road and rail competition across the Channel of the kind present on the continent and would seem to be a clear enough case of a disincentive to European integration.

Education is another major textbook field in which spillovers often justify intervention by the top level of government. Here the case is less applicable to the Community, since benefit leakages through migration between countries is not at present an influence on national education expenditure. An exception is seen in the 14 million UA of expenditure in the General Budget on the "European schools," educating several thousand children of Community employees; in the absence of this expenditure, Brussels might well have been undersupplied with suitable education facilities for polyglot migration-prone

Table 9-3

	1.		2.		3. Price Ratio
Country	International Flights		National Flights		1 ÷ 2
Germany	Brussels–Frankfurt	7.06	Frankfurt–Bremen	6.54	1.1
France	Brussels–Paris	9.15	Paris–Lille	7.37	1.2
Italy	Brussels–Milan	5.69	Milan–Naples	3.77	1.6
U.K.	Brussels–London	9.47	London–Manchester	4.68	2.0

children. There are also problems of inadequate facilities for the children of immigrant workers, especially from nonmember countries, and ideas are being debated in the European Parliament for opening up the European schools to such children.

The opening up of the professions in Europe may give rise to new spillover problems in due course, for example, for doctors; medicine became the first open profession in 1975.

A further clear-cut spillover sector is that of pollution and environmental policy. Community legislation in this area is building up quite fast, although financial intervention by the Community will remain very limited in view of the adoption of the "polluter-pay principle" as the cornerstone of the Community policy.

The principles of spillovers and economies of scale are found together in the field of air-traffic control, for which purpose Eurocontrol has been created (with membership of the Community countries less Italy). While substantial investments in Eurocontrol computer and communications facilities have been made, uncertainties remain as to how far the member countries will implement the original Eurocontrol plans, for reasons *inter alia* of difficulty in integrating civil and military air-traffic control.

In looking for the areas that may offer at present the largest potential economy-of-scale benefits from Community-level activity, one of the most pertinent examples may be the aerospace sector. The costs of disunity in Europe are reflected in the following figures (see *Bulletin of the EC, Supplement* 11/75): in 1973 the U.S. aerospace sector had a turnover of 16,368 million UA; the Community, 5,990 million UA; the U.S. aerospace sector offered nine basic civil aviation models, which had registered 4,613 unit sales; the Community offered ten basic models, which had registered 859 sales. The Community has a full technological and design capacity. United States value-added per capita is double that of the Community. In the military sector, the multiplication of effort and loss of sales are also striking. In the jet-fighter market for the decade ahead, Germany, Italy, and the United Kingdom have jointly developed the MRCA; France and the United Kingdom have jointly developed the Jaguar; France has its own Dassault F1; and none of these aircraft satisfied the needs of Belgium, the Netherlands, Denmark, and Norway, who in 1975 ordered the American F16 after much-publicized negotiations.

The economics of research and development in the aerospace sector, as in the nuclear-energy field, have nonetheless pushed a certain distance in the direction of multinational or Community arrangements. The forms of cooperation that have emerged give a rather complete range of examples to reflect on:

1. Ad hoc intergovernmental clubs: Concorde, Jaguar, helicopters (France, U.K.) Airbus (France, Germany, U.K., Netherlands, and Spain), Alphajet trainer (France, Germany), the MRCA (Germany, Italy, U.K.).

2. Multigovernment public enterprises: nuclear-fuels enterprises URENCO (Germany, Netherlands, U.K.) and EURODIF (France, Belgium, Spain, and Sweden).
3. Multigovernmental agencies: European Space Agency (all the nine, plus Spain, Sweden, and Switzerland), which is commissioning a space launcher, a sky lab, and communication satellites;
4. Community institutions: the Common Research Center (ex-*Euratom*) engaged, among other things, on a 265 million UA project during 1976–1980 on thermonuclear fusion and plasma physics.

The overall result is that in several of these sectors Community countries have been spending significant fractions of their research efforts through multinational clubs of these different sorts, as Table 9–4 shows.

All this provides fertile ground for exploitation of the theory of clubs. In the present European situation, one of transition in the political and economic development of the Community, more analysis is needed of the costs and benefits of the different forms of organization. Ad hoc clubs clearly have the attractions of flexibility and of giving national governments opportunities for assessing the utility of projects and of creating or scrapping any club according to results. The disadvantage is that the more ad hoc and restricted the club, the smaller are the chances for harvesting the potential gains from large-scale production and trade.

These losses can be of two sorts. First there is the lack of marketing muscle in the case of an ad hoc production club. For example, the various ad hoc air-aircraft-production clubs have sometimes failed to capture the European market to the extent that might be expected if there were a Community policy for the aircraft industry (see *Bulletin of the EC, Supplement* 11/75). Second, there is a broader type of loss resulting from the failure of club activities to be fully articulated into the political system for arranging trade-offs of heterogeneous sorts. In the area of advanced-technology industries, this trade-off organization

Table 9–4

Percentage of Public Research and Development Expenditure in Certain Sectors Spent on Bilateral or Multinational Programs in 1972[a]

	Germany	France	Italy	U.K.
Nuclear Research	14.6	9.9	26.5	2.9
Space Research	58.2	37.0	–	62.1
Defense Research (Mainly Military Aviation)	29.2	–	0.6	18.5
Industry and Technology (Including Civil Aviation)	–	57.6	–	42.6

[a]See CREST (1974).

is particularly important, because public procurement is predominant and the achievement of gains from trade is dependent on the functioning of the inter-governmental marketplace.

5. Reallocative and Redistributive Activities

Here we have 23 grant and loan instruments (listed in Tables 9-5 and 9-6), largely in the area of sectoral and regional policies, many of which are amenable to analysis in terms of the theory of intergovernmental grants. The objectives and likely effects of these expenditures can be described in terms familiar to stu-dents of fiscal federalism—their financial conditions, specific-purpose restrictions, matching ratios, and prescribed levels of expenditure eligible for Community reimbursement or financial participation.

The justification for these policies has, in terms of Community legislative language, tended to be along the following lines: to "respond to situations resulting from the functioning of the Common Market" (Social Fund), to "promote a harmonious development in the whole of the Community" (Regional Fund), to avoid "a situation incompatible with the sound functioning of the Community" (Financial Mechanism). In the language of welfare economics, most of these instruments can be interpreted in compensationist terms, and their rationalization can be sought under the concept of Pareto-optimal redis-tribution with respect to gains from trade.

In general, we are looking at the response to the concern—of individuals, sectors, regions, and even national member states—that the fruits of economic integration could be unequally distributed to the point of leaving some groups, in the extreme case, worse off than before. If these fears should be well founded, and in the event that the Community generates large welfare gains in the aggre-gate, the gainers would find it in their interest to redistribute part of the gains to compensate the losers. Optimal compensation, we note, is achieved only in a fully rationalized decision-making process—that is, based on full information— and allows for continuous marginal adjustments. In fact, these optimal condi-tions are not met, either as regards economic information or the decision-making process. To these questions we shall return below. For the time being, however, it can be noted that most of the 23 instruments were introduced under the pressure of decisions to create and enlarge the Community in 1958 and 1973, or under threat of secession in 1974-1975.

It is sometimes argued that this compensationist interpretation should also be applied to some of the instruments already covered above under other headings. The main case in point arose at the birth of the EEC, when France and Italy feared that Germany would benefit most from the industrial common market and insisted on the establishment of the common agricultural market as a *quid pro quo*. While this may have been part of the deal of the day, subsequent

Table 9-5
Principal Community Financial Instruments: Sectoral Allocation and Financial Redistribution in the General Budget

Instrument	Objective / Form of aid	Amount	Terms
FEOGA Guidance Fund: (No. 72/159/EEC)	Modernization of farms with "potential."	46.5 mill. UA in 1975 / 29 mill. UA in 1976 / 82 mill. UA in 1978	25% matching interest-rate subsidy (total up to 6%) or grant, total ceiling of 40,000 UA per farm.
(No. 72/160/EEC)	Cessation of farming, "retirement" annuities, without "potential".	11.0 mill. UA in 1975 / 6 mill. UA in 1976 / 39 mill. UA in 1978	25–65% variable matching grant, total ceiling of 900 UA per married person.
(No. 75/268/EEC)	Subsidy for farms in mountainous and less-favored regions.	– mill. UA in 1975 / 50 mill. UA in 1976 / 85 mill. UA in 1978	25% matching income-maintenance grants; total grants may range from 15 to 50 UA per livestock unit, etc.
Social Fund: (Article 4, agriculture)	*Objective:* Compensating direct consequences of community policies.	60.0 mill. UA in 1975	
(Article 4, industrial-textile)		56.0 mill. UA in 1975	
(Article 4, handicapped workers)		10.0 mill. UA in 1975	
(Article 4, migrant workers)	*Form of aid:* a. Training and retraining of workers, b. Action to increase mobility of labor. c. Income maintenance for subjects of (a) or (b).	35.4 mill. UA in 1975	50% matching grants to total cost of public projects.
(Article 5, regional)	*Objective:* Ease structural disequilibria harmful to Community integration.	189.0 mill. UA in 1975	50% grant to total public (national and Community) contribution to private projects.
(Article 5, where technical progress threatens given industries)		12.0 mill. UA in 1975	
(Article 5, where groups of enterprises are in difficulty)		6.0 mill. UA in 1975	
(Article 5, handicapped workers)		40.0 mill. UA in 1975	

Total Social Fund	369 mill. UA in 1975	
	500 mill. UA in 1976 (Comm.)	
	400 mill. UA in 1976 (Council)	
	470 mill. UA in 1976 (Parlt.)	
	441 mill. UA in 1976 (final decision)	

Regional Development Fund (No. 75/724/EEC):

Aid to investment by enterprises in specific regions.

(Statutory allocation)

300 mill. UA in 1975
500 mill. UA in 1976
500 mill. UA in 1977

Matching grant up to 20% of investment cost and up to 50% of national aid, total ceiling of 100,000 UA investment per new job, etc.

Aid to infrastructure investment by public authorities in specific regions.

Matching grant up to 10 to 30% of investment cost; aid can be through 3% interest-rate subsidy on EIB loan.

Financial Mechanism: (legislation pending)

Reimbursement of disproportionate financing of Community General Budget.

Greater of 250 mill. UA or 3% of Budget.

General-purpose grant to national governments, quasi-automatic macro-economic and fiscal criteria and conditions.

Sources: *Budgets of the European Communities* for 1975, 1976, op. cit.; *Triennial Financial Forecasts 1976/77/78*, op. cit.; *Official Journal of the European Communities*, No. L 131 20/5/1976—Financial Mechanism.

Table 9–6
Principal Community Financial Instruments: Sectoral Allocation and Financial Redistribution in the ECSC and EIB

European Coal and Steel Community:			
(Art. 54, unsubsidized)	Industrial investment for modernization and nationalization of coal, steel, and related sectors.	311.3 mill. UA in 1974	Loans to enterprises on terms reflecting ECSC's capital-market standing, usually 8–10-years duration and not exceeding 30 % of total investment cost.
(Art. 54, subsidized)	Idem, projects of particular Community interest, and environmental investments.	39.7 mill. UA in 1974	Idem, with 3 % interest subsidy on first 5 years of loan.
(Art. 56, unsubsidized)	Structural reconversion, for broad range of industries replacing declining coal and steel plants.	28.5 mill. UA in 1974	Terms as in Art. 54, but projects must first have received national aids.
(Art. 56, subsidized)	Idem.	23.2 mill. UA in 1974	As in Art. 56, unsubsidized, but with 3 % interest subsidy.
(Art. 54,2, own resources)	Subsidized housing loans for employees of coal and steel sectors.		15 to 25 % matching loan, ECSC own resources providing 15–20-year loans at 1 % interest, mixed with national sources of housing finance.
(Art. 54,2, own resources and borrowed funds)	Idem.	4.5 mill. UA in 1974	50 % matching loan ECSC own resources and borrowed funds providing loans at 3½ to 6 % interest, further mixed with national sources of housing finance.
European Investment Bank:			
(Art. 130 (a))	Regional development	540.2 mill. UA in 1974	Loans on terms reflecting EIB's capital-market standing, usually 7–12 years, in range of 2–16 MUA per contribution, not exceeding 40 % of investment cost.
(Art. 130 (b))	Sectoral modernization and conversion.	99.2 mill. UA in 1974	
(Art. 130 (c))	Projects of common interest to several member countries.	344.9 mill. UA in 1974	
Total of above 3 lines:		984.3 mill. UA	
Less double counting of projects under multiple criteria		145.4 mill. UA	
Total EIB member-country loans:		849.7 mill. UA	

Sources: *ECSC Auditors' Report for the Year 1974,* Commission of the European Communities, 1974 (Paul Gaudy, Luxembroug): European Investment Bank, *Annual Report,* 1974 (Luxembourg).

years produced some surprising twists and turns as regards who has been compensating whom. First, in setting the common farm prices, it was in general the German farmer who bid for the highest price levels. The relatively high common prices also did much to create the antimarket lobby in British politics—to the dismay of the British industrialist, who saw large advantages in joining the Community.

Events in recent years have no doubt modified these early political assessments. On the one hand, French industry has been increasing its market shares in Europe, while, as regards the agricultural sector, the first two years of enlarged membership in 1973 and 1974 found the CAP mechanisms protecting the Community consumer from the excess of world-market price fluctuations (see Figure 9-1). To this may be added the effects of the green exchange rates already described above, with the temporary MCA mechanism in effect extending subsidies to the British consumer and the German farmer.

Apart from this broader setting, the Common Agricultural Policy has its own official compensation funds, three of which are listed in Table 9-5—modernization grants, retirement grants, and mountain and least favored areas grants.

The "farm modernization" fund provides investment grants to farms that, according to objective criteria, can potentially support living standards comparable to the nonfarm sector. FEOGA provides a flat 25 percent from member states, with a common ceiling level of total aid (40,000 UA per farm).

The "mountain and least-favored areas" directive is a new program whose introduction was a semicommitment brought through from the enlargement negotiations. The aim is to compensate farmers who are unable to derive an adequate income from the general farm-price policy and are in areas risking depopulation. There is therefore a farm-region map of Europe (see Figure 9-2), and farmers in the designated areas are eligible for a 25 percent flat contribution from FEOGA to recognized programs of national aids. The level of national income maintainance aids must lie between the range of 15 and 50 UA (per livestock unit, or other technical equivalents), in the event the British and German aids are at the high end of this bracket and the Irish and Italian aids are a good deal lower down.

While small, the "retirement grants" program is worth mentioning, for two reasons. First, it is one of the most explicit cases of a Community program aimed at the level of the individual and seeking to compensate the "losers" directly affected by a Community policy. Beneficiaries are farmers between fifty-five and sixty-five years of age whose farms do not have the potential to support an adequate income at Community price levels. Second, this is the only instance so far of a *variable matching* categorical grant. Benefits eligible for FEOGA reimbursement are subject to a Community ceiling of 900 UA. The rate of reimbursement is normally 25 percent, but it is 65 percent with respect to regions where two conditions are simultaneously met: GNP per capita is lower than the Community average, and the working population in agriculture is higher than the Community average. The regions satisfying these criteria are a large part of Italy and about half of Ireland. It was felt that the fiscal capacity of these two countries might cause difficulty in meeting the national counterpart to a flat rate of Community reimbursement.

The *Social Fund* (see *Third Report on the Activities of the New European Social Fund* (1974)], for all its eight operating windows, uses a uniform 50 percent matching-grant rule. The money is mainly spent on vocational training and readaptation. The policy has been to avoid the use of national quotas and, indeed, any "discrimination" among countries in the operation of the fund. Further, the policy has been to identify "Community objectives" and then to finance as far as possible projects that correspond to them. The Community does not apply any fixed minimum or maximum levels of expenditure (per retrained worker, for example) in the application of its 50 percent contribution.

In some areas of operation, the criteria have been sufficiently narrow to avoid an excess supply of eligible project requests in relation to the sums available. This has been the case, for example, for the Article 4 operations for agriculture and textiles, the Article 5 operations for employees of sectors threatened by technical progress, and groups of enterprises in severe difficulty.

In some other areas, however, the criteria have been sufficiently broad to attract an excess demand in relation to the funds made available, notably as regards the Article 5 operations in the regions and for handicapped workers. A choice has then to be made through a combination of committee consensus and management. The Social Fund Committee has certain powers in this area; its membership consists of three "social partners" per country plus three members from the Commission. The voting rules are unusual for the Community institutions: one man one vote, and simple majority decisions. The process of selection, by the joint management of the Commission and the Committee, has been first to evolve priority criteria of a qualitative kind. For example, regional applications for the retraining of young, older, and women workers are favored. The percentage distribution of the regional program of the Social Fund in 1974 was as follows: Italy, 39.7; Ireland, 5.3; United Kingdom, 27.2; France, 17.1; other countries, 11.7. These ratios are in fact quite close to the Regional Fund's quotas (see below).

The excess demand for programs for handicapped workers has led to special procedures. Certain types of program (those giving new and complete services from basic adaptation through to employment) are met, as a first priority, wholly for all countries. As a second priority, programs of this sort that are not new projects are met for Ireland, Northern Ireland, and Italy. This is justified by the objective of maximizing the additionality of the Social Fund interventions; applications from the countries and region mentioned are considered to be more critically dependent on money from the Social Fund.

The *Regional Development Fund* was brought into operation in 1975, with an initial three-year block of funds amounting to 1,300 million UA allocated, in principle, 300 million UA in 1975, and 500 million UA each for 1976 and 1977. In practice, the disbursement of these funds will lag somewhat behind this timetable (see figures in Table 9-1).

The funds are to be spent on projects submitted through national governments, with the following country percentage quotas: Denmark, 1.3; Ireland, 6; Luxembourg, 0.1; Germany, 6.4; Italy, 40; Netherlands, 1.7; France, 15; Belgium, 1.5; United Kingdom, 28. In addition to its 6 percent, Ireland receives 6 million UA per annum, deducted pro rata from the shares of all other countries except Italy.

The funds may be used to help finance (1) investment expenditure of enterprises and (2) infrastructural investment of public authorities. Projects must be within designated areas, that are eligible for certain national aids as well as for the Regional Fund. The matching rules are that, in the case of investment by enterprises, the Regional Fund may contribute 20 percent of the cost of the investment, not exceeding 50 percent of certain national aids to the project. A further ceiling for the fund's contribution is that the above rules apply only to the first 100,000 UA of investment for each new job created or 50,000 UA for each job preserved. In the case of infrastructural investment, the fund's contribution may be between 10 and 30 percent of the cost of the investment (for projects above 10 million UA in total cost).

At the outset, there has been considerable concern about how to ensure the maximum additionality of Regional Fund money. This is not an easy concept to apply at all precisely over a multiyear period. The Regional Fund Committee will have the job of monitoring the fund's contribution in relation to national efforts.

The ECSC and EIB obtain their funds mainly on commercial terms and reallocate the flow of savings and investment into channels that are considered desirable in the Community context and on terms that are implicitly advantageous to the enterprise, regions, sectors, or countries that are most hard pressed.

In the coal and steel sectors, the financial interventions of the ECSC [see *ECSC Financial Report* (1974) and *Auditor's Report* (1974)] are intended to help forward the process of European rationalization and integration, in part by aiding the adaptation of the weaker areas or enterprises. The extent of its financial activities is primarily dependent on the rate of new investment and restructuring activity in the sectors concerned. There are three main operating activities:

1. Financing of investments which fit into a general scheme of rationalization or modernization. Under this heading, 351 million UA were spent in 1974, with some projects of particular Community interest benefiting from a 5-year 3 percent interest-rate rebate, for example, "pioneering" environmental investments and investment to relieve a bottleneck in cokification capacity.

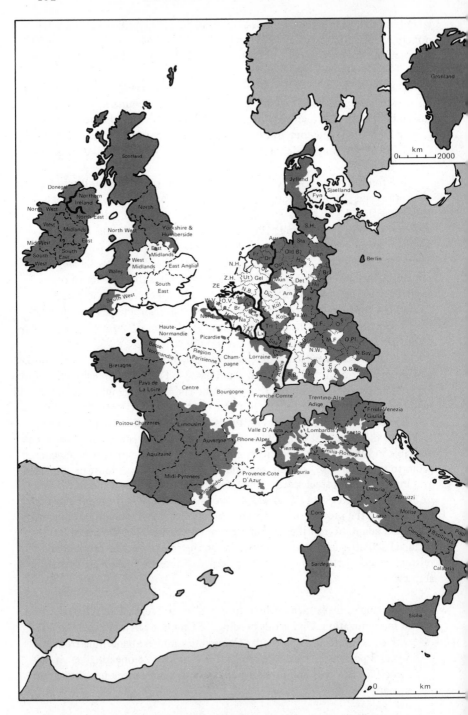

Source: European Documentation 1975/4 '*A New Regional Policy for Europe*', (Commission of the European Communities, Brussels).

Figure 9-2. Regions and Zones Aided by Member States and the Regional Development Fund (shaded areas).

2. Financing of investments in areas suffering from declining coal and steel sectors, the new investments being in a wide range of other sectors. Again, some of these projects benefit from an interest-rate rebate, notably loans to firms reemploying workers made redundant from the coal and steel sectors.
3. Financing, on heavily subsidized terms (1 percent interest), of housing programs for workers in these sectors. The ECSC money is generally highly geared to matching national finance, giving overall terms to the borrowers of between 3½ and 6 percent.

In the case of the *European Investment Bank* (EIB) [see European Investment Bank (1974)], whose activities are not budgeted, the statutory limit on the volume of its lending activities is the rule that its total outstanding loans should not exceed 2½ times its subscribed capital, which is entirely supplied by member governments.

As of December 31, 1974, its subscribed capital amounted to 2,025 million UA; the actual outstanding loans at this time had reached 3,600 million UA (of which 3,411 million has gone to member states, and 189 million to associated countries). The maximum lending limit of 5,062 million UA is considered to be the Bank's global "own resources."

The annual rate of activity has been increasing significantly, reaching a level of 996 MUA loan contracts signed in 1974, compared with 816 million UA in 1973 (the first year of enlarged membership) and 526 million UA in 1972. The EIB's future rate of activity seems likely soon to exceed the 1,000 million UA level of gross loan disbursements.

The EIB has four functions, three within member states and a fourth for development purposes in third countries (which has already been mentioned).

The functions within member states are (a) regional, (b) sectoral, which in practice means in large measure energy, and (c) common-interest projects, i.e., projects that aid the integration of border regions in the Community. The breakdown of the total of 850 million UA loans in member countries in 1974 according to these criteria is given in Table 9-7. Energy projects accounted for 350 million UA, including, for example, cross-border oil and gas pipelines and power stations serving more than one country's electricity grids. Environmental investments of interest to several countries have also attracted EIB financing, for example, the purification of industrial effluent in the upper Rhine.

The EIB lends to industrial enterprises, to independent public authorities, and in some cases in the form of block loans to financial institutions. The EIB's financial contribution is generally in the range of 2 to 16 million UA, with its contribution to total investment costs rarely exceeding 40 percent. The loans are generally of a 7- to 12-year duration, with up to 20 years for infrastructure projects.

The EIB's activities are in numerous ways integrated into the operations of

Table 9–7

Fulfilling Single Criteria		Double		Triple
Regional	372	Regional and Sectoral	64	
Sectoral	–			
Common-interest	274	Regional and Common-interest	132	27
		Sectoral and Common-interest	63	

the other Community instruments, notably the Regional Fund, which can finance a 3 percent interest-rate subsidy on EIB regional loans, and the EDF, where an allocation from the EIB was part of the terms of the Lomé Convention.

The Community's newest instrument of redistribution, and in fact its only instrument of general-purpose financial redistribution between member states, is the Financial Mechanism. While this is an expenditure function, its presentation is best held over to the following section, which deals with the Community's own resources.

Resources

Current Resources

The financing of the budget has been passing through three kinds of system:

1. Systems of purely *political shares* for current contributions, as, for example, under the Treaty of Rome, wheby the early running costs of the Community were financed by identical shares of 29 percent each for France, Germany, Italy, etc. There were other ad hoc contribution keys for various community activities.
2. The above has been replaced by a system of *own resources*, comprising customs duties, agricultural levies, and a share of the revenue to come from a harmonized value-added tax (VAT) base. This was decided in principle in 1970, but with arrangements for a gradual phasing in during the present decade, to which further reference will be made. The main innovation here was to pass to a consolidated financing of the General Budget, with implications for tax harmonization.
3. The partial use of *macroeconomic indicators* (notably GNP shares) for several purposes: (1) funds to substitute for the VAT pending negotiation of the common tax base, (2) points of reference for phasing in the new Three's contributions during their transitional regime in the years 1973–1980, and (3) criteria for redistribution under the Financial Mechanism following the British "renegotiations" of 1974–1975 (see below).

There is no need here to describe in more detail the present system (see *Bulletin of the EC, Supplement* 7/74), which is a complex hybrid of the above elements. It is more interesting, perhaps, to examine some aspects of the own-resource system, which will be the sole source of budget finance in 1978 as regards the Six, and in 1980 as regards the Three.

The most up-to-date forecast of the maximum value of these own resources has been provided in the Commission's 1976–1978 triennial budget forecasts [see *Preliminary Draft General Budget* (1975)]. The following data (in millions of UA) relate to the year 1978, expressed at 1975 prices; data for earlier years are not comparable, since they include some customs duties that are due to disappear:

100% of customs duties	3,404
100% of agricultural levies	1,631
1% of the common VAT base	6,200
	11,235

The forecast financing requirement for 1978, at 1975 prices, is 8,420 million UA. Since the VAT is the marginal source of finance, this would require a rate of VAT levy of 0.55 percent of the VAT base. The average effective VAT rate in the Community is of the order of 10 to 11 percent of the VAT base, which means that the Community's maximum share of this revenue source is in turn on the order of 10 percent.

The philosophy behind the own-resource decision—which is important because it motivates much of the debate in the Community institutions—was broadly as follows. The own resources are intended, according to classical fiscal federal principles, to provide an independent and direct source of funds. From a distributive point of view, the system was intended to be neutral, with the VAT in particular viewed as the most neutral of taxes—and also the least difficult to harmonize. As regards customs duties and agricultural levies, the concepts of incidence and distribution were considered to be irrelevant, on the grounds that these taxes do not relate to the fiscal capacity of member countries since they originate from Community rather than national activities.

These ideas were then confronted in the British "renegotiations" of 1974–1975 by the claim that the United Kingdom would be paying in 24 percent of own resources in relation to a GNP share of 14 percent in 1980 (before this year, the potential outcome of the own-resource system would be restricted by the transitional arrangements for the Three) and that this would be unfair and out of line with ordinarily accepted notions of ability to pay.[5] The Commission, in response, published detailed estimates of the intercountry distribution of the Community budget, including two tables here reproduced as Tables 9–8 and 9–9; these tables showed, with respect to the British case, an estimated 22 percent contribution to own resources alongside a GNP share of 16 percent for

Table 9-8

Simulated Distribution of Relative Shares in the Community Budget and Community Gross Domestic Product, 1973 and 1974

(Current Market Exchange Rates)

	Total Budget Contribution in Million UA		Relative Share in Budget %		Relative Share i Community Gro Domestic Produ	
	1973	1974	1973	1974	1973	197
Denmark	109	120	2.2	2.4	2.6	2.
Germany (FR)	1514	1509	31.0	30.2	33.0	33.
France	897	908	18.4	18.2	23.9	23
Ireland	32	30	0.7	0.6	0.6	0.
Italy	668	662	13.7	13.2	13.2	13
Netherlands	425	389	8.7	7.8	5.8	6.
BLEU. (Belg. Lux.)	264	278	5.4	5.6	4.5	4
United Kingdom	968	1099	19.9	22.0	16.4	15
Community	4877	4995	100	100	100	100

Source: Bulletin of the EC, Supplement 7/74, Table 3.

Note: Tables 9-8 and 9-9 are simulations in that they give estimates of the financing of the budgets of years 1973 and 1974 according to the definitive system of own resources, which is being progressively introduced between 1970 and 1980, and will be completely applicable for the first time in 19

a simulated version of the 1974 budget (i.e., an estimation of what the 1980 own-resource rules would have given if applied in 1974). The Commission acknowledged that "as regards budget charges . . . it does appear that problems could arise in the future" (see *Bulletin of the EC, Supplement* 7/74).

Although the ensuing negotiations, which culminated in the Financial Mechanism agreed at the Dublin Summit of March 1975, were conducted in an atmosphere influenced by the imminent referendum, it is worth noting that the outcome fits reasonably coherently with economic notions of tax incidence.

As regards the VAT part of the problem, it was recognized that while this had been seen as a neutral tax (and indeed would broadly seem to be so in fact as between the Six), it could in certain cases give rise to distributional problems, for example, because investment is exempt from VAT, while investment/ consumption ratios vary substantially between certain member countries. As a result, countries with low investment ratios would have a proportionately higher share of the Community total VAT base than their share of GNP. This imbalance was accepted in the Financial Mechanism, on conditions to which I will return, as an amount eligible for compensatory reimbursement.

As regards the customs duties and agricultural levies, it had long been argued that the country of collection could be a notoriously unreliable guide to incidence. The role of Rotterdam and Antwerp as the ports of entry into the Community for goods destined for German consumption are the obvious exam-

Table 9-9

Simulated Breakdown of the Financing of the Budget under the Definitive Own-Resources System, 1973 and 1974

(Current Market Exchange Rates)

		Agricultural Levies and Sugar Contributions		Customs Duties		VAT		Total	
		Million UA	%	Million UA	%	Million UA	%	Million UA	%
Denmark	1973	5	0.9	39	1.9	65	2.8	109	2.2
	1974	7	2.0	50	2.0	64	2.9	120	2.4
Germany (FR)	1973	144	26.6	621	30.7	749	32.4	1514	31.0
	1974	118	35.4	711	29.0	679	30.8	1509	30.2
France	1973	87	16.1	329	16.3	481	20.8	897	18.4
	1974	72	21.5	371	15.1	466	21.1	908	18.2
Ireland	1973	3	0.7	10	0.5	18	0.8	32	0.7
	1974	3	1.0	8	0.4	18	0.8	30	0.6
Italy	1973	127	23.4	236	11.7	305	13.2	668	13.7
	1974	53	16.0	307	12.5	302	13.7	662	13.2
Netherlands	1973	94	17.4	197	9.7	134	5.8	425	8.7
	1974	22	6.7	239	9.7	128	5.8	389	7.8
BLEU (Belg. Lux.)	1973	30	5.5	130	6.4	104	4.5	264	5.4
	1974	17	5.2	164	6.6	97	4.4	278	5.6
United Kingdom	1973	51	9.4	461	22.8	456	19.7	968	19.9
	1974	41	12.2	606	24.7	452	20.5	1099	22.0
Community	1973	541	100	2023	100	2312	100	4877	100
	1974	333	100	2456	100	2206	100	4995	100

Source: Bulletin of the EC, Supplement 7/74, Table 4.

Note: See note on Table 9–8.

ples generally cited, and this is indeed the reason why the Belgian and Dutch shares of these own resources is much higher than their GNP shares (see Tables 9-8 and 9-9). (In passing, this touches on one of the principles for the selection of taxes for the central as opposed to lower levels of government: to assign to the center those taxes whose incidence is least related to point of collection or, alternatively, where the spillover of incidence would be greatest if the tax were assigned to a lower level of government.) While the British Government did not accept that British collections of these revenues could have any other than British incidence, the rest of the Community refused to allow in the Financial Mechanism the same system of reimbursement as for the imbalance between GNP and VAT shares.

The outcome—the Financial Mechanism—was a system of reimbursement of "excess" payments into the budget (the excess of the share in own resources over the GNP share) subject to the following conditions:

1. GNP per capita had to be beneath 85 percent of the EC average (this covers Ireland, Italy, and the United Kingdom at present).
2. GNP growth per capita had to be beneath 120 percent of the EC average (this allows the above countries a significant margin of GNP catch-up performance before being disqualified).[6]
3. A threshold degree of excess in the share in own resources over GNP was established at 10 percent (this is to allow a further margin for the own-resource system to operate without interference).
4. A scale of progressivity was introduced for the degree of reimbursement, starting at 50 percent and reaching 100 percent when the excess of the share in own resources over GNP reached a ratio of 1:3.

The final refinement to this rather complicated device was to make it more difficult (for reasons already indicated) for countries to benefit from imbalances attributable to customs duties and agricultural levies than from those attributable to VAT. For this purpose, a balance-of-payments criterion was introduced: countries in current-account surplus could receive refunds only with respect to the VAT imbalance; countries in deficit could be compensated with respect to the total own resources.

Where the above criteria are met (for the average of the three preceding years in the case of the economic criteria), the payments under the Financial Mechanism become an automatic general-purpose grant on the expenditure side of the budget. The amounts are not, however, open-ended. A ceiling applies that is the greater of 250 million UA or 3 percent of the budget size.

As already noted, the harmonized VAT base required for levying the third category of own resources has not yet been introduced. Since the 1970 decision of principle, the Community has been laboring to agree on a common VAT base, on the basis of a draft directive from the Commission (see Bulletin of the EC,

Supplement 11/73). These negotiations have led to a seemingly irreducible short list of derogations from the common tax base sought by various member countries (for example, zero rating for food in the United Kingdom, special regimes for agriculture and small enterprises in Belgium and Italy, and the treatment of land in Germany).

After long negotiations attempting to eliminate these proposed derogations, the Council is now (since December 1975) making a revised approach to conclude the affair, which would be to admit under certain conditions a small number of derogations accompanied by an agreed system of financial compensation within the VAT own-resource system matching the admitted derogations.[7]

It was mentioned above that the new European unit of account has not yet been adopted for the General Budget. There are two reasons for this. First, the reform is legislatively complex, particularly since the intent is that the EUA become the standard of value in which the Community will contract with third parties. Second, there are distributive implications as between revaluers and devaluers in the funding of the budget. Under the definitive own-resource system coming into operation in 1978 as regards the Six, and 1980 as regards the Three, the reform of the unit of account would have no significant distributive implications. For the time being, however, for reasons that need not here detain us, there would be a redistribution of the budget burden from revaluers to devaluers, while the growing obsolescence of the present unit of account's exchange rates has had the reverse effect. Unanimity is required to change the unit of account.

Capital Resources

The General Budget has at present no powers to raise loans. The budget has to be in current balance: so much for a macroregulation influence.

Two Community institutions, the ECSC and EIB, do have powers to raise loans, however, and these powers are being used. In 1974 the ECSC raised 528 million UA in long-term bond finance, and the EIB 826 million UA. Both institutions are active on the New York and European capital markets, as well as in member-state capital markets. The uses to which these funds are put have already been indicated. The question now is how far these loan-financing operations imply a redistribution of income (through providing cheaper money to certain member states than they could otherwise have access to) or a reallocation of savings finance into locations that would otherwise have difficulty in attracting the funds.

Both the ECSC and EIB have AAA ratings on the New York stock market, which allows them currently (November 1975) to be raising U.S. dollar 5- to 7-year notes on international capital markets at 9 to 9¼ percent. These funds are then relent to clients in member states on essentially the same terms, with a small markup for service costs but no discrimination between member states or borrowing enterprise according to credit worthiness.

While it is a matter for speculation what terms member governments would obtain at present for equivalent loan operations, Germany and the Benelux countries could probably obtain equivalent finance on no less favorable terms. (Norway, whose international credit rating is presumably as good as anybody's, obtained funds comparable to the cases cited above and at the same time, at 8.85 percent.) Ireland, Italy, and the United Kingdom, however, probably find ECSC and EIB money attractive: these countries have been absent from international capital markets in recent months.

Neither the ECSC nor the EIB carry statutory guarantees of member states of the kind provided in the case of the Euroloan recycling facility. Other factors, however, seem to provide the basis for an equivalent credit rating. The ECSC has powers to raise a levy on all coal and steel output in the Community, and the EIB's lending is limited to 2½ times its share capital, all subscribed by member countries.

A proposal is at present under discussion to give Euratom loan-raising powers to finance investments in nuclear-energy generation. Another institution under consideration—a European Export Bank—would also have needs for long-term finance.

Criteria for Future Developments

In this section I would like to identify the main areas of theoretical analysis and empirical research that might help predict what role the Community's finances should play in the economic and political integration process ahead. Four headings seem relevant: The Allocative Efficiency of Fiscal Federalism; The Macroeconomics of Interregional versus International Balance-of-Payments Financing; Theories of Redistribution at the Interregional Level; and The Influence of Democratic and Decision-Making Procedures.

The Allocative Efficiency of Fiscal Federalism

Under this heading I have little to add to the preceding sections, except to note that the tools of fiscal federal analysis seem in general quite well developed for the purpose of screening what functions may objectively be best assigned to higher or lower levels of government, and how intergovernmental clubs and systems of financial transfers should be analysed to test for their efficiency in carrying out the given objectives. The Community's existing grant and loan programs, while small, may offer more opportunities for useful analysis than is perhaps generally recognized. For the future, it is far from obvious what the

Community tier of government should come to contain from an optimal economic point of view. In some areas, where spillovers are slight, where national programs already meet notions of acceptable minimum standards, or where the existing cross-frontier infrastructure is adequate, the case for Community functions may be limited. In other areas, significant unexploited benefits may stand to be gained. However, this can be evaluated in greater depth, function by function, as experience accumulates and concrete issues arise.

The Macroeconomics of Interregional versus International
Balance-of-Payments Financing

The second heading is a crucial area of analysis that the fiscal federal literature seems to neglect. The need is to clarify what pattern of macroeconomic relations is likely to emerge between the region member states in the budgetary sector if the broad objectives of economic and monetary integration are to be attained. If certain macroeconomic patterns can be identified, the next task is to comprehend how they are achieved through the aggregation of the many partial and microeconomic public-sector functions.

A broad interpretation of the role of interregional budgetary transfers is as follows. Regions do not have independent trade, exchange-rate, and monetary policies but can adjust their balance of payments with the aid of the free movement of labor and capital and budgetary transactions. Nations, at least in the pure type, have independent trade, exchange-rate, and monetary policies but do not adjust with the aid of labor and capital nor with budgetary transactions. The Community region member states are at present in the situation of having largely renounced independent trade policies. Most have de facto lost a good deal of control of monetary policy (to the dominant world capital markets rather than to Community institutions), while the exchange-rate instrument is in some cases partly renounced and in some cases recognized to be of blunted efficiency (here there are important differences that go with the size of the economy). Capital movements are in a state of intermediate freedom of movement. Migration between Community countries, while legally free for the individual, is on a small scale and is seriously limited by linguistic barriers and cultural and political preferences. The Community budget function is, from a macroeconomic point of view, of small importance for the larger member states, although it is already of macroeconomic significance to some small states and regions (for example Ireland, Denmark, and Brittany).

Looking to the future, it seems likely that the effectiveness of exchange-rate and monetary-policy instruments will continue to decline at the region member state level, while it is questionable how far the role of migration as a major equilibrating mechanism is likely to gain political sympathy.

How, in this context, can we assess more precisely the need for a gradual buildup of a Community budgetary function, designed optimally to match the decline in the availability of other instruments of the adjustment process? It would seem to be the first task of the economist to show us how the inter-regional budgetary equilibrating mechanism works in fully integrated economies. At first sight, it may seem surprising that this work has been somewhat neglected in the mature federations (United States, Canada, Australia, Germany). An exception was Hartland's (1949) analysis of how budgetary mechanisms during the 1930s Depression in the United States financed the regional payments deficits of the agricultural regions compared with the industrial areas' surpluses. But this type of analysis has been left aside in the current fiscal federal literature. For example, the regions in Oates's (1972, Appendix to Chap. 1) model on local-government countercyclical policy all have zero trade balances. Regionali-zation of Buchanan's "fiscal residuum" would, however, be relevant.

It may be useful to speculate on the reasons for this neglect. First, of course, there is the lack of regional balance-of-payments data, and there is also the difference between fiscal-incidence and balance-of-payments flow-of-funds concepts. But second, and perhaps more fundamental, is the fact that there is no proposition carrying greater consensus in the present fiscal federal literature than that the budgetary redistribution function should be assigned to the federal or central level of government. This means that the resultant interregional funding of trade imbalances (usually sustaining higher expenditure than output in poorer regions) is entirely taken for granted. This also results from the ten-dency of the North American and Australian literature to concentrate mainly on the case of the mature federations, where the chief issues concern possible devolutions from the top down (as indeed is the case in the debate in some uni-tary states in Europe), rather than on cases of passing functions from the bottom up. Moreover, the North American and Australian historical experiences of early federalism all occurred before the development of the welfare state.

These tendencies, of course, are not very helpful for analyzing the Commu-nity case, where the proposition that the redistribution function should simply be assigned to the top level of government lacks credibility and relevance, since it gives no guidance on cases of intermediate degrees of economic and political integration.

In some European countries, there have nonetheless been developments in these areas of work, starting with the difficult problems of data availability.[8] Analytical contributions have come from Brown (1972) and Buzelay (1975) and are reflected also in the recent report of the Commission's "Marjolin Group" [Marjolin (1974)].

An attempt is currently being made to push this research further ahead in a new Commission Study Group on the role of public finance in European economic integration. The starting point is a comparative study of the regional incidence of public receipts and expenditure in four federations (the United States, Canada, Australia, and Germany) and three large unitary states (France,

Italy, and the United Kingdom). The aim is to combine these regional-incidence studies with data on the regional accounts and, where possible, on the regional balance of payments.

Seeing how the interregional dimension to budgetary integration fits into the pattern of full economic integration in varying constitutional settings may give some guidance to those looking for early steps down this path for the Community.

Theories of Redistribution at the Interregional Level

The idea of an efficiency justification to redistribution is in some ways less difficult to develop in the case of interregional redistribution in a semi-integrated Community than for the entire redistributive function of the modern welfare state. Indeed, much of the modern literature on positive theories of redistribution starts from the concept of Pareto-optimal redistribution with respect to gains from trade. While this concept usually seems inadequate for explaining the much larger-scale redistribution that actually occurs within the modern welfare state, the concept may be more appropriate for the Common Market in its present state of development. For the *locus classicus* one does not have to wait for the Hochman-Rodgers in 1969 and their followers but can go back to Kaldor in 1939. The followers of Hochman-Rodgers are nonetheless of interest— for example, Brennan (1974)—for their attempts to extend the concept of Pareto-optimal redistribution. Brennan's extensions of the concept are aimed at interpersonal redistribution. As regards interregion-member-state redistribution, insurance principles might be applied for the guaranteed maintenance of open markets, for the need to protect the profitability and security of foreign investments, and even for protecting the political system as a whole from the disruptive consequences of too large divergences in economic fortunes.

Very soon, however, these efficiency ideas link in with questions of political objectives. The Community hopes to be a pole of attraction for the Mediterranean countries to the south. Greece is already an applicant for full membership; in Spain there is talk of it eventually. In the pursuit of these objectives, it could be argued that the Community's politicoeconomic system would be a stronger pole of attraction if the Community itself, at the inter-member-state level, expressed more strongly through redistributive policies a reflection of the policies practiced within each member country.

Migration is a further subject where questions of reallocation and redistribution arise, both on efficiency grounds and for reasons linked to the Community's own political and cultural values. While migration has tended, in North America particularly, to be seen as part of an efficient market-adjustment process, it is also apparent that the market can induce much more migration than is optimal. It is argued, for example, by Forte (1975) that migration can be induced by money illusion and by the fact that diseconomies of congestion accrue mainly to the public sector. In the United States it has been noted that even differences in welfare benefits by state can be a determinent of migration, a factor that is not at present a major issue in the Community but could become one. The case for efficient reallocation and redistribution may therefore arise in a number of ways. Then there is the political question of how far it can be expected that the interregional balance-of-payments adjustment process within the Community can be aided by a greater mobility of labor. This may be politically practical in the United States, but, as Scott (1964) has pointed out, it is already less compatible with cultural and political values found in Canada and is even less likely to be the case for the existing Community member countries. This question would become even more acute should some of the currently migration-prone, nonmember Mediterranean countries become full members of the Community. At any event, in an integrated economy, and notably where exchange-rate changes cannot be effectively used, the budgetary consequences of different political preferences on migration are clear: the less the political system tolerates migration, the more the economic adjustment processes have to rely upon budgetary redistribution. On the other hand, a low propensity for inter-member-country migration could be expected to be a factor sustaining the effectiveness of the exchange-rate instrument.

The Influence of Democratic and Decision-Making Procedures

Under this heading I have in mind, of course, the transformation of the Parliament due to take place with direct elections in May or June 1978. The prospect of this reform offers a rare opportunity to political scientists who fancy their skills in predicting how different voting rules and decision-making systems affect the supply of public goods and the redistribution function.

The case is an intriguing one, because the system is due to change from one dominated by a small-number unanimity voting club (which is the Council at present, with qualifications)[9] to one in which the Council will share power with a fully legitimized Parliament of perhaps 284 to 384 members.[10]

According to some schools of political analysis, a change from a small-number unanimity club to a conventional parliamentary democracy will produce major differences in the supply of public goods, particularly of the distributive variety. Under the unanimity club, the redistribution function will be particularly limited [Scharpf's (1975) analysis of "negative coordination," incidentally, is certainly recognizable in the present Community decision-making processes]. Going to the other extreme, it is argued, for example, by Downs, that under majority democratic rule the relatively poor use their political power to obtain transfers from the relatively rich.[11]

Direct election to the European Parliament will not, of course, change the

Community system from one pure type to the other. The Council will doubtless relinquish powers only slowly and gradually. Constitutional ideas at present in circulation tend in any case to advocate a bicameral system, whereby the other chamber would be a Chamber of the States developed on the basis of the present Council.[12] However, it is widely felt that the powers of the European Parliament following direct election will inevitably be increased, and notably in the area of the Community's finances.

Although the present Community budget is small and the present Parliament's power over it is also small, certain recent developments worth noting are illustrated by the passage of the 1976 Community budget through the Commission, Council, and Parliament. The Commission proposed a draft 1976 budget of 7,930 million UA on August 25, which included substantial increases over the preceding year's expenditure on the Social Fund, the Regional Fund, an aid to nonassociated developing countries. The Council on September 29 reduced the total to 7,344 million UA, with the principal cuts falling on the redistributive activities mentioned. On November 11 it was Parliament's turn, and its amendments restored virtually all the cuts made by the Council, the total now being 7,829 million UA. To do this, many parliamentarians found themselves voting contrary to the ministerial representatives of their own parties in the Council. On December 4 it was the Council's turn to amend the Parliament's amendments. In doing this, the Council had to respect the Parliament's "margin of manoeuvre"—a formula-based right to increase certain expenditures (in this case, by 90 million UA). So the fourth budget total became 7,434 million UA, which was then returned for the Parliament's second reading. On December 18 a final budget total of 7,577 million UA was jointly adopted by the two institutions. If, after this, there is still no agreed budget, there must be a joint conciliation session of the Council and Parliament before December 23.

While the amounts of money at stake in this instance are very small, it illustrates the emerging struggle of wills between the two institutions. This struggle is being pursued mainly over questions of Community finances, and it is becoming apparent that the two institutions have rather different inclinations in this area. As direct elections to the Parliament in 1978 approach, questions of how best to organize the decision-making process as between the Community institutions, and of how to allocate functions between the Community and national governments, will come increasingly to the fore. Political and economic scientists are invited to make their contributions to guide this case of embryonic fiscal federalism along the most enlightened path.

Concluding Remarks

The finances of the European Community have been presented in a fiscal federal mold. The expenditure functions are allocative and redistributive in nature;

there is no stabilization function. The allocation functions that have been, or may in the future be, assigned to the Community-level public sector are rationalized in terms of economies of scale and correction for cross-frontier spillovers of costs or benefits; and the redistributive functions are rationalized in terms of compensation for the uneven distribution of the effects of Community policies, notably of the net gains from increased trade.

The role of the redistribution function can also be seen in macroeconomic terms by viewing inter-member-state economic relations in the Community as beginning to move gradually from the realm of international economics to that of interregional economics. In the latter case, interregional budgetary transfers ultimately take over from the exchange rate and demand management as the main instruments of (regional) economic policy. The task is to identify more thoroughly how far and fast these changes in location of instruments of economic policy by level of government should be expected to take place in the Community.

The present decision-making characteristics of the Community, essentially those of a small-number unanimity club, have predictably resulted in only a small-scale redistribution function, with the main initiatives having come from the processes of negotiation in the creation and enlargement of the club and the threatened secession from it. Major changes in these tendencies might be expected as and when the directly elected European Parliament (of 1978 onwards) secures increases in its powers over Community finances. This underlines the need for serious applied economic analysis to identify those areas of public intervention in which Community-level action can give superior economic returns (for reasons of economies of scale, spillovers, etc.), and to clarify the nature and amplitude of the redistribution function that could meet the economic and political demands of the period ahead.

Notes

1. I use the term *fiscal federalism* to follow the conventional language of public-finance literature, as for example in Oates (1972); I do not wish to imply the view that the European Community is on the road to political federation. The political perspective in which this paper is set, taking a positive view of the future of the Community, is more that of an emerging confederal organization.

2. The exchange rates of the three units of account against member-country currencies on January 1, 1976 were:

	UA	EUA	"Green" UA
DKr (Danish krone)	7.5	7.19897	7.57828
DM (German mark)	3.66	3.05362	3.57873

F (French franc)	5.55419	5.21981	5.63317
£Ir (Irish pound)	0.416667	0.575039	0.578322
Lit (Italian lira)	625	797.769	857.000
BF and Lux F (Belgian and Luxembourg francs)	50	46.0606	46.640
f (Netherlands guilder)	3.62	3.13120	3.41874
£ (U.K. pound)	0.416667	0.575973	0.569606

3. The U.K. figure excludes the Adhesion Compensatory Amounts, i.e., further differences which, however, disappear completely on January 1, 1978 at the end of the transitional arrangements for agriculture.

4. The MCAs at present, on January 1, 1976, are +10 percent for Germany, +2.0 percent for Benelux, –4.8 percent for Ireland, and –6.4 percent for the United Kingdom. Denmark, Italy, and France have no MCAs (i.e., they apply Community prices).

5. Mr. Callaghan's speech to the Council of Foreign Ministers in Luxembourg on April 1, 1974.

6. It is interesting to note that among innovations being suggested for U.S. federal grant programs is the introduction of income-growth criteria in addition to the already frequently used income-level criteria [see Mushkin (1974)].

7. A word may be added here on other aspects of the Community's tax-harmonization program, which have recently been summarized in the Bulletin of the EC, Supplement 10/75. The Commission advocates a fairly extensive long-run program of harmonization of the bases and rates of VAT, corporation tax, and excise duties. In the area of corporation tax, the Commission proposes a "partial imputation system," under which the shareholder receives with each dividend a tax credit representing a fraction of the corporation tax, which can then be offset against personal income tax liabilities or claimed back where it exceeds such liabilities.

8. Regional "national" accounts estimates have now been constructed for all the four large Community countries [see INSEE (1966) for France; ISTAT (1973) for Italy; Statistische Landesämter (1975) for Germany; and Woodward (1970) for the United Kingdom].

9. The voting procedures in the Council at present may be summarized as follows: New policies and financial instruments, which are normally proposed by the Commission, have to receive the unanimous assent of the Council. The qualified majority vote is used for specific purposes, including decisions on the budget as a whole and on its individual items. A qualified majority is satisfied with 41 out of 58 votes, where countries' weights are as follows: Germany, 10; France, 10; Italy, 10; United Kingdom, 10; Belgium, 5; Netherlands, 5; Denmark, 3; Ireland, 3; and Luxembourg, 2.

10. Five proposals have so far been tabled for the number and distribution

of seats in the new Parliament, by France (284), Parliament itself (351), the
United Kingdom (355), Italy (361) and Ireland (384).

11. For a summary of the literature in this area, see Culyer (1973).

12. For ideas on possible institutional developments, see the reports on
European Union in the *Bulletin of the EC by the Commission* (Supplement
5/75) and by Tindemans (Supplement 1/76).

References

Brennan, G. 1974. Pareto optimal redistribution: A perspective. *Finanzarchiv* 33.
Brown, A.J. 1972. *The Framework of Regional Economics in the United
        Kingdom.* Cambridge: NIESR Cambridge University Press.
Buzelay, A. 1975. *Le Budget Communautaire: Ses Fonctions de Péréquation
        Financière et de Régulation Economique* (The Community Budget: Its
        Financial Equalization and Economic Regulation Functions). *Revue de
        Science Financière* 1975:73–125.
Commission of the European Communities. *Bulletin of the EC.* Luxembourg:
        Office for Official Publications of the European Communities:
        New Proposals on the Harmonization of VAT. *Supplement* 11/73.
        Inventory of the Communit's Economic and Financial Situation since
        Enlargement and Survey of Future Developments. *Supplement* 7/74.
        Stocktaking of the Common Agricultural Policy. *Supplement* 2/75.
        Report on European Union (by the Community Institutions). *Supplement*
        5/75.
        Harmonization of Systems of Company Taxation. *Supplement* 10/75.
        Action Program for the European Aircraft Industry. *Supplement* 11/75.
        European Union, Report by Mr. Leo Tindemans to the European Council.
        Supplement 1/76.
Commission of the European Communities. 11/1974. *Third Report on the
        Activities of the New European Social Fund.* 1974 Financial Year. Docu-
        ment COM(75)355 final. Brussels.
Commission of the European Communities. 1974. *ECSC Financial Report for
        the Year 1974.* no. 20. Luxembourg.
Commission of the European Communities. 1974. *ECSC Auditor's Report for
        the Year 1974.* Luxembourg: Paul Gaudy.
Commission of the European Communities. 1975. *The Courier, European
        Community–Africa–Caribbean–Pacific.* no. 31, Special issue, March 1975.
        EEC–ACP Convention of Lomé. Brussels.
Commission of the European Communities. 1975. *Preliminary Draft General
        Budget of the EC. Triennial Financial Forecasts 1976-77-78.* Annex to
        Vol. 7, Sec. III. Document COM(75)330. Brussels.

CREST. 1974. Public Expenditure on Research and Development in Community Countries. 1st Report. "Statistics." Brussels.

Culyer, A.J. 1973. *The Economics of Social Policy.* London: Martin Robinson. chap. 4.

European Investment Bank. 1974. *Annual Report.* Luxembourg.

Forte, F. 1975. Regional aspects of migration policies and economic growth. Paper submitted to I.I.P.F. annual congress. Nice, Sept. 1975.

Hartland, P. 1949. Interregional payments compared with international payments. *Quarterly Journal of Economics* 63:392-407.

Hochman, H.H., and Rodgers, J.D. 1969. Pareto optimal redistribution, *American Economic Review* 59:542-557.

INSEE 1966. *Etudes de comptabilité nationale, Regionalisation des Comptes de la Nation* (Regionalization of the National Accounts). No. 9. Paris.

ISTAT. 1973. *Conti Economica Territoriali* (Territorial Economic Accounts), Vol. III, Tomo 11 Edizione 1973. *Annuario di Contabilita Nazionale.* Rome.

Kaldor, N. 1939. Welfare propositions of economics and inter-personal comparisons of utility, *Economic Journal* 49:549-552.

Marjolin, R., et al. 1974. *Report of the study group economic and monetary union 1980.* Brussels: Commission of the EC.

Mushkin, S.J. 1974. New directions in capacity measurement. In *State Aids for Human Services in a Federal System.* Washington, D.C.: Georgetown University.

Oates, W.E. 1972. *Fiscal Federalism.* New York: Harcourt Brace Jovanovich.

Scharpf, F.W. 1975. The Probability of Disagreement in Multi-Level Decisions. Preprint 1/75-31. Berlin: International Institute of Management, Wissenschaftszentrum.

Scott, A. 1964. The economic goals of federal finance, *Public Finance* 19: 241-292.

Statistische Landesämter der BRD. 1975. *Volkswirtschaftliche Gesamtrechnungen der Länder, Heft 5: Entstehung, Verteilung und Verwendung des Sozialprodukts in den Ländern, Standardtabellen 1960-1970* [Origin, Distribution and Spending of the Social Product by Länder, 1960-1970.] Stuttgart: Statistical Offices of the Länder of the Federal Republic of Germany.

Woodward, V.H. 1970. Regional social accounts for the United Kingdom. *Regional Papers I.* Cambridge: NIESR, Cambridge University Press.

Part III
Theoretical and Quantitative Analyses
of Federal Fiscal Structure

10 The Optimality Limits of the Tiebout Model

Pierre Pestieau

One of the main problems in conventional public-goods theory is that of preference revelation. If individuals are charged a tax related to their revealed preferences for public goods, they are tempted to understate their true preferences and efficiency is not likely to result. Tiebout (1956) has argued that this problem holds only for public goods handled at the central-government level and not for those provided by local governments. He considers an economy consisting of various communities offering different packages of public goods combined with the tax rates required to finance them. The consumer-voter chooses among the communities on the basis of his preferences for local public goods, given their tax-price, and moves accordingly. This mobility, well described by the expression "voting with the feet," is then shown to lead to an efficient allocation of resources.

At first glance, Tiebout's model of interregional mobility is attractive: it resolves the delicate problem of the revelation of preferences and it appears relevant in the real world, where the quality of the local public services may be of real importance in the choice of a community of residence. However, as Oates (1972, p. 128) points out, "when we attempt to be more precise about the nature of this model, we find that matters are a good deal more complicated." Reality is seldom consistent with Tiebout's thesis, and his model rests on several restrictive assumptions that usually do not apply.[1] In the past years, there have been several attempts to discuss and to drop some of these assumptions, but there has been neither a formal presentation of the model nor a proof of the efficiency of interregional mobility.

The purpose of this chapter is to fill this deficiency on the basis of a set of assumptions that are essentially already present in Tiebout's original paper. Section 1 introduces the model and its assumptions. Section 2 presents the conditions for an efficient allocation and shows that these can be achieved by interregional mobility. Section 3 appraises the importance and relevancy of each

The basic idea of this chapter, the analogy between the portfolio choice among various risky assets and the act of choosing among communities with different bundles of public goods and taxes, was suggested to me by J. Drèze, to whom I am very grateful. Helpful comments were also received from Maurice Marchand, Dennis Mueller, and Steve Slutsky.

173

assumption and compares them with those of Tiebout. Finally, in section 4 policy implications are discussed.

The structure of the model discussed here is analogous to that of a state-preference model of investor choice, such as the one developed by Drèze (1972, 1974): individuals allocate their lifetime among communities with different bundles of public goods and taxes in the same way that they allocate their wealth among various risky assets.

1. The Basic Model

In this section we present a model of interregional mobility in which, following Tiebout, consumers weigh the benefits from local public goods against the cost of their tax liability in choosing communities of residence. For later discussion, the key assumptions (hereafter, A.1, A.2, etc.) are numbered.[2]

The economy considered here is exhaustively divided into J nonoverlapping communities, indexed $j = 1, \ldots, J$, each offering a different package of public goods and taxes. There are S local public goods, indexed $s = 1, \ldots, S$. The amount of public good s provided in region j is denoted by b_s^j. The taxes imposed in region j are denoted by a_o^j and expressed in terms of a single private good. The public goods supplied in a region do not have external effects on neighboring communities (A.1).

There are I consumers, indexed $i = 1, \ldots, I$. Each consumer i has an income $\bar{x}_o^i$, which can be used for paying taxes or consumed directly as a private good. This income is the same in whatever regions he decides to reside (A.2). His perferences can be represented by a quasi-concave utility function:

$$u^i (\bar{x}_o^i - x_o^i, x_1^i, \ldots, x_s^i, \ldots, x_S^i) \qquad i = 1, \ldots, I \qquad (10.1)$$

where x_o^i denotes the total amount of taxes he pays and x_s^i, his consumption of the public good s. For later use, let

$$u_s^i \equiv \frac{\delta u^i}{\delta x_s^i}$$

Each consumer is fully mobile and can freely allocate his lifetime among several regions (A.3). For example, one can imagine an individual spending his childhood in Chicago, studying in Boston, working in New York, and finally retiring in Florida. The fraction of time that consumer i spends in region j is denoted by θ_{ij}; naturally, $\sum_j \theta_{ij} = 1$.

Consumers are perfectly informed about the various regional fiscal packages (A.4). On that basis, they choose the communities of residence yielding the consumption bundles that best satisfy their tastes. The consumption bundles are indeed a linear combination of the fiscal packages of the regions consumers decide to inhabit. That is,

$$x^i_o = \sum_j \theta_{ij} a^j_o \qquad i = 1, \ldots, I \qquad (10.2)$$

$$x^i_s = \sum_j \theta_{ij} b^j_s \qquad \begin{aligned} i &= 1, \ldots, I \\ s &= 1, \ldots, S \end{aligned} \qquad (10.3)$$

In this model, communities provide impure public goods in the sense that, while the level of consumption is equal for all residents, the quantity consumed per capita depends both on the level of output of the goods and on the population of the community. More specifically, the cost of a given pattern of public goods is assumed to be proportional to the number of consumers enjoying them (A.5). It is thus assumed that a^j_o represents the input cost of providing the vector $[b^j_s]$ to an individual residing full time in region j. If he spends there only a fraction θ_{ij} of his time, the cost will just be $\theta_{ij} a^j_o$. This specification implies that the tax paid by the consumer reflects accurately the cost of the resources he absorbs in consuming the public goods.

Finally, it is assumed that in each region the pattern of public-goods supply is given up to a scale change. That is, the provision of b^j_s is equal to a fixed proportion $\bar{b}^j_s$ of the tax input a^j_o. This implies that each region has access to a single activity: an increase in input leads to equiproportionate changes in the supply of each public good (A.6).[3] Thus, one has:

$$(b^j_1, \ldots, b^j_S) = a^j_o (\bar{b}^j_1, \ldots, \bar{b}^j_S) \qquad j = 1, \ldots, J \qquad (10.4)$$

The fixed coefficients $\bar{b}^j_s$ express the quantity of public good s one gets for one dollar of tax input in community j.

2. Efficiency of Interregional Mobility

Efficiency Conditions

Before examining whether this version of the Tiebout model is efficient, it is necessary to define what is meant here by efficiency. Traditionally, efficiency conditions can be derived by maximizing a weighted sum of individuals' utilities, using arbitrary positive weights with control over all economic variables. In the present setting, however, the control is subject to a geographical constraint: as long as an individual resides in one region, only the public goods provided in this region are available to him. Pareto optimum is thus subject to the constraint that each individual's consumption pattern across the set of local public goods be a linear combination of regions' output patterns. This contraint is expressed by equation (10.3). Thus, instead of controlling the x_s^i's, one controls the θ_{ij}'s.[4]

Our problem can then be formulated as the maximization of a Lagrange function:[5]

$$\sum_i \lambda^i u^i (\bar{x}_o^i - x_o^i, \sum_j \theta_{ij}\bar{b}_1^j a_o^j, \ldots, \sum_j \theta_{ij}\bar{b}_S^j a_o^j) + \beta \sum_i (x_o^i - \sum_j \theta_{ij}a_o^j)$$

where (10.3) and (10.4) are substituted in (10.1), λ^i is the weight given to individual i's utility, and β is a Lagrange multiplier. One can calculate the first-order conditions for an interior maximum by differentiation with respect to x_o^i and θ_{ij}.[6]

$$-\lambda^i u_o^i + \beta = 0 \qquad i = 1, \ldots, I \tag{10.5}$$

$$\lambda^i \sum_s u_s^i \bar{b}_s^j a_o^j - \beta a_o^j = 0 \qquad \begin{matrix} i = 1, \ldots, I \\ j = 1, \ldots, J \end{matrix} \tag{10.6}$$

From (10.5) and (10.6), we obtain:

$$\sum_s \frac{u_s^i}{u_o^i} \bar{b}_s^i = 1 \qquad \begin{matrix} i = 1, \ldots, I \\ j = 1, \ldots, J \end{matrix} \tag{10.7}$$

The LHS of (10.7) gives the overall marginal utility individual i derives from his consumption of publics goods in region j; it is the sum of the marginal utilities of each public good weighted by the amount obtained for one dollar of tax. Equation (10.7) can thus be interpreted as saying that this overall marginal utility should be the same for all individuals and in all regions.

The maximization problem discussed can be viewed as a nonlinear programming problem given the concavity of the maximand (10.1) and the linearity of the constraint (10.4). Thus, from the Kuhn-Tucker theorem, conditions (10.7) are both necessary and sufficient for a maximum. If one can show that the mechanism of interregional mobility leads to an equilibrium satisfying the same conditions, it will have been proved efficient as intuited by Tiebout in his classic paper.

Equilibrium with Interregional Mobility

Consider now an economy where people are free to move among regions. Each region is represented by the fixed-factor technology expressed by (10.4) and by the type of tax-input relationship expressed by (10.2). As initial conditions, one could consider any distribution of the I individuals among the J regions and see how they change their residence so as to maximize utility. Equivalently, one can observe the behavior of an individual coming from abroad and willing to allocate his time optimally among these various regions. This second approach is easier and will be adopted here.

Consider such an individual i seeking to select a "portfolio" of residencies θ_{ij} and an amount of private consumption $(\bar{x}_o^i - x_o^i)$ so as to maximize his utility, subject to the constraint that his private-good supply be exhausted by tax payments:

$$x_o^i = \sum_j \theta_{ij} a_o^j \qquad (10.2)$$

where a_o^j can be viewed as the tax bill he would have to pay in region j if he resided there only. Forming the Lagrangian, one has

$$u_i\left(\bar{x}_o^i - x_o^i, \sum_j \theta_{ij} \bar{b}_1^j a_o^j, \ldots, \sum_j \theta_{ij} \bar{b}_S^j a_o^j\right) + \lambda\left(x_o^i - \sum_j \theta_{ij} a_o^j\right)$$

The first-order conditions for an (interior) maximum are:

$$-u_o^i + \lambda = 0 \qquad (10.8)$$

$$\sum_s u_s^i \bar{b}_s^j - \lambda = 0 \qquad (10.9)$$

Combining (10.8) and (10.9), one gets (10.7), the necessary and sufficient condition for efficiency.

In this somewhat simplified version of Tiebout's model, we have shown his conjecture to be correct: individual mobility suffices to achieve Pareto optimality.

3. Assumptions: Sources of Inefficiencies

In the previous section, the following assumptions were made:

A.1. Absence of interregional spillovers.
A.2. No geographical constraint on individuals' earnings.
A.3. Full mobility.
A.4. Perfect information.
A.5. Tax equal to the true social cost.
A.6. Fixed structure of public-good supply.

In this section, each assumption will be relaxed in turn to see what implications are involved and what type of inefficiency this leads to. Some of these assumptions (A.1, A.2, and A.5) are widely discussed in the theory of local public goods; for these, a brief survey and references are given.

It is interesting to compare these six assumptions with those of Tiebout's classic paper. Assumptions 1, 2, 4, and 6 are explicitly made in Tiebout (1956, p. 419). As pointed out later, instead of A.3, Tiebout assumes that consumers are perfectly mobile once and that there are more communities than types of individuals. Finally, Tiebout makes an assumption similar to A.5 when he discusses a "severe" version of his model (p. 421).

Assumption 1: Absence of Interregional Spillovers

First, it is assumed that the benefits and costs resulting from the consumption of local public goods are internal to the community providing them. Breton (1965) has termed this match between a region and the consumers of the public goods supplied within the region a "perfect mapping." This, however, is frequently not the case. There is virtually no public service that fails to afford some benefits external to the region that provides it.[7] If benefit spillovers are important and those enjoying them do not pay for them, an efficient allocation of resources to the public sector cannot be achieved. To deal with this type of inefficiency, the traditional remedy suggested in the literature is to make interregional grants.[8]

Assumption 2: No Geographical Constraint on Individuals' Earnings

The second assumption is that consumers' private earnings are set regardless of their location decisions; thus, they do "not embody geographical dimensions" [Buchanan and Goetz (1972)]. Tiebout assumed that all consumers are living on dividend income. Thanks to this farfetched assumption, the location in space becomes nicely independent of the allocation of resources in the private sector of the economy. Clearly, relaxing this assumption would make location decisions a function not only of the fiscal packages but also of the earning opportunities offered by the different communities. This leaves unresolved the problem of preference revelation. To overcome this difficulty, Polinsky (1970) and Buchanan and Goetz (1972) have reinterpreted the Tiebout model in the convenient framework of voluntary clubs. Each public good would be supplied by a club to each of its members regardless of his location in space. Such a specification represents quite a drastic departure from the original spirit of Tiebout's argument.

Assumption 3: Full Mobility

The third assumption is that each consumer is free to move at no cost across regions and to spend a portion of his time in several of them. Formally, this implies that the fraction θ_{ij} can take any value as long as it is nonnegative and adds up to one. Dropping this assumption, for example, by supposing that each consumer resides in a single region, is more realistic and conforms to Tiebout's original idea of perfect mobility just once. This, of course, creates problems of nonconvexities by restricting the choice set of consumers. An individual is likely not to be able to find a community which provides the same mix of local public goods as he would purchase if he were allowed to purchase fractional parts of the packages each region supplies. To circumvent this difficulty, Tiebout's original model stipulates an infinite variety of communities, each offering a different package of public goods and tax. However, if all individuals have different incomes and tastes, they will all choose different communities. But then why talk about public goods?

Instead, it is often assumed [see, for example, Stiglitz (1974, p. 61)] that individuals can be grouped in a limited number of types with similar tastes and income. Then Pareto optimality can be achieved if there are as many regions as types of individuals, each region supplying a fiscal package tailored to each type's own tastes. Such a tailoring would not raise any problems of social choice, since there is no individual-preference heterogeneity; it would, however, necessitate a certain flexibility in the public-good supply. This conflicts with Tiebout's idea that "there is no attempt on the part of local government to 'adapt to' the preferences of consumer-voters" (p. 420); it also conflicts with our assumption 6, the relaxation of which implies the possibility of an inefficient mismatching between individuals and communities, as shown below.

Assumption 4: Perfect Information

It is also assumed that consumer-voters have full knowledge of the public-goods pattern supplied and the tax imposed by each community and react to the differences among the fiscal packages. Without such information, "voting with the feet" cannot normally achieve Pareto optimality.

Assumption 5: Tax Equal to the True Social Cost

In our basic model, the cost of the resources needed to provide a given package of public goods is proportional to the number of consumers, each of whom pays a tax price reflecting exactly the cost of the public goods he consumes. When an additional resident enters the community, he pays for the expenditure needed to maintain the specified level of consumption without affecting the welfare of the others. This assumption avoids two sources of difficulties [see Buchanan and Wagner (1970)]. On one hand, we could have dealt with pure public goods, where the cost of production is independent of the number of consumers. Assuming that each community charges each of its residents the same fee, then the arrival of a new resident involves a smaller tax payment for all, and the departure of a resident increases their tax burden. On the other hand, there could be congestion costs attached to the public-goods consumption so that the addition of an extra consumer would dilute the quality of the public goods. Conversely, the departure of a resident would increase the welfare of those remaining behind.

Each consumer, when he envisions moving, considers only changes in his own utility levels and ignores the marginal effects of his move on those he leaves behind and on those he joins. Thus, in either case, inefficiency is likely to result from interregional mobility. Pareto optimality can, however, be restored if each region uses taxes or subsidies to induce those who move out or in to internalize the external costs or benefits their moving entails. This is the remedy suggested by Buchanan and Goetz (1972). Another solution proposed by Flatters et al. (1974) is to charge the central government to make interregional transfers to account for these external effects.

Assumption 5 avoids these difficulties by supposing that the congestion cost inflicted by an individual's move is just offset by the tax-sharing benefit it brings.

Assumption 6: Fixed Pattern of Public-Good Supply

So far, the discussion has been confined to an economy where the pattern of public goods in each region is given. When regions are allowed to modify this output pattern to match the preferences of their residents, two problems arise. First, the Kuhn-Tucker conditions will no longer be sufficient for a maximum; second, if there is some heterogeneity of preferences among residents, a rule of social choice—such as majority voting to determine the level of public goods within each region—will be unlikely to satisfy these conditions.

We now allow the possibility of adjusting production plans so as to modify the pattern of public goods locally supplied. Thus, the transformation function can now be expressed as:

$$G^j (a_o^j, b_1^j, \ldots, b_S^j) = 0 \qquad j = 1, \ldots, J \qquad (10.10)$$

where G^j is to be twice continuously differentiable with $G_o^j \equiv \delta G^j / \delta a_o^j < 0$ and $G_s^j \equiv \delta G^j / \delta b_s^j > 0$. For future use, let $\gamma_s^j \equiv G_s^j / G_o^j$ denote the marginal cost in terms of the private good of producing public goods in region j. In this specification, the levels of both inputs and outputs are control variables. The efficiency problem can now be formulated as the maximization of a Lagrange function:

$$\sum_i \lambda^i \, u^i \, (\bar{x}^i_o - x^i_o, \sum_i \theta_{ij} b^j_1, \ldots, \sum_j \theta_{ij} b^j_S)$$

$$+ \sum_j \mu_j G^j \, (a^j_o, b^j_1, \ldots, b^j_S) + \beta \sum_i (x^i_o - \sum_i \theta_{ij} a^j_o)$$

From the first-order conditions for an interior maximum, one gets

$$\sum_s \frac{u^i_s}{u^i_o} \frac{b^j_s}{a^j_o} = 1 \qquad \begin{matrix} i = 1, \ldots, I \\ j = 1, \ldots, J \end{matrix} \qquad (10.11)$$

and

$$\sum_i \frac{u^i_s}{u^i_o} \theta_{ij} = \gamma^j_s \sum_i \theta_{ij} \qquad \begin{matrix} j = 1, \ldots, J \\ s = 1, \ldots, S \end{matrix} \qquad (10.12)$$

Condition (10.11) is similar to (10.7) and tells us how each individual should allocate his time among different regions. Condition (10.12) states that the marginal cost of supplying public good s in region j for a total period of $\sum_i \theta_{ij}$ must be equal to the sum over all individuals of their marginal rates of substitution between the public good s and the private input, weighted by the fraction of time they spent in region j. This is a natural generalization of Samuelson's conditions for a Pareto-optimal production of public goods. Instead of being simply added, however, the marginal rates of substitution are weighted by the residency fraction.

As shown by Drèze (1972) in the context of stock-market allocations, the problem analyzed here is a nonconvex programming one.[9] Hence, conditions (10.11) and (10.12) are necessary but not sufficient for a maximum. Later we provide an example of an allocation that is inefficient, although it satisfies these two conditions.

We now turn to the concept of equilibrium with Tiebout's mechanism. As before, it implies that no individual wishes to move from his current location and, moreover, that the level of local public goods cum taxes is preferred by a majority over any other level of public goods. An alternative approach is to consider that in each region there is a "dictator" who selects that production plan that maximizes a given regional welfare function.

As in the previous section, one can easily check that the individual's choice of location satisfies our necessary conditions (10.11). In the discussion of the determination of the level of local public goods, each resident of a given region is assumed to have voting rights proportional to his residency fraction, production plans are selected through majority voting, and every individual selects the level of public goods that suits him best given the tax-input requirement. One can then show that the majority voting equilibrium satisfies the necessary conditions (10.12) if, in all regions, the weighted average utility of each public good s in terms of the input

$$\frac{\sum_i \theta_{ij} u_s^i / u_o^i}{\sum_i \theta_{ij}}$$

is equal to the marginal utility of the median voter. Quite clearly, such a coincidence can only be accidental. Turning to a more authoritarian decision-making process would not allow a more optimistic conclusion. We thus end up with the problem of preference revelation that the model was intended to resolve. Moreover, this condition (10.12) that seems so difficult to satisfy is not even sufficient for Pareto efficiency.[10]

Now we shall give an illustration of the latter problem: an allocation conforming to the necessary conditions (10.11) and (10.12), and at the same time inefficient. This example is adapted from Drèze (1974).[11]

We shall consider a highly simplified economy—a country consisting of two regions, c and f (for Colorado and Florida). There are two public goods, m and s (for mountain climbing and swimming facilities). Both regions can produce the two public goods according to the transformation function:

$$G^j (a_o^j, m^j, s^j) = 0 \quad j = c,f$$

For simplicity's sake, $a_o^c = a_o^f$, i.e., both regions start with the same input. These transformation functions are linear and are such that Florida can produce twice as many swimming facilities as Colorado, and vice versa for mountain-climbing facilities. This economy can be depicted with the help of Figure 10-1.

It is conceivable that the Floridians have strong preferences for m and the Coloradians for s. These preferences are represented by the (regional) indifference curves u^f and u^c, respectively, thus assuming the social-choice problem solved. Each community maximizes its utilities with respect to its production constraint; this gives A and B, the optimal production bundles for Colorado and Florida, respectively.

From the figure it is clear that A and B are only local optima and not global optima. With the same inputs in each region, but with the Floridians moving to Colorado and vice versa, the bundles A' and B' could be achieved; that is, the supply of public goods could double at no cost. To achieve such an efficient allocation, one needs not only full information about the production sets of the other regions but also cooperation among the consumers. For example, if one

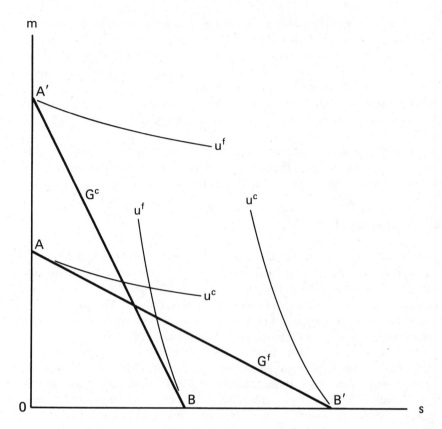

Figure 10-1. Locational Patterns and Welfare Level

Floridian decides to move to Colorado, he will not be able to modify the production pattern of public goods in Colorado and thus he will be worse off than if he had stayed in Florida. The inefficiency of this situation is clear. Each region produces optimally, given the preferences of its residents and regardless of its comparative advantages vis-à-vis other regions. Consequently, it may result in a "mismatching" between the production possibilities of the region and the preferences of its residents.[12]

There are two possible remedies to this situation. First, if the two regions decide to modify their patterns of production and produce the public goods for which they have a comparative advantage, then people will be likely to move so that they can get twice as many public goods at no cost. Second, if people start to move all *together*, they can force the desired adjustment in production plans in both regions.

These two remedies clearly require major changes in residency and production, the initiative for which is unlikely to come from individuals. Hence, this necessitates some form of central direction at least to obtain the optimal distribution of population. Contrary to what Tiebout thought, his decentralized mobility system does not generate the appropriate signals to lead to a global optimum. This failure to generate more than local optima is formally attributable to the nonconvexity of the aggregate production set of the economy (see Figure 10-1).

Finally, one should note that the restrictions in this simple illustration were made only for convenience. Productive inefficiency would also result with more than two regions and two public goods or with concave transformation curves.

4. Policy Implication

In his classic paper, Tiebout argued that preferences for local public goods can be correctly revealed through "voting with the feet" by individuals entering and exiting communities. Though insightful and seemingly plausible, his model has rarely been presented formally or ever been proved correct.[13] This paper attempts to do so. The argument here rests on a number of extreme assumptions, the relaxation of which leads to specific inefficiencies.

It is widely agreed in the literature on fiscal federalism that one of the main roles of the central government vis-à-vis regions is to help alleviate inefficiencies arising at the regional level. Indeed, some of the inefficiencies mentioned above can be dealt with by the central government. Problems stemming from interregional spillovers, tax-sharing benefits, and congestion costs can be solved by intergovernmental payments. To a certain extent, the central authority can also improve mobility, facilitate changes in job location, and improve information concerning the fiscal package of each region. There are, however, inefficiencies, such as those attributable to output substitution and imperfect mobility, for which there appear to be no simple remedy.

Even if Pareto optimality can be achieved by "voting with the feet," it may not be socially desirable in the absence of lump-sum transfers. It is not certain that a world with residential fixity is socially less desirable than a world where people can "vote with their feet". Outmigration by members of upper-income groups to green suburbs and the decline in the fiscal health of many urban areas can have detrimental consequences on the personal income distribution of a nation. There is a snowballing effect in Tiebout: the rich become richer because they enjoy more public goods whose supply is relatively cheaper than the supply of private goods, thanks to tax sharing. The poor become poorer because they cannot afford those public goods whose supply requires a sizable fiscal basis.

Beyond these problems, the Tiebout model raises several serious questions that have been discussed in the literature [see, for example, Mueller (1971) and Samuelson (1958)]. It leads to homogeneous ghettos, whereas heterogeneity and differences have their virtues. It gives little weight to the value of stable communities and close social ties. It favors the attitude "Leave it if you don't like it" over that of "Change it because you like it".

Notes

1. For a divergent view on the empirical value of the Tiebout hypothesis, see Oates (1972, p. 176) and Netzer (1974, p. 372).

2. I am following the notation of Drèze (1974).

3. In the stock-market models, this assumption is known as that of multiplicative uncertainty [see Diamond (1967)].

4. This is a constrained Pareto optimum, following a definition made by Diamond (1967). Pursuing the analogy with the stock-market literature, one may note that this constraint is only binding if there are not as many communities as public goods ($J < S$).

5. We use equality constraints instead of the more general inequality constraints for notational convenience.

6. For any values of $a_o^j, j = 1, \ldots, J$.

7. Similarly, there are few taxes the economic effects of which are entirely confined to the area encompassed by the taxing unit of government. The standard reference is Weisbrod (1964).

8. Break (1967) has developed a theory of optimizing grants designed to deal with the distortion of regional expenditure decisions and hence of resource allocation, occasioned by benefit spillovers.

9. The argument is that conditions (10.3) are not convex if θ_{ij} and b_s^i are both allowed to vary [see Drèze (1974, p. 137)].

10. See Gevers (1974), who shows that the efficiency conditions in a stock-market economy are difficult to implement in practice.

11. After having completed the first draft of this chapter, papers dealing with this point by Stiglitz (1974) and Drèze and Hagen (1975) came to my attention.

12. Let us suppose that we have a fixed coefficient technology: A' is the activity available in Colorado, and B' in Florida. Then there is no mismatching possible; at the equilibrium, all Floridians reside in Colorado and all Coloradians in Florida.

13. With the possible exception of Greenberg (1975), who develops a local-public-goods model within a game-theoretic framework.

References

Break, G.F. 1967. *Intergovernmental Fiscal Relations in the United States.* Washington, D.C.: The Brookings Institution.

Breton, A. 1965. A theory of government grants. *Canadian Journal of Economics and Political Science* 33: 1–14.

Buchanan, J.M., and Goetz, C.J. 1972. Efficiency limits of fiscal mobility: An assessment of the Tiebout model. *Journal of Public Economics* 1:25–43.

Buchanan, J.M., and Wagner, R.E. 1970. An efficiency basis for federal fiscal equalization. In *The Analysis of Public Output,* Margolis, ed. New York: National Bureau of Economic Research.

Diamond, P.A. 1967. The role of a stock market in a general equilibrium model with technological uncertainty. *American Economic Review* 57:759–771.

Drèze, J.H. 1972. A tatonnement process for investment under uncertainty in private ownership economics. In *Mathematical Methods in Investment and Finance*, Szego and Shell, eds. Amsterdam: North Holland.

Drèze, J.H. 1974. Investment under private ownership: Optimality, equilibrium and stability. In *Allocation under Uncertainty: Equilibrium and Optimality,* Drèze, ed. London: Macmillan.

Drèze, J.H., and Hagen, K.P. 1975. Choice of product quality: Equilibrium and efficiency. Core discussion paper 7525. Université Catholique de Louvain.

Flatters, F., Henderson V., and Mieszkowski, P. 1974. Public goods: Efficiency and regional fiscal equalization. *Journal of Public Economics* 3:99–113.

Gevers, L. 1974. Competitive equilibrium of the stock exchange and Pareto efficiency. In *Allocation Under Uncertainty: Equilibrium and Optimality*, Drèze, ed. London: Macmillan.

Greenberg, J. 1975. Pure and Local Public Goods: A Game Theoretic Approach. Working paper. Hebrew University of Jerusalem.

Mueller, D.C. 1971. Fiscal federalism in a constitutional democracy. *Public Policy* Fall: 567–593.

Netzer, D. 1974. State-local finance and intergovernmental Relations. In *The Economics of Public Finance*, A.S. Blinder et al., eds. Washington: The Brookings Institution.

Oates, W.E. 1972. *Fiscal Federalism.* New York: Harcourt Brace Jovanovich.

Polinsky, A.M. 1970. Public Goods in a Setting of Local Governments. Working paper. Washington, D.C.: The Urban Institute.

Samuelson, P.A. 1958. Aspects of public expenditure theories. *Review of Economics and Statistics* 40:332–338.

Stiglitz, J.E. 1974. The Theory of Local Public Goods. Technical report no. 144. Stanford University.

Tiebout, C.M. 1956. A pure theory of local government expenditures. *Journal of Political Economy* 64:416–424.

Weisbrod, B.A. 1964. *External Benefits of Public Education: An Economic Analysis* Princeton, N.J.: Princeton University, Industrial Relations Section.

11

Endogenous City-Suburb Governmental Rivalry through Household Location

Jerome Rothenberg

Introduction

The subject of this chapter is described closely in the title. We construct a model of endogenous local-government decision making for both a central-city and a suburban jurisdiction in a single metropolitan area. In this model the goals of public policy for each can be advanced by competing with the other to attract households—some households—to reside within the jurisdiction. But changes in location behavior by households in turn call for changes in governmental action to realize their goals. Thus, both government behavior and household-location behavior are reciprocally endogenous. The key elements in the model are the specification of policy goals for the two jurisdictions, the submodel by which household location influences government action, and the submodel by which government action influences household location.

Despite notions about governmental goals, the approach is thoroughgoingly individualistic: *public goals* are defined in terms of constituent welfare, and each local government is assumed to be a perfectly responsive representative mechanism. This approach is meant to perform two functions: to characterize behaviorally some real-world complexities affecting the relations between local government and its constituents and among local governments and to contribute to the normative issue of the optimal degree of governmental fragmentation at a metropolitan-area level. The normative issue is part of an extended discussion stemming from the classic Tiebout model[1] in which radical local fragmentation assertedly serves to make the public sector partake of the properties of a purely competitive market system in private goods.

The thrust of the model developed here is that the local public sector is a distinctive system. Its "publicness" is *not* diluted in the context of competitive relationships among governmental decision makers; rather, it impresses a special configuration on the competitive process. The consequences do *not* lead to an easy belief that fragmentation helps to integrate public and private sectors so as more closely to approximate an efficient use of resources. Quite the contrary, fragmentation of public decision making creates a set of "artificial" incentives for households that leads to systematic discrepancies from optimal resource use.

This is established by first developing a model of a single metropolitan government, one in which household-location patterns arise out of pure spatial-distribution considerations. The consequences of such a model are then contrasted with the model of jurisdictional fragmentation, which is the main business of this paper.

The foregoing suggests that this chapter is primarily normative. In fact, it is positive. The chief goal is to throw light on a number of complex relationships between the public and private sectors believed to be operative in metropolitan areas and which have had little systematic exposure. I have deliberately attempted to create a more complicated, richer web of interrelationships than is usual either in local public finance or urban economics. The model in its totality is not tractable for elegant, analytical solutions. It is more amenable to simulation for characterization of overall system outcomes. But several large submodels are detachable and capable of being analytically manipulated to reveal their properties. And certain broad qualitative judgments can be inferred as well for the larger system.

Therefore, this chapter will for the most part elaborate the model informally, explaining the nature of the relationships and their basic function in the overall system. Some qualitative conclusions will, similarly, be informally drawn from the model, results that bear on the normative issue noted above.

Preliminary Assumptions

The metropolitan area is assumed to be divided into two political jurisdictions, a central city and a suburb. The central city is totally surrounded by the suburb and its whole area is developed for urban use. The suburb also has a fixed area, but only part of it is developed for urban use in the initial period. Changes in the urban area depend endogenously on the amount of land that households are willing to buy for urban use.

Each jurisdiction is politically administered by a general form of local government, which provides the variety of so-called local public goods—streets, sewers, police and fire protection, the administration of law, public primary and secondary education, welfare services, health services, recreation, etc. In this model they are assumed to be offered in fixed proportions (with one class of exceptions to be noted below) and so can be treated as components of a single composite public good.

This public good is not a Samuelsonian "pure" public good. It suffers from a generalized form of "crowding." Thus we can distinguish between the provision of the "stock" from which services will be rendered, which is an intermediate good, and the services themselves, which are the final outputs. The level, or quality, of services rendered to each household is equal for all households (except as related to the class of exceptions mentioned above and to be discussed below) and depends on both the size of the stock provided and the number of households who have to share services from it. In general, the quality is a positive function of stock size and a negative function of population size.

In addition to this distinction between intermediate good and output, we make as well a distinction between the input (resource) cost of the intermediate good and the amount of the intermediate good furnished. Thus, unlike most treatments, we do not measure public-service output by input costs; they are separated by both the input cost of intermediate output and the intermediate cost of final output.

Both jurisdictions produce the same composite public services but not necessarily at the same level. Expenditures to provide these services are raised by a set of two different kinds of taxes in the suburban jurisdiction and three different kinds in the central city. Common to both are a proportional tax on household income and an *ad valorem* tax on land. In addition to these, the central-city government uses a set of user charges. The reason for this asymmetry will be discussed below.

Two other public-policy instruments are examined in this model: a business-zoning and a residential-zoning regulation. These are assumed to be possessed by the suburban government but not by the central-city government. The reason for this asymmetry will similarly be discussed below.

Finally, the model concentrates on the local public sector and the location decisions of households, but it also deals—albeit in a deliberately oversimplified way—with the location decisions of businesses. It is assumed that the suburban government designates a maximum permissible business acreage to be allowed in the suburbs—its business zoning, Z^B. In the relevant range of situations dealt with, this represents less land than the metropolitan-area business firms would like to occupy there. The aggregate zoning restriction is therefore binding. If the suburban government wishes more business activity in the suburb, it thus has only to increase the allowable maximum acreage. Business location is thus effectively controlled by suburban-government use of its business-zoning instrument.

The Location Decision of the Individual Household: Abstract Stage

We assume there are N households in the urban area. Throughout this exercise we assume this number unchanged, although the model can easily be developed for changing population size. The purpose of the constant population treatment is to throw maximum light on the determinants of the share of the total that goes to each jurisdiction. The number in the central city is N_1, in the suburbs N_2. Expressed as percentage shares, they are N_1 and N_2, respectively. The total amount of business activity is B, assumed to be distributed spatially in business acres of constant density. Variable density of business concentration is given by percentage of a jurisdiction's acres that are business-occupied, not by differences in business activity per acre. This simple treatment is meant for convenience. Little of substance is involved, so long as the business-location decision is the incomplete one already described. B is divided into B_1 and B_2, the amount of business activity in city and suburb, respectively. The corresponding relative shares of the assumed constant total B are b_1 and b_2.

We assume that all households have the same utility function but differ only with respect to income level. This is tantamount to assuming away differences in demographic structure—size, age, ethnic group, education, job location, special consumption tastes, etc. The reason for abstracting from these known influences on location is to highlight the effect that income alone has and thus to gain some sense of the degree to which observable spatial patterns are understandable in terms of income alone. Further household differences can be superimposed subsequently onto the abstract income treatment to elaborate real-world complexities and thus examine spatial distributions stepwise.

The utility function for household j is

$$u^j = u(H,L,X,G,D) \tag{11.1}$$

H is the amount of housing capital—or structure—consumed. L is the amount of land used as a residence site. H and L together reflect the amount of housing services consumed. These two components of the housing package are separated because some of the public-policy instruments affect the two differently—indeed, are intended to do so. X is the amount of all other private goods consumed, with their relative quantities remaining unchanged (along with their relative prices); the constancy of relative shares enables us to treat X as a composite commodity. G is the quality level of public services consumed.

D is a different kind of "commodity" from any of these others. It is the crowdedness of the "social space." This variable is meant to portray more than simply the average density of land use, i.e., number of structures (or people) per acre. Individuals carry on market, social, and other activities in public places—they use streets, sidewalks, shops, playgrounds, and various public and private facilities. The density of others' intersecting uses of these same spaces contributes to the crowdedness, the press and tempo of the lifestyle of a household. We assume that the tastes of this population make this a negative commodity—on balance people prefer uncrowdedness.[2] Moreover, it is a superior negative good: richer households dislike crowdedness more than poorer households.

Of the five commodities listed, four are location-specific and spatially linked. The two housing components are consumed in one place, and they determine the jurisdiction in which the household resides and thus the local public services that are obtainable only by being a resident. They also determine the home neighborhood and larger community whose character has great influence on the crowdedness of a household's life space. Only X can be consumed anywhere— and in many places within each time period—throughout the urban area.

The household is subject to a budget constraint in making its choice of an optimal budgetary allocation among these commodities. It is as follows:

$$Y_i^j + (P_{L_i} - P_{L_{ji}}) L_{ji} = \tau_i Y_i^j + (tm)_j + P_{L_i}(1 + t_{L_i})L_i + P_H H + P_X X \quad (11.2)$$

Y_i^j is the income level of household j residing in jurisdiction i. Actually, we assume that jurisdictional residence does not itself affect income level. (This is different from the fact that we later establish that there comes to be a systematic income stratification between the two jurisdictions—so that by $self\text{-}selection$ the average income characteristics of the two jurisdictions come to differ.) τ_i is the proportional income tax rate in jurisdiction i. $(tm)_j$ together are the expected total annual travel costs from j's chosen location. t is the travel cost per mile and m the expected annual travel miles. P_{L_i} is the price of land in i, t_{L_i} is the land tax rate in i, and L_i is the amount of land in i consumed. P_H is the price of housing capital per quantity unit and H the amount of housing capital consumed. P_X is the price of the composite private good and X is the amount of that good consumed. Finally, $P_{L_{ji}}$ is the price of land in i at the time when household j first became a resident of i, and L_{ji} is the amount of land bought by j at that time.

The budget constraint says that total purchasing power at the command of household j residing in jurisdiction i is exhausted in outlays due to income tax liability $(\tau_i Y_i^j)$, travel expense $(tm)_j$, land-use costs $[P_{L_i}(1 + t_{L_i})L_i]$, use of housing capital $(P_H H)$, and consumption of the composite private good $(P_X X)$. The income tax rate is a pure rate per dollar of income (τ_i). For travel expense, the expected annual travel miles m depends primarily on work and shopping trips. These depend on the distribution of business activity between central city and suburb (B_1, B_2) and the location of household j's residence—measured in terms of its distance from the nearest point of the central city (k), i.e.,

$$m = m(k, B_1, B_2) \quad (11.3)$$

Travel cost per mile, t, is assumed constant mostly for convenience.[3]

This treatment of location stems from the assumptions that the city has considerably more business activity than the suburb and that, unlike in the suburb, business activity is uniformly distributed. Thus, any location within the city $(k = 0)$ has equal accessibility (expected travel costs) and total expected travel miles depends on distance from this city concentration.

Land-use costs include the annual rental cost of land (an imputed rental, since every household is assumed to own the land it occupies—price per unit

P_{L_i} times amount L_i) and the annual liability of the land tax (tax rate t_{L_i} times price $P_{L_i} \cdot L_i$).

The unusual aspect of this budget constraint is that total available purchasing power in each period is assumed to consist of that period's income earned Y^j *and* that period's share of imputed accumulated capital gains on land. Every household is assumed to own the land that renders it annual services. Capital gains on the land are a product of dynamic adjustments. The model has both a comparative static and a dynamic facet. This stems from a distinction between a short- and long-run adjustment process. This will be discussed below. These capital gains are an important link between constituents' welfare and the use of public policy to influence the long-run location of business and households. It will be seen that locational changes by others have an effect on each household's welfare as a consumer of the commodities listed above (by affecting their size and prices); such changes also affect each household's welfare as owner of the land that makes up the jurisdiction. Such changes in the asset values of households' initial holdings of land increase or decrease their present-period purchasing power over the commodities in their utility function. Since these gains are exempt from the income tax, they directly increase or decrease utility, enhancing consumption.

The capital gains are measured as the difference between present land values in the jurisdiction and those that prevailed when the household first became a resident of the jurisdiction and on the amount of land that the household bought at that beginning period.

In the budget constraint, each of the commodities consumed has a price except for crowdedness of life space (D). In fact, this last has an implicit price as well. We shall discuss it below.

Given these commodity preferences and price-income constraints, household j selects that bundle which maximizes its utility. In selecting a bundle, some elements can be chosen in fine gradations, while others involve an all-or-nothing choice. The composite private good, the amount of land and housing capital can be varied very finely. On the other hand, once a particular piece of land has been selected, a jurisdiction has been selected also. The household then passively has to accept both the one-and-only-one level of crowdedness existing there (by assumption) and the one-and-only-one level of public services provided—both being outside the household's ability to influence.

Thus the choice can be looked on as proceeding from the following two-stage process: household j considers the utility-maximizing combination of goods attainable from a city location (given the budget constraint) and that attainable from a suburban location and then selects that bundle that gives the higher utility level. So the choice in effect simultaneously selects an optimal location and an optimal amount of the different commodities (considering the all-or-nothing constraint on crowdedness and public-service level).

The Location Decision of the Individual Household:
Metropolitan Government

A major thrust of this chapter is to contrast the consequences of metropolitan government and jurisdictional fragmentation. This is begun by examining how the aforementioned household-location decision proceeds under the two situations. For this task, we must clothe the highly abstract procedure above in the particularities of the city-suburb choice.

Under metropolitan government, the level of public services provided and the effective tax rates are the same for all households: i.e., $G_1 = G_2$, $\tau_1 = \tau_2$, $t_{L_1} = t_{L_2}$ (subscripts always use 1 for the city, 2 for the suburb). Moreover, there is no use of zoning to discriminate the use of residential land. Having assumed that business is disproportionately located in the city, the chief basis for selecting a city versus suburban location is simply the choice between the resulting lower crowdedness of the suburb versus the greater accessibility of the city. This depends on the price of lower crowdedness relative to its desirability.

We have not yet spoken of a price for lower crowdedness. Such a price is implicit in the working of the land market. We shall discuss the land market in detail below, but one relevant aspect of it needs to be introduced at this time. Accessibility to desirable destinations is a positive good so long as overcoming distance incurs real costs. Since business destinations are heavily concentrated in the city portion of the area and there is no costless way to increase the supply of land with high accessibility (by increasing accessibility on less accessible land), a gradation of accessibility will come to constitute a dimension of the "quality" of land. Therefore, no one would be willing to pay the same price for an inferior (less accessible) piece of land as for a superior (more accessible) piece. As a result, a competitive process will bid up the price of city land above that of the suburb—and lots in the suburb that differ in accessibility (by k) will have prices that inversely reflect these differences. In short, the land market will capitalize quality differences stemming from accessibility differences.[4]

Differences in accessibility within the suburb—but not within the city (by our earlier assumption concerning k in the city)—will lead to different prices within the suburb. Previously, we have spoken of a single price for land in suburb and city, P_{L_2} and P_{L_1}. While the city does have one price, the suburb has a different one at each accessibility level k. Use of an aggregate refers to the mean for the suburb.

If uncrowdedness is not a valued characteristic of a living area, then city and suburban land will be occupied, but at different prices. The mean difference is $P_{L_1}^o - P_{L_2}^o$, and the population divides with N_1^o in the city and N_2^o in the suburb.[5] This represents a "neutral," base-level price differential. Now suppose uncrowdedness becomes valued. Still at the earlier price differential, suburban residence now looks more attractive, so migration from city to suburb will occur, raising P_{L_2} and lowering P_{L_1} until a new set of price differentials is achieved that balances the attractiveness of higher D with the new lower price differential for the least eager—the marginal—migrant. The new, lower average differential is $P_{L_1}^* - P_{L_2}^*$, and at this level N_2° has increased to N_2^*, N_1° has declined to N_1^*. The decline in the price differential between any lot in the suburb—and thus the average lot—and a lot in the city is a measure of the price of lower crowdedness (i.e., the *difference* between D_1 and D_2):

$$P_D = (P_{L_1}^\circ - P_{L_2}^\circ) - (P_{L_1}^* - P_{L_2}^*) \qquad (11.4)$$

P_D depends, of course, on the size of N_1°, N_2° and the distribution of preferences for D among the whole population (i.e., it depends on the value of the particular differential $D_1 - D_2$ on the part of the marginal mover, both determined simultaneously by the competitive process).

The simple location decision under metropolitan government can therefore be looked on as involving the balance between the attractiveness of less crowded living and the price one has to pay for it. Those households who place a high valuation on noncrowdedness relative to the larger amount of travel cost that becomes uncompensated through capitalization in land prices are likely to move to the suburb. There is some small loss to higher- relative to lower-income households in the lower land-price benefit relative to travel cost, but we assume that noncrowdedness is a commodity with high income elasticity,[6] i.e., utility valuation rises rapidly with income level, so on balance, richer households are highly likely to be the ones who outbid others for noncrowdedness.

This self-selected distribution of the population between city and suburb is in an important sense a "natural" one: it represents the voluntary balance of preference and technical trade-offs between land-use density and accessibility, which represent naturally competitive facets in the deployment of resources over space. Of course, the outcome is not unique. It can be changed by a different distribution of business activity over the area, since this determines the pattern of travel costs and differential crowdedness. This, in turn, can be influenced by a change in business zoning. We shall consider this more specifically in the fragmented-government case to follow.

The Location Decision of the Individual Household: Fragmented Government

City and suburb are now different political jurisdictions. Since public action is deemed to respond to the wants of the constituent population, and since the two jurisdictions can have populations that differ in both tax base and tastes (i.e., differences in relative commodity preferences for households with the same utility function but different income levels), both service levels and effective tax rates can differ. So such differences can now affect household-location decisions, since they enter both into the utility function [equation (11.1)] and the budget constraint [equation (11.2)] . Moreover, these very location decisions will in turn affect the governmental decisions about public-service levels and effective tax rates, since they change tax base and tastes in the two jurisdictions.

The Demand for Public Services

In order to trace the effect of population composition on public choice, we must develop a concept of the demand for public services. We assume a responsive government, one that registers the desires of its electorate by majority rule. Moreover, the single-dimensional expenditure side (the level of public services, G) and the relatively simple tax side of public action seem appropriate to permit the assumption that voter preferences among service level and tax alternatives are single-peaked.[7] This assumption is not essential, but it is convenient in enabling us to express the demand relationship transparently.

Under a set of single-peaked preferences, majority-rule outcomes for a population of some magnitude[8] are in principle completely determinate, and they form a transitive set of social-preference orderings. In explicit or implicit elimination-contest voting procedures, the winning-vote alternative will be that represented by the median most-preferred position (on the compatible spatial array mentioned above).[9] Given the regularity of preferences with income level in our present model, this can be approximated by the most preferred preference position of the median voter—in turn, of the median income recipient in each jurisdiction.

The demand for public-service level by any household is discovered by examining the optimal budget allocation for the household under utility maximization. The hypothetical situation is to suppose that the household is faced with a given price for all of the commodities that enter its utility function, both private and public, and a specified level of D (different amounts cannot be chosen or even directly voted for), and asked how much of each it would buy if it were free to choose any quantity it liked *of every one of them, private and public alike*. This is meaningful for the level of public services because this was defined as the quality of services as experienced by each household, i.e., it represents an "own consumption" level. The hypothetical question is answered by deriving the familiar first-order conditions for utility maximization, which call for marginal rates of substitution (ratios of marginal utilities) equal to price ratios for each pair of commodities. For variations in the prices of own and other commodities, in the level of D and in the household's income level, it traces out the conventional commodity demand function. This demand function, interpreted as the amount of public services a particular household would most favor under each particular configuration of income and prices, is as follows:

$$G_i^j = G(Y^j, P_{G_i}^j, P_X, P_H, P_{L_i}, P_D, D) \tag{11.5}$$

We assume G is a normal good, so that if its price falls or income rises, more of it is wanted. What remains to be defined is the price of public services. It is the amount of total tax liability per unit of public services provided. Since there are two different taxes, this is as follows:

$$P_{G_i}^j = (\tau_i Y^j + t_{L_i} P_{L_i} L_i^j) \div G_i \tag{11.6}$$

Notice that this is a price personal to household j, because the two taxes are weighted by the specific tax bases applicable to household j—its income level and its purchase of land services (remember that every household owns the land it occupies and is thus directly liable to the land tax).

Since L_i is in principle determinate, given the other variables in the demand function, we can substitute (11.6) into (11.5) for the median income recipient in jurisdiction i:

$$G_i = \tilde{G}_i = G(\tilde{Y}_i, \tau_i, t_{L_i}, P_X, P_H, P_{L_i}, P_D, D) \tag{11.7}$$

In general G_i will rise if $\tilde{Y}_i$ rises and will fall if any of the rest rise (D is defined as a negative commodity).

The two tax rates are not unconstrained. In this model it is assumed that the government must balance its budget in every period. Total revenue from given tax rates τ_i and t_{L_i} are:

$$T_1 = \tau_1 \bar{Y}_1 N_1 + t_{L_1} P_{L_1} A_1 \tag{11.8a}$$

$$T_2 = \tau_2 \bar{Y}_2 N_2 + \int_0^K t_{L_2} P_{L_2}(k) a(k) \, dk \tag{11.8b}$$

where: T_1 = total revenue in the city
T_2 = total revenue in the suburb
$\bar{Y}_1, \bar{Y}_2$ = mean household income levels in city and suburb, respectively
A_1 = the total number of privately owned acres in the city
K = the distance from the city border to the suburb border
$a(k)$ = the number of privately owned acres at distance k from the city border.

The formulations differ for city and suburb because by assuming that accessibility is equal for all lots in the city, all have the same price, while lots in the suburb differ in accessibility (as a function of k) and so differ in price correspondingly.[10]

Total expenditures, which must balance total revenues, depend in the general case on two considerations: (1) the quality level of public services provided, G_i,

and (2) the number of households. Public services are neither pure private goods
nor pure public goods, i.e., it is in general inappropriate to assume that total
costs of providing each unit level of services to the total population is either
simply the cost of providing that unit to each member of the population times
the number of members (pure private) or the same regardless of the number of
members (pure public). Consumption of public services is "shared consumption."
Provision of the capacity to provide services to one member constitutes a capacity
to provide services to others as well, since each member's "consumption" does
not exhaust a particular set of resources used exclusively for that member's consumption. So total costs are less than per member cost times number of members. But various forms of "crowding" or interuser interference make the quality
of service fall to each as the same capacity is pressed to provide services to a
larger and larger population. So total expenditures necessary to provide a given
quality level rise as the population size rises.[11]

In addition to the influence of population size, the quality level of services
imparts an unambiguous impact. Higher quality levels require higher total resource costs. So in the general case the total expenditure function (measure of
real resource cost) can be shown as:

$$E_i = E(N_i, G_i)$$

$$(a)\ \frac{\delta E_i}{\delta N_i} > 0 \qquad \frac{\delta E_i}{\delta G_i} > 0 \qquad (b)\ \frac{\delta^2 E_i}{\delta N_i^2} > 0$$

$$(c)\ \delta \frac{E_i}{N_i} \Bigg/ \delta N_i \begin{cases} < 0 \text{ for } 0 < N_i < {}^\circ N_i \\ = 0 \text{ for } N_i = {}^\circ N_i \\ > 0 \text{ for } {}^\circ N_i > N_i \leq N \end{cases} \qquad (11.9)$$

Properties (a) call for rising populations to increase E if some G_i is to be maintained, and quality of services to increase E for any population size. Property
(b) establishes the "crowding" of quasi-public goods as involving (very) small
cost-augmenting impacts for small populations but rising disproportionally as
population increases. Property (c) indicates that there are economies and diseconomies of population scale in providing the quasi-public goods. In the application being presented, we suppose that scale economies are exhausted at a quite
low jurisdiction size (i.e., ${}^\circ N_i$ is small).

Central city and suburb are both subject to this expenditure function. We
assume the budget-balancing procedure to be as follows: at the beginning of the
period, a level G_i is decided upon for a given constituent population, N_i. This
determines an expenditure total to be met out of tax revenues. A prior policy
decision—to be explained below—has set the relative amounts to be raised by income and land taxes. Given the jurisdictional population and its income distribu-

tion, the mean income level is determined and thus the income tax rate necessary to raise the planned amount assigned. Similarly, the population and its income distribution, together with the calculated income tax rate, simultaneously determine the set of optimal demands for land and the land tax rate consistent with this set and with the total revenue goal assigned. Since this depends on the detailed working of the land market and we have not yet spelled that out, we shall not present here the explicit mathematics of this solution process.

Jurisdictional Differences in the Supply of Public Services

What we described above in equation (11.9) was "the general case" of the cost function for public services. In the present model there are special features that distinguish the situation of local-goods provision in a metropolitan area. Built onto the basic land-use asymmetry between city and suburb as described in the metropolitan government case above (namely, the specialized difference in land-use density and distribution of business activity) are a derived set of differences stemming from the existence of jurisdictional fragmentation. They fall into three categories: (1) differences in tax base, (2) differences in welfare load, and (3) differences in interjurisdictional externalities. We shall argue that, in the context of that initial land-use asymmetry, all three create a systematic difference in the same direction between the price of public services in the two jurisdictions.

1. Differences in Tax Base. To facilitate the discussion of tax bases, we note that the proportional income tax base identically and the land tax base indirectly are positive functions of household income level. The higher the income, the higher will be the household's demand for land (as a normal, superior good). The amount of land demanded by the household and, when aggregated, the price of land subjected to increased demand will both rise. Both will increase the household's base subject to *ad valorem* land tax. Thus we can speak of the size of the tax base in terms of income level alone, as though only the proportional income tax were in effect.

Suppose there were two jurisdictions, 1 and 2, with equal populations and equal desired public-service levels. Then total planned expenditures would be the same for both. Suppose also that a proportional income tax were the sole tax source. Assume now that jurisdiction 2 had a total tax base twice as large as jurisdiction 1 because of an average income level twice as large. Then the tax rate required in jurisdiction 2 would be half as large as that required in jurisdiction 1. Nonetheless, every household in the former would pay the same total amount of tax as every household in the latter. So there is no difference in treatment in this original allocation of population. But suppose that households were free to move from one jurisdiction to the other. Any household moving from jurisdiction 1 to jurisdiction 2 would lose a higher tax-rate liability for one that is half as large—

and thus on this particular household the tax base would have a total amount of tax liability one-half as great as previously. This incentive to move does not depend on the income level of the migrant being greater, equal to, or less than that of the destination mean: *every* household beginning in jurisdiction 1 has a similar incentive.

Taken by itself, this systematic migration incentive would increase population in jurisdiction 2 and decrease it in 1. This would increase public-service costs in the former relative to the latter. It would also tend to lower the mean tax base in the former, while its effect on that of the latter depends on which households migrated. On balance, there would be a progressive diminution in the absolute value of the differential tax-rate effect, unless the order of migration actually widened the difference in mean tax base enough to offset the worsening crowding of public-service provision in jurisdiction 2. The initial tax incentive might or might not be eventually wiped out (at small enough sizes of jurisdiction 1, the inefficiencies of small-scale provision of public services would raise their costs as well), but in any event a migration flow would have been elicited from 1 to 2 to take advantage of the tax-rate differential.

In our model, the tax-rate differential makes for a differential in the price of public services in the two jurisdictions and, all other things equal, creates an incentive for households to migrate from the low-tax-base to the high-tax-base jurisdiction. This differential is purely a product of the character of public-sector transactions in contrast to private-sector transactions. Pricing is not based on an exact *quid pro quo* for benefits received by each household, since these are due to services provided with some degree of "publicness." Pricing stems from a communal fund, the tax base, which is—if at all—only remotely related to individual benefits. Thus the jurisdiction's total tax base represents a positive externality for every household in the jurisdiction. Its net benefits from public action is greater the greater is the size of the jurisdictional tax base. It is externalities operating with different magnitude in the two jurisdictions that generate differences in the price of public services and thus differential attractiveness for location.

2. Differences in Welfare Load. Up to now we have spoken about quality level of public services as a flow of benefits going equally to all households in the jurisdiction (although not necessarily with equal utility valuation). Now we introduce an important distinction within the population. Some households are eligible to receive the benefits of various welfare programs. In the real world, this would include relief, food stamps, social-work services, special health-care services, compensatory education and vocational training, etc. In our model world of one composite public commodity, this is approximated by giving those households eligible for "welfare benefits"—*generally* poorer or afflicted households—a supplement to the normal bundle of public services. Thus, while nonwelfare recipients receive G_i, a welfare recipient receives $G_i + \lambda$. For convenience, and because in the real world the welfare supplement is likely to be quite similar in different parts of the same metropolitan area (however dissimilar in different metropolitan areas), we treat this supplement as strictly equal in city and suburb: $\lambda_1 = \lambda_2 = \lambda$.

Suppose now we have two hypothetical jurisdictions, again with equal populations and equal total expenditures. Jurisdiction 1, however, has twice as large a percentage of its population on welfare as does jurisdiction 2. What level of G_i will the same total expenditures finance in the two jurisdictions? Clearly, since each welfare recipient receives $G_i + \lambda$, while nonrecipients receive only G_i, G_2 will exceed G_1: welfare recipients are more expensive and decrease the fund available to produce service quality. Abstracting from the relative size of tax bases and thus of tax rates (which would presumably go in the same direction as what follows anyway), any household in 1 that decided to move to 2 would gain a higher quality level. This holds for welfare recipients and nonwelfare recipients. Even welfare recipients have an incentive to run away from a jurisdiction with many other welfare recipients.

The mechanism here, intrinsic to public-sector transactions, is structurally similar to that for unequal tax bases. Other inhabitants of the jurisdiction draw unequally out of a communal resource pool for providing public services. To participate in a pool with expensive other participants is a negative externality to each. The percentage of participants who are expensive withdrawers is the measure of this negative externality. Different percentages imply different-sized externalities. Since they affect the ratio of quality level to tax levies (via the total expenditure pool), they affect the price of public services in the two jurisdictions.

We are not supposing that only the poorest are eligible for welfare, since the real-world list of services being reflected includes some that go to persons who are *stochastically* distressed and thus not subject to determinate prior identification in terms of income. Nonetheless, the probability that a family will be eligible for welfare in a given period is an inverse function of income. Thus a poorer jurisdiction will have a higher expected proportion of its population as welfare recipients than a richer one. But such a difference will mean that the price of public services is greater in the poorer than in the richer jurisdiction.

Thus tax-base and welfare-load considerations both establish that a poorer jurisdiction will experience a higher price of public services, all other things equal, than a richer. In our analysis of the single metropolitan-area government, the trade-off between travel costs and density suggested that the suburb will become specialized as a residence for wealthier households relative to the rest of the urban area. That initial discrepency in mean constituent income, arising from "natural" spatial considerations, will become the platform for generating a differential in public-service price—thereby creating systematic incentives for additional households to move to the suburbs. The superimposed differential arises entirely out of externalities that are distinctive features of public-sector, as opposed to private-sector, processes.

3. Differences in Interjurisdictional Externalities.[12]   Another vital characteristic of the real-world metropolitan area is that it exists as the counterpart of a very high degree of economic and social interaction: such interaction is the *raison d'être* as well as the consequence of the spatial concentration known as an urban area. Much of the interaction is connected with the carrying out of business activity. The heavy concentration of such activity in the central city means that it is the desirable destination for a large proportion of all trips in the area. When a household moves to the suburb, it does not thereby end all of its presence in the central city. It is likely to continue a significant presence there, as for a job or for specialized shopping, recreation, or cultural activities.

Such presence inadvertently makes use of public services provided in the city, streets and roads, water, sewers, police and fire protection, and special services like libraries, museums, parks, and beaches. Consider the impact of this on roads, for example. Suppose the city government wanted to provide quality level G_1. Since this is an *output*—not input—measure, it implies for roads that a certain trip from A to B should be able to be made in a specified amount of time, with a specified degree of convenience and safety. To determine the input cost of providing this output level, the planners would have to know the expected traffic (since congestion affects all these output dimensions). If only the city residents were expected to use the road system, a certain input cost would be required. But suburbanites would typically want to use the system as well, and it is costly to try to exclude them from the roads. With suburban use, the same capacity would result in lower G for the city residents. So more, wider, and stronger roads would have to be provided—at higher total cost—to achieve the same G_1 in the presence of suburban use. Thus the interactive physical presence of suburbanites in the central city raises the real cost of providing public services to the city residents.

Since the same cost-enhancing effect is present in other types of public services as well, the physical presence of suburbanites in the central city is a negative externality for the provision of public services in the city. It is an interjurisdictional externality, however, since such externalities are not restricted to one direction: the presence of city residents in the suburb should have some of the same effects. There is strong reason to believe, however, that the externalities imposed by suburbanites on the city are greater than those imposed by city residents on the suburb. First, the disproportionate concentration of business, governmental, and nonprofit institutional facilities in the city implies much more per capita suburbanite presence in the city than the reverse. Second, each instance of suburbanite presence in the city is likely to have a larger cost-enhancing (or quality-depressing) impact than the reverse presence of city residents in the suburbs. That results from the fact that the *marginal* crowding effect on public services is greater the greater is the average crowding. This is inferred from properties (b) and (c) of the public-expenditure function (11.9). So the net interjurisdictional externalities imposed on the suburb are likely to be negative, and those imposed on the city positive.

The net increase in cost of public services due to net externalities may be less than suggested by the expenditure function and the differential size of the spillover because there are two potential financial offsets. One is governmental profits on business taxation, the other is the proceeds of special user charges. Since the overconcentration of business in the city is one of the chief causes of the net presence of the suburbanite there, it would seem reasonable to tax that business at rates that yield revenues in excess of the business-induced cost increases. Unfortunately, it is extremely difficult to calculate the business-induced portion of cost increases—i.e., to assign differing liabilities to individual businesses on the basis of their impact on costs. Perhaps even more constraining, however, is that businesses are deemed to be both generally desirable in the urban area and mobile, so that the competitive attractions of alternative areas prevent obviously exploitative tax treatment for fear of losing these valuable mainstays of the urban economy.

Actual treatment of businesses is difficult to evaluate in terms of financial profits or losses relative to interjurisdictional externalities. I have accordingly chosen to exclude this factor from the model, assuming that business taxes are financially neutral: they just equal the marginal cost of providing public services to the business community.

The second financial offset is user charges. These are prices set to compel suburbanites to pay for their use of public services. Some public services are close enough to private goods in their production and distribution that individual instances of consumption and their associated production costs can be reasonably identified, and control of access to use can be restricted at minimal cost. User charges pinpointed to suburbanite use, and approximating marginal costs, are appropriate here. Museums, libraries, swimming pools, and other recreation facilities provide services that fall into this category. But clearly not all public services do: most are *public* services because they violate at least one of these characteristics substantially. Inability to pinpoint and control suburbanite use or to isolate its marginal cost make user charges inefficient. They would often involve a significant real cost to administer, be incapable of accurate calculation, and impinge on city residents as well as suburbanites. Imperfect user charges do not obtain proper financial offsets and impose additional costs on city residents—in extra administrative costs and in the misallocation of resources that results from inappropriate marginal taxation.

Thus, while user charges can be resorted to by the city government to help offset negative net interjurisdictional externalities, they are not a perfect policy instrument. On balance, their use will leave a residual net loss to the city government.

In sum, the asymmetrical presence of interjurisdictional negative externalities in the metropolitan area will increase the real per capita cost of providing any level of G in the central city above that in the suburb and thus the price of public services facing each resident. This increase is superimposed on any differential stemming from the previous two political sources. The differential involved here is not fixed but depends on such variables as the spatial distribution of business and other nonresidential activities, travel costs, and the characteristics of user charges. Of these, in the present model the distribution of business between city and suburb is subject to a policy instrument: business zoning.

Household-Location Choice

We can now summarize the effects of the above differentials for explicit inclusion in the model. The effect of tax base can be directly shown by relating the formation of tax rates to the required expenditure totals and the two tax bases. The effect of welfare load can be shown by introducing the welfare recipient premium, λ, and relating the probability of becoming a welfare recipient to household income level. The interjurisdictional externalities can be treated as a net effect in two respects: for the city but not for the suburban government, and as the residual left after imperfect user charges have been employed optimally (i.e., to minimize the net burden on the city).[13] It can be shown as a complication of the city's—but not the suburb's—public-expenditure function. This is expressed in equations (11.9a$'$) and (11.9b$'$), which also incorporate a variable relating to welfare load (to be explained below):

$$E_1 = E_1\,(N_1,N_2,G_1,B_1,B_2,\phi_1,\lambda) \tag{11.9a$'$}$$

where $(1)\ \dfrac{\delta E_1}{\delta N_2} > 0$ $(2)\ \dfrac{\delta^2 E_1}{\delta N_2^2} < 0$ $(3)\ \dfrac{\delta^2 E_1}{\delta N_2\,\delta N_1} > 0$

$(4)\ \dfrac{\delta^2 E_1}{\delta N_2\,\delta B_1} > 0$ $(5)\ \dfrac{\delta^2 E_1}{\delta N_2\,\delta B_2} < 0$

$$E_2 = E_2\,(N_2,G_2,\phi_2,\lambda) \tag{11.9b$'$}$$

In (11.9a$'$), the E_1 function incorporates the probability that a suburbanite will have a physical presence in the central city. So expenditures rise with total number of suburbanites (via expected total suburbanite presence). This individual probability depends on the distribution of desirable nonresidential trip destinations, so the more they are located in the city the greater is the individual probability and thus the greater is the marginal impact of each suburbanite $[\delta^2 E/(\delta N_2 \delta B_1) > 0]$; the reverse holds for suburban-located business $[\delta^2 E/(\delta N_2 \delta B_2) < 0]$. Trips are made for socializing too, so an increase in absolute size of the suburban population diverts some of such trips away from the city $[\delta^2 E_1/(\delta N_2^2) < 0]$; similarly, a larger city population attracts more such trips, as well as implying a more congested city, thus increasing the marginal crowding impact of each trip on city public services $[\delta^2 E_1/(\delta N_2 \delta N_1) > 0]$.

The variable ϕ_i is the percentage of the population who are welfare recipients.[14] Increase in this variable increases E_i. λ is the per household premium for a welfare recipient.

The overall effect on prices of public services is given as follows:

$$T_i = E_i \tag{11.10}$$

This is the budget-balancing requirement.

$$\tau_i \bar{Y}_i N_i = \Omega_i T_i \quad \text{or} \quad \Omega_i = \frac{\tau_i \bar{Y}_i N_i}{T_i} \tag{11.11}$$

where Ω_i is the public-policy instrument deciding on the percentage of total revenues to be raised by the income tax:

$$E = \bar{W}_E + W_E \tag{11.12}$$

where $\bar{W}_E$ is the total expenditures excluding welfare payments (costs), and W_E is the total welfare payments:

$$W_{E_i} = \lambda \phi_i N_i \tag{11.13}$$

where, as before, λ is the per household premium for a welfare recipient:

$$\phi_i = \phi(\bar{Y}_i, \sigma_{Y_i}) \tag{11.14}$$

where σ_{Y_i} is the standard deviation of the household income distribution in i:

$$\frac{\delta \phi_i}{\delta \bar{Y}_i} < 0, \quad \frac{\delta \phi_i}{\delta \sigma_{Y_i}} > 0$$

$$\tau_i = \frac{\Omega_i E_i}{\bar{Y}_i N_i} \tag{11.15}$$

$$t_{L_i} = \frac{E_i - \Omega_i E_i}{P_{L_i} A_i} \qquad (11.16)$$

where P_{L_i} is the mean value of land per acre in i, and A_i is the total number of private acres in i.

Equations (11.10) and (11.11) simply formalize the budget-balancing requirement and the definition of the policy instrument Ω that determines the relative mix of revenues from the two tax sources. Equations (11.12) and (11.13) show the determination of the costs of the welfare load [(11.12) is purely definitional], and equation (11.14) indicates the probabilistic basis of the welfare load. The higher the mean income the lower the probability; the higher the income dispersion the higher the probability, since for a given mean income a higher dispersion means more people at very low absolute levels—and absolute deprivation is one criterion for welfare eligibility. Equations (11.15) [which is mathematically equivalent to equations (11.10) and (11.11) together] and (11.16) show how the size of the tax base explicitly enters to affect the effective tax rates: both forms of tax base have a negative effect on their corresponding tax rates.

We can now return to the choice situation of the household under fragmented government. Begin at the locational situation established under metropolitan government. N_1^* households reside in the city, N_2^* in the suburb. Mean land prices are $P_{L_1}^*$ and $P_{L_2}^*$; $D = D^*$ and $G = G^*$; and the price of public services is P_G^*. Now every household has the opportunity to face the prices of public services and the service levels resulting from the separate jurisdictional tax bases. From the preceding section and equations (11.5) to (11.16), the initial population distribution establishes a lower public-service price in the suburb than in the city. Every household has at this point a greater incentive to migrate to the suburb than previously. Those who can gain overall by such a move will do so.

To see which households are likely to move, we must examine the nature of the gains now available through political fragmentation. All three sources of advantage operate through a lowered set of tax rates in the suburb relative to that in the city. The absolute size of the money gains is therefore a positive function of household income. Thus, while fragmentation enhances the attraction of the suburb for all, the degree of enhancement is a positive function of income. Since we wish to consider the use of a public-policy instrument in the suburb that generally occurs in the real world only after fragmentation and some subsequent urban development, we shall modify the comparative static "short-run" flavor of the model to construct a fictional dynamics. We suppose that there is a queue of city households in descending order of potential gross gains from migration to the suburb. From the preceding, this queue will isomorphically display decreasing household income levels.

At the start of the fragmentation period, the population is divided between the last (marginal) migrant and the first (marginal) nonmigrant in the queue.

The latter is nearly indifferent between moving and staying, and subsequent members of the queue would lose increasingly the lower the income level (because of the trade-off between crowdedness and travel costs). The political gains from fragmentation will create net gains from migration for households down from the head of the queue. Households will then actually migrate in the same temporal order as the size of these net gains. The net gains will decrease for each subsequent marginal nonmover as households ahead of it migrate, because: (1) the differential crowdedness between the two jurisdictions decreases with higher density in the suburb and lower density in the city, i.e.,

$$D_i = D(N_i, B_i, {}^U\!A_i) \qquad\qquad (11.17)$$

where ${}^U\!A_i$ is the number of private acres in urban use; (2) public services become more crowded in the suburb, less crowded in the city [by equation (11.9)]; (3) the difference between average tax base in city and suburb *may* decline as poorer households move to the suburb (but this depends on the specifics of the income distribution); (4) land prices rise in the suburb and fall in the city, thus raising the price of noncrowdedness (D); (5) the marginal interjurisdictional externality impact falls with the population shift, thereby decreasing the per capita effect on tax rates; (6) whatever the tax-rate differential, the lower income level results in a smaller absolute advantage.

For some household income level, implying as well a certain total of previous migrants, net benefits will be zero, and for lower levels net benefits will be negative. This level establishes the new stable marginal nonmover—and with it the equilibrium population distribution.

Consider the same sequential migration now from the point of view of early migrants (or even those who "hypothetically" became suburbanites under even metropolitan government). Their net gains from residing in the suburb instead of the city are likely to fall as more and more previous city dwellers migrate to the suburb because (1) the D differential falls with population shift; (2) the per household tax base in the suburb declines, thereby raising the tax rate, as unambiguously lower-income households move in (regardless of what happens to the per household tax base *differential*); (3) with lower-income households moving in, the expected percentage of the population on welfare increases, thereby further raising the tax rate.

One force tends to increase gains to the early suburbanites: the population shift raises land prices in the suburb (as it lowers them in the city). This generates capital gains for them. The net effect of these opposing forces depends on the specifics of the relationships described here only abstractly, details of which include the characteristics of the subsequent movers.

Early suburbanites can influence the characteristics of movers so as to increase the probability that capital gains will exceed benefit losses for at least moderate in-migration. By discouraging lower-income households from migrating, they can minimize the losses due to tax-base and welfare-load changes. Moreover, if they can do this while maintaining low density of urban land use despite a larger population, they can minimize the increasing crowdedness of the suburban life space.

Both goals can be accomplished simultaneously by instituting minimum residential-lot zoning in the suburb. Requiring large lot sizes means that any given number of migrants will not seriously increase urban density and will be forced to channel much of the increased total demand for suburban land to the conversion of rural land to urban uses (i.e., increase $^U\!A_2$), leading to similar rises in land prices as if more of the demand were for higher land-use density. Moreover, since the size of lot demanded by a household is positively related to its income, requiring a large lot to be purchased imposes a potentially large utility loss on the poor household by considerably distorting its budgetary allocation— and the loss is greater the lower the income level. Finally, such zoning can be used to control the overall numbers migrating, as well as the composition, by varying its required minimum and thus the whole schedule of losses to potential migrants.

So early suburbanites have a rational incentive for their jurisdictional government to impose minimum residential-lot zoning. This government, assumed to be responsive to their welfare, is therefore assumed to comply. Thus we must include the existence of minimum-lot zoning in the suburb as part of the setting for describing the locational choice of the individual household.[15]

We can now integrate all these elements into the choice situation. The individual household will choose so as to maximize its utility. It does this in two stages: (1) it hypothetically selects the best budgetary allocation for the city and suburb separately; (2) it selects from these two that one which gives higher utility.

Form the indirect utility function V^j for the household (where the achievable utility level is given as a function of the income level and prices of all commodities, as well as the externally determined levels of G_i and D_i):[16]

$$\max U_1^j : V_1^j = V_1 \left[Y^j + (P_{L_1} - P_{L_{j1}}) L_{j_1}, \tau_1, P_{L_1}, t_{L_1}, P_H, P_X, N_1, B_1, G_1, D_1 \right] \qquad (11.18a)$$

$$\max U_2^j : V_2^j = V_2 \left[Y^j + (P_{L_2} - P_{L_{j2}}) L_{j_2}, \tau_2, P_{L_2}, t_{L_2}, (tm), P_H, P_X, L_2^Z, \right. \\ \left. N_2, B_2, G_2, D_2 \right] \qquad (11.18b)$$

where L_2^Z is the minimum-lot zoning requirement in the suburb. Notice that travel costs are included in V_2^j but not in V_1^j because travel costs are zero in the city.

These budget-optimizing allocations will result in an optimal simultaneous choice of $L, H,$ and X in both jurisdictions (G and D being set externally). In the suburb, this optimum is a second best, because the household may be forced to buy more land than it would like in order to satisfy the zoning requirement

$L_2 \geq L_2^Z$. A distortion here means that H and X must in general diverge also from what an unconstrained choice would have warranted. So we characterize the respective choices as follows:

$$\hat{U}_1^j = U(G_1, D_1, \hat{L}_1, \hat{H}_1, \hat{X})$$ (11.19a)

$$\hat{U}_2^j = U(G_2, D_2, L_2^*, H_2^*, X^*)$$ (11.19b)

where $\hat{}$ signifies choice unconstrained except by the budget constraint, and $*$ signifies choice constrained by the minimum-lot zoning requirement, as well as the budget constraint. The net gain from migration to the suburb, π^j, is:

$$\pi^j = V_2^j - V_1^j$$ (11.20)

Equilibrium Population Distribution

We are now able to indicate how individual household-location choice leads to an equilibrium distribution of population between city and suburb. Begin with some $(G_1, G_2, P_{G_1}, P_{G_2}, L_2^Z, P_H, P_X, B_1, B_2, t)$ for the given population of N households. Then all households j with $\pi^j > 0$, when account is taken of their impact on land prices, are assumed to migrate to the suburb; all with $\pi^j < 0$ are assumed to stay in the city. Consider now a sequence of movers and the last household in that sequence, that for which net gains are lowest. Designate this household the marginal mover in the sequence. We express its gains as follows:

$$\pi_{j(N_2,N_1,B_2,B_1)} = \pi^j(N_2,N_1,B_2,B_1) \quad \begin{array}{l} \text{for } j \in N_2 \text{ and } \pi^j \leq \pi^w \\ w \neq j, \text{ all } w \in N_2 \end{array}$$ (11.21)

We define the equilibrium population distribution between suburb and city as that resulting from an equilibrium sequence, which is a sequence of movers to the suburb for which the net gains of the marginal mover is zero:

$$\hat{N}_2, \hat{N}_1 \quad \text{is an equilibrium distribution if} \quad \pi_{j(\hat{N}_2,\hat{N}_1,B_2,B_1)} = 0 \quad (11.22)$$

The analysis can be illustrated by Figure 11-1. Curve π^D shows at each level N_2' the net gains to the marginal mover in the migration sequence equal to N_2' households under metropolitan government (i.e., when only land-use density gains are involved); curve π^{D+J} shows corresponding marginal-mover gains under fragmented government (i.e., when density and jurisdictional gains are involved). Since the array of movers is monotonically decreasing with respect to household income level, this latter scale is shown on the top. The marginal mover at $N_2 = N$ has the lowest income in the population, Y_L; at $N_2 = 0$ it has the highest, Y_H. π^D is flatter than π^{D+J} in the positive and negative sectors: π^{D+J}

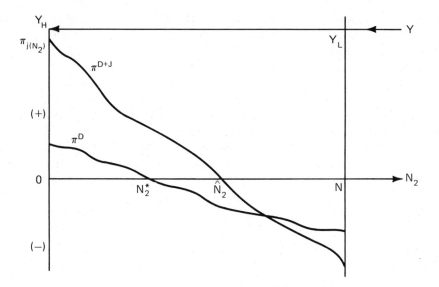

Figure 11-1. Determination of Equilibrium Population Distribution under Metropolitan Government and Fragmented Government.

has bigger potential gains, since jurisdictional benefits can be very substantial for rich households and adds to land-use density gains; it also has bigger potential losses, since in addition to adverse land-price movements with large suburban populations, the presence of minimum-lot zoning makes possible large budgetary distortions for poor households. The equilibrium suburban population is N_2^* under metropolitan government but rises to $\hat{N}_2$ under fragmented government.

The result of jurisdictional fragmentation is (1) a larger suburban population; (2) a lower income for the marginal mover; (3) a price of public services lower than before in the suburb and higher than before in the city ($\hat{P}_{G_2} < P_G^* < \hat{P}_{G_1}$); (4) a higher level of public services than before in the suburb, a lower level than before in the city ($\hat{G}_2 > G^* > \hat{G}_1$); and (5) migration exclusion in the suburb through minimum-lot zoning. So fragmentation has improved the welfare of the richer part of the population—the migrants—while worsening it for the poorer part. This welfare shift in favor of the richer *comes at the expense of the poorer* because it stems heavily from the removal of the wealthier households' tax base from the erstwhile common pool and of their responsibility for tending welfare clients. In effect, fragmentation weakens the ability to use the local level of government to engage in progressive real income redistribution.[17]

The above consequences are predominantly distributional. There is an important resource-allocational consequence as well. The larger suburban population results in (1) a large total of interjurisdictional externalities and (2) a larger total transportation mileage. Externalities drive a wedge between relevant benefits and costs of providing public services. This complicates the problem of balancing resource use between public and private uses and across jurisdictions. This would be especially obvious if we modified our model slightly to allow suburbanites to value the public services they use in the city.

The larger total travel mileage necessary to enable the same population to transact the same total amount of business involves a waste of resources. This is because, while the extra travel cost is presumably the payment for lower-density living, the population does not face the true marginal social cost of the lower-density living, but rather a subsidized, possibly much lower, cost—the offsets through jurisdictional benefits. Thus they are "artificially" induced to buy too much required travel and some of the increase therefore represents a waste of resources.

Both allocational effects decrease the efficiency with which resources are used. Fragmentation therefore has an income-stratifying, regressive distributional impact and a resource-inefficiency impact.

The Working of the Land Market

We argued that under the metropolitan government the land market would operate to permit a balancing of density with travel costs by changing the relative prices of land parcels in accordance with tastes and accessibility. We argued further that under fragmented government jurisdictional benefits are generated just by dint of residing in—and thus owning real property in—the suburb. Since these benefits are specific to particular real property, property that cannot be literally duplicated, shouldn't the land market capitalize these benefits in these particular pieces of land so that, while original owners of the land (farmers and early urban settlers) may benefit, the second and subsequent waves of suburban migrants would find prospective gains to be in fact snatched away before they are realized? If so, the analysis of the last section is wrong, and the impetus to suburbanization is much weaker.

This would occur if favored suburban land were in fact fixed in supply: jurisdictional benefits might then be perfectly capitalized in higher land values. But suburban land is not fixed in supply—there is a positive, price-responsive supply mechanism that prevents land prices from rising enough to wipe out these gains for migrants.

Space will not permit more than the briefest explanation of the land market. There are in fact two land markets, related but different: the city market and the suburban market. The city, being spatially totally encompassed by the suburb, has a fixed land area. Price elasticity of supply is zero here. The price of city land (by assumption homogeneous in everything, including accessibility) is set at that level at which the total demand for city land equals the fixed supply. The demand operates through price. The lower the price, the more land each resident wants to use and the more households want to use it, and vice versa. So total demand shows the conventional inverse relationship to price. If at some price total demand exceeds the fixed supply, price rises until the decreasing amount demanded exactly equals available supply. In this market, increased jurisdictional attractiveness does result in substantial capitalization.

The suburban market is different. For one thing, lots are differentiated by accessibility; for another—and more important—not all the suburb's land is used for urban purposes. Some is under rural use. All land in the suburb is under competition by urban and nonurban users. We assume that the rural opportunity cost—its reservation price—is constant. An increase in urban demand for suburban land is transmitted throughout all developed suburban land in terms of accessibility to the external margin of urban development; the marginal lot used for urban purposes, previously priced equal to the nonurban reservation price, now experiences an increase in price above this level. Urban users can now outbid rural users for land marginally subject to *nonurban* use, at a new price equal to the new price of the previous marginal *urban* lot less the value of differential accessibility between them.

A conversion will therefore occur: additional land will be supplied for urban use, and always at the same price—the reservation nonurban price plus the value of the slight decrease in accessibility relative to the previous margin. This constant supply price is likely to be considerably less than the value of suburban land to at least some new migrants. The competition of new land supplied at the external margin for urban uses prevents all the land in the interior from rising enough to wipe out all prospective migratory gains, since its force is felt by every other lot adjusted only by differential accessibility.

Prospective migratory gains do, however, raise all suburban land prices some, since the newly converted but less accessible land sells at the same price as did the previous marginal land that is more accessible. So price rises everywhere in the interior according to relative accessibility. This set of rises does decrease the prospective gains from migration (without, by itself, wiping them out). At the same time, migration is decreasing both density and jurisdictional gains. The land market thus provides a third mechanism for equalizing net advantages in city and suburb: all three, but not any one of them, reestablish an equilibrium that is disturbed by some new asymmetrical attraction between the two jurisdictions.[18]

Long-Run Public-Policy Adjustment

In analyzing the previous adjustment process, we began by assuming that earlier policy decisions had set the mix of taxes in both jurisdictions and the residential and business zoning regulations in the suburb. The consequent policy adjustment of G, τ, and t_L can be considered a short-run adjustment. We now consider what determines the policy decisions on tax mix and zoning. Adjustment of these constitutes the long-run process.

As noted above, adjustment of business zoning directly influences the distribution of business between city and suburb and, through that, expected travel costs from the suburb, the level of land-use density in city and suburb, the size of interjurisdictional externalities, etc. All these will have some effect on the extent of suburbanization and thus on the size of capital gains for preexisting suburban residents. Thus an adjustment of business zoning is called for in exactly the same way that the short-run service level and tax adjustments were called for, namely, by a majority vote based on utility impacts for constituents. If the median voter experiences utility gain from the capital-gains (density, etc.) consequences, the adjustment will be undertaken.

Adjustment of residential zoning has the same analytic structure: its ability to influence the size, income-level composition, and land-use density of any new migration will have a composite of effects on the components of suburban-voter utility functions. Adjustments will be adopted that positively affect the median voter.

Adjustment of the tax mix is more subtle. Its basis lies in the different kinds of influence a tax on income and a tax on land have on location decisions. While income is mobile and can be completely removed from a jurisdiction's total tax base, land is immobile. It cannot be removed from the jurisdiction. It can lose value, but only in accordance with the working of the land market. It is ordinarily assumed that a rise in a land tax has a smaller disincentive effect on location than a comparable rise in an income tax. In the present model, the consequences are quite complicated, since land-tax capitalization occurs, as does land conversion between urban and nonurban uses, in the suburb but not in the city.

The conversion process, along with the full land-price adjustment mechanism, is too complicated to include in an already overlong paper, but the tax-capitalization process can be briefly noted to help clarify the effect of a change in tax mix on utility.

$$P_{L_i} = P_{L_i}(g_i, t_{L_i})$$
$$\frac{\delta P_{L_i}}{\delta t_{L_i}} < 0 < \frac{\delta P_{L_i}}{\delta g_i} \tag{11.23}$$

where g_i is the value of the services of land excluding the land tax. This function shows that a land tax is shifted back on the owner—the tax is capitalized and subtracted from the selling price. Thus, if a larger share of revenues is assigned by either jurisdiction to the land tax in the hope of attracting more residents so as to produce capital gains for existing residents, the upward impact on land prices of this greater migration is offset to some extent by the backward shifting of the land tax. The net effect depends on specifics of the relationships.

Jurisdictional Rivalry

Given our assumptions of constant population and business in the metropolitan area, every use by a jurisdiction of its long-run policy instruments to gain higher utility for its existing residents by influencing further migration comes *at the expense of the other jurisdiction* (although not necessarily in zero-sum fashion). Moreover, the particular long-run adjustment that will be profitable depends in the general case on the particular levels at which the other jurisdiction's policy instruments stand.

So we may think of a sequential long-run process that begins when one jurisdiction sets its long-run policies. This setting determines where it is worthwhile for the second to set its instruments. But the setting of the second's policies now makes it worthwhile for the first to adjust its instruments. This change in the first's instrument settings changes the second jurisdiction's optimal policies—and so on.

The process is a familiar one of duopolistic strategic interaction. Whether or not the process converges to a joint equilibrium where both long- and short-run adjustments are mutually compatible depends on the particular conjectural variation functions of the two. Analysis of conditions for stability is beyond the scope of this chapter. Two observations can be made about qualitative aspects of the interaction in conclusion, however.

First, the two jurisdictions are not symmetrical in their rivalrous relationship. Because of its spatially enclosed (and fully developed) character and its lower average household income level, encouraging additional migration to the city, starting at any particular situation, is very likely to be beneficial for preexisting city residents, since it bids up city land prices (giving capital gains) and lowers the price of public services. Crowding is worsened but is not a matter for deep concern by the relatively poor population. Thus the city in general wants to become bigger.

For the suburb, additional migration brings a smaller average capital gain because of additional land conversion (the total potential capital gains have to be shared among a larger number of lots). Moreover, although the price of public services rises here too, increasing crowdedness occurs as well, and here it *is* a matter for concern, because the preexisting residents are richer and care more to retain uncrowded conditions. Indeed, the suburb has a specialized function as an area of low crowding. So, while the suburb wants more population in some circumstances, this desire is not unlimited: it has to balance its specialized low-density role with the possibility of more (but marginally falling) jurisdictional advantages and land capital gains.

In this strange game of tug-of-war, then, what one side gains is not always equal to what the other side loses. It is as though as the rope is pulled triumphantly closer, part of it dissolves and part of it grows.

Second, to indicate that the strategic game might in some cases have no harmonious resolution—that it might be unstable—does not thereby disqualify it as a paradigm of the real world. The time scale on which we count the model's so-called short-run responses, not to speak of the long-run responses, is a long one. Over the decades or so necessary for a set of strategic iterations to occur, real-world observations would also presumably show a number of broadly oscillatory movements. It is somewhat presumptuous to judge these movements after a much shorter experience with the modern metropolitan area as reflective of a grand general equilibrium. Our experience of city and suburb has, after all, been one of constant change, not of serene balance.

Notes

1. See Tiebout (1956) and, for example, Boskin (1973), Buchanan and Goetz (1972), Ellickson (1971), McGuire (1971), Oates (1972), and Rothenberg (1970a, 1970b, and forthcoming).

2. In the real world, individual tastes for crowdedness of the social space appear to differ markedly, being a positive good for some. The present treatment is based on the presumed average attitude in postwar urban America.

3. This is tantamount to including only out-of-pocket costs and assuming a single travel mode. This is not so much at variance as it seems with the oft-presumed importance of travel time, with its supposed large utility differences for different income groups. In a system with different travel modes, richer households are likely to choose higher money cost and quicker modes where long trips are involved, poorer households choosing lower money cost but slower modes. Our single, constant "cost" mode represents a fair compromise to this trade-off.

4. This formulation has a classic presentation in Alonso (1964). Other important treatments are Wingo (1961), Muth (1969), Herbert and Stevens (1960), and Kain (1962).

5. The identity of the N_2^o is not random. The trade-off involved is travel costs for land costs. Households buying larger lots are likely to benefit more from the trade than those buying smaller lots and so will be the households migrating under the differential price. Thus each household will be only *marginally* indifferent between city and suburb: everyone would lose if the assignment between city and suburb were reversed.

6. Consistent with many empirical studies [see, for example, Muth (1969), Mills (1970, 1972), and Niedercorn (1971)].

7. Single-peakedness is a property of the *set* of voter preference, such that everyone's preferences can be registered on the *same* single spatial array of alternatives in terms of a most preferred position, and a set of spatial relations, such that relative distances in the same direction from this preferred position are

isomorphic with order of preference, and distance itself becomes a measure of preference intensity. Thus, while all individuals may have different preferences toward a set of alternatives, they all nonetheless share a common perspective about the structure of the differences among these alternatives [see Black (1958) and Arrow (1963)].

8. To avoid strategic misrepresentation of preferences in the course of voting.

9. See Black (1958) and Arrow (1963) for discussion of inferences from single-peaked preference-voting situations.

10. As I noted at the beginning, not all the suburb's area is developed for urban use. Nonurban use does not depend on urban accessibility. Therefore, we assume that from $k = k^*$, the boundary separating urban from nonurban use, to $k = K$, the jurisdictional boundary, land price is not a function of k and can be treated as a constant, P_{L_F}. A more explicit statement of (11.8b) is therefore:

$$T_2 = \tau_2 \bar{Y}_2 N_2 + \int_0^{k^*} t_{L_2} P_{L_2}(k) a(k)\, dk + t_{L_2} P_{L_F} [A_2 - \int_0^{k^*} a(k)\, dk] \qquad (11.8b')$$

A_2 is the total private area of the suburb, so the last term is the revenues from the nonurban portion and the middle term is the revenues from the urban portion.

11. For a discussion of some of the properties of pure-public, pure-private, and quasi-public (mixed) goods, see Samuelson (1969), Musgrave and Musgrave (1976), and Buchanan (1968).

12. See my earlier treatment, e.g., in Rothenberg (1967).

13. Optimal use is achieved when it is expanded to the point where the marginal increase in financial offset just equals the marginal real cost to the city (in administrative cost, resident incidence, and resource allocation).

14. This should more properly be interpreted as the probability that a household in i will be a welfare recipient.

15. Compare this treatment with others in the literature, e.g., Bailey (1959), Davis (1959), Stull (1972), and Siegan (1970).

16. Assume that a household obtains utility only from public services that it consumes in its resident jurisdiction. Those used—impinged on—in the other jurisdiction are deemed to be inadvertent and nonvalued elements of the job or shopping, etc., purpose of the transjurisdictional visits. This could be relaxed but at a cost of some complexity.

17. For a broader perspective on the relationship between jurisdictional fragmentation and the governmental income-redistribution function, see Rothenberg (1970a).

18. Under this treatment, adjacent parcels of land on the two sides of the suburb-city boundary will show a price discontinuity, since not only accessibility (in which they differ very little) but jurisdictional characteristics (in which they

may differ greatly) influence price. This differs from the classic "homogeneous" land-market theories, e.g., Alonso (1964) and Muth (1969). It is more akin to zoning or segregation models, e.g., Stull (1972) and Kain and Quigley (1975).

References

Alonso, W. 1964. *Location and Land Use: Toward a General Theory of Land Rent.* Cambridge: Harvard University Press.

Arrow, K. 1963. *Social Choice and Individual Values*, 2d edition. New York: John Wiley.

Bailey, M.J. 1959. Note on the economics of residential zoning and urban renewal. *Land Economics* 35:288-292.

Black, D. 1958. *The Theory of Committees and Elections.* Cambridge: Cambridge University Press.

Boskin, M. 1973. Local government tax and product competition and the optimal provision of public goods. *Journal of Political Economy* 81:203-210.

Buchanan, J.M. 1968. *The Demand and Supply of Public Goods.* Chicago: Rand McNally.

Buchanan, J.M., and Goetz, C.J. 1972. Efficiency limits of fiscal mobility: An assessment of the Tiebout model. *Journal of Public Economics* 1:25-43.

Davis, O.A. 1959. Economic elements in municipal zoning decisions. *Land Economics* 35:288-292.

Ellickson, B. 1971. Jurisdictional fragmentation and residential choice. *American Economic Review, Papers and Proceedings* 61:334-340.

Herbert, J.P., and Stevens, B.H. 1960. A model for the distribution of residential activity in urban areas. *Journal of Regional Science* 2:21-36.

Kain, J.F. 1962. The journey-to-work as a determinant of residential location. *Papers and Proceedings of the Regional Science Association* 9:137-160.

Kain, J., and Quigley, J. 1975. *Housing Markets and Racial Discrimination.* New York: National Bureau of Economic Research.

McGuire, M. 1971. Group Segregation and Optimal Jurisdictions. Paper presented at the meeting of the Committee on Urban Public Economics. Toronto.

Mills, E.S. 1970. Urban density functions. *Urban Studies* 7:5-20.

Mills, E.S. 1972. *Studies in the Structure of the Urban Economy.* Baltimore: Johns Hopkins University Press for Resources for the Future.

Musgrave, R.A., and Musgrave, P.B. 1976. *Public Finance in Theory and Practice*, 2nd edition. New York: McGraw-Hill.

Muth, R.F. 1969. *Cities and Housing.* Chicago: University of Chicago Press.

Niedercorn, J.H. 1971. A negative exponential model of urban land use densities and its implications for metropolitan development. *Journal of Regional Science* 11:317-326

Oates, W. 1972. *Fiscal Federalism.* New York: Harcourt Brace Jovanovich.

Rothenberg, J. 1967. *Benefit-Cost Analysis of Urban Renewal.* Washington: The Brookings Institution.

Rothenberg, J. 1970a. Local decentralization and the theory of optimal government. In *The Analysis of Public Output,* J. Margolis, ed. New York: Columbia University Press. pp. 31–64.

Rothenberg, J. 1970b. The impact of local government on intrametropolitan location. *Papers and Proceedings of the Regional Science Association* 24:47–81.

Rothenberg, J. Forthcoming. 'Inadvertent' distributional impacts in a provision of public services to individuals. In *Essays in Honor of William Vickrey,* Ronald Grieson, ed. Lexington, Mass.: D.C. Heath.

Samuelson, P.A. 1969. Pure theory of public expenditures and taxation. In *Public Economics*, J. Margolis and H. Guitton, eds. New York: St. Martins.

Siegan, B.H. 1970. Nonzoning in Houston. *Journal of Law and Economics* 13:71–147.

Stull, W. 1972. *An Essay in Externalities, Property Values and Urban Zoning.* Ph.D. dissertation. M.I.T.

Tiebout, C.M. 1956. A pure theory of local expenditures. *Journal of Political Economy* 64:416-424.

Wingo, L., Jr. 1961. *Transportation and Urban Land.* Washington: Resources for the Future, Inc.

12

Intergovernmental Grants: A Review of the Empirical Literature

Edward M. Gramlich

Intergovernmental grants are a newly discovered object of fascination among public-finance economists. At the policy level, grants have become important because they are viewed as a means by which countries can compromise the desire of the central government to expand services, to equalize local incomes, or to make greater use of the central-government tax base without directly assuming the functional spending responsibilities of lower levels of government. Public-finance theorists have followed this interest, giving now much greater attention to such questions as the underlying rationale for different types of grants, analysis of the lower-government budgetary response to grants, and the development of criteria determining how grant money should be allocated to different areas and types of governments.

There has always been a voluminous empirical literature on the budgetary effects of intergovernmental grants. Until five years ago the dominant species was the "determinants" study of local-government expenditures. The typical determinants study consisted of a regression model explaining local-government expenditures, almost always on a cross-section basis for United States' state or local governments, using independent variables, such as income, population, population density, urbanization, and federal grants. The studies generally showed strong and quite significant coefficients for grants, though the results were accepted less than unanimously because of various conceptual and technical problems with the studies—lack of an underlying theory of the behavior of state and local governments, lack of any attempt to distinguish the different effects of different types of grants, lack of any attempt to deal with the possible simultaneous causation of grants and expenditures. In more recent times, the simple determinants study has given way to a somewhat more thorough analysis that shows at least some recognition of these methodological problems and makes at least some attempt to correct them. There have also been a few attempts to strike out in other directions and estimate the budgetary impact of grants in new and different ways. The upshot, as I will attempt to show, is that now the profession should be able to trust most of the broad empirical results of the grants literature—at least for the United States. As empirical studies in economics go, the remaining reservations to some of these results seem relatively harmless. Despite the fact that many of these broad questions seem reasonably well settled, however, there remain many other questions that have not been treated either extensively or well, and where future work could pay large dividends.

This chapter will attempt to summarize the empirical work on the budgetary impact of intergovernmental grants. The summary will necessarily be brief and will not touch on all contributions made in the area—a sheer impossibility given the volume of the literature (in the past 15 years there have been well over a hundred articles and a few books on this topic). The chapter begins where it ought to—with the theory of grants. It examines the underlying theoretical justification for grants, how different types of grants should affect the budgetary behavior of lower levels of government, how this behavior would be altered when these governments are trying to achieve different objectives, and how the effectiveness of grants in achieving central-government objectives should be evaluated. It then examines the empirical literature, assessing the extent to which these findings do or do not corroborate various theoretical points and the extent to which they have or have not addressed all of the relevant and interesting questions. Finally, it concludes with a few thoughts on where future empirical work on grants ought to be headed.

Justification for Grants

There have been several commonly suggested rationales for intergovernmental grants. In general, they fall into two categories—economic justifications, where one can show that the central government could have efficiency, equity, or stabilization objectives that impinge on local governments in various ways, and political or institutional justifications, where it seems more natural to view the lower level of government as agents of central-government policy.

Economic Justifications

The justification most commonly cited in the literature is benefit spillovers. While various authors state the principle in different ways, the general idea is that not all of the benefits of a local expenditure are captured within the community: therefore, other communities, or the central government acting as their agent, should subsidize the first community's purchase of this good or service. This is done by a Pigovian price-reduction grant, according to which the central government will match all state or local expenditures on the project [see, for example, Break (1967) and Thurow (1966)]. To avoid repeating awkward terms, I will call these open-ended matching grants, which alter the relative prices facing lower levels of government, *case A grants*.

A second justification for grants regards, in one way or another, the distribution of income. Since the benefits of the expenditures of lower levels of government accrue more or less proportionately to all income groups, or are even focused on low-income groups somewhat disproportionately [Gillespie (1965)], there is an innate limit to the degree to which local governments can, on their own, impose progressive taxes. If the net of tax revenues paid to lower levels of government less expenditures benefits received from them becomes too large for any business or income group, that group will simply pick up stakes and locate in some jurisdiction that assesses it a less onerous "fiscal residuum" [the term is Buchanan's (1950)]. Thus it makes perfectly good theoretical sense for state and local taxes to be, on the whole, somewhat regressive,[1] and also for the central government, less concerned by any "flight" of its businesses or high-income groups, to try to rectify the distributional implications by imposing progressive taxes of its own and even sharing to some degree the fruits of these taxes with state and local governments. This line of reasoning could justify a program of central-government unconditional grants or closed-end lump-sum transfers to lower levels of government. I will label these grants, which alter the incomes available to lower levels of government but not the relative prices facing them, *case B grants*.

An extension of this argument could justify a revenue-sharing program more focused on poor jurisdictions. As long as the net fiscal residual for high-income groups is greater than that for low-income groups, as it clearly seems to be on average [Netzer (1974)], it will be more advantageous to locate in high-income than low-income communities. In addition to having high incomes and presumably greater spending on public services, households of any income will face lower tax prices for local public services in high-income communities. If these services—health, education, public safety, or whatever—should from a social point of view be provided at equal cost in the two communities, or more cheaply in low-income communities, the central government will also have a reason for redistributing income among communities—giving to low-income communities and taking away from (or not giving to) high-income communities. This would be another justification for case B grants of a redistributive nature [Musgrave (1961)].[2]

A different type of argument regards economic-stabilization considerations. Conventional Keynesian theory dictates using the monetary and fiscal powers of the government to stabilize private spending and employment in a business cycle. If so, why should the central-government budget not also be used to stabilize local-government public spending and employment? If anything, stability in the services offered by the public sector seems a more worthwhile aim than stability in those offered by the private sector. This consideration would again argue for a program of case B grants to lower levels of governments, with the level dependent on the degree of overall unemployment.[3] The same consideration would, of course, argue for taxes on local governments in a boom period, but rare is the real-world central-government politician who would propose such a thing.

Political-Institutional Justifications

While the foregoing arguments have undoubtedly played some role in the development of central-government grant programs as we now know them, a political-institutional justification has probably played an even more important role in most developed countries. There are very good democratic reasons to try to keep power close to the people by having strong and vigorous local governments. At the same time, central governments have increasingly become more ambitious in trying to establish minimum service or spending levels for different government-provided goods and services. A reasonable way to compromise these partially conflicting objectives is for the central government to give closed-ended categorical grants to local governments. This technique preserves local control over the relevant functional category of expenditures but yet allows the central government to upgrade local spending. It does not, however, allow the local government as much freedom as it would have with an open-ended price-reduction grant: the central government maintains control over its own budget by limiting the total amount of funds available to lower governments. The central government will typically also establish rather tight conditions on the uses to which the money can be put, the degree to which local governments can cut back other spending, and so forth. The most natural way to think of these grants then, as argued by Hicks (1968) and Schultze (1974), may be as a device by which local governments are acting as the agents, or contractors, for the central government in carrying out specified tasks. I will call these grants, which can be thought of as affecting both the relative prices and incomes facing lower levels of government, *case C grants*.

The Impact of Different Types of Grants

Standard indifference-curve theory can be used to indicate the effect of these different types of grants on the budgets of lower levels of government [the earliest example is Scott (1952), the most complete is Wilde (1971)]. For case A grants, which simply imply a reduction in the relative price of the grant-aided good, expenditures will increase by an amount depending on the price elasticity of demand: if expenditure demand is price elastic, total (lower plus higher levels of government) expenditures on grant-aided goods will increase by more than the grant, and expenditures on all other goods will decline; vice versa if expenditure demand is price inelastic. In Figure 12–1, if we represent grant-aided goods or public expenditures, along the abscissa and private goods consumed by the

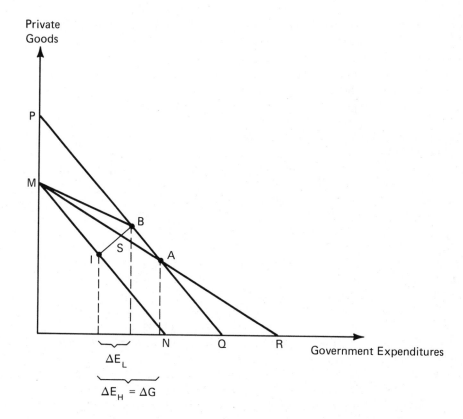

Figure 12–1. The Effect of Grants on Lower-Government Budgets.

community along the ordinate, and if the community was initially located at point I, a reduction in the price of the grant-aided good to MR will increase expenditures by IA, which here is exactly equal to the size of the grant. Thus the partial derivative of expenditures with respect to grants, $\delta E/\delta G$, is equal to unity for this case of a unitary price elasticity of demand. Were price elasticity greater than unity, the community would move to some point along AR and $(\delta E/\delta G) > 1$; were the price elasticity less than unity the community would be on SA and $\delta E/\delta G < 1$; were the price-substitution effect of the change in prices absent, only the income effect would come into play and the community would move along its income-consumption curve to point S. If for purposes of standardization we put everything in terms of a grant of constant size $\Delta G = IA$, the distance ΔE_L (from the income-consumption curve) is the minimum that expenditures should increase in response to an open-ended grant of size ΔG, and ΔE_H is the maximum in the sense that the full price-substitution effect implied by this price elasticity takes place.

Case B grants change the income of the community and not relative prices and, if both public and private goods have positive income elasticities, will move the community to point B. The change in expenditures is again ΔE_L, which will usually be less than the grant so the $0 < (\delta E/\delta G) < 1$. The first inequality will be true as long as there is a positive income elasticity of demand for public goods, the second as long as the same condition holds for private goods. Even though the response of expenditures is smaller, however, the local government still has its freedom and enjoys a higher indifference level than with the same sized grant of type A.

Case C grants represent the intermediate possibility, and the community will go somewhere along the line segment AB for a grant of size ΔG. If the grant of ΔG reduces the price of public goods to MR, the community with unitary price elasticity will go to point A, use up all of the grant funds, and have a value of $(\delta E/\delta G) = 1$. Since the community must match central-government money with its own to get the full grant, the fact that the net value of $\delta E/\delta G$ is only one implies that this community is also reducing spending on public goods it would otherwise have undertaken, a phenomenon known in the literature as the "grant displacement" effect.[4] As the central-government matching provisions become more generous and the price of public goods is reduced to MB, the community wants more of the grant, the constant funds limit allows the community to take less and less advantage of the price reduction, the community is moved from point A to B, and the change in expenditures falls from ΔE_H to ΔE_L. As the price of public goods is reduced even further (angle PMB is reduced toward $90°$), the limit on funds becomes so binding that further price reductions are useless, the community remains at B, and the grant becomes like a case B grant with income effects only. Thus, beginning with relatively unfavorable matching ratios, grants of a constant size ΔG in effect pass from case A to case C to case B types as the matching ratio becomes steadily more favorable and the funds limit steadily more binding, ultimately totally dominating and making irrelevant the price reduction.

The same phenomenon can be demonstrated alternatively, this time holding the price ratio constant at MR and varying the central-government funds limit. If the limit is such that the maximum possible grant can exceed ΔG, the limit obviously becomes irrelevant for this community, it stays at A, and the grant is case A. As the limit is reduced below ΔG, the community moves along line segment SA and the smaller grant would be considered case C. Once the limit on the grant moves the community to S, further reductions push the community along IS and the grant would be considered case B. The result is again that a case C grant can only become a case A grant when the limit is great enough that it is nonbinding and marginal changes in the price become fully operative; and it can only become a case B grant when the limit is tight enough that marginal changes in the price become irrelevant.

Even though this analysis is devoid of any number of real-world complications, it can already have quite complex empirical implications. The impact of grants on the budgetary position of lower levels of government depends on whether grants alter just the income constraint or that plus the relative prices facing local governments. That in turn depends upon the underlying community price and income elasticities of demand for public goods, the degree of relative price reduction, and the maximum size of grant the central government will allow. The only firm prediction of the model is that for any particular type of good, the expenditure impact, $\delta E/\delta G$, will be greatest for case A grants, next greatest for case C grants, and smallest for case B grants. Even this prediction, however, hinges on the underlying assumption that public goods are reasonably homogeneous and that communities are attempting to maximize some vague phenomenon known as *aggregate community welfare.* If these assumptions are relaxed, as they should be, things become even more complex.

The first assumption to be relaxed is that government expenditures are homogeneous. If they are not, it may become physically impossible for the lower government to displace as many expenditures as would be predicted by the above analysis because the expenditures may not be there in the first place. Similar restrictions on displacement could be obtained if the grant came with effective effort-maintenance provisions that tried to preclude displacement. The result is that if case C grants were for new and nondisplacable programs or with effort-maintenance restrictions, they could in principle show larger expenditure inducements ($\delta E/\delta G$) than would case A grants without such side conditions in the same functional area.

In similar fashion, the joint objectives of the community might be more complicated. The indifference-curve, utility-function-maximization approach to state and local behavior [Henderson (1968), Gramlich (1969a), and others] assumes that the community is rationally trying to maximize some concept of utility that can be that of the median voter or the median voter as somehow perceived by politicians. It does not assume a disharmony of interests between politicians and voters. But if some disharmony exists, different results obtain. In the harmonious world, for example, it should not matter whether the central government cuts taxes or gives revenue-sharing funds to local governments. As long as the income-distributional properties are the same, either measure should increase public spending by the income elasticity of demand, with the remainder going into increased private spending [Oates (1972)]. If a central-government tax cut of $1 would raise local spending and taxes by $0.10, central-government revenue sharing of $1 would also raise local spending by $0.10, lower local taxes by $0.90, and raise total local revenues (taxes plus grants) also by $0.10. As classical economists might say, revenue sharing is a veil for the tax cut.

But what if there is disharmony? What if local politicians feel they can fool the people by not cutting taxes the full $0.90 in response to revenue sharing, even though they would only dare raise them $0.10 in response to a central-government tax cut? Then the initial incidence of the money does become important, revenue sharing is not a veil, and the impact of revenue sharing on case B grants cannot be reliably predicted from the response of public expenditures to private incomes. The phenomenon might be called the *flypaper theory of incidence*: money sticks where it hits.[5]

This interesting case has been generalized by Niskanen (1968) and McGuire (1973). McGuire postulates what might be termed a *greedy politicians model*, where local politicians respond to any grant program by spending all they can get their hands on as long as private households are not made worse off in the process. In this case, all types of grants have identical effects—local-government spending rises by slightly more than the full amount of the grant.[6] McGuire neither necessarily believes nor has tested this model, but this line of reasoning does open up additional possibilities by which the response of lower levels of government to various types of grants may not be easily or rigorously predicted from the "theory."

How Should Grants Be Evaluated?

The preceding remarks provide a fairly clear indication of the type of questions any empirical evaluations of grants should deal with. For case A and C grants, the central government is expressly trying to stimulate spending in a certain area. It then becomes logical to ask how much spending was stimulated, whether the displacement effect mitigated the impact of the grant, whether limitations on central-government spending or effort-maintenance provisions were necessary to restrict the outflow of federal funds or to attain a desired degree of spending, whether matching provisions should be altered, and so forth. These questions have all come up in one way or another in the United States in recent years. A first illustration was the attempt of the Nixon administration to fold several categorical case C grants into special revenue sharing—a closed-ended grant program that defines eligible spending very broadly and thus allows so much displacement that it is probably very close to a case B grant; a second is the recently passed public-service employment provision, which again, because of the many types of employment eligible, is likely to turn into a case B grant and frustrate the attempt of Congress to prevent employment displacement.

Beyond this, of course, there are always the fundamental questions. Whether or not grant program X induced displacement, did it achieve its underlying objective of improving education, training workers, cleaning up the atmosphere, or whatever? Introducing these issues raises the vast questions of program evaluation, which I will not go into here in the interest of brevity. Yet to the extent that the data will support it, it should always be pointed out that expenditures and expenditure impacts are not everything, that what this branch of public finance is and should be all about is whether government programs of whatever type are ultimately doing what they ought to.

For case B grants, the relevant questions become both broader and narrower than simply what lower governments are doing with the money. Since the objective of the program is not so much to encourage spending on a particular program or type of program (though people would be less interested in revenue sharing if local governments were not responsible for many "needed" public services) but to modify the distribution of income, there should be less interest in the question of what local governments are doing with the money. Simply knowing that they got it is enough. But since redistribution is a prime goal, the first important question is to ask which governments in fact did get the money and whether they were the ones that should have gotten it. In the United States, this has led into a whole set of articles on the distributional virtues and anomalies of the new general revenue-sharing legislation [see, for example, Nathan, Manvel, and Calkins (1975), Strauss (1974), Reischauer (forthcoming)]. Much interest also attaches to the question of whether general revenue sharing will heighten citizen interest in local government, rationalize or worsen the somewhat haphazard pattern of overlapping local general governments and special districts, improve management, or whatever. Some have even inquired into whether general revenue sharing will "revitalize federalism," a question that seems likely to have some problems at the definitional level.

The Empirical Work on Intergovernmental Grants

To this point, virtually all empirical work on the effect of grants on lower levels of government has been concerned with the United States.[7] Accordingly, this summary will also limit itself to the United States, though it should obviously be recognized that the lessons are of more general relevance. If U.S. empirical work has been successful, scholars in other countries have a leg up in trying to understand their own grants; if U.S. work is not successful, other scholars can avoid making the same mistakes.

Case A Grants

Although most public-finance discussions of grants begin with case A grants—which reduce the relative prices of designated public services provided by local government—examples of these grants in the United States are relatively rare. At the federal level, the only case A grants are for public assistance ($5.4 billion in fiscal 1974) and medicaid ($5.8 billion), now comprising about 25 percent of total federal government grant expenditures. Some state governments also have case A grants in the area of education and other social services.

Since case A grants are open-ended, the level of the grant is determined simultaneously with and as part of the level of expenditures. Most empirical attempts at estimating the impact of public-assistance grants on expenditures have ignored this complication and have simply regressed the level of expenditures on the level of grants across states, in all cases finding $\delta E/\delta G$ to be greater than unity and, implicitly, the price elasticity of demand to be greater than unity also [see Albin and Stein (1971), Osman (1966), Sacks and Harris (1964)]. It is very likely the case, however, that this high estimated effect represents nothing more than simultaneous-equations bias in the coefficient of federal aid and should not be trusted [Oates (1968), Pogue and Sgontz (1968)]. In the one case where federal-assistance parameters were treated properly [Orr (forthcoming)], using an exogenous indication of the true "after-match" price of welfare within the framework of a theoretically consistent model of income redistribution across states and for different dates, the effective price elasticity of demand for public assistance came out to be −0.23 — implying that welfare grants stimulate a relatively small amount of state and local expenditures. With this elasticity, the implied value of $\delta E/\delta G$ in 1970 is only 0.15.

Most indications are that other case A grants are more stimulative. The evidence is very sketchy for medicaid, where there are not even biased regression studies to use as a guide. The only real examination of medicaid was by Gayer (1972), who tested for changes in the ratio of medicaid expenditures to all state and local expenditures or state and local health expenditures between 1965 (before medicaid) and 1968 (after medicaid was introduced). Although this comparison cannot give very fine-grained results, Gayer did find that after correcting for premedicaid upward trends in expenditures, total state and local expenditures seem to have increased as a result of medicaid but not own expenditures. The implied value for $\delta E/\delta G$ is, in other words, not significantly different from unity. Gayer also found that treatment standards among states have not been equalized as a result of medicaid.

Most evidence on the impact of state case A grants on expenditures also suggests values of $\delta E/\delta G$ between zero and unity. Gramlich and Galper (1973) found values ranging slightly above and below 0.8 in a pooled cross-sectional sample of ten large cities for the categories: urban support, social services, and public safety. Fairly similar results were reported by Inman (1971) for a larger cross section of cities. Feldstein (1975) found price elasticities of demand for education of unity or slightly greater in a study of Massachusetts towns aimed at determining how state matching-grant formulas should be written to neutralize the impact of community wealth on local education expenditures. But Ohls and Wales (1972) found negligible price elasticities of demand (in effect, very small values of $\delta E/\delta G$ for case A grants) across states in all areas except highways. Other cross-sectional studies of local governments, not dealing specifically with grants, have found price elasticities of demand for local services in the neighborhood of unity [Borcherding and Deacon (1972)] or closer to zero [Bergstram and Goodman (1973)].

Case B Grants

The second important type of grant program is that which provides lower levels of government with closed-ended unconditional grant assistance—so-called case B grants. Apart from a few very small programs, these grants had not been used at all by the U.S. government until 1972 when the widely discussed general revenue-sharing program began disbursing approximately $6 billion in aid to state and local governments. In fiscal 1974 these case B grants amounted to 14 percent of total federal assistance to states and localities. Case B grants are also used in several other countries—notably Australia, Canada, and West Germany—generally as part of a treaty or other arrangement dividing up taxing powers between different levels of government. There are also many state case B grants to local general governments or school districts.[8]

Because of the newness of general revenue sharing in the United States, there have not been a great number of statistical studies of its budgetary impact [though many are on the way; the National Planning Association (1974) and and the U.S. National Science Foundation (1975)]. One early attempt at "monitoring" revenue sharing by trained field observers in 63 different state or local governments [see Nathan, Manvel, and Calkins (1975)] concluded that 26 percent of the revenue-sharing money led to new spending, another 15 percent to maintenance of programs that otherwise would have been cut, 30 percent to tax cuts or avoiding tax increases, and the remainder into increases in fund balances and/or avoidance of borrowing. These percentages were essentially the same for states and localities, with local governments spending slightly more—possibly because of certain legal requirements attempting to limit spending reductions for local but not state governments. The results are based on survey data and have all the strengths and weaknesses of such studies—they can be more refined and subtle than regression studies, but they can also be less uniform and harder to validate or disprove. They also have the particular disadvantage that they are monitoring only the very short-run impact of revenue sharing on state-local expenditures. It has been argued, for example, that early responses to federal revenue sharing are contaminated by the fact that lower levels of government may have invested extraordinary proportions of the funds in capital projects because of the fear that the program would be cut off.

Concerning the regression studies, Gramlich and Galper (1973) found in time-series regressions for the aggregate state and local sector up to 1972 that the response of expenditures to changes in unconditional budgetary resources of all sorts implied that about $0.43 per dollar of case B grants would go into expenditures in the long run, very close to the spending impact implied by the survey of Nathan et al. This estimate was a prediction of the impact of revenue sharing before the fact—based on the degree to which such "exogenous" budget-ary claims as interest and debt retirement reduced discretionary expenditures—

and while it was not specific to revenue sharing, it also did not have the short-run–long-run problem of Nathan et al. A similar analysis for a pooled cross-sectional sample of 10 large urban governments, this time with some state revenue-sharing money in the budgetary variable, led to coefficients ($\delta E/\delta G$) on the order of 0.25. Other regression estimates in the same general range were made by Feldstein (1975) for state block grants to Massachusetts towns, by Bowman (1974) for West Virginia untied aid to independent school districts, and by Weicher (1972) for untied state school aid to school districts in cities where the district is fiscally independent. At the same time, the coefficients are well below those estimated by Inman (1971) for a panel of cities and again by Weicher for untied aid to municipal governments: both of the latter studies found that almost all case B aid would result in higher expenditures [$\delta E/\delta G$ = 1] with virtually nothing left over for tax reduction. Whether half or all the revenue-sharing money goes into higher expenditures, however, at this point all empirical studies indicate long-run responses appreciably greater than would be implied by the response of expenditures to changes in income—which in vitually all studies comes out to be between 0.05 and 0.10 (implying an income elasticity in the neighborhood of unity). Hence the empirical work to this point strongly suggests that revenue sharing is not a veil for tax cuts—that it does make an appreciable difference in the pattern of expenditures whether the federal government disburses untied aid to state and local governments or makes untied tax cuts benefiting individuals. The results are so striking that the field could well use more theory [perhaps of the Niskanen-McGuire variety] on whether and under what conditions the standard indifference-curve, utility-maximization analysis had better give way to a variant more cognizant of political realities.

In this connection, one of the interesting findings on the probable impact of revenue sharing comes from Weicher (1972). Designers of the general revenue-sharing bill have worried a great deal about which jurisdictions serving a particular area should get the money—should it go to states, counties, towns, villages, overlapping special districts, or whatever? The implication of the veil line of thought is that it does not much matter—if an independent school board gets money, it will lower taxes, allow general governments to raise taxes, and all types of spending will increase; if the school board does not get money, the greater reduction in general government taxes will still allow school boards to raise taxes and again all types of spending will increase. To test hypotheses of this sort, Weicher regressed both municipal and school-district expenditures on a set of variables including cast B state aid to the town and to the other government cross sectionally for 120 large cities with independent school districts. For aid to school districts, he got the expected result that both school and municipal expenditures increase, the former more than the latter, with the total spending coefficient for school aid equal to 0.59—close to that of Nathan et al., Gramlich and Galper, Feldstein, and Bowman. But for untied aid to municipal governments, he found that *school* expenditures increased more, so much so that the total spending coefficient ($\delta E/\delta G$) for case B grants to municipal governments was almost unity. This result, if credible, gives an ambiguous verdict on the veil theory—on the one hand, the theory might be rejected because the net spending impact is so much higher than that for income; on the other hand, it might be accepted because the form of certain types of aid does not appear to matter much. School districts appear to get their cut whether they are or are not directly aided. This finding again should stimulate more examination into the way that governments, particularly overlapping governments, really work.

Case C Grants

Traditionally, the most important type of grant at the federal level has been the closed-ended conditional grant, or case C grant. In fiscal 1974 these grants accounted for $26.8 billion, 61 percent of total grants, in such areas as highways, health, education, manpower, and the environment. The proportion has declined in recent years, however. A few years ago, before the initiation of general revenue sharing and the rapid growth in public assistance and medicaid, it was over 70 percent.[9]

Just as case C grants have received most of the money, they have been the grants ultimately dealt with in most empirical studies of federal aid. The usual approach has been to estimate the spending impact of these grants by regressing the level of total expenditures or expenditures from own funds [as long as one remembers what one is doing, it does not matter which; see Gramlich (1972)] on grants and a set of other independent variables. This technique does not lead to the obvious upward bias in the estimated impact that exists for case A grants, because case C grants are, after all, closed-ended and therefore in principle not simultaneously determined with expenditures. Yet there is a different possible bias relating to the fact that grants are recorded when the money is spent, which is usually the same time that the expenditure is made. There seems to be little question that this type of simultaneous-equations bias led to an excessively high impact of grants on lower-government expenditures in some of the early studies, though more recent studies that have dealt more carefully with simultaneity have not found the bias to be terribly significant [O'Brien (1971) and Horowitz (1968)].

The spending coefficients for federal case C grants on expenditures in 24 recent studies are given in Table 12-1.[10] The estimated values of $\delta E/\delta G$ range between the value of 2.45 for Kurnow, the very first study to use grants as an independent variable, to 0.32 for Bolton, with the mean estimated effect equaling 1.40. If there are any patterns to the results, the early cross-sectional estimates seem to be higher than the later time-series or pooled-cross-sectional estimates and also higher than the amount mandated by the matching formula

Table 12–1
The Impact of Case Grants on Expenditures: Results of Various Regressions Studies for $\partial E/\partial G$

Author	Sample	Date	Dependent Variable	Independent Variable	Result, $\partial E/\partial G$
Kurnow (1963)	48 States	1957	St. Loc. Exp.	Fed. Grants	2.45[a]
Pidot (1969)	81 Large Met. Areas	1962	Met. Exp.	Fed. Grants	2.35
Johnson & Junk (1970)	43 Largest Cities	1967	City Exp.	Fed. & St. Grants	2.02
Osman (1966)	48 States	1960	St. Loc. Exp.	Fed. Grants	1.94
Pogue & Sgontz (1968)	50 States Pooled	1958–64	St. Loc. Exp.	Fed. Grants	1.81[b]
Harlow (1967)	48 States	1957	St. Exp.	Fed. Grants	1.80
Brazer (1959)	462 Cities	1951	City Current Exp.	Fed. & St. Grants	1.74
Petersen (1968)	50 States Pooled	1962–3	St. Loc. Exp.	Fed. current Grants	1.70
Smith (1968)	50 States	1965	St. Loc. Exp.	Fed. Grants	1.66
Booms & Hu (1971)	50 States	1960	St. Loc. Ed. Exp.	Fed. Ed. Grants	1.61
Campbell & Sacks (1967)	48 States	1962	St. Loc. Exp.	Fed. Grants	1.56
Sacks & Harris (1964)	48 States	1960	St. Loc. Exp.	Fed. Grants	1.55
Henderson (1968)	100 Met. Counties	1957	County Exp.	Fed. & St. Grants	1.42
Bahl & Saunders (1966)	48 States	1957–60	St. Loc. Exp.	Fed. Grants	1.36
Horowitz (1968)	50 States	1962	St. Loc. Exp.	Fed. Grants	1.26
O'Brien (1971)	48 States Pooled	1958–66	St. Loc. Exp.	Fed. Grants	1.19
Bowman (1974)	55 W. Va. Counties	1969–70	Loc. Sch. Taxes	Fed. Ed. Grants	1.06[c]
Henderson (1968)	2,980 Non-Met. Counties	1957	County Exp.	Fed. & St. Grants	1.04
Adams (1966)	1,249 Counties	1959	County Taxes	Fed. Grants	0.96[c]
Gramlich & Galper (1973)	76 Quarters	1954–72	St. Loc. Exp.	Fed. Grants	0.90
Ehrenberg (1971)	50 States Pooled	1958–69	St. Loc. Empl. Exp.	Fed. Grants	.79[a]
Gramlich & Galper (1973)	10 City-Counties Pooled	1962–70	Loc. Exp.	Fed. & St. Grants	0.65
Phelps (1969)	16 Years	1951–66	St. Loc. Highway Exp.	Fed. Highway Grants	0.45
Bolton (1969)	40 Quarters	1954–63	St. Loc. Exp.	Fed. Grants	0.32

[a] Estimated in elasticity form and converted to partial derivative using expenditure and grant values for appropriate year.

[b] Regressions were run for each year in the sample. I averaged the seven coefficients, which went as high as 2.04 and as low as 1.31.

[c] Regressions actually used taxes as the dependent variable. In converting to expenditures, I simply added one to the coefficient $[\partial E/\partial G = 1 + \partial T/\partial G]$.

on grants (about 1.3 at present values). These early results are suspect, however, because they imply that not only do federal-grant–supported goods not displace own expenditures at all, they complement own expenditures enough to more than offset the implied reduction resulting from the fact that 0.3 of the grant must be raised from own funds to match it: a possibility that is inconsistent with the fact that the negative income effect of the mandated portion would to some degree reduce expenditures. But even if the very high early estimates of the spending impact are discounted, presumably because of some kind of simultaneous bias, almost all of the regression estimates of the spending coefficients for federal grants remain rather high, usually greater than the estimated effect of case A grants. This in turn implies either that case C grants are given in areas where demand is more price elastic than in the case A grant areas or that grants are given for new types of programs with effective effort-maintenance provisions that prevent much local grant displacement from taking place.

An alternative way of estimating the impact of case C grants on the budgets of state and local governments was developed by Miller (1974). By closely examining highway statistics, he found that all but nine states spend more than is necessary to receive and match closed-end grants under the ABC (non interstate) highway program, indicating that at least small increments in grant funds would not stimulate much spending in all but these nine states. In terms of Figure 12–1, he is finding that the amount of grant funds is so small relative to what states would spend anyway on highways that ABC grants are in effect being converted into case B grants with relatively small spending impacts. This finding does not agree with most of the regression evidence on case C grants. It may not be inconsistent with these findings, however, because the ABC program is much older than most other grant programs and much smaller relative to local expenditures, and it might be natural to expect grant displacement to be much higher. The implication is that if the federal government desires to encourage spending, it can probably do that only by grant programs where the spending output is distinguishable from what the state would have done anyway, where effort maintenance can be effective, and where grants are large relative to existing expenditures. If it wants to encourage somewhat more spending on such areas as highways where states have long been spending large amounts, its grant money will probably get lost in the shuffle anyway and it may as well simply avoid administrative hassles by converting all grants to case B form.

A similar type of finding regards the new U.S. public-service employment program. In some respects, public-service employment might be thought of as a case C grant—it is closed-ended and requires state and local governments to spend in a certain area, i.e., to hire workers. Since the federally funded employment is very small relative to total state and local employment, however, the government may in fact operate much more like a case B grant, because it will be difficult for the federal government to devise effective effort-maintenance provisions insuring that local governments will continue hiring the employees they would have hired otherwise apart from the federal grants (particularly when employment levels are rising over time). The early evaluations of public employment, by Johnson and Timola (1974) and Fechter (1975), indicate that such is the case, that spending and employment propensities are much closer to what might be anticipated under a case B than a case C grant program.

Overall Evaluation

The previous comments suggest the areas where the existing literature is strong and where it is weak. Most of the points have been stressed enough that a detailed recapitulation is not necessary. Yet it is useful to try to put past empirical work into perspective—it has answered this set of questions but not that set. This section indicates very briefly the areas where the work on grants is, in my opinion, reasonably convincing and the areas where there is still much to be done.

Although it is of couse risky to summarize a large number of studies in a few sentences, at the present time empirical work on grants in the United States has basically verified the following four hypotheses:

1. That case A grants generally result in somewhat less spending than the size of the grant, indicating that the price elasticity of demand for most services is probably somewhat less than unity.
2. That case B grants result in some tax reduction and some expenditure increase, with the expenditure increase less than for case A grants, as would be predicted by the theory.
3. That case B grants, on the other hand, stimulate much more spending than central-government tax cuts in the long run, indicating at a minimum the need for some revision in political theories that feature a harmony of interests between bureaucrats and voters.
4. That case C grants stimulate total local spending roughly equal to the grant, generally slightly more spending than is stimulated by case A grants—either because they are given in areas where demand is more elastic, because they are large relative to existing expenditures, or because they come with effective effort-maintenance provisions.

One can always make the claim that researchers on grants should continue working in these areas to refine estimates, test hypotheses in different ways, and so forth. This is as true in the area of grants as in any other area. However, it seems even more important for grant researchers and theorists to extend their investigations into different areas by asking "Why?" and "So what?" The "why" extension would delve into the politicoeconomic theories of bureaucracy indicated in several places. Why does the flypaper theory appear to be correct? Why is the response to central-government grants not as predicted by the harmony-of-interest theory in this case and as predicted by that theory in other cases? Does it or does it not matter whether independent school districts are directly aided, and why? This is an area where it may not be particularly easy to do research, but one can think of many questions regarding grants that can never be convincingly answered without more knowledge of the behavior of government bureaucrats.

A second broad type of extension would move away from the underlying theory and get into questions more relevant for specific legislation. The four hypotheses listed above are broad hypotheses that pertain to grants in general, but they are certainly not universally applicable. Each existing or prospective grant program is obviously unique, and the response of local governments to it will depend on underlying elasticities, the size of the grant, the homogeneity of local expenditures, restrictions on the grant, and any other political factors—in ways that have or have not been laid out above. To get really useful knowledge in this area, legislators must know what specifically will happen with specific changes. The paramount example of the inadequacy of econometric research in this area came recently with the Nixon administration special revenue-sharing proposals: despite all the past work and empirical consensus on the impact of different types of grants, I know of no study that could have convincingly predicted the effects of converting categorical aid to special revenue sharing in any one of the six areas proposed. To predict the effects of this conversion, one simply needed answers to more detailed and specific questions than had been asked before. If econometric research pretends to be policy-relevant, it must extend beyond the broad and general and get into these more specific questions for individual programs.

A third type of extension that also seems warranted is to expand the range of questions asked. To a certain degree, one cannot help but feel that empirical researchers in this area have fallen into the same state of mind that conservative politicians accuse liberal politicians of falling prey to: whereas all liberal politicians can do is "throw money at problems" (this is as alleged but not necessarily my own view), all researchers can do is measure the amount of money thrown. At some point research will have to go beyond the question everybody asks and answers—how much did local spending change—and into some more basic questions, such as whether the right type of spending was encouraged, by the right governments and for the right citizens, and even the ultimate one of whether the spending accomplished its intended objectives. Past empirical work has made a start—it is better to know how much money was spent than nothing—but there is clearly more to grant evaluation.

Notes

1. That they are is shown by Pechman and Okner (1974). When property taxes are allocated according to property ownership, in keeping with the so-

called new view of property-tax incidence, the regressivity is cut markedly. Then state and local property taxes are slightly regressive up to incomes of $20,000, and slightly progressive above that level.

2. If the net fiscal residual were zero for all groups, tax prices for public services would be the same in all communities. But there may still be a reason for case B grants to poorer communities to counter a positive income elasticity of demand for public goods and consequent inequalities of consumption of these goods.

3. The U.S. Congressional Budget Office (1975) has recently made exactly this argument.

4. Sometimes it is called the *substitution effect*, but I use alternative terminology to avoid confusion with the *price substitution effect*.

5. The term was coined by Arthur Okun.

6. Slightly more, because the community is made better off by the increased public spending, and the greedy politicians can then raise taxes slightly without making the electorate either worse off or aware that they are being had.

7. In a few years, it will no longer be possible to make this statement. Expenditure-determinants studies are beginning to appear in Great Britain, though the treatment of grants is still not extensively developed [see Alt (1971) and Ashford (1975)]. The impact of grants on expenditures is also now coming under scrutiny in West Germany, Canada, Australia, and New Zealand.

8. Since school districts cannot easily spend money on, say, highways, there is some doubt as to whether even untied aid to them should be considered a case B grant. In this chapter I do so because school districts still do have the option of lowering taxes in response to case B grants.

9. Strictly speaking, this proportion refers to those grants on which there is a funds limit. Even if there were such a limit, the grant could still be an A grant if undersubscribed. Instances of such undersubscription are, for the United States at least, quite rare.

10. The table omits a few studies that have used either a strange data base or a strange model with some obvious flaw obscuring the effect of grants.

References

Adams, R.F. 1966. The fiscal response to intergovernmental transfers in less developed areas of the United States. *Review of Economics and Statistics* 48:308-313.

Albin, P.S., and Stein, B. 1971. Determinants of relief policy at the subfederal level. *Southern Economic Journal* 37:445-457.

Alt, J. 1971. Some social and political correlates of county borough expenditures. *British Journal of Political Science* 1:49-62.

Ashford, D.E., Berne, R., and Schramm, R. 1975. The expenditure financing decision in British local government. Mimeographed. Cornell University.

Bahl, R.W., and Saunders, R.J. 1966. Factors associated with variations in state and local government spending. *Journal of Finance* 21:523-534.

Bergstrom, T.C., and Goodman, R.P. 1973. Private demand for public goods. *American Economic Review* 63:280-296.

Bolton, R.E. 1969. Predictive models for state and local government purchases. In *The Brookings Model: Some Further Results*, J.S. Duesenberry, G. Fromm, L.R. Klein, and E. Kuh, eds. Chicago: Rand McNally.

Booms, B.H., and Hu, T. 1971. Toward a positive theory of state and local public expenditures: An empirical example. *Public Finance* 26:419-436.

Borcherding, T.E., and Deacon, R.T. 1972. The demand for the services of non-federal governments. *American Economic Review* 62:891-901.

Bowman, J.H. 1974. Tax exportability, intergovernmental aid, and school finance reform. *National Tax Journal* 27:163-174.

Brazer, H.E. 1959. City expenditures in the United States. Occasional paper 66. New York: National Bureau of Economic Research.

Break, G.F. 1967. *Intergovernmental Fiscal Relations in the United States.* Washington, D.C.: The Brookings Institution.

Buchanan, J.M. 1950. Federalism and fiscal equity. *American Economic Review* 40:583-599.

Campbell, A., and Sacks, S. 1967. *Metropolitan America, Fiscal Patterns and Governmental Systems*. Glencoe, N.Y.: The Free Press.

Ehrenberg, R.G. 1973. The demand for state and local government employees. *American Economic Review* 63:366-379.

Fechter, A.E. 1975. Public service employment: Boom or boondoggle? In *Proceedings of a Conference on Public Service Employment.* Washington, D.C.: National Commission for Manpower Policy.

Feldstein, M.S. 1975. Wealth neutrality and local choice in public education. *American Economic Review* 65:75-89.

Fredlund, J.E. 1974. *Determinants of State and Local Expenditures: An Annotated Bibliography.* Washington, D.C.: Urban Institute.

Gayer, D. 1972. The effects of medicaid on state and local government finances. *National Tax Journal* 25:511-520.

Gillespie, W.I. 1965. Effect of public expenditures on the distribution of income. In *Essays in Fiscal Federalism*, R.A. Musgrave, Ed. Washington, D.C.: The Brookings Institution.

Gramlich, E.M. 1969a. State and local governments and their budget constraint. *International Economic Review* 10:163-182.

Gramlich, E.M. 1969b. The effect of federal grants on state-local expenditures: A review of the econometric literature. *National Tax Association Papers and Proceedings* 1969:569-593.

Gramlich, E.M. 1972. A comment on O'Brien's "Grants-in-aid." *National Tax Journal* 25:107-108.

Gramlich, E.M., and Galper, H. 1973. State and local fiscal behavior and federal grant policy. *Brookings Papers on Economic Activity* 1:15–58.

Harlow, R.L. 1967. Factors affecting American state expenditures. *Yale Economic Essays.* Fall 1967:263–308.

Henderson, J. 1968. Local government expenditures: A social welfare analysis. *Review of Economics and Statistics* 50:156–163.

Hicks, U.K. 1968. *Public Finance*, 3d edition. Cambridge: Cambridge University Press.

Horowitz, A.R. 1968. A simultaneous equation approach to the problems of explaining interstate differences in state and local government expenditures. *Southern Economic Journal* 34:459–476.

Inman, R.P. 1971. Towards an econometric model of local budgeting. *National Tax Association Papers and Proceedings* 1971:699–719.

Johnson, G.E., and Timola, J.D. 1974. An evaluation of the public employment program. Technical analysis paper no. 17–A. Department of Labor.

Johnson, S.R., and Junk, P.E. 1970. Sources of tax revenues and expenditures in large U.S. cities. *Quarterly Review of Economics and Business* 10:7–16.

Kurnow, E. 1963. Determinants of state and local expenditures reexamined. *National Tax Journal* 16:252–255.

McGuire, M.C. 1973. Notes on grants-in-aid and economic interactions among governments. *Canadian Journal of Economics* 6:207–221.

Miller, E. 1974. The economics of matching grants: The ABC highway program. *National Tax Journal* 27:221–230.

Musgrave, R.A. 1961 Approaches to a fiscal theory of political federalism. In *Public Finance: Needs, Sources, and Utilization*, National Bureau of Economic Research. Princeton, N.J.: Princeton University Press.

Nathan, R.P., Manvel, A.D., and Calkins, S.E. 1975. *Monitoring Revenue Sharing.* Washington, D.C.: The Brookings Institution.

National Planning Association. 1974. *Proceedings of a Conference on Revenue Sharing Research.* Washington, D.C.

Netzer, D. 1974. State-local finance and intergovernmental fiscal relations. In *The Economics of Public Finance*, A.S. Blinder et al. Washington, D.C.: The Brookings Institution.

Niskanen, W.A. 1968. The peculiar economics of bureaucracy. *American Economic Review, Supplement* (May), 58:293–305.

Oates, W.E. 1968. The dual impact of federal aid on state and local expenditures: A comment. *National Tax Journal* 21:220–223.

Oates, W.E. 1972. *Fiscal Federalism.* New York: Harcourt Brace Jovanovich.

O'Brien, T. 1971. Grants-in-aid: Some further answers. *National Tax Journal* 24:65–77.

Ohls, J.C., and Wales, T.J. 1971. Supply and demand for state and local services. *Review of Economics and Statistics* 54:424–430.

Orr, L.L. 1976. Income transfers as a public good: An application to AFDC. *American Economic Review* 66:359–371.

Osman, J.W. 1966. The dual impact of federal aid on state and local government expenditures. *National Tax Journal* 19:362–372.

Pechman, J.A., and Okner, B.A. 1974. *Who Bears the Tax Burden?* Washington, D.C.: The Brookings Institution.

Peterson, J.E. 1968. The determinants of state and local government capital outlays. Ph.D. thesis. University of Pennsylvania.

Phelps, C.D. 1969. Real and monetary determinants of state and local government capital outlays for highways. *American Economic Review* 59:507–521.

Pidot, G.B. 1969. A principal components analysis of the determinants of local fiscal patterns. *Review of Economics and Statistics* 51:176–188.

Pogue, T.F., and Sgontz, L.G. 1968. The effects of grants-in-aid on state and local spending. *National Tax Journal* 21:190–199.

Reischauer, R.D. 1975. General revenue sharing: The program's incentives. In *Financing the New Federalism*, W.E. Oates, ed. Washington, D.C.: Resources for the Future.

Sacks, S., and Harris, R. 1964. The determinants of state and local government expenditures and intergovernmental flows of funds. *National Tax Journal* 17:75–85.

Schultze, C.L. 1974. Sorting out the social grant programs: An economists criteria. *American Economic Review, Supplement* (May), 64:181–189.

Scott, A.D. 1952. The evaluation of federal grants. *Econometrica*, N.S. 19:377–394.

Smith, D.L. 1968. The response of state and local governments to federal grants. *National Tax Journal* 21:349–357.

Strauss, R.P. 1974. General revenue sharing: How well is it working? *National Tax Association Papers and Proceedings.*

Thurow, L.C. 1966. The theory of grants-in-aid. *National Tax Journal* 19:373–377.

U.S. Congressional Budget Office. 1975. *Temporary Measures to Stimulate Employment: An Evaluation of Some Alternatives.*

U.S. National Science Foundation. 1975. Research applied to national needs: General revenue sharing research program. Mimeographed.

Weicher, J.C. 1972. Aid, expenditures, and local government structure. *National Tax Journal* 25:573–584.

Wilde, J.A. 1971. Grants-in-aid: The analytics of design and response. *National Tax Journal* 24:143–156.

13

Taxation of Multijurisdictional Corporate Income: Lessons of the U.S. Experience

Charles E. McLure, Jr.

1. Introduction

Considerable attention has been devoted recently to improving the income taxation of firms operating in more than one taxing jurisdiction. Some of the increased scrutiny has occurred within federal systems, such as in the United States.[1] But perhaps an even greater reexamination of the principles and practices of income taxation in open economies has taken place in the international sphere.[2] Realization of the free-trade objectives of the European Common Market and (in diminished form) various other regional common markets and free-trade associations has increased the potential for corporate taxation to cause unintended realignment of international economic relations, both among association members and between them and nonmember nations. Another important reason for increased interest in this subject at the international level is doubtless the growing importance of multinational corporations and their far-flung financial, production, and distribution activities. An additional and complementary factor is the growing confrontation between industrialized countries and those of the so-called Third World. Developing countries that feel themselves exploited by the more advanced countries naturally look at altering the taxation of company incomes accruing largely to foreigners as one means of redressing grievances. For their part, the developed countries continue to exhibit some interest in tailoring tax conventions to the advantage of the less developed countries. A final concern is the continuing problem of tax havens.

As currently practiced internationally, the division of tax revenues of a given firm among the various countries in which it operates can be characterized as a two-stage process. First, the tax base, income, must be divided among the various countries in which it originates. Then tax revenues attributable to a given flow of income from source country to residence country must be divided between the two nations, usually via credits granted unilaterally or spelled out in tax treaties.

The author is indebted to Eugene Corrigan, Robert Floyd, Peggy Musgrave, Richard Musgrave, and Carl Shoup for comments on an earlier draft of this chapter. Any remaining errors are solely mine.

241

Virtually all nations employ separate accounting to determine the amount of profits originating within their boundaries, that is, to answer the source-versus-source question posed above.[3] As a result, much of the discussion of potential alterations of income taxation of multinational corporations has been in the context of separate accounting. It has concentrated on refinements of administrative rules for replicating for closely related firms (and even branches) the results of arms-length transactions between unrelated firms so far as prices, interest payments, royalties, etc., are concerned.[4] Relatively neglected is the possibility of moving from the present practice of separate accounting to a system of apportioning profits among countries on the basis of formulas, the general practice employed in the state income taxes in the United States.[5]

The general approach under formula apportionment is to divide the income of a given firm among taxing jurisdictions according to the various jurisdictions' shares in specific economic activities of the firm (commonly sales, payroll, and property). Because there is little residence-based taxation of corporate profits at the state level in the United States, the second problem posed above, division of revenues between states of source and states of residence, never arises.[6]

The purpose of this chapter is to examine experience with formula apportionment in the United States. That experience may be of direct relevance for other countries with federal systems that include source-oriented taxation of corporate income at the subnational level. And, defining horizontal fiscal federalism more broadly, it may be relevant to the discussion of the taxation of multinational corporations, either in or beyond the context of a common market such as the European Community. Because the implications of U.S. experience for other federal systems may sometimes be more obvious than those in the international sphere, emphasis is upon the latter.

It is natural to expect from this discussion a concrete conclusion as to whether separate accounting or formula apportionment is to be preferred for dividing corporate profits among taxing jurisdictions. Yet there is none. Any firm conclusion would simply be premature at this stage, since many complex problems of formula apportionment are almost certainly overlooked here and separate accounting is discussed only in passing. Finally, it should be emphasized that the choice between separate accounting and formula apportionment bears only upon the resolutions of "source-versus-source" claims to tax base. It—and this chapter—says nothing about the issue of division of revenues between source and residence jurisdictions that might arise once the first issue is resolved.

Section 2 describes in general terms the taxation of multistate corporations in the United States, focusing especially upon formula apportionment. Because this is an area of active legislative interest, an entirely timely description may not be possible. Thus it seems better to focus upon basic problems and alternative approaches to their resolution than upon particular statutory provisions. An effort is made in section 3 to evaluate the possibility of adopting and adapting U.S. practices for the taxation of multinational corporations, though many complications are beyond the scope of this paper. Finally, only U.S. practice is covered here because of the author's unfamiliarity with the analogous practices in other federal systems (e.g., Canada, Australia, and Germany).

2. State Corporation Income Taxes in the United States[7]

Before briefly surveying the historical development of corporate taxation of multistate firms in the United States, it will be convenient to describe the kinds of problems that have arisen in this area. The most important of these will be discussed further in Section 3. At that point, particular attention will be devoted to the relevance of U.S. experience for other countries, especially in the international sphere. It should be noted at the outset that many of the potential problems described in the following paragraphs are now much less troublesome in the United States than they were a decade ago.

Determination of Taxable State Income

Before a state can apply its tax to the income of a firm, jurisdictional nexus must be established. Then the firm's total income must be measured and a method (or methods) of dividing income among the states must be settled upon.[8] This part describes briefly American experience in these three areas in order to spotlight the need for uniformity and the difficulties involved in attaining it. In addition, the especially thorny problems of combination and consolidation are previewed.

Nexus Rules. A 1964 congressional study of state taxation of income derived from interstate commerce concluded that nexus rules exhibited little uniformity between states and, perhaps even worse, that the statutes and regulations of most states did not even describe with adequate clarity the conditions under which a firm would be subject to taxation.[9] Such a state of affairs was, of course, intolerable. At the very least, it should be clear whether or not a given activity is sufficient to establish taxable nexus in a given jurisdiction. Beyond that, the nexus rule should not be so severe that only minimal economic association subjects a firm to taxation. Otherwise, administration and compliance will be either very poor or very costly.[10] Nexus rules should be realistic and, given that, enforcement should be serious and compliance a way of life. Finally, there are advantages to uniformity of nexus rules.

Taxable Income. Uniformity of state definitions of taxable income has clear advantages. Gaps and overlaps of interstate taxation will not then result from differences in definitions of taxable income. Moreover, compliance is simplified by the need to master only one set of tax laws and bookkeeping requirements, and the preparation of returns is simplified. Similarly, joint audits are possible, at a saving of the time and expense for both taxpayers and administrators. If, in addition, state definitions of taxable income are patterned after federal provisions, state audits can be based on the results of federal audits and states can rely upon the considerable expertise of the tax technicians who design the complicated provisions of the federal statutes.

Of course, uniformity has its price. First, it is not always easy to attain. Beyond that, if it is attained by adopting the federal tax base, the states may sometimes find themselves with tax provisions they would not have chosen to adopt.[11] Of course, federal law can form the basis for state laws, with each state making whatever adjustments it thinks desirable, but this tends to reduce uniformity and to raise administrative and compliance costs.

Division of Income.[12] Contrary to the situation in the international sphere, *separate accounting* is employed to divide only a small proportion of taxable income among the states. The problems encountered are essentially those that plague use of this device to tax multinational firms: allocation of overhead, transfer pricing, etc. Thus they need not be discussed in detail here.

Specific allocation has been employed by many states for certain kinds of income (primarily that from intangible assets, such as interest, dividends, royalties, etc., and rents and capital gains). Some states simply list the kinds of income to be allocated, while others provide formula apportionment for "business income" and specific allocations only for "nonbusiness income." Needless to say, if states do not agree upon which forms of income to allocate, gaps and overlaps can result.

But the situation is potentially even worse than that, for states need not agree upon where a given item agreed to be allocable should be taxed. First, it must be decided whether income will be allocated to the state in which the income originates, the state in which the taxpayer is located, or the state in which the asset is located. This decision can be crucial in instances where these three tests would give different results, as in the case of interest, royalties, rents, dividends, etc. If taxation is based upon the location of the taxpayer, alternative definitions of location can be offered: state of incorporation, management, and principal place of business. This question is, of course, analogous to the question of residence in the international context. Alternatively, taxation can be based on the location of the income-producing asset. But this is likely to be of little assistance for intangible assets. In short, uniformity in the application of specific accounting is essential if inequities and distortions are to be avoided. Fortunately, states are moving increasingly to apportion all income by formula.

Formula apportionment is used to divide the great bulk of interstate income derived from manufacturing and mercantile activities among the states. Under this approach, a fraction of a firm's total apportionable income equal to the weighted average the state's share in certain activities of the firm (usually sales, payroll, and property) is apportioned to the state. The basic questions then (besides the determination of allocable income) are which factors to use in the formula, how to weight them, and how to measure the selected economic activities for purposes of applying the formulas.[13] Clearly, if states do not agree on the answers to all these questions, overtaxation and undertaxation can result and (especially with regard to the last question) compliance and enforcement costs can be greater than need be. Particularly noteworthy is the fact that apparently similar formulas can be interpreted in quite different ways. This is especially true of the sales factor.

Real property and tangible personal property located in a state form the basis of calculation of the property formula. But whether or not to include rented property, property in transit, transportation equipment, property under construction, and tangible property yielding specifically allocable income must be determined. Beyond that, it is necessary to decide how to value the relevant property; market value, original cost, depreciated basis, and depreciated basis adjusted for inflation being the obvious alternatives.[14]

For the payroll factor, valuation poses little problem, except insofar as fringe benefits are concerned. The primary problems of composition involve compensation of general executive officers and employees producing income that is specifically allocated. Finally, attribution of payroll to states can be based, for example, upon the location of performance of services or upon the location of the place of business to which the employee is attached. Naturally, one can expect considerable variation in the way such general rules are interpreted. A more certain approach is provided by the Uniform Division of Income Tax Purposes Act (UDITPA, to be discussed further below). Under it, attribution is based upon the assignment of employees for contributions to unemployment compensation, which itself is the subject of a preexisting model act.[15]

The sales factor is particularly bothersome. First, it must be decided what kinds of gross receipts should be included in calculating the sales factor. Once this composition question is settled, it is necessary to decide the basis of attribution among states. Besides the obvious and important question of whether to attribute sales to the state of origin or the state of destination, there is the question of how to define either origin or destination. Moreover, some states have actually employed multiple sales factors. Finally, problems of valuing sales among affiliated companies can arise.

Examples of the difficulty of applying the sales factor are worth special note. First, suppose that sales are delivered in one state but received in another. What is the destination? What is the result if the goods are delivered not to the buyer but directly to his customer in another state? How should sales to the U.S. government be treated? Should export sales be excluded from the denominator of the sales factor, or only from the numerator? Finally, should sales made to income tax states that do not have jurisdiction to tax be excluded from the denominator by states employing the destination sales factor? Rather than using such a "throwout" rule, many states employ "throwback" provisions to allow them to tax at origin any such sales, and the practice is sanctioned by the UDITPA.

Consolidated and Combined Returns. Though not a separate issue, the question of consolidated and combined returns has become so important in recent years that it deserves special attention.[16] This is especially true given the relevance of the issue for the taxation of multinational firms, either in the international sphere or within a given country.

Several states provide that two or more closely related firms that are subject to the state's income tax should be taxed as one entity by filing a "consolidated return." Thus, intercorporate transactions, especially dividends, are eliminated. Less common, but more far-reaching, is the practice of "combination." Under this approach, both apportionment factors and income of a given firm are combined with those for related corporations engaged in a "unitary business" for the purpose of determining tax liability to the state requiring combination. Moreover, all intercompany charges are disregarded in the applications of combination.[17] In contrast to the situation under consolidation, not all the firms for which combination is required need even be taxable in the state in question. Rather, combination is intended to measure more accurately the income of the firm over which the state does have taxing jurisdiction in instances in which it is believed that the stated income of the taxable coporation does not accurately reflect income attributable to the state.[18] Combination can produce complicated situations in which activities of foreign affiliates with no taxable nexus in the taxing state, or even in the United States, can be relevant for calculating the taxable income of the unitary business. Not suprisingly, this has produced considerable protest from business spokesmen.

History of State Corporate Taxation

Adoption of the corporation income tax as a form of state revenue has proceeded in spurts. Efforts before the adoption of the Wisconsin tax in 1911 were largely abortive. Between then and 1929, the number of states levying either a corporate income tax or a franchise tax based on income rose to 17. This small number of adoptions, and the prevalance of franchise taxes, reflected the interplay of relatively minor pressures on revenues and the prohibitions against direct taxes found in many state constitutions. (The franchise tax was a means of circumventing the prohibitions.) Revenue demands were greater during the Great Depression, and by 1940 a total of 34 states employed one of these forms of corporate taxation. The 1940s and 1950s saw little action in this field, but the fiscal pressures of the 1960s and early 1970s brought the number of state corporation income taxes to its present 46 (including the District of Columbia).[19]

Despite efforts to achieve uniformity in the definition of taxable income, and especially in methods of dividing income among the states, little progress was made in these areas until the last 10 years. Though a committee of the National Tax Association recommended in 1919 that states base their definitions of taxable income upon the federal definition, no action was taken then and subsequent interest focused upon the division of income. Whereas early attempts at uniformity had been in the context of separate accounting, formula apportionment came to be the preferred method, owing perhaps to the growing integration of business during the 1920s. This preference was called into question when, during the 1930s, separate accounting became the standard approach in the international sphere. But because of the greater integration of interstate corporations relative to their international counterparts, as well as other differences in interstate and international relations, formula apportionment had continued to be the predominant method of dividing income. Only recently has this question been reexamined, this time in the more complex context of the debate over combined reports and consolidated returns of related corporations.[20]

It is probably accurate to say that the so-called Massachusetts formula (based on sales, payroll, and property) became the most popular method of apportioning income. But any appearance of uniformity masked a staggering amount of variety in the application of this principle. Therefore, appeals were made for both federal action and cooperative state action to bring about uniformity in apportionment rules and procedures. But nothing much happened, even when in 1957 the National Conference of Commissioners on Uniform State Laws adopted the Uniform Division of Income for Tax Purposes Act. It was only in response to a series of 1959 Supreme Court cases that distinct moves toward uniformity began to be made.

The particulars of these cases, the most famous of which was *Northwestern States Portland Cement Co. vs. Minnesota*, need not concern us. Basically, the definition of sufficient business activity to incur taxation in a state (the nexus issue) was the focus of the cases. In response to the outcries of businessmen that the nexus definition condoned by the court was unreasonably severe, Congress quickly passed a more liberal stopgap measure.[21] But Public Law 86-272 also contained a potentially more important provision calling for a complete study of state taxation of income derived from interstate commerce to be made for the purpose of recommending proposed legislation that would assure uniformity.

Under this mandate, the House Judiciary Committee's Special Subcommittee on State Taxation of Interstate Commerce undertook an extensive analysis of its assigned topic and produced a four-volume report.[22] In late 1965, the subcommittee's chairman, Edwin Willis of Louisiana, submitted a bill based upon the findings of the study. This bill was revised after further hearings and passed the House of Representatives in 1968 and 1969. However, the Senate failed to act on the House-approved bills, and more recently the House seems to have decided to act no further until action is taken by the Senate Finance Committee.[23]

The main provisions of the Willis bill (the Rodino bill in 1969) were (1) a nexus rule based upon maintenance of a "business location" in the taxing state and (2) an optional apportionment formula containing only property and pay-roll that could be used instead of the state's actual formula by firms with annual incomes for federal tax purposes of less than $1 million. Under the nexus rule, a firm would be subject to tax only if it owned or leased real property, had em-ployees, or maintained an inventory in the state. The optional apportionment formula was meant to protect small firms from inordinate compliance costs.

Many states did not like the federal intervention in state fiscal affairs implied by the congressional response to the *Northwestern* case. Moreover, they feared that nexus rules and apportionment formulas such as those contained in the Willis-Rodino bills could result in competition from out-of-state firms not subject to state corporate income tax and could cause the loss of tax revenue. Thus in 1966 steps were taken that led to the official formation of the Multi-state Tax Commission (MTC) in 1967. As stated in its annual report (1974, p. 87), the purpose of the MTC is:

To bring even further uniformity and compatibility to the tax laws of the various states of this nation and their political subdivisions insofar as those laws affect multistate business, to give both business and the states a single place to which to take their tax problems, to study and make recommendations on a continuing basis with respect to all taxes affecting multistate businesses, to promote the adoption of statutes and rules establishing uniformity, and to assist in protecting the fiscal and political integrity of the states from federal confiscation.

At the beginning of 1976 the MTC contained 21 member states and 15 associate members, or a total of 36 of the 50 states[24] (see Figure 13-1).

The MTC has been instrumental in the achievement of greater uniformity in state income taxes. For example, the Multistate Tax Compact includes verbatim the UDITPA, so that any state joining the MTC as a regular member automatical-ly endorses this uniform law. By the end of 1975, almost 30 states and the District of Columbia had adopted UDITPA, whereas in 1967 only a handful had done so.[25] Moreover, many states are already applying the UDITPA under uniform allocation and apportionment regulations recommended by the MTC only in February 1973.[26] The federal income-tax base now serves as the basis for calculating income for tax purposes in 33 states. Finally, the MTC provides both a program of exchange of information (which has been joined by 21 states) and a program of joint audit. The audit program, while still in its infancy and the subject of litigation in several states, is intended to reduce both administra-tive and compliance burdens and to increase the uniformity of state income tax-ation.[27]

3. Appraisal of U.S. Experience

In appraising U.S. experience in taxing interstate corporations it will be con-venient, if somewhat arbitrary, to divide the discussion into conceptual issues

Source: Multistate Tax Commission Eighth Annual Report, Boulder, Colorado, 1975, p. iv.

Figure 13-1. Multistate Tax Commission Membership, January 1, 1975

and matters of implementation. In addition, much of this discussion is addressed more to issues that arise in the international context than to those that arise within a federal system per se. First, the applicability of the U.S. experience to federalism in other countries may be more direct and therefore in less need of explanation. Beyond that, the higher rates of tax common at the national level may render crucial problems that are only bothersome at the subnational level.[28]

Conceptual Issues

If income of affiliated firms were combined, each jurisdiction would have a tax base in the earnings of a given group of firms that approximated (to the extent that factor apportionment is sensible) income derived within its boundaries.[29] Of course, whether or not the combination of report of affiliates involved in a unitary business is desirable is itself debatable. It can be argued, for example, that this approach is merely the logical extension of the choice of formula apportionment in preference to separate accounting.[30] According to this line of reasoning, profits from unitary businesses should be apportioned on the basis of factors pertaining to that business, regardless of the legal makeup of the unitary business.

Unitary Business. There may, however, be important problems in the implementation of the unitary approach. From a theoretical point of view, it would appear that it may be no easy matter to identify a unitary business. Economic interdependence, the obvious criterion at the conceptual level, would appear not to provide adequate guidance for either taxpayers or tax administrators. Moreover, there is no reason to expect agreement among administrators in different jurisdictions, so there are ample grounds for inconsistencies in the taxation of a given flow of income. Beyond that, the profits of the unitary business must be isolated before factor apportionment can be applied. If a group of affiliated firms carries on more than one unitary business, problems similar to those involved in determining the income of individual firms under separate accounting can arise, namely transfer pricing and division of deductions. That is, transfer prices, for example, between unitary businesses operating in low-tax jurisdictions and those operating in high-tax jurisdictions might be manipulated to minimize taxes. If a group of firms engages in only one unitary business, no such manipulations are possible, since all interaffiliate transactions are ignored in combination.[31] Finally, it is necessary to calculate apportionment formulas based on the activities of the entire unitary business. In some instances, problems similar to those with separate accounting can again arise; that is, sales between affiliates in different unitary businesses can be misstated, and property acquired from related firms can be undervalued or overvalued in the interest of minimizing taxes. There appears to be less latitude for manipulation of the labor factor, so long as a uniform standard is adopted.[32]

Choice of Factors. Just what apportionment factors should be used, and their proper weights, seems to be the object of a relatively sterile debate.[33] One can argue along the following lines, but without much hope of resolving the issue. If the corporation income tax is really a tax on the normal return to equity capital, income should be based upon each jurisdiction's share of a firm's equity capital. But it is generally impossible to distinguish whether a given undertaking is financed from debt or equity (even though there may be easily discernible geographic differences in the undertakings, especially with regard to risk) and apportionment by a property factor may be as sensible as any.

If, on the other hand, the tax is seen as a tax on economic profits, the situation is not so clear.[34] At first glance, it might appear that economic theory tells us to apportion monopoly profits on the basis of sales, since such profits cannot exist without a downward-sloping demand curve. Similarly, it may seem reasonable to attribute monopsony profits to the locus of monopsonized inputs. But, more fundamentally, either kind of profit may be better attributable to whatever restricts entry and prevents a competitive (zero profit) solution. Locating the proper jurisdiction for this kind of attribution would, of course, be difficult in many cases. Moreover, as has often been argued in the interstate literature, no profits, whether normal or economic, can be earned without capital, labor, and sales. Thus perhaps all three factors should be used.[35] But the choice of weights is inherently arbitrary, and it would appear best simply to recognize this.

One important determinant of whether to include sales in the apportionment formula must be the consequences for the distribution of tax revenues between states or nations. Contrary to expectations, it has been found that in the United States the number and choice of factors does not greatly influence the distribution of tax revenues between the so-called industrial states (favored by payroll, property, and sales at origin) and the market states (favored by use of sales at destination) [U.S. Congress (1964, ch. 16)]. The reasons that have been suggested for this anomalous result are worth considering, because they may not be equally applicable in other federal systems or in the international sphere. And, of perhaps equal relevance, they may have implications for the proper definition of the sales factor.

First, sales at destination are not necessarily sales to ultimate consumers. Rather, they are gross receipts. Thus a large fraction of sales at destination go not to market states but to other industrial states, and the distribution of sales at destination does not differ markedly from that of sales at origin. A similar result might well occur in the international context unless sales at destination were defined as retail sales. But then the administration of the corporate income tax would be burdened with the problems common to retail sales taxes.[36] Moreover, many corporations with substantial profits make few retail sales.

Second, if sales made from stocks near markets were to be interpreted as originating where the stocks were located, origin and destination principles would produce similar results in any case. This comment appears to be equally applicable in other countries and in the international context. As in the previous paragraph, the problem is the multiple counting of intermediate transactions.

Third, even final sales tend to be concentrated in the high-income industrial states. This point would be particularly telling internationally. This final reason may be relatively less important internationally than within the United States. The states that would be disadvantaged by heavy reliance on origin-based apportionment formulas do not rely as heavily upon the corporation income taxes as do those that would benefit. The reason may be, however, that these states do not rely heavily on the corporate income tax precisely because they would be disadvantaged by *any* allocation formulas for the reasons mentioned above. Whether a shift from the present system of separate accounting to formula apportionment would adversely affect the revenues of developing countries and the sensitivity of the results to the choice of formula deserves further investigation.[37]

Dividends. Under current international practice, dividends received from foreign subsidiaries are taxed to the parent company (or recipient of dividends on portfolio equity investment), but credits for foreign income taxes are usually allowed (but not for portfolio investors). On the other hand, in the United States treatment of dividends is a hotly debated issue.[38] The MTC, for example, has contended that virtually all intangible income, including dividends, should be apportioned by formula rather than allocated to the site of commercial domicile. Business groups, on the other hand, have argued that portfolio dividends should be allocated and that dividends received from an affiliate should not be taxed, since otherwise the income creating the dividend will be taxed twice. The MTC has countered that interaffiliate dividends should be exempt only if combination is applied. Moreover, it argues, allocation of portfolio dividends to the site of commercial domicile could lead to ruinous competition for home offices of corporations, essentially tax-haven treatment of such income, and loss of revenue.

The interplay of the treatment of dividends with combination and consolidation makes the issue a tricky one. But it does seem that dividends between firms filing combined returns should be exempt.[39] And it is not unreasonable to argue that all dividends should be exempt, in order to avoid double taxation of income. But in the international context that argument must be conditioned by the availability of foreign tax credits not found in the interstate context. Finally, if dividends are to be allocated to commercial domicile, it is clearly necessary to have provisions to prevent passing such dividends through subsidiaries in tax-haven states or countries.

Implementation

The discussion to this point should make clear the need for uniform tax laws, uniformly applied. The feasibility of creating an organization such as the MTC within other countries and the shape it would take would depend upon constitutional conditions in the various countries and is not discussed further here. Turning to the international sphere, we can note that it might be possible to achieve the required uniformity without global cooperation, but the probability of doing so seems quite small. What may be needed, then, is an international counterpart of the Multistate Tax Commission. Whether such an organization should be organized under the auspices of the United Nations or the secretariat of the GATT, for example, or as a separate organization need not concern us.[40] But one thing is clear. It would not be part of a supranational government, so it would not have sovereignty in tax matters. Moreover, it is quite unlikely that nations would surrender fiscal sovereignty, even over the corporation income tax. Thus, as with the MTC in the United States, this organ of fiscal cooperation could have only advisory power so far as uniform statutes and regulations are concerned; that is, model uniform statutes and regulations could be hammered out by the organization, but they would have to be approved by each member country. But, once these were approved, it might be expected that technicians from the international organization could play a large part in the administration of the taxes and especially in the audit of multinational corporations, perhaps in conjunction with administrators from the various interested countries. Joint audits conducted in this way could go far in assuring that the uniformity found in statutes and regulations would be reflected in implementation of the laws.

The logical conclusion of this line of reasoning is that an international court for the settlement of fiscal disputes would be needed. Otherwise, splits among the tax administrators of various countries could threaten to disrupt the activities and agreements of the international tax compact.

Adoption of the idea of international organs for cooperation in taxation would signify important sacrifices of national fiscal sovereignty. But, as indicated by both U.S. and international experience, the alternative may be near fiscal anarchy.

4. Summary and Conclusions

Separate accounting is the accepted way of calculating profits of multinational firms attributable to a given country. Formula apportionment, on the other hand, is the preferred method of dividing the income of interstate firms among the states in the United States. This chapter examines experience in applying state corporation income taxes to interstate firms in the United States. The purpose is not so much to determine which is the better method of dividing income, either among nations or among states. Rather, it is to suggest some of the conceptual and practical advantages and difficulties of formula apportionment. Which is the preferred method can be determined only after further comparison of the pros and cons of the two systems.

Though they are not totally absent, most of the problems that plague separate accounting seem to be much diminished under formula apportionment. This is expecially true if affiliated firms engaged in unitary businesses are required to file combined reports. Moreover, the proper treatment of dividends paid to affiliated firms is greatly simplified under combination, since these, like other transactions between affiliates, are netted out.

Finally, it seems that in the context of either fiscal federalism or international fiscal relations an organization analogous to the Multistate Tax Commission is needed if fiscal anarchy is to be avoided. Ideally such an organization would be supported by courts for settling fiscal disputes between states or countries (or disputes with serious fiscal implications for several countries).

Notes

1. See, for example, U.S. Congress (1964) and the more recent literature cited in McLure (1974).

2. For evidence of this, see the voluminous literature cited in Shoup (1974).

3. Musgrave (1972) distinguishes between "source-versus-source claims to tax base" and the division of revenues between source and residence countries.

4. Another important, and relatively recent, concern is with international coordination of the taxation of corporations and shareholders when some countries provide various degrees of integration of corporate and personal income taxes and others follow the so-called classical or separate-entity approach to taxing corporate profits [see especially van den Tempel (1970) and Sato and Bird (1975)].

5. Among the exceptions are Brannon (no date) and Musgrave (1972).

6. Similarly, no state provides even partial integration of its personal and corporate income taxes, so the problem of coordination analogous to that mentioned in note 4 never arises.

7. This section draws heavily upon McLure (1974), which contains references to basic source literature.

8. Ideally the nexus rules and procedures for attributing income should be consistent. In fact, if all states adopted the same definitions of income and rules for the division of income, nexus would become a redundant issue.

9. For example, any one of as many as two dozen different activities would be sufficient to bring a firm under the taxing jurisdiction of at least one state, but none would do so in all income tax states. There was, of course, near unanimity on some questions: filling orders from mail-order catalogs generally would not draw liability for taxation, but maintenance of a sales office or filling orders from an inventory held in a private warehouse in the state generally would. Events to be described in the next part resulted in substantial clarification and unification of nexus rules. Most states now extend nexus as far as allowed by federal law.

10. The congressional study group found that in each of three size categories at least 25 percent of the state income tax returns filed by multistate firms with gross receipts between $200,000 and $50 million involved less revenue than the estimated costs of preparing them; see U.S. Congress (1964, p. 379). Yet, in total, compliance costs seem not to have been high, primarily because not much effort was made either to comply with the laws or to enforce them. In the words of the congressional investigators (p. 94), "It is . . . a system which

calls upon tax administrators to enforce the unenforceable, and the taxpayer to comply with the uncompliable."

11. State budgetary officials can be expected to take great interest in federal tax legislation, especially that which, for countercyclical reasons, would reduce taxable income. For example, the federal choice between accelerated depreciation, which alters taxable income, and the investment tax credit, which does not, could be of great concern to the states.

12. It will be convenient in what follows to reserve *allocation* for specific allocation and *apportionment* for formula apportionment and to use *division of income* to refer to all the various means of dividing income among the states.

13. An important fourth question, the combination of reports and consolidation of returns of related firms, is treated separately.

14. Most states actually employ original cost. A value equal to eight times rental is commonly used for rented property.

15. This approach has the slight disadvantage, however, of the ceiling on the amount of each worker's annual wages that are taken into account under the unemployment insurance act.

16. Indicative of the importance of this question are the following quotations: "Perhaps 75 percent of the time of the Committee was expended upon the problem of seeking agreement as to how the taxpayer's apportionable income should be determined for income tax purposes; some 80 percent of that time was spent on the subject of consolidation of reports and combination of returns" [Multistate Tax Commission (July 1970), reporting on the activities of an ad hoc committee]. Also, in congressional hearings the California State Franchise Tax Board noted its staff observation that "The central issue with respect to proposed federal interstate tax legislation is the resolution of methods states may use for determining the income of multistate corporate taxpayers which are commonly owned and are conducting their affairs through more than one corporate entity" [U.S. Congress (1973, p. 298)].

17. For a further discussion of combination and its rationale, see Keesling (1974).

18. Under its unitary concept, California has sometimes allowed that for tax purposes the activities of single corporations be split up into separate "unitary businesses." Formula apportionment is then applied to the income of each of the constructively separate businesses, the apportionment being based upon the factors relevant to each of the businesses.

19. Nevada, South Dakota, Texas, Washington, and Wyoming do not levy corporate income taxes.

20. Similarly, Musgrave (1972, p. 407), dealing with the international problem, has written, "The more extensive are business interdependencies, the more necessary it becomes to take a unitary view of the enterprise and to attribute profits on a formula apportionment basis."

21. Public Law 86-272 prohibited imposition of corporate income tax on

a firm whose only activity in the taxing state was soliciting orders or using an independent contractor to make sales within the state. It might be worth noting that the court cases brought more uncertainty to the nexus issue and that uncertainty increased for a period until Public Law 86-272 had been interpreted by the courts. Any new legislation will, of course, lead to a further temporary period of uncertainty.

22. U.S. Congress (1964) and subsequent volumes.

23. The legislation that has been introduced since 1966 is summarized in McLure (1974) and in various annual reports of the Multistate Tax Commission. There is no reason to review these developments in the present context.

24. Note, however, that four of the member states and one associate member do not impose income taxes. Thus 31 of the 45 states that do impose income taxes are affiliated with the MTC. Regular membership requires approval by the state legislature, associate membership requires only action by the governor of the state.

25. Indicative of the latitude for confusion in this area is the disagreement between the Advisory Commission on Intergovernmental Relations (1974, p. 290) and the MTC (1974, p. 27) on the number of states that have adopted the UDITPA. The MTC counts Massachusetts and New Hampshire, even though their formulas or practices depart somewhat from UDITPA, and the ACIR counts West Virginia, even though it applies UDITPA only to allocation of non-business income.

26. Because the MTC has no directory powers, its adoption of uniform regulations can only be advisory. These regulations are contained in Multistate Tax Commission (1974, pp. 64-86).

27. On august 8, 1972, U.S. Steel, Standard Brands, Procter and Gamble, and General Mills filed an unsuccessful suit in U.S. District Court for the Southern District of New York, complaining that the Commission's audit program is illegal and that the Compact itself is unconstitutional. These plaintiffs were subsequently joined by a number of other large corporations. Because the decision was not reached in this case until July 8, 1976, the joint activities of the MTC's New York office have not expanded as one might have expected. The decision has been appealed to the U.S. Supreme Court for final resolution.

The ramifications of the inaction in the New York case can be seen in North Dakota. When International Business Machines and International Harvester Company refused to submit to an MTC joint audit, the state tax commissioner's suit in the state district court was removed to federal court. It was not remanded to the state court and further proceedings were stayed pending resolution of the New York suit. This, of course, had the same effect of preventing MTC audits that an injunction in New York would have had.

A quite different result followed in a similar case in Idaho. There, the federal court ruled that adequate remedy was available in the state court, noting that a stay of proceedings would be tantamount to preliminary injunctive relief. An even more fundamental point was decided in a case heard in the state of Washington. There a county superior court held that the MTC has authority to conduct joint audits, even though Congress has not approved the MTC, and ordered the Hertz Corporation to submit to audit. In so doing, it overruled the request for a stay of action pending settlement of the *U.S. Steel* case in New York. This case is currently before the supreme court of the state of Washington. This description of legal action is from Multistate Tax Commission (1974).

It should be noted that business is not uniformly opposed to the MTC and its operations. In testimony before the Senate Finance Committee, Frank H. Roberts, on behalf of such California-based firms as Standard Oil of California, Del Monte, Bank of America, Southern Pacific, Union Oil, Kaiser, Safeway, etc., supported the MTC because of the perceived uniformity it has brought and could bring in the field of interstate income taxation [U.S. Congress (1973, pp. 219–227); see Capetta (1974) for more on the MTC's joint audit program].

28. Differences in national and subnational tax rates are accentuated by the deductibility of state tax liabilities in calculating taxable income for federal tax purposes. Deductibility, which effectively eliminates about half of any interstate differences, may in fact go far toward explaining why an "intolerable" situation continued so long to be tolerated.

29. But foreign profits of the parent company and its branches would be taxed at home only if a residence-principle rule were grafted onto the basically source-related division of income by formula. Of course, U.S. experience offers no precedent for such an approach, though international experience does.

30. One potential advantage of separate accounting at the state level in the United States is the existence of separate accounting at the national level. States can utilize the expertise of the federal government in enforcing section 482 of the U.S. Tax Code in dividing profits between domestic and foreign (non-U.S.) sources. While this is relevant for any other federal system, it is clearly less relevant for judging which approach to follow at the national level. Moreover, though separate accounting cannot be discussed at length in this paper, it should be noted that the application of section 482 is seen by many as little better than farcical [see, for example, Briloff (1967) Phillips (1970), and Hamlin (1970)]. But the problem of auditing books of affiliated firms residing in other jurisdictions may be more troublesome than in the domestic context.

31. The executive director of the MTC has assured the author [Corrigan (1975)] that this poses no problem in the United States, since hardly ever is one firm or group of firms construed to engage in more than one unitary business. But it is precisely where manipulation is possible that we might expect a request for construction of multiple unitary businesses.

32. The possibilities of manipulation of factors seem to have received little attention in the domestic U.S. context. Because under UDITPA it is based upon attribution of employees for unemployment compensation, the payroll factor should cause little problem. Similarly, original cost of depreciable property (also specified under UDITPA) must, at least in principle, agree with values reported for federal income tax purposes. Sales, on the other hand, could easily be

misstated in transactions at less than arm's length. But there is really room for manipulation of factors only if firms are affiliated but not engaged in only one unitary business, an unusual occurrence in the United States. In the international sphere there is nothing comparable to a higher-level income tax. But sales and property values are likely to be subject to scrutiny by customs officials.

33. This discussion is based on the assumption that the object is to allocate profits for tax purpose to the jurisdictions in which they originate. Other objectives, such as benefit taxation, international equity, and capital export neutrality may require other formulas or residence-based taxation [see also Musgrave (1972 and 1974)].

34. At the national level it is not necessary to distinguish between normal and extraordinary returns to capital because of the use of separate accounting. But the issue cannot very well be ignored in trying to settle the proper choice of apportionment formulas to use in settling source-versus-source claims.

35. Another reasonable candidate for apportionment formulas is value added. But the choice of value added at origin or at destination must be addressed. Payroll, property, and sales at origin are all indicative of origin-principle value added (though one would still need to determine weights). On the other hand, sales at destination reflects destination-principle value added to some extent. (See also the paragraph following in the text.)

36. It might be thought that this would strengthen overall tax administration. But many countries do not now have retail sales taxes. The wisdom of adding the traditional concerns of administrators of retail sales taxes to those of income tax officials is questionable. This would be less of a problem within the United States.

37. For tentative research in this direction see Musgrave (1972) and Brannon (no date).

38. For a more complete discussions and references to literature, see McLure (1974, pp. 96–102).

39. This rule is fairly easy to implement if all the activities of two firms are combined for tax purposes. But in cases in which the unitary business concept controls, it can be argued that, in principle, exemption should extend only to the portion of dividends attributable to the subsidiary's earnings from the unitary business for which a combined return is filed. Implementing such an approach would be difficult indeed. But, as noted in note 31, this would seem to be a minor problem in the United States.

40. In some respects, the Fiscal Committee of the OECD might serve as a prototype for this kind of organization.

References

Advisory Commission on Intergovernmental Relations. 1974. *Federal-State Local Finances: Significant Features of Fiscal Federalism.* Washington: U.S. Government Printing Office.

Brannon, G.M. No date. National shares of multinational company income. Mimeographed.

Briloff, A.J. 1967. The mad, mad, mad, mad world of 482. *Journal of Accountancy* 124:44–53.

Cahoon, C.R., and Brown, W.R. 1973. The interstate tax dilemma: A proposed solution. *National Tax Journal* 26:187–197.

Capetta, F.P. 1974. The joint audit program of the multistate tax commission. *Annual Report of the Multistate Tax Commission.* Boulder, Colorado. pp. 52–63.

Corrigan, E.F. 1975. Letter to Charles E. McLure, Jr. December 30, 1975.

Hamlin, M.L. 1970. Correct allocations under section 482 are still difficult despite new regs. *Journal of Taxation* 358–363.

Keesling, F.M. 1974. The combined report and uniformity in allocation practices. *Annual Report of the Multistate Tax Commission.* Boulder, Colorado. pp. 33–45.

McLure, C.E., Jr. 1974. State income taxation of multistate corporations in the United States of America. In *The Impact of Multinational Corporations on Development and on International Relations.* New York: United Nations, pp. 58–111.

Multistate Tax Commission. Various years. Annual Reports. Boulder, Colorado.

Multistate Tax Commission. July 1970. *Multistate Tax Newsletter.* Boulder, Colorado.

Musgrave, P.B. 1972. International tax base division and the multinational corporation. *Public Finance* 27:394–413;

Musgrave, P.B. 1974. International tax differentials for multinational corporations: Equity and efficiency considerations. In *The Impact of Multinational Corporations on Development and on International Relations.* New York: United Nations. pp. 43–57.

Phillips, C. 1970. The current status of the application of section 482 to foreign related corporations. *Taxes: The Tax Magazine* 48: 472–478.

Sato, M., and Bird, R.M. 1975. International aspects of the taxation of corporations and shareholders. *IMF Staff Papers* 22: 384–355.

Shoup, C.S. 1974. Taxation of multinational corporations. In *The Impact of Multinational Corporations on Development and on International Relations* New York: United Nations. pp. 1–42.

U.S. Congress. Special Subcommittee on State Taxation of Interstate Commerce of the House Committee on the Judiciary. 1964. *State Taxation of Interstate Commerce 1* Washington: U.S. Government Printing Office.

U.S. Congress. Subcommittee on State Taxation of Interstate Commerce of the Senate Committee on Finance. 1973. *State Taxation of Interstate Commerce* Washington: Government Printing Office.

van den Tempel. 1970. *Corporation Tax and Individual Income Tax in the European Communities.* Brussels: Commission of the European Communities.

14 The Economics of Bilingualism

Albert Breton and
Peter Mieszkowski

In many circumstances and for many persons, there are strong economic as well as cultural incentives to acquire skills in a language or languages other than one's mother tongue. For some occupations and activities that involve international interaction or exchange of some sort or other, such as diplomacy, international trade, or international technical ventures, foreign-language skills are almost essential.

It is our aim in this chapter to bring to bear some of the tools of economic analysis on the questions of investment in language in order to illustrate the determinants of the rate of return on this type of investment. One of our objectives is to determine whether investment in language is merely an investment in a particular skill or whether there are novel, unique features to the economics of bilingualism. In particular, we are interested in determining the advantages or disadvantages of being a person whose native language is that of the majority or minority.

The Returns to Language in Simple Competitive Models of Exchange

In this section we consider investment in language as a means of overcoming communication barriers between traders in commodities or in factors of production. This characterization of language is quite general and is analogous to a spatial distance that has to be overcome by transportation expenditures.

To begin, we consider a case where two countries, England and France, have roughly the same populations and national incomes. England specializes in the production of cloth and exchanges it in France for wine. The price of wine in England and cloth in France will exceed the price of wine in France and cloth in England by the cost of transportation plus any other transaction (exchange) costs. Part of the other transaction costs will include a return to investment in

We wish to acknowledge the useful discussions we have had on this subject with Jean-Thomas Bernard, and we are grateful to André Raynauld for commenting on an earlier draft of this chapter.

261

language. Frenchmen may learn English so that they will be able to communicate with English wine wholesalers or retailers. Alternatively, English wholesalers or wine merchants will invest in French and make trips to buy directly from French wine producers.

Owing to the existence of gains from trade, a number of bilingual traders will emerge. Nothing in the structure of this simple situation allows us to predict whether it will be exporters or importers of wine who will invest in the second language. It is very likely that some Englishmen will learn French and some Frenchmen will learn English. When the prices of both commodities are competitively determined in both countries, so will the returns to language, and in the absence of other considerations, this return will be the same for Englishmen and Frenchmen. The market mechanism (i.e., the laws of comparative advantage) will guide traders in making the appropriate investment in language. In such a situation, we say that the returns to bilingualism are *symmetrical* in the sense that the *potential* advantages of learning a second language are the same for the members of the two countries who are trading with each other. The symmetry condition is important, for, as we shall argue below, in many multilingual situations it does *not* hold: the return to investment in English by a native-speaking Frenchman may be higher than the return to investment in French by a native-speaking Englishman. However, the essential point is that those who invest in a second language (the only transaction cost we consider other than transportation costs) will make a profit on international transactions to compensate them for their investment.[1]

The fact that language is a barrier, or a transaction cost, suggests that such costs will be minimized with *perfect sorting*. Unilingual Englishmen should ideally deal with bilingual Frenchmen, while bilingual Englishmen should transact business with unilingual Frenchmen; otherwise, some of the investment in language will not be utilized.

The view of investment in language as an input in the transactions process and/or as a vehicle for communication allows us to make a number of simple predictions. For example, the greater the amount of economic interchange between two nations, the greater will be the investment in bilingualism. Alternatively, we could say that language represents a barrier to trade and economic integration. Further, if we are willing to assume that there is variation in the language component of commodities that enter into international trade, we should observe some corresponding variation in the amount of investment in language depending on the goods that are exchanged. For example, the level of bilingualism, or to put it differently, the degree of fluency in a second language that is needed to trade in wine and cloth may be quite rudimentary, while that necessary to sell and service electronic equipment, automobiles, airplanes, and other "sophisticated commodities" may be much more elaborate. Similarly, the knowledge of a second language that is required to buy and sell bonds across frontiers may be low, while that needed to invest in physical capital in another

linguistic group may be high. If that is the case, the larger the language component of goods that enter into trade, the greater the amount of resources invested
in bilingualism. Alternatively, we could say that the more important is language
as a barrier to trade, the smaller will be the language component of the goods
that are exchanged between countries of different linguistic backgrounds.[2]

If, in addition to the above, we recognize that languages may be more or
less dissimilar, and that the greater the dissimilarity the larger the cost of investment in language, we can predict that *ceteris paribus* the more dissimilar
the languages the less the amount of trade, or the more will trade be biased
towards goods that have a small language component.[3]

The fact that language is a barrier to economic exchange also serves to
explain why economic organization in multilingual societies will tend to be
segregated by language. French-speaking persons will tend to work with other
French-speaking persons and to buy in retail and service establishments staffed
by French-speaking persons, while the English will transact with the English,
the Walloons with the Walloons, the Flemish with the Flemish, and so forth.

We began this section with the example of two unilingual nations, England
and France, and argued that it would be profitable for some Englishmen or
Frenchmen to invest in language as a necessary input in the process of trade.
We suggested that, for the case where the two countries are of equal size, the
returns to investment in language are symmetrical for members of the two
linguistic groups. We now assume that the symmetry condition breaks down and
that certain numbers of Frenchmen, say, learn the English language for reasons
that are unrelated to trade, as would happen if English were learned for cultural
reasons: to read English books, to attend English theater and cinema, and/or to
visit England. In these circumstances, and assuming that the same people who
have learned the second language for cultural reasons also engage in international
trade, the yield on that asset in international wine and cloth trade would be zero
in the specific sense that the prices of both cloth and wine would be lower than
if some individuals had had to invest in a second language for trade reasons.

It is important to note that even though only Frenchmen learn English in
our example, it is not the case that the English get a free ride, since the price of
both commodities is lower than it would otherwise be. The situation is similar
to the one that would obtain if a technological innovation had reduced transportation costs.

The reason why the countries share equally in the gains from the lower cost
of communication is that we have assumed the countries to be of equal size. If,
instead, we assume that one country, say England, is twenty times bigger than
France, we would reach the very different conclusion that all the benefit from
the decrease in the economic cost of communications will accrue to France. The
reason for this is quite simple. By assuming that one of the two nations is very
much larger than the other, we approximate the small-country assumption often
made in the pure theory of international trade. In this case, a small country

faces fixed terms of trade that are determined by demand and supply conditions in the rest of the world (the large country). In moving from a situation of no trade (autarchy) to a free-trade situation, the small country will have only the most marginal effect on the world terms of trade. The benefits of the opening up of trade between a large country and a small country will thus accrue primarily to the small country. For the problem at hand, this implies that "transactions costs," whether due to transportation or to the need to overcome language differences, will be borne by the small country. Consequently, if the transaction costs associated with language barriers (differences) are decreased, either by the adoption of a common language (transition cost aside) or by an increase in investment in language for noneconomic reasons, as discussed above, the benefit resulting from this reduction in costs (where the costs relate to compensation to investment in language) will accrue primarily to citizens of the small country. We also note that trade specialists may not bear the cost of investing in language, since they will be compensated for this investment in the form of higher prices and/or higher wages and salaries. The cost of investment in language is a social cost that is borne by society through a decrease in its real income.

The argument that the small country (or the population speaking the minority language) will bear the communication costs associated with language differences generalizes to situations where the trade is in factors of production rather than in commodities. Consider a case in which both a large and a small country produce the same types of commodities under similar technologies, but assume that trade does not, for some reason, equalize factor prices and that the real return to capital is higher in the small country and the return to labor is lower. Capital will want to flow from the larger to the smaller country, but the flow will be partially impeded by language barriers. Some market agents will have to invest in language so that capital exporters and importers will be able to communicate.

As in the case of trade in commodities, we see no reason why in the absence of other considerations the return to investment in language should not be symmetrical for persons speaking the majority and minority languages. Thus, if the United States is investing capital in Greece, Americans can learn Greek and receive a return for this investment. Someone will have to bear the cost of communications, and it does not matter whether the capital exporters, who speak the majority language (English), learn Greek or are addressed in English. A market agent will receive a return (a wage premium) for investment in language, and if American capital exporters choose not to invest in Greek, then native-speaking Greeks will have an incentive to invest in English.

Although returns to investment in language may be symmetrical for members of the two language groups, the ultimate burden of the cost of this investment may be distributed very unequally between the two groups. Let us suppose that the members of the minority language invest in language training and spend much of their time in language translation and related activities.

A general characterization of this type of activity can be made in terms of the size of the labor force (or the proportion of the stock of human capital) devoted to production. If communication barriers are decreased, then labor services and/or human capital will be freed for work in production. So the removal of, or decrease in, the language barrier will represent an increase in the "effective" labor force of the capital-importing country. Since we are assuming the capital-importing country to be very small relative to the capital-exporting country, the increased capital outflow from the large to the small country will increase by approximately the same percentage as the percentage increase in the effective labor force. As the overall supply of effective labor in the world has increased as a result of the improvement in communications and the decrease in transaction costs, the return to capital will rise.

If, for simplicity, we assume a Cobb-Douglas technology for both countries and also assume marginal-product pricing, the increase in the return to capital will be the increase in the supply of labor multiplied by the share of capital in national income. Consequently, if language barriers are decreased, the gains to capital and some of the gains to labor in the country speaking the minority language will come at the expense of labor speaking the majority language.

It appears, therefore, that when two trading societies are of unequal size, the terms of trade and factor prices essentially will be determined by the endowments and tastes prevailing in the large country. Consequently, the small country must "adjust" to these international prices and so will bear virtually all the transaction costs represented by the language barrier between the two communities. Of course, this argument is really a very general one and applies not only to language but to transportation and any other transaction barriers to trade.

The key assumption on which these arguments are based is that the terms of trade and the return to capital are fixed by market conditions in the large country. When this assumption is weakened, the results become much less definite. A small country may well have terms-of-trade effects under conditions of product differentiation and quality differences within various commodity groups. Many examples can be found where a small country or a group of small- or medium-sized countries supply a substantial proportion of the world consumption of certain commodities. Among the many possible examples are Swiss watches, French wines and fashions, South African diamonds, Latin American coffee and tropical fruit, and various unique tourist attractions in many countries. Consequently, the Hecksher-Ohlin model of international trade, on which the analysis of the few last paragraphs is based, has to be modified and extended to account for various forms of product differentiation.

When supply (cost) conditions in small countries affect the terms of trade in certain commodities, communication barriers will be borne in large measure by the importing countries and a decrease in these transaction costs will benefit the consumers of these products because of the resulting lower prices. We should note once again that different commodities have associated with them varying amounts of transaction or communication costs, and a change in the cost

associated with language will change the relative prices of a country's exports
or imports.

In this section, we have characterized investment in language as an expenditure in overcoming a communication barrier between countries. In the absence of
other considerations, the returns to investment in language should be symmetrical for members of the linguistic majority and of the minority. However,
symmetry does not imply anything about the important question of how the
economic burden of the transaction cost associated with language barriers is
distributed among different communities.

Our basic conclusion on the question of incidence is that the relative size of
various countries is crucial; or more generally, if a country cannot influence,
or has marginal influence on, the international terms of trade, its citizens must
bear the burden of the communication costs. This cost is spread over the general
population in the form of unfavorable terms of trade or lower factor payments.

The Emergence of Dominant Languages and the
Seignorage of Language

When we broaden the set of considerations that bear on the incentives to investment in language, we find, not surprisingly, that certain languages are likely to
become dominant languages, that the return to investment in different languages
will vary, and that symmetry is likely to break down. If English becomes the
dominant language, the rate of return or advantage of learning English by a
typical French person will exceed (perhaps by a substantial amount) the rate of
return to the investment in French by a person whose native language is English.
Also, when a language becomes dominant, it is very likely that persons whose
native language is dominant will earn a premium or seignorage relative to persons
whose native language is not English.

If language dominance is such an important phenomenon, we must devote
some space to a discussion of the factors that give rise to it. Furthermore, since
dominance and the establishment of a language convention are closely related,
we must look into the origin of language conventions and into the nature of the
property rights they confer.

One of the most important, if not the most important, factors in determining the dominance of a language is the absolute size or scale of a nation.
The main reason for this is that power and influence attach to large size. This
is easily seen in the extreme case of a conquering nation that imposes its language on the conquered population. It is less obvious, but still important, in the
case of a large nation that is able to display substantial military power, is willing
to intervene militarily to advance and guarantee its national interest, and is not
too reluctant to interfere diplomatically to ensure its views. There seems to be
little doubt that the current dominance of the English language profited con-

siderably from the appearance of the United States on the world scene as the prevailing military and diplomatic power after the 150 years in which Britain occupied essentially the same position.

Absolute size is important in at least one other respect. If some members of a large nation are preeminent or superior in any endeavor, be it the arts, commerce, science, technology, or fashion, that superiority will contribute to the dominance of language. This last point can be clarified by noting that the contribution to world culture and to scientific knowledge may be much larger on a per capita basis in Norway and Sweden than in the United States, yet the size of the United States is such that the return to investment in the English language will be much higher than the return to investment in the Scandinavian language.

Another very important reason why a few languages become dominant, or why a single language becomes the universal language, or the *lingua franca*, is that there are very strong economic benefits from the adoption of a common means of communication.[4]

Consider a "small"world consisting, initially, of 10 nations of roughly the same size, each with its own distinct language and culture. Each country uses its own language, of course, for internal communication and must invest some resources in a number of foreign languages, perhaps all 9, to engage in international relations.

Under a situation where diplomacy and international trade are carried out in a large number of languages, international relations will be very expensive. Unless economic agents can sort themselves out perfectly, so that they will be using their acquired language skills in communicating with their foreign counterparts, particular language skills will probably be underutilized and the transaction costs of foreign trade will be high, since traders must invest in a large number of languages. The case is analogous to a situation where a person must hold or carry a number of foreign currencies because he cannot be certain which currency will be needed in trade. Although a great deal of investment in languages may take place, the *average* transaction cost per foreign transaction will be high because market agents will be carrying a large, partially underutilized, "inventory" of foreign languages. Thus foreign trade and economic integration will be impeded as a result of the high average costs of overcoming language barriers.

Now, if some of the countries, say England, France, and Germany, become dominant in size and trade, smaller countries will tend to emphasize training and investment in the dominant languages and will begin to deemphasize and cut back their investment in other languages. This will occur because most, if not all, traders will be able to communicate in the dominant languages. Thus, Swedes will transact business with the Dutch in English or German, and the French, Poles, and Hungarians will use French in negotiating trades.

For simplicity, we shall assume that a single *lingua franca* emerges. From a strictly economic standpoint, it is clear that the use of a single language for international transactions will increase the real income of the international community. By investing in a single language (the *lingua franca*), traders can be reasonably assured that they will be able to conduct trade in virtually every country. The larger, partially underutilized, "portfolio" of languages will now be replaced by a single language for international communication.

In analyzing the social or national advantages of having one's native language adopted as the *lingua franca*, we distinguish between the more global, or worldwide, benefits of the development of a *lingua franca* and the specific benefits to the country whose language becomes the international language. We shall consider three "countries": English-speaking countries (England, for short), France, and a number of smaller countries. Imagine that French develops as the international language. Although it is difficult to be very precise about the distribution of the benefits of this "technological innovation" in international communications, a substantial portion of the benefits resulting from the decrease in transaction costs should accrue to the smaller countries. These countries will be less diversified and more specialized than the two larger countries and so will have a great deal to gain from a decrease in transaction costs that promotes international integration and specialization within countries. We speculate that the typical small country is more dependent on foreign trade than are larger countries, so that a decrease in international barriers will benefit smaller countries proportionately more relative to their national income. England and France also benefit from the adoption of a *lingua franca*, as their direct investment in second languages decreases (the investment of France will virtually fall to zero) and the prices of commodities they supply to smaller countries consequently fall.

Next, to appraise the special advantages accruing to the country whose language is the *lingua franca*, we consider the implications of a change in the *lingua franca* from French to English. It may appear that the loss to France of such a change in language convention is self-evident, for a change from French to English will force France to increase her investment in the second language.

However, we argued earlier, in considering trade between two countries of roughly equal size, that the direct expenditure on language communication is irrelevant for the real, or ultimate, distribution of cost burdens. If France and England are of equal size and trade primarily among themselves, the investment in language by France will be partially borne by the English in higher prices of French exports in England. For this case, language investment is akin to transportation cost. It does not matter whether the exporter or the importer "pays" the transportation bill. Also, if for *cultural* (noneconomic) reasons there is an incentive for Frenchmen to learn English, transactions costs will fall, because these persons will work as international specialists with little, if any, *economic* return for their investment in language. Both England and France reap economic benefits from this "technological innovation" (resulting from a cultural basis for

investment in language by the French), and while Frenchmen make the investment in language for cultural reasons, this investment would have been made
even in the absence of trade in more conventional economic goods and in the
absence of exchange in factors of production.

The advantages or benefits to a country of having its language used as the
lingua franca thus arise *primarily* from the existence of a wider international
community (the numerous smaller countries). It is the fact that Italy, Sweden,
etc., invest in English for reasons other than because this language is useful for
economic transactions with England that forms the basis of the "free ride" that
accrues to English-speaking countries. The adoption by the world of a *lingua
franca* represents the development of an international means of communication,
or a public good, that yields benefits to the whole international community.
Yet, while the benefits are distributed generally, the investment cost of creating
this means of communication are borne primarily, if not exclusively, by the
non-English-speaking countries of the world.

Consequently, a change-over from French to English for international
communications will represent a real loss to France and a benefit to England,
since after the change the rest of the world will find it more advantageous to
trade with England than with France at the same terms of trade and France
will be forced to invest in language and/or to suffer a deterioration in its terms
of trade. The change in the language convention means that France is transformed, with respect to world trade, into a small country that has to adjust to
the world terms of trade that have moved against it. Of course, as noted in our
earlier analysis, to the extent that French commodities have special or unique
characteristics, the deterioration in the terms of trade will be moderated, or
could even be quite small.

In general, then, there will be real economic losses associated with a change
in a country's language-dominance status. General de Gaulle's opposition to the
entry of the United Kingdom into the European Economic Community made
sense on economic as well as "nationalistic" grounds if this meant that French
would be replaced by English as the working language of the Common Market
countries. In circumstances of that kind, such a change in language would have
imposed economic costs as well as loss of national prestige on the French.

To analyze the advantages at the level of individual persons of being a
native speaker of the majority language, we first distinguish between the general
or environmental advantages of being a member of a dominant nation or culture
and then relate these advantages to language and the choice of, and change in,
the *lingua franca*.

Suppose that initially all countries are isolated from one another and that
there is no exchange of commodities, factors of production, or technical, liter-
ary, and artistic information between them. Then clearly the persons born in
the nation where the economic system is most developed, whose educational
institutions are the most distinguished, and whose culture is most innovative

will be at a distinct advantage relative to persons who are born in less developed nations. Now, if we allow for exchange of commodities and ideas, the less-developed countries whose native tongue is that of the developed country will be at an advantage relative to individuals in underdeveloped countries, whose native language is not that of the developed one.

Ideas and cultural and technical information will flow more easily if there is no language problem. At the level of the individual in many countries, there will be a strong incentive to acquire, for a variety of reasons, a working knowledge of the dominant language. The cost of the investment in the dominant language will be borne by the individual who makes the investment. The rate of return on that investment, at the level of the individual, will be quite asymmetrical. The returns on an investment in English by a French economist residing in North America is much higher than the returns on the investment in French by an English economist. In part, the asymmetry in rate of return can be explained by scale or size. Suppose there are 50 English-speaking and 5 French-speaking economists; both language groups would gain if all 55 persons could communicate with each other. However, because of diminishing returns to communication, the per capita gains from increased communication to each English-speaking person are likely to be considerably smaller than the per capita gains accruing to each French-speaking person. The French minority will tend to learn English and the English will tend to get a free ride. This is again the seignorage of language, though in a somewhat different form.[5]

Apart from a country's size, innovativeness and superiority in technical and cultural areas will lead to an asymmetry in rates of return to language training. As size and dominance are no doubt related, the general picture that emerges is that persons speaking the dominant language will be at a distinct advantage relative to persons whose native tongue is not dominant. Access to, or importation of, the technical and cultural ideas of the dominant country will depend on investments in language either directly by the individual or by means of translation.

Perhaps the most obvious example of the disadvantages of being a member of a linguistic minority occurs in multilingual societies. Small linguistic and cultural minorities, such as Mexican-Americans or Chinese-Americans, can maintain their economic independence only at the risk of substantial economic cost and restrictions on the economic opportunities of the members of the community. Minority-group members can work in "ethnic work places" and in "ethnic work teams," but when the size of the group is small relative to the overall size of the local economy, ethnic stratification in employment is likely to lead to an overcrowding of minority-group members into certain occupations and industries. The loss in income resulting from restrictions on occupational choice will be especially large for the higher-paying, high-status managerial and professional occupations. Unlike many semi-skilled and unskilled occupations, language proficiency in the majority tongue will almost always be a necessary qualification for higher-skilled occupations in a multilingual society. Consequently, if members of the minority are to qualify for these positions and for access into a more broadly structured economic society, they will have to become bilingual, or unilingual, in the tongue of the majority. In a sense, the position of minority members in a multilingual society is similar, if not identical, to the position of a small country in a larger world community dominated by one or more linguistic groups. The minority group can remain economically and culturally isolated from the rest of the "world," but only at a cost. Typically, many members of this society will find it to their benefit to overcome the language barrier by appropriate language investments so as to be able to qualify for higher-paying employment in the majority language or in order to have access to the commodities and ideas available in other nations.

Conclusion

In this chapter we have considered two broad classes of models. First we looked at simple trade models in which, on the whole, the yield on investment in language is symmetrical and that it is not possible a priori to predict who, of the members of two or more linguistic groups, will acquire a second language. We saw that even in these simple cases the final incidence or burden of the cost of investment may be different from the source or origin of the investment.

We then moved to more complex models in which the yield on investment in language is asymmetrical between two groups because of the existence of a dominant language. That dominance status, we argued, could result from a number of factors, among which we mentioned physical scale, cultural or other kinds of superiorities, and the economic advantages—measured in cost reductions—of a *lingua franca*. For this class of models, we suggested that seignorage or premiums accrue to members of the dominant language group. Initial benefits and final incidence may also differ in these cases.

These models provide us with the broad conceptual apparatus necessary to understand the problems that arise in a world in which the technology of communication and commerce promotes interaction among groups of different languages. However, many specific issues remain to be worked out and elaborated upon. Among these are questions concerning the mimimum size and the characteristics of minorities that can survive linguistically, the magnitudes of the investment involved, and the mechanics of language acquisition (when and how people learn a second language).

In addition, many bilingual situations have idiosyncratic features that necessitate special analysis. In Canada, bilingualism in Quebec represents such a situation. In that province, the English are a minority, though they are a majority in Canada. Yet they have had very little incentive to learn French, in large part because English dominates in the boardrooms and offices of a very substantial part of the Quebec economy. Faced with this situation and with rising French-Canadian nationalism, the government of Quebec has introduced a number of measures to promote the use of French as the "working language" of the province. One of the issues related to this phenomenon on which we have done some preliminary work [Breton and Mieszkowski (1975)] concerns the economic effects of such language policies on the economic status of Quebeckers and of Canadians. The models suggested in this chapter should make such tasks easier.

Notes

1. This simple hypothesis can be generalized to encompass a variety of economic transactions. It serves to explain, for example, why certain hotels in France will employ, at higher wages, bilingual clerks, while other hotels will cater to an exclusively French-speaking clientele. Englishmen who speak French will do well to avoid the "international hotels," as they will be paying a premium to be addressed in their own language. If the French sell wine not only in England but also in Germany, Holland, and Scandinavia, there will be a tendency for hotels to specialize in servicing particular language clienteles, so that in large centers (Paris, for example) one will find "German hotels," "Dutch hotels," and so on.

2. It is difficult to speculate on the size of the language component of commodities, but casual observation seems to indicate that there is some variation in the weight that attaches to this component and that it is related to the extent to which the instructions for the use of the product are important to the nature of the servicing and repair and to other such factors.

3. We can also predict that the returns to bilingualism will vary considerably across occupations, depending upon how much interaction with foreigners a particular individual will have in his occupation or in his economic function. Similarly, in a country such as Canada, composed of two linguistically different groups, the number of bilingual persons will vary across occupational groups. There should, for example, be a much higher return to investment in a second language to politicians and civil servants employed at the national level than to factory workers or laborers who are able to work in isolation with members of their own language group.

4. We owe this important point to a reading of Carr's (undated) paper.

5. We can provide many examples from cultural and intellectual affairs to illustrate the advantages of being a member of the majority and the disadvantages of being a member of the minority. Among the advantages is the greater ease of communication at international conferences, where English is the conventional working language. Among the disadvantages are the need to publish in English, even in journals published in one's native country in order to secure

a wider audience and international recognition, and the lack of recognition for many original contributions. English-speaking economists have made many "unnecessary original contributions" due to their inability to read French, Italian, German, and Swedish. One should also note that there is an interaction between economic and military dominance and cultural dominance. One reason given from the rise of New York and the decline of Paris as the world center for the visual arts is that the preeminence of the United States in noncultural areas immediately after World War II led to the expectation of, and facilitated the acceptance of, American leadership in avant-guarde artistic developments in the postwar period.

References

Breton, A., and Mieszkowski, P. 1975. The returns to investment in language: The economics of bilingualism. Working paper no. 7512. Toronto: Institute for Policy Analysis, University of Toronto.

Carr, J.L. No date. Is English a Natural Monopoly? Manuscript. Toronto: Institute for Quantitative Analysis of Social and Economic Policy, University of Toronto.

15

Quantitative Aspects of Federalism: A Study of Six Countries

Werner W. Pommerehne

1. Introductory Notes

The aim of this chapter is, first, to present a series of statistical data on different countries to describe their federative structures. The countries analyzed for this purpose are Canada, France, the Federal Republic of Germany, Switzerland, the United Kingdom, and the United States. Since most of the statistical data—when they were available[1] —can be easily interpreted, their presentation forms one of the later sections of this chapter (section 4).

Second, using statistical data and empirical studies that have already been carried out (especially on the six countries mentioned), this chapter seeks to demonstrate how relevant the economic approach is to fiscal federalism. This can be done in two ways: we can start with *given* (hierarchically ordered) units and investigate, for example, whether a major redistributional policy is indeed not to be expected at the subcentral governmental level as the economic approach would suggest. Or the assumption of a given federative structure can be dismissed, and we can concentrate our research on the question of which economic, political, and social factors determine the demand for centralization. Since I am considering both approaches in this paper, the sections are arranged accordingly.

Section 2 deals, under the heading of Economic Aspects of Fiscal Federalism, with those branches of fiscal policy that since Musgrave (1959, chap. 1) have been labeled "allocation, distribution, and stabilization." There I do not analyze theoretically one or the other of these branches more closely; this, as far as it concerns their federative aspects, has been done by various authors [see, for example, Oates (1968, 1972) and Musgrave (1969a)] . Rather, the arguments of the economic position are taken as known in their essentials, and I ask how much empirical evidence can be found in the countries mentioned for hypotheses deduced from this position.

Financial support by the Ford Foundation is gratefully acknowledged. The author is indebted to Renate Exner, Thomas Kriedel, Heiner Schuelke, and Hannelore Weck for the extensive bibliographical research underlying this study. He would also like to thank Gebhard Kirchgaessner for his research assistance.

In section 3 the approach is reversed. I investigate which political, social, and economic variables determine the demand for a decentralized fiscal structure. Using quantitative methods (cross-sectional analysis), I attempt to give a tentative answer to this question. As already mentioned, section 4 contains a series of statistical data.

2. Economic Aspects of Fiscal Federalism

Allocational Aspects of Fiscal Federalism

Public Provision of Goods and Services. A first function[2] of the public sector lies in the establishment of an efficient pattern of resource use (i.e., within the framework of a federative structure) to provide defined areas with certain public and private goods and services.[3]

It is well known that the advantage of decentralization of decisions (i.e., the federal fiscal structure) lies in the fact that a variety of demands can be taken into account in a better way than in centralized decisions. But it is also known that the scale on which a good is provided on a certain governmental level tends to depend on the degree to which spillovers can be internalized. If this is not (or only partially) possible on the local level, it must be referred to the decision-making process on the next higher government level, making it possible to take the spatial and external effects (of a positive or negative nature) into account.

But a lack of "fiscal equivalence" (Olson, 1969) does not necessarily mean that the regulation of details and provision of the respective service must take place on the next higher level too. The level of decision making can vary considerably from the level on which the service is provided, either because the respective circumstances can be better dealt with on the subcentral level or that diseconomies of scale occur in the provision. Both the size of spatial external effects and the existence of economies of scale *can* point in the same direction, so that the problem of which level the provision of a good should be decided upon does not arise. However, this is far more difficult in the case of contrasting tendencies, where the advantages and disadvantages of centralization and decentralization must be balanced against each other.[4] From empirical data, however, it is difficult to conclude to what extent the existence of spillovers and economies or diseconomies of scale were decisive for the division of functions and the actual provision of the various services; as an alternative explanation, the central government might provide a certain minimum level of some services deemed to be "merit goods" [see Musgrave (1969b) and Neumann (1971)].

However, certain common traits possibly can be expected in all countries considered here. Thus national defense, the maintenance of international relations, and basic research, for example, will be the responsibility of the central level of a nation because of their nature as public goods. But similar arguments can also be applied, to some extent, to such "goods" as social welfare (with a redistributional goal) and countercyclical policy (with a stabilization goal), as will be pointed out more clearly in the following paragraphs.

On the other hand, the economic approach leads us to expect that services whose beneficiaries are restricted to a locality or region (e.g., law enforcement, public administration, refuse collection) will tend to be decided upon on a local or regional level. Furthermore, it can be expected that decisions on goods and services will not be made mainly at a single governmental level: the responsibilities of higher education, science, and research (especially of the universities and colleges) are being shared more and more by state and federal governments because of their considerable cost and benefit spillovers. We may expect similar tendencies at the state and local levels with such services as police protection, primary and secondary schooling, refuse disposal, and water supply; it could even be the case that these services are regarded as the common responsibility of several local-government units. Finally, because of the manifold goals involved (also of a merit-good nature), questions concerning economic-development projects, the improvement of the traffic network, and the like are decided upon on all levels.

In what follows I will consider the public expenditure of the various government units by function as a rough approximation of the actual functions of each level in order to investigate to what extent this reflects the division of functions described above. For a detailed picture, I take Swiss public expenditures by function and level of government in the years 1969 and 1973 (Table 15-1).[5]

As table 15-1 shows, the economic approach to describing the present federative structure in Switzerland and its development seems successful. The exclusively federal expenditures can be readily explained by the existence of spillovers (national defense) and, as in the case of social-insurance services, by expanded risk-spreading. For functions met by federal and state governments, spillover considerations apply (higher education, university research), as well as technological arguments such as the impossibility of division in production (e.g., airports). The situation is similar for the functions met by the state governments on their own, but in a spatially more restricted sense, with the exception of health services (public health). On the state and local level, economies and (from a certain size on) diseconomies of scale,[6] as well as notions of the state government concerning the minimal provision of certain public services (e.g., primary schooling), seem to be decisive. Not covered by my argument are the expenditures of the social-welfare system. However, it is not a question of the quantitatively important social-insurance services (these are dealt with at the federal-government level), but of relief for the poor (charity) in cases where national insurance affords no assistance. Such aid is steadily decreasing in importance. Most of the exclusively local expenditures are easily justified economically. This applies also to expenditures of which all three levels have a large

Table 15-1

The Federal Economic Structure of Switzerland (Public Expenditure Distribution by Function and Level of Government), 1969 and 1973[a]

Level of Government/Function	Year	Percentage Distribution			Total
		Federal	State	Local	
Federal Government Tasks					
International Relations	1973	100.0	–	–	474
	1969	100.0	–	–	302
Broadcasting System	1973	100.0	–	–	4,863
	1969	100.0	–	–	2,548
Military Defense	1973	97.0	2.1	0.9	2,362
	1969	97.0	2.2	0.8	1,792
Social Insurance	1973	94.1	5.6	0.3	10,087
	1969	94.0	5.5	0.5	8,092
Agriculture (Especially stabiliza-	1973	83.9	13.3	2.8	1,299
tion of farm prices and income)	1969	86.2	10.7	3.1	974
Social Insurance Contributions	1973	69.7	23.2	7.1	3,220
	1969	70.4	22.4	7.2	1,646
Air Transportation	1973	67.8	31.3	1.9	231
	1969	43.4	54.7	1.9	97
Federal and State Government Tasks					
Universities and Basic Research	1973	63.2	36.4	0.4	1,525
	1969	65.2	34.2	0.6	695
Protection from Avalanches,	1973	52.7	34.4	12.9	115
Flooding, etc.	1969	34.1	47.1	18.8	66
State Government Tasks					
Real Value Insurance	1973	–	98.6	1.4	388
	1969	–	98.5	1.5	268
High Schools	1973	4.0	90.4	5.6	796
	1969	3.5	93.6	2.9	368
Health and Hospitals	1973	1.2	82.2	16.6	2,852
	1969	1.5	77.8	20.7	1,512
Public Industrial Utilities	1973	–	80.7	19.3	1,244
	1969	–	80.0	20.0[b]	235
Transportation (Excluding	1973	–	75.0	25.0	322
postal services and railroad)	1969	–	74.6	25.4[b]	191
Contributions to Employee	1973	25.8	60.4	13.8	1,783
Retirement (Insurance trusts)	1969	36.7	47.4	15.9[b]	558
Law Enforcement	1973	15.7	64.2	20.1	585
	1969	11.3	71.2	17.5	379
State and Local Government Tasks					
Police and Fire Protection	1973	2.8	60.7	36.5	925
	1969	2.4	57.1	40.5	543
Social Welfare Payments	1973	2.4	56.5	41.1	886
	1969	0.3	50.8	48.9	520
Forestry, Hunting, Fishing	1973	14.2	49.9	35.9	205
	1969	19.0	71.2	5.8	126
Education (Primary Schools)	1973	1.0	41.4	57.6	3,271
	1969	1.2	43.5	55.2	1,725

Table 15-1 Continued

| Level of Government/Function | Year | Percentage Distribution | | | Total |
		Federal	State	Local	
Local Government Tasks					
Water Supply Service	1973	—	10.5	89.5	251
	1969	—	28.8	71.8	33
Cementery, Public Lavatory	1973	0.3	13.7	86.0	177
	1969	0.2	14.8	85.0	145
Recreational and Cultural	1973	7.3	26.5	66.1	822
Services	1969	8.0	27.2	64.8	444
Sewerage (Including waste	1973	13.2	29.5	57.3	991
treatment facilities)	1969	7.1	46.3	46.6	367
Urban Planning and	1973	4.5	32.6	62.9	104
Development	1969	2.0	20.6	77.4	41
Tasks of All Government Levels					
Public Administration	1973	22.3	35.8	41.9	2,305
	1969	24.0	36.8	39.2	1,283
Education Systems for	1973	21.6	42.6	35.8	769
Employees	1969	19.2	58.1	22.7	392
Roads (Highways included)	1973	37.3	32.3	30.4	5,702
	1969	40.9	32.3	26.8	2,340
Subsidies (Tourism, Industry,	1973	40.4	26.1	33.5	80
Commerce)	1969	39.6	25.2	35.2	34
Housing	1973	43.2	24.4	32.4	301
	1969	24.1	49.3	26.6	104
Civil Defense	1973	52.7	20.9	26.3	500
	1969	55.3	22.8	21.6	271
Total (Without public enterprises)	1973	36.2	36.6	27.2	28,862
	1969	39.4	37.0	23.6	16,247
Total (Including all public enter-	1973	56.1	25.5	18.4	50,750
prises)	1969	60.0	25.6	14.4	27,581

Source: Computed from E.St.A., *Oeffentliche Finanzen der Schweiz* (1969 and 1973); *Statistisches Jahrbuch der Schweiz* (1971), and unpublished materials from E.St.A.

Note: Minor items are excluded; the city expenditures of Basle have been included in the state-government expenditures for statistical reasons; public enterprises comprise the broadcasting system, social insurance, real-value insurance, public industrial utilities, transportation (excluding postal services and railroad), and contributions to employee retirement.

[a]See section 4 for an explanation of the symbols and abbreviations used in tables throughout this chapter.

[b]Estimated

share. These may be either services that are dealt with at the federal level (e.g., public administration) or services of a highly heterogeneous nature (e.g., national and state highways and local roads and streets); statistical data, however, do not clearly differentiate between them.

Most of the other countries considered in this paper present a situation similar to that in Switzerland.[7] This can be seen in Table 15-2.[8] Looking at the

Table 15-2
Distribution of All Governments' Expenditures by Function and Level of Government, 1971[a]

Level of Government and Function	Canada[b]			Germany			Switzerland			United States		
	F	S	L	F	S	L	F	S	L	F	S	L
Federal Level												
Nat. Defense and Int. Relations	100.0	—	—	99.9	0.1	—	90.6	6.1	3.2	100.0	—	—
Federal-State Level												
Public Welfare and Health	55.6	41.1	3.3	54.0	18.4	27.6	32.2	48.3	19.5	31.2	42.6	26.2
Natural Resources and Prim. Industries	63.7	36.3	—	40.6	20.8	38.6	44.9	21.0	34.1	78.1	17.7	4.2
Transport and Communications	25.3	55.7	18.9	44.0	25.6	30.4	42.7	30.5	26.8	20.4	57.1	22.5
State Level												
State-Local Level												
Education	12.3	43.0	44.8	12.5	64.0	23.5	15.0	45.9	39.0	12.7	38.9	48.4
Protection	22.5	35.4	42.1	6.2	77.5	16.3	11.3	57.4	31.3	5.9	22.6	71.5
Housing and Urban Renewal	In Other[a]			10.8	49.1	40.1	In Other[a]			56.6	2.8	40.6
Local Level												
All Levels												
General Government	52.3	24.6	23.1	22.2	38.3	39.5	22.3	35.7	42.0	40.3	27.6	32.1

[a]For detailed terms used for functional breakdown and the sources used here, see Tables 15-15 and 15-17 in section 4.
[b]1968.

problem from a schematic perspective, we find again that the tasks of national defense, the maintenance of international relations, and national development programs are among those services that the federal government handles essentially on its own.[9] Services that fall within the responsibility of both federal and state governments are public welfare, transportation and communication, and higher education, whereas health care is one of the services provided for exclusively at the state level.

What has been said about the state and local and strictly local functions in Switzerland is also valid, on the whole, in the other countries dealt with in this paper. In Table 15-2, however, the expenditure groups are already so strongly aggregated that marked deviations in certain categories and countries become only partially apparent. A detailed study would show, for example, that in Canada the aid to primary industries is mainly a function of the provinces, that in the United States transportation is not a major task of the federal government, and that in France the responsibility for education lies to a large extent in the hands of the central government [see, for example, Delorme (1973b, pp. 15 ff.)].

The full extent to which the various functions are fulfilled by the different governments as well as by all levels together cannot, however, be seen in the structural data presented above. For example, national defense expenditures in the United States constitute a considerable part of federal expenditures (as well as of GNP), whereas in Switzerland they are by comparison insignificant—to a great extent because the fulfillment of this function is for the most part the immediate task of the individual citizens themselves, so that the real costs involved do not appear as *public* expenditures.[10]

Financing Government Activity. In order to see how the provision of publicly supplied goods and services is financed, I start with the public-sector revenue structure of a fictitious federal economic country, which is a composite of the (equally weighted) revenue structures of all six countries dealt with here. This structure would look as follows for the year 1970:[11] approximately 32 percent consumption taxes, approximately 39 percent income taxes (personal and corporation income taxes), approximately 9 percent wealth taxes, and approximately 20 percent other taxes and nontax receipts (especially charges and interest earnings). However, as the Table 15-3 shows, substantial deviations are to be found in the various countries. Especially notable, there is the importance of indirect (consumption) taxes in France and the pronounced direct taxation in the United States.

We can also discern a rough scheme for the distribution of the revenue sources among government levels: Sources exploited solely by the *federal* government are in general (1) customs-duties and (2) general excise duties. Sources exploited *together with the state governments* (either in competition with them or jointly, such as tax sharing) are (1) personal income tax, (2) corporation income tax, and (3) general consumption tax. Sources exploited solely by the *state*

Table 15–3
**Deviations from the Fictitious Composition of the Composite Government
Among the Revenues of the Six Countries, 1970[a]**

Revenue	Canada	France	Germany	Switzer- land	U.K.	U.S.
Consumption taxes		+ +			+	
Income taxes		–		+		+ +
Wealth taxes	+		–			
Other taxes and Nontax revenue }				+		+

[a]$\begin{smallmatrix} + \, +/+ \\ - \, -/- \end{smallmatrix}$ = very strong/strong positive or negative deviation.

government are (1) special consumption taxes, (2) motor-vehicle taxes, and (3) various minor taxes. Sources exploited by *local government* are (1) wealth taxes, (2) various minor taxes, and (3) (often an important source) user charges and fees.

There are various deviations from this scheme that are not restricted solely to differences in the distribution of revenue sources (own-revenue sources, shared-revenue sources) but also to differences in organization, that is, whether the tax exemption represents competition or cooperation between the various government levels. Thus we have in Canada a clear system of separation as far as indirect taxes are concerned and a loose cooperation with direct taxes. In France the opposite is true: local governments have long shared the indirect taxes with the central government, though to a small extent. This method has been extended also to the relations between central governments and states (*départements*) since World War II. In Germany there is complete cooperation among all three levels of government for the three largest and shared tax sources since 1969. In Switzerland indirect taxation is in the hands of the federal government, while all three levels compete in the case of direct taxation. In the United Kingdom tax sources are mainly separated. The central government collects the direct and the consumption taxes, while local governments concentrate on wealth taxes. Nontax revenues also play a major role on the local level. Although the situation in the United States is formally one of complete competition, each of the three levels of government more or less monopolizes some tax sources. Thus, direct taxes go mainly to the federal government and indirect taxes to the state governments, while the communities rely primarily on wealth taxes.

Obviously, the various government levels in each country have different revenue structures, given the differences in the availability of tax sources. This can be seen in Tables 15–24 to 15–27 of section 4.

Finally, intergovernmental grants are a further revenue source of major importance for the subcentral levels of government, as shown in Table 15–4.

As these data show, the central-government level transferred grants in the

Table 15-4

Federal Government Grants-in-Aid to Subcentral Governments[a]

	Canada (1969)	France (1968)	Germany (1969)	Switzerland (1969)	U.K. (1969)	U.S. (1969)
Total (In Millions)	2,473	9,077	11,430	790	2,370	19,947
In % of Federal Gov. Total Expenditure	23.0	6.5	12.0	11.1	14.3	10.0
In % of Subcentral Governments Total Expenditure	31.5	20.0	10.7	10.0	47.7	19.0
In % of GNP	3.5	1.6	1.9	0.9	5.2	2.3

Sources: For Canada, Canadian Tax Foundation, *The National Finances*, 1969–1970; for France, André (1973) and Delorme (1973a); for Germany, St.B., *Finanzen und Steuern, Jahresabschluesse*; for Switzerland, E.St.A., *Bundessubventionen* (1970); for the United Kingdom, C.S.O., *Annual Abstracts of Statistics* (1971); for the United States, Tax Foundation, *Facts and Figures on Government Finance* (1971).

[a]Shared revenues, loans, and repayable advances are excluded.

amount of 1 to 5 percent of GNP to the lower-level units (in most cases, to the state governments). This accounted for between 7 percent (France) and 23 percent (Canada) of central-government total expenditure. In all cases, support from the federal government accounts for one-tenth to one-third of the state governments' total revenue. The same relationship exists for transfers from the states to the local governments. It must be noted, however, that these comparisons have minor importance, since both the conditions and mechanisms vary strongly from country to country. This point will be discussed below.

Intergovernmental Fiscal Relations. As Break (1967, p. 100) and Burkhead and Miner (1971, p. 285) show in more detail, a taxonomy of intergovernmental fiscal relations is not a simple matter; classification is complicated because of the multiple and frequently conflicting purposes of specific intergovernmental fiscal arrangements. Moreover, as a glance at the available statistics reveals, it is most difficult to obtain sufficiently detailed material on specific questions. For this reason I must forgo more detailed comparisons at this point,[12] but I will present the basic characteristics of the intergovernmental fiscal relations of the six countries we are considering.[13]

Canada: Canadian intergovernmental fiscal relations may be characterized as follows:[14] Over the last decade, the federal government has substantially reduced its personal income tax and corporation income tax in order to make room for corresponding provincial taxes. The federal government makes transfers from its own resources to the provinces. The provincial taxes are used to calculate how much the uniformly calculated tax revenue of a province lies below the national average, and this difference is then made up. Conditional grants-in-aid have recently been of increasing importance. This applies to transfers from federal to provincial governments as well as to transfers between the latter and municipalities, whereas the relation between federal and local-level government is of minor relevance. (For a quantitative picture, see section 4.)

France [Delorme (1973, pp. 34 ff.)] is said to be one of the most centralized countries of the developed Western world. First, about 85 percent of total tax receipts (about 80 percent of total government revenue) is collected by the central government; then, the central government exerts its influence on the subcentral units through its grants policy, especially through subsidies for investments. (See the essay by Prud'homme in this book.) Since the investments of subcentral governments are financed to a large extent through loans, and since these loans are granted (by a financial organization controlled by the central government) only after the central-government's subsidy has been approved, the amount of these subsidies is relatively small (about 16 to 20 percent of the total revenue of the subcentral governments). Nevertheless, their influence is huge. If shared (consumption) taxes are added, it can be seen that about 40 percent of the subcentral revenue is under the control of the central government.

Germany [see Haller (1969b), Strauss (1969), and Hunter (1973)] : When the financial reform of 1969 took place, the existing sharing between federal and state governments in the personal and corporation income tax yield was extended to include the value-added tax as well. This means that some 70 percent of the total state and federal tax revenue is collected jointly. The income from the first two taxes mentioned above is divided equally between the two levels, as stipulated in the constitution. The income from the value-added tax is divided between federal and state governments in a ratio of about 70:30.[15] One-quarter of the state share is used for a horizontal equalization, namely to boost the tax revenue of the financially weaker states until it reaches 95 percent of the average of all states (in DM per capita). Further horizontal and vertical equalization effects result from the fact that certain tasks are handled by the federal and state governments together (so-called *Gemeinschaftsaufgaben*), whereby the central government—as part of an effective stabilization and economic-growth policy— gives investment aids to both state and local governments.

In *Switzerland* [see Rohr and Gut (1970), Lehner (1971), and Haller 1969b)] , state and local governments have a relatively large income from taxes, which they impose either jointly or in competition with the other levels of government. However, there are still substantial governmental transfers between federal and state, and state and local, government levels whereby not only vertical-equalization effects are sought but, especially with conditional grants, horizontal-equalization effects as well. [See the Frey essay in this volume.] The latter remain relatively modest, however; these measures, intended to produce a horizontal impact, are probably of less importance than the horizontal effects resulting from agricultural subsidies and welfare payments (national insurance).

Like France, the central government's influence in the *United Kingdom* [Page (1967) and Peacock and Wiseman (1967, pp. 99ff.)] is relatively large, since the local governments receive roughly half their tax revenues in the form of grants from the central government. These transfers, mainly unconditional grants, are used to finance current local expenditures, for the tax on land and buildings, which constitutes the main revenue source (the so-called local rate), seems rather inelastic in relation to local income growth.[16] The central government also has an influence on local capital expenditures, which are financed either out of surpluses of the current budget or by loans, or more recently by bonds and mortgages.

United States [see Break (1967), Ecker-Racz (1970), Maxwell (1969), Wagner (1971), and Netzer (1974)] : As in Switzerland, intergovernmental fiscal relations in the United States are restricted primarily to conditional payments in the form of matching grants to the state governments. (On this issue, see the Reischauer paper in this volume.) That is, a certain amount must be raised by the recipient before the federal government makes such a grant. This is not to any extent an attempt to equalize the burden carried by the states, even when the state tax capacity is considered in determining the apportionment of such grants. Rather, the principle purpose is to encourage state-government initiative in carrying out tasks in which the federal level is strongly interested. Numerous programs have been implemented by the federal government in this context, principally in the field of health and welfare but also for the construction and maintenance of roads and for the school system.

To sum up, nearly all imaginable intergovernmental fiscal relations (and changes) can be found during the last decade in the countries considered in this paper: changes in the allocation systems for tax sources as well as in the sharing systems of jointly levied taxes; changes in the shares of subcentral governments in relation to the federal government's revenues in order to allow for tax increases of the state governments; increases in the number of additional conditional grants; and definitions of tasks of common interest combined with cost sharing of the programs resulting therefrom.

Fiscal Redistribution in Federal Economic Systems

A second function of the public sector is to bring about a socially desired distribution of income, which is mostly interpreted in terms of a more equal distribution of income than that allowed by the market process. As shown in various treatises [Oates (1968, pp. 43, 45), Pommerehne (1975)] , there are a number of reasons why such a redistribution policy is not likely to be carried out on a large scale on the level of subcentral governments:

1. State and local governments often do not have the necessary margin to enforce an aggressive redistribution policy, because the extent to which they can lay down the tax rates is already marked out by the central government, as for example in France.

2. Moreover, because of the mobility of the economic subjects (and other fac-

tors of production), the incentives for such enforcement do not exist on the local- and state-governmental level. A coerced redistribution, say, with the help of simple majority rule might cause the affected individuals to react by migrating to a community or state that is more advantageous to them [see, for example, Negishi (1972)].

If these reflections on the possibilities and incentives for a redistribution policy in federal economic systems are correct, redistribution can be expected to take place mainly through the budget of the central government (Greene, 1970). Furthermore, if the function of the distribution branch is regarded as income insurance, one might argue that only the federal level can take such a risk (Rodgers, 1974, pp. 174–180).

For various reasons, it is not easy to find empirical evidence for (or against) these conclusions. In the absence of market prices, as well as information about the quantities of publicly supplied goods and services (demanded in different amount by members of different income classes), the extent to which members of different income classes draw benefits from public programs can be deduced only on the basis of more or less plausible assumptions. The determination of tax incidence (i.e., of the final resting place of the tax payments and other public receipts), presents a similar problem.

All the same, of late we can find a number of analyses concerning the question of budgetary redistribution in federal states. Some of them proceed not only by looking at the public revenues but by trying, by more or less ingenious criteria, to attach the total costs of public programs to the different income classes. Others choose the realized benefit as a point of reference for the change in the welfare position of the individual, i.e., utility functions are explicitly introduced.

Total Costs as the Point of Departure. In all treatises in the first group, it is (usually tacitly) assumed that every money unit spent by the government represents a money unit worth of benefit to someone.[17] So the main point is to allocate to the income classes taxes and other public receipts, as well as the expenditures of the different levels of governments valued in terms of their costs.

Dodge (1975) has estimated for Canada in 1970, by applying the usual incidence assumptions, that the incidence of state and local taxes and other receipts is regressive [i.e., that the poorer families pay a greater percentage of their income in state and local revenue than rich families (see Table 15–5 and Figure 15–1)].[18] But he also shows that the expenditure programs of state and local governments especially favor the lower-income classes, so that, looked at from a "net" point of view, a slight redistribution in favor of the poorer families can be detected. The analysis of Johnson (1975) shows that this also applies for a single province.[19]

This slight redistribution "to the bottom" is financed by a net charge on the

Table 15-5
Government-Sector Fiscal Incidence by Level of Government, Canada, 1970[a]

Levels of Government		Family Money Income Class (in thousands of Canadian dollars)								
		0–3.0	3.0–5.0	5.0–7.0	7.0–9.0	9.0–11.0	11.0–13.0	13.0–15.0	15.0 and Over	Total
Families	(in thousands)	1,106.9	963.0	946.1	979.9	853.5	633.9	425.8	854.9	6,764.0
	(in %)	16.4	14.2	14.0	14.5	12.6	9.4	6.3	12.6	(100.0)
Broad Income	(in millions)	1,368.2	3,179.1	5,669.1	8,135.7	8,804.2	7,969.2	6,214.2	19,852.3	61,192.0
	(in %)	2.2	5.2	9.3	13.3	14.4	13.0	10.2	32.4	(100.0)
Total State and Local Revenue	(in millions)	553.5	922.7	1,166.9	1,576.3	1,703.6	1,517.2	1,143.3	4,383.7	12,967.2
	(in %)	4.3	7.1	9.0	12.2	13.1	11.7	8.8	33.8	(100.0)
	(in % of Broad Inc.)	40.5	29.0	20.6	19.4	19.4	19.0	18.4	22.1	.
Total State and Local Expenditure	(in millions)	983.8	1,375.3	1,668.4	2,045.7	1,954.0	1,524.8	1,057.0	2,792.5	13,401.5
	(in %)	7.3	10.3	12.4	15.3	14.6	11.4	7.9	20.8	(100.0)
	(in % of Broad Inc.)	71.9	43.3	29.4	25.1	22.2	19.2	17.0	14.1	.
Total Federal Revenue	(in millions)	302.9	724.2	1,198.8	1,639.4	1,773.2	1,619.4	1,224.0	4,381.7	12,863.6
	(in %)	2.3	5.6	9.3	12.7	13.8	12.6	9.5	34.1	(100.0)
	(in % of Broad Inc.)	22.1	22.8	21.1	20.2	20.1	20.3	19.7	22.1	.
Total Federal Expenditure	(in millions)	1,772.9	2,018.4	1,815.3	1,929.3	1,797.8	1,408.9	1,062.1	3,057.2	14,861.9
	(in %)	11.9	13.6	12.2	13.0	12.1	9.5	7.1	20.6	(100.0)
	(in % of Broad Inc.)	129.6	63.5	32.0	23.7	20.4	17.7	17.1	15.4	.
Adjusted Broad Income	(in millions)	3,268.5	4,925.9	6,787.0	8,894.9	9,079.1	7,766.4	5,965.9	16,936.5	63,624.2
	(in %)	5.1	7.7	10.7	14.0	14.3	12.2	9.4	26.6	(100.0)
	(in % of Broad Inc.)	238.9	154.9	119.7	109.3	103.1	97.5	96.0	85.3	.

[a]Computed from Dodge (1975, Table 5, lines 27–33). The broad income concept includes all family money income, adds the family noncash income, and subtracts the government bond interest received and the transfer payments from government to families [see Dodge (1975, pp. 13 ff.) for more detailed comments].

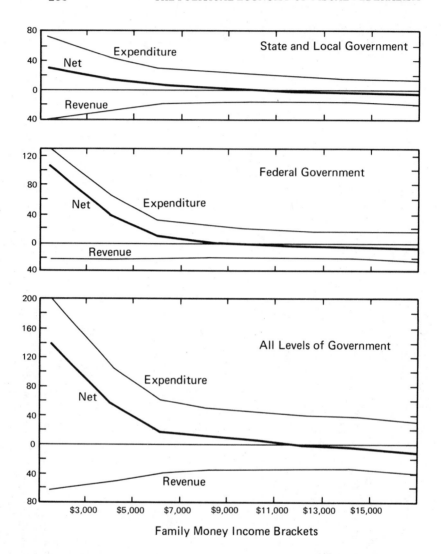

Source: Table 15–5.

Figure 15–1. Government-Sector Fiscal Incidence as a Percentage of Family Broad Income by Level of Government, Canada, 1970.

higher-income groups, while state and local budgets are roughly neutral in terms of their redistributive impact on the members of the middle-income groups. This result is compatible with the thought expressed above that a larger budgetary redistribution can hardly be expected to be accomplished by the local or state levels of government. On the federal level of government, on the other hand, a much more explicit redistribution in favor of the poor can be expected, and this seems to be the case, as shown in Table 15-5. Families with an income over Can $11,000 are in a worse position, while the poorest families, especially, gain. This result coincides with an earlier study by Gillespie (1964, chap. 4) for 1961. Furthermore, as Dodge shows, the result is relatively insensitive to the precise assumptions made about the shifting of taxes and the incidence of expenditures.

Comparable analyses for other countries can be found in Hake (1972) and Hanusch (1976) for Germany; in Gillespie (1965), Tax Foundation (1967), Musgrave, Case, and Leonhart (1974), and Reynolds and Smolensky (1974) for the United States; and in Cartter (1955) and (with restrictions) Nicholson (1964) for the United Kingdom. Table 15-6 condenses the results of the latest studies.[20] It shows that the results for these federal economic systems are very similar to those for Canada.[21]

Cost and Benefit as the Point of Departure. All the fiscal-incidence studies mentioned here do not represent a methodically unobjectionable comparison, because of the manner in which expenditure streams are transferred into fictitious incomes. It is not possible to use different criteria for the estimation of privately and jointly supplied goods and services. On the contrary, a consistent principle must be applied which, like the one used by Aaron and McGuire (1970), transfers the basic idea of the optimization calculus in the analysis of private goods to the publicly provided goods. Including a separable utility function and using the same data and assumptions about the tax incidence that the Tax Foundation study applies, the authors show that the direction and the dimension of budgetary redistribution then depend to a crucial extent on the assumptions about the elasticity of marginal utility of private income (ϵ). Aaron and McGuire choose only two utility functions (with an ϵ of, respectively, -1 and -2) for demonstration purposes and estimate the total fiscal incidence of all governmental levels in the United States.

It seems more interesting to carry out an analysis that (1) distinguishes explicitly between the different levels of government and (2) does not start with values for ϵ chosen in an arbitrary manner or with one—out of many—empirically estimated function of marginal utility,[22] but one that examines what shape the function of marginal utility would have to show if it represented different redistribution hypotheses. Compared with the spectrum of estimated values of ϵ, it is more likely to be able to "prove" to what extent the hypotheses put forth at the beginning of this section hold. Such an attempt can be found—for each level of government—for a Swiss state (Kanton) in Pommerehne (1975).

The main results for local governments are shown in Table 15-7. This table indicates that, on the level of local government, there is in fact no significant redistribution,[23] at least if we assume for ϵ a range between $0 > \epsilon > -1.6$ (a range that comprises the results of nearly all the estimations of the elasticity of marginal utility known to us). If, in addition to the local budget, we take into

Table 15-6
Government-Sector Net Fiscal Incidence as a Percentage of Household Money Income by Level of Government

United States 1970[a]

Household Money Income Class (in thousands of U.S. dollars)

Levels of Government	0-2.0	2.0-3.0	3.0-4.0	4.0-5.0	5.0-6.0	6.0-7.0	7.0-8.0	8.0-10.0	10.0-15.0	15.0-25.0	Over 25.0
State-Local Government	88.1	42.5	24.4	15.9	8.0	5.5	4.2	3.2	1.9	-0.9	-4.2
Federal-Level Government	173.9	87.8	51.2	29.3	15.1	7.5	2.8	-1.0	-3.4	-5.5	-20.2
All Government Total Net Incidence	262.0	130.3	75.6	45.2	23.1	13.0	7.0	2.2	-1.5	-6.4	-24.4

Federal Republic of Germany 1969[b]

Household Money Income Class (in thousands of DM)

Levels of Government	0-7.2	7.2-9.6	9.6-12.0	12.0-14.4	14.4-18.0	18.0-21.6	21.6-30.0	30.0-120.0
Local Government Expenditure	34.7	25.1	20.4	17.2	15.2	14.1	12.9	11.3
State Government Expenditure	31.2	23.4	19.6	17.1	15.6	14.7	13.9	13.2
Federal Government Expenditure	66.3	46.3	35.3	27.7	2.3	20.7	17.8	14.2
Total Government Revenue	40.2	45.1	45.5	44.1	41.9	41.0	38.0	50.9
All Government Total Net Incidence	92.0	49.8	29.6	18.0	-8.7	8.5	6.5	-12.2

[a]Computed from Reynolds and Smolensky (1974, Appendix, Table B-1, line 7; C-1, line 6; C-2, line 7; D-1, line 13; D-2, line 8.
[b]Computed from Hanusch (1976, Appendix, Table 2, lines 1, 2, 8; 13, line 27; 14, line 27; 15, line 27.

Table 15-7
Local-Government-Sector Net Fiscal Incidence as a Percentage of Household Money Income by Alternative Values of the Elasticity of Marginal Utility of Income (ε), 74 Communities of the State Basel-Landschaft (Switzerland), 1969

Value of ε	Household Money Income Class (in thousands of Swiss francs)								
	0–9.0	9.0–13.0	13.0–17.0	17.0–21.0	21.0–25.0	25.0–29.0	29.0–32.0	32.0–37.0	Over 37.0
0.0	51.5	6.2	3.9	2.4	1.0	-0.2	-1.6	-2.8	-6.3
-0.4	24.3	4.6	3.6	2.8	1.8	0.8	-0.4	-1.6	-4.8
-0.6	15.7	3.5	3.1	2.6	1.8	1.0	0.0	-1.1	-4.0
-1.0	5.8	1.0	1.5	1.6	1.4	1.0	0.3	-0.6	-2.1
-1.4	1.6	-1.2	-0.1	0.3	0.5	0.5	0.0	-0.6	0.0
-1.6	0.6	-2.1	-1.0	-0.4	-0.1	-0.1	-0.3	-0.8	1.0
-2.0	-0.3	-3.4	-2.2	-1.6	-1.2	-0.9	-1.0	-1.4	2.9

Source: Computed from Pommerehne (1975, Tables 1, 2).

consideration the budget of state government, the result changes only insignificantly, while the lower- as well as the middle-income groups are a bit better off (see Table 15-8). Only by including the incidence of the central-government budget can we detect bigger changes; the members of the lowest income groups continue to be very considerably better off, while the middle- and the higher-income groups lose in net. It must be added to this result that the state of Basel-Land raises much more in federal taxes than it gets back in the form of expenditure for services rendered by the federal government. In other words, the regional redistribution is added to the personal redistribution. But the poorest households are excluded from this and continue to be in a better position. This corroborates the hypothesis put forth above.

Stabilization Policy in Federal Countries

A third function of the public sector consists in macroeconomie stabilization policy. As shown by different authors [e.g., by Robinson and Courchene (1969); Oates (1968); Kock (1975)], this responsibility also lies with the central government:

1. State and local governments are usually not equipped with the necessary (discretionary) instruments needed for effective countercyclical policy. They cannot, for example, control the money supply; they usually have only restricted access to the capital market; and often they do not have at their disposal revenues and expenditures that are flexibly enough organized, as for example is the case in France and partly in the United Kingdom.[24]
2. Furthermore, there are only weak incentives on the level of subcentral governments to pursue an active stabilization policy. One reason lies in the negative effects of external debt of local governments units, another in the fact that because of the openness of regional or local economies the regional fiscal multipliers can be rather small. So each unit is in danger of bearing the costs of its countercyclical policy without getting back its share of the benefits.

Therefore a subcentral government (especially when of a small spatial and economic size) can hardly be expected to decide to carry out an effective stabilization policy—at least as long as it is not guaranteed that all others will do the same. For a single region, on the other hand, it is rewarding then to break out of any agreement.

Both kinds of restrictions are far less binding at the central-government level. The central government is equipped with important fiscal and monetary instruments. But it is also this authority that is held mainly responsible for the application and the efficacy of the steps taken in stabilization policy.

Table 15-8

Government-Sector Net Fiscal Incidence as a Percentage of Household Money Income by Alternative Values of the Elasticity of Marginal Utility of Income (ε), State Basel-Landschaft (Switzerland), 1969

Value of ε	Household Money Income Class (in thousands of Swiss francs)								
	0–9.0	9.0–13.0	13.0–17.0	17.0–21.0	21.0–25.0	25.0–29.0	29.0–32.0	32.0–37.0	Over 37.0
State and local:									
0.0	123.3	19.4	11.4	7.1	3.5	0.1	-2.7	-5.1	-17.6
-0.5	49.4	14.8	10.5	7.9	5.5	2.8	0.5	-1.2	-13.6
-1.0	16.0	7.9	6.6	5.8	4.8	3.4	1.9	1.0	-8.5
-1.5	4.0	1.8	2.1	2.4	2.4	2.1	1.4	1.3	-3.1
-2.0	0.2	-2.6	-1.9	-1.1	-0.6	-0.3	-0.3	0.1	2.3
All levels:									
0.0	177.9	26.1	10.7	4.9	0.1	-4.6	-7.0	-7.5	-22.8
-0.5	76.7	20.0	9.1	5.8	2.7	-1.0	-2.6	-2.5	-17.2
-1.0	28.3	10.6	3.6	2.7	1.6	0.0	-0.7	0.6	-10.0
-1.5	9.7	1.9	-2.9	-2.3	-1.8	-2.2	-1.4	1.3	-2.1
-2.0	3.5	-4.5	-8.5	-7.3	-6.1	-5.6	-3.8	-0.2	-29.2

Source: Table 15-7 and unpublished data for state and federal government taxes.

This is reflected in numerous laws, for example, in the Employment Act of 1946, which compells the U.S. federal government "to promote conditions under which there will be afforded useful employment for those able, willing, and seeking work, and to promote maximum employment, production and purchasing power." The institutions set up in consequence appear almost more important than the law itself, especially the Joint Economic Committee of the U.S. Congress and the scientific Council of Economic Advisers to the President, which deal with problems of middle- and short-range economic policy in preference to long-range planning. Very similar developments can be shown for most other countries. In Canada, they are the result of the recommendations of the Royal Commission on Dominion-Provincial Relations (1940) and the Dominion-Provincial Agreements Acts of 1942, 1947, 1962 *et seq*., that refer to it. In Germany, they are the result of the budget laws, which since 1960 give legal authority to the federal government "to freeze particular expenditure groups on grounds of cyclical policy," but even more the result of the more comprehensive Law to Promote Stability and Economic Growth of 1967.

The question that interests us here is whether the central government is really the primary agent for stabilizing output and prices and whether these goals are unimportant to the subcentral governments. Hansen and Perloff (1944) provide data to show that subcentral government finance generally was not anticyclical but rather procyclical in the United States during the late twenties and throughout most of the thirties. Smithies (1946) and Brown (1956) reach similar results on the basis of more detailed quantitative analyses, though they point out that the functioning of compensatory finance was not really understood at that time.

Whether these principles were realized and observed or realized but disregarded on the state and local level cannot easily be ascertained for the postwar period. Rafuse (1965) shows that the subcentral governments made a substantial contribution to countercyclical policy in the United States between 1945 and 1961. A closer look shows, however, that this policy had no regard for the state of the economy, as revenues and expenditures simply expanded continuously in this period.

Hansen's (1969, chap. 2 ff.) analysis, which deals with the later period between 1955 and 1965, reaches very similar conclusions, even though slightly different methods of measurement are used to estimate the impact of the government budget. However, all these studies are similarly defective in that they do not really try to quantify the extent of the stabilizing effect of the state and local budget changes and, in a second step, compare them with the stabilizing impact of the changes in the federal budget.

Using the same method as Hansen (1969, chap. 1),[25] Snyder (1970b, 1973) has tried to analyze the *relative* contributions of the state and local government budgets of various countries to stabilization, relative, that is, to the stabilizing impact of the federal government. Snyder first calculates the combination of direct and multiplier effects, or the total effects, of the year-to-year variations in subcentral government budgets and then standardizes them by expressing them as a percentage of GNP. The point of reference used to evaluate the overall effects of subcentral-government budget changes is whether or not the actual growth rate of GNP fluctuates less with their effects than if they had been neutral from year to year. Figure 15-2 shows these relationships for four countries, evaluating the short-run stabilizing effects of state and local governments after accounting for the effects of other government budget changes. Horizontal lines give the average GNP growth rates, solid lines the actual GNP growth rates, and dotted lines the estimates of how GNP might have developed if there had been no effects of the state and local budget changes (but the effects of other government budgets, as well as the combined influence of all other exogenous and endogenous factors, are included). This last line is gained by subtracting the total effects of subcentral-government budget changes from the actual GNP growth rate.

As shown in Table 15-9, the impact of the subcentral budgets of the countries dealt with here has actually been stabilizing, even though to a limited extent, with the exception of Germany, which has comparatively the largest share of state and local expenditures of the GNP.

Changing the *ceteris paribus* assumptions, some public-finance scholars have also used a second base of comparison: the "pure cycle." The *pure cycle* is defined as the variations in GNP growth rates that would have occurred if there had been no changes in the expenditures and revenues of the different governmental units from year to year.[26] It is calculated by subtracting the total stabilizing effects of the general government budget changes from the actual GNP.

In Table 15-9, the "potential stabilization" is given in line 3. Lines 2 and 4 show the net stabilizing effects of the state and local governments respective to the general government. According to the results (in line 5a) Germany and the United States had the largest potential stabilization of general governments and also achieved the strongest net stabilizing effects by eliminating 34 and 40 percent respectively of the potential fluctuations in the pure cycle. The percentage of stabilization in France was substantially less (13 percent), while almost no stabilization was achieved in the United Kingdom.

To evaluate the impact of subcentral budgets on potential stabilization, in Germany and the United States the impact of the state and local budgets was stabilizing under the pure cycle concept (line 2) as well as under the concept used first (line 1).[27] For France and the United Kingdom, the evaluation depends on the norm of comparison used. If the impact of central government is taken as given exogenously, the effects of state and local budgets are generally stabilizing (line 5b), but they were generally destabilizing if the effects of central government are excluded (line 5c).

Although one point of reference may not be generally preferable to the other, Snyder gives some reasons why it appears more appropriate to measure

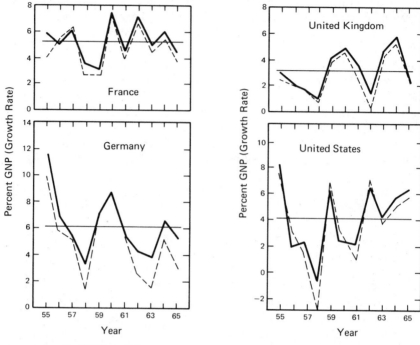

Source: Snyder (1973, p. 204).

Note: Solid and horizontal lines are actual and average GNP (Growth Rate), respectively; dotted lines are the rates without the impact of state and local government budget changes.

Figure 15-2. The Impact of State and Local Government Budget.

net stabilization by the pure cycle concept. He concludes that state and local budgets are generally stabilizing and in France and the United Kingdom have a stronger impact than the general government because of the destabilizing effects of the central government and, in the case of the United Kingdom, of the social security system.[28] For Germany and the United States, which have a rather large subcentral sector, however, the impact of state and local budgets seems smaller than that of the central government.

More interesting, perhaps, is that the impact of state and local government budgets does not vary as much as that of the central government during the cycle. This leads to the supposition that on the subcentral-government level more importance is attached to maintenance of a balanced budget than on national level; i.e., state and local governments do not seem to practice a conscious stabilization policy.[29]

More recent studies for the two other countries, Switzerland [Wagner (1973, pp. 47–49)] and Canada [Curtis and Kitchen (1975)], which are based on a similar method, arrive at the same results; the federal government exerts a policy

Table 15-9

Stabilizing Effects of State and Local Government Budgets, 1955-1965[a]

Stabilizing Effects by Level of Government	France	Germany	United Kingdom	United States
1. Net stabilizing effects of state-local government	0.22	0.50	0.12	0.11
a. Gross stabilizing	0.42	0.77	0.32	0.45
b. Destabilizing	0.20	0.27	0.20	0.34
2. Net stabilizing effects in relation to pure cycle	-0.31	0.28	-0.06	0.35
a. Gross stabilizing	0.15	0.66	0.23	0.56
b. Destabilizing	0.46	0.38	0.29	0.22
3. Potential stabilization for pure cycle	1.29	2.98	1.37	4.37
4. Net stabilizing effects of general government	0.17	1.01	0.07	1.75
5. Percentage potential stabilization achieved:				
a. General government	13	34	5	40
b. State-local government (item 1. : item 3.)	17	17	9	2
c. State-local government (item 2. : item 3.)	-24	9	-4	8

Source: Snyder (1973, p. 206) and own computations. The reader should note that the percentage of potential stabilization achieved by general government (line 5a) is not identical with Hansen's (1969, p. 69) because it excludes the effects of public-enterprise investments and is calculated on a somewhat different basis.

[a]Calculating the stabilizing effect presents no major problem except in cases where the budgetary impact is in the right direction but is greater than the amount necessary to reach the average growth rate. Here the effect must be divided into one part that was stabilizing and another part that was destabilizing. Thus the sum of gross stabilizing effects minus the sum of destabilizing effects—each was divided by the number of years in the period covered by the study—gives the net average stabilizing (destabilizing) impact.

with a more consistent impact on stabilization than do the subcentral governments.[30]

This conclusion is also reached in those studies that measure stabilization policy only in terms of direct effects instead of direct and multiplier effects [see Buschor (1970) for Switzerland, Kock (1975) for Germany, and Lindbeck (1970) for seven OECD countries] or which are based on more extensive econometric models [see, for example, Balopoulos (1967, chaps. 6-8) for the United Kingdom]. It seems that state and local governments are not inclined to execute a countercyclical policy, unless (as was the case for some time in the postwar period) the pursuit of their own goals coincides with the goal of economic stabilization of the whole system. But in times of revenue shortages, this is not to be expected, and in reality it was more or less the central government that gave the correct countercylical impulses.

Any comparison between central and subcentral stabilization policy is rendered more difficult because the central government has often made mistakes,[31] either as a result of misjudging future development, because of an insufficient choice of appropriate instruments and their adequate combination, or because the government had no incentive to pursue a *permanent* countercyclical policy. Indeed, besides the avoidance of forecasting mistakes, the reduction of time lags in the decisionmaking process, and the display of determination and firmness in policy, which are crucial determinants for the effectiveness of any stabilization policy, the central government must be willing to apply countercyclical measures at any time. And this is not to be expected a priori, considering the multiplicity of goals as well as election dates that lie four to five years apart.[32]

3. Political and Social Aspects of Fiscal Federalism: Some Preliminary Findings

Up to now, the federal economic system has been assumed to be exogenously given, and research has been concentrated on the division of functions under aspects of allocation, distribution, and stabilization; now the question is reversed. The federal economic system is no longer assumed to be given; the question is rather how political, social, and economic variables influence it. In other words: What determines the demand for centralization or decentralization of the governmental service and policy complex in the various countries? I will try in the following paragraphs to give a tentative answer with the help of quantitative techniques (cross-sectional analysis).

Another question frequently raised in the social sciences concerns the dynamics of federalism. White (1933, p. 140) said that the "tide of centralization will probably steadily sweep power from the localities to the states, and from the states into the hands of the national authorities." Lord Bryce claimed that federalism is only a transitory form of the state on its way to centralism. Is this indeed the case?

Demand for Decentralization

The Arguments. As the examination of a number of papers on federalism suggests, the dimension in which a decentralization of the governmental complex is desired seems to be determined mainly by the following factors:

1. The *size of the country* (in terms of population) is generally considered an important determinant of demand, for the costs of decision making (including the information costs) rise, as a rule, more than the increasing population; in

other words, the larger the population, the smaller will be the demand for centralization.

2. We find a similar notion for *geographical area*, with the additional argument that the larger the area, the fewer spatial and external effects are produced in the public services.[33] In other words, it can be expected that, *ceteris paribus*, the degree of centralization varies inversely with the geographical extension of a country.

3. This *ceteris paribus* condition does not hold equally for developed and underdeveloped countries, as the latter have to bear higher real costs for decentralization, owing, for instance, to the scarcity of qualified government personnel. To put it the other way round: the higher the wealth of a country measured in *per capita income*, the more likely is a marked decentralization.

4. The *diversity in demands* for publicly provided goods and services is another important determinant, for only the decentralized provision of a public good allows the realization of potential welfare gains for groups with similar demands *within* groups but significant differences in demands *between* groups. The underlying causes of this diversity in demands can be traced back to such factors as differences in language [see, for example, Macmahon (1962) for India], which frequently coincide with differences in religion [as in Canada, see McWhinney (1962)], as well as differences in race (as in Czechoslovakia), and—taken as a whole—differences in culture.[34] But as the demand of an individual for a particular (public or private) good depends on both his tastes and his level of income, we derive a further determinant of the demand for a decentralized governmental structure—the degree of inequality in the distribution of income. It is to be expected that the higher the degree of income inequality, the stronger the demand for decentralized choice, *ceteris paribus*.

5. A last hypothesis touches upon political and institutional constraints on the demand for federalism; in other words, the question of whether the political system is at all prepared and willing to take regional interests into account. We can judge this by observing to what extent there is no authoritarian political system, whether autonomous groups are tolerated in the political field at all, etc. The less this is the case, the less the demand for decentralization can be expected to succeed.

Measuring Centralization. As we have no comprehensive measure of centralization that meets all the requirements of political science, of economics, and of constitutional law, I shall take as an operating measure of "fiscal federalism" the proportion of central-government consumption in the overall governments' consumption expenditures (CGE). The choice of this reference ratio instead of another based on the expenditure or revenue side of the budget is admittedly arbitrary. It is, however, the measure for which we have recourse to relatively reliable sources,[35] where, moreover, the intergovernmental transfers are treated uniformly.[36]

The Results. Equation (15.1) indicates that in conformity with our expectations, the degree of fiscal centralization varies inversely with the size of the country.

$$CGE = 70.68 - 0.07P$$
$$(25.01)\,(2.09)$$

$$N = 50 \quad \bar{R}^2 = 0.05 \quad \overline{CGE} = 68.38 \tag{15.1}$$

where CGE = central-government consumption expenditure as a percentage of all governments' consumption expenditure, 1967–1969
P = population (in millions), 1968. The data are taken from I.B.R.D., World Atlas (1970)
N = sample size
$\bar{R}^2$ = coefficient of determination (adjusted for degrees of freedom)
$\overline{CGE}$ = mean value of CGE.

The numbers in parentheses give the absolute values of the t-statistic for the estimated coefficients: they indicate that in equation (15.1) the influence of population is statistically significant.[37] The explained fraction of the variance in the degree of fiscal federalism is, however, small.
Equation (15.2) adds to (15.1) the geographical size (GS).

$$CGE = 75.59 - 0.05P - 2.58GS$$
$$(25.14)\,(1.37)\quad(2.06)$$

$$N = 50 \quad \bar{R}^2 = 0.11 \tag{15.2}$$

where GS = geographical size (in millions of square kilometers), ca. 1960. The data are taken from F.A.O., F.A.O. Production Yearbook (1965).

This variable, too, is statistically significant and presents the expected (negative) sign. It adds only little, however, to the explanatory power of equation (15.1). One reason for this might be that not only the size of a country but also the spatial settlement of the population, measured, for example, by the degree of urbanization, determines the degree of fiscal federalism [see equation (15.3)]:

$$CGE = 82.04 - 0.05P - 1.18GS - 0.49U$$
$$(20.55)\,(1.71)\quad(0.96)\quad(3.16)$$

$$N = 50 \quad \bar{R}^2 = 0.249 \tag{15.3}$$

where U = degree of urbanization (percentage of population living in cities over

20,000) in 1960; the data are taken from Russett et al. (1967, pp. 51 ff.).

Equation (15.3) shows that this supposition is confirmed: the urbanization variable has the expected sign, it is statistically strongly significant, and it contributes considerably to the explanation of the variation in fiscal centralization.

As equations (15.4) and (15.5) indicate, this is also valid for the variable that is supposed to represent the degree of development of a country, the *GNP* per capita.

$$CGE = 84.22 - 0.06P - 0.16GS - 0.19U - 0.01GNP$$
$$(20.91)\ (2.15)\quad (0.13)\quad (1.06)\quad (3.07)$$
$$N = 50 \quad \bar{R}^2 = 0.359 \tag{15.4}$$

And, excluding the statistically nonsignificant variables *GS* and *U* from equation (15.4),

$$CGE = 82.12 - 0.07P - 0.01GNP$$
$$(26.02)\ (2.48)\quad (5.22)$$
$$N = 50 \quad \bar{R}^2 = 0.383 \tag{15.5}$$

where *GNP* = *GNP* per capita (in U.S. $) in 1968 and, in a few instances, in 1967 or 1969. The data are taken from I.B.R.D., *World Atlas* (1970, 1971).

As was surmised above, the trend to decentralization in public finances is stronger in more prosperous countries than in poorer countries; that is, it appears that the real resources necessary for the institution of a decentralized decision-making structure represent a considerable obstacle in less developed countries.

To investigate the thesis that the differences in demand for publicly supplied goods and services are a relevant determinant of the demand for fiscal decentralization, we estimate first the influence of possible determinants of *differences in tastes*, including a series of dummy variables indicating whether a country is homogeneous or heterogeneous as regards the linguistic, racial, religious, and, as an aggregate of all three, cultural characteristics [see equations (15.6) to (15.9)].

$$CGE = 81.82 - 0.07P - 0.01GNP + 0.35L$$
$$(21.53)\ (2.36)\quad (4.66)\qquad (0.74)$$
$$N = 50 \quad \bar{R}^2 = 0.356 \tag{15.6}$$

where L = dummy variable for the degree of lingual homogeneity: 1 = lingual homogeneity, 0 = lingual heterogeneity. The dummies are computed from Banks and Textor (1963, printout no. 68).

$$CGE = 84.44 - 0.06P - 0.01GNP - 4.60RD$$
$$(19.82)\,(2.31)\quad(4.60)\qquad(0.94)$$

$$N = 50 \qquad \bar{R}^2 = 0.368 \qquad\qquad\qquad (15.7)$$

where RD = dummy variable for the degree of racial differences: 1 = racial homogeneity, 0 = racial heterogeneity. The dummies are taken from Banks and Textor (1963, printout no. 67).

$$CGE = 78.46 - 0.07P - 0.01GNP - 6.12DR$$
$$(18.43)\,(2.48)\quad(4.86)\qquad(1.37)$$

$$N = 50 \qquad \bar{R}^2 = 0.368 \qquad\qquad\qquad (15.8)$$

where DR = dummy variable for the degree of differences in religion: 1 = religious homogeneity, 0 = religious heterogeneity. The dummies are taken from Banks and Textor (1963, printout no. 66).

$$CGE = 81.57 - 0.06P - 0.01GNP + 5.20DC$$
$$(23.07)\,(2.24)\quad(5.19)\qquad(1.00)$$

$$N = 50 \qquad \bar{R}^2 = 0.381 \qquad\qquad\qquad (15.9)$$

where DC = dummy variable for the degree of differences in culture: 1 = cultural homogeneity, 0 = cultural heterogeneity. Cultural homogeneity is assumed if the dummies L, RD, and DR are all unity.

As the equations show, none of the taste variables tested here prove to be statistically significant. In addition, only two variables, L and DC, have the expected (positive) sign. This disappointing result could possibly be explained by the facts that mere dummy variables and not cardinal data were used and that the data used refer to the population as a whole and so do not reflect diversities in geographical groupings of the population.

This latter argument seems to be the more important one, for even when we used cardinal data of the degree of ethnic and linguistic fractionalization and of the degree of religious heterogeneity, a statistically significant influence of these variables did not appear. This is made clear by the following equations (15.10) to (15.12).

$$CGE = 84.55 - 0.06P - 0.01GNP + 8.20LF$$
$$(15.98) \ (1.95) \quad (4.34) \qquad (0.94)$$

$$N = 42 \quad \bar{R}^2 = 0.326 \tag{15.10}$$

where LF = degree of linguistic fractionalization, ranging from 1 (linguistic homogeneity) to 0 (linguistic heterogeneity).

$$CGE = 80.59 - 0.07P - 0.01GNP + 2.39ELF$$
$$(18.16) \ (2.40) \quad (4.80) \qquad (0.31)$$

$$N = 50 \quad \bar{R}^2 = 0.359 \tag{15.11}$$

where ELF = degree of ethnic and linguistic fractionalization, ranging from 1 (homogeneity) to 0 (heterogeneity).

$$CGE = 85.54 - 0.06P - 0.01GNP - 0.05PR$$
$$(4.76) \ (0.82) \quad (5.02) \qquad (0.22)$$

$$N = 35 \quad \bar{R}^2 = 0.395 \tag{15.11}$$

where PR = percent of prevailing religion, ranging from 30 to 100 percent. The data for all equations are computed from Taylor and Hudson (1972, pp. 271–280).[38]

In order to be able to account for the lacking regional aspect, we include a dummy variable (S) in equation (15.5) that indicates in which countries sectionalism is extreme and in which polities the opposite is true.

$$CGE = 86.57 - 0.07P - 0.01GNP - 10.0S$$
$$(19.68) \ (2.14) \quad (4.41) \qquad (1.69)$$

$$N = 32 \quad \bar{R}^2 = 0.434 \tag{15.13}$$

where S = dummy variable for the degree of sectionalism: 1 = sectionalism is extreme, rather than negligible, 0 = sectionalism is negligible, rather than extreme. The data are taken from Banks and Textor (1963, printout no. 112).[39]

As equation (15.13) shows, the admittedly rough indicator for regional differences in tastes just reaches the prescribed degree of statistical significance with the expected negative sign; i.e., countries with strong sectionalism are much more decentralized than those without significant sectional forces. Moreover, this variable also adds to the explanatory power of the previous equations.

A further variable determining the demand for decentralization, which we take now into account, is the degree of inequality in the distribution of income (K):

$$CGE = 47.51 - 0.06P - 0.01GNP - 0.20S + 92.94K$$
$$(2.75)\,(2.25)\quad(1.77)\qquad(0.02)\quad(2.16)$$

$$N = 18 \qquad \bar{R}^2 = 0.483 \tag{15.14}$$

where K = Kuznets-index of household income inequality computed for the case of 20 intervals. The Kuznets-index ranges from 0 (perfect equality) to 1 (perfect inequality).[40] The data are taken from Jain (1974).

Equation (15.14) indicates that—against the expectations voiced in the last paragraph—the greater the inequality in the distribution of income among the households, the greater is the existing fiscal centralization. This is valid in the same way if we investigate the distribution of income among income recipients instead of household incomes, and if for both variables besides the Kuznets-measure we use such measures as the Gini-index and Entropy-measure.[41] Thus the thesis concerning the influence of differing demands for publicly supplied goods and services on the formation and promotion of federative structures seems—at least at the first glance—hardly tenable. Rather, it appears to be the case (in agreement with the results of empirical work on the budgetary redistribution in federal systems mentioned above) that major differences in income give rise to a stronger redistribution through the central government. As measured by our indicator for fiscal centralization, this leads to stronger centralization.

Before we can make this inference, however, there is a possible objection we must consider, namely that the data on household income distribution used here are inadequate and that knowledge of geographical income distribution is necessary. I have attempted to take these considerations into account in equation (15.15).

$$CGE = 10.0 - 0.07P - 0.01GNP - 1.90S + 344.3K - 90.5RID$$
$$(6.29)(2.78)\quad(0.63)\qquad(2.21)\qquad(3.01)\quad(2.13)$$

$$N = 10 \qquad \bar{R}^2 = 0.667 \tag{15.15}$$

where RID = a weighted coefficient of variation measuring the dispersion of the regional income per capita levels relative to the national average, while each regional deviation is weighted by its share in the national population.[42] The data are taken from Williamson (1965, p. 12); they refer in most cases to the early sixties.

As equation (15.15) shows, the spatial distribution of income in a country appears to be of greater importance for the demand for fiscal decentralization; the *RID* variable is statistically significant, it has the expected (negative) sign and adds a large amount to the explanatory power of the last equation. Nevertheless, there is a simple reason why this conclusion cannot be regarded as safely established: our sample sizes (and thus the degrees of freedom) are very small as a consequence of the standard set for the statistical materials used here.

All the estimations I have made up to now account for hardly more than half of the variance in the *CGE*. From this we can conclude that there are, besides the determinants of demand considered so far, certain other factors that influence the division of fiscal activity among levels of government. It is, for example, conceivable that substantial impulses for the strengthening or weakening of fiscal federalism depend on the degree to which the legal framework of a society imposes constraints on decentralization in the decision-making process. Democratically governed countries that have chosen the federative form of decision making in their constitution are more likely to maintain a federal form of government, and they will not be able to oppose a vertical power distribution to the same degree as, for example, in authoritarian political systems. These considerations are integrated into equations (15.16) to (15.18).

$$CGE = 73.24 - 24.32F$$
$$(28.17) \quad (4.18)$$
$$N = 50 \quad \bar{R}^2 = 0.237 \tag{15.16}$$

where F = dummy variable of formal federalism: 1 = formally federal country, 0 = formally nonfederal country. The dummies are computed from Elazar (1968).

$$CGE = 72.3 - 10.64F - 25.48VPD$$
$$(27.10) \,(1.41) \quad (2.55)$$
$$N = 45 \quad \bar{R}^2 = 0.314 \tag{15.17}$$

where VPD = dummy variable for the degree of vertical power distribution: 1 = polity where the regional governments are independent in their respective spheres; 0 = polity where the central and regional governments are coordinate and dependent in their respective spheres [see Banks and Textor (1963, printout no. 165) for more detailed comments and data].

$$CGE = 80.86 - 7.5F - 25.48VPD + 11.69SR$$
$$(13.95) \,(1.00) \quad (2.63) \qquad (1.78)$$
$$N = 42 \quad \bar{R}^2 = 0.353 \tag{15.18}$$

where SR = dummy variable for the status of the regime: 1 = nation where the
status of the regime is authoritarian or totalitarian; 0 = nation
where the status of the regime is constitutional (government conducted with reference to recognized constitutional forms). The data
are taken from Banks and Textor (1963, printout no. 94) and Banks
(1971, segment 1).

Equations (15.16) and (15.17) indicate, as expected, that certain constraints for
the creation or the removal of decentralized fiscal decision making are already
given with the formal framework of a society. As equation (15.18) makes clear,
however, the variable for the degree of formal federalism becomes statistically
insignificant when further political variables are introduced.[43] Still, the sign of
all the variables considered here was, as could be expected, negative, and this
would finally indicate that both forces, the political as well as the economic,
play a role in determining the concrete formation of the federal economic system of a country.[44]

Tendencies in Fiscal Federalism

The question whether federalism is only a transitory form of the state on its way
to centralism cannot be answered with certainty. A number of arguments indeed
speak for an increasing centralization, especially:

1. The extension of the spatial limits for costs and benefits of public activities
    resulting, for example, from improved transportation facilities and the re-
    sulting increase in intranational mobility.
2. The growing demand for a more active redistribution policy, especially in
    economically more developed countries.
3. The mandate for the central government, often anchored in the constitu-
    tion, to ensure a minimal provision of certain goods and services in all re-
    gions of a country.[45]

These facts lead, according to a number of authors, to a stronger dependence of
the subcentral governments, which, they claim, can be seen in the increasing proportion of the total public expenditures carried out by the central government.

   Table 15-10 shows that this does not seem to be the case for the countries
dealt with here (for the postwar period of 1950–1970). No matter how unconditional and conditional grants are treated—whether they are wholly or partially
ascribed to the central or to the subcentral governments—the central-government
share in the total expenditures of all governments considered here has tended to
decrease.[46] But it is nonetheless correct that this development is accompanied
by a relative growth of the conditional grants (as measured in the budgets of the

Table 15-10
Degree of Centralization in Government Expenditure: Percentage Distribution of Total Expenditure, 1950-1970[a]

Canada

Year	Alternative 1 F	Alternative 1 S/L	Alternative 2 F	Alternative 2 S/L	Alternative 3 F	Alternative 3 S/L
1950	52.2	47.8	61.2	38.8	64.5	34.5
1955	59.2	40.8	61.4	38.6	66.5	33.5
1960	50.5	49.5	54.5	45.5	59.7	40.3
1965	43.1	56.9	49.9	50.1	52.6	47.4
1970	38.1	61.9	47.5	52.5	50.0	50.0

France

Year	Alternative 1 F	Alternative 1 S/L	Alternative 2 F	Alternative 2 S/L	Alternative 3 F	Alternative 3 S/L
1950	85.6	14.4	87.5	12.5	87.5	12.5
1955	80.5	19.5	83.3	16.7	83.3	16.7
1960	83.2	16.8	89.7	10.3	89.7	10.3
1965	81.7	18.3	86.6	13.4	86.6	13.4
1970	79.3	20.7	83.3	16.7	83.3	16.7

Germany

Year	Alternative 1 F	Alternative 1 S/L	Alternative 2 F	Alternative 2 S/L	Alternative 3 F	Alternative 3 S/L
1950	48.4	51.6			49.0	51.0
1955	44.3	55.7	46.0	54.0	45.9	54.1
1960	39.9	60.1	44.8	55.2	52.6	47.4
1965	40.3	59.7	.	.	53.5	46.5
1970	37.9	62.1	.	.		

Switzerland

Year	Alternative 1 F	Alternative 1 S/L	Alternative 2 F	Alternative 2 S/L	Alternative 3 F	Alternative 3 S/L
1950	32.9	67.1	37.0	63.0	37.0	63.0
1955	33.4	66.6	36.9	63.1	36.9	63.1
1960	30.7	69.3	33.9	66.1	34.1	65.9
1965	26.9	73.1	30.6	69.4	30.7	69.3
1970	26.2	73.8	30.3	69.7	30.5	69.5

United Kingdom

Year	Alternative 1 F	Alternative 1 L	Alternative 2 F	Alternative 2 L	Alternative 3 F	Alternative 3 L
1950	76.6	23.4	86.0	14.0	87.7	12.3
1955	75.0	25.0	83.2	16.8	84.6	15.4
1960	68.0	32.0	72.2	27.8	80.5	19.5
1965	60.6	39.4	65.0	35.0	75.0	25.0
1970	60.0	40.0	63.7	36.3	75.8	24.2

United States

Year	Alternative 1 F	Alternative 1 S/L	Alternative 2 F	Alternative 2 S/L	Alternative 3 F	Alternative 3 S/L
1950	58.3	41.7	62.2	37.8	62.2	37.8
1955	62.9	37.1	66.0	34.0	66.0	34.0
1960	57.6	42.4	62.8	37.2	62.8	37.2
1965	54.8	45.2	60.9	39.1	60.9	39.1
1970	50.5	49.5	57.5	42.5	57.5	42.5

Sources: Tables 15-11, 15-12, 15-28 and sources therefrom.

[a]Alternative 1 follows the national accounts in treating all transfers as state and local government expenditures. Alternative 2 follows the public-finance statistics in treating unconditional transfers as state- and local-government expenditures and conditional transfers as federal expenditures. In Alternative 3 all transfers are treated as federal expenditures.

receiver units). However, strong assumptions are necessary if we are to conclude from this that the dependence of the subcentral governments has grown. As can be shown using the economic approach, conditional grants frequently became unconditional because of the adaptability of the recipient, and unconditional grants permit the decentralized levels to perform their responsibilities more satisfactorily. This contrasts—*prima facie*—with a further opinion frequently met, which suggests that a continual shift would therefore follow not only of the fiscal resources to the central government but also of the responsibilities themselves. But it is hardly possible to investigate this any further with purely *fiscal* data, for the central government can turn to legislative and administrative measures in such a way that a change in the structure of federal/subcentral decision making takes place that does not appear in our budgetary measure.

4. Development and Structure of Selected Federal Economic Systems

This section presents a compilation of available data on government activity in various developed countries, with particular reference to fiscal federalism.

The problem of the accuracy and reliability of the data in this area is well known. Users of these data are therefore cautioned that the data reported here are not in any sense presented as "reliable" or even "best" estimates. The aim was rather to present a compilation of available statistical information in this field.

In general, I have attempted to trace the original published source of the data as well as prior compilations using those data. However, in many cases neither of them included the data desired; materials contained in unpublished PhD. theses, mimeographed documents, and so on, have therefore also been included. The data are ordered in the following groups:

> Tables 15–11 through 15–14 deal with public expenditure by economic categories and governmental level on a *national-account basis*; i.e., all intergovernmental transfers are treated as a part of the recipient unit. Furthermore, all national-insurance expenditures are excluded, mainly because of the extreme differences among the insurance systems of the countries considered here.
>
> Tables 15–15 through 15–17 comprise public-expenditure data by function and governmental level on a *public-finance–statistics basis*; i.e., the intergovernmental transfers are attributed to the level of the recipient unit as long as they are unconditional and to the donor's level if they are conditional payments. Although national insurance is also excluded, the contributions of the various governmental units to national insurance are included.

Tables 15-18 through 15-22 deal with total employment by all governmental units, as well as with the respective wages bill.

Tables 15-23 through 15-32 comprise a series of data on governmental own revenues, receipts from other governments, and the public debt by level of government.

Throughout these tables, the entry "—" signifies a value not significantly different from zero, while "N.A." means that the information is not available for the year in question. The entry "." means either that it was not clear whether data exist at all or that I have not had access to these data.

Also throughout these tables, the abbreviations F (central level of government), S (state level of government), and L (local level of government) are used. In Canada the state level is the provinces, in France the *départements*, in Germany, the *Laender*, and in Switzerland the *Kantone*. In Canada and the United States the local level is the municipalities, in France the *communes*, in Germany the *Gemeinden* and *Gemeindeverbände*, in Switzerland the *Gemeinden*, and in the United Kingdom county boroughs and counties.

Source references will be found in the notes of the tables; full citations of all public and other documents used may be found in the References and List of Public Documents that follow.

Figures in tables may not add to totals because of rounding.

Table 15-11

All Governments Total Expenditure, 1900-1971[a]

Year	Canada % GNP	Canada Total	France % GNP	France Total	Germany % GNP	Germany Total
1900	9.5	98	15.2	49	14.9	4,852[b]
1910	11.4	244	13.7	58	12.8	6,986[d]
1920	16.1	893	25.1	454	21.3	13,296[f]
1930	18.9	1,084	19.1	752	22.2	17,512
1938	23.1	1,220	26.6	1,011	17.7	13,997[h]
1950	22.1	4,080	34.4	29,365	29.8	25.382
1960	29.7	11,380	40.5	88,190	23.3	64.980
1965	29.7	16,554	40.2	136,021	28.5	114,350
1971	37.7	35,220	37.5	225,293	27.8	167,820[i]

Year	Switzerland % GNP	Switzerland Total	United Kingdom % GNP	United Kingdom Total	United States % GNP	United States Total
1900	N.A.	294	14.4	281	7.7	1,660[c]
1910	N.A.	552[d]	12.7	272	8.2	3,208[d]
1920	N.A.	1,585	26.2	1,592	12.4	9,158[e]
1930	15.9	1,818	26.1	1,145	21.1	12,266[g]
1938	19.2	1,838	30.0	1,587	20.2	17,121
1950	19.9	3,956	39.0	4,539	22.3	63,440
1960	17.7	6,572	31.9	7,285	26.5	133,692
1965	20.9	12,507	32.6	10,362	26.5	180,670
1971	24.3	24,453	37.0	18,117	29.7	311,395

Sources:

For Canada: 1920 and before, Firestone (1958, pp. 66 and 129); thereafter, D.B.S., *National Accounts, Income and Expenditure*, (1926-1956, 1961, 1967, and 1973).

For France: André (1973, pp. 50-52); the French data are given in current NF (nouveau francs).

For Germany: 1938 and before, Andic and Veverka (1964); the GNP data are computed from Hoffmann (1965, pp. 509, 825-826); thereafter, St. B., *Volkswirtschaftliche Gesamtrechnungen* (1969 and 1972), *Statistisches Jahrbuch fuer die Bundesrepublik Deutschland* (1974).

For Switzerland: 1930 and before, Wittmann (1961, pp. 462-465); thereafter, E.St.A., *Nationale Buchhaltung der Schweiz* (several years); *Die Finanzen von Bund, Kantonen und Gemeinden* (1938-1971).

For United Kingdom: 1950 and before, Peacock and Wiseman (1967, pp. 153-154 and 164-166); thereafter, C.S.O., *National Income and Expenditure* (1963-1973, 1970).

For the United States: GNP data for 1922 and before, Kendrick (1961), thereafter, from Tax Foundation, *Facts and Figures on Government Finance* (1973); expenditure data are taken from U.S.B.o.C., *Historical Statistics of the United States Colonial Times to 1957*, *Historical Statistics of the United States Continuation to 1962 and Revision*, thereafter from Tax Foundation, *Facts and Figures on Government Finance* (1973).

Note: The total expenditure used here includes both exhaustive as well as nonexhaustive expenditures, i.e., transfers and subsidies of all governments (see notes of the following tables for more special comments); federal, state, and local governments' contributions to national insurance are included, but national insurance is excluded.

[a]Total = All governments' total expenditure (in millions). [b]1901. [c]1902. [d]1913. [e]1922. [f]1925. [g]1932. [h]1937. [i]1970.

Table 15-12
Distribution of All Governments' Total Expenditure by Level of Government, 1900–1971

Year	Canada			France			Germany			Switzerland			United Kingdom			United States		
	F	S	L	F	S	L	F	S	L	F	S	L	F	S	L	F	S	L
1900	57.1	N.A.	N.A.	70.5	5.8	23.7	39.7	33.2	27.1[b]	20.4	41.2	38.4	64.8		35.2	34.1	8.2	57.7[c]
1910	50.0	27.6	22.4	66.3	8.7	25.0	36.7	27.2	36.1[d]	21.9	40.0	38.1	52.1		47.9	30.1	9.0	60.9[d]
1920	59.2	17.0	23.8	81.5	3.5	15.0	35.3	27.8	36.9[f]	38.9	30.0	31.2	80.1		19.9	39.7	9.8	50.5[e]
1930	32.1	24.6	43.3	71.9	7.1	21.0	40.1	25.1	39.6	26.7	36.7	36.6	63.3		36.7	32.5	16.3	51.2[g]
1938	34.3	36.1	29.6	74.9	10.9	14.2	45.8	19.9	34.3[h]	27.6	36.9	35.5	66.5		33.5	45.5	16.2	38.3
1950	52.2	25.2	22.6	85.6	4.9	9.5	48.4	30.2	21.4	32.9	35.2	31.9	76.6		23.4	58.3	15.2	26.5
1960	50.5	24.1	25.4	83.2	4.7	12.1	39.9	33.2	26.9	30.7	37.7	31.6	68.0		32.0	57.6	13.8	28.6
1965	43.1	28.7	28.2	81.7	5.5	12.8	40.3	30.9	28.8	26.9	41.1	32.0	60.6		39.4	54.8	15.0	30.2
1971	37.1	37.9	25.0	76.9	5.6	17.5	37.9	33.2	28.9[i]	25.0	40.5	34.5	58.1		41.9	48.4	18.6	33.0

Sources: See note to Table 15–11.

Notes: See note to Table 15–1 for general comments. Intergovernmental transfers are recorded at the level of the recipient government in the case of both conditional and unconditional grants.

[a]Percentage distribution:

F = federal government ⎫
S = state governments ⎬ expenditure as a percentage of all governments' total expenditure.
L = local governments ⎭

[b]1901. [c]1902. [d]1913. [e]1922. [f]1925. [g]1932. [h]1937. [i]1970.

Table 15-13
Distribution of All Governments' Exhaustive and Nonexhaustive Expenditure by Level of Government, 1930–1971[a]

Year		Canada				France				Germany				Switzerland				United Kingdom				United States			
		F	S	L	Total	F	S	L	Total	F	S	L	Total	F	S	L	Total	F	S	L	Total	F	S	L	Total
1930	Exh. Exp.	23.8	22.8	53.7	721	75.6		24.4	752	30.8	29.1	40.1	12,340	27.6	36.9	35.5	1,818	33.2		66.2	576	N.A.	N.A.	.	.
	Transf.	47.8	29.2	23.0	356					53.4	13.6	33.0	6,022					93.8		6.2	562	N.A.	N.A.	.	.
	Subsid.	87.7	14.3	–	7													100.0		–	7				
1938	Exh. Exp.	26.4	32.8	40.8	666	78.5		21.5	1,011	35.2	21.8	34.1	11,296[b]	32.9[b]	35.2	31.9	1,838	53.6		46.4	1,041	N.A.	N.A.	.	.
	Transf.	37.0	44.9	18.1	492					52.9	14.7	32.4	2,701[b]					90.9		9.1	529	N.A.	N.A.	.	.
	Subsid.	98.4	1.6	–	62													100.0		–	17				
1950	Exh. Exp.	41.3	24.2	34.5	2,425	84.6		15.4	29,365	43.6	31.6	24.8	17,308	25.3	37.9	36.8	2,823	60.9		39.1	2,508	67.9	9.7	22.4	80,985[d]
	Transf.	66.2	29.6	4.2	492					58.8	27.1	14.1	8,074	51.8	28.5	19.7	1,133	95.2		4.8	1,630	76.1	11.6	12.3	13,374[d]
	Subsid.	95.2	4.8	–	64													100.0		–	401				
1960	Exh. Exp.	39.1	23.5	37.4	6,792	72.2		27.8	60,277	31.7	35.2	33.1	45,990	24.2	39.4	36.4	5,155	61.1		38.9	5,073	56.2	14.6	29.2	110,601
	Transf.	64.7	28.8	6.6	4,345	89.7		10.3	22,502	59.9	28.3	11.8	18,990	54.1	31.7	14.2	1,417	83.0		17.0	1,685	63.0	11.0	26.0	23,091
	Subsid.	88.9	16.3	–	242	94.3		5.7	5,413									86.5		13.5	527				
1965	Exh. Exp.	29.5	32.8	37.7	10,788	69.0		31.0	95,982	32.5	33.0	34.5	81,290	21.2	41.7	37.1	9,738	56.6		45.4	7,477	54.1	14.9	31.0	162,523
	Transf.	54.9	38.5	6.6	5,404	85.5		14.5	28,966	59.6	25.8	14.6	33,060	54.6	40.8	4.6	2,769	73.6		26.4	2,311	61.4	16.1	22.5	18,149
	Subsid.	83.7	16.3	–	362	95.4		4.6	11,073									86.8		13.2	574				
1971	Exh. Exp.	24.8	39.6	35.6	22,101	69.3		30.7	153,281	28.2	36.6	35.2	118,650[c]	19.3	42.6	38.1	17,120	51.5		48.5	12,835	45.0	19.2	35.8	263,537
	Transf.	57.0	35.2	7.6	12,120	85.4		14.6	54,093	61.3	25.1	13.6	49,170[c]	40.0	38.6	21.4	7,333	70.6		29.4	4,346	66.6	15.2	18.2	47,860
	Subsid.	68.5	31.4	–	999	95.6		4.4	17,919									90.0		10.0	936				

Sources: See notes to Table 15-11.

Note: Government *exhaustive expenditures* are outlays for currently produced goods and services. They include extrabudgetary expenditures on goods and services by agencies not treated as government business enterprises, for example, the national and state broadcasting corporations. Sales of goods and services by governments are set against expenditures in order to avoid double counting in the GNP. *Transfers* are payments involving no *quid pro quo* that are made to persons. Interest on the public debt is treated as a transfer payment. *Subsidies* are similar payments made to intermediaries, e.e., business firms.

[a] Exh. Exp. = Exhaustive Expenditures
Transf. = Transfers } As a percentage of the respective total.
Subsid. = Subsidies
Total = All governments' respective expenditure (in millions).
[b]1937. [c]1970. [d]1952.

Table 15-14
Distribution of All Governments' Expenditure on Capital Account and on Current Goods and Services by Level of Government, 1930-1971[a]

Year	Canada				France				Germany				Switzerland				United Kingdom				United States			
	F	S	L	Total	F	S	L	Total	F	S	L	Total	F	S	L	Total	F	S	L	Total	F	S	L	Total
1930 CA	33.8	35.1	31.1	228	·	N.A.	N.A.	·	11.7	15.7	72.6	1,318		N.A.	N.A.	N.A.	4.7		95.3	120	N.A.			·
1930 G&S	19.3	16.6	64.1	493	·	N.A.	N.A.	·	33.1	30.7	36.2	11,022		N.A.	N.A.	N.A.	40.7		59.3	456	N.A.			·
1938 CA	24.7	53.1	22.2	162	·	N.A.	N.A.	·	55.8	17.2	26.9	14,296[b]		N.A.	N.A.	N.A.	25.5		74.5	219	N.A.			·
1938 G&S	27.0	16.6	46.8	504	·	N.A.	N.A.	·						N.A.	N.A.	N.A.	61.1		38.9	823	N.A.			·
1950 CA	15.9	39.4	44.7	497	·	N.A.	N.A.	·	13.5	25.0	61.5	2,413	25.3	37.9	36.8	2,823	7.6		92.4	437	63.7	18.9	17.4	27,388[d]
1950 G&S	47.9	20.3	31.8	1,928	·	N.A.	N.A.	·	48.5	32.7	18.8	14,896					72.1		27.9	2,071	70.1	5.0	24.9	63,597[d]
1960 CA	15.1	40.5	44.4	1,511	47.0		53.0	15,103	18.8	20.6	60.6	9,660	9.8	49.2	41.0	960	29.3		70.7	873	52.7	20.7	26.6	31,946
1960 G&S	45.9	18.7	35.4	5,281	80.7		19.3	45,174	35.1	39.1	25.8	36,330	27.6	37.1	35.3	4,195	67.7		32.3	4,200	55.5	11.7	32.8	81,655
1965 CA	14.4	42.2	43.4	2,430	45.4		54.6	29,351	16.8	19.7	63.5	20,280	5.9	55.7	38.4	2,605	20.0		80.0	1,507	50.3	22.4	27.3	41,608
1965 G&S	33.8	30.1	36.1	8,358	79.4		20.6	66,631	37.7	37.5	24.8	61,010	27.2	36.2	36.6	7,133	63.4		36.6	5,970	55.4	12.3	32.3	120,915
1971 CA	13.9	44.4	41.7	3,714	42.6		57.4	43,284	18.4	20.2	61.4	28,210[c]	6.9	46.8	46.3	5,675	23.0		77.0	2,609	32.1	30.2	37.7	48,824
1971 G&S	27.0	38.7	34.3	18,387	79.8		20.2	109,997	31.2	41.8	27.0	90,440[c]	25.4	40.6	34.0	11,445	58.8		41.2	10,226	47.9	16.7	35.4	214,713

Sources: See notes to Table 15-11.

Note: Government *Expenditure on Capital Account* includes (1) government-built nonrental housing, (2) state and local school and hospital construction, and (3) outlays made directly by government departments. Not included in capital formation are repair and maintenance expenditures. Defense expenditure on construction is included as fixed capital formation; outlays on equipment for the Department of National Defense are excluded. Expenditure on *Current Goods and Services* are calculated as residuals by subtracting the capital series from the exhaustive expenditure series in Table 15-13. This procedure is the same as that used to calculate current expenditures in the national accounts.

[a]CA = Expenditure on Capital Account
G&S = Expenditure on Current Goods and Services } as a percentage of total.
Total = All governments' respective expenditure (in millions).

[b]1937. [c]1970. [d]1952.

Table 15-15
All Governments' Expenditure by Function and Level of Government, 1971

Function	Canada[b] F	S	L	Total	%[a]	France F	S	L	Total	%	Germany F	S	L	Total	%	Switzerland F	S	L	Total	%	United Kingdom F	S	L	Total	%	United States F	S	L	Total	%
Nat. Defense & Int. Relat.	100.0	–	–	1,946	8.2	100.0		–	43,687	17.1	99.9	0.1	–	28,036	12.1	90.6	6.1	3.2	2,857	11.8	100.0		–	3,028	14.0	100.0	–	–	80,910	22.4
Publ. Welfare & Health	55.6	41.1	3.3	7,243	30.4	91.1		8.9	103,853	40.5	54.0	18.4	27.6	57,845	25.1	32.2	48.3	19.5	5,037	20.8	84.4		15.6	8,160	37.6	31.2	42.6	26.2	52,651	14.6
Education	12.3	43.0	44.8	4,807	20.2	94.5		5.5	40,160	15.7	12.5	64.0	23.5	37,315	16.2	15.0	45.9	39.0	5,358	22.1	18.1		81.9	3,224	14.9	12.7	38.9	48.4	90,170	24.9
Transport & Communic.	25.3	55.7	18.9	2,341	9.8	81.8		18.2	9,048	3.5	44.0	25.6	30.4	19,851	8.6	42.7	30.5	26.8	3,624	15.0	40.1		59.9	1,074	5.0	20.4	57.1	22.5	25,920	7.2
Natur. Rec. & Prim. Indus.	63.7	36.3	–	1,084	4.6	76.3		23.7	11,472	4.5	40.6	20.8	38.6	30,359	13.2	44.9	21.0	34.1	2,376	9.8	81.1		18.9	747	3.4	78.1	17.7	4.2	14,374	4.0
Housing & Urb. Renew.	Included in Other					78.2		21.8	6,496	2.5	10.8	49.1	40.1	4,800	2.1	Included in Other					24.7		75.3	999	4.6	56.6	2.8	40.6	6,222	1.7
General Government	52.3	24.6	23.1	1,355	5.7	60.8		39.2	27,875	10.9	22.2	38.3	39.5	12,991	5.6	22.3	35.7	42.0	1,816	7.5	49.3		50.7	616	2.8	40.3	27.6	32.1	7,200	1.0
Protection	22.5	35.4	42.1	1,089	4.6	92.8		7.2	7,799	3.0	6.2	77.5	16.3	9,285	4.0	11.3	57.4	31.3	1,232	5.1	20.5		79.5	682	3.1	5.9	22.6	71.5	8,000	2.2
Debt Charges	60.4	22.0	17.6	1,778	7.5	Included in Other			5,991		39.2	26.7	34.1	8,236	3.6	19.6	30.9	49.4	1,366	5.6	55.6		44.4	2,487	11.5	76.6	8.1	15.3	21,688	6.0
Other	66.0	21.5	12.5	2,162	9.1	89.9		10.1	5,991	2.3	39.1	53.3	7.6	22,094	9.6	48.1	7.8	51.0	526	2.2	87.3		12.7	687	3.2	53.3	15.6	31.1	54,702	15.1
TOTAL	47.5	34.9	17.6	23,805	100.0	88.6		11.4	256,381	100.0	43.7	32.2	24.0	230,812	100.0	35.9	35.0	29.1	24,230	100.0	65.0		35.0	21,704	100.0	49.2	24.6	26.2	361,837	100.0

Sources: See notes to Table 15-17.

Note: The terms used for functional breakdowns in this table are the following: *National Defense and International Relations* seems clear without major elaboration, but it should be mentioned that International Cooperation and Assistance is also included. *Public Welfare and Health* comprises, first, aid to aged, blind, unemployed, and unemployable persons; mothers' allowances; child welfare and other miscellaneous welfare payments; as well as the veterans' pensions and benefits. Second, it comprises general and public health, medical and dental services, and hospital care. *Education* comprises expenditure on schools, universities, and special schools. *Transport and Communication* comprises expenditures on airways, highways, railways, waterways, telephone, telegraph, and radio. *Natural Resources and Primary Industries* comprises expenditures on fish and game, forests, land settlement and agriculture, minerals and mines, and water resources. *Housing and Urban Renewal* comprises low- and moderate-income housing aids, and maintenance of the housing mortgage market. *General Government* comprises executive, administrative, and legislative expenditures, as well as expenditures on research, planning, and statistics. *Protection* comprises law enforcement, corrections, and police and fire protection. *Debt charges* comprises interest, commissions, and discounts. *Other* comprises items that are hard to classify within the above groups (e.g., winter works).

[a]% = Percentage distribution of all governments' total expenditure (Total) by function.
[b]1968.

Table 15-16
Distribution of Government Expenditure by Level of Government and Function, 1971

Function	Canada[a] F	Canada[a] S	Canada[a] L	France F	France S	France L	Germany F	Germany S	Germany L	Switzerland F	Switzerland S	Switzerland L	United Kingdom F	United Kingdom S	United Kingdom L	United States F	United States S	United States L
Nat. Defence and Int. Relat.	17.2	–	–	19.2		–	27.8	–	–	29.8	2.1	1.3	21.3		–	45.4	–	–
Publ. Welfare and Health	35.6	35.8	5.7	41.7		31.5	31.0	14.3	28.7	18.7	28.7	13.9	48.5		17.0	9.2	25.2	14.6
Education	5.2	24.8	51.4	16.7		7.6	4.6	32.1	15.8	9.3	29.0	29.7	4.1		35.2	6.4	39.4	46.0
Transport and Communic.	5.2	15.7	10.6	3.3		5.6	8.7	6.8	10.9	17.8	13.0	13.8	3.0		8.6	3.0	16.6	6.1
Natur. Rec. and Prim. Indus.	6.1	4.7	–	3.9		9.2	12.2	8.5	21.1	12.2	5.9	11.5	4.3		1.9	6.3	2.9	0.6
Housing and Urb. Renew.	Included in Other			2.2		4.8	0.5	3.2	3.5	Included in Other			1.7		10.0	2.0	0.2	2.7
General Government	6.3	4.0	7.5	7.5		37.3	2.9	6.7	9.2	4.7	7.6	10.8	2.1		4.2	1.6	2.2	2.4
Protection	2.2	4.6	10.9	3.2		1.9	0.6	9.7	2.7	1.6	8.3	5.5	1.0		7.2	0.3	2.0	6.0
Dept Charges	9.5	4.7	7.5	Included in Other			3.2	3.0	5.1	3.1	5.0	9.6	9.7		14.7	9.3	2.0	3.5
Other	12.6	5.6	6.4	2.3		2.1	8.6	15.8	3.0	2.9	0.2	0.2	4.2		1.2	16.4	9.5	18.0
Total = 100%	11,300	8,313	4,191	227,029		29,352	100,869	74,442	55,501	8,699	8,490	7,041	14,212		7,492	177,922	89,118	94,797

Sources and Notes: See Tables 15-15 and 15-17.
[a] 1968.

Table 15-17
Distribution of All Governments' Expenditure by Function and Level of Government, 1956–1971[a]

Function and Year	Canada							France				
	F		S		L			F		$S \& L$		
	F_1	F_2	S_1	S_2	L_1	L_2	Total	F_1	F_2	$S\&L_1$	$S\&L_2$	Total
National Defence and International Relations												
1956	100.0	38.9	—	—	—	—	1,855	·	·	N.A.	·	·
1961	100.0	26.4	—	—	—	—	1,716	·	·	N.A.	—	·
1966	100.0	20.9	—	—	—	—	1,698[b]	100.0	18.3	—	—	23,464[b]
1971	100.0	17.2	—	—	—	—	1,946[c]	100.0	19.2	—	—	43,687
Public Welfare and Health												
1956	70.6	25.6	23.4	23.3	6.0	7.9	1,727	·	·	N.A.	·	·
1961	68.4	32.8	28.1	28.8	3.5	4.8	3,109	·	·	N.A.	—	·
1966	62.4	33.8	34.7	30.0	2.9	4.2	4,399[b]	91.5	42.4	8.5	33.2	59,402[b]
1971	55.6	35.6	41.1	35.8	3.3	5.7	7,243[c]	91.1	41.7	8.9	31.5	103,853
Education												
1956	4.6	0.8	43.0	20.9	52.4	33.5	841	·	·	N.A.	·	·
1961	5.2	1.4	46.2	27.7	48.6	39.0	1,821	·	·	N.A.	—	·
1966	10.3	3.7	51.9	29.1	37.8	35.6	2,860[b]	93.8	13.8	6.2	7.8	18,731[b]
1971	12.3	5.2	43.0	24.8	44.8	51.4	4,807	94.5	16.7	5.5	7.6	40,160
Transport and Communications												
1956	21.5	4.5	55.9	32.4	22.6	17.2	1,003	·	·	N.A.	·	·
1961	30.0	6.6	45.9	21.7	24.1	15.2	1,435	·	·	N.A.	—	·
1966	29.4	7.4	49.2	19.7	21.4	14.4	2,035[b]	87.8	5.1	12.2	6.0	7,512[b]
1971	25.3	5.2	55.7	15.7	18.9	10.6	2,341[c]	81.8	3.3	18.2	5.6	9,048
Natural Resources and Primary Industries												
1956	54.2	3.3	45.8	7.6	—	—	288	·	·	N.A.	·	·
1961	66.6	6.2	33.3	6.6	—	—	605	·	·	N.A.	—	·
1966	60.0	5.5	39.4	5.7	—	—	733[b]	84.5	4.4	15.5	6.8	6,648[b]
1971	63.7	6.1	36.3	4.7	—	—	1,084[c]	76.3	3.9	23.7	9.2	11,472

Housing and Urban Renewal												
1956	Included in Other							·	·	·	N.A.	·
1961								·	·	·	N.A.	·
1966								72.9	1.6	27.1	5.2	2,900[b]
1971								78.2	2.2	21.8	4.8	6,496
General Government												
1956	64.9	6.6	14.4	4.0	20.7	7.7	487	·	·	·	N.A.	·
1961	50.3	4.4	23.6	4.4	26.1	6.6	571	·	·	·	N.A.	·
1966	44.1	4.2	27.5	4.2	28.4	7.2	771[b]	67.2	8.7	32.8	36.1	16,643[b]
1971	52.3	6.3	24.6	4.0	23.1	7.5	1,355[c]	60.8	7.5	39.2	37.3	27,875
Protection												
1956	19.7	1.3	30.0	5.3	50.5	11.9	309	·	·	·	N.A.	·
1961	18.1	1.4	29.0	4.6	53.0	11.4	487	·	·	·	N.A.	·
1966	21.9	2.1	30.4	4.4	47.7	11.7	744[b]	91.3	2.8	8.7	2.3	3,942[b]
1971	22.5	2.2	35.4	4.6	42.1	10.9	1,089[c]	92.8	3.2	7.2	1.9	7,799
Dept Charges												
1956	79.4	9.9	9.3	3.2	11.3	5.1	593	Included in Other				
1961	78.4	10.6	9.6	2.8	12.1	4.7	879					
1966	71.3	11.1	11.0	2.7	17.7	7.3	1,258[b]					
1971	60.4	9.5	22.0	4.7	17.6	7.5	1,778[c]					
Other												
1956	61.0	9.0	7.7	3.1	31.3	16.8	705	·	·	·	N.A.	·
1961	55.5	10.1	8.5	3.3	35.5	18.3	1,171	·	·	·	N.A.	·
1966	53.3	11.4	12.4	4.2	34.2	19.5	1,732[b]	90.3	2.9	9.7	2.6	4,122[b]
1971	66.0	12.6	21.5	5.6	12.5	6.4	2,162[c]	89.9	2.3	10.1	2.1	5,991
TOTAL (In % of Total)												
1956	61.0		22.5		16.8	16.8	7,808	·	·	·	N.A.	·
1961	55.0		25.8		19.2	19.2	11,794	·	·	·	N.A.	·
1966	49.9		31.4		18.7	18.7	16,230[b]	89.4	·	10.6	10.6	143,364[b]
1971	47.5		34.9		17.6	17.6	23,805[c]	88.6	·	11.4	11.4	256,381

Table 15-17 Continued

Function and Year		Germany							Switzerland						
		F_1	F_2	S_1	S_2	L_1	L_2	Total	F_1	F_2	S_1	S_2	L_1	L_2	Total
National Defence and Internat. Relations	1956	99.6	24.6	0.4	0.1	—	—	7,378	98.6	42.9	1.1	0.5	0.3	0.1	797[d]
	1961	100.0	27.2	—	—	—	—	13,311	96.9	43.2	1.7	0.8	1.3	0.8	1,084[e]
	1966	100.0	27.6	—	—	—	—	20,209	96.7	36.5	2.4	1.0	0.9	0.5	1,783[b]
	1971	99.9	27.8	0.1	—	—	—	28,036	90.6	29.8	6.1	2.1	3.2	1.3	2,857
Public Welfare and Health	1956	66.6	43.2	17.8	19.5	15.6	24.3	19,356	28.5	45.8	45.3	27.8	26.2	21.3	1,005[d]
	1961	65.6	37.4	17.3	17.8	17.2	22.3	28,136	26.0	13.4	47.4	26.8	26.6	20.5	1,303[e]
	1966	62.1	32.0	17.0	13.3	20.9	23.7	37,738	26.8	14.6	48.6	26.9	22.8	17.1	2,428[b]
	1971	54.0	31.0	18.4	14.3	27.6	28.7	57,845	32.2	18.7	48.3	28.7	19.5	13.9	5,037
Education	1956	3.0	0.7	62.4	42.8	34.6	19.5	7,001	7.2	3.3	53.0	27.3	39.8	27.0	847[d]
	1961	14.8	4.0	56.1	26.7	29.0	17.5	13,081	9.8	5.2	50.5	28.5	39.7	30.5	1,303[e]
	1966	9.4	2.4	62.3	24.5	28.3	16.1	18,957	12.0	3.9	48.6	25.8	39.4	28.3	2,337[b]
	1971	12.5	4.6	64.0	32.1	23.5	15.8	37,315	15.0	9.3	45.9	29.0	39.0	29.7	5,358
Transport and Communications	1956	28.9	3.8	30.6	6.7	40.5	12.6	3,854	19.7	5.2	38.5	11.3	41.8	16.3	488[d]
	1961	33.2	5.1	26.9	7.4	39.9	13.9	7,567	21.5	6.4	42.5	13.7	36.0	15.9	745[e]
	1966	36.4	5.7	31.8	7.6	31.8	11.0	11,459	43.3	20.3	30.2	15.2	26.5	18.0	2,211[b]
	1971	44.0	8.7	25.6	6.8	30.4	10.9	19,851	42.7	17.8	30.5	13.0	26.8	13.8	3,624
Natural Resources and Primary Industries	1956	59.7	8.4	34.4	8.2	5.9	2.0	4,214	59.7	13.0	25.6	6.1	14.7	4.8	398[d]
	1961	44.8	11.3	23.2	10.6	32.0	18.4	12,505	65.2	15.1	24.5	6.1	10.2	3.5	576[e]
	1966	43.5	14.1	23.6	11.6	32.9	23.4	23,700	54.3	13.2	32.1	8.4	13.7	4.8	1,148[b]
	1971	40.6	12.2	20.8	8.5	38.6	21.1	30,359	44.9	12.2	21.0	5.9	34.1	11.5	2,376
Housing and Urban Renewal	1956	44.7	7.0	36.2	9.6	19.1	7.2	4,678			Included in Other				
	1961	36.3	3.8	47.6	9.2	16.1	3.9	5,301							
	1966	22.5	1.6	61.3	6.6	16.2	2.5	5,206							
	1971	10.8	0.5	49.1	3.2	40.1	3.5	4,800							
General Government	1956	26.2	3.3	39.9	8.6	33.9	10.4	3,812	16.2	4.4	37.2	11.1	46.6	18.4	494[d]
	1961	23.1	3.2	37.5	9.2	39.4	12.4	6,752	20.9	4.3	36.0	7.9	43.1	12.9	507[e]
	1966	20.2	2.6	38.8	7.6	41.0	11.6	9,432	14.9	3.6	38.1	9.9	47.0	16.5	1,144[b]
	1971	22.2	2.9	38.3	6.7	39.5	9.2	12,991	22.3	4.7	35.7	7.6	42.0	10.8	1,816
Protection	1956	4.8	0.5	81.3	12.9	13.9	3.1	2,791	9.6	1.4	60.8	10.1	23.6	6.5	274[d]
	1961	7.2	0.6	79.3	11.8	13.5	2.5	4,098	18.7	3.3	57.5	10.8	23.8	6.1	432[e]
	1966	7.0	0.5	81.5	9.1	11.5	1.8	5,326	10.1	1.4	57.2	8.4	32.7	6.5	645[b]
	1971	6.2	0.6	77.5	9.7	16.3	2.7	9,285	11.3	1.6	57.4	8.3	31.3	5.5	1,232

Table 15-17 Continued

	Year														
Debt Charges	1956	58.1	5.1	41.5	6.2	0.4	0.1	2,618	60.6	13.9	22.9	5.8	16.5	5.5	419[d]
	1961	57.6	3.8	42.2	5.0	0.2	—	3,265	43.9	8.8	24.2	5.2	31.9	9.4	498[e]
	1966	40.0	4.8	23.0	4.2	37.0	9.8	8,830	31.1	4.4	28.9	4.4	40.0	8.3	675[b]
	1971	39.2	3.2	26.7	3.0	34.1	5.1	8,236	19.6	3.1	30.9	5.0	49.4	9.6	1,366
Other	1956	23.9	3.4	14.4	3.4	61.6	20.8	4,211	66.7	0.1	—	—	33.3	0.1	9[d]
	1961	40.8	3.6	14.1	2.3	45.1	9.1	4,389	74.7	1.0	—	—	25.6	0.5	32[e]
	1966	44.6	8.6	52.1	15.4	3.4	1.4	14,217	66.7	0.1	—	—	33.3	0.1	3[b]
	1971	39.1	8.6	53.3	15.8	7.6	3.0	22,094	48.1	2.9	7.8	0.2	51.0	0.2	526
TOTAL (In % of Total)	1956	49.8		29.4		20.8		59,913		38.7		34.9		26.4	4,731[d]
	1961	50.0		27.9		22.1		98,408		38.3		35.6		26.1	6,479[e]
	1966	47.4		31.1		21.5		154,668		38.2		35.5		26.3	12,373[b]
	1971	43.7		32.2		24.0		230,812		35.9		35.0		29.1	24,230

Table 15-17 Continued

Function and Year		United Kingdom F_1	F_2	L_1	L_2	Total	United States F_1	F_2	S_1	S_2	L_1	L_2	Total
National Defence and International Relations	1956	100.0	29.7	–	–	1,683^f	100.0	64.8	–	–	–	–	42,680
	1961	100.0	28.5	–	–	1,878	100.0	59.6	–	–	–	–	49,387
	1966	100.0	26.9	–	–	2,433	100.0	64.4	–	–	–	–	60,832
	1971	100.0	21.3	–	–	3,028	100.0	45.5	–	–	–	–	80,910
Public Welfare and Health	1956	86.5	40.2	13.5	16.4	2,636^f	14.6	1.5	44.4	25.0	41.0	11.6	6,924
	1961	85.5	38.7	14.5	16.5	2,975	15.8	2.0	41.8	23.0	42.4	11.9	10,460
	1966	84.7	43.7	15.3	15.6	4,668	17.4	2.8	60.4	18.1	22.2	7.8	15,327
	1971	84.4	48.5	15.6	17.0	8,160	31.2	9.2	42.6	25.2	26.2	14.6	52,651
Education	1956	16.5	2.7	83.5	35.6	929^f	6.6	1.4	15.1	17.4	78.3	45.4	14,161
	1961	18.2	3.1	81.8	35.2	1,123	3.0	0.8	17.9	20.0	79.1	45.2	21,214
	1966	20.0	4.2	80.0	32.9	1,891	4.5	1.6	50.9	34.8	44.6	35.4	34,837
	1971	18.1	4.1	81.9	35.2	3,224	12.7	6.4	38.9	39.4	48.4	46.0	90,170
Transport and Communications	1956	29.4	1.5	70.6	9.1	282^f	1.2	0.1	62.1	35.4	36.7	10.6	7,035
	1961	48.4	3.5	51.6	9.4	475	1.5	0.2	62.3	32.7	36.2	9.7	9,995
	1966	44.7	3.6	55.3	8.8	727	1.0	0.1	80.2	20.3	18.8	5.5	12,895
	1971	40.1	3.0	59.9	8.6	1,074	20.4	3.0	57.1	16.6	22.5	6.1	25,920
Natural Resources and Primary Industries	1956	84.1	5.3	15.9	2.6	359^f	88.4	10.5	8.6	5.4	3.0	1.0	7,810
	1961	85.4	5.8	14.6	2.5	444	88.4	12.2	7.9	4.8	3.7	1.1	11,409
	1966	78.9	3.7	21.1	1.9	421	80.2	8.7	15.2	3.1	4.6	1.1	10,301
	1971	81.1	4.3	18.9	1.9	747	78.1	6.3	17.7	2.9	4.2	0.6	14,374
Housing and Urban Renewal	1956	23.4	1.5	76.6	12.9	367^f	22.2	0.2	–	–	77.8	1.8	598
	1961	22.4	1.4	77.6	12.1	406	28.6	0.5	0.5	–	70.9	2.5	1,320
	1966	13.4	1.2	86.6	15.9	842	41.8	1.1	3.5	0.2	54.7	3.0	2,415
	1971	24.7	1.7	75.3	10.0	999	56.6	2.0	2.8	0.2	40.6	2.7	6,222
General Government	1956	78.2	2.0	21.8	1.4	142^f	30.2	1.0	21.3	3.9	48.5	4.4	2,235
	1961	76.1	1.8	23.9	1.4	155	26.0	1.0	24.0	3.8	50.0	4.1	3,025
	1966	46.1	1.7	53.9	3.9	336	27.5	1.2	25.3	2.2	47.2	4.4	4,105
	1971	49.3	2.1	50.7	4.2	616	40.3	1.6	27.6	2.2	32.1	2.4	7,200
Protection	1956	18.7	0.6	81.3	6.8	182^f	7.1	0.2	7.1	1.3	85.8	7.8	2,224
	1961	19.2	0.6	80.8	7.1	229	5.6	0.2	8.5	1.5	85.9	7.6	3,297
	1966	17.5	0.7	82.5	6.5	360	6.1	0.3	20.2	1.7	73.7	7.4	4,409
	1971	20.5	1.0	79.5	7.2	682	5.9	0.3	22.6	2.0	71.5	6.0	8,000

Debt Charges	1956	75.0	13.9	25.0	12.0	1,048^f	84.4	8.1	4.9	2.5	10.7	2.8	6,297
	1961	73.0	13.7	27.0	12.8	1,239	80.4	9.0	6.3	3.1	13.3	3.3	9,309
	1966	63.4	11.5	36.6	13.1	1,638	78.1	10.1	7.3	1.8	14.6	4.1	12,278
	1971	55.6	9.7	44.4	14.7	2,487	76.6	9.3	8.1	2.0	15.3	3.5	21,688
Other	1956	69.8	2.7	30.2	3.1	222^f	63.2	12.3	8.9	9.1	27.9	14.6	12,699
	1961	70.0	2.8	30.0	3.1	267	61.8	14.5	10.7	11.1	27.5	14.6	19,741
	1966	79.8	2.8	20.2	1.4	317	28.3	9.6	28.8	18.0	42.9	31.3	32,007
	1971	87.3	4.2	12.7	1.2	687	53.3	16.4	15.6	9.5	31.1	18.0	54,702
TOTAL (In % of Total)	1956	72.3		27.7		7,850^f	64.2	12.0			23.8		102,627
	1961	71.6		28.4		9,191	59.6	13.7			26.7		142,157
	1966	66.3		33.7		13,633	49.9	26.6			23.2		189,406
	1971	65.0		35.0		21,704	49.2	24.6			26.2		361,837

Sources:

For Canada: Urquhart and Buckley (1965, p. 207); D.B.S., *Financial Statistics of the Government of Canada* (1961); *Federal Government Finance* (1965); *Financial Statistics of Provincial Governments* (1961); *Provincial Government Finance* (1965); *Financial Statistics of Municipal Governments* (1961); *Municipal Government Finance* (1965); *Consolidated Government Finance* (1968).

For France: André (1974, pp. 1, 4, 61, 64, 66–67, 74–76) and I.N.S.E.E., *Annuaire Statistique de la France* (various years).

For Germany: St.B., *Statistisches Jahrbuch für die Bundesrepublik Deutschland* (various years); St.B., *Wirtschaft und Statistik* (various years).

For Switzerland: E.St.A., *Die Finanzen von Bund, Kantonen und Gemeinden* (1938–1971); *Oeffentliche Finanzen der Schweiz* (various years); *Finanzhaushalt der Kantone* (1930–1971); *Statistisches Jahrbuch der Schweiz* (various years); expenditures for civil defense are included in national defense and international relations.

For United Kingdom: C.S.O., *Annual Abstracts of Statistics* (various years); *Financial Statements and Budget Report* (various years).

For the United States: U.S.B.o.C., *Statistical Abstract of the United States* (various years); *Historical Statistics of the United States, Colonial Times to 1957; Historical Statistics of the United States, Continuation to 1962 and Revisions.*

Note: The figures in Tables 15–15 to 15–17 are based on public-finance statistics, i.e., they refer to the fiscal year, which generally does not end in December; moreover, the classification of expenditures in the public-finance statistics is not identical with the classification used in the national accounts (there is also a somewhat different definition of "government" in both statistics); thus, we will find some differences between data sets (besides the different treatment of conditional intergovernmental transfers). For details of the terms used for functional breakdown in the Tables 15–15 to 15–17, see note to Table 15–15.

^{a}F$_1$, S$_1$, L$_1$ = Percentage distribution of the total expenditure for each function *by level of government.*
F$_2$, S$_2$, L$_2$ = Percentage distribution of the total expenditure of each level of government *by function.*

^{b}1965. ^{c}1968. ^{d}1955. ^{e}1960. ^{f}1959.

Table 15-18
Form of Production and Type of Product

Canada, 1971

Form of Production	Private Goods			Social Goods			Total		
	1	2	3	4	5	6	7	8	9
Public Production	445	12.0	0.6	3,273	88.0	14.8	3,718	100.0	4.0
Private Production	70,693	78.9	99.4	18,896	21.1	85.2	89,589	100.0	96.0
Total Production	71,138	76.2	100.0	22,169	23.8	100.0	93,307	100.0	100.0

France, 1971

Form of Production	Private Goods			Social Goods			Total		
	1	2	3	4	5	6	7	8	9
Public Production	8,784	10.0	1.2	79,334	90.0	56.4	88,118	100.0	9.7
Private Production	754,662	92.5	98.8	61,382	7.5	43.6	816,044	100.0	90.3
Total Production	763,446	84.4	100.0	140,716	15.6	100.0	904,162	100.0	100.0

Germany, 1971

Form of Production	Private Goods			Social Goods			Total		
	1	2	3	4	5	6	7	8	9
Public Production	14,240	16.0	3.0	74,730	84.0	26.8	88,970	100.0	11.8
Private Production	462,750	69.4	97.0	204,380	30.6	73.2	667,130	100.0	88.2
Total Production	476,990	63.1	100.0	279,110	36.9	100.0	756,100	100.0	100.0

Switzerland, 1969

Form of Production	Private Goods			Social Goods			Total		
	1	2	3	4	5	6	7	8	9
Public Production	1,665	28.0	2.5	4,283	72.0	31.9	5,948	100.0	7.3
Private Production	65,845	87.8	97.5	9,137	12.2	68.1	74,982	100.0	92.7
Total Production	67,510	83.4	100.0	13,420	16.6	100.0	80,930	100.0	100.0

Table 15-18 Continued

United Kingdom, 1971

Form of Production		Private Goods			Social Goods			Total	
		1	2	3	4	5	6	7	8	9
Public Production	1	1,649			10,245			11,894		
	2		13.9			86.1			100.0	
	3			4.7			50.5			21.4
Private Production	4	33,590			10,036			43,626		
	5		77.7			23.0			100.0	
	6			95.3			49.5			78.6
Total Production	7	35,239			20,281			55,520		
	8		63.5			36.5			100.0	
	9			100.0			100.0			100.0

United States, 1971

Form of Production		Private Goods			Social Goods			Total	
		1	2	3	4	5	6	7	8	9
Public Production	1	13,100			124,800			137,900		
	2		9.5			90.5			100.0	
	3			1.6			53.6			13.1
Private Production	4	804,500			108,000			912,500		
	5		88.2			11.8			100.0	
	6			98.4			46.4			86.9
Total Production	7	817,600			232,800			1,050,400		
	8		77.8			22.2			100.0	
	9			100.0			100.0			100.0

Sources:

For Canada: D.B.S., *National Accounts, Income and Expenditure* (1973).

For France: S.O.E.C., *National Accounts* (1972).

For Germany: St.B., *Volkswirtschaftliche Gesamtrechnungen* (1972).

For Switzerland: E.St.A., *Nationale Buchhaltung der Schweiz* (1969); *Oeffentliche Finanzen der Schweiz* (1969).

For United Kingdom: C.S.O., *National Income and Expenditure* (1972); *Annual Abstracts of Statistics* (1973).

For the United States: Musgrave and Musgrave (1973, p. 9).

Note: The total (GNP) is broken down according to (1) whether the goods and services are "private" or "social" in nature, and (2) whether they have been produced publicly or by private firms. Total production of *social goods* equals government purchases of goods and services. Public production thereof equals income originating in general government. Private production is residual. Total production of *private goods* equals GNP minus total production of social goods. Public production of private goods equals value added by government enterprise. Private production of private goods is residual. Rows and columns 1, 4, and 7 give the absolute figures (in millions); rows 2, 5, and 8 comprise the percent of total for column; rows 3, 6, and 9 comprise the percent of total for row.

Table 15-19
Total Employment, Unemployment, Civilian Employment and Total Government Employment as a Percent of Total Work Force, 1900–1970[a]

Canada

Year	TE	U	CE	TGE	Total
1900	96.0	4.0	95.7	N.A.	1,861
1910	97.0	3.0	96.9	N.A.	2,801
1920	94.2	5.8	94.1	N.A.	3,318
1930	90.9	9.1	90.7	N.A.	4,066
1938	88.6	11.4	88.5	N.A.	4,595
1950	96.8	3.2	95.9	N.A.	5,210
1960	93.2	6.8	94.6	N.A.	6,531
1965	96.2	3.8	94.6	10.3	7,255
1970	94.2	5.8	92.8	10.8	8,494

France

Year	TE	U	CE	TGE	Total
1900	98.4	1.6	95.6	N.A.	19,900[b]
1910	99.0	1.0	96.1	N.A.	20,240[c]
1920	97.4	2.6	95.4	4.9	20,660
1930	97.9	2.1	95.7	5.5	20,960[d]
1938	96.4	3.6	94.0	5.7	20,220
1950	98.4	1.6	94.9	9.5	19,517[f]
1960	98.8	1.2	94.0	10.9[g]	19,528
1965	98.7	1.3	95.9	11.5[g]	20,381
1970	98.3	1.7	95.7	12.1[g]	21,310

Germany

Year	TE	U	CE	TGE	Total
1900	98.0	2.0	95.6	4.6	26,059
1910	98.1	1.9	95.9	4.9	29,979
1920	93.7	6.3	93.3	3.5	33,112[k]
1930	86.7	13.3	86.3	3.6	35,747
1938	95.6	4.4	94.5	4.8	34,503[e]
1950	91.9	8.1	91.9	2.4	21,950
1960	99.0	1.0	97.9	7.1	26,518
1965	99.5	0.5	97.8	8.5	27,300
1970	99.5	0.5	97.6	9.5	27,353

Switzerland

Year	TE	U	CE	TGE	Total
1900	.	.	.	N.A.	1,587
1910				N.A.	1,783
1920	92.6	7.4	92.6	N.A.	1,872
1930	100.0	0.0	100.0	9.0[g]	1,935[h]
1938	99.9	0.1	99.9	10.2[g]	1,984[i]
1950	99.9	0.1	99.9	11.0	2,156
1960	99.9	0.1	99.9	11.5	2,514
1965	100.0	0.0	100.0	10.4	2,870
1970	100.0	0.0	100.0	13.1	3,005

United Kingdom

Year	TE	U	CE	TGE	Total
1900	97.5	2.5	96.3	N.A.	18,088
1910	95.4	4.6	94.4	N.A.	19,962
1920	98.0	2.0	94.5	N.A.	20,617
1930	90.4	9.6	88.8	N.A.	20,657
1938	92.0	8.0	90.1	N.A.	22,857
1950	98.8	1.2	95.8	24.4	23,526
1960	98.7	1.3	96.7	22.9	25,010
1965	98.9	1.1	97.2	21.5	26,049
1970	97.8	2.2	96.4	21.9	25,675

United States

Year	TE	U	CE	TGE	Total
1900	94.9	5.1	94.0	N.A.	27,766
1910	94.1	5.9	93.7	N.A.	36,580
1920	95.9	4.1	95.1	N.A.	40,625
1930	91.3	8.7	90.8	6.5	50,080
1938	81.1	18.9	80.5	11.2	54,950
1950	94.9	5.1	92.3	12.3	63,858
1960	94.7	5.3	91.2	15.7	72,142
1965	95.6	4.4	92.1	17.5	77,178
1970	95.2	4.8	91.5	18.9	85,903

Sources:

For Canada: Firestone (1958, p. 58); Urquhart and Buckley (1965, p. 61); D.B.S., *National Accounts, Revenue and Expenditure* (1967); *Canada Yearbook* (1972).

For France: Carré, Dubois, and Malinvaud (1972, pp. 121–126, pp. 674 ff.); O.E.C.D., *Manpower Statistics* (1950–1962), and *Labor Force Statistics* (1961–1972).

For Germany: 1937 and before Hoffmann (1965, pp. 237 ff.); thereafter S.O.E.C., Jahrbuch der Sozialstatistik 1968, 1972.

For Switzerland: E.St.A., *Statistisches Jahrbuch der Schweiz* (various years); B.I.G.A., Handbuch der Schweizerischen Sozialstatistik (1973, pp. 63 ff.); the Swiss figures of all government total employment do not comprise military personnel (the armed forces are counted to their civilian profession).

For United Kingdom: 1938 and before Department of Employment and Productivity (1971, pp. 208 ff.). O.E.C.D., *Manpower Statistics* (1950–1962), *Labor Force Statistics* (1962–1972); C.S.O., *Annual Abstracts of Statistics* (several years); National Income and Expenditure (1960).

For the United States: the totals and shares of 1920 and before are based on decennial census data, U.S.B.o.B., *Historical Statistics of the United States Colonial Times to 1957*; thereafter, *Economic Report of the President* (1974).

Note (to Tables 15–19 through 15–22): All government total employment (TGE) refers to full-time equivalent employment; it includes government enterprises and all military personal if not otherwise stated.

[a]TE = Total Employment
U = Unemployment   ⎫
CE = Civilian Employment   ⎬ As a percentage of total workforce.
TGE = All Government Total Employment ⎭

Total = Total workforce (in thousands); total workforce comprises civilian nongovernment employment, civilian government employment, armed forces, and unemployment. Figures for France and Germany exclude government enterprises employment.

[b]1901. [c]1911. [d]1931. [e]1937. [f]1954. [g]Estimated. [h]1929. [i]1940. [k]1925.

Table 15-20
Distribution of All Governments' Total Employment by Level of Government, 1950–1970[a]

Year	Canada				France			Germany				Switzerland				United Kingdom				United States			
	F	S	L	Total	F	S L	Total	F	S	L	Total	F	S	L	Total	F	S	L	Total	F	S	L	Total
1950							1,854				528	41.7	26.1	32.3	238	75.2		24.8	5,724	45.5	13.4	41.1	7,862
1955					75.8	24.4	1,850b				1,004			N.A.		75.2		24.8	6,029	51.2	12.1	36.7	10,367
1960	52.1	26.2	21.7	649c	74.3	25.7	2,220e	26.7	46.1	27.2	1,871	40.5	27.7	31.8	288	69.8		30.2	5,758	43.6	13.5	42.9	11,322
1965	44.6	34.7	20.7	744	67.8	32.2	2,336e	31.0	43.2	25.8	2,324	40.0	28.2	31.8	298	65.4		34.6	5,894	39.9	15.2	44.9	13,312
1970	43.4	36.2	20.4	852d	71.0	39.0	2,570e	30.1	44.3	25.6	2,607	36.8	30.9	32.3	393	63.2		36.8	6,271f	37.4	17.0	45.6	16,216

Sources and Notes: See Table 15-19.

Note also: Federal government employment figures for France and Germany exclude government enterprises employment; Figures for Switzerland in 1970 include part-time employment.

[a] F = Federal government employment
S = State governments employment   } As a percentage of all governments' total employment (total).
L = Local governments employment
Total = All governments' total employment including armed forces (in thousands).

b1954. c1961. d1967. eEstimated. f1968.

Table 15-21
Distribution of Government and Nongovernment Wages Bill, 1950–1970[a]

Year	Canada				France				Germany				Switzerland				United Kingdom				United States			
	TG	CG	NG	Total	TG	CG	NG	Total	TG	CG	NG	Total	TG	CG	NG	Total	TG	CG	NG	Total	TG	CG	NG	Total
1950	12.4	10.8	87.6	8,629	N.A.	.	.	40,320				44,038				10,485	18.6	15.0	81.4	7,603	14.6	11.6	85.4	140,600[b]
1955	15.7	12.7	84.3	13,223	N.A.	.	.	76,100	14.2			81,710				14,100	18.7	15.1	81.3	11,221	16.1	12.1	83.9	224,500
1960	17.9	15.1	82.1	18,245[c]	N.A.	.	.	131,480	13.1			133,610	10.4		83.4	21,420[c]	16.1	11.8	83.9	18,195	16.6	13.2	83.4	294,200
1965	17.9	15.7	82.1	26,179	15.2	13.1	84.8	225,720	16.1			225,810	10.3		89.7	32,090	16.3	12.2	83.7	21,089	17.6	14.5	82.4	393,800
1970	18.3	16.1	81.7	32,389[d]	15.8	13.9	84.2	386,000	17.5			352,140	12.2		87.8	45,017[e]	17.9	13.8	82.1	30,179	19.2	15.9	80.8	599,800

Sources and Notes: See Table 15-19. The civilian government wages bill for France, Germany and the United Kingdom exclude government enterprises employment.

[a]TG = Total Government

CG = Civilian Government　　} Wages bill as a percentage of total government and non-government wages bill (Total).

NG = Nongovernment

Total = Total government and nongovernment wages bill (in millions).

[b]1949. [c]1961. [d]1967. [e]Estimated.

Table 15-22
Distribution of All Governments Total Wages Bill by Level of Government, 1950–1970[a]

Year	Canada					France				Germany				
	FMW	FNW	SW	LW	Total	FMW	FNW	SW LW	Total	FMW	FNW	SW	LW	Total
1950	12.8	31.3	20.0	35.6	1,067	.	.	N.A.	.	.	.	.	.	4,020
1955	18.9	32.0	16.9	32.2	2,076	.	.	N.A.	.	—	7.6	61.4	31.0	11,617
1960	15.6	28.7	18.8	36.9	3,270	.	.	N.A.	.	—	15.1	56.0	28.9	17,560
1965	12.5	26.7	19.7	41.1	4,692	13.9	66.9	19.2	34,323	—	24.3	50.3	25.4	36,396
1970	11.8	27.1	21.0	40.1	5,921[b]	11.9	70.2	17.9	60,912	—	23.7	51.5	24.8	61,484

Year	Switzerland					United Kingdom				United States				
	FMW	FNW	SW	LW	Total	FMW	FNW	SW LW	Total	FMW	FNW	SW	LW	Total
1950	.	.	.	.	N.A.	19.4	44.2	36.4	1,414	20.6	32.3	47.1		20,599[c]
1955	.	.	.	.	N.A.	19.2	44.0	36.8	2,099	24.8	28.0	11.3	35.9	36,145
1960	16.0	.	50.2	33.8	2,217[e]	26.5	28.5	44.9	2,923[d]	20.3	26.8	12.5	40.4	48,710
1965	17.0	.	49.5	33.4	3,312	25.1	29.5	45.4	3,466	17.5	25.1	14.3	43.0	69,228
1970	15.7	.	47.2	37.1	5,482	22.8	29.9	47.3	5,424	17.0	24.2	16.0	42.7	115,042

Sources and Notes: See Table 15–19. Total of Germany refers to Government Nonmilitary Wages Bill only. Totals for France, Germany and the United Kingdom exclude government enterprises employment.

[a] FMW = Federal Government Military Wages Bill
FNW = Federal Government Nonmilitary Wages Bill
SW = State Governments' Wages Bill
LW = Local Governments' Wages Bill
Total = All governments' total wages bill (in millions).

As a percentage of all governments' total wages bill (Total).

[b] 1967. [c] 1949. [d] 1963. [e] 1961.

Table 15-23

Distribution of All Governments' Total Revenue by Sources, 1930-1970[a]

	Canada						France					
Year	IT	WT	CT	OT	NT	Total	IT	WT	CT	OT	NT	Total
1930	9.9	33.4	32.1	5.3	19.3	742[d]	25.6	49.7		0.3	24.4	708[b]
1938	14.9	25.7	36.7	4.5	18.1	1,077[e]	32.5	46.1	–		21.4	767
1950	37.7	10.6	33.9	2.6	15.2	4,440	24.9	47.2	2.1		25.8	34,438
1955	36.7	13.2	33.5	1.0	15.6	6,873	25.2	49.9	2.0		22.9	52,210[f]
1960	38.7	15.3	29.7	1.7	14.7	9,718	27.4	49.4	1.6		21.6	78,356[g]
1965	38.9	13.1	32.3	1.6	14.1	15,353	28.3	52.5	2.3		16.9	137,941
1970	38.3	12.5	29.8	2.2	17.2	32,259	24.8	55.5	2.6		17.1	171,929[i]

	Germany						Switzerland					
Year	IT	WT	CT	OT	NT	Total	IT	WT	CT	OT	NT	Total
1930	.	.	.	.	.	.	.	.	.	N.A.		.
1938	.	.	.	.	.	.	.	.	.	N.A.		.
1950	27.8	6.6	47.6	4.9	13.1	18,583	47.2	26.0	–	26.8		4,226
1955	30.9	5.4	35.8	18.6	9.3	38,785	45.1	28.4	–	26.5		5,137
1960	31.8	3.7	31.2	14.8	18.6	90,139[h]	48.0	29.5	–	22.5		7,356
1965	32.5	3.4	31.8	15.0	17.3	126,144	50.5	30.9	–	18.6		11,767
1970	33.9	3.3	33.4	13.2	16.2	182,224	54.0	27.8	–	18.2		19,839

	United Kingdom						United States					
Year	IT	WT	CT	OT	NT	Total	IT	WT	CT	OT	NT	Total
1930	.	.	.		.	.	11.6	45.2	16.0	4.6	22.5	10,289[c]
1938	30.6	23.0	32.5	–	13.9	1,261	19.5	26.5	22.9	5.1	25.9	17,484
1950	38.8	11.3	41.1	–	8.7	4,664	42.4	11.6	19.8	2.8	23.4	66,679
1955	39.1	11.2	33.6	–	16.1	5,930	46.5	10.6	16.5	2.6	23.8	106,414
1960	38.0	10.7	36.5	–	14.8	7,177	44.1	11.3	16.2	2.4	26.1	153,106
1965	38.2	11.7	35.5	–	14.6	10,512	42.9	12.3	17.3	2.2	25.4	193,583
1970	39.9	9.8	35.5	–	14.8	18,624	43.9	11.1	15.1	2.0	28.0	321,991

Sources:

For Canada: 1955 and before Urquhart and Buckley (1965, pp. 207-210), thereafter D.B.S., *Federal Government Finance* (1960, 1965, and 1970); *Provincial Government Finance* (1960, 1965, and 1970); *Municipal Government Finance* (1960, 1965, and 1970).

For France: Delorme (1973a, pp. 47-51, and Appendix, Tables I-2, A-1.1, A-1.4, and A-1.6); I.N.S.E.E., *Annuaire Statistique de la France. Résumé Rétrospectif*; *Annuaire Statistique de la France* (1972).

For Germany: St.B., *Statistisches Jahrbuch fuer die Bundesrepublik Deutschland* (various years); B.M.F., *Finanzbericht* (various years).

For Switzerland: E.St.A., *Die Finanzen von Bund, Kantonen und Gemeinden* (1938-1971); *Oeffentliche Finanzen der Schweiz* (various years); *Finanzhaushalt der Kantone* (1938-1971); *Statistisches Jahrbuch der Schweiz* (various years).

For United Kingdom: C.S.O., *National Income and Expenditure* (1963-1973); *Annual Abstracts of Statistics* (various years).

For the United States: U.S.B.o.C., *Historical Statistics of the United States Colonial Times to 1957*; *Historical Statistics of the United States, Continuation to 1962 and Revisions*; *Statistical Abstract of the United States, 1972*; unemployment tax is included (classified as nontax receipt).

Table 15-23 Continued

Notes (to Tables 15-23 through 15-26): *Income tax* comprises individual and corporation income tax as well as gift and inheritance taxes; *Wealth tax* comprises property taxes (including taxes on land, buildings, etc.); *Consumption tax* comprises general sales tax as well as selective consumption taxes (on motor fuel, alcoholic beverages, tobacco, etc.) and customs duties; *Other tax* comprises various minor taxes which are hard to classify within the above groups; *Nontax receipts* comprises government enterprises' profit, interest income, fees, charges, various contributions, and other revenue; intergovernmental transfers are excluded in Table 15-23, but included in Tables 15-24 through 15-26; taxes collected under tax rental (sharing) agreements are included with the tax revenue of the renting governmental unit if not otherwise stated.

[a]IT   = Income Tax
  WT   = Wealth Tax
  CT   = Consumption Tax   } As a percentage of all governments' total revenue.
  OT   = Other Tax
  NT   = Nontax Receipts
  Total = All governments' total revenue (in millions).
[b]1929. [c]1932. [d]1933. [e]1939. [f]1956. [g]1959. [h]1961. [i]1968.

Table 15-24
Distribution of Federal Government Revenue by Sources, 1930-1970[a]

	Canada						France					
Year	IT	WT	CT	OT	NT	Total	IT	WT	CT	OT	NT	Total
1930	19.4	–	66.3	0.6	13.7	315[d]	25.1	15.7	46.4	–	12.8	514[b]
1938	25.8	–	63.2	0.4	10.7	524[e]	27.5	12.5	45.6	–	14.4	547
1950	50.7	1.1	39.7	0.6	7.9	3,052	26.6	5.0	43.9	2.5	22.0	21,931
1955	52.2	1.4	38.4	0.4	7.6	4,668	27.6	4.9	48.3	2.5	16.9	41,983[f]
1960	55.8	1.3	34.8	0.1	7.9	6,014	30.4	5.4	46.8	1.9	15.6	63,991[g]
1965	52.3	1.2	38.6	–	8.0	8,715	31.5	5.3	51.1	2.9	9.3	110,285
1970	53.0	0.8	33.8	–	12.4	16,637	27.7	5.9	53.4	3.3	9.8	135,622[i]

	Germany						Switzerland					
Year	IT	WT	CT	OT	NT	Total	IT	WT	CT	OT	NT	Total
1930	.	.	.	.	.	.	41.3	46.7	–		12.0	634
1938	.	.	.	.	.	.	20.6	65.4	–		14.0	500
1950	.	.	.	.	.	.	27.6	55.7	–		16.7	1,827
1955	.	.	.	.	.	.	16.3	64.9	–		18.8	2,137
1960	22.0	–	70.3	7.7	–	30,431[h]	20.5	63.3	–		16.2	3,147
1965	25.8	–	63.5	5.5	5.2	62,151	19.2	69.4	–		11.4	4,762
1970	31.1	–	55.3	8.7	4.5	87,802	23.4	66.8	–		9.8	7,476

	United Kingdom						United States					
Year	IT	WT	CT	OT	NT	Total	IT	WT	CT	OT	NT	Total
1930	.	.	.	.	.	.	39.6	–	27.8	1.4	31.2	2,634[c]
1938	42.3	8.6	45.0	–	4.1	912	41.8	–	28.0	4.2	26.0	7,226
1950	43.3	5.6	45.8	–	5.2	4,184	61.9	–	18.0	0.9	19.2	43,527
1955	44.7	3.5	38.4	–	13.3	5,186	66.1	–	13.3	0.7	19.9	71,915
1960	45.4	–	43.7	–	10.9	5,997	63.9	–	12.6	0.6	22.8	99,800
1965	46.7	–	43.5	–	9.8	8,602	65.9	–	13.7	0.2	20.2	116,833
1970	47.7	–	42.4	–	9.8	15,569	65.5	–	9.4	0.1	25.0	193,743

Sources and Notes: See Table 15-23.
[a] IT = Income Tax
WT = Wealth Tax
CT = Consumption Tax } As a percentage of federal government total own revenue.
OT = Other Tax
NT = Nontax Receipts
Total = Federal government total own revenue (in millions).
[b] 1929. [c] 1932. [d] 1933. [e] 1939. [f] 1956. [g] 1959. [h] 1961. [i] 1968.

Table 15-25
Distribution of State Governments' Revenue by Sources, 1930-1970[a]

	Canada							France						
Year	IT	WT	CT	OT	NT	ROG	Total							
1930	5.3	11.2	19.1	12.5	39.5	12.4	152[c]							
1938	8.9	13.2	22.9	8.9	37.6	8.5	258[d]							
1950	13.4	4.0	28.1	4.8	36.8	12.9	951							
1955	5.2	4.5	28.6	2.5	36.9	21.8	1,611	Included in Local Government						
1960	13.7	2.7	26.3	6.1	30.1	21.1	2,557	Revenue						
1965	27.5	2.3	31.5	4.4	30.0	9.2	5,101							
1970	28.1	2.3	31.6	5.5	22.6	9.8	12,597							

	Germany							Switzerland						
Year	IT	WT	CT	OT	NT	ROG	Total	IT	WT	CT	OT	NT	ROG	Total
1930	.	.	.	.	.	.	.	40.0	5.3	–	36.7	17.1	620	
1938	.	.	.	.	.	.	.	42.7	5.2	–	28.8	23.3	704	
1950	.	.	.	.	.	.	.	54.4	4.8	–	16.2	24.6	1,492	
1955	.	.	.	.	.	.	.	53.1	5.7	–	19.8	21.4	1,907	
1960	82.2	5.1	–	2.0	6.4	4.3	21,573[e]	55.8	6.2	–	17.1	20.9	2,768	
1965	51.9	4.6	2.0	8.6	14.6	18.3	48,269	49.8	5.1	–	14.3	30.8	5,378	
1970	27.2	5.0	1.7	27.3	26.7	14.3	86,186	53.2	5.0	–	12.5	29.3	9,287	

	United States						
Year	IT	WT	CT	OT	NT	ROG	Total
1930	6.0	19.5	35.0	13.9	15.1	10.5	2,541[b]
1938	7.2	8.4	35.2	8.3	28.0	12.9	5,293
1950	9.4	4.9	35.1	7.6	25.5	17.4	13,903
1955	9.3	4,9	36.5	8.2	25.8	15.2	19,667
1960	10.3	4.4	33.1	7.1	24.5	20.5	32,838
1965	11.4	4.1	31.5	6.5	25.4	21.1	48,827
1970	14.5	3.1	30.7	5.6	23.3	22.8	88,939

Sources and Notes: See Table 15-23.

[a]IT = Income Tax
WT = Wealth Tax
CT = Consumption Tax
OT = Other Tax   As a percentage of state governments total revenue
NT = Nontax Receipts
ROG = Receipts from Other Governments
Total = Total revenue (in millions).

[b]1932. [c]1933. [d]1939. [e]1961.

Table 15-26

Distribution of Local Governments' Revenue by Sources, 1930-1970[a]

Year	| Canada IT	WT	CT	OT	NT	ROG	Total	| France IT	WT	CT	OT	NT	ROG	Total
1930	1.4	78.6	–	6.1	13.9	–	294[d]	27.1	16.9		1.0	55.0		194[b]
1938	1.2	75.5	1.6	7.1	13.0	1.6	322[e]	44.9	16.4		–	38.8		221
1950	–	69.6	4.3	9.2	14.3	2.6	575	17.2	39.8		–	43.0		4,835
1955	–	77.3	4.7	1.8	11.6	4.6	988	16.2	36.5		–	47.3		10,227[f]
1960	–	78.6	5.1	0.4	10.1	5.8	1,695	15.3	37.2		–	48.3		14,365[g]
1965	–	77.7	0.3	0.5	9.1	12.4	2,291	16.1	37.1		–	47.2		27,656
1970	–	77.6	–	0.6	13.8	8.0	4,644	14.8	41.4		–	44.1		36,307[i]

Year	| Germany IT	WT	CT	OT	NT	ROG	Total	| Switzerland IT	WT	CT	OT	NT	ROG	Total
1930	.	.	.	.	.	.	.					N.A.		.
1938	.	.	.	.	.	.	.	45.1	0.6	–		54.3		617
1950	.	.	.	.	.	.	.	54.5	0.7	–		44.7		1,244
1955	.	.	.	.	.	.	.	60.1	0.8	–		39.1		1,507
1960	.	.	.	.	.	.	.	52.7	0.8	–		13.2	20.8	2,042
1965	6.2	28.1	–	5.0	28.0	32.7	33,318	60.0	0.8	–		17.1	22.0	3,959
1970	18.8	30.6	–	1.6	13.0	35.6	43,943	59.0	0.4	–		20.0	20.0	6,840

Year	| United Kingdom IT	WT	CT	OT	NT	ROG	Total	| United States IT	WT	CT	OT	NT	ROG	Total
1930	.	.	.	.	.	.	.	–	67.2	0.4	1.4	17.9	13.1	6,192[c]
1938	–	44.0	–	–	28.4	27.6	482	–	57.3	1.6	2.1	16.0	23.0	7,329
1950	–	43.4	–	–	18.4	38.1	776	0.4	34.7	3.0	2.4	22.9	27.5	16,101
1955	–	39.4	–	–	21.9	38.7	1,214	0.6	42.8	3.2	2.6	24.5	26.3	24,166
1960	–	39.3	–	–	20.9	39.8	1,960	0.7	42.3	3.6	1.8	24.5	27.2	37,324
1965	–	38.8	–	–	21.8	39.4	3,168	0.8	40.8	3.9	1.5	24.6	28.4	53,408
1970	–	33.1	–	–	22.4	44.5	5,505	1.8	37.0	3.4	1.3	23.3	33.2	89,082

Sources and Notes: See Table 15-23.

[a] IT = Income Tax
  WT = Wealth Tax
  CT = Consumption Tax
  OT = Other Tax   } As a percentage of local governments total revenue.
  NT = Nontax Receipts
  ROG = Receipts from Other Governments
  Total = Total revenue (in millions).

[b]1929. [c]1932. [d]1933. [e]1939. [f]1956. [g]1959. [h]1961. [i]1968.

Table 15-27
Distribution of All Governments' Tax Revenue by Level of Government, 1930-1970[a]

Canada

Year	F DT	F Total	S DT	S Total	L DT	L Total	Total
1930	21.6	296	33.3	123	2.0	296	542[d]
1938	28.9	439	37.3	201	2.2	279	919[e]
1950	66.0	2,260	33.7	677	0.8	503	3,840
1955	58.3	4,346	23.0	960	1.8	851	6,157
1960	59.2	5,542	35.4	1,688	1.6	1,458	8,688
1965	56.2	7,811	43.7	3,925	1.5	2,134	13,870
1970	71.2	14,015	53.5	9,168	—	3,758	26,941

Germany

Year	F DT	F Total	S DT	S Total	L DT	L Total	Total
1930	19.4	4,782	44.5	3,249	27.5	4,390	12,421
1938	30.5	13,074	40.1	2,219	16.2	4,591	19,884
1950	18.4	9,876	53.4	6,294	.	2,649	18,819
1955	18.6	22,585	72.3	10,794	.	5,627	39,006
1960	20.0	33,809	73.8	21,471	.	8,562	63,842
1965	27.1	59,030	77.4	32,366	.	13,063	104,459
1970	33.0	83,597	54.2	40,482	37.6	18,240	152,319

United Kingdom

Year	F DT	F Total	S DT	S Total	L DT	L Total	Total

France

Year	F DT	F Total	S DT	S Total	L DT	L Total	Total
1930	28.8	448	36.7	30	19.0	58	536[b]
1938	32.1	468	50.0	50	31.2	85	603
1950	34.1	17,115	36.1	840	19.2	1,916	19,871[f]
1955	32.9	34,886	41.2	1,582	29.9	3,807	40,275[f]
1960	35.9	53,999	28.1	2,091	18.4	5,339	61,429[g]
1965	34.6	99,996	27.8	4,411	20.9	10,196	114,603
1970	30.6	122,316	30.5	5,256	24.8	15,038	142,610[i]

Switzerland

Year	F DT	F Total	S DT	S Total	L DT	L Total	Total
1930	47.5	558	88.5	278	98.4	279	1,115
1938	28.2	430	87.8	335	98.6	287	1,051
1950	39.0	1,521	90.3	875	98.7	698	3,094
1955	26.7	1,734	89.2	1,102	98.7	938	3,773
1960	29.0	2,636	88.9	1,684	98.8	1,381	5,700
1965	24.9	4,220	90.2	2,890	98.7	2,473	9,582
1970	31.4	6,746	90.6	5,308	99.4	4,168	16,223

United States

Year	F DT	F Total	S DT	S Total	L DT	L Total	Total

Year													
1930	42.2	774	—	172	946	70.9	1,813	8.1	1,890	—	4,274	—	7,977
1938	43.0	983	—	212	1,195	67.0	5,877	12.2	3,834	—	4,478	—	14,188
1950	50.1	4,170	—	337	4,507	70.9	37,853	16.5	8,958	—	7,988	0.8	54,799
1955	49.4	4,692	—	475	5,167	72.4	63,291	15.8	12,735	—	11,890	1.3	87,915
1960	48.7	5,569	—	771	6,340	68.7	88,419	18.8	20,172	—	18,088	1.4	126,678
1965	43.8	8,048	—	1,228	9,276	64.9	111,231	21.4	29,120	—	25,126	1.7	165,477
1970	50.6	14,702	—	1,824	16,526	66.1	185,670	26.9	51,052	—	38,844	4.2	275,566

Sources:

For Canada: D.B.S., *National Accounts, Income and Expenditure* (1926–1956, 1962, 1967, 1973).

For France: Delorme (1973, pp. 36–37, and Appendix, Tables I–3, II–1); I.N.S.E.E., *Annuaire Statistique de la France* (various years).

For Germany: St.B., *Statistisches Jahrbuch für die Bundesrepublik Deutschland* (various years); *Volkswirtschaftliche Gesamtrechnungen* (1965, 1971).

For Switzerland: E.St.A., *Oeffentliche Finanzen der Schweiz* (various years); *Statistisches Jahrbuch der Schweiz* (various years); *Nationale Buchhaltung der Schweiz* (various years); it should be noted that the share of "direct" taxes also includes wealth taxes for statistical reasons.

For United Kingdom: C.S.O., *National Income and Expenditure* (1963–1973); *Annual Abstracts of Statistics* (various years).

For the United States: U.S.B.o.C., *Historical Statistics of the United States Colonial Times to 1957*; Tax Foundation, *Facts and Figures on Government Finance* (1973).

Note: Direct tax includes both personal and corporation income tax as well as gift and inheritance taxes. Employees' and employers' social security contributions and intergovernmental transfers are excluded from the respective totals; taxes collected under tax rental (sharing) agreements are included with the taxes of the renting government.

[a]DT = Direct tax as a percentage of total federal, state, or local governments' tax revenue.
[b]1929. [c]1932. [d]1933. [e]1939. [f]1956. [g]1959. [h]1961. [i]1968.

Table 15–28
Federal Transfers to Other Governments, 1950–1970

Canada

Year	Unconditional			Conditional			Total
	S	L	Total	S	L	Total	Total
1950	98.9	1.1	125	100.0	–	150	275
1955	98.0	2.0	358	96.6	3.1	92	450
1960	95.6	4.4	562	97.7	2.3	446	1,008
1965	91.0	9.0	422	94.7	5.3	1,147	1,569
1970	96.1	3.9	1,411	98.0	2.0	2,279	3,690

France

Year	Unconditional			Conditional			Total
	S	L	Total	S	L	Total	Total
1950	–		.			548	548
1955	–		.	100.0		1,672	1,672[a]
1960	–		.	100.0		5,751	5,751[a]
1965	–		.	100.0		6,664	6,664
1970	–		.	100.0		9,056	9,056

Germany

Year	Unconditional			Conditional			Total
	S	L	Total	S	L	Total	Total
1950	.	.	.	.	.	.	.
1955	98.8	1.2	1,028	74.1	25.9	3,687	4,715[c]
1960	99.0	1.0	1,256	83.8	16.2	4,528	5,784
1965	99.7	0.3	1,025	88.6	11.4	8,545	9,570
1970	98.3	1.7	630	85.4	14.6	10,800	11,430[d]

Switzerland

Year	Unconditional			Conditional			Total
	S	L	Total	S	L	Total	Total
1950	–	–	–	100.0	–	162	162
1955	–	–	–	100.0	–	164	164
1960	100.0	–	10	100.0	–	213	223
1965	100.0	–	8	100.0	–	465	473
1970	100.0	–	33	100.0	–	830	863

Table 15–28 Continued

| | United Kingdom | | | | |
| | Unconditional | | Conditional | | |
Year	Local	% Total	Local	% Total	Total
1950	75	14.9	428	85.1	503[b]
1955	85	14.4	506	85.6	591
1960	602	66.2	307	33.4	909
1965	1,037	69.3	460	30.7	1,497
1970	2,126	76.9	639	23.1	2,765

| | United States | | | | | | |
| | Unconditional | | | Conditional | | | |
Year	S	L	Total	S	L	Total	Total
1950	.	.	.	91.5	8.5	2,486	2,486
1955	.	.	.	88.2	11.8	3,131	3,131
1960	.	.	.	91.5	8.5	6,974	6,974
1965	.	.	.	89.5	10.5	11,029	11,029
1970	.	.	.	88.1	11.9	21,857	21,857

Sources:

For Canada: D.B.S., *Federal Government Finance* (1965 and 1970); *Historical Review, Financial Statistics of Governments in Canada* (1952–1962); transfers to the Yukon and Northwest Territories, which are regarded as departments of the federal government, are excluded.

For France: André (1973, Appendix A, Table A–II) and Delorme (1973, p. 37); a distinction between federal transfers to states (*départements*) and local governments is not possible for statistical reasons: both governmental levels often are dealt together as "*collectivités locales.*"

For Germany: B.M.F., *Finanzbericht* (various years); St.B., *Statistisches Jahrbuch für die Bundesrepublik Deutschland* (various years).

For Switzerland: E.St.A., *Statistisches Jahrbuch der Schweiz* (various years); *Oeffentliche Finanzen der Schweiz* (various years); Rohr and Gut (1970); federal conditional and unconditional transfers to local governments are included in the grants to state governments (they are, however, of minor importance).

For United Kingdom: C.S.O., *Annual Abstracts of Statistics* (various years); unconditional grants include federal grants, local taxation license duties, and assistance to local authorities whose local tax income (rate income) was heavily reduced by war conditions.

For the United States: U.S.B.o.C., *Historical Statistics of the United States Colonial Times to 1957; Historical Statistics of the United States, Continuation to 1962 and Revisions; Economic Report of the President* (1972); Tax Foundation, *Facts and Figures on Government Finance* (1973).

Note: Taxes collected under tax-sharing agreements are included with the taxes of the renting government unit(s), if not otherwise stated.

[a]Estimated. [b]1953. [c]1961. [d]1969.

Table 15-29

Distribution of Federal Conditional Transfers to State Governments by Function, 1950-1970[a]

					Canada						
Year	*ND*	*W & H*	*E*	*T & C*	*NR & PI*	*H & UR*	*GG*	*P*	*DC*	*Other*	*Total*
1950	–	82.0	2.7	4.7	1.1	–	–	–	–	9.4	150
1955	–	71.0	4.8	18.5	4.4	–	–	–	–	1.2	89
1960	–	78.0	2.0	15.2	1.7	–	–	–	–	3.1	435
1965	–	70.6	15.4	9.1	3.9	–	–	–	–	0.9	1,087
1970	–	70.3	20.4	1.0	6.3	–	–	–	–	2.0	2,234
					Switzerland						
Year	*ND*	*W & H*	*E*	*T & C*	*NR & PI*	*H & UR*	*GG*	*P*	*DC*	*Other*	*Total*
1950	–	11.7	11.3	20.7	18.2	28.2	0.5	9.4	–	–	162
1955	–	7.9	11.7	47.6	27.1	2.0	0.4	3.3	–	–	164
1960	–	4.1	13.2	42.2	34.5	1.9	0.8	3.3	–	–	213
1965	6.3	2.2	11.8	40.1	34.2	0.8	1.0	3.6	–	–	465
1970	10.6	1.5	21.8	28.7	29.6	0.6	1.4	5.8	–	–	830
					United States						
Year	*ND*	*W & H*	*E*	*T & C*	*NR & PI*	*H & UR*	*GG*	*P*	*DC*	*Other*	*Total*
1950	–	48.7	15.2	19.3	–	–	–	–	–	16.9	2,323
1955	–	51.7	10.8	21.5	–	–	–	–	–	16.0	2,762
1960	–	32.1	11.4	45.2	–	–	–	–	–	11.4	6,382
1965	–	31.7	14.1	40.4	–	–	–	–	–	13.8	9,874
1970	–	40.6	23.7	23.0	–	–	–	–	–	12.7	19,252

Note: For more detailed comments, see note to Table 15-15. Data for France are included in federal conditional transfers to local governments; for Germany, not enough data are available.
are available.

[a]ND   = National Defence   GG = General Government
W & H   = Welfare and Health   P   = Protection
E   = Education   DC = Debt Charges
T & C   = Transportation and Communication   O   = Other
H & UR = Housing and Urban Renewal
Total   = Total federal conditional transfers to state governments (in millions).

Table 15-30
Distribution of Federal Conditional Transfers to Local Governments by Function, 1950-1970

					NR	H &					

Canada

Year	ND	W & H	E	T & C	NR & PI	H & UR	GG	P	DC	Other	Total
1950	–	55.6	–	44.4	–	.	–	–	–	–	1
1955	–	17.9	–	42.9	–	.	–	–	–	39.3	3
1960	–	20.3	17.5	44.7	–	.	–	–	–	17.5	10
1965	–	28.7	4.0	8.0	–	.	–	–	–	59.3	61
1970	–	13.6	9.8	21.2	0.1	.	–	–	–	55.3	45

France

Year	ND	W & H	E	T & C	NR & PI	H & UR	GG	P	DC	Other	Total
1950	.	.	.	.	.	.	.	.	.	.	548
1955	.	.	.	.	.	.	.	.	.	.	1,672[a]
1960	.	.	.	.	.	.	.	.	.	.	5,751[a]
1965	.	.	.	.	.	.	.	.	.	.	6,664
1970	.	.	.	.	.	.	.	.	.	.	9,056

United Kingdom

Year	ND	W & H	E	T & C	NR & PI	H & UR	GG	P	DC	Other	Total
1950	–	8.6	57.2	5.8	4.3	11.3	–	9.7	–	3.1	428[b]
1955	–	7.2	59.8	5.9	1.5	13.2	–	9.0	–	3.4	506
1960	–	3.7	24.6	18.6	1.4	26.4	–	20.5	–	4.8	307
1965	–	2.1	25.9	19.8	1.6	23.0	–	24.9	–	2.7	460
1970	–	2.8	4.3	20.4	1.9	34.5	–	33.5	–	2.6	639

United States

Year	ND	W & H	E	T & C	NR & PI	H & UR	GG	P	DC	Other	Total
1950	.	.	.	.	.	.	.	.	.	.	211
1955	.	.	.	.	.	.	.	.	.	.	369
1960	.	.	.	.	.	.	.	.	.	.	592
1965	.	.	.	.	.	.	.	.	.	.	1,155
1970	.	.	.	.	.	.	.	.	.	.	2,605

Note: Data for Switzerland are included in federal conditional transfers to state governments; for Germany not enough data are available.
[a]Estimated. [b]1953.

Table 15-31
Distribution of State Transfers to Local Governments by Function, 1950-1970[a]

Canada

Year	ND	W & H	E	T & C	NR & PI	H & UR	GG	P	DC	Other	Total Cond.	Uncond.	Total
1950	—	5.4	72.7	18.0	0.4	—	—	—	—	3.4	197	27	224[b]
1955	—	6.1	75.1	17.0	0.4	—	—	—	—	1.3	291	37	328
1960	—	10.4	69.5	16.1	0.3	—	—	—	—	3.7	653	70	723
1965	—	6.9	75.2	10.9	0.6	—	—	—	—	6.3	1,301	200	1,502
1970	—	5.9	80.6	9.4	0.8	—	—	—	—	3.4	1,997	289	2,280

Switzerland

Year	ND	W & H	E	T & C	NR & PI	H & UR	GG	P	DC	Other	Total Cond.	Uncond.	Total
1950	·										N.A.	11	
1955											N.A.	17	
1960	—	14.4	69.5	10.2	2.1					13.8	505	24	529
1965	—	16.6	59.6	15.8	2.3					15.7	859	43	901
1970	6.5	27.5	40.9	11.2	2.8	0.4	6.7	3.5		0.5	934	119	1,053

United States

Year	ND	W & H	E	T & C	NR & PI	H & UR	GG	P	DC	Other	Total Cond.	Uncond.	Total
1950	—	21.2	55.0	16.3	—	—	—	—	—	7.5	3,735	334	4,069
1955	—	19.4	58.4	16.9	—	—	—	—	—	5.3	5,395	365	5,760
1960	—	17.2	63.2	14.4	—	—	—	—	—	5.2	8,637	443	9,080
1965	—	18.6	63.9	12.5	—	—	—	—	—	5.0	13,072	656	13,728
1970	—	19.3	65.9	9.4	—	—	—	—	—	5.4	25,934	1963	27,897

Note: For more detailed comments see note to Table 15-8. For France and Germany not enough data are available.

ND	= National Defence	GG = General Government
W & H	= Welfare & Health	P = Protection
E	= Education	DC = Debt Charges
T & C	= Transportation & Communication	O = Other
H & UR	= Housing & Urban Renewal	

Total Cond. = Total state governments' conditional transfers to local governments (in millions).
Uncond. = State governments' unconditional transfers to local governments (in millions).
Total = State Governments' total transfers to local governments (in millions).
[b]1952.

Table 15-32
All Governments' Debt, 1930-1970

Year	Canada				France				Germany			
	F	S	L	Total	F	S	L	Total	F	S	L	Total
1930	58.4	21.1	20.4	7,040[a]	95.6	1.1	3.3	389	42.6	12.1	45.3	22,603
1938	60.8	23.7	15.5	8,410[c]	91.3	2.5	6.2	510	78.6	6.9	14.5	34,584
1950	80.7	13.1	6.2	21,441	96.1	1.4	2.5	4,069	32.6	61.3	6.1	18,776
1960	68.8	18.5	12.7	38,332	86.6	2.9	10.5	98,412	37.6	43.9	18.5	68,224
1970	72.3	13.0	14.7	57,108[e]	78.1		21.9	132,500	33.4	34.4	32.2	142,872

Year	Switzerland				United Kingdom			United States			
	F	S	L	Total	F	L	Total	F	S	L	Total
1930	.	.	N.A.	.	.	.	.	50.4	7.3	42.3	38,692[b]
1938	38.4	40.0	21.6	6,098	.	.	.	65.7	5.9	28.4	56,601
1950	62.3	23.0	14.7	12,760	88.3	11.7	29,510[d]	91.4	1.9	6.7	281,472
1960	44.7	30.3	25.0	14,660	80.9	19.1	34,289	80.4	5.2	14.4	356,286
1970	24.3	44.5	31.2	28,320[f]	68.1	31.9	48,554	72.1	8.2	19.7	514,409

Sources:

For Canada: Urquhart and Buckley (1965, pp. 203-204, 210-211); D.B.S., *Federal Government Finance* (various years); *Provincial Government Finance* (various years); and *Municipal Government Finance* (various years).

For France: 1950 and before in billions AF (*Ancien Francs*), thereafter in millions NF (*Nouveau Francs*); I.N.S.E.E., *Annuaire Statistique de la France, Résumé Retrospectif* (1966); *Annuaire Statistique de la France* (1974).

For Germany: The short-term debt (*Kassenkredite*) is excluded for statistical reasons. 1938 and before St.B., *Bevoelkerungsstruktur und Wirtschaftskraft der Bundeslaender* (1973); thereafter St.B., *Statistisches Jahrbuch für die Bundesrepublik Deutschland* (various years); B.M.F., *Finanzbericht* (various years).

For Switzerland: E.St.A., *Oeffentliche Finanzen der Schweiz* (various years); *Finanzhaushalt der Kantone* (1938-1971); *Statistisches Jahrbuch der Schweiz* (various years); the local debt covers only communities with 5,000 inhabitants and over.

For United Kingdom: C.S.O., *Annual Abstracts of Statistics* (various years).

For the United States: Tax Foundation, *Facts and Figures on Government Finance* (1973).

Note: All governments' debt covers direct debt, i.e., indirect debt (incurred by agencies not included in "government" as defined in most public financial statistics, but nevertheless guaranteed by the government in question) is excluded.
[a]1933. [b]1935. [c]1939. [d]1953. [e]1968. [f]1971.

Notes

1. Very often this was *not* the case, and the collecting and investigating of data was a highly frustrating activity.

2. The terms *first function, second function,* etc., neither state the urgency of the task nor that the different functions are independent.

3. This chapter presupposes institutionally given government units, (i.e., the question concerning the optimal size of a unit is excluded) but see, for example, Tullock (1969) and Bish and Nourse (1975, chap. 5).

4. Considered more closely, the problem becomes even more complicated, because spillovers and economies of scale are not to be regarded as independent factors [see, for example, Boes (1973, pp. 64–65)].

5. In order to be able to take into account the relatively strong influence of the federal government in decision making (not necessarily in actual provision), I shall use data from public-finance statistics and *not* from national accounts. An important difference between the two sources (for a more detailed discussion, see section 4) is that in the national accounts both unconditional and conditional grants are attributed to the respective receiving units. In public-finance statistics, however, at least the quantitatively more important conditional transfers are entered on the side of the grantor (i.e., federal or state government). The latter treatment seems more useful for our purposes.

In order to record approximately the interregional duties—public-finance statistics do not actually attempt this—I make the following arbitrary division: a function will be considered interregional if the proportion of the total expenses carried by the federal (state) government does not diverge strongly from that of the state (local) governments. I limit the span to a maximum of 30 percentage points.

6. For the United States, some evidence is given by Hirsch (1970, chap. 9), and for the United Kingdom by Gupta and Hutton (1968). However, most studies of local-government services estimate economies of scale by a regression of per capita expenditures (instead of a measure of output) on population, among other variables, which does not adequately permit the separation of changes in unit costs from changes in costs resulting from increased service level per capita.

7. I have of necessity given a rather incomplete description of the Swiss federal structure; for a more detailed analysis, see Frey (1974) and Frey, Neugebauer, and Zumbuehl (1975).

8. The United Kingdom is excluded from this comparison because it presents only two governmental levels. France is excluded because of the lack of data. See, however, section 4, Tables 15–7 and 15–9.

9. This last statement is not obvious from the tables, but see, for example, Haller (1969a, p. 146).

10. One could show similar "invisible" federal expenditures for Germany in the period between the wars [see Weitzel (1968, Appendix, Table 11)]. For the

conventional method of measuring the distribution of government activity and functions, see section 4, Table 15-15.

11. Computed from Table 15-23 and further sources cited in the source note.

12. See, however, Tables 15-28 through 15-31 in section 4, which present data on the flow of intergovernmental transfers as well as on the functional composition of conditional grants.

13. I shall concentrate mainly on the differences in federal-state government relations, since those between state and local governments are similar in the countries investigated here (with the exception of the United Kingdom, of course).

14. See Clark (1969), Moore et al. (1966), Sproule-Jones (1974), and Canadian Tax Foundation, The National Finances 1974-1975 (1975, pp. 154ff.) for a detailed picture.

15. This ratio is subject to variation, as it is regulated by law, i.e., not anchored in the constitution.

16. The local government has the power to change the tax base but not the tax rate. Nevertheless, the revenues are not so inelastic as they appear at first glance: the doubling of GNP in money terms during the last 20 years has been accompanied by a threefold increase in the revenue of these taxes.

17. One of the few to mention this assumption explicitly is Tucker (1953, p. 528).

18. The same result is reached for Canada by Maslove (1973) for 1969 and Gillespie (1964) for 1961. This result, incidentally, also applies to most of the federal systems we are concerned with here.

19. See Johnson (1975, especially pp. 70ff.). This analysis—the only one for Canada that distinguishes between provinces and municipal governments—applies only to the province and municipalities of Ontario.

20. A total analysis of this kind has not yet been carried out for Switzerland. The studies of Bobe (1975) and Cazenave and Morrisson (1974) for France refrain from separating federal, state, and local levels of government. The older studies about the countries treated here, as well as studies about other nations, are not mentioned here. But see Windmuller and Mehran (1975, Vol. II, chap. X).

21. This also applies to detailed studies on particular governmental units. See, for example, Eapen and Eapen (1973) for Connecticut, and Hanusch (1975) for the local governments in Germany.

22. For the latter method, see Maital (1973) for the United States.

23. This applies to a consideration of *relative* redistribution effects (relative to money income before state activity). If the focus is on absolute net gains, Table 15-7 shows that the members of the *middle-income groups* are the main winners.

24. For France, see Autin (1972), for the United Kingdom, Hicks and Hicks (1973, p. 145).

25. This method of measuring the impact of various types of budget changes draws from the studies by Brown (1956), Musgrave (1964), and others. The underlying model is simple compared with the large econometric models that have been developed for particular countries. On the whole, a comparison among the different countries by means of these econometric models is very restricted. The approach used by Hansen makes comparison possible.

26. See Hansen (1969, pp. 55–57) for more detailed comments on the pure cycle concept.

27. It is interesting that there is either an extensive autonomy of state and local governments in these two countries (as in the United States) or at least as refers to the expenditure part of the budgets (as in Germany).

28. For the last point, see Snyder (1970c, pp. 268ff.) and Balopoulos (1967, p. 205).

29. A more exact examination would, of course, imply that a distinction be made between automatic stabilizers (in the sense of built-in flexibility) and the impact of discretionary measures of subcentral governments, a distinction that Snyder—as well as most other analysts—does not make. One of the few studies (some prior work is mentioned by Netzer, 1974, p. 362) in which this distinction is made and which also distinguishes between state and local governments is by Robinson and Courchene (1969) for Canada from 1952 to 1965. They come to the conclusion that the impact of the federal sector was countercyclical due to the automatic effects, as well as the impact of discretionary measures, and that the provincial governments, on the other hand, show a slight procyclical policy (due to automatic changes in tax receipts), while municipal budgets seem to be roughly neutral.

30. These studies do not use exactly the same method, and a slightly different measuring concept or point of reference is used, so that we refrain from integrating the results in Table 15–9. For a more detailed theoretical presentation of the different methods of measurement, see Gφrz (1973); a comparative application for the example of Germany is found in Biehl et al. (1973).

31. It is interesting to note that the short-run countercyclical impact of central government was to a great extent the result of automatic stabilizers. See Hansen (1969) and, as concerns studies about built-in flexibility, for example, Ruggeri (1973).

32. See, for example, Lindbeck (1970, pp. 25–30) and Prest (1968, pp. 4–5). For the logical extension of the last idea and the first empirical test of "politico-economic cycles" for Germany, with promising results, see Frey and Schneider (1975).

33. That these factors can play an important part in the elaboration of a constitution has been shown in a slightly different terminology by Brady (1947, p. 124) for Australia, and Macmahon (1962) for India.

34. These are only a few examples, but the list can easily be enlarged considerably under one aspect or another.

35. The ratios are computed from UN Yearbook of National Accounts Sta-

tistics (1970–1973) and, in few instances, from other sources like UN Statistical Yearbook (1970–1973).

36. In addition to this, we have computed various further measures for centralization using as categories both federal expenditures and federal revenue. Since the regressions between them show that they reflect the degree of fiscal centralization about equally well, we confine ourselves to the results of regressions using the measure mentioned above. A more detailed discussion of the difficulties of determining an adequate measure of the degree of fiscal centralization can be found in Musgrave (1969a, chap. 14) and Oates (1972, pp. 195ff.).

37. As level of statistical significance, we take the 95 percent level of confidence. All equations are estimated by ordinary least square (OLS) technique.

38. Similar disappointing results are obtained using data from other sources, e.g., the indexes for ethnic and linguistic fractionalization developed by Muller (1964).

39. *Sectionalism* is defined as "the phenomenon in which a significant percentage of the population lives in a sizable geographic area and identifies self-consciously and distinctively with that area. . . ." [Banks and Textor (1963, p. 88)].

40. Under perfect equality, each 5 percentile group would receive 5 percent of the total income. The absolute deviation $|d|$ of the income share of each 5 percentile group from 5 percent is therefore a measure of inequality. This gives

$$K = \frac{\Sigma \, |d|}{20 \times 9.5}$$

where the division by 9.5 is necessary to standardize the measure to range from 0 to 1 (because the arithmetic average of the 20 absolute deviations ranges from 0 in the case of perfect equality to 9.5 in the case of maximum inequality).

41. Equation (15.14′) gives the results using the latter index:

$$CGE = 60.15 - 0.07P - 0.01GNP - 0.77S + 61.59E$$
$$(4.90) \, (2.28) \quad (1.71) \qquad (0.10) \quad (2.09)$$

$$N = 18 \qquad \bar{R}^2 = 0.473 \tag{15.14′}$$

where E = the entropy measure of inequality of the household incomes, which ranges from 0 (perfect equality) to 1 (perfect inequality); see Jain (1974) for a more detailed definition; the data are taken once again from Jain (1974).

42. More precisely:

$$RID = \frac{\sqrt{\Sigma_i (y_i - \bar{y})^2 \, (N_i/N)}}{\bar{y}}$$

where N_i = population of the ith region

N = national population

y_i = income per capita of the ith region

$\bar{y}$ = national income per capita

It should be noted that the regional breakdown by Williamson is more detailed than usual in the literature. The *RID* value for Italy, for example, is computed from 19 Italian regions.

43. This was also the case with numerous other variables used for characterizing the political systems.

44. A closer investigation of the interdependence was impossible for two reasons: first, the corresponding theoretical approaches are not very well developed, and second, the statistical data that would then be necessary are very likely unavailable [but see, for example, Stephens (1974) concerning this last point].

45. Further reasons follow from the possibly increasing uniformity in individual demands, which in turn results from the increasing uniformity in tastes (with growing equality in the access to information) as well as from equalization in individual income; technical reasons as well (economies of scale) could support this. See, for example, May (1969) and the literature cited therein.

46. Oates (1972, p. 232) got the same results for 12 of 15 countries for which he had data from 1590 to 1965 by contrasting the central-government shares in all governments' current expenditures. See also, Pryor (1968, pp. 70ff.) for similar results.

References

Books and Articles

Aaron, H.J., and M.C. McGuire. 1970. Public goods and income distribution. *Econometrica* 38:907-920.

Albers, W. 1966. *Strukturwandlungen Kommunaler Ausgabenbudgets Waehrend der Letzten Jahrzehnte im Internationalen Vergleich. Archiv fuer Kommunalwissenschaften* 5:239-260.

Andic S., and Veverka, J. 1964. The growth of government expenditure in Germany since the unification. *Finanzarchiv* 23:169-278.

André C. 1973. *La constitution de séries définitives des dépenses publiques de 1872-1971 et une analyse de leur évolution.* In *Etude analytique et numérique de la tendance significative et des facteurs explicatifs de l'évolution des dépenses et recettes publiques francaises au cours de la période 1870-1970*, C. André and R. Delorme, Paris: C.E.P.R.E.M.A.P.

André, C. 1974. *Analyse rétrospective sur la période* 1965-1972 *des dépenses de fonctionnement des administrations selon une nomenclature fonctionnelle.* Mimeographed. Paris: C.E.P.R.E.M.A.P.

Autin, J. 1972. *Vingt ans de politique financière.* Paris: Du Seuil.

Baker, E.M. 1974. *The Federal Polity: A Review and Digest.* Philadelphia: Temple University, Center for Study of Federalism.

Balopoulos, E.R. 1967. *Fiscal policy models of the British economy.* Amsterdam: North-Holland.

Banks, A.S. 1971. *Cross Polity, Time Series Data.* Cambridge, Mass.: M.I.T. Press.

Banks, A.S., and Textor, R.B. 1963. *A Cross-Polity Survey.* Cambridge, Mass.: M.I.T. Press.

Beer, S.H. 1973. The modernization of American federalism. *Publius* 2:49-95.

Benson, G.C.S., and McClelland, H.F. 1961. *Consolidated Grants: A Means of Maintaining Fiscal Responsibility.* Washington, D.C.: American Enterprise Institute.

Biehl, D., Hagemann, G., Juettemeier, K.H., and Legler, H. 1973. Measuring the demand effects of fiscal policy. In *Fiscal Policy and Demand Management*, H. Giersch, ed. Tübingen: Mohr.

Birch, A.H. 1955. *Federalism, Finance, and Social Legislation in Canada, Australia and the United States.* Oxford: Clarendon Press.

Bird, R.M. 1970. *The Growth of Government Spending in Canada.* Toronto: Canadian Tax Foundation.

Bish, R.L., and Nourse, H.O. 1975. *Urban Economics and Policy Analysis.* New York: McGraw-Hill.

Bobe, B. 1975. *Budget de l'état et rédistribution des revenus. Revue Economique* 26:1-35.

Boes, D. 1971. *Eine oekonomische Theorie des Finanzausgleichs.* Vienna: Springer.

Boes, D. 1973. Federalism and intergovernmental problems of urban finance. *Public Finance* 28:56-81.

Bradford, D.F., and Oates, W.E. 1974. Suburban exploitation of central cities and government structure. In *Redistribution Through Public Choice*, H.M. Hochman and G.E. Peterson, eds. New York: Columbia University Press.

Brady, A. 1947. *Democracy in the Dominions.* Toronto: University of Toronto Press.

Break, G.F. 1967. *Intergovernmental Fiscal Relations in the United States.* Washington, D.C.: The Brookings Institution.

Brown, E.C. 1956. Fiscal policies in the "thirties": A reappraisal. *American Economic Review* 46:857-879.

Burkhead, J., and Miner, J. 1971. *Public Expenditure.* London: Macmillan.

Buschor, E. 1970. *Staatshaushalt und Konjunkturpolitik in der Schweiz. Wirtschaft und Recht* 22:77-107.

Canadian Tax Foundation, *Provincial and Municipal Finance.* Annual. Toronto: Canadian Tax Foundation.

Carré, J.J., Dubois, P., and Malinvaud, E. 1972. *La Croissance Française, un Essai d'Analyse Économique Causale de l'Après-Guerre.* Paris: Du Seuil.

Cartter, A.M. 1955. *The Redistribution of Income in Postwar Britain.* New Haven: Yale University Press.

Cazenave P., and Morrison, C. 1974. *La rédistribution des revenus aux Etats-Unis, en France et en Grande-Bretagne. Revue Economique* 25:635-671.

Clark, D.H. 1969. *Fiscal Need and Revenue Equalization Grants.* Toronto: Canadian Tax Foundation.

Curtis, D.C.A., and Kitchen, H.M. 1975. Some quantitative aspects of Canadian budgetary policy 1953-1971. *Public Finance* 30:108-126.

Delorme, R. 1973a. *La constitution de séries de données relatives aux recettes publiques et leur évolution de 1872 à 1971.* In *Etude Analytique et Numérique de la Tendance Significative et des Facteurs Explicatifs de l'Evolution des Dépenses et des Recettes Publiques Françaises au Cours de la Période 1870-1970*, C. André and R. Delorme. Paris: C.E.P.R.E.M.A.P.

Delorme, R. 1973b. *L'évolution des dépenses publiques consacrées à l'enseignement en France au cours de la période 1872-1971.* In *Etude Analytique et Numérique de la Tendance Significative et des Facteurs Explicatifs de l'Evolution des Dépenses et des Recettes Publiques Françaises au Cours de la Période 1870-1970.* C. André and R. Delorme. Paris: C.E.P.R.E.M.A.P.

Department of Employment and Productivity. 1971. *British Labour Statistics.* Historical Abstract 1886-1968. London: Her Majesty's Stationary Office.

Dodge, D.A. 1975. Impact of tax, transfer, and expenditure policies of government on the distribution of personal income in Canada. *Review of Income and Wealth* 21:1-52.

Eapen, A.T., and Eapen, A.N. 1973. Income redistributive effects of state and local fiscs: Connecticut, a case study. *Public Finance Quarterly* 1:372-387.

Ecker-Racz, L.L. 1970. *The Politics and Economics of State-Local Finance.* Englewood Cliffs, N.J.: Prentice-Hall.

Elazar, D.J. 1966. *American Federalism: A View from the States.* Binghampton: Vial-Ballon Press.

Elazar, D.J. 1968. Federalism. *International Encyclopedia of the Social Sciences* 5:353-367.

Firestone, O.J. 1958. *Canada's Economic Development, 1867-1953.* London: Bowes & Bowes.

Frey, R.L. 1974. *Der Schweizerische Foederalismus—Wirtschaftlich Durchleuchtet. Zeitschrift für Schweizerisches Recht* 93:359-378.

Frey, R.L., Neugebauer, G., and Zumbuehl, M. 1975. *Der Schweizerische Foederalismus aus dekonomischer Sicht.* Mimeographed. Basel: University of Basel.

Frey, B.S., and Schneider, F. 1975. On the modelling of politico-economic interdependencies. *European Journal of Political Research* 3:339-360.

Gillespie, I.W. 1964. *The Incidence of Taxes and Public Expenditures in the Canadian Economy.* Ottawa: Queen's Printer.

Gillespie, I.W. 1965. Effects of public expenditures on the distribution of income. In *Essays in Fiscal Federalism*, R.A. Musgrave, ed. Washington, D.C.: The Brookings Institution.

Gørtz, E. 1973. *Measures of the Effects of Economic Policy.* Odense: Odense University Press.

Greene, K.V. 1970. Some institutional considerations in federal-state fiscal relations. *Public Choice* 9:1-18.

Gupta, S.P., and Hutton, J.P. 1968. *Economies of Scale in Local Government Services.* Royal Commission on Local Government in England. Research study no. 3. London: Her Majesty's Stationary Office.

Hake, W. 1972. *Umverteilungseffekte des Budgets.* Göttingen: Vandenhoeck & Ruprecht.

Haller, H. 1969a. *Wandlungen in den Problemen Foederativer Staatswirtschaften.* In *Finanzpolitik*, H.C. Recktenwald, ed. Cologne: Kiepenheuer & Witsch.

Haller, H. 1969b. *Der Finanzausgleich in der Bendesrepublik Deutschland und in der Schweizerischen Eidgenossenschaft. Schweizerische Zeitschrift für Volkswirtschaft und Statistik* 105:121-137.

Hansen, B. 1969. *Fiscal Policies in Seven Countries, 1955-1965.* Paris: O.E.C.D.

Hansen, A., and Perloff, P. 1944. *State and Local Finance in the National Economy.* New York: Norton.

Hanusch, H. 1975. *Einkommensumverteilung durch Kommunale Haushalte. das Beispiel der Bundesrepublik Deutschland 1963 und 1969. Archiv für Kommunalwissenschaften* 14:219-239.

Hanusch, H. 1976. *Personale Verteilung Oeffentlicher Leistungen.* Forthcoming. Göttingen: Vandenhoeck & Ruprecht.

Hauser, H. 1971. *Der Innerkantonale Finanzausgleich.* Bern: Haupt.

Hicks, J.R., and Hicks, U.K. 1973. British fiscal policy. In *Fiscal Policy and Demand Management.* H. Giersch, ed. Tübingen: Mohr.

Hirsch, W.Z. 1970. *The Economics of State and Local Government.* New York: McGraw-Hill.

Hoffmann, W.G. 1965. *Das Wachstum der Deutschen Wirtschaft seit der Mitte des 19. Jahrhunderts.* Berlin: Springer.

Hunter, J.S.H. 1973. *Revenue Sharing in the Federal Republic of Germany.* Canberra: Australian National University.

Jain, S. 1974. *Size Distribution of Income: A Compilation of Data.* Washington, D.C.: World Bank.

Johnson, J.A. 1975. *The Incidence of Government Revenues and Expenditures.* Ottawa: Study prepared for the Ontario Committee on Taxation.

Kendrick, J.W. 1961. *Productivity Trends in United States.* Durham, N.C.: Duke University Press.

Kock, H. 1975. *Stabilisierungspolitik im foederalistischen System der Bundesrepublik Deutschland.* Cologne: Bund.

Leach, R. H. 1972. *Prospects for Federalism in the United States.* Durham, N.C.: Duke University Press.

Lehner, D. 1971. *Der Finanzausgleich Zwischen Bund und Kantonen im Hinblick auf eine Bundesfinanzreform.* Bern: Haupt.

Lindbeck, A. 1970. Fiscal policy as a tool of economic stabilization—comments to an OECD report. *Kyklos* 23:7-32.

Lindbeck, A. 1974. Is stabilization policy possible? Time-lags and conflicts of goals. In *Public Finance and Stabilization Policy*, W.L. Smith and J.M. Culbertson, eds. Amsterdam: North-Holland.

Macmahon, A.W. 1962. The problems of federalism: a survey. In *Federalism, Mature and Emergent*, New York: Russel & Russel.

Maital, S. 1973. Public goods and income distribution: Some further results. *Econometrica* 41:561-568.

Maslove, A.M. 1973. *The Pattern of Taxation in Canada.* Ottawa: Study prepared for the Economic Council of Canada.

Maxwell, J.A. 1969. *Financing State and Local Governments.* Washington, D.C.: The Brookings Institution.

May, R.J. 1969. *Federalism and Fiscal Adjustment.* Oxford: Clarendon Press.

McWhinney, E. 1962. *Die Nuetzlichkeit des Foederalismus in Einem Revolutionaeren Zeitalter.* In *Foederalismus und Bundesverfassungsrecht* 4.

Moore, A.M., Perry, J.H., and Beach, D.I. 1966. *The Financing of Canadian Federalism*. Toronto: Canadian Tax Foundation.

Muller, S.H. 1964. *The World's Living Languages: Basic Facts of Their Structure, Kinship, Location and Number of Speakers*. New York: Ungar.

Musgrave, R.A. 1959. *The Theory of Public Finance*. New York: McGraw-Hill.

Musgrave, R.A. 1964. On measuring fiscal performance. *Review of Economics and Statistics* 54:213-220.

Musgrave, R.A. 1969 a. *Fiscal Systems*. New Haven: Yale University Press.

Musgrave, R.A. 1969b. Theories of fiscal federalism. *Public Finance* 34:521-536.

Musgrave, R.A., Case, K.E., and Leonhart, H. 1974. The distribution of fiscal burdens and benefits. *Public Finance Quarterly* 2:259-311.

Musgrave, R.A., and Musgrave, P.B. 1973. *Public Finance in Theory and Practice*. New York: McGraw-Hill.

Negishi, T. 1972. Public expenditure determined by voting with one's feet and fiscal profitability. *Swedish Journal of Economics* 74:452-458.

Neidhart, L. 1975. *Foederalismus in der Schweiz*. Zurich: Benziger.

Netzer, D. 1974. State-local finance and intergovernmental fiscal relations. In *The Economics of Public Finance*, A.S. Blinder et al., eds. Washington, D.C.: The Brookings Institution.

Neumann, M. 1971. *Zur oekonomischen Theorie des Foederalismus*. *Kyklos* 24: 493-510.

Nicholson, J.L. 1964. Redistribution of income in the United Kingdom in 1959, 1957, and 1953. In *Income and Wealth: Series X*, C. Clark and G. Stuvel, eds. London: Bowes & Bowes.

Oates, W.E. 1968. The theory of public finance in a federal system. *Canadian Journal of Economics* 1:37-54.

Oates, W.E. 1972. *Fiscal Federalism*. New York: Harcourt Brace Jovanovich.

Olson, M. 1969. The principle of fiscal equivalence: the division of responsibilities among different levels of government. *American Economic Review* 59 (May Supplement):479-487.

Page, H.R. 1967. Government grants to local authorities. *District Bank Review*: 3-23.

Peacock, A.T., and Wiseman, J. 1967. *The Growth of Public Expenditure in the United Kingdom*. Princeton: Princeton University Press.

Pluta, J.E. 1974. Growth and pattern in U.S. government expenditures, 1956-1972. *National Tax Journal* 27:71-87.

Pommerehne, W.W. 1975. *Budgetaere Umverteilung in der Demokratie: Ein Empirischer Test Alternativer Hypothesen*. *Zeitschrift für Wirtschafts- und Sozialwissenschaften* 95, 327-364.

Prest, A.R. 1968. Sense and nonsense in budgetary policy. *Economic Journal* 78:1-18.

Pryor, F. 1968. *Public Expenditures in Communist and Capitalist Nations*. London: Macmillan.

Rafuse, K. 1965. Cyclical Behavior of State-Local Finances. In *Essays in Fiscal Federalism*, R.A. Musgrave, ed. Washington, D.C.: The Brookings Institution.

Reagan, M.D. 1972. *The New Federalism*. New York: Oxford University Press.

Reynolds, M., and Smolensky, E. 1974. *The Post Fisc Distribution: 1961 and 1970 Compared*. Madison: University of Wisconsin, Institute for Research on Poverty.; a shorter version with the same title is published in the *National Tax Journal* 27:515-530.

Riker, W.H. 1975. Federalism. In *Government Institutions and Processes*. F.I. Greenstein and N.W. Polsby, eds. Menlo Park: Addison-Wesley.

Robinson, T.R., and Courchene, T.J. 1969. Fiscal federalism and economic stability: An examination of multilevel public finances in Canada, 1952-1965. *Canadian Journal of Economics* 2:165-189.

Rodgers, J.D. 1974. Explaining income redistribution. In *Redistribution through Public Choice*, H.M. Hochman and G.E. Peterson, eds. New York: Columbia University Press.

Rohr, R., and Gut, W. 1970. *Bundesstaatlicher Finanzausgleich in der Schweiz*. Zurich: Redressement National.

Ruggeri, G.C. 1973. Automatic stabilizers, business cycles, and economic growth. *Kyklos* 26:288-306.

Russett, B.M., Alker, H.R., Deutsch, K.W., and Lasswell, H.D. 1967. *World Handbook of Political and Social Indicators*. New Haven: Yale University Press.

Scott, A. 1964. The economic goals of federal finance. *Public Finance* 19:241-288.

Smithies, A. 1946. The American economy in the thirties. *American Economic Review, Papers and Proceedings* 36:11-27.

Snyder, W.W. 1970a. Measuring economic stabilization. *American Economic Review* 60:924-933.

Snyder, W.W. 1970b. Measuring the effects of German budget policies, 1955-1965. *Weltwirtschaftliches Archiv* 104:302-324.

Snyder, W.W. 1970c. Measuring the stabilization effects of social security programs in seven countries, 1955-1965. *National Tax Journal* 23:263-273.

Snyder, W.W. 1973. Are the budgets of state and local governments destabilizing? A six country comparison. *European Economic Review* 4:197-213.

Sproule-Jones, M. 1974. An analysis of Canadian federalism. *Publius* 4:109-136.

Stephens, G.R. 1974. State centralization and the erosion of local autonomy. *Journal of Politics* 36:44-76.

Strauss, F.J. 1969. *Die Finanzverfassung*. Munich: Olzog.

Taylor, C.L., and Hudson, M.C. 1972. *World Handbook of Political and Social Indicators*, 2d ed. New Haven: Yale University Press.

Tax Foundation. *Facts and Figures on Government Finances*. Biennial. New York: Tax Foundation, Inc.

Tax Foundation. 1967. *Tax Burdens and Benefits of Government Expenditures by Income Class, 1961 and 1965*. New York: Tax Foundation, Inc.

Tucker, R.S. 1953. The distribution of government burdens and benefits. *American Economic Review, Papers and Proceedings* 43:518-534.

Tullock, G. 1969. Federalism: Problems of scale. *Public Choice* 6:19-29.

Urquhart, M.C., and Buckley, K.A.H. 1965. *Historical Statistics of Canada*. Toronto: Macmillan.

Wagner, A. 1973. *Die Auswirkung der oeffentlichen Haushalte auf den Konjunkturverlauf in der Schweiz, 1955-1970*. *Schweizerische Zeitschrift für Volkswirtschaft und Statistik* 109:17-57.

Wagner, R.E. 1971. *The Fiscal Organization of American Federalism: Description, Analysis, Reform*. Chicago: Markham.

Weitzel, D. 1968. *Die Entwicklung der Staatsausgaben in Deutschland*. Ph.D. thesis. University of Erlangen-Nuremberg.

White, L.D. 1933. *Trends in Administration*. New York: McGraw-Hill.

Williamson, J.G. 1965. Regional inequality and the process of national development. *Economic Development and Cultural Change* 13:1-84.

Windmuller, T., and Mehran, F. 1975. *Income Distribution and Employment Program: Bibliography on Income Distribution*, 2 Vols. Geneva: International Labour Office.

Wittmann, W. 1961. *Die Entwicklung der oeffentlichen Ausgaben in der Schweiz seit 1900*. *Schweizerische Zeitschrift für Volkswirtschaft und Statistik* 97:461-474.

Wittmann, W. 1971. *Bundesstaatlicher Finanzausgleich: Eine Globalbilanz*. *Zeitfragen der Schweizerischen Wirtschaft und Politik* 101.

Wright, D.S. 1972. The states and intergovernmental relations. *Publius* 1:7-68.

Public Documents

B.I.G.A. (*Bundesamt für Industrie, Gewerbe und Arbeit*). 1973. *Handbuch der Schweizerischen Sozialstatistik* 1932-1971. Berne: *Eidgenoessisches Volkswirtschaftsdepartment*.

B.M.F. (*Bundesministerium der Finanzen*). Annual. *Finanzbericht*. Bonn: B.M.F.

B.M.F. *Die Steuern des Bundes und der Laender*. Annual. Bonn: B.M.F.

B.M.F. 1971. *Gutachten der Steuerreformkommission*, 3 Vols. Bonn: B.M.F.

B.M.W. (*Bundesministerium fuer Wirtschaft*) 1970. *Gesetz zur Förderung der Stabilitaet und des Wachstums der Wirtschaft*. Bonn: B.M.W.

C.E.E.P. (*Centre Européen de l'Economie Publique*). 1973. *Die Entwicklung der oeffentlichen Wirtschaft im Europa der Neun*. Brussels: C.E.E.P.

C.E.E.P. 1975. *Die Bedeutung der oeffentlichen Wirtschaft in der Europaeischen Gemeinschaft*. Brussels: C.E.E.P.

C.S.O. (Central Statistical Office). *Annual Abstracts of Statistics*. Annual. London: H.M.S.O. (Her Majesty's Stationary Office).

C.S.O. *Financial Statement and Budget Report*. Annual. London: H.M.S.O.

C.S.O. *National Income and Expenditure*. Annual. London: H.M.S.O.

D.B.S. (Dominium Bureau of Statistics). *Canada Yearbook*. Annual. Ottawa: Queen's Printer.

D.B.S. 1971. *Consolidated Government Finance: Federal, Provincial and Local Governments' Revenue and Expenditure 1968*. Ottawa: Queen's Printer.

D.B.S. *Federal Government Employment*. Quarterly. Ottawa: Kings' Printer.

D.B.S. *Municipal Government Employment*. Quarterly. Ottawa: Queen's Printer.

D.B.S. *Municipal Government Finance*. Annual. Ottawa: Queen's Printer.

D.B.S. 1962. *National Accounts Income and Expenditure 1926-1956*. Ottawa: Queen's Printer.

D.B.S. *National Accounts Income and Expenditure*. Annual. Ottawa: Queen's Printer.

D.B.S. *Provincial Government Employment*. Quarterly. Ottawa: Queen's Printer.

D.B.S. *Provincial Government Finance*. Annual. Ottawa: Queen's Printer.

Economic Report of the President. Annual. Washington, D.C.: U.S. Government Printing Office (U.S.G.P.O.).

E.St.A. (*Eidgenoessisches Statistisches Amt*). 1974. *Die Finanzen von Bund, Kantonen und Gemeinden 1938-1971*. Berne: E.St.A.

E.St.A. *Bundessubrentionen und Auteile der Kantone an Bundeseinnahmen*. Berne: E.St.A.

E.St.A. 1973. *Finanzhaushalt der Kantone 1938-1971*. Berne: E.St.A.

E.St.A. *Nationale Buchhaltung der Schweiz*. In *Die Volkswirtschaft (Schweizerisches Handelsamtsblatt)*. Annual in the September issue.

E.St.A. *Oeffentliche Finanzen der Schweiz*. Annual. Berne: E.St.A.

E.St.A. *Statistisches Jahrbuch der Schweiz*. Annual. Basle: Birkhaeuser.

E.W.G. (*Europaeische Wirtschaftsgemeinschaft*). 1964. *Die Einnahmen und Ausgaben der oeffentlichen Verwaltungen in den Laendern der EWG* Brussels: E.W.G.

F.A.O. (Food and Agriculture Organization of the United Nations). *Production Yearbook*. Annual. Rome: F.A.O.

I.B.R.D. (International Bank for Reconstruction and Development). *World Atlas*. Annual. Washington, D.C.: I.B.R.D.

I.M.F. (International Monetary Fund). *International Financial Statistics*. Monthly. Washington, D.C.: I.M.F.

I.N.S.E.E. (*Institut de la Statistique et des Etudes Economiques*). 1966. *Annuaire Statistique de la France: Résumé Rétrospectif*. Paris: I.N.S.E.E.

I.N.S.E.E. *Annuaire Statistique de la France*. Annual. Paris: I.N.S.E.E.

I.N.S.E.E. *Données Sociales*. Annual. Paris: I.N.S.E.E.

O.E.C.D. (Organization for Economic Co-Operation and Development). 1974. *Labour Force Statistics 1961-1972*. Paris: O.E.C.D.

O.E.C.D. 1963. *Manpower Statistics 1950-1962*. Paris: O.E.C.D.

O.E.C.D. 1970. *National Accounts Statistics, 1950-1968*. Paris: O.E.C.D.

O.E.C.D. 1974. *National Accounts Statistics. 1961-1972*. Paris: O.E.C.D.

O.E.C.D. 1975. *Revenue Statistics 1965-1972*. Paris: O.E.C.D.

S.O.E.C. (Statistical Office of the European Community). 1969. *National Accounts, 1958-1968*. Luxembourg: S.O.E.C.

S.O.E.C. 1972. *National Accounts, 1961-1971*. Luxembourg: S.O.E.C.

S.O.E.C. *Jahrbuch der Sozialstatistik*. Annual. Luxembourg: S.O.E.C.

St.B. (*Statistisches Bundesamt*). 1973. *Bevoelkerungsstruktur und Wirtschaftskraft der Bundeslaender*. Stuttgart: Kohlhammer.

St.B. *Finanzen und Steuern, Fachserie L, Reihe 1: Haushaltswirtschaft von Bund, Laendern und Gemeinden, II*. Annual. Jahresabschluesse. Stuttgart: Kohlhammer.

St.B. *Statistisches Jahrbuch für die Bundesrepublik Deutschland*. Annual. Stuttgart: Kohlhammer.

St.B. *Volkswirtschaftliche Gesamtrechnungen, Fachserie N, Reihe 1: Konten und Standardtabellen*. Annual. Stuttgart: Kohlhammer.

St.B. 1972. *Volkswirtschaftliche Gesamtrechnungen, Fachserie N, Reihe 3: Sonderbeitraege, Revidierte Reihen ab 1950*. Stuttgart: Kohlhammer.

St.B. *Wirtschaft und Statistik*. Monthly. Stuttgart: Kohlhammer.

U.N. (United Nations). *Demographic Yearbook*. Annual. New York: U.N.

U.N. *Statistical Yearbook*. Annual. New York: U.N.

U.N. *Yearbook of National Accounts Statistics*. Annual. New York: U.N.

U.S.B.o.B. (United States Bureau of the Budget). *The United States in Brief, Fiscal Year . . . .* Annual. Washington, D.C.: U.S. Government Printing Office.

U.S.B.o.C. (United States Bureau of the Census). *Governmental Finances in . . . .* Annual. Washington, D.C.: U.S. Government Printing Office.

U.S.B.o.C. 1962. *Historical Statistics of the United States, Colonial Times to 1957*. Washington, D.C.: U.S. Government Printing Office.

U.S.B.o.C. 1965. *Historical Statistics of the United States: Continuation to 1962 and Revisions*. Washington, D.C.: U.S.G.P.O.

U.S.B.o.C., *Public Employment*. Annual. Washington, D.C.: U.S.G.P.O.

U.S.B.o.C. *State Government Finances*. Annual. Washington, D.C.: U.S.G.P.O.

U.S.B.o.C. *Statistical Abstract of the United States*. Annual. Washington, D.C.: U.S.G.P.O.

List of Contributors

Samuel H. Beer, Harvard University, United States

Albert Breton, University of Toronto, Canada

Michael Emerson, Commission of the European Communities, Brussels, Belgium

René L. Frey, University of Basle, Switzerland

Edward M. Gramlich, Brookings Institution and Cornell University, United States

Jack H. Knott, University of California, Berkeley, United States, and International Institute of Management, Berlin, West Germany

Charles E. McLure, Jr., Rice University, United States

Peter Mieszkowski, University of Houston, United States

Wallace E. Oates, Princeton University, United States

Alan Peacock, University of York, United Kingdom

Pierre Pestieau, University of Liege, Belgium, and Cornell University, United States

Werner W. Pommerehne, University of Konstanz, West Germany

Rémy Prud'homme, O.E.C.D., Paris

Robert D. Reischauer, Congressional Budget Office, United States

Jerome Rothenberg, Massachusetts Institute of Technology, United States

About the Editor

Wallace E. Oates was born in Los Angeles, California, in 1937. He undertook his undergraduate and graduate training in economics at Stanford University. Upon completion of the Ph.D. in 1965, he joined the economics faculty at Princeton University where he is presently Professor of Economics. Professor Oates is author of *Fiscal Federalism* (1972), *The Theory of Environmental Policy* (1974 with William Baumol), and several other books and journal articles. He has served in an advisory capacity on matters of governmental finance to state governments, agencies of the U.S. federal government, and to the European Economic Community.

level of P and the free surface in the tube multiplied by the specific weight of the manometer liquid equals the overpressure at P.

The precision of such a manometer can be seriously impaired if the tube containing the liquid is so small that capillarity comes into play. Furthermore, if the inner surface of the tube near A is clean and near B is dirty or otherwise of different nature, the wetting of the tube surface by the liquid may be so different as to affect seriously the observed pressure reading. For very small pressure differences the ordinary U-tube type of manometer is inadequate.

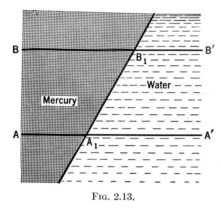

Fig. 2.13.

In some pressure-measuring arrangements different liquids are in contact, for example, water and oil, water and mercury, mercury and alcohol. It is assumed, of course, that the liquids do not mix. Within one kind of liquid the isobars are horizontal planes, and the pressure difference between two planes equals the specific weight times the distance between the planes. It follows that the interface of two fluids can be only a horizontal plane; for if it were inclined as shown in Fig. 2.13, the pressure difference between A and B would be $\gamma_{Hg} \overline{AB}$ and the pressure difference between A' and B' would be $\gamma \overline{A'B'}$ $= \gamma \overline{AB}$. The consequence would be that either at A_1 or at B_1 a pressure difference would exist across the interface. But a pressure difference is impossible in the case of equilibrium. It follows that, if no rigid wall is put between the two fluids, an interface which is not horizontal is physically impossible. This statement may not be true for the part of the fluids very close to a vertical wall, where the fluid interface is usually curved as a result of surface tension.

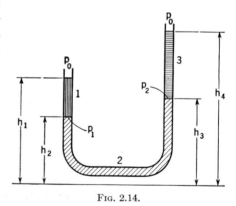

Fig. 2.14.

Let us assume, as shown in Fig. 2.14, that there are three kinds of liquid in a U-tube with respective specific weights γ_1, γ_2, and γ_3. The pressure at the top levels of fluid 1 and fluid 3 is atmospheric, and the pressure at the interface of 1 and 2 is p_1 and at the interface of 2 and 3 is p_2. If h_1, h_2, h_3, and h_4 are the different heights as shown in the figure, the

equilibrium conditions for each of the three fluids supply the following
equations:

$$\frac{p_1 - p_0}{\gamma_1} = h_1 - h_2$$

$$\frac{p_1 - p_2}{\gamma_2} = h_3 - h_2$$

$$\frac{p_2 - p_0}{\gamma_3} = h_4 - h_3$$

Pressure measurements based on the use of a liquid manometer depend
directly on precise knowledge of the weight of unit volume of the fluid used
and on precise observation of the
levels at which the fluid stands.
The measurement of very small pressure differences is obviously difficult,
and various modifications of the
simple manometer have been devised to suit special cases.

a. *Three-liquid Manometer.* In
Fig. 2.15 a manometer is sketched
that contains three nonmiscible liq-
uids of densities γ_1, γ_2, and γ_3. The
unknown pressure p is communi-
cated to a closed vessel by a tube
as shown. The manometer is filled
through the stopcock X.

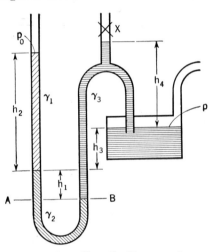

FIG. 2.15. — Three-liquid manometer.

By observing h_1, h_2, and h_3 and
knowing the values of γ_1, γ_2, and
γ_3, p can be computed. Note that the weight of air or other gas that transmits the pressure p to the closed vessel is neglected.

At level AB, pressures are equal in each tube, and hence

$$p_0 + h_2\gamma_1 + h_1\gamma_2 = p + h_3\gamma_3 + h_1\gamma_3$$

and

$$p - p_0 = h_1(\gamma_2 - \gamma_3) + h_2\gamma_1 - h_3\gamma_3$$

b. *Two-liquid Manometer.* If γ_2 represents water γ_w, and γ_1 and γ_3 are
both kerosene γ_k, we can adjust the filling of the manometer to make h_2
equal to h_3 for the pressure to be measured and have

$$p - p_0 = h_1(\gamma_w - \gamma_k)$$

The head h_1 to be measured is now larger than would be the case for a
simple water manometer, $p - p_0 = h\gamma_w$. The amplification is greater the
nearer the two liquids are to the same density.

Note that, when both γ_1 and γ_3 are air γ_a, $\gamma_w - \gamma_a \approx \gamma_w(1 - \frac{1}{800}) \approx \gamma_w$ and the weight of air in the connecting tubes can be neglected.

c. Inclined-liquid Manometer (Draft Gauge). When $p = p_0$, liquid stands at level A (Fig. 2.16). For a pressure difference $p - p_0$, liquid in the inclined tube rises to level B. The change in level of the large reservoir is negligible if its cross section is made very large compared with that of the tube. Provided that the tube is straight,

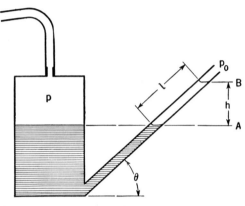

$$p - p_0 = \gamma h = \gamma l \sin \theta$$

The distance l can be observed with precision. The amplification of h is $1/\sin \theta$ for a given liquid. If further amplification is desired, a lighter liquid can be used pro-

Fig. 2.16. — Inclined-liquid manometer.

vided that it makes a clear meniscus with clean glass.

The effect of capillarity in the tube is presumed to be the same at B as at A and not to affect the distance l. The tube is thus assumed to have a uniform bore and surface condition.

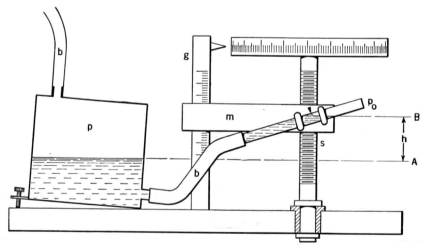

(b)Rubber tubing; (m) metal block carried by screw (s) and sliding on guide post (g)

Fig. 2.17. — Krell, or Prandtl, manometer.

d. Krell, or Prandtl, Manometer. Errors due to capillarity and to change in reservoir level are eliminated by having the liquid meniscus always at the same marked place in the glass tube of Fig. 2.17. The inclined tube is carried parallel to itself by a low-pitch screw with micrometer head. When $p = p_0$, the level is noted at A. When $p - p_0 = \gamma h$, the value of h is read from the micrometer head. Only one reading is necessary to determine h. The inclination of the tube determines the sensitivity of the manometer, and very small deviations from a desired pressure can be detected. The number of turns of the screw needed to bring the meniscus back to a reference mark on the tube measures this deviation.

  e. *Inverted-cup Manometer.* In Fig. 2.18 the pressure difference $p - p_0$ is measured by the force tending to lift the cup,

$$p - p_0 = \frac{b}{a} \frac{F}{A}$$

If the cup is large, a small pressure is measured by a substantial force.

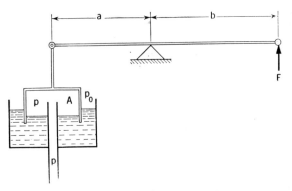

Fig. 2.18. — Inverted-cup manometer.

  f. *Spring-type Gauges.* All such pressure gauges separate two regions of static pressure, p and p_0, by an elastic solid whose deformation depends on the spring constant of the apparatus. These gauges must be calibrated

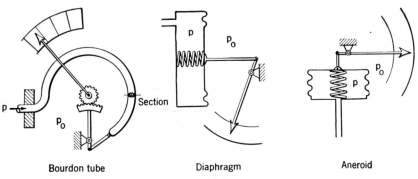

Bourdon tube   Diaphragm   Aneroid

Fig. 2.19. — Spring-type gauges.

against some type of manometer whose indications are based on the hydrostatic equation. Some well-known examples are shown in Fig. 2.19.

2.8. Archimedes' Principle. The theory of flotation and fluid displacement originated with Archimedes, and its formal statement is still called "Archimedes' principle."

Consider the solid body of Fig. 2.20 suspended by a thread below the surface of a liquid. Since the body and all parts of the liquid are at rest, the pressure distribution throughout the liquid and on the surface of the body is described by the hydrostatic equation.

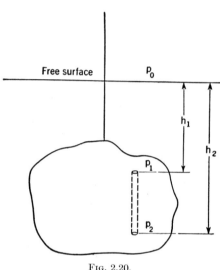

Fig. 2.20.

Assume a small vertical cylinder of cross-sectional area dA cut through the body as shown, extending from depth h_1 at the top to depth h_2 at the bottom. As dA is small, the pressures on the exposed, or wetted, ends of the cylinder may be taken as p_1 and p_2. The force due to the hydrostatic pressure is normal to the surface of each wetted end. The vertical components of these forces are independent of the inclinations of the surfaces and are of magnitudes $p_1\, dA$ and $p_2\, dA$.

Since $p_2 > p_1$, there will be an upward force $(p_2 - p_1)\, dA$ on each element of volume $(h_2 - h_1)\, dA$ and the total lift, or buoyancy, of the hydrostatic pressures all over the wetted surface of the body will be

$$B = \int_A (p_2 - p_1)\, dA = \int_A \gamma(h_2 - h_1)\, dA$$

But the volume of the body is

$$V = \int_A (h_2 - h_1)\, dA.$$

and hence $B = \gamma V$. The weight of the body, if of average specific weight γ_b, is

$$W = \gamma_b V$$

The apparent weight on the suspension is therefore

$$W - B = V(\gamma_b - \gamma)$$

The effect of the horizontal components of the forces on the wetted surface may be dismissed, as the body is hanging at rest. An analogous analytical procedure could be undertaken to show that the pressure forces on the ends of small horizontal cylindrical volume elements are equal and opposite, because they are at the same level. Consequently, the integral over the wetted surface of all horizontal forces is zero.

Archimedes' principle may now be stated thus: A submerged body is subject to a buoyancy equal to the weight of fluid displaced.

A further conclusion of importance can also be drawn. We know that the resultant of the gravity forces on a body passes through a certain point called the center of gravity. Since the buoyancy is the sum of a number of elementary forces, each equal in magnitude to the weight of a small cylindrical portion of fluid, it follows that the line of action of the buoyancy must pass through the center of gravity of the fluid mass which we can imagine put in place of the solid body. In other words, the center of buoyancy is the center of gravity of the displaced fluid.

2.9. Stability of Submerged Bodies. A completely submerged body, such as a submarine (Fig. 2.21), can remain in equilibrium at rest only if the buoyancy B is equal to the weight W and if the center of gravity (C.G.)

Free surface

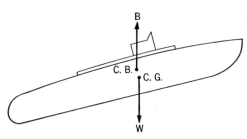

FIG. 2.21.

lies directly below the center of buoyancy (C.B.). Submarines must use balancing tanks to make $B = W$ and trimming tanks to bring the C.B. over the C.G. An airship similarly must use ballast or let out gas to keep in balance and trim as fuel is consumed or weight changed by rain or ice.

The equilibrium of a submerged body is stable with the C.G. below the C.B.; for if the body is rotated through a small angle θ, there is a righting moment, as shown in Fig. 2.22,

$$R = Wa \sin \theta = Wa\theta$$

The body thus tends to return to its original position. In general, an equilibrium position is said to be stable if a small change of this position arouses forces that oppose the change.

The period of the rolling oscillation T evidently depends primarily on the relative magnitudes of the righting moment and the moment of inertia of the body. We might neglect, for a first approximation, the frictional damping of the water. For a given body the righting moment depends on

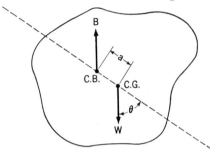

FIG. 2.22.

$Wa\theta$, while $I = (W/g)k^2$, where k is the radius of gyration of the body with respect to the axis of roll. Their ratio is $ga\theta/k^2$, and we assume that T is some function of this quantity, or

$$T = f\left(\frac{ga\theta}{k^2}\right)$$

We might further assume that the function is approximated by

$$T = C\left(\frac{ga\theta}{k^2}\right)^x$$

where C is a constant. But T has dimensions $[T]$ and $(ga\theta/k^2)^x$ has dimensions

$$\left[\left(\frac{L \cdot L}{T^2 \cdot L^2}\right)^x\right] = \left[\frac{1}{T^{2x}}\right],$$

where the brackets indicate that the dimensions only of the enclosed quantity are represented. Consequently, for both sides of the equation to be of the same dimensions, x must equal $-\frac{1}{2}$. Then

$$T = C\frac{k}{\sqrt{ga}}f_1(\theta) = \frac{k}{\sqrt{ga}}f_2(\theta)$$

where $f_2(\theta)$ is an unknown function. Note that the power of θ cannot be determined by balancing the dimensions because θ is already a dimensionless variable. Experiments show that $f_2(\theta)$ is practically constant for small values of θ. It is seen that T is directly proportional to k and inversely proportional to the square root of a.

The equilibrium of a submerged body is unstable if the C.G. lies above the C.B. because the body will tend to move away from its original position if slightly disturbed. The equilibrium is neutral if the C.G. and C.B. coincide.

In general, if the equilibrium is stable, the stability is said to be positive; if the equilibrium is unstable, the stability is negative; and if the equilibrium is neutral, the stability is zero.

2.10. Floating Bodies. Archimedes' principle can be applied to bodies that are partly submerged and floating on the free surface of a liquid. Consider a body as shown in Fig. 2.23 submerged to a certain extent in an incompressible fluid of specific weight γ. Above the free surface the atmospheric pressure is p_0. To find the vertical force exerted by the fluid on the solid body, we proceed as before, subdividing the body into small vertical cylinders of cross-sectional area dA. In this case we find that the

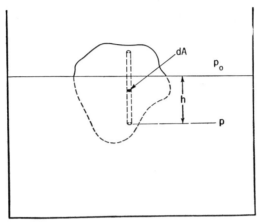

FIG. 2.23.

vertical force acting on each small cylinder whose upper end is above the fluid surface is $(p - p_0) \, dA$. The hydrostatic equation gives $p - p_0 = \gamma h$. Thus we see that the vertical force $\gamma h \, dA$ equals the weight of a fluid cylinder of cross section dA and of height h. The vertical force on a completely submerged small cylinder is the same as in the case of a totally submerged body. The total buoyancy exerted by the fluid upon the solid body has, therefore, the magnitude of the weight of the fluid displaced by the submerged part. The further steps of the argument concerning the horizontal components of the hydrostatic forces and the position of the C.B. can be repeated in exactly the same way as for the case of the fully submerged body. We arrive at the following conclusions: A body partly submerged in an incompressible fluid is subjected to a buoyancy that equals in magnitude the weight of the fluid displaced by the body and that also has the same line of action as this weight.

According to the principle just stated, equilibrium requires that the total weight of the body equal the weight of the displaced fluid and that the C.G. of the body lie on the same vertical line as the C.G. of the displaced fluid.

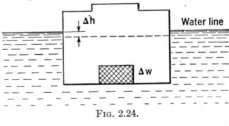

FIG. 2.24.

A floating body to which a weight ΔW is added will sink sufficiently to increase its displacement a corresponding amount (Fig. 2.24). If ΔW is small with reference to the total weight, $\Delta W = \gamma A\ \Delta h$, where Δh is the sinkage caused by ΔW and A is the area of the horizontal section at the water-line plane. With ΔW expressed in tons and Δh in inches, the ratio $\Delta W/\Delta h$ is called by naval architects "tons per inch immersion." This is an important characteristic of a vessel, since it is constant for small changes in draft. The captain, for instance, can check by observation of the change in draft the weight of fuel reputedly placed on board by a contractor.

Consider as an example a short wooden cylinder of circular cross section with radius a and height b floating in water. What is the relation between the densities γ and γ_b and the depth of submergence? First assume that the axis of the cylinder remains vertical. If t denotes the depth of the submerged part, the principle of Archimedes yields the equation $\gamma a^2 \pi t = \gamma_b a^2 \pi b$. Therefore $t/b = \gamma_b/\gamma$. If, for example, the density of the body is one-half that of water, half of the cylinder will be submerged.

2.11. Stability of a Floating Body. A cylinder with a large ratio of length to diameter will not float with axis vertical but will lie flat on the water. Each position of the cylinder, vertical or horizontal, is, however, an equilibrium position. One of the two equilibrium positions is stable, while the other is unstable.

A submerged body is in stable equilibrium when the C.G. lies below the C.B. A floating body, on the contrary, may be in stable equilibrium (against rolling over) when the C.G. lies considerably above the C.B. It is a well-known fact, however, that a vessel has a very limited range of stable locations for the C.G. The criterion of the initial stability of a floating body is the position of a fictitious point, the metacenter, discovered by the French naval architect Bouguer in the eighteenth century to be inherent in the form of the submerged portion of the hull. This portion of the hull is called the "carene."

The concept of the metacenter is illustrated by the pair of sketches of Fig. 2.25. The left-hand sketch represents a cross section of a vessel floating upright at water-line level WL, in equilibrium. The right-hand sketch represents the same vessel inclined through an angle of roll θ and held over at this inclination by some external agency as by a sail. The new water line is marked $W'L'$. For convenience, the former water line and the former vertical axis are also indicated.

The C.G. of the vessel with all weights on board is assumed to be at G. If none of the cargo shifts, the C.G., when the vessel is inclined, will remain at G.

However, the C.B. will not remain fixed with reference to the vessel as it heels over. Recall that the C.B. has been shown to be at the C.G. of the displaced fluid. This is the center of volume of the carene. But the carene has a different shape when the vessel is inclined. The volume of fluid displaced is decreased on the high side by the wedge-shaped portion marked 2 in the figure and increased on the low side by the corresponding wedge marked 1. Since the weight of the vessel is unchanged, the displacement 2 lost on the high side must be equal to the displacement 1 gained on the low side. Consequently, there is a shift of the C.B. to the low side. As the vessel is progressively inclined, the C.B. moves from B to a succession of positions toward the low side and reaches a definite location B' for the

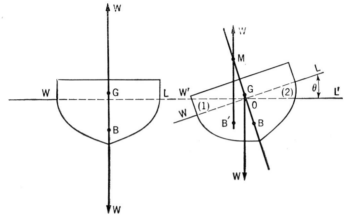

Fig. 2.25.

inclination shown. Note that the location of B' is a function only of θ and the outer form of the hull.

In the upright position, the vessel floats in equilibrium with weight W and buoyancy W, acting along the vertical axis.

In the inclined position, the weight W acts downward through G, but the buoyancy W now acts upward through B', fortunately well to the low side of the vessel. The intersection of the vertical through B' with the axis of symmetry of the vessel (the vertical through B and G in the upright position) is at M. M is named the metacenter.

Now it is apparent that, as long as M lies above G, the couple of the two forces W is of a nature to resist the inclination and to restore the vessel to the upright position. Conversely, if M should fall below G, the couple would roll the vessel over.

The magnitude of the righting moment at a given inclination, or heel, could be readily computed if we knew the location of M. For if the distance $\overline{GM}$ is known, the arm of the couple would be $\overline{GM}\theta$, for a small angle. Then the righting moment would be

$$R = W\overline{GM}\theta$$

2.12. Metacentric Height. Naval architects name the length $\overline{GM}$ the "metacentric height" and make careful estimates of its value under various

conditions of loading and damage before the design of a vessel is accepted.
In the previous section it was noted that the righting moment was proportional to the metacentric height. However, if the righting moment can
be computed without knowledge of the metacentric height, then the
metacentric height can be found.

We observe that the moment of buoyancy of the carene about B in the
upright case is zero, while this moment about the same point becomes
$W\overline{BB'}$ when the vessel is inclined. This change of moment of the buoyant
forces due to a shift of the C.B. from B to B' is caused by a shift of the displacement of wedge 2 on the high side to wedge 1 on the low side. We may
then equate the moment due to the shift of the C.B. to the moment of the
couple due to the shift of displacement from wedge 2 to 1.

Since the moment of a couple is the same for any point in its plane, the
moment of the wedges may be taken about point O for convenience in
computation.

Let V be the volume displaced by the vessel, or $V\gamma = W$. Let x be the
distance from the center line of the vessel to an element of volume as shown
in Fig. 2.26. The element has transverse thickness dx, height θx, and

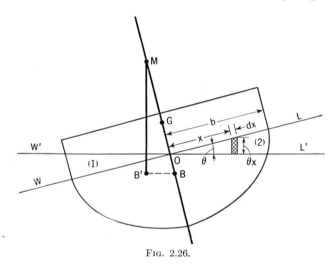

FIG. 2.26.

length l. Assume θ to be a small angle. Then the moment of the displacement of wedges 1 and 2 about O will be the sum of the moments of the
weight of fluid in each such element of volume, $l\theta x\,dx$,

$$\text{Moment of wedges} = \gamma\theta\int_{-b}^{+b} lx^2\,dx = \gamma\theta I$$

where I is the moment of inertia of the water-plane area, the horizontal
section of the vessel cut by the plane of WL.

Since the moment of this couple about O and B is the same, we may, as was mentioned before, equate it to the moment about B due to the shift of the buoyancy from B to B'. Therefore, $W\overline{BB'} = \gamma V\overline{BM}\theta = \gamma\theta I$, and $\overline{BM} = I/V$. Since $\overline{BM} = \overline{GM} + \overline{BG}$,

$$\overline{GM} = \frac{I}{V} - \overline{BG}$$

It is of particular importance to note that we have obtained an expression for the metacentric height that is independent of the specific weight of the fluid γ and of the inclination θ.

The metacentric radius $\overline{BM} = I/V$ depends on the geometry of the vessel and can be computed from its plans. $\overline{BM}$ also depends on the draft, as both I and V change with the water line corresponding to the loading of the vessel. For a vessel of parallel sides, I will remain constant, but V becomes less as load is removed. $\overline{BM}$ should, therefore, increase.

The stability of the vessel, however, depends very much more on the location of the C.G. If cargo is removed from a deep hold, the C.G. in light condition is relatively higher, while at light draft the C.B. is relatively lower. Consequently, $\overline{BG}$ may increase so much at light draft that the metacentric height (and consequently the stability) may vanish.

It is evident from the expression $\overline{GM} = I/V - \overline{BG}$ that to gain stability the C.G. should be low ($\overline{BG}$ small) and the beam wide (I large).

In the discussion of stability in terms of metacentric height, it must be remembered that θ is assumed to be a small angle. Therefore only the initial stability of a floating body is indicated by this analysis.

The initial metacentric height is 1 to 2 ft for passenger steamers and 3 to 4 ft for naval vessels and sailing ships. Experience shows that the period of roll is shorter and rolling is more uncomfortable for a large metacentric height.

2.13. Period of Rolling. The applied moment $W\overline{GM}\theta$ and the mass moment of inertia of the vessel about the axis of roll are the most important factors on which the period of roll depends. The frictional damping is a second-order effect. Denoting the mass moment of inertia by $(W/g)k^2$, where k is the radius of gyration of the vessel, we find by an analysis like the one of Art. 2.9 that the period $T = (k/\sqrt{g\overline{GM}})\phi(\theta)$, where $(\phi\theta)$ is an unknown function. $\phi(\theta)$ is found experimentally to be constant for small values of θ.

We conclude, as has the practical seaman, that large $\overline{GM}$ produces quick rolling. River steamers, not designed for a seaway, customarily have relatively great beam (large I/V), a high C.B. (small $\overline{BG}$), and a metacentric height of as much as 20 per cent of the beam.

A floating cylinder has zero stability; M lies on G, and $\overline{GM} = 0$

(Fig. 2.27). A vertical side or, even better, a flare is required for stability. "Tumble home" as on some whaleback steamers and on submarines awash can give doubtful stability.

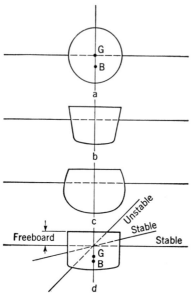

A fair $\overline{GM}$ initially is not enough to give safety, as stability may vanish when the deck edge dips because I decreases abruptly. To preserve a "range of stability" through a large inclination, adequate freeboard is required.

2.14. Inclining Experiment. To determine $\overline{GM}$ experimentally in order to verify the safety of a loaded barge or other vessel is a common precaution. A weight F is moved across the deck a distance x (Fig. 2.28). The change of moment Fx causes an observed heel, or list, θ balanced by a righting moment $W\overline{GM}\theta$. W can be computed from the plans of the vessel corresponding to the observed draft. Then

$$W\overline{GM}\theta = Fx \qquad \text{and} \qquad \overline{GM} = Fx/W\theta$$

Fig. 2.27. — Floating bodies having varying degrees of stability. *a.* Circular cylinder — zero stability. *b.* Hull with flared sides — very stable. *c.* Hull with "tumble home" — doubtful stability. *d.* Range of stability of a typical hull form depends on the freeboard.

2.15. Free-surface Effect. It can be shown, by methods identical with those used to compute the position of the metacenter, that, if any compartment of a ship has a free liquid surface, the metacentric height of the vessel is lowered by an amount equal to i/V, where i is the moment of inertia of the free surface about its center line and V, as above, is the volume of the carene. In damaged condition, a vessel with several compartments open to the sea may capsize before it sinks.

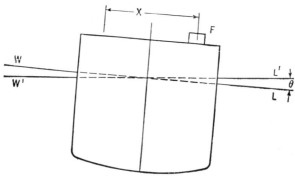

Fig. 2.28.

2.16. Statics of Moving Systems. When the entire continuum is in uniform rectilinear motion, our conclusions regarding the statics of a fluid in the gravity field of force apply without change. This follows from Newton's fundamental concept that force results from change of motion. When there is uniform motion of all particles of a system, there is no change of motion for any of them, and hence no change in the forces that would act on them when at rest.

Consequently, we may ignore a uniform velocity of translation and write as before for the hydrostatic equation.

$$p - p_0 = \gamma h$$

2.17. d'Alembert's Principle. Consider a particle or small portion of fluid of mass m in a continuum, located at x, y, z, and moving at a given time with an acceleration whose components are d^2x/dt^2, d^2y/dt^2, and d^2z/dt^2. The presence of such an acceleration implies, from Newton, that the resultant force acting on the particle has effective components equal to $m(d^2x/dt^2)$, $m(d^2y/dt^2)$, and $m(d^2z/dt^2)$. Now the resultant force acting on the fluid particle is the sum of the external surface and body forces. Let its components be X, Y, Z. Note that the resultant external force is acting in the direction of the resultant acceleration.

The equations of motion for the particle are thus:

$$X = m\frac{d^2x}{dt^2} \qquad Y = m\frac{d^2y}{dt^2} \qquad Z = m\frac{d^2z}{dt^2}$$

or

$$X - m\frac{d^2x}{dt^2} = 0 \qquad Y - m\frac{d^2y}{dt^2} = 0 \qquad Z - m\frac{d^2z}{dt^2} = 0$$

The latter form of the equations of motion is identical in appearance with the three equations of equilibrium for a particle without acceleration. It is therefore obvious that, if a fictitious force with components $- m(d^2x/dt^2)$, $- m(d^2y/dt^2)$, $- m(d^2z/dt^2)$ is considered to act on the particle in addition to the real forces, then this system of fictitious and real forces is in equilibrium. The fictitious force is called the "inertia force," and the fictitious equilibrium is called "dynamic equilibrium."

The principle of d'Alembert is embodied in the last paragraph. It is seen that this principle enables us to reduce a problem of motion to one of equilibrium simply by taking into account the inertia forces which act on the masses involved.

2.18. Uniform Rectilinear Acceleration. Consider the liquid in an open tank moving with constant acceleration a in a horizontal direction as shown in Fig. 2.29. By d'Alembert's principle, we may consider the liquid at rest in the tank in a field of force determined by g units of force per unit mass downward and a units horizontally, toward the left. The resultant force vector is $\sqrt{a^2 + g^2}$ and is directed away from the vertical by $\theta = \tan^{-1} a/g$. The direction and magnitude of the force vector are the same at all points.

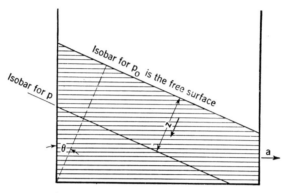

Fig. 2.29.

The force on unit volume of fluid that when at rest is $\gamma = \rho g$ is now $\gamma' = \rho\sqrt{a^2 + g^2}$, and the hydrostatic equation becomes

$$p - p_0 = \gamma' z = \rho\sqrt{a^2 + g^2}\, z = \frac{\rho g z}{\cos\theta} \qquad (2.10a)$$

where z is measured normal to a surface of constant pressure, as shown in Fig. 2.29.

The free surface at $z = 0$ and $p = p_0$ is inclined to the horizontal at an angle $\theta = \tan^{-1} a/g$. If the horizontal acceleration is g, the liquid banks up at a 45-deg angle. The surfaces of constant pressure are parallel to the

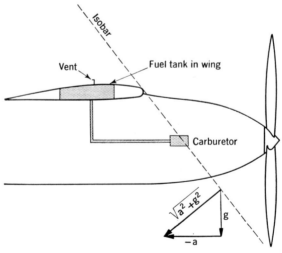

Fig. 2.30. — A catapulted airplane may be momentarily starved of fuel.

free surface. The maximum pressure is at the corner of the tank where z is a maximum.

This type of analysis applies to the design of a tank truck where brakes may be applied roughly or to a tank car for a railway. An interesting example (Fig. 2.30) is furnished by the fuel system of an airplane launched by catapult (with a horizontal acceleration usually greater than g). A gravity feed will not operate; instead, the carburetor may be drained back into the tank, and fuel may pour out of the vent of the main tank. Obviously, a check valve is required, or a pressurized fuel tank.

2.19. Uniform Spin. When a body of fluid rotates uniformly as a whole without relative motion of its parts, each particle moves in a circle as do elements of a rigid body.

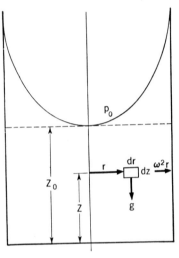

Let the constant angular velocity be ω, and let ρ be the density of the liquid. Choose polar coordinates with z and r as shown in Fig. 2.31. The centripetal acceleration of a particle at radius r is $\omega^2 r$. Consider the dynamic equilibrium of the particle by d'Alembert's principle. In the horizontal plane the pressure must increase radially to balance the centrifugal force $\rho\,dr\,dz\,dn\,\omega^2\,r$. In the vertical plane the pressure must increase with depth to balance the weight $\rho g\,dr\,dz\,dn$, as for a fluid at rest. Therefore,

FIG. 2.31.

$$\rho\,dr\,dz\,dn\,\omega^2 r = \frac{\partial p}{\partial r}\,dr\,dn\,dz \quad\text{or}\quad \rho\omega^2 r = \frac{\partial p}{\partial r}$$

$$-\rho\,dr\,dz\,dn\,g = \frac{\partial p}{\partial z}\,dz\,dr\,dn \quad\text{or}\quad -\rho g = \frac{\partial p}{\partial z}$$

Since p depends only on r and z, we can write that

$$dp = \frac{\partial p}{\partial z}\,dz + \frac{\partial p}{\partial r}\,dr = -\rho g\,dz + \rho\omega^2 r\,dr$$

or

$$p = \int_{z_0}^{z} -\rho g\,dz + \int_{0}^{r} \rho\omega^2 r\,dr = -\rho g(z - z_0) + \frac{\rho\omega^2 r^2}{2} + p_0$$

At the free surface where $p = p_0$, $z = z_0 + (\omega^2/2g)r^2$, a paraboloid of revolution.

Surfaces of constant pressure are similar paraboloids of revolution with common axis,

$$z - z_0 = \frac{\omega^2}{2g} r^2 - \frac{p - p_0}{\rho g}$$

Where $r = 0$, the variation of pressure is as in a fluid at rest,

$$p - p_0 = - \rho g(z - z_0)$$

Note that, for constant z, p increases as r^2. A centrifugal pump and a centrifuge make use of this principle. An enclosed mass of water is whirled rapidly to create a great difference in pressure between its center and its periphery.

2.20. Overshot Water Wheel. On unit mass of water in a bucket as shown in Fig. 2.32, the force field can by d'Alembert's principle be con-

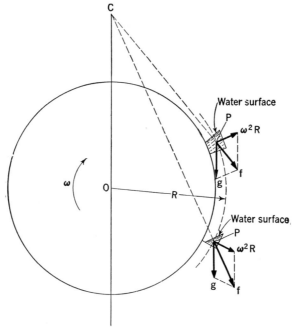

Fig. 2.32. — Overshot water wheel.

sidered as made up of a component g due to gravity and a component $\omega^2 R$ due to centrifugal force as shown. The resultant force f cuts the vertical at C.

$$\frac{OC}{OP} = \frac{OC}{R} = \frac{g}{\omega^2 R}$$

or

$$OC = \frac{g}{\omega^2} = \text{constant}$$

Consequently, C is a fixed point for all buckets, and the water in each is in equilibrium under a force field directed along a line CP. The free surface of water in each bucket will be normal to CP for all positions.

2.21. Statics of Compressible Fluids. The general condition for the equilibrium of a fluid at rest holds for both compressible and incompressible cases, *i.e.*, the pressure gradient equals the specific weight and is directed vertically downward. For the usual coordinate system, with the h axis upward, we have from Eq. (2.7)

$$\frac{dp}{dh} = -\gamma \tag{2.7}$$

The surfaces of constant pressure are horizontal planes as in the case of the incompressible fluid, and p is a function of h alone. From the relation $dp/dh = -\gamma$ we also conclude that γ (or ρg) depends on h. In the incompressible case, density is constant, but for a compressible fluid the density, which obviously decreases with pressure, must also decrease with h and must be constant over each horizontal plane.

If we knew the relation between height and density of the fluid, we could predict the pressure change between level h_1 and a higher level h by integrating the equation to obtain

$$p - p_1 = -\int_{h_1}^{h} \gamma \, dh$$

or

$$h - h_1 = -\int_{p_1}^{p} \frac{dp}{\gamma}$$

2.22. Physical Properties of Liquids and Gases. For practical problems, however, we are usually able to relate density or specific weight only to pressure and temperature. For liquids, the relation between specific weight and pressure is usually given in the form

$$dp = \beta \frac{d\gamma}{\gamma} = -\beta \frac{dv}{v} \tag{2.11}$$

where β, called the "bulk compression modulus," is practically constant over a large range of pressures; and v, the reciprocal of γ, is called the "specific volume."

For water, $\beta = 310,000$ lb per sq in., for usual hydraulic work where temperatures are not near freezing or boiling and pressures are less than 10,000 lb per sq in. Thus for a pressure increase of 1,000 lb per sq in. there is an increase in specific weight or density of 0.32 per cent and a decrease in specific volume of the same amount.

Water is peculiar in its change of density with temperature. For moderate pressures there is an increase in density of about 8 per cent at the change from ice to liquid. There is a further increase to a maximum density at 4 C (39 F) and then a density decrease of about 4 per cent up to the boiling point. At the transition from liquid to steam the density decreases by a factor of 1,700.

The following table shows the variation of specific gravity in the sea as a function of depth. The last column, headed *With compression*, gives the actual specific gravity resulting from the effects of both temperature and pressure. The adjacent column, headed *Without compression*, gives the effect on specific gravity of temperature alone. Note that there is little change in specific gravity (and hence in density) even at immense depths.

Depth, ft	Temperature, deg F	Specific gravity	
		Without compression	With compression
0	80.8	1.02220	1.02220
1,000	40.1	1.02739	1.03215
10,000	36.7	1.02768	1.07123

For engineering purposes, water may be considered incompressible, provided that neither ice nor steam is involved and further provided that it is not subject to severe acceleration giving rise to compression waves (water hammer). Other liquids likewise may be treated as incompressible, and the ordinary hydrostatic equation applied.

$$p_2 - p_1 = - \gamma(h_2 - h_1)$$

For the permanent gases, however, substantial density changes accompany changes of both pressure and temperature. At a height between 3 and 4 miles, where pressure and temperature are considerably lower than at the earth's surface, the atmosphere has but half the density at sea level. The well-known equation of state for a perfect gas is sufficiently accurate for most engineering purposes,

$$pv = RT \tag{2.12}$$

where R is the gas constant for the gas in question and T is the absolute temperature. R has the dimensions of a length divided by a temperature, as shown by Eq. (2.12),

$$[R] = \left[\frac{pv}{T}\right] = \left[\frac{F}{L^2}\frac{L^3}{F}\frac{1}{\theta}\right] = \left[\frac{L}{\theta}\right]$$

A second relationship that applies to the permanent gases is the polytropic equation, connecting specific weight (or volume) and pressure,

$$\frac{p}{\gamma^n} = pv^n = \text{constant} \tag{2.13}$$

where n is a constant. The value of n depends on the process and on the gas. For a process in which friction and heat transfer are negligible (reversible adiabatic process) it is found, to a good approximation, that $n = c_p/c_v$, where c_p and c_v are the specific heats at constant pressure and constant volume, respectively. The ratio c_p/c_v is here denoted by k.

The following table gives the values of R, k, and γ for a few gases:*

Gas	k	R		γ	
		M/deg C	Ft/deg F	Kg/m³	Lb/ft³
Helium..	1.66	212.0	386.5	0.1785	0.01114
Air	1.40	29.27	53.35	1.2928	0.08071
Oxygen..	1.40	26.50	48.31	1.4289	0.08921
Nitrogen.	1.40	30.26	55.20	1.2505	0.07807
Hydrogen	1.41	420.6	766.5	0.08987	0.005611

2.23. Isothermal Equilibrium. The general equilibrium condition for a compressible fluid, $dp/dh = -\gamma$, cannot be integrated to obtain the pressure distribution unless γ can be eliminated. This can be done by means of the equation of state,

$$pv = \frac{p}{\gamma} = RT \quad \text{or} \quad \gamma = \frac{p}{RT}$$

Substituting for γ, we have

$$\frac{dp}{p} = -\frac{dh}{RT} \tag{2.14}$$

For the isothermal case, T is constant. Accordingly, we find by integration of Eq. (2.14), if h is measured above a reference level h_1 where the pressure is p_1, that

$$\left. \begin{array}{c} \log p - \log p_1 = \log \dfrac{p}{p_1} = \dfrac{h_1 - h}{RT} \\[2mm] p = p_1 e^{(h_1 - h)/RT} \end{array} \right\} \tag{2.15}$$

or

This is the pressure distribution for isothermal equilibrium of a permanent gas. It may be noted that it corresponds to and replaces the simpler formula $p = p_1 + \gamma(h_1 - h)$ for an incompressible fluid. The two expressions become identical if $(h_1 - h)/RT$ becomes small, that is, for an elevation of the order of 250 ft. For if x is small, $e^x = 1 + x$ (the first two terms of the power-series expansion for e^x). In this case we can write Eq. (2.15) as

$$p = p_1\left(1 + \frac{h_1 - h}{RT}\right) = p_1 + \frac{p_1}{RT}(h_1 - h) = p_1 + \gamma_1(h_1 - h)$$

substituting $\gamma_1 = p_1/RT$ from the equation of state.

For the measurement of height from a knowledge of the pressures p_1 and p, Eq. (2.15) is put in the form of the so-called "barometric formula." Since barometer heads b_1 and b correspond directly to p_1 and p, we can take $b_1/b = p_1/p$ and write Eq. (2.15) in the form

$$h - h_1 = RT \log \frac{b_1}{b} \tag{2.16}$$

for the isothermal case.

* At 760 mm, 0 C or 29.92 in. Hg, 32 F.

As an example, suppose a mercury barometer is observed to stand at 29.8 in. at the foot of a hill and at 24.6 in. at the top. It is assumed that the average temperature of the air is 50 F. (Note that we neglect the temperature gradient up the hill. For a high mountain this would not be justified.) Then $T = 50 + 460 = 510$ F abs, and from Eq. (2.16)

$$h - h_1 = 53.3 \times 510 \log 1.21 = 2{,}256 \text{ ft}$$

2.24. Lapse Rate in the Atmosphere. In applying the barometer to the measurement of a great altitude, allowance must be made for the decrease in temperature with elevation. For the first few miles above the ground the rate of decrease has been found to be nearly constant. Assume such a constant rate of temperature decrease, and let $dT/dh = -\lambda$, the constant lapse rate.

The equation of state (2.12) and the fundamental condition of equilibrium (2.7) have already been combined to give Eq. (2.14). Eliminating dh by combining Eq. (2.14) with $dT/dh = -\lambda$, we get

$$\frac{dp}{p} = \frac{1}{\lambda R} \frac{dT}{T}$$

The last equation can be integrated to give $\log p = (1/\lambda R) \log T + C$ or

$$\frac{p^{\lambda R}}{T} = C = \frac{p_1^{\lambda R}}{T_1} \tag{2.17}$$

where p_1 and T_1 are an arbitrary pair of values of p and T. Substitution of $p/R\gamma$ for T, from the equation of state, gives

$$\frac{p^{\lambda R} R \gamma}{p} = C$$

or

$$\frac{p}{\gamma^{1/(1-\lambda R)}} = \left(\frac{R}{C}\right)^{1/(1-\lambda R)} = \text{constant} \tag{2.18}$$

Comparison of Eqs. (2.13) and (2.18) shows that the assumption of a constant lapse rate is equivalent to the assumption of a polytropic relation between p and γ for which the exponent

$$n = \frac{1}{1 - \lambda R} \tag{2.19}$$

If n is taken as being equal to k for air, the corresponding value of λ is called the "adiabatic lapse rate,"

$$\lambda_{ad} = \left(\frac{1}{R}\right)\left[1 - \left(\frac{1}{k}\right)\right] = \left(\frac{1}{53.3}\right)\left[1 - \left(\frac{1}{1.4}\right)\right] = 0.00535 \text{ F per ft}$$

or about 5 F per 1,000 ft (1 C per 100 m).

In the real atmosphere the lapse rate is usually about half of this value ($\lambda \approx \lambda_{ad}/2 = 0.0027$ F per ft), and thus the corresponding value of $n = 1/(1 - \lambda R) = 1/(1 - 0.0027 \times 53.3) = 1.17$.

To find the pressure distribution in the atmosphere or the relation between pressure and altitude, we substitute in Eq. (2.17) for T its value from $T - T_1 = \lambda(h_1 - h)$, which is merely the integrated form of $dT/dh = -\lambda$. Thus we find, after solving for $h - h_1$,

$$h - h_1 = \frac{T_1}{\lambda}\left[1 - \left(\frac{p}{p_1}\right)^{\lambda R}\right] \tag{2.20}$$

If the gradient λ and a set of corresponding values of h_1, p_1, T_1 are given, this formula can be used for determining the altitude h from a barometer reading p. If we have for instance at the ground $h_1 = 0$, $T_1 = 540$ F abs, and $p_1 = 29.92$ in. Hg, a barometer reading $p = 17.5$ in. Hg gives, for $\lambda = 0.0027$,

$$h = \frac{540}{0.0027}\left[1 - \left(\frac{17.5}{29.92}\right)^{0.144}\right] = 14,900 \text{ ft}$$

It is evident that the selection of the lapse rate has an important effect on the altitude estimated from Eq. (2.20). An alternative form of the barometric equation requires the selection of a suitable value of n, corresponding to the probable lapse rate.

Substituting in Eq. (2.20) for λ its value from Eq. (2.19), we find

$$h - h_1 = RT_1\frac{n}{n-1}\left[1 - \left(\frac{p}{p_1}\right)^{(n-1)/n}\right] \tag{2.21}$$

This is a general formula for determining height from an observation of two pressures p and p_1 provided that n is known.

A corresponding formula connecting height with temperature drop has already been obtained by integration of $dT/dh = -\lambda$,

$$h - h_1 = \frac{1}{\lambda}(T_1 - T)$$

or

$$h - h_1 = R\frac{n}{n-1}(T_1 - T) \tag{2.22}$$

2.25. Height of the Atmosphere. *a. Adiabatic Case.* Taking $n = k = 1.4$ for dry air, $R = 53.4$ ft per deg F, and $T_1 = 592$ F abs at the ground level, we find from Eq. (2.21) that p will be zero when

$$h - h_1 = RT_1\frac{k}{k-1} = 92,000 \text{ ft}$$

or about 17 miles.

We know that the atmosphere does not stop at 17 miles but extends, with diminishing density, for hundreds of miles. However, we also know that the troposphere, or the part of the atmosphere next the earth, has an approximately adiabatic lapse rate for 6 or 7 miles and that thereafter an isothermal stratosphere extends to a considerable height. Let us examine the extent of a hypothetical isothermal atmosphere to see whether a large extent is compatible with static equilibrium.

b. Isothermal Case. The equilibrium condition for this case is embodied in Eq. (2.15), $h - h_1 = RT \log (p_1/p)$, from which h is seen to be infinite if $p = 0$. An isothermal atmosphere would extend outward indefinitely, as seems to be the case with the actual atmosphere, although it is now known not to be isothermal.

c. Constant-density Case. The height of a column of air of uniform density necessary to create the pressure under which we live, or the "head" of air, can be computed from the hydrostatic equation [Eq. (2.9)]. If the assumed value of density corresponds to $p = 29.92$ in. Hg and $T = 32$ F, the height of the column for $p = 0$ is found to be about 5 miles.

2.26. Remarks on the Equilibrium of the Atmosphere. The lower part of the atmosphere, or troposphere, is constantly being mixed by convection. Water vapor is being taken up and again precipitated, and there are great movements of polar air and of tropical air into the temperate regions. In the tropics, owing to intense heating of the ground, air is rising. This produces a general circulation of air from the temperate regions toward the tropics (trade winds) and a drift near the top of the troposphere from the tropics toward the poles. Cold air aloft settles toward the earth to maintain continuity. This general mixing of the atmosphere is due to unequal heating of the earth's surface, caused by variation of solar intensity with latitude and by unequal heat-absorptive qualities of land and water areas. As a result, the troposphere is kept in some average thermal and mechanical equilibrium whose disturbance we know as weather. This varies from day to day or even from hour to hour in an irregular manner.

Climate is determined by the average weather at a given place over a long period of time. Thus climatology predicts from past records the safe date for planting crops. Meteorology predicts tomorrow's weather from a knowledge of the present condition of the atmosphere near a given locality. The convective mixing of the troposphere tends to establish a stable equilibrium, and there is a certain degree of continuity in our weather.

That the lower atmosphere should have an approximately adiabatic temperature gradient is suggested by the fundamental nature of convection. Air next the ground that is heated more in one locality than elsewhere will rise like warm air in a chimney. Colder and denser air will flow in to take its place. The rising air cools adiabatically, for air is a poor conductor.

It is interesting to observe that the natural temperature lapse rate makes for stability of the lower atmosphere; *i.e.*, an air mass, displaced vertically from any cause, tends to return toward its original level. Consider a mass of air rising by convection because it became slightly unstable at ground level owing to local heating. This air will cool adiabatically 1 C per 100 m. At any level it will be subject to the same pressure as the surrounding atmosphere. Hence, if the atmospheric lapse rate is but 0.6 C per 100 m (the usual case), the displaced air mass will be denser than its surroundings and will tend to fall back.

In general, when the atmospheric lapse rate exceeds the adiabatic rate of 1 C per 100 m, the air is unstable. Under usual conditions the air is stable, and large-scale convection does not occur. Thunderstorms arise in an unstable atmosphere in which the lapse rate is temporarily excessive from abnormal heating of the ground and the lower strata of the air. This condition frequently occurs in summer. In winter, when the ground is covered with snow, the lower strata are cold, the lapse rate is low, and the air is likely to be stable. On a clear summer night the ground cools quickly by radiation, and the lower stratum of air may become cooler than that lying above it. Here the lapse rate may be zero or even reversed. This is called "temperature inversion" and makes for very great stability.

The troposphere is found to extend upward with a fairly constant lapse rate until the temperature has fallen to about −50 C. This temperature may be reached at a height of about 7 miles in our latitude. From there on to 12 or 13 miles, the stratosphere extends as an isothermal blanket.

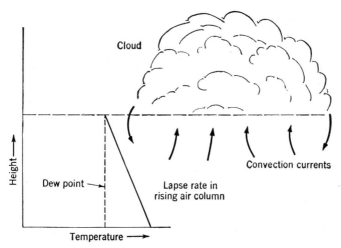

FIG. 2.33. — Cloud formation by condensation of water vapor carried upward in a rising column of air.

Above the stratosphere, there is evidence of a temperature maximum of about 80 C at a level of 30 to 40 miles. Above 50 miles, the atmosphere is strongly ionized and is known as the "ionosphere." It has properties of great importance to radio-wave propagation by reflection. There is evidence from auroral measurements of the presence of an upper atmosphere to 750 miles.

The formation of cumulus clouds and thunderstorms is a result of instability. Warm, moist air next to the ground becomes unstable and rises, cooling adiabatically until the dew point is reached, when condensation of water vapor makes a cloud form (Fig. 2.33). If the initial uprush is violent, the rising air may overshoot its altitude of equilibrium. If there is an inversion or a stable layer of air at this elevation, further upward motion is stopped. However, if the upper air is neutral or slightly unstable, the

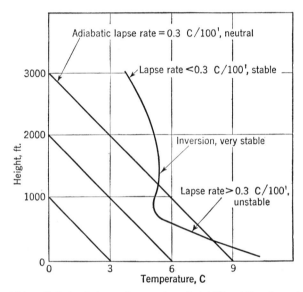

Fig. 2.34. — Relation between lapse rate and stability of the atmosphere.

latent heat released by condensation may be enough to carry the convection current to greater heights. Aviators have occasionally found storm clouds extending to 35,000 ft, but usually the air is clear above 20,000 ft. Figure 2.34 shows how the actual lapse rate may be stable or unstable depending on whether it is greater or less than the adiabatic (neutral) rate.

2.27. Balloons. *a. Taut Balloon.* A balloon is said to be taut if it is completely filled with gas. Since the bag of a balloon can support only negligible internal overpressure, a safety valve is provided, which allows gas to escape as the balloon rises, thus maintaining nearly equal internal and external pressures. If we assume the balloon rises so slowly that the internal and external temperatures are equal at every instant, the equation of state [Eq. (2.12)] yields $\gamma_g/\gamma_a = R_a/R_g =$ constant. Subscript g refers to the gas and subscript a to the atmosphere.

For a balloon of volume V rising at uniform velocity the buoyant force

$V(\gamma_a - \gamma_g)$ is just counterbalanced by the weight W of the structure and load, plus the air resistance D,

$$W + D = V\gamma_g\left(\frac{\gamma_a}{\gamma_g} - 1\right) = V\beta \tag{2.23}$$

As γ_a/γ_g is constant, β will vary as γ_g. The buoyancy of the balloon will therefore diminish as γ_g becomes smaller, $i.e.$, as altitude is increased.

At the maximum height the velocity, and hence the drag D, will be zero, and $\beta = \beta_m = W/V$. Note, however, that, if the balloon overshoots the maximum level by virtue of its kinetic energy, too much gas will be lost and the rest condition cannot be attained. Instead, the balloon will fall under the action of a constant downward force since the weight of gas $V\gamma_g$ will now be constant. The balloon will therefore accelerate downward until the condition $W - D = V\beta$ is satisfied.

If the balloon is anchored to the ground, the drag D of Eq. (2.23) will be replaced by the tension F in the mooring cable. Letting $\beta = \beta_0$ at ground level, we find that $\beta_0 = (W + F)/V$. Therefore, the ratio $\beta/\beta_0 = \gamma_a/\gamma_{a_0} = (p/p_0)^{1/n} = (W + F)/W$. From a table of the standard atmosphere one may pick out h corresponding to any value of p/p_0, or h can be computed from an assumed average temperature change. Hence, for a known value of the ballast necessary to hold a balloon on the ground, one may estimate the height to which it can rise.

b. *Flabby Balloon.* If the balloon is only partly filled at the start, it will rise under the action of a constant buoyant force until it is completely filled, for the weight of gas $V\gamma_g$ remains unchanged. The level at which gas starts to escape is called the "pressure height." For elevations greater than the pressure height the rising balloon is taut and behaves as described above.

2.28. Superchargers. At 20,000 ft the density of air is less than half that at sea level. The oxygen in the air intake per cylinder volume of an airplane engine is therefore only about half that needed to burn the fuel required to develop full power. If a compressor is used to supply air to the engine at sea-level density, the full power is restored. Such compressors, known as superchargers, are gear-driven from the engine or driven by an exhaust turbine. An engine may not safely be supercharged at ground level because the compression ratio is presumably already as high as the fuel will tolerate without detonation.

Human beings resemble the internal-combustion engine in that a fixed lung capacity and a fairly constant frequency of respiration require a fixed amount of oxygen per stroke. Above 12,000 ft human beings need extra oxygen enrichment of the thin air they breathe or else the equivalent of supercharging (supercharged cabin).

CHAPTER III
KINEMATICS AND CONTINUITY

3.1 Relative Motion. Kinematics is concerned only with space-time relationships, without regard to force. We shall deal with a continuum in which there are no voids and such that nowhere in it is fluid either created or destroyed. The mathematical description of the motion is complete if we have an expression which gives, for every point, the magnitude and direction of the fluid velocity at that point, at any instant of time.

Velocity is measured relative to some coordinate system, either fixed or moving. We might choose a coordinate system fixed in space, past which the fluid flows, *e.g.*, an observer sitting on the bank of a stream. Alternatively, we might choose a coordinate system attached to a particular part of the fluid and moving with it, *e.g.*, a swimmer allowing himself to be carried along with the stream. For reasons of simplicity we shall adopt the first system of coordinates, following Euler, and describe fluid velocity V in terms of the time for every point x, y, z, fixed with reference to a stationary coordinate system. Thus $V = f(x,y,z,t)$.

In this connection a type of relativity discussed by Newton will be helpful in keeping our mathematics simple in form. Suppose we are interested in the flow around a solid body moving with velocity V through a large expanse of fluid that is at rest at a great distance from the body. The fluid is disturbed by the passage of the body and, relative to the body, moves past it and closes in behind, preserving the continuity of the fluid. Since the fluid motion is due only to the relative motion of the body and the continuum, the velocities and accelerations relative to the body would be exactly the same at all points in the continuum if we considered the body at rest in an infinite expanse of fluid moving past it with a velocity of $-V$. We shall, in general, consider cases of flow past solid objects as if the object were at rest in a stream of fluid.

We literally adopt this procedure in the wind tunnel, in which a model on a force-measuring balance is exposed to a stream of air. But for testing models of ships, the model is towed through a channel or tank of water at rest. To observe the flow pattern relative to the ship's model it is necessary to fix a camera to the carriage that tows the model. A short time exposure will make a record of the flow pattern, provided that one puts sawdust in the water or otherwise makes visible the motion of individual particles. To observe the flow pattern in the wind tunnel a stationary camera is used to record the appearance of air flow made visible by smoke.

54

With the moving camera in the tank experiment we have in effect chosen a set of coordinates fixed in the body. The camera sees the water as if flowing past the model with a relative velocity equal but opposite to that of the model.

3.2. Streamlines. If we knew the direction of the velocity at each point x, y, z at a given instant of time, we could make a record of the flow by drawing lines everywhere tangent to the particle velocities. Such lines are technically named "streamlines." When we take a short time exposure of the surface of the water in the ship's model tank referred to above, each of the distinguishable particles of water will be represented on the developed plate by a short streak, whose slope indicates the direction and whose length indicates the relative magnitude of the fluid velocity at this point. We can then draw a series of streamlines tangent to these experimentally determined velocity vectors and obtain a streamline picture, or flow pattern.

3.3. Path Lines. If, on the other hand, we take a long time exposure, the long streaks on the plate will register the paths of the different visible particles of fluid. Such lines are called "path lines" (after Prandtl). They do not necessarily give information about the velocity, as they record an observation of the change in the position of particles, which takes place from time t_1 to a later time t_2. Obviously, the streamline picture at time t_2 may be very different from that at time t_1. The path lines may crisscross and present a tangled picture impossible to interpret in terms of velocity.

3.4. Steady Flow. If the velocity at every point remains the same at all times the motion is said to be steady; $V = f(x,y,z)$ and is independent of time, that is, $\partial V/\partial t = 0$ everywhere. For such steady motion, the streamline pattern is "stationary," and all streamline photographs will be identical. Steady motion is often called "stationary flow." In this case, the path lines and the streamlines, as here defined, are identical. Under certain conditions one can show that a steady velocity implies steady pressure, density, and temperature. It will be assumed in all cases that these conditions are fulfilled. A steady flow will therefore be defined as one in which not only velocity but also pressure, density, temperature, and any other fluid property are all independent of time at any fixed point.

3.5. Stream Tubes. Since a streamline is, by construction, everywhere tangent to particle velocities, in steady motion the flow follows the streamlines. Consequently, no fluid crosses a streamline. In an ideal continuum the velocity for steady motion is a continuous function of the space coordinates, and every streamline is a continuous line beginning at an infinite distance upstream and extending an infinite distance downstream. When the continuum is bounded by solid walls, such as is the case in a hydraulic system, we may consider the streamlines as starting in the reservoir where fluid is at rest and extending through the entire system to the ultimate discharge. Streamlines in a steady flow represent the paths of particles; and since matter in the continuum is neither created nor destroyed, a streamline can, theoretically, have no ends. It either extends to infinity in both directions or is a closed line.

Through any point in the fluid only one streamline can be drawn, extending up- and downstream. The streamlines through all points on a closed curve define a stream tube. The fluid inside such a stream tube remains inside the tube since no fluid can cross a streamline. Extending the concept we can imagine the entire flow composed of stream tubes, drawn through some arbitrarily selected net or mesh stretched across the flow.

3.6. Conservation of Mass — Equation of Continuity. The mathematical statement of the fact that fluid is neither created nor destroyed in a

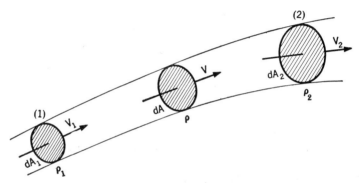

Fig. 3.1. — Flow in a stream tube of infinitesimal cross section.

continuum is called the "equation of continuity." For steady flow in a stream tube of infinitesimal cross section, this equation is

$$\frac{dm_1}{dt} = \frac{dm_2}{dt} = \frac{dm}{dt} = \text{constant}$$

where dm/dt is the rate of mass flow through the stream tube at an arbitrary point. The equation has this form because in steady flow there is nowhere a change in density with time. Hence no accumulation of mass can occur inside the stream tube, and the same amount must pass all cross sections in unit time. Since the rate of mass flow across area dA is equal to $\rho V \, dA$ (Fig. 3.1), the above equation may be written

$$\rho_1 V_1 \, dA_1 = \rho_2 V_2 \, dA_2 = \rho V \, dA = \text{constant} \tag{3.1}$$

For a stream tube of finite cross section this can be integrated to give

$$\int_A \rho V \, dA = \text{constant} \tag{3.2}$$

where dA is normal to the velocity V at every point (Fig. 3.2). If ρ and V are assumed constant over every cross section, Eq. (3.2) reduces to

$$\rho V A = \text{constant} \qquad (3.3)$$

Equation (3.3) is sufficiently exact for many engineering problems. If the fluid can be considered incompressible (as can water in ordinary pipe flow, or air in many aerodynamic problems), Eq. (3.3) becomes

$$V A = \text{constant} \qquad (3.4)$$

We now develop a more general form of the continuity equation, which will apply both to steady and to unsteady flow. The method used here for continuity will be useful in later chapters in the treatment of energy and momentum.

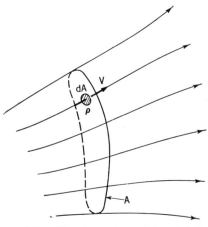

Fig. 3.2. — Flow in a stream tube of finite cross section.

We imagine to be drawn in the fluid a volume of arbitrary shape, which is at rest with respect to a convenient frame of reference. We call this the "control volume" $\mathcal{V}$ and its surface the "control surface" A. Fluid will in general be flowing across some parts of the control surface. At an arbitrary time t_a there is a definite mass m occupying the control volume. This may comprise both fluid and solid bodies, as shown in Fig. 3.3a.

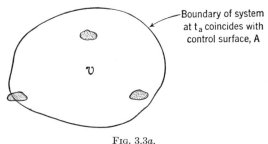

Fig. 3.3a.

After a time interval $dt = t_b - t_a$, the boundary of the mass system will in general no longer coincide with the control surface but will be as shown by the dotted line in Fig. 3.3b.

The mass of that part of the system lying outside of $\mathcal{V}$ at time t_b we call dm_{out}, and the mass of the new matter inside of $\mathcal{V}$ at t_b but not included in the system we call dm_{in}. Representing the entire mass inside $\mathcal{V}$ at any time by m' we can express the mass of the system in two ways, $m = m'_a$ and $m = m'_b + dm_{\text{out}} - dm_{\text{in}}$. Eliminating m and dividing by dt, we get

$$0 = \frac{m_b' - m_a'}{dt} + \frac{dm_{\text{out}} - dm_{\text{in}}}{dt} \qquad (3.5)$$

Equation (3.5) is a general statement of the continuity condition. The first term represents the rate of accumulation of mass inside the control

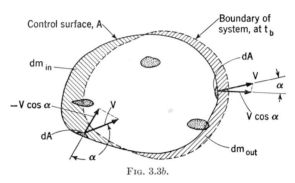

FIG. 3.3b.

volume, while the second represents the net rate of outflow of matter through the control surface.

The special cases already discussed are readily handled by means of Eq. (3.5). If, for example, we let $\mho$ coincide with a section of stream tube (Fig. 3.1), we get

$$\frac{dm_{\text{out}}}{dt} = \rho_2 V_2 \, dA_2$$

$$\frac{dm_{\text{in}}}{dt} = \rho_1 V_1 \, dA_1$$

If, furthermore, the flow is steady relative to $\mho$, the mass inside $\mho$ will not change with time, that is, $m_b' = m_a'$. Equation (3.5) thus reduces to $\rho_2 V_2 \, dA_2 = \rho_1 V_1 \, dA_1$, which is identical with Eq. (3.1).

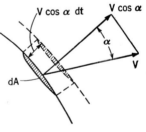

FIG. 3.4.

For future use it will be helpful to express the net rate of mass outflow across the control surface in another form. The mass that crosses an element dA of the control surface in time dt is equal to $\rho V \cos \alpha \, dA \, dt$, where $V \cos \alpha$ is the component of velocity normal to dA (Figs. 3.3b and 3.4). We stipulate that α be the angle between V and the outward-drawn surface normal, so that outward-flowing matter is automatically positive, while inward-flowing matter is negative. Therefore,

$$dm_{\text{out}} - dm_{\text{in}} = dt \int_A \rho V \cos \alpha \, dA \qquad (3.6)$$

where the integral is taken over the entire control surface A. The time interval dt is of course the same for all area elements and has therefore been taken out from under the integral sign. Equation (3.5) thus becomes

$$\frac{m_b - m_a'}{dt} + \int_A \rho V \cos \alpha \, dA = 0 \qquad (3.7)$$

and for steady flow

$$\int_A \rho V \cos \alpha \, dA = 0 \qquad (3.8)$$

It is readily seen also that if the fluid is incompressible ($\rho =$ constant), $m_a = m_b'$ and Eq. (3.7) reduces to

$$\int_A V \cos \alpha \, dA = 0 \qquad (3.9)$$

In most problems, the control surface can be chosen so that $\cos \alpha$ has one of the three values 1, 0, or -1 everywhere on the surface. Furthermore, there will usually be flow across the surface at only a few areas, over each of which the density and velocity can be considered uniform. The integral of Eq. (3.7) or (3.8) thus reduces to the sum of only a few terms. The simplest case has already been discussed, viz., a stream tube or a length of pipe in which the velocity and density can be considered uniform over a cross section. For steady flow in a branched pipe we find, referring to Fig. 3.5 and using Eq. (3.8),

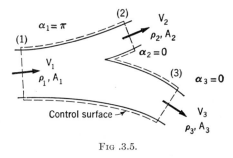

FIG. 3.5.

$$\int_A \rho V \cos \alpha \, dA =$$
$$\rho_2 A_2 V_2 + \rho_3 A_3 V_3 - \rho_1 A_1 V_1 = 0$$

3.7. Two-dimensional Flow. When the flow is identical in all planes parallel to a plane of reference (the plane of the paper in the illustrations that follow), the flow is said to be two-dimensional. For steady motion, $V = f(x,y)$ only. This restriction greatly simplifies the study of many common flow patterns, but the same methods apply to the general case of three-dimensional flow, although a graphical representation is not easy to devise. Consider an incompressible flow in the x, y plane as shown in Fig. 3.6, with identical conditions in every plane parallel to it. Let the flow be represented by a streamline pattern in which the spacing between streamlines is n at any place. Well upstream, if the flow is uniform and parallel there, we might space points a, b, c, d, e at equal intervals, indicating an equal flux entering each rectangular stream tube, of height n_0 in the y direction and of unit width in the z direction normal to the plane of the paper. Let the streamlines through a, b, c, d, e be as shown. Then the

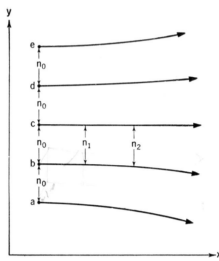

area of each stream tube is numerically equal to n, the spacing of the streamlines. From the condition of continuity for incompressible fluid, $V_0 n_0 = V_1 n_1 = V n$ = constant.

The velocity is thus inversely proportional to the streamline spacing. Where the streamlines are spread apart, the velocity is lower and, where spreading, the flow is slowing down. Consequently, the streamline pattern gives information as to both the direction and the magnitude of the velocity at every point.

Fig. 3.6. — Two-dimensional flow.

The mathematical problem of hydromechanics is to find the function $V = f(x,y)$ that maps the velocity field. We shall, however, find that many simple problems of steady two-dimensional flow of incompressible fluid can be solved approximately by a simple graphical construction.

For example, consider the flow through the square nozzle in Fig. 3.7.

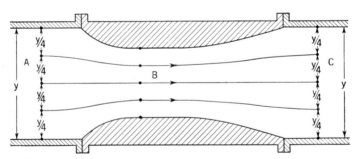

Fig. 3.7. — Flow through a square nozzle treated as two dimensional.

Neglecting friction, the velocity at sections A and C, where the pipe walls are parallel, will be parallel and uniform across the section. We can, therefore, indicate points on several streamlines at each section, as shown. At the throat section B, the velocity is also parallel and uniform across the section. We can thus locate another point on each streamline by dividing the throat section into four equal spaces. The streamlines are then faired through these points. The resulting picture is an approximation only, for but three points on each streamline have been determined. This problem can be solved exactly by use of more advanced methods.

In making a sketch of streamlines based on continuity requirements, we assume a steady flow of a frictionless liquid that follows the boundaries of a solid without separation. For real fluids we may expect the flow picture to be seriously different from the idealized case if the flow is controlled by a body of such abrupt form as to cause the flow to separate from the boundaries. A body of such easy form that a real flow passes smoothly along it is called a "streamline body." The word "streamlining" is popularly applied to efforts to fair, or smooth, surfaces exposed to flow.

CHAPTER IV

DYNAMICS OF AN IDEAL FLUID

The dynamic equations of motion for a fluid particle lead, when integrated, to a generalized statement of the mutual relation between the nature of the flow and the forces acting. The basis for such a relation lies in Newton's second law of motion, which can be stated thus: The component in any direction of the resultant external force acting on a given mass is equal to the product of the mass and the component of its acceleration in that direction. To apply this law to a fluid continuum it will be necessary to choose some particular element or particle of fluid located with reference to time and space coordinates. We must also choose some convenient shape for the volume of this element of fluid. The procedure will be first to determine the external forces acting on the particle and next its accelerations along the axes of the space coordinates and then to write down an equation of motion for each of the axes by the application of Newton's second law.

To facilitate integration of these equations of motion it is necessary to make the simplifying assumption that we deal only with an ideal frictionless fluid. For such a fluid, since there can be no tangential or shearing forces, the only external forces acting are due to pressure and gravity. This assumption, which is fundamental to classical hydrodynamics, has been found by experience to represent to a very fair approximation the behavior of a real fluid in many practical engineering problems.

The development and integration of the equation of motion can be further simplified if we assume steady flow. Again this represents practical conditions in most engineering problems dealing with the steady motion of ships and airplanes and the continuous operation of machinery.

Finally, when the fluid in question is a liquid, it will be permissible to consider the fluid as incompressible. For the flow of air or gas at moderate velocities the assumption of incompressibility, while an approximation, may also be justified.

The circumstances of the case will determine which assumptions should be made. In a later chapter consideration will be given separately to the effect of viscosity on the dynamics of real fluids.

4.1. Accelerations. Consider first a steady flow where the streamline pattern is stationary and each fluid particle moves along a streamline. For this simple case it is possible to state the position of the particle in terms of the distance s that the particle has moved along the streamline, from an original reference position.

The particle is assumed to be at point O initially and to move with the steady flow a distance ds in time dt to point O', as shown in Fig. 4.1. The acceleration of the particle will be the change in its velocity at point O' from its velocity at point O, divided by the infinitesimal element of time dt. It is convenient to choose as space axes the tangent to the streamline at O and the normal to that streamline. Then the accelerations required for the two equations of motion corresponding to these two axes will be the component a_s tangent to the streamline and the component a_n normal to a_s and directed toward the local center of curvature of the streamline.

Let V represent the initial velocity of the particle at O, tangent to the streamline by definition of a streamline. When the particle reaches O', the

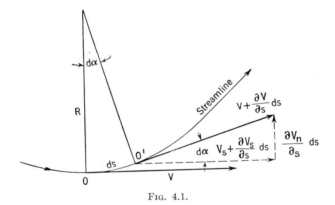

Fig. 4.1.

velocity is tangent to the streamline at that point, its direction having changed through an infinitesimal angle $d\alpha = ds/R$, for which $\cos d\alpha = 1$ and $\sin d\alpha = d\alpha$.

The magnitude of the velocity along the streamline has increased from V at O to $V + (\partial V/\partial s) \, ds$ at point O'. The component of velocity at O' in the direction of the tangent at O is, by geometry,

$$V_s = \left(V + \frac{\partial V}{\partial s} \, ds \right) \cos d\alpha = V + \frac{\partial V_s}{\partial s} \, ds$$

and consequently

$$\frac{\partial V_s}{\partial s} = \frac{\partial V}{\partial s}$$

Taking note that $ds/dt = V$, we can write down the acceleration in the s direction as

$$a_s = \frac{V + (\partial V_s/\partial s) \, ds - V}{dt} = \frac{\partial V_s}{\partial s} \frac{ds}{dt} = V \frac{\partial V}{\partial s}$$

The velocity normal to the streamline at O is zero. From Fig. 4.1, the velocity at O' in this same direction will be

$$V_n = 0 + \frac{\partial V_n}{\partial s} ds = \left(V + \frac{\partial V}{\partial s} ds\right) \sin d\alpha = \frac{[V + (\partial V/\partial s) ds] ds}{R} = V \frac{ds}{R}$$

since $\sin d\alpha = ds/R$ and the term in ds^2 is negligible. Therefore,

$$\frac{\partial V_n}{\partial s} = \frac{V}{R}$$

Then the acceleration in the direction of V_n is

$$a_n = \frac{0 + (\partial V_n/\partial s) ds - 0}{dt} = \frac{\partial V_n}{\partial s} \frac{ds}{dt} = \frac{V^2}{R}$$

For a steady flow, therefore, the two components of acceleration at any point O are

$$a_s = V \frac{\partial V}{\partial s}$$

and

$$a_n = \frac{V^2}{R} \tag{4.1}$$

For an unsteady flow the velocity at a fixed point changes with time, and account must be taken of this fact in computing the acceleration. At a fixed point the rate of change of velocity with respect to time is represented by $\partial(\text{velocity})/\partial t$. At the instant one particle is at O with tangential velocity V, another particle is at O' with velocity components V_s and V_n as discussed for the case of steady flow. After time dt the particle that was at O arrives at O' and then will have velocity components containing an additional term due to the elapsed time dt.

$$V + \frac{\partial V_s}{\partial s} ds + \frac{\partial}{\partial t}\left(V + \frac{\partial V_s}{\partial s} ds\right) dt = V + \frac{\partial V_s}{\partial s} ds + \frac{\partial V}{\partial t} dt$$

$$V_n + \frac{\partial V_n}{\partial s} ds + \frac{\partial}{\partial t}\left(V_n + \frac{\partial V_n}{\partial s} ds\right) dt = \frac{\partial V_n}{\partial s} ds + \frac{\partial V_n}{\partial t} dt$$

where we neglect terms in $ds\,dt$, take $V_n = 0$, but admit that $\partial V_n/\partial t$ need not be zero.

Substituting previously determined values $\partial V_s/\partial s = \partial V/\partial s$ and $\partial V_n/\partial s = V/R$, we find for the acceleration components when the flow is unsteady

$$a_s = V \frac{\partial V}{\partial s} + \frac{\partial V}{\partial t}$$

$$a_n = \frac{V^2}{R} + \frac{\partial V_n}{\partial t} \tag{4.2}$$

4.2. External Forces. To form the equations of motion we must determine the components of the resultant of all external forces in the directions of the accelerations a_s and a_n that they produce. Since the shape of the fluid particle is arbitrary, we choose a rectangular element of volume having an infinitesimal length ds in the direction of s and a height dn in the direction of the normal. The width of the particle (in the direction at right angles to the plane of the paper) is taken as unity, so that the volume is $ds\ dn$, the mass $\rho\ ds\ dn$, and the weight $\rho g\ ds\ dn$.

Figure 4.2 shows the diagram of external forces acting in the s and n

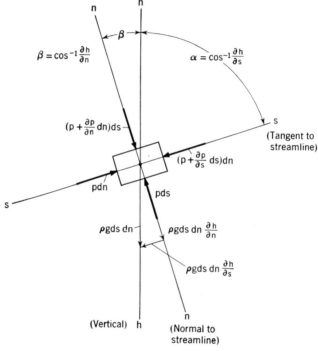

Fig. 4.2.

directions. Recall that we are dealing with a frictionless fluid, so that the only forces are those due to pressure and gravity.

The resultant of pressure forces on the two ends of the particle and the component of the weight along the axis of s give the resultant force in the s direction.

$$F_s = p\,dn - \left(p + \frac{\partial p}{\partial s}\,ds\right) dn - \rho g\,ds\,dn\,\frac{\partial h}{\partial s} = -\left(\frac{\partial p}{\partial s} + \rho g\,\frac{\partial h}{\partial s}\right) ds\,dn$$

In a similar way the algebraic sum of forces in the n direction is made up of the pressure forces on the top and bottom of the particle and the component of the weight in the n direction.

$$F_n = pds - \left(p + \frac{\partial p}{\partial n}\, dn\right) ds - \rho g\, ds\, dn\, \frac{\partial h}{\partial n} = -\left(\frac{\partial p}{\partial n} + \rho g\, \frac{\partial h}{\partial n}\right) ds\, dn$$

The above components of weight are obtained as follows: From Fig. 4.2,

$$s \text{ component} = -\, \rho g\, ds\, dn\, \cos\alpha$$
$$n \text{ component} = -\, \rho g\, ds\, dn\, \cos\beta$$

The change in the height h depends on both s and n. For arbitrary small increments ds and dn, the change

$$dh = dh_s + dh_n = \cos\alpha\, ds + \cos\beta\, dn,$$

as shown in Fig. 4.3. But dh equals the rate of change of h with respect to s times ds plus the rate of change with n times dn.

$$dh = \frac{\partial h}{\partial s}\, ds + \frac{\partial h}{\partial n}\, dn$$

Therefore, $\cos\alpha = \partial h/\partial s$ and $\cos\beta = \partial h/\partial n$, and the components of weight are $-\rho g(\partial h/\partial s)\, ds\, dn$ and $-\rho g(\partial h/\partial n)\, ds\, dn$.

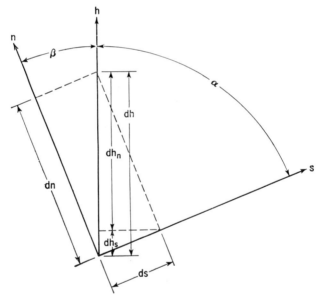

FIG. 4.3.

For clarity in Figs. 4.2 and 4.3, h is shown in the s, n plane although this is not generally true. The expressions for the weight components are not affected by this simplification.

4.3. Equations of Motion. We may now apply Newton's second law by equating these forces to the product of mass and acceleration for the directions s and n.

$$F_s = \rho \, ds \, dn \, a_s$$

and

$$F_n = \rho \, ds \, dn \, a_n$$

Substituting the values found for F_s, F_n, a_s, and a_n, and dividing through by $\rho \, ds \, dn$, we get

$$-\frac{1}{\rho}\frac{\partial p}{\partial s} - g\frac{\partial h}{\partial s} = V\frac{\partial V}{\partial s} + \frac{\partial V}{\partial t} \qquad (s \text{ direction}) \qquad (4.3)$$

$$-\frac{1}{\rho}\frac{\partial p}{\partial n} - g\frac{\partial h}{\partial n} = \frac{V^2}{R} + \frac{\partial V_n}{\partial t} \qquad (n \text{ direction}) \qquad (4.4)$$

4.4 Euler's Equation. If we multiply Eq. (4.3) by ds, an element of length of a streamline at a given instant of time ("instantaneous stream-line"), we can integrate with respect to s and obtain Euler's general equation for the motion of an ideal fluid.

$$\int \frac{\partial V}{\partial t}\,ds + \int V\frac{\partial V}{\partial s}\,ds + \int \frac{1}{\rho}\frac{\partial p}{\partial s}\,ds + g\int \frac{\partial h}{\partial s}\,ds = f(t) \qquad (4.5)$$

or

$$\int \frac{\partial V}{\partial t}\,ds + \frac{V^2}{2} + \int \frac{1}{\rho}\frac{\partial p}{\partial s}\,ds + gh = f(t) \qquad (4.6)$$

It is important to notice that in the derivation of Euler's equation only the restriction to an ideal (frictionless) fluid is involved. The equation, therefore, applies to both steady and unsteady motion and to both compressible and incompressible cases.

Steady flow requires that V, p, and ρ be independent of time. In this case Euler's equation reduces to

$$\left.\begin{array}{l} \dfrac{V^2}{2} + \displaystyle\int \dfrac{1}{\rho}\dfrac{\partial p}{\partial s}\,ds + gh = \text{constant} \\[4mm] \dfrac{V_2^2 - V_1^2}{2} + \displaystyle\int_1^2 \dfrac{1}{\rho}\dfrac{\partial p}{\partial s}\,ds + g(h_2 - h_1) = 0 \end{array}\right\} \qquad (4.7)$$

or

A fluid is said to be homogeneous if the density is a function only of pressure. Experience shows that in most problems of interest to mechanical engineers the working fluid is homogeneous, so that the second term of Eq. (4.7) can be integrated. The so-called "polytropic formula" usually applies, $p/\rho^n = p_0/\rho_0^n$, where n is a constant and p_0 and ρ_0 are the pressure and density at a specified point.

4.5. Bernoulli's Formula. For liquids and for gases where high pressures and velocities are not involved the density can be assumed to remain constant to a good approximation. In the case of steady motion of an incompressible fluid, Euler's equation is further simplified to the relation between velocity, pressure, and elevation attributed to Daniel Bernoulli and known in hydraulics as Bernoulli's formula. Bernoulli is considered to be the father of hydraulics, largely as a result of the clarification of hydraulic phenomena that followed the application of this formula.

Making ρ constant in the steady-flow form of Euler's equation, we find

$$\left.\begin{array}{l} \dfrac{1}{2} V^2 + \dfrac{p}{\rho} + gh = \text{constant} \\[2em] \dfrac{1}{2}(V_2^2 - V_1^2) + \dfrac{p_2 - p_1}{\rho} + g(h_2 - h_1) = 0 \end{array}\right\} \qquad (4.8)$$

or

It should be noted particularly that the Euler equation and the Bernoulli formula as well apply to the one streamline along which the integration is taken. For another streamline the constant may have a different value. In the special case for which the streamlines start in a reservoir where V, ρ, p, and h are the same for all, the constant will be the same for all streamlines. Likewise, in a hydraulic system where all the fluid passes through some region, such as an inlet pipe where ρ, p, h, and V are constant across the section, the same constant applies to all streamlines. In the case of a mass of fluid rotating like a rigid body it will be shown later that the constant varies with the distance from the axis of rotation. Such change is to be expected since both the velocity and the pressure are greater for a greater radius.

4.6. Interpretation of the Equations of Motion. In Eq. (4.7) each term has the dimensions of work or energy per unit mass. Since $-(1/\rho)(\partial p/\partial s)$ is the pressure force on unit mass in the s direction, $-(1/\rho)(\partial p/\partial s)\,ds$ is the work done by the pressure force on unit mass of fluid as it moves a distance ds. Similarly, $-g(\partial h/\partial s)\,ds$ is the work done by gravity on unit mass during the same motion. For steady flow the corresponding change in kinetic energy of unit mass is $V(\partial V/\partial s)\,ds = [\partial(V^2/2)/\partial s]\,ds$. Equation (4.7), therefore, states that in steady flow of an ideal fluid the change in kinetic energy of unit mass between any two positions equals the work done on the mass by pressure and gravity forces. The Bernoulli formula [Eq. (4.8)] is the same statement for unit mass of incompressible fluid.

Since the work done by gravity on a given mass depends only on the initial and final levels, we can assign to the mass a "gravity potential energy," the change in which between any two levels is defined as the negative of the work done by gravity. An alternative statement of Eq. (4.7) is, therefore, that the sum of the changes in kinetic and potential energy equals the work done on the unit mass by the pressure force.

4.7. Applications of Bernoulli's Equation. The examples discussed here are ones in which friction is known from experiment to play only a minor role. Therefore, the results given by Bernoulli's equation require only small corrections, even if high precision is necessary.

a. *Sharp-edged Circular Orifice.* In Fig. 4.4 is shown a tank in which the water level is maintained at a height h above the center of a sharp-edged circular orifice. The cross section of the tank is so large that the velocity is negligible, except near the outlet. Bernoulli's equation [Eq. (4.8)] can be applied between the water surface 1 and the section of minimum jet diameter 2. The result is that

$$V_2 = \sqrt{2gh} \qquad (4.9)$$

which is called "Torricelli's formula," after Torricelli, who discovered it in 1640, a century before Bernoulli's equation was known.

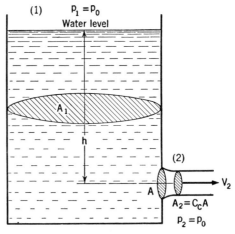

Fig. 4.4. — Steady flow out of a tank.

The jet reaches its minimum cross section, the "vena contracta," at a distance of about one orifice diameter from the outlet. The "contraction coefficient" C_c is equal to A_2/A, by definition. The experimental value of C_c, found by measuring the jet diameter, is about 0.61 or 0.62, which checks well with the value 0.61, obtained by ideal-fluid theory.

If frictional effects were wholly negligible, the discharge rate $Q = A_2 V_2$ would be equal to $C_c A \sqrt{2gh}$. Experiment shows, however, that Q is slightly less than $C_c A \sqrt{2gh}$. It is customary to define a "discharge coefficient" C_d by the formula

$$Q = C_d A \sqrt{2gh} \qquad (4.10)$$

The average of many experiments on water at ordinary temperatures indicates that the best value of C_d is about 0.60, provided that $h \geqslant 1.5$ ft and the orifice diameter $d \geqslant 0.2$ ft. The value of C_d increases if these limits are exceeded or if the kinematic viscosity of the liquid is increased.

Comparison of Eqs. (4.9) and (4.10) shows that a "velocity coefficient" C_v should be introduced into Eq. (4.9) to account for the effect of friction on the velocity.

$$V_2 = C_v \sqrt{2gh} \qquad (4.11)$$

The value of C_v is found to lie between 0.98 and 0.99.

Gravity causes the jet to bend downward soon after leaving the orifice; the path of the stream being approximately a parabola. We have, however, assumed that the effect of gravity on the velocity and pressure in the vena contracta is negligible. This assumption is justifiable only if $d\sqrt{C_c}\, g/V_2^2$ is small compared with unity, as can be shown by writing

Bernoulli's equation for the highest and lowest points of the vena contracta. Experiment shows that errors caused by gravity are negligible provided that $d\sqrt{C_c}\,g/V_2^2 \leqslant 0.2$.

If there is no inflow to maintain the level in the tank constant, the time t needed for the head to be reduced from h_0 to h is found from the fact that $Q = -A_1(dh/dt) = A_2V_2$. The acceleration at a fixed point caused by the decreasing head is very small compared with the acceleration of the fluid approaching the outlet. Thus, although the flow is not perfectly steady, Eq. (4.11) applies, since $\partial V/\partial t$ is negligible. Using the value of V_2 from Eq. (4.11) one finds $-dh/dt = (A_2/A_1)C_v\sqrt{2gh} = (AC_c/A_1)C_v\sqrt{2gh} = (AC_d/A_1)\sqrt{2gh}$. Integrating and solving for t,

$$t = \sqrt{\frac{2}{g}}\frac{A_1}{AC_d}h_0^{1/2}\left[1 - \left(\frac{h}{h_0}\right)^{1/2}\right] \tag{4.12}$$

b. *Pitot Tube.* A small tube pointing directly upstream and connected to a manometer, as shown in Fig. 4.5, provides a means for measuring the velocity anywhere in a straight parallel flow. Such an instrument is called

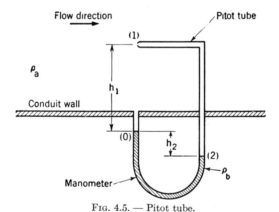

FIG. 4.5. — Pitot tube.

a "pitot tube," after its inventor Pitot, who performed his experiments about the year 1732.

The Bernoulli constant at an arbitrary point 1 is unaffected by the presence of the pitot tube, but the velocity there is reduced to zero (stagnation point). Equating the Bernoulli constants at 1 for the two conditions, with and without the tube, and letting primed symbols represent values with the tube in place, we find

$$\frac{p_1}{\rho_a} + \frac{V_1^2}{2} + gh_1 = \frac{p_1'}{\rho_a} + \frac{V_1'^2}{2} + gh_1$$

whence, since $V_1' = 0$,

$$V_1 = \sqrt{\frac{2}{\rho_a}(p_1' - p_1)} \tag{4.13}$$

By use of Eq. (4.4) the pressure difference $p_1' - p_1$ can be expressed in terms of the manometer reading h_2 and the fluid densities ρ_a and ρ_b. Let the pitot tube be removed from the flow. Then for any direction n, lying in a vertical plane perpendicular to the streamlines and passing through 1, Eq. (4.4) reduces to $(1/\rho_a)(\partial p/\partial n) + g(\partial h/\partial n) = 0$, since the radius of curvature R is infinite.* The pressure is seen to vary hydrostatically over the section. The pressure near the small opening in the conduit wall is unaffected by the pitot tube, and the pressure varies hydrostatically inside the tube and the manometer. The pressure at point 0 is thus equal to $p_1 + \rho_a g h_1$, provided that the manometer-tube opening is flush with the conduit wall, so that no disturbance is set up at this point. The pressure at point 2 is $p_1' + \rho_a g(h_1 - h_2)$; and $p_1' - p_1 = g h_2(\rho_b - \rho_a)$ $= \rho_b g h_2[1 - (\rho_a/\rho_b)]$. Equation (4.13), therefore, becomes

$$V_1 = \sqrt{2gh_2 \frac{\rho_b}{\rho_a}\left(1 - \frac{\rho_a}{\rho_b}\right)} \tag{4.14}$$

If the ratio ρ_a/ρ_b is negligible compared with unity, as for an airflow measured by a water manometer, Eq. (4.14) simplifies to

$$V_1 = \sqrt{2gh_2 \frac{\rho_b}{\rho_a}} \tag{4.15}$$

c. *Pitot-static Tube.* The pitot-static tube shown in Fig. 4.6 has both an impact-pressure opening $1'$ and a static-pressure opening 1. Between 1 and $1'$, differences in level and effects of friction are negligible. At point $1'$ the velocity is zero, while for a properly designed instrument the velocity at 1 is that of the undisturbed stream. Bernoulli's equation yields

$$V_1 = \sqrt{\frac{2}{\rho_a}(p_1' - p_1)}$$

Inside the tube the velocity is everywhere zero, and the hydrostatic equation applies, so that

$$p_1' - p_1 = gh_2\rho_b\left(1 - \frac{\rho_a}{\rho_b}\right)$$

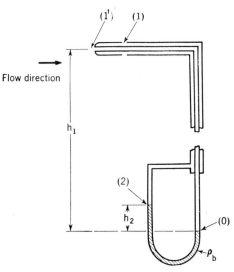

Fig. 4.6. — Pitot-static tube.

* This demonstration is valid only in the absence of friction, since it is based on Eq. (4.4); but the result holds also for a real fluid, as is shown both by experiment and theory.

The relation between the stream velocity and the manometer reading is the same as for the pitot tube.

Equation (4.15), which applies to both the pitot tube and the pitot-static tube, requires no empirical correction. Properly designed instruments can be used without calibration.

4.8. Application of Euler's Equation.   In this article Euler's equation [Eq. (4.7)] will be applied to computation of the pressure at a stagnation

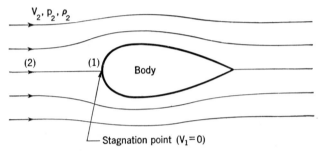

V_2, p_2, ρ_2

(2)   (1)   Body

Stagnation point ($V_1 = 0$)

FIG. 4.7. — Body immersed in a steady parallel flow.

point on a body immersed in a steady flow of compressible fluid that has a uniform parallel velocity distribution far from the body. Changes in elevation will be neglected.

Referring to Fig. 4.7, we see that Eq. (4.7) reduces to

$$\frac{V_2^2}{2} + \int_1^2 \frac{dp}{\rho} = 0 \qquad (4.7a)$$

In this equation the symbol dp is used as an abbreviation of $(\partial p / \partial s)\, ds$ to denote the difference in pressure between two points near together on the same streamline.

It has been found that in such a flow the compression of the fluid is adiabatic and frictionless. In this case the exponent in the polytropic equation is equal to k.

$$\frac{p}{\rho^k} = \text{constant} = \frac{p_2}{\rho_2^k}$$

Combining this equation with Eq. (4.7a) and integrating, we obtain

$$\frac{V_2^2}{2} + \frac{p_2}{\rho_2}\frac{k}{k-1}\left[1 - \left(\frac{p_1}{p_2}\right)^{(k-1)/k}\right] = 0$$

It will be shown in Chap. VII that the square of the sound velocity in the undisturbed stream C_2^2 is equal to $p_2 k / \rho_2$. Making this substitution, solving for p_1/p_2, and expanding by means of the binomial theorem one finds that

$$\frac{p_1}{p_2} = \left[1 + \frac{k-1}{2}\left(\frac{V_2}{C_2}\right)^2\right]^{k/k-1}$$

$$= 1 + \frac{k}{2}\left(\frac{V_2}{C_2}\right)^2 + \frac{k}{8}\left(\frac{V_2}{C_2}\right)^4 + \frac{k(2-k)}{48}\left(\frac{V_2}{C_2}\right)^6 + \cdots$$

$$p_1 - p_2 = \frac{p_2 k}{2}\left(\frac{V_2}{C_2}\right)^2\left[1 + \frac{1}{4}\left(\frac{V_2}{C_2}\right)^2 + \frac{2-k}{24}\left(\frac{V_2}{C_2}\right)^4 + \cdots\right]$$

$$\frac{p_1 - p_2}{(\rho_2/2)V_2^2} = 1 + \frac{1}{4}\left(\frac{V_2}{C_2}\right)^2 + \frac{2-k}{24}\left(\frac{V_2}{C_2}\right)^4 + \cdots \tag{4.16}$$

Equation (4.16) shows, if V_2/C_2 is small compared with unity, that $(p_1 - p_2)/(\rho_2/2) V_2^2 = 1$, which is the result obtained for an incompressible fluid. The ratio V_2/C_2 is known as the Mach number, after one of the pioneer investigators of high-speed gas flow; it will be further discussed in later chapters.

Equation (4.16) may be used to calculate the relation between the pressure difference $p_1 - p_2$, measured by a pitot-static tube, and the velocity of the undisturbed stream V_2. In this connection the following table is of interest; it has been computed from Eq. (4.16) with $k = 1.4$ (the value for air). The table shows that for most purposes compressibility has a negligible effect on the pitot-static tube reading, if the velocity does not exceed two-tenths of the sound velocity.

$\dfrac{V_2}{C_2}$	0.1	0.2	0.3	0.4	0.5
$\dfrac{p_1 - p_2}{(\rho_2/2)V_2^2}$	1.003	1.010	1.023	1.041	1.064

4.9. Curved Streamlines. Many phenomena in fluid mechanics are marked by a whirling of the fluid in circular paths, and typical effects to be accounted for are the high discharge pressure available in a centrifugal pump, the depression in the surface of water at the center of a whirlpool, the tendency of eddies and smoke rings to persist, and the difficulty of forcing a fluid to flow around a sharp corner.

In discussing these phenomena, the concepts of irrotational and rotational motion are indispensable. These ideas will be developed in the following sections for two-dimensional continuous motion of an ideal incompressible fluid.

4.10. Irrotational Motion. The question naturally arises here as to the conditions under which the Bernoulli constant has the same value for all points in a two-dimensional flow. The answer to this question, which is developed below, leads to the very important concept of irrotational motion.

A general criterion for the uniformity of Bernoulli's constant can be developed by combining Eqs. (4.4) and (4.8). For steady flow, Eq. (4.4) reduces to

$$\frac{1}{\rho}\frac{\partial p}{\partial n} + g\frac{\partial h}{\partial n} + \frac{V^2}{R} = 0 \qquad (4.4a)$$

If the Bernoulli constant, or "total head" (dimensions in foot-pounds per pound), is represented by H, Eq. (4.8) becomes

$$\frac{p}{\rho} + gh + \frac{V^2}{2} = gH$$

Differentiate this equation with respect to n, the direction normal to the streamline, bearing in mind that H depends only on n.

$$\frac{1}{\rho}\frac{\partial p}{\partial n} + g\frac{\partial h}{\partial n} + V\frac{\partial V}{\partial n} = g\frac{\partial H}{\partial n} = g\frac{dH}{dn} \qquad (4.17)$$

Combine Eqs. (4.4a) and (4.17).

$$\frac{V}{R} - \frac{\partial V}{\partial n} = -g\frac{dH}{V\,dn} \qquad (4.18)$$

Equation (4.18) shows that the necessary and sufficient condition for H to be constant is

$$\frac{V}{R} - \frac{\partial V}{\partial n} = 0 \qquad (4.19)$$

The expression $(V/R) - (\partial V/\partial n)$ is called the "rotation" of the fluid at a point. Wherever Eq. (4.19) is satisfied, the motion is said to be irrotational; if it is satisfied everywhere, the entire flow is called an "irrotational flow." The reason for the name rotation is given below.

If a short segment of a fluid line is drawn parallel to V, as in Fig. 4.8a, its counterclockwise angular velocity is found to be

$$\omega_{1,2} = \frac{V(ds/2R) + V(ds/2R)}{ds} = \frac{V}{R}$$

Similarly, for the fluid-line segment normal to V in Fig. 4.8b, the counterclockwise angular velocity is

$$\omega_{3,4} = -\frac{(\partial V/\partial n)(dn/2) + (\partial V/\partial n)(dn/2)}{dn} = -\frac{\partial V}{\partial n}$$

The rotation of the fluid at O is defined as the sum of the velocities of the two line segments.

$$\text{Rotation} = \omega_{1,2} + \omega_{3,4} = \frac{V}{R} - \frac{\partial V}{\partial n}$$

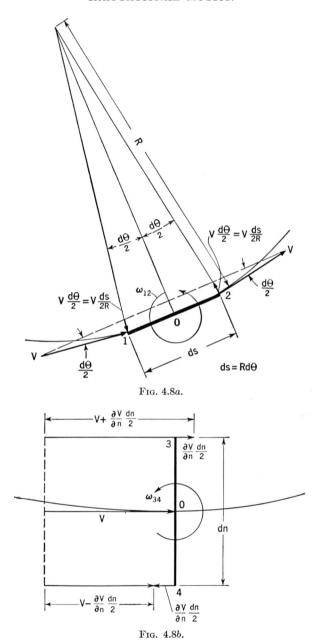

Fig. 4.8a.

Fig. 4.8b.

We note here, without proof, that the rotation has the same value for all pairs of perpendicular line segments drawn in the fluid at O. In other words, it is invariant with respect to orientation of axes. The rotation may therefore be considered as a measure of the angular velocity of the fluid at a point. It is seen that, in general, the net angular velocity may be taken as one-half of the rotation. Equation (4.19) shows that in irrotational motion the two fluid lines turn in opposite directions at equal speeds, so that the particle as a whole is deformed but does not rotate. In other words, its net angular velocity is zero.

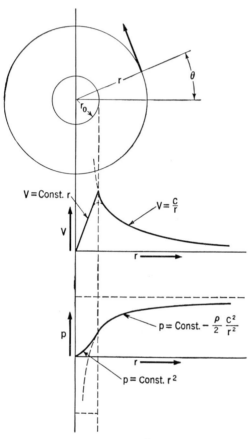

In the application of Bernoulli's equation to flow in ducts and channels in which friction is neglected, the fluid is tacitly assumed to issue from one large reservoir in which the velocity is negligible. The total head H is, therefore, the same for all streamlines, and the motion is irrotational.

4.11. Potential Vortex. One of the most important examples of an irrotational flow is the potential vortex, also called a "free" vortex, since it can exist in a free flow far from any boundaries. A two-dimensional vortex is defined as a whirling mass of fluid with concentric circular streamlines. Continuity shows that the velocity is the same everywhere on one

Fig. 4.9. — Potential vortex.

streamline, because the area of any stream tube is constant along its entire length. The law for the variation of velocity from streamline to streamline is found from Eq. (4.19), as follows:

At an arbitrary point r, θ, in Fig. 4.9, the radius of curvature $R = r$; and $\partial V / \partial n = - \partial V / \partial r = - dV / dr$, since $dr = - dn$ and V is a function of r only. Equation (4.19) reduces to

$$\frac{V}{R} - \frac{\partial V}{\partial n} = \frac{V}{r} + \frac{dV}{dr} = 0$$

whence

$$Vr = \text{constant} = C \tag{4.20}$$

The pressure can be obtained by combining Eqs. (4.8) and (4.20).

$$p + \frac{\rho}{2}V^2 + \rho g h = p + \frac{\rho}{2}\frac{C^2}{r^2} + \rho g h = \rho g H \tag{4.21}$$

If the streamlines lie in a horizontal plane, h is constant, and

$$p = \text{constant} - \frac{\rho}{2}\frac{C^2}{r^2} \tag{4.22}$$

These velocity and pressure distributions are shown in Fig. 4.9.

Since infinite velocities do not occur in nature, the velocity distribution for a free vortex in a real fluid cannot obey Eq. (4.20) near the origin, where friction is dominant. There is a gradual transition from the hyperbolic distribution to a linear one, characteristic of a rotating solid. The zone of transition is usually neglected and the distribution assumed to be as shown by the heavy line in Fig. 4.9. As discussed in Art. 2.19, the pressure distribution in the rotating core (radius r_0) is parabolic.

A tornado is a free vortex set up in the atmosphere. The low pressure in the core gives rise to a waterspout or a "dust devil," depending on whether the tornado moves over water or land.

As will be discussed in Chap. XI, a vortex called a "trailing" vortex is shed from the tip of an airplane wing. If atmospheric conditions are favorable, the low temperature accompanying the low pressure in the core causes condensation of water vapor, so that the core can be seen.

A trailing vortex also appears at the tip of a propeller blade. In a water tunnel for testing model ships' propellers, the low pressure in the cores of the trailing vortices causes air to come out of solution, making the vortex system visible in the water. When viewed by stroboscopic light, a silvery helix seems to spring from each apparently motionless blade tip.

The depression of the surface of a whirlpool is easily explained by use of Eq. (4.21). Atmospheric pressure p_0 exists at the free surface, so that the surface elevation h is

$$h = H - \frac{p_0}{\rho g} - \frac{1}{2g}\frac{C^2}{r^2} = \text{constant} - \frac{1}{2g}\frac{C^2}{r^2} \tag{4.23}$$

Comparison of Eqs. (4.22) and (4.23) indicates that h varies with r in the same way as the pressure at a constant level. A curve of h versus r thus has the same shape as the p versus r curve of Fig. 4.9. It is seen that the finite depth of the depression results from the finite core diameter.

4.12. Rotational Motion. The expression $(V/R) - (\partial V/\partial n)$, which is a measure of the rate of rotation of a fluid particle, is called rotation or "vorticity." The latter term arises from the fact that the angular speed of a free-vortex core, together with the core radius, determines the value of the product Vr, characterizing the vortex.

For rotation like a rigid body the value of $(V/R) - (\partial V/\partial n)$ is every-where the same and equal to twice the angular velocity ω of the fluid. This kind of motion has already been discussed in Chap. II and the pressure distribution shown to be

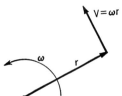

Fig. 4.10.

$$\frac{p}{\rho} - \frac{\omega^2 r^2}{2} + gh = \text{constant}$$

This relation can also be deduced from Eqs. (4.18) and (4.8) and Fig. 4.10 as follows: From Eq. (4.18),

$$\frac{V}{R} - \frac{\partial V}{\partial n} = 2\omega = -g\frac{dH}{V\,dn} = \frac{g\,dH}{\omega r\,dr}$$

Therefore,

$$gH = \omega^2 r^2 + \text{constant}$$

Substituting this value of gH in Eq. (4.8), we get

$$\frac{p}{\rho} + gh + \frac{\omega^2 r^2}{2} = \omega^2 r^2 + \text{constant}$$

or

$$\frac{p}{\rho} + gh - \frac{\omega^2 r^2}{2} = \text{constant} \qquad (4.24)$$

A practical example of such a flow occurs in a centrifugal pump with the discharge valve closed, as shown in Fig. 4.11. The blades constrain the water in the impeller to revolve with the speed ω of the shaft. Neglecting any change in level between the inner and outer radii of the impeller, we find from Eq. (4.24)

$$p_2 - p_1 = \frac{\rho}{2}\,\omega^2\,(r_2^2 - r_1^2)$$

These concepts of vorticity and irrotational and rotational motion will be given further application in the discussions of wing theory and hydraulic machinery.

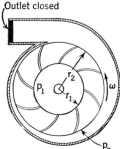

Fig. 4.11. — Centrifugal pump.

CHAPTER V

ENERGY RELATIONS FOR STEADY FLOW

The relationship involving pressure, velocity, and elevation given by Euler or Bernoulli was deduced on the assumption of a frictionless fluid, no account being taken of the frictional effects that actually occur. Nor was the possibility considered of work being done on or by the fluid through the action of moving vanes, as in a pump or turbine.

In many types of apparatus for which the mechanical engineer is responsible both these things must be taken into account. Hydraulic turbines, pumps, fans, compressors, fluid couplings, pipe lines, nozzles, and orifices are familiar examples. In a turbine the flow rotates the runner and causes work to be done on any apparatus connected to the turbine shaft. In a centrifugal pump the flow is the result of work done in turning the pump shaft. Work of this kind will be called "shaft work." In pipe lines, nozzles, or orifices no shaft work is done, but energy is dissipated by the action of viscosity.

Energy considerations are best analyzed in the light of the first law of thermodynamics, which we apply in this chapter to apparatus involving the steady flow of a real fluid. No further assumptions are made as to the nature of the apparatus or as to the character of the flow. As a result of the analysis a steady-flow energy equation is developed that will be found a useful tool in many practical problems of mechanical engineering.

5.1. First Law of Thermodynamics. This law, which, like all the generalizations of science, is based on experience, may be formulated as follows: The difference between the heat added to a system of masses and the work done by the system depends only on the initial and final states of the system.* This difference is, therefore, an attribute or property of the system and is called the "internal energy."

It should be emphasized that neither the heat added nor the work done is a property but depends on the path or process followed, as well as on the end states of the system.

The first law may be written symbolically as

$$\text{Heat} - \text{work} = E_b - E_a \tag{5.1}$$

where *heat* and *work* represent, respectively, the heat added to and work done by a system as it passes from state a to state b and $E_b - E_a$ is the corresponding change in the internal energy of the system.

* For definitions of heat and work, see, for example, reference 2 at the end of this chapter.

As it stands, Eq. (5.1) is difficult to apply to fluid-flow problems. We shall therefore change it to a more convenient form by the procedure used in Art. 3.6 for the equation of continuity.

5.2. Steady-flow Energy Equation. We apply Eq. (5.1) to a mass system defined as the matter lying within a fixed control volume $\mathcal{V}$ at an arbitrary time t_a (Fig. 5.1a). We consider the change in state of this system

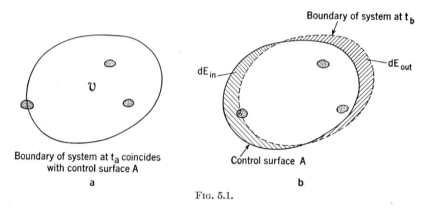

Boundary of system at t_b

dE_{in} — — dE_{out}

$\mathcal{V}$

Boundary of system at t_a coincides with control surface A

Control surface A

a   b

FIG. 5.1.

during a time interval $dt = t_b - t_a$. The boundary of the system at time t_b will, in general, no longer coincide with the control surface A but will be as shown by the dotted line in Fig. 5.1b.

The internal energy of that part of the system lying outside of $\mathcal{V}$ at t_b we call dE_{out}, and the internal energy of the new matter inside of $\mathcal{V}$ at t_b but not included in the system we call dE_{in}. Representing the internal energy of all the matter inside $\mathcal{V}$ at any time by E' we write the initial and final energies of the system, respectively,

$$E_a = E_a' \quad \text{and} \quad E_b = E_b' + dE_{out} - dE_{in}$$

or

$$E_b - E_a = E_b' - E_a' + dE_{out} - dE_{in} \tag{5.2}$$

The change of energy of the system is thus expressed as the sum of the change inside the control volume and the net outflow of energy through the control surface.

Referring to Art. 3.6 and Fig. 3.4 we find that the flow of mass in time dt across an element dA of the control surface is $\rho V \cos \alpha \, dA \, dt$. Multiplication of this expression by the internal energy per unit mass e yields the energy carried across dA by the mass flow in time dt. Accordingly, the net outflow of energy across A is

$$dE_{out} - dE_{in} = dt \int_A \rho e V \cos \alpha \, dA \tag{5.3}$$

Turning next to the work term of Eq. (5.1) we assume a mechanical system, for which we can write

$$\text{Work} = \text{pressure work} + \text{shear work} \tag{5.4}$$

where the terms on the right stand for the work done by the pressure and shearing forces exerted at the boundary on the surroundings. We adopt here the point of view mentioned in Art. 4.6 and take gravity into account through the potential energy of the system. Therefore, gravity work is omitted from Eq. (5.4).

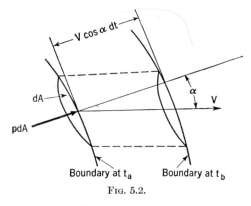

The pressure work done in time dt by a surface element of the system is seen from Fig. 5.2 to be $p\,dA\,V\cos\alpha\,dt$, where $p\,dA$ is the force on the element dA of the boundary at time t_a and $V\cos\alpha\,dt$ is the distance moved by this element normal to itself. The slight change in $p\,dA$ occurring during the motion is of higher order and may be neglected. Since dA is identical with an element of the control surface, the pressure work done by the system over its whole boundary is

$$\text{Pressure work} = dt \int_A pV \cos\alpha\,dA \tag{5.5}$$

Combining Eqs. (5.1) to (5.5) we get, after dividing through by dt,

$$\frac{\text{Heat}}{dt} - \frac{\text{shear work}}{dt} = \frac{E_b' - E_a'}{dt} + \int_A \left(\frac{p}{\rho} + e\right)\rho V \cos\alpha\,dA \tag{5.6}$$

Experience shows that, in the absence of electricity, magnetism, and capillarity, e is the sum of three kinds of energy. Two of these, the potential energy and the kinetic energy, have already been discussed in Art. 4.6. The third kind is called the "intrinsic energy" and is denoted by u (energy/mass).* We may thus write

$$e = gz + \frac{V^2}{2} + u \tag{5.7}$$

where z is the elevation above an arbitrary datum level, so that Eq. (5.6) becomes

$$\frac{\text{Heat}}{dt} - \frac{\text{shear work}}{dt} = \frac{E_b' - E_a'}{dt} + \int_A \left(\frac{p}{\rho} + gz + \frac{V^2}{2} + u\right)\rho V \cos\alpha\,dA \tag{5.8}$$

---

* Changes in the intrinsic energy are explained by atomic theory as changes in the kinetic and potential energy of molecules and of atoms. Measurements of intrinsic energy changes have played an important role in the development of this theory.

Let us consider only systems for which all parts of the control surface not at fixed walls are normal to the velocity of any fluid crossing the surface and to the axis of any shaft crossing the surface. Such a system is shown in Fig. 5.3. The shear work done over the cross section of the rotating

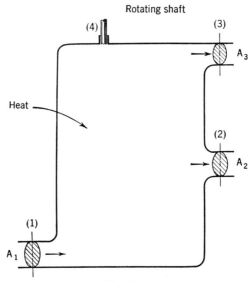

FIG. 5.3.

shaft at 4 is called the shaft work. The shear work done at all other parts of the boundary is zero, because the velocity is either zero or normal to the shearing force. For steady flow $E_b' - E_a' = 0$. Thus, from Eq. (5.8),

$$\frac{\text{Heat}}{dt} - \frac{\text{shaft work}}{dt} = \int_{A_1+A_2+A_3}\left(\frac{p}{\rho} + gz + \frac{V^2}{2} + u\right)\rho V\, dA \qquad (5.9)$$

In the usual case, for which the flow crosses the control surface at only two areas A_1 and A_2, over each of which $(p/\rho) + gz$, V, ρ, and u have uniform values, continuity gives $\rho_1 A_1 V_1 = \rho_2 A_2 V_2$, and Eq. (5.9) becomes

$$q - \mathcal{W}_s = \frac{p_2}{\rho_2} - \frac{p_1}{\rho_1} + g(z_2 - z_1) + \frac{V_2^2 - V_1^2}{2} + u_2 - u_1 \qquad (5.10)$$

where

$$q = \text{heat}/\rho_1 A_1 V_1\, dt \qquad \text{and} \qquad \mathcal{W}_s = \text{shaft work}/\rho_1 A_1 V_1\, dt.$$

The symbols q and $\mathcal{W}_s$ thus stand, respectively, for the heat entering and the shaft work leaving the system, both being referred to unit mass of the flowing fluid.

5.3. Energy Equation for Cyclic Flow. In any machine doing positive or negative shaft work, the flow in the neighborhood of the moving blades or pistons is cyclic, rather than steady. The state of the fluid varies periodically at any fixed point with a period T that is the same throughout the neighborhood.

Select a control surface as described above to eliminate the shear work, and assume as before that conditions are constant where the fluid crosses the control surface. Average Eq. (5.8) over a period by integrating with respect to time between the limits 0 and T and then dividing by T. Since the flow is cyclic, the term

$$\frac{1}{T}\int_0^T \frac{E'_b - E'_a}{dt}\, dt = \frac{E'(T) - E'(0)}{T} = 0$$

and the resulting equation will be similar to Eq. (5.9) or (5.10). These equations are, accordingly, applicable to machines in which the flow is cyclic.

5.4. Relation between the Energy Equation and the Euler Equation. In the stream tube of ideal fluid shown in Fig. 5.4 no shaft work is done. Noting that

$$\frac{p_2}{\rho_2} - \frac{p_1}{\rho_1} = \int_1^2 d\frac{p}{\rho} = \int_1^2 \frac{dp}{\rho} + \int_1^2 pd\,\frac{1}{\rho}$$

where the integration is along the streamline we write Eq. (5.10) as

$$\int_1^2 \frac{dp}{\rho} + \frac{V_2^2 - V_1^2}{2} + g(z_2 - z_1) + \int_1^2 pd\,\frac{1}{\rho} + u_2 - u_1 - q = 0 \quad (5.11)$$

The first three terms of Eq. (5.11) may be set equal to zero by virtue of Euler's equation [Eq. (4.7)].

An observer moving along the stream tube with the fluid would see a

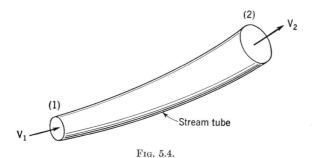

FIG. 5.4.

certain change in state of unit mass during his journey from 1 to 2. The only work done by the ideal fluid would be caused by changes in volume (or density), that is, $\int_1^2 pd\,(1/\rho)$. The apparent energy change would be $u_2 - u_1$, since the fluid would be at rest from the viewpoint of the observer. Consequently, he would write the first law of thermodynamics for unit mass as

$$q - \int_1^2 pd\,\frac{1}{\rho} = u_2 - u_1 \tag{5.12}$$

which is the remainder of Eq. (5.11).

The energy equation is seen to be the sum of two independent equations, one derived from mechanics and the other from thermodynamics.

It may be noted in this connection that the more general equation, Eq. (5.8), can be derived by applying Newton's second law and the first law of thermodynamics to a particle of matter, adding the results, and integrating throughout a finite control volume.

5.5. Applications of the Energy Equation. *a. Frictionless Machine.* Consider for simplicity the type of machine shown in Fig. 5.5, to which

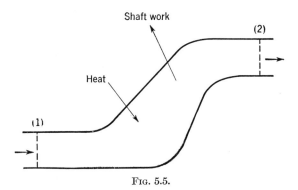

Fig. 5.5.

Eq. (5.10) applies. Breaking up the pressure-work term as in the preceding article and noting that Eq. (5.12) is valid in the absence of friction, we reduce Eq. (5.10) to the form

$$-\mathcal{W}_s = \int_1^2 \frac{dp}{\rho} + \frac{V_2^2 - V_1^2}{2} + g(z_2 - z_1) \tag{5.13}$$

The terms on the right side are those occurring in the Euler equation. In this case, however, instead of being equal to zero, the sum of these terms is the shaft work done on the machine by external means.

It may be mentioned that Eq. (5.13) can be deduced from Newton's laws alone, without reference to the first law of thermodynamics. The derivation is, however, more complicated than the one given here.

For an incompressible fluid, $\int_1^2 dp/\rho = (p_2 - p_1)/\rho$, and Eq. (5.13) states that the shaft work equals the difference between the Bernoulli numbers at exit and entrance.

b. *Machine with Real Working Fluid.* For simplicity we take into account only the friction in the working fluid, neglecting, for example, any bearing friction or windage. We also assume incompressibility.

Referring to Fig. 5.6, consider first the pump, which is lifting fluid

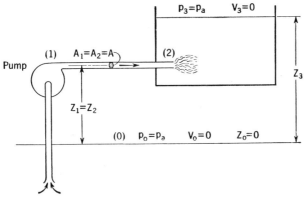

$$P_3 = P_a \qquad V_3 = 0$$

(1) $A_1 = A_2 = A$ (2)

Pump

$Z_1 = Z_2$

Z_3

(0) $P_0 = P_a$ $V_0 = 0$ $Z_0 = 0$

Fig. 5.6.

steadily from one reservoir to another. Equation (5.10) applied between sections 0 and 1 yields

$$- \mathfrak{W}_s = \frac{p_1 - p_a}{\rho} + \frac{V_1^2}{2} + gz_1 + u_1 - u_0 - q_{0,1} \tag{5.14}$$

From Eq. (5.12) or by comparing Eqs. (5.13) and (5.14) we see that $u_1 - u_0 - q_{0,1} = 0$ for a *frictionless* incompressible fluid. The behavior of this expression for a *viscous* incompressible fluid will now be discussed.

For any working fluid * with which we deal we assume that a property, such as internal energy or pressure, is determined when two independent properties, such as density and temperature, have given values. For the incompressible case, therefore, internal energy depends only on temperature. As the working fluid flows through the pump, it undergoes shearing deformation, since the fluid in contact with a solid surface does not slip. Shearing stresses are set up in the viscous fluid as a result of these deformations, and the temperature rises above the value it would have in frictionless flow. This temperature rise tends to increase both $u_1 - u_0$ and the heat $- q_{0,1}$ transferred to the surroundings. The expression $u_1 - u_0 - q_{0,1}$ is, therefore, positive in a flow with friction. It is often referred to as the "loss" and denoted by $g^H{}_{l_{0,1}}$.

It is to be emphasized that these statements concerning $u_1 - u_0 - q_{0,1}$ are restricted to incompressible fluid.

---

* We assume the fluid to be a thermodynamically pure substance. For a definition of such a substance see reference 2 at the end of this chapter.

The efficiency of the pump is defined as the ratio of the shaft work in the frictionless case to that with friction. From Eqs. (5.13) and (5.14) we get

$$\text{Efficiency} = \eta = \frac{[(p_1 - p_0)/\rho] + (V_1^2/2) + gz_1}{-\mathcal{W}_s} = 1 - \frac{u_1 - u_0 - q_{0,1}}{-\mathcal{W}_s} \quad (5.15)$$

The efficiency is less than 1 for a real fluid and equal to 1 in the limiting case of no friction.

Turning now to the flow in the pipe between sections (1) and (2) we get from Eq. (5.10)

$$\frac{p_1 - p_2}{\rho} = u_2 - u_1 - q_{1,2} \quad (5.16)$$

The pressure work done on the fluid in the pipe is entirely used in overcoming the effects of friction.

Finally, applying Eq. (5.10) between sections 2 and 3, we find that $[(p_2 - p_3)/\rho] + g(z_2 - z_3) + (V_2^2/2) = u_3 - u_2 - q_{2,3}$. Furthermore, since the fluid is incompressible, no discontinuity in pressure occurs and the pressure of the jet emerging from the pipe must be the same as that of the surrounding fluid. Consequently, $[(p_2 - p_3)/\rho] + g(z_2 - z_3) = 0$ and

$$\frac{V_2^2}{2} = u_3 - u_2 - q_{2,3} \quad (5.17)$$

All the kinetic energy of the stream at 2 is dissipated in the tank. The surface of discontinuity in velocity that bounds the emergent jet is unstable and breaks down into large eddies, which, in turn, give rise to smaller and smaller eddies, until finally no observable motion remains.

5.6. Energy Equation for Moving Axes. So far in this chapter we have supposed the axes, or frame of reference, to be at rest. Due caution must be observed if the reference frame is moving, since the energy equation is based in part on Newton's laws, which in the form given here apply only for axes at rest or in uniform motion. The energy equations given above are, therefore, valid unless the frame of reference is accelerated.

Only one sort of accelerated frame of reference will be considered in this text, viz., one that rotates at a constant speed about a fixed axis (see Art. 6.8). Applications will be made to rotating machinery.

SELECTED BIBLIOGRAPHY

1. Gibbs, J. W.: "Collected Works," Vol. I, Longmans, Green and Company, New York, 1931.
2. Keenan, J. H.: "Thermodynamics," John Wiley & Sons, Inc., New York, 1940.
3. O'Brien, M. P., and G. H. Hickox: "Applied Fluid Mechanics," McGraw-Hill Book Company, Inc., New York, 1937.
4. Planck, Max: "Thermodynamik," 9th ed., Walter de Gruyter & Company, Berlin, 1930.

CHAPTER VI

MOMENTUM RELATIONS FOR STEADY FLOW

In many engineering problems, the force or torque produced on a solid body by a steadily flowing fluid is of great importance. Familiar examples are the force exerted on a body by a fluid jet; the force on a pipe bend; the lift and drag of an airplane wing; and the thrust and torque of a propeller, turbine, or centrifugal pump.

Newton's laws of motion can be put into a form known as the momentum law, which is especially convenient for dealing with steady-flow problems of this character. Heretofore we have applied Newton's laws only to a single particle of ideal fluid, in setting up Euler's equations of motion. In this chapter we shall apply them in the form of the momentum law, to mass systems including both solid bodies and a stream of fluid. No restrictions will be placed on the fluid; it may be both viscous and compressible so long as the flow is steady.

6.1. Laws of Motion. For an arbitrary direction x, Newton's second law of motion states that the resultant external x force acting on a mass particle is equal to the rate of change of x momentum of the particle. Apply this law to each of several mass particles, and sum the resulting equations. By Newton's third law, action is equal and opposite to reaction, so that any internal forces between particles of the system occur in pairs which cancel out when the forces on all particles are summed. For any mass system, therefore, the relation between force and momentum is the same as that for a single particle, and may be written

$$F_x = \frac{dM_x}{dt} \qquad \boxed{m\,v_x} \qquad (6.1)$$

where F_x stands for the resultant external x force and M_x for the x momentum.

We shall now express this relationship in a form peculiarly suited to the solution of fluid-flow problems. The procedure will parallel that already used in the development of the continuity and energy equations.

6.2. Steady-flow Momentum Equation. We apply Eq. (6.1) to a mass system defined as the matter lying within a fixed control volume $\mathcal{V}$, at an arbitrary time t_a (Fig. 6.1a). For an arbitrary direction x consider the change in momentum of this system during a time interval $dt = t_b - t_a$. The boundary of the system at time t_b will in general no longer coincide with the control surface A but will be as shown by the dotted line in Fig. 6.1b.

87

The x momentum of that part of the system lying outside of $\mho$ at t_b we call $dM_{x_{\text{out}}}$, and the x momentum of the new matter inside of $\mho$ at t_b but not included in the system we call $dM_{x_{\text{in}}}$. Representing the x momentum of all the matter inside of $\mho$ at any time by M'_x, we see that

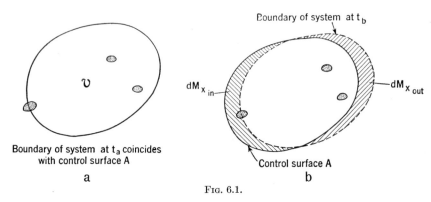

FIG. 6.1.

the initial and final x momenta of the system are, respectively, $M_{x_a} = M'_{x_a}$ and $M_{x_b} = M'_{x_b} + dM_{x_{\text{out}}} - dM_{x_{\text{in}}}$, whence

$$\frac{dM_x}{dt} = \frac{M_{x_b} - M_{x_a}}{dt} = \frac{M'_{x_b} - M'_{x_a}}{dt} + \frac{dM_{x_{\text{out}}} - dM_{x_{\text{in}}}}{dt} \qquad (6.2)$$

The rate of change of x momentum of the system is thus expressed as the sum of the rate of change inside the control volume and the net rate of outflow of x momentum through the control surface.

Referring to Art. 3.6 and Fig. 3.4, we find that the flow of mass in time dt across an element dA of the control surface is $\rho V \cos \alpha \, dA \, dt$. Multiplication of this expression by the x component of velocity V_x (x momentum per unit mass) yields the x momentum carried across dA by the flow in time dt. Accordingly, the net rate of outflow of x momentum across A is

$$\frac{dM_{x_{\text{out}}} - dM_{x_{\text{in}}}}{dt} = \int_A \rho V_x V \cos \alpha \, dA \qquad (6.3)$$

Combination of Eqs. (6.1), (6.2), and (6.3) gives the momentum equation

$$F_x = \frac{M'_{x_b} - M'_{x_a}}{dt} + \int_A \rho V_x V \cos \alpha \, dA \qquad (6.4)$$

The resultant x force on the matter momentarily occupying the fixed volume $\mho$ equals the rate of change of x momentum inside $\mho$ plus the net rate of outflow of x momentum through the control surface.

By reasoning like that in Art. 5.3 it is seen that for steady or cyclic flow Eq. (6.4) reduces to

$$F_x = \int_A \rho V_x V \cos \alpha \, dA \qquad (6.5)$$

In many problems the control volume can be so chosen that fluid enters it at an area A_1 and leaves at area A_2, over each of which ρ, V, and $\cos \alpha$ are uniform. For such a problem, continuity gives $\rho_1 A_1 V_1 \cos \alpha_1 = \rho_2 A_2 V_2 \cos \alpha_2 = \rho_1 Q_1$, and Eq. (6.5) simplifies to

$$F_x = \rho_1 Q_1 (V_{x_2} - V_{x_1}) \qquad (6.6)$$

If Eq. (6.6) is rewritten as

$$F_x - \rho_1 Q_1 V_{x_2} + \rho_1 Q_1 V_{x_1} = 0 \qquad (6.6a)$$

it is seen that the system behaves as if it were in equilibrium under the action of the actual external forces F_x, a force $\rho_1 Q_1 V_{x_2}$ in the negative x direction, and a force $\rho_1 Q_1 V_{x_1}$ in the positive x direction. One can readily extend this result to show that a flux of momentum $\rho Q V$ across an area A has the same effect on the system as a force of magnitude $\rho Q V$ acting at the center of A. This force is parallel to the velocity V but always has an *inward* component, regardless of whether the flow is out or in across the area A. A steady-flow problem can thus be solved by the methods of statics if these effective forces are included with the actual external forces on the system.

6.3. Momentum Equation for Moving Axes. Equations (6.1) to (6.6) are valid when referred to axes moving without acceleration, since the usual form of Newton's laws holds under these conditions.

6.4. Application of the Momentum Equation. A real, compressible fluid flows steadily through the horizontal pipe bend shown in Fig. 6.2. It is desired to find the forces needed to hold the bend stationary. These forces will usually be exerted on the bend by the adjoining pipes and will therefore be distributed over the ends of the bend wall at 1 and 2. For simplicity, we assume that these distributed forces are equivalent to a single concentrated force R.

We choose a control volume to include the bend as well as the fluid, in order that R will be one of the external forces on the system. If the control volume included the fluid only, R would not act on the system and an additional step would be required in the solution of the problem.

In Fig. 6.2 it is seen that $V_{x_2} = V_2 \cos \beta$, $V_{x_1} = V_1$, $V_{y_2} = V_2 \sin \beta$, and $V_{y_1} = 0$. The momentum terms in Eq. (6.6) are therefore readily written down for this problem.

The resultant force on the system is caused entirely by deviations in the stress distribution over the control surface from the uniform atmospheric pressure. (The weight is normal to the plane of flow and does not enter the problem.) We have already seen that R is produced by these deviations

in stress over the ends of the pipe bend at 1 and 2. The only other deviations occur at the fluid surfaces A_1 and A_2. From the axial symmetry of
the flow at these areas it is clear that the shearing forces on either A_1 or A_2

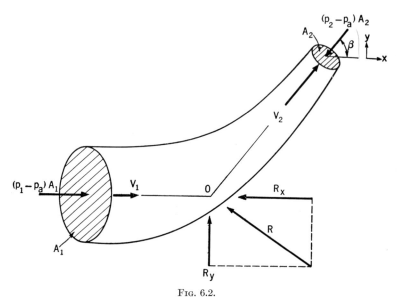

FIG. 6.2.

have a zero resultant. The excess pressure forces at A_1 and A_2 are shown
in Fig. 6.2. The components of the resultant external force, therefore, are

$$F_x = (p_1 - p_a)A_1 - (p_2 - p_a)A_2 \cos \beta - R_x$$
$$F_y = R_y - (p_2 - p_a)A_2 \sin \beta$$

Substitution in Eq. (6.6) of these values of the components of velocity
and force gives

$$R_x = (p_1 - p_a)A_1 - (p_2 - p_a)A_2 \cos \beta - \rho_1 A_1 V_1 (V_2 \cos \beta - V_1) \quad (6.7)$$
$$R_y = (p_2 - p_a)A_2 \sin \beta + \rho_1 A_1 V_1 V_2 \sin \beta \quad (6.8)$$

The pressure and velocity at 2 can be eliminated from these equations if
incompressibility is assumed. The continuity and energy equations for
incompressible flow yield

$$A_1 V_1 = A_2 V_2 \qquad p_2 = p_1 - \frac{\rho}{2}(V_2^2 - V_1^2) - \rho(u_2 - u_1 - q_{1,2})$$

whence

$$R_x = (p_1 - p_a)(A_1 - A_2 \cos \beta) + \frac{\rho}{2} A_1 V_1^2 \left[2 - \cos \beta \left(\frac{A_1}{A_2} + \frac{A_2}{A_1}\right)\right]$$
$$+ \rho(u_2 - u_1 - q_{1,2})A_2 \cos \beta \quad (6.9)$$

$$R_y = (p_1 - p_a)A_2 \sin \beta + \frac{\rho}{2} A_1 V_1^2 \left(\frac{A_1}{A_2} + \frac{A_2}{A_1}\right) \sin \beta$$
$$- \rho(u_2 - u_1 - q_{1,2})A_2 \sin \beta \quad (6.10)$$

The loss terms (on the extreme right) will be zero if the flow is assumed to be frictionless.

6.5. Angular-momentum Law. Newton's second law applied to the mass δm of Fig. 6.3 gives the following results:

$$\delta F_x = \frac{dV_x}{dt} \delta m \qquad \delta F_y = \frac{dV_y}{dt} \delta m$$

where V_x and V_y are the x and y components of velocity. The counter-

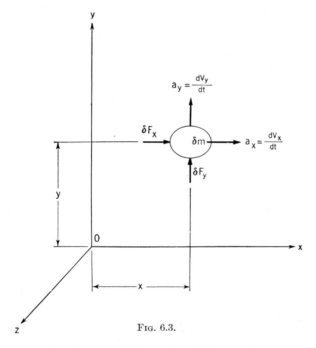

FIG. 6.3.

clockwise moment, or torque, of the external forces about an axis through O perpendicular to the x, y plane (z axis) is

$$\delta T_z = x \, \delta F_y - y \, \delta F_x = \left(x \frac{dV_y}{dt} - y \frac{dV_x}{dt}\right)\delta m$$

By the rules of differentiation

$$\frac{d}{dt}(xV_y - yV_x) = \frac{dx}{dt} V_y - \frac{dy}{dt} V_x + x \frac{dV_y}{dt} - y \frac{dV_x}{dt}$$
$$= V_x V_y - V_y V_x + x \frac{dV_y}{dt} - y \frac{dV_x}{dt}$$

Therefore, since $V_x V_y - V_y V_x = 0$ and δm is constant,

$$\delta T_z = \frac{d}{dt}(xV_y - yV_x)\,\delta m = \frac{d}{dt}[(xV_y - yV_x)\,\delta m] \qquad (6.11)$$

The quantity in square brackets is called the "moment of momentum" or "angular momentum" about the z axis and will be denoted by δH_z. Newton's second law thus leads to the following statement for the mass δm: The resultant external torque about an arbitrary fixed axis (z axis) equals the rate of change of angular momentum about that axis,

$$\delta T_z = \frac{d(\delta H_z)}{dt} \qquad (6.12)$$

Apply Eq. (6.12) to each of several small masses, and sum the resulting equations. By Newton's third law the forces acting between masses of the system occur in pairs whose members are equal, opposite, and collinear. Consequently, the moment of any one internal force is canceled by that of the other member of the pair, and the resultant moment of only the external forces is obtained when the equations are summed. We thus obtain for a system of masses a result identical with Eq. (6.12)

$$T_z = \frac{dH_z}{dt} \qquad (6.13)$$

where T_z represents the resultant external moment about the arbitrary fixed z axis and H_z is the z angular momentum of the system.

It will be noted that, since z is arbitrary, a torque equation for the x or y axis may be obtained from Eq. (6.13) merely by a change of subscript to x or y. The z axis is used in the above development solely because it is customary to refer the flow to the x, y plane.

There is an analogy between Eqs. (6.13) and (6.1) that enables us to write down at once an angular-momentum equation corresponding to Eq. (6.4). For F_x we substitute T_z; for M'_x we substitute H'_z, the z angular momentum of the mass inside the control volume; and we replace the x momentum per unit mass, or x velocity, V_x, by the z angular momentum per unit mass $xV_y - yV_x$ [see Eq. (6.11)].

It is usually convenient to express $xV_y - yV_x$ in terms of V_t and r, defined in Fig. 6.4.

$$xV_y - yV_x = r\cos\theta\,V\sin\phi - r\sin\theta\,V\cos\phi = rV\sin(\phi - \theta) = rV_t \quad (6.14)$$

It is seen that the tangential velocity component V_t is defined as positive for a counterclockwise angular momentum.

Making these substitutions in Eq. (6.4), we get the angular-momentum law

$$T_z = \frac{H'_{z_b} - H'_{z_a}}{dt} + \int_A \rho r V_t V \cos\alpha\,dA \qquad (6.15)$$

The meaning of this equation is analogous to that of Eq. (6.4): The resultant external torque on the matter momentarily occupying a fixed volume $\mho$ equals the rate of change of angular momentum of the matter inside of $\mho$

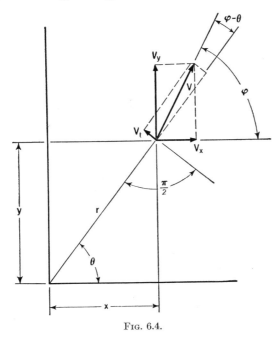

Fig. 6.4.

plus the net rate of outflow of angular momentum through the control surface.

For a steady or cyclic flow, Eq. (6.15) simplifies to

$$T_z = \int_A \rho r V_t V \cos \alpha \, dA \qquad (6.16)$$

which is the analogue of Eq. (6.5).

Assume that the entire flow enters the control volume at an area A_1 and leaves at an area A_2, over each of which ρ, V, and $\cos \alpha$ are uniform. Define $r_2 V_{t_2}$ as the mean value of $r V_t$ over A_2 and $r_1 V_{t_1}$ as the mean value over A_1.

$$r_2 V_{t_2} = \frac{1}{A_2} \int_{A_2} r V_t \, dA \qquad r_1 V_{t_1} = \frac{1}{A_1} \int_{A_1} r V_t \, dA$$

Continuity gives $\rho_1 A_1 V_1 \cos \alpha_1 = \rho_2 A_2 V_2 \cos \alpha_2 = \rho_1 Q_1$, and Eq. (6.16) becomes

$$T_z = \rho_1 Q_1 (r_2 V_{t_2} - r_1 V_{t_1}) \qquad (6.17)$$

which is the analogue of Eq. (6.6).

By rewriting Eq. (6.17) in the form

$$T_z - \rho_1 Q_1 r_2 V_{t_2} + \rho_1 Q_1 r_1 V_{t_1} = 0 \qquad (6.17a)$$

one can show that the moment of the momentum flux across an area A is the same as the moment of a force applied at the center of A and related to the momentum flux as described in Art. 6.2. The methods of statics are therefore applicable here as well as in the case of the linear-momentum law.

6.6. Application of the Angular-momentum Equation. In Art. 6.4 we computed the magnitude and direction of the external force R on a pipe bend. Here we shall find a point on the line of action of R.

In Fig. 6.2, take the z-axis through O, the point of intersection of the center lines of the pipes adjoining the bend. For this axis, it is obvious by inspection that $r_2 V_{t_2} = r_1 V_{t_1} = 0$. From Eq. (6.17), therefore, $T_z = 0$. Since the moments due to the pressure forces are zero, it follows that the line of action of R must pass through O.

6.7. Angular-momentum Equation for a Rotor. Equation (6.17) is

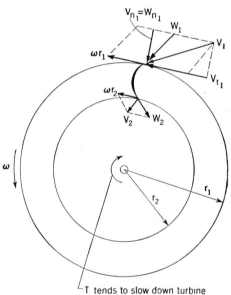

applicable to the rotor of a turbine or compressor since the absolute flow in the interior of the rotor is cyclic and we may assume with fair approximation that ρ, V, and $\cos \alpha$ are uniform over the entrance section 1 and over the exit section 2 (see Figs. 6.5 and 6.6). In the figures, W refers to velocity relative to the rotor (relative velocity), and V, as usual, stands for velocity relative to the earth (absolute velocity). For clarity only one blade is shown.

If we neglect bearing friction, the drag of the fluid on the outside of the rotor, and fluid shearing stresses at 1 and 2, then the external torque T on the shaft equals the *resultant* external torque on either system. For the turbine, however, T is clockwise, while for the compressor it is counterclockwise. Hence, for the turbine,

Fig. 6.5. — Velocity diagrams for a turbine runner.

$$T = \rho_1 Q_1 (r_1 V_{t_1} - r_2 V_{t_2}) \qquad (6.18)$$

and for the compressor,

$$T = \rho_1 Q_1 (r_2 V_{t_2} - r_1 V_{t_1}) \qquad (6.19)$$

It should be emphasized that Eq. (6.16) or (6.17) is not in general applicable to rotating flows. The special case of the turbine or compressor rotor can be handled by Eq. (6.17) only because the flow satisfies the conditions listed at the beginning of this article.

An equation similar to Eq. (6.16) can be developed, however, for any rotating flow, provided merely that it be steady with respect to axes

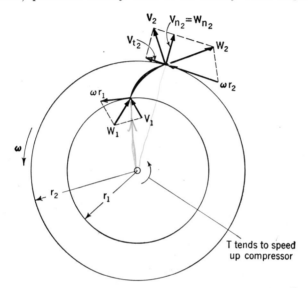

FIG. 6.6. — Velocity diagrams for a compressor or pump impeller.

rotating at a constant angular velocity about a fixed axis. This equation, which can be developed by the control-volume method of Arts. 3.6, 5.2, and 6.2, has the form

$$T_z = \int_A \rho r V_t W \cos \beta \, dA \qquad (6.20)$$

where W is the velocity relative to the rotating axes and β is the angle between W and the outward-drawn normal to the element dA of a control surface that rotates with the axes. For the special case of the turbine or compressor rotor the control volume is merely an annulus concentric with the axis of rotation, so that $W \cos \beta = V \cos \alpha$ and Eqs. (6.16) and (6.20) are identical.

6.8. Energy Equation for a Rotor. To develop the energy equation for this case we retain the assumptions that the absolute flow at entrance and exit of the turbine runner of Fig. 6.5 is steady and uniform and that the absolute flow in the interior is cyclic. We also neglect any work due to fluid shear. Equation (5.10) is therefore applicable to the runner.

$$\frac{p_2}{\rho_2} - \frac{p_1}{\rho_1} + \frac{V_2^2 - V_1^2}{2} + g(z_2 - z_1) + u_2 - u_1 - q + \mathcal{W}_s = 0 \qquad (5.10)$$

Note that $\mathcal{W}_s = T\omega/\rho_1 Q_1$; whence, from Eq. (6.18), $\mathcal{W}_s = (r_1 V_{t_1} - r_2 V_{t_2})\omega$. Substitution of this value of $\mathcal{W}_s$ into Eq. (5.10) gives a term $[V_2^2 - 2\omega r_2 V_{t_2} - (V_1^2 - 2\omega r_1 V_{t_1})]/2$, from which we eliminate the absolute velocities by means of the velocity diagrams of Fig. 6.5.

$$V_2^2 - 2\omega r_2 V_{t_2} = W_{n_2}^2 + (\omega r_2 - W_{t_2})^2 - 2\omega r_2 (\omega r_2 - W_{t_2}) = W_2^2 - \omega^2 r_2^2$$

Similarly,

$$V_1^2 - 2\omega r_1 V_{t_1} = W_1^2 - \omega^2 r_1^2$$

Therefore, the energy equation referred to the rotor is

$$\frac{p_2}{\rho_2} - \frac{p_1}{\rho_1} + \frac{W_2^2 - W_1^2}{2} - \frac{\omega^2}{2}(r_2^2 - r_1^2) + g(z_2 - z_1) + u_2 - u_1 - q = 0 \quad (6.21)$$

A similar development for the compressor impeller shows that Eq. (6.21) applies also to that case.

If friction is negligible, Eq. (5.12) gives $\int_1^2 p\, d(1/\rho) + u_2 - u_1 - q = 0$, so that Eq. (6.21) becomes

$$\int_1^2 \frac{dp}{\rho} + \frac{W_2^2 - W_1^2}{2} - \frac{\omega^2}{2}(r_2^2 - r_1^2) + g(z_2 - z_1) = 0 \quad (6.22)$$

which is Euler's equation for a frame of reference rotating at a constant angular velocity.

In the special case of motion like that of a rotating rigid body ($W = 0$ everywhere), Eq. (6.22) reduces to

$$\int_1^2 \frac{dp}{\rho} - \frac{\omega^2}{2}(r_2^2 - r_1^2) + g(z_2 - z_1) = 0 \quad (6.23)$$

which has already been discussed (for incompressible fluid) in Art. 2.19.

6.9. Recapitulation. It is desirable to set down here the principal results of Chaps. III, V, and VI in order to point out the general pattern to which they all conform. This article will be restricted to a system bounded by a fixed control surface and to the steady-flow case.

The continuity equation [Eq. (3.8)] is

$$0 = \begin{Bmatrix} \text{net rate of outflow of mass} \\ \text{across the control surface} \end{Bmatrix} = \int_A (1)\rho V \cos \alpha \, dA$$

The energy equation [Eq. (5.6)] is

$$\begin{Bmatrix} \text{Heat added} \\ \text{to system} \\ \text{per unit} \\ \text{time} \end{Bmatrix} - \begin{Bmatrix} \text{work done} \\ \text{by system} \\ \text{per unit} \\ \text{time} \end{Bmatrix} = \begin{Bmatrix} \text{net rate of out-} \\ \text{flow of energy} \\ \text{across the con-} \\ \text{trol surface} \end{Bmatrix} = \int_A (e)\rho V \cos \alpha \, dA$$

The linear-momentum equation [Eq. (6.5)] is

$$\begin{Bmatrix} \text{Resultant } x \text{ force} \\ \text{on system} \end{Bmatrix} = \begin{Bmatrix} \text{net rate of outflow} \\ \text{of } x \text{ momentum} \\ \text{across the control} \\ \text{surface} \end{Bmatrix} = \int_A (V_x)\rho V \cos \alpha \, dA$$

The angular-momentum equation [Eq. (6.16)] is

$$\begin{Bmatrix} \text{Resultant } z \text{ torque} \\ \text{on system} \end{Bmatrix} = \begin{Bmatrix} \text{net rate of outflow} \\ \text{of } z \text{ angular mo-} \\ \text{mentum across the} \\ \text{control surface} \end{Bmatrix} = \int_A (rV_t)\rho V \cos \alpha \, dA$$

The factors in parentheses represent, respectively, the mass per unit mass 1, the energy per unit mass e, the x momentum per unit mass V_x, and the z angular momentum per unit mass rV_t. The product of each of these by $\rho V \cos \alpha \, dA$, the rate of mass flow across an area dA of the control surface, gives the rate of flow of each entity across dA. The algebraic sum $\int_A$ of the elementary fluxes then gives the total flux.

It may be remarked that the Euler differential equations [Eqs. (4.3) and (4.4)], on which Chap. IV is based, can be derived from the linear-momentum law by reference to an elementary control surface.

The hydrostatic equation [Eq. (2.7)] is also a special case of the momentum law.

All the problems of steady flow discussed in this book are based on the principles outlined in this article. The method of dimensional analysis, the only other tool that will be used extensively, is presented in the next chapter.

SELECTED BIBLIOGRAPHY

1. von Mises, R.: "Theory of Flight," McGraw-Hill Book Company, Inc., New York, 1945.
2. Prandtl, L., and O. G. Tietjens: "Fundamentals of Hydro- and Aeromechanics," McGraw-Hill Book Company, Inc., New York, 1934.

CHAPTER VII

DIMENSIONAL ANALYSIS AND SIMILITUDE

7.1. Dimensions. In mechanics we deal quantitatively with physical phenomena involving mass, force, momentum, energy, density, viscosity, and many other aspects of nature or entities, to which names have been given. Such an entity can be measured in terms of a selected unit amount of that entity, and we can express its quantity by an abstract number that names the number of times the unit can be contained in it.

7.2. Length. If we choose length as a primary quantity, we can construct area and volume as derived quantities. In this way we give area and volume the dimensions of $[L^2]$ and $[L^3]$. This is a symbolic notation to express the idea of dimensions.

Arithmetic deals with pure numbers, which can be added and otherwise manipulated in accordance with known rules. When we attach dimensional meaning to numbers, we may not follow the rules of arithmetic unless certain restrictions are observed.

For example, if L_1 names the length of a beam and L_0 the length of a stick, we may measure L_1 in terms of L_0 by repeated application of L_0 along L_1. We express the result as $L_1 = nL_0$.

Here n is a pure number expressing the times L_0 is applied to L_1. Now if L_1 and L_0 be each measured in terms of a shorter stick, or unit of length λ, we have

$$l_1\lambda = nl_0\lambda$$

where l_1 and l_0 are pure numbers that express the number of times the unit λ has been applied.

Since λ appears in both terms, $l_1 = nl_0$; and as this expression contains only numbers, the rules of arithmetic apply and we may write

$$\frac{l_1}{l_0} = n = \frac{L_1}{L_0}$$

where L_1 and L_0 are symbols or names for the lengths of two objects.

The important result of this reasoning is the realization that the ratio between two lengths is the ratio between the numbers of units which measure them, regardless of the size of the common unit of length employed.

The justification for the addition and subtraction of lengths follows by similar reasoning. A length $L_0 = l_0\lambda$ applied in continuation of a length

$L_1 = l_1\lambda$ constitutes the addition of two lengths and will be numerically expressed by $l_0 + l_1$ units of length, or

$$l_1\lambda + l_0\lambda = (l_1 + l_0)\lambda$$

We may add measures of length only when the lengths added are expressed in terms of the same unit of length.

7.3. Time. The measurement of time is more difficult than that of length. We know in nature of periodic phenomena that proceed steadily, and we can measure a time interval by counting heartbeats or by watching the sun or a clock. We can select any convenient unit of time based on some such repetition and express a time interval as a number of such units. Since we cannot directly add one time interval to another unless one interval starts when the other ends, we must assume the accuracy of clocks. We are content to add numbers of units of time so long as all time intervals are measured in the same unit.

7.4. Velocity. Velocity might be measured in arbitrary velocity units, as by the Beaufort scale of the sailor, who estimates wind velocity by the appearance of his sails. Thus 5 on the Beaufort scale is "fresh breeze, all sail drawing," and 10 is "whole gale, hove to under storm sail." The sailor has no ready means to measure velocity, and he associates velocity with force, which he can estimate.

Nature does not supply for mechanics a convenient standard unit of velocity. The speed of falling bodies is changing, and the speed of animals uncertain. The velocity of light is convenient for astronomers only. We resolve the difficulty by defining velocity in terms of length and time and making the unit of velocity the ratio between a unit of length and a unit of time. This is a new concept—to divide a length by a time and to call the quotient a velocity. We do this, not as a result of any logical analysis, but purely by our own decision. We choose to define velocity as $V = ds/dt$, where ds is the distance moved in time dt, and, as a consequence, the unit of velocity becomes a derived unit. A simple dimensional equation to express this concept is, in conventional notation,

$$[V] = \frac{[L]}{[T]}$$

where the brackets indicate that the dimensions only of the enclosed quantity are represented.

7.5. Acceleration. Like velocity, acceleration is conveniently derived from length and time, and by definition, is given the dimensions

$$[a] = \frac{[V]}{[T]} = \left[\frac{L}{T^2}\right]$$

7.6. Force. Weight is the most common force, and it is natural that force is universally measured in terms of the weight of a standard block of material. This block is often called a "weight," and the words "force" and "weight" have become confused.

Since prehistoric times, quantities of material have been compared or measured with some form of balance, a convenient standard quantity being used for balance "weights." The convenient unit has usually been of the order of a handful of material—hence our modern pound.

Force is taken as a primary quantity in the so-called "technical" or "gravitational system," and its unit is the weight of a standard block of metal at a place where gravity has a standard value.

7.7. Mass. Mass is quantity of matter. The mass of a standard block is invariant although its weight may vary slightly with location, since gravity is not everywhere the same. The apparent weight of a given mass in an airplane when making a banked turn may be several times normal.

The distinction between weight and mass is primarily a necessity of mechanics. Newton's great generalization for the first time connected force and mass through the statement of his second law. Newton postulated mass as the fundamental entity and described force as a phenomenon whose action could be observed and measured by its effect on the state of motion of a mass. The rate of change in the quantity of motion measures the force acting. In our modern notation this is

$$\text{Force} = \frac{\text{momentum change}}{\text{time of application}} \qquad \text{or} \qquad F = \frac{d(mV)}{dt}$$

with a corresponding dimensional equation

$$[F] = \left[\frac{MV}{T}\right] = \left[\frac{ML}{T^2}\right]$$

which, outside of relativity regions, has been found to express a universal law of nature.

We could, with equal logic, use Newton's second law to define mass in terms of force, length, and time, thus:

$$m = \frac{F}{a} \qquad \text{or} \qquad [M] = \left[\frac{FT^2}{L}\right]$$

It is a matter of convenience whether we choose $[F]$ as a primary quantity and define $[M]$ in a technical system of units or choose $[M]$ as a primary quantity and define $[F]$ in a dynamic system. Both are in general use. The $[M]$ system is usually called the "absolute" system in older texts, but it is now recognized that there is nothing absolute about any system.

7.8. Moment and Work. The dimensions of these entities are symbolically similar although physically distinct. This arises because we define each in terms of a force and a length.

$$[\text{Moment}] = [FL] \qquad\qquad [\text{Work}] = [FL]$$

For example, the moment of a 10-lb force acting with a 10-ft arm is 100 units of moment, where the unit is the moment of one pound acting with an arm of one foot.

The work done by a force of 10 lb acting through 10 ft is also 100 lb-ft. But here work is expressed in terms of a work unit, *i.e.*, the work done by one pound acting along a distance of one foot in the direction of the force. Note that the derived unit of moment is quite different as to the direction of the force with relation to the length. Moment is a vector quantity, while work is a scalar.

7.9. Zero Dimensions. There are quantities that are a ratio of two quantities of the same dimensions. Angles and trigonometric functions are pure numbers and are therefore dimensionless or of zero dimensions. For example, an angle is the ratio of an arc to its radius, which, in dimensional notation, is expressed as

$$[\alpha] = \left[\frac{L}{L}\right] = [L^0]$$

It is a peculiarity of our system of numbers that the zero can have whatever dimensions the other terms of an equation require. For example, consider the physical equation for the law of falling bodies,

$$s = gt^2/2$$

with its dimensional equivalent

$$[s] = [L] = [gt^2] = \left[\frac{L}{T^2} T^2\right] = [L]$$

It is equally valid to write

$$s - gt^2/2 = 0$$

and its dimensional equivalent

$$[s - gt^2/2] = [L] = [0]$$

Zero in this case must have the dimensions of a length.

7.10. Properties of Materials. The dimensions of the common properties of materials can be expressed in terms of the three primary quantities in accordance with their definitions. However, density and viscosity need special attention.

The weight per unit volume of a substance (specific weight) is often erroneously called density. It is recommended to reserve the term "density" in mechanics to mean the mass per unit volume.

$$[\gamma] = \left[\frac{\text{weight}}{\text{volume}}\right] = \left[\frac{F}{L^3}\right]$$

$$[\rho] = \left[\frac{\text{mass}}{\text{volume}}\right] = \left[\frac{M}{L^3}\right]$$

Viscosity was defined by Newton as the force per unit area per unit rate of shear on adjacent layers of a moving fluid. If the thickness of an oil film is h and the relative velocity between the two sides of the film is V, V/h is the rate of shear. The coefficient of viscosity μ is then defined by $F/A = \mu V/h$, where F is the shearing force and A is the area of the oil film. There is a corresponding dimensional equation

$$[\mu] = \left[\frac{Fh}{AV}\right] = \left[\frac{FT}{L^2}\right] = \left[\frac{M}{LT}\right]$$

7.11. Dimensional Systems. A consistent dimensional system is composed of the smallest number of quantities in terms of which all entities and relations in a field of science may be expressed. For mechanics three such "primary" quantities have been found necessary and sufficient, which are usually chosen as $[M]$, $[L]$, $[T]$ or $[F]$, $[L]$, $[T]$.

For thermodynamics a fourth primary quantity is needed, generally taken for convenience as temperature $[\theta]$.

7.12. Units of Force, Weight, and Mass. We have acquired two systems of dimensions, the $[M]$ and the $[F]$, both in the metric system and in the English system.

While force is conveniently measured in terms of weight, a particular sort of force, confusion can develop when forces other than weight are involved, such as occur in dynamics. We accept without question that one pound is the force of the earth's attraction at Greenwich on a particular block of metal. This block of metal is a mass, and it is also called a pound. This "pound" block cannot be at the same time the unit of force and the unit of mass, for one quantity cannot be expressed in terms of the other alone. Their dimensions are not the same.

The difficulty comes from the fact that weight and mass are united by the special relation

$$w = gm$$

with g nearly constant. But g is not a pure number since the equivalence of w and gm would imply an impossible dimensional equation

$$[F] = \left[\frac{ML}{T^2}\right] = [g][M]$$

The two sides of this dimensional equation become reconciled only when g is an acceleration, of dimension $[L/T^2]$.

The "pound" block, if taken as a unit of mass, requires us to name another unit of force, defined from $F = ma$, as the force that gives one pound mass an acceleration of one foot per second per second. This unit of force is $1/g$ times the so-called "pound force." This unusual unit, named the poundal, has never been accepted as useful or convenient by engineers.

Man in general is constantly concerned with weight, rarely with mass. Mass is a quantity necessary to dynamics and may be considered to be a "technical" concept of historically recent origin.

American and British engineers adopt the weight of the pound block measured where $g = g_0 = 32.1739$ ft per sec per sec as the unit of weight, and a mass equivalent to 32.1739 times that of the standard pound block as the unit of mass. This was named the "slug" * by Professor Perry, with sluggishness or inertia in mind, and has been officially adopted for both British and United States government publications. A pound force gives unit acceleration to one slug of mass.

In the metric system, the same care must be taken regarding force and mass units. The unit mass is one gram, and the unit force, called a "dyne," is that force which will impart unit acceleration (in centimeters per second per second) to the gram unit of mass. The dyne corresponds to the poundal. However, the dyne is inconvenient for engineering work and the technical unit of force is taken as the weight of the gram mass measured where $g = 980.665$ cm per sec per sec; the unit of mass is 980.665 times the mass of the gram. Then a gram force gives unit acceleration to this unnamed unit of mass.

7.13. Dimensional Equations. The selection of three primary quantities, such as mass, length, and time, enables us to express the dimensions of all the other quantities of mechanics in terms of these three. The correct definition of a physical quantity implies both an algebraic equation and a dimensional equation.

Suppose a man riding in a car observes a pressure p due to the relative wind of velocity V. He has discovered a physical relation between pressure and velocity that he might assume to have the form

$$p = f(V) = KV^a$$

Since both terms must have the same dimensions, the corresponding dimensional equation, when a and K are pure numbers, would be

$$[p] = \left[\frac{F}{L^2}\right] = \left[\frac{M}{LT^2}\right] = \left[\frac{L^a}{T^a}\right]$$

The dimensional equation is out of balance, and evidently K is not a pure number but must be some function of other variables.

Suppose our experimenter were a more cautious person and assumed

---

* This term is applied only when the foot-pound-second system of British gravitational units is used. In many cases advantage results from using the inch instead of the foot for the linear unit, or what may be called the "inch-pound-second system." In this case the unit of mass is evidently equivalent to 32.1739×12 times that of the standard pound block.

the law of wind force might depend both on the density of the air and on the velocity. Then he would write

$$p = f(\rho, V) = K\rho^b V^a$$

and if he found by experiment that $a = 2$, the dimensional equation would now be

$$[p] = \left[\frac{M}{LT^2}\right] = \left[\frac{M^b}{L^{3b}}\right]\left[\frac{L^2}{T^2}\right]$$

Equating the exponents of M, on both sides of the equality sign, it appears that $b = 1$. Hence $p = K\rho V^2$, where K is an undetermined constant.

This experiment was made by observing the effect of but one variable, velocity; yet the dimensional analysis shows the necessary influence of another variable, density. The fact that p was found to vary as V^2 requires that p also vary as ρ.

Dimensional theory can never determine a numerical coefficient such as K, but it can give the only possible relation among the independent quantities involved. The procedure is first to deduce from dimensional considerations the general relation between the variables assumed to control the phenomenon and then by experiment to check the choice of independent variables and determine the necessary constants.

7.14. Dimensional Homogeneity. Any equation or formulation expressing a relation among physical quantities is actually an algebraic equation in which measurements, or numbers, represented by letters, imply but do not disclose the units in which each of the various quantities has been measured. There is a corresponding dimensional equation that states the dimensions of these units in each term of the algebraic equation. In dealing with physical measurements we may perform the operations of addition and subtraction only with numerical quantities of the same dimensions. The physical equation, therefore, must be dimensionally homogeneous.

This principle of dimensional homogeneity is fundamental to our whole system of physical and engineering mathematics. While pure mathematics is not concerned with dimensions, applied mathematics must deal with numbers that measure physical quantities in units of the same dimensions.

The application of this principle, first stated by Fourier, gives a test of the completeness or of the consistency of any physical equation purporting, as the result of experiment or analysis, to describe a physical phenomenon. It also furnishes a unique dimensional condition that must exist among the physical quantities involved and furnishes a clue to the form of an unknown physical equation describing it. The search for a correct dimensional form for an unknown equation is dignified by the name "dimensional analysis."

7.15. The General Form of Physical Equations. The fact that a complete physical equation must be dimensionally homogeneous can be generalized to develop a formal procedure for analysis of less simple problems. The necessity for a formal procedure arises because for mechanics there are but three primary quantities, while many mechanical relations involve more than three variables. It is not possible to determine the unknown exponents of more than three variables by means of the three simultaneous equations obtained from the exponents of M, L, and T, appearing in the corresponding dimensional equation.

Any complete physical equation expresses the relation among all of the different physical quantities that control the phenomenon in question. Let these quantities be designated by Q_1, Q_2, Q_3, $\cdots$, Q_n. Then we may write the complete physical equation as an unknown function of all of the Q's.

$$\phi(Q_1, Q_2, Q_3, \cdots, Q_n) = 0 \tag{7.1}$$

Assume that Eq. (7.1) may be put in the form of an equivalent power series, each term containing all the quantities Q. A typical term will be of the form $A Q_1^{a_1} Q_2^{a_2} Q_3^{a_3} \cdots Q_n^{a_n}$, where A is a numerical coefficient.

Equation (7.1) may be written as a series of such terms, the number of which may be indefinite,

$$A Q_1^{a_1} \cdots Q_n^{a_n} + B Q_1^{b_1} \cdots Q_n^{b_n} + \cdots = 0 \tag{7.2}$$

Divide through by the first term, and obtain

$$1 + \frac{B}{A} Q_1^{b_1 - a_1} Q_2^{b_2 - a_2} \cdots Q_n^{b_n - a_n} + \cdots = 0 \tag{7.3}$$

By the principle of dimensional homogeneity, it will be observed that each term, including the zero, is dimensionless. Since the numerical coefficients are dimensionless, it follows that the products of the powers of the Q's in each term are also dimensionless.

The dimensional equation corresponding to Eq. (7.3) will express this fact:

$$[Q_1^{x_1} Q_2^{x_2} \cdots Q_n^{x_n}] = [M^0 L^0 T^0] \tag{7.4}$$

where x_1, x_2, $\cdots$, x_n are unknown exponents.

The dimensional equation [Eq. (7.4)], places a restriction on the powers of the Q's in each term of Eq. (7.3), but we cannot determine these exponents by inspection, except for very simple cases.

Since there may be a large number of Q's, it is convenient to deal with a smaller number of products of a few Q's taken together. Let the symbol Π represent a nondimensional product of powers of some of the Q's, and let Π_1, Π_2, $\cdots$, Π_i represent all of such independent products that can be formed by using all the Q's.

Since each Π is dimensionless, the product of any powers of the Π's will also be dimensionless; and since the Π's contain all the Q's, some combination of Π's could represent each term of Eq. (7.3). For example,

$$\frac{B}{A}\, Q_1^{b_1-a_1} Q_2^{b_2-a_2} \cdots Q_n^{b_n-a_n} = N\Pi_1^{y_1}\Pi_2^{y_2} \cdots \Pi_i^{y_i}$$

where N and $y_1, y_2, \cdots, y_i$ are pure numbers.
Therefore, we may replace the unknown function of the Q's [Eq. (7.1)] by an unknown function of the Π's.

$$\psi(\Pi_1, \Pi_2, \Pi_3, \cdots, \Pi_i) = 0 \qquad (7.5)$$

This conclusion means that a complete physical equation, expressed as a function of the physical quantities Q controlling the phenomenon, can be equally well expressed by a function of independent dimensionless coefficients or numerics formed from the Q's. The statement that Eqs. (7.1), and (7.5) are equivalent constitutes the Π theorem.

7.16. Alternative Proof of the Π Theorem. The importance of the Π theorem in experimental fluid mechanics is considered to warrant a second proof, based on a postulate that may appeal to some readers as more nearly self-evident than the principle of dimensional homogeneity.

In order to measure any physical quantity, one must first choose a unit of measurement, the size of which depends solely on the whim of the observer. This arbitrariness of the unit size leads to the following postulate: Any equation describing a physical phenomenon can be so formulated that its validity is independent of the size of the units of the primary quantities. Such an equation is called a "complete physical equation." All the physical equations appearing in this book are assumed to be complete. A line of reasoning through which a physical equation can be simplified by virtue of its completeness is demonstrated in the example below.

A stationary sphere is immersed in a steady flow of incompressible real fluid. The sphere is far from any free surface, so that gravity has no effect on the flow pattern, the weight of every fluid particle being counterbalanced by the static buoyant force. Thus, one may assume that the independent variables determining the flow are the velocity of the undisturbed fluid V, the diameter of the sphere d, and the density and viscosity of the fluid ρ and μ. The force F, exerted on the sphere as a result of the fluid motion, will depend in some unknown way on only these four variables:

$$F = \phi(\rho, V, D, \mu) \qquad (7.6)$$

Several changes of variable are now made, to put Eq. (7.6) in such form that it can be simplified through use of its assumed completeness. The immediate object of these changes is to make all the variables, except one, dimensionless in one of the primary quantities. This dimensional variable can then be deleted, as is shown below.

All the variables except ρ are first made dimensionless in mass. There is no necessity for this particular choice of density and mass, but it will be found convenient. Divide both sides of Eq. (7.6) by ρ, in order to change the dependent variable to F/ρ, which has dimensions $[MLT^{-2}/ML^{-3}] = [L^4T^{-2}]$.

$$\frac{F}{\rho} = \frac{\phi(\rho,V,d,\mu)}{\rho} = \phi_1(\rho,V,d,\mu)$$

The viscosity μ is the only independent variable (besides ρ) that has non-zero dimensions in mass. Divide μ by ρ to get a new independent variable μ/ρ, having dimensions $[ML^{-1}T^{-1}/ML^{-3}] = [L^2T^{-1}]$.

$$\frac{F}{\rho} = \phi_2\left(\rho,V,d,\frac{\mu}{\rho}\right) \tag{7.7}$$

This change from μ to μ/ρ is permissible, for ρ and μ are independent by assumption. One can therefore vary ρ without varying μ/ρ, simply by causing μ to change in proportion to ρ. The practical difficulties would be the same in either case: to keep either μ or μ/ρ constant while ρ were varied would, in general, require a change of fluid as well as a change of temperature.

These changes of variable have no effect on the completeness of the equation. The validity of Eq. (7.7) is therefore unaffected by a change in the size of the mass unit, say from slugs to grams. The value of F/ρ is unaffected by this change, so that the value of $\phi_2(\rho,V,d,\mu/\rho)$ must likewise be unaltered. The values of V, d, and μ/ρ remain the same, but the value of ρ will be different. Consequently, ϕ_2 can depend, not upon ρ, but only upon V, d, and μ/ρ. The density is therefore deleted, and

$$\frac{F}{\rho} = \phi_2\left(V,d,\frac{\mu}{\rho}\right)$$

A similar procedure gives all the remaining variables, except V, zero dimensions in time. Change F/ρ to $F/\rho V^2$, which has dimensions $[L^4T^{-2}/L^2T^{-2}] = [L^2]$; and change μ/ρ to $\mu/\rho V$, which has dimensions $[L^2T^{-1}/LT^{-1}] = [L]$.

$$\frac{F}{\rho V^2} = \phi_3\left(V,d,\frac{\mu}{\rho V}\right)$$

Deleting V by virtue of the completeness of the equation, one gets

$$\frac{F}{\rho V^2} = \phi_3\left(d,\frac{\mu}{\rho V}\right)$$

A third application of the same reasoning leads to

$$\frac{F}{\rho V^2 d^2} = \phi_4\left(d,\frac{\mu}{\rho V d}\right) = \phi_4\left(\frac{\mu}{\rho V d}\right) = \psi\left(\frac{\rho V d}{\mu}\right) \tag{7.8}$$

Equation (7.6), which involves four independent variables, has been simplified by purely dimensional reasoning to Eq. (7.8), which involves only one independent variable. It is clear that experimental data can be correlated more easily by means of Eq. (7.8) than Eq. (7.6).

Equation (7.8) is not the only form obtainable from Eq. (7.6). By operating with μ instead of ρ, or by combining the variables of Eq. (7.8) in an obvious way, one can also get

$$\frac{F}{\mu Vd} = \psi_1\left(\frac{\rho Vd}{\mu}\right) \tag{7.9}$$

It is found, in most applications of these results, that Eq. (7.8) is preferable to Eq. (7.9), for $F/\rho V^2 d^2$ varies less than $F/\mu Vd$ in the practical range of the independent variable $\rho Vd/\mu$.

Consider now any complete physical equation relating a dependent variable to $n - 1$ independent variables:

$$Q_1 = \phi(Q_2, \cdots, Q_n) \tag{7.10}$$

It is clear that the procedure used in the above example can be followed here, to yield a relationship among dimensionless products of the Q's.

$$\Pi_1 = \psi(\Pi_2, \cdots, \Pi_i) \tag{7.11}$$

where i is the number of dimensionless products, or Π's. We thus arrive again at the Π theorem, this time by induction from an example.

To implement the Π theorem one must know how to determine the number of Π's in any given problem. Furthermore, one should have a definite procedure for forming the Π's, once their number has been determined. Finally, one should understand what freedom exists in the choice of alternative Π's. These questions are considered in the following articles.

7.17. Determination of the Number of Π's. Find by trial the largest number of Q's that will not form a dimensionless product, and let this number be k. Usually k will be found to be the same as the number of primary quantities, which in mechanics is equal to three, M, L, and T.

Suppose now that one carries through the transformation of Eq. (7.10) to Eq. (7.11) by means of the procedure of the previous article, using (analogously to ρ, V, and d) any k of the Q's that do not form a dimensionless product. Assume tentatively that the transformation is complete (*i.e.*, that all the products are dimensionless) after $k - 1$ steps. It is seen, however, that one of the products will contain precisely the k Q's from which a Π cannot be made. From this contradiction it follows that at least k steps are necessary to complete the transformation. On the other hand, k steps are sufficient, for in this case every product contains $k + 1$ Q's and is therefore dimensionless.

Referring again to the procedure of the previous article, one sees that the number of Π's, i, is equal to the number of Q's, n, minus the number of steps. Since the number of steps has been shown to equal k, it follows that $i = n - k$. Equation (7.11) can thus be rewritten

$$\Pi_1 = \psi(\Pi_2, \Pi_3, \cdots, \Pi_{n-k})$$

It may be observed for future reference, since the Π's are formed by grouping the same k Q's with each of the other Q's in turn, that $n - k$ is not only the smallest number of Π's which can suffice in Eq. (7.11) but also the largest number of independent Π's which can be made from the Q's.

In the majority of problems, one will find that k is equal to the number of primary quantities. It is easily shown that k cannot exceed this number, but it is possible for k to be less than the number of primary quantities, as in the following example:

Let a steel rod of length l and diameter d be maintained at a temperature T_1 at one end. Let the temperature of the surrounding air at a great distance from the rod be uniform and equal to T_0. For steady conditions, one may assume that

$$q = \phi(T_1 - T_0, l, d, k_s, k_a) \tag{7.12}$$

where q is the rate of heat transfer per unit area at any point on the surface of the rod and k_s and k_a are the thermal conductivities of steel and air, respectively.

There are four primary quantities entering into the six variables of Eq. (7.12)—mass, length, time, and temperature. It is easily found, however, that the maximum number of variables which will not form a Π is only three. There are thus three Π's in this case, rather than two. If $T_1 - T_0$, l, and k_s are chosen to play the role of ρ, V, and d in the example of the sphere, Eq. (7.12) becomes

$$\frac{ql}{k_s(T_1 - T_0)} = \psi\left(\frac{d}{l}, \frac{k_a}{k_s}\right)$$

7.18. Formulation of One Set of Π's. The number of Π's being known, the next step is to formulate explicitly a set of independent Π's for the problem at hand. As already stated, one method is to combine k Q's not forming a dimensionless product with each of the other Q's in turn.

Referring again to the example of the sphere, we find by trial that ρ, V, and d do not form a dimensionless product and that therefore $k = 3$. The number of Q's being $n = 5$, the number of Π's is $n - k = 5 - 3 = 2$. One formulation of the Π's, accordingly, is

$$\Pi_1 = \rho^{a_1} V^{b_1} d^{c_1} F$$
$$\Pi_2 = \rho^{a_2} V^{b_2} d^{c_2} \mu$$

The three unknown exponents in Π_1 are determined from the fact that Π_1 has zero dimensions in each of the three primary quantities M, L, and T. Thus,

$$[\Pi_1] = [M^0 L^0 T^0] = [(ML^{-3})^{a_1}(LT^{-1})^{b_1}(L)^{c_1}(MLT^{-2})]$$
$$[M^0 L^0 T^0] = [M^{a_1+1} L^{-3a_1+b_1+c_1+1} T^{-b_1-2}]$$

Since the unit sizes of M, L, and T can be chosen arbitrarily and independently of one another, this equation implies that

$$0 = a_1 + 1$$
$$0 = -3a_1 + b_1 + c_1 + 1$$
$$0 = -b_1 - 2$$

These three simultaneous equations in three unknowns have a unique solution, $a_1 = -1$, $b_1 = -2$, and $c_1 = -2$, so that $\Pi_1 = F/\rho V^2 d^2$. In the same way it can be shown that $\Pi_2 = \mu/\rho V d$. The result of the analysis can thus be expressed as $\Pi_1 = \psi_1(\Pi_2)$ or $(F/\rho V^2 d^2) = \psi_1(\mu/\rho V d) = \psi(\rho V d/\mu)$.

This method for determination of the exponents is rather lengthy in problems involving many Π's, since the same process must be repeated for every Π. An alternative, quicker method is illustrated in the following example:

Suppose that the torque q which must be applied to a shaft to overcome the friction of a journal bearing depends only on the shaft diameter d; the bearing length l; the diametral clearance, or difference between bearing and shaft diameters, C; the angular speed ω; the oil viscosity μ; the load on the shaft W; and the volume rate of oil flow Q. Thus

$$q = \phi(d,l,C,\omega,\mu,W,Q)$$

It is readily found that d, ω, and W (for example) do not form a dimensionless product. Furthermore, there are only three primary quantities, M, L, and T. We conclude, therefore, that $k = 3$. Since $n = 8$, the number of Π's will be $n - k = 8 - 3 = 5$. These may be formulated as

$$\Pi_1 = \frac{q}{d^{a_1}\omega^{b_1}W^{c_1}} \qquad\qquad \Pi_4 = \frac{\mu}{d^{a_4}\omega^{b_4}W^{c_4}}$$

$$\Pi_2 = \frac{l}{d^{a_2}\omega^{b_2}W^{c_2}} \qquad\qquad \Pi_5 = \frac{Q}{d^{a_5}\omega^{b_5}W^{c_5}}$$

$$\Pi_3 = \frac{C}{d^{a_3}\omega^{b_3}W^{c_3}}$$

To make Π_1 dimensionless, the product $d^{a_1}\omega^{b_1}W^{c_1}$ must have the dimensions of a torque; that is, $[d^{a_1}\omega^{b_1}W^{c_1}] = [ML^2T^{-2}]$. To meet this requirement we write down the dimensions of d, ω, and W and solve for the dimensions of M, L, and T in terms of d, ω, and W.

$$[d] = [L] \qquad [\omega] = [T^{-1}] \qquad [W] = [MLT^{-2}]$$
$$[L] = [d] \qquad [T] = [\omega^{-1}] \qquad [M] = [Wd^{-1}\omega^{-2}] \qquad (7.13)$$

Using Eqs. (7.13), we find that

$$[ML^2T^{-2}] = [(Wd^{-1}\omega^{-2})(d^2)(\omega^2)] = [Wd]$$

whence $\Pi_1 = q/Wd$.

For Π_2, $[d^{a_2}\omega^{b_2}W^{c_2}] = [L]$. But, from Eqs. (7.13), $[L] = [d]$, so that $\Pi_2 = l/d$.

Similarly, it is found that $\Pi_3 = C/d$.

For Π_4, we must have $[d^{a_4}\omega^{b_4}W^{c_4}] = [\mu] = [ML^{-1}T^{-1}]$. Equations (7.13) give $[ML^{-1}T^{-1}] = [(Wd^{-1}\omega^{-2})(d^{-1})(\omega)] = [Wd^{-2}\omega^{-1}]$, so that $\Pi_4 = \mu\, d^2\omega/W$.

For Π_5, $[d^{a_5}\omega^{b_5}W^{c_5}] = [Q] = [L^3T^{-1}] = [d^3\omega]$, so that $\Pi_5 = Q/d^3\omega$.

The analysis thus leads to

$$\frac{q}{Wd} = \psi\left(\frac{l}{d}, \frac{C}{d}, \frac{\mu\, d^2\omega}{W}, \frac{Q}{\omega d^3}\right)$$

This method is quick, because we determine Eqs. (7.13) but once, for Π_1, and then use them for each of the remaining Π's. It is unnecessary to find each exponent individually, as in the first method.

Equations (7.13) bring out the fact that d, ω, and W can themselves be used as primary quantities in this problem. It is thus seen that the greatest number of Q's which will not form a Π is the same as the number of Q's which can themselves be used as primary quantities in a given problem.

7.19. Formulation of Other Sets of Π's. It has already been noted that $n - k$ is the greatest number of independent Π's which can be made from n Q's. If one set of $n - k$ independent Π's be found by the methods of the preceding article, it is obvious that any other Π can be formed by multiplication of powers of two or more members of the given set. Thus all possible sets can be found from a single one. Denote by $\Pi_1', \Pi_2', \cdots, \Pi_{n-k}'$ any such set of independent products.

Suppose that we have determined one nondimensional formulation of some problem,

$$\Pi_1 = \psi_1(\Pi_2, \Pi_3, \cdots, \Pi_{n-k})$$

From this equation it follows that

$$\Pi_1 = \psi_2(\Pi_1^{a_1}\Pi_2^{a_2}\Pi_3^{a_3}\cdots\Pi_{n-k}^{a_{n-k}}, \Pi_3, \Pi_4, \cdots, \Pi_{n-k})$$

where a_1, a_2, a_3, $\cdots$, a_{n-k} are arbitrary exponents. Therefore,

$$\Pi_1 = \psi_2(\Pi_2', \Pi_3, \Pi_4, \cdots, \Pi_{n-k})$$

By progressing in this manner we can readily show that

$$\Pi_1' = \psi'(\Pi_2', \Pi_3', \cdots, \Pi_{n-k}')$$

Any set of $n - k$ independent Π products can thus be used in the non-dimensional expression of a problem.

Dimensional analysis, per se, offers no clue as to which group of Π's may be most convenient in a given problem. Aside from the obvious fact that the dependent variable should be included in only one Π, it is necessary to rely upon previous experience and physical insight in the selection of a useful set of Π's. Considerations of physical similitude, which are helpful in this connection, will be discussed in the next article.

7.20. Physical Similitude. Consider two systems, such as a model and its prototype, that are described by the same equation $\psi(\Pi_1, \Pi_2, \cdots, \Pi_i) = 0$. Physical similitude is said to exist between two such systems if corresponding Π's have the same value.

The identity of corresponding Π's does not mean that corresponding Q's must be equal but does require that they be related by scale ratios such that the Π's which contain them are identical in the two systems.

In general, the model system and the prototype system that it represents will have corresponding quantities Q_1/Q_1', Q_2/Q_2', etc., in certain definite and constant ratios, or scales. The model scales for the several Q's that control the phenomenon are, however, subject to the restriction of the Π theorem. These restrictions can be stated in the form of rules.

1. Provided only that they do not by themselves form a dimensionless product, k of the quantities may have any arbitrary scale ratios between the two systems.

2. The scale ratio for any of the remaining quantities is determined by the fact that the Π which contains it in the model system must equal the corresponding Π in the prototype system.

As a consequence, solid boundaries that control the flow of a fluid will be geometrically similar, and a model must be geometrically similar to its prototype. Corresponding lengths on model and prototype are related by a constant scale ratio. The locations of corresponding points in the two fields of flow can be defined as x/L, y/L, z/L and x'/L', y'/L', z'/L', where L and L' are typical lengths of model and prototype. Then $x/x' = y/y' = z/z' = L/L'$. Geometrical similitude is characterized by a single and uniform scale of enlargement.

Since there is a constant scale ratio for each quantity, it follows that at all pairs of corresponding points the components of velocity bear a constant ratio to each other. Hence the resultant velocities at corresponding points are parallel, and the streamlines are geometrically similar. To transform one flow pattern to the other we need to know only the linear scale of enlargement from model to prototype.

Knowing the velocities at various points in the flow about the model, we can predict the velocities at corresponding points in the flow about the prototype by applying the proper scale of enlargement. This scale of enlargement for velocity may, for convenience, be taken as the ratio of the speeds of advance of model and prototype, V/V'.

Similar considerations lead to the conclusion that, for compressible flow, the densities at corresponding points have a constant ratio equal to the ratio of the densities of undisturbed fluid in the two systems, ρ/ρ'. For incompressible flow, the densities are in this same ratio but are constant everywhere in each system.

In the preceding discussion, steady flow is implied. If the flow is changing with time, particles occupy corresponding positions and have corresponding velocities at corresponding times. The flow patterns will be geometrically similar only at corresponding times.

The particular form of physical similitude for which the corresponding forces have a single scale ratio is called "dynamical similitude." If there be also a single scale of temperatures at corresponding points, we have thermal similitude. For each case, geometrical similitude is a prerequisite.

The requirement of a single scale ratio for forces shows that the polygons of force on corresponding elements in the two systems are geometrically similar.

7.21. Conditions for Dynamical Similitude.   In the general case of flow of a real fluid, the forces acting on an element of fluid are those due to pressure, friction, gravity, and inertia. d'Alembert's principle shows that the vector sum of these forces is zero.

$$F_p + F_f + F_g + F_i = 0$$

Similarity of corresponding force polygons in two flows is obtained if

$$F_f/F_f' = F_i/F_i' \quad \text{and} \quad F_g/F_g' = F_i/F_i' \tag{7.14}$$

since the d'Alembert equation will then ensure that $F_p/F_p' = F_i/F_i'$.

On the other hand, the criterion for dynamical similitude that is obtained directly from the Π theorem is developed as follows, for an incompressible fluid.

Let us represent the quantities controlling the fluid motion by ρ, L, V, μ, and g, where L is any characteristic length, V is the relative fluid velocity at a distance from the object disturbing the flow, ρ and μ are the density and viscosity of the fluid, and g is the acceleration of gravity. Let F represent any force, such as the lift of a wing or the resistance of a ship, whose value is desired in terms of the independent variables. Then,

$$F = f(\rho, L, V, \mu, g)$$

From the Π theorem,

$$\Pi_1 = \phi(\Pi_2, \Pi_3) \tag{7.15}$$

Since inertia forces usually predominate, it has become conventional to select the particular set of Π products beginning with a force coefficient that is independent of μ and g. Thus,

$$\Pi_1 = \rho^{a_1} L^{b_1} V^{c_1} F = \frac{F}{\rho L^2 V^2} \qquad \text{(Newtonian force coefficient)}$$

$$\Pi_2 = \rho^{a_2}L^{b_2}V^{c_2}\mu^{-1} = \frac{\rho VL}{\mu} \quad \text{(Reynolds number)}$$

$$\Pi_3 = \rho^{a_3}L^{b_3}V^{c_3}g^{-1} = \frac{V^2}{Lg} \quad \text{(Froude number)}$$

The criterion for dynamical similitude that is yielded directly from the definition at the beginning of Art. 7.20 is $\Pi_2 = \Pi'_2$ and $\Pi_3 = \Pi'_3$, or

$$\rho VL/\mu = \rho'V'L'/\mu' \quad \text{and} \quad V^2/Lg = V'^2/L'g \quad (7.16)$$

since Eq. (7.15) then ensures that $\Pi_1 = \Pi'_1$.

From the discussion in Art. 7.20, Eqs. (7.14) and (7.16) should be equivalent. Proof of equivalence, which follows below, will shed light on the physical significance of the Reynolds and Froude numbers.

Consider an element of fluid of sides dx, dy, dz, with the x axis parallel to the streamline. The volume of the element is $\mathcal{V} = dx\,dy\,dz$. The steady velocity at the element is in the x direction and will be denoted by u.

The inertia force on this element is by definition equal to the negative of the product of mass and acceleration,

$$-F_i = \rho\mathcal{V}\frac{du}{dt} = \rho\mathcal{V}\,u\,\frac{\partial u}{\partial x}$$

since, for steady motion, $du/dt = u(\partial u/\partial x)$. The ratio of corresponding inertia forces for two systems will be

$$F_i/F'_i = \frac{\rho\mathcal{V}\,u(\partial u/\partial x)}{\rho'\mathcal{V}'\,u'(\partial u'/dx')} = \frac{\rho L^2 V^2}{\rho'L'^2V'^2}$$

because corresponding lengths and velocities have the ratios L/L' and V/V', respectively.

In Art. 1.4 the friction force F acting on the oil film in a concentric bearing was stated to be $F = \mu(V/h)A$, where V is the difference in velocity between the two sides of the film, h is the film thickness, and A is the area of the film. Experiments show that in more complicated flow patterns the friction force on a small fluid surface, such as $dx\,dz$, is given by a formula of this same form, but with V/h replaced by an expression having at most two terms, each of the type $\partial u/\partial y$. Since we are interested only in the ratio of the friction forces acting on corresponding elements of fluid, we may write

$$\frac{F_f}{F'_f} = \frac{\mu(\partial u/\partial y)\,dx\,dz}{u'(\partial u'/\partial y')\,dx'\,dz'} = \frac{\mu VL}{\mu'V'L'}$$

Also, the ratio of corresponding gravity forces is seen to be

$$\frac{F_g}{F'_g} = \frac{\rho g\mathcal{V}}{\rho'g\mathcal{V}'} = \frac{\rho g L^3}{\rho'g L'^3}$$

Substitution of these values into Eqs. (7.14) shows that they are equivalent to Eqs. (7.16).

We see in addition that

$$\frac{F_i/F_f}{F_i'/F_f'} = \frac{\rho V L/\mu}{\rho' V' L'/\mu'} \quad \text{and} \quad \frac{F_i/F_g}{F_i'/F_g'} = \frac{V^2/Lg}{V'^2/L'g}$$

The Reynolds number is thus a measure of the ratio of inertia to friction ratio at any point in the flow, while the Froude number measures the force of inertia to gravity force.

7.22. Friction Forces. The coefficient $\Pi_2 = \rho V L/\mu$ is known as the Reynolds number, in honor of Osborne Reynolds, who first discovered its importance in his classical study of the flow of viscous fluid through pipes.

In order to conduct experiments with a small pipe of diameter D' to predict the flow through a large pipe of diameter D we must arrange to have $\rho V D/\mu = \rho' V' D'/\mu'$. For the same fluid the velocity in the small pipe must be higher than the velocity specified for the large pipe in the ratio D/D'. If this were impracticable, it would be permissible to use some other fluid of much lower viscosity for the model experiment. By the use of the Reynolds number, experiments on smooth pipes (geometrically similar) with various liquids and gases have been reduced to a single curve of $\Pi_1 = f(\Pi_2)$, or

$$\frac{F}{\rho D^2 V^2} = f(R)$$

where F is the resistance to flow and R is the Reynolds number.

It is of practical interest to observe further that for an experiment with a model airplane in air $\rho/\rho' = \mu/\mu' = 1$, $VL = V'L'$. This means that a 5-ft model of a 50-ft wing, expected to operate at 100 mph, should be tested in a wind tunnel at 1,000 mph if frictional effects are to be truly represented. This is clearly impracticable; but if the wind-tunnel air is compressed to 5 atm, the test velocity required for constant R is reduced to 200 mph.

The Reynolds number is frequently written in the form $R = VL/\nu$, where $\nu = \mu/\rho$ is called the "kinematic viscosity" of the fluid. Although water is some 800 times as dense as air, the viscosity of air at ordinary temperatures is relatively high and its kinematic viscosity is some 14 times as great as that of water.

A constant relation between inertia and frictional forces in a given set of experiments is seen to be preserved by constancy of the Reynolds number, but other considerations determine the relative importance of friction in practical cases. Where experiments show that forces vary as $\rho V^2 L^2$, it is permissible to neglect the effect of the Reynolds number. For example, the resistance of a thin plate held normal to a flow is almost entirely due to inertia forces, while the same plate held edgewise to the flow experiences a frictional force due to fluid shear over its wetted surface. In the former position the resistance is independent of the Reynolds number, while in the latter it is not.

The performance of propellers and hydraulic turbines and pumps is found to be mainly dependent on inertia forces. This fact is not unexpected because of the great mass of fluid flowing through the machine and the relatively small wetted surface.

The trajectory of a heavy bomb falling through air or water is largely determined by inertia forces because of the high ratio of mass to surface. On the other hand, the settling of fog particles through air or of sediment through water is controlled by frictional forces because of the low ratio of mass to surface of the individual particles.

7.23. Gravity Forces. Where surface waves are formed, gravity forces are involved, for the weight of an element of fluid near the free surface is not completely counterbalanced by buoyancy, as for one far below the surface. As we have previously seen, the coefficient $\Pi_3 = V^2/Lg$ measures the ratio of inertia to gravity force. This coefficient is known as the Froude number, from the law of comparison discovered by William Froude in 1870 in connection with his pioneering experiments with ship models.

7.24. Compressibility. Similitude between two flows of compressible fluid implies in general not only dynamic similarity but also thermal similarity. Extended consideration of thermal effects is avoided if pressure may be considered a function only of density. This assumption is usually permissible in high-speed flows of technical importance. In such flows one may assume that the changes in density are adiabatic and are uninfluenced by friction (isentropic). It is known that under these conditions there is a relation between pressure and density of the form $p/\rho^k = $ constant, where the exponent k is constant for a given fluid.

If a small mass of fluid, with initial volume equal to $\mathcal{v}$, is compressed isentropically, the first law of thermodynamics shows that its increase in intrinsic energy dU is equal to the work done by the pressure in decreasing the volume,

$$0 = p \, d\mathcal{v} + dU$$
$$dU = - p \, d\mathcal{v}$$

Consider now the change in intrinsic energy dU and the accompanying change in kinetic energy $d(KE)$ as a small fluid mass moves an infinitesimal distance in a high-speed flow. If similarity is to be preserved in a model of this flow, it is necessary that the ratio $dU'/d(KE)'$ for the corresponding mass moving between corresponding points in the model flow be equal to $dU/d(KE)$. This condition may be written

$$\frac{d(KE)}{d(KE)'} = \frac{dU}{dU'} \tag{7.17}$$

Equation (7.17) is a further restriction on the model flow, additional to those given by Eqs. (7.14) or (7.16).

Alternatively, the conditions for similitude in case of compressibility may be developed from the Π theorem if the independent variables controlling the compressibility phenomena are correctly chosen. It is customary to assume that the sound velocity in the undisturbed fluid C is the only variable that need be considered in addition to ρ, L, V, μ, and g. The primary quantities of mechanics thus suffice, and four Π products are indicated. Forming Π_4 in the same way as above, we find that $\Pi_4 = \rho^{a_4} L^{b_4} V^{c_4} C^{-1} = V/C$, Mach number. If the assumption regarding C is correct, we should expect to find that Eq. (7.17) is reducible to

$$\frac{V}{C} = \frac{V'}{C'} \tag{7.18}$$

If this reduction is possible, it will clarify the physical significance of the Mach number. The relationship between Eqs. (7.17) and (7.18) will now be developed.

The change in kinetic energy of a small mass $\rho \mho$ as its velocity changes from u to $u + du$ will be

$$d(KE) = \rho\mho\left[\frac{(u+du)^2}{2} - \frac{u^2}{2}\right] = \rho\mho u \, du$$

The ratio of corresponding kinetic-energy changes will be

$$\frac{d(KE)}{d(KE)'} = \frac{\rho\mho u \, du}{\rho'\mho'u' \, du'} = \frac{\rho L^3 V^2}{\rho' L'^3 V'^2}$$

To evaluate the ratio of intrinsic-energy changes we must develop the relations between the sound velocity, pressure, density, and fluid velocity. Consider a small plane pressure wave propagating from right to left with

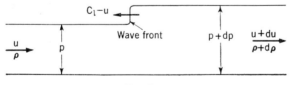

FIG. 7.1.

a velocity C_l relative to the fluid in front of it. If the velocity u of this fluid is toward the right, the absolute speed of the wave will be $C_l - u$ toward the left, as shown in Fig. 7.1. Conditions in the fluid will appear steady to an observer moving with the velocity of the wave front. From this point of view the velocities will be as indicated in Fig. 7.2.

For a stream tube of unit cross-sectional area the equation of continuity yields

$$\rho C_l = (\rho + d\rho)(C_l + du)$$
$$C_l \, d\rho + \rho \, du = 0 \qquad (7.19)$$

Likewise, the momentum equation gives

$$p - (p + dp) = - \rho C_l^2 + (\rho + d\rho)(C_l^2 + 2C_l \, du + du^2)$$

whence, combining with Eq. (7.19), we get

$$dp = - 2\rho C_l \, du - C_l^2 \, d\rho = 2C_l^2 \, d\rho - C_l^2 \, d\rho = C_l^2 \, d\rho$$

$$\frac{dp}{d\rho} = C_l^2 \qquad (7.20)$$

From the assumed relation between p and ρ, namely $p/\rho^k = $ constant,

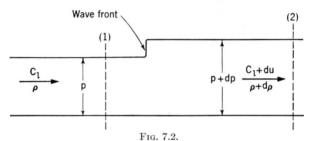

FIG. 7.2.

we find by differentiation that $dp/d\rho = kp/\rho$. Hence, from Eq. (7.20),

$$C_l^2 = \frac{kp}{\rho} \qquad (7.21)$$

The change in intrinsic energy of a mass $\rho \upsilon$ has been shown above to be

$$dU = - p \, d\upsilon$$

But, since the mass $\rho \upsilon$ is constant, its differential is equal to zero, or

$$- d\upsilon = \upsilon \frac{d\rho}{\rho}$$

Therefore, from Eqs. (7.19) and (7.21),

$$dU = p \frac{d\rho}{\rho} \upsilon = - \frac{\rho C_l^2}{k} \frac{du}{C_l} \upsilon = - \frac{\rho C_l}{k} \upsilon \, du$$

Letting p_0, ρ_0, and C represent values in the undisturbed stream, we find that

$$C_l^2 = C^2 \frac{p}{p_0} \frac{\rho_0}{\rho} = C^2 \left(\frac{\rho}{\rho_0}\right)^{k-1}$$

whence

$$dU = - \rho \mho \, du \, \frac{C}{k} \left(\frac{\rho}{\rho_0} \right)^{(k-1)/2}$$

and

$$\frac{dU}{dU'} = \frac{\rho \mho \, du}{\rho' \mho' \, du'} \frac{C}{C'} \left(\frac{\rho}{\rho_0} \right)^{(k-1)/2} \left(\frac{\rho_0'}{\rho'} \right)^{(k'-1)/2} \frac{k'}{k}$$

$$= \frac{\rho L^3}{\rho' L'^3} \frac{VC}{V'C'} \left(\frac{\rho}{\rho_0} \right)^{(k-1)/2} \left(\frac{\rho_0'}{\rho'} \right)^{(k'-1)/2} \frac{k'}{k}$$

Equating these expressions for the kinetic-energy ratio and intrinsic-energy ratio, in accordance with Eq. (7.17), we get

$$\frac{V}{C} = \frac{V'}{C'} \left(\frac{\rho}{\rho_0} \right)^{(k-1)/2} \left(\frac{\rho_0'}{\rho'} \right)^{(k'-1)/2} \frac{k'}{k} \tag{7.22}$$

It is seen that Eqs. (7.17) and (7.18) are equivalent only if $k = k'$. Furthermore, if this condition is fulfilled,

$$\frac{d(KE)/dU}{d(KE)'/dU'} = \frac{V/C}{V'/C'}$$

and the Mach number is a measure of the ratio of kinetic-energy change to intrinsic-energy change, just as the Reynolds or Froude number measures the ratio of certain forces.

The nondimensional quantity k should be included in the general equation as an additional Π. This example illustrates that dimensional analysis is not infallible; if a variable is omitted, the Π theorem cannot indicate the omission unless there are too few quantities to form even one Π product. Ordinarily, k is left out of consideration because model experiments on high-speed flow are usually performed with the same fluid as for the prototype. It is clear that k is important, for it controls the relation between pressure and density. The relation between compressible flows having different values of k may be likened to that between the motions of a linear and a nonlinear spring.

In practice, compressibility is found to be important for high-speed phenomena having Mach numbers exceeding 0.7. Examples are ballistics, rotary compressors, propellers, and high-speed airplanes.

7.25. Special Forms of the Dimensional Equation for Fluid Motion. From the preceding discussion, it will be seen that it is impractical to arrange model experiments to preserve a constant Reynolds number, Froude number, and Mach number. The experimenter, however, is helped by the fact that in practical cases some of the quantities may be neglected.

For example, airplane-model experiments may omit consideration of the Froude number since no free liquid surface is involved and for moderate speeds may ignore the Mach number. However, the drag does involve the Reynolds number, since flight Reynolds numbers are very large.

Efforts are made to test airplane models at as high a Reynolds number as possible by use of compressed air.

For the lift of airplane wings, thrust of propellers, and the delivery of pumps and fans it is found that the effect of friction is much less important than the effect of inertia, and consequently the Reynolds number can be ignored for a good approximation.

The general dimensional equation is therefore not used in complete form but breaks down into

$$\frac{F}{\rho L^2 V^2} = \Pi_1 = \text{constant}$$

where inertia predominates;

$$\Pi_1 = \phi\left(\frac{\rho V L}{\mu}\right)$$

where friction is appreciable;

$$\Pi_1 = \phi\left(\frac{\rho V L}{\mu}, \frac{V^2}{Lg}\right)$$

for ship models;

$$\Pi_1 = \phi\left(\frac{V}{C}\right)$$

for high-speed flows and ballistics. It is to be noted that ship-model experiments require both the Reynolds number and the Froude number to be constant. This, however, is impossible to accomplish.

The naval architect subtracts from the observed model resistance that part due to skin friction, as computed from tests of smooth plates moved edgewise through the water at the Reynolds number of the model test. The remaining, or "residual," resistance F_1 is considered to include the "wave-making" and pressure resistance of the model and to follow Froude's law

$$\frac{F_1}{\rho L^2 V^2} = \phi\left(\frac{V^2}{Lg}\right)$$

When the model is towed at the same value of the Froude number as the ship, or at the "corresponding speed" (proportional to the square root of the length), the ship's residual resistance can be scaled up from the model by the relation

$$\frac{F_1}{F_1'} = \frac{L^2 V^2}{L'^2 V'^2}$$

where primed symbols refer to the model and unprimed ones to the prototype. At this speed the pattern of surface waves made by the model is geometrically similar to the pattern of surface waves created by the ship. Naval architects photograph the wave patterns made by models run at corresponding speeds in order to judge the effect of changes in design.

A 20-ft model of a 500-ft ship, expected to steam at 25 knots, should be towed at a corresponding speed of 5 knots to hold the Froude number constant. Since g in the Froude number is practically constant, naval architects ignore it and use simply the "speed-length ratio" $V/\sqrt{L}$.

Flying boats that do not begin to plane until sufficient speed has been reached must pass through a critical, or "hump," speed where the wave-making resistance is a maximum. This critical speed is a function of the Froude number and can be predicted from model tests. It cannot be computed from first principles.

7.26. Conclusions. The method of dimensional analysis indicates that in experimental and test work the quantities involved may be grouped into a definite number of independent dimensionless coefficients and the results of observation expressed in terms of such coefficients.

For model experiments designed to represent the operation of a proto-type, it is necessary to have some of these coefficients numerically equal for model and prototype.

There appear to be three main uses for dimensional analysis.

1. To obtain comprehensive engineering data from model experiments where only a few of the variables can be changed.

2. To state the conditions, in terms of a few nondimensional coefficients, under which experimental results may be generally applicable.

3. To check the completeness or validity of a physical relation found by experiment or deduced by analysis.

Dimensional analysis is primarily the tool of the designer and the test engineer. Its applications to naval architecture by Froude, to aeronautics by Rayleigh, and more recently to heat transfer, lubrication, and hydraulics have revolutionized these branches of engineering. It is unnecessary to wait for the analytical solution of a problem if a controlled experiment can be arranged to satisfy the conditions of similitude.

SELECTED BIBLIOGRAPHY

1. Bridgman, P. W.: "Dimensional Analysis," 2d ed., Yale University Press, New Haven, 1931.
2. Buckingham, E.: On Physically Similar Systems, *Phys. Rev.*, vol. 4, ser. 2, pp. 345–376, 1914.
3. Buckingham, E.: Model Experiments and the Form of Empirical Equations, *Trans. Am. Soc. Mech. Engrs.*, vol. 37, pp. 263–296, 1915.
4. Gibson, A. H.: The Principles of Dynamical Similarity, *Engineering* (London), vol. 117, pp. 325–327, 357–359, 391–393, 422–423, 1924.
5. Rayleigh, Lord: The Principle of Similitude, *Nature*, vol. 95, pp. 66–68, 1915.
6. Weber, M.: Das allgemeine Aehnlichkeitsprinzip der Physik, *Jahrb. Schiffbautechn. Ges.*, vol. 31, pp. 274–354, 1930.

CHAPTER VIII

INCOMPRESSIBLE FLOW IN CLOSED CONDUITS

Study of fluid flow in pipes not only has yielded information of practical value to the designer of pipe lines but also has broadened our basic knowledge of the mechanism of fluid motion in general.

It has long been known that two distinct kinds of pipe flow occur. The simpler of these, laminar flow, is characterized by motion of the fluid in layers, or laminae, parallel to the pipe axis. The path followed by any small mass of fluid is a straight line. Conditions favorable for laminar flow are high viscosity μ, low density ρ, low mean velocity V, and small pipe diameter D.

Laminar flow in a tube of circular cross section was studied experimentally by Hagen, who published his results in 1839, and independently by Poiseuille, whose work was published between 1840 and 1846. Each deduced from his tests that the volume rate of flow is directly proportional to the pressure drop and to the fourth power of the radius and inversely proportional to the tube length. On this account, the equation relating these quantities to the viscosity is called the "Hagen-Poiseuille law."

In the majority of engineering applications the flow is not laminar but turbulent. In this type of flow only the average motion of the fluid is parallel to the tube axis. The movement of any small fluid mass is highly irregular, random fluctuations being superposed on the average velocity. In a smooth pipe, however, the transverse fluctuations necessarily approach zero in the vicinity of the wall, so that even in a highly turbulent flow a thin laminar film exists next to the wall.

A laminar flow becomes unstable and tends to become turbulent as the mean velocity is increased, other things being equal. Osborne Reynolds, in 1883, showed that the transition from laminar to turbulent motion depends not only on velocity but more generally on the dimensionless quantity $\rho V D/\mu$, which is now known as the Reynolds number R. He showed that if R is below the critical value of about 2,000 the flow is laminar, while at higher values the flow tends to become turbulent. Reynolds also laid the groundwork for the present statistical theory of turbulence.

The twentieth-century developments in our knowledge of pipe flow are in large measure due to Prandtl and von Kármán, and their students. These men, by a remarkable combination of physical intuition, experimental skill, and analytical ability, have developed greatly the theory of turbulent flow in both smooth and rough pipes.

8.1. Entrance and Fully Developed Flow Regions. If an incompressible fluid flows steadily through a horizontal pipe of uniform diameter,

122

the velocity distribution over a cross section will be found to vary with distance from the entrance as shown in Fig. 8.1.   In the tank the velocity is negligible, but in the rounded entrance it increases gradually to give the practically uniform distribution shown at section a.   At the wall the

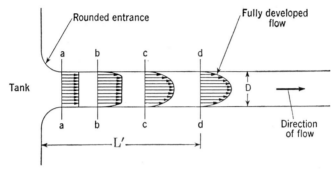

FIG. 8.1. — Development of flow in the entrance length of a pipe.

velocity is zero on account of the viscosity, but the layer of fluid affected by friction is still very thin at a.   This boundary layer grows as the fluid moves along the tube.   Somewhat upstream from section c its thickness is seen to equal the radius of the tube.   The velocity distribution approaches the fully developed form asymptotically, but at section d, a distance L' from the entrance, the maximum velocity has reached 99 per cent of the ultimate value.   This distance is called the "length of transition."

It is found that in laminar flow the ratio L'/D is a function of R.   The theoretical formula

$$\frac{L'}{D} = 0.058 \frac{\rho V D}{\mu} = 0.058R \tag{8.1}$$

due to Langhaar, agrees well with observation.   For $R = 1{,}000$, L'/D is seen to be about 58.

In a turbulent flow it is found that L'/D is less dependent on R than in laminar flow.   Experiments by Nikuradse show that the value of L'/D lies between 25 and 40.

The pressure distribution over a cross section in the entrance length is not uniform, since fluid is being moved toward the center of the pipe.

In fully developed laminar flow the pressure varies hydrostatically over any cross section; in fully developed turbulent flow there is also some variation, but it may not be hydrostatic.   In either case it can be shown that a correct result is obtained for the axial force on a cross section by assuming the pressure to be constant over the section.   It will be convenient to define the symbol p^* as

$$p^* = p + \rho g z \tag{8.2}$$

where z is the elevation of the pipe axis above an arbitrary datum.

In a fully developed flow the momentum law yields a relationship between p^* and the apparent shearing stress acting on a cylindrical surface concentric with the axis. In Fig. 8.2 are shown the external forces acting on the fluid within a cylindrical control surface of cross-sectional area πr^2 and length dx. The apparent shearing stress τ_{app} acting on the lateral surface may be partly real and partly fictitious. The real part is due to

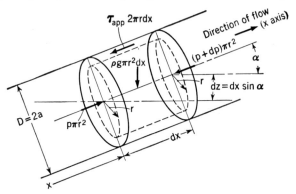

Fig. 8.2. — Forces on a cylindrical mass of fluid.

the viscous stresses exerted by the adjacent fluid, and the fictitious part is actually the net efflux of x momentum per unit area through the lateral surface. Such an efflux will occur only because of turbulent fluctuations; there will be none in a laminar flow. Since the flow is fully developed, there is no net momentum flux through the ends of the cylinder. The momentum law gives

$$p\pi r^2 - (p + dp)\pi r^2 - \rho g\, dx \sin \alpha\, \pi r^2 - 2\tau_{\text{app}}\pi r\, dx = 0$$

or

$$-(dp + \rho g\, dz)\pi r^2 = -dp^*\pi r^2 = 2\tau_{\text{app}}\pi r\, dx$$

or

$$-\frac{dp^*}{dx}\frac{r}{2} = \tau_{\text{app}} \tag{8.3}$$

Since the flow is fully developed, τ_{app} is independent of x and Eq. (8.3) can be integrated with respect to x, say from $x = x_1$ to $x = x_2 = x_1 + L$.

$$-(p_2{}^* - p_1{}^*)\frac{r}{2} = \tau_{\text{app}}\,(x_2 - x_1) = \tau_{\text{app}}L$$

or

$$\frac{p_1{}^* - p_2{}^*}{L}\frac{r}{2} = \tau_{\text{app}} \tag{8.4}$$

If we choose $r = a$, the radius of the tube, τ_{app} becomes equal to the shear stress at the wall, τ_0.

$$\frac{p_1{}^* - p_2{}^*}{L}\frac{a}{2} = \frac{p_1{}^* - p_2{}^*}{L}\frac{D}{4} = \tau_0 \tag{8.5}$$

It is to be noted that all the quantities on the left side of Eq. (8.5) can be readily measured. The equation thus provides a simple means of finding the wall shear stress.

By combining Eqs. (8.4) and (8.5) we find that the apparent shearing stress varies linearly from zero at the pipe center to a maximum at the wall.

$$\tau_{app} = \frac{r}{a} \tau_0 \tag{8.6}$$

8.2. Friction Factor. The motion of a particle of fluid along the tube is independent of gravity because the fluid is incompressible and there is no free surface. Under these conditions the weight of each particle is exactly counterbalanced by the static buoyant force exerted on it by the surroundings. The flow pattern is therefore independent of g, and we may assume for a fully developed flow that τ_0 is a function only of V, D, ρ, μ, and the wall roughness (which is assumed to be uniform everywhere).

Application of the Π theorem to the equation $\tau_0 = \phi_1(V, D, \rho, \mu, \text{rough-ness})$ shows that we may write

$$\frac{\tau_0}{\rho V^2} = \phi_2\left(\frac{\rho V D}{\mu}, \text{ roughness}\right) \tag{8.7}$$

Here ϕ_1 and ϕ_2 represent unknown functions, and the roughness is assumed to be dimensionless. The roughness can be expressed, for example, by a sequence of ratios of various lengths to the diameter D.

Equation (8.7) forms the basis on which pipe-flow measurements have been correlated. So important is it that the dimensionless ratio $\tau_0/\rho V^2$ has been given a name—the friction factor, denoted by f. Usually a numerical coefficient, 2 or 8, is included in the definition of the friction factor. In this text we shall define f as

$$f = \frac{8\tau_0}{\rho V^2} \tag{8.8}$$

The reason for choosing 8 is seen if τ_0 is eliminated from Eqs. (8.5) and (8.8).

$$f = \frac{p_1^* - p_2^*}{L} D \frac{1}{(\rho/2)V^2} \tag{8.9}$$

Equation (8.9) gives f in terms of quantities that are readily measured and contains the familiar factor $(\rho/2)V^2$. It is more convenient for general use in pipe-flow computations than is Eq. (8.8), but the latter should be regarded as defining f, since it shows the intimate connection between the friction factor and the frictional stress on the tube wall.

Equation (8.7) may be written as

$$f = \phi(R, \text{ roughness}) \tag{8.10}$$

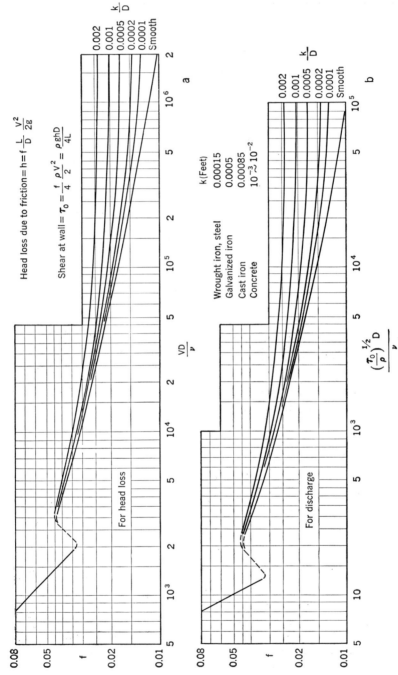

Head loss due to friction $= h = f \dfrac{L}{D} \dfrac{V^2}{2g}$

Shear at wall $= \tau_0 = \dfrac{f}{4} \dfrac{\rho V^2}{2} = \dfrac{\rho g h D}{4L}$

	k (Feet)
Wrought iron, steel	0.00015
Galvanized iron	0.0005
Cast iron	0.00085
Concrete	$10^{-3} \, 10^{-2}$

For head loss

For discharge

$\dfrac{VD}{\nu}$

$\dfrac{\left(\dfrac{\tau_0}{\rho}\right)^{1/2} D}{\nu}$

Fig. 8.3. — Relation between friction factor and other dimensionless parameters for pipes having various values of relative roughness. (*After Moody, reference 10, by permission of American Society of Mechanical Engineers.*)

where R is the Reynolds number $\rho V D / \mu$. This equation has been verified experimentally by many workers. Figure 8.3a shows graphically the form of the relationship for both laminar and turbulent conditions and for smooth tubes and new commercial pipe of various relative roughnesses. It is seen that moderate wall roughness has no effect on f if the flow is

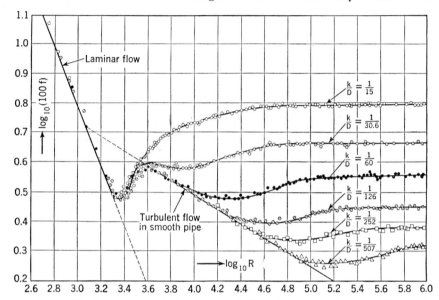

FIG. 8.4. — Relation between friction factor and Reynolds number for artificially roughened pipes.

laminar but has considerable influence for turbulent flow. The curve for laminar flow and the curve for turbulent flow in a smooth pipe are plotted from theoretical equations that will be developed later. The laminar theory is complete, but the turbulent theory requires the experimental determination of several constants whose value the theory cannot yet predict.

Nikuradse [12] * made tests on pipe artificially roughened by a coating of sand grains of uniform size. His results for different values of the relative roughness, k/a, the ratio of sand-grain diameter to pipe radius, are given in Fig. 8.4. In these tests the roughness was adequately described by a single ratio, k/a, as shown by the absence of scatter in the experimental points. The roughness was completely uniform and quite unlike that for commercial pipes.

In Fig. 8.3a are shown curves for commercial pipe of various relative roughnesses. These curves resemble those for the sand-coated tubes of Fig. 8.4, in that they become horizontal at sufficiently large values of R.

* Numbers in [ ] refer to the bibliography at the end of the chapter.

The value of k/a assigned to any kind of commercial pipe is obtained by a direct comparison of the horizontal parts of the curves in Fig. 8.3a with the horizontal parts of Nikuradse's curves.

In the intermediate region in which f depends on both R and k/a the curves for commercial and sand-coated pipes are very different, and one might question whether the roughness of the former can be adequately described by a single parameter k/a. The justification for this procedure is given below in Art. 8.11.

The alternative form of plot shown in Fig. 8.3b can be justified either by Eq. (8.7) and the Π theorem or by suitable intermultiplication of the variables of Eq. (8.10). This plot is useful in case the wall shearing stress (or head loss) is known and the velocity is not.

In the solution of many pipe-flow problems the steady-flow energy equation is useful. In case the fluid is incompressible, as is assumed throughout this chapter, the energy equation [Eq. (5.10)] takes the form

$$\mathcal{W}_s + \frac{p_2 - p_1}{\rho} + \frac{V_2^2 - V_1^2}{2} + g(z_2 - z_1) + gH_{l_{1,2}} = 0$$

where $H_{l_{1,2}}$ stands for $(u_2 - u_1 - q_{1,2})/g$, the energy dissipated per unit weight of flowing fluid.

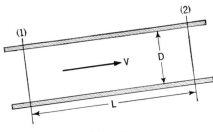

FIG. 8.5.

If sections 1 and 2 are taken in the fully developed flow region of a pipe (Fig. 8.5) $\mathcal{W}_s = 0$ and $V_2 = V_1 = V$, so that

$$\frac{p_2 - p_1}{\rho g} + z_2 - z_1 + H_{l_{1,2}} = 0$$

or

$$\frac{p_1{}^* - p_2{}^*}{\rho g} = H_{l_{1,2}} \qquad (8.11)$$

Combination of Eqs. (8.9) and (8.11) gives the relation between the friction factor and the energy dissipated by friction in the length L of straight pipe.

$$H_{l_{1,2}} = f \frac{L}{D} \frac{V^2}{2g} \qquad (8.12)$$

In complicated problems involving other losses besides those in a straight pipe only that part of the total loss which is due to pipe friction is given by Eq. (8.12). The other losses are added to this part to obtain the total.

8.3. Fully Developed Laminar Flow. The apparent shearing stress in a laminar flow is the actual viscous shearing stress τ, since turbulent transfers of momentum do not occur. Accordingly, Eq. (8.4) reduces to

$$\tau = \frac{p_1{}^* - p_2{}^*}{L} \frac{r}{2} \qquad (8.4a)$$

In order to make further progress we must assume a relation between τ, μ, and the velocity distribution. We base our assumption on the experiment described in Art. 1.4, in which the formula $\tau = \mu V/h$ was found to hold. This formula applies to a thin fluid film of uniform thickness h, between two concentric cylinders, one fixed and one having a peripheral velocity V. In this apparatus the velocity is found to vary linearly across the film, so that at any point in the film $\partial u/\partial y = V/h$,

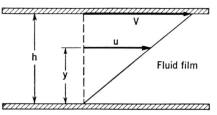

Fig. 8.6. — Linear velocity distribution in a thin film between concentric cylinders (or parallel plates).

where $\partial u/\partial y$ is the rate of change of velocity with distance from the surface (Fig. 8.6). The constant shear stress is in this case equal to $\mu(\partial u/\partial y)$.

For the laminar flow in a pipe we assume that, although the shear stress is not constant, nevertheless it is given by the formula

$$\tau = \mu \frac{\partial u}{\partial y} = -\mu \frac{\partial u}{\partial r} \qquad (8.13)$$

where y is the distance from the pipe wall, as shown in Fig. 8.7. Since τ varies linearly with r, Eq. (8.13) will lead to a parabolic velocity distribu-

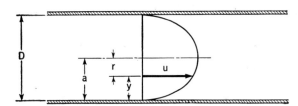

Fig. 8.7. — Nonlinear velocity distribution in a pipe.

tion. Combine Eqs. (8.4a) and (8.13), and integrate with respect to r, noting that $u = 0$ at $r = a$.

$$-\int_{u=u}^{u=0} \frac{\partial u}{\partial r} \, dr = \frac{p_1{}^* - p_2{}^*}{2\mu L} \int_r^a r \, dr$$

$$u = \frac{p_1{}^* - p_2{}^*}{4\mu L} a^2 \left(1 - \frac{r^2}{a^2}\right) \qquad (8.14)$$

and

$$u_{\max} = \frac{p_1{}^* - p_2{}^*}{4\mu L} a^2 \qquad (8.15)$$

It is relatively hard to measure velocity distribution, so that an accurate experimental check on Eq. (8.14) is not easily obtained. We can, however, get an expression for the volume discharge rate Q by using Eq. (8.14).

$$Q = \pi \int_0^a u \, d(r^2) = \pi a^2 \int_0^1 u \, d\left(\frac{r}{a}\right)^2$$

$$= \frac{\pi a^4}{4\mu L}(p_1{}^* - p_2{}^*) \int_0^1 \left[1 - \left(\frac{r}{a}\right)^2\right] d\left(\frac{r}{a}\right)^2$$

$$= \frac{\pi a^4}{8\mu L}(p_1{}^* - p_2{}^*) \tag{8.16}$$

Equation (8.16), which agrees with the measurements of Hagen and Poiseuille as well as with those of more recent investigators, is called the Hagen-Poiseuille law. The accord between Eq. (8.16) and the experimental data justifies the assumption that $\tau = \mu(\partial u/\partial y)$.

Since the mean velocity V is defined as $V = Q/\pi a^2$, it follows from Eqs. (8.15) and (8.16) that in laminar flow

$$V = \frac{u_{\max}}{2} \tag{8.17}$$

Combination of Eqs. (8.9), (8.15), and (8.17) yields the formula for the friction factor in laminar flow, which is plotted in Fig. 8.3.

$$f = \frac{64\mu}{\rho VD} = \frac{64}{R} \tag{8.18}$$

An important engineering application of these equations for laminar flow is the measurement of viscosity. The Hagen-Poiseuille law applied to the apparatus of Fig. 8.8 provides an absolute method of viscosimetry. All the quantities appearing in Eq. (8.16), except μ, are known for the viscometer of Fig. 8.8. Consequently, μ can be calculated. In order that

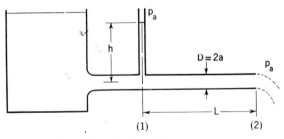

Fig. 8.8. — Capillary-tube viscometer.

Poiseuille's law be applicable it is necessary to measure the pressure difference between two points both of which lie in a region of fully developed flow. Hence, point 1 must be a sufficient distance from the pipe entry [see Eq. (8.1)].

It is difficult to install a manometer in a fine capillary tube such as

must be used to ensure laminar flow. Further, it is hard to measure accurately the diameter of such a tube. Since the fourth power of the radius occurs in Eq. (8.16), a small error in radius will cause a large error in the computed value of μ. For these reasons, this type of viscometer is not widely used for routine measurements; instead, the Saybolt viscometer is ordinarily employed in this country.

This instrument, shown schematically in Fig. 8.9, consists essentially of a reservoir in the bottom of which is a short vertical tube. These are surrounded by a constant-temperature oil bath. A viscosity determination

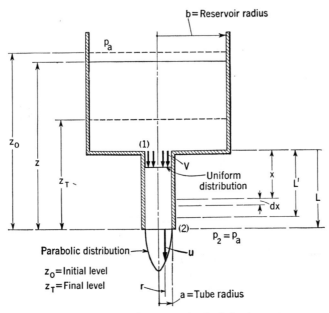

FIG. 8.9. — Essential features of a Saybolt viscometer.

is made by measuring the time required for 60 cu cm of fluid at a known temperature to flow out of the reservoir through the tube, the initial level of the fluid in the reservoir having been previously adjusted to a standard height. From the time measurement (Saybolt seconds) the kinematic viscosity $\nu = \mu/\rho$ of the fluid can be determined through the use of empirical formulas.

It is possible to deduce theoretically a formula that is in fair agreement with the empirical ones. The theory is of interest because it involves both the development of laminar flow in the entrance section of the tube and unsteady flow conditions. It will be given in the next article.

8.4. Development of Laminar Flow. Using the notation of Fig. 8.9, we may write the energy equation for the fluid in the reservoir and tube as

$$z = \frac{1}{\rho g V \pi a^2} \int_{r=0}^{r=a} \frac{\rho u^2}{2} u d(\pi r^2) + H_{l_{0,2}} \tag{8.19}$$

where z is the height of the free surface at any instant. In writing Eq. (8.19) we neglect local changes with respect to time in comparison with space rates of change.

Equations (8.14), (8.15), and (8.17) enable us to express the kinetic-energy term in the simple form V^2/g, but an accurate evaluation of $H_{l_{0,2}}$ is difficult. We neglect losses occurring in the reservoir and consider the only loss to be that in the tube. If we assume the losses there to be the same as in fully developed flow, Eqs. (8.12) and (8.18) give

$$H_{l_{0,2}} = \frac{32\mu}{\rho V a} \frac{V^2}{2g} \frac{L}{2a} = \frac{8\nu L V}{g a^2} \tag{8.20}$$

Since, however, the flow is developing between 1 and 2 in Fig. 8.9, the loss in the transition length will be greater than that for fully developed flow and Eq. (8.20) is an underestimate. Langhaar [7] has developed a satisfactory theory of the laminar transition flow by which one can compute

$$H_{l_{0,2}} = \frac{8\nu L V}{g a^2} + 0.14 \frac{V^2}{g} \tag{8.21}$$

Equation (8.19) now becomes

$$z = \frac{8\nu L V}{g a^2} + 1.14 \frac{V^2}{g} \tag{8.22}$$

The equation of continuity applied to the viscometer gives

$$-\pi b^2 \frac{dz}{dt} = \pi a^2 V$$

or

$$V = -\frac{b^2}{a^2} \frac{dz}{dt} \tag{8.23}$$

where t is the time. Combination of Eqs. (8.22) and (8.23) yields a second-degree differential equation for z, which can be solved for dz/dt in the usual manner for a quadratic. Finally we obtain, after separating the variables,

$$\frac{dz}{1 - \sqrt{1 + (4\beta/\alpha^2)z}} = \frac{\alpha}{2\beta} dt$$

where $\alpha = 8\nu L b^2/g a^4$ and $\beta = 1.14 b^4/g a^4$. This equation is readily integrated to

$$T = \alpha \left(\ln \frac{y_0}{y_T} + y_T - y_0 \right) \tag{8.24}$$

where T = total efflux time

$$y_0 = 1 - \sqrt{1 + \frac{4\beta}{\alpha^2} z_0}$$

$$y_T = 1 - \sqrt{1 + \frac{4\beta}{\alpha^2} z_T}$$

The dimensions of a Saybolt universal viscometer are $a = 0.0883$ cm, $b = 1.488$ cm, $L = 1.225$ cm. The initial height of the fluid $z_0 = 12.50$ cm. The final height is computed from the area of the reservoir and the fact that 60 cu cm flows out: $z_T = 3.86$ cm. The following table shows the theoretical and empirical values of T for different values of ν:

ν, cm²/sec	T [from Eq. (8.24)], sec	T (empirical), sec
0.02	35.2	32.6
0.07	49.3	48.7
0.1	59.2	58.8
1.0	435	462
10.0	4310	4620

For values of ν less than about 0.07 sq cm per sec the computed value of T is too large. This fact can be explained by computation of the average transition length from Eq. (8.1). It is found that the transition length is greater than the length of the tube for $\nu < 0.07$ sq cm per sec. Equation (8.24) is thus an overestimate of T in this range.

For large values of ν, Eq. (8.24) gives a value of T that is too small. This fact is probably due to neglect of friction before the fluid enters the tube.

It is also of interest to determine the amount by which the average wall shearing stress in the transition length exceeds that in fully developed flow. The momentum equation applied to the fluid inside the tube gives

$$\pi a^2 (p_1 - p_a + \rho g L) - \int_0^L \tau_0 2\pi a \, dx = \int_{r=0}^{r=a} \rho u^2 \pi \, d(r^2) - \pi a^2 \rho V^2$$

where τ_0 is the wall shear stress at any point in the tube. The Bernoulli equation can be applied from the free surface to point 1, since friction is neglected there. Hence, $p_1 - p_a + \rho g L = \rho g z - (\rho/2) V^2$. We combine these last two equations and evaluate the integral for momentum efflux and obtain, finally,

$$\rho g \pi a^2 \left(z - \frac{V^2}{2g} \right) - \int_0^L \tau_0 2\pi a \, dx = \pi a^2 \frac{\rho}{3} V^2$$

Let τ_0' be the average value of τ_0 in the transition length L', and note from Eqs. (8.8) and (8.18) that in fully developed laminar flow

$\tau_0 = 4\mu V/a$. Then

$$\tau_0' - 4\mu \frac{V}{a} = \frac{\rho g a}{2L'} \left(z - \frac{5V^2}{6g} - \frac{8\nu V L}{g a^2} \right)$$

Eliminate z and L' by use of Eqs. (8.22) and (8.1).

$$\tau_0' - 4\mu \frac{V}{a} = \frac{0.31 \rho a V^2}{2L'} = \frac{0.31}{2 \times 0.23} \frac{\mu V}{a}$$

Therefore, the percentage excess of wall shear stress in the transition length over that in fully developed laminar flow is constant and equal to

$$\frac{\tau_0' - 4\mu V/a}{4\mu V/a} \times 100 = \frac{0.31 \times 100}{2 \times 0.23 \times 4} = 17\% \qquad (8.25)$$

8.5. Turbulence. Osborne Reynolds [13] first showed that the Reynolds number VD/ν is the criterion for the flow condition in a tube. His apparatus is shown schematically in Fig. 8.10. A fine filament of dye was introduced into the glass tube near its smoothly rounded, trumpet-shaped entrance. At low rates of flow the filament of dye appeared as a straight

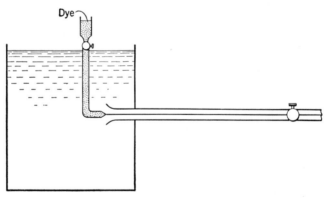

Fig. 8.10. — Reynolds' apparatus for demonstration of laminar and turbulent flow.

line parallel to the tube axis (laminar flow). At a certain critical velocity a sudden breakdown of the laminar motion occurred; the water in the tube became evenly colored by the dye throughout its entire length, except for a portion near the entry.

By performing this experiment with tubes of different sizes and with water at various temperatures Reynolds established the fact that turbulence sets in at a certain value of R. This value he found to be very sensitive to initial disturbances of the water. By allowing the water in the tank to remain undisturbed for some hours before the experiments he obtained the critical value of $R = 13,000$. Other experimenters, by taking elaborate precautions to avoid entry disturbances, have pushed the critical R as high as 40,000.

While there appears to be no definite upper limit to the critical value of R, all experimenters agree that a lower limit exists and that its value is approximately 2,000. If R is below this lower limit, all initial disturbances, no matter how severe, are damped out and the motion becomes laminar at a sufficient distance from the entry. Filaments of dye cannot be used in determining the lower critical R. Reynolds and most of his successors measured the pressure drop in a length far from the pipe entrance and the corresponding rate of discharge.

These results indicate that the laminar motion is unstable if R exceeds 2,000 and that a suitable disturbance will cause the onset of turbulent flow. Reynolds speculated as to the nature of turbulence and suggested that it was a completely random fluctuating motion.

Dryden [4] and others have shown experimentally that Reynolds' assumption of random velocity fluctuations in a turbulent flow corresponds to the facts. These experiments were carried out with a hot-wire anemometer, which consists of a very fine electrically heated platinum wire placed in the fluid stream. Since any change in speed alters the rate at which the wire is cooled, the temperature and consequently the electrical resistance of the wire are changed, so that the voltage drop through the wire varies in a definite way with the local velocity. After amplification, this fluctu-

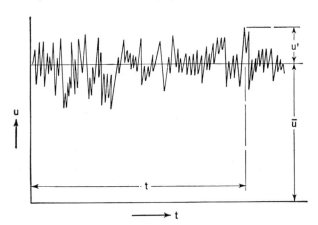

FIG. 8.11. — Random velocity fluctuations in turbulent flow.

ating voltage is applied to a cathode-ray oscillograph. A record of velocity as a function of time can thus be made on a moving photographic film and studied at leisure (Fig. 8.11).

A single hot wire set transversely to the flow will respond primarily to fluctuations parallel to the mean velocity; transverse fluctuations produce only second-order effects. A properly oriented, X-shaped arrangement of two hot wires is needed to measure the transverse fluctuations in a given direction. Fluctuations of the type u', discussed below, are the ones that were first measured by the hot-wire technique.

Let u, v, v_θ be the instantaneous velocity components at any point in a pipe in which the turbulent flow is fully developed. The component u is

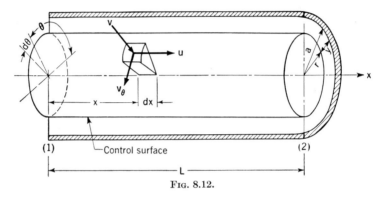

Fig. 8.12.

parallel to the mean flow (x axis); v is parallel to y, where y is measured normal to the wall and increases toward the center of the pipe; v_θ is perpendicular to both u and v. (Fig. 8.12). A photographic record of u, for example, as a function of time would look somewhat like the schematic curve of Fig. 8.11, which is meant to represent a random fluctuation u', superposed on a constant mean value $\bar{u}$. The essential characteristic of u' is that its mean value $\overline{u'}$ is equal to zero. The velocity components v and v_θ are likewise subject to random fluctuations. Therefore, at an arbitrary time t

$$\left. \begin{array}{l} u = \bar{u} + u' \\ v = \bar{v} + v' \\ v_\theta = \bar{v}_\theta + v_\theta' \end{array} \right\} \tag{8.26}$$

where $\overline{u'} = \overline{v'} = \overline{v_\theta'} = 0$.

Obviously, for flow in a pipe of uniform diameter, $\bar{v} = 0$. Also, since we assume there is no spiraling of the flow, $\bar{v}_\theta = 0$.

8.6. Apparent Shearing Stress. In Art. 8.1 the concept of apparent shearing stress τ_{app} was introduced. It was there implied that part of this apparent stress is the average laminar stress and the rest is actually a momentum exchange.

At any surface element, $r\,d\theta\,dx$ of the cylindrical control surface shown in Fig. 8.12 the instantaneous efflux of x momentum is $-\rho uvr\,d\theta\,dx$. Substitute for u and v from Eq. (8.26), noting that $\bar{v} = 0$, and take the average value: $-\rho\overline{uv}r\,d\theta\,dx = -\rho\,(\overline{uv'} + \overline{u'v'})r\,d\theta\,dx$. The average value of $\overline{uv'} = \bar{u}\,\overline{v'} = 0$, but $\overline{u'v'}$ will not be zero if a correlation exists between u'

and v'. Such a correlation is to be expected for flow in a pipe, as will be shown below. Since the flow is fully developed, $\overline{u'v'}$ is independent of x, while by symmetry it does not depend on θ. Therefore, $\overline{u'v'}$ is a function of r (or y) only and is constant over the entire cylindrical control surface.

It may be seen in Chap. VI that an efflux of momentum has the same effect as a force of the same magnitude, applied at the control surface where the efflux occurs, and opposed to the direction of the momentum. Therefore, we can consider $-\rho\overline{u'v'}$ as equivalent to a fictitious shear stress. This fictitious stress is called either the turbulent shear stress τ_{turb} or the Reynolds stress, after Osborne Reynolds, who first pointed out the existence of turbulent momentum transfers. The Reynolds stress is one part of the apparent shear stress τ_{app}.

The other part of τ_{app} is the average laminar shearing stress τ, which, as in laminar flow, is given by the product $\mu(\partial\overline{u}/\partial y)$. In laminar flow there are no fluctuations, so that $\overline{u} = u$.

The apparent shear stress is thus

$$\tau_{\text{app}} = \tau + \tau_{\text{turb}}$$

$$\tau_{\text{app}} = \mu\frac{\partial\overline{u}}{\partial y} - \rho\overline{u'v'} \tag{8.27}$$

It should be pointed out that the laminar shear stress is actually a momentum transfer on a molecular scale. τ_{app} is thus the sum of two momentum transfers, one on a molecular scale, the other on a scale that is appreciable compared with the diameter of the tube. Since in fluid mechanics we ignore molecules and treat fluids as continua, we are content not to delve into the nature of the laminar shear stress. The case of the turbulent shear stress is different, however, for the mechanism of turbulent momentum exchange is one of the fundamental problems of fluid mechanics.

8.7. Zones of Flow in a Pipe. If the pipe wall is smooth, both u' and v' approach zero near the wall, so that there is a thin layer of fluid next to the wall in which τ_{turb} is negligible compared with τ. This layer is called the "laminar sublayer" and its thickness will be denoted by δ. Experiment shows that δ is so small in comparison with the pipe radius that $\partial\overline{u}/\partial y$ may be considered constant for $y \leqslant \delta$. The laminar parabolic velocity distribution in the sublayer is indistinguishable from a straight line, and $\tau = \mu(\partial\overline{u}/\partial y)$ is a constant.

For values of y that are larger than δ but still small relative to the pipe radius, $\mu(\partial\overline{u}/\partial y)$ decreases rapidly. From Eq. (8.4), however, τ_{app} decreases only linearly as y is increased, so that $-\rho\overline{u'v'}$, the turbulent part of τ_{app}, must become appreciable in this range of y values. Direct experiment thus shows that $\overline{u'v'}$ is different from zero and negative in this region. A correlation must, therefore, exist between u' and v'. Such a correlation is to be expected where $\partial \bar{u}/\partial y$ is different from zero, as in this case, for a particle of fluid having a positive v' will move to a region where the mean velocity $\bar{u}$ is greater than that at its first position. Consequently, a negative u' will tend on the average to be associated with a particle having a positive v', and vice versa. At the center of the pipe where $\partial \bar{u}/\partial y = 0$, u' and v' will be uncorrelated.

At some value of y, say $y = \lambda$, the value of $\partial \bar{u}/\partial y$ will be small enough to make $\mu(\partial \bar{u}/\partial y)$ completely negligible with respect to $-\overline{\rho u'v'}$. It is found that λ is small compared with the radius of the pipe.

From the foregoing we are justified in breaking down the flow in a smooth pipe into three zones, as follows:

1. A laminar sublayer lying next to the wall and in which turbulent effects are negligible. $(0 \leqslant y \leqslant \delta.)$

2. A transition zone in which the effects of turbulence and of viscosity are of the same order of magnitude. $(\delta \leqslant y \leqslant \lambda.)$

3. A turbulent core comprising the bulk of the fluid and in which the effect of viscosity is negligible. $(\lambda \leqslant y \leqslant a.)$

For a rough pipe the flow conditions near the wall are in general affected both by viscosity and by roughness. In this case we shall merely distinguish between a wall region and a turbulent core. We shall assume that the turbulent fluctuations in the core are independent of both viscosity and wall roughness.

8.8. Wall-velocity Law. On the basis of experience we may assume that $\bar{u}$ (which from now on will be written u, without the bar) depends on six independent variables, ρ, μ, a, y, wall roughness, and one other. For this sixth variable we might select V, Q, $(p_1{}^* - p_2{}^*)/L$, or τ_0. Of these, τ_0 is the best choice. Accordingly, we assume that $u = f(\rho, \tau_0, a, \mu, y, \text{roughness})$. With ρ, τ_0, and a common to the four independent Π products obtainable from this equation, the Π theorem yields

$$\frac{u}{\sqrt{\tau_0/\rho}} = \phi\left(\frac{\sqrt{\tau_0/\rho}\,a}{\nu}, \frac{y}{a}, \text{roughness}\right) \tag{8.28}$$

where ν is the kinematic viscosity μ/ρ. The roughness is assumed to be dimensionless, as in Art. 8.2. Since $\sqrt{\tau_0/\rho}$ has the dimensions of a velocity, it is convenient to define $u^* = \sqrt{\tau_0/\rho}$, and $R^* = \sqrt{\tau_0/\rho}\,a/\nu$. The ratio y/a will be denoted by ξ. Equation (8.28) becomes

$$\frac{u}{u^*} = \phi(R^*, \xi, \text{roughness}) \tag{8.28a}$$

Equation (8.28a) holds for all values of ξ (or y).

For a smooth pipe it is easy to show that, within the laminar sublayer, the pipe radius a plays no part in determining u. One might, therefore, assume for any type of wall that a has negligible effect also at greater distances from the wall, even as far as the outer part of the turbulent core. An equivalent assumption is that $u = f(\rho,\tau_0,\mu,y,\text{roughness})$. Whence

$$\frac{u}{u^*} = \chi\left(\frac{u^*y}{\nu},\text{roughness}\right) = \chi(R^*\xi,\text{roughness}) \qquad (8.29)$$

Equation (8.29), which is called "Prandtl's wall-velocity law," agrees well with experiments. We shall assume that Eq. (8.29) holds in the range $0 \leqslant \xi \leqslant \xi_1$, where ξ_1 is only slightly greater than λ/a. The function χ will, in general, have different forms in the wall layers and in the outer part of the turbulent core.

8.9. Velocity-defect Law. The difference between the maximum velocity U at the center of the pipe and the velocity anywhere else in the core is called the "velocity defect." From the preceding article it is seen that this defect $U - u$ depends at most on ρ, τ_0, a, μ, y, and roughness. $U - u$ will be determined, however, by the turbulent fluctuations in the core, which have been assumed independent of μ and roughness. Hence $U - u = f(\rho,\tau_0,a,y)$, or

$$\frac{U - u}{u^*} = \psi(\xi) \qquad (8.30)$$

Equation (8.30) is called the "velocity-defect law."

This equation is amply corroborated by experiments, notably those done by Fritsch [2] while working with von Kármán. Fritsch's velocity-distribution curves for a given

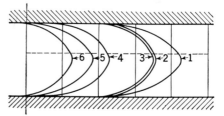

Fig. 8.13. — Turbulent-velocity-distribution curves for pipes having different wall roughness. Curve 1 is for smooth pipe and curves 2 to 6 are for rough pipes. The roughness increases in the order of the numbers of the curves.

value of u^* but for walls of different roughness are reproduced in Fig. 8.13. Curve 1 is for a smooth wall, and curve 6 is for a very rough wall, the other curves being for intermediate roughnesses. Fritsch found that, if the points of maximum velocity are superposed, all the curves are congruent, except in a narrow region near the wall.

If we assume that Eq. (8.30) applies over the whole cross section of the pipe, we find by integration that

$$\frac{U - V}{u^*} = \text{constant} \qquad (8.31)$$

where V is the mean velocity. Experiment shows the wall layers to be so thin that Eq. (8.31) may be used without appreciable error.

8.10. Resistance Law for a Smooth Pipe. From Eq. (8.8), $V/u^* = \sqrt{8/f}$, whence Eq. (8.31) becomes

$$\sqrt{\frac{8}{f}} = \frac{U}{u^*} - \text{constant} \qquad (8.32)$$

Equation (8.28a) indicates that for a smooth pipe

$$\frac{U}{u^*} = \phi(R^*,1) = \Phi(R^*) \tag{8.33}$$

We can, therefore, get f by finding $\Phi(R^*)$.

In the outer part of the turbulent core, where $\lambda/a \leqslant \xi \leqslant \xi_1$, both Eqs. (8.29) and (8.30) are valid. Eliminating u/u^*, we find, for a smooth pipe,

$$\chi(R^*\xi) = \frac{U}{u^*} - \psi(\xi) = \Phi(R^*) - \psi(\xi) \tag{8.34}$$

Differentiation of Eq. (8.34), first with respect to R^* and then with respect to ξ, yields two expressions for $d\chi/d(R^*\xi)$ (which we shall denote by χ').

$$\chi'\xi = \frac{d\Phi}{dR^*}$$

$$\chi'R^* = -\frac{d\psi}{d\xi}$$

provided that $\lambda/a \leqslant \xi \leqslant \xi_1$. From the first of these equations χ' must have the form $f(R^*)/\xi$, since $d\Phi/dR^*$ is independent of ξ. From the second equation χ' must be of the form $f(\xi)/R^*$, since $d\psi/d\xi$ is independent of R^*. Both these requirements can be fulfilled only if $f(\xi) = \text{constant}/\xi$ and $f(R^*) = \text{constant}/R^*$, that is, only if $\chi' = \text{constant}/R^*\xi = A/R^*\xi$, where A is an unknown constant. We thus are led to the following equations:

$$\Phi(R^*) = A \ln R^* + \text{constant} \tag{8.35}$$
$$\psi(\xi) = -A \ln \xi + \text{constant} \tag{8.36}$$
$$\chi(R^*\xi) = A \ln (R^*\xi) + \text{constant} \tag{8.37}$$

Combination of Eqs. (8.32), (8.33), and (8.35) gives

$$\sqrt{\frac{8}{f}} = A \ln (R^*) + \text{constant}$$

Recalling that

$$R^* = \frac{u^*a}{\nu} = \frac{2aV}{\nu}\frac{u^*}{2V} = \frac{DV}{\nu}\frac{\sqrt{f}}{4\sqrt{2}} = \frac{R\sqrt{f}}{4\sqrt{2}}$$

we finally obtain the formula,

$$\frac{1}{\sqrt{f}} = A_1 \log_{10} (R\sqrt{f}) + A_2 \tag{8.38}$$

where A_1 and A_2 are constants to be determined experimentally. Data obtained by Nikuradse, which are plotted in Fig. 8.14, agree exactly with

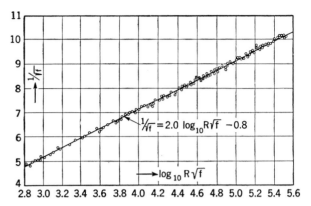

FIG. 8.14. — Resistance law for a smooth pipe.

the straight-line relationship predicted by Eq. (8.38) and lead to the final formula

$$\frac{1}{\sqrt{f}} = 2.0 \log_{10}(R\sqrt{f}) - 0.8 \qquad (8.38a)$$

8.11. Resistance Law for Rough Pipe. If we assume the roughness is so great that viscosity does not affect the flow, and that the roughness depends only on a single length k, a development like that of the last article is possible for rough pipe.

Equation (8.28a) yields in this case, where the nondimensional roughness term is the single ratio k/a,

$$\frac{U}{u^*} = \phi\left(1, \frac{k}{a}\right) = \Phi\left(\frac{k}{a}\right) \qquad (8.39)$$

The wall-velocity law [Eq. (8.29)] becomes

$$\frac{u}{u^*} = \chi\left(\frac{k}{y}\right) = \chi\left(\frac{k}{a}\frac{1}{\xi}\right) \qquad (8.40)$$

so that, in the range $\lambda/a \leqslant \xi \leqslant \xi_1$ Eqs. (8.31), (8.39), and (8.40) yield

$$\chi\left(\frac{k}{a}\frac{1}{\xi}\right) = \Phi\left(\frac{k}{a}\right) - \psi(\xi) \qquad (8.41)$$

Since $\psi(\xi)$ must have the same form as for a smooth pipe, Eq. (8.41) leads to

$$\Phi\left(\frac{k}{a}\right) = -A \ln \frac{k}{a} + \text{constant} \qquad (8.42)$$

$$\psi(\xi) = -A \ln \xi + \text{constant} \qquad (8.43)$$

$$\chi\left(\frac{k}{a}\frac{1}{\xi}\right) = -A \ln\left(\frac{k}{a}\frac{1}{\xi}\right) + \text{constant} \qquad (8.44)$$

Combination of Eqs. (8.32), (8.39), and (8.42) yields

$$\frac{\sqrt{8}}{\sqrt{f}} = -A \ln \frac{k}{a} + \text{constant} = A \ln \frac{a}{k} + \text{constant}$$

or

$$\frac{1}{\sqrt{f}} = A_1 \log_{10} \frac{a}{k} + A_3 \tag{8.45}$$

where A_1 should theoretically have the same value as in Eq. (8.38) and A_3 is an unknown constant.

Nikuradse's experiments on pipe artificially roughened by a coating of sand grains of uniform diameter indicate that the grain diameter k completely characterizes this type of roughness and that for sufficiently large Reynolds numbers

$$\frac{1}{\sqrt{f}} = 2.0 \log_{10} \frac{a}{k} + 1.74 \tag{8.45a}$$

The experiments bear out the prediction that the constant A_1 should have the same value for both smooth and rough pipes.

Nikuradse's results, which are plotted in Fig. 8.4, show that the limiting value of R at which f becomes independent of R varies with a/k. This fact is readily understood if we bear in mind that the importance of the roughness is determined by the ratio k/δ of the grain diameter to the thickness of the laminar sublayer. It will be shown below that δ depends only on R and that $\delta u^*/\nu = 5$. Hence

$$\frac{k}{\delta} = \frac{1}{5} \frac{u^* k}{\nu} = \frac{1}{5} \frac{u^*}{V} \frac{VD}{\nu} \frac{k}{2a} = \frac{1}{10} \frac{\sqrt{f}}{\sqrt{8}} R \frac{k}{a}$$

A plot of Nikuradse's results for $[(1/\sqrt{f}) - 2.0 \log_{10} (a/k)]$ versus k/δ is given in Fig. 8.15. This curve shows that if $k/\delta < 0.8$ the roughness has no effect, that if $0.8 \leqslant k/\delta \leqslant 12$ both viscosity and roughness are important, and that for $k/\delta > 12$ viscosity has no further influence.

It is remarkable that data from numerous sources [10] for new commercial pipes fall approximately on a single curve, as shown in Fig. 8.15. The roughness of any of these pipes is thus adequately described by a single parameter k. At one end this curve approaches asymptotically the straight line for smooth pipes and at the other the horizontal straight line for rough pipes. The formula for this transition curve was suggested by Colebrook [10] and is

$$\frac{1}{\sqrt{f}} = 1.74 - 2.0 \log_{10} \left[\frac{k}{a} \left(1 + 0.658 \frac{\delta}{k} \right) \right]$$

If $\delta/k << 1$, this expression reduces to Eq. (8.45a), while if $\delta/k >> 1$ it becomes $1/\sqrt{f} = 1.74 - 2.0 \log_{10} (0.658\delta/a)$, which, with $\delta = 5\nu/u^*$, is readily seen to be identical with Eq. (8.38a).

In the case of commercial pipes the roughness is seen to affect the friction factor over a much wider range of k/δ than in the case of the sand-coated tubes. The sand grains, being of uniform size and distribution, are all immersed simultaneously in the laminar sublayer and cease to affect

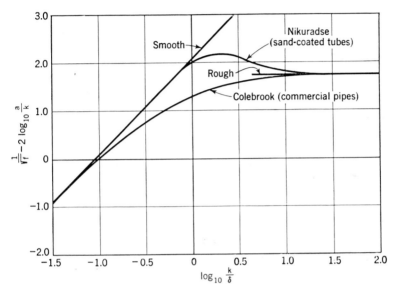

FIG. 8.15. — The friction factor for rough pipes depends on the ratio k/δ of roughness diameter to the laminar-sublayer thickness.

the flow if k/δ is less than about 0.8. The roughness of a commercial pipe, on the other hand, is nonuniform. When most of the irregularities are submerged, occasional large projections may rise clear of the sublayer and exert appreciable influence on f.

8.12. Turbulent Velocity Distribution. Equations (8.29) and (8.37) give the velocity distribution near a smooth wall.

$$u/u^* = \chi(R^*\xi) = A \ln (R^*\xi) + \text{constant}$$

$$= A \ln \left(\frac{u^*y}{\nu}\right) + \text{constant} \qquad (8.46)$$

Equation (8.46) would be expected to hold only in the outer part of the turbulent core, that is, for $\lambda/a \leqslant \xi \leqslant \xi_1$, but experiments by Nikuradse yield the surprising result that the equation is valid nearly to the center of the pipe. The data are plotted on a semilogarithmic scale in Fig. 8.16, from which one finds that in the turbulent core

$$\frac{u}{u^*} = 5.75 \log_{10} \left(\frac{u^*y}{\nu}\right) + 5.5 \qquad (8.46a)$$

It is seen that the points begin to deviate from the straight line of Eq. (8.46a) at a value of $u^*y/\nu = 30$. This value marks the division between transition zone and turbulent core, that is, $u^*\lambda/\nu = 30$.

In the laminar sublayer $\tau_0 = \tau = \mu(du/dy) = \mu(u/y)$, since, as already

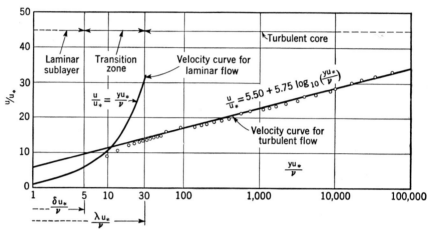

FIG. 8.16. — Velocity distribution in a smooth pipe.

stated, the velocity varies linearly with y. From this equation it follows at once that

$$\frac{u}{u^*} = \frac{u^*y}{\nu} \tag{8.47}$$

provided that $0 \leqslant y \leqslant \delta$. This equation is plotted in Fig. 8.16. Extrapolation of the trend of the test points toward smaller values of yu^*/ν indicates that the limit of the laminar sublayer corresponds to $yu^*/\nu = 5$, that is, $\delta u^*/\nu = 5$.

For roughened pipes Eqs. (8.29) and (8.44) combine to give

$$\frac{u}{u^*} = A \ln \frac{y}{k} + \text{constant} \tag{8.48}$$

for the outer part of the turbulent core. Nikuradse's tests proved, however, that this formula applies from a value $y/k = 1$ practically to the center of the pipe. His data yield

$$\frac{u}{u^*} = 5.75 \log_{10}\left(\frac{y}{k}\right) + 5.85 \tag{8.48a}$$

8.13. Mechanism of Turbulence in Pipes. The above development, which is due to Millikan [9], of the formulas for friction factor and velocity distribution brings out clearly that only two principal assumptions are involved, *viz.*, that the velocity near the wall is independent of the pipe radius and that the velocity defect in the turbulent core is independent of the wall roughness and viscosity. A third assumption, that the wall layers are thin compared with the radius of the turbulent core, is used in justifying Eq. (8.31). Since no detailed picture of the turbulence mechanism is used, the theory cannot be expected to give complete results. Thus, in the formulas for f and u two unknown constants appear. One of these, the constant A, is common to all the formulas and appears to be of a universal nature, but the integration constants are different in every case. Further, the fact that the logarithmic velocity formulas apply nearly to the center of the pipe is entirely unexplained.

Prandtl first proposed a logarithmic velocity distribution law, developing his formula from the following conception of the turbulent process: He idealized the actually continuous mixing by assuming that a mass of fluid retained its original x velocity until it had moved transversely a certain distance l_1 and that it then mixed suddenly and completely with the surrounding fluid. He reasoned that the root-mean-square (rms) of the x velocity fluctuation, $\sqrt{\overline{u'^2}}$, would be proportional to this distance times the average velocity gradient.

$$\sqrt{\overline{u'^2}} \sim l_1 \frac{\partial u}{\partial y}$$

Also, because of the correlation between u' and v',

$$\sqrt{\overline{v'^2}} \sim l_1 \frac{\partial u}{\partial y}$$

The definition of the correlation coefficient is

$$\beta = \frac{\overline{u'v'}}{\sqrt{\overline{u'^2}} \sqrt{\overline{v'^2}}} \tag{8.49}$$

from which the Reynolds stress can be written

$$\tau_{\text{turb}} = -\rho \overline{u'v'} = -\rho\beta\sqrt{\overline{u'^2}}\sqrt{\overline{v'^2}}$$

Prandtl's picture of turbulence thus leads to

$$\tau_{\text{turb}} \sim -\rho\beta l_1^2 \left(\frac{\partial u}{\partial y}\right)^2$$

Prandtl suggested that the factor of proportionality and $-\beta l_1^2$ be absorbed into a single factor.

$$\tau_{\text{turb}} = \rho l^2 \left(\frac{\partial u}{\partial y}\right)^2 \tag{8.50}$$

Since l is a measure of the distance moved by a particle before mixing, Prandtl called it the "mixing length."

In the turbulent core $\tau_{\text{turb}} = \tau_{\text{app}} = \tau_0(r/a) = [(p_1{}^* - p_2{}^*)/L]\,(r/2)$, so that everything in Eq. (8.50) can be determined experimentally, except l. Plots of l/a versus y/a prepared by Nikuradse from his data on pipe flow are given in Fig. 8.17.

Near the wall these curves are approximated by the formula $l = ky$.

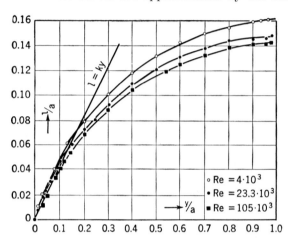

FIG. 8.17. — Mixing-length distribution in smooth and rough pipes.

Since $\tau_{\text{turb}} \approx \tau_0$ in the outer portions of the turbulent core, we get from Eq. (8.50) an approximate expression for the slope of the velocity curve.

$$\frac{\partial u}{\partial y} = \frac{1}{k} \frac{\sqrt{\tau_0/\rho}}{y} = \frac{1}{k} \frac{u^*}{y} \tag{8.51}$$

Noting that u depends only on y, we get by integration

$$\frac{u}{u^*} = \frac{1}{k} \ln y + \text{constant}$$

or, since u^*/ν is constant,

$$\frac{u}{u^*} = \frac{1}{k} \ln \frac{u^* y}{\nu} + \text{constant} \tag{8.52}$$

Comparison of Eqs. (8.46) and (8.52) shows that $A = 1/k$.

If we substitute the exact value of τ_{turb} in Eq. (8.50), we get

$$\frac{\partial u}{\partial y} = \frac{1}{l} \sqrt{\frac{\tau_{\text{turb}}}{\rho}} = \frac{1}{l} \sqrt{\frac{\tau_0}{\rho}} \sqrt{1 - \frac{y}{a}}$$

The plot of experimental data for l given in Fig. 8.17 shows that

$$l \approx ky\sqrt{1 - (y/a)}$$

over the whole range of y values, except very near $y/a = 1$. Combination of these two expressions gives again Eq. (8.51). The surprising accuracy of Eq. (8.52) is thus partly explained, but there is of course no theoretical explanation of the experimental curves of Fig. 8.17.

In 1930 von Kármán [6] suggested that the fluctuations might be kinematically similar over most of the core. In order to use this hypothesis he assumed the fluctuations, and consequently the mixing length, to be on a small scale compared with the pipe radius. Neither of these assumptions is strictly in accord with observation, but the results he obtained are, nevertheless, of interest.

For such small-scale turbulence, according to von Kármán, the value of the mixing length l_1 at any point y_1 will be determined by the local character of the fluctuations. So also will be the change in mean velocity $u_2 - u_1$ occurring between y_1 and any near-by fixed point y_2. Since both l_1 and $u_2 - u_1$ are thus assumed dependent on the same parameters, one may consider l_1 to be a function of $u_2 - u_1$, or vice versa. Now, since $y_2 - y_1$ is small, $u_2 - u_1$ may be represented with sufficient accuracy by a Taylor's series of only two terms, thus:

$$u_2 - u_1 = (y_2 - y_1)\left(\frac{du}{dy}\right)_1 + (y_2 - y_1)^2 \left(\frac{d^2u}{dy^2}\right)_1$$

Therefore, l_1 will be a function of only $(du/dy)_1$ and $(d^2u/dy^2)_1$, $y_2 - y_1$ being a constant previously fixed by the initial choice of y_1 and y_2. If we assume $l_1 = f[(du/dy)_1,(d^2u/dy^2)_1]$, the Π theorem shows that

$$l_1 = \text{constant } \frac{(du/dy)_1}{(d^2u/dy^2)_1} = -k_1 \frac{(du/dy)_1}{(d^2u/dy^2)_1}$$

where the minus sign is used because $d^2u/dy^2 < 0$.

The assumption of kinematically similar fluctuations at all points in the core leads at once to the conclusion that the constant k_1 is the same everywhere. Hence for any value of y in the core

$$l = -k \frac{du/dy}{d^2u/dy^2} \tag{8.53}$$

where k is a universal constant.

Combine Eqs. (8.50) and (8.53) (noting that $\partial u/\partial y = du/dy$).

$$\sqrt{\tau_{\text{turb}}} = \sqrt{\tau_0\left(1 - \frac{y}{a}\right)} = \sqrt{\rho}\,\frac{du}{dy}\left(-k\frac{du/dy}{d^2u/dy^2}\right)$$

$$\frac{d(du/dy)}{(du/dy)^2} = -\sqrt{\frac{\rho}{\tau_0}}\,k\,\frac{dy}{\sqrt{1-(y/a)}} = -\frac{k}{u^*}\frac{dy}{\sqrt{1-(y/a)}} \tag{8.54}$$

In the outer part of the core where $\sqrt{1 - (y/a)} \approx 1$, this equation integrates to

$$\frac{dy}{du} = \frac{k}{u^*} y$$

where the value zero is chosen for the integration constant because this choice has been found to give the best agreement with observation. The equation is seen to be identical with Eq. (8.51). For any point in the core Eq. (8.54) gives

$$\frac{U - u}{u^*} = -\frac{1}{k}\left[\ln\left(1 - \sqrt{1 - \frac{y}{a}}\right) + \sqrt{1 - \frac{y}{a}}\right] \tag{8.55}$$

On the other hand, the logarithmic velocity distribution given by Eq. (8.52) yields

$$\frac{U - u}{u^*} = -\frac{1}{k}\ln\left(\frac{y}{a}\right) \tag{8.56}$$

Although Eq. (8.55) agrees fairly well with experiment, Eq. (8.56) fits the data considerably better. We are thus forced to conclude that von Kármán's hypotheses are not in entire accord with the facts and that the remarkable success of Eq. (8.52) remains to a large extent unexplained.

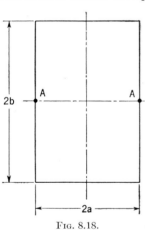

FIG. 8.18.

Burgers and Gebelein have attacked the turbulence problem from the viewpoint of statistical mechanics. More recently, Taylor, von Kármán, and others have also applied statistical methods to turbulence investigations [4]. These researches are outside the scope of this text; it must suffice to state that they have already led to a better understanding of certain turbulence phenomena.

8.14. Flow in Noncircular Conduits. The equations of motion for laminar flow have been solved for tubes of various cross sections, _e.g._, rectangular, triangular, and annular. It is known that these equations are identical mathematically with those for the torsion problem for an elastic bar of the same cross section as the laminar stream. Hence the solutions of the one problem are directly applicable to those of the other [14].

This analogy leads to the following results for a tube of rectangular cross section of sides $2a$ and $2b$ as shown in Fig. 8.18. The maximum shear stress occurs at the mid-points A, A of the long sides of the cross section and has the value

$$\tau_{\max} = k \frac{p_1^* - p_2^*}{L} a$$

where $(p_1^* - p_2^*)/L$ has its usual meaning and k is a numerical factor tabulated below. The discharge rate is

$$Q = k_1 \frac{p_1^* - p_2^*}{4\mu L} (2a)^3 2b$$

where k_1 is a numerical factor given in the following table:

$\dfrac{b}{a}$	k	k_1	$\dfrac{b}{a}$	k	k_1
1.0	0.675	0.141	3	0.985	0.263
1.2	0.759	0.166	4	0.997	0.281
1.5	0.848	0.196	5	0.999	0.291
2.0	0.930	0.229	10	1.000	0.312
2.5	0.968	0.249	∞	1.000	0.333

Experimental results for laminar flow are given by Croft [3].

For turbulent flow it has been found empirically that the relation between the friction factor and the Reynolds number is practically independent of the shape of the cross section, if the proper "equivalent diameter" is used in place of D. The equivalent diameter D_e is four times the hydraulic radius. *i.e.*,

$$D_e = 4 \times \frac{\text{cross-sectional area of flow}}{\text{wetted perimeter}} \tag{8.57}$$

Croft states that for annular sections this substitution gives satisfactory results only if the ratio of inner to outer diameter does not exceed 0.3.

The turbulent fluctuations cause a secondary flow to occur if the cross section is not circular. In a rectangular duct this secondary flow takes the form of a circulation outward at the corners and inward near the midpoints of the sides. The mean velocity near the corners of the section is thus maintained at a relatively high value.

8.15. Flow in Bends. Hofmann [5] has measured the loss H_l, in 90-deg bends of circular cross section. His results are plotted nondimensionally in Figs. 8.19a and b. The expression $2gH_l/V^2$ is seen to depend on the Reynolds number $R = VD/\nu$ and on the ratio of the center-line radius of the bend to its diameter r/D. The velocity V is the mean velocity of the flow through the bend.

The results of Madison and Parker [8] on losses in smooth 90-deg elbows of rectangular cross section are shown in Fig. 8.20. In this figure, "curve ratio" is the quotient of the inner radius by the outer radius of the bend, and "aspect ratio" AR is equal to the width normal to the plane of the bend divided by the difference between the outer and inner radii.

A double-spiral secondary flow occurs in bends. This flow results from

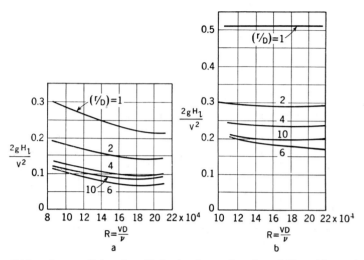

FIG. 8.19. — Loss coefficient in a 90-deg bend as a function of Reynolds number and ratio of bend radius to pipe diameter. (a) Smooth bend. (b) Rough bend. (*After Hofmann, reference 5.*)

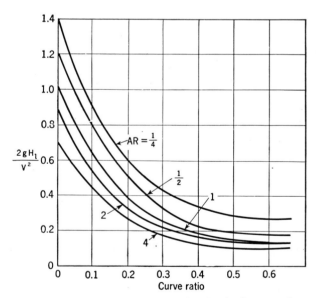

FIG. 8.20. — Loss coefficient for a smooth 90-deg bend of rectangular cross section. Curve ratio = inner radius/outer radius. AR = width normal to plain of bend/(outer radius — inner radius). (*After Madison and Parker, reference 8, by permission of American Society of Mechanical Engineers.*)

he fact that the fluid near the center of the cross section is moving faster than that at the sides, where friction retards it. Hence there is an outward flow in the central plane of the bend and a corresponding inward flow at each side due to the greater centrifugal force on the faster-moving fluid.

Theory shows that in a frictionless fluid rounding a bend the velocity is less at the outer streamlines than at the inner ones, just as in a potential vortex. Consequently, as fluid approaches the mid-point of a bend, the outlying fluid is decelerated and the pressure rises along the outer wall, while the fluid near the inside is accelerated. The reverse process occurs as the fluid leaves the bend, the fluid near the inside being decelerated with an accompanying increase in pressure, while that at the outside is accelerated. Wherever the pressure rises in the direction of flow, there is a rapid thickening of the boundary layer in a real fluid and a tendency for the flow to separate from the boundary. Hence, there may be separation before the mid-point of the bend at the outer wall, followed by a second separation at the inner wall downstream from the mid-point.

8.16. Loss in Pipe Fittings (Turbulent Flow). It has been found that, to a first approximation, the loss H_l in a pipe fitting such as an elbow, tee, valve, or coupling is independent of the Reynolds number of the flow. Therefore, the Π theorem shows that the loss coefficient C, defined by the equation

$$H_l = C \frac{V^2}{2g} \tag{8.58}$$

will be approximately constant. Here V is the mean velocity in the pipe to which the fitting is attached.

The loss in a fitting is also frequently expressed in terms of the length of straight pipe in which an equal loss would occur. This length is called the "equivalent length" for the fitting. Since the loss in a straight pipe is given by $H_l = f(L/D)(V^2/2g)$, the loss in a fitting is

$$H_l = f \frac{L_e}{D} \frac{V^2}{2g} \tag{8.59}$$

where L_e is the equivalent length for the fitting. For purposes of computation all that need be specified is the ratio L_e/D ("equivalent L/D ratio"). This ratio determines the loss in the fitting, provided that f is known or can be estimated. Comparison of Eqs. (8.58) and (8.59) shows that $C = f(L_e/D)$. Since f depends on R and roughness, L_e/D must also depend on the same things if C is a constant. However, the error made in considering both C and L_e/D to be constant for a given fitting is usually negligible, because the loss in the fitting is ordinarily only a small part of the total loss to be considered. Reasonable values of C and L_e/D are given in the following table:

Fitting	C	$\dfrac{L_e}{D}$
Standard 90-deg elbow.....	0.75	35
Standard 45-deg elbow.....	0.35	15
Open gate valve..........	0.15	7
Gate valve ½ closed	4.5	200
Open globe valve	7.5	350
Open angle valve	3.8	170

8.17. Loss at a Sudden Change of Cross Section. For a sudden enlargement a theoretical expression for the loss is easily obtainable. In Fig 8.21 we take section 2 sufficiently far downstream to ensure that the

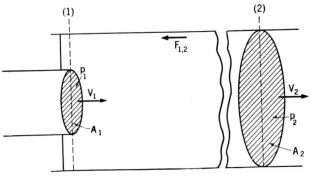

Fig. 8.21.

eddies are practically damped out when the fluid reaches 2. Apply the energy equation between 1 and 2.

$$H_{l_{1,2}} = \frac{p_1 - p_2}{\rho g} + \frac{V_1^2 - V_2^2}{2g} \tag{8.60}$$

$H_{l_{1,2}}$ is the sum of the losses due to the enlargement and to the wall friction.

The momentum equation yields

$$(p_1 - p_2)A_2 - F_{1,2} + \rho A_1 V_1^2 - \rho A_2 V_2^2 = 0 \tag{8.61}$$

where $F_{1,2}$ is the friction force exerted by the pipe wall on the fluid. The assumption is made here that the pressure is uniform over the entire area A_2 at section 1.

Eliminating $p_1 - p_2$ from Eqs. (8.60) and (8.61) and noting that $A_1 V_1 = A_2 V_2$ by continuity, we obtain for the loss due to the enlargement

$$H_l = H_{l_{1,2}} - \frac{F_{1,2}}{\rho g A_2} = \frac{V_2^2}{2g} + \frac{V_1^2}{2g}\left(1 - \frac{2A_1}{A_2}\right) = \frac{V_1^2}{2g}\left(\frac{A_1^2}{A_2^2} - \frac{2A_1}{A_2} + 1\right)$$

or

$$H_l = \frac{V_1^2}{2g}\left(1 - \frac{A_1}{A_2}\right)^2 \tag{8.62}$$

For a sudden contraction a similar analysis can be made, but an unknown contraction coefficient appears in the result. Referring to Fig. 8.22,

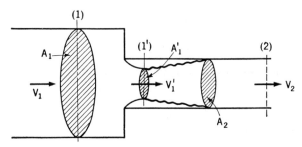

Fig. 8.22.

we can apply Eq. (8.62) between sections 1' and 2.

$$H_l = \frac{V_1'^2}{2g}\left(1 - \frac{A_1'}{A_2}\right)^2$$

Defining $C_c = A_1'/A_2$ and noting that $A_1'V_1' = A_2V_2$, we get

$$H_l = \frac{V_2^2}{2g}\left(\frac{1}{C_c}\right)^2(1 - C_c)^2 = \frac{V_2^2}{2g}\left(\frac{1}{C_c} - 1\right)^2 \qquad (8.63)$$

Values of C_c measured by Weisbach [15] and corresponding values of $[(1/C_c) - 1]^2$ are given in the following table:

$\dfrac{A_2}{A_1}$	0.2	0.4	0.6	0.8	1.0
C_c	0.632	0.659	0.712	0.813	1.0
$\left(\dfrac{1}{C_c} - 1\right)^2$	0.34	0.27	0.16	0.05	0

Equation (8.63) might be improved by taking into account the loss between 1 and 1'. Refinement of either Eq. (8.62) or (8.63) is hardly worth while, however, since the loss at an enlargement or contraction is usually a small fraction of the total. Since variation in velocity over a cross section is neglected in Eqs. (8.62) and (8.63), they will give better results for turbulent than for laminar flow.

8.18. Venturi Meter, Nozzle, and Orifice. These three metering devices are identical in principle, each introducing into the pipe a constriction, which produces a change in pressure. The approximate relation between the pressure change and the rate of flow is easily found if the flow is considered as one dimensional.

Apply the energy and continuity equations between sections 1 and 2 of the Venturi meter shown in Fig. 8.23.

$$\frac{p_2 - p_1}{\rho g} + \frac{V_2^2 - V_1^2}{2g} + H_{l_{1,2}} = 0$$

$$A_1 V_1 = A_2 V_2$$

Combine these, and solve for V_2, the throat velocity.

$$V_2 = \frac{1}{\sqrt{1 - (A_2/A_1)^2}} \sqrt{\frac{2(p_1 - p_2)}{\rho} - 2gH_{l_{1,2}}} \qquad (8.64)$$

It is obvious that, for the same rate of flow (*i.e.*, for the same value of mean throat velocity V_2), the pressure drop $p_1 - p_2$ will be less if the loss

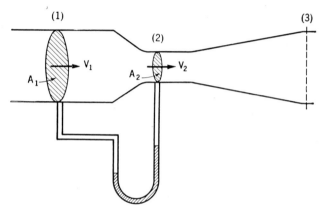

Fig. 8.23. — Venturi meter.

$H_{l_{1,2}}$ is less. The pressure drop that would be required in the limiting, idealized case of no loss would be $(p_1 - p_2)' = p_1 - p_2 - \rho g H_{l_{1,2}}$. Define a coefficient $C_v^2 = (p_1 - p_2)'/(p_1 - p_2)$, the ratio of the ideal to the actual pressure drop. Equation (8.64) can thus be written

$$V_2 = \frac{C_v}{\sqrt{1 - (A_2/A_1)^2}} \sqrt{\frac{2}{\rho}(p_1 - p_2)} \qquad (8.64a)$$

The coefficient C_v is usually called the "velocity coefficient," since it can be interpreted as the ratio of the actual velocity V_2 to that which would occur under the measured pressure drop if there were no loss. However, the interpretation of C_v as the ratio of ideal to actual pressure drop seems to be preferable, because the rate of flow is ordinarily determined by factors external to the measuring device, the pressure drop in the device being the result, rather than the cause, of the discharge rate subsisting in the pipe.

The volume rate of flow Q is equal to $A_2 V_2$; hence

$$Q = \frac{A_2 C_v}{\sqrt{1 - (A_2/A_1)^2}} \sqrt{\frac{2}{\rho}(p_1 - p_2)} \qquad (8.65)$$

Since the pressure drop $p_1 - p_2$ will in general depend on Q, ρ, A_1, A_2, and μ, the Π theorem, together with Eq. (8.65), shows that

$$C_v = \phi_1\left(\frac{\rho Q \sqrt{A_2}}{A_2 \mu}, \frac{A_2}{A_1}\right) = \phi\left(\frac{\rho V_2 D_2}{\mu}, \frac{A_2}{A_1}\right) \qquad (8.66)$$

where D_2 is the throat diameter. The results of tests by several investigators [1] are plotted in Fig. 8.24. The ratio A_2/A_1 varied between $\frac{1}{9}$ and

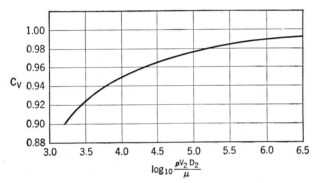

FIG. 8.24. — Coefficient for a Venturi meter as a function of Reynolds number. (*From ASME report on "Fluid Meters," reference 1, by permission of American Society of Mechanical Engineers.*)

$\frac{1}{4}$ in these tests, but there are not enough data available to show the effect of this variable. One is probably justified in concluding from Fig. 8.24 that C_v is independent of A_2/A_1, at least in the range of these tests. There is some evidence from other sources that, at smaller Reynolds numbers, C_v does depend on A_2/A_1, being larger for smaller A_2/A_1 at any given value of Reynolds number.

The purpose of the diverging cone of the Venturi meter is to minify the loss downstream from the throat, by keeping small both separation and wall-friction effects. It has been found that the sum of these two losses is a minimum for a total included angle of divergence of about 6 deg.

The total loss occurring in the Venturi meter is seen from the energy equation to equal $(p_1 - p_3)/\rho g$. The ratio $(p_1 - p_3)/(p_1 - p_2)$ usually has a value between 0.1 and 0.2.

The flow nozzle shown in Fig. 8.25 can be approximately analyzed in the same way as the Venturi meter. It will be noticed, however, that a pressure tap in the pipe wall at section 2 may not yield the pressure at the nozzle throat, because of the eddying that occurs in the dead-water region surrounding the jet. Furthermore, the pressure at the wall upstream from the nozzle varies slightly with distance from the nozzle, owing to the

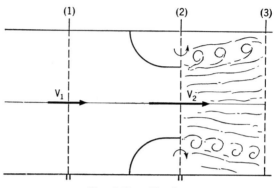

FIG. 8.25. — Nozzle.

curvature of the flow as the stream contracts. For these reasons it is preferable to replace Eq. (8.65) with

$$Q = A_2 C \sqrt{\frac{2}{\rho} \Delta p} \qquad (8.67)$$

where C is called the "discharge coefficient" and Δp is the pressure difference between an upstream and a downstream tap located in any convenient way. The factor $1/\sqrt{1 - (A_2/A_1)^2}$ has for simplicity been absorbed into C.

By reasoning like that which led to Eq. (8.66) we can show that

$$C = \phi \left(\frac{\rho V_1 D_1}{\mu}, \frac{A_2}{A_1} \right)$$

provided that the shape of the nozzle and the location of the pressure taps are arbitrarily fixed.

The Verein Deutscher Ingenieure (VDI) [11] has published curves for the discharge coefficient of the German standard nozzle. The nozzle and curves are shown in Fig. 8.26. By adhering carefully to the specifications for making and installing this standard nozzle one can use it without calibration, by virtue of the curves of Fig. 8.26b.

A third metering device is the plate orifice, such as is shown in Fig. 8.27. The jet contracts after leaving the orifice until it reaches section 2, the vena contracta. The cross-sectional area A_2 is therefore unknown. If we define the contraction coefficient $C_c = A_2/A$, we can rewrite Eq. (8.65) for application to the orifice,

$$Q = \frac{A C_c C_v}{\sqrt{1 - C_c^2 (A^2/A_1^2)}} \sqrt{\frac{2}{\rho} (p_1 - p_2)}$$

Owing to the practical impossibility of determining C_c and C_v separately, as well as the uncertainty in locating pressure taps to measure $p_1 - p_2$, we simplify this equation to

$$Q = AC \sqrt{\frac{2}{\rho} \Delta p} \qquad (8.68)$$

Equation (8.67) for the nozzle and Eq. (8.68) for the orifice have the same

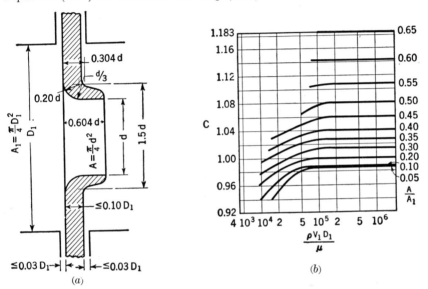

FIG. 8.26. — (a) VDI nozzle. (b) Coefficient for VDI nozzle as a function of Reynolds number and A/A₁. (*From NACA Tech. Men. 952, reference* 11.)

form. The discharge coefficient for the orifice, however, includes the correction for the contraction of the jet. There is no contraction in a well-designed nozzle.

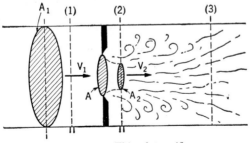

FIG. 8.27. — Thin-plate orifice.

The VDI has also developed a standard orifice, which, together with curves for discharge coefficient, is shown in Fig. 8.28.

There is no guidance of the jet downstream from a nozzle or orifice. Consequently, the over-all loss occurring in either of these instruments is larger than that for a Venturi meter. For either nozzle or orifice, the ratio $(p_1 - p_3)/\Delta p$ has a value of about 0.95 if $A_2/A_1 = 0.04$ and a value of about 0.25 if $A_2/A_1 = 0.80$. As would be expected, the loss in an orifice tends to be slightly greater than that in the corresponding nozzle.

In permanent installations, at least where the loss is a deciding factor,

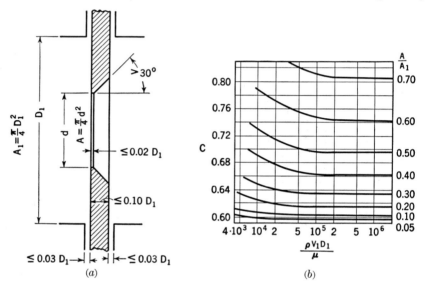

Fig. 8.28. — (a) VDI orifice. (b) Coefficient for VDI orifice as a function of Reynolds number and A/A₁. (*From NACA Tech. Mem. 952, reference* 11.)

the Venturi meter is preferable to a nozzle or orifice. However, the small size and convenience of installation indicate one of the latter instruments for most other applications. The fact that a standard nozzle or orifice can be used without calibration is also an advantage.

SELECTED BIBLIOGRAPHY

1. ASME Research Committee: "Fluid Meters," 4th ed., Part I, p. 56, American Society of Mechanical Engineers, New York, 1937.
2. BAKHMETEFF, B. A.: "The Mechanics of Turbulent Flow," p. 55, Princeton University Press, Princeton, N.J., 1936.
3. CROFT, H. O.: "Thermodynamics, Fluid Flow and Heat Transmission," p. 116, McGraw-Hill Book Company, Inc., New York, 1938.
4. DRYDEN, H. L.: A Review of the Statistical Theory of Turbulence, *Quart. Applied Math.*, vol. 1, pp. 7–42, 1943.
5. HOFMANN, A.: Der Verlust in 90°-Rohrkrümmern mit gleichbleibendem Kreisquerschnitt, *Mitt. hydraul. Inst. T. H. München*, No. 3, Oldenbourg, Munich, 1929.
6. KÁRMÁN, TH. VON: Turbulence and Skin Friction, *J. Aeronaut. Sci.*, vol. 1, p. 1, 1934.

7. LANGHAAR, H. L.: Steady Flow in the Transition Length of a Straight Tube, *J. Applied Mechanics*, vol. 9, pp. 55–58, 1942.
8. MADISON, R. D., and J. R. PARKER: Pressure Losses in Rectangular Elbows, *Trans. Am. Soc. Mech. Engrs.*, vol. 58, pp. 167–176, 1936.
9. MILLIKAN, C. B.: Turbulent Flows in Channels and Circular Tubes, *Proc. Fifth International Congress for Applied Mechanics*, pp. 386–392, John Wiley & Sons, Inc., New York, 1939.
10. MOODY, L. F.: Friction Factors for Pipe Flow, *Trans. Am. Soc. Mech. Engrs.*, vol. 66, pp. 671–684, 1944.
11. N.A.C.A.: Standards for Discharge Measurement (translation of German Industrial Standard 1952), *Tech. Mem.* 952, Washington, 1940.
12. NIKURADSE, J.: Gesetzmässigkeiten der turbulenten Strömung in glatten Rohren, *VDI Forschungsheft*, 356, 1932; Stromungsgesetze in rauhen Rohren, *VDI Forschungsheft*, 361, 1933.
13. REYNOLDS, O.: An Experimental Investigation of the Circumstances Which Determine Whether the Motion of Water Shall Be Direct or Sinuous, and of the Laws of Resistance in Parallel Channels, *Phil. Trans. Roy. Soc. (London)* vol. 174, 1883.
14. TIMOSHENKO, S.: "Theory of Elasticity," p. 263, McGraw-Hill Book Company, Inc., New York, 1934.
15. WEISBACH, JULIUS: "Die experimental Hydraulik," p. 133, J. S. Engelhardt. Freiberg, 1855.

CHAPTER IX

COMPRESSIBILITY PHENOMENA

Compressibility is becoming increasingly important in the problems that mechanical and aeronautical engineers are called upon to solve. There are three general types of problem in which compressibility must be taken into account. First in importance to engineers are high-speed flows, encountered, for example, in the design of aircraft, steam and gas turbines, compressors, jet- and rocket-propulsion devices, and projectiles. These high-speed flows can be divided into those which occur inside of ducts or passages between blades of machines and those which take place around bodies moving relative to the fluid. The designation "high speed" means that the velocities reached are on the order of the velocity of sound propagation through the fluid (see Art. 7.24).

The second type of problem deals with the sound waves set up by accelerated motion of a body in contact with a fluid. This type is characterized by large accelerations rather than by high velocities. Well-known engineering examples are problems in the design of rooms for specific acoustical uses, noise reduction, water hammer, and cavitation.

The third type of problem is concerned with large changes in elevation. The weight of the overlying air layers makes the density of air at ground level several times greater than that a few miles above the earth's surface. Practical application of this type of problem is limited to meteorology.

The remainder of this chapter and later references to compressibility will deal mainly with problems of high-speed flow.

9.1. Motion of a Point Source of Sound. Consider a sphere the radius of which varies periodically with time and which is immersed in a compressible fluid. We assume its radius is small compared with the length of the radiated sound waves, and we call the sphere a "point source" of sound. Suppose first that the source is at rest in the fluid, which extends indefinitely in all directions. Since the wave motion is cyclic, we can choose any convenient point in the wave as the "front." All parts of a wave front move with the same speed C relative

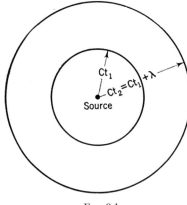

Fig. 9.1.

160

to the fluid. Successive wave fronts are, therefore, concentric spheres having the source as center, and each with radius Ct, where t is the elapsed time since the wave front left the source. The distance between successive

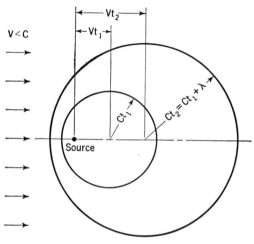

FIG. 9.2.

fronts is the wave length λ. In Fig. 9.1 are shown the circular traces of these spheres in the plane of the source.

If we now suppose that the fluid moves relative to the source with a velocity V less than C, the wave-front spheres are no longer concentric but are related as shown in Fig. 9.2. Each has as center that point in the fluid

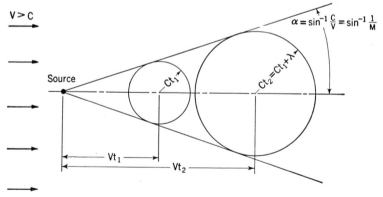

FIG. 9.3.

which coincided with the source at the instant the front left the source.

Finally, assume that V is greater than C. The velocity of wave propagation relative to the fluid is still the same, so that the wave fronts are again spheres, but they no longer surround the source (Fig. 9.3). On the contrary, all wave-front circles are tangent to a line making the angle α with the direction of flow, such that

$$\sin \alpha = \frac{C}{V} = \frac{1}{M}$$

where M is the Mach number, referred to in Chap. VII. This line is the generator of a cone of apex angle 2α; the line is called a "Mach line" and α the "Mach angle."

9.2. Subsonic Motion of a Body. To apply these observations to the steady motion of a rigid body of finite size, such as a projectile or airfoil, consider how the pressure and velocity fields that move along with the body are created. The final velocity of the body can be thought of as the result of a number of small impulsive increases in velocity. Each impulsive change in the motion gives rise to a pressure pulse or sound wave, which emanates from the body. The initial amplitude of the pulse will vary over the surface of the body, since the amplitude at any surface element depends on the component of the acceleration normal to the element. As the pulse passes any point in the fluid, it changes the pressure and velocity there. A positive pulse produces a velocity change having the direction of pulse propagation, while a negative pulse gives a change in the opposite direction. The new pressure and velocity will persist until another wave passes, *i.e.*, until a further acceleration of the body occurs.

A simple example is the one-dimensional motion of a piston in a long cylinder filled with fluid. If the piston is given a small increase in velocity, a pressure pulse will travel down the cylinder with velocity C relative to the undisturbed fluid. As the wave front passes, the fluid acquires the velocity of the piston. This velocity will be maintained until the piston is again accelerated, if no waves are reflected from the far end of the cylinder.

If the velocity relative to a body is everywhere subsonic, it is clear that these pulses will radiate in all directions, so that the pressure and velocity fields accompanying the body extend indefinitely toward front, rear, and sides. These fields die away gradually at some distance from the body, owing to the decrease in amplitude of each pulse as it spreads out. Steady subsonic motion of a body is, therefore, characterized by a continuous pressure and velocity distribution.

As the speed of the body approaches that of sound in the undisturbed fluid, the flow near the body becomes very complex and unsteady, because the local sound velocity is exceeded at certain points. These local disturbances may be of great importance, as, for example, in affecting lift and drag of an airfoil. These things will be discussed in Art. 10.13; here we merely note that, except for certain local regions, the flow will remain subsonic so long as the speed of the body is subsonic, and therefore pressure pulses will be propagated throughout the distant field of flow.

9.3. Supersonic Motion of a Body. In a sequence of positive pressure pulses, each produces a small forward velocity in the fluid through which it has passed and each moves at sonic speed with respect to fluid between it and its immediate precursor. Each pulse, therefore, overtakes ones in front, and it can be shown analytically that the speed of the resultant steep-fronted wave exceeds the sound velocity by an amount depending on its amplitude [5].

Let a body be accelerated from a speed slightly below sound velocity to one slightly above it. The pressure pulses resulting from this small but finite velocity change coalesce into a single steep-fronted wave whose speed is slightly greater than C. Instead of moving indefinitely far ahead of the body, as in subsonic flow, this wave is halted where it reaches essentially undisturbed fluid. The limiting position of the wave marks the practical limit of the pressure and velocity fields established during the subsonic regime.

On the axis, the wave is normal to the relative velocity of the undisturbed fluid. Away from the axis, the magnitude of the wave diminishes, since these parts are farther from the source of disturbance. Hence the

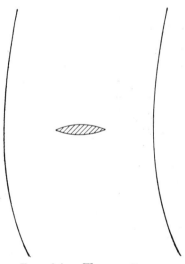

FIG. 9.4. — Wave pattern produced by a body moving at a speed slightly greater than the sound velocity.

propagation velocity of parts farther from the axis is less than that of nearer ones; and at some distance from the axis the amplitude will be so small that the speed is equal to C. The limiting position of the wave is thus not a straight line normal to the axis but a curve that bends slightly backward and approaches a straight line making the Mach angle with the axis. Such a line is indicated in Fig. 9.4. The complex pattern behind the body, caused by the local disturbances referred to above, is suggested by the line at the rear.

If the relative velocity of body and fluid is again slightly increased, a pulse is sent out and the body will move closer to the limiting line until the pulse reaches it. This coalition increases both the size of the pressure jump and its velocity of propagation. Near the axis, the resultant pressure front moves with the speed of the body, while to the sides its amplitude and speed decrease, and it gradually curves backward to make the Mach angle with the axis at some distance from it. It will be noted that the Mach angle corresponding to this new state of motion is less than that previously subsisting.

As the speed is further increased, the pressure front is approached more and more closely by the body and its magnitude becomes greater. Figure 9.5 shows the flow pattern for a tapering body at a Mach number that is considerably greater than unity. In Fig. 9.5 the forward shock is actually in contact with the body. Theory and experiment agree that, for a body with a nose angle that is not too large, there is a limiting value of M below which the nose wave does not touch the body but passes in front of it. If M is above this limit, however, the shock springs from the nose of the body.

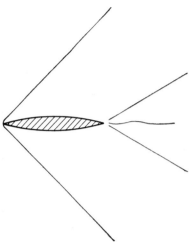

The shock lies ahead of a body having a rounded nose or too large a nose angle, even at very high Mach numbers.

Fig. 9.5. — Wave pattern produced by a body moving faster than in Fig. 9.4.

If the nose wave is detached from the body, as in Fig. 9.4, there is always at least a small subsonic region between the wave and the nose. On the other hand, if the wave springs directly from the nose, as in Fig. 9.5, there may or may not be a region of subsonic flow.

The expansion of the flow along the sides of the body takes place continuously since expansion shocks do not occur (see Art. 9.7). At the rear, however, a second compression shock is formed, where the flow bends back into a parallel stream. This shock originates in the local supersonic regions that develop at the sides of the body while the Mach number of the main flow is still less than unity. These localized shocks gradually move to the rear as the speed increases and eventually assume the form shown in Fig. 9.5. The slope of the tail shock is different from that at the front, because both the magnitude and direction of the velocity entering the shock differ from those in the undisturbed stream.

9.4. Frictionless Flow in a Convergent-divergent Nozzle. It is useful to consider in detail a one-dimensional flow, because the main features of compressibility can be brought out with the aid of relatively simple mathematics. The horizontal passage of Fig. 9.6 will be treated as a single stream tube, *i.e.*, the velocity, pressure, density, and temperature will be assumed uniform over any cross section. For any two sections separated by a distance dx, the continuity and Euler equations are

$$d(\rho A V) = 0 \qquad (9.1)$$

$$\frac{dp}{\rho} + V \, dV = 0 \qquad (9.2)$$

Equation (9.1) is readily transformed to

$$\frac{dA}{A} = -\frac{dV}{V} - \frac{d\rho}{\rho} = -\frac{dV}{V}\left(1 + \frac{V^2 d\rho}{\rho V \, dV}\right)$$

Substituting $dp = -\rho V \, dV$, from Eq. (9.2), we obtain

$$\frac{dA}{A} = -\frac{dV}{V}\left(1 - \frac{V^2}{dp/d\rho}\right) \qquad (9.3)$$

It is seen that $\sqrt{dp/d\rho}$ is a critical value for the velocity. If V is everywhere less than $\sqrt{dp/d\rho}$, the fluid will speed up in the convergent passage, reach a maximum at the throat, and then slow down in the divergent passage. The compressible flow is qualitatively like an incompressible one. It is seen further that V must be less than $\sqrt{dp/d\rho}$ until the flow reaches

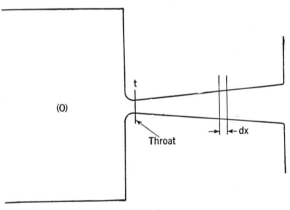

Fig. 9.6.

the throat and that the maximum velocity attainable at the throat is $\sqrt{dp/d\rho}$. If this critical speed is reached at the throat, the velocity in the divergent passage may be either sub- or supercritical. It cannot, however, be equal to $\sqrt{dp/d\rho}$. In the case of supercritical flow the velocity increases along the divergent passage—a behavior opposite to that in subcritical motion.

In Art. 7.24 it is shown, if friction be neglected, that a small plane pressure pulse in a one-dimensional flow moves relative to the undisturbed fluid with a velocity

$$C = \sqrt{\frac{\delta p}{\delta \rho}} \qquad (9.4)$$

Here δp and $\delta \rho$ are the differences in pressure and density that constitute the pulse, as shown in Fig. 9.7. The changes δp and $\delta \rho$ for a gas are found to occur both frictionlessly and adiabatically; that is, $\delta p / \delta \rho$ is derivable from the relation

$$\frac{p}{\rho^k} = \text{constant} \qquad (9.5)$$

where k is the so-called "isentropic exponent" and is constant over a considerable range of pressure. Thus

$$C = \sqrt{\frac{\delta p}{\delta \rho}} = \sqrt{\frac{kp}{\rho}} \qquad (9.6)$$

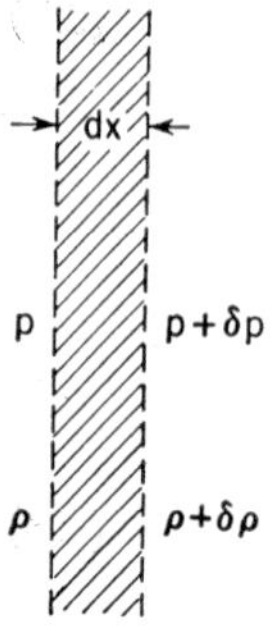

FIG. 9.7.　The sound velocity anywhere in the fluid is seen to depend on the local value of the ratio p/ρ.

If such a pulse is created by some means in the nozzle of Fig. 9.6, it will tend to move relative to the fluid with the velocity $C = \sqrt{kp/\rho}$, where p and ρ are the pressure and density at any section of the nozzle. The pulse can, therefore, be stationary only where the velocity of the fluid is equal to $\sqrt{kp/\rho}$. But the pressure-density relation in a smooth, insulated nozzle is given by Eq. (9.5), so that the critical velocity

$$\sqrt{\frac{dp}{d\rho}} = \sqrt{\frac{kp}{\rho}} \qquad (9.7)$$

In this frictionless adiabatic flow the critical velocity $\sqrt{dp/d\rho}$ and the sound velocity are identical, and the pulse can be stationary only at the throat of the nozzle.

The adiabatic character of sound-wave transmission is practically independent of the temperature of the gaseous medium. That is, negligible heat transfer results from temperature differences associated with a sound wave, regardless of the bulk temperature of the gas. If, for example, the temperature of the gas flowing through a nozzle were maintained approximately constant by heat transfer through the wall, the sound velocity would, nevertheless, be given by Eq. (9.6). The critical velocity, however, would in this case be equal to $\sqrt{p/\rho}$, which is less than the sound velocity $C = \sqrt{kp/\rho}$. A sound wave could, therefore, be propagated upstream through the throat of the nozzle, even though supercritical flow velocities were attained.

With regard to the practically important case of adiabatic flow, the stream velocity can be equal to the local sound velocity only at the throat; upstream from the throat the velocity is less than the local sound speed; and downstream from the throat it may be more or less than the local sonic velocity. This kind of flow will now be further investigated.

9.5. Frictionless Adiabatic Flow in a Nozzle. Combining Eqs. (9.2) and (9.5) and integrating from section 0 in the reservoir, where the velocity is negligible, to any section of the nozzle, we get

$$V = \sqrt{\frac{2k}{k-1}\frac{p_0}{\rho_0}\left[1 - \left(\frac{p}{p_0}\right)^{(k-1)/k}\right]} \qquad (9.8)$$

For given values of k and p_0/ρ_0, the velocity depends only on the ratio p/p_0. The maximum possible velocity, which is attained for $p/p_0 = 0$, is finite and equal to $\sqrt{[2k/(k-1)](p_0/\rho_0)}$ (see Fig. 9.8).

It is of interest to find the sound velocity at the throat C_t in terms of

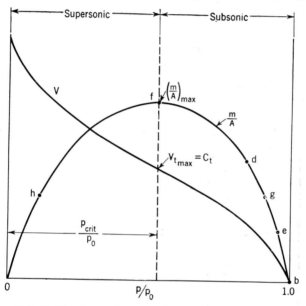

FIG. 9.8. — Velocity V and mass flow per unit area m/A versus pressure ratio p/p_0 for a frictionless adiabatic flow through a convergent-divergent nozzle.

p_0/ρ_0 and k. For this purpose consider the mass flow per unit area m/A, which by continuity equals ρV. Computing the rate of change of m/A with respect to p/p_0 and using Eqs. (9.2), (9.6), and (9.7), we get

$$\frac{d(m/A)}{d(p/p_0)} = \frac{d(\rho V)}{d(p/p_0)}$$

$$= \rho\frac{dV}{d(p/p_0)}\left(1 + V^2\frac{d\rho}{\rho V\,dV}\right)$$

$$= \rho\frac{dV}{d(p/p_0)}\left(1 - \frac{V^2}{C^2}\right)$$

Figure 9.8 shows $dV/d(p/p_0)$ to be negative everywhere, so that $d(m/A)/d(p/p_0)$ is positive for $V > C$, zero for $V = C$, and negative for

$V < C$. Recalling that V can equal C only at the throat, we conclude that the value of p/p_0 at which m/A is a maximum is also the value at which $V = V_{t\,\text{max}} = C_t$. This value of p/p_0 is called the "critical-pressure ratio." Multiplying Eq. (9.8) by ρ and using Eq. (9.5), we get

$$\frac{m}{A} = \rho V = \rho_0 \left(\frac{p}{p_0}\right)^{1/k} V = \sqrt{\frac{2k}{k-1}\rho_0 p_0 \left[\left(\frac{p}{p_0}\right)^{2/k} - \left(\frac{p}{p_0}\right)^{(k+1)/k}\right]} \quad (9.9)$$

which is plotted in Fig. 9.8. Setting $d(m/A)/d(p/p_0) = 0$, we find the critical pressure ratio to be

$$\frac{p_{\text{crit}}}{p_0} = \left(\frac{2}{k+1}\right)^{k/(k-1)} \quad (9.10)$$

The value of $V_{t\,\text{max}}$ or C_t is now determined from Eqs. (9.10) and (9.8).

$$V_{t\,\text{max}} = C_t = \sqrt{\frac{2k}{k+1}\frac{p_0}{\rho_0}} = \sqrt{\frac{2}{k+1}} C_0 \quad (9.11)$$

We shall now consider the theoretical pressure distribution along the divergent part of a nozzle, since it has features that show the limitations

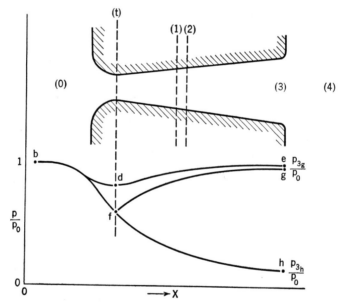

FIG. 9.9. — Pressure distribution along the axis of a convergent-divergent nozzle. (*Reproduced from L. Prandtl, The Flow of Liquids and Gases, in "The Physics of Solids and Fluids," Blackie and Son, Ltd., London and Glasgow.*)

of the one-dimensional frictionless theory and point the way to further investigation. In Fig. 9.9 are shown the pressure distributions along a nozzle of given shape, for both sub- and supersonic flow in the divergent portion. These curves are easily obtained from the m/A curve of Fig. 9.8, since A is a known function of x for a given nozzle. Corresponding points in Figs. 9.8 and 9.9 are labeled with the same letter. If m is chosen small enough, the flow is subsonic throughout and a curve of the type bde is obtained. The maximum possible value of m is the one corresponding to $(m/A)_t = (m/A)_{max}$, which gives either curve bfg or bfh.

It will be observed that in the subsonic regime any value of exit pressure p_3 is allowed such that $p_{3g}/p_0 \leqslant p_3/p_0 \leqslant 1$. The upper limit 1 is approached

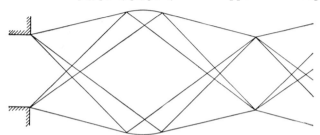

Fig. 9.10. — Wave pattern of emergent jet when receiver pressure is slightly less than at nozzle exit. (*Reproduced from L. Prandtl, The Flow of Liquids and Gases, in " The Physics of Solids and Fluids," Blackie and Son, Ltd., London and Glasgow.*)

as m becomes smaller or A_3 larger. In the supersonic region, however, only a single value of p_3 is allowed, namely, p_{3h}. The question of what happens if the receiver pressure p_4 lies between p_{3g} and p_{3h} is left unanswered by the present analysis.

Experiments show that small, oblique, standing pressure waves occur just outside the nozzle if the receiver pressure is only slightly different from

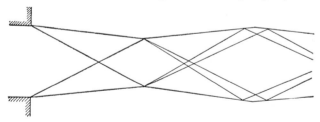

Fig. 9.11. — Wave pattern of emergent jet when receiver pressure is slightly greater than that at nozzle exit. (*Reproduced from L. Prandtl, The Flow of Liquids and Gases, in " The Physics of Solids and Fluids," Blackie and Son, Ltd., London and Glasgow.*)

p_{3h}. These waves are reflected at certain parts of the boundary of the free jet where discontinuities in density occur. Figures 9.10 and 9.11 are from photographs by L. Prandtl of the flow from a two-dimensional nozzle. The first of these shows the expansion if $p_4 < p_{3h}$; the second shows the compression if $p_4 > p_{3h}$.

These pictures were made by the schlieren method, which takes advantage of the fact that a ray of light is deflected if it passes through a medium of nonuniform density. A typical apparatus is illustrated in Fig. 9.12. Light from a source at A is focused near the edge of a plane mirror C. The reflected light traverses a long path to the concave mirror D and back again to a second focus at the knife-edge E, then through a lens system to a

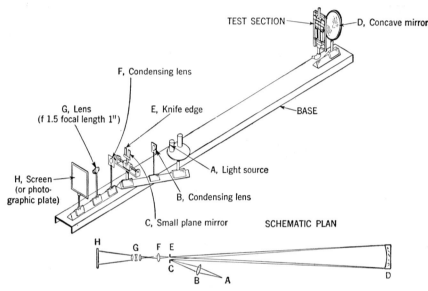

FIG. 9.12. — Schlieren apparatus. (*Courtesy of F. Lustwerk.*)

ground-glass screen or photographic plate H, where an image is formed of a two-dimensional airflow taking place in front of mirror D. The steep density gradients set up in the pressure waves cause the transient light to be bent slightly. Some of these bent rays are cut off by the knife-edge E; and others, which would normally be cut off, pass by the knife-edge and strike the screen. A region in which the density gradient is large thus appears on the screen either as very dark or very light.

A convergent nozzle is a special case of the convergent-divergent passage. If there is no divergent portion, it is readily seen that the flow will be everywhere subsonic so long as the receiver pressure is greater than the critical value. If the receiver pressure is equal to the critical, the throat pressure will also have this value and the throat velocity will be sonic. If the receiver pressure is less than the critical, the throat pressure and velocity will still have their critical values, but after leaving the nozzle the stream will expand suddenly to the receiver pressure.

9.6. Compression Shocks in a Nozzle. If the receiver pressure p_4 of Fig. 9.9 is gradually raised above p_{3h}, schlieren photographs reveal that the waves of Fig. 9.11 move upstream into the interior of the nozzle. The shape of the waves changes also, and the flow downstream from them is considerably disturbed. Figure 9.13, taken from a schlieren photograph, shows oblique pressure waves springing from the wall, followed by a transverse wave extending over a part of the cross section. The flow appears to separate from the wall at these shocks, while downstream there are several smaller transverse shocks. It is found that the flow at the exit is subsonic and that the pressure p_3 is equal to p_4. Upstream from the shocks, however, the flow remains supersonic and entirely unaffected by the rise in receiver pressure.

If p_4 is made still larger, the disturbance becomes very concentrated and moves nearer the throat, as shown in Fig. 9.14. Very little flow separation occurs. Downstream from this

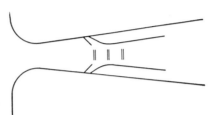

FIG. 9.13. — Disturbances in a nozzle when the receiver pressure is considerably greater than the theoretical value for unretarded flow.

transverse shock the flow is subsonic, while upstream it remains supersonic and unaffected by the changes in p_4. Pressure measurements indicate a sudden rise in pressure at the shock, followed by a further gradual rise to the value p_4 at the exit.

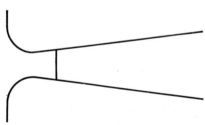

FIG. 9.14. — Transverse shock in a nozzle.

Conditions as shown in Fig. 9.13 are so chaotic that it has so far been impossible to analyze them theoretically, but the concentrated transverse shock of Fig. 9.14 is amenable to theoretical treatment. To carry through such an analysis the shock is assumed to be of infinitesimal thickness, and friction is neglected everywhere, except in the shock itself. It is also necessary to make additional assumptions about the nature of the fluid. For simplicity we assume it to be a "perfect" gas, that is, one that obeys the gas law

$$p = \rho g R T \qquad (9.12)$$

and has constant specific heats. It is shown in thermodynamics texts that, for a perfect gas, the intrinsic energy u depends only on temperature. The specific heats, therefore, are

$$c_v = \left(\frac{\partial u}{\partial T}\right)_v = \frac{\Delta u}{\Delta T} \qquad (9.13)$$

$$c_p = \left\{\frac{\partial [(p/\rho) + u]}{\partial T}\right\}_p = \frac{\Delta [(p/\rho) + u]}{\Delta T} = \frac{\Delta h}{\Delta T} \qquad (9.14)$$

In these equations, R is the gas constant; T is the absolute temperature; h, defined as $(p/\rho) + u$, is the enthalpy; c_p is the specific heat at constant pressure; and c_v is the specific heat at constant volume. For a perfect gas, the ratio of the specific heats is equal to the isentropic exponent.

$$\frac{c_p}{c_v} = k \tag{9.15}$$

It is now supposed that a finite pressure jump occurs between sections 1 and 2 of Fig. 9.9. Since the thickness of this shock is assumed infinitesimal, 1 and 2 may be taken so close together that the difference in their areas and the wall friction force on the narrow strip between them are negligible. The continuity equation, therefore, is

$$\rho_1 V_1 = \rho_2 V_2 = \frac{m}{A_1} \tag{9.16}$$

and the momentum equation [Eq. (6.6)] takes the form

$$p_1 - p_2 = \rho_2 V_2^2 - \rho_1 V_1^2 \tag{9.17}$$

Since the shock is accompanied by frictional effects in the fluid, the Euler equation cannot be used between 1 and 2 but must be replaced by the more general energy equation [Eq. (5.10)], which may be written for this adiabatic flow as

$$h_1 + \frac{V_1^2}{2} = h_2 + \frac{V_2^2}{2} = h_0 \tag{9.18}$$

Here h_0 is the enthalpy in the reservoir. With the aid of Eqs. (9.12) to (9.15), the energy formula becomes

$$\frac{k}{k-1}\frac{p_1}{\rho_1} + \frac{V_1^2}{2} = \frac{k}{k-1}\frac{p_2}{\rho_2} + \frac{V_2^2}{2} = \frac{k}{k-1}\frac{p_0}{\rho_0} \tag{9.19}$$

Combination of Eqs. (9.16), (9.17), and (9.19) yields, finally, the result

$$V_1 V_2 = \frac{2k}{k+1}\frac{p_0}{\rho_0} \tag{9.20}$$

which will be recognized from Eq. (9.11) as equivalent to

$$V_1 V_2 = C_t^2 \tag{9.21}$$

The geometric mean of V_1 and V_2 is equal to the sound velocity at the throat of the nozzle.

It is now readily demonstrated that, if V_1 is supersonic, V_2 will be subsonic. The pressure ratio p_2/p_0 can be found in terms of p_1/p_0, by use of Eq. (9.8) between 0 and 1, where the flow is frictionless, and Eqs. (9.16), (9.17), and (9.20).

$$\frac{p_2}{p_0} = \frac{1}{k-1}\frac{p_1}{p_0}\left[\frac{4k}{k+1}\left(\frac{p_0}{p_1}\right)^{(k-1)/k} - (k+1)\right] \tag{9.22}$$

The dotted curve of Fig. 9.15 is plotted from this equation and gives the

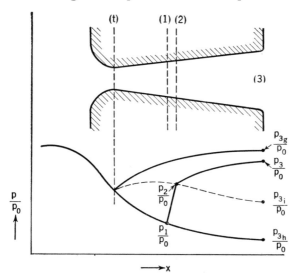

FIG. 9.15. — Theoretical pressure distribution along the axis of a nozzle in the presence of a transverse shock. (*Reproduced from L. Prandtl, The Flow of Liquids and Gases, in " The Physics of Solids and Fluids," Blackie and Son, Ltd., London and Glasgow.*)

pressure jump in a shock for any value of p_1/p_0 in the supersonic range. A little further mathematical juggling yields the relations

$$V_2^2 = \frac{2k(k-1)}{(k+1)^2}\frac{p_0}{\rho_0}\frac{1}{1-(p_1/p_0)^{(k-1)/k}} \tag{9.23}$$

$$C_2^2 = \frac{kp_2}{\rho_2} = \frac{k}{k+1}\frac{p_0}{\rho_0}\frac{[4k/(k+1)]-(k+1)(p_1/p_0)^{(k-1)/k}}{1-(p_1/p_0)^{(k-1)/k}} \tag{9.24}$$

The Mach number at 2 is therefore

$$M_2^2 = \frac{V_2^2}{C_2^2} = \frac{2(k-1)}{k+1}\frac{1}{[4k/(k+1)]-(k+1)(p_1/p_0)^{(k-1)/k}} \tag{9.25}$$

Noting that in the supersonic region p_1/p_0 cannot exceed the critical pressure ratio, we get from Eqs. (9.10) and (9.25)

$$M_2 = \frac{V_2}{C_2} \leqslant 1 \tag{9.26}$$

which was to be proven.

With V_2, p_2, A_2, and A_3 known, one can find p_3 by using the continuity and Euler equations. The theory thus indicates a transverse shock at a definite point in the nozzle for any value of p_3 between the limits p_{3i} and p_{3g} (see Fig. 9.15). The theory does not apply if p_3 is between p_{3h} and p_{3i}. As previously mentioned, a transverse shock is observed to occur only if p_3 is but slightly below p_{3g}. If p_3 lies in this narrow range, there is reasonable agreement between experiment and theory. For lower values of p_3, however, the transverse shock does not fill the entire passage and is preceded by oblique shocks. These complexities are due to the interaction between friction and compressibility and are therefore not predicted by the present theory, which neglects friction except in a region of infinitesimal thickness. These phenomena will be taken up in the next chapter in the discussion of the boundary layer.

The approximate thickness of a shock wave can be calculated if the mechanism of viscous action and of thermal conduction within the shock is taken into account [5]. The thickness of a shock wave in air is estimated to lie between 10^{-5} and 10^{-4} in.

9.7. On the Impossibility of a Rarefaction Shock. Although only compression shocks are observed in nature, none of the preceding work hints at the impossibility of a shock of rarefaction. Proof of such impossibility is based on the second law of thermodynamics, a discussion of which is outside the scope of this book. It may be useful, however, to present a brief treatment of this problem, even though it is impossible to start from first principles. The existence of the entropy will be taken for granted, as well as the fact that the entropy of a system cannot decrease during an adiabatic process. The reader will find these matters discussed in texts on thermodynamics.*

For the adiabatic flow through a nozzle it will be shown that the entropy increases as the gas passes through a compression shock but would decrease in a rarefaction shock. The latter will thus be shown to be impossible.

The change in entropy of unit mass of fluid as it passes from an initial state 1 to an arbitrary final state is defined as

$$s - s_1 = \int_1 \frac{dq}{T} \quad \text{(reversible path only)} \tag{9.27}$$

where dq is the heat transfer to the unit mass during an infinitesimal change and T is the absolute temperature. The integral must be taken along a reversible path, a requirement that is fulfilled in this case if friction is supposed to be absent. The first law of thermodynamics may thus be written as Eq. (5.12), which in differential form is $dq = du + p \, d(1/\rho)$. The change in entropy now becomes

$$s - s_1 = \int_1 \frac{du + p \, d(1/\rho)}{T} = \int_1 \left(\frac{dh}{T} - \frac{dp}{\rho T} \right) \tag{9.28}$$

* See, for example, reference 3 at the end of this chapter.

Using Eqs. (9.12) to (9.15), we get

$$s - s_1 = c_p \ln \frac{T}{T_1} - c_p \frac{k-1}{k} \ln \frac{p}{p_1} \tag{9.29}$$

The change in entropy as the gas passes through a shock is found, after considerable reduction, to be

$$s_2 - s_1 = c_p \ln \left[\frac{V_2}{V_1} \left(\frac{1 - \dfrac{k-1}{k+1} \dfrac{V_2}{V_1}}{\dfrac{V_2}{V_1} - \dfrac{k-1}{k+1}} \right)^{1/k} \right] \tag{9.30}$$

It is readily shown from Eq. (9.30) that the entropy increases if $V_2 < V_1$, and vice versa. Therefore, since a decrease in entropy is not permitted, only a compression shock can occur.

Equation (9.30) is valid only for a perfect gas. Similar results can, however, be obtained as follows for any gas or vapor having known

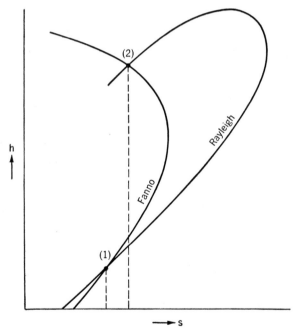

FIG. 9.16.

properties: The continuity and energy requirements of Eqs. (9.16) and (9.18) give a relation between enthalpy and density in a shock.

$$h + \frac{m_2}{2A_1^2 \rho^2} = h_0 \tag{9.31}$$

Since the entropy is a known function of any two independent properties of the gas, such as enthalpy and density, we can eliminate the density by using Eq. (9.31) and obtain a relation between entropy and enthalpy that must be satisfied in the shock. Such a relation is shown schematically in Fig. 9.16, as the curve marked "Fanno line." On the other hand, the continuity and momentum requirements of Eqs. (9.16) and (9.17) yield another relation between enthalpy and density that must be satisfied in the shock. A second curve of enthalpy versus entropy can therefore be drawn independently of the Fanno line. This curve is known as a "Rayleigh line" and is indicated in Fig. 9.16. The points of intersection of the Fanno and Rayleigh lines determine the state of the gas at the beginning and end of the shock. Point 2 at higher entropy is necessarily the final state.

9.8. Adiabatic Flow in a Pipe with Friction. For simplicity we neglect gravity and assume the velocity to be uniform over any cross section.

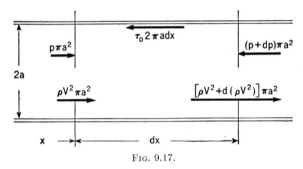

Fig. 9.17.

A relation between pressure drop and wall shearing stress τ_0 is given by the momentum equation applied between the cross sections shown in Fig. 9.17.

$$dp + \frac{2}{a} \tau_0 \, dx + d(\rho V^2) = 0 \tag{9.32}$$

The mass flow per unit area is constant for a pipe of uniform diameter, so that the continuity equation is

$$\rho V = G = \text{constant} \tag{9.33}$$

Combining Eqs. (9.32) and (9.33), we get

$$\frac{dp}{dx}\left(1 - \frac{V^2}{dp/d\rho}\right) = -\frac{2\tau_0}{a} \tag{9.34}$$

and

$$\frac{dV}{dx}\left(1 - \frac{dp/d\rho}{V^2}\right) = -\frac{2\tau_0}{aG} \tag{9.35}$$

Equations (9.34) and (9.35) apply to any sort of pipe flow—adiabatic, isothermal, or other—because they are based only on momentum and continuity. It is seen that $\sqrt{dp/d\rho}$ is a critical value for velocity, just as in a frictionless nozzle flow. If $V < \sqrt{dp/d\rho}$, dV/dx is positive. The velocity will therefore increase; and if it increases faster than $\sqrt{dp/d\rho}$, dV/dx will become larger and larger, approaching infinity as V approaches $\sqrt{dp/d\rho}$. If V should become equal to $\sqrt{dp/d\rho}$ and surpass it in the slightest degree, dV/dx would change from an infinite positive value to an infinite negative one. This physically intolerable fluctuation in dV/dx would persist so long as the flow continued inside the pipe. It is clear, therefore, that V will attain the value $\sqrt{dp/d\rho}$ only at the end of the pipe, if at all.

To determine the critical value of velocity we introduce the assumptions that the flow is adiabatic and the fluid a perfect gas. The energy equation may therefore be written

$$h + \frac{V^2}{2} = c_p T + \frac{V^2}{2} = h_0 = c_p T_0 \tag{9.36}$$

Equations (9.33) and (9.36) and the equation of state [Eq. (9.12)] allow p to be found in terms of ρ, so that $dp/d\rho$ can be computed.

$$p = \rho g R \left(T_0 - \frac{G^2}{2c_p \rho^2} \right) \tag{9.37}$$

$$\frac{dp}{d\rho} = g R T_0 + \frac{G^2}{\rho^2} \frac{gR}{2c_p} = \frac{p_0}{\rho_0} + V^2 \frac{k-1}{2k} \tag{9.38}$$

Equation (9.38) shows that the critical condition $V^2 = dp/d\rho$ is equivalent to

$$V^2 = \frac{p_0}{\rho_0} \frac{2k}{k+1} = C_t^2 \tag{9.39}$$

where C_t is identical with the velocity of sound at the throat of a nozzle [see Eq. (9.11)].

It is of interest to compare the velocity at any point in the pipe with the local sound velocity. For this purpose, recall from Eq. (9.6) that $C^2 = kp/\rho$, and use Eq. (9.37).

$$C^2 = \frac{kp}{\rho} = \frac{kp_0}{\rho_0} - V^2 \frac{(k-1)}{2} \tag{9.40}$$

The following inequalities are now readily established:

$$V^2 > \frac{dp}{d\rho} > C_t^2 > C^2$$

if $V > C_t$, and

$$V^2 < \frac{dp}{d\rho} < C_t^2 < C^2$$

if $V < C_t$. Wherever $V > C_t$, the flow is supersonic; and wherever $V < C_t$, it is subsonic.

The Fanno line of Fig. 9.16 applies to adiabatic pipe flow as well as to a transverse shock, for the cross-sectional area is constant in each case. Since the entropy of the fluid must increase along the pipe in a frictional adiabatic flow, the point of maximum entropy on the Fanno line can correspond only to conditions at the exit end of the pipe. At this point, the slope ds/dh is equal to zero. The differential of the entropy can be computed from Eqs. (9.28), (9.33), and (9.36).

$$ds = \frac{1}{T}\left(dh - \frac{dp}{\rho}\right) = -\frac{dp}{\rho T}\left(1 + \frac{\rho V \, dV}{dp}\right) = -\frac{dp}{\rho T}\left(1 - \frac{V^2}{dp/d\rho}\right) \quad (9.41)$$

If both sides of Eq. (9.41) are divided by dh and it is noted that $dp/dh\rho T \neq 0$, it is seen that $V = \sqrt{dp/d\rho}$ if $ds/dh = 0$. It follows that V can equal $\sqrt{dp/d\rho}$ only at the exit end of the pipe, if at all. This checks the previous conclusion to the same effect.

Points of higher enthalpy on the Fanno line are seen from the energy equation, [Eq. (9.36)] to correspond to subsonic flow in the pipe, and vice versa.

It has been found experimentally that disturbances like those in a nozzle may also occur in supersonic pipe flow. Oblique shocks and separation of the main stream from the wall take place, followed by one or more transverse shocks in the core, which reduce the flow to the subsonic regime.

9.9. Friction Factor for Adiabatic Pipe Flow. A friction factor may be defined for compressible flow in the same way as in Chap. VIII.

$$f = \frac{8\tau_0}{\rho V^2} \quad (8.8)$$

Dimensional analysis shows that, in a pipe carrying compressible fluid, $f = \phi(R, L/D, M)$, where the Reynolds and Mach numbers R and M may be evaluated at any convenient point in the pipe, say the entrance.

The friction factor can be determined experimentally, with the help of the equations previously developed. Substituting Eqs. (8.8) and (9.33) into Eq. (9.32), assuming f to be constant, and integrating between the limits x_1 and x_2, we get

$$\int_1^2 \rho \, dp + \frac{G^2 f}{4a}(x_2 - x_1) + G^2 \ln\frac{\rho_1}{\rho_2} = 0 \quad (9.42)$$

From Eq. (9.37) we find that

$$p = \left(h_0\rho - \frac{G^2}{2\rho}\right)\frac{k-1}{k} \quad (9.43)$$

$$\int_1^2 \rho \, dp = \frac{k-1}{2k}\left[h_0(\rho_2^2 - \rho_1^2) + G^2 \ln\frac{\rho_2}{\rho_1}\right] \quad (9.44)$$

Thus, if the initial state 0 of the fluid is known, together with the mass rate of flow and the pipe diameter, measurements of p_1 and p_2 enable us to

ind ρ_1 and ρ_2 from Eq. (9.43) and, hence, the friction factor from Eqs.
9.44) and (9.42).

Recent experiments on turbulent flow in a smooth pipe show that, for
$L/D > 50$, f is the same function of R as in the incompressible case, regard-
ess of whether the entrance Mach number M is greater or less than
inity [4]. Values of $L/D > 50$ can rarely be attained in supersonic flow,
lowever, so that in this case the relationship between f and L/D is of importance. The experiments appear to show that f passes through several
ninima and maxima in the range $0 \leqslant L/D \leqslant 50$. The relationship be-
ween f and L/D depends on R but is substantially independent of M.
The value of M merely limits the maximum value of L/D attainable in
upersonic flow. It may be that the relationship between f and L/D is the
ame as for an incompressible fluid at the same R. Data on incompressible
low are insufficient to warrant a definite conclusion.

9.10. Isothermal Flow in a Pipe with Friction. If T_1 represents the
constant value of temperature everywhere in the pipe, the equation of
state may be written

$$p = \rho g R T_1 \tag{9.45}$$

Therefore, $dp/d\rho = gRT_1$, so that the critical value of velocity is

$$V = \sqrt{gRT_1} \tag{9.46}$$

The local sound velocity $\sqrt{kp/\rho}$ is equal to $\sqrt{kgRT_1}$ and is constant
throughout the pipe. Supercritical flow is therefore not necessarily supersonic in this case.

9.11. Stagnation Pressure in Supersonic Flow. In contrast to other
aspects of the flow around an immersed body, the stagnation pressure can
be found from one-dimensional considerations.
The treatment given in Art. 4.8, which is
applicable only to subsonic flow, is extended
here to supersonic flow, in which a transverse
compression shock occurs in front of the body,
as indicated in Fig. 9.18. In supersonic flow
the total rise in pressure is conveniently divided into two parts, one due to the shock
and the other due to the frictionless adiabatic compression between the shock and the
stagnation point. Our object, just as in Art.

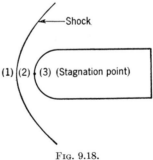

FIG. 9.18.

4.8, is to determine the quantity $(p_3 - p_1)/(\rho_1/2)V_1^2$ as a function of the
Mach number of the undisturbed stream $M_1 = V_1/C_1 = V_1/\sqrt{kp_1/\rho_1}$. For
this purpose, we consider the ratio p_3/p_1, which may be broken into two
factors, $p_3/p_1 = (p_3/p_2)(p_2/p_1)$, the first of which is found either from
Art. 4.8 or Eq. (9.2).

$$\frac{p_3}{p_2} = \left(1 + \frac{k-1}{2k}\frac{\rho_2}{p_2}V_2^2\right)^{k/(k-1)} \tag{9.47}$$

Since the cross-sectional area of the flow is the same on each side of the shock, continuity yields $\rho_1 V_1 = \rho_2 V_2$, and

$$\frac{p_3}{p_1} = \frac{p_2}{p_1}\left(1 + \frac{k-1}{2k}\frac{\rho_1 V_1^2}{p_1}\frac{V_2}{V_1}\frac{p_1}{p_2}\right)^{k/(k-1)}$$

$$\frac{p_3}{p_1} = \frac{p_2}{p_1}\left(1 + \frac{k-1}{2}M_1^2\frac{V_2}{V_1}\frac{p_1}{p_2}\right)^{k/(k-1)}$$

From Eqs. (9.20) and (9.22), V_2/V_1 and p_2/p_1 are obtained in terms of M_1, and

$$\frac{p_3}{p_1} = \left[1 + \frac{k-1}{2}\frac{(k-1)M_1^2 + 2}{k(2M_1^2 - 1) + 1}\right]^{k/(k-1)}\left[1 + \frac{2k}{k+1}(M_1^2 - 1)\right] \tag{9.48}$$

Equation (9.48) is of course valid only if a shock occurs, that is, if $M_1 > 1$. If $M_1 \leqslant 1$, p_3/p_1 is obtained from Eq. (9.47) with subscript 2 replaced by 1.

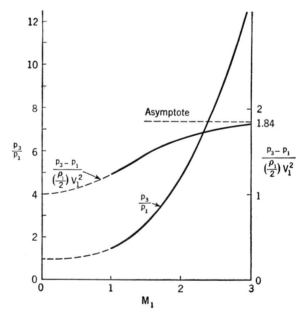

FIG. 9.19. — Stagnation-pressure coefficients for a blunt-nosed body as functions of the Mach number of the undisturbed stream M.

The stagnation-pressure ratio is plotted in Fig. 9.19. The quantity $(p_3 - p_1)/(\rho_1/2)V_1^2$ is easily computed from the formula

$$\frac{p_3 - p_1}{(\rho_1/2)V_1^2} = \frac{2}{kM_1^2}\left(\frac{p_3}{p_1} - 1\right)$$

and is also plotted in Fig. 9.19.

SELECTED BIBLIOGRAPHY

1. BINDER, R. C.: "Fluid Mechanics," Prentice-Hall, Inc., New York, 1943.
2. EWALD, P. P., TH. PÖSCHL, and L. PRANDTL: "The Physics of Solids and Fluids," Blackie & Son, Ltd., Glasgow, 1936.
3. KEENAN, J. H.: "Thermodynamics," John Wiley & Sons, Inc., New York, 1941.
4. KEENAN, J. H., and E. P. NEUMANN: Measurements of Friction in a Pipe for Subsonic and Supersonic Flow of Air, *J. Applied Mechanics*, vol. 13, pp. 91–100, June, 1946.
5. TAYLOR, G. I., and J. W. MACCOLL: The Mechanics of Compressible Fluids, in "Aerodynamic Theory," Vol. III (edited by W. F. Durand), Verlag Julius Springer, Berlin, 1935.
6. ACKERET, J.: Gasdynamik, in "Handbuch der Physik," Band VII, Verlag Julius Springer, Berlin, 1927.

CHAPTER X

DRAG

10.1. Drag and Lift. The force on a body that results from the motion of the body through a real fluid is, in general, inclined to the path direction. The component of this force parallel to the path is called the "drag," and the normal component is called the "lift." The drag does work as the body moves; the lift does no work. The lift is not necessarily vertical; it is defined as normal to the path, which may have any arbitrary direction.

Static buoyant force is excluded from consideration here, since it does not result from the motion of the body.

10.2. Energy and Work. Assume that a body moves at constant velocity through a large mass of fluid that is undisturbed, except by the body. The first law of thermodynamics requires that the work done by the body be equal to the increase in energy of the fluid, provided that the distant boundaries are so far away that nothing is transferred across them. If the body is partly immersed in two fluids, as a surface vessel in water and air, work is done on both fluids.

The energy imparted to the fluid may take one or more of several forms near the body, such as energy of the wake, energy of gravity waves, or energy of compression waves. Ultimately, however, the action of viscosity dissipates all these forms of energy, so that the final effect of the passage of a body is a rise in temperature of the fluid.

10.3. Dimensional Analysis—Drag Coefficient. In general, both friction and gravity forces play a role in the determination of the flow pattern around a body moving at constant velocity. Furthermore, the compressibility of the fluid may have to be taken into account. If all three of these factors are appreciable, the drag D of a body of given shape is a function of ρ, V, l, μ, g, and C, where l is a characteristic length of the body, C is the velocity of sound in the undisturbed fluid, and the other symbols have their usual meanings. Thus,

$$D = \phi(\rho, V, l, \mu, g, C) \tag{10.1}$$

One possible simplification of Eq. (10.1), by means of the Π theorem, is

$$\frac{D}{\rho V^2 l^2} = \phi_1\left(\frac{\rho V l}{\mu}, \frac{V^2}{lg}, \frac{V}{C}\right) \tag{10.2}$$

where the independent variables are seen from Chap. VII to be, respectively, the Reynolds number R, the Froude number F, and the Mach number M.

It is customary to define the drag coefficient as

$$C_D = \frac{D}{(\rho/2)V^2A} \tag{10.3}$$

where the symbol A stands for some area pertaining to the body in question. Equations (10.2) and (10.3) combine to give

$$C_D = \psi(R,F,M) \tag{10.4}$$

Form of body	$\dfrac{l}{d}$	R	C_D
Disk (normal to flow).............	...	$>10^3$	1.12
Tandem disks (l = spacing)			
(normal to flow)...............	0	$>10^3$	1.12
	1	$>10^3$	0.93
	2	$>10^3$	1.04
	3	$>10^3$	1.54
Rectangular plate (l = length)			
(normal to flow)...............	1	$>10^3$	1.16
	5	$>10^3$	1.20
	20	$>10^3$	1.50
	∞	$>10^3$	1.95
Circular cylinder			
(axis parallel to flow)...........	0	$>10^3$	1.12
	1	$>10^3$	0.91
	2	$>10^3$	0.85
	4	$>10^3$	0.87
	7	$>10^3$	0.99
Hemisphere:			
Hollow upstream...............	...	$>10^3$	1.33
Hollow downstream............	...	$>10^3$	0.34
Circular cylinder			
(axis normal to flow)...........	1	10^3 to 10^5	0.63
	5	10^3 to 10^5	0.74
	20	10^3 to 10^5	0.90
	∞	10^3 to 10^5	1.20
	5	$>5 \times 10^5$	0.35
	∞	$>5 \times 10^5$	0.33
Sphere........................	...	10^3 to 10^5	0.47
	...	$>3 \times 10^5$	0.20
Airship hull (model)	...	$>2 \times 10^5$	0.040

In all problems that to date have any practical importance, at least one of the independent variables, R, F, or M, may be neglected. In the case of an immersed body moving through incompressible fluid, neither weight nor compressibility has any effect, and Eq. (10.4) reduces to

$$C_D = \psi(R) \tag{10.5}$$

The remainder of this article and several following ones will deal with the drag problems covered by Eq. (10.5). When a free surface or compressibility is to be considered, the fact will be clearly stated.

In the table on page 183 * are listed approximate experimental values of drag coefficient for various simple shapes. The approximate range of R in which these C_D values apply is also stated.

It will be noted that C_D is independent of R for each of the first five shapes listed, provided that $R > 10^3$. All these bodies have corners, from which the flow separates, and are known as bluff bodies. The next two shapes, the cylinder and sphere, are rounded and exhibit two distinct regimes of flow; that is, C_D has a large value for $10^3 < R < 10^5$ but drops abruptly at a certain critical value of R and then remains approximately constant as R increases. The airship hull is also rounded but is more "streamlined" than the cylinder or sphere and does not exhibit the sudden drop in C_D characterizing those bodies.

Examination of the table thus suggests a classification of shapes as "bluff," "rounded," or "streamlined," the drag coefficient of each class showing a certain typical behavior as the Reynolds number changes.

10.4. Pressure Drag and Friction Drag. It will be found useful to break the total drag into two components, the pressure drag D_p caused by normal stresses, and the friction drag D_f caused by tangential stresses.

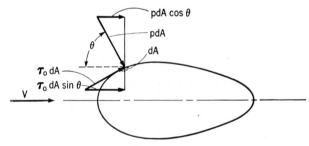

Fig. 10.1.

The normal force on a surface element dA of a body is $p\,dA$, and the tangential force is $\tau_0\,dA$, as shown in Fig. 10.1. The components in the direction of flow of these two forces are, respectively, $p\,dA\cos\theta$ and $\tau_0\,dA\sin\theta$, where θ is the angle between the outward-drawn normal to dA and the upstream direction. Thus the pressure and friction drags are

$$D_p = \int_A p \cos\theta\, dA$$

---

* Adapted from the tabulation in "Fluid Mechanics for Hydraulic Engineers," by Hunter Rouse, McGraw-Hill Book Company, Inc., New York, 1938.

$$D_f = \int_A \tau_0 \sin \theta \, dA$$

An example of the use of these concepts is provided in the explanation of the change in C_D with l/d ratio, for a cylinder with axis parallel to the flow (see the table, page 183). When $l/d = 0$, the pressure-drag coefficient C_{D_p} is large, and the friction-drag coefficient C_{D_f} is zero. As l/d increases, the flow separation from the corners becomes less intense and C_{D_p} gradually decreases. At the same time, however, shearing forces along the cylindrical surface are becoming appreciable, so that C_{D_f} increases. It is seen that these changes cause the over-all coefficient C_D to pass through a minimum when $l/d \approx 2$.

10.5. Drag at Small Reynolds Numbers. It will be recalled from Art. 7.22 that R is a measure of the ratio of inertia to friction force at any point in a flow. Consequently, if R is made sufficiently small, the effect of inertia on the drag may be neglected. In other words, the density of the fluid has no influence on drag at small values of R. In this case Eq. (10.1) simplifies to

$$D = \phi(V,l,\mu)$$

whence, by dimensional analysis,

$$D = \text{constant } \mu l V \tag{10.6}$$

Combining Eqs. (10.3) and (10.6), we get

$$C_D = \frac{\text{constant}}{R} \tag{10.7}$$

The unknown constant appearing in Eq. (10.6) has been evaluated theoretically for certain shapes by means of the equations of motion for a viscous fluid. In the case of a sphere, for example, Stokes found that

$$D = 3\pi\mu V d \tag{10.8}$$

where the diameter d is taken as the characteristic length. The corresponding expression for C_D is

$$C_D = \frac{24}{\rho V d/\mu} = \frac{24}{R} \tag{10.9}$$

Comparison of Eq. (10.9) with experimental values of C_D for a sphere indicates that Stokes' result holds only if $\rho V d/\mu < 1.2$ (see Fig. 10.13). These equations, therefore, are valid only for extremely small spheres and velocities or for very viscous liquids. Practical applications are to dust particles in air and to water droplets occurring in fog or cloud.

The details of Stokes' analysis indicate that the pressure drag of a sphere is one-third of the total, the friction drag accounting for the remaining two-thirds.

10.6. Drag at Large Reynolds Numbers. A large Reynolds number means, in general, that inertia force predominates over friction force. It has been found experimentally that friction can be neglected everywhere in a flow with a large value of R, except in a thin layer of fluid next to the body (called the "boundary layer") and in the wake. This frictional boundary layer is formed because the relative velocity of a real fluid at the body surface is zero, while the velocity a short distance away has a magnitude comparable with that of the undisturbed stream. Consequently, close to the surface, there is a large rate of change of V with respect to n, the outward-drawn surface normal; and the shearing stress $\tau = \mu \partial V / \partial n$ is appreciable, even in a fluid of small viscosity, like air or water.

Inside the boundary layer, the fluid particles are set into rotation by the shearing forces; the motion may be roughly likened to that of rollers in a roller bearing. Outside the boundary layer, however, the friction forces are so small that the motion approximates closely to an irrotational flow of frictionless fluid.

For a streamlined body, the boundary layer remains thin over the entire surface and does not separate, the wake is small, and the streamlines and pressure distribution are nearly the same as for an irrotational flow. Theory shows that the pressure distribution over a body in an irrotational flow always yields a zero value of drag and drag coefficient. Consequently, the pressure-drag coefficient will be small for a streamlined body in a real fluid. It is found that the friction-drag coefficient is of the same order of magnitude as the pressure-drag coefficient.

The flow pattern for a bluff or rounded body differs markedly from an irrotational one, because the boundary layer separates and forms a considerable wake. Close to the body, the wake fluid experiences a violent eddying motion; the mean level of kinetic energy is higher, and the mean level of pressure is less than in the corresponding irrotational flow. Since the pressure over the portion upstream from the separation point approximates to that in irrotational flow, the pressure-drag coefficient will be large if the projected area of the wake is a large fraction of the projected area of the body.

For a bluff body the flow separates at the corners, regardless of R, provided merely that R be sufficiently large. The ratio of the projected areas of wake and body is therefore constant, and so is C_{Dp}. Since $C_{Dp} >> C_{Df}$, the over-all coefficient C_D is likewise nearly constant.

For a rounded body, however, the separation point depends on R and also on other factors, such as the turbulence of the flow approaching the body. The sudden drop observed in C_D at a certain critical Reynolds number is caused by a sudden decrease in the area of the wake, when the boundary-layer flow becomes turbulent. This phenomenon will be discussed in more detail in Art. 10.11.

10.7. Drag in a Nonseparating Flow. In Fig. 10.2 is shown a streamlined body of revolution, together with curves of measured pressure and pressure calculated for an irrotational flow. This is one of several theo-

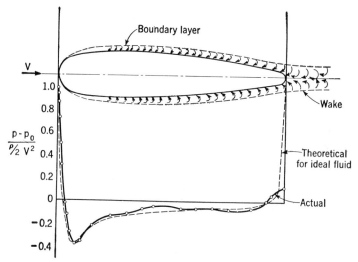

FIG. 10.2. — Theoretical and experimental pressure distributions over a body of revolution. (*After Fuhrmann, reference* 4.)

retically developed shapes tested by G. Fuhrmann [4] in comparing actual and theoretical flows around streamlined forms. It will be noted that the actual and theoretical pressure distributions are nearly the same, except at the tail, where the actual pressure fails to rise to the theoretical stagnation-point value.

The pressure-drag coefficient computed from the measured pressure distribution and based on the projected area of the body was found to be 0.0201. The total drag of the body was simultaneously measured and the over-all drag coefficient found to be 0.0362. The friction-drag coefficient is the difference between these two, *viz.*, 0.0161. It is seen that pressure and friction drags are of the same order of magnitude for a streamlined form.

Figure 10.2 also shows, to an exaggerated scale, the boundary layer formed on the body and the wake shed downstream. There is no appreciable separation of the main flow.

10.8. Boundary-layer Mechanics. Prandtl [6] originated the concept of the boundary layer, early in this century, and he and his associates took the lead in developing both theoretically and experimentally this branch of fluid mechanics. The demand for aircraft capable of ever higher and higher speed has provided a constant stimulus for this development, and many workers have contributed to the field.

This article will be restricted to the simplest case of boundary-layer flow, *viz.*, that on a flat plate parallel to the flow and subject to a uniform pressure. Figure 10.3 shows the two-dimensional flow past one side of such a plate.

The basic assumption is that δ, the thickness of the boundary layer, at any point x be small compared with x. The definition of δ is somewhat arbitrary, because the friction forces die away asymptotically with distance from the surface and the velocity does not quite attain the value V of the

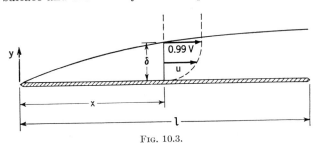

FIG. 10.3.

undisturbed flow. There is, however, practically full recovery of velocity so close to the surface that δ is usually defined as the distance at which the velocity equals 99 per cent of V.

The slowing down of the fluid close to the plate gives rise to a gradual thickening of the boundary layer and to a small velocity component in the y direction, normal to the surface. The main stream thus diverges slightly. This y velocity component is very small compared with u, the x component, and is not shown in the figures.

The main object of a boundary-layer analysis is to set up an expression for the drag coefficient of the plate, since this is the matter of greatest practical interest. Another object is to determine the thickness of the boundary layer.

In the case of a laminar boundary layer the equations of motion of a viscous fluid can be solved, thanks to the simplifying assumption that $\delta \ll x$. Formulas for C_D and δ for the laminar case were obtained by Blasius [3], an associate of Prandtl. They are

$$C_D = \frac{D}{(\rho/2)V^2bl} = \frac{1.33}{\sqrt{Vl/\nu}} = \frac{1.33}{\sqrt{R}} \qquad (10.10)$$

$$\delta = \frac{5.2x}{\sqrt{Vx/\nu}} \qquad (10.11)$$

where D is the drag of one side and b is the width of the plate.

The derivation of these formulas cannot be given here, but an approximation to them will be developed by means of the momentum equation. To use this momentum analysis, which is due to von Kármán [5], one must assume a form for the x-velocity distribution across the boundary layer. The analysis is, therefore, semiempirical, but it has the advantage of being applicable to a turbulent boundary layer, as well as a laminar one. Indeed, since Blasius' exact solution for a laminar layer is available, the momentum analysis is used chiefly for turbulent boundary layers, for which a reasonable velocity distribution can be assumed by analogy with pipe flow.

In Fig. 10.4 is shown an elementary portion of the boundary layer of length dx, at an arbitrary point on the plate. The boundary-layer flow may

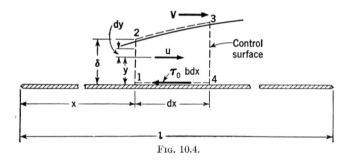

Fig. 10.4.

be either laminar or turbulent. The only external force in the x direction acting on the fluid inside the control surface 1, 2, 3, 4 is $-\tau_0 b\,dx$; there is no pressure force, because the pressure is assumed uniform everywhere. The momentum equation [Eq. (6.6)], gives for this case

$$-\tau_0 b\,dx = \text{net efflux of } x \text{ momentum from the control surface} \quad (10.12)$$

The momentum influx across boundary 1, 2 is seen to be $M = \displaystyle\int_0^\delta \rho u^2 b\,dy$; the difference between the efflux across 3, 4 and the influx across 1, 2 is written as dM. There is also a certain influx of x momentum across boundary 2, 3, which must be subtracted from dM in order to get the net efflux from the entire control surface. This momentum influx is equal to the product of the mass influx across 2, 3 and the velocity V, since 2, 3 marks the limit of the boundary layer, where the x velocity is practically equal to V. By continuity, this mass influx is equal to the difference between the mass efflux across 3, 4 and the influx across 1, 2, which may be written as dm, where m is the mass influx across 1, 2 and is equal to $\displaystyle\int_0^\delta \rho u b\,dy$.

Equation (10.12) thus becomes

$$-\tau_0 b\,dx = dM - V\,dm = d\left(\int_0^\delta \rho u^2 b\,dy\right) - V d\left(\int_0^\delta \rho u b\,dy\right)$$

which, since ρ, V, and b are constant, simplifies to

$$-\tau_0 b \, dx = \rho b V^2 d \left[\int_0^\delta \left(\frac{u^2}{V^2} - \frac{u}{V} \right) dy \right]$$

Changing the variable of integration from y to y/δ, we get

$$\frac{\tau_0}{\rho V^2} = \frac{d}{dx} \left[\delta \int_0^1 \left(\frac{u}{V} - \frac{u^2}{V^2} \right) d\left(\frac{y}{\delta}\right) \right] = \frac{d}{dx} [\delta \alpha] \qquad (10.13)$$

where

$$\alpha = \int_0^1 \left(\frac{u}{V} - \frac{u^2}{V^2} \right) d\left(\frac{y}{\delta}\right) \qquad (10.14)$$

The drag is the summation of the elementary friction forces on the plate.

$$D = \int_0^l \tau_0 b \, dx \qquad (10.15)$$

The drag coefficient is obtained from Eqs. (10.13) and (10.15).

$$C_D = \frac{\int_0^l \tau_0 b \, dx}{(\rho/2) V^2 b l} = \frac{2}{l} \int_0^l \frac{\tau_0}{\rho V^2} \, dx = \frac{2}{l} \delta_l \alpha_l \qquad (10.16)$$

where δ_l and α_l are the values of δ and α at $x = l$.

For a smooth plate the shearing stress at the surface is related to the velocity distribution by the formula

$$\tau_0 = \mu \left(\frac{\partial u}{\partial y} \right)_{y=0} \qquad (10.17)$$

Consequently, if the distribution of velocity across the boundary layer is assumed, one can evaluate α from Eq. (10.14) and then find δ by combining Eqs. (10.13) and (10.17). Finally, the drag coefficient is computed from Eq. (10.16).

To illustrate this procedure assume a linear distribution of velocity across the boundary layer: $u/V = y/\delta$. This is a crude approximation to the actual distribution in a laminar layer. One easily finds that $\alpha = \frac{1}{6}$ and that $(\partial u/\partial y)_{y=0} = V/\delta$. The differential equation for δ obtained from Eqs. (10.13) and (10.17) is

$$\frac{1}{6} \frac{d\delta}{dx} = \frac{\tau_0}{\rho V^2} = \frac{\mu}{\rho V \delta}$$

or

$$\delta \, d\delta = \frac{6\mu}{\rho V} \, dx$$

Noting that $\delta = 0$ at $x = 0$, we get

$$\delta^2 = \frac{12\mu x}{\rho V}$$

or

$$\delta = \frac{3.46x}{\sqrt{Vx/\nu}} \tag{10.18}$$

The drag coefficient is found from Eq. (10.16).

$$C_D = \frac{2}{l}\,\delta_l \alpha_l = \frac{2}{l}\,\frac{3.46l}{\sqrt{Vl/\nu}}\,\frac{1}{6} = \frac{1.16}{\sqrt{Vl/\nu}} \tag{10.19}$$

Equations (10.19) and (10.18) are to be compared with Eqs. (10.10) and (10.11), respectively, the exact formulas for a laminar layer. It is seen that the crude assumption of a linear velocity distribution leads to a value of C_D which is surprisingly near the truth.

The principal use of this momentum analysis is to establish a rational form of expression for C_D in case of turbulent flow in the boundary layer. A reasonable procedure is to assume a velocity distribution in the boundary layer based on measurements of turbulent flow in smooth pipes. In carrying over the pipe-flow data one considers V as the analogue of U, the maximum velocity at the center of the pipe, and δ as analogous to the pipe radius a.

At the time von Kármán first developed this method, it was known that a power law $u/U = (y/a)^{1/7}$ was valid for pipes in the range of Reynolds numbers which had then been investigated. Accordingly, von Kármán assumed that the velocity distribution in the turbulent boundary layer was given by

$$\frac{u}{V} = \left(\frac{y}{\delta}\right)^{1/7} \tag{10.20}$$

The value of α computed from Eqs. (10.14) and (10.20) is $7/72$.

Equation (10.20) does not apply for very small values of y, since it yields an infinite slope for the velocity curve at the plate, where $y = 0$. Actually, this slope is finite because the turbulence dies out close to the smooth surface and gives place to a thin, laminar sublayer. The value of τ_0, therefore, cannot be computed by means of this equation; it is possible, however, to use a formula for τ_0, due to Blasius, which is based on pressure-drop measurements in smooth pipes at moderate Reynolds numbers: $\tau_0 = 0.0228\rho\,U^2(\nu/aU)^{1/4}$. The analogue of this formula for a flat plate is

$$\tau_0 = 0.0228\rho V^2 \left(\frac{\nu}{V\delta}\right)^{1/4} \tag{10.21}$$

Straightforward calculations lead to the flat-plate formulas.

$$\delta = \frac{0.376x}{(Vx/\nu)^{\frac{1}{5}}} \qquad\qquad (10.22)$$

$$C_D = \frac{0.073}{(Vl/\nu)^{\frac{1}{5}}} \qquad\qquad (10.23)$$

It is found that these equations agree with experiments up to a Reynolds number Vl/ν of approximately 2×10^7. Equation (10.23) is plotted in Fig. 10.5.

In the development of Eqs. (10.22) and (10.23), it was assumed that the plate was entirely covered with a turbulent boundary layer. These

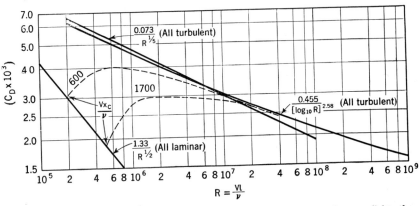

Fig. 10.5. — Drag coefficient C_D versus Reynolds number R for a flat plate parallel to the undisturbed flow.

equations will therefore be incorrect if a laminar layer covers an appreciable part of the plate. It has been found that Eq. (10.23) agrees well with experimental data for a blunt-nosed plate, on which the initial disturbance to the flow causes an early transition to turbulence in the boundary layer. Data on sharp-nosed plates, however, gradually break away from the all-turbulent curve of von Kármán as the Reynolds number decreases, and eventually reach the all-laminar curve of Blasius. An empirically corrected formula that applies in this Reynolds-number range is

$$C_D = \frac{0.073}{(Vl/\nu)^{\frac{1}{5}}} - \frac{\text{constant}}{Vl/\nu} \qquad\qquad (10.24)$$

The constant is determined by the value of Vl/ν at which transition to turbulence occurs at the trailing edge of the plate. This value of Vl/ν is called the "critical Reynolds number" and, for a sharp-nosed plate, depends primarily on the turbulence present in the approaching flow.

With the growth of knowledge about pipe flow, it was found that the power law of Eq. (10.20) did not represent the turbulent velocity distribution at higher Reynolds numbers, and the logarithmic distribution discussed in Chap. VIII came to be accepted as substantially correct. Th. von Kármán repeated his calculations for C_D, using the logarithmic velocity-distribution law and the corresponding expression for τ_0. Since the resulting formula is awkward for numerical computations, an empirical interpolation formula has been developed by Prandtl and Schlichting that agrees with von Kármán's equation up to $Vl/\nu = 10^9$. The Prandtl-Schlichting formula is

$$C_D = \frac{0.455}{[\log_{10}(Vl/\nu)]^{2.58}} \tag{10.25}$$

Equation (10.25) applies only if the boundary layer is all turbulent. To extend its range down to the critical value of Vl/ν, at which the last vestige of a turbulent layer disappears and the plate is completely covered by a laminar layer, the same empirical correction is made as above.

$$C_D = \frac{0.455}{[\log_{10}(Vl/\nu)]^{2.58}} - \frac{\text{constant}}{Vl/\nu} \tag{10.26}$$

The remarks concerning the constant of Eq. (10.24) apply also to this formula.

10.9. Factors Affecting Transition. If the value of Vl/ν is less than the critical, the boundary layer on a flat plate is entirely laminar. If the value of Vl/ν is above the critical, the laminar boundary layer will persist only to a distance x_c back from the leading edge. At this critical distance, transition to turbulence sets in, and the rest of the plate is covered by a turbulent layer. It is found, for a given plate, for given initial turbulence, and in the absence of disturbances, that the value of Vx_c/ν is constant and equal to the critical value of Vl/ν. Thus, as might be expected, the flow at any point is independent of the extent of the plate downstream from that point.

The practical importance of a large value of Vx_c/ν is apparent from Fig. 10.5, in which it is seen that an increase in the fraction of the surface covered by a laminar layer causes a decrease in C_D.

The values of Vx_c/ν indicated in Fig. 10.5 are on the order of 5×10^5. These data were all obtained, however, in wind tunnels having a considerable degree of turbulence. In the motion of a surface through still fluid, as for an airplane wing, the initial turbulence is very small, and the value of Vx_c/ν is larger than that found in a turbulent wind tunnel. For this reason it is important to investigate the behavior of Vx_c/ν under conditions of low initial turbulence and to determine the effect of disturbances on the stability of the laminar layer.

Dryden [2] and his associates [11] at the U.S. Bureau of Standards have developed a tunnel having a very low turbulence. The ratio of the rms of the turbulent component of velocity to the average velocity is used as a measure of the turbulence; the lowest value reached by this ratio is about 0.02 per cent. At this value it is found that Vx_c/ν is approximately 2.8×10^6, while, for a turbulence of 0.32 per cent, Vx_c/ν drops to 1.5×10^6.

The Bureau of Standards group has detected the presence of fluctuations in the laminar boundary layer, which grow until a breakdown of laminar motion takes place. They have found, further, that fluctuations produced artificially by a vibrating metal ribbon are amplified only within a certain band of frequencies. Waves having frequencies outside this range die away without producing turbulence. The existence of such unstable frequency bands was predicted from theoretical considerations of the viscous forces by Tollmien and Schlichting several years before techniques were available for their experimental observation. The experiments have beautifully verified the theory.

It is clear from these results that, for low drag, one should avoid the introduction of vibrations of certain frequencies into the laminar boundary layer. Use of smooth, nonwavy surfaces braced against vibration is indicated. Even engine or propeller noise may promote turbulence, if it contains intense components of the proper frequency.

The above results relate to a flat surface subject to a uniform pressure, whereas in technical applications (e.g., airfoils), the pressure is not uniform. An adverse pressure gradient on a flat surface has been found to widen the band of unstable frequencies and to increase the amplification of the Tollmien-Schlichting viscous waves. Furthermore, dynamic instability is introduced, because the velocity profile develops a reversed curvature or inflection point. By "dynamic instability" is meant one that would be operative even in the absence of friction—in contrast to the viscous instability of Tollmien and Schlichting. The over-all result is that Vx_c/ν is no longer independent of x_c but decreases as x_c is increased.

On the other hand, if the pressure decreases in the direction of flow, it appears that a stabilizing effect is produced and Vx_c/ν may increase with an increase in x_c.

The effect on transition of curvature of the surface has also been studied, with the following general results: In the absence of a pressure gradient, Vx_c/ν appears to be uninfluenced on a slightly convex surface but to be decreased on a concave surface. The destabilizing effect of the latter is due to the introduction of a dynamic instability, and not to viscous instability.

10.10. Low-drag Airfoils. The discussion in the preceding article indicates the desirability of a laminar boundary layer on a body designed for low drag. The National Advisory Committee for Aeronautics (NACA) has developed airfoils that, under test conditions approximating free flight at useful Reynolds numbers, may have a laminar boundary layer over approximately 0.6 of the chord. The minimum drag coefficients obtainable are on the order of 0.003 at a value of $R = (Vl/\nu) \approx 6 \times 10^6$, where l is the chord. Insertion of these values into Fig. 10.5 shows that C_D for these airfoils is down near the value given by Blasius' curve for a flat plate covered by a laminar layer. The minimum C_D for a conventional airfoil is on the order of 0.007.

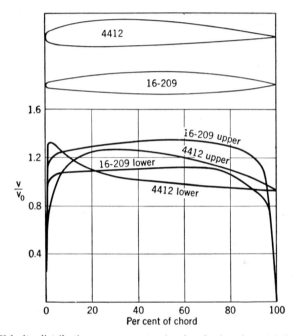

Fig. 10.6a. Velocity distributions over a conventional and a low-drag airfoil, both at a lift coefficient of 0.2.

In Fig. 10.6a is shown one of these "laminar" airfoils, NACA 16–209, together with the theoretical velocity distribution over it at the design lift coefficient of 0.2. For comparison, a conventional airfoil, NACA 4412, is also shown, together with the measured velocity distribution over it at an angle of attack $\alpha = -2$ deg, corresponding to $C_L = 0.2$. It is seen that the NACA 16–209 has the maximum thickness much farther aft than the NACA 4412. This novel shape results in a theoretical pressure distribution that decreases gradually over about 60 per cent of the chord and then rises abruptly at the tail. (The velocity-distribution curves are such that the ordinate is a maximum at the point of lowest pressure and zero at the stagnation pressure.) Tests in a nearly turbulence-free tunnel show that this favorable pressure gradient enables the boundary layer to remain laminar up to approximately the point of minimum pressure, where transition occurs. The formation of a turbulent boundary layer at this point is really advantageous because the air is thereby given enough momentum to follow the rest of the contour more closely than would otherwise be possible. Indeed, in some experiments at lower Reynolds number, transition was so much delayed that the laminar boundary layer separated and stayed separated, the transition coming too late to effect a return of the stream to the surface. Increased drag coefficients were the result.

In contrast to the NACA 16–209, the NACA 4412 has an unfavorable pressure gradient over practically its whole surface. The laminar boundary layer thickens rapidly, therefore, and transition occurs at about 0.3 of the chord. The minimum drag coefficient is greater than 0.007, more than twice the value of approximately 0.003 for the NACA 16–209.

In Fig. 10.6b is shown one of the newest low-drag airfoils. The ordinate, labeled "pressure coefficient," gives the value of $(V/V_0)^2$, instead of V/V_0, as in Fig. 10.6a. For this airfoil a dropping pressure is provided over the first 60 per cent of chord, followed abruptly by a linear rise in pressure over the rest of the surface. A laminar boundary layer is maintained back to the 60 per cent chord point, where the sudden change in pressure gradient causes a quick transition to a turbulent boundary layer. The momentum of the fluid close to the surface is so much enhanced by the turbulence that very little separation occurs.

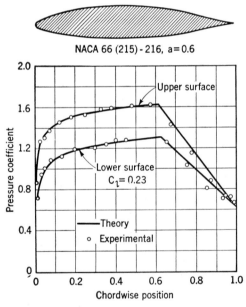

FIG. 10.6b. — Distribution of $(V/V_0)^2$ over a low-drag airfoil.

The theory has been so far developed that it can supply the shape of airfoil to give a desired pressure distribution [12]. This can be accomplished at a useful flight Reynolds number and for a desired range of lift coefficient, provided that both the mean (or design) value of C_L and its range of variation are kept small (both on the order of 0.2). The excellent control of pressure distribution that is possible is illustrated in Fig. 10.6c, which shows the distribution for symmetrical airfoils having the maximum thickness (12 per cent of chord) at 30, 40, 50, and 60 per cent of chord from the leading edge. The subscript 1 indicates that this pressure distribution does not change radically in the range of lift-coefficient values, $C_{L \text{ design}} \pm 0.1$.

The advantage of the low-drag airfoil is brought out in Fig. 10.6d, which gives the C_D versus C_L curves for a conventional section and for two low-

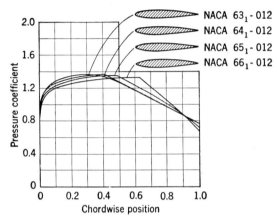

FIG. 10.6c. — Distributions of $(V/V_0)^2$ showing close relationship between point of maximum thickness and point of minimum pressure.

drag sections. The value of $C_{L \text{ design}}$ for both of the latter is 0.2. They differ, however, in the length of the laminar boundary layer, NACA 63_1–212 having 30 per cent of the chord laminar and NACA 66_1–212 having 60 per cent laminar. In the design range of C_L it is seen that NACA

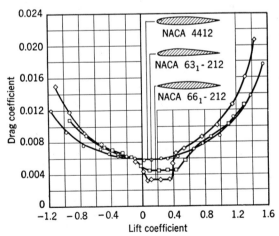

FIG. 10.6d. — Curves of drag coefficient versus lift coefficient for a conventional airfoil and two low-drag airfoils.

66_1–212 has a C_D of about half that of the conventional airfoil. Outside of this range, however, it is the least desirable of the three.

The sudden rise of C_D at each end of the "bucket" in the curve results from a forward shift in the point of minimum pressure and hence of transition.

The importance of restricting the use of a low-drag section to the design conditions is obvious from Fig. 10.6d. It may also be remarked that slight roughness of the airfoil surface can cause transition to occur early and completely vitiate the special low-drag design.

10.11. Drag in a Separating Flow. A flat plate set normal to the distant

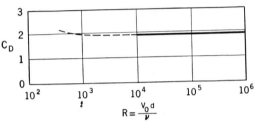

FIG. 10.7. — Drag coefficient C_D versus Reynolds number R for two-dimensional flow past a plate normal to the undisturbed flow and of breadth d. (*After F. Eisner, Das Widerstandsproblem, Third Int. Cong. App. Mech., Stockholm*, 1930.)

velocity is an extreme example of a bluff body. The flow separates at the edges for all except the smallest Reynolds numbers. The entire drag is caused by the pressure difference between the front and back of the plate, since the shearing stresses are all normal to the drag direction. Figure 10.7 gives C_D versus R for two-dimensional flow past a rectangular plate, *i.e.*, flow with negligible end effects. Figure 10.8 shows the dependence of C_D on breadth-to-length ratio d/l for rectangular plates. End effects reduce C_D because the average pressure difference over the surface is less if the flow can close in at the ends.

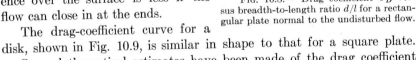

FIG. 10.8. — Drag coefficient C_D versus breadth-to-length ratio d/l for a rectangular plate normal to the undisturbed flow.

The drag-coefficient curve for a disk, shown in Fig. 10.9, is similar in shape to that for a square plate.

Several theoretical estimates have been made of the drag coefficient for two-dimensional flow past a plate. The assumption of a completely irrotational flow yields the obviously erroneous value of zero for the drag coefficient. This is equivalent to the assumption of a scalar "velocity potential" whose gradient at any point is the velocity vector at that point. This type of flow is therefore frequently called "potential flow." It can be shown that the drag of a body of any shape is zero in a potential flow.

Noting that the motion downstream from a plate is highly rotational, Helmholtz and Kirchhoff approximated to the actual wake by a region of dead water or motionless fluid separated from the main stream by an infinitely thin sheet of rotating fluid particles springing from each edge of the plate. (See Fig. 10.10.) Since the fluid in such a "vortex sheet" rotates, there is a jump in velocity from zero in the wake to a finite value in the stream. For this reason the sheet is also called a "surface of discontinuity." The pressure is assumed to vary continuously across the sheet and throughout the flow. In this idealization the flow is divided by the surfaces of discontinuity into two regions, in each of which the motion is irrotational, but which have different Bernoulli numbers. Such a flow pattern cannot be more than

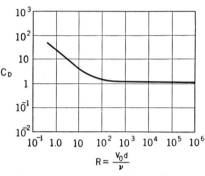

Fig. 10.9. — Drag coefficient C_D versus Reynolds number R for a disk normal to the undisturbed flow. (*After Eisner, Das Widerstandsproblem, Third Int. Cong. App. Mech., Stockholm,* 1930.)

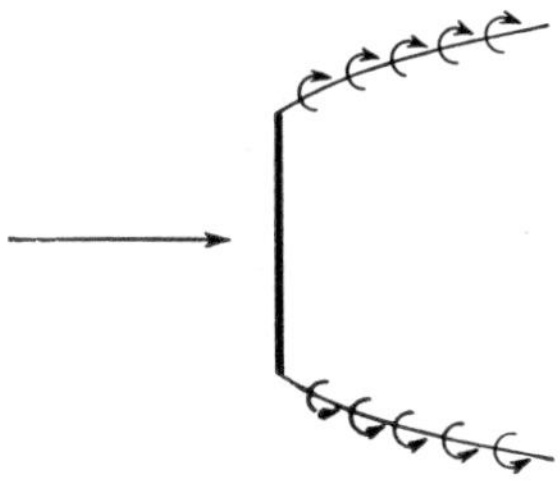

a first approximation to the actual one, because a vortex sheet is unstable in a viscous fluid and tends to break up into scattered vortices, owing to the intense shearing stress accompanying the large (theoretically infinite) velocity change across the sheet.

According to the Helmholtz-Kirchhoff two-dimensional theory, the value of the drag coefficient for the flat plate is

$$C_D = \frac{\text{drag per unit length}}{(\rho/2)dV_0^2} = 0.880$$

Fig. 10.10.

This value is to be compared with the experimental one of 1.8, shown in Fig. 10.7. This theory gives the right order of magnitude for C_D and is evidently a first approximation to reality.

Observation of the wake behind a body shows that under certain conditions vortices are shed alternately from first one edge and then the other at a regular frequency and that they move downstream in two approximately parallel rows. The vortices in one row are staggered with respect to those in the other. Figure 10.11a shows such a well-developed "vortex street" for a cylinder, while in Fig. 10.11b a street is starting to form behind a flat plate. Th. von Kármán has shown theoretically that such a staggered arrangement of vortices in an otherwise irrotational flow is stable only for a certain value of the ratio h/l, where h is the lateral spacing and l is the longitudinal spacing of the vortices. Photographs of actual flows show that the theoretical value of h/l approximates closely the measured ones.

Th. von Kármán has also computed the drag coefficient for this theoretically stable flow in terms of the frequency with which the vortices are shed and their lateral spacing in the wake. Neither the frequency nor the spacing is predicted in the theory, but when experimental values are inserted in the theoretical equations, the computed and measured values of C_D are in good agreement.

Fig. 10.11a. — Vortex formation behind a cylinder.   (*After Prandtl.*)

Fig. 10.11b. — Vortex formation behind a plate.   (*After Prandtl.*)

It should be emphasized that the actual wake ceases to resemble a vortex street if the value of Reynolds number $V_0 d / \nu$ exceeds about 2,500.

Measured values of the drag coefficient (based on projected area) for a cylinder with axis normal to flow and for a sphere are shown in Figs. 10.12 and 10.13, respectively. It has been pointed out in Art. 10.6 that the sudden drop in C_D at a critical value of R is associated with a change in the boundary layer from laminar to turbulent. This effect will here be further discussed for the sphere, which is a representative example of a rounded body.

Near the nose of a sphere the boundary layer is laminar on account of its extreme thinness. Somewhat downstream from the nose the laminar-boundary-layer fluid enters a region where the pressure rises in the direction

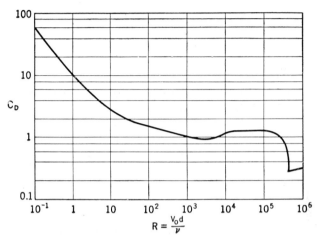

Fig. 10.12. — Drag coefficient C_D versus Reynolds number R for two-dimensional flow past a circular cylinder with axis normal to the undisturbed flow. (*After Eisner, Das Widerstandsproblem, Third Int. Cong. App. Mech., Stockholm,* 1930.)

of flow, so that the fluid is slowed down and eventually halted. Its motion is then reversed, and it is forced away from the surface. If the Reynolds

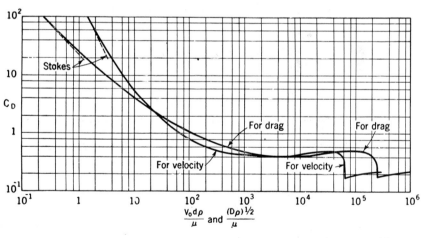

Fig. 10.13. — Drag coefficient C_D versus Reynolds number $\rho V_0 d/\mu$ and $(D\rho)^{\frac{1}{2}}/\mu$ for a sphere.   (*After Eisner, Das Widerstandsproblem, Third Int. Cong. App. Mech., Stockholm,* 1930.)

number is below the critical value, the main stream diverges, or separates, from the body at this point, which thus becomes the separation point. If, however, R is greater than the critical value, the separated laminar layer becomes turbulent and returns to the surface. The increased momentum of the turbulent layer enables it to progress somewhat farther before the adverse pressure again causes it to separate, this time permanently. The

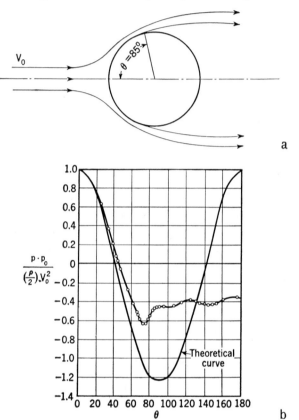

FIG. 10.14. — Measured pressure distribution for subcritical flow past a sphere. The theoretical curve for irrotational flow is also shown. [*From "Modern Developments in Fluid Dynamics" (edited by S. Goldstein), courtesy of the Oxford University Press, publishers.*]

transition from laminar to turbulent flow in the boundary layer thus causes the separation point to be moved toward the rear.

The critical value R_c, below which transition does not occur, depends not only on the shape of the rounded body but also on the turbulence present in the main stream. The greater the turbulence of the approaching flow, the lower the value of R_c, and vice versa.

If $R < R_c$, the separation occurs approximately at the largest cross section of the sphere, as shown in Fig. 10.14a. On the other hand, if $R > R_c$, the separation takes place farther back, where the cross-sectional area is less, as seen in Fig. 10.15a.

In Fig. 10.14b, the measured pressure distribution in subcritical flow is

compared with that for a potential flow, which, from symmetry, is seen to
yield a zero drag. A similar comparison for supercritical flow is given in
Fig. 10.15b. It is obvious from these figures that the pressure-drag coeffi-

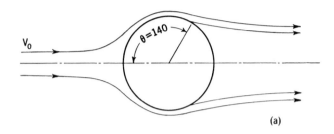

(a)

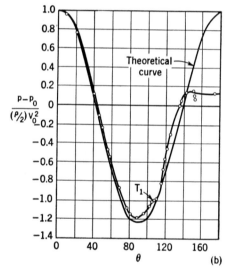

(b)

Fig. 10.15. — Measured pressure distribution for supercritical flow past a sphere. The
theoretical curve for irrotational flow is also shown. [*From "Modern Developments in Fluid
Dynamics"(edited by S. Goldstein), courtesy of the Oxford University Press, publishers.*]

cient is less in supercritical than in subcritical flow. Since the pressure
drag predominates over the friction drag, the over-all coefficient drops as
the Reynolds number surpasses the critical value.

For determination of the terminal velocity of a sphere falling through a
fluid it is convenient to know the drag coefficient as a function of a dimensionless number including the drag, rather than as a function of R, because
D is given, whereas V is unknown. It is seen from Art. 7.19 that the
formula $C_D = \phi(R)$ can be transformed to $C_D = \phi_1(D^{1/2}\rho^{1/2}/\mu)$. This curve
is included in Fig. 10.13.

10.12. Influence of a Free Surface. In this case the general equation for C_D [Eq. (10.4)] takes the form

$$C_D = \psi(R,F) \tag{10.27}$$

The principal application of Eq. (10.27) is to surface vessels, in the design of which the excess over the friction drag, or "residual drag," is an important factor. Offhand, it would appear that the naval architect could test a scale model of a proposed hull at several values of R and F and thereby determine with sufficient precision the C_D surface defined by Eq. (10.27). A difficulty arises, however, because the only practicable liquid in which to carry out towing tests on a model is water. The kinematic viscosity is therefore the same as for the full-scale hull, and it is impossible to fulfill simultaneously the conditions, $R_M = R_P$ and $F_M = F_P$, where the subscripts M and P stand for "model" and "prototype," respectively.

A satisfactory way to carry out and interpret model tests on hull forms was first suggested by William Froude in 1879, as the result of extensive experiments. Stated in modern terms, Froude's basic assumptions are (1) that the friction-drag coefficient is independent of the shape of the hull and is determined completely by the Reynolds number based on the length Vl/ν, and (2) that the residual-drag coefficient is a function of only the Froude number V^2/lg. Thus, Eq. (10.27) becomes

$$C_D = C_{D_f}\left(\frac{Vl}{\nu}\right) + C_{D_r}\left(\frac{V^2}{lg}\right) \tag{10.28}$$

where C_{D_f} and C_{D_r} are the coefficients of friction drag and residual drag, respectively. For the determination of the frictional component, Froude made numerous towing tests on planks, which caused practically no waves, and the drag of which was therefore nearly all due to surface friction. Froude's own friction data have now been superseded by more modern formulations of flat-plate drag, such as the Prandtl-Schlichting equation [Eq. (10.25)].

An example of the Froude method is given in Fig. 10.16. At the left is the curve of C_D for a 20-ft model, obtained from towing tests covering the range of Froude number anticipated for the prototype. Values of the Froude number $F = V^2/lg$ are spotted on this curve. The Prandtl-Schlichting curve for a smooth flat plate covered with an all-turbulent boundary layer is assumed to yield C_{D_f} for either the model or the 400-ft prototype. According to Eq. (10.28) the values of C_{D_r} obtained by subtraction of C_{D_f} from C_D for the model are independent of the Reynolds number and may therefore be added to the C_{D_f} values at the proper Reynolds numbers to get the C_D curve for the 400-ft hull. This curve appears at the right side of Fig. 10.16.

This procedure has been found reasonably satisfactory in the design of vessels. The fact that the shape of the hull is neglected in the determination of the friction-drag coefficient does not lead to serious errors. In practice, however, a correction is added to the Prandtl-Schlichting curve for a smooth plate to take account of the roughness of the full-scale vessel. The empirical correction used depends upon the nature of the surface;

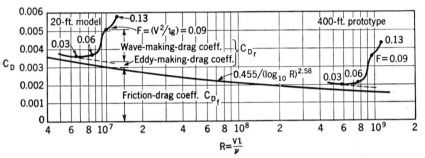

FIG. 10.16. — Drag coefficient, C_D, for a model vessel and its prototype. The dependence on both Reynolds number R and Froude number F is shown. (*After Davidson, reference* 10, *courtesy of the author and the Society of Naval Architects and Marine Engineers.*)

for example, different corrections are employed for riveted and welded hulls or for freshly painted and barnacle-covered surfaces.

The shape of the C_D curves of Fig. 10.16 is of interest in connection with the mechanism of the residual drag. At low values of Froude number ($F < 0.03$) the C_D and C_{D_f} curves are practically parallel; in other words, C_{D_r} is a constant. This fact leads one to suppose that, at low Froude numbers, the residual drag is principally form drag. In support of this conclusion is the observation that no surface waves are set up in this range of F.

The dotted line of Fig. 10.16, parallel to the Prandtl-Schlichting curve, indicates the assumed value of the form- ("eddy-making") drag coefficient at higher values of F.

The upturn in the C_D curve at $F = 0.03$ corresponds with the first appearance of surface waves created by the hull. A train of waves is shed from the bow and another at the stern, both of which increase in amplitude as F increases. The water level around the bow is raised by the presence of the bow wave, while the water level at the stern is lowered by the action of the stern wave. The pressure distribution over the hull is thus changed unfavorably, and the residual-drag coefficient is markedly increased. This increase is called the "wave-making-drag coefficient" and is indicated in Fig. 10.16.

It will be further observed in Fig. 10.16 that the C_D curve has an undulant, or "hump-and-hollow," shape and that this peculiarity is caused by variations in the wave-making coefficient. These variations have been traced to the change in phase between the bow-wave train and the stern-wave train that occurs as F is increased. When the two wave trains are in phase, the water level at the stern is less than it would be in the absence of a bow wave, while the opposite is true when the wave trains are out of phase.

It is obviously desirable to design a hull to operate just at the base of one of the peaks of the C_D curve rather than at the crest. Otherwise, a considerable penalty is paid for a small increase in cruising speed.

10.13. Compressibility at Subsonic and Transonic Speeds. At speeds that are appreciable compared with sound velocity the general drag equation [Eq. (10.4)] takes the form

$$C_D = \psi(R,M) \tag{10.29}$$

The principal application of this equation at Mach numbers less than 1 is to aircraft. Compressibility effects on air propellers have long been recognized, and they are now important also in the flow past wings and control surfaces of high-speed airplanes. If an aircraft exceeds a certain critical velocity (as in a dive), shock waves appear on the wings and control surfaces, which then undergo not only a sudden increase in drag but also a decrease in lift and a shift in the center of pressure.

It is convenient to classify compressible flows as either subsonic or transonic. The former is defined as one in which the velocity is everywhere subsonic, while in the latter there is at least one point where sonic speed is attained or exceeded. The flow past a body moving at subsonic speed can be transonic, because near the body there are regions where the local relative velocities are higher and the local sound velocities are less than those of the distance fluid. The Mach number of the undisturbed stream at which the transition from subsonic to transonic flow occurs is known as the "critical Mach number" M_c.

In general, the Reynolds number and Mach number are both important in determining subsonic flow patterns, but in the transonic regime the Mach number predominates.

Large changes in the drag and lift coefficients of a body are observed to start if the Mach number is increased somewhat above the critical value. These changes are associated with the development of shock waves near the body, resulting from the breakdown of local supersonic flow. There is not yet a satisfactory theoretical value for the Mach number at which the shock waves first appear on a given body. The critical Mach number defined above is obviously a lower limit, since a shock wave can occur only in a supersonic flow. In certain irrotational flows that have been investigated theoretically speeds more than 50 per cent greater than the local sound velocity are attained, together with a continuous deceleration to subsonic speed farther downstream. At higher speed a so-called "limiting line" is found in the theory, beyond which the irrotational flow cannot progress. This line is interpreted as the locus of a shock wave, since these in general introduce rotation into a flow. Little is known of the stability of these theoretical patterns, to say nothing of actual ones, which are further complicated by friction. It seems, however, that the Mach number at which a limiting line theoretically appears is a conservative upper limit to the M value at which a shock will occur in an actual flow.

For subsonic motion the Glauert-Prandtl approximate theory for slender bodies (Art. 11.32) shows that the velocities reached in compressible flow are increased by a factor $1/\sqrt{1 - M^2}$ over those in incompressible flow at the same free-stream velocity. The pressure difference between any two points is also increased in the same ratio, and the drag coefficient may tend to rise, due principally to the thickening of the boundary layer by the larger adverse pressure gradient. This effect is more marked with thick airfoils than with thin ones, as is seen in Fig. 10.17. For the thin airfoil,

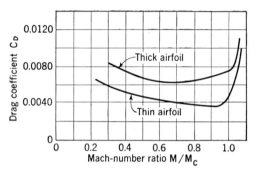

Fig. 10.17.—Drag coefficient C_D versus Mach-number ratio M/M_c for two airfoils.

C_D actually decreases over most of the range of M/M_c, which is attributable to the increasing R.

Figure 10.17 also shows the rapid increase in C_D after the critical Mach number is reached. This change, which dwarfs the small compressibility

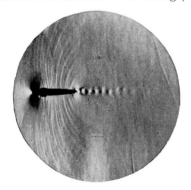

Fig. 10.18. — Schlieren photograph of NACA 0012 airfoil with tail cut off illustrating propagation of disturbances at a Mach number $M = 0.704$. (NACA photograph. Courtesy of John Stack.)

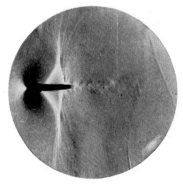

Fig. 10.19. — Schlieren photograph of NACA 0012 airfoil with tail cut off illustrating propagation of disturbances at a Mach number $M = 0.833$. (NACA photograph. Courtesy of John Stack.)

effects in subsonic flow, results from the alterations in the flow pattern produced by shock waves. Schlieren photographs of these flow phenomena are given in Figs. 10.18 and 10.19. An airfoil with the tail cut off was purposely used in these experiments, so that the flow could be interpreted by observation of disturbances set up at the blunt end. These disturbances are shed alternately from one corner and the other, as is seen by their staggered arrangement. In the first picture they can progress upstream everywhere, except in a small region near the widest part of the section, where they are crowded together. The flow is therefore supersonic only in this small region. There is no separation of the stream from the surface.

The Mach number of the flow in Fig. 10.19 is higher than in Fig. 10.18, and a well-developed shock wave springs from both sides of the airfoil. Beyond the ends of the shock the tail disturbances move upstream, indicating that the supersonic region is again only local, although larger than that of Fig. 10.18. The forward end of this region is marked by oblique shocks, which coalesce with the normal shock set up at the downstream end of the region. Noticeable separation occurs, beginning under the oblique shocks and extending the length of the airfoil to form a relatively wide wake.

FIG. 10.20. — Schlieren photograph of separated flow for rear portion of NACA 23015 airfoil at a Mach number $M = 0.691$. Airfoil chord 5 in.; angle of attack 6 deg. (*NACA photograph. Courtesy of John Stack.*)

Another picture of separation is given in Fig. 10.20, which shows a transonic flow over an airfoil at a moderate angle of attack. It is clear that the separation point is just upstream from the first oblique shock. Since there would be no separation of a subsonic flow from this airfoil at this angle of attack, it seems likely that the shock is connected with the separation observed. Measurements of pressure at the surface of the airfoil show a discontinuous rise under the shock, and it is thought that this so thickens the boundary layer that separation takes place. The oblique shocks are believed to be caused by the bending of the supersonic stream into a region of higher pressure, as the supersonic stream flows over the more slowly moving fluid in the boundary layer. The dark line in Fig. 10.20 that extends downstream from the separation point may mark the boundary between sub- and supersonic flow.

The large increase in drag coefficient in the transonic regime is found to be largely due to the separation induced by the shocks, rather than to the losses in the shocks themselves. The defect in total pressure, determined by a wake traverse with an impact tube, is given in Fig. 10.21 for both sub- and transonic flow conditions. The area under each curve is a measure of the corresponding C_D. At the lower Mach number the width of the wake is small, as well as the maximum total-pressure defect. At the higher

Mach number the area under the large peak is attributed to separation and the area under the flatter parts of the curve to the shock. The former area is more than half the total.

It is of interest to compare the measured static-pressure rise on the air-

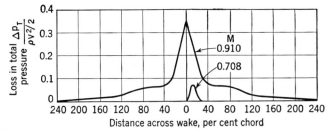

FIG. 10.21. — Wake shape and total-pressure defect as influenced by Mach number. NACA 0012 airfoil at 0-deg angle of attack. (*After Stack, reference 8. Courtesy of the Institute of the Aeronautical Sciences.*)

foil under the shock with the pressure rise computed from the measured total-pressure defect caused by the shock. In Fig. 10.22 are shown the measured pressure distribution over the upper surface of an airfoil and the

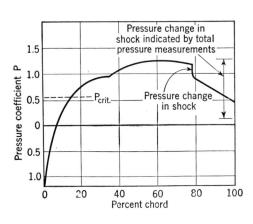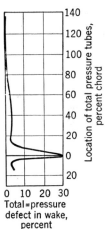

FIG. 10.22. — Measured static-pressure change through shock as compared with calculated change based on total-pressure loss in wake. NACA 4412 airfoil at $\frac{1}{4}$-deg angle of attack. $M = 0.770$. (*After Stack, reference 8. Courtesy of the Institute of the Aeronautical Sciences.*)

total-pressure defect in the wake, together with the pressure jump computed from the height of the flat part of the defect curve. The latter is so much greater than the measured discontinuity that the difference cannot be accounted for by approximations in the theory. A reasonable explanation seems to be that the pressure distribution along the surface is modified by disturbances transmitted upstream through the subsonic boundary layer.

These phenomena of the transonic regime indicate the necessity of a large critical Mach number for an airfoil designed for high subsonic speeds. For a large M_c the excess of the maximum local velocity over the distant velocity must be as small as possible. This condition is met by the NACA 16 series of airfoils, each member of which is designed to have a minimum excess velocity at a definite value of the lift coefficient. In Fig. 10.6a are shown the velocity distributions for an incompressible flow over the NACA 16–209 and NACA 4412 airfoils, each at angle of attack corresponding to $C_L = 0.2$. In Fig. 10.23 are plotted the velocity distributions computed

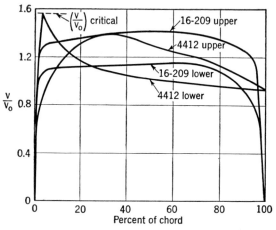

FIG. 10.23. — Velocity distributions for compressible flow over NACA 4412 and NACA 16–209 airfoils, both at the same angle of attack. Compare with Fig. 10.6a.

for a compressible flow over the same airfoils in the same attitude. The only difference between these two figures is in the Mach number: in Fig. 10.6a, $M \approx 0$, while, in Fig. 10.23, $M = 0.6$, which is the critical value for the 4412 at the given angle of attack of -2 deg. It is seen that, under these conditions, the local sound velocity is reached on the lower surface of the 4412 but that the velocity everywhere on the 16–209 is well below the sonic value. The measured critical Mach number for the 16–209 is $M_c = 0.76$.

10.14. Compressibility at Supersonic Speeds. Hitherto, this subject has been of practical importance only in the field of exterior ballistics, but the recent developments in jet and rocket propulsion foreshadow a much more widespread interest. Already, some ballisticians are using their experience with projectiles as the starting point in the rational design of low-drag forms for supersonic motion.

It will be recalled from Chap. IX that a shock wave is formed in front of a body whose velocity exceeds that of sound in the undisturbed fluid. The effect of this nose shock on the drag depends on the intensity of the shock, which in turn is greatly influenced by the shape of the front end of the body. A relatively weak nose wave is associated with a thin airfoil or pointed projectile, while a round-nosed body sets up a bow wave of large amplitude, regardless of the tapering of the tail. A tapering, pointed nose is thus essential for low drag at supersonic speeds.

A drag-coefficient curve for an airfoil is shown diagrammatically in Fig. 10.24. The rapid dropping off of C_D beyond the transonic region is due

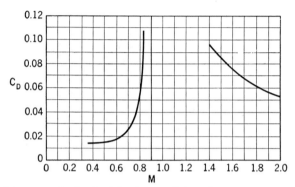

FIG. 10.24. — Diagrammatic sketch of the drag coefficient C_D versus Mach number M for an airfoil.

to the fact that shocks formed on the surface during the critical regime move off the airfoil and to the rear as M increases, the width of the wake being thus reduced. In the supersonic region, C_D is somewhat higher than at subsonic speeds, on account of the shock waves at the nose and tail.

Data on projectiles are illustrated in Fig. 10.25, in which curve a gives

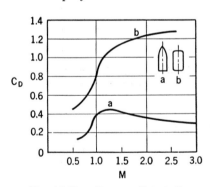

FIG. 10.25. — Drag coefficient C versus Mach number M for a sharp-nosed and a blunt projectile. (*After Ackeret, reference 14.*)

FIG. 10.26. — Wave pattern set up by a bullet at a speed slightly greater than the sound velocity. (*After Ackeret, reference 14.*)

the C_D for a pointed bullet. Critical phenomena similar to those on an airfoil cause a sharp rise in C_D beginning approximately at $M = 0.8$. The local shocks on the bullet for a Mach number slightly greater than 1, where C_D is near its maximum value, are clearly shown in Fig. 10.26.

Curve b of Fig. 10.25, for a blunt-nosed projectile, is quite different from that for the bullet. The effectiveness of the local shocks formed during the transonic motion in increasing the drag coefficient is less than in the previous

Fig. 10.27. — Wave pattern set up by a blunt-nosed bullet at a supersonic speed. (*Photograph made at the Aberdeen Proving Ground. Courtesy of A. C. Charters and R. Turetsky.*)

examples. The probable explanation is that the flow has already separated from the forward corners before the critical conditions are reached. Much of the rise in C_D occurs at supersonic speeds and is largely due to the increased pressure on the nose accompanying the intense head wave. There is pronounced similarity between this C_D curve and the stagnation-pressure curve plotted in Fig. 9.19.

Figures 10.27 and 10.28 are spark photographs that show the striking difference in the nose waves accompanying the blunt and pointed projectiles. It will be recalled from Art. 9.3 that the more nearly normal a shock wave is to the line of motion the greater is its intensity. The nose wave of the blunt projectile is therefore much more intense than that of the pointed one.

At high supersonic speeds the low pressure at the rear has relatively

ittle effect on C_D. The large pressure on the front and the surface friction
are the main sources of drag. The friction increases markedly at high
Mach numbers; it may amount to 75 per cent of the total drag of a well-
designed body at a Mach number of 5.

The frictional heating of the boundary-layer fluid makes the wake

Fig. 10.28. — Wave pattern set up by a sharp-nosed bullet at a supersonic speed.
Photograph made at the Aberdeen Proving Ground. Courtesy of A. C. Charters and R. Turetsky.)

density less than that of the surrounding air, so that the wake is visible
in the photographs.

In line with the growing interest in supersonic motion, tests have recently
been made on spheres [1]. The spheres were fired in place of bullets, and
spark photographs were taken at several stations along the line of flight.
These photographs, made at known times, permitted the calculation of the
drag-coefficient curve of Fig. 10.29. Spheres of $\frac{9}{16}$ in. diameter were used
in most of the tests on which this curve is based, but a few results for $1\frac{1}{2}$-in.-
diameter spheres are also included. These fall on the same curve if $M > 0.8$,
while the dotted line shows their trend at lower values of M.

It is seen that C_D starts to rise at a Mach number of about 0.5, reaches a peak at $M = 1.5$, and then drops gradually with further increase in M. The gradual dropping off of the curve in the supersonic region suggests that the head wave may be intermediate in intensity between those for

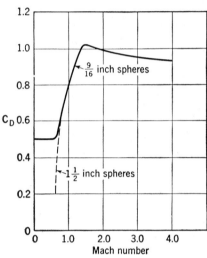

FIG. 10.29. — Drag coefficient C_D versus Mach number M for spheres. (*After Charters, reference 1. Courtesy of the Institute of the Aeronautical Sciences.*)

pointed and blunt objects. The wave pattern of Fig. 10.30 is of interest in connection with this speculation. It is seen that the head wave follows the contour of the surface and hence is steeper (near the axis) than one for a pointed object, but not so steep as one for a blunt body.

Figure 10.31 illustrates the waves at $M = 0.992$. For steady motion there would be no head wave, but for the decelerated motion of the sphere this wave is in process of moving farther ahead and eventually disappearing. In Fig. 10.32, taken a few moments later, the head wave has moved out of the field of view. The value of M for this picture is 0.972.

It is well known that a sphere possesses a critical Reynolds number in incompressible flow. The $\frac{9}{16}$-in. spheres, however, showed no drop in C_D, even though R passed through the range found to be critical for large spheres under conditions of incompressibility. This fact suggests that, at sufficiently large M, the influence of R is secondary.

The dotted line in Fig. 10.29 is good evidence that the larger spheres ($1\frac{1}{2}$ in. diameter) passed through a critical R at a value of M somewhat below 0.6. The fact that the dotted line becomes coincident with the full-line curve at $M = 0.8$ strengthens the conclusion that R is unimportant at large values of M.

SELECTED BIBLIOGRAPHY

1. CHARTERS, A. C.: The Aerodynamic Performance of Small Spheres from Subsonic to High Supersonic Velocities, *J. Aeronaut. Sci.*, vol. 12, pp. 468–476, October, 1945.
2. DRYDEN, H. L.: Turbulence and the Boundary Layer, *J. Aeronaut. Sci.*, vol. 6, pp. 85–100, January, 1939.
3. GOLDSTEIN, S. (Editor): "Modern Developments in Fluid Dynamics," p. 135, Oxford University Press, New York, 1938.
4. *Ibid.*, pp. 24 and 523.
5. *Ibid.*, p. 131.
6. *Ibid.*, p. 117.
7. KÁRMÁN, TH. VON: Compressibility Effects in Aerodynamics, *J. Aeronaut. Sci.*, vol. 8, pp. 337–356, July, 1941.

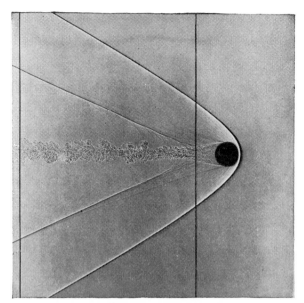

Fig. 10.30. — Wave pattern set up by a sphere at a supersonic speed $M = 2.23$. The vertical black lines are not part of the wave pattern. (*Photograph made at the Aberdeen Proving Ground. Courtesy of A. C. Charters and R. Turetsky.*)

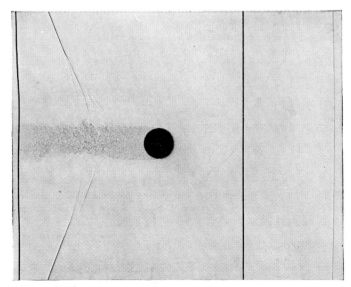

Fig. 10.31. — Wave pattern set up by a decelerating sphere at a Mach number $M = 0.992$. (*Photograph made at the Aberdeen Proving Ground. Courtesy of A. C. Charters and R. Turetsky.*)

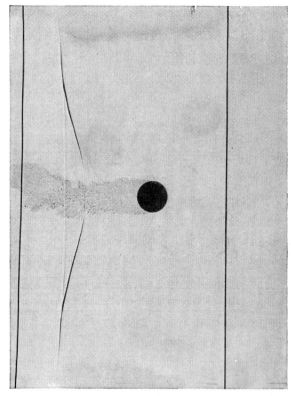

FIG. 10.32. — Wave pattern set up by a decelerating sphere at a Mach number $M = 0.972$. (*Photograph made at the Aberdeen Proving Ground. Courtesy of A. C. Charters and R. Turetsky.*)

8. STACK, JOHN: Compressible Flows in Aeronautics, *J. Aeronaut. Sci.*, vol. 12, pp. 127–148, April, 1945.

9. TOLLMIEN, W.: "General Instability Criterion of Laminar Velocity Distributions," *NACA, Tech. Mem.* 792, 1936.

10. DAVIDSON, K. S. M.: Resistance and Powering, Chap. II in "Principles of Naval Architecture" (edited by H. E. Rossell and L. B. Chapman), Society of Naval Architects and Marine Engineers, New York, 1939.

11. SCHUBAUER, G. B., and H. K. SKRAMSTAD: "Laminar-boundary-layer Oscillations on a Flat Plate," *NACA Rept.*, April, 1943.

12. ABBOTT, I. H., A. E. VON DOENHOFF, and L. S. STIVERS: "Summary of Airfoil Data," *NACA Rept.*, March, 1945.

13. DRYDEN, H. L.: "Some Recent Contributions to the Study of Transition and Turbulent Boundary Layers," *NACA Tech. Note* 1168, April, 1947.

14. ACKERET, J.: Gasdynamik, in "Handbuch der Physik," Band VII, Verlag Julius Springer, Berlin, 1927.

CHAPTER XI

WING THEORY

11.1. Potential Flow. The concept of a potential is familiar from its use in electricity, and in Chap. IV we discussed the potential energy in a gravity field. The potential function for an electric field has the property that its rate of change in any direction gives the magnitude of the force in that direction exerted by the field on unit charge of electricity. The gravity potential function, usually called the "gravity potential energy," has the property that its rate of change in any direction gives the magnitude of the weight force in that direction exerted on unit mass of matter. One can easily verify that the gravity potential energy P has this property, for, from Art. 4.6, P is seen to equal gh, where h is the height above an arbitrary level. The expression, $\partial P/\partial x = g\,\partial h/\partial x$ thus gives the negative of the weight force on unit mass in any direction x.

Each of these potential functions is seen to describe completely the force field to which it applies.

In a somewhat analogous manner, two potential functions, the stream function and the velocity potential, have been found, either of which completely describes the velocity field of a flowing fluid. The reason for introducing them is the mathematical simplification that results and the possibility of finding the theoretical flow patterns about certain shapes.

Here we confine ourselves to the steady flow of an ideal fluid and restrict the discussion to two-dimensional cases.

11.2. Equations of Motion. Any flow pattern is determined by the boundary conditions, which require the boundary streamlines to take a definite form, and by the equations of motion. These include the continuity equation, a purely kinematic relation, and a dynamic equation for each of the dimensions of space.

The continuity equation for a steady flow was shown in Chap. III to be

$$\int_A \rho V \cos \alpha \, dA = 0 \tag{3.8}$$

provided that no source of fluid is included inside the closed surface A. In this equation, α is the angle between the local velocity V and the outward-drawn normal to the surface element, dA. For two-dimensional motion the flow has no component perpendicular to the x,y plane, and the flow patterns in all planes parallel to this are the same. Consequently, the closed surface A can be thought of as a "fence" of unit height whose trace in the x,y plane is a closed curve (Fig. 11.1). In addition to this fence, A will also include two plane-parallel surfaces forming the ends of the cylinder whose side wall is the fence. These planes can be disregarded in the integration indicated in Eq. (3.8), however, since cos α is zero everywhere on them. Equation (3.8) thus can be written as

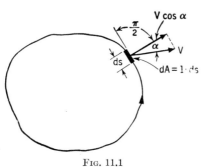

FIG. 11.1

$$\oint \rho V \cos \alpha \, ds = 0 \qquad (11.1)$$

where $\oint$ denotes the integral around the closed curve. By convention, one is said to face along the curve in the positive direction if the region bounded by the curve lies on the left hand. The positive direction is indicated by the arrow on the curve in Fig. 11.1. An observer facing in the positive direction sees the local outward-drawn normal extending from left to right.

The dynamic equations for steady flow of a frictionless fluid are derived for the x and y directions just as in Chap. IV for the directions parallel and normal to the velocity. Here, however, it is convenient to neglect gravity. The components of velocity parallel to x and y are $u(x,y)$ and $v(x,y)$, respectively, and the corresponding accelerations are

$$a_x = \frac{Du}{dt} = \frac{\partial u}{\partial x}\frac{dx}{dt} + \frac{\partial u}{\partial y}\frac{dy}{dt} = u\frac{\partial u}{\partial x} + v\frac{\partial u}{\partial y}$$

$$a_y = \frac{Dv}{dt} = \frac{\partial v}{\partial x}\frac{dx}{dt} + \frac{\partial v}{\partial y}\frac{dy}{dt} = u\frac{\partial v}{\partial x} + v\frac{\partial v}{\partial y}$$

The symbol D/dt denotes differentiation following the motion of the fluid; it is to be noted that here dx and dy are not arbitrary but are the components of the displacement of a particle of fluid, so that $dx = u\,dt$ and $dy = v\,dt$. The components of pressure force per unit mass in the x and y directions are $(-1/\rho)(\partial p/\partial x)$ and $(-1/\rho)(\partial p/\partial y)$, so that Newton's law yields

$$\left.\begin{array}{l} -\dfrac{1}{\rho}\dfrac{\partial p}{\partial x} = \dfrac{Du}{dt} = u\dfrac{\partial u}{\partial x} + v\dfrac{\partial u}{\partial y} \\[2ex] -\dfrac{1}{\rho}\dfrac{\partial p}{\partial y} = \dfrac{Dv}{dt} = u\dfrac{\partial v}{\partial x} + v\dfrac{\partial v}{\partial y} \end{array}\right\} \qquad (11.2)$$

11.3. The Stream Function. The physical principle of continuity, on which is based Eq. (11.1), states that, for a source-free, steady, two-dimensional flow, the net mass efflux across any closed curve is zero.

From Eq. (11.1) we get

$$\int_A^B \rho V \cos \alpha \, ds = -\int_B^A \rho V \cos \alpha \, ds = \int_A^B \rho V \cos \alpha \, ds$$
$$(ACB) \qquad\qquad (BEA) \qquad\qquad (AEB)$$

where ACB and AEB are any two curves joining the points A and B (Fig. 11.2). In words, the mass flux is the same across any curve joining A and B. The mathematical consequences are important, for since the integral $\int_A^B \rho V \cos \alpha \, ds$ is independent of the path, $\rho V \cos \alpha \, ds$ is the differential of some scalar point function. It will be found convenient to define this function by the equation

$$d\psi = \frac{\rho}{\rho_0} V \cos \alpha \, ds$$

or

$$\psi_B - \psi_A = \int_A^B \frac{\rho}{\rho_0} V \cos \alpha \, ds$$

(11.3)

where the constant ρ_0 is the density of the fluid at rest.

The physical meaning of $\psi(x,y)$ is immediate: The difference between the values of ψ at any two points $\psi_B - \psi_A$ is proportional to the mass flux across any curve joining the points. In the case of an incompressible fluid, $\rho = \rho_0$, and $\psi_B - \psi_A$ is the volume flux across any curve joining A and B. For this reason, ψ is called the "stream function."

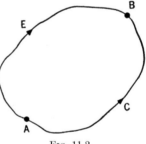

Fig. 11.2.

Only the difference between two values of ψ appears in the definition [Eq. (11.3)]. Therefore, the value of ψ_A, where A is any point in the flow, can be arbitrarily assigned. The values of ψ everywhere else in the flow are then determined by Eq. (11.3).

The stream function has three properties that render it useful, especially in the synthesis of complicated flow patterns from simple ones. The first property is that ψ is constant everywhere on any one streamline. We prove this simply by choosing ds in Eq. (11.3) as an element of the streamline and noting that $\cos \alpha$ is then zero. It follows from Eq. (11.3) that $d\psi = 0$ everywhere along the streamline, or $\psi = $ constant.

The second property is closely related to the first and also follows immediately from the definition. Divide both sides of Eq. (11.3) by ds, and obtain

$$\frac{\partial \psi}{\partial s} = \frac{\rho}{\rho_0} V \cos \alpha$$

(11.4)

where the partial derivative is used to indicate that the change in ψ is that corresponding to a change in s only. The second property can be stated as follows: The rate of change of ψ with distance in an arbitrary direction is proportional to the component of velocity normal to that direction. For

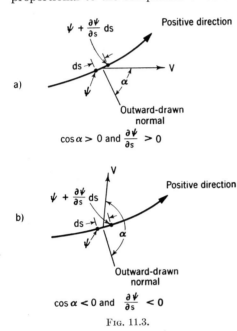

a)

$$\cos\alpha > 0 \text{ and } \frac{\partial\psi}{\partial s} > 0$$

b)

$$\cos\alpha < 0 \text{ and } \frac{\partial\psi}{\partial s} < 0$$

Fig. 11.3.

incompressible fluid, $\rho = \rho_0$, and $\partial\psi/\partial s$ is equal to the normal velocity component. The convention has already been stated in Art. 11.2 that an observer facing in the positive direction along a curve sees the local outward-drawn normal extending from left to right. This convention fixes the sign of $\partial\psi/\partial s$ and is illustrated in Fig. 11.3. For Cartesian coordinates x and y, Eq. (11.4) yields

$$\left.\begin{aligned}\frac{\partial\psi}{\partial y} &= \frac{\rho}{\rho_0} u \\[2mm] \frac{\partial\psi}{\partial x} &= -\frac{\rho}{\rho_0} v\end{aligned}\right\} \qquad 11.5$$

To get the first of these equations, we let $ds = dy$, so that the positive x direction coincides with the outward-drawn normal and $V\cos\alpha = u$. To get the second, we take $ds = dx$, so that the normal points in the negative y direction and $V\cos\alpha = -v$. Similarly for plane-polar coordinates r and θ, we get

$$\left.\begin{aligned}\frac{\partial\psi}{r\,\partial\theta} &= \frac{\rho}{\rho_0} V_r \\[2mm] \frac{\partial\psi}{\partial r} &= -\frac{\rho}{\rho_0} V_\theta\end{aligned}\right\} \qquad (11.6)$$

where V_r and V_θ are the components of velocity in the directions of increasing r and θ, respectively (see Fig. 11.4).

It should be pointed out that, for incompressible fluid, Eqs. (11.3), (11.4), (11.5), and 11.6) all hold (with $\rho = \rho_0$), even in an unsteady

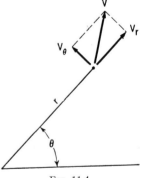

Fig. 11.4.

flow. This follows from the fact that, for incompressible fluid, the continuity equation has the form $\oint V\cos\alpha\,ds = 0$, regardless of whether or not the flow is steady [see Eq. (3.9)].

In this discussion of the stream function, we have so far required merely that the flow be continuous. If we add now the requirement that the fluid be incompressible and consider two flow patterns having stream functions ψ_1, and ψ_2, Eq. (11.4) gives

$$\frac{\partial \psi_1}{\partial s} + \frac{\partial \psi_2}{\partial s} = \frac{\partial (\psi_1 + \psi_2)}{\partial s} = V_1 \cos \alpha_1 + V_2 \cos \alpha_2$$

Since $V_1 \cos \alpha_1 + V_2 \cos \alpha_2$ is the component of the resultant velocity normal to the arbitrary direction ds, we may state the third property of the stream function as follows: The algebraic sum of the stream functions for two incompressible flow patterns is the stream function for the flow resulting from superposition of these patterns.

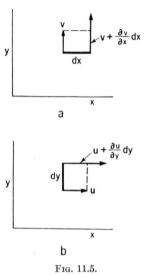

None of the properties of the stream function are of any practical use unless the flow patterns concerned satisfy not only the continuity requirements, but also the dynamical equations [Eqs. (11.2)]. It is possible that two incompressible flow patterns may each fulfill all of these conditions and yet, if they are superposed, their resultant may not satisfy Eqs. (11.2). It is shown below that this difficulty does not arise in case the continuous incompressible flows are assumed to be irrotational.

Fig. 11.5.

The rotation, or vorticity, at a point was defined in Chap. IV as the algebraic sum of the angular velocities of two mutually perpendicular line elements moving with the fluid and intersecting at the point in question. One of the pair of elements there considered was taken parallel to the velocity and the other normal to it. It may be shown, however, that the vorticity at a point is independent of the orientation of the line elements considered, so that the vorticity may be expressed in terms of elements dx and dy, for an arbitrary choice of axes x and y. Figure 11.5a shows that the counterclockwise angular velocity of fluid-line element dx is

$$\frac{v + (\partial v/\partial x)\, dx - v}{dx} = \frac{\partial v}{\partial x}$$

while, from Fig. 11.5b, that of dy is

$$\frac{-[u + (\partial u/\partial y) dy] + u}{dy} = -\frac{\partial u}{\partial y}$$

By convention, the counterclockwise sense is taken as positive. Consequently, the vorticity is

$$\text{Vorticity} = \frac{\partial v}{\partial x} - \frac{\partial u}{\partial y} \qquad (11.7)$$

An irrotational motion is defined as one for which the vorticity is everywhere zero.

$$\frac{\partial v}{\partial x} - \frac{\partial u}{\partial y} = 0 \qquad (11.8)$$

The restriction which the dynamical equations impose on the velocity components is found by elimination of p and ρ from Eqs. (11.2). Assuming ρ to be a function of p only, differentiate the first of these with respect to y, the second with respect to x, and subtract the first from the second.

$$-\frac{\partial p}{\partial y} \frac{d(1/\rho)}{dp} \frac{\partial p}{\partial x} - \frac{1}{\rho} \frac{\partial^2 p}{\partial y \partial x} + \frac{\partial p}{\partial x} \frac{d(1/\rho)}{dp} \frac{\partial p}{\partial y} + \frac{1}{\rho} \frac{\partial^2 p}{\partial x \partial y} =$$
$$\left(\frac{\partial u}{\partial x} + \frac{\partial v}{\partial y} \right) \left(\frac{\partial v}{\partial x} - \frac{\partial u}{\partial y} \right) + \frac{D}{dt} \left(\frac{\partial v}{\partial x} - \frac{\partial u}{\partial y} \right) = 0 \quad (11.8a)$$

It is obvious that, in irrotational flow, Eq. (11.8a) is everywhere satisfied.

Substitution in Eq. (11.8) of $\partial \psi / \partial y = u$ and $\partial \psi / \partial x = -v$, from Eq. (11.5), yields the differential equation that must be satisfied by ψ everywhere in the fluid.

$$\frac{\partial^2 \psi}{\partial x^2} + \frac{\partial^2 \psi}{\partial y^2} = 0 \qquad (11.9)$$

Equation (11.9), known as Laplace's equation, is linear, so that the sum of two solutions is also a solution. Therefore, if two flow patterns are given, having stream functions ψ_1 and ψ_2, each of which satisfies Eq. (11.9), the sum $\psi_1 + \psi_2$ also satisfies the same equation and thus represents the stream function for another irrotational incompressible flow. By the third property of a stream function, discussed above, this flow is the resultant of the two flows in question.

The stream function is thus a powerful tool in the study of irrotational incompressible flows, since complex patterns can be synthesized by algebraic addition of the stream functions of simple patterns. This important application of the stream function is illustrated by the examples below.

11.4. Parallel Flow. As a simple example of a stream function, assume a steady two-dimensional flow parallel to the axis of x and with velocity U. The streamlines are horizontal lines running to the right. Since $\partial \psi / \partial x = -v = 0$ and $\partial \psi / \partial y = u = U$, $d\psi = U\, dy$ and the stream function

$$\psi = Uy \qquad (11.10)$$

completely describes the flow. Note that the x axis is the line $\psi = 0$, and larger values of y correspond to larger numerical values of ψ. If, for example, $y = 5$, $\psi = 5U$ and the discharge between this line and the x axis is $\int_0^5 d\psi = \psi_5 - \psi_0 = 5U$ per unit depth. Note that flow is positive toward the right, by our convention as to signs, so that $5U$ denotes a discharge to the right.

In this example we made the constant of integration equal to zero by arbitrarily setting $\psi = 0$ on the x axis. If we write $\psi = Uy + $ constant, we do not change the flow pattern but merely change the value of ψ on every streamline by an amount equal to the constant. In any flow having a stream function the constant of integration plays the same trivial role, so that in later examples it will usually be set equal to zero.

11.5. Source and Sink. Imagine that, along a line normal to the x,y plane at the origin of coordinates, fluid is being emitted at a constant rate and that it flows away radially from this "line source." In the two-dimensional space of a layer of unit depth the source discharges at a rate of Q units of volume per unit time. At any radius r from the source the velocity V must be, from continuity considerations, $V = Q/2\pi r$. Equation (11.6) applied to this purely radial flow gives

$$\frac{\partial \psi}{r\,\partial\theta} = V = \frac{Q}{2\pi r} \qquad \frac{\partial \psi}{\partial r} = 0$$

Therefore

$$d\psi = \frac{Q}{2\pi}\,d\theta$$

and

$$\psi = \frac{Q}{2\pi}\,\theta \tag{11.11}$$

At the origin, where all the streamlines cross, ψ can have any value whatsoever and is therefore undefined. The origin, where the source is located, is thus a singular point as far as the stream function is concerned. This is to be expected, since a source-free flow was postulated as one essential for the existence of ψ. The stream function for the source is multiple-valued, increasing by Q each time θ increases by 2π.

A sink is the reverse of a source, fluid being abstracted at a rate Q. In this case the radial velocity is $V = -Q/2\pi r$, and the stream function is

$$\psi = -\frac{Q}{2\pi}\,\theta \tag{11.12}$$

The streamlines for both source and sink are radial lines. The product Vr has a constant value in each case, so that the velocity varies hyperbolically along the radius, approaching infinity as r approaches zero and zero as r approaches infinity.

11.6. Combination of a Source and Sink. In Fig. 11.6 are shown a source at B and a sink at A. The two have the same strength Q. The value of the stream function at any point P for the resultant flow is obtained by addition of Eqs. (11.11) and (11.12), with the angles at B and A set equal to θ_1 and θ_2, respectively.

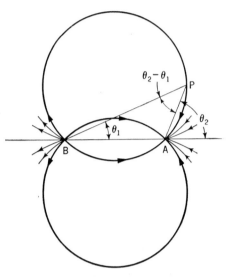

$$\psi = -\frac{Q}{2\pi}(\theta_2 - \theta_1) \quad (11.13)$$

Lines of constant ψ (the streamlines) are lines for which $\theta_2 - \theta_1$ is constant. Thus, by a well-known theorem in geometry, the streamlines are circles passing through A and B.

Fig. 11.6.

11.7. Rankine's Construction for Ship Forms. The stream function for the combination of a source and sink with a uniform flow to the right is

$$\psi = Uy - \frac{Q}{2\pi}(\theta_2 - \theta_1) \quad (11.14)$$

The streamline $\psi = 0$ can easily be shown to be the axis of x, together with an oval enclosing all streamlines running between the source and sink.

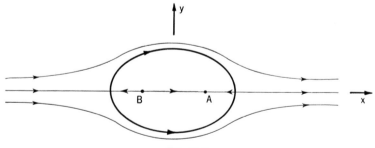

Fig. 11.7.

Outside of this oval is a field of flow consisting of streamlines extending as shown in Fig. 11.7. The oval streamline separates the fluid in the parallel flow from that flowing between the source and sink. The oval may be replaced by a solid body of the same shape, so that Fig. 11.7 may be thought of as the pattern of frictionless flow around such a body. The restriction to frictionless flow is necessary, because the velocity at the oval is not zero. The boundary condition for a viscous fluid is thus violated.

If several sources are combined with several sinks of total aggregate strengths equal, the oval can be elongated or fish-shaped. Rankine de-

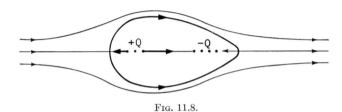

FIG. 11.8.

veloped mathematical forms for ships by this method, using two-dimensional flow, and Fuhrmann developed the forms for early Parseval airships by using a system of three-dimensional sources and sinks (see Art. 10.7).

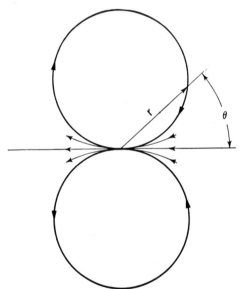

FIG. 11.9. — Streamlines for a doublet.

Such a body, as shown in Fig. 11.8, is an ideal "streamline form," since it is bounded by streamlines in an ideal fluid.

11.8. The Doublet and the Cylinder. If a source at B and an equal sink at A is moved indefinitely close together and their strengths increased so as to maintain $Q\overline{AB}$ finite and constant, the resulting flow is called a "doublet." The streamlines will be circles tangent to the axis of the doublet, as shown in Fig. 11.9. From Eq. (11.13) and Fig. 11.6 the stream function for a source and sink is

$$\psi = -\frac{Q}{2\pi}\frac{(\theta_2 - \theta_1)}{\sin\,(\theta_2 - \theta_1)}\,\sin\,(\theta_2 - \theta_1) = -\frac{Q}{2\pi}\frac{(\theta_2 - \theta_1)}{\sin\,(\theta_2 - \theta_1)}\frac{AB\,\sin\,\theta_1}{r_2}$$

If we let $AB \to 0$, keeping $Q\overline{AB}$ constant, $(\theta_2 - \theta_1)/\sin\,(\theta_2 - \theta_1) \to 1$, $\sin\,\theta_1 \to \sin\,\theta$, and $r_2 \to r$. Therefore, in the limit, the stream function for the doublet is

$$\psi = -\frac{Q\overline{AB}}{2\pi}\frac{\sin\,\theta}{r} = -C\frac{\sin\,\theta}{r} \tag{11.15}$$

where $C = Q\overline{AB}/2\pi$ is a constant. Equation (11.15) can readily be shown to yield the streamline pattern of Fig. 11.9.

If we combine a doublet with a flow parallel to the x axis, the shape enclosed by the external flow is a circle. From Eqs. (11.10) and (11.15),

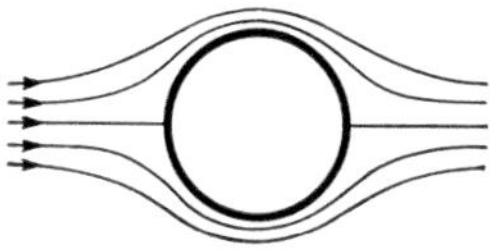

$$\psi = [Ur - (C/r)]\sin\,\theta$$

Let $C = Ua^2$, for convenience, so that

Fig. 11.10. — Combination of a doublet and a parallel flow gives the streamlines for a cylinder.

$$\psi = U\sin\,\theta\left(r - \frac{a^2}{r}\right) \tag{11.16}$$

One can readily show that Eq. (11.16) yields the flow pattern for a transverse flow disturbed by a circular cylinder, as shown in Fig. 11.10.

11.9. Pressure Distribution over a Moving Cylinder. The flow pattern about a cylinder is seen to indicate retarded flow and hence higher pressure at the front and rear of the cylinder and higher velocity and lower pressure over the top and bottom. The symmetry of the flow indicates that there is no force exerted by the pressure on the cylinder in any direction. The pressure distribution over the cylinder is obtained as follows: By Bernoulli's equation, if the pressure and velocity in the undisturbed flow are p_0 and U, we have

$$\frac{p - p_0}{(\rho/2)U^2} = 1 - \left(\frac{V}{U}\right)^2 \tag{11.17}$$

where p and V are the pressure and velocity at any point in the flow. From Eq. (11.16) the components of V are

$$\left.\begin{aligned}
V_r &= \frac{\partial\psi}{r\,\partial\theta} = U\left(1 - \frac{a^2}{r^2}\right)\cos\,\theta \\
V_\theta &= -\frac{\partial\psi}{\partial r} = -U\left(1 + \frac{a^2}{r^2}\right)\sin\,\theta
\end{aligned}\right\} \tag{11.18}$$

At the surface of the cylinder, where $r = a$, Eqs. (11.18) show that $V_\theta = -2U \sin \theta$, and $V_r = 0$. Consequently, Eq. (11.17) becomes

$$\frac{p - p_0}{(\rho/2)U^2} = 1 - 4 \sin^2 \theta \qquad (11.19)$$

This equation is plotted in Fig. 11.11. It is seen that $p - p_0 = 0$ where

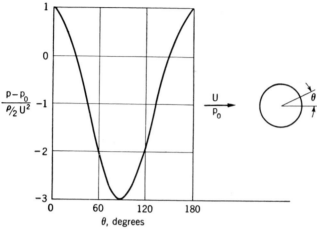

FIG. 11.11. — Pressure distribution over a cylinder.

$\sin \theta = \pm \frac{1}{2}$ and that $p - p_0$ reaches its minimum value $-3(\rho/2)U^2$ where $\sin \theta = \pm 1$.

11.10. Additional Apparent Mass. If on the flow pattern of the preceding article we superpose a general velocity $-U$ from right to left, we get a cylinder moving through a fluid that is at rest at infinity. Since the stream function for a parallel flow from right to left is $-Uy$, or $-Ur \sin \theta$, the stream function for the resultant flow is

$$\psi = U\left(r - \frac{a^2}{r}\right) \sin \theta - Ur \sin \theta = -\frac{Ua^2}{r} \sin \theta \qquad (11.20)$$

The streamlines relative to the fluid are portions of circles, as can be seen by comparison of Eqs. (11.20) and (11.15), and are drawn in Fig. 11.12. The velocity at any point is given by

$$V^2 = \left(-\frac{\partial \psi}{\partial r}\right)^2 + \left(\frac{\partial \psi}{r\,\partial \theta}\right)^2 = \left(-\frac{Ua^2}{r^2} \sin \theta\right)^2 + \left(-\frac{Ua^2}{r^2} \cos \theta\right)^2 = \frac{U^2 a^4}{r^4}$$

Hence the kinetic energy stored in the flow pattern is

$$\int_a^\infty \frac{\rho}{2} V^2 \pi \, d(r^2) = \frac{\pi}{2} \rho U^2 a^4 \left[-\frac{1}{r^2}\right]_a^\infty = \frac{\pi}{2} \rho U^2 a^2 = \frac{1}{2} M'U^2 \qquad (11.21)$$

The virtual mass of the cylinder is thus its own mass M plus an additional apparent mass $M' = \rho\pi a^2$ due to the energy of the flow. Any body in motion through a fluid moves with additional inertia.

Virtual mass affects the motions of balloons and airships, making them slow to accelerate. For airplanes this effect is negligible, as the displacement is relatively small. For ships and submarines virtual mass is important in mooring and docking operations.

11.11. Circulation. The circulation of fluid along any line from A to B is defined by the summation, or line integral, from A to B, at a given instant, of the component of velocity tangent to the line multiplied by

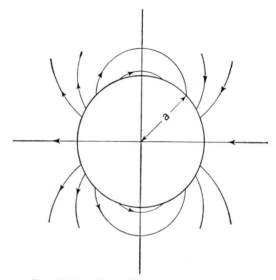

Fig. 11.12. — Streamlines for a moving cylinder.

the corresponding element ds of the line. Expressed in the symbols of Fig. 11.13, the circulation is

$$\int_A^B V \sin \alpha \, ds \qquad (11.22)$$

This definition is analogous to the definition of work as the displacement times the component of force in the direction of the displacement, or

$$\text{Work} = \int_A^B F \sin \alpha \, ds$$

Now we know in mechanics that we may compute work by resolving both the force and the displacement and get, for a two-dimensional case, the work done from A to B as

$$\int_A^B (X\, dx + Y\, dy)$$

where X and Y are the force components in the x and y directions, respectively.

Similarly, the circulation along the line from A to B is the line integral,

$$\int_A^B (u\, dx + v\, dy) \tag{11.23}$$

where u and v are the components of the velocity V in the directions x and y. It should be noted that u and v are functions of x and y and that

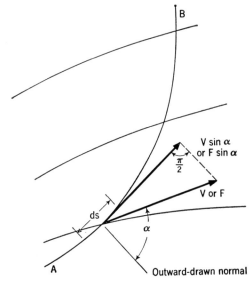

FIG. 11.13.

integration takes place along the line at a given instant. This is space integration, independent of time.

The symbol Γ is generally used to designate the circulation about a closed curve obtained by line integration indicated by the symbol $\oint$.

$$\Gamma = \oint (u\, dx + v\, dy) = \oint V \sin \alpha\, ds \tag{11.24}$$

Consider the circulation about a small rectangular element of area, defined as in Fig. 11.14.

$$d\Gamma = u\, dx + \left(v + \frac{\partial v}{\partial x}\, dx\right) dy - \left(u + \frac{\partial u}{\partial y}\, dy\right) dx - v\, dy$$

$$= \left(\frac{\partial v}{\partial x} - \frac{\partial u}{\partial y}\right) dx\, dy$$

Thus the elementary circulation is expressed in terms of the element of area $dx\, dy = dA$. Any circuit will enclose a number of elementary areas dA.

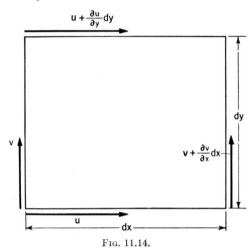

Fig. 11.14.

The sum of the circulations of all the elementary areas is obviously the circulation around the bounding circuit, because every interior line is traversed twice, in opposite directions, and all "internal records" cancel, as indicated in Fig. 11.15.

$$\Gamma = \oint (u\, dx + v\, dy) = \int\!\int \left(\frac{\partial v}{\partial x} - \frac{\partial u}{\partial y}\right) dx\, dy \qquad (11.25)$$

This equation is a special case of Stokes' theorem, discussed in texts on the calculus.

11.12. Velocity Potential. From Eq. (11.7) it will be recognized that $(\partial v/\partial x) - (\partial u/\partial y)$ is the rotation, or vorticity, at any point in the flow. It follows from Eq. (11.25), therefore, that the circulation is zero around any closed curve in an irrotational flow. Consequently, we see by the argument used in Art. 11.3 that the circulation from A to B is the

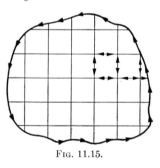

Fig. 11.15.

same along any path joining these points, provided that the flow is irrotational. A scalar point function ϕ can thus be defined as

$$d\phi = V \sin \alpha\, ds$$

or

$$\phi_B - \phi_A = \int_A^B V \sin \alpha\, ds \qquad (11.26)$$

The function $\phi(x,y)$ is called the "velocity potential."

The velocity potential has three properties that are analogous to those of the stream function and that can be demonstrated in the same way. The first property, which follows at once from Eq. (11.26), is that the lines of constant ϕ are normal to the streamlines. A plot of streamlines and equipotential lines thus appears as a mesh having all intersections at right angles.

Dividing Eq. (11.26) by ds and using the partial derivative as in Eq. (11.4), we get

$$\frac{\partial \phi}{\partial s} = V \sin \alpha \qquad (11.27)$$

which gives us the second property: The space rate of change of ϕ in an arbitrary direction s is equal to the component of velocity in that direction. For x, y coordinates we thus find

$$\left. \begin{aligned} \frac{\partial \phi}{\partial x} &= u \\[2mm] \frac{\partial \phi}{\partial y} &= v \end{aligned} \right\} \qquad (11.28)$$

and for plane-polar coordinates

$$\left. \begin{aligned} \frac{\partial \phi}{\partial r} &= V_r \\[2mm] \frac{\partial \phi}{r\, \partial \theta} &= V_\theta \end{aligned} \right\} \qquad (11.29)$$

If we now consider two flow patterns having velocity potentials ϕ_1 and ϕ_2, Eq. (11.27) gives

$$\frac{\partial \phi_1}{\partial s} + \frac{\partial \phi_2}{\partial s} = \frac{\partial (\phi_1 + \phi_2)}{\partial s} = V_1 \sin \alpha_1 + V_2 \sin \alpha_2$$

Since $V_1 \sin \alpha_1 + V_2 \sin \alpha_2$ is the component of the resultant velocity parallel to the arbitrary direction ds, we may state the third property of the potential as follows: The algebraic sum of the potentials for two irrotational flow patterns is the potential for the flow resulting from their superposition.

None of the properties of the velocity potential are of any practical use unless the flow patterns concerned are not only irrotational, but also satisfy the continuity equation [Eq. (11.1), or its equivalent, Eq. (11.4)]. It is possible that two irrotational flow patterns may each satisfy Eq. (11.4) and yet, if they be superposed, their resultant may not do so. It is readily shown, however, that this difficulty does not arise if the continuous irrotational flows are assumed to be incompressible. In this case, Eqs. (11.5), yield the condition that

$$\frac{\partial^2 \psi}{\partial y\, \partial x} = \frac{\partial u}{\partial x} = \frac{\partial^2 \psi}{\partial x\, \partial y} = -\frac{\partial v}{\partial y}$$

or

$$\frac{\partial u}{\partial x} + \frac{\partial v}{\partial y} = 0 \qquad (11.30)$$

Substitution in this equation from Eqs. (11.28) shows that ϕ satisfies Laplace's equation

$$\frac{\partial^2 \phi}{\partial x^2} + \frac{\partial^2 \phi}{\partial y^2} = 0 \qquad (11.31)$$

Since this equation is linear, the sum of the potentials for two different flow patterns is the potential for another irrotational incompressible flow. By the third property of a velocity potential, discussed above, this flow is the resultant of the two flows in question.

The velocity potential can thus be used in place of the stream function in the synthesis of irrotational incompressible flow patterns.

11.13. Thomson's Theorem. An important generalization is Thomson's (Kelvin's) theorem, which states that in a frictionless fluid the circulation along any closed fluid line remains constant as time goes on, provided merely that pressure depends only on density (homogeneous fluid). Consequently, if the motion starts from rest, when the vorticity is everywhere nil, the flow will be irrotational at all times. Thomson's theorem may be proved as follows:

In a continuous two-dimensional flow of fluid (unit thickness normal to xy plane) assume any closed fluid line with P and Q two points on that line: (x,y) and $(x + dx, y + dy)$. The corresponding velocity components are (u,v) and $(u + du, v + dv)$. We neglect gravity for simplicity. From Eq. (11.24) we find that the rate of change of circulation around a closed curve is

$$\frac{D\Gamma}{dt} = \frac{D}{dt} \oint (u\, dx + v\, dy)$$

where the symbol D/dt denotes the rate of change following the motion of the fluid. Since the operations D/dt and $\oint$ are commutative,

$$\frac{D\Gamma}{dt} = \oint \frac{D}{dt}(u\, dx + v\, dy) \qquad (11.32)$$

Consider now the expression

$$\frac{D}{dt}(u\, dx) = u\frac{D}{dt}(dx) + dx\frac{Du}{dt} \qquad (11.33)$$

The points P, Q move with the fluid, so that the x component of the distance separating them, dx, stretches at the rate du, the x velocity of Q relative to P. Thus $(D/dt)(dx) = du$. Reference to Eqs. (11.2) shows that $Du/dt = -(1/\rho)(\partial p/\partial x)$. Therefore, Eq. (11.33) becomes

$$\frac{D}{dt}(u\ dx) = u\ du - \frac{1}{\rho}\frac{\partial p}{\partial x}\,dx$$

The corresponding expression in y and v is

$$\frac{D}{dt}(v\ dy) = v\ dv - \frac{1}{\rho}\frac{\partial p}{\partial y}\,dy$$

Substituting these expressions into Eq. (11.32), we find that

$$\frac{D\Gamma}{dt} = \oint\left[u\ du + v\ dv - \frac{1}{\rho}\left(\frac{\partial p}{\partial x}\,dx + \frac{\partial p}{\partial y}\,dy\right)\right] = \oint\left(d\frac{V^2}{2} - \frac{dp}{\rho}\right)$$

But since $p = f(\rho)$ by assumption, dp/ρ may be written as dP, where P is a function of ρ only.

$$\frac{D\Gamma}{dt} = \oint d\left(\frac{V^2}{2} - P\right)$$

The summation at a given instant around the closed path of the space differential $d\left[(V^2/2) - P\right]$ is obviously zero. Hence we obtain

$$\frac{D\Gamma}{dt} = 0 \qquad \text{or} \qquad \Gamma = \text{constant} \tag{11.34}$$

which was the statement to be proved.*

This proof is readily extended to include gravity and any other body force that has a potential. Consequently, irrotational flow remains irrotational, in the absence of friction, and any flow generated from rest by gravity and pressure forces alone will be irrotational.

We may justly observe that, since pressure and gravity forces cannot act tangentially, no rotation can be set up by them in any element of the fluid. Rotation requires the tangential, or shearing, force of friction, such as exists in real fluids near a solid boundary or near a surface of discontinuity of velocity. The boundary layer of real fluids is therefore rotational and turbulent, after a more or less short initial portion that may be rotational and laminar if the body be smooth and its curvature slight.

Thomson's theorem holds also for a real (viscous) fluid, provided that no vorticity crosses the fluid line. That is, if all particles comprising the fluid line are initially without rotation, the circulation around the line will remain constant so long as the motion of all particles forming the line stays irrotational.

11.14. Potential Vortex. An important example of an irrotational flow is the potential vortex, already discussed in Art. 4.11. It will be recalled

* This may also be proved by using Eq. (11.8a).

that the streamlines are concentric circles and that the product of velocity and radius is the same for all streamlines, Vr = constant. From Eq. (11.24), the circulation about any streamline is

$$\Gamma = \oint V \sin \alpha \, ds = \int_0^{2\pi} Vr \, d\theta = 2\pi \, Vr = \text{constant}$$

Since the value of Γ is different from zero for all curves enclosing the origin, it follows that the motion at the origin is rotational. The origin is thus a singular point in an otherwise irrotational flow. The flow of a real fluid can approximate closely to a potential vortex, except in a core at the center where frictional effects predominate and the motion is like that of a rigid body. The value of Γ can be expressed in terms of the angular velocity ω and cross-sectional area of the vortex core. From the above equation we get

$$\Gamma = 2\pi Vr = 2\pi \omega r_0^2 = 2\omega \pi r_0^2$$

where r_0 is the radius of the core. Γ is thus given by twice the product of angular velocity and cross-sectional area of the core.

Since vortex motion is irrotational except for the origin, or core, a velocity potential exists outside the core. The expression for this potential is obtained by substitution in Eqs. (11.29).

$$V_r = 0 = \frac{\partial \phi}{\partial r}$$

$$V_\theta = V = \frac{\Gamma}{2\pi r} = \frac{\partial \phi}{r \, \partial \theta}$$

whence

$$d\phi = \frac{\Gamma}{2\pi} d\theta$$

or

$$\phi = \frac{\Gamma}{2\pi} \theta \tag{11.35}$$

where the constant of integration is arbitrarily taken as zero. The potential is a multiple-valued function that increases by Γ each time θ increases by 2π.

In a similar manner we may form the stream function for a vortex. Since $\partial \psi / \partial r = - V_\theta = - V$ and $\partial \psi / r \, \partial \theta = 0$, we obtain

$$\frac{d\psi}{dr} = - \frac{\Gamma}{2\pi r}$$

whence

$$\psi = - \frac{\Gamma}{2\pi} \ln r \tag{11.36}$$

Figure 11.16 shows the circular streamlines and the radial equipotential lines for the vortex.

It may be remarked parenthetically that a close analogy exists between a source and a potential vortex. For comparison, the stream function and velocity potential for each are written below:

Source

$$\psi_s = \frac{Q}{2\pi}\theta$$

$$\phi_s = \frac{Q}{2\pi}\ln r$$

Potential Vortex

$$\psi_v = -\frac{\Gamma}{2\pi}\ln r$$

$$\phi_v = \frac{\Gamma}{2\pi}\theta$$

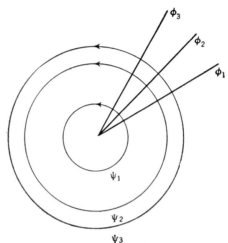

Fig. 11.16. — Streamlines and equipotential lines for a potential vortex.

It is seen that Q, the strength of the source, and Γ, the circulation, play analogous roles; Γ is frequently referred to as the strength of the vortex. The equipotential lines of the source are the streamlines of the vortex, and vice versa. ψ_s and ϕ_v, for each of which the origin is a singular point, are multiple-valued functions, but ψ_v and ϕ_s, for which all points are regular, are single-valued.

11.15. Induced Velocity. Several vortex cores or filaments may be enclosed by a fluid line, in which case the circulation along that line is the sum of the circulations, or strengths, of the enclosed vortex filaments. The velocity at a point in the continuum is the vector sum of the velocities due to each vortex present, $\Gamma_1/2\pi r_1$, $\Gamma_2/2\pi r_2$, ... This velocity is induced by the vortex and is called "induced velocity."

The induced-velocity field due to one or more vortices is similar to the magnetic field induced by one or more conductors carrying electric current. Current strength corresponds to vortex strength.

11.16. Conclusions of Vortex Theory. It can be shown, as by Helmholtz, that for a free potential vortex in an ideal fluid

1. The strength Γ is permanent and is constant along its length.

2. A vortex core must end on a solid boundary, form a closed loop, or extend to infinity.

3. The circulation about any closed curve is equal to the sum of the strengths of the vortex cores enclosed.

4. The velocity distributions induced by several vortices may be superimposed.

5. A vortex moves in a path prescribed by the other vortices in the region.

For example, the following sketches illustrate the nature of the velocity patterns induced by free vortices. For a single vortex, the induced velocity at any point is $V = \Gamma/2\pi r$; it is small at a great distance from the core (see Fig. 11.17a). For a pair of vortices having strengths equal and opposite, the induced velocities are equal and the pair advances, as shown in Fig. 11.17b. The eddies formed at the edges of a paddle are of this character. For a vortex pair having equal strengths, the induced velocities cause the cores to swing around a common center, as shown in Fig. 11.17c. A vortex ring advances in the direction shown in Fig. 11.17d, because of the velocity induced at each element ds by all other elements.

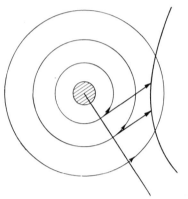

Fig. 11.17a. — Streamlines and velocity distribution for single potential vortex.

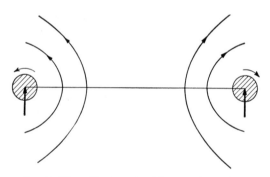

Fig. 11.17b. — Vortex pair with opposed rotations.

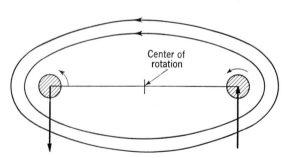

Center of rotation

Fig. 11.17c. — Vortex pair with the same direction.

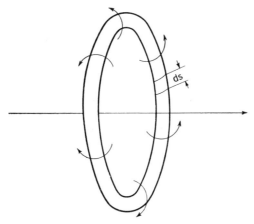

Fig. 11.17d. — Vortex ring.

11.17. Magnus Effect. Consider a circulation about a cylinder, combined with a translation. This combination is approximated in nature by a spinning rod falling or by a sliced golf ball, cut tennis ball, or rotating rifle bullet shot across the wind. Under these conditions a transverse force is produced, known as the Magnus effect.

We have already shown how to develop the stream function defining the flow pattern about a vortex core of strength Γ and the stream function for a circular cylinder moving transversely. We have also shown that stream functions may be added to give the resultant flow. We can thus add the two stream functions and differentiate to find the velocity at any point in the combined flow.

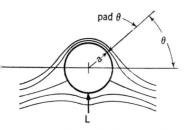

Fig. 11.18. — Combination of a doublet, parallel flow, and vortex gives the streamlines for a cylinder with circulation.

The translation of a cylinder in a perfect fluid gives rise to a symmetrical flow pattern with no resultant force on the cylinder, as shown in Fig. 11.10. However, when the flow appropriate to a clockwise vortex of stream function ψ_2 is superimposed on the flow about a cylinder in translation, given by ψ_1, the induced velocity at every point caused by the vortex produces an unsymmetrical flow pattern, as illustrated in Fig. 11.18. From Eqs. (11.16) and (11.36) the resultant stream function is found to be

$$\psi = \psi_1 + \psi_2 = U\left(r - \frac{a^2}{r}\right)\sin\theta - \frac{\Gamma}{2\pi}\ln r \qquad (11.37)$$

Since the vortex motion has been assumed clockwise, the value of Γ in

Eq. (11.37) is negative, for, by definition, a positive value of Γ is associated with a counterclockwise vortex.

The effect of adding a clockwise circulation is to speed up the flow above the cylinder and to slow it beneath the cylinder. Therefore, from Bernoulli's equation the pressure on the bottom of the cylinder is greater than on the top. Consequently, there must be a resultant upward force, or lift, due to this unsymmetrical pressure distribution. There is no drag, or resistance, to forward motion in irrotational flow, as pointed out in Art. 10.11. Note that the stagnation points S are shifted below the horizontal axis.

The lift per unit length of cylinder can be found from the distribution of pressure around the surface of the cylinder. One computes these pressures by using Bernoulli's equation, in which the velocities are given by the stream function. Differentiating Eq. (11.37) with respect to r, we find for V_θ, the velocity normal to r,

$$V_\theta = - \frac{\partial \psi}{\partial r} = - U \left(1 + \frac{a^2}{r^2}\right) \sin \theta + \frac{\Gamma}{2\pi r}$$

At the cylinder, where $r = a$, there is no radial velocity, and

$$V_\theta = - 2U \sin \theta + \frac{\Gamma}{2\pi a}$$

At the stagnation points $V_\theta = 0$, $\theta = \theta_s$, and

$$\sin \theta_s = \frac{\Gamma}{4\pi a U}$$

By Bernoulli's theorem, the pressure at a point a, θ on the cylinder is

$$p = \text{constant} - \frac{\rho}{2} V^2$$

$$= \text{constant} - \frac{\rho}{2} \left(4U^2 \sin^2 \theta - \frac{2\Gamma U}{\pi a} \sin \theta + \frac{\Gamma^2}{4\pi^2 a^2}\right) \qquad (11.38)$$

From Fig. 11.18 the force on an element of area of unit length and of breadth $a \, d\theta$ is $pa \, d\theta$. The upward component of this force is an element of lift $- pa \sin \theta \, d\theta$. The total lift on unit length of cylinder, L, is the integral,

$$L = - \int_0^{2\pi} pa \sin \theta \, d\theta$$

If we substitute for p from Eq. (11.38), we obtain four terms, the first containing $\sin \theta$; the second, $\sin^3 \theta$; the third, $\sin^2 \theta$; and the fourth, $\sin \theta$. But since

$$\int_0^{2\pi} \sin\theta\, d\theta = 0 \qquad \int_0^{2\pi} \sin^3\theta\, d\theta = 0 \qquad \text{and} \qquad \int_0^{2\pi} \sin^2\theta\, d\theta = \pi$$

all terms drop out except the third, and

$$L = -\rho\Gamma U \tag{11.39}$$

This is an important result and shows that the combination of a circulation with a translation produces a transverse force directly proportional to the strength of the circulation and the speed of advance. Since Γ is negative for the flow pattern of Fig. 11.18, Eq. (11.39) shows that L is positive. Usually we are interested only in the absolute value of L, the direction being obvious. The negative sign in Eq. (11.39), which results merely from the convention regarding a positive circulation, is therefore frequently omitted.

11.18. Kutta-Joukowski Law. Equation (11.39), which was developed for a cylinder, can be shown to hold, regardless of the shape of the body about which the circulation is assumed to take place. This mathematical result was endowed with a semblance of physical reality by Lord Rayleigh and soon after 1900 was given a precise application to the lift of airplane wings by the German Kutta and the Russian Joukowski. Equation (11.39) is now universally known as the Kutta-Joukowski law. It is the basis for the modern vortex, or circulation, theory of the lift of wings, the thrust of fan and propeller blades, or the transverse force on any solid body moving through a fluid in an unsymmetrical attitude.

11.19. Circulation Theory (Wing of Infinite Span). A fundamental consequence of the Kutta-Joukowski law is that, in an ideal frictionless fluid in steady two-dimensional motion, the existence of a transverse force on a wing is associated with a circulation of definite amount. The wing, for purposes of computation, can be replaced by a vortex filament of strength Γ, such that the lift per unit span is given by Eq. (11.39). This imaginary vortex filament has the properties of the free vortex of Helmholtz, except that it does not consist always of the same particles of fluid, is not a fluid line, but is "bound" to the location of the wing rather than drifting away with the transverse flow. It has no physical reality and is called a "bound vortex."

The great contribution of Kutta and Joukowski was the provision of mathematical methods to compute the lift on the wing by adjustment of Γ to give a tangential and thus a finite velocity at the trailing edge. Experiments show that the lift so computed predicts the measured lift with good approximation.

Physical intuition suggests that real fluid streams, separated at the leading edge of a wing and following the contour of the upper and lower surfaces, should join at the trailing edge and flow smoothly away. That circulation about the wing is necessary to accomplish this result is indicated in the sketches of Fig. 11.19, which show successive stages in the development of the steady-state flow pattern around an airfoil from an initial condition of rest. Before the motion starts, the circulation is obviously zero for

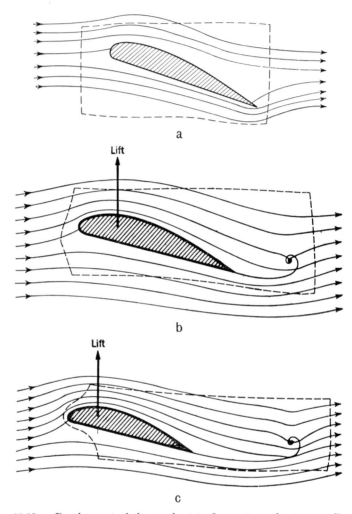

a

Lift

b

Lift

c

FIG. 11.19. — Development of the steady-state flow pattern about a two-dimensional wing. (a) Start of motion: no circulation, no lift, theoretically infinite velocity at trailing edge, stagnation point on back of wing. (b) Formation of starting vortex behind trailing edge (due to high friction where shearing velocity is great); circulation of starting vortex equal and opposite to that about wing. (c) Circulation established about wing sufficient to give smooth tangential flow at trailing edge.

any closed fluid line. Thomson's theorem indicates that the circulation will remain zero for the fluid line shown dotted in the sketches, because no particle in it starts to rotate during the time interval considered.

Figure 11.19a shows the flow pattern observed immediately after motion starts. No rotating particles are yet visible in the flow. Consequently, there can be no circulation around the airfoil. The lift is zero. This flow cannot persist because of the high velocity gradients near the sharp trailing edge. Almost at once, the viscosity causes a counterclockwise vortex to spring from the airfoil, as shown in Fig. 11.19b. A single vortex (called the "starting vortex") is thus created, which has a definite strength (circulation) associated with it. But the circulation around the dotted fluid line is still zero. Hence, an equal and opposite circulation must exist around the airfoil itself, no other vortex being present in the fluid. A lift is therefore set up by virtue of the Kutta-Joukowski relation [Eq. (11.39)].

The flow pattern changes as the circulation around the airfoil increases, until the rear stagnation point has moved to the trailing edge. When this condition is reached, the high velocity gradients no longer exist in the flow, so that the starting vortex cannot continue to grow but travels on downstream, its strength remaining constant. The lift also attains a constant limiting value. This state of affairs is depicted in Fig. 11.19c.

The flow pattern around the wing (and consequently the lift) remains unchanged from this time on. The subsequent history and eventual dissipation of the starting vortex have no effect on the forces acting on the wing.

11.20. Lift Coefficient. For any wing in a two-dimensional incompressible flow, the lift per unit length of span, L, is a function of the chord c, the angle of incidence α, the distant velocity V, and the fluid properties ρ and μ. Dimensional reasoning leads to the result

$$C_L = \frac{L}{(\rho/2)V^2c} = f\left(c, \frac{\rho V c}{\mu}\right) = f(\alpha, R) \qquad (11.40)$$

where C_L is called the "lift coefficient."

We can, to a good approximation, neglect frictional effects on the flow pattern for an airfoil, provided that the angle of incidence is not too large. In other words, the influence of the Reynolds number R is negligible. In this case, C_L depends only on α; it is in fact a linear function of α, as is shown below.

It is easily seen by dimensional reasoning that, if friction is neglected, $\Gamma = Vc\,f(\alpha)$. Therefore, if a wing is fixed parallel to x, as in Fig. 11.20, and the velocity is assumed to be u_0, also parallel to x, the corresponding circulation is $\Gamma_x = u_0 c \Gamma_1$, where Γ_1 is a constant, because the angle of incidence (referred to the tangent to the lower surface of the wing) has the fixed value zero. Similarly, if the velocity is assumed to be v_0, the corresponding circulation is $\Gamma_y = v_0 c \Gamma_2$, where Γ_2 is a constant, because the angle of incidence has the fixed value of $\pi/2$.

If these two flow patterns are superposed, the resultant velocity will be V and the angle of incidence will be α', as in Fig. 11.20. Furthermore, the resultant circulation will be the algebraic sum of the component circulations, since it is a scalar defined in terms of the velocity components $\oint(u\,dx + v\,dy)$.

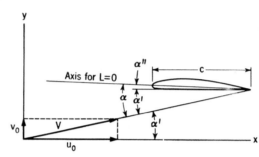

Fig. 11.20.

Thus, $\Gamma = \Gamma_x + \Gamma_y = c(u_0\Gamma_1 + v_0\Gamma_2)$. From Fig. 11.20, $u_0 = V \cos \alpha'$ and $v_0 = V \sin \alpha'$, so that

$$\Gamma = cV(\Gamma_1 \cos \alpha' + \Gamma_2 \sin \alpha')$$

Let $\tan \alpha'' = \Gamma_1/\Gamma_2$; then $\Gamma_1 = \sqrt{\Gamma_1^2 + \Gamma_2^2} \sin \alpha''$, and $\Gamma_2 = \sqrt{\Gamma_1^2 + \Gamma_2^2} \cos \alpha''$

$$\Gamma = cV\sqrt{\Gamma_1^2 + \Gamma_2^2} \sin (\alpha' + \alpha'')$$

It is seen that, for $\alpha' = -\alpha''$, $\Gamma = 0$. The angle $-\alpha''$ is thus the angle of zero lift. Since Γ_1 and Γ_2 are independent of both the magnitude of the velocity and its direction (angle of incidence), we may write, for small angles,

$$\Gamma = \text{constant } (\alpha' + \alpha'')Vc$$

and

$$L = \rho V\Gamma = \text{constant } \rho V^2 c(\alpha' + \alpha'')$$

Introducing the lift coefficient, we get

$$C_L = \frac{L}{\rho V^2 c/2} = \text{constant } (\alpha' + \alpha'')$$

$$= \text{constant } \alpha \qquad (11.41)$$

where α is measured from the attitude of no lift.

This analysis makes the important prediction that for small angles the lift coefficient should vary directly with the angle of incidence, and experiment verifies the prediction. A more elaborate analysis shows that the constant has the numerical value 2π, and experiment shows this to be a close approximation for actual cases. For a wing in air, it is found that

$$C_L = 2\pi\eta\alpha$$

where the correction factor for frictional effects η is of the order of 0.9 for modern airfoil sections. This result, of course, applies only to a wing of infinite span or aspect ratio (two-dimensional flow) inclined at angles well below the stalling incidence.

11.21. Circulation Theory (Wing of Finite Span). While the Kutta-Joukowski concept of a bound vortex replacing the wing predicts the lift per unit span of a wing of indefinite extent, it cannot be applied to the practical case of a wing of finite span, without modification to account for the three-dimensional flow near the tips. According to the rules of vortex motion, the bound vortex cannot end at the wing tips but must continue out into the fluid, either forming a closed loop or extending to infinity. The theory must therefore explain where the unbound portion of the vortex is located. Furthermore, the theory must account for the fact that the lift (and hence the circulation) drops off gradually to zero at the wing tips, even though the circulation of a vortex is constant along its entire length.

Lanchester first suggested that, at each wing tip, there must be a flow of air from the high-pressure region below the wing toward the low-pressure region above it. This flow sets up a vortex that is a continuation of the bound vortex of the wing. The trailing vortex shed from each wing tip is

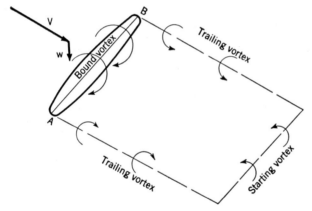

FIG. 11.21. — Vortex system of a finite wing.

thus a free vortex whose core follows the streamlines of the general flow past the wing tip. There is ample evidence of the existence of such trailing wing-tip vortices. When temperature and humidity conditions are favorable, "vapor trails" left by the wing tips of an airplane extend for miles across the sky. The lowered temperature accompanying the lowered pressure at the core of the vortex causes condensation.

The Lanchester concept of a horseshoe-shaped vortex filament extending indefinitely to the rear was developed by Prandtl into the modern

circulation theory of finite wings, by means of which great advances hav
been made in airplane design. In the simplest form of the theory a wing $
replaced by the bound portion of a vortex of circulation Γ, which extend
back from each wing tip to join the starting vortex. Thus we have a close
loop of circulation Γ at all points as the equivalent of the wing (see Fig
11.21).

Within the loop formed by the closed vortex filament, there must be .

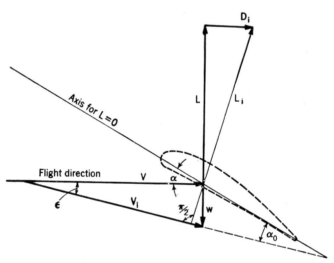

Fig. 11.22.

downward component of velocity, induced by the circulation. The downward momentum imparted to the air as the wing advances is a measure of
the lift, which may be considered to be transmitted to the ground as a
momentary increase of pressure, due to impact of the down-wash.

At any point along the lifting line AB, which replaces the wing, there will
be a horizontal velocity V due to the forward motion of the wing and a
down-wash, or vertical component, of velocity w, due to the horseshoe
vortex. As the starting vortex is far distant or, in a real fluid, quickly
destroyed by friction, the down-wash w is caused by the trailing vortices.
If the wing span were infinite, the trailing vortices would have no effect
and the only velocity would be V. This is, of course, the two-dimensional
case, where the Kutta-Joukowski law applies.

For a finite wing the flow about any section takes place as in the two-
dimensional case except that V has become V_i and is inclined by a small
angle ϵ to the direction of V. The lift L_i, caused by the flow, is normal to
the direction of V_i and is also inclined to L by the angle ϵ. The Kutta-

oukowski law then states, for the case of the finite wing,

$$L_i = \rho V_i \Gamma$$

rom Fig. 11.22, the following relations are evident:

$$\frac{w}{V} = \frac{D_i}{L} = \tan \epsilon = \epsilon$$

$$\frac{L}{L_i} = \frac{V}{V_i} = \cos \epsilon = 1 \qquad L_i = L \qquad V_i = V$$

$$\alpha_0 = \alpha - \epsilon = \alpha - \frac{w}{V}$$

11.22. Induced Drag. The effect of the trailing vortices is, by means
f down-wash, to reduce the effective angle of attack and to rotate the
ransverse (lift) force vector to the rear, so that it has a component D_i in the
irection to oppose the motion. D_i is, in fact, a drag and is given the name
induced drag" because of its origin. ϵ is an induced angle of incidence,
nd w is an induced velocity. Mathematically, w is analogous to mag-
etic-field strength and Γ to current strength for a horseshoe-shaped elec-
ical circuit.

The apparent paradox of drag in a frictionless fluid must be noted.
'his induced drag is represented by the kinetic energy supplied to the trail-
g vortices as they are left behind. In a real fluid there will be an addi-
onal drag due to friction. It should be further noted that the induced
rag is independent of the shape of the wing section or its chord length and
epends only on the section lift. Since lift depends on angle of incidence,
hich in turn determines the circulation necessary to maintain smooth
ow, it is apparent that the induced drag for a given wing will increase
ith the angle of incidence.

It is important to observe that this form of the theory only partly ac-
ounts for the objections first raised. The objection that the bound vortex
ust go somewhere upon reaching the wing tip has been answered by
ostulation of trailing free vortices. The other objection, that the lift
ust drop to zero at the wing tip, has not yet been met, since a single
ortex filament (which must have a constant strength along its entire
ngth) has been assumed to extend across the whole span and to turn
bruptly at the wing tips.

11.23. Lift on Complete Wing. The preceding discussion must be
hought of as dealing with the lift on only the central portion of the total
pan of a wing. To compute the lift on the complete wing, further refine-
ent of the basic concept is required. A single vortex filament of constant
irculation Γ implies a constant lift at every section out to and including

the wing tips. This is obviously impossible, as the lift must fall to zero at the wing tips. Furthermore, the down-wash w, assumed small, varies inversely as the distance from the trailing vortex and becomes large near a wing tip from which a vortex of finite strength is shed.

Prandtl resolved the difficulty by considering that, since circulations about parallel filaments may be superposed, it is immaterial to the Kutta-Joukowski law if we substitute $\int d\Gamma$ for Γ, where Γ is made up of the sum of circulations of a large number of filaments, each of infinitesimal circulation $d\Gamma$. Then he considered, instead of a single lifting line with one pair of trailing vortices, a bundle of such lifting lines of different lengths, each with its pair of trailing vortices. By adjusting the lengths of the elements one can get any desired distribution of circulation along the wing span and hence a corresponding distribution of lift. For each section, $L = \rho V \Gamma$, where Γ is a function of the distance from the axis of symmetry of the wing.

Figure 11.23 illustrates a rough distribution of circulation and lift across the span of a wing. In the limit an infinite number of vortex filaments, each of strength $d\Gamma$, can be imagined, with a trailing vortex sheet behind the wing. Prandtl discovered that an elliptical distribution of lift for a given span gives a constant down-wash at all points along the span and that the total induced drag is a minimum for a given total lift.

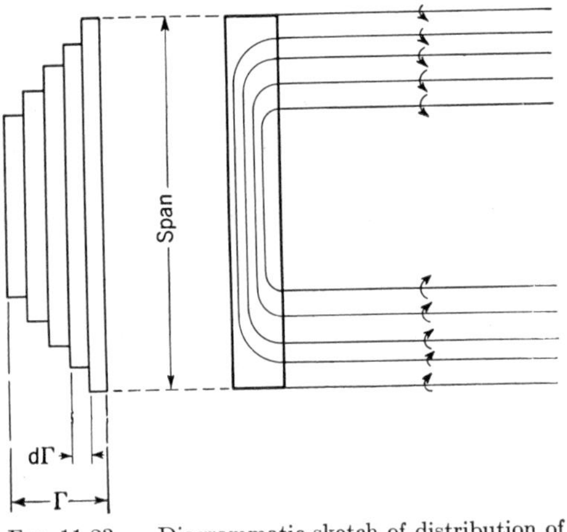

This conclusion from analysis has been of the highest technical utility, as practical wings of elliptical plan form or of conventional taper are found experimentally to have an elliptical lift distribution to a very good approximation.

Fig. 11.23. — Diagrammatic sketch of distribution of circulation along span of finite wing.

For constant down-wash we have similar vector triangles of velocities and forces at all points along the span. Then the induced drag on the whole wing, made up of the sum of section drags, will be

$$\frac{D_i}{L} = \frac{w}{V}$$

We introduce nondimensional lift and drag coefficients, in terms of the wing area S,

$$L = C_L \frac{\rho}{2} V^2 S \qquad D_i = C_{D_i} \frac{\rho}{2} V^2 S$$

and obtain

$$\frac{C_{D_i}}{C_L} = \frac{D_i}{L} = \frac{w}{V}$$

Computations carried out for the elliptical distribution of lift reduce to the following important relation for the necessary down-wash in terms of the aspect ratio A of a wing of span b:

$$\frac{w}{V} = \frac{C_L}{\pi A}$$

where A is defined as $A = \text{span/mean chord} = b/(S/b) = b^2/S$. Furthermore, since $\epsilon = w/V = C_L/\pi A = C_{D_i}/C_L$,

$$C_{D_i} = \frac{C_L^2}{\pi A}$$

and the effective angle of incidence

$$\alpha_0 = \alpha - \epsilon = \alpha - \frac{C_L}{\pi A}$$

where α is the geometrical angle of incidence.

An important conclusion of the theory here outlined is that the induced drag of a wing having a given C_L is reduced directly as the aspect ratio is increased. Modern long-range airplanes, consequently, have narrow wings of the greatest span that can be built in the current state of the art of materials and structural design.

The effective angle of incidence for a finite wing has been shown to be less than for a wing of infinite span by the angle of down-wash induced by the trailing vortices. For a given geometrical angle of incidence, the section lift must be correspondingly less than for the infinite wing, since the lift coefficient varies directly with the effective angle of incidence.

The slope of the lift curve for a wing of infinite span is determined by $C_L = 2\pi\alpha$ from the two-dimensional theory of Kutta and Joukowski. But for the finite wing

$$C_L = 2\pi\alpha_0 \qquad \alpha = \alpha_0 + \frac{C_L}{\pi A}$$

and

$$\frac{d\alpha}{dC_L} = \frac{d\alpha_0}{dC_L} + \frac{1}{\pi A} = \frac{1}{2\pi} + \frac{1}{\pi A}$$

Therefore,

$$\frac{dC_L}{d\alpha} = \frac{2\pi A}{A + 2} < 2\pi$$

The effect of aspect ratio is therefore to flatten the slope of the lift-coefficient curve, as indicated in Fig. 11.24.

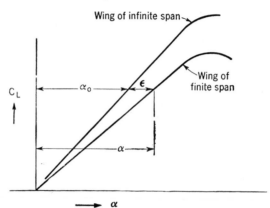

Fig. 11.24. — Diagrammatic comparison of curves of lift coefficient C_L versus angle of incidence α for wings of finite and infinite span.

11.24. Polar Diagram and Profile Drag. For a real wing in a real fluid the total drag at any given attitude is made up of the induced drag D_i, associated with the circulation and lift developed, and, in addition, a drag due to friction of the fluid and defects in the smoothness of flow around the wing section, or profile. This latter portion of the total drag is called "profile drag" because it depends on the shape, or profile, and not on the plan form or aspect ratio of the wing. For infinite span the induced drag is zero, and the total drag is the profile drag, designated by D_0.

We may write in coefficient form,

$$C_D = C_{D_0} + C_{D_i} = C_{D_0} + \frac{C_L^2}{\pi A}$$

where

$$C_{D_0} = D_0/(\rho/2)V^2S$$

We observe that a plot of C_L versus C_{D_i} for given A will be a parabola, and we know from experimental evidence that the profile-drag coefficient C_{D_0} is substantially constant for small angles.

The relative merits of various wing profiles are conventionally displayed by plotting experimentally determined values of C_L versus C_D on a so-called "polar diagram," together with the corresponding angle of incidence. On this polar diagram the induced-drag-coefficient parabola is plotted from $C_{D_i} = C_L^2/\pi A$ to serve as a reference to the ideal case of no friction. The curve of observed values lies to the right of the parabola by the amount of the profile-drag coefficient C_{D_0}, as shown by Fig. 11.25.

For a smooth airfoil at a small angle of incidence the profile drag is nearly equal to the skin friction on a flat plate moving edgewise. However, when a wing or blade is held at too great an incidence or if the curvature is abrupt, the fluid cannot follow the contour, circulation is interfered with, and there is both a loss of lift and a sharp increase in profile drag, due to the formation of a large eddying wake stream. The wing is then said to be "stalled" because of flow separation.

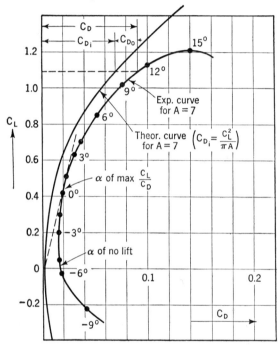

Fig. 11.25. — Polar diagram for an airfoil of finite span. (*After Prandtl.*)

11.25. Section Profile Drag. Airplane wings are usually tapered in plan form, not only to approximate the favorable elliptical distribution of lift and circulation, but also to save structural weight in the design of the cantilever girder. Structural considerations require a thicker wing near the root and a higher profile drag than would otherwise be chosen. Consequently, a designer frequently must estimate the profile drag of a wing having airfoil sections varying from root to tip in some regular manner. Furthermore, in actual construction, the unavoidable roughness of the surface of the wing may increase skin friction (and consequently the actual profile-drag coefficient) considerably above the values reported from wind-tunnel tests with polished models.

The "pitot-traverse" method was developed by Sir Melville Jones to estimate the section profile drag from measurements in flight. The theory is an approximation that has been found to give results within the precision of the experimental observations [5a].

Let a wing move through still air of density ρ. The relative velocity of the air is V, except in a well-defined region behind the wing, where it is less than V. This region is called the "wake" and represents a loss or defect of momentum corresponding to the profile drag. If there were no friction, there would be no wake or profile drag. The plane AA of Fig. 11.26 is normal to V and is sufficiently far behind the wing to have the

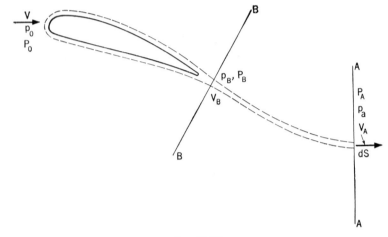

FIG. 11.26.

velocity across the plane sensibly equal to V except in the wake where it is V_A. The static pressure is sensibly equal to that in the undisturbed stream. If dS is an element of area of the plane AA and V_A is the air velocity in the elementary area, the mass of fluid passing per second through a stream tube of section dS is $\rho V_A \, dS$. If there were no wing friction, the velocity of this mass of fluid would be V. There has thus been a change of momentum flux equal to $\rho V_A \, dS(V - V_A)$. The drag of the wing causes the total momentum change in the air passing plane AA, so that

$$D = \int_S \rho V_A (V - V_A) \, dS$$

However, it is not possible to measure V_A in the wake at any considerable distance behind an airplane in flight. Even if we could do so, we should find that the wake had become so diffused and widened by the effects of turbulent mixing that the pitot-tube measurement of velocity differences over the plane AA would be useless. Furthermore, the wakes created by various parts of the airplane could not be identified, as each elementary stream tube leaving the trailing edge of the wing would have mixed with its neighbors.

The assumption is made that it does not matter to the wing how the wake is diffused and that we may replace the real wake by an imaginary one in which stream tubes leaving the wing and passing the plane BB continue unmixed through AA, without further loss of total pressure. In other words, the Bernoulli constant is unchanged behind the wing in this hypothetical wake. At the plane BB, normal to the wake, the mass flow per unit time in a stream tube of section dS' is $\rho V_B \, dS'$. This mass when passing the plane AA has velocity V_A, and the drag of the wing must be

$$D = \int_{S'} \rho V_B (V - V_A) \, dS'$$

The integration is taken across the wake since no other part of the plane AA contributes to the drag. Note that we use BB, the plane of measurement, only to determine the amount of fluid ultimately discharged into the parallel wake where the static pressure is again that of the general stream.

The Bernoulli constant of the undisturbed stream is $P_0 = p_0 + (\rho/2)V^2$, where p_0 is the atmospheric pressure. In the plane of measurements BB, $P_B = p_B + (\rho/2)V_B^2$. In the plane AA the static pressure is again equal to the pressure of the undisturbed atmosphere. Since we assumed no loss of energy between BB and AA, Bernoulli's equation yields

$$P_B = p_B + \frac{\rho}{2} V_B^2 = p_A + \frac{\rho}{2} V_A^2 = p_0 + \frac{\rho}{2} V_A^2$$

whence

$$V^2 = \frac{2(P_0 - p_0)}{\rho} = \frac{2P_0'}{\rho}$$

$$V_A^2 = \frac{2(P_B - p_0)}{\rho} = \frac{2P_B'}{\rho}$$

$$V_B^2 = \frac{2(P_B - p_B)}{\rho}$$

and

$$D = \int_{S'} 2\sqrt{P_B - p_B} \,\left(\sqrt{P_0'} - \sqrt{P_B'}\right) dS'$$

By measuring P_B and p_B with a pitot tube at a number of points in line BB and knowing $P_0' = (\rho/2)V^2$, one can plot values of the function $2\sqrt{P_B - p_B}\,(\sqrt{P_0'} - \sqrt{P_B'})$ in terms of the distance along the line BB. The area hatched in Fig. 11.27 represents the profile drag per unit of span divided by $2P_0'$, the momentum flux through unit cross section of the undisturbed stream.

The profile drag measured in a wind tunnel by the wake-survey method is found to be within 1 or 2 per cent of the profile drag obtained by subtraction of the computed induced drag from the total drag measured by the balance mechanism.

Tests in flight, made with apparatus as shown in Fig. 11.28, on actual airplane wings usually indicate higher section profile drag than polished wind-tunnel models, owing to unavoidable roughness of manufacture. A factory-painted metal wing showed a section-profile-drag coefficient of 0.007, which was reduced to 0.005 by sanding and polishing.

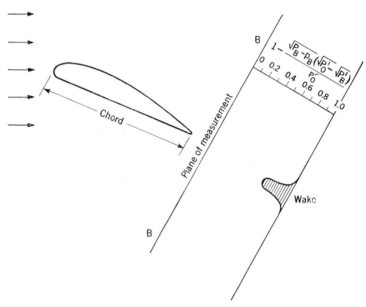

FIG. 11.27.

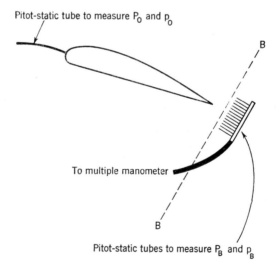

FIG. 11.28. — Diagrammatic sketch of apparatus for wake-survey measurements.

11.26. Boundary Layer. On a solid boundary a real fluid is at rest relative to the body. It was stated in Chap. X that near the boundary there is a strong velocity gradient $\partial V/\partial n$ which decreases to zero at the outside of a narrow boundary layer of fluid, where the velocity of potential flow is reached. In this boundary layer, viscous forces predominate. Outside the boundary layer, viscosity is unimportant because the velocity gradient is small.

The boundary layer is thin initially but becomes turbulent and thickens as the flow progresses along the surface. In order to prevent this layer of

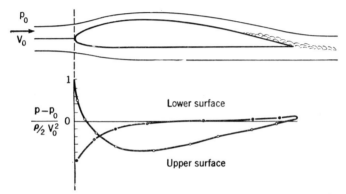

Fig. 11.29. — Pressure distribution over an airfoil at a small angle of incidence.

relatively slow-moving fluid from accumulating, there should be a fall in pressure along the surface in the direction of relative flow. Otherwise there is risk of flow separation.

Figure 11.29 shows a falling pressure at the forward end of an airfoil on the upper surface, and a gradually rising pressure over the lower surface and part of the upper one. This type of pressure distribution corresponds to an angle of incidence giving practically no lift.

11.27. Flow Separation. When the wing is turned to a sufficiently large angle of incidence, the pressure distribution assumes the form given in Fig. 11.30. The boundary layer on the upper surface then thickens and the fluid next the wall moves upstream as a result of the steeply rising pressure. Note that the main flow has separated over the back of the wing and the eddying wake stream is much broader than in Fig. 11.29. The lift of such a wing will be poor because circulation is not good, and the profile drag will be high because energy is lost in the wake.

11.28. Stalling. At a somewhat larger angle of incidence, separation will occur over the entire upper surface, and the drag will be relatively enormous. The wing is now "stalled," as indicated by Fig. 11.31. Circulation has been further interfered with, and the lift may be even less than at a smaller incidence.

The boundary layer contains the key to flow separation and the development of eddies. The lines AB and CD represent "surfaces of discontinuity" as studied by Helmholtz and Kirchhoff. The fluid is continuous in the ordinary sense of having no voids, but the velocity is continuous only in the region outside the wake stream bounded by AB and CD. These surfaces mark a sharp discontinuity in the velocity of fluid particles.

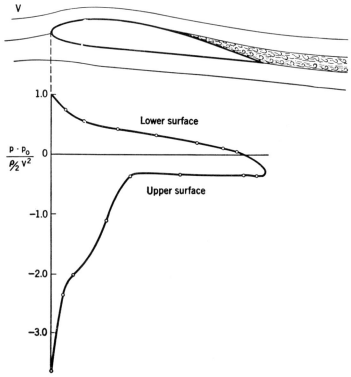

Fig. 11.30. — Pressure distribution over an airfoil at a large angle of incidence.

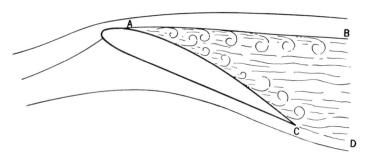

Fig. 11.31. — Streamlines around a "stalled" airfoil.

11.29. Characteristic Curves. The lift and drag at given incidence are found experimentally to vary nearly as the area of the wing, the density of the air, and the square of the velocity of the stream, *i.e.*, the lift and drag coefficients are found to be practically constant. This behavior is found in steady motion, where the velocity at no point in the flow approaches the velocity of sound. More refined experiments bear out the result of dimensional reasoning, that, at given incidence, the lift and drag

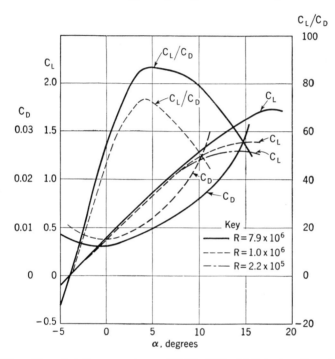

Fig. 11.32. — Characteristic curves for an NACA 4412 airfoil in two-dimensional flow. See Fig. 10.6a for the shape of this airfoil.

coefficients for any particular shape of airfoil depend on the Reynolds number Vc/ν, where c is conveniently taken as the chord. The drag coefficient C_D as a function of the Reynolds number is found to vary rather slowly. C_L for modern wings varies but little with the Reynolds number, indicating that friction plays only a small part in the maintenance of circulation. The ratio C_L/C_D is a measure of the usefulness of a wing. A typical wing has characteristics given by Fig. 11.32. Note that the wing is stalled at about a 15-deg incidence, where C_L reaches its maximum.

11.30. Airplane Mechanics. An airplane in steady level flight has its weight balanced by its lift and its drag by the propeller thrust. Thus

$$W = \text{weight} = C_L \frac{\rho}{2} V^2 A$$

$$T = \text{thrust} = (C_D + C_f) \frac{\rho}{2} V^2 A$$

where C_D is the drag coefficient for the wings and C_f is the parasite-drag coefficient for the rest of the airplane; A is the wing area. The power required is obviously

$$P_R = TV$$

The power available is the engine power P_E times the efficiency of the propeller, or

$$P_A = P_E \eta$$

For a given speed it is necessary that $C_L = 2W/\rho V^2 A$ to support the weight. To this C_L there corresponds a single value of C_D and a corre-

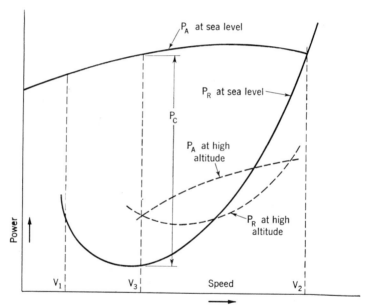

Fig. 11.33. — Power available P_A and power required P_R as functions of speed of an airplane at sea level and at high altitude.

sponding angle of incidence α, which may be found from the characteristic curve for the wing used. C_f, which is nearly independent of α, may then be added to C_D, and P_R computed. Typical speed-power curves for an airplane are given in Fig. 11.33, in which V_1 is stalling speed, V_2 is maximum speed, V_3 is speed of best climb, and P_C is power available for climb.

Note that, at high altitude, the engine power will be much lower (unless supercharged) and that the power required is higher for low speed and

ower for high speed than at sea level. For example, if the density is half
hat at sea level, to maintain a required C_L necessitates a doubled angle of
ncidence at the same speed or a 40 per cent higher speed at the same in-
·idence.   Eventually an altitude may be reached for which the curves of
$^{2}_A$ and P_R become tangent at a certain speed. This is the absolute ceiling
or the airplane with the particular engine installed.

When turning with speed V on a radius r, the airplane must be banked
.t an angle θ such that the centrifugal force

$$F = \frac{WV^2}{gr} = L \sin \theta$$

.nd the weight

$$W = L \cos \theta$$

Ience

$$\frac{F}{W} = \tan \theta = \frac{V^2}{gr}$$

The force diagram is given in Fig. 11.34.

The necessary angle of bank is greater for higher speeds and for sharper

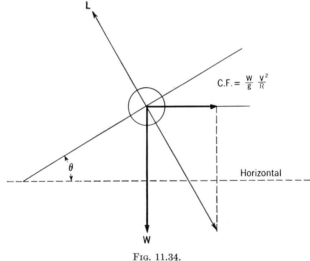

FIG. 11.34.

.urns and is independent of the weight or size of the airplane. Any object,
ncluding the pilot, of weight w experiences a force opposite to the lift
·ector that is the vector sum of weight and centrifugal force, or

$$\text{Apparent weight} = \sqrt{\left(\frac{wV^2}{gr}\right)^2 + w^2} = w\sqrt{\tan^2 \theta + 1} = \frac{w}{\cos \theta}$$

·or a sharp bank the pilot's apparent weight can be several times his
ıormal weight, and serious structural or physiological damage may result.

In a glide with power cut off the component of the weight along the flight path balances the drag D. The lift of the wings L, normal to the flight path, balances the component of W normal to the flight path. The flight path is inclined at an angle θ to the horizon and at an angle α to the wing. For equilibrium, these three forces W, D, and L must meet at the center of gravity (see Fig. 11.35).

$$L = W \cos \theta = C_L \frac{\rho}{2} V^2 A$$

$$D = W \sin \theta = (C_D + C_f) \frac{\rho}{2} V^2 A$$

$$\tan \theta = \frac{D}{L}$$

Since for each angle of incidence α there is one value of D/L (ranging down to about $\frac{1}{15}$), there is also a single corresponding angle of glide θ.

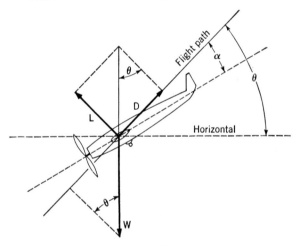

FIG. 11.35.

When $L = 0$, $\theta = 90$ deg and the glide becomes a vertical dive in which $D = W$. The speed of such a dive is called the "terminal velocity."

$$V_{\text{term}} = \sqrt{\frac{2W}{(C_D + C_f)\rho A}}$$

Modern airplanes with high wing loading W/A, low parasite resistance C_f, and flat wings of low C_D may attain dangerous speeds in such a dive.

11.31. Lift at Subsonic and Transonic Speeds. It is found in wind-tunnel tests that the lift coefficient tends to increase with increasing Mach number, other things being unchanged. This rise in C_L continues up to the critical Mach number M_c; but above this value C_L drops off rapidly, and C_D rises. These rapid changes in C_L and C_D are due to the formation of shock waves, as described in Art. 10.13. A typical C_L versus M curve is shown in Fig. 11.36.

This behavior of C_L is important in the flight of an airplane, not only because of the loss of lift, but also because of the changed flow around the

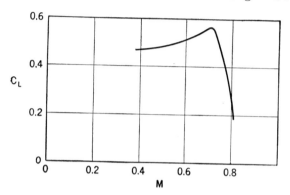

Fig. 11.36. — Lift coefficient C_L versus Mach number M.

control surfaces in the wake of the wing. The decrease in circulation around the wing results in a diminished down-wash, so that the airflow around the control planes is deflected upward from its original direction. The tail thus tends to rise and further to complicate the control problem, which may already be serious, owing to compressibility effects on the elevators themselves.

11.32. Theory of Small Perturbations for Subsonic Speeds. Glauert and Prandtl have developed an approximate theory by means of which the effect of compressibility on the pressure distribution around a thin body can be computed. The basic assumption is that the body be so thin and inclined at such a small angle as to cause only small percentage changes in the velocity of the flow. If U is the undisturbed-flow velocity and u' and v' are the additional components caused by the body, it is assumed that u'/U and v'/U are so small that their squares and products can be neglected. This assumption is obviously not fulfilled in the neighborhood of the stagnation point at the nose of a body; but if the body be thin, this region is small and so is the resultant error.

It is further assumed that pressure and density are related by the reversible adiabatic equation [Eq. (9.5)] $p/\rho^k = $ constant. This, together with the additional assumption of steady irrotational flow, leads to the following equations:

$$p_1 = \left(1 - \frac{k-1}{2} V_1^2\right)^{k/(k-1)} \tag{11.42}$$

$$\rho_1 = \left(1 - \frac{k-1}{2} V_1^2\right)^{1/(k-1)} \tag{11.43}$$

$$C_1^2 = \frac{p_1}{\rho_1} = 1 - \frac{k-1}{2} V_1^2 \tag{11.44}$$

where $p_1 = p/p_0$, $\rho_1 = \rho/\rho_0$, $V_1 = V/C_0$, $C_1 = C/C_0$, and the subscript zero refers to the fluid at rest. Since we are considering only the two-dimensional case, Eqs. (11.5) apply and may be combined with Eqs. (11.28) to give

$$\left.\begin{aligned} \frac{\partial \psi}{\partial y} &= \rho_1 \frac{\partial \phi}{\partial x} \\[2mm] -\frac{\partial \psi}{\partial x} &= \rho_1 \frac{\partial \phi}{\partial y} \end{aligned}\right\} \tag{11.45}$$

Elimination of ψ from these equations, by use of the fact that $\partial^2 \psi / (\partial x\, \partial y) = \partial^2 \psi / (\partial y\, \partial x)$, gives

$$\rho_1 \left(\frac{\partial^2 \phi}{\partial x^2} + \frac{\partial^2 \phi}{\partial y^2}\right) + \frac{\partial \rho_1}{\partial x} u + \frac{\partial \rho_1}{\partial y} v = 0 \tag{11.46}$$

But from Eq. (11.43) one gets

$$\frac{\partial \rho_1}{\partial V_1} = -\frac{\rho_1 V_1}{C_1^2} \tag{11.47}$$

whence

$$\frac{\partial \rho_1}{\partial x} = -\frac{\rho_1}{2C_1^2} \frac{\partial V_1^2}{\partial x} = -\frac{\rho_1}{C_1^2}\left(u_1 \frac{\partial u_1}{\partial x} + v_1 \frac{\partial v_1}{\partial x}\right) = -\frac{\rho_1}{C_1^2}\left(\frac{u_1}{C_0} \frac{\partial^2 \phi}{\partial x^2} + \frac{v_1}{C_0} \frac{\partial^2 \phi}{\partial x\, \partial y}\right)$$

$$\frac{\partial \rho_1}{\partial y} = -\frac{\rho_1}{C_1^2}\left(\frac{u_1}{C_0} \frac{\partial^2 \phi}{\partial x\, \partial y} + \frac{v_1}{C_0} \frac{\partial^2 \phi}{\partial y^2}\right)$$

Substitution of these expressions into Eq. (11.46) yields, finally,

$$\left(1 - \frac{u^2}{C^2}\right)\frac{\partial^2 \phi}{\partial x^2} - \frac{2uv}{C^2} \frac{\partial^2 \phi}{\partial x\, \partial y} + \left(1 - \frac{v^2}{C^2}\right)\frac{\partial^2 \phi}{\partial y^2} = 0 \tag{11.48}$$

Equation (11.48), which is nonlinear since u, v, and C depend on ϕ, must be satisfied in a compressible flow. It replaces the relatively simple linear Laplace equation [Eq. (11.31)] for incompressible fluid, to which it is seen to reduce if u and v are each very small compared with the local sound velocity C.

Introducing now the assumption peculiar to the method of small perturbations, we let

$$u = U + u'$$
$$v = v'$$

where u'/U and v'/U are so small that their squares and products are negligible. The sort of flow considered is shown in Fig. 11.37. Substituting for u and v in Eq. (11.48), noting that $\partial^2\phi/\partial x^2$, $\partial^2\phi/\partial y^2$, and $\partial^2\phi/(\partial x\,\partial y)$ are all on the order of u' or v', and neglecting terms of the order u'^2, we get

$$\left(1 - \frac{U^2}{C^2}\right)\frac{\partial^2\phi}{\partial x^2} + \frac{\partial^2\phi}{\partial y^2} = 0 \qquad (11.49)$$

With the aid of Eq. (11.44) it is readily found that

$$\frac{U^2}{C^2} = \frac{U^2}{C_\infty^2}\left[1 + (k-1)\frac{u'U}{C_\infty^2}\right] = M^2\left[1 + (k-1)\frac{u'U}{C_\infty^2}\right]$$

where C_∞ is the sound velocity and M is the Mach number in the fluid having speed U. Equation (11.49) can thus be written

$$(1 - M^2)\frac{\partial^2\phi}{\partial x^2} + \frac{\partial^2\phi}{\partial y^2} = 0 \qquad (11.50)$$

with negligible error (on the order of u'^2).

It will be noted that Eq. (11.50) applies to either subsonic or supersonic flow, since M may be either greater or less than 1. For the present we are concerned only with the subsonic case, for which $1 - M^2 > 0$. If we introduce a new independent variable $\eta = y\sqrt{1 - M^2}$, Eq. (11.50) reduces to the Laplace equation

$$\frac{\partial^2\phi}{\partial x^2} + \frac{\partial^2\phi}{\partial \eta^2} = 0 \qquad (11.51)$$

in the x,η plane. If, then, we know the value of ϕ at any point x,η in an incompressible flow, we can assign this value of ϕ to the corresponding point x,y of a compressible flow. This procedure may be visualized with the help of Fig. 11.38, in which are shown three values of ϕ in the x,η plane and the same three values at the corresponding points of the x,y plane. From this figure it follows that

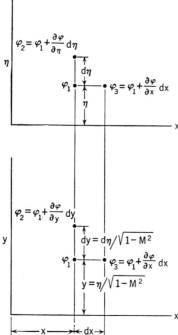

Fig. 11.37.

Fig. 11.38.

or

$$\left.\begin{aligned}\frac{\partial\phi}{\partial\eta} &= \frac{1}{\sqrt{1-M^2}}\frac{\partial\phi}{\partial y}\\[2mm] v_i' &= \frac{1}{\sqrt{1-M^2}}v_c'\end{aligned}\right\} \quad (11.52)$$

and

or

$$\left.\begin{aligned}\frac{\partial\phi}{\partial x} &= \frac{\partial\phi}{\partial x}\\[2mm] U_i + u_i' &= U_c + u_c'\end{aligned}\right\} \quad (11.53)$$

where subscripts i and c refer to incompressible and compressible flow, respectively. The ratio of the slopes of the streamlines at any pair of corresponding points is thus

$$\frac{v_c'}{U_c + u_c'}\frac{U_i + u_i'}{v_i'} = \sqrt{1-M^2} \tag{11.54}$$

It is to be noted that the boundary of the body in the incompressible flow is not mapped into a streamline of the compressible flow. The slope of the line joining these mapped points is increased by a factor $1/\sqrt{1-M^2}$ over that in the x,η plane, while the slope of the *streamline* through any mapped point is reduced by the factor $\sqrt{1-M^2}$ below that through the original point in the x,η plane.

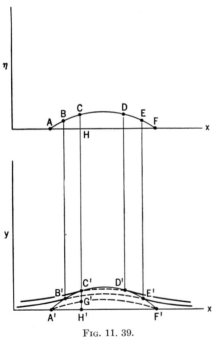

Fig. 11. 39.

The curve $ABCDEF$ of Fig. 11.39 represents the surface of a body in incompressible flow, and $A'B'C'D'E'F'$ is the map of this curve in the x,y plane. The streamlines of the compressible flow obtained from the mapped values of ϕ are shown as heavy lines in the x,y plane. It is seen that between A' and F', B' and E', and C' and D' there are no ϕ values to map, the corresponding points in the x,η plane lying inside the body. The dotted portions of the streamlines are obtained in the following way:

Any distance, such as $G'C'$, between a point on a dotted streamline and the termination of the full streamline directly above it is on the order of δ, the thickness of the original body. This thickness, however, is measured by a mean value of the slope times the length of the body l. Hence

$$\frac{G'C'}{l} \sim \frac{\delta}{l} \sim \frac{v_i'}{U_i} \sim \frac{v_c'}{U_c}$$

Furthermore, $\partial u_c'/\partial x$ is of order u_c'/l. It follows therefore from Eq. (11.50) that $\partial v_c'/\partial y$ is also of this same order of magnitude. The difference between the values of v_c' at G' and C' is thus given by

$$\frac{\partial v_c'}{\partial y} G'C' \sim \frac{u_c'}{l} G'C' \sim \frac{u_c' v_c'}{U_c} \tag{11.55}$$

It can also be shown, from the irrotational nature of the flow, that

$$\frac{\partial u_c'}{\partial y} G'C' = \frac{\partial v_c'}{\partial x} G'C' \sim \frac{v_c'}{l} G'C' \sim \frac{v_c'^2}{U_c} \tag{11.55a}$$

Both these differences are negligible by hypothesis. Hence, at a given value of x, the slopes of all the dotted streamlines are the same as that of an adjacent full streamline.

The dotted streamline $A'G'F'$, which joins the stagnation points A' and F', is a boundary of the compressible flow and thus may be considered as the outline of a body. It is clear from Eqs. (11.54), (11.55), and (11.55a) that any ordinate of this body, such as $H'G'$, is related to the ordinate HC at the same value of x by the equation

$$G'H' = \sqrt{1 - M^2}\, CH$$

It is readily seen from this result that the approximate streamline pattern about a thin airfoil in a subsonic compressible flow can be obtained from that for an incompressible flow about an airfoil of the same length but whose thickness, angle of attack, and camber are all greater by a factor $1/\sqrt{1 - M^2}$ than those of the first airfoil.

Practically, we are interested in knowing the relation between the lift coefficients for these two airfoils. This relation is found as follows:

The lift coefficient for the compressible flow in the x,y plane may be defined as

$$C_{L_c} = \frac{\int_0^l \Delta p\, dl}{\rho_\infty l U_c^2/2} = \frac{\overline{\Delta p}}{\rho_\infty U_c^2/2}$$

where l is the chord, $\overline{\Delta p}$ is the average pressure difference between the lower and upper surfaces of the profile, and ρ_∞ is the density and U_c is the velocity of the distant fluid. The Euler equation [Eq. (4.7)] reduces in this case to

$$\int_{p_\infty}^{p} \frac{dp}{\rho} + \frac{(U_c + u_c')^2 + v_c'^2 - U_c^2}{2} = 0$$

which, together with the formula $p/\rho^k = $ constant, yields

$$\frac{p}{p_\infty} = \left(1 - \frac{k-1}{C_\infty^2} U_c u_c'\right)^{k/(k-1)} = 1 - \frac{kU_c u_c'}{C_\infty^2}$$

or

$$p - p_\infty = -\frac{kp_\infty}{C_\infty^2} U_c u_c' = -\rho_\infty U_c u_c'$$

where terms of the order $u_c'^2$ have been neglected. Therefore

$$\overline{\Delta p} = -\rho_\infty U_c \overline{\Delta u_c'}$$

and

$$C_{L_c} = -\frac{2\overline{\Delta u_c'}}{U_c} \qquad\qquad (11.56)$$

The lift coefficient for the incompressible flow around the profile in the x,η plane is found by similar methods to be

$$C_{L_i} = -\frac{2\overline{\Delta u_i'}}{U_i}$$

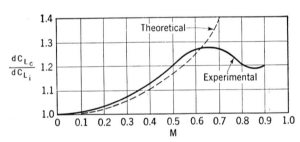

Fig. 11.40. — Ratio of the slopes of the lift-coefficient curves for compressible and incompressible flow dC_{L_c}/dC_{L_i} versus Mach number M. (*After R. von Mises, reference* 4.)

Thus the ratio of lift coefficients is

$$\frac{C_{L_c}}{C_{L_i}} = \frac{\overline{\Delta u_c'}}{\overline{\Delta u_i'}} \frac{U_i}{U_c} \qquad\qquad (11.57)$$

Since Eqs. (11.53) apply at all pairs of corresponding points, they hold far upstream where $u_i' = u_c' = 0$. Hence $U_i = U_c$, $u_i' = u_c'$, and $\overline{\Delta u_i'} = \overline{\Delta u_c'}$. Therefore, using Eqs. (11.55a) and (11.57), we find that

$$C_{L_c} = C_{L_i}$$

It is easily seen that the lifts and pressure distributions, also, are the same for these two airfoils, provided that ρ_∞ is the same of both.

The question now arises as to the effect of compressibility on the lift coefficient of a given profile at a given angle of attack. It is found that in this case

$$\frac{C_{L_c}}{C_{L_i}} = \frac{1}{\sqrt{1 - M^2}} \qquad (11.58)$$

The details are left to the reader (see problem 11.19).

The theoretical formula, Eq. (11.58), is found to agree well with experiment for M less than about 0.6, as shown in Fig. 11.40. Here the measured value of dC_{L_c}/dC_{L_i} is compared with that computed from Eq. (11.58), at different values of M. The computed value is, obviously, $1/\sqrt{1 - M^2}$. The increasing divergence between experiment and theory for values of M greater than 0.6 is due to the fact that variations in the local Mach number and its approach to 1 in certain regions can no longer be ignored.

11.33. Lift at Supersonic Speeds. The flow pattern around a wing at supersonic speeds is characterized by the nose and tail shock waves already discussed in Art. 10.14. An idealized example, the two-dimensional flow around a thin flat plate in an unsymmetrical attitude, is given in Fig. 11.41. The approaching flow remains unaffected by the plate until the fluid reaches the lines oa and oc. On the upper side the fluid expands and turns gradually until at the line ob it is moving parallel to the plate. It then flows in a straight path to the line $o'c'$, where the stream is suddenly deflected back to its original direction. On the lower side the stream turns suddenly at the line oc, moves parallel to the surface, and then gradually returns to its original direction between $o'a'$ and $o'b'$. The pressure and velocity are constant over both the upper and lower surfaces, the pressure being greater underneath than above. It is thus a relatively simple matter to compute the lift and drag of the plate.

The theoretical flow pattern of Fig. 11.41 is based on the assumption of two-dimensional irrotational flow. It is found that a solution of the equations of motion exists which satisfies these postulates and which yields the flow patterns for the expansions around the sharp corners, *i.e.*, it gives the streamlines and pressure distributions in the wedges aob and $a'o'b'$. A second solution is known which gives the oblique shock lines oc and $o'c'$ by which the fluid is turned and suddenly compressed. Schlieren photographs of the flow of air past a plate are practically identical with the theoretical pattern.

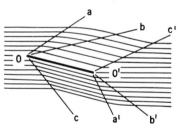

FIG. 11.41. — Supersonic flow past a flat plate at a small angle of incidence.

The occurrence of drag in this two-dimensional compressible flow is at first sight even more baffling than that in the three-dimensional incompressible flow around a wing of finite span. For the wing of finite span the origin of the drag is the continual introduction of rotation into the fluid by the trailing vortices. In the present problem, on the other hand, the flow near the plate is entirely irrotational. It will be observed, however, that the lines oc and $o'a'$ extended will intersect. Since $o'a'$ represents a wave of rarefaction, its junction with the shock line oc will result in a decrease in the pressure jump across oc. The shock line will thus become more oblique and will eventually intersect all the rays from o', after which it will have disappeared completely, since the pressure rise at the leading edge is exactly equal to the pressure drop at the trailing edge. It will be shown below that rotation is introduced into the flow along that part of the shock line beyond the point of intersection with $o'a'$, where the conditions cease to be the same at all points on the shock. The drag thus results from the continual input of rotational kinetic energy into the fluid at some distance from the plate.

11.34. Theory of Small Perturbations for Supersonic Speeds. As already mentioned, Eq. (11.50) of the Glauert-Prandtl theory is applicable to supersonic flow. In this case, since $M > 1$, the equation is written

$$(M^2 - 1)\frac{\partial^2 \phi}{\partial x^2} = \frac{\partial^2 \phi}{\partial y^2} \tag{11.59}$$

It is readily shown by direct substitution that a solution of this equation is

$$\phi = Ux + f(x - \sqrt{M^2 - 1}\,y) + F(x + \sqrt{M^2 - 1}\,y) \tag{11.59a}$$

where f and F are arbitrary functions of their respective arguments.

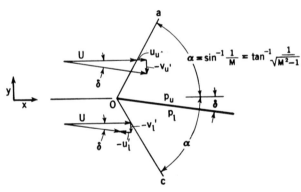

FIG. 11.42.

Equation (11.59a) will be applied to the supersonic flow around a small angle, as shown in Fig. 11.42.

Ux is the velocity potential for the undisturbed flow approaching the angle. The function $f(x - \sqrt{M^2 - 1}\,y)$ is the potential for an additional flow superposed on the main stream. Since the argument of f is constant along a straight line of slope $1/\sqrt{M^2 - 1}$, both f and its derivatives

$\partial f/\partial x = u'$ and $\partial f/\partial y = v'$ are also constants along such a line. Therefore, the additional velocity is normal to this line and has a constant value everywhere along it. We can accordingly build up a supersonic flow pattern that is theoretically correct by choosing suitable additional velocities to turn the stream through an angle δ when it reaches the straight lines oa and oc. The angle $\alpha = \sin^{-1} 1/M = \tan^{-1} 1/\sqrt{M^2 - 1}$ that these lines make with the x axis will be recognized as the Mach angle. The lines oa and oc, known as "Mach lines," represent standing disturbances or wavelets; the component of the approaching velocity normal to the wavelets is $U \sin \alpha$, which is equal to C_∞, the sound velocity in the undisturbed flow.

The potential $F(x + \sqrt{M^2 - 1}y)$ gives disturbance velocities along lines of slope $- 1/\sqrt{M^2 - 1}$. In the present example, however, the boundary conditions are satisfied without any such wavelets, and F must be put equal to zero.

Figure 11.42 may be considered as the flow around a flat plate. It is a simple matter to compute the lift coefficient for the plate from the theory presented above. We note that the velocity (and hence the pressure) is constant over the upper and lower surfaces of the plate. The lift coefficient is easily expressed in terms of these constant pressures: $C_L = [(p_l - p_u)/(\rho_\infty/2)U^2] \cos \delta \approx (p_l - p_u)/(\rho_\infty/2)U^2$. The Euler equation has here the form given on page 263, since terms in u'^2 are assumed negligible. Accordingly, $p_l - p_u = \rho_\infty U(u_u' - u_l')$ and $C_L = (2/U)(u_u' - u_l')$. The velocity diagrams of Fig. 11.42 yield the relations

$$\frac{u_u'}{U} = \frac{\delta}{\sqrt{M^2 - 1} - \delta} \qquad \text{and} \qquad \frac{- u_l'}{U} = \frac{\delta}{\sqrt{M^2 - 1} + \delta}$$

so that

$$C_L = \frac{4\delta}{\sqrt{M^2 - 1}} \qquad (11.60)$$

The drag is equal to the resultant force multiplied by δ. Hence, the drag coefficient is $C_D = C_L\delta/\cos \delta$ or (with $\cos \delta \approx 1$)

$$C_D = \frac{4\delta^2}{\sqrt{M^2 - 1}} \qquad (11.60a)$$

which is of order δ^2 and is here neglected.

The flow pattern around a thin body, such as is shown in Fig. 11.43, may be determined by the Glauert-Prandtl method if the continuously curved surface is replaced by a number of straight segments. At each corner formed by the junction of two consecutive segments a Mach line is drawn, at every point of which the velocity direction changes by the same amount. Compression occurs only at the nose and tail; along the whole surface the flow expands. It will be noted that in this approximate theory all the Mach lines are parallel, since changes in the Mach number are assumed negligible. An exact theory must take into account the fact that

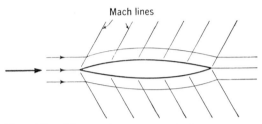

FIG. 11.43. — Glauert-Prandtl approximate supersonic flow pattern past a thin body.

neighboring Mach lines diverge in a region of expansion and converge in a region of compression.

11.35. Flow around a Corner (Expansion). To develop such a theory we observe that the Glauert-Prandtl theory is exact for an expansion of an initially parallel stream around an infinitesimal corner and that the flow downstream from the corner is again parallel but has a higher velocity and smaller Mach angle. The further expansion of this flow around another infinitesimal corner can be handled just as that around the preceding one; the new values of approach velocity and Mach angle must, however, be used. In an expanding flow, such as that over the body of Fig. 11.43, we can thus approximate as closely as we please to the exact solution, by replacing the continuously curved outline with a number of straight segments and applying the Glauert-Prandtl approximation to each corner so formed, using in every case, the appropriate velocity and Mach angle. Obviously, the greater the number of segments used, the better will be the approximation.

In a flow that is being compressed, the Mach angle increases at succes-

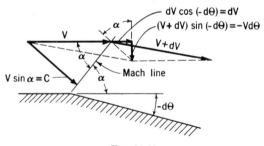

FIG. 11.44.

sive corners, and the Mach lines converge and eventually come together. Such coalescence results in the formation of a finite pressure jump, or shock, in which the changes in pressure and density are not of the reversible adiabatic type postulated in the development of the Glauert-Prandtl theory. If, however, the total compression is small, the above method may be used with only a small error. An outline of this method, which was developed by Prandtl and Busemann, follows:

In Fig. 11.44, V is the velocity of a parallel flow approaching a corner at which the direction changes by an infinitesimal angle $-d\theta$; α is the local Mach angle; and $V + dV$ is the velocity after the flow turns the corner. By the Glauert-Prandtl theory, conditions are uniform all along the Mach line, and the disturbance velocity is normal to the Mach line. The velocity diagram of Fig. 11.44 thus yields the equation

$$\frac{dV}{V\, d\theta} = -\tan \alpha = -\frac{1}{\sqrt{(V^2/C^2) - 1}} \tag{11.61}$$

where C is the local sound velocity. In this equation, terms of second

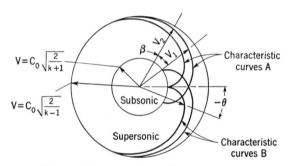

FIG. 11.45. — Characteristic curves for synthesis of supersonic flow patterns.

order are neglected. With the aid of Eq. (11.44), Eq. (11.61) can be transformed to

$$\frac{dV}{V\, d\theta} = -\frac{\sqrt{1 - [(k-1)/2]\,(V^2/C_0^2)}}{\sqrt{[(k+1)/2]\,(V^2/C_0^2) - 1}} \tag{11.62}$$

where C_0 is the sound velocity in fluid at rest.

An integral curve of Eq. (11.62) is conveniently plotted in polar coordinates for which the radius vector is the velocity V and the polar angle is the angle of turn θ. This plane is appropriately called the "hodograph plane." It is seen from Eq. (11.62) that, in these coordinates, an integral curve is radial ($dV/V\, d\theta = \infty$) where $V = \sqrt{2/(k+1)}C_0$, which is the value of the local sound velocity [see Eq. (9.11)]. This lower limiting value of V is represented by a circle in the hodograph plane, as shown in Fig. 11.45. Furthermore, an integral curve is normal to V (that is, $dV/V\, d\theta = 0$) where $V = \sqrt{2/(k-1)}C_0$, which will be recognized from Eq. (9.8) as the maximum attainable velocity (corresponding to $p = 0$). This upper limiting value of V is given by the outer circle in Fig. 11.45. In the supersonic region lying between these two limits it can be shown from Eq. (11.62) that an integral curve (characteristic curve) is generated by a point on a circle rolling on the inner circle and touching the outer one. The characteristics are thus epicycloids.

It is obvious that if the flow expands through a positive (counterclockwise) angle $d\theta$ we shall get Eq. (11.62) without the negative sign. There are therefore two families of characteristic curves A and B, as sketched in Fig. 11.45.

If the flow expands from any initial supersonic velocity V_1, around a corner (or series of corners) of total angle β, the final velocity V_2 is uniquely determined by the appropriate characteristic curve (see Fig. 11.45). But from Eqs. (11.42) and (11.44) the pressure and sound velocity are determined (for given p_0 and C_0) when the velocity is known. The final condition of the flow is therefore known. It is apparent from Fig. 11.45 that there is a maximum angle through which a stream can turn and that this angle depends on the initial velocity. The greatest value of this angle, which occurs if the flow is initially just sonic, is 129.3 deg [9].

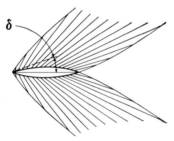

A graphical method, based on the characteristic diagram of Fig. 11.45, has been evolved, by which supersonic two-dimensional flow patterns are readily constructed.* The flow determined by this method around the lenticular body of Fig. 11.43 is shown in Fig. 11.46. Since the nose and tail angles of the body are small, the method is satisfactory even for the compression of the flow in these regions. For example, one determines the magnitude of the velocity on the upper surface immediately downstream from the nose by following in the counterclockwise sense through a polar angle δ the appropriate characteristic of family B of Fig. 11.45.

FIG. 11.46. — Shock waves and Mach lines for a supersonic flow past a thin body. (*Reproduced from L. Prandtl, The Flow of Liquids and Gases, in " The Physics of Solids and Fluids," Blackie and Son, Ltd., London and Glasgow.*)

11.36. Flow around a Corner (Compression). If the flow is compressed and turned suddenly through an angle that is not small, the method of characteristics is not even approximately correct and a new analysis is required. It is assumed that a parallel irrotational flow of a perfect gas is turned through a finite angle by means of a straight oblique shock, along both sides of which conditions are uniform. The irreversible changes that occur as the fluid crosses the shock preclude the use of the Euler equation between points on opposite sides of the shock, and it is necessary to use the energy equation [Eq. (9.19)]. The analysis is similar to that given in

* For further information see references 1 and 9 at the end of this chapter.

Art. 9.6 for a transverse shock, the only new feature being the inclusion of a velocity component parallel to the shock.

The velocity diagrams and control surface used in the analysis [9] are shown in Fig. 11.47. The upper and lower sides of the control surface are streamlines, and the other two sides are parallel to the shock. For convenience the areas at the ends of the control surface, through which fluid enters and leaves, are taken as unity. The continuity equation thus gives

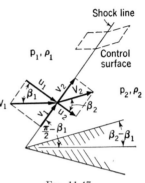

Fig. 11.47.

$$\rho_1 u_1 = \rho_2 u_2 \qquad (11.63)$$

The momentum equation applied normal to the shock yields, when combined with Eq. (11.63),

$$p_1 - p_2 = \rho_1 u_1 (u_2 - u_1) \qquad (11.64)$$

while, when applied parallel to the shock, it gives $\rho_1 u_1 (v_2 - v_1) = 0$ or $v_2 = v_1$. The energy equation [Eq. (9.19)] therefore takes the form

$$\frac{k}{k-1}\left(\frac{p_2}{\rho_2} - \frac{p_1}{\rho_1}\right) = \frac{u_1^2 - u_2^2}{2} \qquad (11.65)$$

From Eqs. (11.63), (11.64), and (11.65) we obtain, finally, the expressions

$$\frac{\rho_2}{\rho_1} = \frac{(k+1)p_2 + (k-1)p_1}{(k-1)p_2 + (k+1)p_1} \qquad \text{and} \qquad u_1^2 = \frac{p_1}{2\rho_1}\left[(k-1) + (k+1)\frac{p_2}{p_1}\right]$$

Noting that $u_1 = V_1 \cos \beta_1$ and that the Euler equation may be applied between section 0 upstream where the velocity is zero and section 1 to give

$$V_1^2 = \frac{2k}{k-1}\frac{p_1}{\rho_1}\left[\left(\frac{p_0}{p_1}\right)^{(k-1)/k} - 1\right]$$

we find

$$\cos^2 \beta_1 = \frac{[(k-1) + (k+1)(x/y)](k-1)}{4k\,[(1/y)^{(k-1)/k} - 1]} \qquad (11.66)$$

and

$$\frac{\tan \beta_2}{\tan \beta_1} = \frac{(k+1)(x/y) + (k-1)}{(k-1)(x/y) + (k+1)} \qquad (11.67)$$

where $x = p_2/p_0$ and $y = p_1/p_0$.

The curves of Figs. 11.48 and 11.49 are a convenient means of representing Eqs. (11.66) and (11.67). Figure 11.48 gives two values of β_1 for a given value of y and the angle of deflection $\beta_2 - \beta_1$. Only the smaller of these two values of β_1 is found to occur in experiments. This figure also shows that no solution of this type exists if the stream is turned through an angle greater than about 45 deg. It is further seen that no solution of this type exists, even for $\beta_2 - \beta_1 < 45$ deg, if β_1 is too small. This condition on β_1 is equivalent to the stipulation that the Mach number at 1, V_1/C_1, cannot be too small. Experiments show that, if this type of solu-

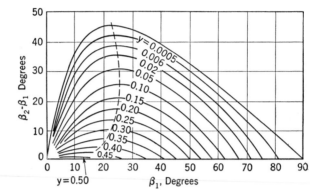

FIG. 11.48. — Curves for synthesis of a shock wave. (*Courtesy of Sir Geoffrey Taylor.*)

tion fails for either of these reasons (nose angle too great or V_1/C_1 too small), the shock wave does not have the shape shown in Fig. 11.47, nor

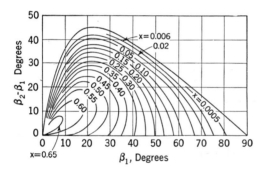

FIG. 11.49. — Curves for synthesis of a shock wave. (*Courtesy of Sir Geoffrey Taylor.*)

does it touch the nose of the body; instead, it is curved and passes in front of the nose, as described in Art. 9.3.

As an example of the use of these curves, suppose that the angle $\beta_2 - \beta_1$ is given, together with the flow conditions at 1 and 0. Figure 11.48 then gives the value of β_1, from which the slope of the shock is found, while from Fig. 11.49 the value of $x = p_2/p_0$ is determined.

A similar analysis has also been made for the axially symmetrical flow over a cone [9].

11.37. Shock Waves and Rotation. In Art. 11.33 it was pointed out in connection with Fig. 11.41 that the drag on a two-dimensional object in supersonic flow results from the introduction of rotation into the fluid behind shock waves. If we refer to Fig. 11.47 it is clear that, in the region *abd* of Fig. 11.50, there is no rotation, since the flow conditions are uniform throughout this region. Between points *b* and *c*, however, the shock intensity gradually diminishes to a negligible value owing to the action of the rarefaction wavelets emanating from corner *d*. The flow downstream from this segment of the shock wave is rotational, as is shown below.

The definition of rotation given in Art. 4.12 is

$$\text{Rotation} = \frac{V}{R} - \frac{\partial V}{\partial n}$$

where R is the radius of curvature of the streamline, and the normal direction n is considered positive toward
the center of curvature (Fig. 11.51).
Since the fluid is assumed frictionless
in this region and gravity is neglected,
Euler's differential equation for the
pressure change normal to the stream-
line [Eq. (4.4)] is valid: $(1/\rho)(\partial p/\partial n)$
$= - V^2/R$. Furthermore, the flow is
supposed to be adiabatic everywhere
and to be uniform upstream from
the body, so that the energy equation takes the form of Eq. (9.18):
$h + (V^2/2) = $ constant, or $(\partial h/\partial n)$
$+ V(\partial V/\partial n) = 0$. The expression for rotation thus becomes

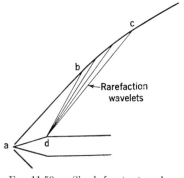

Fig. 11.50. — Shock front set up by a body with a wedge-shaped nose.

$$\text{Rotation} = \frac{1}{V}\left(-\frac{1}{\rho}\frac{\partial p}{\partial n} + \frac{\partial h}{\partial n}\right)$$

This equation can, however, be expressed in terms of the entropy change
normal to the streamlines, with the aid of Eq. (9.28), differentiation of
which leads to $T(\partial s/\partial n) = (\partial h/\partial n) - (1/\rho)(\partial p/\partial n)$. The rotation,
therefore, is

$$\text{Rotation} = \frac{T}{V}\frac{\partial s}{\partial n} \tag{11.68}$$

According to Eq. (11.68) there must be rotation downstream from segment
bc of the shock, because the entropy jump through
the shock is different for different streamlines.

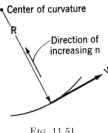

Fig. 11.51.

11.38. Hodograph Method. The theoretical
methods so far discussed yield solutions if the flow
is entirely subsonic or if it is entirely supersonic
but fail if the flow contains both sub- and supersonic regions. The equation of motion for a compressible fluid in the form of Eq. (11.48) is practically
impossible to handle because it is nonlinear. The
Russian mathematician Chaplyguine, however, dis-
covered that this equation becomes linear if expressed in terms of V and θ
as independent variables, instead of x and y. (See Art. 11.35 for the definition of V and θ.) The great advantage of a linear equation is that solu-

tions may be added to obtain another solution, so that a technique similar to that used for an incompressible fluid can be developed. This superposition method is limited to the V, θ (hodograph) plane in the case of a compressible fluid, and a great deal of labor is involved in the transfer of the solutions to the x,y (physical) plane. The differential analyzer has been used [8] to obtain certain solutions in the hodograph plane and to transfer them to the physical plane.

Perhaps the most important result of the limited investigations so far made by the hodograph method is the fact that a continuous transition from sub- to supersonic flow and back again is possible, at least in frictionless fluid. It may be, therefore, that an airfoil can in future be designed such that over part of its surface there is supersonic flow but a complete absence of shock waves. The critical speed of such an airfoil would be considerably nearer the sound velocity than that of the best sections developed to date (see Fig. 10.23). It is, of course, impossible to avoid shocks if the speed of the airfoil itself is supersonic.

11.39. Some Factors in High-speed Flight. The flow conditions on a thin wing in actual flight approximate to those assumed in the Glauert-Prandtl theory of small perturbations (Arts. 11.32 to 11.34). The results of this theory are useful in demonstrating the adverse changes in wing characteristics that occur, say, between the flight Mach numbers of 0.8 and 1.2. Such demonstration can be expected to be only a rough guide since both these values of M are fairly close to 1.

As a simple example, consider the changes in lift coefficient C_L of a thin flat plate. Potential theory of incompressible flow [2] yields the formula $C_L = 2\pi\delta$, for a small angle of incidence δ. The effect on C_L of compressibility at subsonic speeds is given by Eq. (11.58), from which we find, for $M = 0.8$, $C_L = 2\pi\delta/\sqrt{1 - 0.64} = 10.5\delta$. In the supersonic range, on the other hand, the flow pattern has changed completely, and C_L is obtained from Eq. (11.60). It is found, for $M = 1.2$, that $C_L = 4\delta/\sqrt{1.44 - 1} = 6.0\delta$.

The change in the drag coefficient is also adverse. In subsonic motion the only source of drag in a two-dimensional flow over a plate is the skin friction, and measurements indicate that C_D is approximately 0.01 under these conditions. In supersonic motion, on the other hand, there is an additional component of drag, which is given by Eq. (11.60a). For $M = 1.2$, the incremental drag coefficient is found to be $\Delta C_D = 4\delta^2/\sqrt{1.44 - 1} = 6.0\delta^2$. If, for example, $\delta = 2$ deg (0.04 radian), $\Delta C_D = 0.009$. The drag coefficient is thus approximately doubled in the supersonic flow.

In the immediate neighborhood of $M = 1$ the Glauert-Prandtl theory is inapplicable, but the experimental results shown in Figs. 10.24 and 11.36 demonstrate the extremely undesirable changes encountered in the transonic region.

It is apparent from these two-dimensional considerations that flight at
ransonic or supersonic speeds offers
many difficulties in connection with wing
lesign. These difficulties are moder-
ted, however, if a third-dimensional
omponent is introduced into the rela-
ive flow by use of a wing swept back at
n angle greater than the flight Mach
ngle. The basis for this improvement
s the fact that the wing characteristics
lepend primarily on the component of
low normal to the leading edge of the
ving. Thus, if the sweepback angle is
greater than the Mach angle, the normal
omponent is subsonic and the wing
haracteristics are nearly the same as
hose at this subsonic speed [11].

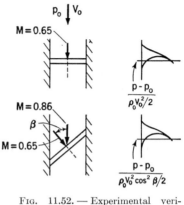

Fig. 11.52. — Experimental veri-
fication of the effect of sweep in a two-
dimensional flow. Pressure distribution
over mid-section depends only on normal
component of flow.

Consider a wing of infinite aspect
atio in a subsonic flow normal to the leading edge. It is evident, if fric-
ion be neglected, that motion of the wing parallel to its leading edge
will have no effect on the pattern of the
normal flow. The relative velocity of air and
wing can theoretically be given an arbitrarily
high value without effect on the wing characteristics. Experiments made under two-
dimensional conditions verify the theory, as
shown in Fig. 11.52. The pressure distribution along the chord of the normal wing is
seen to be practically the same as for the
swept-back wing, even though the Mach
numbers of the resultant flows are quite different.

The finite length of an actual wing will
modify this conclusion somewhat, owing not
only to the tip but also to the "wall effect"
of the fuselage. The latter effect is peculiar
to a swept-back wing and results from the
following phenomenon:

The resultant streamlines for an infinite
swept-back wing are not straight in the plan
view but are slightly curved, as shown in
Fig. 11.53. This bending results from the

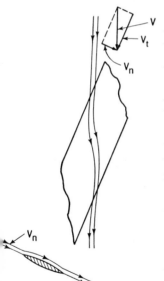

Fig. 11.53. — Streamlines near
swept-back wing in two-dimen-
ional flow. (*After Jones, refer-
nce 11.*)

uperposition of a constant velocity component V_t, parallel to the leading edge, and a variable component V_n, normal to the leading edge. The normal component V_n is slightly reduced near the leading and trailing edges and increased near the middle of the chord, as seen from the shape of the stream tube in the sectional view of Fig. 11.53. The introduction of a wall, such as a fuselage surface, parallel to the distant flow will thus result in a changed pressure distribution, since the streamlines are thereby constrained to be parallel to the wall.

Another effect of the finite length that tends to reduce the benefit from sweepback comes into play if the Mach angle approaches the sweepback angle. In this case an air particle is undisturbed by the wing until it has practically reached the leading edge, and the flow pattern over the forward part of the wing must differ from that in subsonic motion.

These unfavorable effects of the finite length are not of first importance, however, as is evident from the fact that at supercritical Mach numbers the drag coefficient for a wing swept back at a 45-deg angle may be less than half that of an unswept wing.

The effect of sweep on stability of a wing is also important. Although, at low speed, sweep may have an unfavorable influence, at high speed it is beneficial [12]. The characteristics of control surfaces at high speed are also improved by sweepback.

In summary, it may be said that the problem of transonic and supersonic flight may not be so formidable as might be expected from the purely two-dimensional considerations of previous articles. The study of three-dimensional compressible flow is just beginning, but it has already led to important practical developments [13].

SELECTED BIBLIOGRAPHY

General:

1. Ewald, P. P., Th. Pöschl, and L. Prandtl: "Physics of Solids and Fluids," 2d ed., Blackie & Son, Ltd., Glasgow, 1936.
2. Glauert, H.: "The Elements of Aerofoil and Airscrew Theory," Cambridge University Press, London, 1930.
3. Goldstein, S. (Editor): "Modern Developments in Fluid Dynamics," Vol. I, Oxford University Press, New York, 1938.
4. von Mises, R.: "Theory of Flight," McGraw-Hill Book Company, Inc., New York, 1945.
5. Rouse, Hunter: "Fluid Mechanics for Hydraulic Engineers," McGraw-Hill Book Company, Inc., New York, 1938.
5a. Cambridge University Aeronautical Laboratory: "Measurement of Profile Drag by the Pitot-traverse Method," R. and M. 1688, Aeronautical Research Committee, London, 1936.

Compressible Flow:

6. Emmons, H. W.: Shock Waves in Aerodynamics, *J. Aeronaut. Sci.*, vol. 12, no. 2, pp. 188–194, April, 1945.

7. KÁRMÁN, TH. VON: Compressibility Effects in Aerodynamics, *J. Aeronaut. Sci.*, vol. 8, no. 9, pp. 337–356, July, 1941.

8. KRAFT, H., and C. G. DIBBLE: Some Two-dimensional Adiabatic Compressible Flow Patterns, *J. Aeronaut. Sci.*, vol. 11, no. 4, pp. 283–298, October, 1944.

9. TAYLOR, G. I., and J. W. MACCOLL: The Mechanics of Compressible Fluids, in "Aerodynamic Theory," Vol. III (edited by W. F. Durand) Verlag Julius Springer, Berlin, 1935.

0. JACOBS, E. N.: "Preliminary Report on Laminar-flow Airfoils and New Methods Adopted for Airfoil and Boundary-layer Investigation," *NACA Rept.*, June, 1939.

1. JONES, R. T.: "Wing Plan Forms for High-speed Flight," *NACA Tech. Note* 1033, March, 1946.

2. SOULÉ, H. A.: "Influence of Large Amounts of Wing Sweep on Stability and Control Problems of Aircraft," *NACA Tech. Note* 1088, June, 1946.

3. KÁRMÁN, TH. VON: Supersonic Aerodynamics, J. Aeronaut. Sci., vol. 14, no. 7, pp. 373–402, July, 1947.

CHAPTER XII

HYDRODYNAMIC LUBRICATION

12.1. Introduction. All machinery depends for its useful operation on slippery surfaces between moving parts. The limitation on our ability to maintain slippery surfaces has always constituted an effective bar to materially higher performance. The difficulty of lubricating the hot pistons of high-powered airplane engines now limits their output, and one of the apparent advantages of the combustion gas turbine is the elimination of this restraint.

From long experience with oils and greases the term "oiliness" has come into use to indicate the slippery quality of a lubricant on a smooth surface, although no single physical property of the lubricant to measure oiliness has ever been found. It is obvious that, while maple sirup may resemble a mineral oil in appearance, it certainly does not resemble it in oiliness.

Perfect lubrication presupposes the presence of a fluid completely separating the rubbing parts and substituting fluid friction for solid friction. Perfect lubrication, therefore, becomes a matter of fluid mechanics and is often referred to as hydrodynamic lubrication. Since the solid parts do not touch, there can be no wear, and the viscosity of the fluid determines the friction. It will be shown that no oiliness consideration is required by the theory and that in special cases water or even air may afford perfect lubrication.

Hydrodynamic lubrication cannot occur if the rubbing surfaces are pressed too tightly together, as when a machine has to be started from rest. The bulk of the fluid lubricant is squeezed out in such a case and only an adherent surface film remains. This film may be only a few molecules thick but can still prevent seizure and permit sliding. The adherent film of lubricant is bound to the metal by molecular forces of great intensity and has evidently lost its fluid properties.

Under very severe conditions even the adsorbed film may be burned or scraped off. In such cases the dry friction of the metal surfaces may be avoided by the use of a solid lubricant that shears easily, such as graphite, or a chemically formed coating such as an oxide or sulfide of the metal of one of the rubbing surfaces.

Severe conditions under which perfect lubrication is impossible are classed as conditions of imperfect or boundary lubrication, and the properties of the metal surfaces in relation to the physical and chemical properties of the lubricant become of primary importance.

The limiting case of no lubricant at all implies the occurrence of dry friction and failure of the bearing. Wear, galling, and seizure are associated with dry friction. Whether or not a bearing is easily destroyed by partial or temporary failure of the lubrication has been found to depend on the combination of metals paired in the design.

Boundary lubrication is intimately concerned with the nature of the rubbing surfaces and of the lubricant, while perfect lubrication is concerned primarily with the viscosity of the lubricant. However, as a practical matter, a bearing operates sometimes under conditions of perfect lubrication and at other times under conditions of boundary lubrication. Furthermore, practical bearing surfaces are only technically smooth, clearance and alignment are not exact, the lubricant may contain abrasive dirt, and the lubricant may oxidize and change in character at high temperature. Many practical considerations combine to limit the period of perfect lubrication and to incite failure. As a result of long experience, certain metals have been found suitable for use in bearings, and other substances— fluids, plastics, and solids—have been found suitable for use as lubricants with them.

The use of ball and roller bearings avoids some of the complications of the lubrication art but introduces other difficulties inherent in high-pressure rolling contact. Rollers and balls in effect take the place of a lubricant by separating the rubbing surfaces.

12.2. Historical. The art of lubrication is at least as ancient as the greasing of Egyptian chariot wheels and axles with tallow. The launching ways of shipbuilders were greased with animal fats until very recent times. Lard oil is still used in machine shops as a "cutting" fluid to lubricate the chip coming off the tool point. Sperm oil is still highly prized by clockmakers. The early airplane engines required castor oil as a lubricant, and it was not until 1918 that the American Liberty engine demonstrated that mineral oil could be successfully employed under severe operating conditions. These references to animal and vegetable oils with good oiliness characteristics imply an empirical art in which bearing design evolved slowly with the machinery for which lubrication was essential.

The ideal, or perfect, lubrication by which moving parts are completely separated by a fluid film is a recent concept and is associated exclusively with smooth, accurate parts, continuous motion, and high speeds. In other words, the concept is associated with modern machinery.

The axle of a heavy wagon is rough and loosely fitted; the motion is slow; stopping and starting are frequent. Any lubricating fluid would be squeezed out. The case is obviously one of imperfect lubrication, and a stiff grease or even wet clay could be more effective than an oil. The pressure at the point of the cutting tool of a lathe or at the bit of a drill press is too great to permit a fluid film to separate the cutting tool from the metal being cut. The early airplane engines already mentioned ran too hot, had inadequate bearings, and consequently suffered from imperfect lubrication. Castor oil, having superior oiliness characteristics, established tolerable boundary lubrication for a short time and helped out a defective design.

The concept of perfect lubrication evolved at about the same time, but independently, in England and Russia. Beauchamp Tower conducted

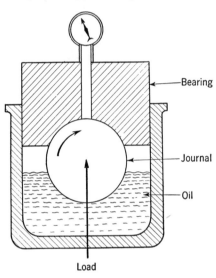

experiments to determine the friction of the journal of a railway-car wheel. Such a journal runs in a partial bearing pressing down from above and is supplied with lubricant by a wick or pad of waste which wipes against the journal as it turns. Tower obtained erratic results until he ran the journal in an oil bath, so ensuring a copious supply of lubricant (see Fig. 12.1). Then he observed a stream of oil being discharged from an oilhole in the top bearing. The journal and bearing acted as a pump, and attempts to hold a plug in the oilhole indicated a very high pressure. Tower drilled other holes through the upper bearing and measured the distribution of pressure in the oil

Fig. 12.1. — Schematic diagram of Beauchamp Tower's apparatus for detecting high pressure in a partial journal bearing.

between journal and bearing, reporting his results to the British Institution of Mechanical Engineers in 1885.

Professor Osborne Reynolds of the University of Manchester reported in the next year the results of his analysis of Tower's experiments. He showed that application of the principles of fluid mechanics would account for the pressures observed by Tower. His analysis was formulated as a differential equation requiring as parameters only the viscosity of the lubricant, the speed of rotation, and the dimensions. Reynolds in this paper really established the modern theory of perfect lubrication although its significance was not recognized until much later.

About this same time N. Petroff in Russia was experimenting with bearings lubricated with mineral oil from the newly opened Russian oil fields. A paper in the *St. Petersburg Engineering Journal* for 1883 indicated that Petroff also had the modern concept of perfect lubrication by means of a separating fluid film. He explained how the friction of the bearing could be entirely accounted for by shearing forces in the viscous film of lubricant.

Petroff established fluid shear as the source of frictional resistance to rotation in the form of an equation involving viscosity, speed, and the dimensions. Reynolds proved that the pressures depended on the same parameters. Reynolds's name is recalled in the Reynolds number, the non-dimensional criterion of dynamical similitude in fluid motion. Petroff is remembered by the Petroff equation for the coefficient of friction of a journal bearing.

Reynolds's theory of the journal bearing was subsequently further developed by Sommerfeld in Germany in 1904. His name is preserved in the "Sommerfeld parameter," which will later be shown to control the performance of similar bearings. Michell of Australia and Kingsbury of New Hampshire State College independently extended Reynolds's theory of the pressure-sustaining property of a converging oil film to the design of thrust bearings. A plane bearing surface was divided into separate segments, or shoes, each free to adjust itself to a small angle of inclination to the opposite rubbing surface. Because of the pressure developed in the wedges of oil so formed, metal-to-metal contact was prevented, and a large thrust load could be transmitted. These pivoted-shoe thrust bearings are necessary for large hydroelectric and marine power plants.

The theory of perfect lubrication may be considered to be in a very satisfactory state. Engineers can design bearings with full confidence in their predicted performance under specified conditions. Unfortunately, the same assertion cannot be made for boundary lubrication. Here the phenomena are much more complicated: properties of the oil other than viscosity are involved, as well as the physical and chemical condition of the surfaces.

12.3. Properties of Lubricants. Oils and greases are the most widely used lubricants. While viscosity is the most important single property involved in lubrication, in engineering applications many other properties, both physical and chemical, become important under special conditions. A voluminous literature exists regarding the specification and testing of the various properties of lubricants, but only brief mention of their nature need be made here.

12.4. Viscosity. For a fluid lubricant of Newtonian characteristics shear stress τ is directly proportional to rate of shear, that is,

$$\tau = \mu \frac{\partial u}{\partial y}$$

where μ is the coefficient of viscosity (or simply viscosity), u is relative velocity in the direction parallel to the sliding surfaces, and y is measured across the fluid film. Experiments both with bearings and with flow through capillaries indicate that Newton's law may safely be relied on for bearing design both with fatty and with mineral oils in liquid state.

Furthermore, there is abundant evidence that there is no slip between the fluid and the solid surfaces at the boundary. For extreme cold or extreme pressure, however, oils may solidify and in such condition do not behave as true fluids.

Viscosity can be measured by determining the rate of flow through a capillary tube and using Poiseuille's formula [Eq. (8.16)]. Another method is to measure the force required to rotate a cylinder mounted concentrically within an outer cylindrical shell, the space between being filled with oil. From the measured force and the rate of shear, which is known from the relative velocity and the clearance between the cylinders, viscosity can be calculated.

Common commercial practice in this country expresses the viscosity of an oil in "Saybolt universal seconds," meaning the time taken for a standard volume of liquid to flow out through the short tube of the standard Saybolt instrument. Such a measure of viscosity may be useful in purchasing oil but for engineering purposes has to be converted to absolute viscosity by means of tables.

The poise is the cgs unit of viscosity, named for Poiseuille, and is the viscosity of a fluid maintaining a shearing stress of 1 dyne per sq cm for a rate of shear of 1 cm per sec per cm thickness. The poise is thus equivalent to 1 dyne-sec per sq cm. The centipoise is one-hundredth of the cgs unit. In this country, the usual engineering unit is named after Reynolds; it is called a "reyn" and is equivalent to 1 lb-sec per sq in.

Hersey [7] gives the following conversion table:

VISCOSITY UNITS

1 poise, or dyne-sec/cm^2 = 1.02×10^{-2} kg-sec/m^2
1 poise, or dyne-sec/cm^2 = 2.09×10^{-3} lb-sec/ft^2
1 poise, or dyne-sec/cm^2 = 1.45×10^{-5} lb-sec/in.^{2}
1 poise, or dyne-sec/cm^2 = 2.42×10^{-7} lb-min/in.^{2}

1 kg-sec/m^2 =	98 poises
1 lb-sec/ft^2 =	479 poises
1 lb-sec/in.^{2} =	69,000 poises
1 lb-min/in.^{2} =	4,140,000 poises

The viscosity of a gas rises slowly with increasing temperature, about as the four-fifths power of the absolute temperature. The viscosity of the common lubricating oils, like that of most liquids, falls rapidly with rising temperature and may be approximately expressed by the formula

$$\mu = \mu_0 e^{b/(T+\theta)}$$

where T is temperature and b and θ are empirical constants. θ has been found to be nearly constant for most lubricating oils.

The degree to which the viscosity depends on temperature is called the "viscosity index" (V.I.) of the oil. Oils from Pennsylvania crudes, which show the smallest change with temperature, have been arbitrarily assigned a V.I. of 100, and those from California crudes, which show the greatest change, have a V.I. of zero. This scale has little physical significance, as additives often raise this index above 100. A high V.I. is desirable for machinery that must be started cold and is especially necessary for the working fluid of hydraulic control systems exposed to extreme ranges of temperature.

The dependence of viscosity on pressure is given by the equation

$$\mu = \mu_T e^{cp}$$

where p is the gauge pressure, μ_T is the viscosity at temperature T and atmospheric pressure ($p = 0$), and c is an empirical constant. This increase becomes appreciable at pressures greater than 1,000 lb per sq in. At a sufficiently high pressure the oil solidifies. The pressure at which this occurs for a given oil depends on the temperature. At atmospheric pressure the temperature at which solidification occurs is called the "pour point" of the oil. The effect of both temperature and pressure is more pronounced on the viscosity of mineral than fatty oils, but the fatty oils solidify more readily.

12.5. Density. The density of an oil has no direct influence on its lubricating value, but experience has indicated that, for oils made by similar methods from similar stock, viscosity increases with density. Hence there has grown up a popular classification by density of so-called "heavy" and "light" oils, although it is possible for two oils of the same density to be of substantially different viscosity.

Each industry that uses hydrometers to measure specific gravity generally devises some convenient but arbitrary scale. The petroleum industry has in the past used two so-called "Baumé scales" for liquids lighter than water but standardized in 1921 on the American Petroleum Institute (API) scale, defined by the relation

$$\text{Deg API} = \frac{141.5}{\text{specific gravity at } 60/60 \text{ F}} - 131.5$$

Degrees API are equivalent to a uniform scale of specific volume. Specific gravity is here defined as the ratio of the density of oil at 60 F to the density of water at 60 F as indicated by the symbol 60/60 F.

12.6. Acidity. The chemical test for acidity is of use to the lubrication engineer to detect deterioration of oil or to detect the presence of fatty acids as addition agents. Fatty acids in very small concentrations may be desirable for certain applications to increase oiliness but in general are dangerous in causing corrosion, sludges, and emulsions. At high temperatures the oiliness gain may be lost and several bad effects exaggerated. The acidity of a fatty oil will increase with decomposition at high temperature. The standard ASTM test rates acid content by a "neutralization number."

12.7. Oxidation. There is no generally accepted standard for testing the oxidizing characteristics of an oil, and recourse is usually had to testing in the actual machine for which it is intended. Carbon, gum, and varnish deposits are likely to be found in all types of internal-combustion engines where the oil is in contact with air at high temperature.

12.8. Flash Point. Though usually of no effect on lubricating value, the flash point is often cited as a characteristic of an oil. It is the temperature at which a flash appears when a test flame is placed near the surface of oil in an open vessel. It measures the degree to which light petroleum fractions have been removed in refining and should never be less than 300 F.

12.9. Emulsification. Tests of emulsification indicate the time required for an emulsion of oil and water to separate. Emulsions are undesirable for general lubrication as they retain dirt, interfere with circulation, and promote corrosion. However, for metal cutting, emulsions may be of advantage because their water content gives them a relatively large specific heat.

12.10. Foaming. Entrainment of air bubbles, bubbles of gas coming out of solution, and bubbles of water vapor may appear at high temperature and low pressure. Foaming is an especially dangerous phenomenon for airplane engines at high altitudes. The designer of the lubricating system must provide against entrainment of air and for the segregation of foam. Water in the oil tends both to increase the volume of foam and to stabilize the bubbles.

A "foam meter" is an apparatus to convert a sample of oil to foam and to note its rate of collapse. Antifoaming chemicals are frequently added to lubricating oils to cause segregated froth to collapse and submerged bubbles to coalesce. Such chemicals are generally ineffective above 212 F.

12.11. Specific Heat. This property is important in cooling a bearing by means of oil circulating through it. The specific heat of lubricating oil is about 0.45 times that of water.

The specific heat of petroleum oils, given in the following Bureau of Standards table, is calculated from the equation

$$c = \frac{1}{\sqrt{d}} (0.388 + 0.00045T)$$

in which c is the specific heat in Btu per pound per degree Fahrenheit, d is the specific gravity at 60/60 F, and T is temperature in degrees Fahrenheit. This formula does not take into account latent heat of fusion, vaporization, or reaction (cracking).

SPECIFIC HEAT OF PETROLEUM OILS

(Btu/lb deg F)

Temperature, deg F	Deg API at 60 F							
	10	20	30	40	50	60	70	80
	Specific gravity at 60/60 F							
	1.000	0.934	0.876	0.825	0.780	0.739	0.702	0.670
0	0.388	0.401	0.415	0.427	0.439	0.451	0.463	0.474
100	0.433	0.448	0.463	0.477	0.490	0.504	0.517	0.529
200	0.478	0.495	0.511	0.526	0.541	0.556	0.570	0.584
300	0.523	0.541	0.559	0.576	0.592	0.609	0.624	
400	0.568	0.588	0.607	0.625	0.643	0.661		
500	0.613	0.634	0.655	0.675	0.694			
600	0.658	0.681	0.703	0.724				
700	0.703	0.727	0.751					
800	0.748	0.774	0.799					

12.12. Thermal Conductivity. Experimental data on thermal conductivity of petroleum liquids are represented approximately by the following equation:

$$K = \frac{0.813}{d}[1 - 0.0003(T - 32)]$$

in which K is the thermal conductivity in Btu per hour per square foot per degree Fahrenheit per inch, d is the specific gravity of liquid at 60/60 F, and T is temperature in degrees Fahrenheit.

THERMAL CONDUCTIVITY OF PETROLEUM OILS

(Btu in./hr ft² deg F)

Temperature, deg F	Liquids						Solids	
	Deg API at 60 F						Asphalt	Wax
	10	20	30	40	50	60		
	Specific gravity at 60/60 F							
	1.000	0.934	0.876	0.825	0.780	0.739		
0	0.82	0.88	0.94	1.00	1.05	1.11	1.2	1.6
200	0.77	0.83	0.88	0.94	0.99	1.05	For temperature range	
400	0.72	0.77	0.83	0.88	0.93	0.98	from 32 F to melting	
600	0.67	0.72	0.77	0.82			point	

12.13. Perfect Lubrication. Assume two sliding surfaces separated by a film of fluid lubricant. The motion of the fluid can be considered laminar because, although the speeds involved may be high, the thickness of the film is very small. The Reynolds number for the system stays well below the critical value. In this discussion we assume the usual boundary condition in fluid mechanics, that the relative velocity of the fluid adjacent to

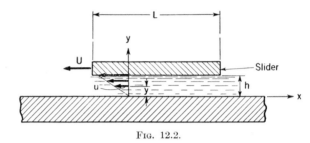

Fig. 12.2.

either solid surface is zero. We also assume the fluid to be incompressible, continuous, and of viscosity defined by the Newtonian relation

$$\tau = \mu\,\frac{\partial u}{\partial y}$$

Consider first the physical aspects of the problem. Let a flat slider, or slipper, of length L and width B slide on a much larger flat surface upon which is spread a copious supply of fluid lubricant as indicated in Fig. 12.2. If the two surfaces are parallel, the shear stress in the lubricant is

$$\tau = \mu\,\frac{\partial u}{\partial y} = \mu\,\frac{U}{h}$$

since experiment shows that the velocity is a linear function of y. Then the absolute value of the shearing force or friction force on the slipper will be

$$F = \tau BL = \mu\,\frac{U}{h}\,BL$$

If the two surfaces are parallel, the system will support no transverse load, since it can be shown that the pressure everywhere in the oil film equals atmospheric pressure. If, however, the surfaces are inclined to each other as shown in Fig. 12.3, a pressure is built up in the film by the motion. The upward force due to this pressure balances the normal load applied to the slider.

If the supported load W is to be large, it is necessary that the slider be wide (B/L large) to minimize the pressure-relieving effect of leakage of fluid at the sides. It is also necessary that the minimum thickness of the film be small. It is obvious that, for a given speed and fluid, the upper limit of W will be reached when the slider is pressed down to make h

vanish. Then there will be metal-to-metal contact at high spots of the plate by the heel of the slider, and imperfect lubrication with attendant wear and risk of seizure.

The velocity of the slider should be high, in order to develop sufficient pressure to support the load. In starting from rest a condition of boundary lubrication obtains until the slider reaches some minimum velocity.

It is also reasonable to conclude that high viscosity will impede the

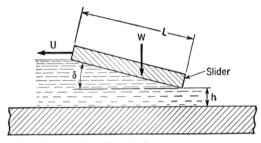

Fig. 12.3.

escape of fluid from beneath the slider and so contribute to the development of pressure in the wedge-shaped film of lubricant. Furthermore, the angle of inclination δ and the length L must play a direct part in the determination of the amount of load that can be supported.

The density of the fluid is known to be of first-order importance in the dynamic lift of airplane wings or turbine blades, but in the case of a slider inclined at a small angle and moving on a wedge-shaped film of oil the inertia effects are negligible. Density, therefore, plays no part in these phenomena.

From this consideration of the physical aspects of the problem we may name the independent variables as L, B, δ, U, μ, and h, with W as a dependent variable whose magnitude is determined by a particular set of values for the six independent quantities. Thus

$$W = \phi_1(U,B,\mu,\delta,L,h)$$

The Π theorem shows that this equation is equivalent to one involving four dimensionless products of the above variables, since there are three primary quantities. These products, or Π's, can be chosen in any way, provided only that they are independent of one another.

Let

$$\Pi_1 = \frac{\mu U L}{W}$$

$$\Pi_2 = \frac{h}{L}$$

$$\text{II}_3 = \delta$$

$$\text{II}_4 = \frac{B}{L}$$

Then

$$\frac{\mu U L}{W} = \phi_2\left(\frac{h}{L}, \delta, \frac{B}{L}\right) \tag{12.1}$$

The maximum load that can be carried safely by a bearing is of paramount importance. Equation (12.1) enables us to discuss this matter in a qualitative way. For given values of δ and B/L, $\mu U L/W$ is determined by the value of h/L. For geometrically plane surfaces, h might theoretically decrease to zero, but in actual practice there is a lower limit to h that is governed by the roughness of the surfaces and the probable size of grit and other adventitious solid particles in the lubricant. If these particles cannot pass out under the trailing edge, they will collect under the rider and score the surfaces.

This minimum value of h/L determines some corresponding minimum value of $\mu U L/W$ that, for a given slider and oil, determines a maximum value of W. This is the load capacity of the lubricated system and is of great practical importance in all design work. Since the minimum value of $\mu U L/W$ is fixed, we see that, if either viscosity or speed is doubled, the load capacity is also doubled.

If δ is increased for given h/L and B/L, the ratio of the entrance cross section to exit cross section for the oil is increased and more oil tends to collect under the slider with a resultant increase in oil pressure and load capacity.

Finally, if the slider is made quite narrow (B/L small) with δ and h/L fixed, more of the lubricant escapes from the sides and the oil pressure is decreased. This reduces the load capacity.

We have so far assumed that δ, the angle of inclination, can be fixed at will. But since δ must be small and consequently difficult to maintain accurately in practice, it is customary to pivot the slider on its support and allow it to take its own inclination. It is shown in Art. 12.16 that a pivoted slider is inherently stable.

Another point of interest in connection with a bearing is the size of the friction force. Let F be the friction force between the fluid and the supporting lower surface, when W is the total transverse load applied across the fluid film. The conventional coefficient of friction is defined as

$$f = \frac{F}{W}$$

The concept of the friction coefficient has been carried over from the study of dry friction between two solid bodies, where it has long been known that f is essentially independent of the load and speed.   Actually in fluid friction f is independent of neither.   It has little fundamental signifi-cance, but long usage has made it the commonly accepted measure of performance.

We now consider f as the dependent variable and, as before, take L, B, δ, U, μ, and h as independent variables.   Then

$$f = \phi_3(L,B,\delta,U,\mu,h)$$

Inspection shows that no dimensionless product can be formed with μ or U in combination with any of the other variables.   The Π theorem therefore leads to

$$f = \phi_4\left(\frac{h}{L}, \delta, \frac{B}{L}\right) \qquad (12.2)$$

If the flow is assumed to be two dimensional, $i.e.$, if side leakage is neglected, B has no influence on f and Eq. (12.2) becomes

$$f = \phi_4\left(\frac{h}{L}, \delta\right) \qquad (12.3)$$

We shall see later what form is taken by the undetermined function ϕ_4, but the dimensional reasoning shows that the coefficient of friction for a

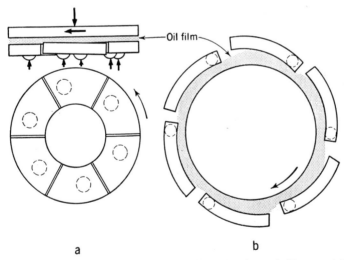

a   b

FIG. 12.4. — Schematic drawing of (a) segmental thrust bearing and (b) segmental journal bearing.

family of geometrically similar bearings (h/L, B/L constant) depends only on the inclination of the slider and is independent of speed and the kind of oil used.

A thrust bearing is designed to take an axial load on a rotating shaft. In its primitive form it consists merely of a flat plate pressing against the squared end of the shaft. Since the moving surfaces are parallel, the formation of a wedge of lubricant is impossible and the load capacity is very low. In the bearings of Michell and Kingsbury the thrust plate is cut up into segments each of which is pivoted so that it can tilt as shown in Fig. 12.4a. In this way a fluid wedge is formed under each segment as discussed in the case of the plane slider, and the load capacity of the bearing is increased many times. The same principle can also be applied to journal bearings as shown in Fig. 12.4b for unidirectional motion. Bearings can be designed so that the pivot shifts as the direction of rotation is changed.

12.14. Reynolds's Pressure Distribution. A clearer appreciation of how pressure is produced in a wedge-shaped film of fluid under the action

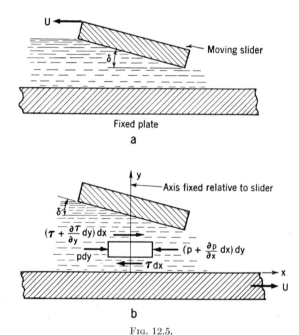

Fig. 12.5.

of viscous shear forces may be gained by a discussion of the fluid mechanics involved.

Figure 12.5 represents a slipper bearing for the two-dimensional case. It is assumed that the angle of inclination δ is small. The lubricant is a viscous incompressible fluid in laminar flow. Figure 12.5a shows the slider moving with a steady velocity U toward the left and the base plate fixed. In Fig. 12.5b the slider is at rest, and the base plate is moving toward the right with velocity U. Though the slider may actually be the moving element, it is more convenient for purposes of analysis to consider the motion relative to the slider as shown in Fig. 12.5b. Newton's laws can be applied in the usual form to the relative motion because U is a constant velocity.

In Fig. 12.5b is shown an element of fluid of dimensions dx, dy and of unit depth normal to the x,y plane. The x forces on the element are as indicated. It can be shown that, since δ is a small angle, the pressure is independent of y and the inertia effects are negligible. Consequently, $\partial p/\partial x = dp/dx$, and the sum of the x forces is zero. The statement of the latter relation is

$$p \, dy - \left(p + \frac{dp}{dx} \, dx\right) dy = \tau \, dx - \left(\tau + \frac{\partial \tau}{\partial y} \, dy\right) dx$$

or

$$\frac{dp}{dx} = \frac{\partial \tau}{\partial y} \tag{12.4}$$

Substituting for τ from the Newtonian definition of viscosity

$$\tau = \mu \frac{\partial u}{\partial y} \tag{12.5}$$

we obtain

$$\frac{dp}{dx} = \mu \frac{\partial^2 u}{\partial y^2} \tag{12.6}$$

On integration, Eq. (12.6) becomes

$$\frac{\partial u}{\partial y} = \frac{1}{\mu} \frac{dp}{dx} y + f_1(x) \tag{12.7}$$

and

$$u = \frac{1}{2\mu} \frac{dp}{dx} y^2 + y f_1(x) + f_2(x) \tag{12.8}$$

where f_1 and f_2 are functions that can be evaluated from the boundary conditions $u = U$ when $y = 0$ and $u = 0$ when $y = h$. The quantity h is the thickness of the film at x. Then $f_2 = U$, $f_1 = -(h/2\mu)(dp/dx) - (U/h)$, and

$$u = \frac{1}{2\mu} \frac{dp}{dx} (y - h)y + U \frac{(h - y)}{h} \tag{12.9}$$

The velocity at any point y in a cross section of the oil film at x is seen to consist of two terms, and we may therefore consider the velocity u of Eq. (12.9) to be made up of two components, u_1 and u_2, such that

$$\left. \begin{aligned} u_1 &= \frac{1}{2\mu} \frac{dp}{dx} (y - h)y \\ u_2 &= U \frac{(h - y)}{h} \end{aligned} \right\} \tag{12.9a}$$

The first term u_1 represents a parabolic distribution of velocity as shown in Fig. 12.6a. Note that the velocity u_1 is zero for $y = 0$ or $y = h$.

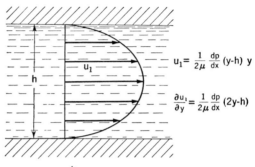

$$u_1 = \frac{1}{2\mu} \frac{dp}{dx} (y-h) \, y$$

$$\frac{\partial u_1}{\partial y} = \frac{1}{2\mu} \frac{dp}{dx} (2y-h)$$

$\frac{dp}{dx}$ is assumed negative in the figure

a

FIG. 12.6a. — Parabolic velocity distribution for laminar pressure flow between fixed parallel planes.

and the flow pattern is that which would occur between stationary parallel surfaces in response to a pressure gradient dp/dx falling along the direction of the x axis.

The second term u_2 represents a linear distribution of velocity such as would occur in a layer of fluid between two parallel surfaces separated by a distance h and moving relative to each other with velocity U as indicated in Fig. 12.6b.

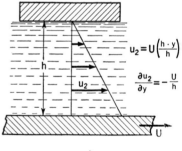

$$u_2 = U\left(\frac{h \cdot y}{h}\right)$$

$$\frac{\partial u_2}{\partial y} = -\frac{U}{h}$$

Let Q represent the volume rate of flow per unit width of slider. Then, from continuity, Q is the same at all cross sections. By using Eq. (12.9), we can express Q as follows:

FIG. 12.6b. — Linear velocity distribution for laminar flow at constant pressure between parallel planes, one fixed and one moving.

$$Q = \int_0^h u \, dy = \frac{Uh}{2} - \frac{h^3}{12\mu} \frac{dp}{dx} \quad (12.10)$$

We thus obtain a form of Reynolds's fundamental equation for the pressure gradient,

$$\frac{dp}{dx} = 6\mu U \left(\frac{1}{h^2} - \frac{2Q}{h^3 U}\right) = 6\mu U \left(\frac{1}{h^2} - \frac{k_1}{h^3}\right) \quad (12.10a)$$

Another form of this result, which is useful in some applications, is obtained by computing dQ/dx from Eq. (12.10a) and setting it equal to zero by virtue of continuity.

$$\frac{d}{dx}\left(\frac{h^3}{\mu}\frac{dp}{dx}\right) = 6\frac{d}{dx}(Uh) \qquad (12.10b)$$

The constant $k_1 = 2Q/U$ of Eq. (12.10a) can be evaluated, after an integration, from the fact that the pressures at entrance and exit are atmospheric. Note that the pressure gradient depends only on the viscosity of the lubricant μ, the speed of the slider U, and the thickness of the film h. This equation was derived without any assumption as to the shape of the surface of the slider, and, as we shall see in Art. 12.22, this equation can be applied to the developed oil film in a journal bearing.

Equation (12.10a) cannot be integrated until h is expressed as a function of x. To accomplish this in the present case the surface of the slider is taken as a plane. Let h_1 represent the film thickness under the toe, or

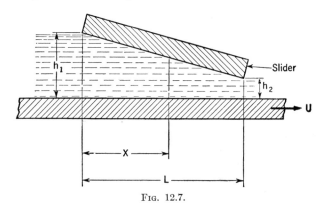

FIG. 12.7.

entrance, and h_2 the film thickness under the heel, or exit, from the slider. Let the slider be of length L in the direction of motion, and let x be measured in the direction of motion as shown in Fig. 12.7.

The film thickness h is obviously a linear function of x, with the inclination of the slider as the determining parameter. Using the method of Norton * we may write

$$h = h_1 - \frac{x}{L}(h_1 - h_2)$$

It is convenient to use, in place of x, a length coefficient $l = x/L$ such that at the toe of the slider $l = 0$ and at the heel $l = 1$. Similarly, a non-dimensional slope coefficient $s = h_1/h_2$ determines the inclination of a slider of given length. Changing the notation to correspond, one finds $h = h_2(s - sl + l)$.

Substitution of the above expression for h and Ll for x in Eq. (12.10a) yields

* See p. 72 of reference 8 of the bibliography at the end of the chapter.

$$\frac{dp}{dl} = \frac{6\mu UL}{h_2^2}\left[\frac{1}{(s - sl + l)^2} - \frac{k_1}{h_2(s - sl + l)^3}\right] \tag{12.11}$$

Integration with respect to l along the length of the slider gives

$$p = \frac{6\mu UL}{h_2^2}\left[\int_0^l \frac{dl}{(s - sl + l)^2} - \frac{k_1}{h_2}\int_0^l \frac{dl}{(s - sl + l)^3}\right]$$

and

$$p = \frac{6\mu UL}{h_2^2}\left[\frac{-1}{(1 - s)(s - sl + l)} + \frac{k_1}{2h_2(1 - s)(s - sl + l)^2}\right] + k_2$$

The constants of integration, which are determined from the condition

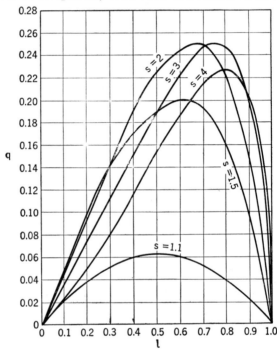

Fig. 12.8. — Theoretical pressure-distribution curves for a slipper bearing. (*After Norton*, *reference* 8.)

that $p - p_0 = 0$ ($p_0 = $ atmospheric pressure) when $l = 0$ or 1, are

$$k_1 = \frac{2s}{s + 1}h_2 \qquad k_2 = \frac{6\mu UL}{h_2^2}\frac{1}{1 - s^2} + p_0$$

Substitution of the constants leads to

$$p - p_0 = \frac{\mu UL}{h_2^2}q \tag{12.12}$$

where

$$q = \frac{6(s - 1)(1 - l)l}{(s + 1)(s - sl + l)^2} \tag{12.13}$$

The quantity $\mu U L / h_2^2$ has the dimensions of pressure, and q is a non-dimensional function called the "pressure function."

It is important to observe that, at the toe and heel of the slipper where $= 0$ and $l = 1$, the pressure function $q = 0$. The pressure function also becomes zero when $s = 1$, indicating as would be expected that the pressure is atmospheric throughout the film when there is no inclination of the slipper.

It remains to consider how the fluid pressure is distributed in such a manner that a transverse load can be supported. The point of maximum pressure can be found by setting $dp/dx = 0$. With the nondimensional notation used before we find that this point is at

$$l_{\max} = \frac{s}{s+1} \tag{12.13a}$$

and, substituting this in Eq. (12.12),

$$p_{\max} - p_0 = \frac{\mu U L}{h_2^2} \left[\frac{1.5(s-1)}{s(s+1)} \right] \tag{12.14}$$

The distribution of pressure as given by Eq. (12.13) is shown by the computed values of the pressure function q plotted in Fig. 12.8.

12.15. Bearing Load. Any transverse load carried by the slider must be borne by hydrostatic pressure in the fluid film. Since the inclination of the slider is small, the external load can be equated to the total normal force on its surface. For a longitudinal section of unit width the total load will be

$$W = \int_0^L p \, dx = L \int_0^1 p \, dl$$

By using Eq. (12.12) for p and integrating, we find

$$W = \frac{\mu U L^2}{h_2^2} C_w \tag{12.15}$$

where

$$C_w = \frac{6}{(s-1)^2} \left[\ln s - \frac{2(s-1)}{(s+1)} \right] \tag{12.16}$$

Both W and the quantity $\mu U L^2 / h_2^2$ have the dimensions of force per unit of width, while C_w is a nondimensional load factor. It is to be noted that for a given bearing the load factor depends entirely on the inclination, and where $s = 1$ no load is supported by hydrostatic pressure.

12.16. Center of Pressure. For a practical bearing it is necessary to support the slider by means of a pivot located somewhat behind the center of pressure, in order that the slider may adjust itself to an inclination appropriate to the given values of W, μ, U, L, h_2.

Using the notation of Fig. 12.7, let x_1 be the distance of the center of pressure from the toe of the slider. Take moments about the origin, and get $x_1 W = \int_0^L xp\, dx$. Substitution of the value of p from Eq. (12.12) and W from Eq. (12.15), a straightforward manipulation, which need not be detailed here, yields $x_1 = LC_p$, where C_p represents a nondimensional support factor that is found to be a function of slider inclination alone. Calculation of C_p for a series of values of the inclination $s = h_1/h_2$ discloses that the center of pressure lies behind the mid-point of the slider and moves to the rear as the inclination is increased, as indicated in the following table:

$\dfrac{h_1}{h_2}$	1	2	3	4	5	Ratio of film thickness at entrance to thickness at exit
C_p	0.50	0.56	0.61	0.64	0.66	Center of pressure, % of slider length from toe

It is fortunate that the center of pressure shifts to the rear as the inclination is increased since this makes for stability. For example, suppose the pivot placed at the 56 per cent point to balance the estimated load with $h_1/h_2 = 2$. If the slider turned to a greater inclination, say to $h_1/h_2 = 3$, the center of pressure would move back to the 61 per cent point, giving a moment about the pivot tending to reduce the inclination. Correspondingly, any decrease of inclination from the equilibrium position for $h_1/h_2 = 2$ would cause the center of pressure to move ahead of the pivot and to restore the designed inclination.

12.17. Frictional Force. The force necessary to move the plate along under the slider is equal to the friction of the fluid on its wetted surface, or

$$F = \int_0^L \tau_0\, dx \qquad (12.17)$$

where F is the frictional force on the plate per unit width and τ_0 is the shear stress at the plate surface.

Combination of Eqs. (12.5) and (12.9) gives the expression for τ at any point in the fluid film. On the surface of the plate $y = 0$, $\tau = \tau_0$, and

$$\tau_0 = -\mu \left(\frac{h}{2\mu} \frac{dp}{dx} + \frac{U}{h} \right)$$

But from Eq. (12.10a) an expression for dp/dx is available. Substituting for τ_0 in Eq. (12.17) and integrating, we obtain the result in the form

$$F = \frac{\mu U L}{h_2} C_f \qquad (12.18)$$

where C_f is a nondimensional friction factor that is a function of the inclination. As might be expected, the friction factor becomes somewhat smaller as the inclination increases, dropping from about 0.85 for $h_1/h_2 = 1.5$ to 0.62 for $h_1/h_2 = 5.0$.

The average coefficient of friction for the bearing as a whole can be found from Eqs. (12.15) and (12.18).

$$f = \frac{F}{W} = \frac{(\mu UL/h_2)C_f}{(\mu UL^2/h_2^2)C_w} = \frac{h_2}{L}\frac{C_f}{C_w} \tag{12.19}$$

Equation (12.19) is to be compared with Eq. (12.3), which was based on dimensional analysis. Since h_2 in Eq. (12.19) is identical with h in Eq. (12.3) and C_f/C_w is a function of $s = 1 + \delta(L/h_2)$, the two equations are in complete agreement. Dimensional reasoning alone cannot, of course, yield as complete information as the analysis leading to Eq. (12.19).

Note that the coefficient of friction is independent of the viscosity of the lubricant. This results from the fact that the transverse force W is caused by hydrostatic pressure that in turn is caused by viscous shear. [Recall that in Eq. (12.4) shearing forces were balanced against pressure forces in the horizontal plane. Since hydrostatic pressure is independent of direction, the same pressures cause an upward force on the slider to support the load W.] Hence both W and F are the direct result of fluid shear stress, owing to viscosity. Their ratio is therefore independent of the

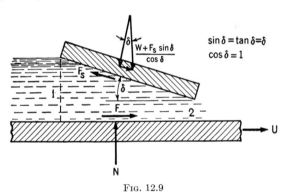

$$\sin\delta = \tan\delta = \delta$$
$$\cos\delta = 1$$

FIG. 12.9

lubricant, provided that it is a true fluid and provided that h_2 has a finite value. Obviously, if h_2 becomes zero, the load is taken by contact at the heel of the slider and the theory is invalid.

The friction force F exerted by the oil on the lower plate is equal to the force of the oil on the slider. This is true because the acceleration of the oil film is negligible. The forces acting on it are therefore in equilibrium. From Fig. 12.9

$$F_s = W\delta + F$$
$$N = W - F_s\delta = W(1 - \delta^2) - \delta F = W$$

It is permissible to let $N = W$ since $\delta^2 \ll 1$ and, from Eq. (12.19), F is on the order of $W\delta$.

It is apparent from the foregoing that the work done per second on unit width of oil film in moving either the slider or the plate at a constant speed U is equal to FU.

12.18. Energy Balance. Apply the energy equation [Eq. (5.8)] to the oil film under the slider of Fig. 12.9, assuming a steady two-dimensional flow, and neglecting heat transfer. Inertia effects and gravity are ignored, as in the rest of this chapter. Noting that the shear work per second done by the oil is $- FUB$, where B is the width of the slider, and recalling the definition of enthalpy $i = (p/\rho) + u$, we find from Eq. (5.8) that

$$FUB = (i_2 - i_1)\rho Q = \rho c \Delta T Q \tag{12.20}$$

where c is the specific heat of the oil, ΔT is its temperature rise as it passes under the slider, and Q is the volume rate of flow. Substitution of F from Eq. (12.18) yields

$$\rho c \Delta T Q = \frac{\mu U^2 L B}{h_2} C_f \tag{12.21}$$

Equations (12.9a) show that the velocity distribution across the oil film is linear at the section where $dp/dx = 0$. At this section the average velocity will be $U/2$, and consequently $Q = UBh_0/2$ where h_0 is the film thickness. Since, from Eq. (12.13a), $l_{\max} = s/(1 + s)$, $h_0 = h_2(s - sl_{\max} + l_{\max}) = 2h_2s/(1 + s)$. Substitution of this value of h_0 in the expression for Q gives $Q = UBh_2s/(1 + s)$. From Eq. (12.21) the temperature rise is found to be

$$\Delta T = \frac{\mu U L}{\rho c h_2^2} \frac{s + 1}{s} C_f \tag{12.22}$$

The quantity h_2 is, of course, extremely difficult to measure and is generally unknown. Consequently, Eq. (12.22) is of little practical interest. However, h_2 can be eliminated by substituting its value from Eq. (12.15), and we obtain in place of Eq. (12.22)

$$\Delta T = \frac{W}{L} \frac{1}{\rho c} \frac{s + 1}{s} \frac{C_f}{C_w} \tag{12.23}$$

In specialized texts on lubrication,* graphs are given for values of the several nondimensional coefficients C_w, C_f and others appearing in the equations for the principal operating characteristics. These nondimen-

* See p. 76 of reference 8.

sional coefficients are each functions of the inclination $s = h_2/h_1$. The designer wishes to make the load capacity as large as possible but without letting h_2 become too small for perfect lubrication and without excessive temperature rise. Fundamentally, the designer's problem involves seven quantities of which six must be fixed to determine the seventh.

The above analysis assumed that the viscosity was constant throughout the whole extent of the film. Since the rate of shear will vary with the film thickness, the work done in shearing the oil film will vary, and hence the temperature. As a result, the viscosity will vary. Christopherson [1] has investigated this problem and solved the resulting equations, which are somewhat more complicated than those given above. Comparison of the constant-viscosity theory and of the more exact theory shows that the discrepancies are small, less than 5 per cent. It is therefore justifiable to use the constant-viscosity theory for ordinary calculations. Constant viscosity will be assumed in the remainder of this chapter.

12.19. Cylindrical or Journal Bearings. This common type of bearing is designed to take the radial load on a rotating shaft or journal. We define the following quantities (see Fig. 12.10):

D = diameter of shaft or bearing

L = axial length of bearing

C = diametral clearance, or difference in diameters of bearing and shaft

N = speed of journal in revolutions per unit time

P = load per unit projected area = W/LD

μ = viscosity of the lubricant

Q = volume rate of lubricant flow through the bearing if it has forced lubrication

By dimensional reasoning any dimensionless ratio involving the following dependent operating variables,

h_0 = minimum film thickness

e = eccentricity, or separation of the centers of shaft and bearing
   = $(C/2) - h_0$

ϕ = aspect of the journal, or the angle between the line of centers and the line of the applied load

F = friction force on journal or bearing

can be expressed in terms of four Π functions.

$$\Pi_1 = \frac{\mu N}{P}$$

$$\Pi_2 = \frac{D}{C}$$

$$\Pi_3 = \frac{L}{D}$$

$$\Pi_4 = \frac{\mu Q}{C^3 P}$$

Specifically, we define

$$\eta = \frac{e}{C/2} = 1 - \frac{h_0}{C/2} = \text{eccentricity ratio}$$

$$f = \frac{F}{W} = \frac{F}{PLD} = \text{friction coefficient}$$

These quantities, together with ϕ, completely specify the system for any given conditions of operation.

12.20. Petroff Equation. If the shaft is unloaded and the speed is high, it runs concentrically, as shown in Fig. 12.10. If the shaft and bearing are absolutely concentric, the film thickness is everywhere the same and as in the case of the plane slider the bearing supports no load. However, even in this case there is a finite friction force that can be calculated if the space between shaft and bearing is assumed to be completely filled with lubricant.

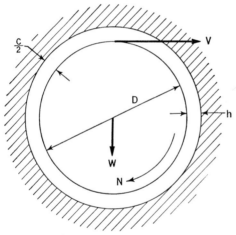

Since $C/2$, the average film thickness, is always very much less than D, the curvature in the path of flow of the lubricant can be neglected and, for laminar flow, the average shearing stress will be $\tau = \mu(V/h) = F/A$, where F is the total tangential force on the bearing of wetted area A. But V, the linear speed of the journal surface, is equal to πDN, $h = C/2$, and $A = \pi DL$. Therefore, the friction force exerted by the journal on the bearing will be $F = \tau A = \mu[\pi DN/(C/2)]\pi DL$. Hence the friction coefficient is given by the relation

Fig. 12.10. — Definition sketch of a concentric journal bearing.

$$f = \frac{F}{W} = \frac{F}{PDL} = 2\pi^2 \frac{\mu N}{P} \frac{D}{C} \qquad (12.24)$$

This is generally known as Petroff's equation. Experiments verify this relation with great precision. If the shaft is *very lightly loaded* and running at high speed, it will remain *almost* concentric in its bearing so that this equation still applies.

In the deduction of this equation, end effects (that is, dependence on L/D) have been ignored. However, the value of f depends on the dimensionless parameters $\mu N/P$ and D/C, identical with Π_1 and Π_2 of Art. 12.19. Petroff's formula thus agrees, as far as it goes, with the more general results of dimensional reasoning. Petroff's equation does not allow for the effect of forced lubrication as indicated by the term $\mu Q/C^3 P$.

Equation (12.24) is valuable, however, aside from its historical interest in embodying the concept of hydrodynamic lubrication, because it supplies a simple means of estimating journal friction. Furthermore, the running clearance C is very difficult to measure after a bearing is assembled, and it is often better to determine the friction coefficient from a torque measurement and to compute the clearance by Petroff's equation.

12.21. Loaded Journal Bearings. If the journal and bearing are not concentric, there is a converging wedge through one-half of the oil space as shown in Fig. 12.11 and we have the necessary physical condition for building up pressure in the oil film and ability to support a transverse load. The analysis of the problem will follow exactly that of the plane slider, but the steps will only be indicated, for they are mathematically involved. We begin by recalling Eq. (12.10a).

$$\frac{dp}{dx} = 6\mu U \left(\frac{1}{h^2} - \frac{k_1}{h^3} \right)$$

giving the derivative of the pressure in the oil film at every point. We recall that this equation was derived without any assumption as to the shape of the slider. As in the case of the plane slider, in order to integrate this equation we must express the film thickness h in terms of its position x. We neglect the curvature in the direction of motion and hence develop the oil film so that the surface of the bearing is taken as plane and use

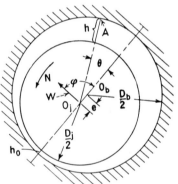

FIG. 12.11. — Definition sketch of an eccentric journal bearing.

its thickness as h in the above equations. Bearing in mind that both h and C are much smaller than D, we see from Fig. 12.11 that

$$O_j A = h + \frac{1}{2} D_j = \frac{1}{2} D_b + e \cos \theta = \frac{1}{2} D_j + \frac{C}{2} + e \cos \theta$$

whence $h = (C/2) + e \cos \theta$. Here θ is measured counterclockwise from the point of maximum film thickness. Also $x = \frac{1}{2}D\theta$; whence $dx = \frac{1}{2}D\,d\theta$.

Substituting in Eq. (12.10a), noting that $U = \pi Dn$, and integrating, we find that

$$p = p_0 + 12\pi \left(\frac{D}{C}\right)^2 \mu N \frac{\eta(2 + \eta \cos \theta) \sin \theta}{(2 + \eta^2)(1 + \eta \cos \theta)^2} \qquad (12.25)$$

Here p_0 is the pressure at the point $\theta = 0$, and the constant k_1 has be
determined by the condition that the pressure returns to its original val
when θ has increased by 2π. This pressure distribution is plotted in F
12.12, and it is seen that the pressure rise $p - p_0$ increases from zero at t
point of maximum film thickness to a maximum on the converging si
and then falls to zero at the point of closest approach, as in the case of t

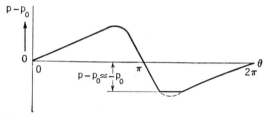

Fig. 12.12. — Theoretical pressure distribution for a two-dimensional journal bearing.

plane slider. On the diverging side the reverse is true, and the different:
pressure falls to negative values. If a liquid could support a tension und
the conditions existent in a bearing, the pressure would follow the dott
curve, which is symmetrical with the portion on the converging sic
Actually, however, the oil film breaks near zero absolute pressure as shov
by the full line. Cavitation and foaming can occur under unfavorat
conditions, with consequent failure to maintain continuity of liquid in t
clearance space.

This suggests a cautious approach to the question of the location
oilholes and oil grooving in a bearing. Since the maximum pressure in t
oil film may be some thousands of pounds per square inch it is obvious
unwise to put an oilhole for the purpose of introducing oil in the hig
pressure region. The oil will probably be forced out rather than in, ar
the maximum pressure in the film decreased. Oilholes should preferab
be located on the low-pressure, or suction, side of the bearing. Oil groov
are often used to lead fresh oil from the inlet to different parts of the bea
ing and are also expected to collect grit, which might otherwise lodge at t
line of minimum running clearance and score the surfaces. The introdu
tion of any oil grooves whatever should in general be viewed with suspicio:
The designer should avoid connecting by grooves regions of high pressu
with ones of low pressure. The oil may be drained from the high-pressu
area with a resultant drop in load capacity.

To obtain the total load that can be carried by the bearing when it ha
an eccentricity ratio η we must integrate the pressure over the whole c
film. We shall assume that p_0 is maintained so high that the oil film
continuous and follows the dotted line in Fig. 12.12. Let us resolve th
force $W = PDL$ that is exerted by the load on the journal into component
parallel and normal to the line of centers. These must equal the respectiv

components of the film pressure integrated all around the journal. The equation for the parallel component is

$$PDL \cos \phi = \int_0^{2\pi} Lp \cos \theta \, \frac{D}{2} \, d\theta$$

where ϕ is the angle between the load direction and the line of centers, as shown in Fig. 12.11. On substituting for p from Eq. (12.25) and integrating one finds that the integral is zero. Hence $\cos \phi = 0$ or $\phi = 90$ deg. This means that the resultant force due to the film pressure is always at right angles to the line of centers; in other words, the journal so positions itself in the bearing that the line of centers is always at right angles to the direction of the load. This holds true even when the effect of side leakage is taken into account. On the other hand, it does not hold if the oil film is incomplete, if oil is fed into the bearing through an oilhole in such a manner that its pressure either partly supports or depresses the journal, or if there is any metal-to-metal contact.

To determine on which side of the load line the center of the journal will lie one should bear in mind that it is the oil pressure in the *converging* wedge which supports the load and that it is the sense of rotation of the shaft which determines the converging side. The position of the journal is then as shown in Fig. 12.11. It is to be noted that this position is opposite to that which would obtain if the bearing were dry and the journal were mechanically rolling on it.

One obtains the expression for the load component normal to the line of centers (resultant load) by substituting for p in the equation

$$PDL \sin \phi = \int_0^{2\pi} Lp \sin \theta \, \frac{D}{2} \, d\theta$$

and integrating, remembering that $\phi = 90$ deg,

$$PDL = 12\pi^2 DL \left(\frac{D}{C}\right)^2 \mu N \, \frac{\eta}{(2 + \eta^2)(1 - \eta^2)^{\frac{1}{2}}}$$

or, rearranging,

$$\frac{\eta}{(2 + \eta^2)(1 - \eta^2)^{\frac{1}{2}}} = \frac{1}{12\pi^2(D/C)^2(\mu N/P)} = \frac{1}{12\pi^2 S} \qquad (12.26)$$

The dimensionless quantity S is often called the "Sommerfeld variable" after the eminent German mathematical physicist who first derived the above equation. This equation gives the journal position, or eccentricity, in terms of the operating conditions of the system and checks our dimensional result. Both η and its complement $h_0/(C/2)$ are plotted in Fig. 12.13.

It is seen that when the shaft is practically concentric, that is, when $h_0/(C/2) \approx 1$ or $\eta \approx 0$, S is very large and only a small load can be supported. When $h_0/(C/2)$ decreases, or η approaches unity, S decreases, finally becoming zero theoretically when the shaft and bearing touch. Before this point is reached, however, a limit to practical operation is set by other factors, which are difficult to take account of mathematically. Even at eccentricity ratios appreciably less than unity, metal-to-metal contact may occur owing to roughness of the surfaces, vibration, shaft deflection under load, misalignment, dirt in the oil, etc. Metal-to-metal contact, if prolonged, will cause excessive heating and initiate a train of events leading ultimately to failure of the bearing. The eccentricity ratio at which this begins to occur therefore sets a safe limit to practical operation, which according to Fig. 12.13 sets a lower limit to S. (As we shall see below, the side leakage is also a factor in determining this value of S.) The maximum safe value of the eccentricity ratio varies greatly for different bearing assemblies and is determined largely from experience. Under the worst conditions it may be as low as 0.5; under good conditions it may be as high as 0.9.

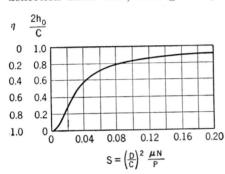

FIG. 12.13. — Eccentricity ratio η and minimum relative film thickness $2h_0/C$ versus Sommerfeld variable S for a two-dimensional journal bearing.

12.22. Friction Loss in a Loaded Journal Bearing. To obtain the friction loss in a journal bearing running eccentrically we combine Eqs. (12.5) and (12.9) to obtain the shearing stress at any point in an oil film between two solid surfaces in relative motion.

$$\tau = -\frac{\mu U}{h} + \left(y - \frac{h}{2}\right)\frac{dp}{dx}$$

Substituting for dp/dx from Eq. (12.10a) and expressing h and x in terms of θ, we can integrate the shearing stress over the whole surface of the journal $(y = 0)$ to obtain the friction force and hence the friction coefficient on the journal, or

$$f_j = \frac{F}{W} = \frac{1}{PDL}\int_0^{2\pi} L\tau_j\frac{D}{2}\,d\theta$$

When this integration is carried out and S is eliminated from the result by using Eq. (12.26), we obtain

$$\frac{D}{C}f_j = \frac{1 + 2\eta^2}{3\eta} \tag{12.27}$$

Performing the same operations at the surface of the bearing $(y = h)$, we obtain for the friction coefficient on the bearing

$$\frac{D}{C}f_b = \frac{1-\eta^2}{3\eta} \tag{12.27a}$$

Note that, as in the case of the plane slider, f depends only on the position η of the journal. Also note that the two coefficients are different. This is because the oil pressure in the converging wedge exerts a certain tangential component of force, which must be balanced. This force is responsible for the shaft's eccentric position. η can be eliminated from these expressions and Eq. (12.26) to give the friction coefficients as a function of S. The resulting equations are plotted in Fig. 12.14. The dotted line is the Petroff equation [Eq. (12.24)], which is approached by both the friction coefficients for large values of S.

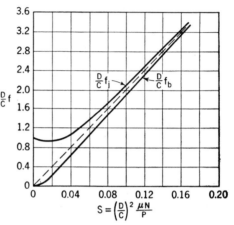

Fig. 12.14. — Friction coefficient for a journal f_j and for a bearing f_b versus Sommerfeld variable S for a two-dimensional journal bearing.

12.23. Effect of Side Leakage. In the above analysis we neglected the effect of leakage of oil from the ends of the bearing, or rather we assumed the bearing to be so long compared to its diameter that this effect was not appreciable. In most bearings, however, it *is* appreciable, the pressure varying in the axial direction somewhat as shown in Fig. 12.15. Obviously, if this is taken into account, the load capacity is reduced since the contribution of the oil pressure near the ends is reduced; hence the same eccentricity ratio is reached at a larger value of S. The derivation in Art. 12.14 of Reynolds's equation for the pressure distribution in the oil film assumed flow only in the x direction. If in addition there is flow in the transverse, axial, or z direction, then Eq. (12.10b) becomes

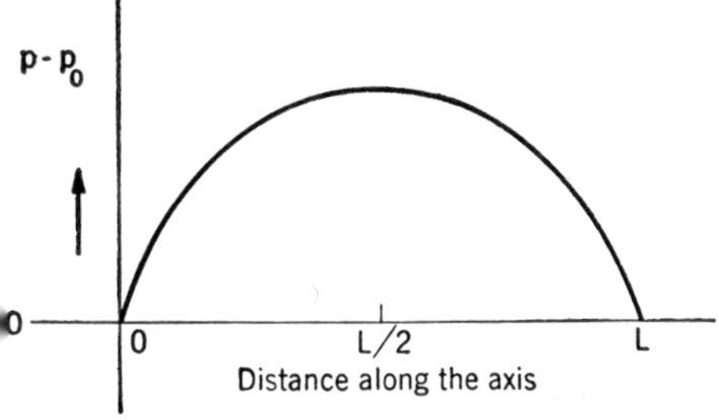

Fig. 12.15. — Diagrammatic sketch of axial pressure distribution in a three-dimensional journal bearing.

$$\frac{\partial}{\partial x}\left(\frac{h^3}{\mu}\frac{\partial p}{\partial x}\right) + \frac{\partial}{\partial z}\left(\frac{h^3}{\mu}\frac{\partial p}{\partial z}\right) = 6\frac{\partial}{\partial x}(hU) + 6\frac{\partial}{\partial z}(hW)$$

where W is the velocity of the moving surface in the z direction, which is this case is zero.*

This problem is complicated mathematically but it has been attacked by Kingsbury [2] using an electrical analogy and by Muskat and Morgan [3] for a limited range of η using a method of successive approximations. The results are conveniently expressed as factors by which the value of S for the two-dimensional bearing, denoted by S_∞, must be multiplied to give the value of S for the bearing of finite length having the same eccentricity ratio. In the table below, this factor in the form of S_∞/S is given for $\eta = 0.6$ for a number of length-diameter ratios. Obviously, $S_\infty/S = P/P_\infty$, or the relative load capacity.

$\dfrac{L}{D}$	$\dfrac{S_\infty}{S}$
0.2	0.025
0.4	0.075
0.5	0.115
0.8	0.24
1.0	0.31
1.6	0.50
2.0	0.59
3.2	0.73
4.0	0.78

While these factors vary with η, the dependence is not extreme and they can be used for the whole range of safe limiting values of η generally employed in bearings.

12.24. Journal Bearings with Dynamic Loading. In Arts. 12.19 to 12.23 we have investigated the steady-state solution of the journal bearing, assuming a constant load in a fixed direction. In a great many important practical cases, however, notably in all reciprocating engines, the load is constant neither in magnitude nor in direction. In such cases there is in addition to the pressure built up in the oil film due to the relative tangential motion of the two surfaces an additional pressure in the film produced by the relative motion of the surfaces toward and away from each other. This is the type of pressure normally developed in hydraulic recoil mechanisms and dashpots and responsible for the action of all hydraulic damping forces. Reynolds's equation [Eq. (12.10b)] must therefore be rewritten to take account of fluid velocities in the y direction,

$$\frac{\partial}{\partial x}\left(\frac{h^3}{\mu}\frac{dp}{dx} - 6hU\right) = 12V \tag{12.28}$$

where V is the velocity of any point x, h on the moving surface normal to the plane of the two surfaces. Now since the load will in general be varying

---

* For the derivation of this equation see any standard text on fluid mechanics, such as H. Lamb, "Hydrodynamics," 6th ed., Chap. XI, Cambridge University Press, London, 1932.

in both magnitude and direction, we can no longer assume the position of the journal center fixed with respect to that of the bearing. Hence U will no longer equal simply πDN, but both U and V will have components of motion due to the component velocities of the journal center, $(C/2)(d\eta/dt)$ and $(C/2)\eta(d\phi/dt)$. These can be evaluated; and, repeating the identical steps as for the case of a constant load, we finally arrive at expressions for the two components of the load, parallel to and normal to the line of centers. These may be written, respectively,

$$\left.\begin{array}{c} \dfrac{1}{(1-\eta^2)^{3/2}}\dfrac{1}{2\pi N_j}\dfrac{d\eta}{dt} = \dfrac{1}{12\pi^2 S}\cos\phi \\[3mm] \dfrac{\eta}{(2+\eta^2)(1-\eta^2)^{1/2}}\left[1-\dfrac{2}{2\pi N_j}\dfrac{d}{dt}(\phi+\alpha)\right] = \dfrac{1}{12\pi^2 S}\sin\phi \end{array}\right\} \quad (12.29)$$

Here all the quantities are as previously defined; t is the time, and α is the instantaneous angle between the load line and some reference direction fixed with respect to bearing (see Fig. 12.16). In general, both α and S will be functions of the time depending on how the load varies. Note that the line of centers is now no longer in general normal to the load line.

It is interesting to note that even here the running position of the journal still depends on the operating variables of the system as combined in the Sommerfeld variable S, with the exception of the rotational speed of the journal N_j, which appears in addition but always in combination with the time and which would in theory at least disappear on performing the integration with respect to time and substitution of the limits. Furthermore, although we spoke of the varying load as the reason for this analysis, it was nowhere explicitly assumed and Eqs. (12.29) require only that S be a function of time.

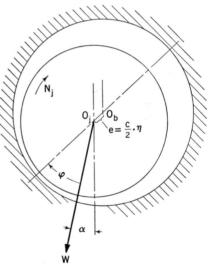

Fig. 12.16. — Definition sketch of a journal bearing with dynamic load.

Hence cases where the speed or the viscosity varies with time can also be solved by use of these equations. To perform the last integration of Eqs. (12.29) the dependence of S and α on the time must be known. For most cases of practical interest it is not possible to carry out the integration, and resort must be had to numerical methods. However, some qualitative discussion of certain of these cases is worth while. (This discussion follows in part that given by Swift [4].)

In the case of a steady state under constant load, if we take the two time derivatives to be zero, the equations reduce to the Sommerfeld equation [Eq. (12.26)].

In the case of a constant load revolving at constant speed (N_f) the equations reduce to the single one

$$\frac{\eta}{(2 + \eta^2)(1 - \eta^2)^{1/2}} \left(1 - 2\frac{N_f}{N_j}\right) = \frac{1}{12\pi^2 S} \qquad (12.30)$$

This equation is similar in form to that of Sommerfeld. If $N_f < \frac{1}{2}N_j$, the point of minimum film thickness will lie 90 deg ahead of the load line, as in the static case, but the bearing will have less load capacity (that is, a larger value of η for a given value of S) than in the static case. If $N_f = \frac{1}{2}N_j$, the bearing will support no load, which explains the phenomenon of oil whirl. If $N_f > \frac{1}{2}N_j$, the point of minimum film thickness lies 90 deg behind the load line. In particular, if $N_f = N_j$, the bearing has the same load capacity as in the static case. This is reasonable since the physical situation is the same as if the shaft were fixed and the bearing were rotating in the opposite direction. If $N_f > N_j$ or is in the opposite direction to N_j, the load capacity can become arbitrarily large as the magnitude of N_f increases.

The term $d\eta/dt$ represents the load capacity arising from a radial motion of the journal in the bearing sometimes called a "squeeze film." There will also in general be a tangential motion of the journal center, described by the term in $d\phi/dt$. If this is in the same direction as the rotation of the journal, as it generally is, it may decrease the load capacity arising from the rotation ("wedge film") alone. It is thus not generally true that dynamic loads, producing motion of the journal center in the bearing, will necessarily increase the load capacity over the static case. In fact under certain types of loading there will be a net decrease in load capacity.

For the general solution of the problem of a constant load, including the transient condition when the load is first applied, dt can be eliminated from the two original equations to yield a single differential equation in η and ϕ, which can be integrated to give

$$\sin \phi = \frac{12\pi^2 S}{5\eta(1 - \eta^2)^{1/2}} + \frac{c(1 - \eta^2)^{3/4}}{\eta} \qquad (12.31)$$

where the constant c depends on the initial conditions, *i.e.*, the position of the journal when the load is first applied. This equation, together with the two original ones, shows that, even under a constant load, periodic motion of the journal center takes place. Its path is a closed orbit, surrounding the equilibrium position as given by the Sommerfeld equation. Thus during part of its orbit the journal is nearer the bearing wall than if it were stationary in the equilibrium position. The physical existence of these orbits has not been established. If they do not exist in practice, then they must be damped out by some force, such as solid friction, not taken account of in this analysis.

A general analytical solution of these equations for any type of dynamic loading has not been possible to date, but numerical integration has been carried out for the case of a simple reciprocating load

$$P = P_0 \sin 2\pi N_f t$$

where N_f is the frequency of the loading and P_0 is its maximum value. Under this type of loading the journal center moves in a path resembling

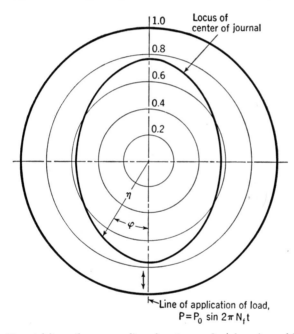

Line of application of load,
$P = P_0 \sin 2\pi N_f t$

Fig. 12.17. — Eccentricity ratio η versus line-of-centers angle ϕ for a journal bearing with a reciprocating load.

an ellipse, in the same direction as the rotation of the journal as shown in Fig. 12.17. The maximum eccentricity in this path is taken to determine the load capacity. Here again, as in the case of the constantly rotating load, if $N_f < \frac{1}{2}N_j$, the maximum eccentricity is greater and the load capacity is correspondingly less than in the static case. In this instance the minor axis of the path is parallel to the line of action of the reciprocating load. If $N_f = \frac{1}{2}N_j$, there is evidence, although it has not been proved analytically, that the bearing will support no load at all. (This is of interest since four-cycle internal-combustion engines all have a large half-period load component.) If $N_f = N_j$, which is the case of greatest practical importance, there is a definite increase in load capacity over the static case. In this case the major axis of the path is parallel to the line of action of the load, and the same maximum eccentricity is achieved with a 74 per cent greater load than under a static condition, for which bearings are conventionally designed. If $N_f > N_j$, there are even larger increases in load capacity. This 74 per cent increase in load, while quite appreciable, is smaller than that sometimes observed in bearings loaded in this manner. This may be due to the fact that the maximum eccentricity, corresponding to this load, is reached only twice every cycle. At other times the eccentricity is considerably less, so that a better measure of the load capacity might be obtained from the average eccentricity over the cycle, which would give a greater estimated load capacity. Still another explanation might be the fact that in actual unidirectionally loaded bearings the oil film is seldom complete on the unloaded side, while in the present case it may be more nearly so owing to the pumping action of the journal motion.

Finally, in the limiting case of a reciprocating load with no journal rotation, the first of the two original equations vanishes; and if ϕ is taken as 0 deg, the second one integrates to

$$\frac{\eta}{(1 - \eta^2)^{1/2}} = \frac{1}{12\pi^2 S_0'} \qquad (12.32)$$

where $S_0' = (D/C)^2(\mu N_f/P_0)$ and $P = P_0 \sin 2\pi N_f t$. Comparison of this with the Sommerfeld equation,

$$\frac{\eta}{(2 + \eta^2)(1 - \eta^2)^{1/2}} = \frac{1}{12\pi^2 S}$$

shows almost a threefold increase in the load capacity if N_f replaces N_j.

12.25. Oil Flow through a Journal Bearing. In many bearing assemblies the oil is introduced into the bearing through a hole or groove under pressure and flows through the bearing, finally emerging from the ends. A large volume of oil may thus be circulated through the bearing. Oil in excess of the amount required to keep the clearance space filled performs the useful function of carrying away the heat generated in shearing the oil film and hence keeps the bearing cool. For this reason it is useful to know the rate of oil flow through the bearing, a problem in fluid mechanics for which we have already derived the basic equations.

First consider the rate of flow circumferentially around the shaft. Equation (12.10) is the general expression for the rate of oil flow per unit width across any section of the film, which, since the fluid is incompressible, is the same across all sections. Hence for convenience we may consider the section where dp/dx or $dp/d\theta$ is zero. From Eq. (12.25) it an be found that at this section $\theta = \cos^{-1}[-3\eta/(2+\eta^2)]$. Then since $= (C/2)(1 + \eta \cos \theta)$, at this point $h = C[(1 - \eta^2)/(2 + \eta^2)]$ and the xpression for the total circumferential flow through a bearing of width L becomes

$$QL = \frac{\pi}{2} DLCN \frac{1 - \eta^2}{2 + \eta^2} \qquad (12.33)$$

The dimensions of this flow are volume per unit time. Note that it is a maximum when the shaft and bearing are concentric and decreases with ncreasing eccentricity.

For flow in the axial direction we must refer to Eq. (12.9), the expression or the velocity at any point in a cross section of a viscous film. In the case of flow in the axial, or z, direction, $\partial p/\partial x$ must be replaced by $\partial p/\partial z$, nd u by w. Since the relative velocity of the two surfaces in this direction is zero, $U = 0$. Equation (12.9) thus becomes

$$w = \frac{1}{2\mu} y(y - h) \frac{\partial p}{\partial z}$$

nd the average velocity across the section is

$$\bar{w} = \frac{1}{h} \int_0^h w \, dy = -\frac{h^2}{12\mu} \frac{\partial p}{\partial z} \qquad (12.34)$$

Consider a circumferential groove around the center of a journal bearing of which the length L is large compared with the breadth of the groove and which is supplied with oil at a pressure p_s above atmospheric. Equation (12.34) applies to this flow, which is to be thought of as superposed on the axial component of flow already described in Art. 12.23. Such superposition is legitimate because the equations of motion are linear. The symbols $\bar{w}$ and p in Eq. (12.34) thus do not represent resultant quantities but components superposed on those already present by the addition of the circumferential source. Since the flow from this source is uniformly distributed around the periphery, the p component in Eq. (12.34) is a function of z only. Also, by virtue of continuity, $\bar{w}$ is independent of z. Equation (12.34) thus shows that $\partial p/\partial z$ is constant. The value of this constant must be $2p_s/L$. Since $h = (C/2)(1 + \eta \cos \theta)$, the total flow due to the source out of both ends of the bearing is given by

$$Q_s = 2 \int_0^{2\pi} \bar{w}h \frac{D}{2} \, d\theta$$

$$= \frac{1}{48\mu} \frac{DC^3}{L} p_s \int_0^{2\pi} (1 + \eta \cos \theta)^3 \, d\theta$$

$$= \frac{\pi}{24} \frac{DC^3 p_s}{\mu L} \left(1 + \frac{3}{2} \eta^2\right) \qquad (12.35)$$

The dimensions of this flow are also volume per unit time. (This should be compared with the expression for Π_4 in Art. 12.19.) Note that in this case the flow increases with increasing eccentricity and varies inversely with the L/D ratio. In Art. 12.23 it was shown that a reduction in L/D decreases the load capacity. But here we see that a reduction in L/D also increases the oil flow and hence the rate of cooling. The viscosity will thus become larger, and the reduction in load capacity with L/D will not be so great as in a bearing without forced circulation.

12.26. Criteria for Journal-bearing Operation. We are now in a position to consider the criteria for determining the safe hydrodynamic operating conditions for a journal bearing. As we have already seen, one condition is that the minimum film thickness h_0 should never be less than a certain value, which in turn determines a safe minimum value of S, denoted $S_{\min}$, from Eq. (12.26).

The second condition is that the operating temperature T should never exceed a certain maximum value $T_{\max}$; otherwise, deterioration of the oil will be produced, corrosion of the bearing surfaces by the oil will be accelerated, and in some cases softening of the bearing materials will result.

Expressing the necessary relations analytically, we have

$$S = \left(\frac{D}{C}\right)^2 \frac{\mu N}{P}$$

whence

$$P = \left(\frac{D}{C}\right)^2 \frac{\mu N}{S} \tag{12.36}$$

(This S includes the factor to allow for side leakage.)

We also eliminate η from Eqs. (12.26) and (12.27), and obtain the friction coefficient as a function of S.

$$f = \Psi(S) \tag{12.37}$$

Now the operating temperature of the bearing is that temperature at which the sum of the rates of heat dissipation and net enthalpy efflux is equal to the power input to the bearing. Heat is carried away from a bearing by conduction through the supporting members, while the net rate of enthalpy efflux depends on the rate of oil flow and the temperature rise of the oil in the bearing. The sum of these quantities is thus

$$BA(T - T_R)^a + \rho Q c(T_2 - T_1)$$

where A is the area of the oil film πDL, T_R is the ambient or room temperature, B and a are empirical constants, Q is the rate of oil flow, ρ and c are the density and specific heat of the oil, respectively, and T_1 and T_2 are the entrance and exit temperatures of the oil. T_2 is directly dependent on the temperature of the bearing T and in many cases may be taken equal to T.

T_1 may also depend on T if the oil cooler is limited in capacity. If the oil-circulating system maintains a constant pressure, Q will depend on the viscosity and the clearance space in the bearing, according to Eq. (12.35). Both a and B have been determined empirically in some classical experiments by Lasche [5] and more recently investigated by Muskat and Morgan [6]. The value of a generally lies between 1 and 2.

Now the power input to the bearing is given by

$$FU = fPDL\pi DN$$

so that for equilibrium [compare Eq. (12.20)]

$$fPDL\pi DN = B\pi DL(T - T_R)^a + \rho Qc(T_2 - T_1) \qquad (12.38)$$

In particular, if the Petroff equation is assumed,

$$FU = 2\pi^3 \frac{D}{C} \mu N^2 D^2 L$$

Finally, of course, the viscosity of the oil is markedly dependent on the temperature so that

$$\mu = \mu_0 \beta(T) \qquad (12.39)$$

where μ_0 is the viscosity at some standard temperature and hence represents the grade of the oil. $\beta(T)$ is a function of the temperature that for petroleum oils is fairly independent of the grade. As pointed out in Art. 12.4, $\beta(T)$ is approximately exponential and may be expressed as $e^{b/(T+\theta)}$. It should be remembered that μ may also depend on the pressure if the latter is high.

We now have four equations [Eqs. (12.36) to (12.39)] in the quantities μ, f, S, and T. When these quantities are either eliminated or assigned limiting values, there results an expression involving the speed, the load, and the grade of oil for a given bearing. For instance, we can assume a safe minimum value for S such as S_{min} and then eliminate μ, f, and T from the four equations and obtain a relation among P, N, and μ_0. Alternatively, we can assume a safe maximum temperature T_{max}, eliminate μ, F, and S,

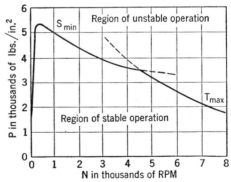

Fig. 12.18. — Plot of the two stability criteria for a journal bearing.

and obtain a second relation among P, N, and μ_0. Representative curves giving the relation between P and N for a given grade of oil are shown in Fig. 12.18.

The region lying below the curve of constant S_{min} corresponds to values of S which satisfy the condition that S never be less than S_{min}. The region lying below the curve of constant T_{max} satisfies the second condition that the operating temperature of the bearing never exceed T_{max}. Hence, in the region lying below both curves, both conditions are satisfied, and any combination of load and speed that lies in this region represents conditions of possible operation. All the rest of the region represents impossible operating conditions. Hence the full curve in Fig. 12.18 gives the load capacity at any speed of the bearing using a given grade of oil, under the limitations originally imposed.

A similar analysis can be made to select the proper grade of oil for a bearing whose operating speed and load are known. A lighter oil will in general result in a cooler-running bearing because the rate of doing work is not so high. Indeed, it turns out in a great many practical cases that the viscosity of the light oil at its operating temperature is about the same as that of the heavy oil at *its* operating temperature. Hence, for a given load and speed, the value of $(D/C)^2(\mu N/P)$ is not lowered by using a lighter oil, yet the bearing will be much cooler. As a result, it is generally advantageous, under hydrodynamic operating conditions, to use the lightest possible oil.

SELECTED BIBLIOGRAPHY

1. CHRISTOPHERSON, D. G.: A New Mathematical Method for the Solution of Film Lubrication Problems, *J. Proc. Inst. Mech. Engrs.*, vol. 146, pp. 126–135, 1942.
2. KINGSBURY, A.: On Problems in the Theory of Fluid-film Lubrication, with an Experimental Solution, *Trans. Am. Soc. Mech. Engrs.*, vol. 53, pp. 59–75, 1931.
3. MUSKAT, M., and F. MORGAN: Theory of Thick-film Lubrication of Flooded Journal Bearing, *J. Applied Phys.*, vol. 10, pp. 398–407, 1939.
4. SWIFT, H. W.: Fluctuating Loads in Sleeve Bearings, *J. Inst. Civil Engrs.*, vol. 5, pp. 161–195, 1937.
5. LASCHE, O.: On Bearings for High Speeds, *Traction and Transmission*, vol. 6, pp. 33–64, 1903.
6. MUSKAT, M., and F. MORGAN: Temperature Relations in Journal-bearing Systems, *J. Applied Mechanics*, vol. 10, pp. A131–A138, 1943.
7. HERSEY, M. D.: "Theory of Lubrication," John Wiley & Sons, Inc., New York, 1936.
8. NORTON, A. E.: "Lubrication," McGraw-Hill Book Company, Inc., New York, 1942.

CHAPTER XIII

BOUNDARY LUBRICATION

The theoretical friction coefficient for a journal bearing behaves, according to Sommerfeld, somewhat as curve A in Fig. 13.1 However, experimental friction curves resemble B or C. They follow the theory closely in the region of perfect lubrication and high values of S but turn up sharply near some minimum value of S that depends on the particular bearing. This is the minimum permissible value S_{min}, discussed in the preceding chapter. The region near this minimum for any particular bearing is called the region of "imperfect" or "boundary lubrication." The region to the left of the minimum, where the friction coefficient increases as S is diminished, represents unstable operation, and here bearings generally fail by seizure.

For well-designed bearings, boundary lubrication occurs in the vicinity of $S = 0.003$ and the conditions of operation here are quite different from those in the hydrodynamic range. For this condition the load is too great

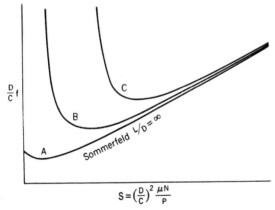

Fig. 13.1. — Schematic curves of friction coefficient f versus Sommerfeld variable S for a journal bearing.

or the speed too low to maintain fluid separation of journal and bearing by building up adequate pressure in the converging oil wedge. The load on the shaft is apparently taken on the bearing by direct contact. The viscosity of the oil is no longer of primary interest, but rather the nature of the rubbing surfaces and whatever oil film may remain to keep them slippery.

A journal operates under boundary lubrication when starting or when the oil supply fails, but many machine elements such as gears and cams normally operate under such conditions.

Boundary lubrication is notoriously marginal, and slight variations from previously successful practice are likely to cause failure. The ability of a bearing to operate under conditions of boundary lubrication has been found to depend upon a combination of physical properties, *viz.*,

1. Nature of the lubricant.
2. Finish of the rubbing surfaces.
3. Material of the rubbing surfaces.
4. Lubricant supply.
5. Temperature.

13.1. Oiliness. Experience has indicated a marked superiority at moderate temperature in the ability of certain animal and vegetable oils to keep smooth surfaces slippery, as compared with mineral oils of the same viscosity. This ability has been called "oiliness." Despite its somewhat vague character, the term is useful in denoting that quality of a lubricant which makes it effective under conditions of boundary lubrication where viscosity is not important.

That marked differences exist in the lubricating value of various oils was recognized as early as 1902 by Kingsbury [1] in experiments on an oil-testing machine where lard oil and mineral oils were compared at loads beyond the range of effective hydrodynamic lubrication. It was found that under these conditions the lard oil ran with much less friction, qualitatively resembling curve *B* in Fig. 14.1, as compared with the mineral oil, which followed a curve similar to *C*.

Oiliness may be defined as the ability of an oil to give a lower coefficient of friction in the boundary region than another at a given value of *S*. Machines have been devised to test empirically for this so-called "property," but no physical property of a fluid has been found to correlate with the results of oiliness tests. It is therefore necessary to seek an explanation in the chemical nature of the oils in question. What follows may be somewhat speculative but appears to be consistent with observed facts.

13.2. Molecular Structure. The majority of lubricants are oils that are compounds of carbon and hydrogen with sometimes a small amount of other elements. There are two main categories, mineral oils, which are derived from petroleum, and fixed oils, which are derived from animals and vegetables. The mineral oils are composed solely of carbon and hydrogen. The molecules are generally in the shape of long chains of carbon atoms with hydrogens attached or of rings with long side chains such as are shown in Fig. 13.2.

The structure of the molecule is responsible for the properties that we generally consider typical of oil. The relatively high viscosity that oils

possess can be pictured physically as due to the entangling and inter-
meshing of their very long chains.   Another result of their shape is a tend-

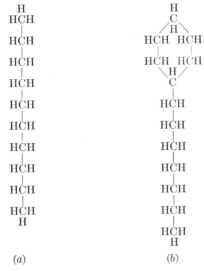

(a)   (b)

Fig. 13.2. — Structural formulas for (a) a straight-chain hydrocarbon, and (b) a ring hydrocarbon with side chain.

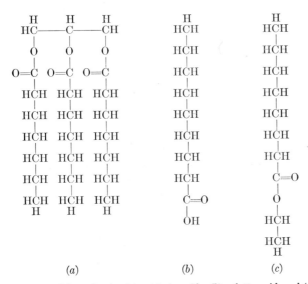

(a)   (b)   (c)

Fig. 13.3. — Structural formulas for (a) a tri-glyceride, (b) a fatty acid, and (c) an ester.

ency under certain conditions to align themselves parallel to one another
and to pack closely together to form, in two dimensions, a relatively dense
and rigid layer on a solid surface.   This tendency is greatly accentuated

by the addition of small amounts of other types of oil to the pure hydrocarbon.

The fixed oils are a mixture of a wide variety of substances. The major portion consists of triglycerides with three long carbon chains hooked through a carboxyl linkage to a nucleus of three carbons, as in Fig. 13.3a, with lesser amounts of straight-chain hydrocarbons having a hydroxyl, —OH, or a carboxyl, —COOH, radical on one end, as shown in Fig. 13.3b. The latter are called "fatty" alcohols or acids. Other constituents are represented by the ester shown in Fig. 13.3c. All these compounds occur naturally in animal and vegetable oils and can be removed or concentrated by refining. There are other compounds that behave in a similar manner chemically and can be used in the same way, but they do not occur in nature and must be synthesized. They may contain a halogen, —Cl or —Br, or an amine, —NH₂, radical, as shown in Fig. 13.4a; or the short hydrocarbon chain in Fig. 13.3c may be replaced by a metal atom as shown in Fig. 13.4b to produce a metallic soap.

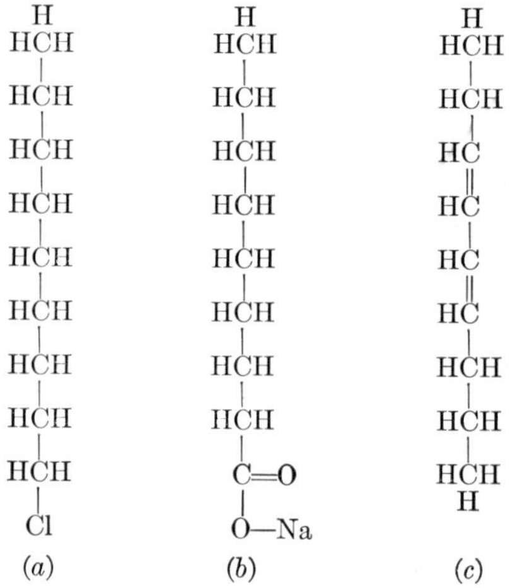

Fig. 13.4. — Structural formulas for (a) a chlorine substitution product, (b) a sodium soap, and (c) an unsaturated hydrocarbon.

Often some of the carbon atoms in the chain are not bonded to as many hydrogen atoms as possible so that double bonds between two carbons are formed, as in Fig. 13.4c. Such molecules are said to be unsaturated. Unsaturation often occurs in the fixed oils, while the mineral oils are more generally saturated. The region of the double bond is chemically active and will pick up other molecules, notably oxygen from the air if the oil is heated, as in an automobile engine. This activity has two results. (1) It generally produces acidity of the oil and leads to severe chemical attack of the bearing surfaces. (2) Oxidation produces gum and varnish deposits, which are generally harmful in engines.

13.3. Surface Chemistry. The above discussion of the molecular structure of the possible constituents of practical lubricants is necessary in order to elucidate their mechanism and to understand why they are made with their present-day compositions. A glance at the structures shown in Figs. 13.2 to 13.4 shows that all have the feature in common of a long chain. This point is important. As will be shown below, all these molecules tend, when in the vicinity of a solid surface, to orient themselves so that they are standing more or less normal to the surface, with one end attached to it. This being the case, it is obviously desirable to have a long chain so as to provide the maximum physical separation of the two bearing surfaces. This view has been partly substantiated in tests which show that for a homologous series of compounds, be they straight hydrocarbons, alcohols, or fatty acids, the friction within a given series decreases with increasing chain length up to a certain point.

Another property of these long-chain molecules in contact with a solid surface is their tendency to adhere in clusters. If a sufficient number is present, they will completely coat the surface with a monomolecular film of great lateral strength. This film is to all intents and purposes a solid in two dimensions. The rigidity is due to the chemical affinity between the CH_2 groups in the adjacent hydrocarbon chains. This rigid structure has been confirmed by electron-diffraction evidence.

The third structural characteristic of the molecule that is conducive to the formation of a strong adherent film is its possession of an active radical. So far we have discussed properties common to the mineral oils and the fixed oils alike, but now we reach a point of significant difference. As opposed to the pure mineral oils the molecules of a fixed oil and of a synthetic additive have an active radical on one end. This asymmetry in the otherwise symmetrical structure of the molecule, as shown in Fig. 13.3b, disarranges the normal symmetrical distribution of electric charge so that one end becomes predominantly positive and the other end negative. Such a molecule is said to be "polar."

The radical end of a polar molecule has a strong affinity for a metal surface. This end, therefore, attaches itself to such a surface, while the rest of the molecule tends to stand out more or less normal to the surface. The affinity of the active end varies both with the type of radical and with the length of hydrocarbon chain. It can be designated quantitatively as the free energy of adhesion and can be measured in a variety of ways [2]. It is a function of both the oil and the surface but is believed to depend principally on the nature of the oil. It is the work necessary to pull a unit area of oil away from a solid surface and, consequently, has the dimensions of energy per unit area. The polar and nonpolar liquids differ greatly in their energy of adhesion to metals, but a given oil has about the same energy of adhesion for all the usual bearing metals. An everyday illustration of a difference in energies of adhesion is the fact that water will stand up in droplets on a greasy surface, whereas it will spread in a thin uniform film on a clean one. The force of adhesion tends to draw the water over the surface and increase the mutual area of contact, while the surface tension of the droplet holds it back. The attraction between the water and the greasy surface is less than the surface tension and the water is held back, whereas the attraction of the clean surface is great enough to overcome the surface tension. Furthermore, the waterdrop on the greasy surface, on being rolled around, leaves a dry area behind it, so little is its attraction for the grease. On the clean surface, however, the water never recedes from an area that it has once wetted. This property of spreading, which is the result of a high adhesion energy, is obviously desirable for a boundary lubricant.

13.4. Film Formation. Long-chain molecules with lateral attraction for other chains and an active radical group at one end tend to form an adherent film on a bearing surface. Oils that have molecules of this type are superior to other fluids of the same viscosity under imperfect, or boundary, lubrication conditions. The function of the film is to separate two metal surfaces so that on rubbing they do not gall or seize. Furthermore, the film permits the surfaces to slide over each other with much less friction since the tops of the films are composed of CH_3 radicals, which are chemically saturated and have very little attraction. The situation has been likened to a stand of wheat firmly rooted to the ground. If a half-inch steel ball were magnified to the size of the earth, the thickness of the monolayer of oil on its surface would equal the height of the wheat. (This analogy to a wheat field is not quite exact since it ignores the mutual cohesive forces among the closely packed carbon chains.)

This strong monomolecular film exists only below a certain temperature, characteristic of the particular lubricant molecule *and* the particular metal surface. As the temperature increases, thermal agitation of the oil molecules decreases the attractive tendency between them. Above a certain temperature, called the "transition temperature," attraction and orientation cease entirely, and the molecules that were in the surface layer disperse themselves through the bulk lubricant much as a liquid vaporizes to a gas. This phenomenon is reversible on cooling.

Transition temperatures vary for the different classes of compounds. They are lowest for the pure hydrocarbons, which experiments by Bowden [3] and his coworkers have shown are effective as boundary lubricants only when they are solid, that is, at temperatures below their bulk melting points. As is well known, the melting point, and hence the transition temperature, increase with increasing chain length. For molecules of the same chain length the transition temperature is higher for the polar molecules since it takes more thermal agitation to tear the active radical loose from the bear-

ng surface. Some typical transition temperatures are given in Table I,
aken from Bowden's work.

TABLE I.—TRANSITION TEMPERATURES OF ORGANIC COMPOUNDS

Compound	Temperature, Deg C
Docosane, $C_{22}H_{46}$	43
Octadecane, $C_{18}H_{38}$	28
Lauryl alcohol, $C_{12}H_{25}OH$	23
Octadecanol, $C_{18}H_{37}OH$	59
Lauric acid, $C_{11}H_{23}COOH$	44
Stearic acid, $C_{17}H_{35}COOH$	69
Copper laurate, $Cu(C_{12}H_{23}O_2)_2$	110
Sodium stearate, $NaC_{18}H_{35}O_2$	290

For even the most active polar compound, such as a fatty acid, there is a
definite temperature above which it will not adhere to the bearing surface
in a rigid monolayer. As may be seen from Table I, this temperature for
he fatty acids is not so high as that often reached by high-performance
automobile and aircraft engines. It was found experimentally, however,
hat lauric acid on copper behaved as a good boundary lubricant up to a
temperature of about 100 C, while on platinum it ceased to be effective
above about 43 C. Similar results have been obtained with other fatty
acid-metal combinations. The explanation lies in the fact that the lauric
acid reacts slightly with the copper surface to form a thin, adherent film of
copper laurate, whose transition temperature is much higher than that of
he pure acid. On platinum, however, the lauric acid is completely un-
reactive.

Such chemical reactions should be generally desirable, so long as the
attack is not severe enough to change the surface contour.

13.5. Additives. We have seen that the best structure for a boundary
lubricant consists of a long straight hydrocarbon chain with an active
radical at one end. Compounds having such a structure occur naturally
in the animal and vegetable oils, or they may be synthesized, but they do
not occur in the mineral oils.

These compounds often have certain impractical aspects that make
them undesirable for commercial use. For instance, the naturally occurring
fixed oils, being unsaturated chemically, tend to oxidize at engine temper-
tures to produce acidity and chemical attack of the bearing surfaces.
Further oxidation produces gummy deposits that cause stuck piston rings
and clogged drains.

Fortunately, there is an easy way out of this difficulty. It has been
found that a small percentage of an active polar compound when added to
straight mineral oil renders the product as efficacious a boundary lubricant
as the pure additive and yet does not appreciably affect the bulk properties
of the mineral oil. This is explained by the fact that the additive, having

a great affinity for the surface, migrates to it, forming its characteristi[c]
strong monolayer or chemical coating, to the exclusion of the mineral-o[il]
molecules. Only a small fraction of 1 per cent of additive is required t[o]
coat the surface. The residue remains in solution in the mineral oil, wher[e]
it is almost instantly available to repair areas of the film worn away b[y]
rubbing. In this connection Table II is of interest, which gives som[e]
measurements by Burwell [4] of the friction coefficient under boundar[y]
conditions between two ground and hardened steel surfaces for variou[s]
concentrations of oleic acid in mineral oil.

TABLE II

Lubricant	Friction Coefficient
Pure mineral oil	0.360
2% oleic acid in mineral oil	0.249
10% oleic acid in mineral oil	0.198
50% oleic acid in mineral oil	0.198
Pure oleic acid	0.195

This table shows that although a fractional percentage of oleic aci[d]
should be sufficient to cover the surfaces completely, the friction coefficien[t]
continues to decrease up to 10 per cent concentration of the acid. Pre[-]
sumably, molecules of the acid are forced more rapidly to a break in th[e]
surface film if the concentration of additive is increased, but this effect i[s]
less marked at high concentration than at low.

The concentration of additive beyond which no improvement in per[-]
formance is noted depends on a number of factors, notably the speed an[d]
severity of rubbing, the affinity of the additive for the bearing surface, it[s]
relative solubility in the bulk lubricant, and the difference between th[e]
temperature of operation and the transition temperature.

We conclude that a lubricant for general service where boundary condi[-]
tions may be expected should consist of a mineral oil of appropriate vis[-]
cosity, to which has been added a small percentage of a polar substance[,]
preferably either a fatty acid or a metal soap. The requirements for suc[h]
a "film-strength" additive are

1. The molecule should contain an active radical to give high adhesio[n]
to the bearing surfaces.

2. The molecule should be of the long straight-chain type, the activ[e]
radical being at one end.

3. The additive should be present in a concentration of at least a fe[w]
per cent, but not in sufficient quantity to contribute its disadvantageou[s]
bulk properties to the lubricant.

4. Either its own transition temperature or that of its reaction produc[t]
with the bearing surface should be above the anticipated operatin[g]
temperature.

Good commercial practice is in line with the above. Generally the
ctive substance is added in the form of an easily procurable commercial
il, such as lard, sperm, or castor oil. A few petroleum crudes naturally
ontain a small fraction of such substances, and, from this standpoint, it
s possible to overrefine a mineral oil. In the extreme-pressure (E.P.)
ubricants used for gears, where the loading of the film is extremely high
wing to the small areas of contact, the metallic soaps are generally used.

In the case of commercial oils for automobile engines where the service
equirements are complicated by the necessity for exposure to extreme
ransient temperatures and the products of combustion, other addition
gents are also used for various other purposes. Next in importance to
he film-strength additives are the oxidation inhibitors. These prevent
he unsaturated molecules that are inevitably present in all commercial
ils from becoming oxidized. The inhibitors act principally by taking up
hemically all the oxygen present and thus forming harmless materials.
)ther additives are employed as detergents, which enable the oil to keep in
suspension finely divided solids, such as sludge and metal particles, and
prevent their adhesion to the metal surfaces. Other agents are sometimes
ised for more specialized requirements such as raising the viscosity index
and depressing the pour point.

13.6. Chemical Polishing Agents. These are used to prevent galling
and seizure in the running in of new bearings. As a class, the chemical
polishing agents are hydrocarbon compounds containing a metalloid atom
such as sulfur, phosphorus, or arsenic. Tricresyl phosphate is an example
of one that is used commercially. Beeck [5] has explained the action of
these compounds as follows:

They are stable at room temperature but at elevated temperatures
decompose and release the free metalloid atom. Thus they do not attack
the bearing surfaces at the temperature of normal operation; but where
metal-to-metal contact occurs, the local temperature rises and the resultant
decomposition of the agent releases some of the metalloid, which then attacks the metal over the rubbing area to form a thin, easily sheared coating
of the compound of the metal and metalloid, e.g., the metal sulfide or phos-
phide. This coating alloys with the metal to lower its melting point, so
that the high spot is worn away and the local temperature is reduced.

A chemical polishing agent ceases to function after running in is complete and the true bearing area has reached its maximum value. Hence it
may be removed, and plain oil used thereafter. The film-strength additive,
on the other hand, must of course be retained in the oil throughout the life
of the bearing.

13.7. Other Lubricants. All the discussion so far has centered in the
hydrocarbon family of compounds. However, their somewhat considerable
drawbacks and the urgent requirements of the Second World War prompted

a search for other families of compounds suitable for lubricants and hydraulic fluids. To date the most interesting that have been evolved are the silicones. These are synthetic substances characterized by long chains composed of alternate silicon and oxygen linkages, as shown in Fig. 13.5.

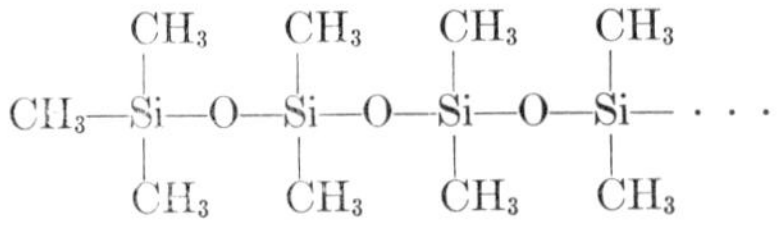

$$CH_3—Si—O—Si—O—Si—O—Si— \cdots$$

with CH_3 groups above and below each Si.

FIG. 13.5. — Structural formula for a silicone.

A silicone molecule may also contain active radicals. Silicones are superior to the hydrocarbons in having a higher viscosity index and in being noninflammable, so that they have found important use as hydraulic fluids, particularly in airplanes and naval vessels. They have not yet been developed as good boundary lubricants, but there is promise in this direction.

For specialized purposes other fluids may be used. Water is used to lubricate the rubber bearings that support the propeller shafts of vessels. Air is used for high-speed centrifuges and grinders where the clearance space is small, the speed is high, and the load is light.

Important lubricants for certain applications are the greases. They are mixtures of mineral oil and soaps either with or without a solid filler. The mixture forms a gel that is semisolid at room temperature. The base may be a sodium, a calcium, or a lead soap. Greases are never so good from a lubrication point of view as oils, but they are used under the following conditions:

1. Where the clearances are excessive, owing either to poor design or to extreme wear.

2. In dusty or dirty surroundings in order to trap dirt and grit and keep them out of the bearings.

3. In places such as weaving and food machinery where dripping oil would damage the product.

4. In inaccessible locations or where the servicing of the moving parts is likely to be infrequent.

5. At high temperatures, where the grease may be liquid at the operating temperature and behave like an ordinary oil.

For very high loads and low speeds or frequent reversals of motion a solid lubricant is effective, either alone or added to oil. The solid friction between the two metal surfaces is replaced by the friction of shearing the solid lubricant, so that galling is prevented. Graphite is advantageous since it shears easily and yet is hard enough in the direction normal to the plane of shear to support an appreciable load. There is also indication that it is wetted by oil. It can withstand high temperatures and so can be used where ordinary oils cannot, *e.g.*, in bake-oven, glassmaking, die-casting, and other hot machinery. It is used as a colloid in either oil or water. Other solid lubricants are talc, soapstone, and mica.

13.8. Oil Supply. Wherever possible, there should be a copious supply of lubricant. Inadequate supply of oil, improperly delivered to the bearing surfaces, is probably the most common cause of bearing failure. It is always desirable to operate hydrodynamically, but this is impossible unless there is sufficient oil. Furthermore, if the oil is circulated through the bearing, a high rate of oil flow performs the very important function of cooling the bearing, as discussed in Art. 12.25. Lack of an adequate supply may in a few cases be intentional as in the case of piston rings, where it is desirable to leave as little oil on the combustion walls as possible, or in the case of textile machinery, where spoilage of the product is to be avoided.

The lubricant can be supplied to bearings and other rubbing surfaces by a number of methods. These include drop- and wick-feed oilers, hydrostatic lubricators, ring, chain, and collar oilers, mechanical force-feed oilers, and centralized appliances and circulating systems employing oil pumps and coolers. These will not be discussed further here, but reference may be made to any standard text on practical lubrication [14, 15].

13.9. Surface Finish. From the preceding discussion it follows that boundary lubrication depends largely on a joint property of the liquid and the metal surfaces, involving the maintenance of an adsorbed film over the sliding areas of contact.

Figure 13.6 indicates in a general way the nature of the contact between two supposedly flat surfaces pressed together with an oil film between them. They touch only at A and B, and the true area of contact is very

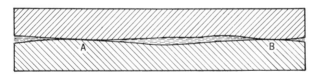

Fig. 13.6. — Schematic cross section through the contact area in boundary lubrication.

much less than the wetted area used in the theory of perfect lubrication. Boundary lubrication is characterized by the dominance of the true area of contact. As the surfaces slide over each other, they are separated at A and B by an oil film of molecular dimensions. Whether or not this oil film breaks down and metallic seizure takes place will depend on the intensity of the pressure (which in turn is governed by the areas of A and B), on the temperature rise at the local contact spots, and on whether or not the oil film is renewed from the reservoirs of oil in the hollows between contacts. Obviously the contours of the metal surfaces must determine the ability of a given film to support the load, and hence a knowledge of surface rough-ness is essential.

By surface roughness is meant the small-scale geometrical profile that is imparted to bearing surfaces by the usual commercial finishing operations. It may be defined as recurrent or random irregularities in a surface that have the form of small waves or bumps. The American Standards Association (ASA) has arbitrarily set the upper limit of their spacing at about 0.01 in. This limitation excludes waviness due to looseness or chatter in the finishing machine and also dimensional deviations from shape. In these cases the wave length is relatively long and can ordinarily be measured with a dial gauge. The lower limit of height of the roughness that can be conveniently detected at present is a fraction of a wave length of light or a few millionths of an inch. This is still several hundred molecular diameters and unfortunately leaves a region of surface contour about which we know little.

There are a great many ways to measure surface roughness. One way is to take a cut perpendicular to the bearing surface, polish the section, and examine the profile under a microscope. One can also use the optical properties of the surface as a measure of its roughness or smoothness. The higher the ratio of the specularly reflected light to the diffusely reflected light from a given source, the smoother the surface. In practice, however, a mechanical-tracer type of instrument has been most commonly employed. It is similar in construction to a phonograph pickup. The vertical displacement of a stylus as it passes over the surface is amplified either by mirrors or electrically, and a magnified image of the surface profile is drawn on a moving tape. Alternatively, the electrical impulse may be fed into an a-c meter, which automatically reads the rms average of the deviations of the surface from some median plane. Surface roughness is usually specified as this rms value in microinches (μin.), or millionths of an inch. A turned surface may measure 100 μin. or more and a ground surface about 20 μin. Honing or superfinishing with abrading stones or lapping with loose abrasive may give 2 to 8 μin., while metallographic polishing can give a surface profile of less than 1 μin.

It is obviously a great oversimplification to attempt completely to describe such a complex geometrical surface by a single number. This inadequacy becomes apparent if one compares the lubrication performance of two bearing surfaces having the same rms roughness but finished by different methods. It is often found that their performance differs markedly. To describe this situation better it has been suggested that a second quantity such as the rms of the first derivative of the surface, *i.e.*, its slope, be defined also.

The directional quality of surface profile is another characteristic that distinguishes surface finishes. Turned and ground surfaces possess this

uality, while honed, superfinished, and grit-blasted surfaces do not.   This
ʀoperty is important since bearing performance depends on the relation
ꜰ scratch direction to the direction of motion.

Finally, the finishing operation itself may produce metallurgical changes
ᴉ the surface material.   This is discussed in the following section.

That lubrication performance does in fact depend on surface roughness
ꜱ illustrated by the results of two experiments, the first of which was per-
ᴏrmed under conditions of boundary lubrication.   In Table III are shown
ᴀlues of friction coefficient for surfaces of different roughness.   The
ᴜbbing surfaces were crossed cylinders in the form of standard automobile
ᴉiston pins.   The roughness readings are rms values and were read with a
ʀacer-type profilometer.   The interesting fact appears that the friction
ᴉncreases with roughness up to about 20 μin., after which it remains essen-
ᴉally constant.   Values for grit-blasted surfaces are appreciably less than
ᴉhose for ground surfaces of the same roughness.   This may be the fault
ꜰf the roughness measurement and may substantiate the need for a second
ꜰuantity besides the rms roughness to compare surfaces prepared in differ-
ᴺt ways.   It may be further noted that, the smoother the surface, the less
ᴉe improvement effected by the addition agent.   Possibly the incentive
ᴏr producing improved addition agents in the oil industry would have
ᴮeen less if our rubbing surfaces had always had good surface finish.

TABLE III

Lubricant	Surface roughness, μin., rms				
	Super-finished 2	Ground 7	Ground 20	Ground 50	Grit-blasted 55
ᴍineral oil................	0.128	0.189	0.360	0.372	0.212
ᴍineral oil + 2% oleic acid	0.116	0.170	0.249	0.261	0.164
ꝺleic acid................	0.099	0.163	0.195	0.222	0.195
ᴍineral oil + 2% sulfonated sperm oil................	0.095	0.137	0.175	0.251	0.165
ꜱAE 30 oil................	0.119	.....	0.252	0.253	0.192

The second category of experiments [6,7] employed full journal bearings
ᴡith flooded lubrication in which journals finished in different ways to
ᴠarious roughnesses were run against a number of bearing metals.   Under
ᴴeavy loading it was found that in the region of boundary lubrication the
ꜱeizure tendency was substantially reduced as the roughness of the journal
ᴡas reduced from 10 down to 1 μin.   The load just prior to seizure was
Ꝉ00 per cent greater for the smoothest journal than for the roughest.

13.10. Materials of the Bearing Surfaces.   We now consider the solid
ᴍaterials of which the rubbing, or bearing, surfaces are composed.   Good

performance depends on certain physical and chemical properties of the surfaces as well as on a number of bulk properties of the bearing materials. Furthermore, the properties of the two surfaces must be properly matched to one other. A material that is satisfactory in rubbing against one surface may be unsuitable for use against a surface of a different material. In the case of rotating parts the shaft usually must be designed for mechanical strength, so that steel should be used for the shaft, regardless of its rubbing properties. Hence, bearings must be chosen that will operate satisfactorily against steel. Furthermore, one of the two surfaces generally wears more and must be replaced sooner. In most machinery the easier part to replace is the bearing, which further justifies the practice of making the shaft out of a hard material like steel. In other situations, such as the piston-ring-cylinder problem, there is some flexibility in the choice of materials for both surfaces.

There are several empirical rules followed in selecting materials for the two bearing surfaces. The first is that the two should not be made of similar material. If metal-to-metal contact occurs locally, two like metals tend to weld together owing to the frictional heat and pressure. When they break away, portions of one surface are left adhering to the other surface. This will in turn cause more metal pickup until the galling has become severe enough to produce failure.

In general, both surfaces should not be hard if the speed is to be high. If both are hard, the abrasion produces unnecessary friction and heat. If the speed is very low or intermittent, as in the jewel bearings of watches, two hard bearing surfaces are advantageous, as the wear is slight and little looseness develops in the parts. For the speeds that commonly occur in machinery, however, one surface should be soft enough to yield and conform to the other, to relieve the high local pressures due to misalignment. On the other hand, it must not be so soft as to yield under the normal operating load or deform under shock. Such deformation may change the shape of the converging oil wedge and impair its load-carrying capacity. A further advantage of softness is an ability to embed adventitious grit so completely that it will not scratch or grind the hard surface.

These somewhat conflicting requirements as regards hardness and strength cannot easily be achieved in a homogeneous material. As a result, practical experience has led to bearing-material compositions of a duplex nature, containing one hard constituent that mechanically supports the load and a soft constituent that conforms to the shaft and shears at a low temperature. (This mechanism is discussed further in Art. 13.11 below.) These constituents may be disposed in a number of ways. There may be hard particles embedded in a soft matrix as in the case of the babbitts; there may be soft areas in a hard matrix as in the copper-lead alloys and the lead bronzes; or the soft constituent may be a continuous thin layer ᴠer the hard one as in the case of lead-coated and lead-indium-coated ilver. This duplex structure is not universal, however, bronze and cast ᴛon being commonly used for bearings where light loads are encountered.

An important property for bearing metals to be used in internal-com-ᴜstion engines is corrosion resistance. In the airplane engine, tempera-ures today are high and are still increasing. In gas turbines, they may ᴄe excessive. As a result, the oil, in spite of addition agents to increase tability, often becomes partly oxidized and acidic. Lead is particularly usceptible to acid attack. While a certain amount of chemical activity on he part of bearing materials improves performance under boundary condi-ions, there must be a compromise between this requirement and destruc-ive corrosion.

Whenever alternating or shock loads are present, the fatigue resistance ᴏf the materials becomes important. Alternating loads are obviously ᴐresent in all reciprocating engines. For high-speed operation where the ᴇvolution of heat becomes a problem the thermal conductivity of the ᴐearing material is important. Metals have a great advantage over non-ᴍetallic materials and coatings in this respect. Hardness is an essential ᴐrerequisite to good wear resistance.

Pure lead, tin, cadmium, and indium are the softest bearing materials ᴀnd are in many cases the most satisfactory. They are given the necessary ᴍechanical strength by coating them on steel or other strong backing ma-ᴛerials, the layers being quite thin, often less than 0.010 in. Lead has the ᴅrawback of great susceptibility to corrosion. To increase their mechanical strength these metals may be alloyed in a number of ways. Such alloys ᴀre the babbitts, the first to be developed commercially. They originally ᴄonsisted of about 90 per cent tin and the remainder copper and antimony, ᴛhe latter elements forming hard crystalline intermetallic compounds with ᴛhe tin, and being embedded in the soft matrix of the tin-rich eutectic. For ᴇconomic and strategic reasons lead has recently been used to replace the ᴛin, either partly or entirely. Mechanically it is just as satisfactory, but its corrosion resistance is poor. The babbitts as a class have poor fatigue ᴛesistance. The cadmium alloys are similar in structure to the babbitts ᴀnd are coming into general use.

If somewhat greater mechanical strength is desired, the copper-lead al-loys and lead bronzes are used. The copper-lead alloys and the lead bronzes are a dispersion of lead droplets in the copper or bronze, the lead being completely insoluble in them, even in the liquid state. On running, the lead smears over the hard matrix, which otherwise has poor resistance to galling. The depressions left by the lead serve as oil reservoirs. The copper-lead alloys still require steel backing for strength; but the bronzes, whether containing lead or not, and particularly the phosphor bronzes, are strong enough to be used as complete bushings. These are generally used where the loads are not severe, the alignment is good, and long life without replacement is desired. Copper and its alloys may be attacked by traces of sulfurous acid left in the oil from the refining process.

A somewhat ingenious use of bronze is to form by a powder-metallurgy process a bushing containing voids. When soaked in oil, such a bushing will take up about 30 per cent of its volume and can then be used with little or no external oiling since it furnishes its own lubricant.

For more severe service, silver is coming into widespread use. It is fatigue resistant and has a low elastic modulus (10,000,000 lb per sq in.), while its low hardness (25 Brinell) affords some opportunity for grit to become embedded under its surface. Also, its thermal conductivity is high and results in a cool bearing. It has some tendency to gall and seize, possibly owing to its chemical inertness to additives, but this can be counteracted by plating a film of lead over the silver surface. The corrosion of the lead is prevented by coating it with a still thinner film of indium and diffusing it into the surface by heat treatment.

A hard metallic bearing material is cast iron. It has been in use for a long time, but only where light loads, high speeds, and good alignment are encountered. A good example is the supporting bearings for grinding-machine spindles. Superficially it would appear to violate all our rules as a good material to run against steel. It is as hard or harder than the steel shaft and chemically of the same composition. It has now been shown, however, by electron-diffraction examination that a cast-iron bearing surface after running is coated with graphite flakes, which are dragged out of the cast-iron matrix and smeared over the surface. This may account for its good operation.

Another very hard material having unique bearing properties is chromium plating. Its great chemical dissimilarity to copper and its alloys is evidenced by the chromium-copper phase diagram, which shows practically no solid solubility even at 1000 C. This lowers the tendency to gall. The smoothness of electroplated chrome surfaces is probably helpful also, although there is some indication that interrupting this smooth surface with small pits, or depressions, will improve the performance still further, particularly for engine-cylinder walls. Several processes for preparing such surfaces have been developed.

Some bearing surfaces today are chemically treated to improve their performance. This may be an oxidizing, a sulfidizing, or a phosphate treatment. It is maintained that the coating of these compounds acts as an antiwelding agent between the metal surfaces.

It is probable that bearing surfaces composed of the same material may differ in their lubrication performance owing to metallurgical differences, often produced by the forming or finishing operation. For instance, Wulff [8] has shown that grinding, honing, and lapping induce the transformation from austenite to ferrite in 18–8 stainless steel. Since these differ in crystal structure, they may be expected to differ in properties that influence rubbing performance. It is well known that any such mechanical operations will distort the metal grains in the surface and reduce their size. When this is carried to an extreme degree as in a very highly polished metal surface, it has been found that such a surface is chemically more active than an undisturbed surface. Also, thermal and mechanical stresses induced in surfaces by grinding have been found greatly to increase the rate of corrosion. These surface layers may be only 0.0001 in. deep, but that is quite sufficient to change the surface properties. Shaping operations such as hot- or cold-rolling and -drawing will produce a preferred orientation of the grains, especially near the surface. It can be expected that the different crystal faces which are thus exposed may have somewhat different chemical properties with respect to the lubricant, particularly in metals the crystal structures of which are relatively anisotropic, such as zinc, antimony, or white tin. Burnishing, peening, and cold-rolling may produce high compressive surface stresses, which are advantageous for fatigue strength since they counteract the stress-raising effect of local cracks, flaws, and notches. Carburized parts also have compression in the carburized surface layer; but if this layer is removed by grinding, the new surface may be in tension and be liable to crack or check (e.g., wrist pins, ball-bearing races, gear teeth).

Mention should also be made of some nonmetallic bearing materials that have value for certain special applications. The very hard wood lignum vitae has been traditionally used to line the outboard bearings that support the propeller shafts of ships. It is sufficiently hard, it will not gall the shaft, it is not injured by sea water, and there is a certain amount of natural oil in the wood. Rubber also is a very good bearing material where water is the lubricant and is gaining increasing use in ships. Certain plastic-impregnated materials such as textolite and micarta are proving satisfactory as supports for the roll necks in steel-rolling mills. Here also the antigalling property is valuable.

13.11. Dry Friction. Logically we should, proceeding still farther to the left on the curves of Fig. 13.1, next take up the phenomena of seizure and wear that occur when boundary lubrication fails. For this, it is essential that we have some knowledge of the elements of dry friction.

Results of experiments on the friction between rubbing surfaces were published by Amontons in 1699 and by Coulomb in 1779. These showed that the friction force F was proportional to the load W applied normal to the surfaces, or

$$F = kW \qquad (13.1)$$

Over a large range the coefficient k was found to be independent of W, of the relative velocity of the two surfaces, and of the apparent area of contact.

It appeared at first to be a physical constant typical of the materials if the surfaces were carefully cleaned.

It was further observed that its static value, measured when the two surfaces were at rest, was almost always greater than the kinetic value when the surfaces were in relative motion. This law of proportionality at first suggested the explanation of dry friction as due to the mechanical interlocking of the asperities on the two surfaces. It can be seen from simple geometry that, if this were the case, k would equal tan θ, where θ is an average angle of slope of the asperities. The friction coefficient should, accordingly, decrease with increasing smoothness, as was found to be the case in the range of moderate roughness; but with fairly smooth surfaces the coefficient approached a constant finite value and never reached zero. This simple theory, therefore, is inadequate.

The work of subsequent investigators, climaxed by that of Bowden and his collaborators [9], of Ernst and Merchant [10], and of others, has succeeded in formulating a picture of the mechanism of dry friction which, although still tentative and with some significant gaps, does qualitatively explain most of the facts observed to date. According to this picture the total friction force consists of three terms. The first is due to the interlocking of the surface roughnesses as explained above; but since the average slope of well-ground surfaces is only a few degrees and that of honed and polished surfaces is even less, tan θ is very small and for most cases this term is negligible.

The second term in the friction force arises when the two surfaces are of unequal hardness and is due to the plowing out of the softer material by the protuberances on the harder surface. This term is equal to the flow pressure of the softer material multiplied by a constant that is dependent on the geometric shape of the plowing protuberance. For simple geometric shapes it can be easily calculated. This may or may not be an appreciable part of the whole friction force.

The third term is based on the hypothesis that when two surfaces are in apparent contact the load is in fact carried by the few points on the surfaces which actually come into contact, as indicated in Fig. 13.6. That this area is only a small fraction of the apparent area of contact has been confirmed by measurements of the electrical conductance between two metal bodies in contact. Owing to the very small contact area, the local pressures are extremely high, so that prominences flow plastically until the local pressure no longer exceeds the flow pressure of the softer material. (In this operation the *apparent* area of contact has not changed.) It is further hypothesized that another result of these high local pressures is to cause adhesion and welding of the two surface materials over these true contact areas. Hence a portion of the friction force is due to the shearing of these junctions, which are alternately made and broken as sliding proceeds.

To the effect of pressure in forming these local welds is added that of temperature. If the sliding velocity is appreciable, the work done by this shearing component of the friction force is expended over a very small area and there is a local temperature rise. That these temperatures become appreciable has been shown in a classic experiment by Bowden and Ridler [11] in which the two rubbing surfaces were made of dissimilar metals and acted as the elements of a thermocouple. It was found that the temperature often rose to the melting point of the lower melting metal.

The third term in the friction force is equal to the shear strength of the welded junction times the true area of contact. This shear strength is difficult to calculate from the other physical properties of the materials. If the two materials are the same or similar, so that they have a high mutual solid solubility, the junction formed will generally have shear strength as great as or greater than that of the softer material and the shear will take place in the latter, thus leaving particles of the softer material adhering to the harder surface. This has been established experimentally both by electrochemical development of the foreign material on gelatine-coated paper [12] and also by making the softer surface radioactive and measuring the activity picked up by the harder material after rubbing [13]. In such cases we can use the shear strength of the softer material, which is well known, although it may be raised somewhat by work hardening. If, on the other hand, the two materials are quite dissimilar and do not tend to weld easily, the shear strength of the junction may be small.

Summarizing the above quantitatively we can say that the friction force is given by

$$F = W \tan \theta + cp + sA \qquad (13.2)$$

where W is the normal force between the two surfaces, θ is the average slope of the surfaces, p is the flow pressure of the softer metal, c is a constant dependent upon the geometrical shape of the slider, s is the shear strength of the welded junction, and A is total *true* area of contact, *i.e.*, the sum of the areas of all metallic junctions.

For bearing surfaces, θ is small, and the first term can be neglected. The relative importance of the other two terms will depend on the shapes of the protuberances and the relative hardness of the two surfaces. If, for instance, the protuberances on the harder surface are imagined as spade shaped, with very little area projected on the nominal plane of contact but capable of plowing out or pushing ahead a large cross section of the softer material, then the second, or plowing, term will strongly predominate. In this case the friction may rise during the sliding owing to the softer metal piling up ahead of the spade-shaped protuberance and because p may increase owing to work-hardening. This second effect should increase with velocity, as has been found experimentally to be the case [9].

If, on the other hand, the protuberances on the harder surface are well rounded and the materials of the two surfaces tend to form junctions of high strength, then the last term, the shearing term, will predominate. In general, the load will then determine the true area of contact by causing plastic flow of the softer metal until the true area of contact has increased to a point where the local pressure no longer exceeds the flow pressure of the metal. Hence $A = W/p$. Substitution for A in Eq. (13.2) gives for the coefficient of friction of a smooth pair of surfaces

$$\frac{F}{W} = k = \frac{s}{p} = \frac{\text{shear strength of junction}}{\text{flow pressure of softer metal}} \tag{13.3}$$

It should be noted that this makes k a function of the bulk properties of two metals, and hence k itself is a property of the metal pair. It has not been possible to find metal combinations having extremely small coefficients of dry friction (below $k = 0.1$) since for most metals s and p are somewhat proportional. Graphite, however, is an example of a material having a fairly high indentation hardness and yet a very low shear strength within itself.

Equation (13.3) provides an explanation of the observed fact that in certain instances the friction force is proportional to the applied load.

TABLE IV.—FRICTION COEFFICIENT OF A SPHERICAL STEEL RIDER
ON VARIOUS MATERIALS

Material	k
Steel.........................	1.0
Copper........................	0.9
Copper film on steel............	0.3
Lead..........................	1.2
Lead film on steel..............	0.3
Lead film on copper............	0.18
Copper-lead alloy..............	0.17
Indium........................	2.0
Indium film on steel............	0.08
Silver.........................	0.55
Indium film on silver...........	0.1

That this is due to the influence of the load on the true area of contact, and not to the load per se, has been confirmed by Bowden [9] in some ingenious experiments in which the friction coefficient of a hard slider rubbing over a soft metal in bulk was compared with that of the same slider rubbing over the same metal in the form of a thin film deposited on a very hard base. Here s, characteristic of the soft metal, remained the same, but p was much greater and hence A much less in the latter case, owing to the support of the hard base. In particular, it was found that thin films of lead and indium on copper and steel gave remarkably low coefficients of dry friction as shown in Table IV, taken from Bowden's paper.

It was concluded therefore that the friction force is actually proportional to the true area of contact and depends on the applied load only through the latter's influence on the true contact area.

This table suggests the reason for the efficacy of copper-lead bearings and lead-indium-coated silver as well as partly substantiating the old picture of the mechanism of the babbitt materials. The lead or indium provides a low shear strength, and the silver or copper has a high hardness or flow pressure.

The concept of local welding also serves to explain why static friction is usually larger than kinetic. When the surfaces are at rest, all the junctions that can form have an opportunity to do so. When the surfaces are in motion, a certain fraction (statistically speaking) of the junctions are being made and broken. If a finite time is required to form a junction, then these do not make their full contribution to the friction force. Although this explanation seems probable, it has not been positively established.

We have already seen that, by using the artifice of a thin film of a soft metal on a hard base, the value of k may be lowered. A similar effect may occur if there are foreign films present. Such a film may be adventitious as the oxide film formed on most metals in the presence of air or water vapor; or it may be due to the chemical action of a constituent of the lubricant such as sulfur, phosphorus, or arsenic; or the film may be purposely prepared for antiseizing purposes; or it may be the oiliness or boundary additive in a commercial lubricant. These films serve to reduce the shear strength at the junctions since these nonmetallic materials do not weld strongly to the metal.

At the other extreme, the static-friction coefficient of extremely clean metal surfaces that have been outgassed and measured in a vacuum may reach values as high as 6.

When the friction is due primarily to the breaking of the welded junctions and the shearing term predominates, it is generally observed that the motion proceeds intermittently. This is familiar as "chattering," or "squealing." Careful investigation has demonstrated that one surface does indeed move over the other by a series of sticks and slips. Mathematical analysis of the mechanics show that this will occur if the static coefficient of friction is higher than the kinetic, which it generally is, and if there is any elasticity in the supporting members, which is always the case. In the case of similar metals or when actual galling occurs, the motion proceeds smoothly, presumably owing to the continuous plastic deformation of the bulk material.

In the machining of metals all the conditions obtain for the welding of one surface to the other. The surface of the chip is perfectly clean and not even exposed to air at the tip of the cutting tool; the cutting edge has been wiped free of all films by the chip rubbing over it; and there is no lubricant present at the cutting edge, the fluid being used solely for cooling. Owing to frequent starting and stopping, static friction produces incipient stick-slip action, which often results in chattering. This problem has been studied by Ernst and Merchant [10].

It need not be assumed that both materials are metallic, since friction occurs universally. However, most of the careful experimental work has been done with metals, the mechanism of local welding being most easily understood in this instance.

13.12. Seizure and Wear. The above picture of the mechanism of dry friction permits some deductions to be made about the observed phenomena of seizure and wear, since both are either extremely exaggerated instances or the integrated effect over a long period of time of the minute phenomena that contribute to dry friction under moderate conditions.

Seizure is initiated by the welding of a local junction as described above. If the two metals are similar and not too hard, they form a local weld of relatively great strength over a large area. As a result, the metal breaks, not at the weld but generally on one side or the other, so that a spot that was originally slightly high is now made higher because of metal from the other surface adhering to it. This rubs even more severely, producing higher temperatures and pressures and welding momentarily over larger areas. This process builds up until the driving force is no longer able to break the weld that has formed. Seizure is prevented by making the rubbing surfaces of dissimilar materials so that low-shear-strength junctions are formed, by keeping the true area of contact small through using hard materials or hard backing, by coating the surfaces with antiwelding films, and by use of a copious supply of a good boundary lubricant.

Wear, on the other hand, represents the long-time summation of the individual small effects of dry friction, both abrasion and welding. Another contribution to wear may be from chemical corrosion and the subsequent rubbing off of the loose compound formed, which may in itself be abrasive, as in the case of chemical polishing agent, extreme-pressure lubricants, or water vapor. Automobile-cylinder wear is thought to be due in large part to corrosion aided by moisture of condensation from the combustion products.

The same general factors that prevent seizure will also minimize wear, but with some modifications. For wear prevention the emphasis should be on hardness of both surfaces. Hence both surfaces are often made of hardened steel even though by so doing one sacrifices the desirable feature of dissimilarity of material. This difficulty can be remedied somewhat and the surfaces made even harder by carburizing, nitriding, or chrome-plating one or both surfaces. Examples are gears, cams and rollers, and piston rings and cylinders. Smooth surface finish is also important in decreasing wear by reducing the local pressures.

Antiwelding films over the hard surfaces will reduce wear so long as the
ms remain intact and are not in themselves abrasive. A tin or cadmium
ısh on new pistons is often used as a temporary antiwear agent while a
·rmanent coating is being built up during running in.

Evaluation of wear resistance is best obtained through a simulated
rvice test of the actual assembly or a scale model. Wear-testing ma-
ıines may test the relative merits of lubricants but are generally mis-
ading for machine design because of exaggeration of service conditions.
, is better to use more precise methods of measurement than to accelerate
ıe rate of wear.

The process of running in is generally classed as a beneficial wear
ıenomenon. It was originally thought that the running of newly as-
·mbled parts at reduced loads and speeds produced greater conformance
ï the surfaces through gradual wear of the offending high spots so that
ltimately the system would be able to carry a greater load than would
therwise be the case. That a better performance will result from this
ractice is well established, but its explanation is not clear. Dayton [6]
nd others [7] have measured the metal worn off during running in, through
ıicrochemical analysis of the oil, but the amounts are either very small or
uite inappreciable and disappear even while the running in is still in-
reasing the load capacity. The changes in surface profile are too small to
·e measured by an instrument although the surfaces often look smooth
nd bright to the eye after running in. These changes can be accentuated
·y the use of the chemical polishing agents described in Art. 13.6. It is
rue, however, that a very slight smoothing of sharp roughnesses may
epresent a large increase in the effective load-supporting area. The im-
·rovement is generally greatest with the harder bearing materials and
east with babbitt. Running in of the harder bearing materials generally
·roduces a glazed appearance, particularly in the case of piston rings and
·ylinders, and there is some evidence that this appearance indicates the
·resence of a very thin surface layer, having altered chemical and metal-
urgical properties. The nature of these changes has not yet been deter-
nined.

It therefore seems probable that the beneficial effects of running in are
due in part to a change in surface profile and in part to the formation of a
wear-resistant layer, at least on the harder materials.

13.13. Rolling Friction. The so-called "antifriction" bearings, ball and
roller bearings, substitute rolling friction for sliding friction. Rolling friction is very much less than sliding friction under any conditions of boundary
lubrication, particularly in starting from rest; but where perfect fluid
lubrication can be assured, the coefficient of friction of a plain journal
bearing can be made lower than that of ball or roller bearings.

Rolling friction arises entirely from the elastic deformation of the two
surfaces. It is distinguished by the fact that the maximum stress in the

metal is at a small but finite depth below the surface and failure is due, not to surface adhesions or galling or wear, but to fatigue cracks starting in the region of maximum stress and causing small pieces of the surface to flake, or spall, out. A metal of high fatigue resistance is important here. Where sliding is added to the rolling, as in the case of gear teeth, the region of maximum stress is raised nearer the surface. The total stress may be increased, but the wear is more of the surface type, a less harmful kind. Extreme-pressure lubricants cut down the sliding or surface wear but can do nothing for the subsurface or fatigue type of failure.

The use of any large quantity of fluid lubricant in antifriction bearings is to be avoided. A fluid can have no effect on the fatigue of a metal, and the churning of the oil by the balls or rollers will increase the friction and operating temperature. Hence there is no real lubrication problem for these bearings except between the balls or rollers and their cages. However, grease should be used to keep out dust and grit, which are extremely harmful, and also to prevent rusting of the surfaces.

13.14. Lubrication of Piston Rings and Cylinders. The lubrication of the pistons and piston rings of high-duty internal-combustion engines presents today the most critical problem of boundary lubrication. A combination of conditions unfavorable to lubrication conspires to defeat the designer's efforts to develop more power per unit of piston displacement.

The piston rings are subjected to high temperature, a doubtful supply of lubricant, high gas pressure behind the rings, and intermittent motion. The lubricant trapped in the rings is liable to break down chemically under high piston temperature and to deposit carbon, gum, and hard varnish. The usual oiliness agents are ineffective at such high temperatures, but chemical addition agents are frequently used as oxidization inhibitors and as detergents.

The case of the piston is peculiar in that the side thrust of the connecting rod is taken on a line contact with the cylinder wall, with motion in the direction of the line. Gear teeth also make line contact, but the rubbing is transverse to the line, and there is some chance to form an oil wedge. The lubrication of gears is also favored by the generally continuous nature of the motion.

Piston rings are usually made of cast iron and are carefully run in against a smooth cylinder liner of hard steel, sometimes nitrided. Where dust and grit are present, as in desert operation, wear is rapid. Chromium-plated steel rings, grooved rings, and other expedients to minimize wear are active subjects of research. Cast-iron pistons have a distinct advantage for boundary lubrication from the graphite content but are too massive for very high-speed engines because of high dynamic forces.

High-speed diesel engines often use thin-walled steel pistons designed to block the flow of heat from the crown to the rings. Airplane engines

enerally use thick-walled aluminum-alloy pistons, which, although light,
ᴿe especially unfavorable to lubrication since they conduct heat too well
ᴿom the crown to the rings. The lubricant, therefore, must be copiously
ɪpplied to the inside of the pistons, to cool them, thus necessitating oil
ᴵdiators and an elaborate circulating system. Extreme precautions are
ᴛken in running in new pistons to avoid seizure before good boundary-
ɪbrication conditions are established.

13.15. Summary. We may summarize this chapter by the statement
ᴵat the performance of sliding surfaces operating under conditions of im-
ᴇrfect, or boundary, lubrication depends on a large number of factors,
ᴵany of which are difficult to evaluate. Some of them are

The molecular structure of the lubricant and its addition agents.
The chemical properties of the lubricant and its addition agents.
The supply of lubricant.
The surface properties of the bearing materials.
The bulk properties of the bearing materials.
The physical structure of the bearing materials, *i.e.*, whether homo-
ᴇneous, duplex, or thin film.
The roughness of the surfaces.

The problem of selecting the best materials for boundary operation is
ɴe that can be treated only qualitatively at the present time and usually
ᴇquires some compromise among the factors listed above. Further in-
ᴇstigation of the mechanism of dry friction and of the physics and
ʰemistry of the metal-lubricant interface is needed to give a better under-
ᴛanding of the subject.

SELECTED BIBLIOGRAPHY

1. Kingsbury, A.: A New Oil-testing Machine and Some of Its Results, *Trans. Am. Soc. Mech. Engrs.*, vol. 24, pp. 143–160, 1903.
2. Adam, N. K.: "The Physics and Chemistry of Surfaces," 2d ed., Chap. V, Oxford University Press, New York, 1938.
3. Bowden, F. P., J. N. Gregory, and D. Tabor: Lubrication of Metal Surfaces by Fatty Acids, *Nature*, vol. 156, pp. 97–101, 1945.
4. Burwell, J. T.: Role of Surface Chemistry and Profile in Boundary Lubrication, *S.A.E. J.* (*Trans.*), vol. 50, pp. 450–457, 1942.
5. Beeck, O., J. W. Givens, and E. C. William: Wear Prevention by Addition Agents, *Proc. Roy. Soc.* (*London*), ser. A, vol. 177, pp. 103–118, 1940.
6. Dayton, R. W., H. R. Nelson, and L. H. Milligan: Surface Finish of Journals, *Mech. Eng.*, vol. 64, pp. 718–726, 1942.
7. Burwell, J. T., J. Kaye, D. W. van Nymegen, and D. A. Morgan: Effects of Surface Finish, *J. Applied Mechanics*, vol. 8, pp. A49–A58, 1941.
8. Wulff, J.: Proc. MIT Summer Conferences on Friction and Surface Finish, June, 1940, p. 13.
9. Bowden, F. P., A. J. W. Moore, and D. Tabor: Ploughing and Adhesion of Sliding Metals, *J. Applied Phys.*, vol. 14, pp. 80–91, 1943.

10. ERNST, H., and M. E. MERCHANT: ASM Symposium on Surface Treatment of Metals, October, 1940, p. 299.
11. BOWDEN, F. P., and K. E. W. RIDLER: The Temperature of Sliding Metals and Lubricated Surfaces, *Proc. Roy. Soc. (London)*, ser. A, vol. 154, pp. 640–656, 1936.
12. BOWDEN, F. P., and A. J. W. MOORE: Adhesion of Lubricated Metals, *Nature*, vol. 155, pp. 451–452, 1945.
13. SAKMANN, B. W., J. T. BURWELL, and J. W. IRVINE: Measurements of the Adhesion Component in Friction, *J. Applied Phys.*, vol. 15, pp. 459–473, 1944.
14. CLOWER, J. I.: "Lubricants and Lubrication," McGraw-Hill Book Company, Inc., New York, 1939.
15. THOMSEN, T. C.: "The Practice of Lubrication," 3d ed., McGraw-Hill Book Company, Inc., New York, 1937.

CHAPTER XIV

HYDRAULIC TURBINES

The purpose of a hydraulic turbine is to convert gravity potential nergy of water into shaft work. Experience teaches that all such energy ould be so converted by an ideal turbine in which friction was absent. .n actual turbine is arranged by artifices of design to alter the momentum f a stream of water as it passes through some sort of wheel having buckets r vanes. The forces resulting from this sustained momentum change ause the wheel to turn against an external load and thus perform work. he inevitable friction causes such a machine to fall somewhat short of he ideal, but the modern hydraulic turbine is one of the most efficient rime movers in existence.

The difference between the initial and final water levels, known as the head," differs greatly from one installation to another. In mountainous ountry a head amounting to many hundred feet may be available, while lsewhere the head may be as low as 10 ft or even less. The amount of rater available also depends on location and in general is small for high eads and large for low heads. These natural differences in the conditions f operation have given rise to three principal types of turbine, the impulse urbine, the radial- and mixed-flow reaction turbine, and the axial-flow, r propeller, reaction turbine. The first type is suited to high head and mall discharge, the second covers the intermediate range, while the third andles a large volume under low head.

In an impulse turbine one or more nozzles direct jets of water at atmosheric pressure against buckets on the rim of a wheel. Most of this kinetic nergy is utilized by the wheel, the discharge having just enough velocity ·ft to move clear of the buckets before falling into the low-level reservoir, r "tail water." The water thus loses kinetic energy as it passes through n impulse wheel but enters and leaves at the same pressure.

In a reaction turbine, on the other hand, the flow through the wheel, r runner, is completely enclosed, and both the pressure and velocity at xit are different from those at entrance. The terms "radial flow" and axial flow" refer to the direction of water movement through the runner.

14.1. Impulse Turbine. The impulse turbine is represented by the ²elton wheel, shown in Fig. 14.1, developed in California about 1880 to tilize the high heads available in the mountains. As already stated, the ιead of the supply water is converted into one or more high-velocity free ets which are directed against buckets mounted on the rim of a wheel.

These buckets are spoon shaped, with a central ridge dividing the impingin‹ jet into halves, which are deflected backward relative to the bucket throug‹ an angle of about 165 deg. The spouting velocity of the water is ver; high for high heads, but with a large-diameter wheel only moderate speed‹

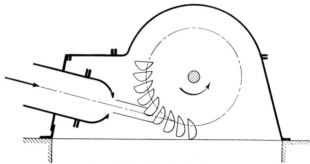

Fig. 14.1. — Impulse turbine.

of rotation are required. Present practice, for heads greater than 1,000 ft is to use the Pelton turbine exclusively. It is also frequently employe‹ for lower heads where insufficient water is available to operate any othe‹ type of turbine at good efficiency. Since the maximum practicable je‹ diameter is limited, the volume of water that can be handled under a lo‹ head is much less than that for a reaction turbine. Hence the Pelton whee‹ is essentially a high-head low-discharge machine. The highest head s‹ far used is 5,800 ft in Switzerland, where a wheel with a single jet develop‹ 30,000 hp. There are numerous installations in California, one of whic‹ has two double units, each of 56,000 hp. The highest efficiency obtaine‹ to date with a Pelton turbine is approximately 91 per cent, but for mos‹ installations the efficiency is between 85 and 90 per cent.

The runaway speed of an impulse turbine may be nearly double th‹ normal operating speed. The runner and any machine connected to th‹ turbine should be built to withstand the centrifugal stresses caused b; removal of the load.

The resultant external torque on the system comprising the wheel an‹ shaft and the water between sections 2 and 3 of Fig. 14.2 can be compute‹ by means of the angular-momentum law. For this purpose we refer t‹ the velocity diagrams of Fig. 14.2b, which gives an end view of a singl‹ bucket, such as would be presented to an observer in the plane of th‹ wheel and looking toward the axis of rotation. We assume (1) that th‹ absolute velocities V_2 and V_3 are uniform over sections 2 and 3 and ar‹ independent of time, (2) that the absolute flow on the buckets is cyclic‹ and (3) that the tangential velocity components V_2 and V_{t_3} have the sam‹ moment arm r. Equation (6.17) thus yields

$$\text{Resultant clockwise torque} = \rho Q r (V_2 - V_{t_3})$$

his resultant exceeds the useful shaft torque T by the amount of the
orques due to bearing friction and windage. It is therefore convenient

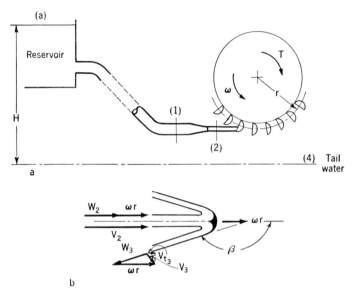

IG. 14.2. — (a) Schematic side elevation of impulse turbine.   (b) Section through bucket;
sectioning plane normal to radius at radius r.

o define a mechanical efficiency η_m by the formula

$$\eta_m = \frac{\omega T}{\omega(\text{resultant torque})} \tag{14.1}$$

o that

$$T = \eta_m \rho Q r (V_2 - V_{t_3}) \tag{14.2}$$

Equation (14.2) can be put into a more useful form with the aid of the
nergy equation. Since we have assumed the absolute flow to be cyclic,
e could use Eq. (5.10), which refers to fixed axes. It is much simpler,
owever, and the same result is obtained if the relative flow is assumed
teady during the time each bucket is operative and Eq. (6.22), for rotating
xes, is employed. Neglecting fluid friction on the buckets and any change
1 level between 2 and 3, we thus find that $W_2 = W_3$. This relation, to-
ether with the velocity diagrams of Fig. 14.2b, permits the torque to be
xpressed as

$$T = \eta_m \rho Q r (V_2 - \omega r)(1 - \cos \beta) \tag{14.3}$$

The output power P is equal to ωT; hence, by Eq. (14.3),

$$C_P = \frac{P}{(\rho/2)QV_2^2} = \eta_m 2x(1 - x)(1 - \cos \beta) \tag{14.4}$$

where $x = \omega r/V_2$ and C_P is a dimensionless power coefficient. If, as a first approximation, η_m is assumed to be a constant, Eq. (14.4) shows that, for any given value of β, C_P is a maximum for $x = \frac{1}{2}$, and that

$$C_{\text{Pmax}} = \eta_m \frac{1 - \cos \beta}{2} \tag{14.5}$$

In an actual turbine, the optimum value of x is about 0.45, instead of $\frac{1}{2}$, owing, in large measure, to the variation of η_m with x and, to a lesser extent, to friction in the flow over the buckets.

The efficiency of any hydraulic turbine is defined as the ratio of the actual shaft work to that which could be done in a frictionless machine. The frictional effects in the inlet duct are omitted in this definition, the inlet duct not being considered part of the turbine. Furthermore, in the case of the Pelton turbine, the slight difference in level between the nozzle exit 2 and the tail-water level 4 is disregarded. The energy equation [Eq. (5.10)] gives $\mathcal{W}_s = gH - (u_4 - u_0 - q_{0,4})$, where, since the fluid is incompressible, $u_4 - u_0 - q_{0,4}$ is the energy dissipated by friction. Using the notation introduced in Chap. VIII, namely, $gH_{l_{0,4}} = u_4 - u_0 - q_{0,4}$, we have $\mathcal{W}_s = g(H - H_{l_{0,1}}) - gH_{l_{1,4}}$. The efficiency is thus

$$\eta = \frac{\mathcal{W}_s}{g(H - H_{l_{0,1}})} = \frac{\mathcal{W}_s}{\mathcal{W}_s + gH_{l_{1,4}}} \tag{14.6}$$

where $H - H_{l_{0,1}}$, the total head minus the loss in the inlet pipe, is called the "effective head."

We obtain an expression for efficiency that is more useful in the present case, by writing Eq. (5.10) between sections 1 and 4 (neglecting the slight difference in height between these two sections).

$$\mathcal{W}_s = \frac{p_1 - p_4}{\rho} + \frac{V_1^2}{2} - gH_{l_{1,4}} \tag{14.7}$$

Noting that $\mathcal{W}_s = P/\rho Q$, we find from Eqs. (14.6) and (14.7)

$$\eta = \frac{\mathcal{W}_s}{[(p_1 - p_4)/\rho] + (V_1^2/2)} = \frac{C_P}{[2(p_1 - p_4)/\rho V_2^2] + (V_1^2/V_2^2)} \tag{14.8}$$

This equation is true in general and is not restricted by the assumption of frictionless flow over the buckets or through the nozzle. It is interesting to note that, in case the nozzle is assumed frictionless, the denominator of Eq. (14.8) reduces to 1 and $\eta = C_P$. If, further, friction of the water on the buckets is neglected, Eq. (14.4) may be used, and

$$\eta = \eta_m 2x(1 - x)(1 - \cos \beta) \tag{14.9}$$

Under these idealized conditions, the maximum value of η is equal to $\eta_m[(1 - \cos \beta)/2]$, η_{max} being less than η_m solely because β must be less than

π to enable the flow to clear the buckets. For $\beta = 165$ deg and $\eta_m = 0.97$, $\eta_{max} = 0.953$. As already mentioned, the maximum efficiency attained in practice is approximately 0.91.

The relationship between the efficiency and the output power measures the performance of a turbine over a range of operating conditions. According to the idealized equation (14.9), the efficiency of an impulse turbine of given blade angle β depends only on the ratio $x = \omega r/V_2$, regardless of the power output. Actually, there is some variation of η as P is changed with x constant. The discharge rate and hence P are usually controlled by means of a needle valve, which changes the effective cross-sectional area of the nozzle without much change in the velocity. Figure 14.3 gives an example of such an η versus P curve.

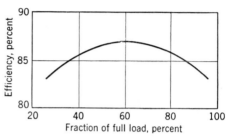

FIG. 14.3. — Efficiency versus output power for an impulse turbine.

14.2. Radial- and Mixed-flow Turbines. A turbine of this type is shown in Fig. 14.4. The flow, which is totally enclosed, enters the guide vanes directly from the inlet duct. These guides impart a tangential velocity and hence angular momentum to the water before it enters the revolving runner, in which its angular momentum is reduced. This change in angular momentum of the water as it passes through the runner gives rise to the driving torque of the turbine. From Fig. 14.4 it is clear that this type of turbine, known as the Francis turbine after J. B. Francis, who developed it in 1849, can handle a greater volume of flow than can an impulse turbine. Individual designs of runner include not only the purely radial-flow type, which is suited to relatively small volumes and high heads, but also the mixed-flow types shown in Fig. 14.5, which work efficiently with larger volumes and lower heads. On account of these wide design variations it has been possible to build Francis turbines to run at heads as low as 15 ft and as high as 750 ft. Installations up to 150,000 hp have been made, with efficiencies in the neighborhood of 94 per cent.

The resultant external torque on the system comprising the runner and shaft and the water inside the runner between sections 2 and 2' of Fig. 14.4 can be computed from the angular-momentum law [Eq. (6.17)].

$$\text{Resultant clockwise torque} = \rho Q(r_2 V_{t_2} - r_{2'} V_{t_{2'}})$$

This resultant exceeds the useful shaft torque T by the amount of the torques due to bearing friction and the water drag on the shroud of the runner. Defining the mechanical efficiency as in Eq. (14.1), we get

$$T = \eta_m \rho Q(r_2 V_{t_2} - r_{2'} V_{t_{2'}}) \tag{14.10}$$

In the case of the radial-flow turbine of Fig. 14.4, $r_{2'}$ and $V_{t_{2'}}$ are both uniform over 2', so that Eq. (14.10) has a definite meaning. On the other hand, for mixed-flow runners as in Fig. 14.5, both $r_{2'}$ and $V_{t_{2'}}$ vary over 2', and the meaning of Eq. (14.10) is not clear. There is no difficulty, however, if we consider only operating conditions near the design point, where the

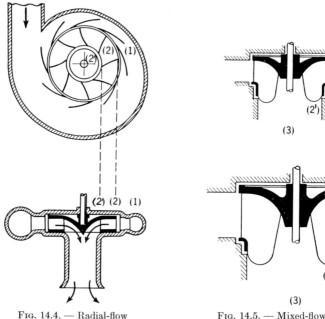

Fig. 14.4. — Radial-flow turbine.

Fig. 14.5. — Mixed-flow runners.

maximum efficiency obtains. Under these conditions it is shown below in Art. 14.4 that the blades must be designed to make $V_{t_{2'}} = 0$ everywhere, so that Eq. (14.10) reduces to $T = \eta_m \rho Q r_2 V_{t_2}$. For operation away from the design point it is desirable that $r_{2'} V_{t_{2'}} = \text{constant}$ everywhere, but this condition is practically impossible to fulfill with a mixed-flow runner. Further discussion is deferred to Art. 14.4.

We define the efficiency as in Eq. (14.6), including as part of the turbine everything between sections 1 and 5 of Fig. 14.6. Noting that $\mathcal{W}s = T\omega/\rho Q$, we combine Eqs. (14.6) and (14.10), to get

$$\eta = \eta_m \frac{\omega(r_2 V_{t_2} - r_{2'} V_{t_{2'}})}{g(H - H_{l_{0,1}})} \qquad (14.11)$$

which is sometimes referred to as Euler's turbine equation; it is of basic importance in turbine design.

Referring to Fig. 14.6, we break up the losses into several kinds.

a. Friction losses between 0 and 1 in the inlet pipe.

b. Friction losses between 1 and 2 in the guides.

c. Entrance losses and friction losses between 2 and 3 in the runner.

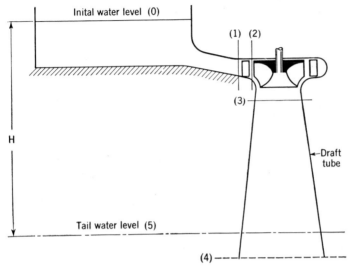

Fɪɢ. 14.6. — Schematic side elevation of a mixed-flow turbine.

Entrance losses occur if the speed, discharge rate, and guide-vane setting are improperly related, causing the relative velocity at 2 not to be tangent to the leading edge of the runner blade.

The condition shown in Fig. 14.7a is corrected in Fig. 14.7b by a de-

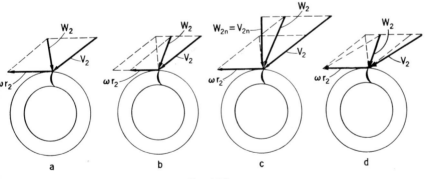

Fɪɢ. 14.7.

crease in ω, in Fig. 14.7c by an increase in Q (= $2\pi r_2 b_2 V_{n_2}$, where b_2 is the thickness of the runner at its periphery), and in Fig. 14.7d by a change in the setting of the guides, which control the direction of V_2.

d. Friction and separation losses between 3 and 4 in the draft tube.

e. Shock losses between 4 and 5 produced by the sudden enlargemen of the cross-sectional area of the flow at the draft-tube exit. Since the area changes from a finite value at 4 to a practically infinite one, it is clea that all the kinetic energy of the flow at 4 will be dissipated by viscosity in the tail water. This conclusion can be checked by reference to Eq. (8.62)

14.3. Draft Tube. The purpose of the divergent draft tube is to make the sum of the losses between sections 3 and 5 of Fig. 14.6 smaller than would otherwise be possible. Both the exit loss and the loss in the draft tube depend on the area ratio A_4/A_3. Since the exit loss is merely the kinetic energy of the flow at 4, we may define an exit-loss coefficient as $C_{4,5} = 2gH_{l_{4,5}}/V_3^2 = V_4^2/V_3^2$. By continuity,

$$C_{4,5} = \frac{V_4^2}{V_3^2} = \frac{A_3^2}{A_4^2} \qquad (14.12)$$

The combined friction and separation loss in a conical diffuser has been studied experimentally by several investigators. Their results [3] are

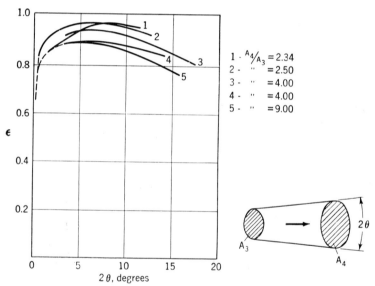

FIG. 14.8. — Diffuser efficiency ϵ versus diffuser angle 2θ for various exit-to-entrance-area ratios. (*After Patterson, reference 3. Courtesy of Aircraft Engineering.*)

conveniently expressed in terms of a diffuser efficiency ϵ, defined as $\epsilon = [p_4 - p_3 + \rho g(z_4 - z_3)]/(\rho/2)V_3^2[1 - (A_3/A_4)^2]$. Experimental values of ϵ as a function of the diffuser angle 2θ and the area ratio A_4/A_3 are plotted in Fig. 14.8. It is seen that, to a first approximation, the maximum value of ϵ is 0.9 for all values of A_4/A_3 tested and that it occurs at a value of 2θ approximately equal to 6 deg. The shape of these curves is easily ccounted for in terms of familiar concepts. For any given area ratio the ength of the diffuser becomes so great at small values of θ that the flow s essentially like that in a straight tube and the wall friction is excessive. As the angle of flare increases beyond the optimum value, however, the dverse pressure gradient associated with the deceleration of the fluid becomes big enough to cause a rapid thickening of the boundary layer and

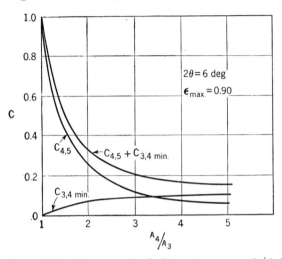

FIG. 14.9. — Loss coefficient C versus ratio of exit to entrance area A_4/A_3 for a diffuser.

separation of the flow from the wall. From the definition of ϵ, the equation of continuity, and Eq. (5.10), we find that

$$\epsilon = 1 - \{2gH_{l_{3,4}}/V_3^2[1 - (A_3/A_4)^2]\}.$$

Defining the loss coefficient for a diffuser (draft tube) as $C_{3,4} = 2gH_{l_{3,4}}/V_3^2$, we get

$$C_{3,4min} = \frac{2gH_{l_{3,4min}}}{V_3^2} = (1 - \epsilon_{max})\left[1 - \left(\frac{A_3}{A_4}\right)^2\right] \qquad (14.13)$$

Values of $C_{4,5}$ and $C_{3,4min}$, computed from Eqs. (14.12) and (14.13), respectively, are plotted against A_4/A_3 in Fig. 14.9. It is seen that the sum of the draft-tube and exit-loss coefficients decreases rapidly as A_4/A_3 is increased from 1 to 3 but that little is gained by use of a larger area ratio. If an area ratio $A_4/A_3 = 3$ is used, the corresponding diameter ratio is $d_4/d_3 = 1.7$; and the length-diameter ratio is $(z_3 - z_4)/d_3 = 6$, since the total flare angle $2\theta = 6$ deg.

14.4. Conditions for Efficient Operation. There are two conditions of operation that must be met if the efficiency of a turbine is to be a maximum. (1) The speed, discharge, and guide setting must be adjusted to ensure shockless entry of the water into the runner. (2) The outflow from the draft tube must have no tangential velocity component. Such a component is undesirable since it plays no role in getting the water out of th draft tube but merely increases the kinetic energy of the outflow and thu the exit shock loss. To translate this condition into one that applies a section 2′ of Fig. 14.6, we neglect friction and use the angular-momentum equation between sections 2′ and 4. Since the efflux of angular momentum at 4 is zero by assumption and no torque acts on the fluid, the angular momentum crossing 2′ must also be zero, that is, V_t must be zero everywhere over section 2′. This requirement can be fulfilled at the design conditions of operation by use of properly shaped runner blades.

For operating conditions away from the design point there will be non zero values of V_t at section 2′ and, consequently, everywhere in the draft tube, angular momentum being conserved. In order that this tangential velocity may not, through centrifugal effects, cause intermingling of the stream tubes and thus give rise to eddy losses, it should be distributed in a definite way along the radius. To determine this distribution, we consider first section 3 and assume that there the axial velocity component is uniformly distributed and the radial component is zero. We also neglect friction and assume the blades to be so shaped that any element of the discharge dQ flows through a vase-shaped stream tube, as in Fig. 14.10,

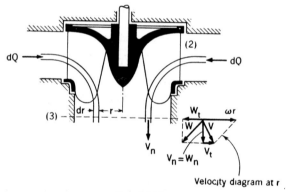

Velocity diagram at r

Fig. 14.10.

not mingling with other elements. In the figure, dQ is the volume that at 3 passes through the annulus of radius r and width dr. Neglecting for simplicity any change in level between 2 and 3, we may write the energy equation for rotating axes [Eq. (6.22)] in the form

$$p + \frac{\rho}{2} W^2 - \frac{\rho}{2} \omega^2 r^2 = p_2 + \frac{\rho}{2} W_2^2 - \frac{\rho}{2} \omega^2 r_2^2$$

where the symbols without subscript refer to any point of section 3. Conditions are assumed uniform at 2, so that the right-hand side of the equation is the same for all stream tubes and

$$p + \frac{\rho}{2} W^2 - \frac{\rho}{2} \omega^2 r^2 = \text{constant} \qquad (14.14)$$

he further condition, that the radial pressure change balance the cen-
rifugal force at 3, is obtained from Eq. (4.4) by the substitution of
$- \partial p / \partial r$, V_t, and r in place of $\partial p / \partial n$, V, and R, respectively.

$$\frac{\partial p}{\partial r} = \rho \frac{V_t^2}{r} \qquad (14.15)$$

Differentiate Eq. (14.14) with respect to r, substitute for $\partial p / \partial r$ from
Eq. (14.15), and use the fact that $W^2 = W_t^2 + W_n^2 = (\omega r - V_t)^2 + V_n^2$.

$$\rho \frac{V_t^2}{r} + \frac{\rho}{2} \frac{\partial}{\partial r} [(\omega r - V_t)^2 + V_n^2] - \rho \omega^2 r = 0$$

ince V_n is independent of r by assumption, we finally get

$$\left(\frac{V_t}{r} + \frac{\partial V_t}{\partial r} \right)(V_t - \omega r) = 0 \qquad (14.16)$$

'or blades designed to give $V_t = 0$ at the design point the second factor
of Eq. (14.16) is in general not equal to zero. It is therefore necessary that
he first factor be zero. The differential equation thus obtained is

$$\frac{1}{V_t} \frac{\partial V_t}{\partial r} dr + \frac{dr}{r} = 0$$

which integrates to $r V_t = $ constant. It thus appears that, if V_t is not everywhere zero, it should be distributed like the velocity in a potential vortex,
o that the resultant flow at 3 is the sum of an axial motion and a vortex
motion with its axis at the center of rotation (see Arts. 4.11 and 11.14).
n the absence of friction the angular momentum of the fluid is conserved,
and the circulation, or strength, of this vor-
ex, $\Gamma = 2\pi r V_t$, will be constant throughout
he draft tube.

It may be remarked that the stability condition $r V_t = $ constant is not in general fulfilled in a mixed-flow turbine, except for a
imited range of operating conditions. In a
purely radial-flow turbine, however, this condition is satisfied if the entrance to the draft
tube is properly designed. For in this case
the flow is assumed uniform at the runner

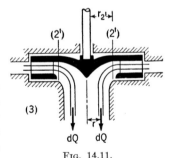

Fɪɢ. 14.11.

exit at radius $r_{2'}$ (Fig. 14.11). In the absence of friction, no torque is exerted on the fluid in any stream tube between sections 2′ and 3, so that the
angular-momentum law [Eq. (6.17)] gives $dT = 0 = \rho \, dQ(r V_t - r_{2'} V_{t_2})$ or
$r V_t = r_{2'} V_{t_{2'}} = $ constant.

14.5. Axial-flow Turbine. An axial-flow (or propeller) turbine, such as is shown in Fig. 14.12, is able to handle a larger volume on a given diameter than other types, since the discharge is relatively unrestricted by the

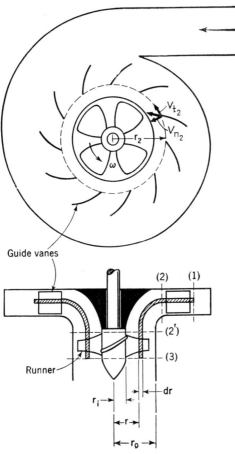

wheel. The modern low-head turbine of the propeller type is usually fitted with blades that can be adjusted to suit operating conditions, a feature due to Dr. Viktor Kaplan of Czechoslovakia. It is of more compact construction than the Francis type, runs faster, and has a higher partial-load efficiency, owing to the adjustable pitch of the blades. The Francis wheel may have some 16 blades and an outer shroud ring. The Kaplan turbine usually has but 4 to 6 blades and no shroud ring, so that the surface subjected to high water speeds is comparatively small, and so are the frictional losses. An efficiency above 92 per cent is practical with units up to 60,000 hp capacity.

As shown in Fig. 14.12, the guide vanes for a Kaplan turbine are arranged in the same way as for a Francis turbine and serve the same purpose, *viz.*, to impart angular momentum to the flow. Before entering the runner, however,

FIG. 14.12. — Diagrammatic sketch of an axial-flow turbine.

the stream turns through a right angle and is assumed to have no radial velocity component as it passes through the runner. It is further assumed that the axial component of velocity is uniformly distributed over the cross-sectional area of the stream at sections 3 and 4. Both these assumptions can be realized by suitable design of the passages and runner blades.

The resultant external torque on the system comprising the runner, the shaft, and the fluid between sections 2′ and 3 is readily obtained by familiar methods. The argument of the last paragraph of Art. 14.4 can be applied etween sections 2 and 2' of Fig. 14.12 to show that, at 2', rV_t = constant $= r_2V_{t_2}$. Furthermore, the analysis leading to Eq. (14.16) is valid between ections 2' and 3 of Fig. 14.12 and indicates that the blades should be designed to give, at 3, rV_t = constant (preferably zero). From the angular-momentum law we thus get

$$\text{Resultant torque} = \rho Q(r_{2'}V_{t_{2'}} - r_3 V_{t_3})$$

nd if the mechanical efficiency is defined as in Eq. (14.1), the useful shaft orque is

$$T = \eta_m \rho Q(r_{2'}V_{t_{2'}} - r_3 V_{t_3}) \qquad (14.17)$$

The discussion of efficiency, losses, and draft tube given in connection ith the Francis turbine is equally valid for a Kaplan turbine.

A rational method of blade design, based on wind-tunnel data on air-oils, is possible for an axial-flow machine. Since the flow is assumed to ollow annular stream tubes, as in Fig. 14.12, the blade elements of length dr in one stream tube can be designed without reference to adjoining ele-nents. The essentially two-dimensional flow over a blade element at adius r is conveniently represented by unrolling of the annular stream ube onto a plane, as in Fig. 14.13. The local velocity diagrams are deter-nined by over-all requirements of ead, discharge, efficiency, speed, and ub and casing diameters, together ith the condition that the product V_t be independent of radius. If, in ddition, the lift and drag coefficients or two-dimensional flow over the pro-ile are known, it is not difficult to letermine with a useful degree of ac-uracy the chord length and angle of the element. A detailed discussion of

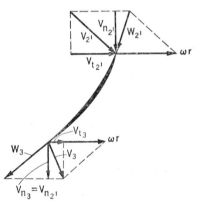

FIG. 14.13. — Velocity diagram at radius r of an axial-flow turbine.

the theory is deferred to Chap. XV; for the present it is sufficient to re-mark that the blade angle must decrease toward the blade tip.

14.6. Dimensional Analysis of a Turbine. Two important uses of dimensional theory in connection with a turbine are (1) to determine what type of turbine will operate most efficiently under given conditions of head, speed, and power; and (2) to predict the performance of a prototype from tests on a model.

We begin the analysis by listing, on the basis of experience, the inde-pendent variables ρ, μ, g, H, Q, D, and ω, for a turbine of given design. The runner diameter D is here chosen as a convenient measure of size.

This list can be simplified if we notice that the incompressible flow in a reaction turbine is totally enclosed, except at the surfaces of the initial and tail-water reservoirs. The gravity field, therefore, affects the flow only in connection with the over-all potential-energy change gH, the flow pattern being otherwise independent of g. The same is true also of an impulse turbine, because the velocity of the free jet is so high that g has no influence on it (see Art. 4.7a). We may accordingly express the output power and efficiency as functions of six independent variables.

$$P = f_1(\rho, D, \omega, Q, gH, \mu) \qquad (14.18)$$

$$\eta = f_2(\rho, D, \omega, Q, gH, \mu) \qquad (14.19)$$

At this stage it is advisable to test whether the variables in parentheses are really independent, as assumed. Consider, for example, a change in gH. By suitably readjusting a valve, or gate, in the system and changing the load, we can keep ω and Q constant. The other variables will be unaffected, except possibly by slight temperature changes, which are disregarded. Similarly, it can be shown that each variable can be altered independently of the other five. That no important variable has been omitted can only be decided by experiment or detailed analysis.

Applying the Π theorem to Eqs. (14.18) and (14.19) and including ρ, D, and ω in each of the four independent Π products, we get

$$\frac{P}{\rho \omega^3 D^5} = f_3 \left(\frac{Q}{\omega D^3}, \frac{gH}{\omega^2 D^2}, \frac{\rho \omega D^2}{\mu} \right) \qquad (14.20)$$

$$\eta = f_4 \left(\frac{Q}{\omega D^3}, \frac{gH}{\omega^2 D^2}, \frac{\rho \omega D^2}{\mu} \right) \qquad (14.21)$$

Experiments show that, in the usual range of speed and size, the flow is highly turbulent and the viscosity has only a secondary influence on the behavior of a turbine. Variations in speed or size large enough to cause a change from turbulent to laminar conditions must of course be ruled out if μ is to be neglected. Subject to this restriction, we may write

$$\frac{P}{\rho \omega^3 D^5} = f_3 \left(\frac{Q}{\omega D^3}, \frac{gH}{\omega^2 D^2} \right) \qquad (14.22)$$

$$\eta = f_4 \left(\frac{Q}{\omega D^3}, \frac{gH}{\omega^2 D^2} \right) \qquad (14.23)$$

Equations (14.22) and (14.23) are useful in the application of test data from a model to a prototype. Model data plotted in terms of these dimensionless quantities are immediately applicable to a prototype, provided that the influence of viscosity is negligible, as we have assumed. These equations also show that, if H, ω, ρ, and D are all constant (i.e., if the head and speed of a given hydraulic turbine are held fixed), P and η are functions of Q only, so that Q may be eliminated and η plotted against P. Such a curve for a Pelton turbine is given above in Fig. 14.3, while curves for several reaction turbines are shown in Fig. 14.14. The efficiencies of the fixed-blade machines, especially the Francis turbine, are seen to be excellent at the design point, but they drop off rapidly if the load changes, because the blade shape is then incorrect, the flow is much disturbed, and eddy

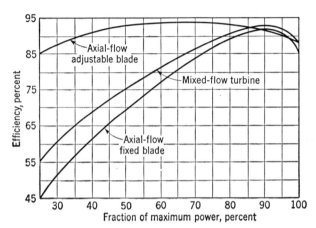

Fig. 14.14. — Curves of efficiency versus power for mixed- and axial-flow turbines. (*Courtesy of G. E. Russell.*)

losses occur. The efficiency of the Kaplan turbine, however, is maintained nearly constant over a wide range of load by means of a hydraulic servo-motor that automatically adjusts both the guides and blades to the optimum setting.

The behavior of geometrically similar turbines operating at maximum efficiency is of interest, especially in connection with the choice of a turbine to run under given conditions of head, speed, and power. It is found that the efficiency is a maximum for only one pair of values of the two independent variables of Eq. (14.23). Thus, if $\eta = \eta_{\max}$,

$$\frac{Q}{\omega D^3} = \text{constant} = C_1 \qquad (14.24)$$

$$\frac{gH}{\omega^2 D^2} = \text{constant} = C_2 \qquad (14.25)$$

where the values of C_1 and C_2 depend on the design of the turbine. Equation (14.22) then yields

$$\frac{P}{\rho \omega^3 D^5} = \text{constant} = C_3 \qquad (14.26)$$

These three equations indicate the effect of changes in ρ, ω, or D on Q, H and P of a given type of turbine running at maximum efficiency. Further-more, Eqs. (14.25) and (14.26) are the basis of the widely used "specific speed," which is discussed below.

Eliminate D from Eqs. (14.25) and (14.26), and get

$$\frac{\omega P^{\frac{1}{2}}}{H^{\frac{5}{4}}} = \frac{C_3^{\frac{1}{2}}}{C_2^{\frac{5}{4}}} \rho^{\frac{1}{2}} g^{\frac{5}{4}} \quad \text{or} \quad \frac{N\text{HP}^{\frac{1}{2}}}{H^{\frac{5}{4}}} = \frac{C_3^{\frac{1}{2}}}{C_2^{\frac{5}{4}}} \rho^{\frac{1}{2}} g^{\frac{5}{4}} \frac{60}{2\pi} \frac{1}{550^{\frac{1}{2}}}$$

where N is the speed in rpm, IP is the output horsepower, and H is the head in feet. The right-hand side of this equation has a definite constant value for a turbine of given design operating on water. This constant is called the specific speed N_s, so that

$$N_s = \frac{N\text{HP}^{\frac{1}{2}}}{H^{\frac{5}{4}}} \tag{14.27}$$

The name specific speed comes from the fact that, if a "specific turbine" be imagined that at maximum efficiency develops 1 hp under a 1-ft head, N_s is numerically equal to the speed, in rpm, of this turbine. The specific speed is used in the selection of the type of turbine best suited to operate at a given speed under a given head and produce a given horsepower. These three factors are determined by the characteristics of the site chosen for the installation and by the use to which the turbine is to be put. Experience shows that the range of allowable values for each of the principal types of turbine is as follows:

Kind of Turbine	Specific Speed N_s
Pelton (single jet)............	Not over 6
Pelton (multiple jet)..........	Not over 10
Francis.....................	10–110
Kaplan.....................	100–215

Computation of the specific speed is thus the first step of the designer. He is then able to decide on the general type of turbine required for an efficient installation and can proceed with the details of the design.

14.7. Cavitation. The pressure everywhere in a turbine must be above a certain critical value if the continuity of the liquid is to be preserved. Otherwise, cavities of air and vapor will form, and the flow conditions will change, to the detriment of the efficiency. It has been found by tests on model turbines [6] that the formation of bubbles of air brought out of solution through lowering of the pressure has but a slight effect on the efficiency. The efficiency begins to be seriously affected only after bubbles of vapor start to form, i.e., only after the vapor pressure has been reached somewhere in the flow. In the following discussion, the critical pressure will, accordingly, be identified with the vapor pressure:

The formation of vapor bubbles in a liquid through lowering of the pressure is called "cavitation." It is inherently an unstable phenomenon. In a flowing liquid, vapor bubbles form, grow and simultaneously move downstream, and ultimately collapse upon reaching a zone of higher pressure. The collapse causes a pressure wave, which spreads outward with the speed of sound relative to the liquid. If the zone of collapse is close enough to the place where the cavities form, the wave raises the pressure there above the critical value and cavitation ceases momentarily. The wave dies away very quickly, however, so that the phenomenon is repeated with a frequency that may be as high as several thousand cycles per second, depending on the apparatus involved. There may be no regular frequency associated with the cavitation if the collapse point is far downstream from the point of formation.

Cavitation is undesirable for two reasons. (1) The efficiency η decreases if a sufficient volume of cavitation is present. (2) Even though there may not be enough cavitation to affect η, the collapse of localized cavitation produces repeated impacts so intense that the blades may be seriously damaged. With this mechanical damaging action may be combined electrochemical effects, which accelerate the destruction.

According to the first paragraph of this article, the occurrence of cavitation depends on the value of the expression $p_m - p_v$, where p_m is the minimum pressure in the turbine and p_v is the vapor pressure of the water at the operating temperature. If $p_m - p_v > 0$, cavitation will not take place; but if $p_m - p_v = 0$, cavitation will, in general, occur. The efficiency thus depends on $p_m - p_v$ in addition to the other independent variables listed in Eq. (14.19).

$$\eta = f_1(\rho, D, \omega, Q, gH, \mu, p_m - p_v) \qquad (14.28)$$

Measurement of p_m is ordinarily not feasible, since it usually occurs on the runner blades. It is therefore necessary to express p_m in terms of measurable quantities. This is done by means of the energy equation, as follows: Referring to Fig. 14.6 and using Eq. (5.10), for fixed axes, we find

$$p_2 - p_0 + \frac{\rho}{2}(V_2^2 - V_0^2) + \rho g(z_2 - z_0) + \rho g H_{l_{0,2}} = 0$$

and from Eq. (6.21), for rotating axes,

$$p_m - p_2 + \frac{\rho}{2}(W_m^2 - W_2^2) + \rho g(z_m - z_2) + \rho g H_{l_{2,m}} + \frac{\rho}{2}\omega^2(r_2^2 - r_m^2) = 0$$

Combining these equations, noting that $V_0 = 0$ and $p_0 = p_a$, we get

$$p_m - p_a + \frac{\rho}{2}[W_m^2 - W_2^2 + V_2^2 + \omega^2(r_2^2 - r_m^2)] - \rho g(H - h) + \rho g H_{l_{0,m}} = 0$$

where $h = z_m - z_5$, the height of the minimum-pressure point above the tail-water level. Since the velocities and frictional effects upstream from the point m, where cavitation starts, depend only on ρ, D, ω, Q, and μ the last equation can be written

$$p_m = p_a - \rho g h + f(\rho, D, \omega, Q, gH, \mu) \qquad (14.29)$$

Equation (14.28) thus becomes

$$\eta = f_2(\rho, D, \omega, Q, gH, \mu, p_a - p_v - \rho g h)$$

Neglecting μ, as in Art. 14.6, and applying the Π theorem, we find as one possible rearrangement of this equation

$$\eta = f_3 \left(\frac{Q}{\omega D^3}, \frac{gH}{\omega^2 D^2}, \frac{p_a - p_v - \rho g h}{\rho \omega^2 D^2} \right)$$

or, alternatively,

$$\eta = f_4 \left(\frac{Q}{\omega D^3}, \frac{gH}{\omega^2 D^2}, \frac{p_a - p_v - \rho g h}{\rho g H} \right) \qquad (14.30)$$

The form of the cavitation number, $(p_a - p_v - \rho g h)/\rho g H$, given in Eq. (14.30) is due to D. Thoma of Munich and is in general use as a cavitation criterion for hydraulic machinery [5]. It is denoted by the symbol

$$\sigma = \frac{p_a - p_v - \rho g h}{\rho g H} \qquad (14.31)$$

We should expect σ to have no effect on η, so long as $\sigma > \sigma_c$, a critical value corresponding to the starting condition for cavitation. This expecta-

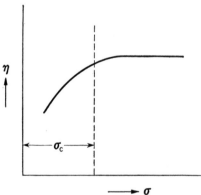

tion is borne out by experiments as shown schematically in Fig. 14.15. Since the value of σ_c determined from tests on a model turbine is equal to that for a prototype, the turbine builder can tell whether or not a certain design will be free from cavitation under all operating conditions.

The obvious means to eliminate cavitation is to reduce the height h of the turbine above tail water, since as shown by Eq. (14.29), reduction of h increases p_m. Lowering of the turbine is, however, frequently im-

FIG. 14.15. — Schematic curve of turbine efficiency η versus cavitation number σ.

possible for reasons of accessibility or structural soundness. In such a case improved blade design may serve to increase p_m above the danger point. For example, in Kaplan turbines, which employ blades of airfoil section, it is common practice to use a profile that has a practically uniform pressure

istribution along the chord. A small region of excessively low pressure is
hus avoided. A profile of this type developed by the NACA for other
pplications is shown in Fig. 10.6a.

Even with the most advanced design it may be impossible to avoid
avitation under all operating conditions, such as, for example, an exces-
ively low tail-water level at certain seasons of the year. In such a case,
lamage to the blades can be reduced if the endangered areas are coated
vith a welded-on layer of resistant material like stainless steel.

SELECTED BIBLIOGRAPHY

, Addison, H.: "Applied Hydraulics," 2d ed., John Wiley & Sons, Inc., New York,
 1938.
. Lowy, R.: Efficiency Analysis of Pelton Wheels, *Trans. Am. Soc. Mech. Engrs.*,
 vol. 66, pp. 527–538, Aug., 1944.
. Patterson, G. N.: Modern Diffuser Design, *Aircraft Eng.*, vol. 10, pp. 267–273, 1938.
. Russell, G. E.: "Hydraulics," 5th ed., Henry Holt and Company, Inc., New York,
 1942.
, Thoma, D.: Experimental Research in the Field of Water Power, *Trans. 1st World
 Power Conf.*, vol. 2, pp. 536–551, Lund Humphries, London, 1925.
. Vuskovic, I.: Experiments on the Influence of Air Content on Cavitation (German),
 Escher Wyss Mitt. vol. 13, pp. 83–90, 1940; (English) *R.T.P. Translation* 2387, re-
 printed by Durand Reprinting Committee, California Institute of Technology,
 Pasadena, Calif.

CHAPTER XV

PUMPS, FANS, AND COMPRESSORS

The purpose of a pump, fan, or compressor is to convert mechanical work into energy of a fluid; it is thus the inverse of a turbine. In this chapter we shall discuss only hydrodynamic machines, leaving positive displacement apparatus out of consideration. Hydrodynamic machines are divided into radial-flow, or centrifugal, and axial-flow types, according to the motion of the fluid as it passes through the impeller. In a pump the working fluid is a liquid, while in a fan or compressor it is a gas. Fans are distinguished from compressors by the fact that, in the former, the working fluid suffers no appreciable density change, while in the latter the density is considerably increased.

15.1. Centrifugal Pump and Fan. A centrifugal pump consists essentially of a bladed wheel, the impeller, which rotates inside a casing, as shown in Fig. 15.1. Liquid enters the impeller near the axis and flows

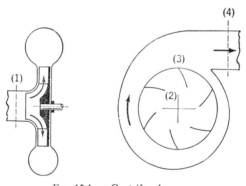

FIG. 15.1. — Centrifugal pump.

normal to the axis out along the blades into the casing and thence to the discharge pipe. Centrifugal force acting on the revolving liquid in the impeller produces the flow.

Tangential velocity is necessarily imparted to the liquid by the impeller, since the applied torque gives rise to a flux of angular momentum. The tangential velocity plays no part in transporting the liquid into the discharge pipe and is dissipated in shock losses unless guide vanes or a vortex chamber be fitted to reduce the whirl gradually. A pump with guide vanes, known as a turbine pump, has a high efficiency over only a limited range of speed and discharge and is more expensive than one without guides. A vortex chamber, which reduces the tangential velocity simply by allowing the fluid to move farther from the center of rotation before entering the outflow pipe, adds to the over-all diameter of a pump. For these reasons the type most widely used is the simple volute pump, illustrated in Fig. 15.1.

The maximum head against which a single impeller works is ordinarily

360

about 300 ft of water, although several single-stage pumps have been built
to pump against heads as high as 2,000 ft. If a high head is needed, it is

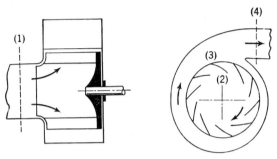

Fig. 15.2. — Centrifugal fan.

usual to build a pump with several impellers connected in series. Six such
stages is the normal maximum number. Discharge rate and power vary
between wide limits. The maximum efficiency of a centrifugal pump has
been made as high as 92 per cent but is usually about 85 to 88 per cent.

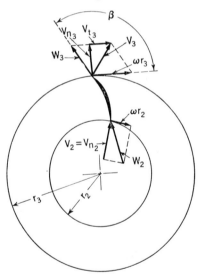

A centrifugal fan (Fig. 15.2) is
essentially the same as a centrifugal
pump as long as the pressure rise is
limited to 10 or 15 in. of water. Otherwise the density change in the air being handled becomes appreciable and
the machine must be treated as a centrifugal compressor or supercharger,
under quite different design procedures.

The resultant torque on the impeller and on the fluid between sections
2 and 3 of Fig. 15.1 or 15.2 is obtained from the angular-momentum
equation [Eq. (6.19)].

Resultant torque $= \rho Q(r_3 V_{t_3} - r_2 V_{t_2})$

where Q is the volume rate of flow and
the velocities and radii are as shown

Fig. 15.3. — Velocity diagrams for a
centrifugal pump or fan.

in Fig. 15.3. This resultant includes
the applied torque T of the driving motor, as well as the torques due to
bearing friction and the drag of the fluid on the shroud. We define the
mechanical efficiency as

$$\eta_m = \frac{\omega(\text{resultant torque})}{\omega T} \tag{15.1}$$

and get

$$T = \frac{\rho Q(r_3 V_{t_3} - r_2 V_{t_2})}{\eta_m}$$

The flow at 2 has no tangential component if the inlet piping has bends in only one plane or if a suitable straightener is installed near the entrance. For this reason, the expression for T is simplified to

$$T = \frac{\rho Q r_3 V_{t_3}}{\eta_m} \tag{15.2}$$

The efficiency η is defined as the ratio of the input power that would be needed for a frictionless machine to that actually required. Since the flow is incompressible, the steady-flow energy equation [Eq. (5.10)] can be written between the entrance and exit sections in the form

$$-\mathcal{W}_s = \frac{p_4 - p_1}{\rho} + \frac{V_4^2 - V_1^2}{2} + g(z_4 - z_1) + gH_{l_{1,4}}$$

where $-\mathcal{W}_s$ is the work done by the driving motor per unit mass of fluid and $H_{l_{1,4}}$ is the sum of all the losses between sections 1 and 4 of Fig. 15.1 or 15.2. The efficiency is thus

$$\eta = \frac{\rho Q(-\mathcal{W}_s - gH_{l_{1,4}})}{\rho Q(-\mathcal{W}_s)} = \frac{[(p_4 - p_1)/\rho] + [(V_4^2 - V_1^2)/2] + g(z_4 - z_1)}{-\mathcal{W}_s} \tag{15.3}$$

Noting that $-\mathcal{W}_s = \omega T/\rho Q$ and combining Eqs. (15.2) and (15.3), we get Euler's equation for a pump or fan.

$$\eta = \eta_m \frac{[(p_4 - p_1)/\rho] + [(V_4^2 - V_1^2)/2] + g(z_4 - z_1)}{\omega r_3 V_{t_3}} \tag{15.4}$$

The head developed is defined as the shaft work that would be needed in the frictionless case per unit weight of fluid. Thus the head is

$$H = \frac{p_4 - p_1}{\rho g} + \frac{V_4^2 - V_1^2}{2g} + z_4 - z_1 \tag{15.5}$$

Equation (15.4) is frequently written in terms of H.

$$\eta = \eta_m \frac{gH}{\omega r_3 V_{t_3}} \tag{15.6}$$

This equation is analogous to Eq. (14.11) for a turbine.

The losses in a pump or fan are similar to those in a turbine but are necessarily larger, for the flow takes place against an increasing pressure. The adverse pressure gradient leads to thicker boundary layers and possibly to separation.

It should be mentioned that Eq. (15.3) is a slight overestimate of the efficiency, for in practice some recirculation of fluid occurs through the clearance spaces between shroud and casing. This effect, which results from the adverse pressure gradient, will be disregarded here.

To determine whether a pump or fan will suit a particular application it is useful to have an experimental characteristic curve, *i.e.*, a curve of H versus Q. Several common shapes of characteristic curve are shown in Fig. 15.4. The shape depends on whether the blades are radial or curved, as will be shown below. The characteristic curve also depends on the speed ω, so that several curves are needed to show the performance over a range of speed.

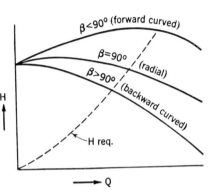

The head required to force a given quantity Q through the pipe, or duct, system to which the machine is attached is, in general, roughly proportional to Q^2, since the Reynolds number is usually high. It is clear that the pump or fan should be chosen so that its charac-

Fig. 15.4. — Characteristic curves for centrifugal machines. β is the blade angle at exit from the impeller (see Fig. 15.3).

teristic curve will intersect the head-required curve at the desired value of Q. A typical head-required curve is shown dotted in Fig. 15.4.

In the range of discharge values for which the efficiency is approximately constant, the slope of the characteristic curve depends on the value of β, the blade angle at the exit from the impeller (Fig. 15.3). Using the velocity diagrams of Fig. 15.3, we get H from Eq. (15.6) in the form

$$H = \frac{\eta}{\eta_m} \frac{\omega^2 r_3^2}{g} \left(1 + \frac{V_{n_3}}{\omega r_3} \frac{1}{\tan \beta} \right) \tag{15.7}$$

Since V_{n_3} is proportional to Q, it follows that, at constant speed, H would vary linearly with Q, provided that η/η_m were constant. Since the latter varies somewhat, the actual curves are like those of Fig. 15.4. The general trend over the operating range is seen to depend on β, but all three curves drop off at both ends of the diagram, owing to the decrease in η/η_m.

Backward-curved blades are preferred in many applications, for the following reasons: (1) The absolute exit velocity is less than for other blade shapes, so that the shock loss at impeller exit can be kept small without the use of a large-diameter casing or guide vanes. (2) The negative slope of the characteristic curve over a large range of discharge rate makes possible the stable operation of two machines in parallel over this range.

It is also useful to have curves of efficiency and input power versus discharge rate, so that the power requirements can be easily determined. A typical set of curves for a pump with backward-curved blades is shown in Fig. 15.5.

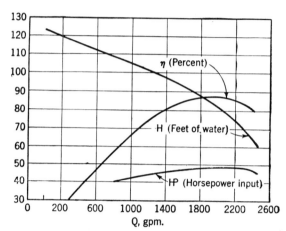

Fig. 15.5. — Head H, efficiency η, and input horse-power IP versus discharge rate Q, for a centrifugal pump with backward-curved blades.

15.2. Axial-flow Pump and Fan. Axial-flow pumps are built in a wide variety of sizes for use where a large discharge rate is required under a relatively low head. The unrestricted passage through such a pump adapts it to handling solids in suspension. Typical applications are to sewage disposal, irrigation, and drainage.

Axial-flow fans, like pumps, are best adapted to delivering a large volume under a low head. These fans are used for many ventilating applications, such as in mines, buildings, and vessels.

The fan shown in Fig. 15.6 is mounted at the entrance to a duct, but it is obvious that such a unit can be mounted anywhere in a duct system. The guide vanes shown in the figure serve their usual purpose, *viz.*, to remove from the fluid the angular momentum imparted by the impeller, thus eliminating the superfluous tangential velocity and increasing the pressure rise through the fan.

The blades and guides are designed so that no radial flow occurs between sections 1 and 3 of Fig. 15.6. The bell mouth and the hub fairing are shaped to give a uniformly distributed, purely axial velocity at 1. Since the casing and hub diameters are uniform between 1 and 3 and no radial flow occurs, continuity requires a uniform distribution of axial velocity at 3. There is no tangential velocity at 3. The tapering of the hub increases the cross-sectional area of the flow, thus reducing the velocity and increasing the pressure. Section 4, at which the diffusing action is complete and conditions are uniform across the duct, is taken as the downstream end of the fan.

The resultant torque on the blade elements and fluid within the annular stream tube between 1 and 2 at radius r is found from the angular-momentum law [Eq. (6.19)] to be

$$\text{Resultant torque} = \rho r(V_{t_2} - V_{t_1})\, dQ$$

where dQ is the volume flow through the stream tube, and V_{t_2} and V_{t_1} are the tangential velocity components at radius r at 2 and 1, respectively. If

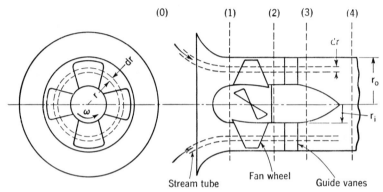

(0)   (1)   (2)   (3)   (4)

FIG. 15.6. — Axial-flow fan.

we neglect friction, we can show by the method of Art. 14.4 that the product rV_t is constant over section 2; and, by assumption, $V_{t_1} = 0$. Summing over the entire cross section, we get, therefore

$$\text{Resultant torque} = \rho Q r V_{t_2}$$

Introduction of the mechanical efficiency from Eq. (15.1) leads to

$$T = \frac{\rho Q r V_{t_2}}{\eta_m} \tag{15.8}$$

where T is the torque applied to the shaft by the driving motor. This equation is identical with Eq. (15.2) for a centrifugal machine.

The efficiency and head are defined just as for a centrifugal fan and can be expressed by Eqs. (15.3) to (15.6). It is customary, however, in the case of a fan mounted at the entrance to a duct, to include the bell mouth as part of the fan. If this is done, the expression for the head becomes

$$H = \frac{p_4 - p_0}{\rho g} + \frac{V_4^2}{2g} + z_4 - z_0 \tag{15.9}$$

section 0 being taken in front of the fan where the velocity is zero. Since the losses between 0 and 1 are small, there is practically no difference between Eqs. (15.5) and (15.9).

The characteristic curve of H versus Q is useful for an axial-flow

machine, just as for a centrifugal one. A typical curve, together with curves
of power input and efficiency, is shown in Fig. 15.7. The dip in the charac
teristic curve is caused by "stalling," *i.e.*, by separation of the flow from
the blades. This separation begins near the hub, where the operating

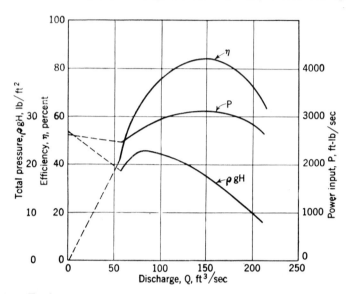

Fig. 15.7. — Total pressure, efficiency, and input power versus discharge rate for an axial-flow
fan. (*After Keller, reference 7.*)

conditions are less favorable than near the blade tips, owing to the lower
speed at the hub.

15.3. Dimensional Analysis of a Pump or Fan. Dimensional analysis
is used in the same way for these machines as for a hydraulic turbine
(see Art. 14.6).

Three important quantities in connection with the design or selection
of a pump or fan are the head produced H, the power input required P,
and the efficiency η. For a machine of given design, each of these is a
function of the following independent variables: ρ, ω, D, Q, and μ. Here D
represents the impeller diameter, chosen as a convenient length characteristic of the machine. The head H depends also on g, since H represents
shaft work per unit *weight* of fluid. The product gH, however, or the shaft
work per unit *mass* of fluid, is independent of g, because the flow through
the machine is totally enclosed and the fluid incompressible. Accordingly,
we write, for a given design,

$$gH = f_1(\rho,\omega,D,Q,\mu)$$
$$P = f_2(\rho,\omega,D,Q,\mu)$$
$$\eta = f_3(\rho,\omega,D,Q,\mu)$$

Applying the Π theorem and letting ρ, ω, and D be common to the three independent Π products of each of these equations, we get

$$\frac{gH}{\omega^2 D^2} = f_4 \left(\frac{Q}{\omega D^3}, \frac{\rho \omega D^2}{\mu} \right)$$

$$\frac{P}{\rho \omega^3 D^5} = f_5 \left(\frac{Q}{\omega D^3}, \frac{\rho \omega D^2}{\mu} \right)$$

$$\eta = f_6 \left(\frac{Q}{\omega D^3}, \frac{\rho \omega D^2}{\mu} \right)$$

Experiment shows, as for turbines (Art. 14.6), that the viscosity has only a secondary effect on the performance of a pump or fan. Hence, for a given design,

$$\frac{gH}{\omega^2 D^2} = f_4 \left(\frac{Q}{\omega D^3} \right) \tag{15.10}$$

$$\frac{P}{\rho \omega^3 D^5} = f_5 \left(\frac{Q}{\omega D^3} \right) \tag{15.11}$$

$$\eta = f_6 \left(\frac{Q}{\omega D^3} \right) \tag{15.12}$$

Equation (15.10) indicates that the characteristic curves at various speeds for a series of geometrically similar machines will all coalesce into a single curve when plotted nondimensionally, with $gH/\omega^2 D^2$ as ordinate and $Q/\omega D^3$ as abscissa. Similar conclusions can be drawn from Eqs. (15.11) and (15.12) regarding the power and efficiency. These statements are of course valid only over the range of size and speed for which changes in Reynolds number $\rho \omega D^2 / \mu$ have a negligible effect on the flow.

Equations (15.10) to (15.12) are useful also in indicating the effect of changes in size or speed on the performance at maximum efficiency η_{max}. If $\eta = \eta_{max}$, Eq. (15.12) shows that $Q/\omega D^3$ has a definite constant value. Therefore,

$$\frac{Q}{\omega D^3} = C_1 \tag{15.13}$$

$$\frac{gH}{\omega^2 D^2} = C_2 \tag{15.14}$$

$$\frac{P}{\rho \omega^3 D^5} = C_3 \tag{15.15}$$

In words, Q is proportional to ωD^3, H is proportional to $\omega^2 D^2$, and P is proportional to $\rho \omega^3 D^5$.

The concept of specific speed is applied in the selection of a pump to satisfy known operating conditions, just as in the case of a hydraulic turbine (Art. 14.6). The discharge Q, the head H, and the speed ω are usually required to have certain values in any proposed installation. A dimensionless product of these quantities that has a definite value for a machine of given design operating at maximum efficiency is obtained from Eqs. (15.13) and (15.14).

$$\frac{\omega Q^{\frac{1}{2}}}{(gH)^{\frac{3}{4}}} = \frac{C_1^{\frac{1}{2}}}{C_2^{\frac{3}{4}}} = \text{constant}$$

For pumps, the speed N is usually expressed in rpm and the discharge in gallons per minute (gpm). The head H is expressed in feet. From the above relation we can define

$$N_s = \frac{N(gpm)^{\frac{1}{2}}}{H^{\frac{3}{4}}} \tag{15.16}$$

where N_s, the specific speed, has a definite value for a pump of given design operating at maximum efficiency. For single-stage centrifugal pumps the values of N_s range between 500 and 5,000, while for single-stage axial-flow pumps N_s lies between 5,000 and 10,000.

A similar definition of N_s can be used in connection with fans. The discharge, however, is measured in cubic feet per second instead of gpm.

15.4. Design of an Axial-flow Machine. The blades and guide vanes of an axial-flow machine can be rationally designed if it be assumed that wind-tunnel data on lift and drag coefficients C_L and C_D are applicable to each element of a blade or guide vane. In the analysis leading to the design equations we consider only that part of the machine between sections 1 and 3 of Fig. 15.6. In case two or more stages are required, we consider only the part between the entrance to the first and the exit from the last stage and assume the pressure rise through each stage to be $\Delta p/N$, where Δp is the total pressure rise and N is the number of stages.

The given quantities on which a design is to be developed are (1) the discharge Q, (2) the pressure rise Δp, (3) the speed ω, (4) the radius of the casing r_o, (5) mechanical efficiency η_m, and (6) one or more blade forms having known values of ϵ (= C_D/C_L) and C_L. We wish to determine the required number of stages N, a hub radius r_i that will give a high value of efficiency, and the width and angle of the blades and guides at any radius. We begin by discussing, for a single stage, the blade and guide-vane elements of length dr at an arbitrary radius r, as follows:

Differentiation of Eq. (15.8) with respect to r gives (since rV_{t_2} is independent of r)

$$\eta_m \, dT = \rho r V_{t_2} \, dQ$$

where $\eta_m \, dT$ is the external torque transmitted from the shaft through the blades to the blade elements, or, since these elements move at constant speed, the torque exerted on the fluid by them. Since the velocity V_1 at section 1 is assumed axial and uniform, $dQ = V_1 2\pi r \, dr$, and

$$\eta_m \, dT = Z \, dF_t r = \rho r V_{t_2} V_1 2\pi r \, dr \qquad (15.17)$$

where Z is the number of blades and dF_t is the tangential component of the force acting between one blade element and the fluid, as in Fig. 15.8. Application of the momentum principle [Eq. (6.6)] to the control volume

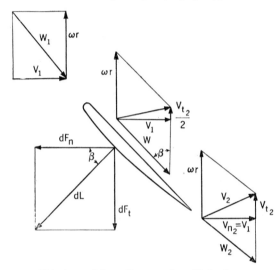

FIG. 15.8. — Velocity and force diagrams for a blade element at radius r.

formed by the annular stream tube and sections 1 and 2 of Fig. 15.6 yields

$$Z \, dF_n = (p_2 - p_1) 2\pi r \, dr \qquad (15.18)$$

where dF_n is the axial component of the force acting between the fluid and blade element.

In the idealized frictionless case, the resultant force on the blade element is the lift dL, which makes an angle β with the axial direction (Fig. 15.8). To determine β, we use Eqs. (15.17) and (15.18).

$$\tan \beta = \frac{dF_t}{dF_n} = \frac{\rho V_1 V_{t_2}}{p_2 - p_1}$$

The energy equation for rotating axes [Eq. (6.22)] yields

$$p_2 - p_1 = \frac{\rho}{2} \left(W_1^2 - W_2^2 \right)$$

since $r_1 = r_2 = r$ and changes in level are ignored. The velocity diagrams of Fig. 15.8 give

$$W_1^2 - W_2^2 = W_{t_1}^2 + W_{n_1}^2 - W_{t_2}^2 - W_{n_2}^2 = \omega^2 r^2 - (\omega r - V_{t_2})^2 = 2V_{t_2}\left(\omega r - \frac{V_{t_2}}{2}\right)$$

and, therefore,

$$\tan \beta = \frac{V_1}{\omega r - \dfrac{V_{t_2}}{2}} = \frac{\phi}{1 - \lambda} \tag{15.19}$$

where $\phi = V_1/\omega r$ and $\lambda = V_{t_2}/2\omega r$.

The diagram for the mean relative velocity W based on this value of β is shown in Fig. (15.8). It will be assumed that wind-tunnel data on single airfoils can be applied to the fan-blade element if the lift and drag coefficients are referred to this relative velocity W. Thus,

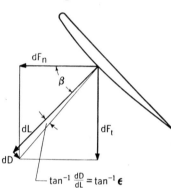

$$\left. \begin{aligned} dL &= C_L \frac{\rho}{2} t W^2 \, dr \\[2mm] dD &= C_D \frac{\rho}{2} t W^2 \, dr \end{aligned} \right\} \tag{15.20}$$

FIG. 15.9. — Forces exerted by the fluid on a blade element at radius r.

where t is the chord of the element. The data should, of course, be corrected to conditions of two-dimensional flow, since no trailing vortices are shed from the element (see Art 11.21). In the actual case of flow with friction the forces are thus as shown in Fig. 15.9, and the ratio of tangential to normal force is

$$\frac{dF_t}{dF_n} = \tan (\beta + \tan^{-1} \epsilon) = \frac{\rho V_1 V_{t_2}}{p_2 - p_1} \tag{15.21}$$

A similar analysis for the corresponding element of the guide vane (Fig. 15.10) yields

$$\tan \beta_g = \frac{2V_1}{V_{t_2}} = \frac{\phi}{\lambda} \tag{15.22}$$

$$\frac{dF_{tg}}{dF_{ng}} = \tan (\beta_g + \tan^{-1} \epsilon_g) = \frac{\rho V_1 V_{t_2}}{p_3 - p_2} \tag{15.23}$$

The efficiency η' of the blade and guide-vane elements combined is obtained by application of the energy equation between sections 1 and 3.

$$\eta' = \frac{1}{\eta_m} \frac{\text{shaft work (frictionless)}}{\text{shaft work (actual)}} = \frac{p_3 - p_1}{\eta_m \rho(- \mathcal{W}_s)} = \frac{\Delta p}{N \rho(- \mathcal{W}_s)\eta_m}$$

But since $- \mathcal{W}_s = \omega \, dT/\rho \, dQ = \omega r V_{t_2}/\eta_m$,

$$\eta' = \frac{\Delta p}{N \rho \omega r V_{t_2}} = \frac{p_3 - p_1}{\rho \omega r V_{t_2}} = \frac{p_3 - p_2}{\rho \omega r V_{t_2}} + \frac{p_2 - p_1}{\rho \omega r V_{t_2}} \tag{15.24}$$

By use of Eqs. (15.21) and (15.23)

$$\eta' = \frac{V_1}{\omega r}\left[\frac{1}{\tan(\beta + \tan^{-1}\epsilon)} + \frac{1}{\tan(\beta_g + \tan^{-1}\epsilon_g)}\right] \quad (15.25)$$

and from Eqs. (15.19) and (15.22)

$$\eta' = \phi\left[\frac{1 - \lambda - \epsilon\phi}{\phi + \epsilon(1 - \lambda)} + \frac{\lambda - \epsilon_g\phi}{\phi + \epsilon_g\lambda}\right] \quad (15.26)$$

For simplicity we assume that the drag-lift ratio is the same for both blade

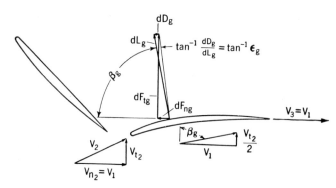

FIG. 15.10. — Velocity and force diagrams for a guide-vane element at radius r.

and guide-vane elements, that is, $\epsilon_g = \epsilon$. The efficiency is thus a function of three independent variables ϕ, λ, and ϵ.

Substitution of $\epsilon_g = \epsilon$ and reduction of Eq. (15.26) yield

$$\eta' = \frac{\phi[\phi(1 - \epsilon^2) + 2\epsilon(\lambda - \lambda^2 - \phi^2)]}{\phi^2 + \phi\epsilon + \epsilon^2(1 - \lambda)\lambda} \quad (15.27)$$

differentiation of which with respect to λ and setting of $\partial\eta'/\partial\lambda = 0$ show that the optimum value of λ is $\frac{1}{2}$. It will be shown below that, if wind-tunnel data on single airfoils are to be applicable, λ should not exceed about $\frac{1}{4}$. The conclusion is, therefore, that λ should be kept as near this upper limit as possible.

Since ϵ is small (usually about 0.025) and since ϕ is on the order of unity ($\phi = V_1/\omega r$), Eq. (15.27) can be written with good approximation as

$$\eta' = \frac{\phi + 2\epsilon(\lambda - \lambda^2 - \phi^2)}{\phi + \epsilon} \quad (15.28)$$

where terms in ϵ^2 have been omitted. In Fig. 15.11, which is computed from Eq. (15.28), η' is plotted against ϕ for several values of λ and ϵ. It will be observed that the η' curves are practically flat in the range $0.5 < \phi < 0.7$ and that, within this range of ϕ and for $0.10 < \lambda < 0.25$,

η' can be maintained constant by means of small variations in ϵ. This is a fortunate circumstance, since Eq. (15.24) shows that η' must be the same at all radii, both $p_3 - p_1$ and rV_{t_2} being assumed independent of r. Values of ϵ will therefore be chosen to give a uniform distribution of η' along the radius.

As the first step in the design it is convenient to select a value of ϕ

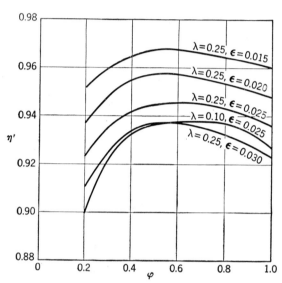

FIG. 15.11. — Efficiency of blade and guide-vane element combined η' versus flow coefficient ϕ for various values of the rotation and friction parameters λ and ϵ.

in the neighborhood of 0.5 to apply at the outer radius r_o. Let this value be ϕ_o. The hub radius r_i is next found from the relation

$$\frac{Q}{\pi(r_o^2 - r_i^2)} = V_1 = \phi_o \omega r_o \qquad (15.29)$$

A tentative value of η' is then chosen, based on inspection of Fig. 15.11.

Before further progress can be made, a maximum allowable value for λ must be selected. A criterion for this choice is developed as follows:

It is found from experience that the "solidity" $Zt/2\pi r$ should not exceed about 1.1, if wind-tunnel data on single airfoils are to apply to the blade elements. We obtain a relation between the solidity and ϕ, ϵ, and λ by using Eqs. (15.17) and (15.20) and Figs. 15.8 and 15.9.

$$dF_t = \rho V_1 V_{t_2} \frac{2\pi r \, dr}{Z} = dL \, (\sin \beta + \epsilon \cos \beta)$$

$$dL = C_L \frac{\rho}{2} tW^2 \, dr = C_L \frac{\rho}{2} t \frac{V_1^2}{\sin^2 \beta} \, dr$$

whence, after considerable reduction,

$$C_L \frac{Zt}{2\pi r} = \frac{2V_{t_2}}{V_1}(\sin\beta + \epsilon\cos\beta) = \frac{4\lambda}{\sqrt{\phi^2 + (1-\lambda)^2}[1+\epsilon(1-\lambda)/\phi]} \qquad (15.30)$$

By substitution of simultaneous values of ϕ and ϵ from Fig. 15.11 it is easily shown that $C_L(Zt/2\pi r) \approx 1$ for $\eta' \approx 0.94$ and $\lambda = \frac{1}{4}$. The solidity $Zt/2\pi r$ will be approximately unity also, since $C_L \approx 1$. The maximum allowable value for λ is therefore about $\frac{1}{4}$. The maximum value of λ will occur at the hub, since $\lambda = rV_{t_2}/2\omega r^2 = \text{constant}/r^2$. The value of λ at the hub is denoted by λ_i.

Having chosen a tentative value for λ_i, we can determine the number of stages N by using the definition of η' [Eq. (15.24)].

$$\eta' = \frac{\Delta p}{N\rho\omega r V_{t_2}} = \frac{\Delta p}{2N\rho\omega^2 r_i^2 \lambda_i}$$

whence

$$N = \frac{\Delta p}{2\rho\omega^2 r_i^2 \lambda_i \eta'} \qquad (15.31)$$

The value of λ_i is to be adjusted to make the right-hand side of Eq. (15.31) equal to an integer.

The use of airfoil data begins at this point. The values of η', ϕ_i, and λ_i being known, ϵ_i can be found from Fig. 15.11 or Eq. (15.28). The data plotted in Fig. 15.12 give ϵ versus C_L for the NACA 4412 airfoil, at various values of Reynolds number $R = Wt/\nu$. Figure 15.12 is to be used in conjunction with Eq. (15.30) to determine reasonable values for t_i and Z. Two conditions are to be fulfilled: (1) $Zt_i/2\pi r_i$ should be less than 1.1; and (2) ϵ_i, C_{L_i}, and Wt_i/ν should correspond to a single point in Fig. 15.12.

To illustrate this procedure let the following numerical values be given, on the basis of which it is required to design a suitable fan wheel.

$Q = 200 \text{ ft}^3/\text{sec}$
$\Delta p = 20 \text{ lb/ft}^2$
$\omega = 180 \text{ radians/sec}$
$r_o = 1.00 \text{ ft}$
$\rho = 2.3 \times 10^{-3} \text{ lb-sec}^2/\text{ft}^4$
$\nu = 1.6 \times 10^{-4} \text{ ft}^2/\text{sec}$

Assuming $\phi_o = 0.50$, we find from Eq. (15.29) that $r_i = 0.540$ ft. Since this appears to be a reasonable hub radius, we proceed, assuming tentatively, on inspection of Fig. 15.11, that $\eta' = 0.95$. From Eq. (15.31) it is then found that, if N be chosen as 2, $\lambda_i = 0.243$. Referring to Fig. 15.11 we find that $\epsilon_i \approx 0.020$, whence, from Eq. (15.30), $C_{L_i}Zt_i/2\pi r_i = 0.805$.

Assuming now that $C_{L_i} = 0.80$, we see that $Zt_i/2\pi r_i = 1.01$, which is less than the allowable maximum of 1.1. To determine t_i we note from

Fig. 15.12 that the Reynolds number at the hub $W_i t_i / \nu \approx 3 \times 10^5$, from which it follows that $t_i \approx 0.36$ ft. It is now readily found that $t_i = 0.38$ ft if $Z = 9$. Both these values appear to be satisfactory.

At the outer radius $r_o = 1.00$ ft, the value of ϵ_o is found from Eq. (15.28)

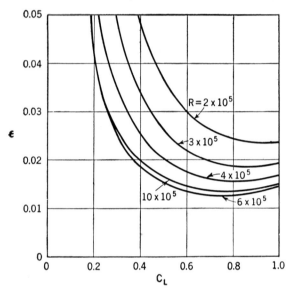

FIG. 15.12. — Drag-lift ratio ϵ versus lift coefficient C_L, for the NACA 4412 airfoil. The Reynolds number is defined as $R = Wt/\nu$.

to be 0.019, since $\eta' = 0.95$ and $\lambda_o = \lambda_i (r_i/r_o)^2 = 0.071$. Equation (15.30) yields $C_{L_o} t_o = 0.179$. A tentative value of t_o may now be assumed and the corresponding value of Reynolds number computed. If the values of C_L found from Eq. (15.30) and Fig. 15.12 do not agree, the process is repeated until a check is obtained.

A preferable method of determining t and C_L is to consider the behavior of the fan in the *neighborhood* of the design point [5]. We have seen that for stability it is necessary that the product rV_{t_2} be independent of radius, not only at the design point, but for all operating conditions. In order to fulfil this requirement, at least for a small range of speed near the design value, the chord t must be a definite function of r. To find this relation between t and r we assume that the velocity at entrance V_1 is held constant and uniform while ω is allowed to vary. In this approximate analysis we neglect friction and rearrange Eq. (15.30) to get

$$rV_{t_2} = \frac{tZV_1}{4\pi} \frac{C_L}{\sin \beta} \qquad (15.30a)$$

The restriction which we wish to impose is that the rate of change of rV with respect to ω be the same at all radii. This will ensure that rV_{t_2} is constant over the fan disk at values of ω near the design point. Noting that

$$\frac{\partial(rV_{t_2})}{\partial\omega} = \frac{\partial(rV_{t_2})}{\partial\beta}\frac{d\beta}{d(\tan\beta)}\frac{\partial(\tan\beta)}{\partial\omega}$$

we find

$$\frac{\partial(rV_{t_2})}{\partial\beta} = \frac{tZV_1}{4\pi}\frac{1}{\sin\beta}\left(\frac{\partial C_L}{\partial\beta} - \frac{\cos\beta}{\sin\beta}C_L\right)$$

$$\frac{d\beta}{d(\tan\beta)} = \cos^2\beta$$

$$\frac{\partial(\tan\beta)}{\partial\omega} \approx \frac{\partial(V_1/\omega r)}{\partial\omega} = -\frac{V_1}{\omega^2 r}$$

The expression $\partial C_L/\partial\beta$ can be rewritten as $\partial C_L/\partial\beta = (dC_L/d\alpha)(\partial\alpha/\partial\beta)$, which, since the blade angle $\alpha+\beta$ remains fixed, can be expressed as $\partial C_L/\partial\beta = -dC_L/d\alpha = -C_L'$. This substitution is advantageous, because C_L' is practically constant over the useful range of angle of attack.

We thus get

$$\frac{4\pi\omega^2 r\tan\beta}{ZV_1^2}\frac{\partial(rV_{t_2})}{\partial\omega} = t\cos\beta\left(C_L' + \frac{\cos\beta}{\sin\beta}C_L\right)$$

The approximation used above, namely, $\tan\beta \approx V_1/\omega r$, is equivalent to the assumption that $r\tan\beta$ is independent of r. The right-hand side of the last equation can thus be considered independent of r, so that

$$t\cos\beta\left(C_L' + \frac{\cos\beta}{\sin\beta}C_L\right) = t_i\cos\beta_i\left(C_L' + \frac{\cos\beta_i}{\sin\beta_i}C_{L_i}\right)$$

The unknown C_L can be eliminated by means of the relation $tC_L/\sin\beta = t_iC_{L_i}/\sin\beta_i$, which follows from Eq. (15.30a). The final result is

$$\frac{t}{t_i} = \frac{\cos\beta_i}{\cos\beta} + \frac{C_{L_i}}{C_L'}\frac{\cos\beta}{\sin\beta_i}\left(\frac{\cos^2\beta_i}{\cos^2\beta} - 1\right) \tag{15.32}$$

Values of t and C_L at several stations along the blade are to be determined from Eqs. (15.30) and (15.32). The angle of attack α can then be found from airfoil data, such as Fig. 11.32, and the total blade angle determined as the sum $\alpha+\beta$.

We are now able, by means of Eq. (15.32), to determine the width of the blade tip for the example discussed above. Recalling that $\tan\beta \approx V_1/\omega r$, we get $\cos\beta_i \approx \omega r_i/\sqrt{V_1^2 + \omega^2 r_i^2} = 0.737$, $\sin\beta_i \approx V_1/\sqrt{V_1^2 + \omega^2 r_i^2} = 0.682$, and $\cos\beta_o \approx \omega r_o/\sqrt{V^2 + \omega^2 r_o} = 0.895$. From Fig. 11.32 an approximate value of C_L' is seen to be $C_L' \approx 0.095$ per deg $= 5.45$ per radian. Substitution in Eq. (15.32) yields $t_o/t_i = 0.763$; whence $t_o = 0.290$ ft. From the previous result that $C_{L_o}t_o = 0.179$ it follows that $C_{L_o} = 0.617$.

A check on the value of ϵ_o is obtained by computation of $W_o t_o/\nu$, which is found to be 3.65×10^5. Reference to Fig. 15.12 shows that these values of C_{L_o} and $W_o t_o / \nu$ correspond to $\epsilon_o \approx 0.019$, the value previously found. Failure to check approximately here would indicate either a different airfoil at the tip or a new start on the entire computation.

Values of β at root and tip are obtained from Eq. (15.19), and the values of α corresponding to the known values of C_L are found from Fig. 11.32.

The following table gives the results already discussed, together with values at an intermediate radius:

Given: $Q = 200$ ft^3/sec $\nu = 1.6 \times 10^{-4}$ ft^2/sec
$\Delta p = 20$ lb/ft^2 $\rho = 2.3 \times 10^{-3}$ lb-sec^2/ft^4
$\omega = 180$ radians/sec   4412 airfoil
Results: Number of stages $N = 2$
Number of blades $Z = 9$

r, ft	C_L	t, ft	β, deg	α, deg	$\alpha + \beta$, deg
0.54 (root)..	0.80	0.36	50.7	4.5	55.2
0.80........	0.70	0.31	35.1	3.3	38.4
1.00 (tip)...	0.62	0.29	28.1	2.5	30.6

The design of the guide vanes can be carried out by a similar method.

For fans in which the solidity $Zt/2\pi r$ is somewhat in excess of unity the same method can be used, but data on airfoil grids must be substituted for those on single airfoils. The chief effect of the increased solidity is found to be a reduction in C_L below the value measured for a single airfoil [6]. This reduction is largely attributable to the decrease in relative velocity of the fluid as it passes through the grid.

15.5. Centrifugal Compressor. These machines are widely used to compress air and other gases; they are simple in construction and can be built to operate under a wide variety of conditions. The ratio of outlet to inlet pressure does not ordinarily exceed a value of about 3, for a single stage. Efficiencies on the order of 75 per cent are commonly reached.

Referring to Fig. 15.1 or 15.2, we express the driving torque as in Eq. (15.2).

$$T = \frac{mr_3 V_{t_3}}{\eta_m} \tag{15.33}$$

where ρQ is replaced by m, the constant mass flow through the machine.

The efficiency is defined as the ratio of the power input for a frictionless compression to the actual power input. If leakage is neglected, the efficiency can be written as the ratio of the shaft works. If gravity is ignored, the energy equation for the frictionless case [Eq. (5.13)] reduces to

$$-\mathcal{W}_s = \int_1^3 \frac{dp}{\rho} + \frac{V_3^2 - V_1^2}{2} \tag{15.34}$$

while, in the actual case, the energy equation gives

$$- \mathcal{W}_{s_a} = \frac{p_3}{\rho_{3_a}} - \frac{p_1}{\rho_1} + \frac{V_{3_a}^2 - V_1^2}{2} + u_{3_a} - u_1 - q_{1,3_a}$$

where the subscript a is used to denote actual values. The pressure p_3 is considered the same in both cases, since the machine is supposed to develop an assigned output pressure. If the flow is assumed to be adiabatic, Eq. (9.5) is applicable to the frictionless case and Eq. (15.34) becomes

$$- \mathcal{W}_s = \frac{k}{k-1} \frac{p_1}{\rho_1} \left[\left(\frac{p_3}{p_1} \right)^{1-(1/k)} - 1 \right] + \frac{V_3^2 - V_1^2}{2} \qquad (15.35)$$

The actual work under adiabatic conditions is

$$- \mathcal{W}_{s_a} = h_{3_a} - h_1 + \frac{V_{3_a}^2 - V_1^2}{2} \qquad (15.36)$$

where the enthalpy h is defined as $(p/\rho) + u$. For adiabatic flow, the efficiency is thus

$$\eta = \frac{- \mathcal{W}_s}{- \mathcal{W}_{s_a}} = \frac{[k/(k-1)](p_1/\rho_1)[(p_3/p_1)^{1-(1/k)} - 1] + [(V_3^2 - V_1^2)/2]}{h_{3_a} - h_1 + [(V_{3_a}^2 - V_1^2)/2]} \qquad (15.37)$$

If the fluid is assumed a perfect gas, Eqs. (9.12) to (9.15) apply and Eq. (15.37) reduces to

$$\eta = \frac{c_p T_1 [(p_3/p_1)^{1-(1/k)} - 1] + [(V_3^2 - V_1^2)/2]}{c_p (T_{3_a} - T_1) + [(V_{3_a}^2 - V_1^2)/2]} \qquad (15.38)$$

An alternative expression for the efficiency is obtained by use of Eq. (15.33), together with the fact that $- \mathcal{W}_{s_a} = (\omega T/m)$.

$$\eta = \eta_m \frac{c_p T_1 [(p_3/p_1)^{1-(1/k)} - 1] + [(V_3^2 - V_1^2)/2]}{\omega r_3 V_{t_3}} \qquad (15.39)$$

This is the analogue of Eq. (15.4) for a pump or fan.

If we assume for the moment that both η and η_m are unity, Eq. (15.39) can be used as a guide in the development of a convenient form for the plotting of experimental results. We assume further that the compressor has blades which are radial at the exit section 3, so that $V_{t_3} = \omega r_3$. We thus have

$$\omega^2 r_3^2 = c_p T_1 \left[\left(\frac{p_3}{p_1} \right)^{1-(1/k)} - 1 \right] + \frac{V_3^2 - V_1^2}{2}$$

Furthermore, $V_3^2 = V_{t_3}^2 + V_{n_3}^2 = \omega^2 r_3^2 + V_{n_3}^2$ and continuity gives $A_3 \rho_3 V_{n_3} = A_1 \rho_1 V_1$, from which

$$V_{n_3} = V_1 \frac{A_1}{A_3} \frac{\rho_1}{\rho_3} = V_1 \frac{A_1}{A_3} \left(\frac{p_1}{p_3} \right)^{1/k}$$

Therefore,

$$\frac{\omega^2 r_3^2}{2} = c_p T_1 \left[\left(\frac{p_3}{p_1} \right)^{1-(1/k)} - 1 \right] + \frac{V_1^2}{2} \left[\frac{A_1^2}{A_3^2} \left(\frac{p_1}{p_3} \right)^{2/k} - 1 \right]$$

which, by use of the equations $C^2 = (k-1)c_p T$ and $C_1^2/C_3^2 = (p_1/p_3)^{1-(1/k)}$ can be reduced to

$$M_1^2 = \left(\frac{V_1}{C_1} \right)^2 = \frac{(\omega r_3/C_3)^2 - [2/(k-1)][1 - (p_1/p_3)^{1-(1/k)}]}{(A_1^2/A_3^2)(p_1/p_3)^{1+(1/k)} - (p_1/p_3)^{1-(1/k)}} \quad (15.40)$$

Here C is the local sound velocity. The pressure ratio is thus expressed in terms of M_1, $\omega r_3/C_3$, and A_1/A_3. It can be shown by means of Eqs. (9.1), (9.5), and (9.8) to (9.10) that the value of M_1 determines the ratio m/m^*, where m^* is the mass flow when the sound velocity is reached at 1. The ratio m/m^* cannot exceed unity.

$$\frac{m}{m^*} = M_1 \left[\frac{k+1}{2 + (k-1)M_1^2} \right]^{1/(k-1)} \quad (15.41)$$

It thus appears that p_3/p_1 is a function of m/m^*, $\omega r_3/C_3$, and A_1/A_3, in

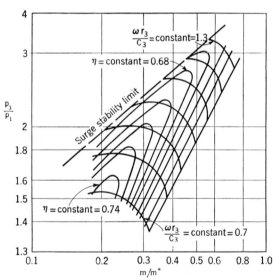

FIG. 15.13. — Pressure ratio p_3/p_1 versus relative mass flow m/m^* for a centrifugal compressor.

this idealized case. It is possible to plot experimental results in terms of these independent variables, as shown in Fig. 15.13 for a supercharger.

15.6. Dimensional Analysis of a Compressor. A form of plot similar to Fig. 15.13 can be developed by means of dimensional analysis. We assume that, for a compressor of given design, any of the three dependent variables p_3, η, or input power P depends only on ω; on the impeller diameter D; on the properties of the fluid at entrance ρ_1, C_1, and μ_1; and on the mass flow m.

The dependent quantities will, in general, be functions also of k and of the heat transfer through the casing, but these are ignored under the assumption that k is the same for all the operating fluids (diatomic gases) and that the flow is adiabatic.

It is convenient to change the independent variables ρ_1 and C_1 to p_1 and c_pT_1, respectively, because p_1 and T_1 are directly measured in compressor tests. These changes are legitimate, since $(kp_1/\rho_1) = C_1^2 = c_p(k-1)T_1$. Thus

$$p_3 = f_1(c_pT_1,D,p_1,\omega,m,\mu_1)$$

Applying the Π theorem and grouping c_pT_1, D, and p_1 in each of the three Π products, we get

$$\frac{p_3}{p_1} = f_2\left(\frac{\omega D}{\sqrt{c_pT_1}}, \frac{m\sqrt{c_pT_1}}{p_1D^2}, \frac{p_1D}{\mu_1\sqrt{c_pT_1}}\right) \qquad (15.42)$$

Similarly, η and $P/p_1\sqrt{c_pT_1}D^2$ are functions of the same three variables.

Experiment shows that the third independent variable of Eq. (15.42),

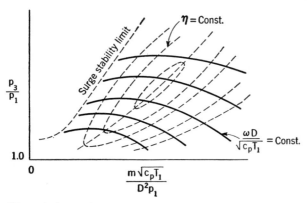

Fig. 15.14. — Dimensionless performance curves for a centrifugal pump. (*After Del Mar, reference* 1. *Courtesy of the American Society of Mechanical Engineers.*)

viz., that containing μ_1, is of negligible importance, viscosity playing only a minor role in determining the flow through the compressor [1]. Figure 15.14 shows schematically how test results appear when plotted in these coordinates.

The "surge stability limit" marked in Figs. 15.13 and 15.14 is the locus of points at which the operation becomes unstable. Suppose that the compressor is running at a constant value of $\omega D/\sqrt{c_pT_1}$ and that m is decreasing. So long as the operating point lies to the right of the limiting line, the pressure p_3 developed by the machine drops less rapidly with decrease in m than does the pressure characteristic of the attached system. Operation is therefore stable. To the left of the limiting line, however, the pressure p_3 drops more rapidly with decrease in m than does that of the system, and instability, or "surging," is the result.

SELECTED BIBLIOGRAPHY

1. DEL MAR, B. E.: Presentation of Centrifugal Compressor Performance in Terms of Nondimensional Relationships, *Trans. Am. Soc. Mech. Engrs.*, vol. 67, pp. 483–490, 1945.
2. KEARTON, W. J.: "Turbo-blowers and Compressors," Sir Isaac Pitman & Sons, Ltd., London, 1926.
3. PATTERSON, G. N.: "Ducted Fans: Design for High Efficiency," *Rept.* ACA-7, Australian Council for Aeronautics, July, 1944.
4. SORG, K. W.: Supersonic Flow in Turbines and Compressors, *J. Roy. Aeronaut. Soc.*, vol. 46, pp. 64–85, 1942.
5. TROLLER, TH.: Zur Berechnung von Schraubenventilatoren, *Abhandl. Aero. Inst. Tech. Hochschule Aachen*, no. 10, pp. 43–47, Verlag Julius Springer, Berlin, 1931.
6. WISLICENUS, C. F.: A Study of the Theory of Axial-flow Pumps, *Trans. Am. Soc. Mech. Engrs.*, vol. 67, pp. 451–470, 1945 (see especially the discussion by Th. Troller on p. 468).
7. KELLER, C.: "Axial-flow Fans," McGraw-Hill Book Company, Inc., New York, 1937.

CHAPTER XVI

PROPELLERS AND JETS

A propeller adds momentum to the fluid passing through it and so develops an axial force, or thrust. The fluid in the wake of the propeller is called the "race" or "slip stream," and the relative increase of velocity there is called "slip," from analogy with a screw. If a portion of propeller blade, the face of which was a helical surface of pitch p, worked in a firm nut, without slip, it would advance a distance p for one complete revolution. The helix angle at radius r would be $\tan^{-1} (p/2\pi r)$. Actually a propeller proceeding ahead at speed V advances in the time $1/n$ taken for one revolution of the propeller a distance V/n which is less than p. The slip, therefore, is $p - (V/n)$. This definition of slip is arbitrary, based on the geometry of the propeller. Its physical significance is not very clear, but for a higher-pitch propeller we should naturally expect more slip and more thrust. For no slip (when $p = V/n$) we should expect no thrust, since no fluid is accelerated. Modern propellers may have blades for which the pitch is not uniform over the face. The common practice is to have the pitch increase somewhat toward the blade tips. The pitch at three-quarters radius is usually taken as the approximate specification of the "mean geometrical pitch" of a propeller.

The common propeller-type ventilator, or fan, set in a wall or window, without an entrance pipe, operates like a propeller. Here the thrust of the fan is not the essential feature, but the velocity of flow that can be maintained. Obviously, fluid is given axial momentum by the fan. Such fans are cheap, quiet, and efficient where a large diameter can be allowed.

16.1. Momentum Theory of a Propeller. For purposes of analysis the

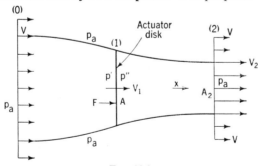

FIG. 16.1.

actual propeller is replaced by a hypothetical "actuator disk," which accelerates the flow axially without imparting any whirl to the slip stream.

381

The fluid is assumed to be frictionless. A surface of discontinuity in velocity is assumed to separate from the surrounding fluid the fluid that passes through the actuator, as shown in Fig. 16.1. The pressure is atmospheric everywhere on the surface, as well as at sections 0 and 2, which are stationary with respect to the disk and at which the streamlines are parallel and straight. The velocities indicated in this figure are taken relative to the disk. The undisturbed fluid is assumed to be at rest with respect to the earth, so that the actuator has an "absolute" velocity of magnitude V, from right to left.

If the actuator is considered as attached to an airplane or other load, the latter will exert a force F on the disk, as shown. This thrust is the only external x force on the system comprising the actuator and the fluid in the slip stream between sections 0 and 2. The momentum equation [Eq. (6.6)] thus gives

$$F = m(V_2 - V) \tag{16.1}$$

where m is the mass rate of flow through the actuator.

If the assumption of incompressibility is introduced here, the velocity immediately in front of the disk is seen to be the same as that just behind it, since the area of the stream is the same at both sections. The product of this velocity and the thrust, FV_1, gives the work per second done by the actuator on the fluid. This is identical with the power input to the actuator, since the latter is assumed 100 per cent effective. The shaft work done on the actuator is found by application of the energy equation [Eq. (5.10)] to the system comprising the disk and the fluid of the slip stream between sections 0 and 2,

$$-\mathcal{W}_s = \frac{(V_2^2 - V^2)}{2} \tag{16.2}$$

whence

$$FV_1 = -\mathcal{W}_s m = m\,\frac{(V_2^2 - V^2)}{2} \tag{16.3}$$

Combination of Eqs. (16.1) and (16.3) gives

$$V_1 = \frac{V + V_2}{2} \tag{16.4}$$

The velocity V_1 at the disk is thus the arithmetic mean of V and V_2, half of the velocity change taking place upstream and half downstream from the disk.

The efficiency of the actuator is defined as the ratio of the useful work done by it to that done on it. The useful work per second (power output) is the product of the thrust and the forward speed of the disk with respect to the earth, FV, while, from Eq. (16.2), the power input to the actuator is $m(V_2^2 - V^2)/2$. The efficiency for this idealized case, called the "ideal" or "Froude" efficiency, is thus $\eta_i = 2FV/m(V_2^2 - V^2)$, which, with the aid of Eq. (16.1), is reduced to

$$\eta_i = \frac{2V}{V + V_2} \tag{16.5}$$

or

$$\eta_i = \frac{1}{1 + (\Delta V/2V)} \tag{16.5a}$$

where $\Delta V = V_2 - V$.

It is to be noted that Eq. (16.5) or (16.5a) is based only on the definition of useful power and on Eqs. (16.1) and (16.2). All three of these are valid regardless of the compressibility of the fluid or the form of the actuator. Equation (16.5) or (16.5a), therefore, applies quite generally to any propulsive jet, whether produced by a propeller or other jet-propulsion device utilizing the atmosphere as the material of the jet.

The effect of each of the several variables on η_i is seen if a thrust coefficient is introduced, defined as $C_F = 2F/\rho V^2 A$. The efficiency is readily expressed in terms of C_F: $\eta_i = 2/(1 + \sqrt{1 + C_F})$. This relation, which is plotted in Fig. 16.2, shows that η_i increases with increase in V, ρ, or A but decreases with an increase in thrust. It is therefore desirable to make C_F small for an actual propeller, in order that the ideal upper limit to the efficiency may be high. Since the thrust, speed, and density are usually fixed by other considerations, it follows that the propeller diameter should be made as large as possible.

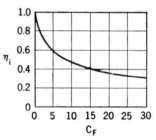

Fig. 16.2. — Ideal propeller efficiency η_i versus thrust coefficient C_F.

The ideal efficiency cannot be reached by an actual propeller, for the following reasons:

1. Some energy of whirl is left in the slip stream.
2. Tip and hub losses (eddies) always exist.
3. There are friction losses on the blades.
4. Owing to the finite number of blades the flow is not steady but pulsates.
5. The entire disk area is not utilized, there being no flow near the hub.
6. The propeller race is not an ideal jet bounded by a cylindrical surface of discontinuity but breaks up into eddies.

The actual efficiency can, however, approach the ideal quite closely, ordinarily being about 85 per cent of η_i. For airplanes, however, the actual efficiency itself may be as high as 85 per cent. For ships, owing to restrictions on diameter, efficiencies on the order of 60 per cent are more common.

16.2 Blade-element Theory of a Propeller. The momentum theory of the previous article applies to an idealized actuator disk the mechanism of which is unspecified. A more detailed theory is therefore needed to investigate the performance of an actual propeller. The blade-element theory, which is commonly used for this purpose, is similar to that already described for an axial-flow fan in Art. 15.4. There are, however, certain differences between the fan and propeller, as regards both construction and purpose, which lead to modifications of the fan theory. The principal differences are pointed out below.

In the fan the product rV_{t_2} (or $Z\Gamma/2\pi$, where Γ is the circulation about one of the Z blades) is constant along the blade, since, by virtue of the housing and hub, no trailing vortices are shed. The flow immediately downstream from the fan is thus made up of a potential-vortex motion superposed on an axial translation and is irrotational (except for the frictional wakes from the blades), since the hub replaces the vortex core. The guide vanes take out the tangential velocity before the hub tapers away to zero diameter, so that no rotation appears in the flow downstream from the fan.

The flow through a propeller, on the other hand, is complicated by the absence of a housing. As already noted in the momentum theory, there is a contraction of the slipstream, which causes the relative axial velocity at the propeller to be higher than the velocity of advance. There is also a radial component of velocity near the tips, but this is so small under normal operating conditions that it is neglected in propeller theory. The principal effect of the exposed blade tips is the three-dimensional flow produced, with its accompaniment of trailing vortices, which are shed downstream in helical paths. Similar conditions exist at the blade roots. The slip stream of a propeller thus contains much rotation (even though friction on the blades be neglected). This vorticity is distributed throughout the stream but shows considerable concentration in two thin cylindrical shells, one springing from the tips and the other from the roots of the blades. The situation is similar to that on a finite wing, described in Arts. 11.21 to 11.23.

The theory of the finite wing shows that the circulation around the wing decreases toward the tip, as the trailing vortices are shed. The gradual dropping off of the circulation around the propeller blades to zero at the tips means that the thrust and torque per unit length do likewise. To see that this is so we refer to Figs. 15.8 and 15.9 and Eqs. (15.17) to (15.21), which are applicable to an element of a propeller blade.

From Eq. (15.17) we get, by substituting $rV_{t_2} = Z\Gamma/2\pi$,

$$\frac{dT}{dr} = \frac{\rho V_1 Z\Gamma}{\eta_m}\, r \qquad\qquad (16.6)$$

while, from Fig. 15.9,

$$Z \, dF_n = Z \, dF_t \cot (\beta + \tan^{-1} \epsilon) = \eta_m \frac{dT}{r} \cot (\beta + \tan^{-1} \epsilon)$$

$$= \rho V_1 Z \Gamma \cot (\beta + \tan^{-1} \epsilon) \, dr$$

Hence, the thrust per unit length of all the blades at radius r may be written

$$\frac{dF}{dr} = \frac{Z \, dF_n}{dr} = \rho V_1 Z \Gamma \cot (\beta + \tan^{-1} \epsilon) \qquad (16.7)$$

Starting from Eqs. (16.6) and (16.7), one can develop expressions for dT/dr and dF/dr from which can be computed the torque and thrust distributions for a propeller of given design and size operating at a given speed of advance V and rotational speed ω [2]. The details of this development will not be given here, since they are similar to those of Art. 15.4. Typical computed curves are shown schematically in Fig. 16.3.

From Eq. (16.6) one sees, if Γ is independent of r, as for a fan in a housing, that dT/dr varies linearly with r. For comparison with a propeller such a curve is shown dotted in Fig. 16.3.

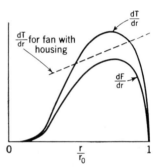

Fig. 16.3. — Schematic representation of torque and thrust grading along a propeller blade. The dotted line indicates the torque grading for a propeller in a duct.

Since the purpose of a propeller is to do work at rate FV, the blade-element efficiency is defined as $\eta' = V dF / \eta_m \omega \, dT$, which with the aid of Eqs. (16.6) and (16.7) becomes

$$\eta' = \frac{V}{\omega r} \frac{1}{\tan (\beta + \tan^{-1} \epsilon)} \qquad (16.8)$$

In contrast to that of a ducted fan, the blade-element efficiency of a propeller varies along the radius, the value at three-quarters of the outer radius ($0.75 r_o$) being approximately equal to the over-all efficiency.

16.3. Dimensional Analysis of a Propeller. On account of the complexity of the flow over the blades, theory alone cannot at present indicate the most efficient design for a propeller intended to perform under specified conditions. For this reason, model experiments, correlated and interpreted by dimensional analysis, are widely used in propeller research and development.

The input power P and the efficiency η of a propeller of given design are usually desired as functions of the independent variables ρ, ω, D, V, μ, and C. Here D is the propeller diameter, V is the velocity of advance, and C is the sound velocity in the undisturbed air. (This last variable is

important only in case of very high velocity of the air relative to the pro
peller blades.   The tips are the first part of the blades to be affected b
compressibility because their velocity is highest.)   It is thus assumed tha

$$P = f_1(\rho,\omega,D,V,\mu,C)$$

$$\eta = f_2(\rho,\omega,D,V,\mu,C)$$

Application of the Π theorem to the first of these equations, with ρ, ω
and D included in each of the four Π products, yields

$$\frac{P}{\rho\omega^3D^5} = C_P = f_3\left(\frac{V}{\omega D}, \ \frac{\rho\omega D^2}{\mu}, \ \frac{V}{C}\right) \qquad (16.9$$

where C_P is called the "power coefficient."   Similarly, it can be shown tha
η is a function of the same three variables.

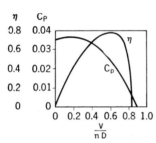

Since $V/\omega D$ (or V/nD, where $n = \omega/2\pi$
determines how fast a given propeller is being
turned relative to the speed of advance, o
how actively it is being worked, it is a fai
assumption to regard V/nd as the primary
parameter and to expect that the effects o
viscosity (in the Reynolds number $\rho\omega D^2/\mu$
and compressibility (in the Mach numbe
V/C) are secondary and in the nature of cor

FIG. 16.4. — Power coeffi-
cient C_P and efficiency η versus
slip coefficient V/nD. (After
Weick, reference 2.)

rections.   This assumption is borne out by
wind-tunnel tests.   A typical set of curves fo:
a family of geometrically similar propellers i:
given in Fig. 16.4.

The Reynolds number is found to have an appreciable effect on the
efficiency curve, the maximum value of η being larger and occurring at a
higher value of V/nD for a full-scale propeller than for a model.

The Mach number has little or no effect on full-scale propeller per
formance until values of V/C on the order of 0.7 are reached.   For stil
higher Mach numbers the efficiency drops off rapidly, and C_P increases
The thinner the blades of the propeller, the less marked are these effects
Special thin airfoil sections have been developed for use on high-speed
propellers.   One of these is shown in Fig. 10.6a; they are also referred to
near the end of Art. 10.13.

It is common practice to test a series of propellers that are identical
except for the ratio of pitch to diameter (pitch ratio), the pitch being
measured at three-quarters radius.   The effect of this change in design is
indicated in Fig. 16.5, which shows that the maximum value of η increases
with increase in pitch ratio.   At larger values of pitch ratio than those
shown the maximum efficiency is found to decrease again.

For a propeller to perform satisfactorily on a given airplane or vessel, it must fulfill definite requirements as to input power, speed, velocity of advance, and fluid density. The problem is usually to select from a series of propellers of different pitch the one that will have the highest efficiency at the given conditions of operation. The diameter D and efficiency η are to be determined as functions of ρ, V, n, P, and p, it being assumed that the effects of μ and C are negligible. The Π theorem thus leads to

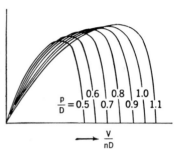

$$\frac{V}{nD} = f_3\left(\frac{\rho V^5}{P n^2}, \frac{p}{D}\right) \qquad (16.10)$$

$$\eta = f_4\left(\frac{\rho V^5}{P n^2}, \frac{p}{D}\right) \qquad (16.11)$$

FIG. 16.5. — Efficiency η versus slip coefficient V/nD, for various values of pitch ratio p/D. (*After Weick, reference 2.*)

It has been found convenient to plot V/nD and η against $(\rho V^5/Pn^2)^{\frac{1}{5}}$, which is called the "speed-power" coefficient C_s. Typical curves for airplane propellers are shown in Fig. 16.6.

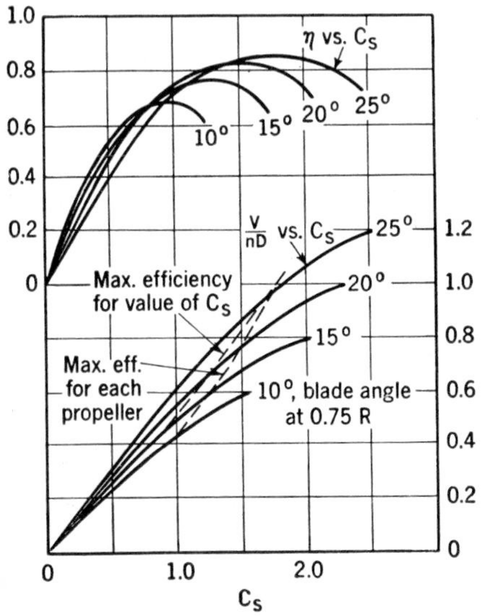

16.4. Momentum Theory of a Windmill. Just as a propeller adds momentum to a stream of fluid passing through it, a windmill takes momentum out of the wind blowing through it. From continuity considerations, the fluid passing through a propeller must form a jet of reduced diameter in the rear of the propeller. The windmill, on the contrary, has a wake, or slip stream, of reduced velocity and larger diameter.

Assuming steady flow of an ideal, incompressible fluid through a windmill, we select a control volume, with pressures and velocities as shown in Fig. 16.7. By reasoning like that for the propeller (Art. 16.1) we reach a conclusion identical with Eq. (16.4), viz.,

FIG. 16.6. — Design curves for a typical family of airplane propellers. (*After Weick, reference 2.*)

$$V_1 = \frac{V + V_2}{2} \qquad (16.12)$$

The energy equation [Eq. (5.10)] shows that in this ideal machine the power output is

$$\mathcal{W}_s \rho A V_1 = \rho A V_1 \frac{(V^2 - V_2^2)}{2}$$

The efficiency of the ideal windmill η_i is defined as the ratio of the output power to the kinetic energy, which, in the absence of the windmill, would

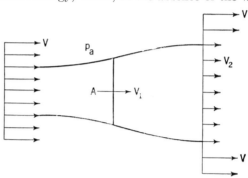

Fig. 16.7.

pass per second through an area A. Thus,

$$\eta_i = \frac{\rho A V_1 (V^2 - V_2^2)/2}{\rho A V^3/2}$$

With the aid of Eq. (16.12) the ideal efficiency can be expressed as

$$\eta_i = \frac{1}{2}\left(1 + \frac{V_2}{V} - \frac{V_2^2}{V^2} - \frac{V_2^3}{V^3}\right) \tag{16.13}$$

Differentiate Eq. (16.13) with respect to V_2/V, and set the derivative equal to zero to find the condition for a maximum of η_i: $\partial\eta_i/\partial(V_2/V_1) = \frac{1}{2} - (V_2/V) - \frac{3}{2}(V_2^2/V^2)$. The optimum value of V_2/V is found to be $\frac{1}{3}$; hence

$$\eta_{i\max} = {}^{16}\!/_{27} \approx 0.59 \tag{16.14}$$

Dutch windmills of very large diameter are said to approach 20 per cent in efficiency. Modern propeller-type windmills are more efficient.

The thrust on the windmill is, of course, of interest to the builder, and it will be zero theoretically when $V = V_2$, a condition that implies some sort of magic feathering of the blades in an ideal fluid, such that the wind is not impeded at all. On the other hand, when V_2 is very small compared with V, we have the case of a many-bladed windmill that nearly stops the wind. The thrust will then be high, and the ideal efficiency about 50 per cent. Practically, such a windmill is likely to be blown over in a storm and means must be provided to feather the blades and govern the rotative speed.

16.5. Jet Propulsion. There are many ways to produce propulsive jets for aircraft, missiles, and rockets by means of the thrust reaction to the force required to increase the rearward momentum of a stream of gas. The conventional engine-propeller combination is a jet-propulsion device to increase the momentum of the air passing through the propeller-swept area, as shown by Eq. (16.1). Some additional thrust can be obtained by leading the engine exhaust through nozzles directed toward the rear. The additional thrust due to exhaust jets may amount to 10 per cent in a fast airplane.

If the propeller is driven by a gas turbine, the total thrust is the sum of the contributions of the propeller and of the turbine exhaust. Such a gas turbine must develop not only the power to drive the propeller but also the power necessary to drive a compressor to supply air to the combustion chamber where the fuel is burned. The relative proportions of total thrust due to the turbine exhaust and due to the propeller may be arbitrarily chosen by the designer.

For very-high-speed airplanes, where propeller efficiency is low owing to the effects of compressibility, the designer may omit the propeller and depend on the turbine exhaust entirely. This arrangement is known as a "turbojet."

The Germans, for their "buzz bombs," developed an intermittent jet that simplified the compressor–combustion chamber–turbine combination to a simple combustion chamber and tail pipe. Air, in great excess over the amount needed for combustion, is admitted through spring-closed non-return flap valves in the nose. Ignition of the fuel causes a volume increase and pressure rise, closure of the admission valves, and the ejection of hot gas as a jet. The ram pressure $\rho V^2/2$ (due to the speed of flight) then reopens the admission valves to admit a fresh charge of air. By proper tuning of the valve-closing springs and the proportions of the combustion chamber and tail pipe, firing occurs some forty times per second. This device is not effective at very low speeds and has to be launched by a powerful catapult.

A further simplification of the same idea, eliminating the admission valves and the intermittent character of the jet, can be applied at very high speeds, when the ram pressure is substantial. Such a "ram jet" takes combustion air from a forward opening through a diffuser, to decrease its relative velocity and to increase its pressure, into the combustion chamber, where fuel is burned continuously. The heated air and combustion products are ejected through the tail pipe as a steady jet.

A ram jet has certain drawbacks that partly offset its simplicity. In the first place, it has to be got up to high speed before it will operate. Furthermore, combustion is difficult to maintain, both because the flame will blow out if the local air velocity is too great and because the fuel-air ratio near the ignition region must be kept within practical limits for a wide range of speeds and altitudes.

The rocket is the oldest as well as the simplest device for jet propulsion. The difficulties of an adequate compressed-air supply are eliminated, as well as all questions of fuel-air ratio, mixing, vaporization, flame velocity, and air flow. The rocket carries its own oxygen, so that combustion is independent of both altitude and speed. However, the penalty for these advantages is severe; for 80 to 90 per cent of the weight of the rocket propellant is due to the oxidant, and the propulsive efficiency is low, owing to the small diameter and high speed of the jet. Consequently, rocket propulsion is practicable only for a short operating time.

Applications of rocket propulsion have been made with success to the launching of airplanes and missiles, to self-propulsion of shells and bombs, and to give an airplane a short burst of speed.

The combustion of a solid propellant cannot be turned off and on, but with liquid fuel and liquid oxidant excellent control is possible. The great advantage of rocket propulsion comes from the fact that the thrust is the same at any speed and at any altitude. It has peculiar advantages under extreme conditions, e.g., for a standing start or for supersonic flight in the upper atmosphere where other jet-propulsion means are relatively ineffective.

16.6. Jet-propulsion Comparisons. The utility of any type of jet propulsion depends, not only on the Froude, or ideal, efficiency of the jet proper (propulsive efficiency), but also on the thermal cycle efficiency of the means employed to create the jet. As a consequence, there appear to be certain operating conditions favoring one type and other operating conditions favoring another. As technological improvements are made, the relative merits of the various types may change. Therefore, comparisons based on the existing state of the art should be considered tentative and subject to the light of possible developments and the shadow of inherent limitations.

16.7. Ideal Efficiency of a Jet. In Art. 16.1 expressions for the ideal, or Froude, efficiency and for the thrust of a propulsive jet were given as Eqs. (16.5a) and (16.1), respectively. For easy reference these are reproduced here.

$$\eta_i = \frac{1}{1 + (\Delta V / 2V)} \tag{16.5a}$$

$$F = m(V_2 - V) = m \, \Delta V \tag{16.1}$$

For a propeller the jet is large and ΔV small. Hence $\Delta V/2V$ is small, and the Froude efficiency rises as the speed of flight increases. For a turbojet, on the other hand, the jet is necessarily restricted, and to obtain a given thrust for a small m the velocity increase ΔV must be large. It is apparent from the Froude efficiency equation that any small high-speed jet having a high value of $\Delta V / V$ is inherently less efficient than systems which utilize a large mass flow and a small value of $\Delta V / V$.

A propeller giving a constant thrust gains rapidly in ideal efficiency with forward speed, because m increases directly with V, causing ΔV to diminish. The result is a doubly rapid reduction of $\Delta V / V$. On the other hand, turbojets and other small high-speed jets give approximately constant ΔV. Therefore, $\Delta V / V$ diminishes with flight speed, although more slowly than for the propeller.

The straight jet, made without a propeller, can in practice closely approach its ideal efficiency even at high flight speeds, whereas the propeller is subject to additional energy losses due to rotation of the wake, nonuniformity of radial-thrust distribution, and the drag of the propeller blades. Furthermore, the blade-drag losses become serious at high speeds, as a consequence of compressibility effects. The actual efficiency of the propeller thus starts to fall off at a flight speed corresponding approximately to a Mach number $M = 0.7$; and near the speed of sound, that is, for $M = 1$, the actual propulsive efficiency of the propeller may be very low.

16.8. Engine-propeller System, Turbojet, Ram Jet. In this section, the computed efficiencies * of three types of jet propulsion at an altitude of 30,000 ft are based on the following assumptions:

Engine-propeller System:
    Rotational tip speed corresponding to $M = 0.8$
    Blade-drag loss, and rotation of wake 7% at $M = 0.6$, increasing to 40% at $M = 1.0$
    Compression ratio of engine............................... 7.5
    Ideal thermal efficiency.................................. 44%
    Actual thermal efficiency................................. 25%

Turbojet:
    Maximum temperature at end of combustion................. 1500 F abs
    Compression ratio 5.0
    Compressor efficiency.................................... 80%
    Turbine efficiency....................................... 75%
    Combustion-chamber pressure loss......................... 8%

Ram jet:
    Maximum temperature at end of combustion................. 2960 F abs
    Effective pressure in combustion chamber................. 88% of ideal ram

a. Propulsive Efficiency. At flight Mach numbers up to 0.7 (476 mph at 30,000 ft) the propeller has a far higher Froude, or propulsive, efficiency than the jet units. Above $M = 0.7$, however, a rapid loss for the propeller occurs owing to compressibility effects on blade drag, while the turbojet continues to gain in efficiency with speed. Reliable test data on propeller efficiencies above $M = 0.7$ are not available, and the dotted curve of

* Made by John V. Becker of the NACA.

Fig. 16.8 is an estimate. In spite of this uncertainty, Fig. 16.8 indicates that turbojet and propeller propulsive efficiencies approach equality before $M = 1.0$.

For the ram jet at $M = 0.45$, the jet velocity becomes equal to the flight velocity, so that $\Delta V = 0$. The propulsive efficiency of 100 per cent for this case is of no significance, since the thrust is zero.

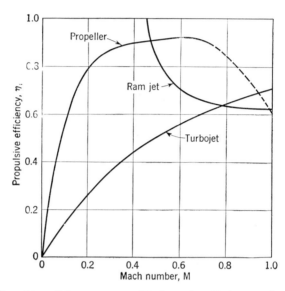

Fig. 16.8. — Propulsive efficiency η_i versus Mach number M, for propeller, turbojet, and ram jet.

b. Cycle Efficiency. The efficiency of the thermodynamic cycle of the engine is of equal importance with the propulsive efficiency in establishing the over-all or thermopropulsive characteristics of the system. Figure 16.9 shows that the thermodynamic cycle efficiency for the turbojet is not greatly lower than that of the internal-combustion engine, even at low flight speeds. Owing to the increased compression resulting from ram the turbojet cycle efficiency improves with flight speed, becoming about equal to that of the internal-combustion engine at $M = 1.0$. The cycle efficiency for the ram jet in the subsonic speed range is extremely low in comparison with the other systems. At a supersonic speed of the order of $M = 1.3$ the ram-jet cycle efficiency becomes about equal in magnitude to that of the turbojet.

c. Over-all Efficiency. The over-all efficiency is the product of the propulsive and the cycle efficiencies. Figure 16.10 indicates that the turbojet is considerably inferior to the propeller-engine system for Mach numbers up to at least 0.7, where the turbojet efficiency is only 0.13 as compared

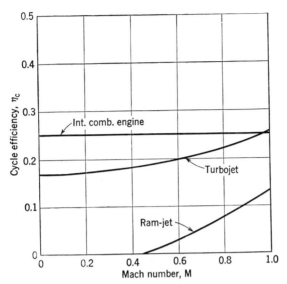

FIG. 16.9. — Cycle efficiency η_c versus Mach number M, for a conventional internal-combustion engine, turbojet, and ram jet.

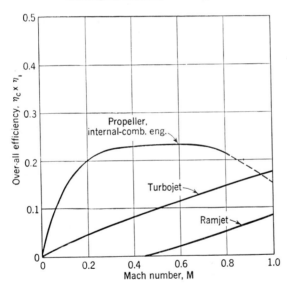

FIG. 16.10. — Over-all efficiency $\eta_i \eta_c$ versus Mach number M, for propeller-engine, turbojet, and ram jet.

with 0.23 for the propeller-engine system. At Mach numbers approaching unity, however, the performance of the two systems is about equal. The ram jet, because of poor cycle efficiency, has a very low over-all efficiency at subsonic speeds. The only practical advantage of this system at subsonic speeds, aside from its obvious simplicity, is the absence of the maximum-temperature restriction imposed on the turbine in turbojet systems.

The increasing use of the turbojet for propulsion of aircraft whose high speed lies in the Mach-number range of 0.7 to 0.8 is justified by the feasibility of employing extremely high fuel rates. By this means, thrusts much higher than those obtainable with current engine-propeller systems can be achieved in spite of the lower over-all efficiency of the turbojet at these flight speeds. Other advantages are mechanical simplicity, light weight, and less bulk.

16.9. Trends of Development. Present airplane propellers under favorable conditions operate at an actual efficiency of the order of 85 per cent, which is close to the ideal efficiency. Research is devoted to the development of blade forms that postpone the advent of serious drag losses as the speed of sound is approached. Considerable success toward this end has been obtained by use of wide and thin blade profiles, swept-back leading edges, and other artifices. While it may be possible to retain a good efficiency up to a rotational-speed Mach number of unity, there will eventually occur a serious drop in efficiency as compressibility effects become predominant. Consequently, it is fair to state that, while the propeller as a propulsive means is highly efficient, it is inherently limited to subsonic flight speeds. There is little prospect of radical change in this situation.

The internal-combustion engine is also a highly efficient machine. With present high compression ratios and high-octane gasoline, fuel consumption may be as low as 0.4 lb per bhp-hr, and with laboratory fuels now available this figure can be further reduced. An additional gain in economy is possible by recovery of wasted power from the exhaust by use of an exhaust gas turbine geared to the crankshaft. Such a compound engine might have a fuel consumption of 0.3 lb per bhp-hr.

The great advantages of the internal-combustion engine are its high state of development and its high efficiency as a compressor and combustion device. Its disadvantages are that it is complicated and costly, limited in maximum power output, and must be used with a propeller of some form. The engine-propeller combination can be improved in over-all efficiency to a useful degree but is inherently limited to subsonic flight and to moderate altitudes.

A propeller driven by a gas-turbine unit and assisted by the exhaust jet of the turbine is lighter and simpler, but the fuel consumption may be of the order of 0.5 to 0.8 lb per bhp-hr. Since the turbine cannot withstand an excessive temperature, it is necessary to compress much more air than that necessary for the combustion of the fuel. Also, the art of compressor design limits the compression ratio. Consequently, the cycle efficiency is inferior to that of the internal-combustion engine but is subect to substantial improvement whenever higher compression ratios are easible. By the use of regeneration, heat exchangers to permit hot exaust gases to warm the incoming air, a gain in economy can be had at he expense of extra weight and bulk. However, the propeller-turbine ombination suffers from the inherent limitations of the propeller.

16.10. Turbojets. The turbojet unit, by omission of the propeller, reaks away from the inherent propeller limitations. Here the gas turbine upplies only the power for the compressor. Such units developed for military purposes show a specific fuel consumption of about 1 lb per hr per b of thrust. At 375 mph this corresponds to 1 lb of fuel per propulsive horsepower-hour. Since thrust is substantially independent of speed, the power economy improves with speed. A thrust of 4,000 to 5,000 lb is practicable at present, while the weight per unit thrust (specific weight) averages about 0.4.

It should be appreciated that the gas turbine was made possible by the availability of metals able to withstand high operating temperatures. The temperature of the turbine blades closely approaches the ambient-gas temperature, while in the Otto-cycle engine extremes of temperature are only momentary and the average temperature of the parts is much lower. Continuous operation at high temperature results in rapid loss of strength and high creep and corrosion rates.

Arrangements to cool the blades with compressed air entail a loss of efficiency and a higher specific fuel consumption and specific weight. German turbojets developed during the Second World War were inferior in these respects to British and American designs of the same period. German designers were short of cobalt, nickel, chromium, molybdenum, and other desirable alloying elements and resorted to somewhat elaborate cooling means. It can be expected that, as better heat-resisting alloys become available, important improvements in the gas turbine and therefore in the turbojet will follow.

Already materials are known having a useful service life at 1500 F, and other types would be usable at 3000 F if brittleness and corrosion could be overcome. Ceramics, sintered powdered metals, and their combinations have possibilities. Metallurgical research can be expected to produce improved heat-resisting materials, with a corresponding opportunity to raise the cycle efficiency of the gas turbine.

As the cycle efficiency is increased, separation and shock effects in the flow through the compressor and turbine become relatively more important. Thus, when the rate of pressure rise along a blade surface is too rapid, the boundary layer does not flow into the high-pressure region and separation takes place, with considerable energy loss. This problem of a rising pressure gradient is more serious in the compressor than in the turbine.

Adverse pressure gradients may arise from a compressibility shock with abrupt transition from supersonic to subsonic flow and a consequent sharp pressure rise along the surface.

The fluid mechanics of flow separation for a three-dimensional rotating blade system is not well understood, nor are methods available for postponing the occurrence of compressibility shock. Consequently, the design of both compressors and turbines is based on conservative approximations, and maximum efficiency and compactness are not realized.

Owing to the fact that the turbojet requires combustion air, it is not effective above a limiting altitude. Because of expense, it is unlikely to be used to propel short-range missiles where rocket propulsion will suffice.

None of the readily available organic fuels offers the possibility of any significant improvement over petroleum products. The light combustible metals, such as magnesium, possess higher heating values per unit of weight or volume, but magnesium oxide would be discharged through the turbine. This appears to be intolerable.

In conclusion it should be pointed out that increased thrust resulting from higher combustion temperature is accompanied by decreased propulsive efficiency, with a resultant drop in over-all efficiency. Higher temperature is nevertheless desirable, because a higher power output can thus be obtained, despite the sacrifice in over-all efficiency.

16.11. Ram Jets. The intermittent ram-jet or buzz-bomb engine developed by the Germans had a specific fuel consumption of about 3 lb per hr per lb. Analysis indicates that this figure could be reduced to one-third of the above value if more rapid combustion could be achieved. To do this requires a fuel system with a burning time of a few thousandths of a second. Were such an improvement to be made, the intermittent ram jet could compete with the internal-combustion engine at subsonic flight speeds.

Since the intermittent ram-jet engine is extremely simple and cheap, it is the ideal propulsive system for an expendable missile. Its best operating speed is from 400 to 500 mph, and from the standpoint of over-all weight its range should be somewhat less than 500 miles. Operation at flight speeds greater than 600 mph is questionable because of difficulties of air supply and valving.

The true ram jet is relatively undeveloped but appears to be the most promising propulsive device for supersonic long-range missiles. Its efficiency increases with speed, as ram pressure rises. At subsonic speeds its thrust is too low to be of interest, but at supersonic speeds it should be very effective. Ram-jet missiles must use some other source of power, such as a rocket, to bring them to a flight speed above 400 mph, at which the ram jet can take over. At a flight speed corresponding to $M = 2$, a ram jet should show a fuel consumption of about 0.8 lb per hp-hr.

The supersonic ram jet presents a host of aerodynamic and combustion problems that are not yet solved, and there appear to be two inherent limitations, *viz.*, low thrust at subsonic speeds and low thrust at low air density (high altitude).

16.12. Rocket Mechanics. The propulsion of a rocket is due to the reaction of its jet. Let the jet velocity be designated by W relative to reference axes moving with the rocket, and let e represent the energy content of the propellant per unit mass (foot-pounds per slug or square feet per square second). In this reference system, unburned propellant has no kinetic energy. The burning of propellant in the rocket will convert a fraction η_0 of its energy into kinetic energy in the jet.

$$\eta_0 e = \frac{W^2}{2}$$

or

$$W = \sqrt{2\eta_0 e} \qquad (16.15)$$

Let propellant be burned at the mass rate of m slugs per sec. Then the reaction, or thrust, of the jet will be the rate of increase of momentum in the jet, relative to the moving axes,

$$T = mW = m\sqrt{2\eta_0 e} \qquad (16.16)$$

Now refer to axes fixed on the earth, and let the "absolute" velocity of the rocket be V. Observe that the rocket's original energy supply is being used up at the rate of $m[e + (V^2/2)]$, as propellant of mass m is ejected every second. The useful work of the thrust in moving the rocket is done at the rate of $TV = mV\sqrt{2\eta_0 e}$. The over-all efficiency of the rocket η_R in the fixed reference system is therefore

$$\eta_R = \frac{mV\sqrt{2\eta_0 e}}{m[e + (V^2/2)]} = 2\eta_0 \frac{W/V}{(W/V)^2 + \eta_0} \qquad (16.17)$$

Setting the derivative $\partial \eta_R / \partial (W/V) = 0$, one finds that η_R is a maximum if

$$\frac{W}{V} = \sqrt{\eta_0} \qquad (16.18)$$

and that, consequently,

$$\eta_{R\max} = \sqrt{\eta_0} \qquad (16.19)$$

For perfect conversion of energy of combustion, that is, for $\eta_0 = 1$, the over-all efficiency would be 100 per cent, and W would equal V. The exhaust material would thus be ejected at rocket speed and left without kinetic energy relative to the reference system in which work was being done. Usually η_0 is found to be about 0.25, giving $\eta_R = 0.5$ as the maximum over-all efficiency. However, this efficiency is of secondary interest to the designer, who must utilize the greatest amount of energy from the initial mass of propellant.

The energy usefully applied per unit mass of propellant is

$$\eta_R\left(e + \frac{V^2}{2}\right) = V\sqrt{2\eta_0 e} \approx \frac{V}{\sqrt{2}}\sqrt{e}$$

For a given kind of propellant this quantity increases directly with rocket speed. From Eqs. (16.18) and (16.15) it is seen that, for given speed V, the highest efficiency is attained for $V = W/\sqrt{\eta_0} = \sqrt{2e}$, or $e = V^2/2$. For example, at low speed, say 400 ft per sec, the best efficiency would be obtained from a propellant having an $e = 80,000$ sq ft per sq sec. The overall efficiency would thus be 0.5, and the useful work per unit mass would be $\eta_R[e + (V^2/2)] = 80,000$ sq ft per sq sec.

A mixture of gasoline and oxygen, on the other hand, for which $e = 3,300,000g$ would be utilized at an over-all efficiency [Eq. (16.17)] of only 2.7 per cent at this speed, but the useful energy per unit mass would be 2.96×10^6 sq ft per sq sec.

Consequently, it appears that for starting rockets, and low speeds generally the high-energy propellants are best in spite of low efficiency.

A rocket is handicapped for long range by having to carry its own oxidant as well as the fuel, but the ram jet uses the atmosphere as oxidant. The following simplified comparison brings out the advantage of the ram jet:

It can be shown for a ram jet, as in problem 16.7, that the relative kinetic energy of the jet is equal to the relative kinetic energy of the incoming air plus that part of the energy of the fuel which is converted to kinetic energy by the combustion process. Thus, under the assumption that 15 slugs of air combine with 1 slug of fuel, $16W^2/2 = (15V^2/2) + \eta_0 e$. Hence,

$$W = \frac{1}{4}\sqrt{2\eta_0 e + 15V^2} \tag{16.20}$$

Refer now to axes fixed in space. Let m_f represent the mass of gasoline burned per second. The net thrust, resulting from the burning of fuel at this rate in $15m_f$ slugs of air per second, will be

$$T = m_f W + 15m_f(W - V) = m_f(16W - 15V) \tag{16.21}$$

For a rocket burning its propellant at m_r slugs per sec, the corresponding statement is, from Eq. (16.16),

$$T = m_r\sqrt{2\eta_0 e_r} \tag{16.22}$$

where e_r is the energy per unit mass of propellant. Elimination of T from Eqs. (16.21) and (16.22) gives $m_r/m_f = (16W - 15V)/\sqrt{2\eta_0 e_r}$, while substitution for W from Eq. (16.20) yields

$$\frac{m_r}{m_f} = \frac{4\sqrt{2\eta_0 e + 15V^2} - 15V}{\sqrt{2\eta_0 e_r}} \tag{16.23}$$

Taking $e = 15 \times 10^6 g$, $e_r = 3.3 \times 10^6 g$, and $\eta_0 = 0.25$, we find the ratio
[fuel rates to be

$$\frac{\text{Rocket fuel rate}}{\text{Ram-jet fuel rate}} = \begin{cases} 7.1 \text{ for } V = 800 \text{ ft/sec} \\ 5.8 \text{ for } V = 1{,}600 \text{ ft/sec} \end{cases}$$

The possibility of sending rockets to very great altitudes has prompted
)eculation about leaving the earth [9]. A very great quantity of propellant
ould be required, and the arrangement
ould have to convert quickly a large
ortion of the energy of the propellant
ito kinetic energy of the rocket. Work
one in raising the weight of unburned
•opellant to a great height is wasted.
'he rocket should be accelerated to a
igh velocity in the shortest possible
istance.

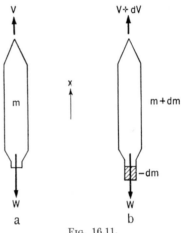

Consider the system of mass m shown
1 Fig. 16.11a, comprising a rocket and
he propellant inside it at an arbitrary
ime. The rocket has an instantaneous
pward (x) velocity V relative to the
arth, and the motion of the burning pro-
•ellant relative to the rocket is steady.

Fıg. 16.11.

'he constant relative velocity of the jet at exit is denoted by W.

By Newton's second law the change in x momentum of this system in
ime dt is equal to the product of the resultant x force F_x and dt. During
his time interval an observer moving with the rocket would see a
eduction $- dm$ in the mass of unburned propellant and a movement of
.n equal mass of gas out the tail pipe, with relative velocity W (Fig.
6.11b). He would see no change in the relative velocity of any part of
he remaining mass, $m + dm$. The change in "absolute" velocity
)f this remaining mass is therefore dV, and its momentum change is
$m + dm)\, dV$. The initial absolute velocity of the mass $- dm$ is V, and
ts final velocity is $V + dV - W$. Its momentum change is therefore
$- dm(V + dV - W - V)$ or $- dm(dV - W)$. The change in momentum
)f the entire system is thus known, and

$$F_x \, dt = (m + dm)\, dV - dm(dV - W) = m\, dV + W\, dm \qquad (16.24)$$

It may be remarked parenthetically that Eq. (16.24) is equivalent to
Eq. (16.16), for uniform motion of the rocket $(V = \text{constant})$. In this
:ase, $F_x - W(dm/dt) = 0$ [which in the notation of Eq. (16.16) is
$\mathcal{F}_x + Wm = 0$]. In words, the system behaves as if, in addition to the actual
•xternal force F_x, it were acted upon by a forward thrust $T = - W(dm/dt)$.

This notion of the effective thrust T of the jet can also be applied to th accelerated system. For Eq. (16.24) can be rewritten as $F_x - W(dm/d = m(dV/dt)$ or $F_x + T = m(dV/dt)$. At any instant, therefore, the system behaves as if it had a constant mass m and were acted upon by a thrust in addition to the actual external force F_x.

If now the air resistance of the rocket be neglected, the only force c the system is its weight mg, acting in the negative x direction. Equation (16.24) thus becomes $- W(dm/m) = dV + g\,dt$, which, with W and g con stant, integrates to

$$\ln\frac{m_0}{m} = \frac{V}{W} + \frac{gt}{W} \tag{16.25}$$

where m_0 is the mass of the rocket and propellant at the start of the motion when $V = 0$ and $t = 0$. If t be the time required to burn all the propellant m and V will be the values of mass and velocity at "all burnt."

The jet velocity W for a given propellant and a given η_0 can be deter mined from Eq. (16.15). If the velocity V required to carry the rocket ou of the earth's gravitational field is found, the ratio m_0/m of starting mas to all-burnt mass can be computed from Eq. (16.25). In the absence of an data on burning time, gt may, as a first approximation, be assumed negli gible compared with V. Both this approximation and the neglect of ai resistance tend to give a smaller value for m_0/m than the actual one; the both err on the optimistic side.

To find the initial velocity required to carry a body outside the earth' gravitational field (with air resistance neglected) we use the Newtonian law of gravitation,

$$F = \frac{- Gmm_E}{r^2} \tag{16.26}$$

where F is the force between a mass m and the earth of mass m_E, r is the distance between the earth's center and m, and G is the gravitational con stant. The negative sign indicates that F acts in a direction opposite t that of increasing r.

The work done by F on m as m moves away from the earth's surface (where $r = r_E$) to infinity is

$$\int_{r_E}^{\infty} F\,dr = - Gmm_E \int_{r_E}^{\infty} \frac{dr}{r^2} = \frac{- Gmm_E}{r_E}$$

This work is equal to the difference between the final and initial kineti energies of the mass m. The smallest initial kinetic energy which suffice to get the mass away from the earth is that corresponding to a final kinetic energy of zero. Thus $- Gmm_E/r_E = 0 - (m/2)V^2$. Noting that at the earth's surface $F = - mg$, we get, from Eq. (16.26), $gr_E = Gm_E/r_E$, so tha

$$V = \sqrt{2gr_E} = 36{,}700 \text{ ft/sec} \qquad (16.27)$$

here the value $r_E = 20.9 \times 10^6$ ft has been substituted.

An approximate value of m_0/m is now found, for a propellant of gasoline and oxygen ($e = 3.3 \times 10^6 g$ sq ft per sq sec) and for $\eta_0 = \frac{1}{4}$, by combination of Eqs. (16.15), (16.25), and (16.27)

$$\ln \frac{m_0}{m} = \frac{1}{\sqrt{2\eta_0 e}} \, (V + gt) \qquad (16.28)$$

$$\ln \frac{m_0}{m} = \frac{36{,}700 + 0}{\sqrt{3.3 \times 10^6 \times 32.2/2}} = 5.03$$

$$\frac{m_0}{m} = 155$$

$$\frac{m_0 - m}{m_0} = 0.993 \qquad (16.29)$$

he mass of propellant is thus more than 99 per cent of the total, and rocket ight to other planets is impracticable with gasoline and oxygen.

The picture is completely changed, however, if one considers the eventual possibility of using a propellant such as the uranium isotope U–235, which derives energy from nuclear changes rather than from ordinary combustion. For U–235, the value of e is $2.44 \times 10^{13} g$ sq ft per sq sec [4], which s 0.74×10^7 times larger than that for gasoline and oxygen. With this value of e, Eq. (16.28) yields

$$\frac{m_0 - m}{m_0} = 0.0019 \qquad (16.30)$$

The mass of propellant is only about 0.2 per cent of the initial mass and is practically negligible.

Even though a source of nuclear power is theoretically available, the problem of its utilization at a reasonable efficiency (η_0) remains to be solved. This problem is referred to again at the end of this chapter.

The feasibility of a space rocket is one aspect of the general question of the range of a simple rocket without wings. In this connection it is of interest to compare the results of Eq. (16.25) with information now available concerning the German V–2 rocket. The estimated maximum velocity V of this rocket was 3,500 mph or 5,130 ft per sec. The propellant, alcohol and liquid oxygen, should have given a jet velocity W of about 6,500 ft per sec. The burning time t was 60 sec. Equation (16.25) thus yields $m_0/m = 2.95$. The reported initial weight of the V–2 was 13.5 tons, including some 9 tons of propellant, so that actually $m_0/m = 13.5/4.5 = 3.0$.

In view of the uncertainty in several of the figures used, the very close

agreement between the actual and computed values of m_0/m is large|
accidental. It is clear, however, that Eq. (16.25) gives a good approxima
tion to the truth.

It is obvious that the V–2 type of rocket would have greater range
more fuel were burned, but this would require a vehicle of increased $m_0/$
ratio. In view of the necessity for at least a ton of explosive, elabora|
control mechanisms, and a powerful pumping system for the liquid pro
pellant, it would be difficult to bring this ratio much beyond 3.

Discussion of the effect of adding wings to the missile to prolong i|
trajectory by gliding under the pull of gravity is beyond the scope of thi
text.

All rocket propellants now in use have roughly the same energy pe
unit mass or per unit weight. The following values of energy are quote
to indicate that all are of the same order of magnitude:

Propellant	e/g, Ft-lb/lb
Hydrogen and ozone...........	5,500,000
Hydrogen and oxygen..........	4,500,000
Gasoline and oxygen..........	3,300,000
TNT.......................	2,500,000
Guncotton.................	1,500,000

The merits of a propellant may also be judged on the basis of the impuls
per unit weight or per unit volume, which is called the "specific impulse."
The specific impulse, which is merely the thrust divided by the weight o
volume of propellant burned per unit time, can be computed from Eq
(16.16). Values for several propellants are tabulated below.

Propellant	Specific impulse		W, ft/sec
	Lb-sec/lb	Lb-sec/gal	
Solid (Ballistite).............	210	2,850	6,750
Fuming nitric acid and aniline.	240	2,750	7,700
Liquid oxygen and hydrogen ..	340	1,300	11,000

Note that the oxygen–hydrogen pair is inferior, on a volume basis, be
cause of the low density of the hydrogen.

To improve the performance of rockets substantially it would be neces
sary to increase jet temperature or to employ gas of lower molecular weight
Neither of these means offers great promise [8]. Temperature is already
of the order of 4000 to 5000 F, and the weight of metal required to with
stand the pressure is substantial. The exit nozzle is difficult to keep coo
enough to prevent rapid erosion and erratic flight.

To make a major improvement in rocket missiles, some method o
acceleration of the jet material other than pressure expansion is needed

Discoveries in the field of nuclear power may some day provide means for accelerating electrons or gaseous ions, but there will still remain the problems of a material to withstand an extremely high rate of energy release in a confined space and of a working fluid to be ejected. The difficulties may be appreciated from the following comparison of the velocities involved:

The velocity W obtained with the best of the present propellants is on the order of 10^4 ft per sec. If a nuclear propellant were to be utilized at roughly the same efficiency, a velocity one thousand times greater would be attained—on the order of 10^7 ft per sec.

Present rocket research is concerned with propellants giving a high spontaneous energy release that are, at the same time, nontoxic, noncorrosive, stable in manufacture and storage, and insensitive to impurities or ordinary temperature changes. Besides the propellants mentioned previously the following have been found useful: hydrogen peroxide with permanganate catalyst, hydrogen peroxide, and hydrazine hydrate.

SELECTED BIBLIOGRAPHY

Propellers:

1. Glauert, H.: "Aerofoil and Airscrew Theory," Cambridge University Press, London, 1926.
2. Weick, F. E.: "Aircraft Propeller Design," McGraw-Hill Book Company, Inc., New York, 1930.

Jets:

3. Sänger, E.: "Raketen Flugtechnik," R. Oldenbourg, Munich and Berlin, 1933.
4. Tsien, Hsue-Shen: Atomic Energy, *J. Aeronaut. Sci.,* vol. 13, pp. 171–180, April, 1946.
5. Westinghouse Electric and Manufacturing Company: The Day Dawns for Jet Propulsion, *Westinghouse Eng.,* March, 1945; also *Reprint* 4123.
6. Zucrow, M. J.: Jet Propulsion and Rockets for Assisted Take-off, *Trans. Am. Soc. Mech. Engrs.,* vol. 68, pp. 177–188, April, 1946.
7. Various articles that have appeared during recent years in *Aviation* (see especially vols. 44 and 45, 1945 and 1946).
8. Ackeret, J.: Zur Theorie der Raketen, *Helv. Phys. Acta,* vol. 19, pp. 103–112, 1946.
9. Malina, F. J., and M. Summerfield: The Problem of Escape from the Earth by Rocket, *J. Aeronaut. Sci.,* vol. 14, pp. 471–480, August, 1947.

CHAPTER XVII

FLUID COUPLINGS AND TORQUE CONVERTERS

Fluid couplings and torque converters are power transmissions whose operation depends on the dynamics of fluid motion. A coupling consists of only two elements, the primary, which is a centrifugal pump; and the secondary, which is a reaction turbine driven by the pump. Both these elements are enclosed in one casing, in order to make the efficiency as large as possible. Since torque is applied to the coupling only at the primary and secondary shafts, these two torques are equal under steady running conditions.

A torque converter comprises the same two elements as a coupling, but interposed between them is a set of guide vanes, fastened to the casing. By suitable design the torque reaction on these stationary vanes can be given any desired value. The output torque at starting can thus be made several times greater than the input torque.

17.1. Description of a Fluid Coupling. In Fig. 17.1 is shown a typical fluid coupling. The primary and secondary runners are identical; each

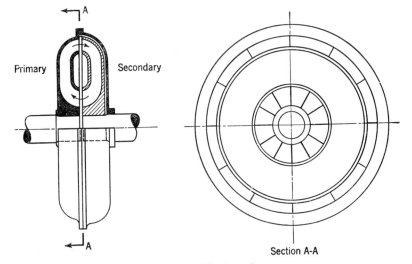

Primary   Secondary

Section A-A

Fig. 17.1. — Fluid coupling.

has straight, radial blades so that it resembles half of an orange with the pulp removed. There is no mechanical connection between the runners.

The coupling is wholly or partly filled with liquid (usually oil), so that

404

hen the primary is rotated, the oil in it acquires moment of momentum
)out the axis and also tends to move radially outward through the passages
etween the blades. Oil thus flows from primary to secondary at the pe-
phery and, by virtue of continuity, from secondary to primary at the
ib. This circulation of oil continues as long as the secondary rotates
iore slowly than the primary, i.e., as long as slip occurs. If the speeds
·e equal (zero slip), the centrifugal effects balance each other and no oil
ows.

The moment of momentum of the oil leaving the primary is greater than
iat of the oil entering, for the tangential velocity is greater at the periphery
ian at the hub. Under steady conditions the net efflux of moment of
.omentum from the primary is equal to the driving torque, by virtue of
:q. (6.19). Similarly, the net influx to the secondary equals the load
)rque on the driven shaft. The torque transmitted by a given coupling
·ill therefore depend both on the speed of the primary and on the slip.
·or zero slip, no torque is transmitted, regardless of the speed. It will be
hown below that for a given slip the torque is practically proportional to
he square of the primary speed. Hence a coupling is best adapted to high-
peed operation.

The efficiency is defined as the ratio of output to input power. Since
he power equals the product of torque and angular velocity and input
nd output torques are equal, the efficiency reduces to the ratio of secondary
o primary speed. At normal loads and speeds the efficiency is high,
isually more than 95 per cent.

The smallest couplings in use handle about 1 hp and the largest, about
·6,000 hp.

The principal advantages of the fluid coupling lie in its unsteady-state
haracteristics. It provides low starting torques on electric motors and
nternal-combustion engines having high-inertia loads and smooths out
orsional vibrations originating either at the prime mover or at the load.

Under steady conditions the coupling will provide a smoothly variable
;peed from a constant-speed prime mover. We accomplish this variation
)y changing the amount of oil in the coupling and thus controlling the
imount of slip. By this means, flexibility is gained at the expense of
:fficiency, since slip and efficiency are related by the equation

$$\text{Slip} = s = 1 - \frac{\omega_s}{\omega_p} = 1 - \eta \qquad (17.1)$$

·vhere ω_s and ω_p are the secondary and primary speeds, respectively, and
η is the efficiency. Such speed control is obviously unsuited to constant-
power applications or to prolonged operation at reduced speed if efficiency
is important.

Fluid couplings have been found particularly useful for automotive drives; marine, railroad, and industrial diesel drives; electric-motor drive and variable-speed conveyer operation.

17.2. Steady-state Analysis of a Fluid Coupling. A dimensiona analysis of a coupling may be made, as follows: We assume that the torqu T is a function only of ρ, ω_p, D, s, $\mathcal{v}$, and μ, for a coupling of given design

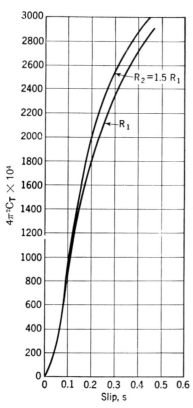

Here $\mathcal{v}$, ρ, and μ are the total volume density, and viscosity, respectively, (the operating fluid, ω_p is the primar speed, and D is the coupling diametei In applying the Π theorem we may le ρ, ω_p, and D be common to all four I products. We get

$$C_T = \frac{T}{\rho\omega_p^2 D^5} = \phi\left(s, \frac{\rho\omega_p D^2}{\mu}, \frac{\mathcal{v}}{D^3}\right) \quad (17.2$$

Tests at a fixed value of $\mathcal{v}/D^3$ wer performed at the Massachusetts Insti tute of Technology on an automotiv type of coupling. Some of the result are shown in Fig. 17.2, from which th effect of slip is seen to be much mor important than that of the Reynold number $R = \rho\omega_p D^2/\mu$. This behavio is not surprising, since it will be re called from earlier chapters that th minor influence of R is typical of hy drodynamic machinery. The meanin of these curves is clarified by the fol lowing approximate analysis of th mode of operation of a coupling:

Fig. 17.2. — Torque coefficient versus slip for a fluid coupling. The measurements were made at two values of Reynolds number R, and for a constant volume of oil in the coupling.

Application of Eq. (6.19) to th primary runner of the coupling of Fig 17.3 shows that the primary torqu equals the net efflux of moment o momentum from the primary. In th notation of Fig. 17.3 the efflux of moment of momentum is $\rho Q\omega_p r_2^2$, an the influx is $\rho Q\omega_s r_1^2$. Thus, the torque is

$$T = \rho Q(\omega_p r_2^2 - \omega_s r_1^2) \quad (17.3$$

To render this equation useful, we eliminate the unknown factor Q b means of the following considerations:

The difference between the input and output power $T(\omega_p - \omega_s)$ is du to the losses in the coupling, which arise in two ways.

1. As oil enters either the primary or secondary runner, the tangential velocity component of the oil suffers an abrupt change, owing to the difference between ω_p and ω_s. Eddies are thus set up because the main flow tends to separate from the leading edges of the blades. The energy of these eddies, which is called the "shock loss," is eventually dissipated

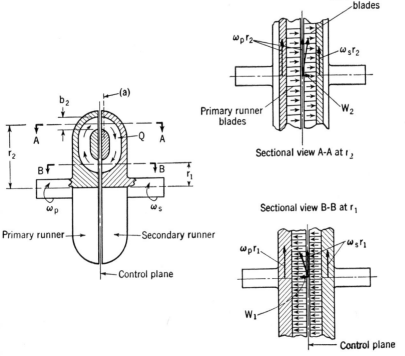

FIG. 17.3. — Velocity diagrams for a fluid coupling.

by viscosity and, under the steady conditions here assumed, appears as a heat transfer to the surroundings.

To estimate the shock loss at entrance to the secondary we use the steady-flow energy equation referred to axes rotating with the secondary [Eq. (6.21)]. In this rotating frame of reference no shaft work appears to be done on the fluid between the control plane and an adjacent section a just inside the secondary runner (see Fig. 17.3). Neglecting any change in pressure, we get from Eq. (6.21) that the energy of the eddies at a must be equal to the change in the average kinetic energy of the fluid as it moves from the control plane to a.* In a coupling having thin, radial blades,

* The momentum law shows the pressure change to be small, since the friction forces on the elementary lengths of blade are small and, by continuity, the axial momentum is constant.

practically all the tangential velocity component at the control plane $(\omega_p - \omega_s)r_2$ has disappeared at section a. The axial velocity is constant by continuity, so that the energy per unit mass converted into eddies is $(\omega_p - \omega_s)^2 r_2^2/2$ sq ft per sq sec. Similarly, at the entrance to the primary the energy per unit mass of the eddies is $(\omega_p - \omega_s)^2 r_1^2/2$ sq ft per sq sec.

The shock losses can be reduced by use of blades having well-rounded leading edges. Such refinement is not usually worth while, however, for at the same value of ω_p, the same torque can be transmitted with equal efficiency by a coupling of slightly larger diameter and having the usual sheet-metal blades.

2. The second cause of loss in the coupling is the frictional drag of the fluid on the walls of the passages between the blades. These are similar to pipe-friction losses and may be expressed in the form $\lambda Q^2/2A^2$, where A is the cross-sectional area of the flow at an arbitrary point in the circuit. The ratio Q/A is thus a measure of the oil velocity relative to the passage walls. The dimensionless factor λ is analogous to the pipe-friction factor. The effect of the ratio of length to effective diameter is, however, included in λ.

With the aid of these formulas for the losses the power dissipation can be expressed as

$$T(\omega_p - \omega_s) = \frac{\rho}{2} Q \left[(\omega_p - \omega_s)^2 (r_1^2 + r_2^2) + \lambda \frac{Q^2}{A^2} \right] \qquad (17.4)$$

Eliminating Q by combining Eqs. (17.3) and (17.4), we find the torque to be

$$T = \rho \omega_p^2 r_2^5 s^{1/2} \frac{A}{r_2^2} \sqrt{(2 - s)\left(1 - \frac{r_1^2}{r_2^2}\right)} \frac{1 - (1 - s)(r_1^2/r_2^2)}{\lambda^{1/2}} \qquad (17.5)$$

This equation, in conjunction with the experimental curves of Fig. 17.2 shows that, at small values of s, λ decreases rapidly as s increases, but, at larger values of s, λ becomes approximately constant. This behavior of λ is what might be expected from the friction-factor chart (Fig. 8.3) since at small slips the flow in the coupling will be laminar, while at large slips it will be very turbulent, owing to the shock losses. In the laminar range λ decreases rapidly as s increases, while, in the turbulent range, λ is nearly constant.

17.3. The Fluid Coupling as a Vibration Absorber. Consider an engine whose shaft has a vibratory twisting motion (torsional vibration) at the end to which a load is to be attached. To couple the driven shaft to the engine in such a way that the former turns at a uniform speed the coupling must transmit only the steady component of the driving torque and absorb the vibratory component. A *fluid* coupling is well adapted to this use. The primary runner can oscillate freely about a mean position without influencing seriously the steady circulation of oil in the coupling. The secondary thus feels an essentially steady driving torque.

Even the small fluctuating torque unavoidably transmitted may have serious effects, however, if the load system has a natural frequency close to that of the pulsating torque. In this case the coupling may be ineffective, for the small exciting torque tends to set up resonant vibrations of the load system. To remedy this situation one can obviously change the natural frequency of the load. If such change is impracticable, it will be necessary to attach the coupling to the driven system at a node, where the amplitude of resonant vibration is a minimum. The pulsating applied torque will thus have a minimum tendency to excite the system.

Sinclair [6] has described experiments in which torsiograms were made for both primary and secondary shafts of a fluid coupling connected to a diesel engine. Even under resonant conditions, he found that the amplitude of vibration transmitted to the secondary was only about 2 per cent of the amplitude at the primary.

Eksergian [3] has analyzed in detail the vibratory characteristics of several systems involving a fluid coupling.

17.4. Description of a Torque Converter. In Fig. 17.4 is shown a side view of a torque converter. It will be seen that both primary and secondary runners lie in the left-hand half of the casing, while the entire right-hand half is taken up by the stationary guide vanes, or reaction stage. The converter illustrated has only a single-stage secondary (turbine) runner. Converters are in use that have three turbine stages and two reaction stages. These converters have a good efficiency over a wider operating range than the simpler type. The blades are not radial in a converter but are curved so as to give the desired relationships between the input and output torques and speeds.

The principle of operation of a converter is much like that of a fluid coupling. Oil is forced by centrifugal action out of the primary runner and into the turbine. From the turbine the oil enters the guide vanes, which are curved so as to alter the moment of momentum of the oil before it is discharged once more into the primary. This change in moment of momentum causes an external torque reaction on the housing. Under steady conditions the secondary torque must equal the sum of the primary and reaction torques, that is,

$$T_s = T_p + T_g \qquad (17.6)$$

where the subscripts s, p, and g stand for secondary, primary, and guide vanes, respectively.

The efficiency of a converter is defined as the ratio of output to input power.

$$\eta = \frac{\omega_s T_s}{\omega_p T_p} \qquad (17.7)$$

The maximum efficiency is less than that attainable in a fluid coupling on account of the greater complexity of a converter. It is usually about

85 to 87 per cent, but values as high as 89 per cent have been reported.

The first torque converters were built before 1914, by Dr. H. Föttinger of Hamburg, Germany. They had a speed ratio of 5 to 1 and were used to connect high-speed steam turbines to low-speed marine propellers. They were later displaced in this application by helical reduction gears, which

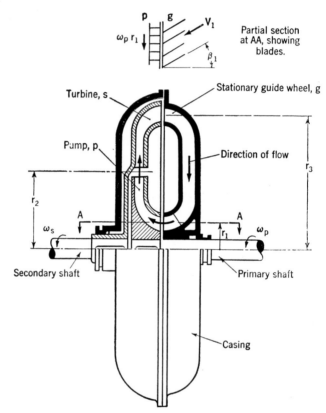

Fig. 17.4. — Torque converter.

have a higher efficiency and lower cost. In recent years, converters have come into use for automotive service, especially on trucks and busses operating in heavy traffic. The converter eliminates the frequent gear shifting that would otherwise be needed.

17.5. Analysis of a Torque Converter. For a given design of converter, filled to a fixed percentage of its total volume, we may assume that T_p, T_s, and η are functions only of ρ, ω_p, ω_s, μ, and D, the converter diameter. Application of the Π theorem leads to

$$C_p = \frac{T_p}{\rho \omega_p^2 D^5} = \phi_1\left(\frac{\omega_s}{\omega_p}, \frac{\rho \omega_p D^2}{\mu}\right) \tag{17.8}$$

$$C_s = \frac{T_s}{\rho \omega_p^2 D^5} = \phi_2 \left(\frac{\omega_s}{\omega_p}, \frac{\rho \omega_p D^2}{\mu} \right) \qquad (17.9)$$

$$\eta = \phi_3 \left(\frac{\omega_s}{\omega_p}, \frac{\rho \omega_p D^2}{\mu} \right) \qquad (17.10)$$

Dividing Eq. (17.9) by Eq. (17.8), we get

$$\frac{T_s}{T_p} = \phi_4 \left(\frac{\omega_s}{\omega_p}, \frac{\rho \omega_p D^2}{\mu} \right) \qquad (17.11)$$

Experiments show that, to a first approximation, the effect of the Reynolds number $R = \rho \omega_p D^2 / \mu$ can be neglected in comparison with that of the speed ratio. Typical experimental curves are plotted in Fig. 17.5.

Theoretical expressions for the torque ratio and efficiency that are in

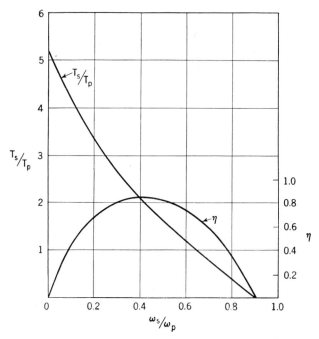

FIG. 17.5. — Torque ratio T_s/T_p and efficiency η versus speed ratio ω_s/ω_p, for a torque converter. (*After Spannhake, reference 8. Courtesy of the Society of Automotive Engineers.*)

substantial agreement with these curves can be set up with the aid of a few simplifying assumptions. Although the pump and turbine blades must be curved for good efficiency, we assume straight radial blades for these elements and take curvature into account only at the exit from the reaction stage. We assume also, on the basis of experience, that Eq. (17.8) will reduce to $C_p =$ constant. Finally, we assume the cross-sectional area of the flow A to be the same everywhere in the circuit.

Referring to Fig. 17.4 and using Eqs. (6.18) and (6.19), we get

$$T_p = \rho Q(\omega_p r_2^2 - V_1 \sin \beta_1 r_1) \tag{17.12}$$

$$T_s = \rho Q(\omega_p r_2^2 - \omega_s r_3^2) \tag{17.13}$$

Noting that $V_1 = Q/A \cos \beta_1$, we transform these two equations to:

$$C_p = \frac{T_p}{\rho \omega_p^2 r_3^5} = \frac{Q}{\omega_p r_3^3}\left(\frac{r_2^2}{r_3^2} - \frac{Q \tan \beta_1}{A \omega_p r_3}\frac{r_1}{r_3}\right) \tag{17.14}$$

$$C_s = \frac{T_s}{\rho \omega_p^2 r_3^5} = \frac{Q}{\omega_p r_3^3}\left(\frac{r_2^2}{r_3^2} - \frac{\omega_s}{\omega_p}\right) \tag{17.15}$$

The torque ratio is thus

$$\frac{T_s}{T_p} = \frac{(r_2^2/r_3^2) - (\omega_s/\omega_p)}{(r_2^2/r_3^2) - (Q \tan \beta_1/A \omega_p r_3)(r_1/r_3)} \tag{17.16}$$

and the efficiency is

$$\eta = \frac{T_s\omega_s}{T_p\omega_p} = \frac{[(r_2^2/r_3^2) - (\omega_s/\omega_p)](\omega_s/\omega_p)}{(r_2^2/r_3^2) - (Q \tan \beta_1/A \omega_p r_3)(r_1/r_3)} \tag{17.17}$$

From the second assumption made above and from Eq. (17.14) it follows that $Q/\omega_p r_3^3$ is constant. Consequently, Eqs. (17.16) and (17.17) show that T_s/T_p is a linear function of ω_s/ω_p and that η varies parabolically with ω_s/ω_p. At maximum efficiency, T_s/T_p has one-half of its initial value.

It is clear from Fig. 17.5 that these calculated results are in approximate agreement with observation. The discrepancies between the two can be ascribed to variations in $Q/\omega_p r_3^3$ and to curvature of the pump and turbine blades. Eksergian [3] has developed a more refined theory, which takes these factors into account through an energy balance like that for the coupling, in Art. 17.4.

17.6. Torque Converter — Coupling Unit. A combination of torque converter and fluid coupling appears to offer one solution to the problem of power transmission in passenger cars. In such a combination the reaction stage is at rest so long as the primary torque is less than that required at the secondary. The unit thus functions as a converter. As soon as the primary and secondary torques become equal, however, the reaction stage automatically starts to rotate with the secondary and the unit becomes a coupling. This action is obtained through the use of two overrunning clutches.

Dimensionless characteristic curves for such a unit are shown as full lines in Fig. 17.6. The broken extensions of these curves apply to the converter or coupling individually. Combination of the two elements makes it possible to use each one in a favorable operating range.

An alternative scheme is to use a torque converter for torque multiplication and to change over automatically to direct drive when the primary and secondary torques become equal [2]. With this arrangement the

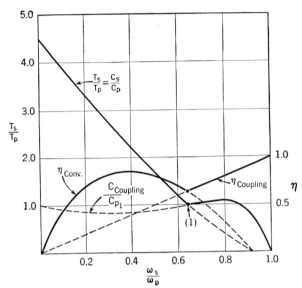

FIG. 17.6. — Torque ratio $T_s/T_p = C_s/C_p$ and efficiency η versus speed ratio ω_s/ω_p, for a combined converter and coupling. (*After Spannhake, reference* 8. *Courtesy of the Society of Automotive Engineers.*)

clutch must, of course, slip momentarily until the primary and secondary speeds are equalized.

SELECTED BIBLIOGRAPHY

1. Alison, A. L., R. C. Olson, and R. M. Nelden: Hydraulic Couplings for Internal-combustion-engine Applications, *Trans. Am. Soc. Mech. Engrs.*, vol. 63, pp. 81–90, February, 1941.
2. Deimel, A. H.: Hydraulic Transmissions for Motor Vehicles, *S.A.E.J.*, vol. 53, pp. 10–18, January, 1945.
3. Eksergian, R.: The Fluid Torque Converter and Coupling, *J. Franklin Inst.*, vol. 235, pp. 441–478, May, 1943.
4. Föttinger, H.: Die hydrodynamische Arbeitsübertragung, *Jahrb. Schiffbautechn. Ges.*, vol. 31, pp. 171–214, 1930.
5. Haworth, H. F., and A. Lysholm: Progress in Design and Application of the Lysholm-Smith Torque Converter, *Proc. Inst. Mech. Engrs.*, vol. 130, pp. 193–230, 1935.
6. Sinclair, H.: Recent Developments in Hydraulic Couplings, *Proc. Inst. Mech. Engrs.*, vol. 130, pp. 75–190, 1935.
7. Sinclair, H.: Some Problems in the Transmission of Power by Fluid Couplings, *Proc. Inst. Mech. Engrs.*, vol. 139, pp. 83–182, 1938.
8. Spannhake, W.: Hydrodynamic Power Transmission for Motor Cars, *S.A.E.J.*, vol. 45, pp. 433–443, October, 1939.

CHAPTER XVIII

HYDRAULIC TRANSMISSIONS AND CONTROLS

Hydraulic positive-displacement transmissions and controls are basically different from hydrodynamic machines. In the latter the pressure and velocity are interrelated, while in the former the working fluid is confined between two pistons and maintained at an arbitrary pressure level by the external forces on the pistons, regardless of the velocity. This fundamental difference is brought out by reference to Art. 17.5, in which it is stated that, for a torque converter, the primary-torque coefficient C_p is approximately constant. The input torque is thus nearly proportional to ω_p^2. For a hydraulic transmission, on the other hand, the input torque is substantially independent of the speed of the input shaft.

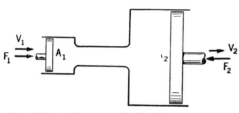

Fig. 18.1. — Elementary hydraulic transmission.

A primitive example of a positive-displacement transmission is the hydraulic press, described in Art. 2.6. The power input to the small piston is transmitted through the confined liquid to the load attached to the large piston (see Fig. 18.1). If dynamic effects and friction are neglected, the ratio of the forces equals the ratio of the piston areas.

$$\frac{F_2}{F_1} = \frac{A_2}{A_1}$$

Also, if leakage and compressibility of the liquid are neglected and the boundaries are assumed perfectly rigid, continuity requires that $A_1V_1 = A_2V_2$, or

$$\frac{V_2}{V_1} = \frac{A_1}{A_2}$$

Under these idealized conditions the input and output powers are equal $(F_1V_1 = F_2V_2)$ and the efficiency is 100 per cent, regardless of the value of either F_1 or V_1. The two components of power, force and velocity, are completely independent of each other in this ideal positive-displacement transmission.

It is frequently required to transmit power from one rotating shaft to another turning at a different speed and/or at a distance from the first. Many forms of positive-displacement transmission have been developed for this purpose, but they are all basically the same as the hydraulic press.

414

The single driven piston of the press is replaced by a pump that has a shaft turned by an electric motor or other prime mover and that provides a more or less continuous flow of liquid (usually oil) under pressure. This liquid flows through suitable pipes to a hydraulic motor, which replaces the single output cylinder and piston of the hydraulic press. The work done by the oil on the motor is converted by it into shaft work.

There are three principal types of pump, multiple-piston pumps, vane pumps, and gear pumps. The first two types are readily built with a variable displacement, so that the rate of oil flow can be continuously varied from a maximum in one direction to a maximum in the opposite direction. A gear pump has a fixed displacement, so that a by-pass must be used to get a controlled rate of oil flow, in one direction only.

Hydraulic motors are similar to multiple-piston or gear pumps. Vane-type motors are not used, for the vanes are held in position by centrifugal force and do not operate satisfactorily at low speeds.

These two primary elements, the pump and the motor, together with auxiliary devices, such as valves and accumulators, are connected to form a hydraulic circuit, which may take any one of a variety of forms, depending on the special function of the transmission. The design of a complex hydraulic circuit is a highly specialized task, especially when the circuit is incorporated in a servomechanism.

Hydraulic power transmission is in many respects similar to electrical. The liquid flow is analogous to the flow of electric current. Pressure may be likened to potential. Hydraulic and electrical connecting circuits are much alike. Hydraulic valves and electrical switches perform much the same functions.

Because of their similarity the two systems may be used in equivalent applications; and almost identical analyses may be applied to them. However, hydraulic transmissions have greater power-carrying capacity and greater shaft torques for given unit sizes. They also respond more exactly to control. Hydraulic-machine speeds are somewhat lower than the electrical. Distance of transmission is more limited. The efficiencies of the two types are about the same.

In consequence of certain advantages over mechanical or electrical apparatus, the hydraulic transmission is becoming a significant factor in the solution of power problems. It is applied principally to perform the following functions:

1. To provide positively controlled stepless adjustable speeds from a constant-speed prime mover.

2. To provide controlled variable driving torques or forces by manual or automatic direction.

3. To provide damping of driving shocks or pulsations.

4. To give servocontrol or power "follow-up" response to small control efforts.

5. To reduce equipment size and cost for equivalent duty.

6. To simplify design.

7. To lower maintenance costs.

Various industrial machines, such as presses, planers, and broaching machines, which require automatic speed variations during the operating cycle, are frequently fitted with hydraulic drives.

Steering engines for ships, automatic pilots for aircraft, and fire-control apparatus for naval and antiaircraft guns are among the more spectacular uses of hydraulic elements in servomechanisms.

During the war, precision-made motors and pumps of small size were developed, which handle extremely high power for their weight. One such pump or motor unit, which may easily be held in the palm of the hand, is rated at 2 hp.

18.1. Hydraulic Circuits. There are three principal types of circuit, variable speed, controlled torque, and controlled power. The first of these, shown diagrammatically in Fig. 18.2, consists of a variable-displacement

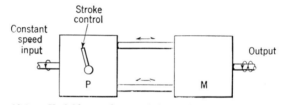

Fig. 18.2. — Variable-speed transmission with variable-stroke pump.

pump P connected to a constant-displacement motor M. For the sake of clarity, important details such as relief and replenishment valves, replenishment pump, and oil reservoir are not shown. The speed of the hydraulic motor is continuously variable from zero to a maximum in either direction. The maximum torque obtainable is independent of speed and is proportional

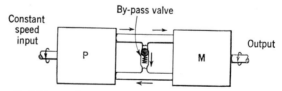

Fig. 18.3. — Variable-speed transmission with fixed-stroke pump and by-pass valve.

to the maximum pressure difference developed, which is limited by a safety relief valve. The maximum power obtainable is thus proportional to the speed.

An alternative form of this circuit, sketched in Fig. 18.3, employs a constant-displacement pump and a by-pass valve instead of a variable-displacement pump. The arrangement shown is obviously limited to uni-directional operation. This scheme is simpler and cheaper than that of Fig. 18.2 and is usually preferred for low-power applications. For high power the low partial-load efficiency resulting from by-passing of the oil becomes important, and a variable-displacement pump is indicated.

A controlled-torque circuit is illustrated in Fig. 18.4. The displacement control of the pump is automatically adjusted to maintain a constant pres-

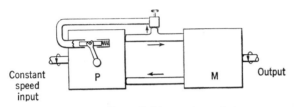

Constant speed input   P   M   Output

Fig. 18.4. — Controlled-torque transmission.

sure difference across the motor, and hence a constant torque, regardless of the output speed. The circuit of Fig. 18.3 will perform the same function if a spring-loaded automatic by-pass valve is employed.

The controlled-power circuit of Fig. 18.5 utilizes a constant-displacement pump and a variable-displacement motor. The output speed is

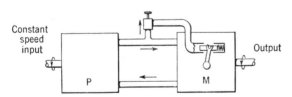

Constant speed input   P   M   Output

Fig. 18.5. — Controlled-power transmission.

automatically adjusted to maintain a constant pressure difference across the pump. The torque applied to the constant-speed input shaft is there-fore constant, and so is the transmitted power.

It is clear that modifications of these elementary circuits can be made to give an output torque or power which is practically any desired function of speed.

18.2. Radial-piston Machines. The pistons of hydraulic machines are arranged either radially or axially. The construction of a typical radial variable-displacement pump or motor is shown in Figs. 18.6, and 18.7. The cylinder block turns on a pintle, which acts also as a porting mechanism. The outer ends of the pistons bear against a reaction ring forming part of the rotor, which is free to revolve with the cylinder block. The center of rotation of this ring can be adjusted relative to that of the cylinder block by means of the handwheel shown in Fig. 18.6. The discharge can thus be varied from zero to a maximum in either direction. A sectional view showing the slide block in one extreme position is given in Fig. 18.7.

The pistons are free to rotate about their own axes. No sliding occurs

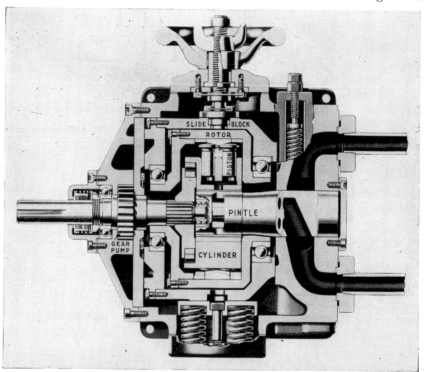

Fig. 18.6. — Radial-piston variable-stroke pump. (*Courtesy of The Oilgear Company.*)

between the pistons and the ring, but only a slight oscillating rotary motion of the pistons. Wear is thus reduced.

The gear pump mounted on the drive shaft is used to keep the hydraulic system full of oil and to operate hydraulic controls.

A fixed-displacement unit of the radial type is shown in Fig. 18.8. It is identical in construction with the variable-displacement unit, except for the omission of the displacement control and the auxiliary pump.

Radial pumps and motors are available in ratings between 2 and 150 hp. Pressures are usually on the order of 1,000 to 2,000 lb per sq in., but some models can operate intermittently at 3,000 lb per sq in. Maximum rotational speed is approximately 1,000 rpm.

FIG. 18.7. — Radial-piston variable-stroke pump.   (*Courtesy of The Oilgear Company.*)

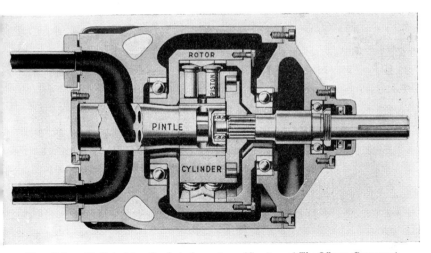

FIG. 18.8. — Radial-piston fixed-stroke motor.   (*Courtesy of The Oilgear Company.*)

Representative performance curves are given in Fig. 18.9. It is seen that the over-all efficiency of a complete transmission exceeds 80 per cent over two-thirds of the speed range. The maximum efficiency approximates to 85 per cent.

Radial transmissions are used principally in industrial applications,

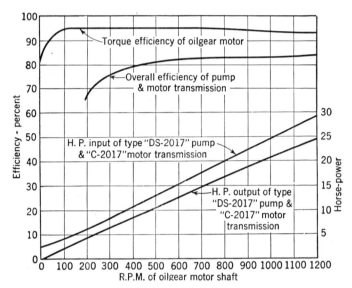

FIG. 18.9. — Performance curves for a radial-piston transmission. (*Courtesy of The Oilgear Company.*)

where precise control and durability are required, but where weight and bulk are not of paramount importance.

18.3. Axial-piston Machines. An example of a fixed-displacement unit of this type is given in Fig. 18.10. The cylinder block rotates about an axis set at an angle with respect to the drive shaft. The piston rods are attached by ball-and-socket joints to the pistons and to a plate carried on the drive shaft. A double universal joint serves to lock the drive shaft and cylinder block into synchronism. None of the load torque is transmitted through this shaft, only the small friction torque.

A variable-displacement unit is similar in all essentials to that just described. The cylinder block is mounted on trunnions, however, in such a way that the angularity between its axis and the drive shaft can be easily adjusted. The discharge can thus be varied at will.

Axial-piston machines are available in ratings between 2 and 300 hp. Pressures are usually on the order of 1,000 to 2,000 lb per sq in., but some models can operate at 3,000 lb per sq in. Rotational speeds for small pumps used on aircraft may exceed 4,000 rpm; maximum speeds of large units range down to 850 rpm.

Performance curves are similar to those of Fig. 18.9 for radial-piston machines.

Axial-piston transmissions are used in numerous industrial applications. In addition, they are well adapted to use in aircraft hydraulic

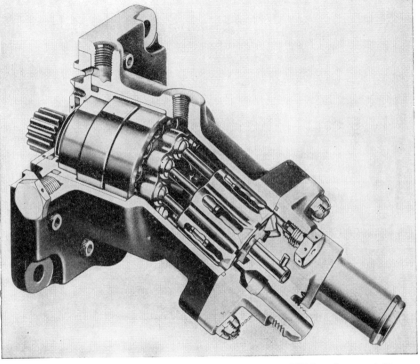

Fig. 18.10. — Axial-piston fixed-stroke pump. (*Courtesy of Vickers Incorporated.*)

systems, since the small-diameter bearings can operate at high speed and the units are compact, weighing less than 1 lb per hp.

18.4. Gear-type Machines. A hydraulically balanced gear unit is shown in Fig. 18.11. The symmetrical layout of the ports eliminates bearing loads caused by the pressure change in the machine. All gear units are of the fixed-displacement type. A gear pump must therefore be used with a by-pass valve to obtain a variable flow rate.

These machines are inherently limited to low pressure and small power, for ample clearance must be provided to prevent contact of gears and housing at all operating temperatures. The leakage can be kept within reasonable limits only if the pressure is less than 1,000 lb per sq in. and the power is below about 25 hp. Even within these limits, the efficiency is apprecia-

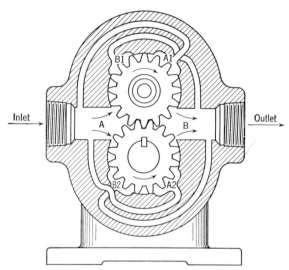

Fig. 18.11. — Hydraulically balanced gear pump.   (*Courtesy of Vickers Incorporated.*)

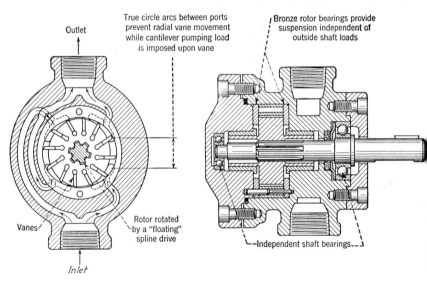

Fig. 18.12. — Hydraulically balanced vane pump.   (*Courtesy of Vickers Incorporated.*)

bly less than that of a piston unit, but their relative simplicity and low cost justify the use of these machines in many applications.

18.5. Vane Pumps. These may be of either the fixed- or variable-displacement type, as shown in Figs. 18.12 and 18.13. The former has the advantage of simplicity and hydraulic balance to offset its lack of flexibility.

Vane pumps are subject to the same limitations as gear units with regard to pressure and power [8, 9].

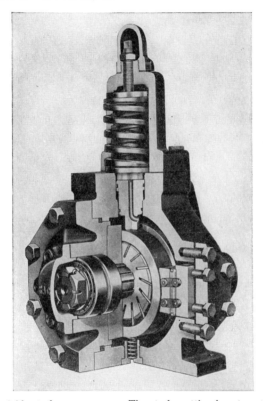

Fig. 18.13. — Variable-stroke vane pump. The stroke setting is automatically adjusted to maintain a constant output pressure. (*Courtesy of Racine Tool and Machine Company.*)

18.6. Auxiliaries. A detailed discussion of auxiliary apparatus is beyond the scope of this book [2, 4]; all that will be attempted is a mention of the principal items.

There are many kinds of controls available for variable-displacement machines, from a simple handwheel to highly complicated automatic power control.

By-pass valves are used in conjunction with fixed-displacement pumps. Ingenious designs have been developed, by means of which any desired flow may be obtained by setting of a graduated dial. The flow is independent of pressure and temperature over a considerable range.

Relief valves are essential to any hydraulic circuit, to prevent overload. Designs range from a simple spring-loaded ball, which permits large pressure variations around the nominal maximum, to a balanced valve, which limits the pressure accurately to a preset value, regardless of the volume handled by the valve.

Some hydraulic systems, notably in aircraft, are used only intermittently but are supplied by a constant-displacement pump, running continuously. An unloader valve and accumulator incorporated into such a circuit ensure a supply of high-pressure fluid at all times, yet permit the pump to run idle, except when the system is actually doing work or when the accumulator needs recharging [2]. An aircraft accumulator is simply a hollow steel sphere divided into halves internally by a flexible diaphragm, on one side of which is introduced compressed air at a predetermined pressure. To charge the accumulator the pump forces oil from the hydraulic system into the sphere, thus further compressing the air on the opposite side of the diaphragm. When the desired pressure has been reached, the unloader valve automatically opens a by-pass, allowing the oil to be circulated freely between pump and reservoir until the pressure in the system drops below the minimum permissible level. The unloader valve then reconnects the pump into the circuit and closes the by-pass.

The oil reservoir is an important element of a hydraulic circuit. A reservoir of sufficient capacity must be included to allow for adequate cooling of the oil and to permit air bubbles to escape. Entrained air is obviously detrimental to performance, especially where rapid and precise response is essential.

The clearances permissible in hydraulic apparatus are so small that extreme care must be taken to ensure clean operating fluid. This is especially true in small-size equipment for high pressures. A filter, usually incorporated in the reservoir, is therefore an indispensable part of a hydraulic circuit.

18.7. Hydraulic Fluids. For hydraulic service a fluid is required to be practically incompressible (*i.e.*, to be a liquid), to flow easily, to be chemically stable, and to be a good lubricant. To satisfy the last requirement, not only must the viscosity be above some lower limit, but also the other properties must be such as to prevent appreciable wear under boundary-lubrication conditions. Petroleum oils have so far best satisfied these requirements. For apparatus that operates near room temperature any highly refined turbine-type of oil is satisfactory. The kinematic viscosity of such an oil is approximately that of an SAE 20 grade (340 Saybolt universal seconds, 74 centistokes, or 0.11 sq in. per sec, at 100 F).

For equipment that is required to function over a wide range of temperature, such as that of an aircraft, the effect of temperature on viscosity is a prime consideration. A fluid that is satisfactory under normal conditions may be too thin to lubricate properly at 150 F and may congeal at − 20 F. The effect of high temperature on the stability of the fluid is also mportant. Some oils break down rapidly at high temperature, forming gummy deposits on working surfaces and clogging the system with sludge.

The following table gives the kinematic viscosity, in centistokes, of several hydraulic fluids as a function of temperature.

Temperature, deg F	Petroleum oil I V.I. = 101 Pour point = −20 F	Petroleum oil II V.I. = 145 Pour point = −50 F	Silicone A V.I. = 156	Silicone B V.I. = 170
210	9.5	18	30	18
130	37	57	56	36*
100	80	103	74	43*
0	8,270	2,330	275	160
−20		6,100	390	260*
−40			600	360

* Approximate value interpolated on Chart *A* of ASTM Standard D341.

Petroleum oil I is, by ordinary standards, an excellent oil, having a V.I. of 101, which is as good as can be obtained without special treatment (Art. 12.4.). Petroleum oil II is especially prepared for hydraulic service; its V.I. of 145 permits an extension of the operating range in both directions. The pour point is lowered to − 50 F. Silicones A and B are examples of the recently developed dimethyl-silicone-polymer fluids (Art. 13.7). Silicone B is especially remarkable, having a kinematic viscosity equal to that of Petroleum oil II at 210 F but less than 5 per cent of it at − 20 F.

From the viscosity-temperature standpoint, these silicones appear to be ideal hydraulic fluids. Another advantage is their noninflammability. As already mentioned, however, the boundary-lubrication characteristics of the fluid must be adequate. Recent tests on silicone A [3] have shown that it lubricates satisfactorily, provided that proper combinations of metals are used for the rubbing surfaces. Steel and bronze, for example, appear to function well, but the mating of two ferrous surfaces is to be strictly avoided. If the apparatus is suitably designed in this respect, very little wear occurs. Furthermore, the silicone fluid is exceptionally stable, showing practically no discernible change in viscosity or other properties, even after some hundreds of hours of operation.

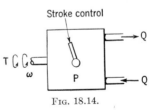

Fig. 18.14.

18.8. Basic Formulas for Hydraulic Transmissions. If both friction and leakage are neglected in the pump shown schematically in Fig. 18.14, the steady-flow energy equation [Eq. (5.10)] yields

$$- \mathscr{W}_s = \frac{p_2 - p_1}{\rho}$$

To obtain an expression for the ideal torque T_{ideal} applied to the pump shaft we notice that $T_{\text{ideal}}\,\omega = -\,\rho Q \mathbb{W}_s$ and $Q = \omega DS$, where D is the displacement per radian at full stroke and S, the stroke setting, is the ratio of stroke to full stroke. Substitution in the energy equation gives

$$T_{\text{ideal}} = -\,\frac{\rho Q \mathbb{W}_s}{\omega} = (p_2 - p_1)DS \tag{18.1}$$

We define the torque efficiency of the actual pump as the ratio of the ideal torque to the actual torque required to produce a given pressure rise $p_2 - p_1$.

$$\eta_{TP} = \frac{T_{\text{ideal}}}{T_{\text{actual}}} \tag{18.2}$$

Combination of Eqs. (18.1) and (18.2) gives for the actual torque

$$T_P = \frac{\Delta p_P D_P S_P}{\eta_{TP}} \tag{18.3}$$

where the pressure rise is conveniently denoted by Δp, and the subscript P indicates a pump.

The over-all efficiency of the pump is defined as the ratio of the ideal input power to the actual input power needed to produce a given pressure rise Δp_P and rate of flow Q_P. The ideal power input is readily seen to be $\Delta p_P Q_P$, while the actual power input is $\omega_P T_P$. With the aid of Eq. (18.3) the over-all pump efficiency is found to be

$$\eta_P = \frac{\Delta p_P Q_P}{\Delta p_P D_P \omega_P S_P}\,\eta_{TP} = \eta_{TP}\,\frac{Q_P}{D_P \omega_P S_P} = \eta_{TP}\eta_{VP} \tag{18.4}$$

where $\eta_{VP} = Q_P/D_P\omega_P S_P$ and is called the "volumetric efficiency" of the pump, since it is the ratio of the actual to the ideal discharge rate.

A similar development for a hydraulic motor yields the following:

$$\eta_{TM} = \frac{T_{\text{actual}}}{T_{\text{ideal}}} \tag{18.5}$$

$$T_M = \eta_{TM}\,\Delta p_M D_M S_M \tag{18.6}$$

$$\eta_M = \eta_{TM}\frac{D_M\omega_M S_M}{Q_M} = \eta_{TM}\eta_{VM} \tag{18.7}$$

where the subscript M indicates a motor. It will be noted that the actual output torque is less than the ideal for a given pressure drop Δp_M, so that η_{TM} is less than unity.

The torque efficiency of a radial-piston motor over a range of motor speed is shown in Fig. 18.9.

The over-all efficiency of a complete transmission is defined as the ratio of output to input power,

$$\eta = \frac{T_M \omega_M}{T_P \omega_P} \tag{18.8}$$

Substituting from Eqs. (18.3) and (18.6), we get

$$\eta = \eta_{TP} \eta_{TM} \frac{D_M \omega_M S_M}{D_P \omega_P S_P} \frac{\Delta p_M}{\Delta p_P} \tag{18.9}$$

which from Eqs. (18.4) and (18.7) becomes

$$\eta = \eta_P \eta_M \frac{Q_M}{Q_P} \frac{\Delta p_M}{\Delta p_P} \tag{18.10}$$

It is obvious that Q_M/Q_P and $\Delta p_M/\Delta p_P$ represent, respectively, the effect of leakage from and friction in the pipes connecting pump and motor.

From continuity, the total leakage from the system Q_l must equal the difference between the displacements per unit time of pump and motor.

$$Q_l = D_P \omega_P S_P - D_M \omega_M S_M \tag{18.11}$$

Equation (18.9) can thus be expressed in terms of the total leakage.

$$\eta = \eta_{TP} \eta_{TM} \left(1 - \frac{Q_l}{D_P \omega_P S_P}\right) \frac{\Delta p_M}{\Delta p_P} \tag{18.12}$$

The maximum allowable speed of a piston-type machine is limited by dynamic stresses. Assuming that, for a given design, the maximum allowable stress s_0 depends only on the density of the material, ρ_m, on ω_{max}, and on D, we get by dimensional reasoning

$$\frac{s_0}{\rho_m \omega^2_{max} D^{2/3}} = \text{constant}$$

Both s_0 and ρ_m may be considered constant, to a good approximation. Experience indicates a good working rule to be

$$\omega_{max} = \frac{187}{D^{1/3}} \tag{18.13}$$

where ω_{max} is in radians per second and D is in cubic inches per radian.

The above relationships are useful in the discussion of various types of hydraulic circuits. In the following we shall assume, for simplicity, that $D_P = D_M = D$ and neglect the pressure drop in the connecting lines, i.e., assume $\Delta p_P = \Delta p_M = \Delta p$. Consider, for example, the circuit of Fig. 18.2, which includes a variable-displacement pump and fixed-displacement motor. The continuity equation [Eq. (18.11)] enables us to plot the motor speed as a function of S_P, the stroke setting of the pump. Noting that $S_M = 1$, we get

$$\frac{\omega_M}{\omega_P} = S_P - \frac{Q_l}{\omega_P D}$$

If we assume for the moment that $Q_l = 0$, we get the straight line aob of Fig. 18.15. Equation (18.3) shows, however, that the pressure drop across the system, Δp, varies directly with the applied torque T_P. Since

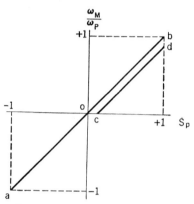

in an actual system there is some leakage whenever Δp (and hence T_P) exceeds zero, the line aob is the limit approached as $T_P \rightarrow 0$.

Actually, of course, there is some pressure rise across the pump and some leakage whenever oil is being displaced, i.e., whenever $S_P \neq 0$. Suppose that initially $S_P = 0$ and that it is gradually increased. The motor shaft will not turn until S_P surpasses a critical value corresponding to a Δp great enough to produce the required starting torque, in accordance with Eq. (18.6). The entire discharge of the pump goes into leakage, that is, $S_P = Q_l/\omega_P D$, so long

Fig. 18. 15. — Speed ratio ω_M/ω_P versus pump stroke setting S_P, for the transmission of Fig. 18.2.

as this value of Δp is not exceeded. The critical value of S_P is reached at point c in Fig. 18.15. If it is assumed that Q_l remains constant as S_P is further increased, the straight line cd is followed. The horizontal distance oc between the lines ob and cd is equal to the ratio of the constant leakage to the displacement rate of the pump, $Q_l/\omega_P D_P$.

In a well-designed unworn system the clearances are small, and the leakage flow is laminar. The leakage rate is found to be very nearly proportional to the pressure drop Δp and to be essentially independent of speed. According to Eq. (18.6), therefore, $Q_l \sim T_M/\eta_{TM}$; and since η_{TM} is nearly constant over a wide range of speed, it follows that $Q_l \sim T_M$. The straight line cd in Fig. 18.15 thus corresponds approximately to the case of constant output torque.

The circuit of Fig. 18.5 is intended to yield a constant output power over a wide range of output speeds. To this end, the pressure drop Δp is automatically held constant. To analyze this circuit we apply the continuity equation [Eq. (18.11)] and find

$$\frac{\omega_M}{\omega_P} S_M = 1 - \frac{Q_l}{\omega_P D} \qquad (18.14)$$

Neglecting leakage, we get $\omega_M S_M/\omega_P = 1$, the speed ratio varying hyperbolically with the motor displacement (see Fig. 18.16). From Eq. (18.6), the output power is found to be $P_M = T_M\omega_M = \Delta p D \eta_{TM}\omega_M S_M$, whence $P_M/\Delta p D \omega_P \eta_{TM} = 1$. The output power is thus approximately constant if Δp is closely regulated and variations in η_{TM} are small.

To take the laminar leakage into account it is assumed, for geometrically similar systems, that Q_l depends only on Δp, D, and μ (the viscosity). Dimensional analysis then yields

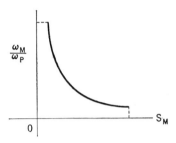

$$\frac{Q_l \mu}{D\,\Delta p} = \text{constant} = C_l \quad (18.15)$$

where C_l is the "leakage coefficient." From Eqs. (18.14) and (18.15),

$$\frac{\omega_M S_M}{\omega_P} = 1 - \frac{C_l\,\Delta p}{\mu\omega_P}$$

Fig. 18.16. — Speed ratio ω_M/ω_P versus motor stroke setting S_M, for the transmission of Fig. 18.5.

so that the power output becomes

$$P_M = \omega_M T_M = \Delta p D \omega_P \eta_{TM}\left(1 - \frac{C_l\,\Delta p}{\mu\omega_P}\right)$$

The only effect of leakage is, therefore, to reduce both the speed ratio and the power output; the character of the curves is unchanged, provided that the viscosity is constant.

18.9. Servomechanisms. A manually controlled transmission requires an operator whose function is to observe the output, note any deviation from the desired behavior, and adjust the control so as to return the output to the value wanted. He thus acts to keep small the difference between the desired output and that actually existing. This difference is called the "error."

It is possible to feed back, mechanically, electrically, or otherwise, the actual output to a device which compares it with that called for by some input signal and which automatically adjusts the control in such a way as to reduce the error. Such a feed-back linkage is an essential feature of a servomechanism. A second feature is the amplification of power achieved in a servomechanism. The power level of the input signal is usually very low compared with the output. For our purposes a servomechanism may be defined as an error-controlled power amplifier. We shall be concerned principally with hydraulic servomechanisms, but much of the following applies to other types as well.

Servomechanisms may be electrical, mechanical, pneumatic, hydraulic, or some combination of these. Their use is growing rapidly; present applications, aside from industrial, include automatic piloting of vessels and aircraft, fire control of guns, and power steering of heavy vehicles.

There are three aspects of the behavior of a servomechanism that must be considered in design or analysis. Since a source of energy for producing the power amplification is an essential part of a servomechanism, the operation may be unstable. The question of stability is therefore of primary concern.

In addition to the requirement of stability, a servomechanism must respond rapidly and accurately to the applied signal, *i.e.*, its "transient response" must be satisfactory. Under this heading are included the time lag of the output behind the input signal, the amount of overshoot, and the time required for any oscillations to die down to a given fraction of their initial amplitude.

Finally, the "steady-state error" must be taken into account, *i.e.*, the error subsisting an indefinitely long time after application of a signal. The steady-state error depends on the type of signal. For example, it may be zero for a signal consisting of a certain constant *displacement* of the input member, but this error may be finite if the input member is given a constant *velocity* or *acceleration*. Servomechanisms are sometimes described according to their steady-state error, as of the "zero-displacement-error," "zero-velocity-error," or "zero-acceleration-error" type.

There are two categories of servomechanisms, linear and nonlinear. The differential equation of a linear servomechanism is linear and has constant coefficients. The differential equation of a nonlinear servomechanism is unrestricted.

The theory of linear servomechanisms is highly developed, two methods being available for analysis or design. The transient-response method involves solution of the differential equation of the system for one or more types of input step signal. (A step signal is one that changes discontinuously from a constant zero value to some other constant value. Those usually considered are displacement, velocity, and acceleration step signals.) The behavior of the system can be completely determined by this means, but the method has two disadvantages: (1) It is tedious and cumbersome to apply to complex systems. (2) The results usually do not show how a system should be changed if its behavior deviates too greatly from a prescribed pattern.

The second method applicable to a linear system is the frequency-response method. Essentially, it involves determination of the response of a system to a sinusoidal signal of any frequency within the range of interest. It is unnecessary to obtain the general solution of the equation of the system in order to predict its behavior closely enough for design purposes. This method is relatively simple, even for complicated systems. It is especially useful in design, since the results indicate the effect on performance of a change in any one of the design parameters. Unfortunately, its use is restricted to linear systems.

No general theory is available for nonlinear servomechanisms. The differential equation must be solved in every individual case, as outlined above for the transient-response method. This task is in general much more difficult than that of solving a linear equation with constant coefficients.

18.10. Ideal Hydraulic Servomechanism. The hydraulic transmission shown in Fig. 18.17 is assumed to have "proportional control," that is, a

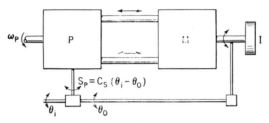

FIG. 18.17. — Hydraulic servomechanism.

feed-back linkage whereby the pump stroke control S_P is made proportional to the error. In this case the desired output-shaft position is the same as that of the signal shaft, so that the error is simply $\theta_i - \theta_o$, where θ_i and θ_o stand for the instantaneous angular displacements of the signal and output shafts, respectively. The feed-back linkage thus ensures that

$$S_P = C_s(\theta_i - \theta_o)$$

where C_s is a constant whose value depends on the nature of the linkage. If, for example, the feed-back circuit is purely mechanical, C_s will be determined by the gear ratios employed. The following additional assumptions are also made:

$$\omega_P = \text{constant}$$
$$D_P = D_M = D$$
$$S_M = 1 \text{ (fixed-displacement motor)}$$
$$Q_l = 0$$

The fluid is incompressible.
The boundaries do not deform.

The continuity equation [(Eq. (18.11)] thus gives

$$\omega_M D = \frac{d\theta_o}{dt} D = S_P \omega_P D$$

into which the expression $S_P = C_s(\theta_i - \theta_o)$ is substituted.

$$\frac{d\theta_o}{dt} + \omega_P C_s \theta_o = \omega_P C_s \theta_i \tag{18.16}$$

In order to discuss this equation we shall presuppose an elementary knowledge of the complex variable and of linear differential equations with constant coefficients.

A standard procedure for solving a linear equation with constant coefficients is to solve first for the "complementary function," which in the case of Eq. (18.16) is the solution obtained for $\theta_i = 0$. It is well known that the complementary function is the sum of exponential terms of the form Ce^{zt}, where both C and z may be complex constants.

The second step in the procedure is to determine a particular solution of the equation as originally given [that is, for a nonzero value of θ_i in Eq. (18.16)]. The complete solution is the sum of the complementary function and the particular solution. It is called "complete" because it contains just enough arbitrary constants to satisfy any given boundary conditions.

Suppose that no signal is applied to the system ($\theta_i = 0$) and that arbitrary initial conditions of displacement, velocity, etc., are imposed on the output shaft by suitable external means. (The number of initial conditions that can be arbitrarily chosen is equal to the order of the differential equation of the system. In the present case, only the initial displacement is arbitrary.) The servomechanism is said to be stable if, when the external actions on the output shaft are removed, the shaft eventually comes to rest. The stability of a linear servomechanism can be investigated by means of the complementary function since nonzero values of θ_i are not involved. The system will be stable if none of the exponents z has a positive real part, since in this case all terms of the complementary function remain finite as the time t approaches infinity. It is possible for the output shaft to oscillate indefinitely at a finite amplitude if one of the z's is pure imaginary. In this case the system would be neither stable nor unstable. Such a neutral system is relatively unimportant and will not be further considered.

It may be remarked that an actual system is at most linear over only a certain range of motion. If the system is unstable, either the motion will build up to the point where the apparatus destroys itself or the nonlinearity will limit the motion to a safe value. This latter behavior is not to be confused with the neutral oscillations of a linear system mentioned in the previous paragraph.

To check on the stability of the ideal system of Fig. 18.17 we assume $\theta_i = 0$, $\theta_o = C_o e^{zt}$ and substitute in Eq. (18.16).

$$C_o e^{zt}(z + \omega_P C_s) = 0$$

Ruling out the trivial solution $C_o = 0$, we get

$$z + \omega_P C_s = 0 \qquad (18.17)$$

om which it is obvious that the apparatus is stable, since $z = -\omega_P C_s$, hich is a negative real number.*

The next question of interest is the response of the system to a step gnal. Three types are commonly used in the study of servomechanisms: isplacement, velocity, and acceleration step signals. We shall consider nly the first type, which may be defined by

$$\left.\begin{array}{l} \theta_i = 0 \quad \text{for } t < 0 \\ \theta_i = C_i \quad \text{for } t \geqslant 0 \end{array}\right\} \tag{18.18}$$

ubstituting this expression into Eq. (18.16) we get, if $t \geqslant 0$,

$$\frac{d\theta_o}{dt} + \omega_P C_s \theta_o = \omega_P C_s C_i$$

particular solution of this equation is readily seen to be $\theta_o = C_i$. The omplete solution of Eq. (18.16) is thus the sum

$$\theta_o = C_o e^{-C_s \omega_P t} + C_i = C_o e^{-\alpha_0 t} + C_i$$

f the boundary condition is arbitrarily chosen as $\theta_o = 0$ at $t = 0$, $C_o = C_i$ nd

$$\theta_o = C_i(1 - e^{-\alpha_0 t}) \tag{18.19}$$

The response curve is plotted in Fig. 18.18, from which it is seen that here is no overshoot and hence no oscillation. Furthermore, $\theta_o/\theta_i \to 1$ s $t \to \infty$, so that the error ultimately ecomes zero.

The parameter $\alpha_0 = \omega_P C_s$, which as the dimensions of angular velocity, s seen from Eq. (18.16) to equal the atio of the output angular velocity to he error. It is thus a measure of the peed with which the system responds. urthermore, if a displacement step

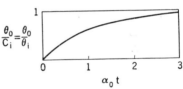

Fig. 18.18. — Response of an ideal hydraulic servomechanism to a displacement step signal.

ignal is applied to the servomechanism, it follows from Eq. (18.19) that ./α_0 is the time required for the error to drop to one eth of its initial value. α_0 is usually called the "time constant" of the system.

It is convenient to introduce the term "rise time," which is defined as he time required for θ_o/θ_i to rise from, say, 0.1 to 0.9. We observe that he rise time is reduced if the time constant α_0 is made larger. For this deal servomechanism α_0 is the only parameter at our disposal; it should clearly be made as large as possible, to ensure a good transient response.

---

* C_s might, of course, be made negative, by means of a suitable feed-back linkage. The system would then be unstable.

If θ_i is assumed to be a velocity step signal, it will be found as before that there is no overshoot or oscillation, but the steady-state error will be different from zero. This type of servomechanism is therefore better adapted to positioning the output shaft than to driving it at a constant velocity. For the latter function a device with a zero velocity error would be selected.

The above method of determining the transient behavior (*i.e.*, solving the equation when θ_i is a suitable step function) is not feasible for complex systems. We shall therefore illustrate for our ideal system an alternative method of attack, the frequency-response method. For this purpose we assume that the signal θ_i is a sinusoidal function of t, having an angular frequency ω.

$$\theta_i = C_i e^{i\omega t} \tag{18.20}$$

where C_i and ω are real.* It is easily demonstrated that, for this signal, a particular solution of Eq. (18.16) is

$$\theta_o = C_o e^{i\phi} e^{i\omega t} \tag{18.21}$$

where C_o and ϕ are both real. This is the steady-state response to a sinusoidal signal, *i.e.*, the response that will obtain after the signal has been applied for a long (theoretically infinite) time.

It is well known that θ_i and θ_o can be represented as vectors drawn from a common origin and rotating at the constant angular velocity ω. The constant angle ϕ maintained between them is called the "phase angle." C_i and C_o are the lengths, or "absolute values," of θ_i and θ_o, respectively. The absolute values are also denoted by $|\theta_i|$ and $|\theta_o|$.

To show that Eq. (18.21) is a solution of Eq. (18.16), we substitute in the latter.

$$C_o e^{i\phi} e^{i\omega t}(i\omega + C_s \omega_P) = C_s \omega_P C_i e^{i\omega t} \tag{18.22}$$

$$\frac{C_o}{C_i} e^{i\phi}\left(1 + \frac{i\omega}{C_s \omega_P}\right) = 1$$

$$\frac{C_o}{C_i} \sqrt{1 + \frac{\omega^2}{C_s^2 \omega_P^2}} \, e^{i[\phi + \tan^{-1}(\omega/C_s \omega_P)]} = 1$$

Since the left-hand side must be real, the exponent of e is equal to zero, or

$$\tan \phi = -\frac{\omega}{C_s \omega_P} = -\frac{\omega}{\alpha_0} \tag{18.23}$$

and

$$\frac{|\theta_o|}{|\theta_i|} = \frac{C_o}{C_i} = \frac{1}{\sqrt{1 + (\omega^2/C_s^2 \omega_P^2)}} = \frac{1}{\sqrt{1 + (\omega^2/\alpha_0^2)}} \tag{18.24}$$

---

* The symbol i in $e^{i\omega t}$ here has its usual meaning, *viz.* $i^2 = -1$. Do not confuse this symbol with the subscript i. The latter indicates a quantity associated with the input, or signal, shaft.

$_o$ and ϕ are thus determined in such a way that Eq. (18.16) is satisfied. A similar demonstration can be made for any linear differential equation with constant coefficients.

The dimensionless parameter ω/α_0 represents the ratio of the angular frequency of the applied signal to the time constant of the system. When this ratio is small, it is found that the system responds more faithfully to an applied signal than when the ratio is large.

A plot of Eq. (18.24) is given in Fig. 18.19. The same qualitative information can be gleaned from this figure as from Fig. 18.18. We notice first that, since the curve exhibits no resonance peaks, the system will not oscillate at any frequency and hence cannot overshoot. Furthermore, the value of $|\theta_o|/|\theta_i|$ is close to unity only for small values of ω/α_0. Hence the response at high frequencies will be improved if α_0 is made larger. Since a system that will not respond accurately to a high-frequency sinusoidal signal will obviously have a

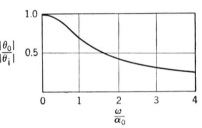

FIG. 18.19. — Amplitude response of an ideal hydraulic servomechanism as a function of frequency.

poor response to a step signal, we conclude that, the larger the value of α_0, the better will be the transient response. This conclusion is rigorously justified by the theory of transients in linear systems, in which it is shown that a step signal can be considered as a suitable summation of sine waves of all frequencies.

The value of the rise time cannot be determined from Fig. 18.19 alone; but if this curve is supplemented by an empirical rule, the rise time can be found with sufficient accuracy for most design purposes. This rule is

$$\omega_c t_r = \pi \tag{18.25}$$

where t_r is the rise time and ω_c is the angular frequency of "cutoff," defined as that ω at which $|\theta_o|/|\theta_i|$ has one-half its value at zero frequency.

To determine the order of the approximation to be expected from Eq. (18.25) we compare the value of t_r computed from it with the value found from Eq. (18.19). The cutoff angular frequency is first obtained from Eq. (18.24).

$$\frac{|\theta_o|}{|\theta_i|} = \frac{C_o}{C_i} = \frac{1}{2} = \frac{1}{\sqrt{1 + (\omega^2/\alpha_0^2)}}$$

whence

$$\frac{\omega_c}{\alpha_0} = \sqrt{3}$$

Equation (18.25), therefore, yields

$$\alpha_0 t_r = \frac{\pi}{\sqrt{3}} = 1.82$$

The exact value of $\alpha_0 t_r$ is obtained from Eq. (18.19).

$$\alpha_0 t_r = \alpha_0(t_{0.9} - t_{0.1}) = \ln\frac{1}{0.1} - \ln\frac{1}{0.9} = 2.20$$

where $t_{0.1}$ and $t_{0.9}$ stand for the times at which C_o/C_i equals 0.1 and 0.9 respectively. The approximate value of $\alpha_0 t_r$ is seen to be about 20 per cent too low.

In many applications the phase angle ϕ is also important. Equation (18.23) is accordingly plotted in Fig. 18.20.

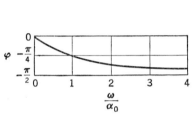

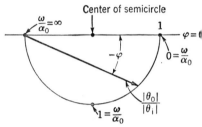

FIG. 18.20. — Phase-angle response of an ideal hydraulic servomechanism as a function of frequency.

FIG. 18.21. — Vectorial form of the frequency response of an ideal hydraulic servomechanism.

The information given by Figs. 18.19 and 18.20 can be combined into the single polar curve of Fig. 18.21, in which $|\theta_o|/|\theta_i|$ is plotted as the radius vector from the origin at an angle ϕ. Values of the parameter ω/α_0 are spotted on the curve. It is readily shown by means of Eqs. (18.23) and (18.24) that in this example the curve is a semicircle of radius $\frac{1}{2}$ and center at $|\theta_o|/|\theta_i| = \frac{1}{2}$, $\phi = 0$. The proof of this is left to the reader.

18.11. The Transfer Function. The results of the frequency-response analysis, which are presented in Eqs. (18.23) and (18.24) and plotted in Figs. 18.19 and 18.20, can also be obtained graphically, by means of the "transfer function" ζ. Use of the transfer function simplifies the analysis of complicated systems, for which the algebra leading to results corresponding to Eqs. (18.23) and (18.24) would be extremely involved. The conditions under which a system will be stable can also be easily determined by means of ζ.

The transfer function is defined, in general, as the ratio of the steady-state response to the error when a sinusoidal signal is applied. In symbols,

$$\zeta = \frac{\theta_o}{\theta_i - \theta_o} \tag{18.26}$$

where θ_o is the steady-state response and θ_i is a sinusoidal signal. Substituting into this equation the values of θ_i and θ_o from Eqs. (18.20) and (18.21), we get

$$\frac{\zeta}{\zeta + 1} = \frac{\theta_o}{\theta_i} = \frac{C_o}{C_i} e^{i\phi} \tag{18.27}$$

Or, if we put $\zeta = |\,\zeta\,|\,e^{i\psi}$ and $\zeta + 1 = |\,\zeta + 1\,|\,e^{i\chi}$

$$\frac{|\,\zeta\,|}{|\,\zeta + 1\,|} = \frac{C_o}{C_i} \tag{18.28}$$

and

$$\psi - \chi = \phi \tag{18.29}$$

It is clear from Eqs. (18.28) and (18.29) that, if ζ is known as a function of ω, C_o/C_i and ϕ can be readily determined graphically. The procedure is easily visualized from Fig. 18.22, which shows a hypothetical curve followed by the ζ vector as ω changes. For any value of ω, C_o/C_i is found from the ratio of the measured lengths of ζ and $\zeta + 1$, while ϕ is obtained from measurements of χ and ψ.

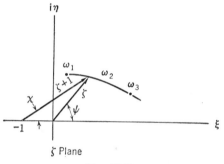

Fig. 18.22.

The problem of making a frequency-response analysis is thus reduced to that of finding the transfer function. As a simple illustration of a general method for getting ζ, revert to the ideal hydraulic servomechanism already discussed. Combining Eqs. (18.22) and (18.27), we find that

$$\frac{\zeta + 1}{\zeta} = \frac{\theta_i}{\theta_o} = \frac{C_i}{C_o e^{i\phi}} = \frac{i\omega}{C_s \omega_P} + 1 = \frac{i\omega}{\alpha_0} + 1 \tag{18.30}$$

from which $\zeta = \alpha_0/i\omega = -i\alpha_0/\omega$. Since ω is real and positive, $i\omega$ is positive imaginary and ζ is negative imaginary, as shown in Fig. 18.23. An arbitrary point g on the $i\omega$ axis of the z plane is carried over to g' in the ζ plane. The results expressed in Eqs. (18.23) and (18.24) are embodied completely in Fig. 18.23b.

Consider now a more general form of hydraulic servomechanism for which the differential equation is

$$\alpha_n \frac{d^n\theta_o}{dt^n} + \cdots + \alpha_1 \frac{d\theta_o}{dt} + \alpha_0\theta_o = \beta_0\theta_i \tag{18.31}$$

where the coefficients are all constant. This equation is adequate to describe the behavior of practically any linear servomechanism having proportional control [that is, $S_P = C_s(\theta_o - \theta_i)$].

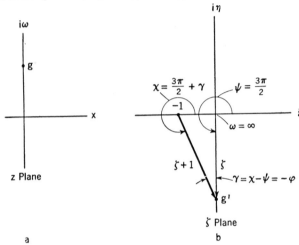

FIG. 18.23. — Transfer function for an ideal hydraulic servomechanism.

Assuming as before that θ_i and θ_o are given by Eqs. (18.20) and (18.21), we get from Eq. (18.31)

$$C_o e^{i\phi} e^{i\omega t}(\alpha_n i^n \omega^n + \cdots + \alpha_1 i\omega + \alpha_0) = \beta_0 C_i e^{i\omega t}$$

whence, introducing ζ from Eq. (18.27),

$$\frac{\zeta + 1}{\zeta} = \frac{\theta_i}{\theta_o} = \frac{C_i}{C_o e^{i\phi}} = \frac{\alpha_n i^n \omega^n + \cdots + \alpha_1 i\omega + \alpha_0}{\beta_0} \qquad (18.32)$$

In any given case the coefficients $\alpha_0, \ldots, \alpha_n$, and β_0 are known, and ζ can be found from Eq. (18.32). The graphical determination of C_o/C_i and ϕ then proceeds as already described.

The stability of a servomechanism can also be investigated by means of the transfer function. It will be recalled from Art. 18.10 that the stability is determined from the complementary function, which describes the behavior of the system when there is no impressed signal. To get the complementary function for Eq. (18.31), we set $\theta_i = 0$ and $\theta_o = Ce^{zt}$. Substituting in Eq. (18.31), we find that

$$\alpha_n z^n + \cdots + \alpha_1 z + \alpha_0 = 0 \qquad (18.33)$$

whence

$$\theta_o = C_1 e^{z_1 t} + \cdots + C_n e^{z_n t} \qquad (18.34)$$

where $z_1, \ldots, z_n$ are the n roots of Eq. (18.33). It is clear from Eq. (18.34) that, if none of the z's has a positive real part, θ_o will remain finite, no matter how great the value of t. In other words, the system will be stable

We now observe that Eq. (18.32) defines ζ as a function of z when z is restricted to purely imaginary values, $i\omega$, and that ζ is not yet defined for complex values of z. We may therefore extend the definition of ζ in any way that does not contravene Eq. (18.32). A useful extension is that in which $i\omega$ in Eq. (18.32) is replaced by z.

$$\frac{\zeta + 1}{\zeta} = \frac{\alpha_n z^n + \cdots + \alpha_1 z + \alpha_0}{\beta_0} \qquad (18.35)$$

Comparison of this with Eq. (18.33) shows at once that the roots of the latter are also the roots of the expression $(\zeta + 1)/\zeta$. This expression can be zero, however, only when the numerator $\zeta + 1$ is zero. We thus conclude that the roots of $\zeta + 1$ are the $z_1, \ldots, z_n$ of Eq. (18.33) or (18.34). We may therefore state that, if $\zeta + 1$ has no roots with a positive real part, the servomechanism is stable.

A great simplification results from this use of ζ, for, in general, it is difficult and tedious to determine the roots of an nth-degree equation. Such determination can be avoided by use of the following theorem: Let a function $f(z)$ be analytic [that is, let $f(z)$ have a continuous derivative] for all values of z in and on the boundary of a region R, and let $f(z)$ be different from zero for all z's on the boundary curve S. Then, if the vector z traces out S, the vector $f(z)$ will trace out a closed curve S' in the $f(z)$ plane, as indicated schematically in Fig. 18.24. It can be shown

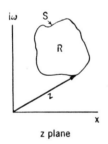
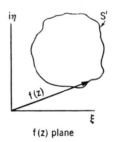

z plane   f(z) plane

Fig. 18.24.

that the net number of counterclockwise revolutions made by the vector $f(z)$ in tracing out S' is equal to the number of roots of $f(z)$ inside the region R.*

In applying this theorem to the stability problem we take the curve S as shown in Fig. 18.25a, so as to include in the limit the entire right-hand half plane and thus all z's with positive real parts. The function $f(z)$

* A proof of the theorem is outside the scope of this book. A proof is given in E. C. Titchmarsh, "Theory of Functions," 2d ed., pp. 115–116, Oxford University Press, New York, 1939.

$= \zeta + 1$ is the one to be investigated. All the expressions for $\zeta + 1$ tha we shall meet satisfy the requirements for $f(z)$ listed above.

For the ideal hydraulic servomechanism, Eq. (18.32) reduces t Eq. (18.30), so that, if $i\omega$ is replaced by z, $\zeta = \alpha_0/z$. The curve S' in th ζ plane corresponding by this expression to S in the z plane is shown i Fig. 18.25b. The points a' and d' at the origin in the ζ plane correspond t

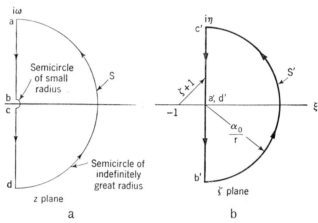

FIG. 18.25. — Stability diagram for an ideal hydraulic servomechanism.

a and d, infinitely far from $z = 0$, while the radius $\alpha_0/r \to \infty$ as $r \to 0$. It i seen therefore that, as the tip of the z vector moves around the boundar S of the right-hand half plane, the vector $\zeta + 1$ will not make a complet revolution about its point of origin -1, and the system will be stable.

While quite superfluous in the present example, this method of in vestigating stability is simple and rapid, even for complex systems. I will be noted that a rough sketch of S' is sufficient, since the only informa tion needed is the number of revolutions made by $\zeta + 1$ as it traces out th curve S'. The advantage of this method is brought out by the exampl of the next article.

18.12. Hydraulic Servomechanism with Leakage and Elasticity. Th apparatus considered here is the same as that of Fig. 18.17. We neglec for the moment any elastic deformation of the system and deal with th leakage, which we treat as in Art. 18.8, assuming Q_l to be proportional t the pressure drop Δp.

$$Q_l = \frac{C_l D \, \Delta p}{\mu} \tag{18.15}$$

The continuity equation [Eq. (18.11)] thus gives

$$\frac{d\theta_o'}{dt} = \omega_P S_P - \frac{C_l}{\mu} \Delta p \tag{18.36}$$

where θ_o' represents the angular displacement of the output shaft of the rigid system.

We now take the elastic deformation of the system into account in the following approximate way: The sole effect of the elasticity is assumed to be a change in angular position of the output shaft that is proportional to the output torque T_M. Since T_M is a load torque, its effect is to compress the fluid and expand the pipes, so that the actual output-shaft position θ_o, will be somewhat less than θ_o'. The elastic constant of the system, C_e, is therefore defined as

$$T_M = C_e(\theta_o' - \theta_o) \tag{18.37}$$

The torque T_M is expressible in terms of the moment of inertia I and the angular acceleration of the load mass, by virtue of Newton's second law.

$$T_M = I\frac{d^2\theta_o}{dt^2} \tag{18.38}$$

Here it is assumed that T_M is the only external torque on the load mass.

Another expression for T_M is given by Eq. (18.6), which may be applied to nonsteady flow if the mass of all other moving parts is assumed negligible relative to the load mass.

$$T_M = \Delta pD \tag{18.39}$$

For simplicity, η_{TM} has been set equal to unity.

Combining the last four equations and introducing as before the assumption that $S_P = C_s(\theta_i - \theta_o)$ we get, after some reduction,

$$\frac{I}{C_e}\frac{d^3\theta_o}{dt^3} + \frac{C_lI}{\mu D}\frac{d^2\theta_o}{dt^2} + \frac{d\theta_o}{dt} + \omega_P C_s\theta_o = \omega_P C_s\theta_i \tag{18.40}$$

The primary question is again that of stability, to answer which we proceed as before to investigate graphically the zeros of the complementary function. Assume, as usual, that $\theta_i = 0$, $\theta_o = Ce^{zt}$, and introduce the symbols $\alpha_0 = \omega_P C_s$, $\alpha_2 = C_lI/\mu D$, and $\alpha_3 = I/C_e$. Equation (18.40) thus yields

$$\alpha_3 z^3 + \alpha_2 z^2 + z + \alpha_0 = 0$$

which will be recognized as the special form of Eq. (18.33) for this system. Comparison of Eqs. (18.31) and (18.40) shows that here $\beta_0 = \alpha_0$, so that Eq. (18.35) reduces to

$$\frac{\zeta + 1}{\zeta} = \frac{\alpha_3 z^3 + \alpha_2 z^2 + z}{\alpha_0} + 1$$

whence

$$\zeta = \frac{\alpha_0}{\alpha_3 z^3 + \alpha_2 z^2 + z} \tag{18.41}$$

It is obvious that $\zeta \to 0$ as $z \to \infty$, so that points a and d of Fig. 18.25a are mapped into the origin of the ζ plane. Also, $\zeta \to \alpha_0/z$ as $z \to 0$. Hence, if z traces out a semicircle of very small radius (Fig. 18.25a), ζ will describe a very large semicircle. The behavior of this ζ is therefore the same as that of the previous example, for either very large or very small values of z.

To determine the path followed by ζ for pure imaginary values, $z = i\omega$ (where $-\infty < \omega < \infty$), we substitute this value of z in Eq. (18.41) and get, after reduction,

$$\zeta = -\frac{\alpha_0\alpha_2}{\alpha_2^2\omega^2 + (1 - \alpha_3\omega^2)^2} - \frac{i\alpha_0(1 - \alpha_3\omega^2)}{\alpha_2^2\omega^3 + \omega(1 - \alpha_3\omega^2)^2} \qquad (18.42)$$

We notice that, as ω decreases from very large positive values, the imaginary part of ζ is first positive, becomes zero at $\omega^2 = 1/\alpha_3$, and then ap-

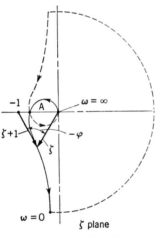

proaches $-\infty$ as $\omega \to 0$. Furthermore, the real part of ζ $[R(\zeta)]$ is never positive: $R(\zeta) \to 0$ if $\omega \to \infty$, and $R(\zeta) = -\alpha_0\alpha_2$ at $\omega = 0$. The positive imaginary axis, therefore, is mapped somewhat as shown by the full-line curve of Fig. 18.26. The rest of the boundary S of Fig. 18.25a maps into the dotted curve. The map of the negative imaginary z axis is simply the mirror image of the full-line curve with respect to the real axis of the ζ plane.

It will be recalled that the criterion for stability is that the vector $\zeta + 1$ make zero complete revolutions as it traces the entire closed curve of Fig. 18.26. The system will thus be stable if the point A lies to the right of the point -1, that is, if $R(\zeta) > -1$. From Eq. (18.42) we have already seen that $\omega^2 = 1/\alpha_3$ at point A. Therefore, $R(\zeta) = -\alpha_0\alpha_3/\alpha_2$ at A, and the stability condition is

Fig. 18.26. — Transfer function for a hydraulic servomechanism with leakage and elasticity.

or

$$\left.\begin{array}{c} \dfrac{\alpha_0\alpha_3}{\alpha_2} < 1 \\[2ex] \dfrac{\omega_P C_s\mu D}{C_e C_l} < 1 \end{array}\right\} \qquad (18.43)$$

It was shown above for the ideal servomechanism that the larger $\omega_P C_s$ the more rapid the response. Here we see that there is actually an upper limit beyond which $\omega_P C_s$ cannot go without destroying the stability. An in-

-rease in either the stiffness or the leakage coefficient C_e or C_l improves he margin of stability.

The transient response of the servomechanism is the next point of nterest. Since Eq. (18.40) is of the third order, one must solve a cubic equation to get the complementary function and hence the complete solution for a step signal. This difficulty is avoided (unless exact results are necessary) by use of the frequency-response method. The value of ζ can be found from Eq. (18.41) if z is replaced by $i\omega$. Whence

$$\frac{\zeta}{\zeta + 1} = \frac{\theta_o}{\theta_i} = \frac{C_o e^{i\phi}}{C_i} = \frac{\alpha_0}{-\alpha_3 i \omega^3 - \alpha_2 \omega^2 + i\omega + \alpha_0}$$

$$= \frac{\alpha_0/(-\alpha_3 i \omega^3 - \alpha_2 \omega^2 + i\omega)}{1 + \alpha_0/(-\alpha_3 i \omega^3 - \alpha_2 \omega^2 + i\omega)} \tag{18.44}$$

The full-line curve of Fig. (18.26) can be used to obtain graphically the value of C_o/C_i and ϕ corresponding to any given ω. In this example, however, it is relatively simple to get algebraic expressions for C_o/C_i and ϕ, so that a resort to graphical methods is unnecessary. Reduction of Eq. (18.44) yields

$$\frac{\theta_o}{\theta_i} = \frac{C_o e^{i\phi}}{C_i} = \frac{e^{-i \tan^{-1}\{(\omega/\alpha_0)[(1-\alpha_3\alpha_0^2)(\omega^2/\alpha_0^2)/(1-\alpha_2\alpha_0)(\omega^2/\alpha_0^2)]\}}}{\sqrt{[1 - \alpha_2\alpha_0(\omega^2/\alpha_0^2)]^2 + (\omega^2/\alpha_0^2)[1 - \alpha_3\alpha_0^2(\omega^2/\alpha_0^2)]^2}}$$

from which it follows that

$$\frac{C_o}{C_i} = \frac{1}{\sqrt{[1 - \alpha_2\alpha_0(\omega^2/\alpha_0^2)]^2 + (\omega^2/\alpha_0^2)[1 - \alpha_3\alpha_0^2(\omega^2/\alpha_0^2)]^2}} \tag{18.45}$$

and

$$\tan \phi = -\frac{(\omega/\alpha_0)[1 - \alpha_3\alpha_0^2(\omega^2/\alpha_0^2)]}{1 - \alpha_2\alpha_0(\omega^2/\alpha_0^2)} \tag{18.46}$$

These are seen to reduce to the corresponding equations for the ideal system [Eqs. (18.23) and (18.24)] if $\alpha_2 = \alpha_3 = 0$.

Each of the dimensionless parameters of Eqs. (18.45) and (18.46) has a physical significance. The basic parameter ω/α_0 has already been shown to represent the ratio of the forcing frequency to the time constant of the ideal system. The parameter $\alpha_3\alpha_0^2 = I\omega_P^2 C_s^2/C_e$ is a measure of the ratio of inertia to elastic effects; the greater the stiffness of the system relative to the inertia of the load, the smaller this parameter. Similarly, $\alpha_2\alpha_0 = I\omega_P C_s C_l/\mu D$ measures the ratio of load inertia to the viscous forces opposing leakage.

The stability criterion [Eq. (18.43)] states simply that $\alpha_3\alpha_0^2/\alpha_2\alpha_0 < 1$, or that the ratio of viscous force to stiffness must be less than a certain upper limit. It is obvious physically that, the greater the resistance to leakage relative to the stiffness of the system, the greater the tendency for continued oscillation, i.e., the smaller the margin of stability.

Plots of Eq. (18.45) for several values of $\alpha_3\alpha_0^2$ and $\alpha_2\alpha_0$ are given i**
Fig. 18.27. Curve a, for the ideal case of infinite stiffness and zero leakage
is the same as Fig. 18.19.

Curve b, for large stiffness and low leakage, has several desirable char**
acteristics. The resonance peak is very small and occurs at a high valu**
of ω/α_0, so that the amplitud**
response is better at high fre**
quencies than in the ideal case**
The low value of the pea**
means that there will be ver**
little overshoot in the respons**
to a step signal. Furthermore**
the occurrence of the peak a**
a large ω/α_0 boosts the cutof**
value of ω/α_0 from about 1.**
for curve a to 2.4 for curve b**
Equation (18.25) thus indicate**
a rise time for b only about 7**
per cent of that for a. Th**
stability number $\alpha_3\alpha_0/\alpha_2$ is wel**

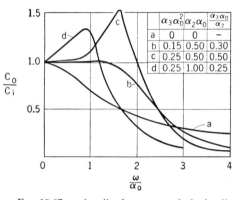

	$\alpha_3\alpha_0^2$	$\alpha_2\alpha_0$	$\frac{\alpha_3\alpha_0}{\alpha_2}$
a	0	0	–
b	0.15	0.50	0.30
c	0.25	0.50	0.50
d	0.25	1.00	0.25

Fig. 18.27. — Amplitude response of a hydraulic
servomechanism with leakage and elasticity.

below unity, so that the time required for oscillations to damp out should
be satisfactorily small.

Curve c shows what happens if the stiffness is decreased without change**
in the leakage parameter. The amplitude ratio at resonance is 1.56, a**
value that is found to give undesirably large overshoot in the response to a
step signal. The maximum amplitude ratio that can be tolerated is found
by experience to be about 1.35. Thus, although the rise time is about the
same as for b, curve c is unsatisfactory. Another count against c is the
relatively large value of the stability number, which means decreased
damping of the oscillations.

Curve d shows the effect of an increased leakage if the stiffness is kept
the same as for c. The amplitude ratio at resonance drops to 1.35, which
is reasonable, and the margin of stability is improved. The increased rise
time, accompanying the lowered resonant frequency, may, however, be a
serious drawback.

The phase-angle response corresponding to each of the curves of Fig.
18.27 has been computed from Eq. (18.46) and plotted in Fig. 18.28. The
most notable feature is that the presence of leakage and elasticity increases the maximum phase shift from $-\pi/2$ to $-3\pi/2$. There is little
to choose among curves b, c, and d, but curve b seems on the whole to be
the best. The dotted curve is included to show that the maximum phase
shift is equal to $-\pi$ if the system is assumed to be rigid but to have a
finite leakage.

The results of Figs. 18.27 and 18.28 can be combined on a single polar diagram like that of Fig. 18.21. This is left as an exercise for the reader.

The steady-state error for a displacement step signal is readily seen from physical considerations to be zero, since the load has been assumed to be entirely due to inertia. For, so long as the error is different from zero, Δp cannot be zero, and hence, from Eqs. (18.38) and (18.39), the load mass will have some angular acceleration. θ_o will thus continue to change until it equals the constant value of θ_i.

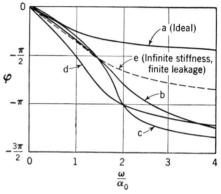

The same thing can be shown theoretically from the fact that the full-line curve of Fig. 18.26 approaches infinity along the negative imaginary axis. Furthermore, if this curve approached infinity along the negative real axis, the servomechanism would have a zero velocity error [1]. Proof of these statements is beyond the scope of this book.

FIG. 18.28. — Phase-angle response of a hydraulic servomechanism with leakage and elasticity.

It is clear physically that the steady-state displacement error will not be zero if there is applied to the output shaft an external torque which does not vanish with the angular velocity or acceleration, $d\theta_o/dt$ or $d^2\theta_o/dt^2$. For, in such a case, the steady-state pressure difference across the motor must suffice to counterbalance this torque. On account of the leakage, this pressure difference cannot be maintained without a finite steady-state error.

18.13. Linear Servomechanisms: Concluding Remarks. The examples discussed above are intended to illustrate the two methods available for analysis and design of hydraulic (or other) linear servomechanisms and to bring out the relative simplicity and power of the frequency-response method.

In both these examples the feed-back circuit has been assumed to give proportional control, that is, $S_P = C_s(\theta_i - \theta_o)$. It is frequently advantageous to employ more complicated feed-back arrangements, to give, for example, "proportional plus derivative control" or "proportional plus integral control," that is,

$$S_P = C_s(\theta_i - \theta_o) + G_s \frac{d}{dt}(\theta_i - \theta_o)$$

or

$$S_P = C_s(\theta_i - \theta_o) + H_s \int_0^t (\theta_i - \theta_o)\, dt$$

Discussion of such systems cannot be undertaken here. The reader is re ferred to problems 18.12 and 18.13, and to the literature [1].

18.14. Valve-controlled Servomechanisms. If a translatory motion is to be controlled by a hydraulic servomechanism, the simplest scheme is to use a hydraulic cylinder connected through a four-way valve to a source of high-pressure oil, as shown schematically in Fig. 18.29. . Such an apparatus has many applications, for example, in machine tools, control of aircraft, and power steering of heavy vehicles.

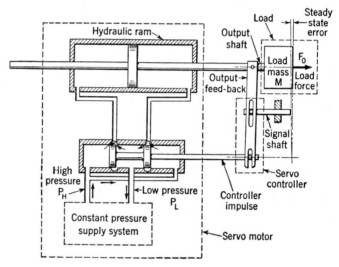

Fig. 18.29. — Schematic diagram of a valve-controlled hydraulic servomechanism. (*Courtesy of C. E. Grosser.*)

Study of Fig. 18.29 shows that, if the signal shaft is moved, say, to the left and then held stationary, the valve will open in such a way as to admit high-pressure oil to the right end of the cylinder and permit the low-pressure oil to flow out of the left end. The piston will then move to the left, and the feed-back link will tend to close the valve.

It will be observed that a given position of the signal shaft implies, ideally, a single corresponding position of the power shaft. Actually, however, if the mechanism is initially at rest and the signal shaft is displaced, the power-shaft position will fail momentarily to correspond to that called for, *i.e.*, an error will be produced. It is the creation of this error that opens the valve, thus causing the power shaft to move so as to reduce both the error and the valve opening.

The differential equation of a valve-controlled servomechanism is based on the energy principle [Eq. (5.6)] and will involve, *inter alia*, the hydraulic losses occurring in the system. To a first approximation, the losses in the pipes and fittings can be neglected, as was done previously, by virtue of the assumption that $\Delta p_P = \Delta p_M = \Delta p$. The loss in the valve of Fig. 18.29 will, however, become of prime importance as the valve nears the closed position. The loss per unit mass of oil varies as the square of the oil velocity through the valve, which in turn depends on the product of the area of the valve opening and the piston velocity. The resulting equation is nonlinear and must be integrated by special methods, such as a step-by-step technique [4], or by means of a differential analyzer.

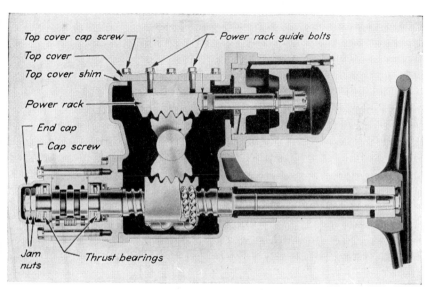

Fig. 18.30. — Valve-controlled hydraulic steering booster. (*Courtesy of F. W. Davis.*)

A detailed discussion of this servomechanism cannot be given here. It exhibits, however, a behavior which is qualitatively like that of a linear servomechanism, *i.e.*, if subjected to a displacement step signal, it has a certain rise time, overshoot, natural oscillation frequency, and decay time. The corresponding steady-state error is zero for a pure inertia load, as may be seen from a physical argument like that of Art. 18.12. If, however, a static force is applied to the output shaft, the leakage necessitates a slight opening of the valve to maintain the required pressure difference across the piston. A steady-state error results, which is greater the greater the leakage.

The servomechanism of Fig. 18.29 is operated from a constant-pressure source of oil. This may be supplied in several ways, for example, by a fixed-displacement pump and relief valve or unloader valve, together with an accumulator, as described in Art. 18.6.

In some applications, such as power steering of a truck, it is desirable to dispense with the complication of the accumulator and the associated valves. This simplification has been accomplished in one type of steering booster by use of a control valve that under static conditions is open instead of closed [10]. This booster is shown in Fig. 18.30. Oil from a gear pump driven at engine speed circulates freely through the open valve unless a considerable steering effort is required. If only a small torque is needed to turn the wheels, the valve is unaffected, the booster does not operate, and steering is done manually in the usual way. If, however, the torque on the steering wheel exceeds a predetermined amount, the end thrust suffices to move the steering column slightly lengthwise, through compression of centering springs. The valve spool, which moves with the steering column, is thus displaced from its neutral position, oil is forced to the appropriate side of the piston, and the booster functions.

In addition to its relative simplicity, this type of booster has the advantage that the steering effort required of the operator is readily adjustable. Some operator effort has been found advisable for safety reasons, since a certain "feel" of the road is thereby obtained, which is absent if the entire steering load is taken by the booster.

SELECTED BIBLIOGRAPHY

1. BROWN, G. S., and A. C. HALL: Dynamic Behavior and Design of Servomechanisms, *Trans. Am. Soc. Mech. Engrs.*, vol. 68, pp. 503–524, July, 1946.
2. FIELD, HOWARD, JR.: An Introduction to Aircraft Hydraulic Systems, *Trans. Am. Soc. Mech. Engrs.*, vol. 66, pp. 569–576, October, 1944.
3. FITZSIMMONS, V. G., D. L. PICKETT, R. O. MILITZ, and W. A. ZISMAN: Dimethylsilicone-polymer Fluids and Their Performance Characteristics in Hydraulic Systems, *Trans. Am. Soc. Mech. Engrs.*, vol. 68, pp. 361–369, May, 1946.
4. GROSSER, C. E.: Hydraulic Control Affords Design Flexibility, *Machine Design*, vol. 12, pp. 37–40, 120–122, December, 1940 (see also several other related articles that appeared during 1941).
5. HERMAN, DALE: Evolution of the Hydraulic Pump as Applied to Aircraft, *Trans. Am. Soc. Mech. Engrs.*, vol. 66, pp. 583–588, October, 1944.
6. HERMAN, K. R.: Modern Hydraulic Units for Machine Tools, *Mech. Eng.*, vol. 60, pp. 823–828, November, 1938.
7. MacCOLL, L. A.: "Fundamental Theory of Servomechanisms," D. Van Nostrand Company, Inc., New York, 1945.
8. PIGOTT, R. J. S.: Some Characteristics of Rotary Pumps in Aviation Service, *Trans. Am. Soc. Mech. Engrs.*, vol. 66, pp. 615–623, October, 1944.
9. WILSON, W. E.: Rotary-pump Theory, *Trans. Am. Soc. Mech. Engrs.*, vol. 68, pp. 371–384, May, 1946.
10. DAVIS, F. W.: Power Steering for Automotive Vehicles, *S.A.E.J.* (*Trans.*), vol. 53, pp. 239–256, 1945.

APPENDIX

MECHANICAL PROPERTIES OF FLUIDS

Values of fluid properties are given at several places in the text. These places are listed below for easy reference.

Art. 2.22. Bulk compression modulus of water. Specific-heat ratio, gas constant, and specific weight of gases.

Art. 8.4. Kinematic viscosity: relation between Saybolt seconds and centistokes.

Art. 12.4. Conversion factors for viscosity.

Art. 12.5. Specific gravity of oils.

Art. 12.11. Specific heat of oils.

Art. 12.12. Thermal conductivity of oils.

Art. 18.7. Kinematic viscosity of hydraulic fluids.

The following tables give the density ρ, the viscosity μ, and the kinematic viscosity ν as functions of temperature for several liquids and gases. The first two tables are for water and air, since these are the fluids most commonly used in engineering practice.

PROPERTIES OF WATER AT ATMOSPHERIC PRESSURE *

Temperature		Density		Viscosity		Kinematic viscosity	
Deg C	Deg F	G/cm³	Slug/ft³	Dyne-sec/cm²	Lb-sec/ft²	Cm²/sec	Ft²/sec
0	32	0.99987	1.940	1.794×10^{-2}	3.746×10^{-5}	1.794×10^{-2}	1.930×10^{-5}
4	39.2	1.00000	1.941	1.568	3.274	1.568	1.687
5	41	0.99999	1.941	1.519	3.172	1.519	1.634
10	50	0.99973	1.940	1.310	2.735	1.310	1.407
15	59	0.99913	1.940	1.145	2.391	1.146	1.233
20	68	0.998	1.937	1.009	2.107	1.011	1.088
30	86	0.996	1.932	0.800	1.670	0.803	0.864
40	104	0.992	1.925	0.654	1.366	0.659	0.709
50	122	0.988	1.917	0.549	1.146	0.556	0.598
60	140	0.983	1.907	0.470	0.981	0.478	0.514
70	158	0.978	1.897	0.407	0.850	0.416	0.448
80	176	0.972	1.885	0.357	0.745	0.367	0.395
90	194	0.965	1.872	0.317	0.662	0.328	0.353
100	212	0.958	1.858	0.284	0.593	0.296	0.318

* Data from the "International Critical Tables" (abbreviation I.C.T.), McGraw-Hill Book Company, Inc., 1930.

APPENDIX

PROPERTIES OF AIR AT ATMOSPHERIC PRESSURE *

Temperature		Density		Viscosity		Kinematic viscosity	
Deg C	Deg F	G/cm³	Slug/ft³	Dyne-sec/cm²	Lb-sec/ft²	Cm²/sec	Ft²/sec
0	32	1.293×10^{-3}	2.510×10^{-3}	1.709×10^{-4}	3.568×10^{-7}	0.1322	1.427×10^{-4}
50	122	1.093	2.122	1.951	4.074	0.1785	1.921
100	212	0.946	1.836	2.175	4.541	0.2299	2.474
150	302	0.834	1.619	2.385	4.980	0.2860	3.077
200	392	0.746	1.448	2.582	5.391	0.3461	3.724
250	482	0.675	1.310	2.770	5.784	0.4104	4.416
300	572	0.616	1.196	2.946	6.151	0.4782	5.145
350	662	0.567	1.101	3.113	6.500	0.5490	5.907
400	752	0.525	1.019	3.277	6.842	0.6246	6.721
450	842	0.488	0.947	3.433	7.168	0.7035	7.570
500	932	0.457	0.887	3.583	7.481	0.7840	8.436

* Data from the I.C.T.

PROPERTIES OF LIQUIDS AT ATMOSPHERIC PRESSURE *

Temperature		Density		Viscosity		Kinematic viscosity	
Deg C	Deg F	G/cm³	Slug/ft³	Dyne-sec/cm²	Lb-sec/ft²	Cm²/sec	Ft²/sec
Carbon Tetrachloride							
0	32	1.633	3.170	1.34×10^{-2}	2.80×10^{-5}	0.82×10^{-2}	0.88×10^{-5}
20	68	1.594	3.094	0.97	2.02	0.61	0.65
40	104	1.555	3.018	0.74	1.54	0.48	0.52
Castor Oil							
20	68	0.960	1.863	9.86	2.059×10^{-2}	10.27	11.05×10^{-3}
40	104	0.946	1.836	2.31	0.482	2.44	2.63
Ethyl Alcohol							
0	32	0.806	1.564	1.790×10^{-2}	3.738×10^{-5}	2.221×10^{-2}	2.390×10^{-5}
20	68	0.789	1.531	1.716	3.583	2.175	2.340
40	104	0.772	1.498	1.647	3.439	2.133	2.295
60	140	0.756	1.467	1.581	3.301	2.091	2.250
Glycerol							
30	86	1.255	2.436	3.8	7.9×10^{-3}	3.0	3.2×10^{-3}
75	167	1.226	2.380	0.24	0.50	0.20	0.22
Glycol							
25	77	1.110	2.154	0.174	0.363×10^{-3}	0.158	0.170×10^{-3}
Mercury							
0	32	13.60	26.40	1.66×10^{-2}	3.47×10^{-5}	0.122×10^{-2}	0.131×10^{-5}
20	68	13.55	26.30	1.54	3.22	0.114	0.123
40	104	13.50	26.20	1.47	3.07	0.109	0.117
100	212	13.35	25.91	1.26	2.63	0.094	0.101
Methyl Alcohol							
0	32	0.810	1.572	0.808×10^{-2}	1.687×10^{-5}	0.998×10^{-2}	1.074×10^{-5}
20	68	0.791	1.535	0.593	1.238	0.750	0.807
40	104	0.773	1.500	0.449	0.938	0.581	0.625
60	140	0.753	1.462	0.349	0.729	0.463	0.498
White Mineral Oil (SAE 10)							
15.5	60	0.875	1.698	1.29	2.69×10^{-3}	1.47	1.58×10^{-3}
49	120	0.855	1.660	0.236	0.493	0.276	0.297
93.5	200	0.835	1.621	0.062	0.129	0.074	0.080
White Mineral Oil (SAE 30)							
15.5	60	0.885	1.718	3.70	7.73×10^{-3}	4.18	4.50×10^{-3}
49	120	0.865	1.679	0.414	0.864	0.479	0.515
93.5	200	0.845	1.640	0.88	0.184	0.104	0.112

* Data for castor oil from "Smithsonian Physical Tables," 8th ed., Smithsonian Institution, 1933. All other data from I.C.T., except for the white mineral oils. For these the density was furnished by the supplier, and the kinematic viscosity was measured at M.I.T.

The viscosity of a gas can be obtained from Sutherland's formula, as follows:

$$\mu = \mu_0 \frac{273 + C}{T + C}\left(\frac{T}{273}\right)^{\frac{3}{2}}$$

where μ_0 = viscosity at $T = 273\ C$ abs
$\quad\ \ C$ = constant characteristic of the gas
Values of μ_0 and C for several gases are as follows:

	μ_0		C
	Dyne-sec/cm²	Lb-sec/ft²	
Air *	1.71×10^{-4}	3.57×10^{-7}	120
Carbon dioxide	1.42	2.97	240
Helium	1.89	3.95	80
Hydrogen	0.867	1.81	72
Nitrogen	1.66	3.47	110
Oxygen	1.89	3.97	131

* Data for air from I.C.T. All other data from "Smithsonian Physical Tables," 8th ed., Smithsonian Institution, 1933.

Plots of kinematic viscosity versus temperature are given below for air and water to facilitate computation of the Reynolds number.

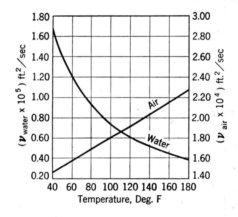

PROBLEMS

Chapter II

2.1. The motor for the hydraulic testing machine shown is capable of producing a thrust of 400 lb. It is desired to produce a stress of 150,000 lb per sq in. (based on initial area) in a standard tensile test specimen of 0.505-in. diameter. What must be the area ratio of the two pistons A and B?

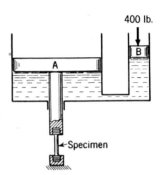

PROBLEM 2.1.

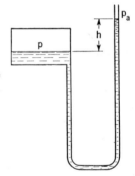

2.2. The gauge pressure $p - p_a$ at the liquid surface in the closed tank is 3.0 lb per sq in. Find h if the liquid in the tank is (a) water; (b) methyl alcohol; (c) mercury.

PROBLEM 2.2.

2.3. If the pressure difference between the two tanks is $p_a - p_b = 142$ lb/ft² and $z_1 = 36$ in., $z_2 = 30$ in., $z_3 = 26$ in., $z_4 = 29$ in., find the specific weight of fluid X.

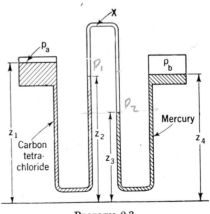

PROBLEM 2.3.

453

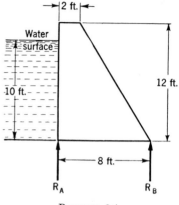

2.4. If the specific weight of concrete is 150 lb per cu ft, find the vertical reactions R_A and R_B for a unit length of the concrete dam.

PROBLEM 2.4.

2.5. A gate 3 ft square in a vertical dam is exposed to the atmosphere on one side. It is located so far below the level of the water surface that the center of pressure is 1 in. below the center of gravity of the gate. How far is the top of the gate below the water surface?

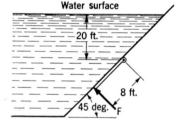

2.6. A rectangular gate 4 by 8 ft, located in a slanting wall is held shut by a force F. If the gate weighs 500 lb, find F.

PROBLEM 2.6.

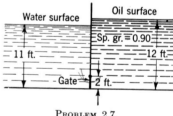

2.7. A rectangular gate 3 ft wide and 2 ft high is hinged at the top. Find the direction and magnitude of the moment tending to turn the gate about the hinge.

PROBLEM 2.7.

2.8. A container for liquid is made up of two hollow quarter cylinders hinged together along the edge OO and held by a strap at each end along the horizontal diameter. If the semicylindrical container is completely filled with liquid of density ρ, find the tension T in each strap.

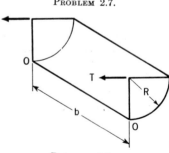

PROBLEM 2.8.

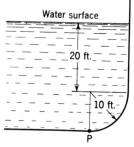

PROBLEM 2.9.

2.9. A dam is composed of a straight vertical section 20 ft high and a quadrant of 10-ft radius. Find the moment about P of the water forces on unit length of the dam.

2.10. Find the force per unit length F required to keep the gate closed. Neglect bearing friction and weight of gate.

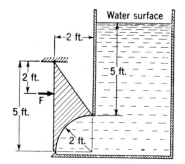

PROBLEM 2.10.

2.11. Determine the horizontal force per unit length F required to keep the S-shaped gate closed. Neglect friction in bearing O.

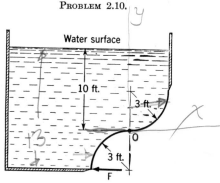

PROBLEM 2.11.

2.12. The specific gravity of the right circular cylinder shown is 0.9. (a) Find the specific gravity of the unknown fluid, assuming the system to be in equilibrium as shown. (b) Why is not this system in stable equilibrium? (c) When the system reaches equilibrium, where will the top of the cylinder be relative to the interface between liquids?

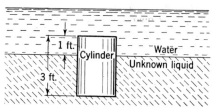

PROBLEM 2.12.

2.13. A rectangular body of specific gravity $\frac{2}{3}$ has length a, width b, and height c $(a > b > c)$. Determine the maximum value of c for stable flotation in water.

2.14. A long prism (specific gravity s) the cross section of which is an equilateral triangle of side a is assumed to float in water with one side horizontal and submerged to a depth t. (a) Find t/a as a function of s. (b) Find the metacentric height for small angles of tilt if $s = \frac{3}{4}$.

2.15. A river barge of rectangular plan and cross section 60 ft long and 20 ft wide is loaded to a uniform depth of 4 ft with sand of specific weight 94 lb per cu ft. The unloaded barge weighs 50,000 lb, and its center of gravity is 2 ft above the center of its bottom. Find (a) the depth of immersion of the bottom of the barge; (b) the metacentric height for small angles; (c) the righting moment for a 1-deg angle of tilt.

2.16. A block 3 ft long, 2 ft wide, and $\frac{1}{3}$ ft high floats submerged half in water and half in oil of specific gravity 0.86. Find the specific gravity of the block and the metacentric height for small angles of tilt.

2.17. A rectangular block of specific gravity $\frac{1}{2}$ is 4 ft long and has the cross section shown. Find the righting moment when the block is tilted as indicated.

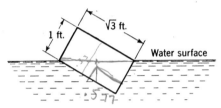

PROBLEM 2.17.

2.18. Find the pressure at an elevation of 9,000 ft if the lapse rate of the atmosphere is constant and equal to $\frac{1}{300}$ F per ft. The ground-level temperature is 60 F, and the barometer reading is 29.8 in. Hg. (The gas constant for air is 53.4 ft per deg F.)

2.19. The temperature of air at ground level $T_0 = 520$ F abs, the pressure $p_0 = 15$ lb/in.^{2} abs (psia). The lapse rate of the troposphere $\lambda = \frac{1}{300}$ F/ft. The height of the troposphere is 7 miles. (a) Find the heights above ground level at which $p = p_0/2$ and $p = p_0/10$. (b) Find the temperature at each level asked for in part (a).

2.20. A balloon filled with hydrogen (gas constant = 767 ft/deg F) reaches a maximum height of 6 miles above the earth. The following are known:

W = weight of balloon, gondola, etc. (excluding gas), lb............ 2,000
L_0 = initial lift force (or the tension in mooring cable), lb...........   200
T_0 = ground-level temperature, deg F abs.......................   525
p_0 = ground-level pressure, psia.................................   15
λ = atmospheric lapse rate, deg F/ft........................... $\frac{1}{300}$

Assuming that, at any elevation, the pressure and temperature of the hydrogen are the same as those of the surrounding air, find the volume of hydrogen in the balloon at take-off and at the maximum height.

2.21. A balloon 6 ft in diameter is filled with hydrogen at ground-level pressure and temperature and sealed. The weight of balloon and load is 4 lb. (a) Neglecting any change in volume of the balloon and using the pertinent data of the preceding problem, find the maximum height reached by the balloon. (b) Assuming the temperatures of the hydrogen and air to be the same, find the difference between the internal and external pressures.

2.22. A tank containing water slides down an inclined plane under the action of gravity. The angle between the plane and the horizontal is α. Find the angle between the water surface and the horizontal (a) if the surface is frictionless; (b) if the coefficient of friction between tank and surface is μ.

2.23. An automobile manufacturer claims for his car an acceleration from 15 to 50 mph in 13 sec in high gear. If a glass U-tube with vertical legs 2 ft apart is partly filled with water and used as an accelerometer, what is the difference in level of the two legs for this constant acceleration? For an initial speed of 15 mph, how fast would the car be going at the end of 13 sec if the difference in level were $\frac{1}{2}$ in. larger? If it were $\frac{1}{2}$ in. smaller?

2.24. A vertical cylindrical tank 2 ft in diameter and 4 ft in height contains a water layer 2 ft deep and an oil layer 1 ft deep. The specific gravity of the oil is 0.86. (a) At what rotational speed will the oil just reach the rim of the tank? (b) What is then the pressure at the intersection of the wall and the bottom?

2.25. A vertical cylindrical tank 2 ft in diameter and 5 ft in height is half full of water. (a) Find the maximum speed with which it can be rotated without spilling any water. (b) If the same tank has a cover with a pinhole in the center, is completely filled with liquid of specific gravity 0.89, and is turned at 100 rpm, find the gauge pressure at the periphery of the top and bottom and at the center of the bottom.

2.26. A U-tube containing water rotates about the vertical axis CA. (a) If the atmospheric pressure is 14.7 psia, find the pressure at A for 100 rpm. (b) Assuming the vapor pressure to be zero and neglecting the volume of liquid vaporized, find the height of the liquid surface in the vertical legs at 950 rpm. (c) What are the levels in the legs if the tube rotates about axis BD at 200 rpm?

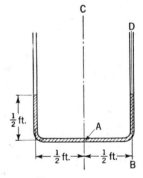

PROBLEM 2.26.

2.27. An open can 1 in. in diameter is filled with mercury to a depth of 10 in. and whirled at constant angular velocity at the end of a wire. The bottom of the can is outermost and describes a circle of 3-ft radius in a vertical plane. If the minimum tension in the wire during a revolution is equal to zero and the weight of the can is neglected, find (a) the angular velocity; (b) the location and magnitude of the minimum gauge pressure in the mercury.

Chapter III

3.1. The magnitude of the relative velocity at the surface of a cylinder in two-dimensional incompressible flow is given by $W = 2W_0 \sin \theta$, where W is tangent to the surface and W_0 is the velocity of the distant fluid. At points A and B construct the vector diagram of the relative and absolute velocities.

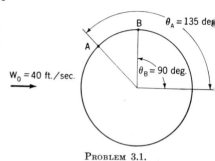

PROBLEM 3.1.

3.2. A pipe 10 in. in diameter carries an unsteady flow of incompressible liquid. The pipe terminates in a nozzle 6 in. in diameter. Find the velocity and acceleration of the parallel stream leaving the nozzle at the instant when the velocity and acceleration in the pipe are 12 ft per sec and 2 ft per sq sec.

3.3. A gas following the law $p = $ constant ρT flows steadily in a horizontal pipe of constant cross-sectional area A. If the flow is isothermal and the ratio of the pressures at two sections is $p_2/p_1 = \frac{3}{4}$, find the velocity ratio V_2/V_1.

3.4. (a) Incompressible fluid flows radially outward in all directions from a point source. Assuming that the velocity depends only on r, the distance from the source find V as a function of r. (b) Do the same for the axially symmetrical flow from a line source.

3.5. (a) A uniform parallel flow of velocity V_0 is superposed on the flow from a point source discharging at a rate Q. Where is the resultant velocity equal to zero? (b) Answer the same question if the parallel flow is superposed on a line source of strength Q.

3.6. Show that the rate of change of mass inside a control volume $\mathcal{U}$ can be expressed as $\int_{\mathcal{U}} \frac{\partial \rho}{\partial t} d\mathcal{U}$.

3.7. Standing waves are set up in a compressible fluid contained in a rigid pipe of constant cross-sectional area A. The density is uniform over every cross section but varies with time t and distance along the pipe axis x, according to the law

$$\rho = \rho_0 = (\rho_m - \rho_0) \sin \left(\frac{2\pi ct}{\lambda}\right) \sin \left(\frac{2\pi x}{\lambda}\right)$$

where ρ_0 is the average density, ρ_m is the maximum density, c is the velocity of wave propagation in the fluid, and λ is the wave length. Find the net rate of mass flow at any instant out of the length of pipe bounded by the planes $x = 0$ and $x = \lambda/4$.

Chapter IV

4.1. Water flows steadily at a rate of 0.6 cu ft per sec through a horizontal cone-shaped contraction the diameter of which decreases from 4.0 to 3.0 in. in a length of 1.2 ft. Assuming that conditions are uniform over any cross section find the rate of change of pressure in the direction of flow at the section 0.6 ft from the ends of the contraction.

4.2. A two-dimensional duct contains a straight-sided contraction. At a certain time the flow per unit width is 4.0 sq ft per sec and is increasing by 3.0 sq ft per sec^2. Assuming the velocity to be uniform over any cross section find the acceleration at the section $x = 0.75$ ft.

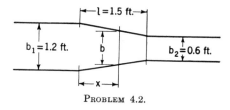

PROBLEM 4.2.

4.3. Find $p_1 - p_2$ and A_1/A_2 in terms of $z_1 - z_2$, h, ρ_a, ρ_b, and V_1.

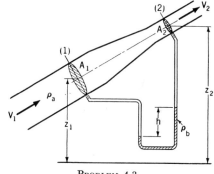

PROBLEM 4.3.

4.4. Air of density 2.38×10^{-3} slug per cu ft flows in the working section of a wind tunnel, in which the pressure is atmospheric. One leg of a U-tube containing alcohol of specific gravity 0.79 is attached to an impact tube inside the tunnel. The other leg of the U-tube is open to the atmosphere. Find the difference in the alcohol levels corresponding to a velocity of 90 mph in the working section.

4.5. (a) Determine the ratio h_p/h_q. (b) Repeat for a slanted pipe.

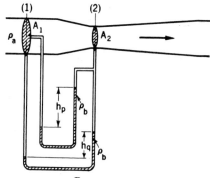

PROBLEM 4.5.

4.6. Water flows from a large open reservoir and discharges horizontally into the air, striking the ground a distance x from the nozzle.

$$z_1 = 30 \text{ ft} \qquad d_2 = 5 \text{ in.}$$
$$z_2 = 20 \text{ ft} \qquad d_3 = 3 \text{ in.}$$

Neglecting friction, find (a) velocity V_3 at nozzle exit; (b) velocity V_2 and pressure p_2 in the pipe near the nozzle; (c) x (assuming parabolic path).

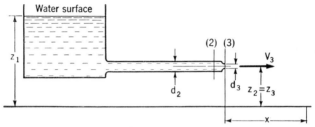

Water surface

(2) (3)

V_3

z_1

d_2

d_3 $z_2 = z_3$

x

PROBLEM 4.6.

4.7. Water flows through the system shown.

$$z_1 = 30 \text{ ft} \qquad d_3 = 3 \text{ in.}$$
$$z_5 = 7 \text{ ft} \qquad d_2 = d_5 = 5 \text{ in.}$$
$$h_5 = 1.6 \text{ ft} \qquad d_6 = 2.5 \text{ in.}$$

The fluid in the manometers is mercury. Neglecting friction, find (a) discharge rate Q; (b) h_3; (c) h_4.

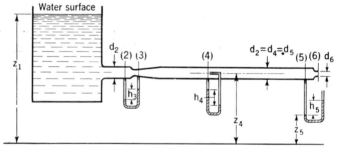

Water surface

d_2 (2) (3)   (4) $d_2 = d_4 = d_5$ (5) (6) d_6

z_1

h_3 h_4 h_5

z_4

z_5

PROBLEM 4.7.

4.8. Air flows steadily from a 2-in.-diameter convergent nozzle in a large tank out into the atmosphere. The velocity in the tank far from the nozzle is negligible and the pressure there is 50 per cent greater than atmospheric pressure. The relation between pressure and density anywhere in the flow is $p/\rho^{1.4} = \text{constant}$. At the nozzle outlet, the pressure is atmospheric and equal to 14.7 psia, and the density is 2.4×10^{-3} slug per cu ft. Find the mass rate of flow through the nozzle.

4.9. Water in an open cylindrical tank 10 ft in diameter discharges into the atmosphere through a nozzle 2 in. in diameter. Neglecting friction and the unsteadiness of the flow, find the time required for the water in the tank to drop from a level 16 ft above the nozzle to the 8-ft level.

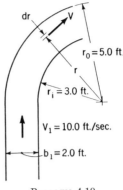

4.10. An irrotational two-dimensional flow leaves a straight duct and enters a bend of the same width. Assuming a velocity distribution in the bend like that in a potential vortex (Vr = constant), find the velocities at the inner and outer walls of the bend.

PROBLEM 4.10.

4.11. At a distance of 3 in. from the axis of a whirlpool the velocity is 13.1 ft per sec. At radii of 6 in. and 12 in. find the depression of the free surface below the level of the distant fluid.

4.12. A paddle wheel 6 in. in diameter rotates at 200 rpm inside a closed circular concentric tank 2 ft in diameter completely filled with water. Assuming two-dimensional flow in a horizontal plane, considering the water inside the wheel to move as a forced vortex and that outside to move as a free vortex, find the difference in pressure between the rim of the tank and the center of the wheel.

Chapter V

5.1. Water flows through the system shown. Neglect all friction losses except those occurring at sections 2 (reentrant pipe), 3 (open globe valve), 5 and 6 (90° elbows), 7 (sudden enlargement). Each loss in head is expressed as $CV^2/2g$.

$z_1 = 20$ ft	$D_2 = D_6 = 3$ in.	$C_6 = 0.75$
$z_2 = 5$ ft	$D_8 = 5$ in.	$C_7 = 0.41$ (based on velocity
$z_4 = 2$ ft	$C_2 = 1.0$	in 3-in. pipe)
$z_6 = 9$ ft	$C_3 = 7.5$	$p_1 = p_a = 15$ psia
$h_4 = 0.8$ ft		

Find V_8 and p_8.

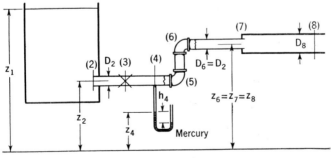

PROBLEM 5.1.

5.2. A pump discharges water at a constant rate of 0.80 cu ft per sec. The total length of pipe between 2 and 6 is $L = 600$ ft, and the uniform diameter $D = 3$ in. The loss due to friction in the straight pipe is given by $Hl_{pipe} = 0.02 \ (L/D)V^2/2g$, where V is the velocity in the pipe. The loss coefficients for the elbows and valve are the same as in the preceding problem, while the loss coefficient for the sudden enlargement at 6 is 1.0. (a) Find the gauge pressure at 2. (b) Neglecting losses in the inlet pipe and assuming a pump efficiency of 80 per cent, find the power input to the pump.

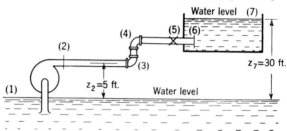

PROBLEM 5.2.

5.3. Frictionless incompressible fluid is pumped steadily at a rate of 0.8 cu ft per sec by the apparatus shown. The density of the fluid is 1.6 slug per cu ft. At section 2, the pressure is 10 lb per sq in. gauge (psig), the velocity is 9.5 ft per sec, and the area $A_2 = 0.04$ sq ft. At section 3, the pressure is 30 psig, and the area $A_3 = 0.03$ sq ft. If the heat transfer to the apparatus is 100 Btu per min (1 Btu = 778 ft-lb), find the power input at the shaft.

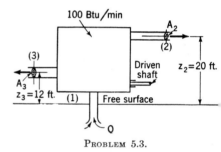

PROBLEM 5.3.

5.4. An axial-flow fan absorbing 0.54 hp discharges 5,000 cu ft per min of air having a specific weight of 0.0765 lb per cu ft. A water-filled manometer attached to the duct downstream from the fan shows that the static pressure at that point exceeds atmospheric by ¼ in. of water. If the air taken into the fan is drawn from a large room where the air is at rest at atmospheric pressure, find the loss upstream from the point where the manometer is attached. (Duct diameter = 2 ft.)

5.5. An incompressible fluid flows past one side of a flat plate, as shown. The velocity at the leading edge of the plate is uniform and equal to V_0, while the x component u at the trailing edge is distributed linearly across the thickness δ_2. Find the sum of the rates of heat transfer and intrinsic-energy transport out of the control surface $abcd$. The result is to be given in terms of ρ, V_0, and δ_2.

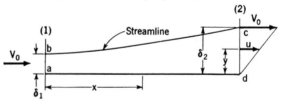

PROBLEM 5.5.

5.6. The efficiency of the hydraulic turbine η_T is defined as the ratio of the actual power output to that which would subsist if $H_{l_{BC}}$ were zero. The efficiency of the pump η_P is analogously defined in terms of $H_{l_{FG}}$.

$$\eta_P\eta_T = 0.85$$
$$Q_P = 0.354 \text{ ft}^3/\text{sec}$$
$$Q_T = 0.500 \text{ ft}^3/\text{sec}$$
$$H_{l_{AB}} = H_{l_{CD}} = H_{l_{EF}} = 5 \text{ ft}$$
$$H_{l_{FG}} = 9 \text{ ft}$$
$$H_{l_{GH}} = 3 \text{ ft}$$

Find (a) z; (b) power output of turbine; (c) loss in the turbine, $H_{l_{BC}}$.

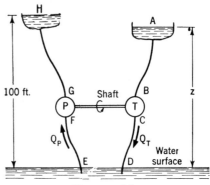

PROBLEM 5.6.

5.7. Water flows between the three reservoirs as shown.

$$Q_{AB} = 0.15 \text{ ft}^3/\text{sec}$$
$$Q_{BE} = 0.05 \text{ ft}^3/\text{sec}$$
$$H_{l_{AB}} = 30 \text{ ft}$$
$$H_{l_{CB}} = 10 \text{ ft}$$
$$H_{l_{CD}} = 20 \text{ ft}$$

(a) Find $H_{l_{EB}}$. (b) What is the efficiency η_T of the turbine T? (η_T is defined as in Prob. 5.6). (c) What is the power output of the turbine?

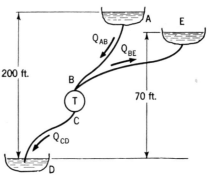

PROBLEM 5.7.

5.8. For the turbine installation shown $H_{l_{AB}} = H_{l_{BC}} = H_{l_{ED}} = 2$ ft, $H_{l_{DC}} = 4$ ft. Find (a) velocity at B; (b) power output of turbine; (c) efficiency of turbine η_T, defined as in Prob. 5.6 (all pipe 2-in. diameter).

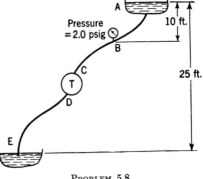

PROBLEM 5.8.

5.9. Consider the machine in Prob. 5.8 to be a pump with all losses the same and the same reading on the pressure gauge as there given. If water is pumped from E to A, find (a) velocity at B; (b) power input to pump; (c) efficiency of pump.

Chapter VI

6.1. A two-dimensional jet of incompressible fluid strikes a plane surface. Neglecting friction and gravity, find V_2, V_3, b_2, and b_3 in terms of ρ, V_1, b_1, and β. Find also the direction and magnitude of the force per unit length needed to hold the plate stationary.

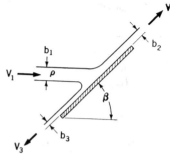

PROBLEM 6.1.

6.2. Find the force F needed to prevent rotation of this pipe about the vertical axis O.

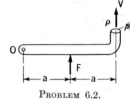

PROBLEM 6.2.

6.3. A locomotive pulls a tender at a constant velocity $V = 59$ ft/sec. The combined wind and wheel resistance is $D = 400$ lb. Water is being scooped up at a constant rate $Q = 10$ ft³/sec from a trough between the tracks. (a) Find the pull F exerted by the locomotive on the tender. (b) Find the horsepower developed by the locomotive.

6.4. Incompressible fluid flows steadily through a two-dimensional series of fixed vanes, a few of which are shown. The velocity and pressure are constant all along sections 1 and 2. Find the reactions per unit length R_x and R_y necessary to keep one vane in its fixed position. Neglect gravity and friction.

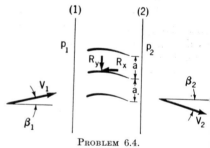

PROBLEM 6.4.

6.5. Find R_x and R_y for the preceding problem if a loss $H_{l_{1,2}}$ occurs between sections 1 and 2.

6.6. Water flows steadily through the horizontal pipe bend shown.

$A_1 = 0.1$ sq ft $\beta = 45$ deg
$A_2 = 0.2$ sq ft
$V_1 = 20$ ft/sec
$p_1 = 20$ lb/in.² abs
$p_0 = 15$ lb/in.² abs
$H_{l_{1,2}} = 6.0$ ft-lb/lb

(a) Find R_x and R_y. (b) Show that, if no external moment is exerted on the pipe, R must act through P, the intersection of the lines of V_1 and V_2.

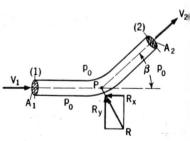

PROBLEM 6.6.

6.7. Ideal incompressible fluid of density $\rho = 1.94$ slugs/ft³ flows steadily with respect to axes rotating in a horizontal plane at a constant rate $N = 200$ rpm. The relative velocities at two points on the same relative streamline are $W_1 = 20$ ft/sec and $W_2 = 15$ ft/sec, the flow going from 1 to 2. The normal distances from the axis of rotation are $r_1 = 1.6$ ft and $r_2 = 1.0$ ft. If the two points are at the same elevation, find $p_1 - p_2$.

6.8. Repeat the preceding problem if a loss of energy $H_{l_{1,2}} = 2.50$ ft-lb/lb occurs between points 1 and 2.

6.9. Water flows through the impeller of a centrifugal pump as shown. Find the torque exerted on the impeller and the power required to drive it. The absolute velocity of the water at the entrance has no tangential component.

$Q = 2$ ft³/sec
$\omega = 100$ radians/sec
$r_1 = 2$ in.
$r_2 = 6$ in.
$b_2 = \frac{1}{2}$ in.
$\beta_2 = 120$ deg

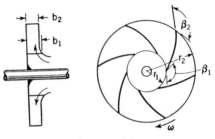

PROBLEM 6.9.

6.10. Two horizontal fluid jets strike a flat plate, which is held in equilibrium by forces whose horizontal components are F_a and F_b. Find F_b and b in terms of ρ_1, ρ_2, A_1, A_2, V_1, V_2, a, c, and F_a.

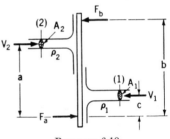

PROBLEM 6.10.

6.11. Gasoline is burned in this thrust augmenter at one-thirtieth the mass rate of air inflow at 1. The density and velocity of the air far in front of the augmenter are 2.4×10^{-3} slug per cu ft and 200 ft per sec. $A_1 = 1.5$ sq ft. The mean density of the combustion products at 2 is 0.86×10^{-3} slug per cu ft. Assuming $p_1 = p_2 = p_a$ and neglecting friction upstream from 1, find the external force F on the augmenter.

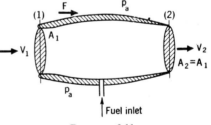

PROBLEM 6.11.

6.12. Water flows past one side of a flat plate. The velocity is uniform at the leading edge and parallel to the plate, while at the trailing edge the parallel component varies linearly with y, $u = ky$ for $y \leqslant h$. For $y > h$, $u = V$. Assuming steady two-dimensional flow, find F, the parallel component of the supporting force per unit width.

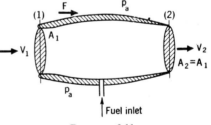

PROBLEM 6.12.

6.13. Water flows from the nozzle in this tank.

$$A_1 = 1.0 \text{ sq ft} \qquad z_1 = 5.0 \text{ ft}$$
$$A_2 = 0.02 \text{ sq ft} \qquad z_2 = 0.5 \text{ ft}$$
$$a = \tfrac{1}{3} \text{ ft} \qquad \beta = 60 \text{ deg}$$

Neglecting friction and the weight of the tank (but not that of the water), find the supporting forces R_1, R_{2x}, and R_{2y}.

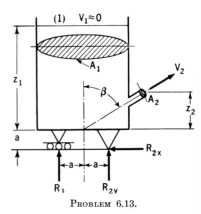

PROBLEM 6.13.

6.14. Neglecting friction, compute the axial force produced at flange 1 when water is discharged from this nozzle at 100 gpm.

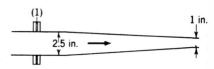

PROBLEM 6.14.

6.15. Water flows steadily through this closed tank. No force is transmitted by the flexible union at 1. Neglecting friction, find the rate of flow and R_{ax}, R_{ay}, and R_b, if

$$A_1 = 0.03 \text{ sq ft} \qquad b = \tfrac{2}{3} \text{ ft}$$
$$A_2 = 0.04 \text{ sq ft} \qquad d = 2 \text{ ft}$$
$$h = 2 \text{ ft} \qquad p_1 - p_a = 10 \text{ lb/in.}^2$$

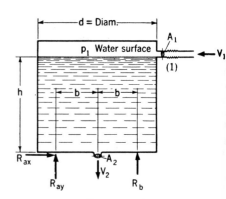

PROBLEM 6.15.

6.16. Liquid flows steadily out of the reentrant (Borda) nozzle in the wall of this tank. Neglecting friction, find the ratio of the jet area to the nozzle area a/A (contraction coefficient).

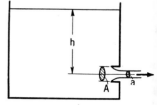

PROBLEM 6.16.

6.17. Water having a constant velocity V_1 strikes a vane moving with constant velocity U in the same direction. Neglecting friction and gravity, find R_x and R_y, the external forces on the vane, and the power output if

$V_1 = 40$ ft/sec $U = 30$ ft/sec
$A_1 = \pi/144$ sq ft $\beta = 20$ deg

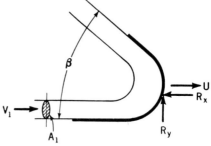

PROBLEM 6.17.

6.18. Water flows through the bend and discharges into the atmosphere at 2. Neglecting friction and gravity, find the supporting force and moment transmitted to the bend at the flange 1 if $Q = 10$ ft³/sec, $A_2 = 0.10$ sq ft, $A_1 = 0.25$ sq ft, $h = 5$ ft.

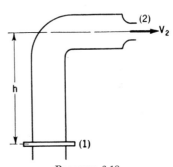

PROBLEM 6.18.

6.19. A piston at 2 is at rest at time $= 0$ and is accelerated toward the right by the pressure of the fluid in the cylinder. It is required that F be constant at all times. (*a*) Find ΔF at time $t = 1$ sec, assuming that friction and compressibility are negligible and that the x component of velocity is uniform over any area normal to the x direction, such as A. ΔF is to be expressed in terms of

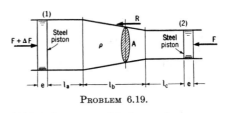

PROBLEM 6.19.

Fluid density, $\rho = 1.6$ slugs/ft³	$F = 100$ lb
Steel density, $\rho_s = 15$ slugs/ft³	$\dfrac{dV_2}{dt} = 10$ ft/sec²
Area of piston 1, $A_1 = 0.03$ sq ft	$l_a(0) = 2$ ft, $l_b = 1$ ft
Area of piston 2, $A_2 = 0.01$ sq ft	$l_c(0) = 2$ ft, $e = 1$ in.

(*b*) Find the external supporting force R needed to hold the cylinder stationary. (*c*) Compare the values for ΔF and R with those obtained for steady flow, assuming $V_2 = 10$ ft/sec.

6.20. Air flows steadily at a rate of 1.082 slugs per sec with an upward component in a pipe 4 in. in diameter tilted at an angle of 30 deg to the horizontal. At section 1, the pressure is 100 psia and the density is 0.0155 slug per cu ft. At section 2, 50 ft downstream, the pressure is 98 psia, and the density is 0.0152 slug per cu ft. Assuming the average density of the air between 1 and 2 to be the arithmetic mean of ρ_1 and ρ_2, find the friction force exerted by the air on the wall of the 50-ft length of pipe.

Chapter VII

By means of dimensional analysis simplify Probs. 7.1–7.5.

7.1. The period of a pendulum T is assumed to depend only on the mass m, the length l, the acceleration of gravity g, and the angle of swing θ.

7.2. The velocity of propagation V of surface waves on shallow liquid is assumed to depend only on the depth of the liquid h, the density ρ, and the acceleration of gravity g.

7.3. A mass m is mounted on a massless spring of spring constant k and subjected to a damping force proportional to the velocity. The damping constant is C. If the mass vibrates steadily under the action of a periodic force of amplitude F_0 and frequency f, the maximum displacement x_0 is assumed to depend only on m, k, C, f, and F_0.

7.4. The velocity of sound propagation C in a liquid is assumed to depend only on the density ρ, the viscosity μ, and the bulk compression modulus β [see Eq. (2.11)].

7.5. The thrust T of a propeller is assumed to depend only on the diameter D, the fluid density ρ, the viscosity μ, the revolutions per unit time n, and the velocity of advance relative to the distant fluid V.

7.6. A ship 340 ft long moves in fresh water at 60 F at 30 mph. Find the kinematic viscosity of a fluid suitable for use with a model 12 ft long, if dynamical similarity is to be attained.

7.7. (a) The height h to which a liquid will rise in a small-bore tube owing to surface forces (the capillary rise) is a function of the specific weight of the liquid γ, the radius of the tube r, and the surface tension of the liquid σ. By dimensional analysis, find an expression for h involving nondimensional variables only. (b) If the capillary rise for liquid A is 1 in. in a tube of radius 0.010 in., what will be the rise for a liquid B having the same surface tension but four times the density of A in a tube of radius 0.005 in.?

7.8. A test on a 12-in.-diameter model ship propeller indicates 50 per cent increase in the relative water speed behind the screw when the towing speed is 10 ft per sec and the rotational speed is 1,000 rpm. (a) Estimate the corresponding thrust on the model propeller shaft. (b) If the prototype propeller is to operate at 200 rpm at a forward speed of 25 ft per sec, what will be the thrust on the prototype shaft when operating at the same efficiency as the model? The fluid (water) has the same density for model and prototype.

Chapter VIII

8.1. Oil of kinematic viscosity $\nu = 4 \times 10^{-4}$ ft²/sec at room temperature flows through an inclined tube of ½ in. diameter. Find the angle α between the tube and the horizontal plane if the pressure inside the tube is constant along its length and the delivered quantity of oil $Q = 5$ ft³/hr. The flow is laminar.

8.2. Find the quantity Q, the mean velocity V, and the maximum velocity V_{max} of an oil of kinematic viscosity $\nu = 14 \times 10^{-3}$ ft²/sec at room temperature flowing through an inclined tube of 1 in. diameter when the lost head per unit of length $H_l/l = \frac{1}{2}$. The flow is laminar.

8.3. A positive-displacement pump forces oil at a constant rate $Q = 425$ in.³/min through a copper tube, as shown, and into a bearing. The pressure p_3 where the oil enters the bearing is required to be 10 psig. The oil properties are $\rho = 1.6$ slugs/ft³ and

$= 5.0 \times 10^{-4}$ ft²/sec. The velocity is constant across the cylinder diameter (section 1) and across the tube diameter at entrance (section 2). Effects of friction between 1 nd 2 are neglected. (a) Show that the flow in the tube is laminar. (b) Find the power utput of the pump. (c) Find the percentage error in power for each of the following ases: (1) The difference in levels $z_3 - z_2$ is neglected. (2) The correction for development of the laminar flow pattern between 2 and 3 is neglected.

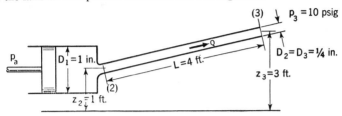

PROBLEM 8.3.

8.4. A steady laminar two-dimensional flow takes place between parallel fixed plates. (a) Assuming the velocity to be parallel to the plates, the pressure to be independent of y, and that

$\tau = \mu \, \partial u / \partial y$, show that

$$u = \frac{p_1 - p_2}{2\mu L} \left(\frac{h^2}{4} - y^2 \right)$$

(b) Show that the volume flow per unit depth is

$$Q = \frac{h^3(p_1 - p_2)}{12\mu L}$$

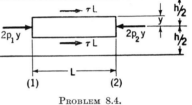

PROBLEM 8.4.

8.5. A horizontal crack 0.01 in. wide and 10 in. long extends completely through a wall that is 10 in. thick. Water at 70 F stands on one side of the wall; the other side s open to the atmosphere. If the water surface is 10 in. above the crack, estimate the leakage rate through the crack.

8.6. Find Reynolds number for water at 50 F flowing (a) in a capillary tube of $\frac{1}{4}$ in. diameter with a velocity of 4 in. per sec; (b) in a pipe of 8 in. diameter with a velocity of 3 ft per sec; (c) in a pipe of 5 ft diameter with a velocity of 6 ft per sec.

8.7. What is the velocity for each of the three cases of the preceding problem when the flow changes from turbulent to laminar?

8.8. In order to obtain the same friction factor for water of 60 F flowing through a certain pipe and for air at the same temperature and at atmospheric pressure flowing through the same pipe, what must be the ratio of the volume rates of discharge?

8.9. Water flows steadily through a smooth circular pipe lying horizontally. The discharge rate is 1.5 cu ft per sec; the pipe diameter is 6 in. Find the difference in pressure between two points on the pipe separated a distance of 400 ft if the water temperature is 60 F.

8.10. Repeat the preceding problem assuming that the pipe is tilted upward in the direction of flow at an angle of 10 deg with the horizontal.

8.11. A new steel pipe 4 in. in diameter and 100 ft in length is attached to a large reservoir. The pipe slopes downward at an angle of 15 deg to its free end, which is 50 ft below the water level in the reservoir. Neglecting all losses except those due to

pipe friction, find the rate of discharge. The water temperature is 50 F. A trial
and-error method must be used.

8.12. A fan is required for delivering 100 cu ft per sec of air at the upper end of
vertical smooth-walled duct 18 in. in diameter and 40 ft in length. Neglecting all
losses except those due to pipe friction in the duct and assuming the fan to be located
in a room in which the air is at atmospheric pressure, find the necessary power input to
the fan. The air temperature is 80 F. What error is made if variation of atmospheric
pressure with height is neglected?

8.13. Two pipe lines are connected to a large water reservoir and have free discharge at the outlet ends. One is 6 in. in diameter and 1,000 ft in length, with outlet
12.5 ft below the reservoir water level. The other is 8 in. in diameter and 2,000 ft in
length. The combined discharge rate is 2.00 cu ft per sec. Assuming that $f = 0.013$
for each pipe and neglecting entrance losses, find how far the end of the 8-in. pipe is
below the water level in the reservoir.

8.14. Solve the preceding problem if the 8-in. pipe is terminated by an open-gate
valve and contains three standard 90-deg elbows, while the 6-in. pipe terminates in an
open globe valve. The over-all discharge rate is assumed to be the same.

8.15. A smooth rectangular duct, 12 by 24 in. in cross section and 150 ft long, contains two 90-deg bends with a 16-in. inside radius. The free end of the duct is 15 ft
higher than the inlet end. Find the reading (inches of water) of the water-filled U-tube
attached as shown, if the discharge rate is 75 cu ft per sec of air at 85 F.

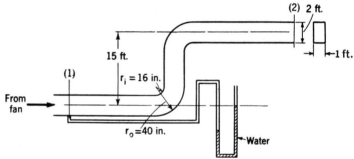

PROBLEM 8.15.

8.16. Water flows uniformly through
the rectangular open channel, as shown.
The channel is made of finished concrete,
for which the friction factor $f = 0.0217$.
Find angle of slope β.

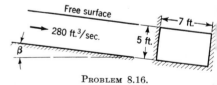

PROBLEM 8.16.

8.17. Two identical parallel pipes leave a reservoir at a distance H below the water
surface. Each pipe has length L, diameter D, and friction factor f. Two cross connections are located a distance αL apart. The
length αL of one pipe lying between the connections is closed, the flow being as shown in the
figure. Find the percentage decrease in discharge if $D = 6$ in., $f = 0.020$, $L = 2,000$ ft,
$\alpha = \frac{1}{4}$. Neglect all minor losses and losses In
branches.

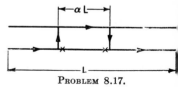

PROBLEM 8.17.

8.18. Water at 72 F is pumped rough cast-iron pipes to reservoirs A nd B. The discharge at the pump is cu ft per sec, while 0.8 cu ft per sec ws into B. Neglect friction loss in the take pipe CD and other minor losses.) Find the head imparted to the water the pump. (b) Find the head lost at lve X.

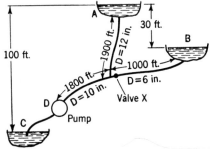

PROBLEM 8.18.

8.19. A straight 10-in. pipe 2 miles long runs between two reservoirs of surface evations 450 ft and 200 ft. A parallel 12-in. line 1 mile long is laid from the mid-int of the 10-in. line to the lower reservoir. Neglecting all minor losses and assuming friction factor of 0.02 in both pipes, find the increase in discharge rate caused by the ldition of the 12-in. pipe.

8.20. An 18-in. pipe divides into 8- and 6-in. branches, which rejoin. If the 6-in. ranch is 5,000 ft long, how long must be the 8-in. branch for the flow to divide equally hen 5 cu ft per sec flow in the 18-in. pipe? The 8-in. branch is cast iron, and the in. branch is smooth. The water temperature is 65 F.

8.21. The pressure p_2 at a distance L down-ream from a sudden enlargement is equal to p_1, e pressure at the enlargement. Assuming D_2 $\sqrt{2}D$ and a friction factor of 0.02, find L/D_2.

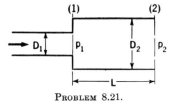

PROBLEM 8.21.

8.22. Ethanol at 65 F flows in this cast-iron pipe.

$$p_1 - p_2 = 3,500 \text{ lb/ft}^2$$
$$z_2 - z_1 = 30 \text{ ft}$$
$$L = 150 \text{ ft}$$
$$D = 3 \text{ in.}$$

nd Q.

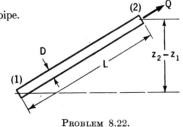

PROBLEM 8.22.

8.23. A gauge at 2 reads 78 lb per sq in. The measured torque on the pump shaft 32.8 ft-lb, and the speed is 1,625 rpm. The discharge pipe is smooth and contains vo 90-deg elbows. Neglecting loss in the short entrance pipe, find the pump efficiency.

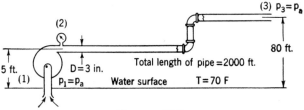

PROBLEM 8.23.

8.24. A pump that is capable of delivering any desired volume of water at 60 ps is connected by a horizontal 2-in. steel pipe 1,000 ft long to a machine requiring wat at 20 psig. What is the maximum volume that can be delivered at 65 F?

8.25. An oil having a kinematic viscosity of 60 Saybolt universal seconds and specific gravity of 0.86 flows through a 3-in. standard orifice in a 5-in. pipe. If the pre sure drop across the orifice is 40 lb per sq in., find the rate of discharge.

8.26. Two horizontal pipes of equal length carry air and water, respectively, i 30 F at velocities such that the Reynolds numbers and pressure drops for each are t same. Find the ratio of the mean air velocity to that of the water.

8.27. Water flows in turbulent fashion through a smooth pipe of diameter D ar a square pipe of area D^2. In which pipe will the pressure drop per unit length be great if the discharge rates are the same? Explain.

Chapter IX

9.1. Air leaves a reservoir in which the pressure and density are p_0 and ρ_0 and e pands isentropically through a convergent-divergent nozzle. The exit velocity V_3 1.70 times as great as the sound velocity in the reservoir. Find the ratio of the ex diameter to that at the throat d_3/d_t, p_3/p_0, and ρ_3/ρ_0.

9.2. Suppose that a transverse shock occurs in the nozzle of the preceding proble at a section 2 where $d_2/d_t = \sqrt{2}$. (a) Find V_1/C_0 and V_2/C_0, where V_1 and V_2 a the velocities immediately above and below the shock and C_0 is the sound velocity the reservoir. (b) Find V_3/V_2, ρ_3/ρ_0, and p_3/p_0, where subscript 3 refers to the nozz exit.

9.3. Derive Eq. (9.21).

9.4. Air leaves a reservoir in which the pressure and density are p_0 and ρ_0 ar expands isothermally through a convergent-divergent nozzle. The exit velocity $= 1.70\sqrt{p_0/\rho_0}$. (a) Find p_t/p_0, the ratio of the throat pressure to that in the reservo (b) Find d_3/d_t, the ratio of exit to throat diameter. (c) Find d_s/d_t, where d_s is the c ameter where the local sound velocity occurs.

 9.5. (a) If the friction factor f is assumed to be constant in an isothermal flow gas through a horizontal tube, show that

$$\frac{fl}{d} = \frac{2}{G}\left[\frac{p_1^2}{2GgRT_1}\left(1 - \frac{p_2^2}{p_1^2}\right) - ln\frac{p_1}{p_2}\right]$$

where d and l are the diameter and length of the tube, G is the mass rate of flow p unit area, and subscripts 1 and 2 refer to the upstream and downstream ends of t tube, respectively. (b) If the critical velocity is reached in the tube, show that t above expression reduces to

$$\frac{fl}{d} = \frac{p_1^2}{p_2^2} - 1 + \frac{2\sqrt{gRT_1}}{p_1}\frac{p_1}{p_2}ln\frac{p_2}{p_1}$$

9.6. (a) For an isothermal flow of air through a horizontal smooth pipe 0.1 ft in d ameter, $T_1 = 540$ F abs, $p_1 = 30$ lb/in.^{2}, and $p_2/p_1 = 0.5$. The critical velocity is reach in this flow. Assuming the relation between friction factor and Reynolds number be the same as for incompressible flow, find the length of the pipe. (b) Using t arithmetic mean of the initial and final velocities, estimate the time required for sound wave to be propagated from the downstream to the upstream end of the pip and vice versa.

9.7. What would be the maximum length of the pipe of the preceding problem if the mass flow per unit area were 1.5 times larger and p_1 and T_1 were unchanged?

9.8. For an isothermal flow of air through a horizontal smooth pipe 0.1 ft in diameter, $T_1 = 700$ F abs, $p_1 = 1.0$ lb/in.²abs, and $p_2/p_1 = 1.1$. Assuming the critical velocity to be reached in this pipe and that subcritical speeds do not occur in it, find the length of the pipe.

Chapter X

10.1. Find the terminal velocity of a steel sphere of specific weight $\gamma_s = 0.28$ lb/in.³ and 0.0175 in. diameter, falling freely in oil of specific weight $\gamma_o = 0.032$ lb/in.³ and viscosity $\mu = 7.0 \times 10^{-6}$ lb-sec/in.²

10.2. A solid spherical particle of radius a and density ρ_s is whirled in a horizontal circular path of radius r with a tangential velocity V_t by means of an inwardly spiraling flow of air of density ρ and viscosity μ. Assuming that Stokes's law applies, find the inward radial component of air velocity V_r. Assume that $\rho_s = 6.0$ slugs/ft³, $a = 8.0 \times 10^{-6}$ ft, $V_t = 150$ ft/sec, $\mu = 3.6 \times 10^{-7}$ lb-sec/ft², $r = \frac{3}{4}$ ft.

10.3. A disk 6 in. in diameter is set normal to the velocity of an air stream. The measured drag of the plate is 0.89 lb when the air velocity is 60 ft per sec and the air temperature is 80 F. Find the drag of a disk 15 in. in diameter similarly arranged in a flow of water having a velocity of 15 ft per sec and a temperature of 50 F.

10.4. Find the steady-state angular velocity ω of the four-cup anemometer. Consider only the position shown, that is, arm 1-2 normal to V_0 and arm 3-4 parallel to V_0. Neglect any torque exerted by cups 3 and 4. $V_0 = 60$ ft/sec, $\rho = 2.4 \times 10^{-3}$ slug/ft³.

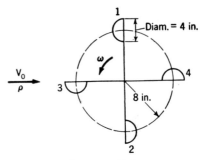

PROBLEM 10.4.

10.5. A rising spherical weather balloon 6 ft in diameter is filled with hydrogen of specific weight 0.00416 lb per cu ft. The specific weight of the surrounding air at that level is 0.0600 lb per cu ft. If the combined weight of the rubber envelope plus instruments is 6 lb, find the rising velocity V. (Temperature = 500 F abs.)

10.6. A sphere 8 in. in diameter is found to have a drag of 1.80 lb in air at 80 F having a relative velocity of 150 ft per sec. (a) Find the velocity at which the drag of a 2-ft sphere immersed in water at 50 F can be determined from the above data. (b) What is the drag of the 2-ft sphere for the velocity found in a?

10.7. If the vertical component of the landing velocity of a parachute is equal to that acquired during a free fall of 6 ft, find the diameter of the open parachute (hollow hemisphere), assuming the total weight to be 250 lb and an air density of 2.4×10^{-3} slug per cu ft.

10.8. A rectangular billboard 10 ft high by 50 ft long is erected on an open scaffold some distance above the earth's surface. A 100-mph gale strikes the board normally. If the air density is 2.4×10^{-3} slug per cu ft, find the total force due to wind pressure.

10.9. A bracing wire $1/20$ in. in diameter is found to vibrate at 930 cps when the speed of the airplane is 60 mph. If the natural frequency of the strut is 500 cps, at what speed is the amplitude of vibration likely to become dangerously large?

10.10. A flat plate 2 ft long is set parallel to a flow of air at a temperature of 70 F. The velocity of the air far from the plate is 40 ft per sec. (*a*) Find the maximum thickness of the boundary layer. (*b*) Find the over-all drag coefficient. (*c*) Find the total drag per unit width of the plate if the air covers both sides.

10.11. Repeat the preceding problem if the plate is immersed in water at 60 F, assuming the Reynolds number to be unchanged.

10.12. A flat plate 10 ft long is immersed in water at 60 F, flowing parallel to the plate with a velocity of 20 ft per sec. Neglect the laminar part of the boundary layer. (*a*) Find the approximate boundary-layer thickness at $x = 5$ ft and $x = 10$ ft, where x is measured from the leading edge. (*b*) Find the over-all drag coefficient. (*c*) Find the total drag per unit width of the plate if the water covers both sides.

10.13. A flat plate 4 ft long is immersed in air at 70 F flowing parallel to the plate at a speed of 50 ft per sec. Assume the critical Reynolds number is 5×10^5. (*a*) At what distance from the leading edge does transition occur? (*b*) Plot the local drag coefficient $2\tau_0/\rho V^2$ as a function of Vx/ν. (*c*) Find the total drag per unit width of the plate.

10.14. Find the ratio of the friction drags of the front and rear halves of a plate of total length l if the boundary layer is completely turbulent and follows the one-seventh-power law of velocity distribution.

10.15. A ship 160 ft long requires 200 hp to overcome the resistance to motion at 20 ft per sec. Find the friction and residual drags if the wetted area is 4,000 sq ft. Assume $\rho = 1.94$ slugs/ft^3 and $\nu = 1.2 \times 10^{-5}$ ft^2/sec.

10.16. A model vessel having a submerged surface area of 8.0 sq ft and length 7.0 ft has a total drag of 0.95 lb when towed at a velocity of 5.14 ft per sec. Assume the friction drag of the submerged part of the hull to follow the same law as a flat plate of the same length, set parallel to the velocity, and covered with a completely turbulent boundary layer. The density and kinematic viscosity of the water are the same as in the preceding problem. (*a*) Find the friction drag of the model hull. (*b*) Find the total drag of a geometrically similar hull 25 times as long as the model when moving at corresponding speed.

Chapter XI

11.1. Given the stream function $\psi = Vy$. (*a*) Plot the streamlines. (*b*) Find the x and y components of velocity at any point. (*c*) Find the quantity flowing between the streamlines $y = 1$ and $y = 2$.

11.2. Find the stream function for a parallel flow of uniform velocity V making an angle β with the x axis.

11.3. Given the stream function $\psi = Axy (A > 0)$. (*a*) Sketch several streamlines. (*b*) Find the x and y velocity components at 0, 0; 1, 1; ∞, 0; 4, 1. (*c*) Find the quantity crossing any line joining points 0, 0 and 1, 1; points 1, 3 and 7, 5.

11.4. Given the stream function $\psi = 3x^2y - y^3$. Express this in polar coordinates, recalling that $\sin 3\theta = 3 \sin \theta \cos^2 \theta - \sin^3 \theta$. Sketch the streamlines, and determine the magnitude of the velocity at any point.

11.5. A fluid flows along a flat surface parallel to the x direction. The velocity u varies linearly with y, the distance from the wall, that is, $u = ky$. (a) Find the stream function for this flow. (b) Determine whether or not the flow is rotational.

11.6. The flow in a laminar boundary layer on a flat plate is given approximately by the stream function

$$\psi = V_0\left[y + \frac{(\delta - y)^2}{3\delta^2}\right] \text{ for } 0 \leqslant y \leqslant \delta$$

where V_0 is the velocity outside the boundary layer, δ is the boundary-layer thickness, and y is the coordinate normal to the plate. Variation of δ with x is neglected. (a) Sketch the streamlines. (b) Determine the velocity, rotation (vorticity), and shearing stress at any point if the viscosity is μ.

11.7. Show that in polar coordinates the rotation, or vorticity, is given by the expression

$$\frac{\partial V_\theta}{\partial r} + \frac{V_\theta}{r} - \frac{1}{r}\frac{\partial V_r}{\partial \theta}$$

11.8. Given: $V_r = \dfrac{A}{r}$, $V_\theta = \dfrac{A}{r}$ $(A > 0)$. Find ψ, and sketch a few streamlines.

11.9. In Prob. 11.1 to 11.4, find the velocity potential, and sketch lines of constant ϕ.

11.10. Given the velocity potential $\phi = A\theta$ $(A > 0)$. (a) Sketch lines of $\phi = $ constant. (b) Find the velocity components at any point (r,θ). (c) Find ψ, and sketch a few streamlines.

11.11. Given the stream function $\psi = (\frac{2}{3})r^{\frac{3}{2}} \sin (\frac{3}{2})\theta$. ($a$) Plot the streamline $\psi = 0$. (b) Find the velocity at $r = 2$, $\theta = \pi/3$ and $r = 3$, $\theta = \pi/6$. (c) Find the velocity potential ϕ.

11.12. A two-dimensional flow of ideal incompressible fluid is composed of a parallel flow of velocity V_0, a source of strength Q, and sink of strength $-Q$, separated by a distance b in the direction of the parallel flow, the source being upstream from the sink. (a) Find the resultant stream function and velocity potential. (b) Find the distance from the upstream stagnation point to the source.

11.13. Find the stagnation points on a cylinder of 1-ft radius if the velocity in the undisturbed stream $V_0 = 15$ ft/sec and circulation $\Gamma = -90$ ft²/sec.

11.14. (a) In order to have a lift force of 5 lb per ft of length on the cylinder of the preceding problem, how large must be the circulation if $V_0 = 15$ ft/sec and the density is 2.4×10^{-3} slug per cu ft? (b) Find the points of maximum and minimum pressure on the cylinder. (c) Plot the pressure distribution on the cylinder.

11.15. A cylinder of radius $a = 0.5$ ft is submerged in a flow of ideal fluid having a velocity $V_0 = 60$ ft/sec. If $2(p - p_0)/\rho V_0^2 = -8$ at the top of the cylinder, find the velocity at this point and the circulation.

11.16. A long cylinder of radius a is immersed in air having velocity V_0 and is rotated clockwise with an angular speed ω such that the observed flow pattern resembles the theoretical pattern in which the stagnation points coincide. (a) Find the theoretical lift coefficient. (b) Find ω, assuming that the peripheral speed of the cylinder equals the maximum theoretical velocity of the fluid at the surface of the cylinder.

11.17. In a two-dimensional flow of ideal fluid past a cylinder of radius a the maximum velocity is 6 times that of the undisturbed stream V_0. (a) Show that the maximum velocity occurs on the cylinder. (b) Find the circulation and the distance of the stagnation point from the center of the cylinder.

11.18. A ship having a water-drag coefficient of 3.55×10^{-3} based on the wetted area of 1,000 sq ft has (in place of sails) two identical 20-ft-high cylinders, or rotors, each of which spins about a vertical axis. The ship moves on a fresh-water lake at a constant speed V_s, which is parallel to the resultant force of the wind on the rotors. The absolute wind velocity is V. Assuming that $V_s = V/2$ and that the lift and drag coefficients based on the projected rotor area are 10 and 5, respectively, find the radius a of the rotors. Assume the density of air to be 2.38×10^{-3} slug/ft^3.

11.19. Let ϕ_c and ϕ_i be the velocity potentials for compressible and incompressible flow, respectively, about a given thin profile in a given altitude; ϕ_c satisfies Eq. (11.50), and ϕ_i satisfies Eq. (11.51). (a) Show that Eqs. (11.50) and (11.51) are satisfied if $\phi_i = k\phi_c$, where k is an arbitrary constant. (b) Using the condition that the slope of a streamline at the profile surface must be the same in both compressible and incompressible flow, show that k must equal $U_i\sqrt{1 - M^2}/U_c$, where U_i and U_c are the velocities of the distant fluid. (c) Verify Eq. (11.58).

11.20. An airfoil moves with a speed of 550 ft per sec at a given angle of attack, at sea level and at a 10,000-ft altitude. Taking the gas constant for air as 53.3 ft per deg F and assuming a sea-level temperature of 50 F and a lapse rate of $\frac{1}{300}$ F per ft, estimate the ratio of the lift coefficients and the ratio of the lifts.

11.21. A two-dimensional parallel flow of air is deflected by a flat plate set at an angle of 20 deg to the undisturbed flow. The stagnation temperature and pressure of the air are 60 F and 14.7 psia. The Mach number of the undisturbed flow is 2.02. (a) Find the pressure of the undisturbed flow. (b) Find the pressure on the high-pressure side of the plate and the angle of the shock wave set up at the leading edge of the plate. (c) By plotting an epicycloid, as in Fig. 11.45, find graphically the velocity on the low-pressure side of the plate. (d) Find the normal force per unit area of the plate.

11.22. From Eqs. (11.2) show that

$$\frac{\partial v}{\partial x} - \frac{\partial u}{\partial y} = -\frac{(dp/\rho) + dV^2/2}{V \sin \beta \, ds} = -\frac{(dp/\rho) + dV^2/2}{dQ}$$

where ds and β are as shown. Explain how this result proves the rotation to be independent of the choice of axes.

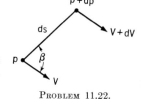

PROBLEM 11.22.

11.23. (a) Using the result of Art. 11.3 that $(D/dt)[(\partial v/\partial x) - (\partial u/\partial y)] = 0$, show that, although $\psi_1 = k_1 y^3/3$ and $\psi_2 = k_2 x^2/2$ both satisfy Eqs. (11.2), their sum does not.

Chapter XII

12.1. A thrust bearing supports a total thrust of 3,000 lb. There are four slippers, each having $l = b = 3.00$ in. The point of support of each slipper is at a distance of 6 in. from the axis of the shaft and 1.83 in. from the leading edge. The shaft turns at 750 rpm, and the oil viscosity is 6×10^{-6} lb-sec per sq in. Assuming that the flow under each slipper is the same as that for a two-dimensional slipper bearing with sliding velocity equal to that under the point of support, find the angle of tilt of the slipper and the minimum film thickness.

12.2. The fixed shoe of a slider bearing is 2 in. long (in the direction of motion) and 4 in. wide and is fixed at an inclination of 4 min. The oil to be used has a viscosity of 40 centipoises at the operating temperature. The speed of the moving slider is 30 ft per sec. What load can the bearing carry if the minimum film thickness is not to be less than 0.002 in. for safe operation?

12.3. Calculate the friction coefficient and total power requirements for the two bearings of a grinder, assuming the shaft and bearings to be practically concentric. Length of each bearing is 5.00 in., shaft diameter is 2.50 in., clearance ratio is 1 part per thousand, shaft speed is 1,500 rpm, total load on both bearings is 1,100 lb, oil viscosity is 5.84×10^{-4} lb-sec per sq ft.

12.4. The load capacity for a perfectly lubricated journal bearing can be defined as the load at which the minimum film thickness is half the radial clearance between shaft and bearing. The corresponding value of the Sommerfeld variable is 0.034. What is the load capacity of each of the bearings of the preceding problem if the effect of side leakage is neglected?

12.5. A full journal bearing 6.4 in. long, 2 in. in diameter, and having 0.0018 in. diametral clearance runs at 800 rpm. If the minimum film thickness for safe operation is not to be less than 0.0005 in., what oil viscosity at the operating temperature is required to carry a load of 3,000 lb? What is the power consumption? Neglect the effect of side leakage.

12.6. If account is taken of side leakage in the bearing of the preceding problem, what oil viscosity will be required?

12.7. The following are given for a journal bearing: shaft diameter $D = 1.00$ in., bearing length $L = 2.00$ in., clearance ratio $D/C = 1,000$, speed $n = 50$ rps, room temperature $T_0 = 80$ F, specific weight of the oil $\gamma = 0.0314$ lb/in.^{3}, specific heat of the oil $c = 193$ Btu-in./lb sec^2 F, oil viscosity $\mu = 0.0250/T$ lb-sec/in.^{2}, where T is oil temperature in degrees Fahrenheit. Assuming that Petroff's equation applies and neglecting any heat transfer from the bearing to the surroundings, determine the rate of oil flow needed to limit the oil temperature to 150 F. The oil enters the bearing at room temperature.

12.8. The friction coefficient for a journal bearing is given by

$$\frac{D}{C}f = 15\left(\frac{D}{C}\right)^2 \frac{\mu n}{P} + 5.0$$

provided that $(D/C)^2(\mu n/P)$ is not less than 0.006. If $(D/C)^2(\mu n/P)$ is less than 0.006, the bearing seizes. The viscosity of the oil is $\mu = 3.60/T^2$ lb-sec/ft^2, where T is in degrees Fahrenheit. The rate of heat transfer from the bearing is $\alpha \pi D L(T - T_0)$ Btu per sec, where T and T_0 are the temperatures of the oil and the surroundings, respectively. The following are known: $n = 15$ rps, $D = 0.17$ ft, $L = 0.12$ ft, $D/C = 1,000$, $T_0 = 80$ F, $\alpha = 1.50 \times 10^{-3}$ Btu/sec ft^2 F. There is no appreciable flow of oil through the bearing. Assuming the maximum allowable oil temperature to be 220 F, find the maximum allowable value of P, the load per unit projected bearing area.

12.9. The friction coefficient for a journal bearing is the same as for the preceding problem; the limits on $(D/C)^2(\mu n/P)$ are also the same. The following are known: $P = 800$ lb/in.^{2}, $n = 15$ rps, $D = 0.17$ ft, $L = 0.12$ ft, $D/C = 1,000$, $\alpha = 1.60 \times 10^{-3}$ Btu/sec ft^2 F, $T_0 = 70$ F, oil density $\rho = 1.73$ slugs/ft^3, specific heat of oil $c = 16.1$ Btu/slug F, rate of oil flow through bearing $Q = 4.0 \times 10^{-5}$ ft^3/sec. Assuming that the maximum oil temperature cannot safely exceed 180 F, find the maximum and minimum allowable values of viscosity.

12.10. A 3-in. shaft rotating at 2,000 rpm carries an assembly that is free to rotate about it and is driven in the same direction by a 2.5-to-1 gear reduction. The assembly carries an eccentric weight that applies a centrifugal load equivalent to 5,000 lb at this speed. The oil has a viscosity of 3 centipoises at the operating temperature. How long should each of the two shaft bearings be made if the safe minimum film thickness is 0.0002 in.? Follow the usual design practice of taking the clearance ratio as 1 part in a thousand. Neglect side leakage.

Chapter XIV

Mechanical efficiency $\eta_m = 1.00$ in all problems for this chapter.

14.1. A Pelton turbine has a diameter of 78 in., a speed of 300 rpm, and a bucket angle $\beta = 165$ deg (see Fig. 14.2, page 343). The exit diameter of the nozzle is 8 in., the base diameter is 12 in., and C_v and C_c are 0.97 and 0.80, respectively. (See pages 154 and 156 for definitions of C_v and C_c.) (a) Find the maximum power output, neglecting loss at the buckets. (b) Find the efficiency of the turbine (wheel and nozzle combined).

14.2. The velocity diagrams for the runner of a Francis turbine are shown. The discharge is 159 cu ft per sec, the head is 350 ft of water, the speed is 410 rpm, $r_1 = 2.0$ ft, $\alpha_1 = 18$ deg, $V_1 = 117$ ft/sec, and the tangential component of the absolute velocity at the runner exit V_{t_2} is zero ($\alpha_2 = 90$ deg). Find β_1, the torque, the output power, and efficiency.

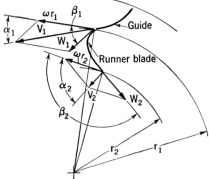

PROBLEM 14.2.

14.3. At 240 rpm the pressure at the entrance to a hydraulic-turbine runner is 27.5 psia, while that at exit is 4 psia. Referred to the figure of Prob. 14.2, the other data are

$$\alpha_2 = 90 \text{ deg} \qquad r_1 = 3.0 \text{ ft} \qquad W_1 = 55 \text{ ft/sec}$$
$$\beta_2 = 160 \text{ deg} \qquad r_2 = 2.5 \text{ ft} \qquad z_1 = z_2$$

Compute the loss in the runner $H_{l_{1,2}}$.

14.4. Referred to the figure of Prob. 14.2, the data for a Francis turbine are

$$Q = 113 \text{ ft}^3/\text{sec} \qquad \omega = 4.50 \text{ radians/sec}$$
$$r_1 = 4.67 \text{ ft} \qquad \text{Width of runner} = b = 0.97 \text{ ft}$$
$$r_2 = 4.00 \text{ ft} \qquad \text{Loss in runner} = H_{l_{1,2}} = \frac{0.20W_2^2}{2g} \text{ ft}$$
$$\alpha_1 = 12 \text{ deg}$$
$$p_2 = 5 \text{ psia}$$
$$V_{t_2} = 0$$

Find the pressure p_1 at the runner entrance, and $H_{l_{1,2}}$.

14.5. A Pelton water wheel is 10 ft in diameter and operates at 250 rpm. (a) When operating at the theoretical condition for maximum efficiency, what head of water will be required at the inlet to the nozzle if the outlet diameter of the nozzle is 6 in., $C_v = 0.98$, and $C_c = 0.85$? (b) If the specific speed of this turbine is 2.7, what is its over-all efficiency?

14.6. A Francis turbine operates under the following conditions (see the figure of Prob. 14.2):

$$W_1 = 5 \text{ ft/sec}$$
$$W_2 = 20.3 \text{ ft/sec}$$
$$\omega = 5 \text{ radians/sec}$$
$$r_2 = 4 \text{ ft}$$
$$r_1 = 5 \text{ ft}$$
$$\alpha_2 = 90 \text{ deg}$$
$$\text{Width of runner} = 1 \text{ ft}$$

(a) Find the flow through the turbine. (b) Find the torque.

14.7. A turbine develops 640 hp at an efficiency of 86 per cent under head of 40 ft when fitted with a cylindrical draft tube 5.0 ft in diameter. Determine the increase in power and efficiency if a conical draft tube 7.5 ft in exit diameter is substituted for the cylindrical one. Assume the discharge, head, and speed to remain the same and that the losses in both draft tubes are the same. Assume that $V_t = 0$ for each tube.

14.8. A vertical cone-shaped draft tube 23 ft long is 6 ft in diameter at the top (section 1) and 8.4 ft in diameter at the bottom (section 2). The lower end of the tube is 5 ft below the tail-water level. The discharge rate is 810 cu ft per sec. Assume the loss in the tube to be $H_{l_{1,2}} = 0.6(V_{n_2}^2/2g)$ where V_{n_2} is the axial velocity component at the exit. (a) If the circulation in the draft tube is zero, find the gauge pressure at the wall at 1. (b) If there is in the draft tube a free vortex with a core of constant radius r_c and a constant circulation Γ, show that the kinetic energy resulting from the tangential velocity components that crosses section 2 per unit time is

$$\rho Q \frac{\Gamma^2}{4\pi^2 r_2^2}\left(\frac{1}{4} + \ln\frac{r_2}{r_c}\right)$$

(c) Find the gauge pressure at the wall at 1 if $\Gamma = 200$ ft²/sec and $r_c = 0.50$ ft, assuming that all the kinetic energy at 2 is dissipated. Use Eq. (5.9).

14.9. A Kaplan turbine has a casing diameter of 16 ft, a hub diameter of 6 ft, a speed of 120 rpm, and a discharge of 7,000 cu ft per sec. The circulation just upstream from the runner is 240π sq ft per sec and is zero in the draft tube. (a) Assuming shockless entry of the water into the runner, find the entrance and exit blade angles at a 5-ft radius. (b) Find the power output.

14.10. What type of turbine will be required in order to develop 6,500 hp at 530 rpm under a head of 650 ft? If only 850 hp is to be developed, what type of turbine should be used?

14.11. A model of a Francis turbine one-fifth of full size develops 4.1 hp at a speed of 360 rpm under a head of 5.9 ft. Find the speed and power of the full-size turbine when operating under a head of 19 ft. Assume that both model and full-size turbine are operating at maximum efficiency.

14.12. In the development of the power of a certain river, it is found that the mean annual discharge is 6,000 cu ft per sec and the mean head is 40 ft. What type of turbine should be selected if it is to run at 180 rpm, use half of the water available, and have an efficiency of 85 per cent?

14.13. (a) Assuming that the maximum relative velocity on the blades of the turbine of Prob. 14.9. is 1.2 times as great as the relative velocity at the runner entrance, determine whether cavitation will appear first at the root or tip of the blades. (b) Neglecting the loss in the guide vanes and runner blades, assuming that the hydraulic efficiency η/η_m is 94 per cent, and taking atmospheric pressure as 14.7 psia and the vapor pressure as zero, find the maximum allowable height of the turbine runner above the tail-water level.

Chapter XV

Mechanical efficiency $\eta_m = 1.00$ in all problems for this chapter.

15.1. The following are known for a centrifugal water pump (see figure of Prob. 6.9):

$$r_1 = 2 \text{ in.} \qquad r_2 = 6 \text{ in.}$$
$$b_1 = 0.75 \text{ in.} \qquad b_2 = 0.50 \text{ in.}$$
$$\beta_1 = 120 \text{ deg} \qquad \beta_2 = 150 \text{ deg}$$
$$N = 1,800 \text{ rpm}$$

The gauge pressure is 45 lb per sq in. at a point on the discharge pipe which is 6.0 ft above the water level in the reservoir from which the pump draws water. The diameter of the discharge pipe is 6.0 in. Neglect losses in the entrance pipe, assume shockless entry of water onto the blades at 1, and take $V_{t_1} = 0$. (a) Draw the entrance and exit velocity diagrams. (b) Determine the discharge rate. (c) Find the shaft horsepower. (d) What is the efficiency?

15.2. A centrifugal pump operates at 150 radians per sec and requires 294 hp. Determine the flow through the pump if the absolute velocity of the water at the entrance has no tangential component and

$$r_2 = 8 \text{ in.}$$
$$b_2 = 1 \text{ in.}$$
$$\rho = 1.94 \text{ slugs/ft}^3$$
$$\beta_2 = 135 \text{ deg}$$

(See figure of Prob. 6.9)

15.3. A 10-bladed axial-flow fan with guide vanes, hub, and housing draws in air from a room in which the air is at rest (see Fig. 15.6). The casing radius is 1.0 ft, the hub radius is 0.5 ft, the speed is 2860 rpm, $p_3 - p_1 = 14$ lb/ft^2, and the air density is 2.38×10^{-3} slug per cu ft. At a radius $r = \frac{5}{6}$ ft the absolute tangential velocity of the air at 2, $V_{t_2} = 26.3$ ft/sec, and the angle between the relative air velocity W_1 and ωr is 15 deg. (a) Find the discharge rate. (b) Find the tangential force per unit length on one blade at $r = \frac{5}{6}$ ft. (c) Find the total torque exerted on the fan wheel. (d) What is the efficiency of the fan?

15.4. For the fan of the preceding problem, compute that part of the kinetic energy passing section 2 per second which results from the tangential velocity V_{t_2}. Assume, as usual, that rV_t is independent of r. Note that, if the guide vanes are removed, all this kinetic energy will be wasted. Show then that, if friction in the guides is neglected,

$$\eta_{NG} = \eta_G - \frac{V_{t_2,0}}{\omega r_o} \frac{ln(r_o/r_i)}{1 - (r_i/r_o)^2}$$

where η_{NG} is the efficiency without guides, η_G is the efficiency with guides for the same input power and discharge, $V_{t_2,0}$ is the tangential velocity at 2 at the casing, and ω is the angular velocity.

15.5. A certain water pump tested at 2,000 rpm discharges 6.0 cu ft per sec against a head of 340 ft. At this capacity, the efficiency is 88 per cent. If a geometrically similar pump of twice the size runs at 1,500 rpm, find its discharge, head, and power for the same efficiency.

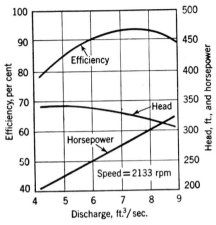

15.6. The curves shown refer to a centrifugal pump A discharging water. A geometrically similar pump B having a diameter 50 per cent greater than that of pump A and discharging oil of specific gravity 0.84 operates at 1,750 rpm. Neglecting the effect of friction, find the head developed and the necessary horsepower input for pump B at its maximum efficiency.

PROBLEM 15.6.

15.7. The following test data apply to a centrifugal water pump having impeller diameter $D = 0.875$ ft and running at $n = 24.2$ rps.

Discharge, Ft³/sec	Head, Ft of water	Efficiency, %
2.23	70	72
2.67	67	77
3.12	64	84
3.57	60	88
4.02	55	86
4.46	44	78

Geometrically similar pumps having impeller diameters of 0.750 and 0.667 ft are available. Either of these can run at 29.2, 24.2, or 19.2 rps. (a) Select from among these the most suitable combination for a pump that is to produce a head of 51 ft of water at a discharge rate of 1.90 cu ft per sec. (b) Compute the power input required for the pump chosen in part a.

15.8. The following are given for an axial-flow fan: Discharge rate = 20 ft³/sec, pressure rise = 5.0 lb/ft², speed = 1,200 rpm, casing radius = 0.60 ft. Air pressure and temperature are 14.7 psia and 70 F. The blades are to have NACA 4412 sections. Assuming that blades and guide vanes have the same value of ϵ, the drag-lift ratio, determine a suitable hub radius, number of stages, number of blades, C_L, t, α, and $\alpha + \beta$ at hub and tip. (These symbols are defined in Art. 15.4.)

15.9. Derive Eq. (15.41).

15.10. Referring to the notation of Fig. 15.1, assume that a centrifugal compressor has blades which are radial at exit 3. Assume further that the flow is isentropic and the fluid a perfect gas. Using the results of Art. 15.5, plot p_3/p_1 as a function of m/m^* for several constant values of $\omega r_3/C_3$. Consider the following ranges of the variables:

$$1.4 \leqslant \frac{p_3}{p_1} \leqslant 2.0 \qquad 0.7 \leqslant \frac{\omega r_3}{C_3} \leqslant 0.9$$

Take $A_3/A_1 = \sqrt{3}$ and $k = 1.4$. Compare your plot with Fig. 15.13.

Chapter XVI

16.1. A 6-ft-diameter ship propeller develops a thrust of 4,000 lb in fresh water when the velocity of the ship is 25 mph (a) What is the ideal efficiency? (b) What is the absolute velocity of the slipstream at some distance from the propeller?

16.2. A propeller of the series shown in Fig. 16.6 is to absorb 1,000 hp at 1,200 rpm and a speed of 225 mph at sea level. (a) Determine the blade angle at the ¾-radius point, the efficiency, and the diameter. (b) Find the thrust and ideal efficiency.

16.3. A three-bladed propeller 18 ft in diameter absorbs 3,000 hp at 800 rpm when moving at 400 mph at a 25,000-ft altitude. The efficiency is 0.81. (a) Find the thrust F_n and the torque T. (b) If, at the ¾-radius point, $dF_n/dr = 130$ lb/ft and $dF_t/dr = 145$ lb/ft, find dL/dr and dD/dr at this point. Neglect any additional velocity caused by contraction of the stream. (c) Assuming a lapse rate $\lambda = \frac{1}{300}$ F/ft, ground-level pressure and temperature of 14.7 psia and 60 F, and a lift coefficient of 0.35, find the blade width (chord) at the ¾-radius point. What is the drag coefficient of this blade element?

16.4. A model propeller 3 ft in diameter is tested in a wind tunnel having an airstream speed of 300 ft per sec. The pressure and temperature of the air are 14.7 psia and 60 F. At a rotational speed of 40.5 rps, this propeller absorbs 31.8 hp and produces a thrust of 47.0 lb. (a) What is the efficiency of the propeller? (b) A geometrically similar propeller 12 ft in diameter moves at 400 ft per sec relative to the undisturbed air. At what rotational speed can the power and thrust of this propeller be computed from the above model data if friction and compressibility are neglected? (c) Find the power and thrust of the 12-ft propeller if it operates at a 25,000-ft altitude. Assume ground-level conditions as above and a lapse rate of $\frac{1}{300}$ F per ft.

16.5. Assuming steady flow with respect to a ram jet traveling at constant velocity through the atmosphere, find, by use of the momentum theorem, the force that must be exerted on the ram jet to enable it to pick up air at a constant mass rate m. What work is done on the ram jet per unit time by this force?

16.6. The velocities of liquid propellant and gaseous combustion products relative to a steadily moving rocket are shown in the figure. To a good approximation, W_3^2 can be neglected, and the heating value of the propellant e_p can be taken equal to h_3, the enthalpy per unit mass of propellant entering the combustion chamber at 3. Show by applying the steady-flow energy equation that

PROBLEM 16.6.

$$\frac{W_2^2}{2} = e_p - h_2 = \eta_0 e_p$$

where h_2 is the enthalpy per unit mass of (burned) propellant at 2 and η_0 is defined by the equation

$$\eta_0 = \frac{e_p - h_2}{e_p}$$

16.7. The velocities and mass rates of flow of air, gas, and liquid fuel relative to a steadily moving jet-propulsion unit are shown in the figure. To a good approximation, W_3^2 can be neglected, and $e_f m_f = h_1 m_a + h_3 m_f$ where h_1 and h_3 are enthalpy per unit mass at 1 and 3, respectively. (a) Show by applying the steady-flow energy equation that

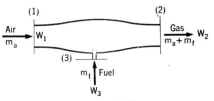

PROBLEM 16.7.

$$\frac{W_2^2}{2} = \frac{W_1^2}{2}\frac{m_a}{m_a + m_f} + e_f\frac{m_f}{m_a + m_f} - h_2 = \frac{W_1^2}{2}\frac{m_a}{m_a + m_f} + \eta_0 e_f\frac{m_f}{m_a + m_f}$$

where η_0 is defined by the equation

$$\eta_0 = \frac{e_f m_f - h_2(m_a + m_f)}{e_f m_f}$$

(b) Show that this definition of η_0 is identical with that given in the preceding problem. (Note that $e_f m_f = e_p m_p$ for a given fuel.)

16.8. (a) If the efficiency η of a jet-propulsion unit is defined as the ratio of the useful power output to the energy per unit time supplied by the fuel, show (with the aid of the results of the preceding problem) that

$$\eta = 2\eta_0\frac{(1 + \alpha)x - 1}{(1 + \alpha)x^2 - 1 + \alpha\eta_0}$$

where $x = W_2/W_1$ and $\alpha = m_f/m_a$. (b) Noting that to a good approximation α can be neglected in comparison with unity, plot η/η_0 as a function of x.

16.9. Assuming the maximum velocity of a V-2 rocket to be 5,130 ft per sec and neglecting air resistance and any variation in g, find the height to which the rocket will rise above the point where the maximum velocity is attained.

16.10. (a) Assuming that the initial and final weights of a V-2 rocket are 27,000 lb and 9,000 lb, respectively, that the relative jet velocity is constant and equal to 6,500 ft per sec, and that propellant is discharged at a uniform rate, find the height above the earth reached by the rocket at the end of the burning time of 60 sec. Neglect air resistance and variations in g. (b) What is the total height attained? (See preceding problem.)

16.11. A jet-propulsion unit uses 40 lb of air per pound of fuel at an over-all efficiency of 15 per cent when moving at a velocity of 800 ft per sec. Assuming a value of $\eta_0 = 0.25$, find the specific impulse (thrust per unit weight of fuel).

Chapter XVII

17.1. A radial-bladed fluid coupling has the characteristic curve of Fig. 17.2 corresponding to the larger value of Reynolds number. The specific gravity of the oil is 0.89. (a) What diameter must the coupling have to transmit a torque of 200 ft-lb at 3,000 rpm and a slip of 5 per cent? (b) If the slip is doubled, what is the necessary diameter?

17.2. An automobile has the following characteristics: Total weight is 3,000 lb; maximum engine brake torque is 150 ft-lb over a speed range of 1,000 to 3,600 rpm; reduction ratio in differential is 4 to 1; tire diameter is 28 in.; a 1-ft-diameter fluid coupling having the upper characteristic curve of Fig. 17.2. is attached to the engine shaft. (a) What car speed is attained at an engine speed of 3,600 rpm if the torque transmitted is three-quarters of the maximum? (b) What is the approximate efficiency of the coupling under these conditions? (c) Assuming a constant engine speed of 3,600 rpm and that the over-all drag of the car varies as the square of the car speed, find the engine torque, coupling efficiency, and car speed when the car climbs a grade of 4 per cent.

17.3. The torque coefficient of a fluid coupling of given design is found to follow the law

$$C_T = \frac{T}{\rho \omega_p^2 D^5} = 0.0080\left(1 - \frac{\omega_s}{\omega_p}\right)^{\frac{1}{2}}$$

where T is the torque, ρ is the density of the operating fluid, ω_p and ω_s are the angular speeds of the primary and secondary shafts, respectively, and D is the diameter. Find ω_p for a coupling 1 ft in diameter filled with oil of density 1.65 slugs per cu ft if the output is 15 hp and the efficiency is 98 per cent.

17.4. A fluid coupling having diameter $D = 1.20$ ft transmits a torque $T = 194$ ft-lb at a slip of 3 per cent when connected to an engine shaft turning at 2,000 rpm. A geometrically similar coupling is to be used to deliver 20,000 hp to a propeller shaft turning at 600 rpm. Find the diameter of this coupling if it operates on oil of the same density as the other.

17.5. A certain automotive hydrodynamic torque converter having the characteristics of Fig. 17.5 develops an output torque of 300 ft-lb at an output-shaft speed of 1,000 rpm when operating at maximum efficiency. (a) What are the input torque and speed under these conditions? (b) What is the efficiency? (c) If the input torque and speed are held constant and the output torque is doubled, what will be the output-shaft speed?

17.6. Two torque converters of the same design having diameters D and D run at maximum efficiency. Both use the same kind of oil and are filled to the same fraction of the total volume. Neglect frictional effects, and assume that $\omega_p = 2\omega_p$ and $D' = D/2$. (a) How do the torque ratios T_s/T_p and T'_s/T' compare? (b) What is the value of T'_s/T_s?

17.7. A torque converter is to be designed which is similar to that described in Art. 17.5 and shown in Fig. 17.4, except that the trailing edges of the primary and secondary blades are curved backward, instead of being normal to the direction of blade motion. The trailing edges of the primary vanes make an (acute) angle β_2 with the tip velocity $\omega_p r_2$. The trailing edges of the secondary vanes make an (acute) angle β_3 with the tip velocity $\omega_s r_3$. The guide vanes are the same as in Fig. 17.4. The converter is to give a torque ratio $T_s/T_p = 2.2$ when the shock losses are zero. Under these conditions it is assumed that the friction losses amount to 14 per cent of the power input, i.e., the efficiency is 86 per cent. If $r_1 = 2.50$ in., $r_3 = 7.00$ in., $\beta_1 = 45$ deg, $A = 57$ sq in., $\omega_p = 200$ radians/sec, and the specific weight of the oil is 0.0298 lb per cu in., find r_2, β_2, β_3, and the input horsepower.

17.8. A torque converter is identical with that shown in Fig. 17.4 and has $r_1 = 2.50$ in., $r_2 = 5.42$ in., $r_3 = 7.00$ in., $\beta_1 = 45$ deg, and $A = 57$ sq in. (a) Taking only shock loss into account, set up an expression for the efficiency; combine this with Eq. (17.17) to determine $Q \tan \beta_1/A\omega_p r_3$ as a function of ω_s/ω_p. (b) What is the percentage variation of $Q \tan \beta_1/A\omega_p r_3$ from a mean value? Is the assumption that this expression is constant justifiable as a first approximation in computing the optimum value of ω_s/ω_p, as in Art. 17.5? (c) Find the approximate value of the maximum efficiency.

Chapter XVIII

18.1. A rotary displacement pump is tested at constant speed and full stroke by throttling the discharge to produce different values of Δp, the pressure rise across the pump. If the friction torque T_f is constant, find the torque efficiency and power input in terms of Δp, D_P, T_f, and ω_P.

18.2. A hydraulic transmission consists of a variable-stroke pump and a fixed-stroke motor, having equal displacements, $D_P = D_M$. Assume a constant over-all torque efficiency of 90 per cent and a constant leakage rate of 5 per cent of the pump displacement per unit time ($Q_l = 0.05 D_P \omega_P$). Plot the over-all efficiency as ordinate, using as abscissa (a) pump stroke and (b) percentage of maximum motor speed.

18.3. A hydraulic transmission comprising a constant-displacement pump and variable-displacement motor is to do work at a uniform rate of 20 hp over an output-speed range of 800 to 1,800 rpm. Assuming a pressure rise of 1,700 lb per sq in. at the pump and reasonable values for the efficiencies involved, determine the approximate displacement per revolution of the hydraulic motor.

18.4. Calculate the leakage flow rate past a stationary piston if the piston length is 1.00 in., piston diameter is 1.00 in., pressure difference between the ends of the piston is 1,500 lb per sq in., viscosity of oil is 2.00×10^{-6} lb-sec per sq in., uniform radial clearance between piston and cylinder is 0.0010 in. Assume fully developed laminar flow throughout clearance space.

NOTE: Equation (12.10) is the starting point for the solution of this problem. The clearance is so small compared with the radius of the piston that the flow may be considered identical with that between parallel planes.

18.5. Solve the preceding problem if the piston has a constant velocity of 10 ft per sec in the direction of the pressure drop.

18.6. A dashpot consists of a piston of diameter D and piston rod in a closed cylinder through both end plates of which the piston rod extends. The cylinder is completely filled with oil of viscosity μ, which flows through four small holes of diameter d drilled axially through the piston, when the piston moves along the cylinder. The length of the piston is l, and its mass is m. Neglect leakage, friction force on the piston, and compressibility; and consider both the cross-sectional area of the piston rod and that of the four holes to be negligible compared with $\pi D^2/4$. (a) Assuming that Poiseuille's law applies to the flow through the holes in the piston and neglecting the mass of the oil and piston rod, set up the equation of motion of the piston under the action of an external force F_0. (b) Show that the solution of this equation is

$$x = \frac{F_0}{m\alpha^2}(e^{-\alpha t} - 1 + \alpha t)$$

if the displacement and velocity, x and dx/dt, are both zero at $t = 0$. The constant α is to be expressed in terms of known quantities μ, l, m, d, and D.

18.7. The following are given for an elevator driven by an electric motor through a hydraulic-displacement transmission:

$$\text{Limiting acceleration of cab} = \pm \frac{g}{5}$$

$$\text{Limiting velocity of cab} \quad = \pm 500 \text{ ft/min}$$

$$\text{Distance between stops} \quad = 17 \text{ ft}$$

Assume a variable-stroke pump and a fixed-stroke motor, with $D_P = D_M$. Neglect leakage. (a) What is the relation between the stroke-control setting S_P and the speed of the motor shaft, ω_M? (b) If the hydraulic-motor shaft is automatically geared to the stroke-control shaft at a distance h before a stop, determine h and the time required for the cab to travel a distance $0.99h$. Assume that the cab is traveling initially at its limiting speed and that the initial deceleration has its limiting value. (c) Sketch the velocity-distance and velocity-time diagrams for single-floor operation.

18.8. The following additional information is given for the elevator of the preceding problem:

Weight of cab, W . . . . 2,500 lb
Weight of counterweight, W_1 . . . . 2,250 lb
Radius of drum for cable, r . . . . 15 in.
Leakage constant $Q_l/\Delta p \omega_P D_P$ . . . . 5 × 10⁻⁵ in.²/lb
Displacement $D_P = D_M$ . . . . 3.67 in.³/radian
Pump speed $N_P = \omega_P 60/2\pi$ . . . . 600 rpm
Motor torque efficiency η_{TM} 1.00

(a) Find the speed of the hydraulic motor at a cab speed of descent $dz/dt = -500$ ft/min. (b) Assuming that the cab just fails to oscillate when it is brought to rest and that the initial deceleration and velocity are $d^2z/dt^2 = 0$ and $dz/dt = -500$ ft/min, find the value of h. (c) Compute the maximum deceleration.

18.9. Assuming that the stopping period for the elevator of the preceding problem begins at $t = 0$ and that the values of height, velocity, and acceleration at $t = 0$ are $z = h = 10.8$ ft, $dz/dt = -500$ ft/min, find the time required for z to reach the value $h/100 = 0.108$ ft. Also determine the maximum deceleration during the stopping period.

18.10. An ideal displacement servomechanism with proportional control has the following characteristics: Moment of inertia of load is 0.350 lb-in. sq sec, pump speed is 1,800 rpm, displacement of pump or motor is 2.00 cu in. per radian, pinion to ring-gear ratio of differential is 1 to 4, gear ratio from output shaft to differential is 1 to 1, pump stroke-control shaft turns 30 deg from neutral to full stroke, motor has a fixed stroke. (a) Compute the time constant α_0. (b) Plot $\alpha_0 \theta_o/\omega_i$ against $\alpha_0 t$ when a velocity step signal $d\theta_i/dt = \omega_i = $ constant is applied at $t = 0$ and maintained for all later times. Assume $\theta_o = d\theta_o/dt = 0$ at $t = 0$.

18.11. The servomechanism of the preceding problem is no longer supposed to be ideal but to have a leakage of 5 per cent of the maximum displacement of the pump when the pressure rise across the pump is 1,000 lb per sq in. The viscosity of the oil is 2.0×10^{-6} lb-sec per sq in. (a) Compute the leakage coefficient C_l defined in Eq. (18.15). (b) Determine the value of the elastic coefficient C_e [Eq. (18.32)] at which the system becomes unstable. (c) If C_e has twice this limiting value, plot the response curve, as in Fig. 18.27.

18.12. An ideal linear hydraulic servomechanism has proportional-plus-derivative control, i.e.,

$$S_P = C_s(\theta_i - \theta_o) + G_s \frac{d}{dt}(\theta_i - \theta_o)$$

(a) Show that the transfer function ζ for this servomechanism is expressible in the form

$$\frac{1+\zeta}{\zeta} = \frac{z/\omega_P G_s}{z + C_s/G_s} + 1$$

(b) Make a rough plot of this transfer function, similar to Fig. 18.25, and determine therefrom the stability criterion and the approximate form of the frequency-response curve. What is peculiar about the limiting value of the response as the frequency increases? (c) Compute the transient response to a displacement step function $\theta_i = C_i$.

18.13. An ideal linear hydraulic servomechanism has proportional-plus-integral control, i.e.,

$$S_P = C_s(\theta_i - \theta_o) + H_s \int_0^t (\theta_i - \theta_o)\, dt$$

(a) Show that the transfer function ζ for this servomechanism is expressible in the form

$$\frac{1+\zeta}{\zeta} = \frac{z^2}{\omega_P(C_s z + H_s)} + 1$$

(b) Make a rough plot of this transfer function, similar to Fig. 18.25, and determine therefrom the stability criterion and the approximate form of the frequency-response curve. (c) Determine the transient response to a velocity step signal $d\theta_i/dt = \omega_i$ = constant, and show that the steady-state error is zero. (Note the statement at the end of Art. 18.12 regarding steady-state error and shape of the transfer-function curve.)

INDEX